new makers of modern culture

New Makers of Modern Culture is the successor to the classic reference works *Makers of Modern Culture* and *Makers of Nineteenth-Century Culture*, published by Routledge in the early 1980s. The set was extremely successful and continues to be used to this day, as a result of the high quality of the writing, the distinguished contributors, and the cultural sensitivity shown in the selection of those individuals included. *New Makers of Modern Culture* takes into full account the rise and fall of reputation and influence over the last twenty-five years and the epochal changes that have occurred: the demise of Marxism and the collapse of the Soviet Union; the rise and fall of postmodernism; the eruption of Islamic fundamentalism; the triumph of the Internet.

Containing over eight hundred essay-style entries, and covering the period from 1850 to the present, New Makers includes artists, writers, dramatists, architects, philosophers, anthropologists, scientists, sociologists, major political figures, composers, film-makers and many other culturally significant individuals and is thoroughly international in its purview.

Next to Karl Marx is Bob Marley, next to John Ruskin is Salmon Rushdie, alongside Darwin is Luigi Dallapiccola, Deng Xiaoping rubs shoulders with Jacques Derrida, Julia Kristeva with Kropotkin. Once again, Wintle has enlisted the services of many distinguished writers and leading academics, such as Sam Beer, Bernard Crick, Edward Seidensticker and Paul Preston. In a few cases, for example Michael Holroyd and Philip Larkin, contributors are themselves the subject of entries.

With its global reach, *New Makers of Modern Culture* provides a multi-voiced witness of the contemporary thinking world. The entries carry short bibliographies and there is thorough cross-referencing throughout. There is a comprehensive index and a list of entries by contributor to aid the reader.

Justin Wintle's many books include *Romancing Vietnam, Furious Interiors: Wales, R.S. Thomas and God* and *The Rough Guide History of Islam*. His latest book is *Perfect Hostage*, the biography of the Burmese Nobel Peace Prize winner Aung San Suu Kyi (2007).

new makers of modern culture

edited by
justin wintle

volume 2
L–Z

Routledge
Taylor & Francis Group

LONDON AND NEW YORK

First published 2007
by Routledge
2 Park Square, Milton Park, Abingdon, Oxon OX14 4RN

Simultaneously published in the USA and Canada
by Routledge
270 Madison Avenue, New York, NY 10016, USA

Routledge is an imprint of the Taylor and Francis Group, an informa business

© 2007 Justin Wintle

Typeset in Bembo by Taylor & Francis Books
Printed and bound in TJ International Ltd, Padstow, Cornwall

British Library Cataloguing in Publication Data
A catalogue record for this book is available from the British Library

Library of Congress Cataloging in Publication Data
A catalog record for this book has been requested

ISBN10: 0–415–33831–X (set)
ISBN10: 0–415–42547–6 (vol. 1)
ISBN10: 0–415–42553–0 (vol. 2)

ISBN13: 978–0–415–33831–8 (set)
ISBN13: 978–0–415–42547–6 (vol. 1)
ISBN13: 978–0–415–42553–7 (vol. 2)

contents

volume 1

volume 2

L

LACAN, Jacques

1901–81

French psychoanalyst

In the second half of the twentieth century, Jacques Lacan was the psychoanalyst who perhaps did most to confirm the importance and the utterly revolutionary character of **Freud's** discovery of the unconscious. If, despite all of the controversies surrounding its allegedly unscientific character, psychoanalysis is today still widely practised and if its theory continues abundantly to influence many academic disciplines, this is to a great extent due to Lacan's multi-faceted ability to update both Freudian clinics and conceptual models by means of the most recent elaborations of structural linguistics (**Saussure, Jakobson**), structural anthropology (**Lévi-Strauss**) and post-Hegelian philosophy (Kojève, **Heidegger**).

Lacan was born in Paris to a prosperous, middle-class Roman Catholic family, studied medicine and then specialized in psychiatry; his doctoral thesis on self-punishing paranoia, published as *De la psychose paranoïaque dans ses rapports avec la personnalité* (1932), enjoyed a great success in avant-garde literary circles for its treatment of human knowledge as essentially paranoiac and resulted in Lacan's becoming a contributor to the surrealist journal *Le Minotaure*. In the same years, he also began his psychoanalytic treatment with Rudolph Loewenstein and assiduously attended Alexander Kojève's influential lectures on Hegel together with other French intellectuals such as **Georges Bataille** and **Raymond Queneau**. He made his first appearance on the psychoanalytic scene as early as 1936 when he presented a paper on the so-called 'mirror stage' of a child's development at the 14th Congress of the International Psycho-analytic Association. Although his articles from the 1930s and 1940s were already highly original contributions to Freudian theory (see among others, 'Le temps logique' and 'Propos sur la causalité psychique', now in *Écrits*, 1966), as well as 'Les complexes familiaux dans la formation de l'individu', now in *Autres écrits*, (2001), it was nevertheless only in 1953, with the beginning of his famous 'seminar' – which he held uninterruptedly until 1979 – and his first rupture with the psychoanalytic establishment, that his controversial thinking captivated the intellectual world of the time.

The fact that Lacan's principal published work – provocatively entitled *Écrits* ('Writings') – mostly consists of written re-elaborations of earlier lectures suggests that his teaching was first and foremost oral. In the 1970s he assigned his son-in-law the task of establishing the text of his annual seminars on the basis of existing shorthand notes, but so far only eleven volumes have been published in French and only six of these have been translated into English; this means that the transmission of Lacanian psychoanalysis continues to rely principally on the circulation of unauthorized transcripts. What clearly transpires from both the openness of the work-in-progress of the seminars and the notoriously cryptic recapitulations offered by the *Écrits* is the fact that Lacan's systematic 'return to Freud' is never finally settled but is constantly subjected to the most radical critical scrutiny.

While it is crucial to emphasize that Lacan tends to rehabilitate every 'old' theory within the framework of a 'new', increasingly complex elaboration, it is nevertheless possible to divide his work into three consecutive stages.

The first is characterized by a predominant interest in the order of the Imaginary. This is the realm of instinctual life which presides over animal sexuality and should be regarded as fundamentally disrupted in human beings. An animal is instinctively predisposed to recognize the image of the body of another animal of the same species; on the other hand, man identifies himself with the completeness of the image of another human body, and thus alienates himself in it, in order to compensate for his original helplessness – a baby cannot walk and is absolutely dependent on adults to carry out every one of its basic vital tasks. These considerations led Lacan to consider the ego as a paranoiac construction made up of a succession of alienating identifications with the image of the other: thus, at this stage, the role of psychoanalysis is to dis-alienate the subject's unconscious desire from these identifications. In this way, Lacan stood diametrically opposed to mainstream post-Freudian theories which understood psycho-analytic treatment as a means of enabling the ego to 'colonize' the unconscious and consequently aimed at assisting the patient's adaptation to society. Lacan scrutinizes these topics in articles such as 'The Mirror Stage as Formative of the Function of the I' (1949) and 'Aggressivity in Psychoanalysis' (1948), as well as in *The Seminar. Book I* (1987).

The second stage in Lacan's development began in the early 1950s, as he devoted himself to a more precise discussion of the Freudian unconscious and proposed that its nature is essentially symbolic. Not only does the subject undergo an imaginary alienation but is also (unconsciously) 'spoken' by language understood as a structure. The unconscious is structured like a language: hence, far from simply being identifiable with sheer irrationality, it follows a specific logic which manifests itself in phenomena such as dreams, bungled actions, slips of the tongue and psycho-somatic symptoms. In his seminal article 'Function and Field of Speech and Language' (1953), Lacan suggested that alie-nation in language could be overcome; this overcoming would in turn enable the subject to overcome his imaginary alienation. At this stage, Lacan thus appeared to believe that unconscious desire can fully be realized: it is enough for it to be recognized by the Other (subject) through psychoanalytic treatment, since desire is basically the desire to be desired by the Other (subject). The key reference for Lacan here was Hegel's dialec-tical notion of desire as propounded by Kojève. On the other hand, a few years later, in his article 'The Agency of the Letter in the Unconscious' (1957) – as well as in *Le Séminaire, livre IV* (1994) and *Le Séminaire, livre V* (1998), from 1956 to 1958 – Lacan realized that alienation in language is unsurpassable. The subject's individual desire is irremediably subjected to the universal field of language and to its laws. Here Lacan's key reference – which allowed him to rethink the Freudian notion of the Oedipus complex in structural terms – was Saussure's linguistics (largely in the form of Jakobson's re-elaboration).

Although Lacan's name is often associated with the movement of structuralism and although the notion of structure undoubtedly played a significant role in his theories, we should remember that, in opposition to structuralist and post-structuralist talk of a 'death of the subject', for Lacan the notion of subjectivity was an essential precondition of psychoanalytic experience. The impossibility of reducing his thought to structuralism becomes clearer if we take into consideration the work that he carried out in the 1960s and 1970s in which the order of the Real acquires increasing pre-eminence. This pre-eminence characterizes the third stage in Lacan's develop-ment. Here the unconscious structure – and, similarly, language *tout-court* – is considered as inherently limited by a non-assimilible non-symbolic remainder which is at the same time a prerequisite for the very functioning of the unconscious. Lacan identifies this 'real' dimension with the psycho-sexual pleasure-in-pain of enjoyment (*jouissance*): this notion results from a reworking of Freud's idea – rejected by many of his followers – that human tendencies also include a masochistic death drive. The aim of psychoanalysis is now to allow the subject to adopt a different stance in relation to his unconscious enjoyment. During this period, the clinical and theoretical study of enjoyment obliges Lacan to examine the ethical and political implications of psychoanalysis: he carries out these investigations most thoroughly in *The Seminar. Book VII* (1992) – held in 1959–60 – and *Le Séminaire, livre XVII* (1991) – held in 1969–70.

It is indubitably Lacan's work on the Real which today dominates Lacanian practice and has had the most profound repercussions for the most advanced formulations of philosophy and political theory (including Alain Badiou), as well as cultural studies and film theory – especially through the pioneering comparative readings of Slavoj Žižek who is also largely responsible for Lacan's recent academic fortune in the Anglophone world.

While Lacan remains more widely known for his theoretical achievements, it is nevertheless important not to underestimate a series of innovations that he introduced to the conception and conduct of psychoanalytic treatment: (1) the lack of distinction between 'training analysis' and 'therapeutic analysis': analysands who enter analysis in order to become analysts should not be treated differently from analysands who enter analysis with a view to being cured of a given symptom; (2) the institution of the 'passe': an analysand logically ends his analysis only when he is able convincingly to transmit the meaning of what he has achieved within it; (3) the variable length of the sessions; (4) the reformulation of the transference–countertransference phenomenon in terms of the relationship established between the demand for interpretation

that the analysand presents to the analyst – whom he sees as a 'subject supposed to know' – and a complementary 'desire of the analyst' which is a desire without object.

Further reading

Other works include: *Écrits: A Selection*, 1977, retranslated with major changes in 2002; articles mentioned above whose title is translated into English appear in this selection while those whose title is left in the original French do not. Those of Lacan's seminars which have been published in book form and are not mentioned above are the following: *The Seminar. Book II* (1988); *The Seminar. Book III* (1993); *The Seminar. Book XI* (1977); *The Seminar. Book XX* (1998); other seminars which have been published in French but remain as yet untranslated are *Le Séminaire, livre VIII* (1991) and *Le Séminaire, livre X* (2004). The most popular account of Lacan's life remains Elisabeth Roudinesco's *Jacques Lacan* (1997). Bruce Fink's volumes *The Lacanian Subject. Between Language and Jouissance* (1995) and *A Clinical Introduction to Lacanian Psychoanalysis* (1997) are good general introductions to Lacanian theory and practice.

LORENZO CHIESA

LAFORGUE, Jules

1860–87

French poet

Six years after Jules's birth in Montevideo, most of the Laforgue family moved to Tarbes in France and then returned to Uruguay in 1867. Jules and his older brother Émile stayed on in Tarbes, for their education at the *lycée* (these schooldays form the background of *Stéphane Vassiliew*, published 1946). The rest of the family were back in France in 1875 and settled in Paris the following year. Jules pursued his education at what is now the Lycée Condorcet, but never brought it to a successful conclusion, failing the *baccalauréat* three times and thus denying himself access to a professional career. Laforgue's mother, pregnant for the twelfth time, died in 1877, and Jules was left in Paris with his eldest sister, Marie, when his father returned to Tarbes in 1879. In these months of loneliness and poverty, Jules read widely in poetry and philosophy, in particular Schopenhauer and Eduard von Hartmann's *Philosophy of the Unconscious* (French trans. from German, 1877), and made valuable personal contacts: Paul Bourget, Gustave Kahn, Charles Henry. The year 1881 found him attending the course in aesthetics given by **Taine** at the École des Beaux Arts and in the employment of Charles Ephrussi, art-collector and later editor of the *Gazette des Beaux-Arts*, as a secretary, sharing his employer's enthusiasm for the Impressionists. Before the end of the year, Bourget and Ephrussi had secured for Laforgue the post of French reader to the Empress Augusta of Germany. For the next five years, Laforgue followed the empress in her annual progress from Coblenz to Berlin to Baden-Baden, each year spending two months of the summer with his family in Tarbes. Laforgue's agenda of 1883 indicates an ill-defined affair with a member of the imperial entourage, R. His literary energies were devoted to art journalism and poetry – *Les Complaintes* appeared in 1885, as did *L'Imitation de Notre-Dame la Lune*. In 1886, Laforgue took English lessons in Berlin with Leah Lee, whom he married on 31 December. In the meantime, Kahn had founded a review, *La Vogue*, and was pleased to publish anything that Laforgue sent him; to be singled out among Laforgue's contributions are his translations of **Walt Whitman** and his free-verse poems, arguably the first free verse in France, later collected as *Derniers vers* (1890). But Laforgue's health was rapidly deteriorating; he died on 20 August 1887, of tuberculosis, the illness that killed his wife the following year.

Although in sympathy with Taine's deterministic thinking, Laforgue could not consent to his aesthetic idealism, or to his belief in the moral utility of art. For Laforgue, the determining force is in part Schopenhauer's blind and aimless Will, the force of appetite, driving humankind pointlessly on to a pointless end; the only remedies are to be found in the contemplative equilibrium of Art or a life-denying asceticism that produces nirvana. Hartmann's Unconscious has nothing to do with Freudian notions – though Laforgue's submarine and foetal imagery moves in that direction – and is Schopenhauer's Will recast in fashionable physiological and neurological terms: a synthetic and relativized Absolute, individual and collective, a compound of unconscious idea and unconscious will. Aesthetically, the Unconscious had positive attractions for Laforgue, was an invitation to let himself go, to write associatively, capriciously, as the Unconscious 'dictated'; in practical terms, the Unconscious justified a nihilistic fatalism, reducing man to a set of reflexes, a plaything of pre-ordained patterns of instinct. The difficulty of Laforgue's relationships with women is ascribable to his fear of love's inevitable degradation to reproductive processes, and to his conviction that woman was the agent of sexual mindlessness, though he recognized that her enslaved condition was to blame for her sexual hypertrophy. He aspired to a more fraternal relationship with women, without ulterior motive or self-abandonment.

In a world in which sexuality and instinct are incurable illnesses, the sun, source of life and fertility, is shunned. Laforgue looks, rather, to the moon, the principle of sterility, total suspendedness, pure contemplation, the 'navel of Nothingness'. Anaemic and tubercular, the moon is a call to love which is a mockery of love. The spleen of the lunar nihilist is concentrated in Sunday, the idle day, the provincial day, dedicated to bourgeois ritual and complacent, illusory metaphysics, when the untouchable *communiantes* disguise their bodies in exercises of spiritual hygiene. These *communiantes* are the same girls who play the piano in suburban streets, practising their pieces to the metronome of their own existences. Laforgue's instrument is the barrel-organ, the Don Quixote and the fall-guy of music, the instrument of the *complainte*, mechanical enough to capture the metrical naiveties of popular song, but dissonant and uneven enough to be self-ironic. Not surprisingly, the two *personae* who dominate Laforgue's work are Hamlet and Pierrot. Hamlet, as he appears in the prose burlesques *Moral Tales from Jules Laforgue* (*Moralités légendaires*, 1887, trans. 1928), is the brother of Yorick, impulsive but undecided, never in possession of himself, finding in words all necessary evasions and yet a route, too, to transcendence, discouraging Ophelia from unavoidable self-depravation. Pierrot, masked beyond knowledge, is caught in the limbo between spurned day-to-dayness and ideals desired but not believed in, an acrobat in attitudes, a juggler with concepts; moon-lover, his expressionless floured face is a measure both of his ironic detachment and total vulnerability.

The kind of poetry that could cope with the beckonings of the Unconscious, with the succession of masks assumed by the hyper-trophic dandy and dilettante, will-less, afloat in the fluid, ungraspable present, had to be peculiarly available, available to changes of tone and register, to sudden deviations, tan-gents, after-thoughts, and above all uncom-mitting, anticipating nothing. And yet it had also to be sufficiently poised, in a formal sense, to maintain its self-reflexive quality and to give leverage and discipline to its irresis-tible ironies. After the derivative, philoso-phical eloquence of the early poems of *Le Sanglot de la terre* ('The Lament of the Earth', collected 1901), Laforgue moved into the multivocal, contrapuntal, heterostanzaic and heterosyllabic structures of *Les Complaintes*, oscillating, with their vocalic elisions, false liaisons, ungrammaticalness, often impar-isyllabic lines, neologisms, exploration of savant vocabularies, between colloquial care-lessness and learned meticulousness ('I possess my language in a more minute, more clownish way'). These are poems of mono-logue and dialogue, involving the reader as a potential interlocutor, so that processes of self-identification with the text are impossible for him. Instead, he is totally without privilege and *point de repère*, as subject to manipulation and textual double-cross as any *personae* within the text. Furthermore, because the text is ventriloquial, quotational, intertextual, it is already a metalanguage; there are no situations to penetrate through to, no person behind textual 'personality'; one can get only

as far as the changing disguises, the shifts between different kinds of situation denoted by different kinds of text, in an infinitely recessive allusiveness. In the *Derniers vers*, ('Last Poems') although the text is still highly allusive and wobbles between the urgency of exclamation and the shrugs of *points de sus-pension*, there is more tonal coherence, more consistency of stance. Laforgue's free verse is never far from regular structures and the atti-tudes embedded in them; it leans on the ready-made, the better to make it only approximate, vulnerable to corrosive innuendoes; and rhyme, now irregular and improvised, operates both as the motor of association of ideas and as a constant cue to the text for merciless self-scrutiny.

If Laforgue has left his mark on the work of **Apollinaire**, Fargue, Toulet, Deréme, Supervielle, it is the Anglo-American world that owes him most. In the 1928 Introduction to **Pound's** *Selected Poems*, **Eliot** speaks of **Laforgue** as 'if not quite the greatest poet after Baudelaire ... certainly the most important technical innovator', and admits that the free verse he began to write in 1908 or 1909 'was directly drawn from the study of Laforgue together with the later Elizabethan drama'. *Prufrock and Other Observations* (1917) abounds in Laforguian echoes, but most commentators on the connection find in Eliot a greater control, a greater ability to break out of the prison of personality, a greater sustainedness in the development of idea and utterance, less sheer verbalism, than in Laforgue. Pound claimed that Eliot's respect for Laforgue was less than his own. In his essay 'Irony, Laforgue and some Satire' (1917), Pound praises Laforgue for being nine-tenths critic, for making a poetry out of literary poses and clichés which act, none-theless, as vehicles for personal emotion. Elsewhere, he speaks of Laforgue's redis-covery of logopoeia, 'the dance of the intel-lect among words', a use of language which foregrounds usage and in which the meaning of words lies in the ideological assumptions of their habitual contexts. Textual borrowings are harder to trace, but the 'Hugh Selwyn

Mauberley' cycle has many Laforguian turns. Laforgue's presence is also to be found in the poems of **Aldous Huxley** (*The Burning Wheel*, 1916), Edith Sitwell, **Hart Crane** and **Wallace Stevens**.

Further reading

See: M. Collie, *Jules Laforgue* (1977); J.-L. Debauve, *Laforgue en son temps* (1972); M.-J. Durry, *Jules Laforgue* (1952); E.J.H. Greene, *T.S. Eliot et la France* (1951); L.Guichard, *Jules Laforgue et ses poésies* (1950); W. Ramsey, *Laforgue and the Ironic Inheritance* (1953); D. Arkell, *Looking for Laforgue: An Informal Biography* (1979); Anne Holmes, *Jules Laforgue and Poetic Innovation* (1993).

CLIVE SCOTT

LAING, Ronald David

1927–89

Scottish psychiatrist

Born in Glasgow in a three-room tenement, R.D. Laing attended school in that city before going on to read medicine in his local university. He graduated as a doctor in 1951 and spent the next two years in the British army before returning to Glasgow for three years' further training as a psychiatrist. In 1957 he moved to London and joined the Tavistock Clinic, and was director of the Langham Clinic from 1962 to 1965. From 1961 to 1967 he was involved in research into psychiatric disturbance in families with the Tavistock Institute of Human Relations as a Fellow of the Foundations Fund for Research in Psychiatry. In 1964, Laing founded the Philadelphia Association, a registered charity concerned with establishing a network of households where people in extreme mental distress might spend some time without having to undergo orthodox forms of psychiatric treatment. He also set up a private practice as a psychoanalyst.

Laing burst into prominence with the publication of his first book, *The Divided Self* (1960). In the preface to the first edition, he acknowledge his debt to the phenomenologists **Jaspers** and Binswanger and to the existentialists Kierkegaard, **Heidegger** and **Sartre**. The book set out to demystify madness, break down the divide between the sane and the insane and provide an understanding of so-called 'mad' communication and behaviour. In particular Laing explored the role of the schizophrenic patient as 'outsider', estranged from self and society, and portrayed him as the inventor of a false self with which to cope and keep at bay the outside world and the inner despair. Such a model of madness envisaged schizophrenia as the final state of personal disintegration involving a total 'splitting' between the negated inner 'real' and the external 'false' self.

Laing subsequently wrote *Sanity, Madness and the Family* (1964), with Aaron Esterson, and *The Self and Others* (1961), in which he examined patterns of communications within the families of schizophrenic patients and focused particularly on the potential role of Gregory Bateson's notion of the 'double-blind'. However, it was the publication of *The Politics of Experience/The Bird of Paradise* (1967) which marked a radical departure in Laing's thinking and elevated him into the role of a guru of the 1960s. In that book, Laing turned from the exploration of individual pathology to social sickness and the human condition in general. A conspiratorial model took shape in which the psychotic patient became both a scapegoat, driven into madness by a mechanistic and dehumanizing world, and a voyager, engaged in a semi-mystical journey of self-exploration, transcendence and growth. The book uncannily reflected ideas and passions prevalent in society at the time and contributed to the bracketing of the psychotic patient with the criminal, the racial outcast and the political dissident in a coalition of oppressed bearers of an authentic statement concerning the human condition. It also became a crucial text in the growing 'anti-psychiatry' movement by virtue of its portrayal of psychiatrists as agents of social control, psychiatric institutions as centres of degradation, and psychiatric treatment as a process of invalidation and the re-establishment of a state of 'pseudo-sanity'.

Shortly afterwards, Laing went to Ceylon and India to meditate and familiarize himself with Buddhist and Hindu philosophy. His influence within psychiatry was less extensive than it has been outside – the widespread notion of the 'schizophrenogenic' mother driving her offspring mad, epitomized in the film *Family Life* (1971), owed much to Laing, and his views on the value of hallucinatory experience were marshalled to support moves to legalize cannabis.

In recent years, Laing became interested in the experiences of pre-natal life and birth itself and their impact on subsequent development of the person. He made a film that was highly critical of current obstetrical techniques and practices and in *The Facts of Life* (1976) explored the notion that in adult life we are haunted by and re-enact our conception, foetal life and birth, the loss of the placenta and cord.

The overall impact of Laing's writings on psychiatry seems likely to be judged in terms of the emphasis he placed on the *experience* of madness at a time when psychiatry was more preoccupied with its *form*. It is his first book which remains a seminal work for its uniquely rich and imaginative exploration of the content of psychopathology.

Further reading

Other works include: *Reason and Violence* (with David Cooper, 1964); *Interpersonal Perception* (with H. Phillipson and A.R. Lee, 1966); *Knots* (1970); *The Politics of the Family* (1971). See also: Edward Z. Friedenberg, *Laing* (1973); Andrew Collier, *R.D. Laing: The Philosophy and Politics of Psychotherapy* (1977); Daniel Burston, *The Wing of Madness: Life and Work of R.D. Laing* (1996); John Clay, *R.D. Laing: A Divided Self* (1997); Bob Mullan, *R.D. Laing: A Personal View* (1999).

ANTHONY W. CLARE

LAMPEDUSA, Giuseppe Tomasi di

1896–1957

Italian writer

At the age of sixty, an obscure teacher of English literature in the Sicilian capital Palermo, with almost no experience of writing or publishing, completes his first novel, but dies soon after the work is rejected by a leading Italian publisher. Issued a year later by another firm, the book is hailed as a masterpiece, soon achieving classic status among the great novels of the world. Its author's reputation, although undoubtedly enhanced by subsequent publication of three short stories and a memoir, rests firmly on the critical impact of this single major work.

The case of Giuseppe Tomasi di Lampedusa – author of *Il Gatorade* (1958, translated as *The Leopard* 1960) – is unique in the annals of literature. He was certainly not brought up to be a writer. Living in their ancestral palace in Palermo, where he was born on 23 December 1896, his father, the Duke of Palma, and his mother, Beatrice Tasca Filangeri di Cuto, were both members of a vast feudal aristocracy created over many centuries by Sicily's various rulers. Though complex local inheritance laws had already much reduced the family's income, Giuseppe was raised in a style appropriate to a young nobleman, the only child in a household full of bachelor uncles and spinster aunts. The major annual event during his early years was the removal of the Lampedusas and their servants each summer to the country estate belonging to his maternal grandparents at Santa Margherita in western Sicily, a journey which later furnished one of the key episodes in *Il Gattopardo*.

Though Giuseppe wished to study literature at university, his father, who had now inherited the title of Prince of Lampedusa, ordered him to enrol in a law faculty. His student career, first in Turin and then in Genoa, was interrupted, however, by the Great War. Having joined an infantry regiment, he was captured after the battle of Caporetto in 1917, but soon managed to escape. A somewhat aimless existence following demobilization was transformed by several visits to England, where an uncle served as Italy's ambassador in London. Already imbued with an Italian aristocrat's typical Anglophilia, Giuseppe developed an intense admiration for British political institutions and an encyclopaedic knowledge of English literature from Anglo-Saxon poetry to **T.S. Eliot**. While in London, he met and fell in love with his uncle's step-daughter Alexandra Wolff, known as Licy. A Baltic baroness with a castle in Latvia, she was a woman of strong character, who never took kindly to living in Sicily and clung to the Russian-speaking culture in which she had been brought up. The attachment between the pair was genuine and lasting, though there were no children and most of their affection was lavished on their numerous dogs.

After World War II, when the already decaying and half-abandoned Palazzo Lampedusa suffered irreparable damage during the Allied bombing of Palermo, the couple settled in a smaller palace and the Prince of Lampedusa, as Giuseppe now was, began teaching an English literature course to private pupils. At the same time he started revisiting various scenes of his childhood, but an initial plan to write an autobiography never got beyond an enchanting memoir of his early years. Instead he transmuted the experience of a generation of ancestors into a novel set in Sicily during Garibaldi's invasion of the island in 1860.

Death, in one form or another, begins and ends *Il Gattopardo*, and the narrative gained much of its power from Lampedusa's awareness of his own mortality. A heavy smoker, he died of lung cancer on 23 July 1957, while the book still awaited publication. A year later, after being seen through the press by Giorgio Bassani, himself an outstanding novelist, it appeared to general acclaim beyond Italy's borders and furious critical controversy within them. Its portrait of a vanished world, presented unsentimentally and with uncanny sharpness of detail, was framed by the author's undeniably pessimistic view of Sicily itself as an ancient, seemingly insoluble human problem. Once the dust had cleared among those who condemned it for spiritual nihilism, reactionary political views or stylistic conservatism, *Il Gattopardo* was seen for the complex literary organism it truly

was, a work combining the author's detached view of his own social echelon and a cunningly extended historical perspective with genuine fictional artistry, epic breadth and poetic sensibility offset by an engagingly sardonic sense of humour. The hugely successful film treatment made by **Luchino Visconti** soon after the book's publication emphasized the powerful definition of characters such as the handsome opportunist Tancredi, his bewitchingly earthy fiancée Angelica and, of course, the Prince of Salina himself, through whose increasingly weary and disillusioned gaze we watch the narrative unfold. *Il Gattopardo* as we have it is not an entirely finished product: had Lampedusa survived, a notably different book might have emerged. What exists is nevertheless a masterpiece, in which the wisdom, authority and technical accomplishment of the writing make it more like a final testament than a first novel.

Further reading

Other work include: *Two Stories and a Memory* (1963) and *The Siren and Selected Writings* (1996). See: A.Vitello, *I Gattopardo di Donnafugato* (1963); David Gilmour, *The Last Leopard* (1991).

JONATHAN KEATES

LANG, Fritz
1890–1976
German/US film director

Lang, the most important film director to make a successful transition from the German silent cinema of the 1920s to Hollywood in the 1930s, was born into a bourgeois Catholic family in Vienna in 1890. His early studies in architecture, encouraged by his father, a municipal architect, conflicted with his own interests in the visual arts, particularly the work of **Klimt** and Schiele, and in 1911–12 he left home to globe-trot before settling in Paris in 1913. Here he scraped a living as a commercial artist and became interested in the new art of the cinema. With the outbreak of the Great War, Lang escaped home to

Vienna, where he joined up, was promoted to officer, and was wounded and decorated on more than one occasion. In military hospital he began to write film scenarios – three of them known to have been brought to the screen by Joe May during 1917 – and as an actor came to the attention of Erich Pommer's company Decla, which Lang joined in Berlin in 1919. Here he read and wrote scripts and also did some editing and bit-part acting before moving promptly into direction with *Half-Caste* (1919). In this first year with Decla Lang also directed *The Master of Love*, *Hara-Kiri*, *The Wandering Image* and the two-part adventure melodrama *The Spiders*, his first surviving work of the period. In 1920, rapidly emerging as a major young director, Lang married the writer Thea von Harbou, with whom he was to write the majority of his German films, and who also turned several of their scripts into successful novels.

Following *Four Around a Woman* (1920, now lost) Lang directed eight films before fleeing **Hitler's** Germany in 1933. Two of these deal with historical fantasy and legend. *Destiny* (1921) tells its stories of lovers separated by the Angel of Death through a triptych of flashbacks – to the Arabian Nights, to Renaissance Venice, and to Imperial China – while an epic German version of *The Niebelungen* is retold in Lang's two-part film, *Siegfried* and *Kriemhild's Revenge* (1924). Two of Lang's silent films of the 1920s deal on the other hand with futuristic fantasy in the science fiction genre. The spectacular and costly *Metropolis* (1926) recounts the story of a workers' revolt in a visionary city of the future, while *Woman on the Moon* (1928) presents a comic-strip account of a rocket trip to prospect for lunar gold. The other four films of the period draw from the contemporary world of criminality and post-war angst. The two parts of *Dr Mabuse* – *Dr Mabuse the Gambler: A Picture of the Times* and *Inferno: Men of the Times* (1922) – enact the exploits of an unscrupulous master criminal with skills in hypnotism and disguise. His talents are later transferred to his psychiatrist

in *The Last Will of Dr Mabuse* (1932–3). Lang's other two chief criminals of the period are the master spy in *The Spy* (1928), and the pathetic child-murderer hunted down by both police and criminals in Lang's first sound-film, *M* (1931).

The Last Will of Dr Mabuse, drawing links between criminality, dictatorship and mind-control, was immediately banned by Goebbels, but Lang was nonetheless offered charge of the Nazi film industry on the basis of Hitler's admiration for *Metropolis*. Fleeing overnight to Paris, Lang was once more hired by fellow émigré Pommer, now with Fox, to make his only French film, *Liliom* (1933), a tragi-comic fantasy of fairground life starring Charles Boyer. Espoused to National Socialism, however, Thea von Harbou remained in Germany, and divorced Lang. After *Liliom* Lang joined the central European exodus to the United States, where he joined MGM. Here, on the basis of sophisticated work in the popular genres, he was rapidly to become established as one of the leading Hollywood directors and as one of the key *auteurs* discovered by emerging generations of film critics in the 1950s and 1960s in America and Europe.

The bulk of Lang's twenty-two Hollywood films are crime thrillers. These commence with the anti-lynching drama of his first American film, *Fury* (1936), and his drama of the consequences of wrongful conviction, *You Only Live Once* (1937), and then re-emerge in the middle and later 1940s with his celebrated murder dramas in the *film noir* style, full of narrative and visual panache and complexity and frequently reworking some of his German themes such as the 'guilty innocent' and the *femme fatale: The Woman in the Window* (1944), *Scarlet Street* (1945), *Secret Beyond the Door* (1948), *House by the River* (1949), *The Blue Gardenia* (1952), *The Big Heat* (1953), *Human Desire* (1954), *While the City Sleeps* (1955) and *Beyond a Reasonable Doubt* (1956).

In the 1940s Lang also directed a group of films dealing with the experience of war – *Man Hunt* (1941), from Geoffrey Household's novel *Rogue Male, Hangmen Also Die* (1943), co-written with **Brecht**, a version of **Greene's** novel *Ministry of Fear* (1941), *Cloak and Dagger* (1946) and *An American Guerrilla in the Philippines* (1950). He made only three Westerns – *The Return of Frank James* (1940), *Western Union* (1941) and *Rancho Notorious* (1952). His more off-beat work in Hollywood included the anti-realist musical romance with music by **Weill**, *You and Me* (1938), his version of **Odets's** fishing melodrama, *Clash by Night* (1951), and *Moonfleet* (1955), a smuggling yarn set in Britain, his first film in Cinemascope and one of his rare films in colour.

Lang's career as a director ended, as it had begun, in Germany, and consisted of a return to some of his early German themes. *The Indian Tomb* (1958) remade the two films written by Lang for Joe May in the early 1920s – *The Tiger of Bengal* and *The Indian Tomb* itself. His last film, *The Thousand Eyes of Dr Mabuse* (1960), similarly, extends the 1920s Mabuse theme to the contemporary world of industrial intrigue. In 1963, signalling his importance for filmmakers of the new European cinema, the patriarchal Lang appears as himself in **Godard's** film industry love-tragedy, *Contempt*.

Further reading

See: Siegfried Kracauer, *From Caligari to Hitler* (1947); Peter Bogdanovich, *Fritz Lang in America* (1967); Paul M. Jensen, *The Cinema of Fritz Lang* (1969); Lotte H. Eisner, *Fritz Lang* (1976); Steve Jenkins (ed.) *Fritz Lang* (1981); Patrick McGilligan, *Fritz Lang: The Nature of the Beast* (1997); Tom Gunning, *The Films of Fritz Lang* (2000).

PHILIP DRUMMOND

LARKIN, Philip Arthur

1922–85

English poet

Poet and novelist, born in Coventry, educated at St John's College, Oxford – in a generation *mirabilis* that included also John Wain and **Kingsley Amis** – who has deliberately embraced an ordinary, provincial life (working as a university librarian in Belfast, then in Hull) and cultivated a principled provincialism of outlook and practice in his writing. His two novels, *Jill* (1946, rev. 1964, written in 1943–4 when he was only twenty-one) and *A Girl in Winter* (1947), both rightly rejected by their author as juvenilia, are of little interest now except as early indicators of Larkin's sense of the provincial self (*Jill* is about a northern working-class boy up at Oxford) and of the stimulus the bleaker, wintrier aspects of English life grant him. The poems of *The North Ship* (1945), a juvenile *mélange* soon as toughly denigrated by their author as his novels, indicate rather more clearly Larkin's maturer direction. For among the soothing echoes of the earlier **W.B. Yeats** and odd hints of a young poet too overpowered by **Dylan Thomas** there appear clearly the formal polishings of Robert Graves and the adjectival precisions that come from having attended carefully to **W.H. Auden**:

> Who can confront
> The instantaneous grief of being alone?
> Or watch the sad increase
> Across the mind of this prolific plant,
> Dumb idleness?

Larkin's emerging personal voice, however, only achieved its complete definition much later, with *The Less Deceived* (October 1955) and *The Whitsun Weddings* (1964). Larkin lacks, of course, the prolific output frequently associated with major poets, and there is a marked levelling-out in his *High Windows* volume (1974), but *The Less Deceived* and *The Whitsun Weddings* poems have achieved for him a central, even *the* central position, among English poets of the middle twentieth century.

Larkin's mature style is consciously in an English tradition. His poetry was considerably inspirited by his discovery (he dates it 1946) of **Thomas Hardy's** poetry, his realization of the possibilities of the best

Georgian poets, particularly (though no doubt Georgianism was also filtered through Robert Graves and William Empson) **Edward Thomas**. Larkin has rejected influences from overseas. He points to the failure of authors who 'change countries' ('Look at Auden'). He believed the styles and fashions imported and popularized by **Pound** and **Eliot** to be regrettable intrusions into the English tradition. Modernism of all kinds – in painting and music as well as in literature – he rejected (see his volume of jazz reviews, *All What Jazz*, 1970, whose Introduction is his major anti-modernist tract). He blamed the academic industry of literary study for supporting much pretentious literary and critical nonsense (see, for example, 'Posterity' in *High Windows*).

Larkin has been accused of standing for the impoverished achievement, the cowardly practice of a retreating islanded minimalism. His *Oxford Book of Twentieth-Century English Verse* (1973), with its carefully garnered harvest of the provincial and minor, its large welcome to the likes of Hardy, **Betjeman** and Walter de la Mare, was seized on to illustrate the meagreness of his stand. Admittedly, Larkin's modernist targets are the very largest ones ('whether ... **Parker**, Pound or **Picasso**: it helps us neither to enjoy nor endure'). Granted, too, that the pervasive negativism so frequently noticed by his readers (his fondness, for example, for words beginning with *un-*, *in-* and *dis-*) settled in *High Windows* into a sometimes dismaying drizzle of envious hostility towards the young and freer ('They fuck you up, your mum and dad'; 'Sexual intercourse began/In nineteen sixty-three/(Which was rather late for me)'). But the gains for his poetry purchased by Larkin's dedicated hostility to the modernistic macrocosm were impressively positive. He became the laureate of the common bloke, the unheroic man in bicycle clips (see 'Church Going' in *The Less Deceived*), the quiet narrator of life in back-street digs on Saturday afternoons as seen from the railway train ('An Odeon went past, a cooling tower,/And someone running up to bowl': lines from 'The Whitsun Weddings' sometimes hailed as the essence of the so-called 'Movement' of the 1950s), the voice of the ordinary chap who would rather stay at home, listen to his Sidney Bechet records and ponder death (see 'Vers de Société' in *High Windows*). 'I love the commonplace,' he said, 'I lead a very commonplace life. Everyday things are lovely to me.' This means accepting ordinariness – the truth of 'a real girl in a real place' that he celebrates in 'Lines upon a Young Lady's Photograph Album' (*The Less Deceived*). It entails paying attention to the vernacular of 'Mr Bleaney' and his landlady (*The Whitsun Weddings*), to people who like bottled sauce, do the football pools, go to Frinton in the summer and have sisters in Stoke. It's an impressive refusing not to face our common mortality (see, for example, 'Dockery and Son' in *The Whitsun Weddings*). And its success depended on a lovingly close regard (and Larkin wrote some very fine love-poems) for the intransigent stuff of the day-to-day – a quotidian reality that Larkin's language constantly animates as it unflaggingly presents us with toughly bitten-off metonymic gobbets of it for our continual delight and illumination.

Further reading

See: Anthony Thwaite (ed.) *Selected Letters of Philip Larkin 1940–85* (1992); David Timms, *Philip Larkin* (1974); Blake Morrison, *The Movement* (1980); Andrew Motion, *Philip Larkin* (1982); D. Salwak, *Philip Larkin: The Man and His Work* (1989); Anthony Thwaite (ed.) *Further Requirements: Interviews, Broadcasts, Statements and Reviews, 1952–85* (2002); A.T. Tolley (ed.) *Early Poems* (2005); Richard Bradford, *Then Fear: The Life of Philip Larkin* (2005).

VALENTINE CUNNINGHAM

LARTET, Edouard Armand Isidore

1801–71

French palaeontologist and prehistoric archaeologist

Although in his early years Lartet made major contributions in palaeontology, some of which helped create the atmosphere for the acceptance of the antiquity of man, and while he continued to make contributions in the field until his death, it is for the role that he played, in the last ten years of his life, in the establishment of prehistoric archaeology that he is remembered. Born into relative affluence at St-Guiraud (Gers) he trained as a lawyer at Toulouse, where he moved in circles interested in natural history, and sympathetic to the search for 'fossil man', and at Paris, where he neglected the law for lectures at the Natural History Museum. Returning to Gers he established himself as a lawyer at Auch, giving with the generosity that was to mark his whole life free consultations to the poorer peasants. These repaid him by bringing in curiosities from their fields amongst which were the fossil bones that led him to the discovery of the Miocene palaeontological site of Sansan.

In 1834 he gave up the law to excavate full time at Sansan. Here in 1837 he made a major discovery – the first find of a fossil primate, *Pliopithecus (Protopithecus) antiquus*. This contradicted the influential Cuvier, who, in arguing against the existence of fossil man, had stated that no other fossil primates would be found either.

The find, published in the *Comptes rendus de l'Académie des Sciences* (t. 4, 1837, p. 85), established Lartet as a palaeontologist, particularly of the late Tertiary and Quaternary. In 1851 he wrote his final account of Sansan, moving to Toulouse, and two years later to Paris. While he continued with palaeontological study and publication, his early work had prepared him for the contribution he was to make to prehistoric archaeology.

Since the 1830s Boucher de Perthes had been arguing, with scant success, for the acceptance of worked flints from the river gravels of north France as the work of man and contemporary with the bones of extinct animals. In 1858 and 1859 visits by the Englishmen Falconer, Sir **John Evans** and Prestwich brought general acceptance to the finds of de Perthes, and in 1859 Lartet joined forces with him to defend the finds in France.

While publishing his defences of de Perthes in Geneva and London, access to the *Comptes rendus de l'Académie des Sciences* being closed to him by his opponents, Lartet turned to the study of finds being reported from the caves of south-west France. In 1857 he had been sent details of excavations in the late Palaeolithic cave of Massat in the Pyrenees, which he presented via Geoffroy-Saint-Hilaire to the Academy in the same year, coupled with a tribute to the work of de Perthes. In 1860 he visited Massat where he recognized and established the Palaeolithic dating of the mobiliary art – engraved and decorated bones and tools – previously considered Celtic.

On his return he paused to excavate the cave of Aurignac, discovering important Palaeolithic material beneath Neolithic burials. He published the results in May 1861 in the *Annales des Sciences naturelles* (Zoologie, 4e série, t. 15, p. 177), stressing the role of human agency in the accumulation of cave sediments, and establishing the antiquity of the archaeological material, which he illuminated by comparisons with ethnographic material. Influential as a text, the paper became a manifesto, and the foundation stone of a new discipline – prehistoric archaeology.

In 1863, in association with Henry Christy, an English banker interested in American ethnography, he turned his attention to the Dordogne where the list of their excavations is a roll-call of famous sites: Le Moustier, Laugerie-Haute, La Madeleine, Gorge d'Enfer. The startlingly rich material recovered was published in 1864 in the *Revue Archéologique*, then in detail in the serial publication *Reliquiae Aquitanicae*, which appeared in London between 1865 and 1875, not being completed until after the deaths of both Christy (1865) and Lartet. Beside details of the excavations and an extensive iconography, further comparisons, to American ethnographic material, were made by Christy.

It was in the 1864 paper, however, that the major theoretical contributions were made. Here was propounded the first explanation for Stone Age art, the simple 'art for art's sake' theory that corresponded to contemporary opinion of all art; and also the sketch of the first scheme for subdivision of the Old Stone Age, a scheme established at the Paris Universal Exhibition of 1867. This suggested an 'Epoch of the Hippopotamus' representing the Lower Palaeolithic finds from the river gravels of northern France, and a 'Cave Bear and Mammoth Epoch' and 'Reindeer Age' covering four recognized divisions in the material from the caves of south-west France, and equivalent to the Mousterian, Aurignacian, Solutrean and Magdalenian of later terminology. Although the palaeontological nomenclature was replaced by that of de Mortillet from 1869, and although Lartet himself was not clear about whether the divisions should be regarded as chronological, they do represent those that still provide the outline structure for Palaeolithic finds in Western Europe.

Although prehistoric archaeology entered a period of intellectual decline after the glorious decade 1860–70, the work of Lartet in discovery and observation, in the publication of finds, and in systematization, provided a solid foundation for the future, and marked out many paths that have been taken up again more recently.

Appointed a professor at the Natural History Museum at the age of sixty-nine, Lartet did not live to teach formally. Weighed down by the Prussian invasion, and by fears for the safety of his son Louis, he retired to Gers in 1870, where he died the following year.

Further reading

See: *Origines de l'archéologie préhistorique en France* (1964). No complete biography exists, but the early years are well dealt with by L. Meroc in 'Aurignac et l'Aurignacien', *Bulletin de la Société méridionale de Spéléologie et de Préhistoire*, vols VI–IX (1956–9). Notices published after the death of Lartet were collected in *Vie et travaux de Edouard Lartet* (1872), the most useful of which are those of E. Hamy (with bibliography) and J. Prestwich.

MARTIN HEMINGWAY

LAUTRÉAMONT, Comte de (Isidore-Lucien DUCASSE)

1846–70

French prose poet

Ducasse exerted no influence on the nineteenth century. His two books, the rambling *Les Chants de Maldoror* (1869) and the terse, polemical *Poésies* (1870, trans. 1978), were only scrappily published in his lifetime. He died at the age of twenty-four in a Paris hotel, from unknown causes and with no reputation. A freak offspring of the age of **Berlioz** and Delacroix, it took the convulsion of the Great War to make of his passionate, delinquent art something comprehensible to a wider sensibility. He was rediscovered, reprinted and extolled as a great precursor by **André Breton**, who found the germ of Surrealism in *Les Chants* at the moment when the beauty of a boy is described as being like 'the chance meeting on a dissecting table of a sewing-machine and an umbrella!' From this was derived a literary theory of automatic writing and random imagery, a *reductio ad absurdum* – as Mario Praz pointed out in *The Romantic Agony* – of the idea of inspiration.

Born in Montevideo, the only child of a minor French diplomat, Ducasse was an outsider by birth as well as by temperament. His mother died in his second year. At thirteen he travelled to France and was educated at *lycées* in Gascony. Just one photograph exists, a fine angry face without self-pity. *Les Chants*, complete, was published in Brussels in 1869 at the author's expense and under the pseudonym 'Comte de Lautréamont' (a name by which he is still identified). One of only three contemporary notices describes it as 'a series of visions and reflections in bizarre style, a sort of Apocalypse whose meaning it would be futile to guess'.

This is a reasonable description of the strangest product of post-Byronism, a long quasi-autobiographical meditation from Maldoror-Ducasse which reconnoitres the twilit zone between the conscious and unconscious, wakefulness and sleep, sanity and lunacy, in pursuit of 'meaning', an enterprise that is doomed in this region of grotesque and mercurial apparitions where absolute meanings cannot apply. *Les Chants* is a prismatic text whose meanings depend largely on how it is turned and by whom, a prose poem of blasphemy, guilt, lyricism and painful frustration. The form is rhapsodic but the texture is extremely self-conscious, full of parodies, puns, collages, thefts, jokes, abrupt shifts and personal interruptions, a style without kin until the twentieth century. For Ducasse the line between inspiration and self-intoxication has vanished. He has discovered a form for psychic explosion.

As a revolutionary delinquent, Ducasse is less successful than **Rimbaud** (that is, more anarchic, less nourishing to read) because he is less certain of what he is doing. Rimbaud's attempt to endow his frustrations with significance succeeds through superior artistry and its powerful links with the mythic universe, whereas with Ducasse the same desire often reveals him as laying claim to a sophistication and experience he did not possess. Mercuriality can become chronic indecision, extravagance mere ostentation, the whole insufficiently realized even within its own outlandish terms. The extent to which his mystification is deliberate is always debatable. Thus *Les Chants* has become a labyrinth not so much of meanings as of motives.

Ducasse's alienation was social and sexual. The young man's failure to exorcize the father through financial independence, extending to a general revolt against prevailing values, seeks solace in the status of aristocrat. It is the perfect solution to his predicament, an elevation above the mass which confers the freedom to despise, yet without loss of social incorporation. More: the cult of transgression which in a poor clerk would be criminality or madness becomes in the case of the nobleman a glamorous experiment in personality. Ducasse's primary purpose in *Les Chants*, and in *Poésies* also, is not the manufacture of a work of art but the construction of an identity for himself. This narcissistic tendency for art to be the

by-product of the artist's concern with his own identity has characterized much avant-garde art since Ducasse, except that what was self-dramatization in the nineteenth century became in the twentieth self-analysis.

The vehemence of his passion for words as texture, his incestuous intercourse with other authors (abductions from the Bible, Homer, Dante, Shakespeare, **Baudelaire**, for example), the obsessional repetitions, his screams for attention, and lascivious addresses to the reader – a collection of mannerisms which resurfaces with a theory behind it in the books of **William Burroughs** – suggest that to an exceptional degree the character of his work derives from blocked sexuality. It is against this entrapment of his own flesh within words that he is fighting with such elaborate fury. Like all outsiders, Ducasse is churned by the tension between an animal, emotional yearning for acceptance, and an aristocratic and intellectual scorn of it. The first reaches out, the second twists the contact into a variety of perversions. Being a young man, he has neither detachment nor guile, and so the writing is sentimental and belligerent by turns. But Ducasse's youth gives this torture an exquisiteness which, when all the theoretical argument has fallen quiet, is his work's abiding beauty.

Further reading

Other works include: *Oeuvres complètes*, ed. Hubert Juin (1973). See: Peter Nesselroth, *Lautréamont's Imagery* (1969); Michel Philip, *Lectures de Lautréamont* (1971); Alex De Jonge, *Nightmare Culture* (1973); Claude Bouche, *Lautréamont due lieu commun à la parodie* (1974); Maurice Blanchot, *Lautréamont and Sade* (1949, trans. 2004).

DUNCAN FALLOWELL

LAWRENCE, David Herbert

1885–1930

English novelist, poet, playwright and artist

The reputation of D.H. Lawrence has suffered many vicissitudes but he is now placed among the greatest English writers. Condemned as a reactionary in the Marxizing 1930s, he became a major influence on English writing during the regionalist revival of the 1950s, largely on the strength of his third novel, *Sons and Lovers* (1913). This therapeutic venture into psychological realism, admired now for its exploration of adolescent sexuality, vivid dramatization of family conflicts (influenced by **Freud**), the scrupulous authenticity of its local colour (the mining country of Nottinghamshire and Derbyshire where Lawrence grew up), and the new intensity it imparted to the genre of the *Bildungsroman*, earned Lawrence abuse as well as praise from his contemporaries, whose repeated accusations of 'formlessness' derived, as Lawrence well knew, from class resentment and sexual prudery. Much rewritten and in many places painfully confessional, *Sons and Lovers* is the record of a personal struggle between the son and the (bourgeois) mother and (working-class) father in a style which Lawrence himself criticized almost immediately as 'hard and violent' and 'full of sensation and presentation', no doubt referring in this way to the moral over-determination of certain episodes. The novel represented, however, a major artistic and personal breakthrough for its author, being much less self-consciously literary than his two earlier novels, *The White Peacock* (1911), a technically insecure work, the main interest of which lies in the way it prefigures the key motifs of his last novel, *Lady Chatterley's Lover*, and *The Trespasser* (1912), a **Wagnerian** mythological romance with a **Dostoevskian** finale, the product of an intense artistic sensibility working with second-hand materials.

Only when Lawrence had exorcized the 'cultured' mother and come to terms with his psychological problem, which he was able to do in *Sons and Lovers* with the help of Frieda, wife of his German tutor at Nottingham University College, with whom he eloped in 1912, could he mature as man and artist. A prolific poet, influenced by **Whitman** and praised by **Pound** for his 'modernity' of image and movement, Lawrence, whose poems were very personal right up to the posthumous *Ship of Death* (1933), recorded his sense of liberation in the significantly entitled collection *Look! We Have Come Through!* (1917), his third volume of verse. This maturation coincided with the First World War and a growing sense of disintegration and disorientation in European civilization. In 1913 he began writing *The Sisters*, a work of epic proportions charting the evolution of a family generation by generation from a mythic Genesis to an Apocalypse corresponding more or less with the war. In the first part of this work, *The Rainbow* (published in 1915 and suppressed at once as immoral on sexual and political grounds), Lawrence builds up a massive cyclical interpretation of history in which the organic rhythms of the life of a farming family within a rooted community are shown responding and reacting to the pressures of industrialization, with a consequent intensification, atomization and individuation of consciousness as well as growing ideological conflicts. The emergence of a recognizably 'modern' (i.e. sharply individuated and explicit) expression of sexual desire and sexual anxiety, the search for a sexual identity, embodied above all in the novel's ultimate protagonist and heroine, Ursula, are accompanied by experimentation in the presentation of character which Lawrence, in a famous letter of 1914, compared to the techniques of the Italian Futurist poets and painters. **F.R. Leavis's** high praise of the novel helped to establish it as a classic in direct relation to the English 'great tradition'; but it has more in common with Emily Brontë than with **George Eliot** and should in any case be read in relation to its 'sequel' (the continuation of the projected *Sisters* novel) *Women in Love* (1921), in which the intricately woven 'rainbow' of history and myth is unwoven, painfully and obsessively, and discontinuous, fragmentary, imagistic 'illuminations' take the place of God's covenantal bow in the clouds as the correlatives of modern consciousness, if and when this elusive entity can be discovered. The moralized landscapes of Lawrence's earlier work have receded (there are apocalyptic visions instead), together with *The Rainbow's* apparatus of Victorian interpretation explicitly derived from Ruskin and others, though the quest for the sources of life persists, especially in the characters of Ursula (recognizably continuous with the Ursula of *The Rainbow*) and Birkin (a new, deliberately intermittent and 'unfinished' character). Through Birkin's anguished and self-contradictory scrutinizing of himself and others, and his complex theory of the two rivers, of 'life' and of 'dissolution', a 'polarization' of male and female principles is advanced as the antidote to the neurosis of the modern world.

As Keith Sagar remarked, marriage might seem to have been the end of the quest, and many critics have taken this to be the case: but the novel itself makes this reading impossible, as do those which follow. Virtually an exile, Lawrence gave his wanderings literary form in a sequence of works (novels, short stores, travel writing, poetry) which constitute a loose synthesis of genres: journalistic commentary and travelogue go arm-in-arm with political philosophy and poetic descriptive writing, while through the whole runs a bitterly satirical note, often (as in *Women in Love*) implicating living persons. Italy engendered *Aaron's Rod* (1922), Australia *Kangaroo* (1923), and Mexico *The Plumed Serpent* (1926). Seldom have geographical exploration and literary improvisation gone so closely together. In the course of this 'third' phase of his career Lawrence returned to painting, the rudiments of which he had mastered as a boy and which he often wrote about, brilliantly if idiosyncratically. He regarded his own paintings as improvisations; influenced by Cézanne, whom Lawrence greatly admired and tried to 'rescue' from English art historians in his *Introduction to These Paintings*, they celebrate, in bold colours and forms, what Lawrence liked to call the 'phallic', which might be understood as a veneration for sexual desire and sexual tenderness liberated from dictatorial will.

Lawrence's last novel, *Lady Chatterley's Lover*, unpublishable in England during Lawrence's lifetime, is wholly shaped by the 'phallic' faith of the now impotent and ill Lawrence (the rejected title of his late story 'The Man who Died', which was originally 'The Escaped Cock', makes explicit the connection between resurrection and the phallus). All three versions of the text are characterized by an intense eroticism (though Lawrence himself characteristically eschewed this word). In the later rewritings, however, the political and naturalistic elements of the earlier are restructured as myth and symbol in close touch with folklore and fairy-tale. **W.B. Yeats** spoke of the use of dialect by the aristocratic lady and her gamekeeper lover (a device related to the use of the infamous 'four-letter words') as 'a forlorn poetry uniting their solitudes, something ancient, humble, and terrible'. The national scandal of the prosecution of Penguin Books in 1960 for finally publishing the uncensored text in England was a major cultural event. *Lady Chatterley's* victory signalled a new 'permissiveness' in life and letters, and for a time Lawrence became a cult hero of sexual liberation. This misrepresents him to the extent that the context of Lawrence's phallic religion is an apocalyptic radical Puritanism (Bunyan and Blake are among his forebears), and the apocalyptic eroticism of *Lady Chatterley's Lover*, which defied literary and moral convention, is consistent with Lawrence's essentially religious veneration for the act of love as the core of what, for want of a better word, he called 'Life'.

Lawrence's output was as large as it was diverse. His short stories alone would have commanded a reputation. In recent years increased attention to his writings on art and his paintings, his plays (very effectively staged), his poetry, his very distinguished literary criticism, as well as the philosophizing he self-deprecatingly called 'pollyanalytics', has gone hand-in-hand with a new awareness of the dominant place he occupies in what is now called Modernism. The immensely rich and complex *Women in Love*, for example, now looks no less impressive and central in its way than **Joyce's** *Ulysses*.

Further reading

Other works include: Novels: *The Lost Girl* (1920); *St Mawr* (1925); and *The Virgin and the Gypsy* (1930). Short stories: *The Prussian Officer and Other Stories* (1914); *England, My England and Other Stories* (1922); *The Ladybird* (1923); *The Woman Who Rode Away and Other Stories* (1928). *The Collected Poems* (2 vols) were published in 1964. His *Letters* (ed. Aldous Huxley, 1932, and again in two vols by Harry T. Moore, 1962) are indispensable. Critical studies include: F.R. Leavis, *D.H. Lawrence: Novelist* (1955); Graham Hough, *The Dark Sun* (1956); Julian Moynahan, *The Deed of Life* (1963); H.M. Daleski, *The Forked Flame* (1965); George H. Ford, *Double Measure* (1965); Keith Sagar, *The Art of D.H. Lawrence* (1966); Colin Clarke, *River of Dissolution* (1969); Frank Kermode, *Lawrence* (1973). The standard biography is Harry T. Moore, *The Priest of Love* (1975), although the earlier three-volume *D.H. Lawrence: A Composite Biography* (1957–9) remains important. See also: J. Worthen, *D.H. Lawrence: The Early Years, 1885–1912* (1991); M. Bell, *D.H. Lawrence: Language and Being* (1992); A. Fernihough, *D.H. Lawrence: Aesthetics and Ideology* (1993); D. Ellis, *D.H. Lawrence: Dying Game, 1922–1930* (1998).

G.M. HYDE

LE CARRÉ, John (David John Moore CORNWELL)

1931–

English novelist

John le Carré's writing career is now in its fifth decade, a remarkable achievement for a writer ostensibly working in a genre (the spythriller) which is seen both as inherently secondrate and as having lost its *raison d'être* with the end of the Cold War. Where his early novels, particularly *The Spy Who Came in from the Cold* (1963), were initially seen as a reaction against the macho glitz of **Ian Fleming's** James Bond or the classless cool of Len Deighton, le Carré's subsequent work has shown a capacity to transcend genre limitations and a sheer perseverance which ally him to Eric Ambler or **Graham Greene**.

Like Greene, le Carré has always cultivated a somewhat mysterious persona. By his own account, his father was a charming con man whose rackety life and associates inspired several of the dubious figures who populate his novels, for example *A Perfect Spy* (1986). Born David Cornwell, he was educated (unhappily) at Sherborne School and later at Berne University and Lincoln College, Oxford, where he read Modern Languages. He taught at Eton before joining the Foreign Office and serving in Bonn, which provides the backdrop for *A Small Town in Germany* (1968). Le Carré – the writing pseudonym was necessary because of his simultaneous diplomatic career – is rather cagey about the extent of his involvement with the intelligence services but the presumed association has always given his books their apparent authenticity.

His first two novels, *Call for the Dead* (1961) and *A Murder of Quality* (1962), were fairly standard mysteries, but *The Spy Who Came in from the Cold* catapulted le Carré into bestsellerdom and enabled him to leave the Foreign Office and write fulltime. More importantly, *Spy* announced the arrival of a distinctive new voice in espionage fiction, one that was unheroic and unillusioned. The central figure, British agent Alec Leamas, is treated as a pawn by his own side in a complex game of betrayal and dissimulation. At ground level, in the grey world of moles and double agents, there did not seem to be that much difference between the freedomloving West and the duplicitous East.

Le Carré's most enduring and endearing character was introduced on the first page of *Call for the Dead*. George Smiley is utterly unremarkable or, more properly, unremarked – in a characteristic flourish the author describes him as travelling 'without labels in the guard's van of the social express' – and so ideally suited for undercover work. Smiley, memorably played by Alec Guinness for television, is the central figure in a trilogy of novels, most famously *Tinker, Tailor, Soldier, Spy* (1974), in which he is given the task of unmasking a double agent at the heart of the 'Circus', the author's name for the Secret Service. Smiley sifts through files, listens to the tales of superannuated spies and arrives at the truth through an unshowy display of patience. In the next two books, *The Honourable Schoolboy* (1977) and *Smiley's People* (1980), Smiley brings about the defeat and defection of his opposite number at 'Moscow Centre', a shadowy figure known as Karla. In the duel between the two there is a touch of other, more sensational fictional confrontations – one thinks of Holmes and Moriarty, or of Bond and Blofeld – although le Carré's attitude is one of weary ambivalence.

A similar contradiction marks le Carré's treatment of the British establishment, always a central factor in his work. On the one hand, there is a grudging relish for the mores of the commonroom and the club. Singlehanded, the author created a lexicon of spying terms ('control', 'lamplighters', 'scalphunters') reflecting his attraction to closed, secretive societies. On the other hand, there is his impatience with the snobbish obstructions and evasions of the intelligence hierarchy, and above all with Britain's postimperial delusions and its dependence on the USA. In a sense the greater part of le Carré's work can be interpreted as an attempt to open the reader's eyes to the 'reality [which is] a poor island with scarcely a voice that would carry across the water' (*Tinker, Tailor*). It is revealing that *Absolute Friends* (2003), a kind of résumé of the later stages of the Cold War and the beginnings of the socalled War on Terror, should climax with the betrayal and death of the central character at the hands of American special forces.

Recent events may have given an angry zest to le Carré's work but in the years which followed the crumbling of the Berlin Wall (always a key location in his work) he produced a series of novels, such as *The Night Manager* (1993) or *The Constant Gardener* (2001), which showed a switch of focus from traditional espionage to the murkier areas of business and industry. Le Carré is in for the long haul and it is always interesting to see where this author, with his global concerns and his insider's touch, will next direct his attentions.

PHILIP GOODEN

LE CORBUSIER (Charles-Édouard JEANERET)

1887–1965
Franco-Swiss architect and painter

Of all the great architects of the Modern Movement, Charles-Édouard Jeaneret (Le Corbusier) had, perhaps, the most unlikely origins. He was born in La Chaux-de-Fonds, which as he liked to point out is over 1,000 metres above sea level, the centre of the Swiss Jura watchmaking industry. His mother was a musician and his father, a stalwart of the town industry, had Jeaneret apprenticed at the age of thirteen as a watchmaker and engraver. However, he detached the retina of his left eye by drawing at night and his resulting bad eyesight (enshrined in his uniform of heavy glasses) prevented him pursuing this vocation: at the age of seventeen he gave it up to study building (in the local technical school) and to undertake some minor architectural commissions.

Early in the twentieth century he set out on a series of apparently aimless but serendipitous tours: to Budapest, Vienna and Berlin, and later to Greece and Turkey, where the architecture profoundly impressed him. In Vienna and Berlin, his *wanderlust* paid off when he found work with the Vienna Werkstätte and in Peter Behrens's office, where Ludwig Mies **van der Rohe** and **Walter Gropius** were his contemporaries.

In between these two trips he worked in Paris with that great pioneer in concrete, the engineer-contractor and family friend Auguste Perret, and then in northern France designing houses, sluice-gates and other waterway architecture for the local Waterways Board. Jeaneret was always rather proud of his lack of conventional architectural training, and, in later years, was one of the only three 'unqualified' architects licensed to practise in France.

In 1919 he moved to Paris, where he lived the rest of his life, and set up a small office with his cousin, Pierre Jeaneret, who had undergone a more conventional architectural training. Perret introduced him to **Fernand Léger** and Amedée Ozenfant and the transformation from Jeaneret to Le Corbusier had begun. The name 'Le Corbusier' Jeaneret chose under the direction of Ozenfant to distinguish clearly his new architectural self from the old. It refers to an annual task undertaken in the Middle Ages by the Jeaneret family of cleaning the crows' nests out of the local church steeple, probably their only previous architectural connection. With its adoption came a rigorously maintained lifestyle (painting and 'visual researches' before lunch, then a role change to the besuited, bespectacled after-lunch architect), and a complete change in his persona, for before this time he had never painted, and his architecture had generally been of little interest with the exception of the Dom-Ino concrete housing system (1914), where six columns, arranged as on a domino tile, support flat concrete slabs, thus allowing a special freedom of spatial division.

On Le Corbusier the painter and visual artist (as he now was), Léger's work left a profound mark. Le Corbusier painted, and later sculpted and designed murals and tapestries, within the 'Purist' style of post-Cubism, broadening his approach and using brighter, plainer colours and strong, almost crude forms, sometimes with a particularly symbolic intention (e.g. his frequent use of the open hand). His painting is not particularly significant except in regard to his architecture. Indeed, it is almost as though his paintings, failing to live in two dimensions, take on life and vitality in the three-dimensional world of the built form, where the concrete realization of the crude forms and bright colours could flourish as massive monuments.

Le Corbusier's work as an architect may be divided into three categories: his building; his town-planning projects; and his theorizing. One of the earliest and clearest theoretical statements he made of his intentions was in a manifesto he composed with his partner-cousin (who is usually, and quite inexplicably, neglected) in 1926, and called *Almanach de l'architecture moderne* (translated as *Almanac of Modern Architecture*). In this, they call for five 'principles' in the new architecture: free supports, that is to say a column structure which lifts the building off the ground ('pilotis'); roof gardens, i.e. using the new flat roof as a resource and a viewing platform; a free plan (as in the Dom-Ino house, where the walls may move freely within the space without being confined by the structure); horizontal windows, which 'express' the non-structural character of the external walls; and the free design of the façades of the building. (These five principles became Le Corbusier's operations manual and, together with his early experience of concrete and industrial buildings, essentially account for his architecture.) The five principles, and Le Corbusier's other theoretical works of the 1920s – he also wrote several other manifesto-type statements, especially in the magazine *L'Esprit nouveau*, and many justifications of his ideas and buildings – constituted a revolutionary architectural statement, a realization in architecture of a new aesthetic of particular honesty and utility which had its origin in the fragmented picture plane of the 'Cubists', and the novel consequent interpretation of the concept of transparency and thus spatial definition. Its effect was profound: it was almost as though Le Corbusier had single-handedly invented the Modern Movement – particularly that part of it we now call the Heroic Period of the International Style – and his importance and influence were enormous. Indeed, it was through his work that the foundation of the Congrès Internationaux d'Architectes Modernes (CIAM), the formative architectural association of the century, came about, in which internationalist group of architects Le Corbusier was the energetic and highly esteemed flag-bearer.

He also wrote several books, the earlier statements of architectural theory being very polemical, as in *Towards a New Architecture* (*Vers une architecture*, 1923, trans. 1946), which espouses the 'Machine Aesthetic', and *When the Cathedrals were White* (*Quand les cathédrales étaient blanches*, 1937, trans. 1947). In later years, his theorizing became somewhat more ascetic and less polemical, culminating in the publication of *The Modulor* (*Le Modulor*, 1949, trans. 1954), an account of his proportional system. This book had a wide influence among architects in the 1950s, but was founded on a most peculiar view of mathematics and absolute size standards. Nevertheless, its Fibonacci series of related lengths did provide variety in the somewhat sterile environment of the post-war pre-fab.

His building work can be assembled in four groups: the first consists of individual villas which he built for rich clients and in which he could explore some of the spatial freedom demanded in the *Almanach*, using freestanding walls and double volume spaces, and experimenting with roof gardens, an exploration that gave play to his machine aesthetic and which generated his famous aphorism 'A House is a Machine for living in'. (His meaning of Machine was more Platonic xthan ours, and his comment is mainly about aesthetics.) Of these, the villas Vaucresson (about which he said, 'Until the house at Vaucresson, he [i.e. Le Corbusier] had no creative ambitions of any kind'), La Roche, Stein and Savoye (now a French national monument), all built in the 1920s, are the most interesting. For these houses he also designed his famous furniture, some of it still in production.

The second group, social housing, actively involved Le Corbusier for most of his lifespan. Here he tried to express his vision of the contemporary city and lifestyle of what **Reyner Banham** has called the 'First Machine Age'. Essentially he developed the large housing block, containing the street in the sky and the vertical street. These blocks were developed from about 1930, starting with the Pavillon Suisse in Paris and including

his Salvation Army building, finding their most exact form in the 'Unité d'Habitation' built in Marseilles and duplicated elsewhere. These schemes almost all had strong town-planning overtones.

The third group includes the projects in what may be thought of as urban compositions (as opposed to town-planning). Le Corbusier had a megalomaniac streak, which not only led to a massive self-righteousness but let him enjoy designing the largest of urban buildings. The first of these, in the 1920s, was the project for the League of Nations which, he tells us, was the competition jury's preferred scheme but was disqualified because it was not drawn in Indian ink. He followed this with the (unbuilt) Palace of Soviets which included an auditorium for 14,000, which he claimed rather simplistically 'was acoustically faultless (tested by light-waves)'. Other schemes include a sports stadium project, the Ministry of Education in Rio de Janeiro, and the initial planning of the United Nations building in New York: but the most celebrated is the new provincial capital Chandigarh in the Punjab, where Le Corbusier designed and built the whole administrative and juridical complex around a vast pool of water.

The final aspect of his building is a number of extremely individualistic one-off jobs. The most impressive of these (and they are superb) are the pilgrimage church at Ronchamp in the Vosges mountains, noted for its scrolled roof and windows puncturing the massive walls; the Dominican Training Monastery at La Tourette with its randomly articulated façade; and the Philips Pavilion built for the Brussels World Fair, the home of one of the world's first 'total art' shows. (These last two were largely designed by **Iannis Xenakis**, better known as a composer for his stochastic music.)

One cannot conclude an account of Le Corbusier without discussing his town-planning projects. It was largely he who put forward and developed the ideas adopted by CIAM for the contemporary city. His was the driving force behind the vision of the vast separated blocks in the Elysian Fields that was the modernist's dream. These ideas he developed through various projects, for 'La Ville contemporaine' – the initial design as an isolated new town for three million people – to proposed applications involving large-scale rebuilding of several distinguished towns, including Paris (the Plan Voisin), Stockholm and Barcelona. None of these schemes was built, much to his chagrin, for they aroused great public anger; but they had an enormous influence on architects and planners and their effects can be seen in the vandalized tower blocks situated in seas of asphalt that are all too familiar nowadays. However, it is hardly fair to Le Corbusier to judge his ideas on these realizations, for they are not only unpleasant and extraordinarily bad buildings, they are also appallingly executed travesties of his ideas. Whether such ideas, attacked by some as megalomaniac and totalitarian, could ever work, we are unlikely now to find out.

Le Corbusier built himself a pair of small 'primitive huts' on the Mediterranean coast where he went for privacy and contemplation. It was while there, swimming, in 1965 that he had a heart attack and drowned. He was married but had no children.

Further reading

See: C. Jencks, *Le Corbusier and the Tragic View of Architecture* (1973); C. Blake, *Le Corbusier* (1964); Carol Palazzolo and Riccardo Vio (eds) *In the Footsteps of Le Corbusier* (1991). W. Boesiger, *Le Corbusier* (1999) is an eight-volume chronological record of Le Corbusier's work.

RANULPH GLANVILLE AND SAM STEVENS

LE FANU, Joseph Thomas Sheridan

1814–73

Irish novelist

Brought up in a County Limerick parsonage during a period of bitter agrarian unrest, Le Fanu's education at Dublin University (Trinity College) brought him in contact with dissident Tories who expressed themselves in cultural terms through the *Dublin University Magazine* and in political terms through such groups as the Irish Metropolitan Conservative Association. By 1840 he was contributing actively to both, and by 1875 he had published his first novel, *The Cock and Anchor*, in which the influence of romantic nationalism is cautiously admitted. The rebellion of 1848, however, alarmed Le Fanu, and his story of that year 'Richard Marston' is a grim tale of self-betrayal and retribution.

Political reverses and marital unhappiness worked to keep Le Fanu's literary talents safely in the channels of anonymous journalism until 1863, when he resumed novel-writing with *The House by the Church-yard*. *Wylder's Hand* and *Uncle Silas*, the best of his so-called 'sensation' novels, followed in 1864. He continued to publish roughly a novel a year, together with some rather better tales, until his death. Much of this work appeared in the *Dublin University Magazine* which he owned and edited between 1861 and 1869.

The recurring theme of Le Fanu's work is guilt, usually portrayed in the repetition of past offences in the present. *Wylder's Hand* appears to offer a more harmonious vision of man, society and history, but its optimism is entirely cancelled in *Uncle Silas* where a tightly knit symmetrical structure extends the predestined fates of the characters virtually to a metaphysical level – Le Fanu's use of Swedenborgian symbolism anticipates **W.B. Yeats** in this respect. Though the novels from 1864 onwards are set in contemporary England, the real locus of energy is the Irish eighteenth century, the legacy of that proud Protestant hegemony being visited upon latter-day villain-victims. In the tales and short stories, Le Fanu effectively employs supernatural conventions to explore similar themes.

Pressed for money in a society where the middle class felt obliged to play the part of a dowdy aristocracy, Le Fanu wrote too much and on uncongenial terms. His work is very uneven, and with the exception of *Checkmate* (1871) none of the late novels deserves attention. The tales, however, are almost all marked in their style by an effective blend of tension and confidence: the most important collections are *Chronicles of Golden Friars* (1871) and *In a Glass Darkly* (1872), together with some of the posthumously gathered *Purcell Papers* (1880).

Seen as precursor to the Anglo-Irish Revivalists, Sheridan Le Fanu must be ranked as their inferior. Yet his subversive challenge to the myth of a noble 'protestant ascendancy' in the Augustan Age had its influence on Yeats, while *The House by the Church-yard* was incorporated into the referential structure of **Joyce's** *Finnegans Wake*.

Further reading

Uncle Silas is available in an annotated edition with an introduction by W.J. McCormack (1981). The short stories and tales have been comprehensively treated in two collections edited by E.F. Bleiler, *Best Ghost Stories* (1964) and *Ghost Stories and Mysteries* (1975). The standard biography is W.J. McCormack, *Sheridan Le Fanu and Victorian Ireland* (1980). See also: Michael H. Begnal, *Joseph Sheridan Le Fanu* (1981).

W.J. MCCORMACK

LEACH, (Sir) Edmund Ronald

1910–89

English anthropologist

Edmund Leach was born in 1910 and educated at Marlborough and at Cambridge, where he read engineering. He worked briefly in China, then returned to England to study anthropology under **Malinowski** at the London School of Economics. A short field-study in Kurdistan in 1938 resulted in a slight monograph which, however, foreshadowed his concern with the constancy of change and flux. In 1939 he travelled to Burma to study the Kachin. Caught up in the war, he served with Kachin irregulars until 1945. His field notes were lost, but combining his field experiences with the study of secondary sources he wrote a doctoral thesis, later published in revised form as *Political Systems of Highland Burma* (1954), by common consent

his masterpiece. A later field-study in Sri Lanka provided the basis for a second major study, *Pul Eliya* (1961). At some stage in the 1950s Leach came under the influence of **Lévi-Strauss's** work (which incidentally provided a new model of Kachin social organization). He was one of the first and perhaps the most important critics and interpreters of the new structuralist movement, contributing important analyses in his own right.

Leach always enjoyed challenge and controversy, and tried, perhaps not altogether successfully, to shock the British bourgeoisie in his pro-youth, pro-machine and anti-God Reith lectures, *A Runaway World?* (1968). A serious atheist, he was for some time president of the Humanist Association. His polemical and critical posture within the discipline was a source of constant stimulation and controversy, and can in part be recaptured through a reading of his collection of essays, *Rethinking Anthropology* (1961).

Leach held teaching positions at the LSE (1947–53) and Cambridge (1953–78), where he became Provost of King's College and was responsible for the admission of women and the abolition of High Table. In 1972 he was created Professor by personal title and elected to the British Academy, and in 1975 he was knighted.

Leach's two major monographs, on the Kachin and on the Sinhalese village he calls 'Pul Eliya', were presented as challenges to the sociological mood of British social anthropology represented by **Radcliffe-Brown** and his followers. Leach felt that they took too positivistic and static a view of the shifting and unsystematic flow of social relations, and too mechanistic a view of ritual and ideology. Social order was rooted in the ecological realities, which endured and imposed themselves upon the actors; and in the ideological or ritual language in which the actors struggled to make sense of whatever actual arrangements they were constrained to form with one another. The actors, constrained by material factors but not by ritual or ideology, competitively pursued their basic interests, these being variously and never closely defined. The language of ritual permitted them to explain themselves to themselves.

Developing these ideas partly as a series of polemics against the Radcliffe-Brown school of thought, Leach was not always consistent or even entirely coherent as a theorist; but he was usually suggestive, original and stimulating. The analysis of the interplay of lions and foxes, *gumlao* and *gumsa*, anarchy and state, among the Kachin has proved to have repercussions for our understanding of a whole series of political societies. A related essay on the political implications of Kachin marriage provided a vital rider to Lévi-Strauss's alliance theory and a model for numerous analyses by others.

In his later work Leach was dominantly concerned with explaining, criticizing and adapting Lévi-Strauss's theories of classification and of myth. Despite Lévi-Strauss's own methodological reservations, Leach produced several analyses of biblical episodes which have been influential. Never an easy follower, Leach and Lévi-Strauss were often critical of each other; but despite various disclaimers, Leach became inappropriately generally labelled a structuralist.

This protean, energetic and idealistic man increasingly came to dominate British social anthropology in the 1970s, becoming both intellectually and institutionally recognized as the leader of the profession. His outstanding students include such important senior figures as Fredrik Barth, Nur Yalman and S.J. Tambiah, as well as several of the ablest younger anthropologists.

Further reading

See: *Genesis as Myth* (1970); his characteristically impatient *Lévi-Strauss* (1970); and *Culture and Communication* (1976) which provides an introduction to structuralist analysis in social anthropology. A discussion of his career and contribution is to be found in Adam Kuper, *Anthropologists and Anthropology* (1975); Stanley J. Tambiah, *Edmund Leach: An Anthropological Life* (2002).

ADAM KUPER

LEAN, (Sir) David
1908–91
English film director

David Lean made only fifteen films as sole director, but they include a half-dozen that deserve inclusion in any history of the cinema as an expressive art form. One of the few British filmmakers to realize the potential of film as both a narrative and a visual medium, Lean was responsible for some of the most memorable moments in cinema history: the poignant railway-station farewell of *Brief Encounter* (1945), the rain-lashed Gothic orphanage that opens *Oliver Twist* (1948), the parched desert panoramas of *Lawrence of Arabia* (1962) and the snowy vistas of revolutionary Russia in *Doctor Zhivago* (1965). Yet for all his accomplishments, Lean has been criticized for an obsessive perfectionism that meant his oeuvre was small in comparison with those of Britain's other two greatest film talents, **Alfred Hitchcock** and Michael Powell.

Lean was born in South Croydon, London, the son of staunchly Quaker parents whose disapproval of picture houses as 'dens of vice' did nothing to dampen his youthful ardour for the cinema. He followed the usual apprenticeship for a budding filmmaker by working his way up through the British studio system of the 1930s from tea-boy, messenger and clapper-loader to editor. It was the combination of his technical proficiency and his intuitive understanding of film narration that by the outbreak of the Second World War had earned for Lean the reputation as the best editor in the industry. Having turned down opportunities to direct supporting features, Lean's entry into direction came in 1941 when **Noël Coward** approached him to act as co-director of Coward's patriotic naval flag-waver *In Which We Serve* (1942). The success of this film marked the beginning of a four-picture collaboration between Lean and Coward. *Blithe Spirit* (1945) was a lightweight supernatural fantasy in the style of René Clair, but it was Lean's sensitive direction of *This Happy Breed* (1944) and *Brief Encounter* that demonstrated his ability both to represent realistic social environments on screen and to draw moving, understated performances from his actors.

Lean came to prominence at a time of unprecedented artistic creativity and cultural visibility for British cinema. *This Happy Breed* and *Brief Encounter*, especially, were prominent examples of what contemporary critics referred to as 'the quality film', praised for the realism and emotional restraint that differentiated them from the tinselled melodramas of Hollywood. This was a time when a genuinely British national cinema can be seen to have emerged and Lean was one of the directors whose films were, to quote Roger Manvell, 'bound to the national life of Britain'.

It was also a time when the Rank Organization was investing heavily in films that were the antithesis of either economic or cultural conservatism. Lean's two **Dickens** adaptations were part of an ambitious attempt by Rank to open up the American market for British films, though in the event *Oliver Twist* was released in a truncated version in the United States due to perceived anti-Semitism in its characterization of Fagin. Nevertheless, these two films represent probably the peak of Lean's visual powers and narrative skill. The opening sequence of *Great Expectations* (1946) on the Essex marshes, for instance, includes a bravura example of suspenseful editing that owes much to the montage principles of **Sergei Eisenstein**.

Lean's critical standing declined in the 1950s, when his films, like so many products of the British film industry during that period, were more workmanlike than artistic. His first colour film, the romantic drama *Summertime* (1955), shot on location in Italy, indicated that Lean was ready to leave the drab austerity of British cinema behind. It was the acclaimed prisoner-of-war drama *The Bridge on the River Kwai* (1957) that restored Lean's reputation (he won the first of his two Academy Awards for Best Director) and set him on the path of expensive, visually sumptuous epics. *Kwai*'s narrative of intense psychological drama against the background of

war was repeated to even greater effect in *Lawrence of Arabia*, garnering Lean's second Academy Award, while his adaptation of **Boris Pasternak's** *Doctor Zhivago* was the biggest box-office success of his career.

Lean's meticulous working methods meant that the periods between his films became longer. The inevitable critical backlash came with *Ryan's Daughter* (1970), an over-long love story set during the Irish Uprising of 1916, though its reputation as a sincerely acted pastoral drama has since improved. It was fourteen years until Lean directed his next, and last, film, a literate and well-received adaptation of **E.M. Forster's** *A Passage to India* (1985). Lean was honoured in his later years by a knighthood (1984) and by the American Film Institute's Lifetime Achievement Award (1990). At the time of his death in 1991 he was working on an unrealized film of **Joseph Conrad's** *Nostromo*.

The career of David Lean highlights issues that are central to any assessment of film as an art form rather than a mere entertainment medium. That, for most of his career, he enjoyed relative creative autonomy free from the philistinism of studio executives would seem to lend substance to the *auteur* theory which sees the history of film in terms of its visionary directors. Certainly Lean experienced little of the disruption that blighted **Orson Welles's** career. That so many of his most successful films, however, were literary adaptations (Coward, Dickens, Pasternak, Forster) might call into question the autonomy of film from other art forms. Lean always had a strong visual sense, though his later films were criticized for their overly pictorialist style and languorous pace. Nevertheless, as a director whose films won both critical and popular acclaim, Lean deserves to be regarded as one of cinema's outstanding talents.

Further reading

Other works include: *The Passionate Friends* (1949), *Madeleine* (1950), *The Sound Barrier* (1952) and *Hobson's Choice* (1954). See: Roger Manvell, *Film*

(1946); Alain Silver and James Ursini, *David Lean and His Films* (1974; rev. 1991); and Kevin Brownlow, *David Lean: A Biography* (1996).

JAMES CHAPMAN

LEAR, Edward

1812–88

English draughtsman, illustrator, watercolourist, nonsense-writer

Lear's claim that his grandfather was Danish, and spelled his name Lør, is probably a piece of fanciful embroidery. On the other hand, his claim to remember (aged three and wrapped in a blanket) the illuminations that celebrated the victory of Waterloo may not be simply the work of an exceptionally vivid imagination. However, the fact that he was the twentieth child of Anne and Jeremiah Lear is not open to question, nor the fact that his general perception of himself was both acute and wryly self-deprecatory:

> How pleasant to know Mr. Lear!
> Who has written such volumes of stuff:
> Some think him ill-tempered and queer,
> But a few think him pleasant enough.
> His mind is concrete and fastidious,
> His nose is remarkably big;
> His visage is more or less hideous,
> His beard it resembles a wig.

If Lear was not endowed with good looks or good health (he suffered all his life from asthma, bronchitis and epilepsy), he had an extraordinary gift for making and keeping friends. But his congenial humanity seems to have excluded any passionate sexual love.

His affections concentrated on a number of men he admired, and on his cat Foss, with whom he shared seventeen years of faithful companionship. With children, in his happiest role of 'Adopty Duncle', he was at untrammelled ease – the endearing, slightly dotty, conspiratorial inventor of fantasy words and worlds, of amazing alphabets, limericks, puns and outrageous recipes.

The limerick was not Lear's original invention, but his impromptu private entertainments for children developed the form for a popular audience (his first *Book of Nonsense*, 1846, went into thirty editions during his lifetime), and also established it as a literary style.

From the age of eighteen, however, when he earned himself a reputation as an ornithological draughtsman, Lear's chosen career was that of artist. His industry was indefatigable, but his sales were occasional. Lear was no businessman, and throughout his life depended on private patronage. As a topographical watercolourist in perpetual pursuit of the picturesque, his nomadic travels took him from the comparatively civilized delights of the Mediterranean to more intrepid romantic views in Egypt, Albania, the Near East and, at the age of sixty, on a physically debilitating trip to India and Ceylon. This last year-long journey was undertaken at the invitation of the then viceroy, Lord Northbrook, in exchange for one or two decorative scenes!

For the last thirty-five years of his life he nursed a project that would compliment and complement his friend **Tennyson's** lyric 'genius for the perception of the beautiful in landscape'. But the planned series of 200 line and colour illustrations was never completed, and Tennyson did not particularly like what he saw.

Lear suffered more than his fair share of disappointments, but was able to transform his sense of gloom and isolation into triumphant comic absurdity in his writing. Sometimes the words remain uncompromisingly unintelligible, as in a letter to a friend which begins: 'Thrippy Pilliwinx-Inkly Tinksy pooblebookle abblesquabs? Flosky? beebul trimble flosky!'

But when sounds are made sense, as with his verse creations of creatures like the Quangle Wangle, the Jumblies, the Pobble and the Dong with a Luminous Nose, Lear combines surreal comedy with a haunting, underlying personal sadness. In these verses, a mix of quirky and commonplace vocabulary with hypnotic rhythms produce what Maurice

Baring has praised extravagantly as 'architectonic music'. An inspired accompaniment was provided by the caricature 'doodles'. All the precise, painstaking draughtsmanship of his 'Landskip' work was jettisoned in favour of more crude, but 'spontegetatinous' imaginative design.

In his voluminous journals, Lear never refers to his comic writing and drawing. But of his landscapes he records every detail of progress, subjects, hours worked, prices, frames, exhibitions and even the comments of friends. Lear's place in the English watercolour school may be assured, but his immortality and true originality endure in his Nonsense.

Further reading

Other works include: *Journals of a Landscape Painter in Albania, etc.* (1851); *Journals of a Landscape Painter in Southern Calabria, etc.* (1852); *Journal of a Landscape Painter in Corsica* (1870); *Nonsense Songs, Stories, Botany and Alphabets* (1871); *More Nonsense, Pictures, Rhymes, Botany, etc.* (1872); *Laughable Lyrics* (1877). See: Angus Davidson, *Edward Lear: Landscape Painter and Nonsense Poet* (1938); Vivien Noakes, *Edward Lear: The Life of a Wanderer* (1968); John Lehmann, *Edward Lear and His World* (1977); V. Noakes (ed.) *Selected Letters* (1988); P. Levi, *Edward Lear* (1995).

PAUL SIDEY

LEARY, Timothy

1920–96

US cult figure

Born in Springfield, Massachusetts, Leary rejected the parental insistence of being trained at West Point military academy, studied psychology in the University of California at Berkeley, served in an army hospital in the Second World War, became assistant professor of psychology at the San Francisco School of Medicine, and finally lectured in psychology at Harvard University. While he was working in the Center for Research in Personality, Harvard sacked him in 1963; the faculty discovered he had

become the leader of a group of researchers and volunteers working with psilocybin, a chemical derived from a mushroom sacred for many centuries to certain Amerindians. Leary had taken the mushroom at the behest of a University of New Mexico scientist at Cuernavaca in 1960, and the experience changed his attitudes towards consciousness and religion. Then he began to concentrate research on the uses of lysergic acid (LSD), and other drugs, towards forms of expanded consciousness, psychedelic experience and religious illumination.

During the 1960s Leary became one of the most powerful influences on American youth, particularly those of the campuses deeply engaged in critical action against the official imperial and domestic wars into which they had grown up. Leary's psychedelic messianism became part of American cultic life, contributing strongly to the breaking up of fixed inherited patterns of behaviour. In the mid-1960s, the LSD 'trip' was featured in every newspaper and magazine. In 1963, *Esquire* ran an article on the work of Leary and Richard Alpert at Harvard, quoting the former's beliefs that drugs provided the consumer with 'transcendence of space–time, of subject–object relations, and the ego or identity'; they were thought to be 'mental vitamins, or mental health foods'. The first issue of the *Psychedelic Review*, organ of the International Foundation for Internal Freedom, appeared the same year, and Leary's Center was investigated by the Food and Drug Administration. *Playboy* magazine published a panel discussion on the issues, whose members included **William Burroughs**, Leslie Fiedler, Alan Watts and Harry J. Anslinger, for thirty-three years commissioner of the Bureau of Narcotics. By 1966, two thousand people could pack a New York theatre for Leary's 'Psychedelic Celebration No. 1', presented by the League for Spiritual Discovery. At the same time Leary's centre at Millbank, New York, was raided. Subsequent charges, however, were dismissed. In his 'Death of the Mind Service', Leary preached 'the biochemistry' of the body bringing about 'a state of grace', and followed this up with 'The Reincarnation of Jesus Christ' and an 'LSD Mass', a performance in which he proclaimed, 'I am here to lead the broken-hearted', and so on, in Christ-like style. The same year he told a Senate subcommittee on juvenile delinquency that the use of LSD had run out of control and that a third of the nation's college students were experimenting with it. His slogan 'Turn On. Tune In. Drop Out' (in an article syndicated by a widely distributed underground press organization) appeared everywhere – he intended good advice: 'Do not routinely and blindly expose yourself to stupor-producing, symbol-addicting environments.'

In 1968, the state declared him 'a menace to the community'. A year later he said a kind of farewell at the Village Gate Theatre in New York, backed by **Allen Ginsberg** and Paul Krassner, among others. In 1970 Leary was sentenced to ten years' imprisonment (Lawrence Ferlinghetti's City Lights press published his 'Memorandum' for bail), but escaped through the Weatherman Underground, and issued a statement from hiding calling on Americans to resist the Third World War waged by the government against its own people (he had been arrested an estimated fourteen times on drug charges). In 1971 his *Jail Notes* appeared with a preface by Ginsberg excoriating both the narcotics laws and Harvard University.

Leary next turned up in Beirut in 1970, hoping to contact Al Fatah, and then emerged in Algiers in 1971, hoping to ally with **Eldridge Cleaver** there, but the Black Panther leader arrested him as a dangerous influence on the black revolt – 'we cannot afford to jeopardize our work toward revolution in Babylon', and in any case Leary's mind 'has been blown by acid'. In 1973, after a spell in Switzerland and Afghanistan, Leary was back in jail in Los Angeles.

His cult status is best described by Ginsberg: 'a hero of American consciousness'. He began as a sophisticated academician, he encountered discoveries in his field which confounded him and his own technology, he pursued his studies where attention commanded, he arrived beyond the boundaries of public knowledge.' This is indeed the basis of his messianic politics, extended in jail to the necessity for 'worldwide ecological religious warfare'. *High Priest* (1968) speaks of the need to break fixed, trained motivation, attitude and preconception by transformation in personal consciousness. The book is a record of 'a psychedelic scholar-politician', a contribution to 'the psychedelic revolution ... a religious renaissance of the young', and he includes important meetings with **Charles Olson** and **Arthur Koestler**, Ginsberg and **Burroughs**, and other highly influential figures. The change came for him in 1961 when, under acid, he had to confront the stereotypical pointlessness of his family's life, and then, under an overdose, to realize the void in his own life and his own responsibility for change. He concluded later that 'psychedelic research is experimental philosophy, empirical metaphysics, visionary science ... The discovery of LSD is as important to philosophy and psychology and religion as the discovery of the microscope was to biology.' In 1962, after a trip in a Vedānta *ashram* in Boston, he began 'the slow invisible process of becoming a guru, a holy man'. The Harvard project became 'an ontological conspiracy' – 'the course of social conflict is usually neurological. The cure is biochemical.' Such is his basis for 'the religious, scientific quest', 'the great plan', through which we are to find courage to recognize new forms of energy (*The Politics of Ecstasy*, 1969). The notorious 'generation gap' is in fact 'an evolutionary lurch ... a species mutation'. The LSD lesson was to mean you have to re-enact the evolutionary drama, 'go through the *whole* sequence yourself'. Leary admitted to over three hundred acid trips in order to 'suspend' social conditioning (but, he adds, Herman Kahn had taken acid, so that there is no guarantee of any radical identity change for the better ...). Leary's faith lay with the young: 'No one over the age of fifty should be allowed to vote' and 'voting should be by the extended family . . . We must return – advance to – the tribal unit of society.' The prelude to a better society is to be found in 'the retracing of genetic memories back down through the myriad, multi-webbed fabric of RNA-DNA memories'. Freedom from symbol systems addiction comes through 'cellular wisdom'. Leary's advice to the youthful reformer is 'become your own priest . . . your own doctor . . . your own researcher on consciousness', and to 'love God and every living creature as thyself'. In addition, he claimed, in the famous *Playboy* interview (reprinted in *The Politics of Ecstasy*), that 'LSD is the most powerful aphrodisiac ever discovered by man' – a highly disputable assertion, apparently. He totally denied that LSD led to any harmful effects on the body–mind system – again a disputed claim. Reviewing both these books in the *New York Times Book Review* in 1969, Rollo May, the American psychotherapist, observed that it was not surprising that hallucinogenic drugs should appeal to a younger generation 'beset with malaise and apathy'; and 'when the prospect of discovering God is combined with the joy of escape that drugs promise, you have a power whose attraction is great indeed'. May concludes that while drugs do 'clear away debris, the false faiths, the conventional hypocrisy', you still have to 'move on to something more complete'. Leary himself seems never to have discovered that condition beyond the *ashram*.

Leary's last two decades before his death of prostate cancer at his Beverley Hills home were eventful in another way: he became a yet more prolific writer and lecturer. After arrest in Afghanistan in 1973, and parole after three years, the books poured from him, prominent among them *What Does Woman Want?* (1976), *Exo-Psychology* (1977), *The Game of Life* (1979), his detailed and illuminating autobiography *Flashbacks* (1983), *Chaos and Cyber-Culture* (1994) in which his preoccupation with death as integral to life is explored, and a run of posthumous collected work to include *Design for Dying* (1997) and *The Delicious Grace of Moving One's Hand: The Collected Sex Writings* (1998). Throughout this period he flirted with the Libertarian Party; worked a highly lucrative lecture circuit with G. Gordon Liddy, the Watergate burglar who had once arrested him in Texas; ran a Multimedia Show called *How to Operate Your Brain*; and even made his own dying into a cyber-performance in which his last moments were telecast. As the figure Richard Nixon once called 'the most dangerous man in America' and **Ken Kesey**, not unironically, a 'psychedelic wiseman', he observed of his cancer, 'I am looking forward to the most fascinating experience in life, which is dying.' Vintagely loved and hated, the guru and the ogre, yet always a true counter-culture name, it may be appropriate that his very last words were 'Why not?'

Further reading

See: Leary, with R. Metzner and R. Alpert, *The Psychedelic Experience* (1964); Leary, G.M. Weil and R. Metzner (eds) *The Psychedelic Reader* (1965); Leary, *Psychedelic Prayers* (1966).

ERIC MOTTRAM
(REVISED AND UPDATED BY A. ROBERT LEE)

LEAVIS, Frank Raymond
1895–1979
English critic

Cambridge-born literary critic, whose lectures, seminars and tutorials in the Cambridge English School, combined with a stream of books and articles, especially articles in the periodical *Scrutiny* which he and his wife Q.D. Leavis conducted (1932–53), not only put Cambridge English studies on the map (after William Empson left for the Orient and I.A. Richards for Harvard, Leavis *was*, in most people's eyes, Cambridge English), but also dominantly influenced the assumptions and aims of teachers, especially schoolteachers of English literature, in the middle years of the century. Personally extremely kind, Leavis was nonetheless always tough and frequently venomous in the conduct of his critical discourse. Like **Matthew Arnold** he had a sharp sense of the power and pervasiveness of the enemy. The opposition was entrenched in the narrow-minded mediocrity of some senior members of the Cambridge English Faculty (who went on black-balling his wife and only slowly and grudgingly let him into a permanent university post), in the civilized glibnesses of Oxford literary criticism represented most annoyingly by the aristocratic gentilities of Lord David Cecil, in the entire London literary world as represented in and about Bloomsbury and the organs of British cultural exchange (the *Times Literary Supplement*, the BBC, the *New Statesman*, serious Sunday newspapers) and in the steady march of a technological culture. The old sore tone, the ancient grudges, did tend to rankle on long after many of Leavis's more personal struggles had been won – when practically no academic pulpit was closed to him (he became Reader in Cambridge, was 1967 Clark Lecturer at Cambridge, became a Professor at York, was frequently invited to Oxford), when the periodicals he derided would have snapped up even his most unconsidered trifles, when youthful audiences were only bemused by still sharp sneers at Professor E.M.W. Tillyard or Kingsley Martin, once editor of the *New Statesman*. But then, Leavis and his wife *had* early suffered real academic ostracism; the piano-seller's son had had a long struggle to get his voice heard over the suaver, though intellectually feebler, tones of the privileged members of the converging intellectual and social establishments; the 'persecution mania' of which he was often accused was rooted in *real* persecution when in the mid-1920s he was pursued by the Cambridge police, the Public Prosecutor and (Leavis thought) the Home Secretary himself, for challenging the then ban on **Joyce's** *Ulysses* by discussing it in his lectures. And, of course, what Leavis called 'technologico-Benthamite' industrial civilization showed no signs of abating. All the more reason, then, for the unrelenting verbal sharpness of eighteenth-century satire (some

of Leavis's best essays were on Swift and Pope) and the steady moral determination of Dr Johnson (one of Leavis's most kept-up heroes). 'I believe,' Leavis quotes **Henry James** as saying (it's an epigraph to one of Leavis's collections of *Scrutiny* essays, *The Common Pursuit*, 1952),

> only in absolutely independent, individual and lonely virtue, and in the serenely unsociable (or if need be at a pinch sulky and sullen) practice of the same; the observation of a lifetime having convinced me that no fruit ripens but under that temporarily graceless vigour.

Leavis came to feel increasingly close, in fact, to William Blake (see *Nor Shall My Sword: Discourses on Pluralism, Compassion and Social Hope*, 1972).

The promptings and sources of Leavis's earliest critical work are not particularly original ones. The strength, though, of his early signposting essays in *New Bearings in English Poetry: A Study of the Contemporary Situation* (1932) and *Revaluation* (1936) lies in the vigour with which he adapts and promotes **T.S. Eliot's** classical position on poetry. And, very shortly, Leavis was to be found pursuing literary quality where Eliot (and Practical Criticism) had been reluctant to venture – in the realm of the novel. It is a major part of Leavis's distinction as a critic that he added, so to speak, Henry James to Arnold and T.S. Eliot, and was arguing for the central moral and social importance of great fiction while much of literary criticism was still stuck fast in increasingly routine and often decreasingly important 'Practical Critical' exegeses of poems. *The Great Tradition: George Eliot, Henry James, Joseph Conrad* (1948) was followed by *D.H. Lawrence: Novelist* (1955: this represented a severe departure from Eliot's views), by *Dickens the Novelist* (with Q.D. Leavis, 1970: a departure, in fact, from the Leavises' earlier, shared reluctance over **Dickens's** greatness), and by *Thought, Words and Creativity: Art and Thought in Lawrence* (1976).

The novel, and some novelists in particular – there was a steadily mounting concentration on the earlier works of **D.H. Lawrence** – were represented as performing literature's chief function: conveying a sense of enriching 'life', of moral seriousness, of personal maturity; in short of virtue, weighed with a modern puritanism's determination. Just as many writers, lost leaders, fell from grace (Eliot and **Auden** to name no others), so many novelists were considered too nasty and/or trifling ever to have made the grade. Lofty critical standards were justified as necessary, however, because the moral education of readers, and so the only hope of resisting the swamping onrush of technology, were at stake. To be sure, from his pamphlet *Mass Civilisation and Minority Culture* (1930) onwards, Leavis could sometimes sound altogether too Luddite for his ideas to seem even remotely practicable. His pleas for the mythic 'organic community' of the English village (hence the attractions of the sentimental villager in D.H. Lawrence, and the cult of T.F. Powys in the younger Leavis's circle) are in the end impossibly and wistfully unreal. What is more, his case for the élitist role of culture in society, as well as his developing stance on the unique centrality of English studies in the university (see *Education and the University: A Sketch for an 'English School'*, 1943), can seem as wilfully (even megalomaniacally) narrow as some of his literary preferences. Nevertheless, Leavis's passionate concern for the culture of England, especially as reflected in works of literature the educated common reader could be expected readily to respond to ('And I am English, and my Englishness is my very vision': a favoured quotation from Lawrence), his stern insistence on the intelligent play of the critical mind, his high-minded defence of the centrality in education of the humanities, particularly English literature (it earned him obloquy as well as fame when he rebutted C.P. Snow's glib assertion in the 1959 Rede Lecture at Cambridge that there were 'Two Cultures', a scientific as well as a humane), all this made Leavis one of the twentieth-century's most powerful as well as one of its most attractive educators. As a force for the conservation of the best of the English past he takes his place in a long tradition of a very English kind of radicalism. Despite his having early on rejected **Marx** and what Leavis called 'Marxizing', his teaching nevertheless runs deep – especially as refracted by the Cambridge-educated Marxist **Raymond Williams** – into English (literary) Marxism. And it now seems not at all absurd to add him to the distinguished list of corrosive, prophetic, crankily conservative English radicals: Bunyan, whom he loved; Swift, the twists and turns of whose prose he dissected so tellingly; Cobbett and Blake; D.H. Lawrence himself.

Further reading

Other works include: *'Anna Karenina' and Other Essays* (1967); *English Literature in Our Time and the University: Clark Lectures 1967* (1969); *Lectures in America*, with Q.D. Leavis (1969); *Letters in Criticism*, ed. John Tasker (1974); *The Living Principle: 'English' as a Discipline of Thought* (1975). See also: *The Importance of Scrutiny*, ed. Eric Bentley (1948); *A Selection from Scrutiny*, compiled by F.R. Leavis (2 vols, 1968). See: Francis Mulhern, *The Moment of 'Scrutiny'* (1979); M. Bell, *F.R. Leavis* (1988); A. Samson, *F.R. Leavis* (1992); I. Mackillop, *F.R. Leavis* (1995); G. Day, *Reading Leavis: Culture and Literary Criticism* (1996).

VALENTINE CUNNINGHAM

LÉGER, Fernand

1881–1955

French painter

More than any other major twentieth-century painter, Fernand Léger reacted with delight and enthusiasm to the new optimism expressed in the machine aesthetic. But he also had first-hand experience of the harsh realities of the trenches during the First World War and it was this that turned him away from the dry Cubist manner of the pre-war years and led him to evolve a more deliberately simple method that he knew might be readily understood by simple people. He no longer thought of an art for an elite. His art would not be of the studio but of the street, and would be quite acceptable to the man and woman in that street. In the trenches he had met ordinary people under extraordinary conditions and he was quite convinced of their worth.

Fascinated by the ever-changing urban scene, his belief that the new dynamism of the new century was to be found in the city led him to renew his interest in architectural space, and he well understood the complexities of modern building as part of his early training had been in an architect's office. His sense of decoration led to an art of contrast with the freely flowing forms of smoke and clouds used to accentuate the stark rigid metallic character of the frames used in the new construction.

The contemporary world around him was his starting point, though a careful study of the late works of **Cézanne** gave him a sound framework into which he could introduce the almost robot-like figures that were to become his trademark. They first appear in the important *Card Players* of 1917 (Kröller-Müller, Otterlo) reminiscent in subject-matter of Cézanne but treated here with steel-like precision reflecting both the character of soldiers at war and the machinery with which they fight that war. Man and machine act as one, and Léger merges them into a total unity epitomizing the essence of the new optimism.

Throughout his long life Léger's theme rarely strayed from the basic premise that man ought to be at one with the world that he has made and that he must learn to live in the present and not in the past. Like the Futurists, for whom he had much sympathy, he was a man of his time, though unlike the Futurists he approached everyday life with his feet firmly on the ground. The large painting *The Constructors*, painted in 1950 (Musée Nationale Fernand Léger, Biot), typifies this attitude of mind. The men who are building this electricity pylon are dwarfed by the vast metal structure but it is they who are responsible for it. Standing in infinite space, clouds drift through the structure as it rises still higher into the sky. The men are dwarfed not only by the pylon but also by the forces of nature that surround them. But they are confident in their work and confident in the new technology that makes it possible. They take their obvious strength for granted. They are the heroes of the new century and Léger is their spokesman.

Further reading

See D. Cooper, *Fernand Léger* (1949); *Léger and Purist Paris* (exhibition catalogue with texts by J. Golding and C. Green, Tate Gallery, London, 1972). See also: Nicholas Serota and Joanna Skipwith (eds) *Fernand Léger: The Later Years* (1988); D. Kosinski (ed.) *Fernand Léger: The Rhythm of Modern Life* (exhibition catalogue, 1994); Serge Fauchereau, *Fernand Léger* (1994).

JOHN FURSE

LEMKIN, Raphaël

1900–59

Polish/Jewish jurist

In his 1944 book *Axis Rule in Occupied Europe: Laws of Occupation, Analysis of Government, Proposals for Redress*, Raphaël Lemkin created the term 'genocide'. He was also the prime mover in the discussions that led to the 1948 UN Convention on the Prevention and Punishment of the Crime of Genocide.

Lemkin was born in Bezwodne, a village near present-day Vaulkovisk, a small city in what is now Belarus. In his unfinished autobiography 'Totally Unofficial Man', Lemkin recalls that from childhood he was stirred by historical accounts of extermination. He read about the destruction of the Christians by Nero; the Mongols overrunning Russia, Poland, Silesia, and Hungary in 1241; the persecution of Jews in Russia by Tsar Nicholas I; the destruction of the Moors in Spain; the devastation of the Huguenots. He confides that from an early age he took a special delight in being alone, so that he could feel and think without outer disturbances, and that loneliness became the essential condition of his life.

Lemkin studied philology at the University of Lvov, then decided on a career in law. In 1933, the year of **Hitler's** election to government in Germany, Lemkin sent a paper to a League of Nations conference in Madrid on the 'Unification of Penal Law'. He proposed the creation of the crimes of barbarity and vandalism as new offences against the law of nations. Acts of barbarity, ranging from massacres and pogroms to the ruining of a group's economic existence, undermine the fundamental basis of an ethnic, religious or social collectivity. Acts of vandalism concern the destruction of the cultural heritage of a collectivity as revealed in the fields of science, arts and literature. Lemkin argued that the destruction of any work of art of any nation must be regarded as an act of vandalism directed against 'world culture'.

Lemkin always regretted that the 1933 conference did not enact his proposals in international law. He felt that if they had been ratified by the thirty-seven countries represented at Madrid, the new laws could have inhibited the rise of Nazism. In 1939 Lemkin fled Poland and reached Stockholm in Sweden, where he did extensive research on Nazi occupation laws throughout Europe. In April 1941 he arrived in the United States via Japan. He thought help for European Jewry, including his own family, could only come from the USA, which he saw as a nation born out of moral indignation against oppression, and a beacon of freedom and human rights for the rest of the world. Yet he also records that as he travelled by train to take up a teaching appointment at Duke University, he saw on the station at Lynchburg, Virginia, toilet signs saying 'For Whites' and 'For Coloreds'. An ambivalence about the moral history of the United States remained to his last days, especially revealed in his unpublished papers.

What was notable about Lemkin's 1933 proposals concerning barbarity and vandalism was the width of his formulations. In similar spirit, eleven years later, chapter nine of *Axis Rule in Occupied Europe* proposed his new concept of 'genocide', derived from the Greek word *genos* (tribe, race) and Latin *cide* (as in tyrannicide, homicide, fratricide). Genocide is composite and manifold: it signifies a co-ordinated plan of different actions aiming at the destruction of the essential foundations of life of a group. Such actions can but do not necessarily involve mass killing. They involve considerations that are political, social, legal, intellectual, spiritual, economic, biological, physiological, religious and moral. Such actions involve considerations of health, food and nourishment, of family life and care of children, and of birth as well as death. Such actions involve consideration of the honour and dignity of peoples, and the future of humanity as a world community.

In 1933, Lemkin had focused on what he would later call genocide as an episode or act or event. In 1944 he saw genocide as also a process. 'Genocide has two phases,' he wrote:

> one, destruction of the national pattern of the oppressed group; the other, the imposition of the national pattern of the oppressor. This imposition, in turn, may be made upon the oppressed population which is allowed to remain, or upon the territory alone, after removal of the population and the colonization of the area by the oppressor's own nationals.

In the post-war years Lemkin worked tirelessly in the fledgling UN circles to persuade relevant committees to pass a convention banning genocide. At the same time, he was writing a history describing many examples of genocide in history, which he could submit as memoranda to influential delegates. For this research, Lemkin gained financial assistance from various sources, including the Viking Fund and the Lucius N. Littauer Foundation, as well as from the Yale Law School, which provided him with an office and research support.

This book remained unfinished and unpublished when Lemkin died in 1959. Yet the various manuscript chapters and research notes and cards are now being explored. The work kept expanding, taking in examples from antiquity to modernity. In particular, Lemkin pursues the linking of genocide with colonization to include European colonizing around the world, including of the Americas, by the Spanish from 1492 and later in North America by the English, French and post-independence Americans. He is highly critical of Columbus as an 'egregious genocidist' who set the historical example for the future of Spanish colonization in the Americas, instituting slavery and catastrophic loss of life. He develops a sophisticated methodology that permits the possibility of multifaceted analyses of settler-colonial histories in relation to genocide. He carefully distinguishes between cultural change and cultural genocide. He points out that the relationship between oppressor and victim in history is always unstable, and that in world history there are many examples of genocidal victims transforming into genocidists. He points to recurring features in historical genocides: mass mutilations; deportations under harsh conditions often involving forced marches; attacks on family life, with separation of men and women and taking away of the opportunity of procreation; removal and transfer of children; destruction of political leadership; death from illness, hunger and disease through overcrowding on reserves and in concentration camps.

Lemkin's views on humanity and violence were double-edged, both pessimistic and optimistic. He argued that genocide has followed humanity through history, that it occurs in relations between groups with a certain regularity as homicide takes place between individuals. Yet he also hoped that international law could restrain or prevent genocide.

In retrospect, we can see Lemkin's historical conceptions and legal thinking emerging from a 1930s and 1940s context where émigré intellectuals were attempting to reprise and develop traditions of cosmopolitanism and internationalism which they saw being engulfed by Nazism, itself a culmination of nineteenth-century nationalism and colonialism. Figures like **Walter Benjamin**, **Freud**, Lemkin, **Hannah Arendt**, **Erich Auerbach**, Leo Spitzer and their heir **Edward Said** were concerned that humanity should establish a duty of care to all the world's peoples and cultures. Central to Lemkin's thought were notions of world culture and the oneness of the world, valuing the variety and diversity of human cultures.

Lemkin's wide-ranging definition of genocide and his linking of genocide with colonization have proved increasingly productive and influential since his death. The resurgence of genocide in Cambodia, the former Yugoslavia and Rwanda was followed by an expansion of international law concerned with crimes against humanity, as in the International Court of Justice and the International Criminal Court. There has also been an explosion of research, writing, special issues of journals, and conferences concerned to explore Lemkin's seminal insight linking genocide and settler-colonialism, including relating Nazi colonizing plans, projects and practices to previous European colonization.

Genocide has proven to be a protean concept: it inspires thought at the limits of what humanity as a species might be.

Further reading

James Fussell conducts an invaluable website, http://www.preventgenocide.org, that features Lemkin's essays. Lemkin's autobiographical essay 'Totally Unofficial Man' is in Samuel Totten and Steven Leonard Jacobs (eds) *Pioneers of Genocide Studies* (2002). *Patterns of Prejudice*, Vol. 39, No. 2 (2005) reproduces an unpublished essay by Lemkin on Tasmania, edited and introduced by Ann Curthoys. The opening chapters of Samantha Power, *'A Problem from Hell': America and the Age of Genocide* (2002), evoke Lemkin's involvement in the drafting of the 1948 UN genocide convention. See also Dirk Moses (ed.) *Genocide and Colonialism* (2005) for new directions in genocide studies inspired by Lemkin.

JOHN DOCKER

LENIN (Vladimir Ilyich ULYANOV)

1870–1924

Russian revolutionary, statesman, publicist and theoretician

Lenin was born in 1870 at Simbirsk in the heart of Russia. He came from an educated and enlightened family: his father was a schoolteacher and so too was his mother for a while. Lenin was the second son in a family of six children and received the usual middle-class schooling of his time. Lenin's elder brother, Alexander, was a romantic revolutionary; he was executed for plotting to murder the then Tsar. Lenin was seventeen then and the execution left a deep impression on him. Lenin's elder sister, too, was active in the revolutionary movement. Soon after his brother's death Lenin enrolled as a law student in the provincial university of Kazan. His university career, however, did not last for long; he was sent down and confined to his mother's estate for playing a leading role in a demonstration against the government regulations to which students were subject. Lenin did eventually qualify as a lawyer but only to practise for a year or so. Throughout his life he remained a professional revolutionary.

Lenin embarked on his eventful political career by joining in the revolutionary groups which had started to develop all over Russia. After a couple of years of political activities in provincial towns he moved to St Petersburg, then the capital of Russia – also the main industrial city and naturally the hub of anti-government political activities. It was there that Lenin in 1894 published his first major political work: *Who the Friends of the People Are and How They Fight the Social Democrats* (*Chto Takoye 'Drusya Naroda', kak oni voyuynt protiv Sotsial-Demokratov?*, trans. 1946). The tract is a blistering attack on the Narodniks (populists in Russian) and has all the features which characterize Lenin's voluminous writings: written by way of a political intervention with a view to drawing specific conclusions to guide political activity. Lenin's style is to combine didactic arguments with withering polemics.

Lenin was not allowed to remain free to participate in political activities for long. After a year of imprisonment he was exiled to Siberia for three years; it was there that he married a fellow revolutionary, Krupskaya. Lenin used his period of imprisonment and exile to write his monumental *Development of Capitalism in Russia* (*Razvitiye Kapitalizma v Rossi*, 1899, trans. 1956). Though the work is scholarly in content as well as in style, it is nonetheless political. It is, like most other pre-1900 writings of Lenin, directed against the Narodniks.

To start with, Narodism covered a heterogeneous group opposed to the autocratic political and economic order in Russia. But by the 1890s the label came to be applied exclusively to non-**Marxists** who saw in the village commune the foundation of the future Russian society. They regarded capitalism – large-scale manufacturing industry and modern farms – as an alien import grafted on to Russian society.

What Lenin argued against the Narodniks was that capitalism was not only firmly implanted but also rapidly growing, both in the Russian cities and in the countryside. The village commune which was to serve as the foundation of the Narodniks' future Russia, Lenin demonstrated, was no longer a community of equal individuals. On the contrary it was stratified; a small minority of richer peasants (*kulaks*) prospered while the rest were becoming progressively poorer and forced to work for wages. From this Lenin drew the political conclusion that Russia, contrary to the Narodnik thesis, would not follow a path of economic and social changes radically different from the one already traversed by Western European countries. The implication was that in Russia, as in the rest of Europe, the leading political force was the working class and the appropriate form of political organization a Social Democratic Party, similar to those which had already developed in Western Europe.

From 1900 onwards one may divide Lenin's life and activities into three phases: (1) the period up to 1907; (2) the period of exile from 1907 to 1917; and finally (3) the period of revolution and the establishment of the Soviet Union from 1917 till his death.

The Social Democratic Party was founded when Lenin was still in Siberia, and it grew very rapidly in size and influence soon after its formation. During the period 1900–7 the question of differences between Marxism and Narodism was no longer important. The two main issues which occupied Lenin during this period were, first, the nature of the impending revolution, and second, the aim and the organization of the Social Democratic Party.

Lenin was convinced of the imminence of revolution and so too were other Russian revolutionaries. There was a nationwide uprising again the Tsarist autocracy and feudal lords in 1905 – an event which Lenin later termed the full dress rehearsal of the 1917 revolution. In his *Two Tactics of Social Democracy* (*Dve taktiki Sotsial-Demokraty v demokrat icheskoy revolyutsi*, 1905, trans. 1935) Lenin argued that the impending revolution would be bourgeois rather than socialist in character. For, according to him, the working class and the Social Democratic Party, because of conditions specific to Russia could not carry through the revolution to victory on its own and thus realize a socialist economy. That, Lenin went on to argue, did not mean that Social Democrats could not play a leading role in the impending revolution; on the contrary, it was necessary for them to do so in order to make sure that all vestiges of autocracy and feudalism were wiped out. Thus for Lenin, though it may seem paradoxical, the impending bourgeois revolution was to be led by the socialist party rather than by bourgeois parties.

Within five years of its establishment the Social Democratic Party split into two factions, the *Bolsheviks* (majority, in Russian) and the *Mensheviks* (minority) – the labels which later came to designate two separate socialist parties. Lenin became the leader of the former and it was the Bolsheviks who led the October Revolution of 1917. The immediate cause of the split was the difference of opinion on the nature of the party, its internal organization and the condition of its membership. Lenin argued for the establishment of a tightly knit party led from the centre, and which restricted its membership to only those who actively participated in its activities. The Mensheviks, in contrast, wanted the Russian party to develop like other European Social Democratic parties – a mass political party covering a wide political spectrum which was willing to admit a variety of individuals ranging from active participants to sympathizers. Lenin managed to win over the majority by a very slim margin. His conception of the party has become a legacy of the communist movement and it came in for criticism from diverse quarters, including Trotsky and Rosa Luxemburg.

The 1905 revolution shook the existing political and economic order but did not overthrow it. It led to the persecution of leading revolutionaries; Lenin like other Russian revolutionaries was driven abroad. He left Russia in 1907 to return to it in 1917 and spent most of his exile in Switzerland.

The Tsarist government, shaken by the 1905 uprising, tried to introduce a modicum of reforms: the commune was abolished and there was a half-hearted attempt on the part of the government to grant more power to the feeble assembly of elected representatives. The outbreak of the First World War soon put a stop to the process of economic and political reforms, and it was that which was decisive in shaping the course of events up to the October Revolution.

The outbreak of the war confronted the European socialist movement with the awkward problem of what attitude to adopt towards the war. Earlier, the Second International, as the socialist movement was then named, had decided that in the event of a war it would stand aside, leaving the ruling classes of belligerent countries to fight it out. This was not, however, what the majority of socialists did when the war was declared. In Germany the majority of Social Democratic members of parliaments voted funds for the war. The war split the socialist movement and put an end to the Second International.

Lenin argued that socialists should stand aside and refuse to take any part in the conduct of the war. For, as he explained, the war was an imperialist war – by that he meant that it was not the national boundaries of the leading European combatants but the division of Africa and Asia into colonies which was the main issue in the war. Therefore the war was not worthy of support by socialists for patriotic reasons. Lenin's theses on imperialism, publicized in his pamphlet *Imperialism* (*Imperializm*, 1917, trans. 1933), had a dual political significance. Apart from indicating to socialists the right attitude towards the war, they were based on the postulate that imperialism was a particular stage of capitalism. He analysed imperialism as a product of the internal dynamics of capitalism and went on to argue that imperialism had turned the whole world into a unified and interdependent system. From this Lenin drew the political conclusion that revolutions could no longer be regarded as just national affairs; and that socialist revolutions in advanced capitalist countries, bourgeois revolutions in semi-capitalist countries like Russia and the struggles of national liberation in colonized regions were all interlinked. This was an important innovation; because till then the prevalent conception was that socialist revolution would first take place in advanced capitalist countries like Germany and then later in other countries, depending on the development of capitalism in those countries.

The war, which was opposed by all sections of Russian Social Democracy, sapped the Russian state of all its power. In February 1917 – when Lenin was still in Switzerland – an almost bloodless revolution ended the Tsardom. The political power then passed into the hands of not one but two governments: one formal in the shape of the provisional government (dominated by conservative and liberal parties), the other informal and founded on the Soviets – a revolutionary council of workers' representatives. Of them the St Petersburg Soviet was the most important; such assemblies had been established before, during the 1905 revolution.

Lenin arrived in Russia in April of 1917 and he argued for the transfer of all power to the Soviets, thus ending the situation of dual power which existed then. At that time it was not the Bolsheviks but the Mensheviks and the Social Revolutionaries (heirs of the Narodniks) who dominated the Soviets. With the two governments the political situation was balanced on a knife-edge. It was the attempt by a General Kornilov to capture political power which finally shifted the balance in favour of the Soviets, because it was they who frustrated the attempted *coup d'état*. By the beginning of October 1917 the leadership of the Soviets had passed into the hands of the Bolsheviks. It was then that Lenin called for an immediate seizure of power. Lenin's call was initially opposed by the majority of Bolshevik leaders, but, as in so many other situations in 1917, he managed to have his way. Thus within a year Russia went through two revolutions: one bourgeois democratic (the February Revolution) and the other socialist (the October Revolution).

After the October Revolution, Lenin became an undisputed leader of Russian socialism and also of a substantial section of the European socialist movement. The centre of revolution shifted from Germany to Russia; Lenin went on to establish the Third International (the international organization of communist parties) to replace the already fissured and demoralized Second International.

The new Soviet state had to fight a civil as well as an external war against Germany. It survived both of them, but at a very heavy cost. The war lasted for two years and it was the period of what was then termed War Communism – meaning a strict regimentation of citizens and the direct administrative control of industrial production and of distribution. The war and the War Communism led to a near collapse of the Russian economy. In order to avert that, Lenin boldly suggested rolling back the frontiers of the communist economy. This he did by proposing what has come to be known as the New Economic Policy. Lenin did not live long enough to see the construction of the first socialist economy in the world. He died after being bedridden for a year and a half.

The significance of Lenin and the Russian revolution are intertwined; both of them left a decisive imprint on the politics of the twentieth century. The Leninist political legacy consisted of three main elements: his conception of the revolutionary party, his refinement of the art of political calculation, and his conception of the state.

It could almost be said that Lenin spent all his political life determining what is possible and calculating what is needed to realize the chosen possibility. It was Lenin who made revolutions objects of calculation; it was in this respect that he added an entirely new dimension to Marxist politics.

Lenin's ideas on the state are elaborated in his famous *The State and Revolution* (*Gosudarstvo i revolyutsiya*, trans. 1919) which he wrote in the midst of revolution in 1917. In it he treated democracy and dictatorship as complements rather than as mutually exclusive alternatives. He argued that parliamentary democracy of capitalist countries was, nonetheless, a dictatorship of the capitalist class. Further, that the aim of a socialist revolution was to replace the dictatorship of the capitalist class with the dictatorship of the proletariat – a phrase which acquired an ominous meaning during the mass purges of the **Stalin** era.

Further reading

See: *Collected Works* in forty-five volumes (English translation, Moscow 1960–70); the three-volume *Selected Works* (1967). See also: Adam B. Ulam, *Lenin and the Bolsheviks* (1965); Robert Conquest, *Lenin* (1972); Neil Harding, *Lenin's Political Thought* (1977); Christopher Hill, *Lenin and the Russian Revolution* (1978); Robert Service, *Lenin* (2000); Christopher Read, *Lenin: A Post-Soviet Re-evaluation* (2005).

ATHAR HUSSAIN

LEO XIII (Gioacchino Pecci)

1810–1903

Pope

On 7 February 1878 Pope Pius IX died, bringing to an end the longest reign in the history of the papacy. His election in 1846, in succession to the ultra-conservative Gregory XVI, had provoked Metternich, the Austrian chancellor and guardian of the traditional order in Europe, into his well-known remark that he had 'allowed for everything except the accession of a liberal Pope'. By the time of his death, however, 'Pio Nono' had long lost his early radical reputation. The revolutionary events in Rome in 1848 and 1849 had convinced the pope that there could be no compromise between the Catholic Church and faith and the principles of the French Revolution, represented in Italy in their most uncompromising form by Mazzini. The process of Italian unification further increased the distrust and distaste which he felt for the direction history was taking. The territory of the Papal States was steadily eroded by the aggression of the Piedmontese, whose king was determined to be the first monarch of a reborn Italian nation. By the time Rome itself was seized in 1870 the estrangement of Pius IX from the modern world, symbolized by the 1864 *Syllabus of Errors* which anathematized eighty propositions, seemed complete. Its ringing final condemnation denounced the idea that 'The Roman Pontiff can and ought to reconcile himself to, and agree with progress, liberalism and civilization as lately introduced'. As E.E.Y. Hales points out, the *Syllabus* can only be properly understood in the context of Italian politics – the liberalism of Mazzini was not that of **Gladstone** or **J.S. Mill**, however fondly English radicals may have imagined it to be – but the general point remains. Not only was Pio Nono hostile to the political developments of his day but his positive contributions to the development of church doctrine, the proclamation of the dogmas of the immaculate conception of the Virgin Mary and of Papal Infallibility, though long implied in Catholic theology, seemed to fly in the face of the spirit of the age.

The election of Cardinal Pecci as Pope Leo XIII led to a fundamental change in the relationship between the church and the surrounding world. There is a widespread tendency to see Leo's reign, marked as it is by the revival of Catholic philosophy in its Thomist form and the great social encyclicals, *Rerum Novarum* (on the rights and duties of labour and capital, 1891) above all, as a creative reversal of the stands taken by his predecessor. This is at best a half-truth and was certainly not the way contemporary Catholics saw matters. The denunciations and dogmatic pronouncements of Pius IX and the elaboration of a positive social doctrine by Leo XIII were part of the same process by which the Catholic Church, deprived in so many parts of Europe of the traditional support of Christian monarchies, found itself having to make explicit the concept of social order which had previously been inherent in its teaching. The reign of Pius IX marked an essential period of self-definition necessary before the enunciation of a positive programme of restoration. If Pio Nono had made it plain what Catholic thought was not, Leo XIII concerned himself with showing what it was and how relevant it was to the concerns of the modern world.

In the encyclical *Aeterni Patris* (1879), the new pope recommended the study of the work of St Thomas Aquinas in Christian schools and universities. This was the beginning of the Thomist revival which was to exert a considerable influence on the development of European intellectual life. Catholic intellectuals, many of them converts, played a prominent part in the late nineteenth-century reaction against positivism and materialism, and in this they were encouraged by a pope who was himself a noted scholar. But more significant still was the interest which Leo XIII took in social and economic affairs. The doctrine which he developed and the policies he recommended endorsed neither the unrestrained free-market policies of contemporary liberalism nor the revolutionary alternative of socialism. The doctrine of *Rerum Novarum*, carried further in *Graves de Communi* (1901), set the discussion of economy and society in the context of a Christian conception of the duties owed by men to each other. It provided the inspiration for the

policies of the new Christian democratic and trade union movements which were growing up in many parts of Europe, and stands at the beginning of the long line of social encyclicals which extends into the present day.

In contrast to his predecessor, Leo XIII, a skilled diplomat, encouraged the full participation of Catholics in the politics of liberal states. Anti-clericalism in France and Germany had to be fought on the battleground of parliamentary politics as well as by diplomatic pressure. It was this rather than any particular affinity for the republican form of government that led the pope to advise the predominantly monarchist Catholics of France to reconcile themselves to the republic. His attitude, as Philip Hughes has put it, was that

> Liberalism having come to stay, Catholics must be shown how to live in a Liberal world, and yet live by their Catholic principles; they must learn, not only how they could survive in such a world, but how to be active loyal citizens of the liberal states.

If Leo XIII is one of the greatest of the modern popes it is because, from the beleaguered and isolated throne to which he was called, he turned a tide that seemed to threaten the survival of the Catholic Church as an effective force in the world. He renewed Catholic confidence in philosophical thought as well as in social and political action. He left the Catholic Church with the strength to face the pressures of the new century in a positive spirit.

Further reading

Pope Leo XIII's major encyclicals are collected in *The Church Speaks to the Modern World*, ed. Etienne Gilson (1959). See also: *Leo XIII and the Modern World*, ed. E.T. Gargan (1961); E.Soderini, *Il pontificato di Leone XIII* (3 vols, 1932–3). For Pius IX see: E.E.Y. Hales, *Pio Nono* (1954).

DAVID J. LEVY

LEVI, Primo

1919–87

Italian writer

When Primo Levi committed suicide, many refused to see this as simply the last desperate act of a man in the throes of profound depression and dogged by physical illness. Two of his most distinguished contemporaries among Italian writers, Natalia Ginzburg and **Alberto Moravia**, believed that it was the enduring memory of his years in the concentration camp at Auschwitz which had finally overwhelmed him. Several close friends, on the other hand, attributed his profound gloom to worries as to the health of his mother, to whom he was profoundly – some felt abnormally – attached. Others feared the effect of hostile criticism directed at his complex response to the Holocaust, of which he was so eloquent a survivor.

If, for some of these detractors, Levi had never seemed sufficiently Jewish, this was because the community into which he was born in 1919 appeared more assimilated than others throughout Europe at the time. Primo's parents belonged to the prosperous bourgeoisie of Turin, one of northern Italy's fastest-growing industrial cities, which welcomed **Mussolini's** 1922 seizure of power as a guarantee of social stability. Levi was encouraged to join the Fascist youth movement, becoming an enthusiastic skier and mountaineer, passions which later enabled him to survive the bitter winters of Auschwitz. School and university studies, focused on science, were threatened by the issue, in 1938, of the notorious Racial Laws, under which Jews were excluded from public education and barred from state employment.

Managing, with the help of sympathetic Gentile professors, to circumvent restrictions on Jewish students, Levi was able to complete a chemistry course at Turin university, gaining first-class honours. After the fall of the Fascist government in 1943 and the subsequent German occupation of Italy, he joined the Resistance, but was taken prisoner,

along with a group of Jewish fugitives, at an inn near Aosta and sent to an internment camp before being transferred to Auschwitz. By no particular irony, Levi's scientific expertise made him too valuable to be exterminated forthwith, and he became a 'specialist slave' working in the IG Farben chemical laboratory close to the camp. His luck held when an attack of scarlet fever confined him to an isolation ward just before the Germans evacuated Auschwitz in January 1945, as Russian armies advanced into Poland. Eight months later, via several Russian transit camps and a journey across Romania and Hungary to the Italian border, Levi returned to Turin, to find his mother and sister still alive, though one-fifth of Italy's Jewish population had fallen victim to the Nazis.

The trauma of Auschwitz was exorcised for him, if only partially, by the writing of his memoir *If This is a Man* (*Se questo è un uomo*, trans. 1959). On its publication in 1947 the critics were puzzled by the notable avoidance of vindictiveness and accusation in its overall tone, as well as by an elegance of style unfashionable in post-war Italy. Temporarily abandoning his literary ambitions, Levi resumed work as an industrial chemist. It was another twenty years before genuine critical recognition greeted him on publication of *The Truce* (*La Tregua*, 1963, trans. 1987), an account of his experiences between leaving Auschwitz and returning to Italy. The book was widely translated, film rights were sold, and the writer gained several major Italian prizes.

Levi soon retired from his job at a Turin enamelling plant and began a writing career in earnest.

The Periodic Table (*Il sistemo periodico*, trans. 1984), a remarkable sequence of portraits, sketches and stories all inspired by the various chemical elements and their properties, appearing in 1975, confirmed his status among Italy's major authors. Less successful was *If Not Now, When?* (*Se non ora, quando?*, 1981, trans. 1985), an attempt at novel-writing to which Levi's talents were unsuited. In *The Drowned and the Saved* (*I sommersi e i salvati*,

1986, trans. 1987) he returned to the subject of Auschwitz via a series of essays more gloomy and questioning in tone than any of his earlier work.

The delayed impact of his wartime ordeal now made itself felt both physically and mentally. Levi's depressions, exacerbated by his mother's illness from cancer, were made worse by attacks on his integrity, whether as a Jew, an anti-Fascist or a writer, launched in the American press. Increasingly haunted by memories of the concentration camp and outraged by revisionist historians who sought to diminish its significance, Levi equated his mother's suffering with 'the faces of men stretched out on their Auschwitz plank-beds'. On 11 April 1987 he left his apartment to throw himself down the stairwell.

Primo Levi remains the most admired and effective of all writers on the Holocaust, not simply for his dignity of utterance but for his refusal to deal in blanket condemnations, sentimental rhetoric or crude demands for revenge. He himself observed, in his introduction to the German edition of *If This is a Man*, that his only clear aim was 'to bear witness, to have my voice heard'. If the horrors of Auschwitz contributed in the end to his self-extinction, they had also, by no special irony, shaped his purpose as a literary artist.

Further reading

Other works include: *The Wrench* (*La chiave a stella*, 1978, trans. 1987) and *Other People's Trades* (*Altrui mestiere*, 1985, trans. 1985). See: Mirna Cicioni, *Primo Levi: Bridges of Knowledge* (1995); Myriam Anissimov, *Primo Levi: Tragedy of an Optimist* (1999); Carole Angier, *The Double Bond: Primo Levi: A Biography* (2002); Ian Thomson, *Primo Levi: A Life* (2003).

JONATHAN KEATES

LÉVI-STRAUSS, Claude

1908–

French social anthropologist

A central exponent of Structuralism, Claude Lévi-Strauss was born in Brussels. His secondary education was acquired in Paris at the Lycée Janson de Sailly. In 1931 he graduated in law and in philosophy. After two years as a philosophy teacher in small country towns he left France for Brazil, where he lectured at the University of São Paulo (1934–9). During his stay he became interested in social anthropology and started travelling in the Matto Grosso and the Amazon. He returned to France in 1939, but left again after the settling of arms in 1940, this time for the USA. In New York, Lévi-Strauss lectured at the New School for Social Research, then, with other exiled French intellectuals, founded the École Libre des Hautes Études de New York. After a brief return to Paris at the end of the war he became Cultural Counsellor at the French Embassy in Washington (1945–8). Back in Paris he was appointed Associate Curator of the Musée de l'Homme (1949), Director of Studies at the École Pratique des Hautes Études (1950–74), and, from 1959, Professor of Social Anthropology at the Collège de France. A member of the Académie Française since 1973, Professor Lévi-Strauss is the recipient of many awards, and a member of British, American, Dutch and Norwegian Academies.

Lévi-Strauss's remarkable autobiographical travel account, *Tristes Tropiques* (1955, translated as *A World on the Wane*, 1961, and as *Tristes Tropiques*, 1973), is littered with references to overcrowding and congestion of every sort. Time and again he exposes 'those outbreaks of stupidity, hatred and credulousness which social groups secrete like pus when they begin to be short of space'. The cardinal virtues Lévi-Strauss appreciates are discretion and good manners. Only Buddhism is allowed to qualify as an acceptable moral and intellectual system, although Amerindian myths share his own concern for privacy: they regard the world as overcrowded as soon as a man has got a brother or a woman a sister. For 'as the myths explain, a brother can be a hardship … his social function being usually limited to that of potential seducer of their sibling spouse.' This establishes Lévi-Strauss's claimed affinity with

Rousseau, who wrote: 'The ancient times of Barbarity were the Golden Age, not because men were united, but because they were separated.'

Although Lévi-Strauss does not propose a global system of interpretation of the world, there is a remarkable consistency in his approach to widely different domains of human culture. His epistemological framework can be briefly described. Recent interpretations of the fate of the human race hesitate between two explanatory schemes: either the human environment, natural and cultural, is shown as a near-perfect clockwork wherein any part of the system is strictly constrained by the others and every event occurs necessarily; or constraints are shown to be few and human cultures have repeatedly to face choices between various alternatives. Sociobiology and the other varieties of cultural materialism belong to the first scheme, while Lévi-Strauss's system belongs to the second. However, to him the great diversity of human culture is not arbitrary; it exhibits combinations which result from the interplay of two types of constraints: the constraints which lie in the outer world and the constraints of the inner world, what Lévi-Strauss calls 'l'esprit humain', the human mind. The human mind is not a metaphysical entity, it is a material object: man's nervous system. Cultures result from the interplay between the outer world and the possibilities of man's nervous equipment. This is why Lévi-Strauss regards structural anthropology as a variety of psychology: anthropology is necessarily 'cognitive' anthropology.

Although Lévi-Strauss has sometimes claimed to be a **Marxist**, his conception of history is essentially anti-historicist. To him there are no laws to history: history is a probabilistic process which he compares to roulette; favourable sets of throws will allow some cultures to engage in cumulative sequences, while unfavourable throws will mean for others stagnation or cultural regression. The presence of culturally variegated neighbours acts here as a stimulus towards added sophistication; isolation, on the contrary,

entails a risk of cultural regress. But as history is unpredictable it is therefore capital to keep a record of it, as accurately as circumstances allow. History provides the only experiments the anthropologist has at his disposal. This is one of the differences between the 'Sciences de l'homme' and the other natural sciences. Another difference is that the natural sciences restrict their level of apprehension to that of *explanation*, while a Science of Man cannot do so without tackling also the level of *understanding*, otherwise it would be meaningless. But very seldom does the anthropologist know whether he is dealing with *explanation* or with *understanding*. Therefore the Sciences of Man cannot state propositions which are falsifiable like propositions in physics. Lévi-Strauss distinguishes, however, the Sciences of Man from the social sciences (law, economics, political science, social psychology, etc.), which are 'in cahoots' with their object.

A hypothesis which pervades most of Lévi-Strauss's work is that of exchange, or rather of gift and counter-gift as it was defined by **Marcel Mauss**. Humankind is constituted of a collection of groups socially defined in kinship on the basis of natural reproduction. To a large extent the social tissue results from these groups refraining from using for their own sake their own women, their own words and their own commodities.

The Elementary Structures of Kinship (*Les Structures élémentaires de la parenté*, 1949, trans. 1969) rests on 'the structuralist hypothesis ... that in every society, even where marriage seems to result only from individual decisions dictated by economic or emotional considerations foreign to kinship, definite *types* of cycles tend to get constituted' (D. Sperber, *Le Structuralisme en anthropologie*, 1973). Elementary structures appear in societies where men refrain from marrying their own women (incest prohibition) for the benefit of other men who belong to other groups but are nevertheless traceable kinsmen of a particular kind, e.g. the bridal pair is of cross-cousins, children of siblings of different gender. Lévi-Strauss introduced as a conceptual tool the opposition between 'restricted' and 'general-ized exchange'. In restricted exchange, two exogamous groups exchange women, the men of A marry women of B, while men of B marry women of A. In generalized exchange, men of A marry women of B, while men of B marry women of C, etc. Another contribution of *The Elementary Structures* and later texts is the emphasis on the 'atom of kinship'. Kinship can only be ana-lysed if the unit considered is not the nuclear family (parents and children) but an atom where the wife-giving group is taken into account. The representatives of the wife-giving group might be one mother's brother, but also any other suitable representatives (e.g. the mother's mother's brother in a society where men marry their mother's mother's brother's daughter's daughter).

The Elementary Structures is a vast survey of the societies where prescriptive marriage with definite kin is in force. Many critics have discovered inaccuracies in the ethnography whereon Lévi-Strauss's argument rests; others have insisted that formalization in such mat-ters leads to a neglect of essential sociological features of the marriage systems described: for instance, alternative choices or infringements on the rules. Whatever the case, *Les Structures élémentaires* became a reference book of Anglo-Saxon anthropology long before it was translated into English, a rare achievement.

The exchange scheme is visible in other spheres of social life: some gift-cultures of the Pacific have established a kind of exogamous economy – I give all I have produced and I only consume what I have been given. In many ways verbal taboo is also giving my 'words' for others to use. Lévi-Strauss shows the exchange scheme as having a high operational value; castes appear, for instance, as reversed totemic groups: castes keep their women for themselves but exchange goods and services, while totemic groups exchange women but consume their own products (*La Pensée sauvage*, 1962, trans. as *The Savage Mind*, 1966).

Lévi-Strauss's near fascination for the formal properties of his object of enquiry has often upset his critics. Indeed, once he has estab-lished the possible combinations, the 'group of transformations', of a particular social phenomenon, not only is he not much con-cerned in determining why this possibility has been chosen preferably to others (this is rela-ted to his probabilistic view of history), but he is not prepared to privilege empirical actuality over mere logical possibility. His reply to critics in a slightly different context on this latter point is disarming:

> What does this matter? For if the final aim of anthropology is to contribute to a better knowledge of objectified thought and its mechanisms, it is in the last resort immater-ial whether in this book the thought pro-cesses of the South American Indians take shape through the medium of my thought, or whether mine take place through the medium of theirs.
>
> (*Le Cru et le cuit*, 1964; translated as *The Raw and the Cooked*, 1969)

If in his enquiry of kinship Lévi-Strauss was preceded by anthropologists like **L.H. Morgan** or **W.H.R. Rivers**, this is not the case for mythology; only the Russian formalist Vladimir Propp can be regarded as a fore-runner of the French anthropologist's approach. The four volumes of *Mythologiques* (1964–72; *Introduction to a Science of Mythology*, 1969–79) constitute the illustrative pro-gramme, on Amerindian myths, of Lévi-Strauss's method of analysis. Myths are not to be deciphered, there is no latent message lurking behind their manifest meaning. Rather, the meaning of a myth resides in the fact that there are other myths. The myths of a particular culture constitute a mythological system, and it is possible to discover the rules that account for the transformation of one myth into another. Similarly, there are rules which account for the differences between two versions of the *same* myth in different cultures. The existence of such rules explains why for Lévi-Strauss there is no authentic version of a myth: the set of all possible ver-sions constitute a group of transformations. Any version is as good as any other as long as it is felt by the native listener that 'it tells properly the same story': 'Therefore, not only Sophocles, but **Freud** himself, should be included among the recorded versions of the Oedipus myth on a par with earlier or see-mingly more "authentic" versions' (*Anthro-pologie structurale*, 1958; *Structural Anthropology*, 1963). The function of a myth is neither to be a charter – Lévi-Strauss regards this idea as a platitude – nor to *explain* the origin of things. It is true that myths often mention when such and such an animal or plant appeared for the first time, but this is not the function of the myth. Plants and animals are actors in myths, not the things to be explained. The function of myths – if there is any such thing – is to account for categories. The world seems to be torn apart by the contradiction between irreducible opposites like near and remote, right and left, up and down, nature and culture, etc. Myths are a reflection on the conceptual puzzles and attempts at mediation. Mediation might succeed, for instance by showing that it is possible to bridge the opposition by 'stuffing' the conceptual gap with intermediaries, or it might fail, 'either that the mediator joins one of the two poles and gets completely dis-juncted from the other (and then not always from the same one), or that it gets disjuncted from both'. Although Lévi-Strauss's venture in *Mythologiques* is undoubtedly impressive critics have been very embarrassed at appraising it. His reading is obviously con-sistent, but as his own method entails, it is but one among many. Moreover, the limitations of the method show conspicuously when it is used by anthropologists less gifted than Lévi-Strauss himself.

It is tempting to locate Lévi-Strauss in a straight line of descent from **Durkheim** via Mauss, but as he himself repeatedly stressed, he owes much more to Anglo-Saxon social anthropology than he does to the French school of sociology. In particular, Durkheim's 'attempt to use sociology for metaphysical purposes' is not congenial to him. Time and again Lévi-Strauss praised Rivers's, **Radcliffe-Brown's** or Robert Lowie's contributions to anthropology. But most of all he has underlined his personal debt towards **Boas**. This particular assertion of filiation does not seem to have been taken seriously by most reviewers, probably because of the discrepancy between Lévi-Strauss's theoretical achievements and Boas's con-spicuous unpretentiousness in theoretical matters. But as Lévi-Strauss noted, it is Boas's excessive demands towards theory which prevented him from contributing decisively to it. The development of anthropology during the fifty years which separate Boas's and Lévi-Strauss's works might explain their different attitudes to theory.

But Lévi-Strauss's most decisive contribu-tions seem to have resulted from outer influences, especially those of structural pho-nology (**Jakobson**) and cybernetics (**Wiener**) with which he became familiar through personal contact during his New York days. Later writings reveal his constant concern of keeping in touch with the latest develop-ments in the natural sciences, particularly with neurophysiology.

Lévi-Strauss's influence on recent anthro-pology is so considerable that it is difficult to evaluate it properly. Among the anthro-pologists who have best understood Lévi-Strauss's lesson and have applied it to other objects in their own way are, in Britain, **Edmund Leach** and **Rodney Needham**; in France, Pierre **Bourdieu** and Dan Sperber; and in the United States, Marshall Sahlins.

In the early 1960s in France, Lévi-Strauss's works became very fashionable. *The Savage Mind* in particular was read by a large public of laymen. A trend called Structuralism flourished then before it receded dramatically after the May 1968 'events' which resulted in a renewed interest in Marxist studies. Not all the stars of Structuralism were noticeably influenced by Lévi-Strauss. **Jacques Lacan**, the psychoanalyst, borrowed the concept of 'symbolic function', and constituted his own topology of 'The Real', 'The Imaginary' and 'The Symbolic'. **Roland Barthes** found some inspiration in Lévi-Strauss's approach to myth, especially visible in his *Système de la* *mode* (1967) and *S/Z* (1970). **Foucault's** '*épistème*', the spirit of the time in natural and human sciences, functions much like a Lévi-Straussian 'group of transformations'. **Jacques Derrida** discovered in Lévi-Strauss's reading of Rousseau matter for his reflection on the role of writing in the constitution of modern metaphysics (*De la grammatologie*, 1967).

Aiming to bridge C.P. Snow's 'two cultures', Lévi-Strauss has managed to combine the talent of an acclaimed writer with the skills of a properly scientific mind, mesmerized by the human endeavour's infinitely kaleidoscopic nature. Often impatient with mathematical formalization, which he regards as de-humanizing and simplistic, he has shown time and again his own aptitude at grasping underlying structures in a quasi-algebraic fashion. Lévi-Strauss's students were struck by the contrast existing between the severe style of his lecturing, self-absorbed and rarely if ever turning towards the audience, and the captivating manner of his chairing of the seminar he led at the Collège de France. Respectfully interrupting the invited speaker, he would often bring order to the chaos of his guest's original account with his own definitive and glowing abstract

Lévi-Strauss's original work is often seen as the disincarnated report of a coroner. But such interpretations miss altogether what is probably one of the distinctive qualities of his work: the very ethical premises whereon his whole approach rests. His sympathy for Buddhism is everywhere endemic, and his use of the conceptual opposition of nature and culture can only be understood in the light of his play 'L'Apothéose d'Auguste' (Chapter 37 of *Tristes Tropiques*). The true meaning of his work appears clearly in his reply to the question: what should be deposited in a coffer for the benefit of archaeologists in the year 3000?:

> I will put in your time-vault documents relative to the last 'primitive' societies, on the verge of disappearance; specimens of vegetable and animal species soon to be destroyed by man; samples of air and water

not yet polluted by industrial wastes; notices and illustrations of sites soon to be ravaged by civil or military installations.

> (*Anthropologie structurale 2*, 1973; trans. as
> *Structural Anthropology 2*, 1976)

Further reading

Other works include: *Race et histoire* (1952); *Le Totémisme aujourd'hui* (1962, translated as *Totemism*, 1969); *Du miel aux cendres* (1966, translated as *From Honey to Ashes*, 1973); *L'Origine des manières de table* (1968, translated as *The Origin of Table Manners*, 1978); *L'Homme nu* (1971, translated as *The Naked Man*, 1980); *La Voie des masques* (1975); *Le Regard éloignéI* (1983, translated as *The View from Afar*, 1985); *La Potière jalouse* (1985, translated as *The Jealous Potter*, 1988); *Regardez, écouter, lire* ('Look, Listen, Read!', 1993); *Saudades Do Brasil. A Photographic Memoir* (1994, 1995). See also: Edmund Leach, *Lévi-Strauss* (1970); Catherine Clément, *Lévi-Strauss* (1970); E. Nelson Hayes and Tanya Hayes, *Claude Lévi-Strauss: The Anthropologist as Hero* (1970); Raymond Bellour and Catherine Clément, *Claude Lévi-Strauss* (1979); R.A. Champagne, *Claude Lévi-Strauss* (1987).

PAUL JORION

LEVINAS, Emmanuel

1906–95

French philosopher

Emmanuel Levinas was a major philosopher in the European phenomenological tradition: his abiding and central interest was in ethics and in Judaism. His influence has can be seen in the work of a huge range of figures who are as diverse as **Jacques Derrida** and **Pope John Paul II**.

Born in Kovno in Lithuania, his family was part of the large Jewish community. In 1923 he went to study philosophy in France, and then in 1928 studied in Germany, where he was exposed to the work of **Martin Heidegger**. In 1930 he married, became a French citizen, did military service and took a job teaching for the Alliance Israélite Universelle in Paris. Drafted into the army in 1939, he was captured by the Germans in 1940 and imprisoned in a camp for Jewish prisoners of war. While his wife and daughter were hidden in France, his family in Lithuania were murdered by the Nazis or by Lithuanian nationalists. After the war, he returned to France and became director of the École Normale Israélite Orientale. Mixing in philosophical circles in Paris, Levinas published papers on a number of themes connected to ethics. He also began a study of the Talmud with an enigmatic but influential master, Monsieur Chouchani, and from then took an active interest in and involvement with Jewish intellectual life. His first book, *Existence and Existents* (*De l'existence a l'existant*, trans. 1978) was published in 1947. However, the first of his two most important books *Totality and Infinity* (*Totalite et infini, essai sur l'exteriorite*, trans. 1969), was not published until 1961. In 1964 he was appointed Professor of Philosophy at Poitiers, and then in 1967 at Paris-Nanterre and in 1973 at the Sorbonne. His second major book, *Otherwise than Being* (*Autrement qu'être ou au-dela de l'essence*, trans. 1981), was published in 1974. Though he retired in 1976, he continued teaching and writing. Many conferences were held on him and his work in the 1980s and 1990s; he received many honours, including being made an *Officier de la Légion d'honneur* in 1991. After a long illness, he died in 1996.

Levinas's work, while taking much from **Husserl** and Heidegger, is centrally concerned with the experience of ethics. His aim is not to offer a new ethical system or moral rules: rather it is an attempt to understand how our obligations to others arise, and what this means. In a key moment of *Otherwise than Being*, he asks why 'does the other concern me? What is Hecuba to me? Am I my brother's keeper?' His answer to these question is to suggest that they

> have meaning only if one has already supposed the ego is concerned only with itself, is only a concern for itself. In this hypothesis, it indeed remains incomprehensible that the absolute outsideofme, the other, would concern me. But in the 'prehistory' of the ego posited for itself speaks a

> responsibility, the self is through and through a hostage, older than the ego, prior to principles.

He is suggesting that before we think of ourselves as ourselves, we are already responsible for the others who people the world. We are, to use one of his many terms for the experience of obligation, their hostages; and their very otherness – rather than some shared quality, such as national identity – imposes this burden on us. One of his key terms for this experience of the ethical stems from 'the face': by this he means that, when we face someone, before we decide how to respond (to give or not to give a beggar money, to wish someone 'good morning' or to turn away) we are already put into a relationship with them. This unconditional responsibility is not something we take on or a rule by which we agree to be bound: instead, it exists before us and we are 'thrown' into it, without any choice.

Further reading

Other works include: *Emmanuel Levinas: Basic Philosophical Writings* (1996) ed. Adriaan Peperzak. There is an excellent short interview with Levinas in Richard Kearney (ed.) *States of Mind: Dialogues with Contemporary Thinkers* (1995); and a longer series of interviews in Levinas, *Ethics and Infinity: Conversations with Philippe Nemo* (1985), which make good introductions to his thought. See also: Marie-Anne Lescourret, *Emmanuel Levinas* (1994); and *The Cambridge Companion to Levinas* (2002), edited by Simon Critchley and Robert Bernasconi.

ROBERT EAGLESTONE

LEWIS, Henry Sinclair

1885–1951

US novelist

Sinclair Lewis was born in Sauk Center, Minnesota, and educated at Oberlin College, Ohio, and Yale. After graduation, he worked as a journalist and in various publishing houses. His first novel, *Our Mr Wrenn*, appeared in 1914. Lewis's early work (1914–19) bridged the gap between the two kinds of novel then prevalent in America: the sentimental gentility of Booth Tarkington and the 'Hoosier' school, and the stark naturalism exemplified in the novels of **Theodore Dreiser** (who had a lasting influence on Lewis's writing). But the early fiction was greeted with little acclaim. Unimaginative in its allegiance to traditional American values and ideals, it gave little indication of the talent which was to make Lewis famous.

Recognition came with the publication, in 1920, of *Main Street*, which mockingly anatomized the provincialism of the small town in the American Middle West. The central themes of the novel – the philistinism and complacency, cant and hypocrisy of a vulgar and meretricious society – were those which were to preoccupy Lewis throughout the next decade. The novel enjoyed a *succès de scandale*, and secured for Lewis a reputation as iconoclast, and as America's foremost satirist. He was quickly classed with **Hemingway**, **Fitzgerald**, Sherwood Anderson and H.L. Mencken (the latter a formative influence on Lewis) as one of the leaders of a generation of American writers in revolt. In *Babbitt* (1922), Lewis turned his attention to the urban middle class. He captured the idioms and rendered the lifestyle of the American bourgeois with a derisive exactitude which has since caused Babbitt's name to be enshrined in the dictionaries as a synonym for smug conformity. In *Arrowsmith* (1925), the satire was respectably offset by a new strain of idealism. But *Elmer Gantry* (1927), Lewis's scathing portrayal of the corruption of religious life in America, provoked outrage still more extreme than that generated by *Main Street*.

With fame came prosperity, the life of a celebrity in Washington, New York and Europe, and, in 1930, the Nobel Prize in Literature, which marked the climax of Lewis's career. Ten novels followed over the next two decades. The concern with a variety of social and political issues remained – prison conditions, organized philanthropy, the Negro question, the labour unions, communism and fascism. But the tone of the satirist yielded increasingly to that of the pamphleteer. The later novels failed to meet with the success of the major work, and critics have commonly agreed that they are inferior productions.

During the 1920s, Lewis was thought by many to be the leading American novelist. His impact was immense. To a massive reading public, at home and abroad, he seemed to offer a precise diagnosis of the cultural and moral ills of America – the malaise inseparable from the new materialism of the postwar years. His reputation has since waned, and his subsequent influence has been slight. His importance is now often judged to be chiefly historical. Accurate and pungent at its best, his satire is not distinguished by its subtlety. Its triumphs are easily come by. In so far as his work has a redeeming complexity, it is the result of a latent orthodoxy which was present in Lewis from the outset, and conflicts with the iconoclastic and ostensibly enlightened attitudes of the major novels. It draws him into sympathy with the very objects of his satire, and allows him to perceive the frustration and despair that lie beneath the jejune enthusiasms and vacuous pieties he otherwise mocks so vigorously.

Further reading

Other works include: *The Trail of the Hawk* (1915); *The Job* (1917); *Free Air* (1919); *Mantrap* (1926); *The Man Who Knew Coolidge* (1928); *Dodsworth* (1929); *Ann Vickers* (1933); *Work of Art* (1934); *It Can't Happen Here* (1935); *The Prodigal Parents* (1938); *Bethel Merriday* (1940); *Gideon Planish* (1943); *Cass Timberlane* (1946); *Kingsblood Royal* (1947); *The God-Seeker* (1949); *World So Wide* (1951). On Lewis: D.J. Dooley, *The Art of Sinclair Lewis* (1967); M. Light, *The Quixotic Vision of Sinclair Lewis* (1975); M. Schorer, *Sinclair Lewis: An American Life* (1971); M. Schorer (ed.) *Sinclair Lewis: A Collection of Critical Essays* (1962); Martin Bucco, *Sinclair Lewis as Reader and Critic* (2004); Richard R. Lingeman, *Sinclair Lewis: Rebel from Main Street* (2005).

ANDREW GIBSON

LEWIS, John Saunders

1893–1985

Welsh patriot and writer

The son of a Welsh Presbyterian minister, Saunders Lewis was born in Wallasey, Cheshire (England). Although he attended school and university in Liverpool, his life and work were overwhelmingly concerned with Wales, to the extent that by many he is ranked alongside David Lloyd George (British prime minister from 1916 to 1922) as the foremost Welshman of the twentieth century, and by some as the greatest Welshman since Owain Glyndwr in the fourteenth century, his principal achievement being to revive the Welsh nationalist cause, notably through the institution of a cultural politics based on the Welsh language.

In the Great War Lewis served as an officer, first in Flanders, then in military intelligence in Athens. During this period he began reading the works of Maurice Barrès, particularly *Le Culte du moi*, which stressed the need to be faithful to one's roots. Although Barrès was French, what he said echoed Lewis's father's admonition that no good would come of him until he 'returned' to Wales. When the war finished, Lewis completed his degree at Liverpool University, in French and English Literature, then enrolled as a lecturer at University College Swansea.

By then Lewis was already courting his Irish wife-to-be, Margaret Gilcriest. The two had corresponded throughout the war, and both were heavily influenced by the Irish nationalist 'Easter' uprising of 1916. Largely as a result of this liaison Lewis became interested in the Irish literary renaissance, and in such writers as **W.B. Yeats** and **J.M. Synge**. His wife was also instrumental in Lewis's abandonment of Welsh Calvinism and his conversion to Catholicism, in 1932.

Welsh had always been spoken in his childhood home, and at Swansea Lewis began steeping himself in Welsh literature, at the same time turning his mind to politics. In 1924 he published *A School of Welsh Augustans*, a study of the extent to which Welsh writers in the eighteenth century were affected by their English counterparts. The following year he co-founded the Welsh Nationalist Party, originally called the Plaid Genedlaethol Cymru, but more famously known as Plaid Cymru, becoming its president in 1926 – a position he retained until 1943, when Lewis 'resigned' from politics, claiming that his Catholicism had become a hindrance to the party's progress.

As Plaid Cymru's leading theorist, Lewis called for Welsh autonomy, or 'home rule', within a renegotiated 'union' with the rest of Britain; but significantly Lewis did not seek to dissolve Wales's allegiance to the Crown, and his views about militant action were at best ambiguous.

For ten years Plaid Cymru made little progress in winning hearts and minds, but the situation was transformed in 1936, when, together with the Rev. Lewis Valentine and D.J. Williams, Saunders Lewis staged what became known as the 'Fire in Llŷn'. The three men set fire to some empty huts at the site of a proposed Royal Air Force bombing school at Penyberth on the Llŷn Peninsula, then promptly gave themselves up to the police. The proposed facility had already excited widespread opprobrium in Wales, for religious and pacifist as well as nationalist reasons, but when the 'Penyberth Three' were sent for trial in London after a Welsh court failed to secure their conviction, it became a *cause célèbre*.

In the event, Lewis, Valentine and Williams were sentenced to a modest nine months' imprisonment, but this was sufficient to turn them into martyrs. In retrospect, Penyberth was a masterstroke of civil protest. Henceforward Welsh sentiments could not be ignored. Yet ironically, for Lewis himself, the event marked a turning away from overt participation in public life. Sacked by University College Swansea, he devoted his energies instead to creating an astonishing corpus of literary works, nearly all in Welsh, and including twenty-one plays as well as several volumes of verse and criticism – an oeuvre widely regarded as the century's outstanding achievement in Welsh.

Like the French Catholic philosopher Jacques Maritain, Lewis believed in the primacy of the spiritual, yet was astute enough to know that in literary matters things had to be somewhat different. He abhorred moralistic writing, particularly that of his nineteenth-century nonconformist compatriots. For him, artistic endeavour had nothing to do with categorical imperatives, and everything to do with creative play – fishing in the subconscious, as he described it in 1977: fashioning original characters and images in the search for significant form. As his close friend the poet David Jones had said, art had to do with the gratuitous in life.

Lewis perhaps attained his apogee as a religious poet, counterpointing the paradoxes inherent in the twin sources of knowledge affecting a Christian – revelation and reason. Wary of presenting religious truth as fact, he could make fine poetry out of the seeming absurdities of faith, echoing Søren Kierkegaard in such lines as 'walking as if one saw, and experiencing the night of the blind, is the perpetual life of the Faith'. While another line, given in one of his plays to a would-be Marxist assassin frustrated by his wife's concern for his soul, is: 'She loves me as if eternity existed.'

That was how Saunders Lewis loved Wales. After 1943 he increasingly eschewed the polemical. Notwithstanding, in 1962 he delivered a coruscating radio broadcast – *Tynged yr Iaith* ('The Fate of the Language') – in which he castigated his fellow countrymen for allowing Welsh as a spoken language to wither. As a result the Welsh Language Society (Cymdeithas yr Iaith Gymraeg) was founded, with Lewis himself as its honorary president; and shortly afterwards Plaid Cymru enjoyed its first electoral successes.

Lewis died in Cardiff, in 1985. Twelve years later the British government conceded limited autonomy in Wales through the creation of a Welsh National Assembly. While this may not be everything Lewis dreamed of, his particular brand of cultural politics may be said to have greatly helped it happen. Regarded by some non-Welsh-speaking Welsh as retrogressive and reactionary – notoriously he advocated neutrality in the 1939–45 war against **Hitler** – Lewis can nonetheless claim credit for helping to rehabilitate a 'minority' Celtic language, both through his own writings, and for the encouragement he gave such other Welsh authors as Islwyn, Gwenallt and Waldo Williams, and also the English-language poet **R.S. Thomas**.

Further reading

See: Saunders Lewis, *Selected Poems*, trans Joseph P. Clancy (1993); A.R. Jones and Gwyn Thomas (eds) *Presenting Saunders Lewis* (1973); Bruce Griffiths, *Saunders Lewis* (1989); Harri Pritchard Jones, *Saunders Lewis* (1990); Ioan Williams, *A Straitened Stage* (1991)

HARRI PRITCHARD JONES

LEWIS, Percy Wyndham

1882–1957

Anglo-American painter, novelist, critic

Of mixed British and American parentage, Wyndham Lewis was born on a yacht off Nova Scotia, and was educated at Rugby, the Slade School of Art, and privately as an art student in various European cities, including Paris and Munich. Originally primarily a painter, Lewis began writing in order to do justice to what he felt he must keep out of his painting to prevent it from being too 'literary'.

Lewis early developed an absurdist view of life, with the body seen as a primitive and 'wild' machine, to which an essentially alien mind was attached. This condition can be seen as either comic or tragic. The early writings on the theme were revised and collected in *The Wild Body* (1927). The stories concern peasant life in Brittany, and rigorously exclude sentiment. Early pictures, executed in a style derived from Cubism and as satires on Fauvism, depict primitives, but in a way that prevents sentimental identification with their mindless self-absorption; one can be a spectator or a participant, but not both.

This theme is also the subject of Lewis's first novel, *Tarr* (1918). The unillusioned artist Tarr is unable to organize his life, and is no less absurd than the deluded German romantics Bertha and Kreisler, who live the myth of Bohemia.

Tarr satirizes romantic social conventions, but Lewis recognized that without shared values and myths life is mechanical and worthless. He felt that technology gave people control over their lives as never before, and that the artist should bring this revolution to public consciousness. Lewis criticized Cubist pictures for restricted subject-matter which detracted from major formal innovations, whereas Futurist pictures lacked formal rigour and evinced too uncritical an adulation of the machine. Breaking away from Roger Fry's Omega Workshops in 1913, Lewis founded the Vorticist movement and edited its magazine *Blast* (2 issues, 1914 and 1915).

Lewis's Vorticist pictures are geometric abstractions from mechanical and architectural forms, conveying both the violence and excitement of the modern city. They are anti-formalist (in opposition to Fry) and exploit discords in colour and unpleasant paint texture (e.g. *Workshop* and *The Crowd*, both in the Tate Gallery). Vorticism was destroyed by the war, in which Lewis served on the Western Front and as an artist. The hatred of war and violence he acquired can be seen in his war pictures, which adapt the harsh and angular vocabulary of Vorticism for more realistic ends.

Lewis's revolutionary enthusiasm survived the war briefly, and it took some years to adapt his artistic means to his new sense of the world. The main achievements of the transition period (1919–25) are pencil portraits and figure studies that show his skill as one of the century's finest draughtsmen.

It seemed to Lewis in the 1920s that, instead of controlling their lives, people were passive and fatalistic, despite living in a largely man-made world. In a series of books he analysed this failure of will in the fields of philosophy, politics, popular culture and literature (*The Art of Being Ruled*, 1926; *Time and Western Man*, 1927; *Paleface*, 1929; *Doom of Youth*, 1932). *The Childermass* (1928), a fantasy of life after death, is a fictional presentation of the same theme, as is *The Apes of God* (1930) – a satirical and pessimistic masterpiece of the same order as Pope's *Dunciad*.

Lewis's reputation was permanently damaged during the 1930s. Fearful of another war, he wrote antiwar books showing sympathy to Fascist regimes and policies. But the coldness or 'brutality' of Lewis's style has been too readily equated with an authoritarian temperament; *The Revenge for Love* (1937), a novel, is humane and moving: one of the profoundest 'political' novels since **Conrad**.

Lewis now tried to re-establish his reputation as a painter, with an exhibition (1937) of oils produced, despite serious illness, since 1933. The pictures express the same tragic sense of life evident in *The Revenge*, and show the influence of **de Chirico** and the Surrealists. Together with the essays on art in *Wyndham Lewis the Artist* (1939), they influenced the generation of British painters then emerging. The oil portraits of 1937–9, notably of **T.S. Eliot**, **Ezra Pound** and of the artist's wife, are among the finest of the last century.

Lewis spent the war in the USA and in Canada, unwilling to watch Europe destroy itself again. Fantastic watercolours concerned with violence and creativity are the main result of this unhappy period, which forms the background of a fine tragic novel, *Self Condemned* (1954). Despite going blind in 1951 Lewis continued to write criticism and fiction, and some critics have seen this late work as his best. *The Human Age: Part II* (1955), ostensibly a continuation of the unfinished *Childermass*, explores the tragic consequences of Lewis's absurdist view of life in a time of mass violence and genocide. Lewis had always seen himself as a 'detached' intellectual, though not an unconcerned one; without rejecting that role he now measured its human consequences. He died in 1957 before he could write the final volume of *The Human Age*.

Lewis's work is difficult to evaluate, partly because of its immense scope. He is of major importance independently in each of the following areas: painting; art criticism and theory; literary criticism; fiction. Some critics have considered him of importance as a poet. His influence has been hidden but enormous, felt by figures as diverse as El Lissitsky and **Graham Sutherland**, **Marshall McLuhan** and **George Orwell**, **Samuel Beckett** and **Anthony Powell**, David Storey and **Saul Bellow**. His best work shows an incomparably energetic accuracy in the use of the medium, in presenting its subject and in embodying a unique and forceful personality.

Further reading

Other works include: Fiction: *Snooty Baronet* (1932); *The Vulgar Streak* (1941); *Rotting Hill* (1951); *The Red Priest* (1956); *Unlucky for Pringle*, ed. C.J. Fox and R.T. Chapman (1973); *Collected Poems and Plays*, ed. A. Munton (1979). *Blasting and Bombardiering* (1937) and *Rude Assignment* (1950) are autobiographical. Literary criticism: *The Lion and the Fox* (1927); *Men without Art* (1934); *The Writer and the Absolute* (1952); *Enemy Salvoes*, ed. C.J. Fox (1975). Art criticism: *The Demon of Progress in the Arts* (1954); *Wyndham Lewis on Art*, ed. C.J. Fox and W. Michel (1969). Walter Michel's *Wyndham Lewis: Paintings and Drawings* (1971) is the most comprehensive work on Lewis's paintings. Critical studies include: Hugh Kenner, *Wyndham Lewis* (1954); William H. Pritchard, *Wyndham Lewis* (1968); Robert T. Chapman, *Wyndham Lewis: Fictions and Satires* (1973); Geoffrey Meyers, *The Enemy: A Biography of Wyndham Lewis* (1980); Paul O'Keeffe, *Some Sort of Genius: A Life of Wyndham Lewis* (2000); Paul Edwards, *Wyndham Lewis: Painter and Writer* (2000). *A Bibliography of the Writings of Wyndham Lewis* by B. Morrow and B. Lafourcade was published in 1978.

PAUL EDWARDS

LIBBY, Willard Frank

1908–80

American scientist

Willard F. Libby's receipt of the Nobel Prize in Chemistry in 1960 acknowledged the significance of the development of radiocarbon dating, first announced in 1949. Thanks to his imagination and tenacity in the laboratory, fundamental changes in the past of humanity – such as the adoption of farming by hunter-gatherers, or the emergence of urban civilizations – were placed on a sound chronological footing. Furthermore, since proxy evidence for climatic change (such as plant remains recovered from ancient soils and peat bogs) can also be dated by the radiocarbon technique, we can place changes in human societies into a wider environmental context. The creation of an independent chronological framework means that the time before historical records (prehistory) now has dates of comparable reliability to those derived from written sources. Archaeologists can now concentrate on explaining changes in sites and artefacts in terms of human behaviour, rather than classifying them in an antiquarian manner in the hope of guessing their age.

By the eighteenth century, few scientists still accepted calculations from the Bible that dated the Creation of the Earth to 4004 BC. Nineteenth-century biblical scholarship, combined with archaeological discoveries in Egypt and Mesopotamia, traced literate civilizations back to around 3000 BC. However, it remained impossible to estimate the duration of the 'prehistoric' cultures that preceded them, let alone the time our ape-like ancestors took to evolve into humans (according to **Darwin**). Evolutionary thinking reinforced Charles Lyell's emphasis upon the great depth of geological time, but it was only in the early twentieth century that geologists began to obtain reliable estimates of the age of the Earth from techniques based on radioactivity. However, they were derived from lead isotopes which measured time in millions of years, whereas the adoption of agriculture and the growth of civilizations had taken place since the end of the last Ice Age in less than 12,000 years.

Libby realized that the half-life of the radioactive isotope carbon-14 (^{14}C) lasted thousands rather than millions of years, and that new ^{14}C was continuously formed in the atmosphere by cosmic radiation. Most important, freshly formed isotopes were added to the carbon contained in all living plants and animals until their death. At this point a 'radioactive clock' started ticking: the age of a sample of ancient wood, textile or bone could be estimated by measuring how much of its original radioactivity remained, and by using the known half-life of ^{14}C to work out how many years it would have taken to fall to the observed level.

Libby worked on the chemistry of carbon before the Second World War, but during the war took part in the Manhattan Project which produced the atom bomb. After the war he refined radiocarbon dating by testing samples of known age. Suitable organic material up to 5,000 years old was available from Egypt, preserved in dry conditions and dated by inscriptions. Once a good correspondence between ages known from tree rings or historical records and radiocarbon estimations had been established, the technique could be applied to undated prehistoric samples. This 'first radiocarbon revolution' provided a way of dating sequences of cultural development anywhere in the world *and* relating them to unconnected developments elsewhere.

Libby lived to see a second radiocarbon revolution. Continuous sequences of annual tree rings taken from timber preserved in arid conditions or in bogs were gradually extended beyond the oldest dated material from Egypt into prehistoric times. Samples taken from annual growth rings revealed fluctuations in cosmic radiation that meant that radiocarbon dates underestimated real 'calendar' age before 1000 BC by an increasing margin. A calibration curve was constructed to correct the error, with the result that stone monuments such as Stonehenge and megalithic chambered tombs around the Atlantic coast now predated the first stone architecture in Egypt and around the Aegean. As a result, the long-held belief in the 'diffusion' of ideas and technology from Near-Eastern civilizations to prehistoric Europe collapsed, requiring completely new explanations of independent social and technical innovation.

A third radiocarbon revolution took place after Libby's death. Accelerator mass spectrometry (AMS) was introduced for measuring small amounts of ^{14}C more precisely, allowing samples back to around 50,000 years old to be counted with reasonable margins of error. This made it possible to date phenomena such as the replacement of Neanderthals by 'modern' humans in Europe around 35,000 years ago, the unexpectedly early colonization of Australia at least 50,000 years ago, and the comparatively recent first occupation of New Zealand around AD 1200.

Further reading

See W.F. Libby, *Radiocarbon Dating* (1952 and subsequent editions). A straightforward modern explanation can be found in S. Bowman, *Radiocarbon Dating* (1990) or in more detail in M.J. Aitken, *Science-based Dating in Archaeology* (1990). See also: Colin Renfrew, *Before Civilization: The Radiocarbon Revolution and Prehistoric Europe* (1973); J. Gowlett and R. Hedges (eds) *Archaeological Results from Accelerator Dating* (1986). Papers on many topics and geographical areas can be found in R.E. Taylor *et al.* (eds) *Radiocarbon after Four Decades: An Interdisciplinary Perspective* (1992).

KEVIN GREENE

LICHTENSTEIN, Roy

1923–97

US painter

Fascinated by American popular mythology and by the language of mass visual communication, Lichtenstein was central to the American Pop Art movement of the 1960s – even if it was **Warhol**, not he, who was its most celebrated exponent. His pre-war paintings had frequently depicted a certain side of his native New York: jazz musicians, Coney Island, etc. In 1949–50 his favoured subjects had been cowboys, Indians and all aspects of the Western myth. But it was only in 1961 that his painting style, hitherto mostly loose and expressionistic, changed into the impersonal, hard-edged look for which he is famous and which was the perfect tool for his ironic semantic analysis.

His first properly called Pop paintings were of **Walt Disney** characters but he soon switched for his material to comic books like *Armed Forces at War* and *Teen Romance*, whose subject-matter was more emotionally charged. With deliberate humour he exploited the powerful narrative impact of such images. At first sight, his paintings appear merely as massively enlarged reproductions; only then does the difference appear between his purpose and that of the 'originals'. Rather than storytelling, his aim is the creation of a unified work of art, in an almost Classical sense. From his student days at Ohio State University, he learned the central importance for art of 'organized perception'. What one happens to be looking at is far less important than 'building a unified pattern of seeing'. His work testifies that this is possible even from the most unpromising material and in so doing opens up hitherto unsuspected perspectives on that material, in terms of both technical and wider social factors.

Particularly successful is his painting *Whaam!* (1963), whose overt subject is aerial combat but whose real subject is the exploration of one sign-system by means of another. Like many of Lichtenstein's pictures, this features an explosion, the attraction of which lies in the contrast between the amorphousness of the phenomenon and the concreteness of its conventionalized representation. He even made solid sculptures of explosions. In the same spirit, he produced paintings of Expressionistic brushstrokes in which the calm deliberateness of their making gently mocked the convention by which wild brushstrokes were taken as evidence of creative spontaneity and authenticity; again later concretizing this in three dimensions, for example in the aluminium sculpture *Brushstrokes in Flight* (1984). Almost his trademark was the Benday dot, the commercial printing technique for simulating halftones, to whose artificiality attention is drawn by its being transferred, in his work, to a vastly larger scale than that for which it was intended.

It was his use of comic book imagery which made Lichtenstein famous but already in 1963 he had painted *Woman with Flowered Hat* (1963) parodying **Picasso**; and after 1965 he turned primarily to pastiches of high art, especially various Modernist styles, including Cubism and Futurism, as well as both German and Abstract Expressionism. Without aggressively negating the significance of earlier styles of art, he nevertheless drew attention to their abstract and formal properties at the expense of their content. A natural semiotician, he stressed the importance of the signifier rather than the signified. Thus, as Robert Hughes pointed out in an obituary, he can be seen as 'a postmodernist before the term got going'. While underneath the cool exterior of Warhol's work it is not hard to discern an element of turmoil and pain, emotional as well as existential anxiety is entirely absent from Lichtenstein's, even if, as he himself once pointed out, the cool 'lack of sensibility' in it does perhaps relate to that 'kind of brutality' and 'aggressiveness' which he believed characterized the 'world outside largely formed by industrialism or by advertising'.

Further reading

See: Lawrence Alloway, *Roy Lichtenstein* (Modern Masters Series, Vol. 1, 1983); Janis Hendrickson, *Lichtenstein* (2001); and his own book *Roy Lichtenstein: All About Art* (2004), published posthumously. There is a celebrated video (also DVD in USA and Canada) *Roy Lichtenstein* (1991) directed by Chris Hunt.

GRAY WATSON

LIGETI, György Sándor

1923–

Hungarian composer

Born to Jewish parents in Dicsöszentmárton, Transylvania, Ligeti studied music in Kolozsvár and Budapest, but his early artistic development was shaped as much by political forces as by formal training. His first decade as a composer was spent not only in the shadow of World War II, during which most of his family died at Auschwitz, but also in the severe cultural confines of communist Hungary, where experimental music was banned and composers were expected to work within the aesthetic parameters of social realism. Despite these circumstances, Ligeti's early years yielded some impressive music, much of it characterized by melancholy wistfulness and the influence of **Bartók**, whose folk-inspired idioms were considered permissible by the authorities. Though Ligeti focused mainly on choral music in this period, he also wrote some highly innovative instrumental pieces, among which *Musica ricercata* (1951–5) – a cycle of short piano pieces built from limited numbers of pitches – stands out as a highly original and compelling composition.

In December 1956, after the Hungarian Uprising was crushed by Soviet military invasion, Ligeti and his wife fled to Austria, where the young composer was finally free to study the works of his contemporaries and tread a more radical musical path. Settling in Cologne, he became acquainted with **Karlheinz Stockhausen** at the city's Studio for Electronic Music, where he wrote a handful of works including the darkly comic *Artikulation* for quadraphonic tape. He also started teaching at the Darmstadt summer school, but retained a typically dissenting view about total serialism, the rigorous compositional approach advocated by **Pierre Boulez**, Stockhausen and Luigi Nono, the school's dominant figures. Ligeti viewed serialism as overly dogmatic and restrictive, and pioneered an alternative texturalist style based on slow-changing musical 'clouds', often dense musical meshes woven from masses of overlapping melodic and rhythmic fragments – a technique that he named micropolyphony.

With his international reputation secured by *Apparitions* (1958–9) and *Atmosphères* (1961), his first major 'cloud' works, Ligeti entered a more surrealist phase, writing *Poème symphonique* (1962) for a hundred out-of-sync clockwork metronomes, and two extravagantly theatrical vocal pieces based on the

texts of meaningless syllables: *Aventures* (1963) and *Nouvelles aventures* (1962–5). These radical approaches soon resurfaced in more impressive micropolyphony works. Clockwork-like rhythm was integrated into the orchestral textures of *Lontano* (1967), while experimental vocal writing formed the basis of two astonishingly dark and imposing works for choir: the *Requiem* of 1963–5 and *Lux aeterna* of 1966 (today widely known from its use in **Stanley Kubrick's** film *2001*).

In the ensuing years, which he spent in Berlin and Vienna, Ligeti focused on orchestral formats, and introduced more clearly defined melodies and transparent rhythms into his music – even occasional hints of tonality. The results included the Cello Concerto (1966), the *Chamber Concerto* (1969–70), *Melodien* (1971) and the Double Concerto for flute and oboe (1972), all remarkable works that alternate scintillating, frenzied movement with static and ethereal beauty. This penchant for varied textures would soon develop into full-blown eclecticism with *Le Grande Macabre*, Ligeti's only major music-theatre piece to date, written for Stockholm Opera between 1974 and 1977. Premiered in 1978, and revived all over Europe, *Le Grande Macabre* is an extraordinary, multifaceted work that draws together Ligeti's previous approaches in a kaleidoscopic patchwork of musical sincerity and surrealism, parody and grotesquery – car horns and ragtime jostling with disfigured quotes from the classical canon.

After *Le Grande Macabre*, Ligeti composed almost nothing for a number of years. When he eventually resurfaced in 1983, his music had a new sense of nostalgia about it – for the modalities of Hungarian folk in two unaccompanied choral works, and for earlier art-music forms in the elegiac *Horn Trio*. Since then, however, the most dominant feature of his work has been complex interlocking rhythm, inspired partly by recordings of music from Central Africa and the Caribbean. This polyrhythm lies at the heart of the Piano Concerto (1985), parts of the Violin Concerto

(1992) and the extraordinary *Études* for piano, which have appeared in two 'books' (1985 and 1993), with a third still in progress. Dazzlingly virtuosic and shot through with an electric energy, the *Études* exploit an immense range of dynamics and timbres, and provide a distilled example of something that underpins and unites much of Ligeti's seemingly disparate output: the building of complex forms from simple processes.

Though he has always stood apart from any single school or doctrine, Ligeti is widely recognized as one of the most significant figures of post-war music. His work, more than that of any other avant-garde composer, appeals not just to musicians and music historians but also to general listeners. This is perhaps because in Ligeti's music – despite his having what one commentator described as the 'mindset of a scientist' – intellectual concepts have never taken precedence over direct communicative power.

Further reading

Other works include: Sonata for Cello Solo (1953); String Quartet No. 1 (1954); *Volumina* (1962); String Quartet No. 2 (1968); *Continuum* (1968); *Ramifications* (1969); *Clocks & Clouds* (1973); *San Francisco Polyphony* (1974); *Monument, Selbstportrait, Bewegung* (1976); *Magyar Etüdök* (1983); *Drei Phantasien* (1983); Viola Sonata (1994). See: Paul Griffiths, *György Ligeti* (1997); Richard Toop, *György Ligeti* (1999); Richard Steinitz, *György Ligeti: Music of the Imagination* (2003).

DUNCAN CLARK

LIN, Maya Ying

1959–

US architect and designer

Born in Athens, Ohio, of Chinese stock, Maya Lin shot to international prominence at the age of twenty-two when she won a nationwide competition for the design of a memorial to commemorate those Americans who died or were reported missing in action in Indochina during the Vietnam War of 1962–73, for a site in Washington DC. At the time she was still a student, in her final year at the University of Yale School of Architecture, but her design was chosen against over 14,000 other entries, exhibited in an aircraft hangar.

The inspiration for the competition belonged to Jan C. Scraggs, a war veteran who felt that the ordeals experienced and sacrifices made by those Americans who had fought in Vietnam had never been adequately honoured, particularly in the nation's capital. Lin's simple but elegant solution, almost for the first time involving elements of modernism in a public monument in America, was duly raised and dedicated in 1982. Consisting of a hinged monolith, its concave surface is inscribed with the names of the dead. By some it is perceived as a type of boomerang, reflecting the nature of a conflict that 'came back to haunt' the superpower that perpetrated it.

Known as the Vietnam Veterans' Memorial, Lin's ground-breaking work attracted immediate controversy and has remained the most visited site in Washington ever since. Part of the controversy, stoked by some veterans as well as by social and political conservatives, had to do with Lin's own identity, and was both sexist and racist. How could such a young Sino-American woman have the capacity to respond to the complex of emotions aroused by the activities of white and black soldiers fighting for America in a non-Chinese part of East Asia? Much more though, controversy centred on the design itself. Unlike other large war memorials, nothing about it sought to glamorize either war of the military, or for that matter the nation. Memorably, having visited the site during construction, Lin had opted to leave the surrounding park intact, as a place where visitors could relax and play.

Debate was sufficiently heated to prompt the US Fine Arts Commission to install a thoroughly conventional, 'realistic' sculpture and flag close by Lin's monument. Lin's initiative, however, permanently changed public art in America, opening the way for diffused use of modernist techniques and conceptualization. Significantly, following the destruction of the twin towers of the World Trade Center by al-Qaeda in September 2001, submissions for memorializing features to be installed at New York's 'Ground Zero' nearly all showed striking similarities to Lin's 1982 composition. Lin herself participated in the judging of the entries, and it has been contended that the final selection closely resembled a sketch previously submitted by her to the *New York Times*.

After 1982, Lin found herself in constant demand as an architect-designer, and she has continued to produce monumental work, notably the Civil Rights Memorial (1989) in Montgomery, Alabama, inspired by the assassination of **Martin Luther King**. At the centre of this is a granite table upon which are inscribed the names of forty-odd individuals together with brief descriptions of the events leading to their deaths, and over which water flows from a central wellspring. Adjacent to this table is a curved wall bearing a quotation from King, over which water also cascades.

Less immediately striking, but equally effective, is *The Wave Field* (1995), on the campus of the University of Michigan at Ann Arbor. Here, fifty grass waves arranged in eight rows spread over 10,000 square feet. Drawing on scientific, environmental and art historical sources, this work provides, and is intended to provide, an area of green space for student relaxation.

While not averse to taking on residential and commercial commissions, Maya Lin has consistently sought to engage the viewer and user in a modernist, even postmodernist, relationship with her constructs. The notion that a public monument must do more than simply commemorate and celebrate is by no means hers alone, yet her influence in this regard has been profound. In addition, her studio produces furniture and other non-monumental artefacts.

Further reading

Other writing include: accompanied by extensive illustrations, *Boundaries* (2000), and the 1995 film *Maya Lin: A Strong Clear Vision* provides perhaps the best appreciation of her output.

ANNE K. SWARTZ

LINCOLN, Abraham

1809–65

Sixteenth president of the United States

Born on 12 February 1809 in Kentucky, Lincoln arrived in Illinois at the age of twenty-one, having lived the previous fourteen years in Indiana. The northwest, and Illinois in particular, was growing more rapidly in population and in the means of producing wealth than was any other region in the United States. It was a good location for an able and ambitious man. Engaging in a variety of occupations before making his reputation as a lawyer, Lincoln entered politics as a Whig: that is, as a member of the political party most committed to the idea of a strong central government in a nation defined by its regional and sectional diversity. By the time he entered national politics in the 1840s it was sectionalism and its associated problem of slavery which dominated the national political scene, and Lincoln's own political career was shaped by it and was ultimately dedicated to the search for a reconciliation between the needs of the nation and the diversity of its components.

After serving a single undistinguished term in Congress during the Mexican War Lincoln was thrust into the political wilderness by the partial eclipse of the Whig Party in Illinois. He returned to the fray with renewed enthusiasm in 1854 as a result of the Kansas–Nebraska crisis. Douglas's plan for the settlement of Kansas and Nebraska attempted to take the associated issue of the expansion of slavery out of national politics by making it a matter for local self-determination. Pro–and anti-slavery forces hastened to confront each other in the new Territory and the continued turmoil in Kansas became a reference point for the emergence of a new set of political alignments. The Republican Party, opposed to the spread of slavery, replaced the Whig

Party in the North while the Democratic Party, purged of its northern anti-slavery elements, and reinforced by southern Whigs, upheld the equal rights of slavery. Over the course of the next six years Lincoln emerged as the leader of the Republican Party, and it was the positions he took which came to define the central ground within that party. Those positions will best be understood, perhaps, when contrasted with those of his principal opponent, Stephen A. Douglas.

Both Lincoln and Douglas were nationalists but their nationalism differed. Douglas equated nationalism with expansion and democracy; the latter he conceived of in terms of the spread of American democratic institutions and of popular sovereignty: that is, local self-determination. Lincoln was less expansionist because he recognized that in the context of the mid-nineteenth century it involved less the expansion of the nation than that of its sections. His commitment to democracy was, moreover, more complex than that of Douglas. It was never for him merely a matter of majority rule and certainly not one of local majorities. It was the content of politics which mattered, not merely its operations. The American Union was defined for Lincoln by its commitment to certain goals and principles. These had been enshrined in the Declaration of Independence at the moment the nation was conceived. It was the moral content of American democracy which concerned Lincoln, and at the centre of a web of moral propositions was the idea of equality. He refused to contemplate the implication of Douglas's position that slavery and freedom shared an equal moral status depending upon the whims of local majorities. He also refused to contemplate the abdication of the central government from a determination of national issues in the interest of political quiet. Lincoln's sense of the past, his insistence that the Constitution be read in the light cast upon it by the Declaration of Independence, was complemented by a sense of history as an ongoing process. American ideals were belied by American practice but Lincoln conceived of a nation in which they would converge.

The slavery issue was a crucial test of the national commitment to such a vision. Arguing that the Founding Fathers had been prepared to compromise their principles with respect to slavery only because they assumed its inevitable demise, Lincoln denied the possibility that the nation could survive on the basis of a permanent co-existence of slavery and freedom. Yet the course of events in the 1840s and 1850s pointed towards a commitment in the South to the permanence of slavery and, indeed, towards a vigorous promotion of its interests. Lincoln's response was to invoke the Declaration of Independence on behalf of black as well as white Americans. Equality was a universal right. His concept of the meaning of equality was narrow when compared to that prevailing in the late twentieth century, and even when compared to some radical spirits in his own day, but it was well in advance of the majority of his compatriots. His ability, after coming close to defeating Douglas in the 1858 senatorial contest, to make his own position that of the centre of his party testifies to his political skill. It was around his ideas that the Republican Party coalesced, and fought and won the presidential contest in 1860 which sparked off the secession of the South from the Union. What Lincoln posited, in essence, was the interpendence of white and black freedom. Pressing Congress in 1862 to agree to his scheme of voluntary and compensated emancipation in the loyal states, he insisted that 'in *giving* freedom to the slave, we *assure* freedom to the free'.

It was his recognition that the future of the Union, as he conceived it, and the future of slavery were inextricably linked that enabled Lincoln to embark upon a political course that always carried with it the risk of civil war. It was only because the Union contained a profound moral quality that the risk was worth taking. Lincoln clearly underestimated the risk, and he equally clearly had no conception of the cost of the struggle to preserve the Union, but even with greater foresight he might have been willing to pay the price to preserve the 'last, best hope of earth'.

Lincoln's extraordinary political skill was exhibited during the Civil War in his ability to maintain the integrity of his administration, and the commitment of his party to the war, in the face of fierce opposition and of continued and severe reverses on the battlefield. The eventual collapse of the Confederacy ensured the final abolition of slavery. Lincoln's assassination, only days after Lee's surrender, on Good Friday 1865, left the even more difficult task of reconstruction in other hands, but Lincoln's work was done. In great part through the force of his own character and determination he had preserved the Union, thereby guaranteeing the unity and great power of a major part of the North American continent. He had played an important role in the release from servitude of some four million human beings. Above all, perhaps, his commitment to an American purpose, to the idea of the United States as embodying certain principles, had a decisive effect, if only because of its association with the Civil War, in moulding a continued sense of American idealism. Often crass, but sometimes noble, that commitment has had a profound effect upon subsequent world history.

Further reading

The literature on Lincoln is enormous. Larger biographies include: Carl Sandburg, *Abraham Lincoln: The Prairie Years* (2 vols, 1926) and *The War Years* (4 vols, 1939); and James G. Randall, *Lincoln the President* (4 vols, 1945–55). The best one-volume biographies are: Benjamin Thomas, *Abraham Lincoln* (1952); and Stephen B. Oates, *With Malice Toward None: The Life of Abraham Lincoln* (1977). His speeches and letters can be found in Abraham Lincoln, *Collected Works*, ed. Roy P. Basler (9 vols, 1953–5). See also: David Herbert Donald, *Lincoln* (1996); Joshua Wolf Shenk, *How Depression Challenged a President and Fueled His Greatness* (2006).

DUNCAN MACLEOD

LISTER, Joseph

1827–1912
English surgeon

Lister came from a pious Quaker family and his lifelong meticulousness, industriousness and self-questioning bear witness to his childhood. He remained devoted to his father, Joseph Jackson Lister, a wealthy wine merchant who contributed substantially to the perfection of the objective lens system of the microscope and who also fostered his son's early interest in science. In 1844 Lister registered at the only English university open to a Quaker, University College, London. In 1848 he suffered a nervous breakdown, but eventually resumed his studies and received his MD degree and fellowship of the Royal College of Surgeons in 1852. Already by this time Lister was resolved to be a surgeon, and was pursuing microscopical researches in his spare time.

In 1853 Lister moved to Edinburgh. Here he was befriended by the famous surgeon James Syme. In 1854 he became Syme's house surgeon and the following year married Syme's eldest daughter Agnes. It was at this time, as worldly success began to come his way, that he resigned his membership of the Society of Friends. By 1860 his lecturing and research on inflammation had brought sufficient reputation for him to be elected a fellow of the Royal Society. In 1860 he became Regius Professor of Surgery in Glasgow and entered into the most intellectually fruitful period of his life.

Victorian hospitals were essentially centres for the treatment of the poor. Cleanliness and nutrition were often inadequate and in surgical wards mortality could be very high. The main cause of death was 'hospitalism', the post-operative development of sepsis and gangrene in wounds. This problem had become particularly acute by the 1860s, for anaesthesia had been introduced in the late 1840s and had resulted in a rise in the number of operations performed and an increase in operating time.

Lister, fascinated by the attendant question of inflammation, was also preoccupied by the theoretical and practical issues surrounding suppuration. Already by 1865 he was doubting the prevalent view propounded by Justus von Liebig that putrefaction was simply a form of combustion occurring when moist organic substances make contact with oxygen. In the same year his attention was drawn to the claims of **Louis Pasteur** that putrefaction was essentially a fermentative process produced by living organisms. Over the next two years Lister began using carbolic acid as an agent to protect accidental and surgical wounds against infection. The wound was both cleaned with the acid and covered with a dressing impregnated with it. His results were remarkable. In eleven cases of compound fracture, nearly always a fatal injury, nine patients recovered. The new technique and Lister's claims for its success were described in a series of reports in the *Lancet* (1867) – 'On a New Method of Treating Compound Fracture, Abscess, etc., With Observations on the Condition of Suppuration'.

Lister's ideas and methods were by no means immediately accepted by the medical profession. To begin with, most surgeons had their own favoured methods of dealing with sepsis, and second, carbolic acid treatment was unpleasant for the surgeon and its action on the wound delayed healing. In the long term, acceptance was eventually assured by the gradual establishment of the germ theory, associated with **Robert Koch**, in the 1880s. The growth of antiseptic treatment was also closely associated with Lister's own personality. His indefatigable lecturing, research and European and American propagandizing helped convert the younger generation of surgeons.

Over the years he gradually extended his technique to cover all bacteriological exigencies. Innovations included a 'donkey engine' and then a 'steam spray' to atomize carbolic acid over the operative area. Eventually, however, he abandoned these. Towards the end of the century other surgeons began to advocate aseptic as opposed to antiseptic surgery. This technique involved scrupulous presterilization of the skin, the

operating area and all instruments in contact with the wound. It remains the basis of modern surgery. Lister, although he recognized the theoretical basis of the procedure, always doubted whether it was practically effective. Antiseptic surgery, however, had made such a concept possible.

For Lister himself, the triumph of antiseptic surgery brought great personal fame, enormous wealth, and finally a baronetcy. It might be said that his contribution to the modern heroic mythology of the surgeon was as great as his achievement in surgical practice.

Further reading

See: Lister's works are collected as *The Collected Papers of Joseph Baron Lister* (2 vols, 1909). See: Rickman J. Godlee, *Lord Lister* (1917); Richard Fisher, *Joseph Lister 1827–1912* (1977); Martin Goldman, *Lister Ward* (1987).

C.J. LAWRENCE

LISZT, Franz
1811–86
German/Hungarian composer and pianist

One of the foremost musicians of the Romantic period, Liszt was born into a German-speaking family, being the son of a steward on the Esterhazy estate where Haydn had previously served as *kapellmeister*. As a youth he received piano tuition from Carl Czerny and composition lessons from Salieri, the teacher of Beethoven and Schubert. After his first public appearance at the age of eleven, which met with high critical acclaim, he gave up lessons and embarked on a course of self-instruction lasting five years. Afterwards he lived exclusively on his earnings as an international virtuoso pianist until early retirement in his mid-thirties. In 1823 he settled in Paris, though during the next decade he travelled extensively, visiting Russia, Portugal and Turkey as well as England and the rest of Europe. In 1848, having abandoned most of his performing activities, he took up permanent residence at the court of

Weimar as musical director. By now he had all but given up the concert stage and instead applied himself to the task of composing orchestral works and directing operatic music. His friendship with **Wagner** at this time produced piano transcriptions of *Tannhäuser*, *Lohengrin* and new scores by **Berlioz**, whose music he had always championed. These performances realized a life-long ambition to publicize the many unrecognized compositions of his contemporaries; however, he eventually clashed with the court authorities and resigned his post in 1859. Soon afterwards Liszt moved to Rome where in 1865 he took up orders as a minor canon of the church. From then on until his death in 1886 his time was divided travelling between Rome, Weimar and Budapest, where he spent his remaining years both as a teacher and promoter of new music.

Aptly described as a truly international artist, Liszt had a unique musical style which reflects a vast interest in the literary eclecticism of the Romantic period: such philosophical inquiries were frequently expressed in the formal and harmonic experiments within his works. Though the composer himself wished to be thought of primarily as a Hungarian with strongly nationalistic traits, his early training in Vienna brought him in touch with more classical concepts via the music of Bach and Beethoven, which during the 1820s was considered out of favour. However, his move to Paris added the new dimension of Romantic thought to the conception of his compositions and concert performances. This new exposure led him to meet not only the writers **Victor Hugo**, Lamartine, Sainte-Beuve and George Sand, but also the painter Delacroix, whose creations were the embodiment of Romantic imagery. Liszt's early interest in the church can be traced to this period, when he was to study the spiritual writings of Lamennais and Saint-Simon whose philosophies of Christian socialism and the advocation of art as a means of attaining moral perfection were to colour the composer's religious attitudes in later life. Such influences explain the strongly programmatic and spiritual elements in most of his output.

Besides these literary considerations, more musical influences must also be taken into account. Liszt's meeting with Berlioz, Chopin and Paganini in the early 1830s offered new opportunities for experiment in his many piano works of the period. The recent success of Berlioz's *Symphonie fantastique* caused Liszt to transcribe it for piano solo and also enabled him to champion the Frenchman's later works, many of which rarely met with the public's approval. The programmatic elements of Berlioz's scores together with their frequent use of a cyclic musical thread of *idée-fixe* did much to shape Liszt's own thinking in terms of a similar 'thematic metamorphosis' within his own larger compositions. It was Chopin who offered Liszt new approaches to the treatment of sonority and pianistic effect together with singing melodic lines derived from the lyrical operatic arias of Bellini. Liszt assimilated these characteristics into his own style by further extending their emotional content via more rubato, dynamic range and rhythmic interest. The addition of folk rhythms from central Europe, advanced chords and particularly distant modulations to unrelated keys made him the most daring of composer-performers.

During this period the development of orchestral instruments lagged well behind that of the piano, and this is the main reason why Liszt preferred a medium over which he had total personal control. Probably the greatest contribution to his art was that of Paganini, whose violin recitals he attended in Paris in 1831. Though much less a composer than a performer, Paganini gave the young musician the impetus to study and perfect a kind of showmanship and extroversion unknown during this period and yet so typical of the Romantic spirit. Liszt was not only impressed with the violinist's daring performances but was determined to emulate this method of musical sorcery, both with the inception of a new kind of pianistic virtuosity and by way of its presentation.

Liszt's compositions spanned seventy years, and though a large proportion are original works for piano, he also made many transcriptions and arrangements of songs, orchestral works and symphonies for the medium. Added to this there are over a dozen symphonic poems, the programmatic *Faust* and *Dante* Symphonies (1856), concert pieces and two piano concertos (1856, 1861), together with many choral compositions and songs. The mature piano works are well represented in the *Études d'exécution transcendante* (1851), many of whose titles convey the particular technical device or mood to be exploited. Of less difficulty are the three sets of short pieces called the *Années de pèlerinage* (Vols 1 and 2, 1850; Vol. 3, 1867–77) and reflect his impressions as a visitor to Switzerland and Italy. The brilliant Sonata in B minor (1853), an extended movement on four interrelated themes, exploits the process of thematic metamorphosis by subjecting the material to constant variation in tempo, texture and mood as it unfolds: similar procedures are to be found in the piano concertos and in many of the symphonic poems. These descriptive works, though generally rather short, exploit a similar cyclic use and follow the train of thought in some work of poetry or painting that provided the creative inspiration: their essentially programmatic nature is displayed in such titles as *Les Préludes* (1848), *Mazeppa* (1851), *Hamlet* (1858) and many others which like *Hungaria* (1854) are strongly nationalistic. Similar preoccupations can be seen in the nineteen *Hungarian Rhapsodies* written between 1846 and 1886: these are again free in conception, taking the czardas as their formal basis, and contrast many sections of tempo changes, melodic variations and virtuoso devices.

Although Liszt gave up a virtuoso career at the age of thirty-five he continued to write for the piano until his death. These late works were only heard by a close circle of friends and pupils who appeared reluctant to reveal their existence. Their availability now shows that Liszt was constantly paring down his musical materials to a minimum and that his experiments were to be responsible for shaping the outlook of many composers at the beginning of this century. This process of economy invariably mixed with advanced chromatic treatment appears in the early *Années de pélerinage* and in the *Malédiction* for piano and strings sketched as early as 1830. Similar practice with roving harmonies and obscure key centres can be seen in the two great organ works *Fantasia and Fugue on Bach* (1855) and in his Meyerbeer arrangement on the choral *Ad nos, ad salutarem undam* (1850): both works foreshadow the heavy chromaticism of **Richard Strauss** and Max Reger by nearly fifty years. Though the above mentioned are rather severe in style, many of the lighter piano pieces also look to the future as in the four *Valses oubliées* (1881–6), the three *Mephisto Waltzes* (1860, 1881, 1883) and especially the *Fountains of the Villa d'Este* (1877) which strongly influenced the Russian school of pianists and the impressionist works of **Debussy** and **Ravel**. The majority of these late works reflect the composer's obsession with his own mortality, though their melancholy feeling can often be explained by Liszt's increasing use of exotic scales derived from folk song: good examples of this effect can be seen in the *Czardas obstiné* (1884), *Czardas macabre* (1882) and the little-known *Hungarian Portraits* (1885). The aphoristic style of these piano pieces, together with the *Lugubre Gondola* (1882), *R.W. – Venezia* (1883) and *Am Grabe Richard Wagner's* (1883) memorial fragments were to be a major influence on the harmonic experiments of **Busoni** and **Bartók**. Many were just sketches conceived for optional performance as chamber music for solo strings with harmonium or piano accompaniment, as can be seen in the enigmatically titled *Dark Star, Sleepless, Sinister* or *Grey Clouds*: their economy of melodic and rhythmic material may well convey the composer's spiritual disappointment and resignation to the 'idle uselessness that frets me'. Likewise, other strange essays of this period reflect a similar state of mind: the meditation *Via Crucis* for chorus and organ (1878) and the final symphonic poem, *From the Cradle to the Grave* (1881–2).

The position of Liszt as a composer of major importance went unrecognized in his own time, and for a long while Wagner was considered to be the sole prophet of new developments in twentieth-century music. Though both men were fully involved with a creative means of expression which encompassed traits of nationalism and Romanticism in the nineteenth century, it befell Liszt to anticipate the importance of a later internationalism in music of the future.

Further reading

See: C. Wagner, *F. Liszt* (1911); E. Newman, *The Man Liszt* (1934); H. Searle, *The Music of Liszt* (1954); B. Szabolcsi, *The Twilight of Liszt* (1956); *Franz Liszt, the Man and His Music*, ed. Alan Walker (1970); A. Walker, *Liszt* (1974) and *Reflections on Liszt* (2005).

MICHAEL ALEXANDER

LIVINGSTONE, David

1813–73

Scottish explorer

In the year of David Livingstone's death **Florence Nightingale** referred to him as 'the greatest man of his generation'. He was a missionary who only made one convert, an impassioned opponent of the slave-trade who was often dependent for the necessities of life on the slavers, and an explorer whose discoveries were rendered worthless in his own eyes by their failure to live up to his expectations – the Zambesi was not God's Highway to Central Africa, Lakes Nyasa and Moero were not the sources of the Nile, the Victoria Falls were awesomely beautiful but inconvenient. But for all his failures he was intemperately loved and revered. His life-story is so incomprehensible in terms of worldly motivations that his contemporaries believed him to be a saint. It suited his sponsors, the Society of Missionaries and the Royal Geographical Society, and his would-be

saviour **H.M. Stanley**, to promote his legend, but the circumstances of his solitary explorations were enough to make him a figure of romance. He was a hero custom-made for Victorian Britain. Not only did he typify their most admired qualities, he provided them, before they even needed it, with a moral justification for imperialism.

He was born in 1813 at Blantyre, near Glasgow, and grew up in a room 10 feet by 14 in which he, his parents and his five siblings cooked, ate, read (those of them who could) and slept. At the age of ten he went to work as a cotton-piecer. His working hours were from six in the morning until eight at night, after which he went on to study for two hours at a local school and to teach himself Latin in the remaining hours of the night. His qualifying himself to enter, at the age of twenty, a medical training school for missionaries is one of the most impressive of all his remarkable feats. It was achieved at some cost. To study so intensely in that crowded room he had to learn to distance himself from those around him; he was never again fully at ease with the members of a white race.

He sailed to South Africa in 1840. Disappointed by the realities of missionary life he quarrelled with colleagues and took every opportunity to push further and further away from other settlements, 'to work beyond other men's lines'. He married the daughter of Robert Moffat, the leader of the South African missionaries, but in 1852 he sent her and their children back to England. He had already travelled further north into the interior than any European before him. Now, walking or riding an ox, he made his way across deserts, through rain-forests and past the territory of hostile tribes to the west coast at Luanda. Realizing that his own journey had been too fraught with danger and difficulty to be feasible for others but still determined to find a route through which the word of God and Western civilization could penetrate Central Africa, he retraced his steps and continued along the River Zambesi to the east coast. In four years of appalling hardship he had crossed Africa.

He returned to England a national hero. **Queen Victoria** laughed at one of his ponderous jokes. He was invited to lecture and to write a book. He was eager to explain himself. He had been met at the mouth of the Zambesi by a letter from the Missionary Society pointing out that his wanderings had little bearing on his supposed calling. The criticism hurt; he had, as his journals show, already been considerably exercised to justify his actions.

He respected the tribal institutions of those among whom he had spent so many years. His experiences had shown him how contact with Europeans distorts and corrupts that organization. He knew that to Africans, who worked only to feed themselves and had no concept of capitalism, the industrial revolution had little to offer. Worst of all, he already guessed, and soon would know with certainty, that his explorations opened up new routes, not for missionaries but for slavers. Yet he was driven by a desire which went beyond reason to see Africa 'civilized'. To this end, he argued, explorers should open the way for traders. Commerce would rapidly destroy the generous co-operative responsibility which was the essential premise of tribal life. This was regrettable but necessary. The African, isolated by the erosion of familiar social structures, would more readily convert to Christianity. Meantime legitimate trade would make the native prosperous enough to resist the slavers. Trade was to be the underpinning of the new Africa, the winning of converts and the abolition of slavery its twin justifications.

Livingstone returned to Africa in 1860 as Her Majesty's Consul for Civilization and Commerce. The expedition was disastrous. His five European companions and the mission which, responding to his inspirational last lecture in Cambridge, followed them out suffered from famine, malaria, the hostility of slavers and the dangers of tribal warfare. Watching Livingstone attempting to navigate unnavigable rivers and to settle forbiddingly hostile terrain, some of them concluded he was mad.

Some biographers have agreed with them. Livingstone was probably a manic-depressive, the extremity of his moods being increased by his belief in divine providence. He believed that he was appointed to do God's work and that he was therefore invulnerable. When things went well he was fearless and fanatically energetic, but setbacks of any kind unnerved him. A sandbank was not just an annoyance, it was a sign that God had withdrawn his protection. At such times he would try to throw off his depression by means of violent physical exertion and he had no sympathy for other people's weaknesses. The Zambesi expedition ended inconclusively, leaving many, including Livingstone's wife and the man who was to have been the first bishop of Central Africa, dead.

He embarked on his last journey in 1866. His official purpose was to find the source of the Nile; his private justification for such an ungodly exercise was that it might provide him with opportunities at least to hinder the slave trade. For seven years he wandered, increasingly infirm and despondent. His geographical discoveries were momentous but they meant little to him. In all his travels he kept copious notes, recording details of flora and fauna and compiling vocabularies of tribal languages. His maps are almost unbelievably precise; he was once known to take over 2,000 sightings to establish one position. He was a gifted geographer and natural scientist but his conscience would not allow him to devote his life to the pursuit of mere knowledge.

He was now in almost constant pain from internal bleeding, from ulcers and from the shoulder which, twenty years before, had been crushed by a lion. He had repeated attacks of malaria. His ready sympathy with any non-European made him tolerant of the slavers. He wrote that they should be judged 'by the standards of an East African Moslem, not by ours', but his frequent dependence on their charity demoralized him. In 1871 he witnessed the massacre of about 400 Africans by slavers at Nyangwe and after that he would accept no Arab kindness. By the time he was found by Stanley he was close to destitution, but he refused to return to the coast.

By now the sources of the Nile had assumed a mystical significance for Livingstone. He yearned to find those twin fountains of which Herodotus and Ptolemy had written, to trace the river back to the Mountains of the Moon. He set off once again. His chronometer had been damaged; his miscalculations proved fatal. After wading for days through mud which sometimes reached their armpits, the African porters woke up one day to find their leader dead.

Livingstone's life was not as fruitless as he despairingly imagined it to be. His account of the Nyangwe massacre provided the abolitionists with essential ammunition. Within two years of his death the slave-market at Zanzibar was closed and thereafter the East African slave-trade withered away. He had opened up vast tracts of previously uncharted territory. More profoundly, his equation − commerce and the attendant disruption of tribal life = civilization = Christianity and the end of slavery − was to give those who, in the subsequent generation, carved up Africa a high and holy excuse for doing so.

Further reading

Other works include: *Missionary Travels and Researches in South Africa* (1857) and *Narrative of an Expedition to the Zambesi and Its Tributaries* (1865). Other published writings include: *Some Letters from Livingstone 1840–1872*, ed. D. Chamberlain (1940); *Livingstone's African Journal 1853–1856*, ed. I. Schapera (1963); *The Last Journals of David Livingstone in Central Africa*, ed. H. Waller (1874). See: Tim Jeal, *Livingstone* (1973); Oliver Ransford, *David Livingstone* (1978); Meriel Buxton, *David Livingstone* (2001).

LUCY HUGHES-HALLETT

LODGE, David

1935–

English novelist and critic

Like his friend and fellowacademic Malcolm Bradbury (1932–2000), David Lodge has from the beginning of his career combined fiction and literary criticism in an especially

fruitful way, illuminating each with the practice of the other. Almost all of Lodge's professional life has been spent at the University of Birmingham −the city appears under the name of Rummidge in his novels − and he is now the Emeritus Professor of English Literature there. With Bradbury, Lodge was among the first to realize the comic and satiric potential of the 'campus novel' as a means of exploring cultural and social shifts in the world beyond the university as well as in academia. Most of his early fiction is in the realist mode that reached its apogee at the beginning of the 1960s, and draws on Lodge's own life, particularly *Out of Shelter* (1970) which its author describes as 'probably the most autobiographical of my novels'. The book recounts the journey of a sixteenyear-old to Heidelberg where, courtesy of his sister, he is introduced to a world which is doubly foreign: a Germany newly defeated and still under supervision by American occupying forces. This template − of the sensitive and enquiring outsider in a semialien landscape − appears also in his National Service novel, *Ginger, You're Barmy* (1962) and *Changing Places* (1975), about a teacherexchange between British and American academics. But the sophistication and complexity of this and the later campus novels, which include *Small World* (1984), *Nice Work* (1988) and the more recent *Thinks . . .* (2001), show how far Lodge has moved from the social realism of his early work. *Nice Work*, for example, is an oblique tribute to **Elizabeth Gaskell's** *North and South* (1855), with its opposition between the aggressive world of industry and the softer province of learning, both of them under threat in the financial climate of the 1980s.

The other strand to Lodge's novels, and one which sets him apart from comparable academic satirists like Bradbury or **Kingsley Amis**, is Catholicism. Religion is central to one of his best works, *How Far Can You Go?* (1980), which traces the progress of a group of Roman Catholics through three decades, and it is a significant aspect of a novel like *Therapy* (1995), detailing the midlife crisis of a sitcom writer. Lodge does not wear an anguished heart on his sleeve, in the style of **Graham Greene**, nor does he tread the **Waughpath** of converts and censers. The spiritual in Lodge's world is – paradoxically – much more mundane, the element in which many of his characters move, something which is frequently questioned but never treated as melodrama or camp.

The accessibility which Lodge grants his readers to these two worlds – the academic and the religious – is reflected in his literary criticism, which in terms of volume alone does not fall far behind his fiction. In the preface to *Consciousness and the Novel* (2002) Lodge explains how in the 1970s and 1980s he 'absorbed and domesticated some of the concepts and methods of Continental European structuralism'. The key word here is 'domesticated'. Without quite drawing the teeth of theory, Lodge nevertheless renders it less alarming for a general readership notoriously shy of such things. Indeed, he is quite capable of incorporating into his fiction dialogue dealing with semiotics (*Nice Work*) or theories of consciousness (*Thinks ... *). Lodge's pragmatic, undoctrinaire approach is well illustrated in his nutsandbolts guide to writing, *The Art of Fiction* (1992), which grew out of a weekly column in the *Independent on Sunday* and which deals – very usefully, it should be said – with topics like 'Fancy Prose' and 'Intertexuality'. Equally, Lodge is a generous judge of others' work, always readable and enlivening.

Goodhumoured, balanced, lucid: the same terms apply to Lodge's fiction as to his criticism. They characterize his style, too, and his writing on theory is a reproach to the impenetrability of much academic discourse. Evenness of tone and pleasure in exposition make of Lodge a very ordered writer, one in whom the roles of entertainer and instructor are attractively balanced.

Further reading

See also: Kingsley Amis; Elizabeth Cleghorn Gaskell; Graham Greene; Evelyn Arthur St John Waugh.

PHILIP GOODEN

LONDON, Jack (John Griffith)

1876–1916
US novelist

The illegitimate son of an astrologer, Jack London was born in San Francisco and brought up by his mother and step-father, keeping the latter's name. Throughout his adult life he worked hard, like **Hemingway** after him, to create a myth of himself and the short episodes experienced as an adolescent: working as an oyster pirate and on the Fishery Patrol, joining Coxey's Army in its march of protest on Washington against unemployment, going to the Arctic on a sealer, or to the Klondike rush for gold. These experiences became exaggerated into the major episodes in his life, and out of them emerged an ambitious writer of short stories and novels who worked in short bursts and spent the rest of the time with his friends and hangers-on, accumulating debts which had to be paid for by hackwork. The myth he clung to and disseminated was that of the self-made man, rising from drudgery and criminality to a hard-living outdoor man, traveller and intellectual, absorbing all the latest theories and combining radical socialism with evolutionism and determinism.

The fusion of the ideas of **Herbert Spencer**, **Marx** and **Nietzsche** with the stylistic influences of **Kipling** and **R.L. Stevenson** produced vivid adventure stories riddled with philosophizing, wildly inconsistent and yet hauntingly revealing of the dilemmas and nightmares of the time. Captain Wolf Larsen in *Sea Wolf* (1904) is a Nietzschean superman, immensely strong, resourceful, intelligent and articulate, who propounds a belief in the supremacy of power as the only meaning in the universe, and yet is defeated by a brain tumour and a bourgeois greenhorn whom he kidnaps. Similarly, in the semi-autobiographical *Martin Eden* (1909), the seaman hero becomes a successful author only to reject the possibility of marriage into the middle classes and instead, in disgust and despair, he commits suicide. Such self-defeat suggests that evolution, conceived as a competition to find the fittest, is a metaphor inadequate to our life as a species, and that the elitism it entails is empty because it is nihilistic; there is no obvious purpose in power except the exercise of it.

London's best writing works by under-cutting itself and hence suggesting further depths. His renowned animal stories, *The Call of the Wild* (1903), in which a pet dog becomes a sledge-dog and thence the leader of a wild pack, and *White Fang* (1906), in which a wild dog enters into a close but ambiguous relationship with a man, explore his ambivalent attitude towards predatory and aggressive drives. This takes the form of both an admiration for them and a fear of the ruthless and unstable consequences. Closer to contemporary problems, his documentary account of the poverty of the East End of London, *The People of the Abyss* (1903), alter-nately sees the inhabitants as social victims and as dregs, the evolutionarily unfit; *The Iron Heel* (1907) is a distopic vision of the future of Chicago under a totalitarian dictatorship. The underlying contradictions of London's time emerge here with a commitment to competitive individualism and also a fear of centralized power. Even the socialism of the time stressed the efficiency of nationalization and centralization, and yet London could only conceive this as the result of individual initiative. This is illustrated in *The Dream of Debs* (1914) or the posthumously completed *The Assassination Bureau* (1963), where socia-list millionaires use force and violence to bring about universal peace and justice.

The underlying despair, most clearly visible in London's account of his alcoholism, *John Barleycorn* (1913), where an inner 'white logic' argues against all purpose or meaning, seems to have underpinned most of his life, and his death was at least partially caused by his own indulgence in drink and drugs.

Further reading

See: *The Son of the Wolf* (1900), *Children of the Frost* (1902), *South Sea Tales* (1911) and *The Scarlet Pla-gue* (1915). Other novels include: *Before Adam* (1907); *The Valley of the Moon* (1913). See also: Dale Walker and James E. Sisson III, *The Fiction of Jack London: A Chronological Bibliography* (1972); Charmian London, *The Book of Jack London* (1921); Joan London, *Jack London and His Times* (1939); Irving Stone, *Sailor on Horseback* (1938); Earle Lubor, *Jack London* (1974). James I. McClintock, *White Logic* (1976) is a critical study of the stories.

DAVID CORKER

LONGFELLOW, Henry Wadsworth
1807–82
US poet

Few poets, nineteenth-century American or otherwise, can have enjoyed the quite stu-pendous esteem given by his age to Long-fellow, or subsequently have suffered so decisive a reversal of critical favour. On both sides of the Atlantic popular taste eulogized him as America's national laureate, the poet of familiar and loved Victorian domestic themes and of the founding Puritan and Indian legends. His suitably genteel choices of subject, metrical virtuosity and admired public demeanour suggested the very incar-nation of the high-toned man of letters, an American equivalent of **Tennyson** or **Browning**. If there were dissenters, and Poe was one of them, easily more typical was the praise which came from every hand estab-lishing him as the pre-eminent of the New England 'Fireside Poets'.

Victor Hugo spoke for many Europeans in judging him the epitome of New World eloquence. English Victorian stalwarts from Tennyson to **Gladstone** to **Victoria** herself fêted him. In 1869 Oxford and Cambridge both gave him honorary doctorates and in 1884 a bust was unveiled to him in Poets' Corner. To his fellow New England *literati* – **Emerson**, **Lowell**, **Holmes**, Whittier, Pre-scott and others – he was additional testi-mony, if it were needed, to the hereditary cultural wealth of their Boston and Cam-bridge world. Like them he came to repre-sent the Brahmin class, another educated voice of WASP New England and a Harvard professor and respected European linguist and translator. From the outset, perceptibly enough, he was not without his advantages – affluent American birth, the means to pursue extensive private European travel and study, early academic position, stunning acclaim and sales of his poetry, and an unaffected patrician ease of manner which apparently endeared him everywhere. In private, the evidence suggests, he was a more complex figure than his stately, benign general image, on occasion deeply self-doubting and no stranger to personal and family tragedy. At his funeral, it was appropriately Emerson, another ancestral New England voice and nearing death himself, who spoke for the almost universal fine regard in which Longfellow was held when he described him as 'a sweet and beautiful soul'.

By the starkest contrast, to a later vantage-point shaped by the modernism of **Pound**, **Eliot, Stevens** and **William Carlos Williams** and accustomed to thinking **Whitman** and **Emily Dickinson** the best of the nineteenth-century American poets, Longfellow seems almost painful, typically the mannered versifier of *Hiawatha* (1855). Where read at all, it tends to be as part of the history of taste, an exemplar of what Victorian Americans thought 'poetic'. Undoubtedly Longfellow was lavishly over-praised in his time, understood little of the central historical currents of America, and cannot now be thought other than minor. But he by no means deserves the usual instant obloquy. His claims are several: the few strong poems, his kindly literary encouragement of others, and his efforts in translating and teaching Dante, Goethe and a range of important Spanish, German and other European poetry by which he hoped to widen American horizons. In this latter, if in no other respect, he especially deserves acknowledgement.

Born into a prosperous leading family of coastal Maine (the sea becomes a recurring allusion in his poetry), he attended Bowdoin College (1822–5), where **Hawthorne**, and a future president, Franklin Pierce, were classmates; he studied in Europe (1826–9), experiences recalled in his Irvingesque

Outre-Mer (1835), before returning to Bowdoin as Professor of Modern Languages (1829–35); and in 1831, married, with enormous happiness, a Portland, Maine, girl, Mary Storer Potter. Four years later, while again in Europe to prepare for the Harvard Chair of Languages he had been offered in 1835, Mary Longfellow died in Rotterdam of a miscarriage. Longfellow assuaged his grief in work, as a Harvard teacher, and in the writing which flowed from his pen – *Hyperion* (1839), a thinly veiled prose narrative about his love for Frances Appleton who, though at first offended, married him in 1843; *Voices of the Night* (1839), his first full-length book of poetry; *Ballads and other Poems* (1841), the collection which includes the best known of his early poems like 'A Psalm of Life', 'The Wreck of the Hesperus' and 'Excelsior'; *Poems on Slavery* (1842), tepid, abolitionist verse which lacks the commitment of Whittier's anti-slavery poems; *The Spanish Student* (1843), an ineffectual blank verse play based on Cervantes and Thomas Middleton; and his oddly lethargic anti-war poem 'The Arsenal at Springfield'. In all these, Longfellow's technical competence rarely is at fault: rather, the poetry lacks committed imaginative life. Increasingly he now turned to longer verse narrative, each, it has to be recognized, a laboured metrical confection: *Evangeline* (1847), an allegorical history of America told in the form of the Acadian flight from Newfoundland to Louisiana; *The Golden Legend* (1851), a medieval fable to do with the quest for faith; the two New England compositions on which his reputation has seemingly come to rest, *Hiawatha* and *The Courtship of Miles Standish* (1858); and *Tales of a Wayside Inn* (1863), which includes the immensely popular 'Paul Revere's Ride' and poems like 'The Saga of King Olaf'. In these latter, Longfellow treats American history as if it were pageant of a sort, almost operatic chronicle. They also, *Hiawatha* especially, reflect to quite tiresome, and unintendedly comic, effect Longfellow's interest in trochaic and other metrical experiment, notably in the Finnish *Kalevala* and Scandinavian oral-formulaic verse. In 1849, he attempted his only novel, *Kavanagh: A Tale*, which explores liberal Unitarian theology and the making of an American literature derived from European tradition.

Longfellow was also to suffer a further major family tragedy. In Craigie House, the gift of his second wife's father and with which he is habitually associated in later photographs and portraits, he witnessed Frances's death when her hair caught fire and she was engulfed in the flames. The event almost unhinged Longfellow. But he won through, eventually, turning more than ever to religion in both his life and poetry. He worked principally on his translation of *The Divine Comedy*, an assiduous but finally undistinguished rendering, which saw publication in 1867–70. The later poems include his attempted *magnum opus, Christus: A Mystery* (1872), a compendious, often top-heavy, verse sequence which includes earlier work like *The Golden Legend* and *The New England Tragedies* (1868), and in which he sought to depict divine good intentions in epic form. The result is thin, cumbersome, hardly of a kind with his professed models in Dante, Milton and Goethe. In later life, Longfellow's achievement rests principally upon his sonnets, together with the series for which he served as editor, *Poems of Places* (1876–9), work like *Keramos and other Poems* (1878), *Ultima Thule* (1880) and his last, reconciliatory volume, *In the Harbor* (1883). His posthumous fragment, *Michael Angelo* (1883), usefully recapitulates many of his views about art, poetry, the meaning of belief and the heritage of Dante.

Further reading

See: Lawrance Thompson, *Young Longfellow (1807–1843)* (1938); Edward Wagenknecht, *Longfellow: A Full-Length Portrait* (1955); Newton Arvin, *Longfellow: His Life and Work* (1963); Edward Hirsh, *Henry Wadsworth Longfellow*, University of Minnesota pamphlet (1964); Cecil B. Williams, *Henry Wadsworth Longfellow* (1964); Bonnie L. Lukes, *Henry Wadsworth Longfellow: America's Beloved Poet* (1998); Robert L. Gale, *A Henry Wadsworth Longfellow Companion* (2003).

A. ROBERT LEE

LORCA, Federico García
1898–1936
Spanish poet, dramatist

Born in Fuente Vaqueros, Granada, Lorca achieved mythic status as a symbolic sacrificial victim of fascism with his murder in 1936. His work, status and worth have been buried under layers of interpretation and exegesis; his versatility and difficulty have attracted every sort of criticism – the reason for his murder (his homosexuality, his politics, his notoriety?) being a good example of this.

Lorca was a mercurial figure in whose enigmatic work several different elements can be identified. Central to all was the theatrical, sometimes histrionic but always dramatic nature of his life and work. He wrote many experimental plays from folk tragedies to surrealist farces, from puppet plays to almost naturalistic dramas and can be considered Spain's foremost twentieth-century playwright: he incorporated children's songs and games, surrealist devices, symbolic scene settings in his main plays from *Mariana Pineda* (1925) to *When Five Years Pass* (*Así que pasen cinco años*, 1931), *The Public* (*El público*, 1933) to the celebrated trilogy *Blood Wedding* (*Bodas de sangre*, 1933), *Yerma* (1934) and *Bernarda Alba* (*La casa de Bernarda Alba*, 1936). He was at the height of his skill as a ceaselessly inventive dramatist when he was killed. His poetry could also be anecdotal and dramatic (with events and characters), even self-dramatic, as in the posthumously published *Poet in New York* (1940). A narrative thread links his famous *Gypsy Ballads* (*Romancero gitano*, 1928), binding the brilliant images together. Lorca loved declaiming his verse aloud.

Lorca was also a painter (he exhibited in Barcelona in 1927) and was an early friend of **Salvador Dali**. His naive, colourist and whimsical paintings underline the power of his poetic imagery by drawing attention to their visual, plastic and sensual basis. For Lorca the image was at the origin of all language; the image was a transposition of the senses, the poet being the 'teacher of the five body senses'. This points to the emotionally vivid way his writing deals with the external world.

A friend of the composer Manuel de Falla, Lorca was also a proficient musician; he collected folk songs and possessed an acute ear for rhythm and sound, which, allied with visual acuity, underscores all his writing. He often incorporated lullabies, popular songs, *cante jondo*, into his work.

Lorca's receptivity to the aural, visual and dramatic was the mainspring of his art. Although he began a formal education (law at Granada University) he never graduated. He was a humorous, provocative and deliberately childish anti-intellectual (he avoided self-analysis, explanation, definitions of poetry), though his critical effort in his generation's revival of Góngora is revealing. Lorca had a strong sense of craft and tradition but always experimented.

By 1927 (with *Book of Poems*, *Poem of the Cante jondo*) he was already considered as a major poet. But his famous *Romancero gitano* (1928) brought him the kind of instant popularity usually denied to modern poets. In these updatings of medieval ballads (*romances*) Lorca used the gypsy (the romantic outcast, primitive, still tied to elemental forces) as a myth on which to bind his often difficult and private but always sensual images in poems dealing with fundamental passions (sex, death, violence, pain). The following year Lorca left Spain (for the first time) for New York (part failed love affair, part escape from popularity) where the extreme culture shock produced Lorca's most difficult poems (*Poeta en Nueva York*). He hated Anglo-Saxon culture, but found sympathy with the blacks and **Walt Whitman**. It is from these explosive, private and surrealistic poems that Lorca started out on another burst of creativity. He founded a student drama group (La barraca) to bring theatre back to the people in the

villages (he was always a populist). In 1935 he published his moving and beautifully controlled *Lament for Ignacio Sánchez Mejías (Llanto por I.S.M.)*, a bullfighter friend killed, and his last collection heralding yet another direction, the *Diván del Tamarit* (1936).

His sudden violent death seemed to many to be the death of a certain kind of carefree artist-child; a quality that most witnesses to Lorca's life selected as essential to his personality (his charm, spontaneity, his mimetic qualities). As a poet it is the literally enchanting way in which Lorca makes the reader participate in the work, combining seductivity with a pressure to communicate. Lorca's identification with the gypsy as persecuted outcast, with the sterile mother, with doomed passionate lovers, with passion, death and violence, could all be metaphors of his own life, but that would be to psychologize his gift, his fertility, what he called the *duende* (the magical, dionysiacal source of art, close to 'blood', 'death' and found in music, dance and oral poetry).

Further reading

See: *Obras completas* (1963). Best translations include *Poet in New York*, trans. Greg Simon and Steven F. White (1988); and Christopher Maurer (ed.) *Selected Poems* (1997). There are numerous translation of the plays, See also: *Selected Letters* (1984); Leslie Stainton, *Lorca: A Dream of Life* (1988); Ian Gibson, *Federico García Lorca. A Biography* (1989); C. Brian Morris, *Son of Andalusia: The Lyrical Landscapes of Federico García Lorca* (1997).

JASON WILSON

LORENTZ, Hendrik Antoon
1853–1928
Dutch physicist

Although Lorentz never lived outside of the Netherlands, he was a truly international figure who was widely known both within and beyond the scientific community. Lorentz received his education at the University of Leiden, where he was awarded his doctoral degree in 1875. As early as 1878 he was appointed Professor of Theoretical Physics in Leiden and until his death he remained connected with the University of Leiden. Because of his outstanding contributions to physics he became a leader in his field to whom many physicists turned for help and advice. In recognition of his achievements Lorentz received many honours and prizes, the most important of which was the Nobel Prize (1902). During the first part of his career, Lorentz led a fairly secluded life, but after 1900 he travelled extensively, both inside and outside of Europe. Everyone who met him was impressed by his mild and well-balanced personality, his integrity and his concern for his fellow-men. Albert Einstein, who often visited Leiden and who became very attached to Lorentz, wrote in 1953: 'For me personally he meant more than all the others I have met on my life's journey.'

During and after the First World War, Lorentz used his influence to promote the cause of peace and to re-establish the international scientific contacts that had been severely disrupted by the war. He gained much respect and recognition because of his activities towards this goal in several international organizations, in particular in the International Committee on Intellectual Cooperation of the League of Nations, of which he was first a member and later the chairman.

Nationally, Lorentz also played an important administrative role as a member of several government committees. He contributed to the reform of the Dutch university system and, on a more practical level, he almost single-handedly carried out the calculations for the enclosure of the Zuiderzee by a dike.

Although his fifty-year long career spanned equal periods in the nineteenth and twentieth centuries, Lorentz may be considered one of the last great representatives of 'classical' nineteenth-century physics. It is true that he also contributed to several of the revolutionary developments that took place in physics during the first two decades of the twentieth century (relativity theory, quantum theory), but his most important achievements date from before 1900. Or one might say that his fundamental contributions prepared the way for the creation of modern physics.

Around 1870, much confusion existed in the field of electromagnetic theory, the theory describing electric and magnetic phenomena. Concepts such as electricity were not used in a consistent way and opinions varied widely on the nature of the ether, the medium in which the electromagnetic phenomena presumably took place. Lorentz's fundamental contribution to this field consists of the idea that ether and matter should be considered separate entities. In a series of publications, the first of which was his thesis (1875), Lorentz applied this idea to electromagnetic theory, combining it with the atomistic view of matter. The resulting theory reached its final form in 1904 and is known as the 'electron theory'. According to Lorentz, electromagnetic phenomena are caused by charged particles − electrons − creating a condition of 'stress' in the ether. This condition is propagated through the ether with the speed of light and causes the mutual interactions of charged particles such as the attractive forces between charges of opposite sign.

At first, the ether was treated by Lorentz as a material medium, but in the course of the development of the electron theory it lost most of its material properties. The one property it retained was the property of immobility, and as a consequence absolute motion, understood as motion with respect to the ether, remained a meaningful concept within the framework of the electron theory. This feature distinguishes the electron theory from **Einstein's** theory of relativity (1905), to which it is mathematically almost identical. By abandoning the notion of absolute motion Einstein had eliminated the ether altogether. Lorentz had never been able to take this step; until his death he clung to the concept of the ether. Nevertheless, his idea of a separation between ether and matter and his application of it to electromagnetic theory have been immensely fruitful and clarifying. The modern concept of the electromagnetic field as an entity distinct from, but caused by, charged matter derives directly from Lorentz's work. The only difference is that today the field is not treated as a state of the ether, but as an independent entity.

Further reading

Other works include: *Collected Works* (9 vols, 1934–9). See: *H.A. Lorentz: Impressions of His Life and Work*, ed. G.L. de Haas-Lorentz (1957); R. McCormmach, 'Lorentz, Hendrik Antoon', in *Dictionary of Scientific Biography*, ed. C.C. Gillispie, Vol. VIII (1973).

A.J. KOX

LORENZ, Konrad Zacharias

1903–89

Austrian ethologist

Konrad Lorenz's father was an eminent surgeon who invented a method of curing a congenital hip disorder, as a result of which he was proposed for (but did not receive) the Nobel Prize. Konrad himself graduated in medicine at Vienna University, but was already more interested in animal behaviour (ethology). He did his best work at the family home in Altenberg during the 1930s. His first major academic post was a chair of philosophy at Königsberg which he held for a year until conscripted. After being a prisoner of war in Russia until 1948 he worked mainly at Buldern. In 1956, together with his geese, he moved to Seewiesen, where he stayed until retiring back to Altenberg in 1973, in which year he shared the Nobel Prize with **Niko Tinbergen** and Karl von Frisch.

Although **Darwin**, among others, had made important observations of animal behaviour, Lorenz is aptly referred to as 'the father of ethology' because it was he (and Tinbergen) who first formulated many of the problems of ethology and who, both directly and through his many students, inspired much subsequent work. His naturalistic approach is apparent from the descriptions of jackdaws, geese and other animals in his ever-popular *King Solomon's Ring* (*Er redete mit dem Vieh, den Vögeln und den Fischen*, 1949, trans. 1952). Lorenz recognized that behaviour, just like anatomy, is organized into units, such as distinct sequences of movements. He called these units 'fixed action patterns' and studied their function and evolution by comparing them in different species. His 'theory of instincts' explained how fixed action patterns are 'released' in response to stimuli ('releasers') or sometimes occur spontaneously.

Lorenz tended to dichotomize animal behaviour into the innate and the learned. This was strongly criticized because 'innate' behaviour is demonstrably dependent on the environment during its development, though in different ways from learning. In his *Evolution and Modification of Behaviour* (1965), Lorenz said that he meant the dichotomy to apply to the animal's 'sources of information' about its environment, not to development. Lorenz also stressed that learning is adaptive and so cannot be independent of the genes (i.e. there must be 'innate teaching mechanisms').

After 1960 Lorenz increasingly concentrated on human behaviour. Much human behaviour, he argued, is the product of evolution ('phylogenetically acquired'). For example, in *On Aggression* (*Die sogenannte Böse*, 1963), he argued that aggression is 'instinctive' in humans and in many other animals; aggression will appear spontaneously in humans unless 'redirected' to some less destructive pursuit. The subsequent controversy was exacerbated by his bold, assertive literary style which makes him liable to misrepresentation. In *Civilized Man's Eight Deadly Sins* (1974), in addition to rehearsing the themes of environmentalism, Lorenz repeated his fear that civilization causes genetic deterioration. (He had previously written on this in a paper of 1940 replete with Nazi jargon later on retracted; a mistranslation led to Lorenz's being falsely accused of racism.) His fear that civilization is dysgenic may have been aroused by his father's work on congenital disorders.

In addition Lorenz was interested in the consequences of evolutionary theory for epistemology; early in his life he identified his idea of 'innate' with Kant's a priori. *Behind the Mirror* (*Die Rückseite des Spiegels*, 1973) further explores this theme.

Further reading

Other writings include: *Man Meets Dog* (*So kam der Mensch auf den Hund*, 1950); *Darwin hat recht gesehen* ('Darwin Has Seen Correctly', 1964); *Motivation of Human and Animal Behaviour* (*Antriebe tierischen und menschlichen Verhaltens Gesammelte Abhandlungen*, 1968); his collected papers, *Studies in Animal and Human Behaviour* (2 vols, London 1970 and 1971); *Vergleichende Verhaltensforschung* ('Comparative Ethology', 1978). See also: R.W. Burkhardt, *Patterns of Behavior: Konrad Lorenz, Niko Tinbergen, and the Founding of Ethology* (2005); F.M. Wuketits, *Konrad Lorenz: Leben und Werk eines grossen Naturforschers* (1990); *Konrad Lorenz: The Man and His Ideas* (1975), ed. R.I. Evans; A. Nisbett, *Konrad Lorenz* (1976).

MARK RIDLEY

LOSEY, Joseph Walton

1909–84

US film director

Born in La Crosse, Wisconsin, into a middle-class family of declining wealth and influence, Joseph Losey abandoned his medical studies at Dartmouth College on the eve of the Depression and the New Deal in order to pursue an interest in the theatre. In a classical reaction against an upbringing in which culture and liberalism were offset by snobbery and prejudice, he worked throughout the 1930s almost exclusively on Leftist plays or such agit-prop ventures as 'The Living Newspaper'.

In Hollywood, from 1948 to 1951, Losey made five feature films, which included a charming fantasy designed as a call to peace (*The Boy with Green Hair*, 1948), a powerful but conventional indictment of racial intolerance (*The Lawless*, 1948 – *The Dividing Line* in the UK), and a classic thriller in the *film noir* mode (*The Prowler*, 1951). It was during this period, troubled by a sense of uselessness and by the anomaly of his position in Hollywood,

that Losey joined the Communist Party. As a result, he was obliged to go into exile, in anticipation of being blacklisted for 'un-American activities'.

In England, from 1954 until *The Servant* brought him worldwide recognition in 1963, there ensued a long and difficult period in which Losey was forced to work on subjects which held little interest for him, over which he did not exercise control, and to which he was initially prevented by the blacklist from signing his name. The result was the birth of what has been called Losey's baroque style, evident in the symbolic role played by explosive camera movements and Goya's painting of a bull in characterizing the tyrannical father in *Time Without Pity* (1957), or in the systematic use of mirror images and serpenting camera movements to suggest the ebb and flow of a marital relationship in *Eve* (1962).

Although frustration led to some over-elaboration while Losey was re-establishing his reputation, this 'baroque' style was brought under perfect control from *The Servant* onwards. Essentially it derives from two complementary factors at the root of all Losey's work. First, a theatrical conception of character – pre-rehearsal before filming begins enables the actors to work in depth, while the pursuing camera allows them to develop characterization in continuity – and second, an acute awareness of the role played by settings as reflectors or elucidators of behaviour.

First with the animator John Hubley in America, then with the artist Richard Mac-Donald in England, Losey established a method of 'pre-designing' his films: with the aid of sketches, details of setting, lighting and movement were pre-planned so that the filmed images would yield *only*, and *precisely*, the impression required by the director's conception. In *The Prowler*, for example, a policeman enviously eyes the spacious archways and elegant white walls of a rich man's Spanish-style house to which he is summoned to investigate reports of a prowler; but as he becomes sexually involved with the lady of the house and contemplates murder for gain, one begins to see the house itself somewhat differently, as a cheap and shoddy imitation, a snare for consumers of the American dream. An even more striking example occurs in *Blind Date* (1959), where the same room looks entirely different when viewed first through the eyes of a young man in love, then again when he is beginning to suffer disillusionment.

It is this exactness of perception which made masterpieces of later Losey films like *The Servant, Accident* (1967) and *The Go-Between* (1971), all three superbly scripted by **Harold Pinter**. Here, the roles played (respectively) by the town house foundering into decadence as the master is taken over by his servant, by the dreaming spires and Oxford lawns where the academics are faced with their own inadequacies, by the country mansion bathed in endless summer which tempts a boy to venture disastrously out of his social depth, are absolutely crucial to the barbed analysis of a lingeringly moribund English social system.

The Servant, cold, calculating and glitteringly witty, was generally hailed as the insight of an outsider casting an acidly dispassionate eye on an alien society. But the warmth, the nostalgia even, that infuses *Accident, Secret Ceremony* (1968), *The Go-Between* and much of *Mr Klein* (1976) suggests that in these films Losey was also coming to terms with his own background, one of wealth and privilege remarkably similar to the Middle Western family whose past grandeurs and present decadence are chronicled with a bittersweet mixture of malice and regret in **Orson Welles's** *The Magnificent Ambersons*.

Further reading

Other works include: *M* (1951); *The Sleeping Tiger* (1954); *The Gypsy and the Gentleman* (1957); *The Damned* (1962); *King and Country* (1964); *Modesty Blaise* (1966); *Boom* (1968); *Figures in a Landscape* (1970); *The Assassination of Trotsky* (1972); *A Doll's House* (1973); *The Romantic Englishwoman* (1975); *Les Routes du Sud* (1978); *Don Giovanni* (1979); *Steaming* (1984). See: Tom Milne (ed.) *Losey on Losey* (1967); James Leahy, *The Cinema of Joseph Losey* (1967); Michel Ciment (ed.) *Le Livre de Losey* (1979); David Caute, *Joseph Losey: A Revenge on Life* (1996); Colin Gardner, *Joseph Losey* (2004); James Palmer and Michael Riley, *The Films of Joseph Losey* (1993).

TOM MILNE

LOVELOCK, James Ephraim

1919–

English chemist and environmentalist

James Lovelock, inspired by the first images of the earth from the moon, proposed the hypothesis of 'Gaia', the living earth, which has engendered controversy ever since. Contrary to his popular image as an environmentalist visionary, he began his professional career as a chemist. Brought up in Brixton, London, Lovelock was 'repelled by formal schooling', but read avidly and found a school-leaver's job as a laboratory assistant. He then enrolled as an evening student at Birkbeck College, and completed his studies in Manchester during World War II, when he registered as a conscientious objector.

A chemist among biologists, he spent twenty years at the National Institute for Medical Research, London, working on subjects as diverse as clotting in blood, protecting cells from freezing, and the common cold. It was here Lovelock began developing inventions such as his 'electron capture detector', which could determine the presence of a chemical in minute quantities (such as a femtogram, a thousand million millionth of a gram). This device helped provide insight into pollution levels, detecting, for example, PCB pesticides and chlorofluorocarbons (CFCs) in the natural environment. It also generated a good income as Lovelock visited labs advising on its use, and enabled him to come into contact with many diverse scientists to discuss his ideas on Gaia. In 1963, Lovelock came back to the UK after a spell in the USA, to devote himself to his research as an independent scientist.

Always a lateral thinker, Lovelock proposed while working as a consultant for NASA that rather than going all the way into space, he could determine the likelihood of life on Mars by observing its atmosphere from the earth using data from an infra-red telescope. Living creatures, by adding and subtracting gases, tend to alter the balance of the earth's atmosphere away from what would be expected by chance. If Mars had life, its atmosphere might be expected to show such a property.

He then took a leap of thinking to suggest that these alterations on earth were due to the behaviour of the living earth as an organism, regulating conditions to make them optimal for life. The influence, for example, of marine shoreline algae on the global sulphur cycle; the balance of oxygen in the atmosphere held at exactly the right range, above which living beings would spontaneously ignite, below which they would be unable to respire, breathe and therefore live. Something, Lovelock urged, must be regulating the oxygen at exactly the right quantities. These ideas were incorporated into various papers and eventually three books: *Gaia: A New Look at Life on Earth* (1979), *The Ages of Gaia* (1988) and *The Practical Science of Planetary Medicine* (1991), followed by the autobiographical *Homage to Gaia: The Life of an Independent Scientist* (2000).

The idea of the earth having an overriding regulatory system was enthusiastically greeted by new age hippies and many in the environmental movement who felt at last a scientist had lent credence to their sense of wonder and unity of the earth. The downside was that for scientists, in the words of Margulis and Sagan (see below), Gaia can seem like 'the latest deification of the earth by nature nuts'. Throughout, Lovelock's greatest conundrum has always been his quest for scientific credibility, contradicted by his success as a guru for new age 'Mother Earth' worship.

The original Gaia hypothesis, that life controls planetary processes, became known as the 'strong Gaia'. Few scientists are willing to support it. Among notable objections are: first and most widespread, experiments can't be designed to test it. Second, Lovelock's use of the term 'Gaia' and the idea of the earth maintaining a global optimal environment for life, guarding her offspring benignly and consciously planning, has been difficult to reconcile with current evolutionary thinking. **Darwinian** biologists, notably Richard Dawkins, arch-proponent of the Selfish Gene concept, have suggested that if the earth is an organism and she falls within current biological paradigms, she must exist as part of a reproducing population of planets, or how did she evolve? These and many other concerns remain.

Gradually though, a form of the Gaia hypothesis has achieved scientific credibility. Further research has firmly established as true Lovelock's brilliant insight that life influences planetary processes. This idea has become known as the weak (or influential) Gaia hypothesis. Most scientists support this notion, which forms the basis of a new 'earth systems science' (what Lovelock refers to as geophysiology). The late and brilliant evolutionist William Hamilton compared Lovelock to Copernicus, the astrologer who suggested that the earth moves round the sun. He had a big idea that others found hard to accept, and was waiting for his Newton to explain how it could all work.

James Lovelock is the author of approximately 200 scientific papers on medicine, biology, instrument science and geophysiology. He has received many awards and accolades for his work among them: Fellow of the Royal Society of Science (1974); the Amsterdam Prize for the Environment (1990);the Volvo Prize for the Environment (1996); the Blue Planet Prize (1997). He has also received many honorary doctorates, and was made a Companion of the British Empire in 1990.

Further reading

See: L. Margulis and D. Sagan, *Slanted Truths: Essays on Gaia Symbiosis and Evolution* (1997); J. Turney, *Lovelock and Gaia, Signs of Life* (2003).

SASHA NORRIS

LOWELL, Amy

1874–1925

US poet

T.S. Eliot called her the 'demon saleswoman of poetry'; **D.H. Lawrence** felt that she was 'much nicer, finer, bigger' as a person than as a poet; **Ezra Pound** held her responsible for turning the fertile Imagist movement into that much feebler phenomenon 'Amygism'. The verdicts of these three major figures have not helped Amy Lowell's reputation. She is remembered today chiefly for her personal eccentricities: the Manila cigars, the nocturnal work schedule, the bed of many pillows. And if she is read at all, it tends to be in anthologies, where she looks one of the least impressive of the Imagists. Yet Amy Lowell was a more complex person, and a very different kind of poet, than is popularly imagined. The poet who could help **Robert Frost** as well as write a book on French Symbolism, and who used long narrative modes as well as miniaturist ones, was more than the narrow and bullying self-promoter that she is sometimes said to have been. Though a follower rather than a leader, she played an active and influential part in the development of Modernist poetry.

Amy Lowell grew up in Brookline, a well-to-do suburb of Boston, and spent most of her life in her parents' house 'Sevenels' (its garden was a source for many of her poems). Educated privately, she left school at seventeen determining to teach herself. A rigorous reading course followed, and a lifelong admiration for Keats – about whom she was later to write a two-volume biography– **Tennyson** and Walter Scott. These Romantic influences were evident in her first, undistinguished collection *A Dome of Many Coloured Glass* (1912), published when she was in her late thirties. The lukewarm reviews might have deterred a less ambitious writer, but when the following year she discovered the poetry of H.D. and others in Harriet Monroe's magazine *Poetry*, Amy Lowell became convinced that she was part of a wider movement (as she put it, 'Why I, too, am an Imagiste'). The conviction led her to London, where she met Pound, Richard Aldington and their colleagues, and within two years, much to Pound's displeasure, she had put together the first of her three Imagist anthologies. She continued to champion Imagism and *vers libre* until her death – notably in her critical study *Tendencies in Modern American Poetry* (1917).

Though a zealous promoter of Imagism, Amy Lowell was not by nature a poet of terseness and 'essentiality'. True, her second collection *Sword Blades and Poppy Seed* (1914) had a new power and conciseness; and later, in *Fir-Flower Tablets* (1921), she collaborated with Florence Ayscough in translations of Chinese poetry (an attempt to compete with Pound's *Cathay*). But her instinct was towards looser forms: 'the long flowing cadence of oratorical prose', or as she put it in a more self-deprecating moment 'whirling afflatus'. Collections like *Men, Women and Ghosts* (1916) and *Legends* (1921) contain many ballads and long narratives. *Can Grande's Castle* (1918) is a sustained experiment in what she called 'polyphonic prose'. *A Critical Fable* (1922) provides an extended satirical assessment of her poetic contemporaries. Only in what is perhaps her best collection, *Pictures of the Floating World* (1919), did she properly come to grips with miniaturist forms. The central image of 'Middle Age', for example, is not picturesque, but disturbing and authentic:

> Like black ice
> Scrolled over with unintelligible patterns by
> an ignorant skater
> Is the dulled surface of my heart.

In this and a handful of other poems ('Patterns', 'In a Garden', 'The Basket', 'Sisters'), Amy Lowell seems a genuine talent rather than a mere camp follower. Her own prediction – 'She'll be rated by time as more rather than less' – may seem unduly genial, for even as a publicist she made mistakes, allowing personal rivalries to obscure her critical judgement (how else could she have preferred John Gould Fletcher to Ezra Pound?). But she did much to overcome popular resistance to modern poetry, had a shrewd eye for the healthy and new, and fought her battles on a surprisingly broad front.

Further reading

See: *The Complete Poetical Works of Amy Lowell* (1955). See also: F.C. Flint, *Amy Lowell* (1969); Jean Gould, *Amy: The World of Amy Lowell and the Imagist Movement* (1975).

BLAKE MORRISON

LOWELL, James Russell

1819–91

US author and diplomat

'A New Englander ... of acute discursive mind and deft literary fingering' – so William Rossetti, introducing a British popular edition of the collected poems, characterized Lowell. His account was at once shrewd and usefully to the point. Like the other 'Fireside Poets' with whom his name is associated – Bryant, **Longfellow**, **Holmes** and **Whittier** – Lowell was, before he was anything, a hereditary New Englander, another nineteenth-century high American Brahmin and scholar whose family had been eminent in the affairs of Boston and the eastern seaboard since the earliest years of the Puritan settlement. To contemporaries, both in America and across the Atlantic, he ranked as a major representative American figure, not only as poet, essayist, satirist, editor and Longfellow's successor in the Smith Professorship of Modern Languages at Harvard, but as a seasoned diplomat and ambassador. Lowell's writing no longer commands any extensive readership, except perhaps for *The Biglow Papers* (1848, 1862–3) and 'A Fable For Critics' (1848), but it was rarely other than agile – 'deft' in Rossetti's terms – the expression of a versatile, well-stocked but ultimately limited mind. **Henry James**, who met frequently with Lowell in Europe and

developed a complex, almost filial, relationship with him, once revealingly spoke of him as the 'oddest' mixture of 'the infinitely clever and unspeakably simple'.

Born in Cambridge, Massachusetts, and educated at Harvard, Lowell first thought of a career in the law, but the verse he had been writing since boyhood convinced him that his was a literary vocation. By 1839–40 he was contributing poems to the *Dial*, **Emerson's** Transcendentalist quarterly, and to the *Southern Literary Messenger,* which Poe had briefly edited. In 1841, he published his first collection, *A Year's Life,* genteel lyric and occasionally ironic pieces, and from then on, his confidence established, wrote voluminously, appearing in a range of contemporary periodicals – among others, *Boston Miscellany*, *Graham's Magazine, Massachusetts Quarterly*, *Putnam's* and the *U.S. Magazine and Democratic Review.* In 1843, he founded his own magazine, the *Pioneer*, which, though it ran for only three issues, served notice of his editorial flair; in 1844, he married Maria White, a considerable minor versifier in her own right who eased him away from his instinctive political conservatism, especially toward abolitionism; and from 1848 to 1852 he edited and contributed to the *National Anti-Slavery Standard* and the *Pennsylvania Freeman*, both leading anti-slavery periodicals. The climax of his editorial career came with his appointment as editor from 1857 to 1861 of the *Atlantic Monthly,* where he built a deserved and widely influential reputation, and to the *North American Review,* which he co-edited with Charles Eliot Norton, founder of the *Nation* and a Harvard Professor of Fine Art. Lowell's work as an editor merits recognition. He had a genuine shaping role to play in the creation and dissemination of an American national literature through the journals, and in making available to his countrymen a tradition of European writing.

The two other principal phases of Lowell's career were his Harvard professorship and his diplomatic appointments. When he succeeded Longfellow in the Smith Chair, he turned increasingly to literary criticism, reading

widely in European literature (he was a skilled linguist) which led to a run of worthy if
uncontentious essay collections, *Fireside
Travels* (1864), *Among My Books* (first and
second series, 1870, 1876), *My Study Windows*
(1871), *Latest Literary Essays and Addresses*
(1891) and *The Old English Dramatists* (1892),
all, for the most part, informed, easily digested introductory surveys and annotation. In
1877, although his Harvard appointment
nominally continued, Lowell was appointed
minister first to Madrid (1877–80), then to
London (1880–5), by the conservative Hayes
administration whose policies he felt drawn
to (his *Political Essays, 1888*, are worth consulting), thereby continuing the American
habit of rewarding men of letters with distinguished diplomatic office and in which he
joined Irving, **Hawthorne** arid **Howells**. In
his later years, with Longfellow, he was
widely taken to represent the high spirit of
literature in America, an international name
and almost yearly visitor to Europe to whom
Oxford and Cambridge gave honorary
degrees. He knew, and was warmly respected
by, almost every leading English writer of the
age. In 1890, venerable, a voice from an earlier, patrician phase of New England and
American literary life, he saw through the
presses a ten-volume collection of his work.

Lowell's best poetry was written when
young. Principally, his claims rest upon 'A
Fable for Critics', no *Dunciad* to be sure but a
gently *satiric jeu d'esprit* (Lowell's phrase) in
couplet-form which shrewdly depicts the best
known of his American fellow *literati* –
Emerson, Bryant, Holmes, Hawthorne,
Cooper, Poe ('There comes Poe, with his
raven, like Barnaby Rudge,/Three fifths of
him genius, and two fifths sheer fudge') and
Irving. From the five volumes of poetry he
published, *A Year's Life, Miscellaneous Poems*
(1843), *Poems: Second Series* (1848), *Under the
Willows and Other Poem* (1868) and *Heartsease
and Rue* (1888), and the poems he contributed to the journals, among the likeliest to
endure are 'The Vision of St Launfal' (1848), an
inventive retelling of the Grail legend; 'After
the Burial' (1850), written in remembrance of

the death of his second child; the 'Harvard
Commemoration Ode' (1865), a eulogy to
Lincoln and to the university's dead, and
worthy in parts of comparison with
Whitman's 'When Lilacs Last in the Dooryard Bloom'd'; 'The Cathedral' (1869), his
tribute to Chartres and a statement of his own
religious feelings; and the 'Ode to Agazziz'
(1874), a touching remembrance of the
Swiss-born naturalist. Lowell's other claims
tie with *The Biglow Papers* (first series, 1848;
second series in the *Atlantic Monthly, 1862–
3*), the dialect sayings and opinion in both
prose and verse of Hosea Biglow, a wry
Yankee farmer. Lowell's versatility was rarely
more evident. In Biglow's voice he was able
to take aim at the Mexican War, slavery,
secession and the threat to the Union. Whether Lowell's own reputation has been secure
or not, he has enjoyed a species of reflected
glory in two later scions of the family, **Amy
Lowell**, the pioneer imagist poet, and
Robert Lowell, whose 'confessional' poetry
perhaps most strikingly marks the difference
between us and the American nineteenth-
century genteel tradition.

Further reading

See: Leon Howard, *A Victorian Knight Errant: A
Study of the Early Career of James Russell Lowell*
(1952); Martin Duberman, *James Russell Lowell*
(1966); Claire McGlinchee, *James Russell Lowell*
(1967).

A. ROBERT LEE

LOWELL, Robert
1917–77
US poet

The scion of an old Boston family, Lowell
was descended from the poet **James Russell
Lowell** and related to the Imagist ('Amygist')
Amy Lowell. After entering Harvard, he left
to study under **John Crowe Ransom** at
Kenyon College, Ohio, where he also came
under the influence of the poet Allen Tate.
The move was a symbolic one, a reaction

against the suffocating civilization of money he had inherited in New England which he sought to correct with the classicism and decorum of the Southern tradition. While growing up, as he himself said, as 'Northern, disembodied, a Platonist, a puritan', he grew to despise the values of his forefathers. In 1943 Lowell served five months in prison for refusing military service, and during the 1960s was an active spokesman in both the Civil Rights Movement and in the campaign against the war in Vietnam.

His work shows a three-part movement, as the critic Thomas Parkinson puts it, 'from Roman Catholicism to general Christian piety to a kind of agnostic existentialism'. He in fact entered the Catholic Church in 1940 and seceded from it in 1950. *Land of Unlikeness* (1944), *Lord Weary's Castle* (1946) and *The Mills of the Kavanaughs* (1951) contain studied poems, sometimes clotted with allusiveness and rigid with metaphor, burdened with his sense of the war and a profound alienation from traditional Christian consolations. His principal subject, as he himself glossed it, was 'struggle, light and darkness, the flux of experience'. Another chief theme he found in his personal antagonism towards Boston as a city representative of commercialism. He associated the notions of dread and death and materialism as sterile misconceptions of spirituality, engrossed himself in the works of **Hawthorne**, **Melville**, Bunyan, Hooker and Jonathan Edwards, and accordingly took the stance of an anti-Calvinist. In an Introduction to *Land of Unlikeness*, Allen Tate pin-pointed the concern with a 'memory of the spiritual dignity of man now sacrificed to the mere secularization and a craving for mechanical order'. A number of the early poems are in a sense spoiled by being forced towards a position of religious affirmation. Though some end with strident, rhetorical appeals for divine intercession in the affairs of humankind, however, perhaps most of them succeed in expressing Lowell's keen apprehension of religious vacuity, desolation and determinism. We must allow in the early work for two strains: the spirit of violence

and doom which he loathed in Calvinism, and the sense of grace he perceived as a possibility of his Catholicism. The best-known of the early works is 'The Quaker Graveyard in Nantucket', a powerfully achieved elegy for his cousin Warren Winslow who was killed at sea.

After losing his faith, it was eight years before Lowell brought out another volume, *Life Studies* (1959). A sequence which Stephen Spender has cruelly but pertinently called Lowell's 'Family Album', *Life Studies* has likewise been inappositely labelled 'Confessional' verse, although the volume was assuredly a new departure towards loose verse forms detailing the poet's feelings of dispossession. The prevailing mood is one of pathos: Lowell defines himself through an ironic inspection of his memories and impressions of childhood and close kin. He discovers both destitution, sometimes comic and ineffectual, and new dignity. Subdued, conversational, and yet strictly controlled in form despite their apparent looseness, the poems can be affectionate and indulgent, as in the close of 'My Last Afternoon with Uncle Devereux Winslow', or directly satirical, as in the portrait of his father 'Commander Lowell'. More emphatically personal is 'Man and Wife', though perhaps the most important and exciting poem is 'Skunk Hour', which moves from satire, through sardonicism, to what Lowell himself called 'affirmation, an ambiguous one'. Throughout *Life Studies*, in fact, there runs an ambiguous statement of personal integrity; the affirmation of human affections ironically characterizes the remainder of Lowell's work.

For the Union Dead (1964) is in many ways more painful than *Life Studies*: a volume of post-Christian poems largely concerned with the failure of personal relationships, its tone is self-condemning. Although the poet is no less morally alert, the poems seem to lack morale and a substitute for the Christian sanction which suffused the earlier work.

Near the Ocean (1967) contains a number of translations, but precedes them with a group of fine poems about the ambiguous moral order Lowell has ascertained. They combine wistfulness with a sense of theological disease; their uncanny poise of tone is undercut by a terrifyingly severe indictment of a land which has lost spiritual values, as in 'Waking Early Sunday Morning' where the earth is figured as 'a ghost/orbiting forever lost/in our monotonous sublime'. The tenor of the poems veers between bitterness at Man's estate and a growing faith in existential consolation.

History (1973) consists of serried blank-verse sonnets. The volume reworks, expands and puts into chronological order an earlier volume called *Notebook* (1969) and is presumably modelled on *Les Trophées* (by José-Maria de Heredia), a sequence which, just like Lowell's, attempts to chart and evoke the foci of succeeding civilizations, from Greece through Rome and the Renaissance to the landscapes and impressions of its own times. Lowell found the period from 1967 to 1972, during which he seems to have written mainly unrhymed sonnets, a time of happy reversion to his ideal of 'formal, difficult' poetry.

The Dolphin (1973) represents perhaps the happiest marriage possible between the studied, formal and evasive mode that he indulged for so long in *Notebook* and *History* and a treatment of personal experience that he had cultivated earlier. Exploring a symbol of succour, lovingness and constancy, *The Dolphin* makes available the best devices that may be recovered from the Symbolists, raising personal emotion to a level of suggestiveness and immutability.

Day by Day (1977) represents a wilful regression to free verse, 'a way of writing I once thought heartless'. Although these last verses continue Lowell's serial autobiography, they lack the proven fierce rhetoric and syntax of his earlier decades. The prevailing mood is elegiac, rehearsing old friendships and mismanaged love, and indeed the rue and melancholy of certain poems about lost relationships often have an intense poignancy. The finest poems continue to illustrate Lowell's porcelain sensitivity. Lowell clearly regretted leaving behind the grand and formal manner. His last poems demonstrate contemplation and achieved art, though the evidence of fresh insight is disconcertingly weak. Tender-hearted, enduring without demanding, several poems do still touch to magic moments, whimsies, a sense of transience, and the pathos and incorrigibility of the poet's own life.

Further reading

Other works include: *Phaedra* (1961); *Imitations* (1961); *The Old Glory* (1965); *Prometheus Bound* (1969); *For Lizzie and Harriet* (1973). The *Collected Poems* were published in 2004 and *The Letters of Robert Lowell*, ed. Saskia Hamilton, in 2005. See: John Crick, *Robert Lowell* (1974); Hugh B. Staples, *Robert Lowell: The First Twenty Years* (1962); Jonathan Price, *Critics on Robert Lowell* (1974); Patrick Cosgrave, *The Public Poetry of Robert Lowell* (1970); and Alan Williamson, *Pity the Monsters: The Political Vision of Robert Lowell* (1974); Steven Axelrod and Helen Deese (eds) *Robert Lowell: Essays on the Poetry* (1996); Peter Davison, *The Fading Smile: Poets in Boston from Robert Lowell to Sylvia Plath* (1996); Ian Hamilton, *Robert Lowell: A Biography* (1998).

JOHN HAFFENDEN

LOWRY, Laurence Stephen

1887–1976

English artist

L.S. Lowry – he was always known only by his initials – is widely known as the creator of 'matchstick men', and is often assumed to be a naïve artist. The first is a facile reference to the hundreds of tiny human figures that populate his haunting pictures of the now largely vanished industrial north-west of England of the mid-twentieth century. The accusations of naivety and being 'a Sunday painter' came largely from other artists who lacked his popular recognition and his burgeoning commercial reputation.

That he was a somewhat eccentric human being is undeniable, and that too coloured his reputation. Despite his wealth – he could afford to buy works of art by **Rossetti** and

Lucian Freud – he lived in a modest, even primitive, stone cottage in Mottram in Longdendale, near Manchester. He had lived with his mother until her death, when he was fifty-two, and earned a modest living as a rent collector in Salford, the city next to Manchester whose City Art Gallery built up a three-hundred strong collection of his works, transferred in 2000 to be the centrepiece of the large Salford art centre called, simply, the Lowry.

Yet, despite the day job, Lowry attended various Manchester art schools and, so far was he from being a 'naïve' painter, he once famously applied seven coats of his favourite white paint to a piece of cardboard and then stored it in a light-excluding drawer for seven years. At the end of that time he took another piece of card to which he also applied seven coats of white and only then did he open the drawer to remove the first cardboard to study the effects of time on his work.

Lowry never married and there is no record of any sexual relationship. The woman with glossy black hair and a centre parting who appears in several paintings and is sometimes referred to as 'Ann' is a fantasy figure, and Lowry, when asked about his fascination with Rossetti in particular and exotic pre-Raphaelite women in general, said: 'I'm fascinated by the paintings of his ladies. Nothing else. They're not real women, they are dreams.'

Lowry accepted membership of the Royal Academy because it was recognition by his peers but declined several proffered decorations and a knighthood on the grounds that he did not believe in such baubles. He was much admired by critics and art historians as diverse as Herbert Read, who pointed out that Lowry: 'accepts the industrial revolution and makes the most of it', and E.H. Gombrich: 'He did not try to be original, he just was original. He never tried to follow fashion or to be ahead of his time. In this way he became an individual and great artist.'

Lowry, in his industrial scenes of factory gates, mills with their vast chimneys, crowds of people going to a football match, etc., had no truck with Blakean visions of dark Satanic mills. For him it was 'purely pictorial. The industrial buildings are the backgrounds for the people.' Lowry's pictorial sense, always acute, was frequently focused on the inter-relationship of cityscape and inhabitants, the contrast between the mighty chimneys and the minuscule people.

The people, lightly dismissed as matchstick men, are in fact tiny miracles of painterly compression. They are not identical models stamped out by an artistic template, but are, for the most part, scrupulously individual with almost as infinite a variety as humankind itself.

Lowry always had a keen sense of compassion for his human figures, no matter how diminutive, a compassion he extended even when painting a picture like *The Cripples* of 1949, with its rich assortment of grotesques and the afflicted. This is done in an entirely nonvoyeuristic spirit and is both comical and moving. When Lowry turned, as he often did, to individual people as opposed to crowds, his reportorial skill and his understanding of character were both acute and as sophisticated as any of the distinguished portrait painters of his day.

Lowry was also a painter of mountain landscapes and, particularly, of the sea, with which he frequently communed during long visits to the north-east coast. But above all he was a painter of wonderfully elaborate crowd scenes, teeming with men, women, children, animals and perambulators against a background of factories, churches, municipal lakes full of little rowing boats, busy roads and railway lines – in short, everything that contributed to an industrial landscape of endless vitality, seen through Lowry's jaundiced-coloured spectacles.

Further reading

See: Michael Leber and Judith Sandling, *L.S. Lowry* (1987); Shelley Rohde, *A Private View of L.S. Lowry* (1979); Michael Howard, *Lowry: A Visionary Artist* (2000).

T.G. ROSENTHAL

LU XUN (ZHOU SHUREN)

1881–1936

Chinese writer

Lu Xun (pen-name of Zhou Shuren) was born to a privileged scholar-gentry family in Shaoxing. While still a boy he experienced the bitterness of a precipitous decline in familial wealth and prestige when his grandfather, holder of the most advanced degrees the civil service examination system could offer, was deprived of his offices after he had been caught accepting bribes from the families of junior candidates. Then, in his teens, Lu Xun saw his father, an opium smoker and general failure, die spitting blood. After a classical education at home he went to Nanking, where in 1901 he was a member of the first and only graduating class of the School of Mines and Railroads attached to the Jiangnan Army Academy. He was subsequently sent to Japan as a government-sponsored student. There he attended the K?bun College in Tokyo (1902–4), where he was taught Japanese and the rudiments of science, and then the medical school at Sendai. His motives for wanting to be a doctor were twofold: he had been deeply disillusioned by the failure of traditional Chinese medicine to cure his father (who had even been prescribed ink); and he was aware that the rapid modernization of Japan was associated with the introduction of Western medicine. Like Japan, China was being subjected to an onslaught of Western influences, and Lu Xun saw that the Confucian tradition was wholly inadequate for the new challenge.

During his second year at Sendai a slide of a Chinese prisoner about to be executed was shown at the end of a class. What struck Lu Xun were the uncaring expressions on the faces of the Chinese bystanders. It was at that point that he decided that his countrymen's spiritual sickness was a far more pressing concern than their physical health. The treatment he came to propose was a difficult one: it amounted to nothing less than the remoulding of the Chinese personality, and in particular the remoulding of his own scholar-gentry class. Quitting his studies, he dedicated his life to literature. He also turned rebel to his own class, asserting that the scholar-gentry blamed China's backwardness on the 'inherited superstitions' of her common people as a ploy designed to absolve their own irresponsibility. The way to cope with Western culture, he reasoned, was neither to shun it by praising the glories of Chinese antiquity, nor to embrace it wholeheartedly, but rather to learn to look out on it, so that China might take her place as one civilization among many. His writings, which were mainly devoted to this end, may be divided into three groups: his translations, his stories, and his essays, or *zawen*.

During the early part of his stay in Japan, when he still thought that China might solve her problem through the adoption of Western science, Lu Xun translated two of **Jules Verne's** novels into Chinese; but after leaving Sendai to devote himself to writing he deliberately sought out literature from weak and oppressed countries, for example the stories of Leonid Andreyev and Vsevolod Garshin. It was not until after he had gone back to China (in 1909, becoming a science teacher at the Zhejiang Normal School in Hangzhou) that he began writing his own fiction. His first short story, 'Remembrances of the Past' (*Huaijiu*), was composed in classical Chinese on the eve of the Republican Revolution of 1911. In it a strict, hypocritical and slow-witted Confucian teacher is contrasted by the narrator with a pair of warm, honest and quick-witted family servants. It was not, however, until six years after the Republic was established, and six years after he had accepted a sinecure with the Ministry of Education, that he joined ranks with the cultural revolution then afoot in Peking and Shanghai, with the publication of 'Diary of a Madman' (*Kuangren riji*, 1918). This was the first *literary* short story to be written in the vernacular; previously only commercial fiction writers had switched from classical Chinese, a purely written language spoken by no one. Borrowing both title and form from Gogol, Lu Xun used them to voice his radical and unflattering view of Chinese society. The sixth entry of the 'Diary' reads:

> Pitch black, don't know if it's day or
> night.
> The Zhao family's dog has started barking
> again.
> Fierce as a lion, timid as a rabbit, and crafty
> as a fox.

The dog clearly referred to the Chinese character as Lu Xun envisaged it: a lion before inferiors, a rabbit before superiors, and a fox when the other's social status was uncertain. Like the madman in his story, Lu Xun saw Chinese society as a cannibalistic feast in which the strong devour the weak, the educated the unlettered, and the old the young. Those not directly involved merely stand around, like the bystanders in the slide that had left such a lasting impression upon him.

In all Lu Xun wrote only twenty-five vernacular stories, collected in 'Outcry' (*Nahan*, 1923) and 'Wandering' (*Panghuang*, 1926). In each of them the oppressed, be they women, children or members of the working classes, are illiterate, and hence innocent of Confucianism. Formally, with only one exception, the stories were each strongly influenced by foreign models. The exception – 'The True Story of Ah Q' (*Ah Q Zhengzhuan*) – is the most famous. In this rambling tale, first published serially in a newspaper, Lu Xun employs the diction and structure of traditional popular fiction in an attempt to sum up the weaknesses of the Chinese people in the person of the vagabond ne'er-do-well Ah Q. Of all Ah Q's defects the most serious is his inability to face up to the here and now of reality. Instead he escapes, either into a past where his ancestors are rich and powerful, or into a future peopled by his as yet unborn children; and when temporal evasion is impossible, Ah Q simply rationalizes failure into success, transforming each setback into a 'psychological victory'. Such was the impact of the story that 'Ah Q-ism' and 'psychological victory' passed immediately into everyday conversation. Chinese scholars who boasted complacently about China's history while disdaining the Johnny-come-lately accomplishments of the West were now dismissed as victims of 'Ah Q mentality'.

In addition, and in a few deft strokes, 'The True Story of Ah Q' also exposed the Republican Revolution for what it was, a superficial and deceptive change in the form of government that left the fabric of Chinese society virtually intact: the common people remained outside the effective political structure. Beginning in 1925 personal and political events conspired to radicalize Lu Xun still further, so that he gradually moved away from fiction towards a more direct form of criticism, the political essay. The personal events centred mainly on Xu Guangping, a student twenty years his junior who had attended his classes at the Women's Normal College in Beijing, and who subsequently began writing to him in 1925. Soon after initiating the correspondence (preserved in 'Letters from Two Places', *Liangdi shu*, 1933) she became leader of a student movement organized to oppose appointments made by the Ministry of Education. Siding with the students, Lu Xun was temporarily dismissed from his own post at the ministry. Then, in 1926, the police fired into a crowd of people demonstrating against China's weakness in the face of foreign aggrandizement, killing forty-seven of them, including another of his students. This drew forth some of Lu Xun's most vitriolic compositions, for which he earned a place on an arrest list of fifty 'radicals'. After a period of hiding he was forced to flee Beijing, accompanied by Xu Guangping. Together they found teaching posts in Guangzhou (Canton), where in April 1927 they witnessed at first hand Chiang Kai-shek's bloody purge of communists from the Guomindang – a party Lu Xun had previously held out some hope for. Now he turned to communism as the only solution to China's problems. At the same time he moved, with Xu Guangping (who now became his wife) to Shanghai, the most cosmopolitan and revolutionary city in China. There he was to spend the last nine years of his life.

In Shanghai he devoted prodigious energies to cultivating younger writers, fostering the 'woodcut movement' (of the Eighteen Society, whose slogan was 'out of the salon and into the streets'), translating, founding short-lived publishing houses, lecturing, and campaigning for the simplification and eventual elimination of Chinese ideographs (to be replaced by an alphabetic system). At the same time he composed score upon score of *zawen*, directed mainly at the Guomindang and its rightist sympathizers. No contemporary was able to match him in this essay form, either in clarity of thought or in brilliance of style. Constituting the bulk of his creative work during the last decade of his life, the incisiveness of Lu Xun's satire ensured the survival of his *zawen*, so that they became valued by critics in the later People's Republic above his other writings, as contributing more to both literature and revolution. Praised by **Mao Zedong** as 'a hero without parallel in our history', Lu Xun the iconoclast became himself an idol.

Yet Lu Xun's status as a national hero of Chinese Communism is perhaps deceptive. Above and beyond being a great writer he was an internationalist. His translations (which continued throughout his Shanghai period, until his death from tuberculosis, when he was working on the second part of Gogol's *Dead Souls*) were outstanding because Lu Xun himself set great store by them. He continually urged his fellow-writers to spend more time rendering foreign works into Chinese, for, as he argued, translations make a larger contribution than shoddy original work. In the burgeoning of left-wing literature in the wake of the 1927 purges he translated several important pieces of Soviet criticism expressly to raise the prevailing level of discourse. In addition he also argued for a higher level of self-criticism among writers. In 1931, noting that no contemporary left-wing writer actually came from peasant or worker stock, he said that the

best they could do was to produce novels of exposure, against their own classes. Because he scorned those who pretended to know how peasants thought and felt, he was sometimes attacked by the left as well as the right. He was therefore a more isolated figure, and his politics more critical, than his posthumous reputation in China suggests. Passionate in his concern for social justice and in his vision of China as a member of a world community of nations, Lu Xun has, even in translation – left a rich legacy to share with his fellow men.

Further reading

Lu Xun's complete writings (10 vols, 1956–8) and complete translations (10 vols, 1959) have been published in Peking. Recommended translations: *Ah Q and Others: Selected Stories of Lusin* (Wang Chi-chen, 1941); *Selected Works of Lu Hsün* (Yang Hsien-yi and Gladys Yang, 4 vols, 1956–60); *A Brief History of Chinese Fiction* (also the Yangs, 1959); *Silent China: Selected Writings of Lu Xun* (Gladys Yang, 1973). See also: William A. Lyell, *Lu Hsün's Vision of Reality* (1976); Merle Goldman (ed.) *Modern Chinese Literature in the May Fourth Era* (1977); Lin Yü-Sheng, *The Crisis of Chinese Consciousness – Radical Anti-traditionalism in the May Fourth Era* (1979); V.I. Semanov, *Lu Hsün and His Predecessors* (trans. 1980); David Pollard, *The True Story of Lu Xun* (2002).

WILLIAM LYELL

LUHMANN, Niklas

1927–98

German sociologist

Born in Lüneburg, Niklas Luhmann studied law at the University of Freiburg, then worked as a consultant (*Referent*) for the ministry of education in Lower Saxony. Among other duties he took charge of applications for redress with respect to 'unlawful' decisions of the fallen Nazi regime. In 1960–1 he studied administrative sciences and sociology at Harvard University with **Talcott Parsons**. Returning home, he worked at the University for Administrative Sciences at Speyer, the Institute for Social Research at the University of Dortmund, and the

University of Münster. In 1968 he became Professor of Sociology at the newly founded University of Bielefeld, where he taught until he was given emeritus status in 1993.

Luhmann's significance lies in his application of new developments in general systems theory to sociology, and in his elaboration of a particular sociological theory of society. More specifically, he revised Talcott Parsons' notion of social systems and conceived of social systems as self-referential, autopoietic social systems consisting of temporary elements, i.e. events, taking form as communication. To modern cognitive sciences he contributed the notion of a strict separation of mental systems and social systems, the former being based on the emergence of human awareness, the latter on the emergence of communication, and both being structurally, yet not operationally, coupled by language.

Luhmann's sociology describes modern society as functionally differentiated into such subsystems as the economy, politics, law, science, religion, arts and education. However, society does not exhaust the realm of social systems. There exist small systems called interactions based on the distinction of presence from absence, and formal systems called organizations based on the distinction of members from non-members, which both have their own codes of communication distinct from those of the society. With respect to society, Luhmann extended Parsons' theory of generalized media of interchange to a theory of communication media showing how media such as money, power, law, truth, belief, beauty or love account for the modern type of a dynamically stable society.

Together with **Jürgen Habermas**, for many years his favourite intellectual rival, Luhmann defined the cultural situation of Germany in the last quarter of the twentieth century. Like Habermas, he was dissatisfied with **Heidegger's** and **Adorno's** approaches to post-Nazi Germany, Heidegger being silent about his engagement with Nazi ideology, and Adorno desperately restricting himself to a critique of the administrated, i.e. false, world. Luhmann and Habermas developed new ways of dealing with the shock of Germany having succumbed to Fascism. But whereas Habermas opted for Reason, and developed a social technology of unwavering and relentless pedagogy of *Aufklärung*, which is still the dominant political, and politically correct, culture of Germany, Luhmann accepted the notion of Complexity, which describes systems as necessarily, yet contingently, so, insisting on a viable reduction of complexity. Scope and reduction are terms he borrowed from Kenneth Burke to describe a society which should be able to control and judge its scope with respect to its reductions.

Luhmann's sociological output focused on modern society as a functionally differentiated society. He wrote a whole series of papers, published as *Gesellschaftsstruktur und Semantik: Studien zur Wissenssoziologie der modernen Gesellschaft* ('Social Structure and Semantics: Studies in a Sociology of the Knowledge of Modern Society', 4 vols, 1980, 1981, 1989 and 1995), exploring how such a society first came about, in the seventeenth and eighteenth centuries, when the effects of the introduction of the printing press became apparent and social systems were forced to deal with a relentless and uncertain social world. One system after another ascribed to the idea of an opaque future as the organizing principle of social order, first perhaps in love (considered as uncertain because passionate), then in the economy (where property, wealth and profit depend on constant re-evaluation), in politics (where democracy means that nobody knows whether he will be re-elected or not), in science (where all answers lead to new questions) and in education (where status is replaced by intelligence).

Luhmann devoted the last chapter of his two-volume chef d'oeuvre *Die Gesellschaft der Gesellschaft* ('The Society of the Society', 1997) to the ingenious devices modern society has invented to describe itself, chief among them the concepts of subject, class and nation. Yet the general idea behind his endeavour to give an account of modern society's complexity was the feeling that its 'old-European' methods of understanding the world are about to vanish due to the invention and introduction of the computer. Luhmann considered writing, the printing press and the computer as the most important distribution media of communication to have been invented. Each in its own way has manufactured new kinds of social order – broadly the civilization of the Jews and Greeks, the modern society of Europe and, slowly emerging, a global society we remain to this day uncertain of. By describing modern European society, Luhmann sought to indicate possible solutions to the sort of societal problems that now have to be reconsidered.

Further reading

Other works include: *Risk: A Sociological Theory* (1993); *Social Systems.* (1995); *Art as a Social System.* (2000); and *Law as a Social System.* (2004). See also William Rasch, *Niklas Luhmann's Modernity: The Paradoxes of Differentiation* (2000)

DIRK BAECKER

LUKÁCS, Georg

1885–1971

Hungarian philosopher and literary critic

Gyorgy Szegedy von Lukács, considered by many to be the foremost **Marxist** thinker of his times, was born in Budapest of a wealthy Jewish family. His father was a self-made banker ennobled by the Hapsburg crown. The Lukácses (originally Löwingers) were thoroughly German in their culture, and their son, who once said he could hardly philosophize in Hungarian, wrote most of his books in German. After a training in law Lukács, eager to learn philosophy and social science, departed for Berlin in 1906, and again in 1909, when he attended the lectures of **Georg Simmel**. During this period he began his long and distinguished career as a literary critic, contributing to *West*, a journal strongly opposed to the conventional nationalism of the Magyar establishment while

receptive to modernist attitudes in art. From 1912 to 1915 he lived in Heidelberg, continuing his philosophical studies under Heinrich Rickert, a leading neo-Kantian with a stark anti-naturalist bias. There he became acquainted with the charismatic Stefan George circle, made friends with Emil Lask and the Marxist utopian Ernst Bloch, impressed Max Weber as an intense, near Tolstoyan youth, and wrote his most influential piece of literary essayism, *The Theory of the Novel* (1916, trans. 1971). Soon after the outbreak of the First World War he returned to Budapest. Dreading a German victory, he was filled with equal dismay at the prospect of the triumph of Western capitalism and its utilitarian values; nor, having sympathized with the anarcho-syndicalism of Georges Sorel since his schooldays, could he at first welcome the October Revolution. Nonetheless, within a week of its foundation in 1918, he joined the Hungarian Communist Party, and served as commissar for public education in the short-lived coalition government headed by the communist Béla Kun, fleeing to Austria after its overthrow by right-wing forces in the summer of 1919.

For the next decade he settled in Vienna, devoting himself to the survival of communism in the West, editing an ultra-leftist journal and remaining largely oblivious of such Vienna-based developments as psychoanalysis and logical positivism. Instead, his overwhelming concern at the time was the philosophical understanding of political revolution. Between 1919 and 1922 he wrote eight essays that together make up *History and Class Consciousness* (*Geschichte und Klassenbewusstsein*, 1923, trans. 1971), his major contribution to Marxist theory.

In 1931, after a year at the Marx-Engels-Lenin Institute in Moscow, Lukács moved to Berlin, where he started writing Marxist literary criticism, engaging in a two-front polemic – against avant-garde formalism on the one hand, and Stalinist propaganda literature on the other – that was to continue for the rest of his life. Forced to return to Moscow by the rise of **Hitler**, he was admitted as a researcher to the Institute of Philosophy of the Soviet Academy of Sciences, where, in addition to some remarkable studies of the European novel, he produced a study of the early thought of Hegel. During the years of the popular front policy (1935–9) his prestige in the Soviet Union was considerable; yet this did not protect him from harassment by **Stalinist** hard-liners, nor from a spell of imprisonment in 1941. At the end of the Second World War he returned to Budapest, where he was appointed a professor at the university and sat in the national assembly, despite continuing attacks on his publications. Wisely he refrained from any significant political activities while **Stalin** lived, preferring to busy himself with the completion of his Marxist history of modern philosophy, *The Destruction of Reason* (1954). Following the thaw, however, he lent his authority to the restless meetings of the Petöfi Circle, an ideological prelude to the Uprising of 1956. Appointed Minister of Culture in the Nagy government, Lukács was duly deported to a Romanian spa following the Russian invasion. Although he was soon allowed to return to Hungary, he was not readmitted to the Party until 1967. The important works of his last years were the lengthy, though unfinished, summas: *Die Eigenart des Aesthetischen* ('The Peculiarity of Aesthetics', 1963) and *Zur Ontologie des gesellschaftlichen Seins* ('The Ontology of Social Existence', 1971–3).

Although it is possible to divide Lukács's output into literary criticism and his aesthetics and social theory, the one continuous throughout his career, the other only intermittent, the two are peculiarly mortgaged to each other. As a thinker this was both his strength and his weakness. In so far as the point of *History and Class Consciousness* is the elucidation of the purpose and meaning of the social world, this Marxist *opus magnum* may be said to descend from the existential preoccupations of Lukács's early, pre-Marxist literary criticism (see below). Technically speaking, its theme is the spelling out of the genuine sense of Marxism. In Lukács's view,

orthodox Marxism does not consist in any allegiance to specific tenets, but in its faithfulness to a method: the dialectic. Method as dialectic means not so much a set of rules, but a way of thinking based on the awareness that true thought at once grasps the world and changes it. In this Lukács was emphasizing the Hegelian roots of Marxism, for Hegel had argued that true reason does not fully understand reality until it realizes that the very act of understanding also belongs to reality, that proper thought is itself a function of the world, which it not only mirrors but *is*. This uniting of the cognitive and the normative is reflected in the way that Lukács's dialectic works as *praxis*, as opposed to contemplation. Above all, dialectical thought implies a sense of *totality*: it requires viewing the social universe as a dynamic, directional whole, existing and acting beyond any given set of mere facts. Facts, indeed, are viewed as 'Momente', partial aspects of the ever-changing whole. For this reason Lukács's 'totality' is pre-eminently characterized by the future, a future both foreseen and created. However, to be concrete, totality needs 'mediations', directional links connecting it with particular phenomena. Without mediations it would be an abstract ideal, and not the concrete historical movement in its substance. Moreover, totality as praxis is self-activated: its nature is that of a *subject*. Again, like Hegel's *Geist*, totality must be an 'identical subject-object', both an objective reality and the subject that knows it, and in so doing also knows itself as an active part of it.

Thus, in praxis, knowledge is action, and action knowledge. The subject of this totality, however, must be a collective one, namely a social class, because only a social class can both penetrate social reality and change it. But of the social classes there is only one possible candidate: the proletariat. Only the proletariat can know itself as both a subject and an object, because only workers, realizing that their labour is simultaneously a commodity and their own life, can experience an objective reality stemming, as a source of collective effort, from debased human activity. The worker's very wretch-edness forbids him to 'know' the world in any contemplative fashion, and this compels him to self-consciousness *as an object*. Fur-thermore, the proletariat is a revolutionary class and therefore only it can call on totality as the meaning of future history. (The bour-geoisie is disqualified because it is incapable of dialectical knowledge: rather, its thought is characteristically contemplative, detached. The habit of bourgeois rationalism is 'reifica-tion', a term Lukács borrows from Simmel and equates with one of the senses Marx adopted for 'alienation'; human attributes are mistaken for things and thing-like abstractions, which prohibits the praxis of totality.)

History and Class Consciousness was written to provide a historico-philosophical justifica-tion of revolutionary socialism as it emerged in Russia in 1917. Disillusioned by the failure of proletarian uprisings outside Russia, Lukács had turned away from his erstwhile Luxemburgism (i.e. the cult of spontaneous revolution and workers' councils) towards a **Leninist** stress on the rule of the revolu-tionary party as the vanguard of the masses. Notwithstanding this, the book was con-demned by the Comintern in 1924, and ten years later Lukács himself repudiated it. In regard to classical Marxism as codified by Engels and Lenin, several core tenets of *History and Class Consciousness* were heretical. Having described totality as a subject in history, Lukács ruthlessly ruled out Engels's notion of a dialectic of nature. Similarly, no room was allowed for Lenin's 'reflection' theory of knowledge. Again, he bluntly stated that the decisive difference between Marxist and bourgeois thinking is not the primacy of economic causes in historical explanation, but the viewpoint of totality. Indeed, he went as far as to say that historical materialism should be subjected to a critique analogous to that which Marx had performed on bourgeois economics.

In his early, pre-Marxist literary criticism, Lukács had placed himself as far as possible from aestheticism and the idea of 'art for art's sake', making his own Arnold's dictum about literature as a 'criticism of life'. He firmly opposed tendentious literary formulae on the grounds that the political meaning of litera-ture should organically emerge from its artistic qualities instead of being simply juxtaposed to them. Even the early *Soul and Form* (1911, trans. 1974), with its near-existentialist response to the meaning of tragedy, regarded literary works as moral gestures, in which an author attempts to give form to his 'soul', and thus define a basic attitude towards life. Similarly *The Theory of the Novel* is concerned with the ethical values of literature, con-ceived historically. Whereas the ancient epic presented human life in thorough mean-ingfulness, its heroes always organically linked to their communities, the novel is seen as an essentially bourgeois form representing a desperate bid on the part of the author to recapture a sense of existence amidst a meaningless world. Accordingly the novel's hero is characterized as a solitary seeker, in constant opposition to his social environ-ment. He is prone to abstract idealism, as in *Don Quixote*, or to romantic disillusionment, as in **Flaubert's** *Éducation Sentimentale*: only in utopian novels like Goethe's *Wilhelm Meister*, or in fleeting glimpses of a natural harmony outside society, as in **Tolstoy**, can he find happiness or peace of mind. Novelists are the 'negative mystics' of 'godless epochs'.

During the 1930s Lukács broadened and refined the concept of 'critical realism', a staple category of official Marxist aesthetics in the USSR. In particular it came to denote a sub-tle version of historical consciousness on the part of bourgeois novelists, past and present. Flaubert, **Dostoevsky**, Balzac and **Mann** are among those writers Lukács describes as transcending the class-bias of the bourgeois mind, albeit unwittingly. *The Historical Novel* (written 1938, published in 1955, trans. 1962), perhaps his finest modulation of rea-lism into historico-stylistic terms, cogently relates the birth of historical fiction in Walter Scott to the changes in attitude towards his-tory that attended the French Revolution. In addition Balzac is interpreted as the first major novelist to succeed in depicting 'the present as history', so achieving a higher level of 'realism', paradoxically through his romantically melodramatic characterization.

The fulcrum of Lukácsian realism is the idea of characters as *types*, a concept which he inherited from the poetics of the Enlightenment as well as from classical Marxism, and which he radically historicized. These types are defined by their breadth of characterization, by their self-awareness in times of turmoil, and, most importantly, by their historical representativeness, or the way they are enhanced above the mere average of their age and social class. In other words a realist hero need not be heroic; but what he must convey is an intimation of the historical process as a *totality*. Thus while a handful of 'socialist realists' like the later **Gorky** and **Sholokhov** are admired for achieving a sense of historical perspective without descending to trivial moralizing, bourgeois naturalism, modernism and Stalinist 'revolutionary romanticism' are each rejected for being 'departures from realism'. In this respect at least Lukács broke with his earlier criticism: instead of envisaging literature as a negative mysticism, he now praised certain selected parts of it for its realistic power of rendering the historical saga of humankind.

The underlying concern with the Hegelian idea of totality survived into Lukács's old age. The great *Aesthetics* is comprised of four main conceptual elements: totality; the primacy of content over form; reflection as mimesis; and the idea of the wholeness of man. While the first two derive from Hegel, the role of reflection comes from Engels and Lenin's theory of knowledge (with which he at last became reconciled) skilfully combined with Aristotle's mimetic theory of art; and the 'whole man' theme incorporates the lofty ethico-aesthetical ideals of Weimar classicism. Above all, art embodies man's self-awareness: 'art is the self-consciousness of humanity', and so, if it fulfils its ideal, it cannot help but be historically minded. In being outrightly anthropomorphic, art differs from science; in being resolutely inner-worldly, it differs from religion; and by its comprehensiveness of

vision, by dropping the normative focus on positive paradigms, it is marked off from ethics. By 'overflowing into ethics', however, art as an inner-worldly anthropomorphism endowed with cognitive powers and productive of a cathartic effect acts at an equal distance from disinterested contemplation and practical life; and so prepares man for higher forms of existence. In short, aesthetic knowledge is a necessary mediator between individuality and universality – but only universality in the sense that it is synonymous with 'totality'.

Taking his work as a whole, Lukács strove to restore the rich philosophical heritage of Marxism; and to the extent that it is no longer possible to take at face value Marx's dictum about 'standing Hegel on his feet' he was successful. By stressing Lenin's emphasis on the subjective factor in history as a conquest extending the limits of classical Marxism he laid bare the prophetic and eschatological drive in Marxist thought, together with its pursuit of a logic of history hinging on class conflict and redemptive revolutions. Because of this he has been much criticized for unabashed historicism; but a greater sin was perhaps his inflation of dialectics at the expense of historical materialism in its awareness of social determinisms – an inflation that entailed the identification of science *as such* with 'bourgeois ideology'. Because his dialectics method, which as praxis engulfs history, is self-grounded and submits to no real criteria of objective truth, Lukács the fierce anti-irrationalist can never be entirely free from the taunt that he was himself irrational. He cast a long shadow on Western Marxism, dooming it to be far more speculative than empirical in content. Thus, for example, the 'critical theory' of the Frankfurt School (*vide* **Horkheimer**, **Adorno**) amounts to *History and Class Consciousness* minus the faith in revolutions. Often a first-rate literary critic, his search for a total meaning sometimes led him to stray from the discipline of critical reason. It is perhaps of some relevance that Thomas Mann, in *The Magic Mountain*, portrayed Lukács as Naphta, an intelligent Jesuit in dire need of authority.

Further reading

See: Lukács's *Collected Works*, in seventeen volumes, are being published by Luchterhand in West Germany (from 1962). Other translations include *The Young Hegel* (1975); *Studies in European Socialism* (1964); *Goethe and His Age* (1968); *Essays on Thomas Mann* (1964); *The Meaning of Contemporary Realism* (1963); and *The Ontology of Social Being, I, Hegel* and *II, Marx* (1978). See: G.H.R. Parkinson (ed.) *Georg Lukács: The Man, His Work and His Ideas* (1970); I. Meszaros, *Lukács' Concept of Dialectic* (1972); chapters in M. Merleau-Ponty, *The Adventures of the Dialectic* (1973); L. Colletti, *Il Marxismo e Hegel*, (1969); F. Jameson, *Marxism and Form* (1971); S. Avineri (ed.) *Varieties of Marxism* (1977); L. Kolakowski, *Main Currents of Marxism*, Vol. III (1978); Mary Gluck, *George Lukács and His Generation, 1900–1918* (1985); Ernest Joos (ed.) *George Lukács and His World* (1987); Judith Marcus and Zoltan Tarr (eds) *George Lukács* (1989); Arpad Kadarkay, *Georg Lukács* (1991).

J.G. MERQUIOR

LUTOSŁAWSKI, Witold

1913–94

Polish composer

As with Chopin and **Szymanowski**, the two other indisputably great art music composers to have emerged from Poland's molten cultural topography, Witold Lutosławski's life and work appear inextricably intertwined. He was born in Warsaw in 1913, and his early years included episodes of unquestionably stark drama – visiting his father Józef in a Moscow prison just hours before his execution by the Bolsheviks in 1918, escape from the Wehrmacht as a prisoner of war during World War II, brushes with the Nazis during the occupation of Warsaw. Later on, **Stalinism**, Communism and Poland's struggle for democracy all impinged on his artistic consciousness, and Lutosławski never entirely denied the impact on his work (albeit unwanted and perhaps unconscious) of life's often tragic intrusions. As a latterday romantic humanist, however, he viewed his music as an attempt to transcend the turmoil of everyday existence, designing his works to open channels of communication between individuals in an ideal world of sound.

Lutosławski's first great achievement was a unique modernist voice. Rather than embracing abstractionism, and not too self-absorbed to countenance fresh takes on established musical conventions, he fashioned a stylistic continuum ranging between the riches of contemporary compositional thinking and deeper currents of expressivity. Consequently, his post-1960 music is justly prized for its harmonic riches (Lutosławski was one of the twentieth century's masters of harmony), its animation of texture through carefully delimited chance procedures, and its distinctive take on large-scale musical forms. But it must also be celebrated for its gestural verve, expressive shaping and masterly control of atmosphere. Even the evolution of his original voice, however, pivoted around politically mediated circumstances – the brief thaw in Polish cultural life during the late 1950s, which permitted art music to surge into experimental territories forbidden to most other artists under the post-war Stalinist then Communist regimes. Beforehand, Lutosławski had worked within the constraints of Poland's robustly pungent take on musical neo-classicism. His soundworld at this stage was inspired by **Debussy**, **Ravel** and early **Stravinsky**, but in the 1930s the course on classical forms taught at the Warsaw Conservatory by his teacher Witold Maliszewski encouraged a spirited fusion of French–Russian sonorities with Austro-German symphonism. The inventiveness, panache and punch of his early music – whether in the assured Symphony No. 1 (1941–7), countless songs, suites, dance tunes and didactic works, or magnificent Concerto for Orchestra (1950–4), the finest Polish composition to admit traces of socialist-realist ideology through its symphonic treatment of folk materials – marked him out as the outstanding Polish composer of his generation.

Lutosławski's post-1960 output is generally split into middle and late periods, although there was no further evolution comparable to the one separating his neo-classical and modernist styles. Indeed, in his post-1979 'late' style, increasingly transparent textures permitted a revitalizing of melody that, fascinatingly, brought his modernism stylistically parallel to his earlier neo-classicism. For instance, the linguistic and expressive similarities between the *Poco adagio* of his First Symphony and 'La Belle-de-Nuit', the first song in *Chantefleurs et Chantefables* (1989–90), a delightful cycle of Robert Desnos settings for soprano and chamber orchestra, are as arresting as the differences. So wit, energy and invention are traits of the later music too. They shine through the pathos of his Symphony No. 3 (1981–3), the drama of which revolves around its material's search for a unified melodic voice (perhaps the work's most compelling claim to being connected, albeit obliquely, to the emergence of Solidarity), and are abundant in both *Chain 2* for violin and orchestra (1984–5), which the always modest Lutosławski considered to be his least imperfect work, and the enchanting Piano Concerto (1987–8). His crowning late achievement, however, Symphony No. 4 (1988–92), brought the often lighter tone and textures of the later works into conflict with a darker mood more prevalent in the music of his middle period.

All of Lutosławski's works of the 1960s contain riches, particularly his String Quartet (1964) and *Paroles tissées* (1965), a setting of Jean-François Chabrun poems for tenor and chamber ensemble. But the chain of works inaugurated by *Livre pour orchestre* (1968) and including the Cello Concerto (1969–70), *Les Espaces du sommeil* (1975–76) and *Mi-parti* (1976) are Lutosławski's finest triumphs. On the one hand, these are his most ravishing sonic tableaux. Few composers could match the exquisiteness of *Livre*'s iridescently textured opening sonorities, *Les Espaces du sommeil*'s central dreamscape of luminously refracting harmonies, or *Mi-parti*'s infinitely poised and poignant close. On the other hand, they reveal a mastery of musical plotting filtered through a modernist's gift for subverting conventional expectations. Almost operatic in their initially tragic impact, in

each of these works a catastrophic rupture releases, in turn, transcendence – elegiac in the codas of *Livre*, *Les Espaces* and *Mi-parti*, defiant in the Cello Concerto's Petrushka-like resurrection of its protagonist after the soloist's battle with an oppressive orchestra. Lutosławski himself was no puppet of contemporary events, still less of political regimes, and his music will always resist crude allegorical readings. Yet it will also continue to electrify and intrigue, as much for the multivalent resonances of its dramatic symbolism as for its rarely surpassed sonic beauty.

Further reading

See: recordings directed by Esa-Pekka Salonen and Antoni Wit are highly commendable, alongside the composer's own readings. See Charles Bodman Rae, *The Music of Lutosławski* (1999) for an accessible and cogent survey of Lutosławski's entire life, stylistic evolution and oeuvre.

NICK REYLAND

LYOTARD, Jean François
1924–98
French philosopher

Jean François Lyotard was born and died in Paris. He taught in Paris universities and in the United States. His best-known contribution to modern culture concerned the idea of the postmodern. With the timely appearance of his *La Condition postmoderne* (1979, translated as *The Postmodern Condition*, 1984), he provided its most philosophical account. The book was widely followed and criticized. It was also widely misunderstood in a series of narrow and illinformed interpretations, notably from the Frankfurt School, on the left, and from a more liberal American pragmatism.

The misunderstanding still holds some sway. Its basis lies in confusion about Lyotard's attitude to postmodernism, postmodernity and the postmodern. Postmodernism is a movement in the arts, politics, philosophy, sociology and the sciences. It claims that a monolithic and hegemonic modern era should be brought to an end and replaced by a fragmented set of competing and irreducibly heterogeneous views and products. Different demands and values can then be held together loosely through a mix of capitalism and liberal democracy.

Lyotard was never party to this postmodernism and to its claim that history could come to an end. It was his life's work to find ways of resisting the illusion of a benign mix of capital and debated opinions. He sought to preserve the 'honour of thought' away from modern idealism, with its justifications for violence in the name of future peace, and away from postmodern collaboration or political naivety. In resisting both he coined the new term 'differend': a difference that could be testified to but never resolved.

This relation between feeling and justice is a constant in Lyotard's work. For him, postmodern works are shocking and uncomfortable. They innovate and hence trigger feelings that show the limits of current beliefs and practices. Such works are therefore not bound to a postmodern era; rather, the postmodern and the avantgarde can be found in all times, in the quattrocento, impressionism or surrealism.

In his book *Le Différend* (1983, translated as *The Differend*, 1988), he claimed that differends are as much part of liberal democracy and capitalism as of any other system. They occur, for example, with the insistence on 'proper' forms of representation, despite the fact that some wrongs cannot be expressed in these forms, or with the practice of assigning a value to all things, even those which may be beyond measure – ethical obligations, for instance.

Postmodernity is supposed to be an epoch where postmodernism achieves its goal. Society becomes fragmented and a plurality of cultures co-exist relatively peacefully. A very superficial reading of one of Lyotard's main claims – on 'the end of grand narratives' – can lead to a belief that he had diagnosed the arrival of postmodernity and welcomed it. This is a misunderstanding of his relation to time and to history.

For Lyotard, there is no final passing of epochs. Instead, there are competing ideas about each epoch in terms of its relation to the future. Ideas can only provide us with guiding threads for narratives – such as, science and open societies will lead us to a povertyfree new world order or freedom comes through the dictatorship of the proletariat. These grand unifying accounts can never be truthful, since reality is an unsteady relation of forms of knowledge and novel events that destabilize them. His best account of this state of reality is in the deliberately shocking but beautiful book *Economie libidinale* (1974, translated as *Libidinal Economy*, 1993), where structures are described as concealing and thriving off libidinal intensities. Lyotard's libidinal work owes much to **Nietzsche** and to Spinoza. It is also part of Lyotard's 'drift away' from **Marx** and **Freud**.

Earlier, in *Discours, figure* (1971), his great deconstruction of structuralism and phenomenology, Lyotard had argued for a different kind of event: the figural, or an event in language and art where sensation and discourse meet and evolve, but where neither dominates. In his later works, *L'Inhumain: causeries sur le temps* (1988, translated as *The Inhuman*, 1991) and *Moralités postmodernes* (1993, translated as *Postmodern Fables*, 1997), he drew on Kant to argue for sublime events that make us aware of the limits of knowledge but that also drive us to seek ways of showing that there are events beyond it: beyond the known human and into the inhuman.

Lyotard deployed irony against overblown and simplifying projects. He sought the thoughtprovoking quality of the essay, rather than the impregnability of theory. He invited readers to think anew, rather than tell them what they should think. Not everyone has an ear for his laughter and wit. Some search for more serious and permanent truths. He saw this quest as a sign of a nihilistic need to impose transcendence on a more fluid and truthful existence.

Further reading

Other works include: *Signé Malraux* (1996, translated as *Signed, Malraux* 1999) and on art, for example on Cézanne, in *Des dispositifs pulsionnels* (1973).Works on Lyotard include

Geoffrey Bennington, *Lyotard: Writing the Event* (1988), Bill Readings, *Introducing Lyotard: Art and Politics* (1991) and Simon Malpas, *JeanFrançois Lyotard* (2002).

JAMES WILLIAMS

M

MacDIARMID, Hugh (Christopher Murray GRIEVE)

1892–1978
Scottish poet

Hugh MacDiarmid was born Christopher Murray Grieve in the little Scottish border town of Langholm, the son of a rural postman. The family lived in the post office building beneath the local library and young Grieve had access to a collection of some 12,000 books which he claimed to have read by the age of fourteen. He attended Langholm Academy, then went to Edinburgh to study at the university and train as a schoolteacher at Broughton Junior Students' Centre, but when his father died in 1911 he abandoned all idea of a steady career. As he explained in *Lucky Poet* (1943):

> I was very early determined that I would not 'work for money', and that whatever I might have to do to earn my living, I would never devote more of my time and my energies to remunerative work than I did to voluntary and gainless activities.

In the First World War, Grieve served with the Royal Army Medical Corps and was invalided home from Salonika suffering from cerebral malaria. In 1918 he married Margaret Skinner and the couple moved to Montrose where Grieve became chief reporter of the weekly *Montrose Review*, the father of two children, a Labour member of the town council, a Justice of the Peace, and also a founder of the Scottish Centre of P.E.N., the National Party of Scotland, and two magazines. The first of these, *Northern Numbers*, was a fairly conventional Georgian publication to which Grieve contributed poems in English. As editor of the *Scottish Chapbook*, though, Grieve introduced his readers in 1922 to the work of 'Hugh MacDiarmid'. The first MacDiarmid lyric, 'The Watergaw', was a memory of his dead father and brought a new intellectual element to Scots poetry, for the poet had combined the strength of oral Scots with the range of Scots words preserved in Jamieson's *Etymological Dictionary of the Scottish Language*. The result was variously termed 'Lallans' (Lowland Scots), 'synthetic Scots' and 'aggrandized Scots'; whatever the label there was no doubt that MacDiarmid had shaken the Scots language to its linguistic roots and that the heather was about to be set on fire.

MacDiarmid's early lyrics were published in *Sang-schaw* (1925) and *Penny Wheep* (1926), and spectacularly broke with the Burns tradition. MacDiarmid replaced Burns's Standard Habbie Stanza (which had been *de rigueur* in Scots poetry since the eighteenth century) with concise and sensuous quatrains that packed a philosophical punch; his characteristic method was to isolate a particular image, then seek out its cosmic implications. Although he used the slogan 'Dunbar – Not Burns!' in the 1920s, MacDiarmid was not confined to Scottish precedents. He was fully aware of developments in European poetry and alive to the linguistic innovations contained in two key works published in 1922 (the *annus mirabilis* of modernism): **Eliot's** *The Waste Land* and **Joyce's** *Ulysses*. In 1926 he made his own supreme contribution to the century's literature with his long poem *A Drunk Man Looks at the Thistle* (1926).

With this masterpiece MacDiarmid virtually remade Scotland in his own image. The narrative was, basically, a functional vehicle for MacDiarmid's views. A drunk man, during his unsteady odyssey to the bed of his beloved Jean (a folk equivalent of Homer's Penelope), stumbles on a hillside and there, by the light of the full moon, considers the thistle as a rugged symbol of Scotland's past and potential. As the alcoholic spirit wears off it is replaced by a deep psychological spirituality and the drunk man's sobriety is penetratingly expressed in verse of great dignity. Scotland is no longer treated as a country with defeatist obsessions but a nation with a glorious future:

> The thistle rises and forever will,
> Getherin' the generations under't.
> This is the monument o' a' they were,
> And a' they hoped and wondered.

Although MacDiarmid had immortalized modern Scotland in the verse published in the 1920s, he was to find himself a prophet without honour in his own country. In 1929 he had gone to London to edit *Vox*, a radio magazine, which collapsed after three months. The poet almost collapsed with it. He left his wife in London while he worked as a publicity officer in Liverpool; after a disastrous year there he returned to London to be divorced in 1932. He then married a Cornish girl, Valda Trevlyn and, with their baby Michael, the family moved to an abandoned cottage on the Shetland island of Whalsay in 1933. Economically impoverished, MacDiarmid was still poetically and politically active. His *First Hymn to* **Lenin** *and Other Poems* (1931) had initiated the political poetry of the 1930s and during that decade MacDiarmid, who joined the Communist Party in 1934, moved from Scots to a deliberately didactic poetry in English. His island exile also inspired him to introduce geological data into poems like 'On a Raised Beach' from *Stony Limits and Other Poems* (1934).

When he did leave Whalsay, at the age of forty-nine, it was to do a war job: first as a fitter on Clydeside, then as a deckhand on a Norwegian ship. When the war ended he was again technically unemployed, though his poetic output was prolific and his creative energies were directed to the epic and erudite English poetry subsequently collected under titles like *In Memoriam James Joyce* (1955) and *The Kind of Poetry I Want* (1961). Widely recognized as the poetic equal (and perhaps superior) of Dunbar and Burns, he was far from settling down as a mellow Grand Old Man. In 1951 he obtained a derelict, rent-free cottage in Biggar, Lanarkshire, and remained there for the rest of his life (with frequent trips all over the world). His political opinions continued to give offence: he had been expelled from the National Party in 1933 for his communism and expelled from the Communist Party in 1938 for his nationalism. In 1957 he encountered great hostility by rejoining the Communist Party in the wake of the Soviet suppression of the 1956 Hungarian Rising.

MacDiarmid created modern Scots poetry and attracted dozens of disciples, so that the contemporary Scottish poet has a bilingual choice to make between Scots and English (and a further choice between conventional English and the highly cerebral English favoured by the mature MacDiarmid). He was a great creative artist who also delighted in polemics (his hobby, as listed in *Who's Who*, was 'Anglophobia'). Yet there were two sides to the man, a private Chris Grieve and a public Hugh MacDiarmid. This contrast startled all who knew him and could observe his ability to shift from a cosy chat to a shatteringly incisive discourse.

Further reading

Other works include: *Complete Poems 1920–1976* (2 vols, 1978) and his memoirs and opinions are gathered in *Lucky Poet* (1943) and *The Company I've Kept* (1966). See: Alan Bold (ed.) *The Letters of Hugh MacDiarmid* (1984). See also Kenneth Buthlay, *Hugh MacDiarmid* (1964) and Duncan Glen, *Hugh MacDiarmid and the Scottish Renaissance* (1964); Alan Bold, *Hugh MacDiarmid: A Biography* (1985).

ALAN BOLD

MACH, Ernst

1838–1916

Austrian scientist, historian and philosopher of science

Although Mach had wide-ranging scientific interests and contributed to various fields, especially sound and physiology of perception, these contributions were not perhaps of the first importance, and his lasting influence has been based largely on his work in the history and philosophy of science. This work was widely known in Vienna at the end of the nineteenth century and beginning of the twentieth (Mach spent the last six years of his working life at the University of Vienna) and his very strict positivist views undoubtedly strongly influenced **Wittgenstein** and the members of the Vienna Circle – indeed, the public organization formed by several members of the circle was given the name Ernst Mach Verein (the 'Ernst Mach Society').

Mach was born in 1838 in Chirlitz-Turas, near Brno, Morovia (now part of Slovakia). His father played the central role in his early education, instilling in him a particular love of 'nature study'. Mach spent five years studying mathematics, physics and philosophy at the University of Vienna, obtaining his doctorate, with a dissertation on electrical discharge and induction, in 1860. The wide range of his scientific interests is to some degree reflected in the variety of his subsequent university titles. He was Professor of Mathematics and then of Physics at Graz (in fact he spent most of his time there working on 'psychophysics' – on what we would now call the psychology and physiology of perception). In 1867 he became Professor of

Experimental Physics at Charles University, Prague. And finally he returned to Vienna as Professor of the History and Theory of the Inductive Sciences in 1895. He retired in 1901, becoming in that same year a member of the upper house of the Austrian parliament. He died in 1916.

His name is remembered in the theory of perception for the so-called 'Mach bands' which he studied and described, and in supersonics for the 'Mach numbers' (based on the ratio of the speed of an object to the speed of sound in the undisturbed medium in which the object is travelling).

The general philosophical position that he developed was an extreme version of empiricism, reminiscent in certain respect of Berkeley's view. Its fullest exposition appears in his book *The Analysis of Sensations* (*Die Analyse der Empfindungen und das Verhältnis des Physichen zum Psychischen*, 1886, 9th edn, trans. 1914). He insists that 'the world consists only of our sensations'. Talk of physical objects, independent of ourselves and causing these sensations, is not to be interpreted realistically. More generally, our scientific theories are not to be regarded as hypothesizing a reality hidden behind the phenomena – *only the phenomena are real* – the role of theories is simply to codify and schematize the phenomena in a convenient and economical way. The aim of theoretical science is not to explain, but to introduce 'economy of thought' through the construction of functional relationships between entities ultimately denoting the elements of sensation. His general philosophical position led Mach to the view that the barriers between the various sciences are purely artificial: there are no differences of subject-matter – all the sciences study our sensations.

Although Mach's phenomenalism has been very influential, there are certain rather obvious difficulties with it (such as the problem of other minds, the fact that it flies in the face of the realist beliefs of the overwhelming majority of scientists, etc.) to which Mach produced no very convincing reply. And, indeed, although twentieth-century Anglo-Saxon philosophy in the main tended towards a positivism of a more or less Machian kind (**Russell's** 'neutral monism', for example, owes much to Mach), there have been notable philosophers who have reacted strongly against this mainstream view, and have subjected Mach's position to attack. One famous attack was launched from the viewpoint of dialectical materialism by **Lenin** in his 1909 book *Materialism and Empirio-Criticism: Critical Comments on a Reactionary Philosophy*. Later, **Karl Popper** was a consistent critic of positivism in general and of Mach's position in particular.

Perhaps the most fundamental *internal* difficulty in Mach's views is this: on the one hand he taught that no concept was admissible in science unless it is firmly rooted in (definable in terms of) 'experience'; on the other hand, he saw the role of science as that of maximizing 'economy of thought'. What guarantee have we that these two ideas do not clash? Why may not the theory producing the most economical representation of the phenomena involve highly theoretical or metaphysical concepts which are *not* 'reducible' to experience? Mach's famous opposition to the atomic-kinetic theory (discussed below) highlights this difficulty.

The idea that the world consists only of our sensations was never very influential within science itself. But Mach's claim that concepts which cannot be 'reduced' to experience must be eliminated from science *was* widely discussed by scientists. Because of his vigorous advocacy of this claim, Mach is usually cast in the strange dual role of dogmatic reactionary concerning one scientific revolution, and visionary progenitor of another.

Not surprisingly, Mach was very much opposed to invisible atoms and molecules, and this translated itself into near life-long opposition to the atomic-kinetic theory of heat. Despite his opposition, this theory underwent a most fruitful revival during the second half of the nineteenth century. The theory, developed by **Clausius**, **Boltzmann**, **Maxwell** and others, held that gases, for example, are made up of molecules moving around randomly at high velocities. Heating the gas gives a greater mean velocity to the molecules, and in fact the temperature of the gas is a measure of the mean kinetic energy of its constituent molecules. Mach insisted that no good could come of hypothesizing such invisible entities and advocated that scientists stick more closely to the direct phenomena of heat – to so-called phenomenological thermodynamics. There were undoubtedly real difficulties in the kinetic theory to which Mach could point, but most scientists preferred to tackle these difficulties rather than reject the whole theory on dogmatic anti-atomist grounds. Their attitude was vindicated when the atomic-kinetic theory turned out to have new consequences which were dramatically confirmed experimentally.

It seems that Mach's insistence that all scientific concepts be experimentally definable and his consequent crusade against atoms at least partially blinded him to the possibility that the kinetic *theory* could be scientifically superior to its rivals. Indeed, this superiority would be explained on Mach's own terms if the atomic theory turned out to classify more phenomena more 'economically' than other theories. This illustrates the main difficulty in Mach's views alluded to above.

Although his anti-atomism was very much out of tenor with mainstream scientific thought, Mach's similarly based opposition to certain mechanical notions is held by many commentators to have helped instigate the Einsteinian relativity revolution.

In many ways Mach's most impressive work was his *The Science of Mechanics: A Critical and Historical Account of its Development* (*Die Mechanik in Ihrer Entwicklung historisch-kritisch dargestellt*, 1883, trans. 1942). He there charts the history of mechanics – principally with a view to conceptual analysis of its foundations. Pursuing his overall objective to rid science of any concept not firmly rooted in experience, Mach strongly criticized Newton's notions of absolute time, space and motion. According to Newton there is, as well as motion relative to some more or less arbitrarily chosen 'fixed' point, *absolute motion* – motion 'relative' to space ('God's sensorium') itself. Moreover, according to Newton, there is no need to refer time to anything in our experience – time too is absolute, 'flowing uniformly without regard to anything external'.

Mach had no time for such metaphysical notions – for example, all motion is, for him, relative, because only if it is observed can it exist and motion can only be observed relative to some chosen co-ordinate system.

The most distinctive feature of the special theory of relativity which **Einstein** proposed in 1905 as a rival to, and replacement for, Newtonian mechanics, is its insistence that all motion is indeed relative to a frame of reference. Moreover, according to relativity theory, the time interval too is frame-dependent; two events which are simultaneous in one frame of reference may not be simultaneous in another frame moving relatively to the first. It is no surprise, then, that Mach is regarded as having played an important role in the genesis of relativity theory – especially as Einstein himself admitted that Mach had influenced his early thought.

Mach is also attributed a role in the development of *general* relativity theory, which yields Einstein's account of gravitation and which was proposed in 1914. In the *Science of Mechanics*, Mach had criticized not only Newton's treatment of motion but also his treatment of *mass*. Newton had characterized this as 'quantity of matter' – much too metaphysical an idea for Mach since it is not firmly grounded in experimental procedures. Mach proposed a different characterization of the mass of a body, which has, as a consequence, the proposition that a single body in an otherwise empty universe would exhibit no resistance to acceleration, i.e. have no mass. Einstein christened this proposition 'Mach's principle'. Its precise consequences and its role in the genesis of general relativity theory have ever since been matters of heated debate. (Although the principle could well have been suggestive for Einstein, it does *not* follow from his general theory, as he eventually realized.)

We have Einstein's word for it that Mach's views influenced him, but whether these views played a really significant role in the relativity revolution is open to doubt. Certainly other factors (internal factors from within science itself) played a more important role; and certainly the idea that the relativity breakthrough consisted chiefly of ridding science of some excess metaphysical baggage is greatly exaggerated – relativity theory is, in its own way, just as 'absolutist' as its Newtonian predecessor. Einstein himself later came to realize the untenability of Mach's positivism; and as for Mach, he always disclaimed any responsibility for relativity theory, which he *explicitly* rejected.

Further reading

Other works include: *Knowledge and Error* (*Erkenntnis und Irrtum* 1905, trans. 1926, 1976); and two important historical works: *The Principles of Physical Optics* (*Die Principien der Physikalischen Optik. Historisch und Erkenntnis-psychologisch entwickelt*, 1921, trans. 1926) and *Die Principien der Wärmelehre: Historisch-kritisch entwickelt* (1896). See: John Blackmore (ed.) *Ernst Mach: A Deeper Look: Documents and New Perspectives* (1992); Erik C. Banks, *Ernst Mach's World Elements: A Study in Natural Philosophy* (2003).

JOHN WORRALL

MACHADO DE ASSIS, Joaquim Maria
1839–1908
Brazilian writer

Unanimously reckoned as the foremost name in Brazilian literature and one of the very greatest masters of fiction in Portuguese, Joaquim Maria Machado de Assis was born a poor mulatto on a Rio hill, where his parents lived under the protection of the widow of an empire grandee. He was brought up by a kind stepmother, a negress. Still in his teens, the self-taught boy, who learnt French from the Gallic bakers of the Court district, S. Cristóvão, was helped by a Dickensian figure, the printer and bookseller Paula Brito, to enter the world of journalism and of the belated Latin-American Romanticism; he spent most of his twenties as a drama critic, a translator (notably of **Hugo** and **Dickens**) and a parliamentary reporter deeply attached to liberal causes. His status improved at thirty, when he became a government official and when he married Carolina, the mature and learned sister of his friend, a minor Portuguese poet named Faustino Xavier de Novaes. A tough social climber, he turned his back on everything connected with his humble past, including his stepmother. Machado had suffered for long from epilepsy, though of a milder kind than **Dostoevsky's**. Shortly before he was forty, a major crisis forced him to a protracted convalescence in a mountain resort near Rio. The result was a baffling transformation of the outlook of his work, issuing in the unique prose works which earned him his enduring glory. By the closing years of the century, he led, with the critic José Verissimo, the group of the Revista Brasileira, cradle of the Brazilian Academy, whose chairmanship he was offered by general consensus. Remote as he was to everything smacking of edifying literature, he died as the living symbol of institutional fine letters, widely acclaimed yet scarcely understood. The subsequent heroic age of the avant-garde entailed further misunderstandings; the noisy Dionysiac nationalism of 'modernismo' was indeed a far cry from the subtle shadows of Machadian art.

Machado first reached consistent literary quality as a poet. In *Americanas* (1875) he added moral probing to the staple Romantic subject-matter of *indianismo*; the *Ocidentais* (written *c.* 1880) yield philosophical musings in impeccable Parnassian technique. The beginnings of the storyteller were also romantic. Like the founder of Brazilian novel, José de Alencar (1829–77), who befriended him, Machado was alive to the dialectic of love, money and ambition in well-to-do urban settings of mid-century Brazil; on the other hand, he still sticks to the Victorian versions of values such as honesty, self-sacrifice and the work ethic. But he shows remarkable skill in drawing female characters and eventually, in his fourth novel, *Iaiá Garcia* (1878), eschews melodramatic language for the sake of natural dialogues and deeper psychological analysis.

Yet it was the short story that harboured his final break with Romanticism. The novelette 'The Alienist', a masterpiece where Swiftian humour is enhanced by anachronism, portrays the toils of Dr Simon Bacamarte, a paragon of moral and scientific integrity who, having started a thorough research on human folly as 'an island lost amidst the ocean of reason', fatally begins to suspect it is rather like a continent. Madness, and especially madness *qua* vice, is universal; man is most often a predatory animal, and men slaves to opinion. Coming back to one's senses actually means coming back to *others'* senses, says the story, which theorizes about selfhood as the 'external soul'.

The significance of Machado's later novels lies in their ability to project this wry cast of mind on the formal level. Thus *Epitaph of a Small Winner* (*Memórias póstumas de Brás Cubas*, 1881, trans. 1952), originally entitled 'Posthumous Memoirs of Brás Cubas', technically amounts to a wilful return from **Flaubert** to Laurence Sterne – a Sterne purged of sentimentality. This odd book, written 'with a mocking pen and melancholy ink', re-enacts an old genre: the Menippean satire, the comic-fantastic brand of philosophical narrative. Machado is a modern Lucian who put the Menippean within the crazy autobiographical framework of a 'dead author', Brás Cubas, a wealthy, selfish *fainéant* with a few amours and much spleen, who deems nature a plague and history a catastrophe. The background of his erratic memoirs discloses the misery and sadism of slave-owning elites ever hankering after lust and power. Machado writes as a disillusioned French moralist well acquainted with Schopenhauer, who cannot help caricaturing philosophical optimism ('humanitism') as sheer nonsense. Nevertheless, unlike other late nineteenth-century pessimists, he is by no means a determinist, and does not seem to hold too tragic a view of humankind. Instead, he keeps a sense of *lusus naturae*, and defines man as 'a thinking erratum'.

Most of Machado's later *contos* (short stories) are in keeping with this poetics of disillusion. Although he was also an excellent *conteur à la* **Maupassant**, as well as a master of the apologue, Machado's favourite focus fell on the painting of characters in the La Bruyèrean sense: taken together, his *contos* present a magnificent moral pageant, rendered with a command of narrative technique unsurpassed in the Iberian countries until Borges. Machado's characters are not, like those of Naturalism (which he opposed), *described* – rather, they *betray* themselves, caught, as it were, in the net of nimble sentences fraught with witty, revealing tropes.

The *Epitaph*'s sequel, *Philosopher or Dog* (*Quincas Borba*, 1891, trans. 1954), is also told in short chapters, but in the third person and with the humorous authorial interventions made more organically related to the plot. The anti-hero, Rubião, far less eccentric than Cubas, is a humane fool, a *loco cuerdo* enriched by an inheritance and – as a victim of megalomania – an easy prey to the cupidity of those he helped or saved. With *Dom Casmurro* (1899, trans. 1953), Machado returned to the first-person novel, but this time with fewer characters. Dom Casmurro – 'the Brazilian Othello', as an American critic described him – is an unsocial widower trying to relive the green paradise of youthful love. He is obsessed with Capitu, the sensuous brunette who embodies the 'life is treason' theme, not the least because their son grows into a startling resemblance of the couple's best friend. The 'impregnation' motive – the idea that a woman can lend her child the looks of her beloved even though the latter has not fathered it – was already present in Goethe's *Elective Affinities* (1809) and at the centre of young **Zola's** *Madeleine Férat* (1868); but Machado tackles it with a wonderful, truly **Jamesian** impressionistic sensibility, particularly apt at grasping the feeling of time.

The novels of maturity are crowned by *Esau and Jacob* (1904, trans. 1966), again in the first person, but with a positively self-effacing narrator, the retired diplomat Ayres. Allegory prevails throughout, especially around Flora, a Botticellian beauty who proves foreign to the world of passion and appetite (and the rivalry of two brothers) because she is in love with the absolute. Since the action of *Epitaph for a Small Winner* harks back to pre-Independence Brazil, and *Esau and Jacob* comments on the first decade of the Republic, with a novel like *Iaià Garcia*, set in the days of the war with Paraguay, in the middle, one might say that Machado's chronicle of Brazilian life covers the whole of his century. In spite of his conscious avoidance of 'social' fiction, no other novelist provides more insight into the national mind of the age. In an oblique way, Machado often showed the huge gap between progressive bourgeois ideology and the grim realities of Brazilian class structure. His book-length farewell to fiction, *Counsellor Ayres' Memorial* (*Memorial de Aires*, 1908, trans. 1973), goes beyond misanthropy in the purest music of Machadian prose. Some see in his language – a faultless balance of high and low, old and new usage – his most precious bequest to Brazilian literature; its expressive powers also shine in a modest but most popular genre, the *cronica*, which was established by Machado. Perhaps the biggest paradox about Machado de Assis is that such a profound writer, in whose hands Brazilian letters outgrew the age of naive consciousness, should also be the least solemn of authors.

Further reading

Other works include: *The Psychiatrist and Other Stories* (trans. 1963). Important studies include: Augusto Meyer, *Machado de Assis* (1958); Eugenio Gomes, *Machado de Assis* (1958); Helen Caldwell, *Machado de Assis: The Brazilian Master and His Novels* (1970); Dieter Woll, *Machado de Assis – die Entwicklung seines erzaehlerischen Werkes* (1972); Roberto Schwarz, *Ao Vencedor as Batatas* (São Paulo, 1977); R. Magalhães Jr, *Vida e Obra de Machado de Assis* (4 vols, 1981); Maria Luisa Nunes, *The Craft of an Absolute Winner: Characterization and Narratology in the Novels of Machado de Assis* (1983); Maria Manuel Lisboa, *Machado de Assis and Feminism* (1996); Roberto Schwarz, *A Master on the Periphery of Capitalism: Machado de Assis*, trans. John Gledson (2001).

J.G. MERQUIOR

MacINTYRE, Alasdair

1929–

British philosopher

An original thinker who had a strong influence on the development of moral philosophy in the late twentieth century, MacIntyre was born and educated in Britain and taught at a number of universities, mostly in the USA. His early work *Marxism: An Interpretation* (1953) included a critical examination of the relationship between the **Marxist** and the Christian worldviews, and his *Short History of Ethics* (1967) emphasized the culturally embedded nature of ethical theory (against the then dominant ahistorical view of moral reasoning). His masterpiece, *After Virtue* (1981), contributed powerfully to the revival of so-called 'virtue ethics' in the closing decades of the twentieth century.

In *After Virtue*, MacIntyre argued that the 'Enlightenment project' of providing a universal rational justification for morality not only failed, but inevitably had to fail. The philosophers of the eighteenth century and their successors had attempted to find a universal rational basis for their moral beliefs, but failed to recognize their own peculiar historical and cultural situation, which made them inheritors of 'incoherent fragments of a once coherent scheme of thought and action'. Thus, although they invoked concepts such as duty and obligation, these were nothing more than 'ghosts of conceptions of divine law ... quite alien to the metaphysics of modernity'. In the Enlightenment world of secular rationality, religion could no longer provide the required shared background and foundation for moral discourse. And the resulting failure of philosophy 'to provide what religion could no longer furnish' was an important cause of philosophy 'losing its central cultural role and becoming a marginal, narrowly academic subject'.

Following on from the collapse of the Enlightenment project, MacIntyre pointed to the twentieth-century rise of 'emotivist' and other deflationary accounts of ethics as showing that our culture had succumbed to a nihilistic **Nietzschean** vision, which reduced moral discourse to the arbitrary assertion of raw desire or will. In place of this dead-end, however, MacIntyre proposed a return to the older conception of an ethics of the *virtues*, of the kind which Aristotle had championed, and which had subsequently been developed by Aquinas. But instead of the questionable idea underpinning traditional virtue theory – that of a determinate goal (or *telos*) based on the essential nature of humankind – MacIntyre proposed a reworking of Aristotelian virtue in terms of more socially and historically mediated notions. The virtues, on this revised conception, are defined by MacIntyre as qualities necessary to achieve the *goods internal to certain human practices*. Understanding the relevant goods does not depend on a timeless conception of human nature; rather, they 'can only be elaborated and possessed within an ongoing social tradition'.

One of the recurring ideas behind this picture is that our grasp of morality, and indeed all human action, depends on locating its elements within an intelligible *narrative*. The idea of a narrative might at first suggest an individual piece of storytelling; but for MacIntyre we are, necessarily, socially located creatures who do not write the script from scratch, at best only 'co-authors' of our own history. 'Man is, in his actions and practice, essentially a story-telling animal ... But I can only answer the question *What I am to do?* if I can answer the prior question *Of what story or stories do I find myself a part?*'

One problem with this idea is the complexity of modern culture, which seems to have been shaped and influenced by many differing and often competing worldviews: locating ourselves within a Marxist story, for example, may give a very different account of how we should live than locating ourselves within the narrative structures of Catholic Christianity. And a further complication, if we are faced with a choice between competing narratives, is that the standards of rationality and justification may themselves varying significantly within different traditions. In *Whose Justice? Which Rationality?* (1988), MacIntyre attempts to address this issue, arguing that any given conception of the good life stands or falls by how well it grows and adapts to tackle the crises which it has to face; and in *Three Rival Versions of Moral Enquiry* (1990) he moves towards a more explicit defence of the merits of the Catholic Thomist tradition in sustaining a viable conception of the good for humankind. His later work *Dependent Rational Animals* (1999) continues to develop a virtue-based account of human flourishing, but in a way that gives new emphasis to something often overlooked by moral theorists – the fundamental vulnerability and dependency of the human condition.

In all his writings, MacIntyre has brought a deep historical understanding to the enterprise of ethical theory. Against the often prevailing academic tendency to render the subject ever more abstract and artificial, he has contributed significantly to making it a more humane discipline, integrally connected to the rest of our intellectual and moral culture.

Further reading

Other works include: *Three Rival Version of Moral Enquiry* (1990). See also: J. Horton and S. Mendus (eds) *After MacIntyre* (1994); D. Statman (ed.) *Virtue Ethics* (1997); S. Darwall (ed.) *Virtue Ethics* (2003).

JOHN COTTINGHAM

MACKINTOSH, Charles Rennie

1868–1928
Scottish architect and designer

Standing halfway between the English Arts and Crafts Movement and European Art Nouveau, Mackintosh is a unique figure, part of both the nineteenth and the twentieth centuries. He combines, in his designs for architecture, interiors and furniture, extreme decoration with extreme functionalism, evolving an aesthetic idiom which is very much his own.

Born in Glasgow in 1868, Mackintosh's first love was for two dimensions and he spent much time up until 1900 and again in the last decade of his life with decorative graphic work – pencil sketches and watercolours – producing designs, in the early period, which are reminiscent of **Aubrey Beardsley** and the Dutch symbolist painter Jan Toorop. Simplified stylizations of natural forms, particularly flowers and their stems, appear in these designs and recur throughout his career. Mackintosh's architectural training was broad, and in the same year as he was articled to the Glasgow architect John Hutchins (1884) he signed on as an evening student at the Glasgow School of Art to study painting and drawing. He moved in 1889 to the firm Honeyman and Keppie as a draughtsman but left temporarily in 1891 to travel to Italy on the scholarship he had won. It was at Honeyman and Keppie that he met another draughtsman, Herbert McNair, who was to introduce him to two sisters, Margaret and Frances MacDonald. The group soon became known as 'The Four' publishing their graphic designs in periodicals at home and abroad.

In the late 1890s Mackintosh began designing furniture for various tearooms in Glasgow with simple, stylized pieces of furniture. He is best known for the high-backed ladder chairs and white painted chairs with an abstracted rose motif. The interiors were total environments with the same shapes and motifs echoed throughout. In 1898 Mackintosh started work on his design for a new building for the Glasgow School of Art – his best-known piece of architectural work. The form of the building, completed in 1909, is dictated entirely by its internal function and plan, and the large, unembellished windows look forward to the Modern Movement.

Other architectural projects of the following decade reflect the same progressive attitude combined with attention to detail and a smattering of controlled decoration. In 1899

Mackintosh designed Windyhill and, in 1902, Hill House. His reputation abroad grew when a design for a room was exhibited at the 1902 Turin exhibition and in the same year he was commissioned to design a music room in Vienna. Links with the Vienna Sezession group were strong, particularly with Josef Hoffmann.

After 1910 Mackintosh's work declined rapidly and in 1914 he moved with his wife, Margaret MacDonald, whom he married in 1900, to Suffolk and subsequently to the south of France, where he returned to watercolours for the last five years of his life. Although Mackintosh's designs are few in number they are striking in their originality and have influenced many designers who came after him both in Britain and in Europe.

Further reading

See: T. Howarth, *Charles Rennie Mackintosh and the Modern Movement* (1952); R. Macleod, *Charles Rennie Mackintosh* (1968); Alan Crawford, *Charles Rennie Mackintosh* (1995); William Buchanan, *Mackintosh's Masterwork: The Glasgow School of Art* (2004); J. Macaulay, *Charles Rennie Mackintosh: A Biography* (2005).

PENNY SPARKE

MacNEICE, Frederick Louis

1907–63

Northern Irish poet

The son of a Protestant clergyman – later a bishop – and his first wife, 'Lily', both from Connemara, Louis MacNeice was born the youngest of three children in Belfast, and spent his childhood in Carrickfergus, a little town on the north shore of the Belfast Lough. The death of his much-loved mother when he was seven haunted his childhood and his poetry, and is movingly described in *The Strings are False* (1965), MacNeice's autobiography. But he was educated in England, first at Sherborne Preparatory School, then at Marlborough and at Merton College, Oxford. Regularly he won scholarships and

distinctions, apparently without much effort: 'I was a natural examinee, an intellectual window-dresser.' He lectured in Classics at Birmingham University, and later at Bedford College, London University, and in 1941 joined the Features Department of the BBC as a highly successful and distinguished scriptwriter. Always attractive to, and attracted by, women, he was twice married and had many love affairs.

His life-long friend John Hilton wrote of the Marlborough schoolboy:

> Louis was a ribald seer, an anarchic and mocking seeker after the deep springs of action and faith or at least hope or at least mythology which would keep hope alive in a world always transient and mostly trivial, sordid and brutal.

A 'ribald seer' he remained: it is the ribald side of his personality that allowed him to accept authority and yet reject it on his own terms. 'Marlborough,' he wrote, 'unlike many public schools, has a strong highbrow tradition; there was always a group amongst the older boys that was openly against the government, and mocked the sacred code and opposed to it an aesthetic dilettantism'. Anthony Blunt, the art historian exposed as a Soviet spy, was a contemporary (as was **John Betjeman**).

Yet MacNeice himself was always wary of joining any cause. 'I will escape, with my dog on the other side of the Fair,' he wrote in 'The Individualist Speaks'. It is ironic therefore that this most uncommitted of poets should have been the object of so many attempts to claim him for one or other of the 'movements' to which writers in the 1930s were so addicted and which he so adroitly evaded: 'Macspaunday', linking him to **Auden**, Stephen Spender and Cecil Day Lewis, was really a figment of the South African poet Roy Campbell's pugnacity, though it is true that MacNeice was a great admirer of Auden's work and on varying terms of friendship with the other two. His reply to the Left Review's pamphlet 'Authors Take Sides on the Spanish Civil War' was sympathetic but characteristically laconic; he never joined the Communist Party, though his personal instincts were to the Left; as he wrote, 'the strange appeal of the Communist Party was that it demanded sacrifice; you had to sink your ego'; and this, of course, he persistently refused to do.

His relationship with Ireland is even more complex – a mixture of love and exasperation would seem the best summary of his feelings. In a radio discussion on modern poetry, accused by the Irish poet F.H. Higgins of neglecting the Irish 'blood-music', MacNeice replied: 'I think that one may have such a thing as one's racial blood-music, but that, like one's subconscious, it may be left to look after itself.' Yet he has been a major influence on modern Northern Irish poetry.

Auden had, by 1939, come to regard the 1930s as a 'low dishonest decade'; MacNeice perceived the modern malaise as 'the mess that is caused everywhere by wishful thinking'. 'The public-school boy, after a few years of discomfort, has all the answers at his fingertips – he does not have to bother with the questions.' But it was the 'questions' that fascinated MacNeice. He had, from his time at Sherborne, been captivated by Malory and Spenser and the Quest for the Grail, and in his last term at Marlborough he had been 'swept away by Heraclitus, by the thesis that everything is flux and fire is the primary principle'. See 'Variations on Heraclitus', for example, or 'Reflections'.

But Horace was his greatest love, for his 'grain of salt' and his 'tidiness', for his combination of detached observation and underlying melancholy. He also praised **Baudelaire** for his 'concentration' and a 'fine balance between wit and inspiration'. For much the same reason he admired George Herbert, whose 'Sighs and Grones' was to inspire his own 'Prayer before Birth'. To MacNeice the poet was not so much a teacher as a maker: 'the community's conscience, its critical faculty, its generous instinct ... No one except the poet can give us poetic truth.' He mistrusted poetry that was too clever or wilfully obscure: his main

preoccupation was to be honest with himself and others; he agreed with Alexander Pope that the 'proper study of Mankind is Man', and had little time for any theory of art that diminished the central importance of the human: '"Significant form", on any analysis, ought to mean significant of something outside itself', and he found reading Edwin Muir's poems 'like walking through a gallery of abstract paintings'. This was not intended as a compliment.

Unquestionably, *Autumn Journal* (1939) is one of MacNeice's finest achievements, not unworthy to stand with **Tennyson's** *In Memoriam* as an expression of the anxieties of his time: the sense of an intelligent, liberal-minded man in a world inevitably moving towards catastrophe is miraculously caught in its artless-seeming, casually brilliant verse, reminiscent of A.H. Clough's *Amours de Voyage*.

In *The Poetry of W.B. Yeats* (1941) MacNeice writes that **Yeats**

> was like Lancelot who nearly saw the Greal [sic]. He believed in the Greal, *divining* its presence (to use Plato's metaphor), he made great efforts to achieve direct vision. But it was perhaps just because he lacked this direct vision that he was able to write poetry. Would not Lancelot have been able to give a better account of the Quest than Galahad? Galahad, I feel, would have lost his human feelings in that superhuman experience.

MacNeice's writings too are a record of a Quest. Sometimes he seems to lose his way – his middle-period poetry has its *longueurs* – but towards the end he found the road again. Such poems as 'Selva Oscura', 'The Wiper', 'Charon' and 'Thalassa' have a determination and grim, purposeful tread, as does his celebrated pioneering radio drama *The Dark Tower* (first broadcast 1946, with music by **Benjamin Britten**), inspired by **Robert Browning's** *Childe Roland*. 'The Sin against the Holy Ghost – What is it?' was a question that always haunted him. He may not have found an answer but, like Lancelot, he better than most, can give an account of the Quest; and that to him mattered most. Modern society could learn a great deal from that.

Further reading

Other works include: *The Collected Poems of Louis MacNeice,* ed. E.R. Dodds (1966, revised 1979); *Letters from Iceland* (with W.H. Auden, 1937); *The Strings are False: An Unfinished Autobiography,* ed. E.R. Dodds (1965). Jon Stallworthy, *Louis MacNeice* (1995) is a fine biography. See also: Robyn Marsack, *The Cave of Making: A Study of the Poetry of Louis MacNeice* (1982); Edna Longley, *Louis MacNeice: A Study* (1988); Valentine Cunningham, *British Writers of the Thirties* (1988).

JOSEPH BAIN

MAETERLINCK, Mauritius Polydorus Maria Bernardus

1862–1949
French/Belgian dramatist and essayist

Bilingual in Flemish and French, Maurice Maeterlinck grew up in Ghent, later the centre of the Belgian Symbolist movement, to which he contributed along with his poet friends Charles van Lerberghe and Grégoire le Roy. After the Parisian stir occasioned by his first play *La Princesse Maleine* (published in 1890 but never staged), Maeterlinck became a controversial figure in his native country, where new departures in the arts were not encouraged. By 1897, he had moved to France, where he took up residence for the rest of his life in a succession of picturesque retreats, including a medieval abbey and a converted casino near Nice to which he gave the fairy-tale name of Orlamonde. Apart from an early liaison with the actress Georgette Leblanc, his later marriage, his wartime exile in the United States (1940–7) and the various literary honours that accrued to him, Maeterlinck's life was outwardly uneventful, being rather a series of adventures of the spirit pursued in a comfortable privacy.

Maeterlinck's first publication was a collection of Symbolist poems entitled *Serres chaudes* ('Hothouse Blooms', 1889). These comprise on the one hand poems in regular quatrains which sound a wistful and naively folkloric note; and on the other several innovatory free-verse pieces. These evoke typically Symbolist moods of ennui or melancholy: their originality lies in the wilful strangeness of their oddly juxtaposed images, in which indeterminate references transmit connotations of unrest, doubt, poignant enigma. It is as though, imbibing the poetic influence of **Whitman**, Poe and **Rimbaud**, Maeterlinck had made an intuitive leap into an idiom of hallucinatory landscaping which even anticipates some of the bizarre visions of Surrealism, as witness these lines from 'Cloche à plongeur' ('Diving-bell'):

> Take heed! the shadows of great schooners
> are cruising over the dahlias in the forests
> beneath the sea!
> And for a moment I fall in the shadow of
> whales as they head for the Pole!
> At this very instant, the others are doubtless
> unloading ships laden with
> snow in the harbour!
> There was still a glacier left amid the July
> meadows!
> They are swimming backwards in the
> green waters of the bay!
> At noon they enter gloomy grottoes!
> And breezes from the open sea are fa
> ning the terraces!

Maeterlinck had hit on a formula for eliciting waves of indefinite yet powerful association by the oblique presentation of people doing simple yet unexplained things in strange and empty places. The essence of his Symbolist procedure lies in this poetic structuring of moods of uncertainty and foreboding, and it is out of this that he developed the successful style of his early dramatic work. *Les Aveugles* ('The Blind', 1890) is a one-act dialogue between thirteen blind people who stand in a grim Nordic forest scarcely lit by faltering moonlight, waiting with varying degrees of impatience for a nameless stranger who never shows up. The play is entirely static, consisting merely of the speeches of these practically disembodied voices, which comment in hollow tones on the emptiness of life and the hopelessness of the human condition. Nothing happens or can happen: existence seems to have seized up. The play is a remarkable early manifestation of absurdist paralysis in the theatre, anticipating **Beckett's** *Waiting for Godot* (1955) by over six decades.

In comparison, *Pelléas et Mélisande* (1892, trans. 1894) resembles a colourful melodrama in its collation of extravagant themes, including adulterous passion, attempted and actual fratricide, and the heroine's final tragic death. Yet for all its essential Romanticism, Maeterlinck shapes the play in a decisively discrepant way, deliberately depriving the action of any colour or energy. The plot advances with scarcely any perceptible stress, the characters speaking abstractedly *past* rather than *to* one another – or else speaking on one level while listening in on another. They give the impression of being 'somewhat deaf somnambulists who keep getting dragged out of a painful sleep', in the dramatist's own rather rueful words. As if caught in a cycle of hypnotic repetition, the characters enact another allegory of doomed waiting, borne down by a horrifying fatality that stifles all personality and initiative. *Pelléas et Mélisande* is a play which compulsively shies away from explanation. Who exactly is Mélisande? What are her true feelings towards Golaud? Why does she lose her wedding-ring in the fountain? How is it that Pelléas fails to realize he is falling in love with her? Does Golaud act consciously or in a state of maddened automatism when he kills Pelléas? Maeterlinck allows no answers: the texture of the action is all murmur and mystery, a drift into darkness. As such, the play's affinities lie less with drama proper than with the wordless suggestivity of music, and the play indeed inspired fine incidental music by **Fauré** (1889) and **Sibelius** (1905), as well as **Debussy's** *drame lyrique Pelléas et Mélisande* (1902), where spellbound recitative and shimmering orchestral textures exactly match Maeterlinck's minimally accented portrayal of human helplessness.

'It should never be supposed that language ever serves as a true communication between people' is a disturbing aphorism from 'Le Silence', in Maeterlinck's first book of essays, *The Treasure of the Humble* (*Le Trésor des humbles*, 1896, trans. 1897). But what might at first be construed as a watchword of pessimism, the recognition of man's irreducible solipsism and consequent irredeemable solitude, soon emerges in more positive light as Maeterlinck, under the influence of Georgette Leblanc, goes on to speak of the intuitive non-verbal contact that links sensitive people together. Maeterlinck speaks of an 'active silence' through which man can divine his position within the unspeaking world of nature. And far from sticking to the bleak fatalism of the early plays, Maeterlinck will argue his way forward in a long cycle of major essays composed throughout the rest of his life, in search of a position of ultimate serenity, fascination and sense of belonging in the world. It is true, Maeterlinck contends, that we are unable to articulate the deeper meanings of existence, so that the world appears to lack final explanation. Yet we should not abandon hope, for our intuitive understanding of the ineffable mysteries is advancing all the while.

A sedulous observer of phenomena like sleeping and dreaming, and an ardent student of telepathy and other aspects of parapsychology, Maeterlinck adumbrates a poetic metaphysics which is as confident as it is ultimately unfalsifiable. In it he shows himself to be an heir to the mysticism of his countryman Ruysbroeck (whose *Adornment of Spiritual Marriage* he translated in 1889) and of the German Romantic Novalis (whom he translated in 1895), as well as to the occult tradition at large, which he surveyed in *Le Grand Secret* ('The Great Secret', 1921).

Though Maeterlinck had a keen interest in the natural sciences, it usually played second string to his poetic fancy. In *The Life of Space* (*La Vie de l'espace*, 1928, trans. 1928), he addresses himself to the poetic implications of the idea of a fourth dimension: 'The problem of the fourth dimension is not only a mathematical problem; it is a problem integral to real life.' The book is a highly speculative gloss on post-**Einsteinian** hypotheses, and is in some measure indebted to the ideas of Ouspensky. Maeterlinck's broad intention in his metaphysical essays is to reconcile the two ways of the spiritual and the material: 'It is probable that where there is matter, there is equally spirit, since they are in all likelihood two aspects of the same substance, matter ending with the beginning of spirit, and spirit beginning with the end of matter.'

The oracular lyricism of such propositions is balanced by a cycle of essays about observable natural phenomena – the life of insects and plants. In *The Life of the Ant* (*La Vie des fourmis*, 1930, trans. 1931), Maeterlinck describes with the patient delight of a Fabre the complex habits of the insect, while also allowing himself occasional divagations on such topics as the immortality of the ant and the 'totemism' which he sees as underlying the religious structure of its collectivized community. In *L'Araignée de verre* ('The Glass Spider', 1932), he reports in close detail his personal observations of the *Argyroneta aquatica*, the water-spider which creates its own underwater air supply, contenting himself here with the straightforward description of a marvel in order implicitly to underline the point that Nature is more inventive and mysteriously consistent than man normally recognizes. In *The Intelligence of Flowers* (*L'Intelligence des fleurs*, 1907, trans. 1907), he is at pains to list the incredible variety of plant forms, the subtleties of their smells, their many far-fetched modes of reproduction. The moral is again uplifting: if such a colourful exhibition of oddities and monstrosities can be shown to have purpose, then all creation must surely have meaning – there is no phenomenon which does not function in the universal teleology.

The essays are sometimes flawed by sententiousness and aphoristic glibness, as well as by sentimentality and a rather naive approach to themes like reincarnation and human immortality. Maeterlinck is manifestly a poet rather than a philosopher: even so, his essays on existence have a lingering charm, deriving mainly from his recourse to poetic analogy, and especially the notion of a harmony between inner and outer reality, wherein he manifests his fundamental kinship with nineteenth-century and specifically Romantic currents of thought.

Maeterlinck's reputation was at its peak in the 1890s, during the period of his first theatrical productions. It remained small but even through the next few decades when, withdrawn from public life, he released a steady stream of meditative essays to the world. But in a post-war period coloured by discussions of existentialism and political commitment, the quietistic colouring of his work could no longer have any impact. His death in 1949 passed unnoticed in France, and although in recent years his reputation has been assiduously promoted in his native Belgium, the 1911 recipient of the Nobel Prize for Literature is today practically unknown within European culture at large.

Further reading

Other works include: *La Mort de Tintagiles* (1894, trans. *The Death of Tintagiles*, 1899); *Ariadne et Barbe-bleue* ('Ariadne and Bluebeard', 1902); and the best-selling fairy-play *L'Oiseau bleu* (1908, translated as *The Blue Bird*, 1909). The early Symbolist plays (1889–1902) have been reissued as *Théâtre Complet* (1979). The two-score volumes of his essays also include: *La Vie des abeilles* (1901, translated as *The Life of the Bee*, 1901); *Le Temple enseveli* ('The Buried Temple', 1902); and *La Grande Porte* ('The Great Doorway', 1939). There is also a volume of childhood reminiscences, *Bulles bleues* (1948, translated as *Blue Bubbles*, 1949). His poetry is collected in *Poésies complètes* (1965). English translations of Maeterlinck were a commonplace up until the 1930s, but today very little remains in print. See: May Daniels, *The French Drama of the Unspoken* (1953); W.D. Halls, *Maurice Maeterlinck* (1960); *Maurice Maeterlinck 1862–1962*, ed. J. Hanse and R. Vivier (1962); Alex Pasquier, *Maurice Maeterlinck* (1963); Marcel Postic, *Maeterlinck et le symbolisme* (1970); W.D. Halls, *Maurice Maeterlinck: A Study of His Life and Thought* (1989); Patrick McGuinness, *Maurice Maeterlinck and the Making of Modern Theatre* (2000).

ROGER CARDINAL

MAGRITTE, René-François-Ghislain

1898–1967

Belgian artist

The Belgian surrealist painter René Magritte may be said to have cultivated a career of minimal incident, electing to spend most of his life in a neat house in the suburbs of Brussels with his wife and a succession of pet Pomeranian dogs. Out of this unimpeachably respectable existence – typified by Magritte's perennial bowler hat and businessman's suit – came forth some of the most disquieting images in modern painting.

Magritte's premise is that 'the world is a defiance of common sense'. Our everyday surroundings are fraught with mystery – a mystery as potent as it is, in essence, banal. Where other Surrealists go to great lengths to document complex dream versions of reality, Magritte worked from the things around him in an unruffled, deadpan style, pursuing a few fundamental ideas in the manner of a speculative philosopher. Painting was for him a medium in which to explore intellectual puzzles, and his work as a whole represents a kind of elegant treatise on certain problems of consciousness.

In particular, Magritte was fascinated by questions of perception and conception, the ways in which our sightings of phenomena and our images thereof are oddly disjunct. *Familiar Objects* (1927–8) portrays five men with blank stares, each with a different object suspended before his eyes – a lemon, a sponge, a pitcher, a knotted ribbon, a seashell in which may be discerned the form of a naked female body. Are these to be interpreted as obsessional delusions? It may be that Magritte is simply dramatizing the hypothesis that at any given moment our perception of a material object turns into a mental concept, the object proper being emptied of its corporeality: we unconsciously seek to project this phantom form from conceptual space back into the external world.

In thus addressing himself to the gap between the mental and the material, Magritte established that 'there is little relation between an object and that which represents it'. Our conventional sign-systems, whether verbal or pictorial, are inadequate to the task of truly isolating what is singular in the object, since 'whatever its manifest nature may be, every object is mysterious'. Magritte often went about a picture by asking himself in what way a given object might be represented so as to demonstrate this intrinsic mystery. Each object, he thought, possesses just one property or aspect which will, if exposed, illuminate its singularity. Rejecting the usual Surrealist practice of arbitrary association, Magritte purported to calculate *exactly* the one correct answer to 'the problem of the object'. 'He has a thirst for precise mysteries,' commented his friend Louis Scutenaire.

Magritte's calculations led to the invention of a whole set of devices to defamiliarize the object and so force the spectator to witness it under the bright light of visual surprise. In *Homesickness* (1941), a recumbent lion poses next to a gentleman with wings leaning against a parapet, lost in thought. Neither protagonist appears concerned about the bizarreness of the arrangement. In *The Heart of the Matter* (1928), Magritte offers an enigmatic collocation in the manner of **de Chirico**, evoking a lingering sense of profundity shorn of explanation: a burly woman with a cloth over her face stands beside a tuba and a closed suitcase. A clue to this image derives from one of the few details in Magritte's bland biography: one night his mother was drowned and her body recovered from the local river with her nightgown wrapped round her head. But the tuba and the suitcase remain a perfect mystery.

Elsewhere the artist tampers with the rules of physical plausibility. In *The Listening-Room* (1952), he shows us an apple so huge as to occupy all the space in a room. He paints a sky built of solid azure cubes, a petrified lightning-flash, a granite bird on the wing, a cloud slumped to the ground, a door key which bursts into flames. In *Not to be Reproduced* (1937), a man with his back to us stands before a mirror in which he is reflected not full-face, but *still* with his back to us. Hybrid forms – a chair with a tail, a mountain shaped like an eagle, a carrot turning into a bottle, a cigar-fish (or fish-cigar!) – enact propositions about the compatibility of alien entities. All this is done with a perfectly cool sense of logic. Thus the creature depicted in *Collective Invention* (1935) is an anti-mermaid – a woman's lower body with the upper body and head of a fish. It is a typical example of Magritte's system: he has taken the proposition *mermaid* and scrupulously reversed its terms. In so doing he has not created something counter-mythical, but rather something *doubly* unreal. Nevertheless the soberly academic paintwork encourages the feeling that this chimera is somehow 'a matter of fact'.

These paradoxical images, with their deliberately unhelpful titles, have done much to imprint a certain image of Surrealism upon the popular consciousness. While Magritte has had an influence on the visual arts, notably on painters in the orbit of Pop Art such as **Oldenburg**, Dine and **Johns**, his deepest impact has been in the field of commercial art. An American television network adopted as its emblem Magritte's image of an eye with the iris composed of a section of sky with clouds (*The False Mirror*, 1929); the publicity brochure of an international airline exploits his image of a soaring cut-out bird superimposed on a seascape (*The Large Family*, 1947). The repertoire of Magrittian devices of surprise is regularly exploited in magazine ads across the globe. Their inventor, who himself once worked for an advertising agency, designing illustrations for a furrier's catalogue, might have been amused by this further paradox of an idiosyncratic approach to the 'problem of the object' being made into a 'collective invention' – though it must be said that the products Magritte advertised in his paintings are rather less congenial than those promoted by commercial pastiche.

Further reading

Other works include: *Manifestes et autres écrits* ('Manifestos and Other Texts', 1972). On Magritte: P. Nougé, *René Magritte ou Les Images défendues* ('René Magritte or The Forbidden Images', 1943); P. Waldberg, *René Magritte* (1965); D. Sylvester, *Magritte* (1969); S. Gablik, *Magritte* (1970); A.M. Hammacher, *Magritte* (1974); H. Torczyner, *Magritte: Ideas and Images* (1977); D. Sylvester, *Magritte* (1992).

ROGER CARDINAL

MAHLER, Gustav
1860–1911
Austrian composer

The second of fourteen children, Mahler studied music at the Vienna Conservatoire under Robert Fuchs and Franz Krenn and at the University of Vienna with **Anton Bruckner**. He began his career as a conductor at Linz in 1880 and returned to the Linz Opera as one of its two chief conductors in 1886, having spent the intervening years as conductor at the Cassel Opera, the Prague Opera and elsewhere. The First Symphony (1888), the *Lieder eines fahrended Gesellen* (1884) and *Das klagende Lied* (1880) belong to this early period of his creative career.

In 1888 Mahler was appointed director of the Budapest Opera and in 1891 the chief conductor of the Hamburg Opera. For the ten years from 1897 to 1907 Mahler was conductor and general director of the Vienna Opera and also occasional conductor of the Vienna Philharmonic. In 1901 he married Alma Schindler. During these years as conductor of the Vienna Staatsoper he composed Symphonies 4–8 and the *Rückert Songs*.

Following his resignation from the Vienna Opera in 1901 Mahler left Europe to take up a post in America as conductor of the Metropolitan Opera and the New York Philharmonic. He returned to Europe in the early months of 1911 and died in Vienna in May of that year.

Despite the bitter controversy surrounding his appointment and tenure of office as the director of the Vienna Staatsoper – a controversy which eventually led to his leaving Vienna – Mahler was generally acknowledged to be one of the finest conductors of his generation. Composing was almost entirely confined to the summer months, when the opera was closed, with what little free time was available during the rest of the year being devoted to copying and scoring the works.

Apart from a number of songs for voice and piano or voice and orchestra, Mahler's creative output consists entirely of symphonies. Mahler's symphonies can be conveniently divided into three chronological and stylistic groups: (1) the first four symphonies, all of which employ material from Mahler's settings of poems from the *Das Knaben Wunderhorn* collection of German folk poetry (Symphonies 2, 3 and 4) or from the *Lieder eines fahrenden Gesellen* song cycle (Symphony 1). With the exception of the First Symphony all the works in this group employ voices: a single soprano voice in the Fourth Symphony; soloists and a large chorus in Symphonies 2 and 3; (2) the three purely instrumental middle period symphonies (Nos 5, 6 and 7); (3) the works of the final years including the vast Symphony No. 8, the so-called 'Symphony of a Thousand' (the performance of which requires a double mixed chorus, a children's chorus and eight solo voices as well as a large orchestra), *Das Lied von der Erde*, a 'symphony' for tenor and alto soloists and orchestra, the instrumental Ninth Symphony and the unfinished Tenth Symphony.

In many respects Mahler's symphonies can be seen as the final products of the tradition of the Austro-German symphony during the Romantic period. Like most nineteenth-century German composers, Mahler felt that Beethoven had established the symphony as the supreme musical form and consequently regarded it as being the only form suited to the expression of sustained, serious musical-philosophical thought. Many of the characteristics of Mahler's musical style are a logical extension of the features to be found in the work of his immediate predecessors. Thus, for example, Mahler's time scale springs from that of the **Wagnerian** music drama, his use of large choral and instru-

mental forces in a symphony from the example of Beethoven's Choral Symphony, his fondness for simple folk-like melodies and for folk dances such as the Ländler from Schubert and Weber and his discursive and frequently leisurely developmental technique from Schubert. On a less purely musical level many of those features that appear to be peculiarly Mahlerian – his love of the grotesque, the demoniacal and the sinister, his view of the artist as an individual isolated from society, his feeling for nature and for natural sounds and his occasional triumphant visions of the possibility of redemption – are equally typical of much of the artistic work and thought of the German Romantics. Although Mahler expanded both the time scale of the individual movements and the number of movements in a work, his formal designs are those traditionally employed in the German symphony, the weight of the musical argument being concentrated in the sonata form first movement and in the last movement of the work (which may also be a sonata form), with the central movements (often, in Mahler, a collection of three or four short movements) forming a lighter, more relaxed episode.

Alongside such traditional and characteristically late-Romantic elements, however, can be found many techniques and an aesthetic outlook that now strike us as peculiarly modern and forward-looking. Like **Berlioz**, the other great virtuoso composer-conductor of the nineteenth century, Mahler had an unerring ear for instrumental timbre. By employing his large forces less to create big 'massed' effects than as a means of obtaining a wide variety of instrumental colour, Mahler created a new 'unblended', chamber music-like texture (achieved by bringing together clearly differentiated solo timbres) that was to have a great influence on those composers who followed him. To some extent this handling of the orchestra was a result of Mahler's equally forward-looking conception of music as being essentially polyphonic, the harmonies resulting from the coming together of a number of separate melodic lines. In the Ninth and Tenth Symphonies the individuality of the parts, coupled with the large leaps and the extreme chromaticism that spring from the desire for maximum emotional expression, creates a harmonic structure that frequently borders on the edge of atonality.

Equally significant as a pointer to future musical developments are the aesthetic implications of Mahler's style. In Mahler's works intensely emotional and deeply felt passages exist alongside music which seems deliberately to question and undermine this emotional ardour; the folk songs give way to tortuous chromatic lines, the simple dance melodies to biting dissonance, the naive to the sardonic, the noble and elevated to the banal and trivial. The characteristically late-Romantic yearning is, thus, coupled with a bitter acceptance of the impossibility of recapturing the tonal and moral innocence towards which much of the music seems to reach. It is this emotional ambiguity, the ironic detachment which enables Mahler to confront his own emotional response and his own illusions, that makes him such an influential figure in the development of twentieth-century music. A typically Mahlerian use of the cheap and trivial can be found in works as different as **Berg's** *Wozzeck*, **Britten's** *Peter Grimes* and **Vaughan Williams's** Fourth Symphony as well as in much of the music of **Shostakovich** and **Peter Maxwell Davies**. To the extent that Mahler's irony is also a means of creating a music which questions its own premises – a means, that is, of creating a music about music – Mahler's work not only looks forward to the themes of such apparently antithetical works as Berg's *Lulu* and **Stravinsky's** *The Rake's Progress* but anticipates one of the basic concerns of much twentieth-century art.

Further reading

See: *Mahler, Memoirs and Letters*, to Alma Mahler, ed. Donald Mitchell (1973); *Selected Letters of Gustav Mahler*, ed. Knud Martner (1979); Bruno Walter, *Gustav Mahler* (1941); Donald Mutchell, *Gustav Mahler; The Early Years* (1958) and *Gustav Mahler; The Wunderhorn Years* (1975); Henry-Louis de la Grange, *Mahler* (Vol. 1, 1974); Natalie Bauer-Lechner, *Recollections of Gustav Mahler* (1980); J. Carr, *The Real Mahler* (1997); D. Mitchell and A. Nicholson (eds) *The Mahler Companion* (1999); Stuart Feder, *Gustav Mahler: A Life in Crisis* (2004).

DOUGLAS JARMAN

MAILER, Norman
1923–
US novelist

Mailer was born in New Jersey, but his family moved to Brooklyn, New York, when he was four. He graduated from Harvard in 1943 and married for the first time in 1944, shortly before being drafted into the army to serve in Leyte, Luzon and Japan. In his long and uneven career as a novelist, commentator on the American political scene, poet and film writer/producer, the central theme of his work has always been to relate the large-scale economic, political and institutional events of the national to the inner spiritual condition, the lifestyles and the choices of individuals, in their sexual bodily existences.

In his first novel, the highly successful *The Naked and the Dead* (1948), the army is an organism which feeds off the repressed and channelled energies of those it has swallowed. The soldiers' thoughts are predominantly about sex and money, and yet these seemingly private realms are the very sources of the competitive masculine energy which will ensure that they conform, outperform each other, and excel in courage or control of others. Even the general, Cummings, finds the battle won in his absence, so that we see that his personal weight and authority derive from the army and not from his will. The ambiguous hero-figure, Hearst, is a liberal whose beliefs in high-mindedness and detachment are impotent to intervene in the situation, to control it, or to prevent his death.

Mailer's second novel, *Barbary Shore* (1951), similarly translates the struggle between **Marxist** and capitalist ideologies into personal terms, as the again ex-communist, McLeod, tries to atone for his own bloody past yet to reaffirm his own relationship to ideals of justice and progress. His adversary, the FBI agent Hollingsworth, is, by contrast, an adolescent figure who keeps his role at a distance from his personality, and thereby grants to authority an empty zombie.

Clarifying his ideas under the influence of **Wilhelm Reich's** psychology with its equation of political and sexual repression, and various existentialist ideas. Mailer produced a volume of fragments and essays. *Advertisements for Myself* (1959), with its key essay 'The White Negro', an attempt to define authentic behaviour without involving morality or sanctions. This line of speculation was continued in *Cannibals and Christians* (1966) in the essay 'Metaphysics of the Belly', where he explores the idea that the soul can die, indeed that it lives only by those of our acts which nourish it, and that, having died, only empty forms of spirits exist. Even the way we eat, digest and excrete are indicative of our acceptance or avoidance, the guilt, fear or courage with which we face our lives. The clearest fictional expression of these ideas is his *American Dream* (1965) in which the hero, Rojack, war hero, television personality, ex-Senator and academic, finally rejects the swollen image from which he derives his status by killing his wife. The divorce of his true and false selves started in the war, when, by shirking the challenge in the eyes of those he was killing, he chose to identify himself with an image of bravery and success. He and his father-in-law, Kelly, become materially successful by identifying with and allowing themselves to be used by those institutionalized forces which run the country. This is seen as a form of black magic, selling one's soul in return for material power, and in the process becoming larger than life, bloated with non-human, social power.

The other side of the coin is explored in *Marilyn* (1973), a rather weak account of Marilyn Monroe's tragic attempts to come to terms with the enormous power she wielded as the nation's sex-queen, tapping the energy from the fusion of personal beauty and generalized desires.

Much of Mailer's critique of American society stems from his belief that the leaders in particular, and the population at large, refuse to perceive these collective energies even though they identify with them and consume them via the media. This refusal to see he calls 'the plague' or 'totalitarianism', and is re-created in a concentrated form in *Why are We in Vietnam?* (1967), in which the hip-talk of a bear-hunting disc-jockey embodies all the psychoses and aggressions pent up in the American psyche. *A Fire On the Moon* (1970), on the other hand, laments the effect of this blindness in totally depriving the moon-shot of any human significance or poetry, making it into a piece of technological common sense.

At one point in the **Kennedy** administration, Mailer thought that decisive leadership could awaken the nation to the struggle for the possession of its own souls, and he cast Kennedy in that role in *The Presidential Papers* (1963), but Kennedy's death and the Vietnam War placed Mailer on the side of the protesters, and in *The Armies of the Night* (1968, Pulitzer Prize winner for non-fiction) he champions the power of those marching on the Pentagon to outflank the embedded military mind by acting in a spontaneous and natural way. His own image in these books, however, is that of a muddled and puzzled participant, somehow left behind the march of events in a way reminiscent of **Henry Adams** in *The Education of Henry Adams* (1918).

In 1969 Mailer's failure to be elected mayor of New York City heralded what seemed at the time a decline in his writing abilities. Not until *The Executioner's Song* (1979, Pulitzer Prize winner for fiction) – a 'non-fiction novel' about Gary Gilmour, the first man to be executed in the USA in twenty years – were his immense powers as a natural journalist not afraid to resort to raw aggression seen to revive. Since then this prolific, but also at times wearyingly prolix, author has seldom laid aside his pen, for all that he simultaneously attempted to sustain his career as a film director. *Ancient Evenings* (1983) is a big novel set in Egypt of three thousand years ago, followed quickly by a conventional thriller, *Tough Guys Don't Dance* (1984). In the same year he visited the Soviet Union, which he percipiently reported not as a commensurate antagonist in the Cold War, but as an underdeveloped place unlikely to last much longer. Then in the following decade appeared arguably Mailer's most ambitious novel, *Harlot's Ghost* (1992), a chronicle of the CIA set against a backdrop of the Cold War, followed by *Oswald's Tale* (1995), another 'non-fiction novel' that reconstructs the life of Kennedy's assassin, Lee Harvey Oswald, including the two years he spent in Russia.

Nothing on the same scale or of the same quality has appeared since, though it would be unwise to write Mailer off as long as breath remains in his body. *The Gospel According to the Son* (1997) is an idiosyncratic life of Jesus. *The Time of Our Time* (1998) is a compendium of previously published writings, while *The Spooky Art* (2004) gives Mailer's version of the writer's craft. Lacking the finesse of his literary contemporary **Gore Vidal**, the self-consciously virile Mailer is likely to be considered a heavyweight for a while to come, for all that he is sometimes regarded as a master of the importunate. That he's also led an entertaining life has sustained his reputation: six wives, one of whom (Adele Morales) he attacked with a knife, in 1960; arrest as a peace protestor during the Vietnam War; and an unfortunately successful campaign to gain the release of a convicted murderer, Jack Abbot, in 1980. Not long afterwards Abbot murdered someone else.

Further reading

Mailer has published over forty books. Other titles include: *The Deer Park* (1955); *Deaths for the Ladies* (1962); poems, *The Idol and the Octopus* (1968); *Miami and the Siege of Chicago* (1968); *The Prisoner of Sex* (1971); *On the Fight of the Century* (1971); and a film script, *Maidstone: A Mystery* (1971). See: Donald L. Kaufman, *Norman Mailer: The Countdown* (1969); Richard Poirier, *Mailer* (1972); H. Mills, *Mailer: A Biography* (1982); Nigel Leigh, *Radical Fictions and the Novels of Norman Mailer* (1990); J. Michale Lennon, *Critical Essays on Norman Mailer* (1986); Barry H. Leeds, *The Enduring Visions of Normal Mailer* (2002).

DAVID CORKER
(REVISED AND UPDATED BY THE EDITOR)

MALCOLM X (Malcolm LITTLE/El Hajj Malik EL-SHABAZZ)

1925–65

US racial leader

Malcolm Little was born in Omaha, Nebraska, the son of a West Indian mother and black American father. His father, a Baptist minister and follower of Marcus Garvey, moved the family to Lansing, Michigan, when Malcolm was very small. His father's black nationalist beliefs were very unpopular in this overwhelmingly white community; the family home was burned and his father murdered. Malcolm, however, moved relatively easily among whites. It was not until he visited an older half-sister in Boston in 1940 that he discovered the sub-culture of black ghetto life. He was never the same again. After finishing the eighth grade, he left school and Michigan behind and moved to Boston. He quickly acquired a fascination for street life and became immersed in a world of 'hustling' – drugs, night life, theft and prostitution. He operated in Harlem during most of the Second World War, but in 1945 he returned to Boston, was soon arrested for burglary and sentenced to prison. He was not yet twenty-one years old.

Malcolm Little's first reaction to prison was blind rage. His anger began to take focus, however, when members of his family in Detroit began writing to him about their discovery of the 'natural religion of the black man'. From them he learned of the teachings of **Elijah Muhammad** and the small black religious sect known as the Nation of Islam. Muhammad taught a version of history in which black Americans had a central and dominant role. The racial degradation which

Malcolm had experienced was explained as being the work of the white devil (all whites in Western civilization). Malcolm now came to realize that his lifestyle and those of black Americans had been inhibited by self-hate and shame over their blackness. Complete rejection and withdrawal from whites was the answer, and this could only be accomplished by adhering rigidly to the Nation of Islam's programme of disciplined personal behaviour. Malcolm Little now had an explanation for his anger and a programme of redemption.

He was released from prison in 1952 and joined his family in Detroit where he applied formally for admission into the Nation and threw himself into the activities of the local mosque. He went to Chicago where Elijah Muhammad personally trained him as a Muslim minister and gave him the name Malcolm X. In 1953 he was sent east and quickly developed a reputation as a dynamic speaker who attracted new converts to the teachings of Muhammad. Malcolm X built a growing base of support in New York and founded the Nation's newspaper, *Muhammad Speaks*. As America's news media responded to the spreading Civil Rights Movement in the late 1950s, it also became more interested in other phenomena in black America. Malcolm saw this as an opportunity to put more blacks in touch with the saving teachings of Elijah Muhammad. His charismatic personality drew large crowds, and his message of hatred and rejection served as a stinging antithesis to the sermons of love and forgiveness being popularized by **Martin Luther King**, Jr. He was soon the best-known black Muslim – more widely quoted and sought after than Elijah Muhammad. This popularity began to arouse jealousy in other Muslim leaders, however, and when Malcolm X sought to make the Nation of Islam more responsive and active in organizing among black communities, Elijah Muhammad consistently held him back. Distance appeared between prophet and minister. Finally, after an intemperate response to **John F. Kennedy's** assassination in November 1963, Malcolm X was ordered to be 'silent' in public, and by

March 1964 pressure on him had reached the point that he knew he could no longer function nor was he wanted in the Nation of Islam. This was a shattering blow, for he always maintained that he owed his very salvation as a human being to the message and guidance of Elijah Muhammad.

Malcolm struggled to find a new perspective on his religious beliefs and his commitment to mass action by blacks. He made a pilgrimage to Mecca, meeting many leaders of the African and Arab nations and never escaping the international spotlight. His exposure to orthodox Islam deepened his spiritual devotion, but drew him away from the doctrinal and social narrowness of the 'Black Muslims'. He returned to the USA more open to the possibility of reconciliation with whites (but only by maintaining separate groups) and committed to non-sectarian mass action. He formed the Organization of Afro-American Unity and had just begun to project a new mission for himself when he was assassinated by three members of the Nation of Islam at a public meeting in New York on 21 February 1965. Malcolm left his wife (whom he married in 1958), four children, and a vacuum in the black struggle for dignity and opportunity in America. He had an asset that no other black leader of the time had: he was from the masses, had suffered their plight, and had conquered the depths. After encountering Malcolm X's mass appeal other black leaders were forced to deal with some hard racial truths in America regarding their integrationist goals. He forced them to recognize the validity of a growing demand for 'black power'.

Further reading

See: Malcolm X (with Alex Haley), *The Autobiography of Malcolm X* (1964); C. Eric Lincoln, *The Black Muslims in America* (1961); and John Henrik Clarke, *Malcolm X: The Man and His Times* (1969); Bruce Perry, *Malcolm: The Life of the Man Who Changed Black America* (1991); William Stickland, *Malcolm X: Make It Plain* (1994); Robert L. Jenkins and Mfanya Donald Tryman (eds) *The Malcolm X Encyclopedia* (2002).

LESTER C. LAMON

MALEVICH, Kazimir

1878–1935

Russian artist

Initiator of Suprematism (a radical 'hard-edged' abstractionism in painting), and generally one of the pioneers in twentieth-century art, Malevich developed his talents and theories slowly, not reaching the climax of his evolution until his late thirties. In this he resembles **Kandinsky** – the other internationally famous abstract innovator in modern Russian art – though in almost every other respect their ideas and careers make an instructive contrast.

Born near Kiev of humble parents (many of the leaders of the Russian 'modern movement' were provincials), he lived successively in Kursk, from 1902 in Moscow (where he managed to get some art education), in Vitebsk (from 1919) where he joined the art college headed by **Chagall** – whom he quickly ousted and superseded – and finally (from 1922) in Petrograd/Leningrad. His earliest surviving works, from the first decade of the century, have Art Nouveau elements; after *c.* 1908 his style evolves rapidly through several well-defined stages. Heavily outlined, powerful, lumbering peasant figures characterize a primitivistic phase in which curvilinear rhythms dominate the canvas; subsequent developments take him close (though not derivatively so) to Italian Futurist methods, to geometricized figures reminiscent of **Legér**, to a Cubist dissection of the object: always his bold colour sense plays a primary role in the organization of the composition. By *c.* 1913 the 'alogism' that was to form a main plank of his aesthetic theory is discernible in works (e.g. the famous *Englishman in Moscow*) that outstrip any Western European analogues in their anti-rational daring and fragmentation.

Malevich was close to other representatives of the second (post-Symbolist) phase of modernism: notably to the literary Futurists, who similarly developed the concept of *sdvig* (dislocation) as a prime element of their aesthetic. He illustrated various Futurist books, and designs for the Futurist opera *Victory over the Sun* (1915) opened the path to Suprematism. Suprematist paintings were first shown late in 1915, and caused a furore within the avant-garde (notably a violent quarrel with Vladimir Tatlin). Unlike Kandinsky's – though with no less spiritual verve – his abstractionism 'liberated' the painting from any connection with representationalism, creating a universe of free-floating, geometrically simple monochrome shapes against a white background suggestive only of limitless space. Though a vigorous controversialist, his aim was not shock for its own sake, but a breakthrough on behalf of the autonomy and cognitive status of art, informed by an intense awareness of beauty as an independent category.

From *c.* 1920 painting occupied him less, and he devoted himself more and more to educational endeavours, to writing and – with his disciples (notably El Lissitzky) at the art group Unovis – to devising ideal architectural models (*planity*), whose lack of functionalism emphasizes how remote his concerns were from the post-Revolutionary Constructivists, on whom his innovations nevertheless had an impact. In 1927 he travelled to Germany with a substantial exhibition of his works; these remained in the West and are the source of the major public collection at the Stedelijk Museum, Amsterdam. His short book of the same year, *The Non-Objective World,* was influential at the Bauhaus and beyond. However, the atmosphere in the USSR was already turning against his approach to art, and his last years (though he remained a focus for modernist endeavours in Leningrad) were passed in obscurity. The paintings and drawings of this period, sometimes unjustly impugned as a 'sell-out', are extremely interesting: Suprematist elements are combined with a pervasive cross motif in a 'classicizing' return to recognizable subject-matter, notably the transcendentally simplified human figure.

When Malevich died and was buried in his Suprematist-decorated coffin, the anti-modernist reaction in the USSR (even indeed outside it) was in full swing. For years his heritage was publicly ignored; only in the 1970s did Western and Soviet scholarship begin tentatively to explore it and a small proportion of the works to emerge from museum store-rooms. It lived on, however, not only through the force of his example on his many followers, but as a crucial formative element in much modern design, and above all as one of the noblest modern expressions of an anti-utilitarian, anti-romantic justification of the autonomy and spiritual purpose of art.

Further reading

Other works include: *The Non-Objective World, Essays in Art,* ed. T. Andersen (1968 onwards). See: C. Gray, *The Russian Experiment in Art* (1971); S. Compton, *The World Backwards: Russian Futurist Books 1912–16* (1978); T. Andersen, *Malevich* (Stedelijk Museum, Amsterdam, 1970); W. Simmons, *Malevich: Black Square* (1981); G. Demosfenova (ed.) *Malevich: Artist and Theoretician* (1990); C. Douglas, *Malevich* (1994); J. Milner, *Kazimir Malevich and the Art of Geometry* (1996).

ROBIN MILNER-GULLAND

MALINOWSKI, Bronislaw Kaspar

1884–1942

Polish/British anthropologist

Bronislaw Malinowski, one of the most influential scholars in modern British social anthropology, was born in Cracow and died in New Haven, Connecticut. He obtained his PhD at Cracow University in 1908 in physics and mathematics, but illness prevented him from pursuing these subjects. While convalescent he turned to the study of anthropology, notably **Frazer's** *Golden Bough*, and, after studying at Leipzig, he came to London as a postgraduate student at the London School of Economics. His publications on the Australian Aborigines (1913) and the Mailu of New Guinea (1915) earned him a DSc degree in 1916, but a major breakthrough in his career had already occurred in 1914, when, with the support of Professor

C.G. Seligman, he attended the meeting of the British Association for the Advancement of Science in Australia. He then undertook fieldwork in New Guinea for much of the next four years. It was his fieldwork in the Trobriand Islands which was decisive in shaping his approach to what he conceived, in effect, as a new discipline, social anthropology.

Malinowski was closely linked with the LSE from 1920 to 1938. He was appointed Lecturer in Social Anthropology for 1922–3, becoming Reader in 1924 and Professor of Anthropology in 1927. By 1938 his health was not good and he went to the USA for a sabbatical year. Following the outbreak of the Second World War he became a visiting professor at Yale until 1942, when he was appointed to a permanent professorship, an appointment cut short by his death. In the relatively short period of intense academic work between the wars Malinowski, more than any other individual in Britain, changed the leading ideas and fieldwork strategies of his subject away from preoccupations with comparative ethnology and cultural evolution towards the study of contemporary non-Western societies. His influence was notable in three main areas: fieldwork, theory and methods of teaching.

Malinowski's fieldwork was characterized by its depth, care for detail, a balance of quality against quantity, and a concern for the apparently inconsequential imponderabilia of life – collected as far as possible in the vernacular. This gave his ethnography a richness unusual for his time, which enabled him to demonstrate the close contextual (i.e. functional) interrelationship of many aspects of social behaviour. He was not, of course, the first functionalist in British anthropology, but in his hands functionalism became an analytical tool at several levels of abstraction. First, the function of an institution was seen in terms of its effects on other institutions, from which principles of social organization could be induced. Second, the study of function included 'an analysis of the effects of an institution on the maintenance of specific relationships and the achievement of specific ends as defined by the members of a particular community' (Kaberry, in Firth, 1957). Third, Malinowski saw function 'as the part played by an institution in promoting social cohesion and the persistence of a given way of life or culture in a given environment' (Kaberry, ibid.). Thus his insistence on the need for prolonged and detailed fieldwork was the concomitant of his championing of the functionalist theory. In a series of books on aspects of his Trobriand fieldwork published between 1922 and 1935 these concepts were elaborated and refined. Concurrently he was developing a theory of needs which he defined as follows:

> By need, then, I understand the system of conditions in the human organism, in the cultural setting, and in the relation of both to the natural environment, which are sufficient and necessary for the survival of group and organism. A need, therefore, is the limiting set of facts. Habits and their motivations, the learned responses and the foundations of organization, must be so arranged as to allow the basic needs to be satisfied.
>
> (*A Scientific Theory of Culture*, 1944)

Malinowski's seminars at the LSE have acquired an honoured place in the history of anthropology, partly because they attracted many able students who subsequently attained positions of importance in the discipline and developed many of his ideas. The seminars were notable for their scope, rigour, polemical character and wit. Indeed, the manuscript of *Coral Gardens and Their Magic* (1935) was there subjected to page-by-page scrutiny. Many of his students have testified to the stimulation, sense of inspired leadership and strong affection which Malinowski gave them. Not surprisingly, there were elements of messianic dedication in his teaching and research which stamped the character of social anthropology for many years after his death. His writings retain an important place in anthropological literature and show no sign of being consigned to 'history'. On the

other hand, his work has inevitably generated much criticism, aspects of which must be mentioned briefly.

The functional concept is self-evidently limited in analytical value. Moreover, despite his debt to **Durkheim**, Malinowski used it more for the study of culture than of society. His empiricism led him to this position. But to give the study of culture the central place in anthropological theory was, in the eyes of many scholars, to preclude an effective comparative study of social institutions regardless of their particular empirical character. Similarly, these theoretical constraints limited his studies of economics, magic and religion.

Malinowski's work, because it was so clearly directed against accepted prevailing attitudes within anthropology, bears plainly the marks of his time. But if one discounts these, there is still an enormous amount of ethnographic information and analysis in his writings worthy of careful study. As a fieldworker he remains a major exemplar, and as an analyst his insights can still stimulate, while an understanding of his career is necessary to appreciate the character and interests of British social anthropology.

Further reading

Other works include: *Argonauts of the Western Pacific* (1922); *Crime and Custom in Savage Society* (1926); *Sex and Repression in Savage Society* (1927); *The Sexual Life of Savages in North-Western Melanesia* (1929). See also: R. Firth (ed.) *Man and Culture: An Evaluation of the Work of Malinowski* (essays, 1957); M.W. Young, *The Ethnography of Malinowski: The Trobriand Islands 1915–18* (1979); M.W. Young, *Malinowski: Odyssey of an Anthropologist, 1884–1920* (2004).

PETER GATHERCOLE

MALLARMÉ, Stéphane

1842–98

French symbolist poet

Mallarmé trained as a teacher of English and settled in Paris in 1871, where he led a Jekyll and Hyde existence as a conscientious if unenthusiastic *lycée* teacher by day and, by night, a toiling insomniac passionately devoted to the construction of a revolutionary poetic language which remains his distinctive and monumental contribution to poetry. His uneventful public life was chequered only by four brief visits to England. Yet Mallarmé lived cocooned rather than secluded. He took seriously his role as the head of a family and valued greatly the company of the fellow-artists who came to pay him court at his famous Tuesday-evening gatherings in the rue de Rome. The rarefied and often ritualistic character of Mallarmé's social encounters (it is reported that he would allow the reading of poetry to begin only after the room was saturated with cigar smoke) perhaps represents a psychic compromise struck between a fear of loneliness and a Baudelairean abhorrence of 'real' life: 'The proper occupation of any self-respecting man is to contemplate the blue sky while dying of hunger.'

If this unlusty outlook needs an explanation more specific than that afforded by the general nature of poetic sensibility, then it is probably attributable to the series of bereavements and separations which punctuated Mallarmé's life. His mother died when he was a child, as did his beloved sister, Maria; and his own son died at the age of eight. But whatever their origins in his personal experience, the notions of 'nothingness' and death came to loom large in the mature poet's thinking about the creation and the mode of being of the poetic universe: 'I found nothingness, then I found beauty.' He held that the imitation of death in life was a prerequisite for the evocation of the spiritual realm to which poetry must aspire; and the conjuring up of this realm presupposes the linguistic destruction of the detail of the real world, in order that its 'pure notion' be released into the fall-out atmosphere of the world's 'vibratory disappearing', and sensed in or through the musical quasi-substantiality of the destructive language itself. Death, which 'speaks' in this language, is thereby defeated, by being not cancelled out but

transvalued. Poetry redeems when it demonstrates that it is 'nothingness which is the truth': it is the brother who, as a living person, is in a deficient state of being relative to the dead sister, so that his biological death holds out hope of reunion with her in the truth of non-being, which for Mallarmé is not a void but the impersonal 'silent music' revealed and guaranteed by poetic language.

Mallarmé was never tempted to transpose this aesthetic credo into a religious faith, but the ease with which this could have been done attests to the literalness with which he believed, with **Proust**, that art alone effects salvation. His daily devotion to art, moreover, may be properly described as religious, for Mallarmé laboured endlessly and anxiously over a relatively small poetic output which, in a deathbed gesture of characteristic perfectionism, he instructed, unavailingly, to be burned.

The first phase of his output consists in poetry written in a lyrical-descriptive Parnassian vein between 1857 (the year of his sister's death) and 1862. These technically conventional juvenilia, in which the influence of Poe, Banville and Gautier is apparent, show a marked talent for the kind of lyrical composition which Mallarmé soon came to regard as facile, but which continued to tempt him throughout his later striving to develop the austere 'cerebral' poetry to which he owes his fame and influence. The first batch of this mature poetry appeared in the *Parnasse contemporain* of 1866, and thanks mainly to the publicizing efforts of **Verlaine** and of **Huysmans**, **Mallarmé** came to prominence in the mid-1880s as the leader of the Symbolist movement. By this time his oeuvre was becoming increasingly hermetic, a tendency which culminated in the seeming obscurantist hocus-pocus of his typographical poem 'Un coup de dés jamais n'abolira le hasard', which attempts to emulate the capacity of music to express meanings simultaneously rather than in the linear sequence enforced by typographical conventions.

This notorious hermeticism has two aspects. The first, which may be described as the 'obscurity' of the poetry, arises mainly from his philologically erudite use of words and, more bewilderingly, from a private symbolism, the origin and development of which is not made clear in its context of use, as it is in Proust. The words 'wing', 'window', 'glory', 'dream', among others, simply appear on the page bearing meanings that lie outside the fields of normal semantic connotation and even 'sophisticated' cultural association. It has been pointed out that the meanings attributed to those words in the complex poems may be made clear by studying their use in simpler contexts. Thus L.J. Austin says that 'the aim must be to make the utmost use of the documents available – earlier versions, parallel texts in prose, correspondence'. But it might well be felt that poetry loses its vitalizing cultural function when it becomes the preserve of scholars in possession of the necessary documents.

The other, more justifiable aspect of Mallarmé's hermeticism may be described as the 'difficulty' of the poetry, and this is distinct from its obscurity both in that it results from formal complexities and in that these largely do yield to sustained analytical and imaginative attention. For the most part, this difficulty is intrinsic in the new poetic language which Mallarmé spent his life developing. It is accordingly more pervasive and obstructive of easy understanding than the elements of obscurity. The difficulty of this language is organically connected with its aesthetic productivity: it is contrived to yield to pressure and not to yield univocally. But what is new and exquisite is that the residual indeterminacy appears as the mystery of the reader's process of *creating* meaning rather than as a background of missing intelligibility against which assimilated meaning is set. The result is the 'bright darkness' of the poem, the glimpsing of the darkness that the process of dispelling darkness is for itself.

The purpose of Mallarmé's language was to express what he variously called his Dream, the Idea, the Ideal, or Literature, although it is perhaps his description of poetry as the 'musician of silence', or of reading it as a 'solitary silent concert', which best conveys the flavour of the aesthetic experience to which these abstractions refer. Language must be made to create or present a universe envisaged as a dynamic or musical system of analogic relations accessible to the imaginative intelligence rather than to the senses. For Mallarmé 'Poetry ... is Musique *par excellence.*' Where for **Baudelaire** the system of universal analogy was still material, and apprehended in synaesthesia, with Mallarmé it is refined into pure spiritual structure or 'silent' music. He was dogmatically convinced that this spiritual music can be played only by poetry, and that it is 'more divine', by reason of its silence and pure form, than the 'public or symphonic expression' given by the orchestra. 'It is not from the elementary sonorities of the brass, string or wood instruments, but from the intellectual word that ... Music, as the totality of relations existing in the universe, must result.' The suggestion seems to be that it is the *propositional* structure of language, present in poetry as in prose but absent from music, which, suitably cast and effectively interacting with patterns of word-music (rhythm, assonance and alliteration), supplies the vital ingredient that makes poetry alone capable of expressing the music of the spheres.

Be this as it may, propositional meaning is an essential part of Mallarmé's poetic language. This fact is important, first because it implies that the syntax of the poems was meant to be and can be understood, although understanding here is usually a matter of winning from the syntax a dialectic of tentative proposals as opposed to a set of mutually confirming confident propositions. Second, the ballast given by ordinary propositional meaning prevents the aesthetic meaning of the poem from being monopolized by word-music, in the manner of some Surrealist poetry. His method is not to allow word-music to take over from propositional meaning, but to produce silent music by bringing the two into suggestive modes of contact through the 'artifice of dipping words by turn in sonority and in sense'. The sound-system, instead of being merely confirmatory, inflects, deflects and even contradicts the acquisitions of the propositional (syntactical) system; a word or phrase will change colour when 'dipped' in some dimension of the sound-system, an effect which acquires a special poignancy in a poetry that playfully treads the tightropes of philosophical dilemmas (do Platonic Ideas exist objectively or only in the imagination?) relevant to the nature and aspirations of literary creativity. Syntactical commitments entered into in the penultimate tercet of a sonnet condemn an anticipated object not to exist. Inexorably the syntax snakes its way down to the final line of the poem where it names and annihilates its victim: a rose indwelt by night. But the protective isolation in which this image is placed by the short octosyllabic line, allowing room for it and for not a syllable more, reinforced by the self-sufficient beauty of the image, confers on the rose a kind of absolutism which liberates it from the control of the ambient negative forces that logically ought to destroy it. Audio-visual effects afford the fleeting illusion of the rose blossoming at the moment of its obliteration by syntax. The same sonnet begins with the title-line 'Surgi de la croupe et du bond', a literally meaningless phrase which strikes the reader as a garbled version of the more plausible 'Surgi de la coupe et du fond'. But this is as Mallarmé intends: the printed line causes the reader to follow through with his mind's eye the movement of a vase springing into being, while the more plausible line implants spectral submeanings which later reveal their connections with the declared themes of the poem. This interplay of meaning-systems accounts for a pervasive and distinctive characteristic of Mallarmé's poetry: the disproportion between tininess of linguistic cause and colossalness of metaphysical effect.

The immediate obstacle confronting the reader of a Mallarmé poem is its contorted syntax, which is rich in suggestivity quite apart from its transactions with the sound-system. Without actually dislocating it, Mallarmé bends and twists syntax, pulls it out of true and recasts it with about the same degree of deviation from the norm as **Cézanne** imposes on the contours of surfaces. Ambiguities are courted, expected affirmations tortuously deferred, linear developments give way to vertical imbrications of syntactical units, by means of long parentheses, contrapuntal contrivances and far-flung appositions. A given stretch of words often belongs to more than one syntactical pattern. The result is a multiplicity of meanings 'flickering' among themselves, and the emergence of the poem as an autonomous linguistic world in which meaning constantly makes and unmakes itself. The sound-system is contrived to the same end. Mallarmé likes to think of verbal sounds as facets of precious stones exchanging reflections and refractions. His use of words in oblique senses evoking strange but revealing associations is also a factor here. But for the main it is ordinary language which these techniques transform into a keyboard. The guiding intention is to ensure that the reader 'no longer receives the impression of anything external'; by their play of verbal mirrorings, words 'no longer appear to have their own colour, but to remain only as the transitions of a gamut'.

Mallarmé's syntactical convolutions have led many people to describe his poetry as 'intellectual'. Others, more impressed by its phonetic qualities, see it as pure musical substance. The first of these emphases is inadequate because it neglects the sensuous quality of the poetry, the second because it assumes that this sensuous quality consists in word-music alone. But it lies just as much in visual imagery imported from the real world. This imagery is 'poetic' in so far as it is 'unreal', and to purify it of real denotation is the function of the referential aspect of his language. The problem of reference, and so of sensuous imagery, may be stated as follows: on the one hand, the creation of a poetry in which the unworldly Dream might seem to be realized calls for a language where meaning is separated from existential reference, since this ties meaning to the real world: on the other hand, words which did not *somehow* refer to the real world would have no value as bearers of images, forming a trivial realm of analytical discourse. (What would absent flowers be without real flowers?) It follows, therefore, that the only relation which Mallarmé's language can tolerate with the world is one in which reference is restricted to distilling the spiritual structure of sensuous experience. Things are referred to (inevitably), but in a way which yields up their latent spiritual content by means of obscuring their real existence – a kind of verbal equivalent of **Husserl's** transcendental reduction. Poetry practises the art of suggestion when its language simultaneously combines these positive and negative functions. It must 'paint, not the thing but the effect it produces'. The negative condition of the poem's being able to capture the inwardness of things is that it should never name them. 'To name a thing is to destroy three-quarters of the pleasure of the poem.' And in order to suggest without naming, Mallarmé dispenses with titles, spins elaborate periphrases, besets his terms with privations and restructions, keeps his metaphors implicit, all of which adds to the difficulty of the poetry.

'My art is an impasse.' Mallarmé's prophetic words explain and correctly predict the scope of his influence. The limits of intelligibility had been reached. The literary contingent of the flock of artists who came to his 'Tuesdays' are today nearly all great names, including Proust, **Gide**, **Verlaine**, **Maeterlinck**, **Claudel**, yet wisely none of them attempted to emulate him. But his *ideas* on poetry have had a profound and far-reaching impact, immediately and personally through his illustrious friends and subsequently through the established position he now occupies in the theory of poetry. He was the major impetus behind the emergence of the short-lived Symbolist Theatre in France; however, it is as a poet and poetic theorist that his international stature has steadily grown, casting its shadow over all future innovators. Perhaps the most revealing reflection on Mallarmé's existence is that Verlaine, his admiring fellow-poet, should have almost equalled him, with the sonorous joys of a new simplicity.

Further reading

Other works include: *Oeuvre*, collected in the Bibliothèque de la Pléiade edition (1945), edited and annotated by Henri Mondor and G. Jean-Aubry. Most of Mallarmé's mature poems are collected in *Poésies* (1965). An English edition of *Poésies* in the original French, accompanied by translations, is A. Hartley, *Mallarmé* (1965). See: J. Seherer, *L'Expression littéraire dans l'oeuvre de Mallarmé* (1947); G. Davies, *Les Tombeaux de Mallarmé* (1950); G. Delfel, *L'Esthétique de Stéphane Mallarmé* (1951); L. Cellier, *Mallarmé et la morte que parle* (1959); K.G. Kohn, *Towards the Poems of Mallarmé* (1965); Emilie Noulet, *Vingt Poèmes de Stéphane Mallarmé, Exégèses* (1967); M. Bowie, *Mallarmé and the Art of Being Difficult* (1978); Richard Pearson, *Unfolding Mallarmé: The Development of a Poetic Art* (1996); Michael Temple (ed.) *Meetings with Mallarmé* (1998); Rosemary Lloyd, *Mallarmé: The Poet and His Circle* (1999).

ROGER MCLURE

MALRAUX, André
1901–76
French novelist, essayist and political activist

Malraux was born and educated in Paris, but his early years are not well documented. In the early 1920s, his interest in archaeology took him to the Far East, where he also came into contact with revolutionary politics – in Laos, for example, as well as in China. After his return to France in 1927, he became involved with anti-fascist activities, and 1936 saw him in Spain, as a member of the International Brigade, fighting for the Republican cause. After escaping from imprisonment in the Second World War, he joined the Resistance and in due course became a tank commander. In the post-war world his political activities were bound up with the career of General **de Gaulle** – as a minister in de Gaulle's 1945–6 administration, as an active member of the Gaullist RPF (Rassemblement du peuple français), and again as a minister (of culture) after de Gaulle's return to power in 1958.

In a sense, the whole of Malraux's work – whether as novelist or philosopher of art, autobiographer or political figure – is a single expression of his reflection upon his experience of life. His novels, for example, are closely linked to the political and social reality of which he had direct knowledge, with the exception of his first work, *Lunes de papier* ('Paper Moons', 1920, described by the author himself as *farfelu* – hare-brained). The words 'hero', 'action', 'history' recur constantly in discussions of Malraux's work, and not without reason, whether in *La Tentation de l'occident* ('Temptation of the West', 1926), carrying events and the action they demand on to the metaphysical plane; *The Conquerors* (*Les Conquérants*, 1928, trans. 1929), set in Guangzhou (Canton) at the time of the general strike of 1925; *The Royal Way* (*La Voie royale*, 1930, trans. 1935), showing Perken in his search for temples lost in the depths of the jungles of Asia; *Man's Estate* (*La Condition humaine*, 1933, trans. 1948), Malraux's most famous novel (for which he was awarded the Prix Goncourt), portraying the revolutionary events in Shanghai in 1927; *Days of Contempt* (*Le Temps du mépris*, 1935, trans. 1936); *Days of Hope* (*L'Espoir*, 1937, trans. 1938), arising directly out of his activity in the Spanish Republican cause; or *The Walnut Trees of Altenburg* (*Les Noyers de l'Altenburg*, 1943, trans. 1952). Faced with the need to participate in events related to major conflicts, but in a world where human existence has no obvious justification, characters seek to give meaning to their life, not only through their action and the sense of community which comes from acting together for a cause (often revolutionary), but also through their death, or rather, perhaps, the manner of their dying.

In the post-war world, his writing is represented by two major works: in *Voices of Silence* (*Les Voix du silence*, 1951, trans. 1953), Malraux's reflection turns from action to art for evidence that man may transcend his contingency through artistic creation; while the *Antimemoirs* (*Antimémoires*, 2 vols, 1967 and 1974, trans. 1968) are a meditation upon the experience of a lifetime, and more particularly upon Malraux's significant encounters with some of the major world figures.

Malraux's importance is considerable, not only for any lasting value his writing might have, but also – and more especially – for the impact of his work upon the rising generation of the 1930s. It might indeed be held that *Man's Estate*, along with **Céline's** *Journey to the End of the Night*, is a key work in the decade preceding the Second World War.

Further reading

See: D. Boak, *André Malraux* (1968); P. Galante, *Malraux* (1971); C. Jenkins, *André Malraux* (1972); J. Lacouture, *André Malraux, une vie dans le siècle* (1973); A. Madsen, *Malraux* (1977); Herman Lebovics, *Mona Lisa's Escort: André Malraux and the Reinvention of French Culture* (1999); Olivier Todd, *Malraux: A Life* (2005).

KEITH GORE

MANDELA, Nelson
1918–
South African statesman

Nelson Mandela, born in a remote Xhosa village in South Africa's Transkei, became quite simply one of the most famous people in the world, and not just famous but near-universally admired, respected and, by many, loved. He was president of South Africa from 1994 to 1999 after spending twenty-seven years of his life in the apartheid jails of white-supremacist South Africa. It was he who was responsible more than anyone for leading his country not just to majority rule but, even more important, achieving this while averting racial conflict and possibly civil war in what Archbishop Desmond Tutu had dubbed 'the rainbow nation'.

Although he came from a royal Xhosa family his childhood was modest – he herded cattle, underwent the tribal initiation, and fled his clan when his guardian arranged an unattractive marriage. He went to Johannesburg and eventually became a lawyer, with his life-long friend Oliver Tambo.

He joined the African National Congress and quickly became dissatisfied with the quietism of its older leaders at a time when the National Party government was institutionalizing apartheid. Convinced of the hopelessness of the plight of the African majority, he embraced civil disobedience, was 'banned', arrested, imprisoned, banned again. At the 'Treason Trial' in Pretoria, 1959–61, he and his colleagues were eventually found not guilty, but after the Sharpeville Massacre in 1960 he went underground and became a 'Black Pimpernel', travelling in disguise for a year. He had reluctantly agreed that non-violence was a futile policy and that he had no option but to agree to an 'Armed Struggle' in which he was commander-in-chief of Umkhonto we Sizwe, the ANC's military arm. His sentence to five years' jail in 1962 was overtaken by the 'Rivonia Trial' (1963–4) of most of the Umkhonto leadership.

Sentenced to life imprisonment, Mandela delivered one of the most memorable speeches of the century:

> During my lifetime I have dedicated myself to this struggle of the African people. I have fought against white domination, and I have fought against black domination. I have cherished the ideal of a democratic and free society in which all persons live together in harmony and with equal opportunities. It is an ideal which I hope to live for and to achieve. But if needs be, it is an ideal for which I am prepared to die.

He was sent to South Africa's Alcatraz, Robben Island, off-shore from Cape Town, where he was forced to break rocks in a quarry. But as the years passed, conditions were slowly improved a little, as Mandela won the allegiance of his fellow prisoners and even the respect of some of the warders. The government gradually realized that these very years of the Island were giving Mandela a charisma, at home and also abroad, where the 'Free Mandela' campaign gathered momentum.

It was a secret at the time but the government, from the mid-1980s, began to make tentative approaches to him. He had been moved to the mainland, to much better, even comfortable, conditions. He kept his negotiations secret even from his own party-in-exile, and later said that 'it was time to talk'. The breakthrough came in February 1990 when the new white president, F.W. de Klerk, bravely decided to release the ANC prisoners and Mandela emerged to worldwide acclamation.

The ANC suspended its Armed Struggle. Mandela, determined on a reconciliation between South Africa's racial groups, agreed to a Government of National Unity in which he associated himself with the National Party which had imprisoned him for so many years. These years had succeeded in destroying his marriage to the flamboyant Winnie Mandela, who had tended the flame while he was in prison. They separated in 1992 and he later wrote, 'She married a man who soon left her, the man became a myth, and then the myth returned home and proved to be just a man after all.'

President Mandela was sworn in on 10 May 1994, saluting the courage of F.W. de Klerk. The two men had shared the Nobel Peace Prize in 1993. As president, he deliberately held back from the minutiae of Cabinet government: his overwhelming concern was to promote reconciliation in his nation. He made many gestures of forgiveness and friendship to the whites who had near-destroyed his life. In this he had a great gift for what can only be described as public relations – most famously when South Africa won the World Cup rugby competition in 1995, the traditional game of the country's Afrikaners, and he went on to the field wearing a Springbok jersey and embraced the (white) captain. Most South African whites became convinced that they were fortunate that he had emerged as their leader.

He always understood that the first five years of majority rule would be critical for future multi-racial harmony, but he stuck to his plan to step down at the first election, in 1999. In these years he was often candid to admit the failures and shortcomings of his administration – with the exception of the country's horrifying AIDS epidemic which, he afterwards admitted, he had been slow to acknowledge and publicize. He made up for this in retirement, when he did not hesitate to confront his successor, Thabo Mbeki, who was turning a blind eye on the scourge. His ghosted autobiography, *Long Walk to Freedom* (1994), was a brilliant success, a worldwide best-seller.

In old age Mandela was extraordinarily active, particularly on the international stage, where his reputation was unique and where his diplomatic skills were in constant demand. No longer the official leader of his own country, he had in effect become the single most respected elder statesman of the developing world.

There was a final achievement of a normal life when 'Madiba', as he was known at home, in 1998 at the age of eighty married Graca Machel, widow of the late president of Mozambique. In his homes in the Transkei and in Johannesburg the world's best-known political prisoner is approaching his end surrounded by a large extended family. His beaming smile, his fancy shirts and his curious, rather high-pitched voice had become famous throughout the world, symbols of his iconic status.

Further reading

See: Anthony Sampson, *Mandela: The Authorised Biography* (1999).

J.D.F. JONES

MANDELSTAM, Osip Emilievich

1891–1938

Russian poet

Mandelstam was born in Warsaw, but grew up in a Jewish family in St Petersburg. He spent much of the period from 1907 to 1910 as a student in Western Europe. His first volume of poems, *Stone* (*Kamen*), appeared in 1913. After the Revolution he remained in Russia, and in 1919 began to live with Nadezhda Yakovlevna Khazina, with whom he was formally married some years later. From this time until his death he lived in many different places, suffering increasing hardship as he was progressively excluded from serious literary work. In 1934 his authorship of satirical verses about **Stalin** brought him three years of exile in the town of Voronezh. Shortly after his return, he was again arrested and sent to a labour camp. By now he was a very ill man; he is reported to have died in a transit camp near Vladivostok.

One may see the primary poetic impulse in Mandelstam as the struggle against chaos. His earliest poems show clearly the influence of the poet Fyodor Tiutchev, who saw day as a golden cover thrown over the chaos of night, and almost all his writing – in this respect very much the product of St Petersburg – speaks of the fragility of human culture. This note becomes more intense in his later, more tragic work.

In opposition to chaos, his first book, with its significant title of *Stone*, celebrates the ordering impulse which is seen in civilization, and particularly in great works of architecture. In this stress on the positive, building spirit, Mandelstam is at one with the Acmeist school, who praised the real, physical world as against the other-worldly longings of the Symbolists. In his view Acmeism was the 'nostalgia for world culture' and his conception of poetry was one of *recognition*; the poets of all ages echoed one another, the poetic word was an enduring living force. He wrote some remarkable essays on the poetry of the past and present, notably his *Conversation about Dante* (*Razgovor o Dante*, written in 1933, published in Moscow in 1967). Far more than most Russian poets he saw the civilization of the Mediterranean as the summit of human achievement; a recurrent notion in his writing is that 'Hellenism' succeeded in domesticating chaos and providing an area of human warmth for life in the world. This he saw as the continuing task of the poet, particularly in the barbarian modern age.

In keeping with these beliefs, Mandelstam's poems often refer explicitly to poets and artists of earlier centuries: Bach, Racine, Ovid, Petrarch and many others. The verse of the first two books also shows a striking ability to create harmonious and rich verbal constructs – the sound of the verse embodies the beliefs. But it would be wrong to imagine him, even in his earlier work, as a simple classicist; even in *Stone*, and much more so in the aptly named *Tristia* (1922), the dominant note is one of loss. Happiness lies in recognition and recovery, but this is generally denied to the modern poet. A characteristic poem in this respect is one written in 1920 and beginning, 'I have forgotten the word I wanted to say.' Mandelstam tended to write clusters of poems in which images and themes recur, and in the group to which this poem belongs the central motifs are the swallow (a brief visitor to the dark North), Psyche, Persephone and the underworld of shades, all of them expressing fragility, negativity and emptiness. The formal order of the poem only emphasizes by contrast the real disarray that lies at the heart of it.

The feeling of loss, which was clearly provoked in part by Mandelstam's understanding of the Revolution, is even more apparent in the small body of poems written between 1921 and 1925 and published in 1928 – almost his last published poetry. In such magnificent pieces as 'The Slate-Pencil Ode' ('Grifelnaya Oda') and 'January 1st 1924', he expresses a tragic vision of his age, likened to an animal with a broken backbone. These are fragmentary, broken odes (comparable in their way to **T.S. Eliot's** work of the same period), poems of great and often puzzling richness whose main theme is the difficulty or impossibility of writing odes in the great tradition which stretches back through the eighteenth-century poet Derzhavin to Pindar.

After 1925 the difficulty of writing forced Mandelstam into a period of poetic silence which was only broken in the 1930s and particularly in the 'Notebooks' written in Voronezh between 1935 and 1937. Here all the bridges are down; the poems are more intensely tragic than anything that he had written before. They are a strange mixture of clarity and obscurity. Mandelstam now sees his destiny very clearly, and many of the poems express a lucid courage and even acceptance, but at the same time the fear of chaos and cruelty and the poet's inner turmoil often

force the writing into a jagged, elliptical and hermetic form which contrasts sharply with the first two books. This is particularly true of the menacing and defiant 'Verses about the Unknown Soldier' ('Stikhi o neizvestnom soldate'), the oblique result of an unavailing attempt to write an ode in praise of Stalin.

Officially the importance of Mandelstam's poetry was only very grudgingly recognized in the Soviet Union, but for many readers both there and in the West his reputation eclipsed even that of **Pasternak**. To a certain extent this was perhaps an elite cult which fed on Mandelstam's difficulty, but it seems beyond doubt that he was one of the three or four great Russian poets of his century.

Further reading

Mandelstam's collected works have been published in Russian, edited by G.P. Struve and B.A. Filippov, 3 vols (1964–71). Translations include *Selected Poems* (trans. C. Brown and W. S. Merwin, 1973); *Poems* (trans. J. Greene, 1977); *The Prose of Osip Mandelstam* (trans. C. Brown, 1965); *Selected Essays* (trans. S. Monas, 1977). The best general study of Mandelstam is C. Brown, *Mandelstam* (1973). See the two volumes of memoirs by Mandelstam's widow, N. Mandelstam, *Hope against Hope* (trans. M. Hayward, 1971) and *Hope Abandoned* (trans. M. Hayward, 1974). See also: Nancy Pollak, *Mandelstam the Reader* (1995); Clare Cavanagh, *Osip Mandelstam and the Modernist Creation of Tradition* (1995).

PETER FRANCE

MANET, Edouard

1832–83

French painter

Although he was a reluctant rebel, Manet played a leading role around the middle of the nineteenth century in formulating a new and modern style of painting in opposition to the outworn conventions of academic painting. He was a friend of **Monet** and **Degas**, but while his innovations were to have a decisive influence on the Impressionists he refused to be associated with the group and never contributed to their exhibitions. It was Manet's ambition to achieve success within the official art establishment, but ironically his work was repeatedly rejected by the Salon and castigated by the critics, even after he had established a reputation as the leader of the modern school.

Manet was the son of a magistrate and it was only after twice failing the entrance examinations to the Naval Academy that his father permitted him to enrol, in 1849, at the École des Beaux Arts, where he studied under Thomas Couture. From his master he imbibed a love of Venetian art and a vigorous painterly technique. But the pupil's methods were too radical for the teacher, and after quarrelling with Couture, Manet left his studio in 1856 to complete his education by copying in the Louvre and travelling in Italy, Germany and Holland. His first entry for the Salon, in 1856, *The Absinthe Drinker*, was rejected, in spite of Delacroix's support, but in 1861 a portrait of his parents and *The Spanish Guitar Player* were shown at the Salon and he was at once hailed by young painters and progressive critics as a leader. During the next decade the pattern continued, with major works being rejected or creating scandal in the press, but with such writers as Astruc, **Baudelaire** and **Zola** rallying to his defence. At the Café Guerbois, artists and critics gathered to hear Manet speak, and his Paris studio became a meeting place for artists. In Fantin-Latour's painting of 1870, *A Studio in the Batignolles*, Manet is shown surrounded by **Renoir**, Monet, Bazille, Zola, Scholderer and Maître, at work on a portrait of Astruc.

Manet was surprised at the official response to his work since he regarded himself as a traditionalist. He greatly admired the Spanish masters, and his broad handling and rich, dark colouring, with a liberal use of black, are derived from Velazquez, Ribera and Goya. A number of his early works also treat Spanish themes, such as bullfights and Spanish dancers. His chief entry for the Salon of 1863, *Le Déjeuner sur l'herbe*, was rejected and created a scandal at the special Salon of rejected works – the so-called 'Salon des Refusés'. It derives its composition from an engraving by Marcan-

tonio Raimondi after a lost Raphael painting, and transposes into a modern idiom the arcadian idyll of Titian's early *Fête champêtre* in the Louvre. But critics were appalled by the sight of naked women beside men in contemporary dress, and, furthermore, attacked Manet's style. In looking back to the example of Velazquez, Manet rejected the detailed finish, polished surface and laborious modelling of academic painting for a rapid execution and bold colouring. In order to preserve the vitality of his visual impressions he simplified what he saw, encompassing figures in bold outlines and eliminating the carefully modulated halftones favoured by the academic masters.

Manet daringly applied this radical technique to contemporary themes. In 1863, at an exhibition of his work at the picture dealer Martinet's, he showed a painting of fashionably dressed Parisians, among them his friends, parading in a park. *A Concert in the Tuileries Gardens* is a landmark because it treats modern life in a spontaneous style, in a composition that is apparently so unpremeditated as to be almost haphazard. At the Salon of 1865 Manet caused yet another scandal with his *Olympia*. The picture is a reinterpretation of Titian's *Venus of Urbino*, but the reclining female nude is defiantly modern, so much so that she outraged the public. The model, as in *Le Déjeuner sur l'herbe*, was Victorine Meurend, but here she is more abrasively erotic, brazenly staring at the spectator, naked except for a pair of slippers and a black velvet lace around her neck.

It is impossible to determine how much of the air of worldliness and vulgarity in *Olympia* is intentional. Manet denied that he intended to shock, but in transposing a Renaissance Venus into a nineteenth-century boudoir she became a prostitute, and Manet's intuition and honesty as an observer prevent him from denying the fact. He is the painter of modern life *malgré lui*, and it is precisely his keen sense of the flavour of modern life that earned him the admiration of Baudelaire and Zola.

Not until 1865 did Manet in fact visit Spain and encounter the work of Velazquez and Goya in quantity, and in 1867 he painted a large picture of *The Execution of the Emperor Maximilian*, inspired by Goya's *Third of May*. That same year he exhibited some fifty paintings at the Exposition Universelle but with little success. During the Franco-Prussian War he served as a staff officer in the National Guard, but under the Commune of 1871 he retired to the country with his family. He travelled in Holland in 1872 and *Le Bon Bock*, which was a great success at the Salon of 1873, shows the strong influence of Frans Hals.

The next phase of Manet's career shows him turning increasingly to modern themes, and even, under the influence of the Impressionists, painting out of doors. It was through Berthe Morisot, his pupil since 1868, and one of the models for *The Balcony* (Salon 1869), that he became intimate with Monet and Renoir. During the summer of 1874 he joined Monet at Argenteuil and painted river scenes and regattas in a lively Impressionist technique. Such pictures as *Boating* (1874) and *Monet Painting in His Floating Studio* (1874) are more brilliant in colour and more loosely painted than his earlier work, but still retain some touches of the black of which he was so fond.

The association with the Impressionists did nothing for Manet's reputation, and he suffered more Salon rejections in 1876 and 1877. Nor did his paintings of modern life help. From the mid-1870s he began a dazzling series of pictures, close in spirit to the work of his friend Degas, of bars, concert-halls and prostitutes which includes *Nana* (1877) and *La Servante de Bocks* (1878, two versions), and culminates in the masterful *Bar at the Folies-Bergère* (1881). This late work, completed less than two years before his death, defines the type of the modern female, in her glance, her pose, her dress, and in her habitat, the brash, noisy and mysterious world of the café-concert reflected in the mirror behind her.

In the summer of 1879 Manet first began to feel the effects of the illness (*locomotor ataxia*) that was to lead to his death. Over the next four years he retreated increasingly to the seclusion of the country around Paris, to Bellevue, Versailles and Rueil. In semi-retirement his work took on a lighter and more domestic character, with paintings of women sitting in his garden, and pastel portraits of such lady friends as the actress Méry Laurent. Even his chief Salon exhibits of these years, *In the Conservatory* (1879) and *At Père Lathuille's* (1880), are like vignettes of modern life, comedies of manners in a light, romantic vein. From this period also date many of Manet's still-lifes. It was above all in this genre, in small canvases of peonies or asparagus, that he displayed his keen colour sense and virtuoso brushwork.

Manet's influence in his own lifetime and since has been enormous. His early disciples included Monet, Berthe Morisot and Eva Gonzales, but his process of bold simplification of form was to determine the approach of most of the Post-Impressionists, as well as the early **Picasso** and **Matisse**. But he also created the genre of contemporary social themes which was taken up by **Toulouse-Lautrec**, and also debased by many fashionable painters of the latter part of the century, such as Boldini, Carolus-Duran and Émile Blanche. The aspect of Manet's achievement that is most often neglected is his psychological insight. Because his understanding of the modern human animal is so much more subtle than Renoir's, for example, he avoids the latter's excesses of sentimentality. In his pictures of men and women meeting, conversing, at a bar or a ball, over lunch or dinner, he creates a drama which, though calculated understatement, evokes with great intensity the spirit of the era.

Further reading

See: Julius Meier-Graefe, *Edouard Manet* (1912); Etienne Moreau-Nelaton, *Manet raconté part lui-même* (2 vols, 1926); George H. Hamilton, *Manet and His Critics* (1954); Pierre Courthion, *Manet* (trans. 1962); Anne Coffin Hansen, *Edouard Manet* (1967); Pierre Schneider, *The World of Manet* (1968); K. Adler, *Manet* (1986).

MICHAEL WILSON

MANN, Jonathan Max

1947–98

US epidemiologist

Jonathan Mann was an epidemiologist and public health physician. His legacy (his life was cut short in the crash of Swissair flight 111 in September 1998 when he was only fifty-one) is his impact on the world's approach to HIV. Appointed to lead the first WHO (World Health Organization) programme on AIDS in late 1986, he raised the world's consciousness of the epidemic in a remarkably short time – and increased the budget for the programme tenfold in less than two years. By the time of his death, he had deeply influenced the way that HIV was approached by the UN, by governments and by NGOs globally.

After starting his career as an epidemiologist studying bubonic plague in New Mexico, Mann moved to Kinshasa, Zaire (now the Democratic Republic of Congo) in 1984 to work with the US Centers for Disease Control investigating the new phenomena of HIV/AIDS. His research was an important part of the early scientific study of HIV in Africa, and he avoided contributing to the sensationalism of many reports about AIDS in Africa at the time. His experience and the diplomatic skills he developed in Zaire stood him in good stead when he was appointed head of the new Special Programme on AIDS (soon to become the Global Programme on AIDS or GPA) by Dr Halfdan Mahler, the then UN Secretary-General.

Mann stayed in Geneva until 1990, when disagreements with the new WHO chief, Dr Hiroshi Nakajima, came to a head and he resigned. During his four years at Geneva he addressed the General Assembly of the UN in 1987, leading to the first UN resolution concerning a specific disease, and in 1988 brought together 117 ministers of health to the London Summit of Ministers in London. He was adept at media relations and his success and public profile probably contributed to the breakdown of relationships with Nakajima.

From the start, he made an effort to include NGOs and people living with HIV in GPA meetings and discussions. Perhaps partly because of these contacts, he developed the conviction that human rights must form the basis of public health policy, especially in relation to HIV. The virus was linked to homosexuality, prostitution and drug use, and discrimination against both those with the disease and the marginalized groups associated with HIV was rampant. Mann argued that such discrimination would drive HIV underground, and thus help it to spread faster. He spoke of the three epidemics – the silent spread of the virus, the sickness and death which followed, and the third epidemic, that of social and cultural responses, stigma and discrimination.

After leaving WHO, Mann joined the Harvard School of Public Health and set up a new group, the Global AIDS Policy Coalition. In 1992, with colleagues who had left WHO with him, the Coalition produced a vast book, *AIDS in the World: A Global Report*, which estimated much higher rates of HIV infection than had been proposed by WHO. From 1993 until his death Mann served as the first François-Xavier Bagnoud Professor of Health and Human Rights, and Director in the newly established FXB Center for Health and Human Rights. He was co-founder of the Center with Countess Albina du Boisrouvray: built with three-quarters of her family fortune, it was named after her son who died in a helicopter crash at the age of twenty-four.

Mann recognized that disease is determined by social, cultural and economic factors, and concluded that respect for human rights and dignity is the key to the prevention of epidemics such as HIV. His analysis, although taking into account the influence of society and culture, was based on a mainly European and American world view, in which the rights of the individual tend to be paramount. This was combined with the early GPA policy of introducing a global strategy on HIV/AIDS, adopted by seventy-five countries in Asia, Africa and Latin America. The key elements were IEC (information, education and communication), care and surveillance. This

986 MANN, Luis Heinrich

was a top-down analysis from Geneva, focusing on health services. Information programmes were superficial, frequently with messages of fear and death. There was little attempt to involve people in finding their own solutions.

Mann's major legacy is the emphasis on human rights in health policy. His influence encouraged a humane approach of inclusion and compassion and prevented the hideous and pointless alternative of quarantine, incarceration and discrimination. Moreover, human rights have become an obligatory part of any programme addressing the epidemic. However, rights are often interpreted narrowly and individualistically, and this continuing focus has contributed to the prioritizing of a service-based, commodity-led response. The notion of individual rights to life and health, and therefore to condoms, treatment and health services, has been adopted at the expense of understanding how community-led responses can change societal attitudes and norms. The few success stories, notably Thailand and Uganda, demonstrate not only respect for people and political leadership but also, crucially, community involvement and community-determined change.

We will never know if Mann's strategies curbed the epidemic or represented a missed opportunity. What we do know is that since the first case was described in 1981, the number of people being infected, living and dying with HIV has risen inexorably. The latest estimates are that more than 40 million people are currently infected. There is no cure or vaccine. Infections are still increasing, in both rich and poor parts of the world.

Biennial International AIDS Conferences now attract more than 14,000 delegates: at the Bangkok conference in 2004, the lack of leadership was a constant theme. Whatever his effect on the epidemic, Jonathan Mann undoubtedly provided global leadership at a time when it was much needed.

Further reading

See: J.M. Mann *et al.*, 'Natural History of HIV Infection in Zaire', *Lancet*, Vol. ii (1986), pp. 707–

9; Jonathan Mann, Daniel J.M. Tarantola and Thomas Netter (eds) *AIDS in the World: A Global Report* (1992); Laurie Garrett, *The Coming Plague* (1994).

SUE LUCAS

MANN, Luis Heinrich
1871–1950
German writer

The eldest son of a prosperous Hanseatic merchant, and brother of **Thomas Mann**, Heinrich Mann was born in Lübeck in the same year as **Bismarck's** creation, the second German Empire, which was to furnish the subject-matter and concern of the novels and essays of his maturity. He was intended to follow his father into the family firm, and at the age of thirteen was sent, as part of his preparation for this, to visit trading relatives in St Petersburg. But the journal the boy kept of the journey shows rather the precocious talent of the born writer, and an early gift for drawing. Sharing his generation's sense of being late-comers to the achievements of the nineteenth-century bourgeois protestant ethic, Heinrich struggled to free himself from his inheritance until his father recognized the inevitable, and made a will dissolving the family firm and enabling Heinrich and Thomas to live the life of literary *rentiers* in the last years of the century. Heinrich never returned to Lübeck. Ill-health, a love affair with a failed opera-singer, a deep attachment to his actress sister Carla and no fixed abode all went to make up a typical literary lifestyle of the time.

Fontane, the Naturalists and above all Heine were the writers he first admired. But he soon turned to the differentiated psychology of Hermann, Bahr and Paul Bourget, who left their mark on his first, tentative novel *In Einer Familie* (1894). Bourget's pessimistic conservatism, adapted to German affairs, can also be traced in his brief editorship of *Das zwanzigste Jahrhundert, Blätter für deutsche Art und Wohlfahrt* (1895–96), a journal devoted to the monarchist, militarist, anti-democratic and anti-semitic views of the threatened petty bourgeoisie. This is a curious episode, less of a false start than in retrospect it might seem. It represented a first attempt to put *l'art pour l'art* attitudes behind him and engage critically with his society. It gave way to a programmatic realization that what Germany lacked was a tradition of the social novel as a means to social self-knowledge. Suddenly discovering his talent as a satirical novelist while in Italy, he set about making good this lack. His first novel of any stature, *In the Land of Cockaigne* (*Im Schlaraffinland*, trans. 1929), appeared in 1900. It tells the tale of the rise and fall of an unscrupulous young man on the make – the model is **Maupassant's** *Bel Ami*. All the figures, from the kept women to the bought newspaper editors, are the creatures of the grand capitalist J.J. Turkheimer. Three characteristics show themselves in this novel which were to become Mann's hallmark: the theme of power (and the intellectual's relationship to it); the impersonal 'dramatic' presentation, with a cast of thousands; and the set-piece of a theatrical performance as the touchstone of social values – in this case the radical chic of an expensive audience getting its thrills from a dire Naturalist drama about the Plight of the Workers, a brilliant parody on elements from Hauptmann's *Die Weber* and **Zola's** *La Bête humaine*. There is as yet no unspoken moral basis for this satire on capitalism abounding beyond a worldly anti-bourgeois fastidiousness. His next novels, the trilogy *Die Göttinnen oder die drei Romane der Herzogin von Assy* ('The Goddesses or the Three Novels of the Duchess von Assy', 1903), are symptomatic of his ambivalence. On the one hand he is overtly critical of decadent aestheticism; on the other, Mann's intense, florid prose, and the extravagance of his heroines' lifestyles indicate that he is as much fascinated by as critical of the current **Nietzschean** vitalism. But from now on the criticism prevails, not only of the compensatory psychology of decadence (*Pippo Spano*, 1905), but also of the compensatory psychology of power (*Professor Unrat oder das Ende eines Tyrannen*, 1905,

translated as *Small Town Tyrant*, 1944). Concurrently with these Mann wrote his major essay *Flaubert und George Sand* (1905), a subtle study of the socially alienated artist. The degree of both criticism and identification in this essay marks a stage in his development towards the sense of social commitment for which his later work is known.

A real signal came with his rhetorical manifesto *Geist und Tat* ('Mind and Action', 1910), which exhorted German intellectuals to abandon their remote and acquiescent attitude towards the institutions of power, and to look to the French style, where a politically responsible public could demand (and get) a political responsibility from its writers. The man of letters is understood as the public conscience of his country. Increasingly, he came to define his position as that of the French republican democrat. The two novels he was at work on are in tune with this declaration. *The Little Town* (*Die kleine Stadt*, 1909, trans. 1931) is a happy return to the Italy of Mascagni and **Puccini** and memories of **Garibaldi**: a stagnant Italian town is brought to comic, democratic life by the upheavals and self-knowledge provoked by the disturbing visit of an operatic troupe. The satirical, negative counterpart to this Utopian idyll is the famous novel for which he had been gathering material since 1907: *The Man of Straw* (*Der Untertan*, 1918, trans. 1947). The scene is the ugly little German town of Netzig in the 1890s, the tale the rise of the characteristic figure of the period, the hollow bully Dietrich Hessling, whose aggressive posturings are modelled on those of his histrionic master Kaiser Wilhelm II. To tell 'the inner history of the period' is its purpose, and Mann's old insight into the psychology of compensatory aggressiveness out of impotence is developed to interpret a whole generation: his own generation of sons, the empty-handed inheritors of an older generation's achievement. Role-playing, performance, is now endemic to the entire society, from monarch to subject: 'Theatre, and not even good theatre' – the tawdry pretentiousness of **Wagner's** theatre. The defeat of the old liberal tradition of 1848 forms the novel's climax – and, given that the book was finished in 1914, a prophetic one.

The First World War was the occasion of a fundamental estrangement, private and public, between the two brothers. Thomas Mann's response to the outbreak had been the traumatic discovery, in his own terms, of Germany and patriotism. Heinrich, with his French republican allegiance, came out with a major essay, *Zola* (1915); the passionate rhetoric of **Zola** accusing the French Second Empire on behalf of the wronged Dreyfus acts as a figure for Mann's own opposition to Germany's initiation of the war. His denunciation of Zola's time-serving literary contemporaries stung Thomas into a complex self-justification, in *Betrachtungen eines Unpolitischen* (1918). The classic dispute between Heinrich's Utopian republicanism and his brother's sceptical conservatism was not resolved until 1922 when the two Manns reunited in a sustained defence of the vulnerable Weimar Republic.

The years that followed were the years of Heinrich's greatest fame and political activity, from his funeral speech at the grave of the assassinated Kurt Eisner in 1919 to his turning away from Germany, in *Bekenntnis zum Übernationalen* ('Commitment to the International Idea', 1932), to Coudenhouve-Kalergi's hope for a united Europe. The rich harvest of political essays is the work of this decade for which he will be remembered (*Macht und Mensch*, 'Power and Humanity', 1919; *Diktatur der Vernunft*, 'Dictatorship of Reason', 1923: *Sieben Jahre*, 'Seven Years', 1929). The works of the imagination are frailer. *The Chief* (*Der Kopf*, 1925, trans. 1925), set in high government places, was intended to be the social novel of the Republic as *Der Untertan* had been for the Empire; but caught in the daily battle of criticizing and sustaining the Republic in reality, he could not find a suitable form to present it in fiction.

An energetic advocate of all good liberal causes, he moved further left in his views as the National Socialists took hold of Germany. Dismissed as President of the Literary Section of the Prussian Academy of Arts in 1933 (he had been appointed in 1931), he crossed into France only days before the burning of the Reichstag. As the father of the German intellectual left he became chairman of the Schutzverband deutscher Schriftsteller, writing for the many German journals-in-exile, and moving progressively nearer the Communist position, which attacked not so much Nazism as a German phenomenon but Fascism as the instrument of international capitalism. Exile stimulated his imagination as well, and these years saw two of his finest novels: *King Wren* (*Die Jugend des Königs Henri Quatre*, 1935, trans. 1937) and *Henri IV King of France* (*Die Vollendung des Königs Henri Quatre*, 1938, trans. 1938), an image in historical terms of the power struggles and hopes of his own time.

In 1940, with the invasion of France, he fled again, to the USA by way of Spain. His last years were spent in straitened circumstances in California, writing unproduced film scripts and the novels *Der Atem* ('Breath', 1949) and *Empfang bei der Welt* ('The World Receives', 1956). The major work of this last, and saddest period of his life (his second wife Nelly Kröger killed herself) was his autobiography, the historical, impersonal account of a life in his time: *Ein Zeitalter wird besichtigt* ('An Age is Viewed', 1945). He died as preparations were being made to welcome him back to the new German Democratic Republic.

Heinrich Mann was a prolific and uneven novelist. Apart from *Der Untertan* and *Henri Quatre* there is still no consensus on what constitutes the canon of his major works, and his reputation has fluctuated since his death almost as much as when he was alive. Although he was always regarded as an established classic in the DDR, post-war Western Germany of the *Wirtschaftswunder* seemed ready to forget him, at least until the revival of the old wish for social responsibility in the novel restored his stock and led to a wider recognition of his pre-war importance.

Further reading

Other works include: novels: *The Poor* (*Die Armen*, 1917, trans. 1917); *Kobes* ('Kobes', 1925); drama:

SchausPielerin (The Actress', 1911); *Die grosse Liebe* ('Great Love', 1912); *Madame Legros* (1913); essays: *Das öffentliche Leben* ('Public Life', 1932); *Der Sinn dieser Emigration* ('The Meaning of this Emigration', 1934); *Es kommt der Tag* ('The Day Will Come') (1936); biography: Klause Schröter, *Heinrich Mann* (1967). See: David Roberts, *Artistic Consciousness and Political Conscience: The Novels of Heinrich Mann* (1971); Nigel Hamilton: *Brothers Mann: The Lives of Heinrich and Thomas Mann* (1978).

JOYCE CRICK

MANN, Thomas

1875–1955

German novelist

Son of a prosperous north German grain merchant and a mother of partly Brazilian origins, Thomas, younger brother of **Heinrich Mann**, was born in Lübeck. He began writing early and was fortunate enough, on leaving school, to be able to devote most of his time to it. In 1893 Mann left Lübeck for Munich, which became his home for the next forty years. His marriage to Katia Pringsheim in 1905 resulted in six children, a number of whom were to become distinguished in their turn as writers or scholars. In 1929 Mann was awarded the Nobel Prize; in 1933 the rise of Nazism forced him and his family into exile, first in Switzerland, then in the USA where he was held in high honour, his home in Pacific Palisades, California, becoming something of a place of pilgrimage. After the war he returned to Switzerland and settled there for the remainder of his life.

At the age of only twenty-six, Mann achieved immediate success with his first novel, *Buddenbrooks* (1901, trans. 1924). This surprisingly mature work is the history of four generations of a family of grain merchants from prosperity and full integration into the Hanseatic community in which they live to final alienation and decline. The single-minded vitality of the Buddenbrook clan is able, in its great days, to assimilate and control its rogue members with their dangerous traits of fecklessness or lethargy: but

these elements are gradually reinforced by a more powerful and complex strain – that of the imagination with its tendency to question and even subvert the stolid self-assurance of the practical life. In proportion as imagination, art and the probing intellect assert their claims, the Buddenbrook hold on life diminishes until, in the musically gifted but physically feeble Hanno, the last of the line, it disappears altogether.

The tendency, supported by Mann's reading of Schopenhauer, to view the imagination as a force essentially hostile to the crude vitality of life is one which fuels much of Mann's earlier fiction, notably the novellas *Tonio Kröger* and *Tristan* (1903), both in their different ways studies in the predicament of the writer. In Mann's possibly most famous work, *Death in Venice* (*Der Tod in Venedig*, 1911; translated in *Three Tales*, 1929), the protagonist, Gustav von Aschenbach, is a mature and renowned writer who has subjugated the moral dubieties of the imagination to the demands of a classicizing art of intransigent ethical and aesthetic rigour. But Aschenbach's (in Nietzsche's term) Apolline solutions are undermined and finally obliterated: on a journey to Venice he encounters the Polish boy Tadzio whose almost perfect beauty, though seeming at first a confirmation of Aschenbach's classical ideals, gradually tempts him into sensual indulgence, Dionysian disintegration and finally death. *Death in Venice*, then, is concerned with the essential paradox of the artistic endeavour: the ethical and aesthetic realms which Aschenbach has thought to reconcile with one another prove in the end to be warring elements: and the story itself, which is constructed with consummate artistry, thus implicitly calls its own very virtuosity in question.

The Magic Mountain (*Der Zauberberg*, 1922, trans. 1927) was originally conceived as a comic pendant to *Death in Venice*, but grew to a novel of considerable length. It is, ironically, a *Bildungsroman*: ironically because its hero, the innocent young Hans Castorp, is educated to life not, like the traditional hero of the German novel of education, via life itself, but in the hermetically sealed environment of a Swiss tuberculosis sanatorium whose entire *raison d'être* is disease and death. Does disease heighten the sensibilities, ennoble the personality? Hans Castorp is at first romantically disposed to think so, but finds himself disenchanted by the relentlessly trivial preoccupations of most of the sanatorium's denizens. More deeply demanding are the claims on his consciousness of a small number of characters who act as educators or at least as perpetrators of particular, exclusive viewpoints: Hans Castorp's cousin Joachim, devoted to a Prussian ethics of duty; Settembrini, an Italian rationalist and humanist; Naphta, a Jew turned Jesuit turned Marxist, advocate of a reviving terror; Dr Krokowski, adherent of psychoanalysis; Claudia Chauchat, bearer to Hans Castorp of the darkly irresistible attractions of Eros in a diseased body; and Mynheer Peeperkorn, the aged and tragically impotent apostle of vitalism. Hans Castorp, representative of Germany, pays respectful heed to all these mentors, but does not unequivocally decide for any of them. History, in the shape of the First World War, erupts into his timeless dream and precipitates him on to the fields of Flanders: perhaps, the narrator reflects in the book's final sentence, Love will rise from this universal carnage. Both here and in his earlier vision in the chapter entitled 'Snow', Hans Castorp rejects the enticing darknesses of experience in favour of health and life: but it is possible to feel that Castorp's options remain somewhat abstract, unrealized and in context unrealizable against the author's obvious enthralment by the forces of decay.

In addition to other preoccupations, *The Magic Mountain* is much concerned with the problem of time, and in particular with the disjunction between consciousness and chronology. Mann's next major work, the tetralogy *Joseph and His Brothers* (*Joseph und seine Brüder*, 1933–43, trans. 1934–44), extends this theme further to probe the relationship between time and myth and to investigate the patterns formed by a mythic appropriation of history – many of the characters in the first volume, *The Tales of Jacob* (*Die Geschichten Jakobs*), are prone to see themselves as types in whom time-bound particularization is of far less importance than their mythical status. But Joseph, the story of whose rejection by his brothers, slavery and rise to favour and administrative genius in Egypt is the subject of the other three volumes, is of a more modern, sophisticated turn of mind: unabashed by his knowledge of his place in the scheme of things, he adapts this knowledge to his own ironic purposes, seeing myth in terms of psychology and highly conscious of the fact that he is 'in a story'. The young Joseph, handsome, gifted, egoistic and something of a rogue, undergoes a long process of education in which he is twice cast into the pit and twice resurrected to become finally adviser to Pharaoh and provider during the great famine; as in Genesis, he is ultimately reconciled with his father and brothers. Like *The Magic Mountain*, the Joseph tetralogy is a kind of *Bildungsroman* depicting the progress both of its protagonist and also, as Mann himself indicated, of the human race as a whole to arrive at a point where myth becomes fruitfully integrated into history and egoism gives place to responsibility.

The writing of the Joseph tetralogy was almost exactly contemporaneous with the rise and fall of the **Hitler** regime, and it was part of Mann's intention to oppose to the crude racist mythologizing of the Nazis a treatment of myth which should be light, lucent and ultimately humanistic. In *Doktor Faustus* (1947, trans. 1948), however, the light mood disappears to make room for Mann's fullest treatment of the suspect and demonic nature of the imagination. The devil grants to Mann's Faust, the composer Adrian Leverkühn, the traditional twenty-four years of heightened existence, at the end of which he shall succumb, via the syphilis he has already contracted, to the hell that awaits him. Leverkühn's creativity shall be intensified and he shall find, in his music, the true passion which, according to this highly sophisticated devil, can, at this late stage of men's culture, inhere only in ambiguity and irony. But a clause is attached to the pact — the eschewal of love. Hence, Leverkühn's genius, the devil goes on to say, will be that of sickness, a type of genius which life loves far more than the plodding progress of health. But Leverkühn's story is transmitted to the reader via a narrator for whom the composer's genius, however great its fascinations, is essentially suspect: the scholar Serenus Zeitblom, a representative of the humanistic tradition submerged and silenced during the Nazi era. Zeitblom writes his account of Leverkühn's life during the last two years of the war, ending as the Allied troops are marching into Germany: and he develops during the time of that narration from a bumbling, slightly absurd figure into a figure of moving dignity as he laments the fate of his country. Above all, Zeitblom is a *decent* man; and although Mann attempts no crude equation between Leverkühn's career and the course of Nazism, he does, by setting the decent against the damned, limited order against creative chaos, achieve the effect of a dialogue between the forces at work in the German — and, indeed, the human — psyche. Mann reverts here to his early theme of the contrast between the man of imagination and the man of the practical life — but the contrast here is far more subtly differentiated and has a far greater resonance.

In *Confessions of Felix Krull* (*Bekenntnisse des Felix Krull*, begun 1911, resumed 1951, published 1954, translated 1955), however, the man of imagination makes his last and most light-hearted appearance. The long line of Mann's artist figures, stretching from Hanno Buddenbrook and Tonio Kröger via no less a figure than Goethe (in *Lotte in Weimar*, 1940) to Leverkühn, culminates in Felix Krull, the artist as illusionist. Blessed with a combination of extreme good looks, quick wits and a flawless acting technique, Krull in effect makes his life his material, rising from obscure beginnings to the pleasures of assumed aristocracy and justifying his roguery with a paradoxical evaluation of himself as a practitioner of high moral self-discipline. In comic form, the novel is concerned with the moral dubiety of the aesthetic enterprise. But Mann only completed the first half of this parodistic exercise in the picaresque: completion in the traditional pattern would have had to involve Krull in some form of remorse and penitence — as it is, he leaves us in the full flush of triumph.

And this, perhaps, has its own appropriateness. Mann's ultimate stance is that of the humanist, concerned to explore those forces by which the health of life is threatened. Yet many readers have felt that the health of life fails to engage the full weight of Mann's creative interest, but is merely implicitly posited somewhere outside the text, theoretically deferred to but never imaginatively realized. Other serious disagreements have arisen: is Mann's famous irony an expression of balance and mature judgement or does it too often function as a means of evading the issues involved? Does his frequent play with paradox result in revealing perceptions or only in a kind of higher glibness? Are his novels over-schematized? These are problems which continue to be discussed: but discussed in the context of the realization that Mann's commanding stature as a novelist — his range, creative energy and sustained technical mastery — can hardly be seriously questioned.

Further reading

See: *Gesammelte Werke* (12 vols, 1960). Other translations include: *The Holy Sinner* (1951); *The Black Swan* (1954); *Stories of Three Decades* (1936). See also: E. Heller, *The Ironic German* (1958); R. Gray, *The German Tradition in Literature* (1965); T.J. Reed, *Thomas Mann: The Uses of Tradition* (1974); T.E. Apter, *Thomas Mann: The Devil's Advocate* (1978); Nigel Hamilton: *Brothers Mann: The Lives of Heinrich and Thomas Mann* (1978); Herbert Lehnert and Eva Wessell (eds) *A Companion to the Works of Thomas Mann* (2004).

CORBET STEWART

MANNHEIM, Karl

1893–1947

German sociologist

Karl Mannheim, a founder of the sociology of knowledge (*Wissenssoziologie*), was born in

Budapest, studied at the universities of Budapest, Berlin, Paris and Freiburg, had academic posts at Heidelberg, Frankfurt, the London School of Economics and the University of London, and died in London. His biography, which is one of intellectual and geographical migration, falls into three main phases: Hungarian (to 1920), German (1920–33), British (1933–47). Among the most important early intellectual influences upon Mannheim are the Hungarians **Georg Lukács**, Béla Zalay, Bernhard Alexander and Geza Revesz, and the Germans **Georg Simmel**, **Edmund Husserl**, Heinrich Rickert and Emil Lask. Mannheim was also strongly influenced by the writings of **Karl Marx**, **Max Weber**, Alfred Weber, Max Scheler and **Georg Dilthey**. Through these and other writers, German historicism, Marxism, phenomenology, sociology and – much later – Anglo-Saxon pragmatism became decisive influences upon his work.

The writings of Karl Mannheim's Hungarian phase – primarily on literary and philosophical themes – remain largely untranslated. His essay *Lélek és Cultura* ('Soul and Culture', 1918) – which shows the influence of Georg Simmel's philosophical ideas – is a notable and interesting exception. It demonstrates Mannheim's first, tentative attempts to go beyond the German idealist view of history and society. In the German phase, Mannheim's most productive, he gradually turns from philosophy to sociology although he never abandons philosophical questions and concerns himself particularly with the investigation of the possible social roots of culture and knowledge. Many of his essays on methodological, epistemological and substantive aspects of the new sociology of knowledge – as theory of the existentiality of thought – have become sociological classics. In this period, Mannheim writes on the interpretation of *Weltanschauung*, on the structural analysis of epistemology, on historicism, on the ideological and sociological interpretation of intellectual phenomena, on conservative thought, on the problem of generations, on competition as a cultural phenomenon, and

on the nature of economic ambition. Two early essays (1922–4) posthumously published and translated as *Structures of Knowledge* (1980) and particularly Mannheim's most influential work, *Ideology and Utopia* (*Ideologie und Utopie*, 1929, trans. 1936), were also written during this period. All these writings testify to Mannheim's ambitious attempts to prepare the ground for and carry out a comprehensive sociological analysis of the structures of knowledge. In *Ideology and Utopia*, he tries to show that all mental structures with the exception of the knowledge of the natural sciences are context-dependent and therefore different in distinct social and historical settings. The sociology of knowledge, as developed here by Mannheim, though founded upon the analysis of ideology, abandons its original Marxist formulation, according to which ideology is 'necessarily false consciousness'. Mannheim reformulates the problem of ideology and distinguishes between two conceptions of ideology: (1) the 'particular conception', in which the total mental structure of an asserting subject is *not* yet called into question or seen as determined by its social and historical location; and (2) the 'total conception', in which the subject's entire categorical apparatus is related to, and derived from, the social and historical situation. The sociology of knowledge, as an exponent of the total conception of ideology, is thus concerned with the ways in which objects present themselves to the subject according to the differences in their social location. Mannheim argues that this reformulation of the concept of ideology has created a thoroughly new situation, analogous to a transformation of quantity into quality; as soon as suspicion of ideology is asserted about one's own situation, i.e. with the emergence of the 'general-total conception of ideology', the simple theory of ideology develops into the sociology of knowledge, and the whole noological structure is seen as 'ideological', as determined by the social and historical location of individuals and groups. As a sociologically oriented history of ideas, the sociology of knowledge makes the existentiality of thought its research focus, and investigates the specific expressions of this existentiality together with the different structures of consciousness which are its result. The sociology of knowledge thus relates the entire thought structure of the asserting subject in two ways to the social and historical situations: (1) by attempting to show when and to what extent the structures of social location participate in the production of mental and intellectual phenomena; and (2) by inquiring if and in what sense thought is concretely influenced by 'social existence'.

Ideology and Utopia and its related essays on the sociology of knowledge became the centre of attention of a vigorous intellectual dispute in Germany towards the end of the Weimar Republic, in part because of the, as many critics argued, 'relativistic' implications of Mannheim's argument. (Mannheim, however, never accepted this charge of relativism but claimed that, on the contrary, his brand of 'relationism' prepared the ground for a new comprehensive 'perspective' capable of transcending heretofore fragmented and partial social and political perspectives; the 'socially unattached' intelligentsia, he maintained, had an instrumental role in developing such a synthetizing perspective.) The sociology of knowledge dispute was concerned with the most important epistemological and methodological issues confronting German sociology and, though involving a considerable range of theoretical and philosophical traditions, centred eventually on the relationship between Marxism and the sociology of knowledge, with Marxists and Critical Theorists alike often linking the latter's sudden popularity to a neutralization and betrayal of Marxism.

Mannheim's British phase was in some ways foreshadowed by the more pragmatic and practical orientation already evident in his writings prior to his emigration from Germany, in particular *Die Gegenwartsaufgaben der Soziologie* ('Present Tasks of Sociology', 1932). The comprehensive analysis of the structure of modern society must, Mannheim argues, be the task of applied sociology, especially through democratic social plan-

ning, in which education must occupy a central role. These new emphases in Mannheim's thought developed and matured rapidly, under the influence of Anglo-Saxon pragmatism, after he settled in Great Britain. Three books are of particular importance here: *Man and Society in an Age of Reconstruction* (*Mensch und Gesellschaft im Zeitalter des Umbaus*, 1935, trans. 1940), *Diagnosis of Our Time* (1943) and the posthumously published essays *Freedom, Power and Democratic Planning* (1959). During this period, reflecting Mannheim's intellectual and practical concerns, he founded Routledge and Kegan Paul's 'International Library of Sociology and Social Reconstruction'.

The original themes of the sociology of knowledge were formulated in Germany during a period of major social crisis, and may be seen, as Mannheim himself saw them, as the product of one of the greatest social dissolutions and transformations, accompanied by the highest form of self-consciousness and self-criticism. The renewed interest in the problems posed by the sociology of knowledge today, often accompanied by a fascination with Weimar Germany's experience of political, social and cultural achievements and dissolutions, perhaps reflects the experience of a similar crisis in our own period and may therefore be said to owe more to the course of events than to the course of analytical progress.

Further reading

Other works include: *Essays on the Sociology of Knowledge* (1952); *Essays on Sociology and Social Psychology* (1953); *Essays on the Sociology of Culture* (1956); *Systematic Sociology: An Introduction to the Study of Society* (1957); *An Introduction to the Sociology of Education* (with W.A.C. Stewart, 1962). See also: David Kettler, *Marxismus und Kultur: Mannheim und Lukács in den ungarischen Revolutionen 1918/19* (1967); Gunter W. Remmling, *The Sociology of Karl Mannheim* (1975); A.P. Simonds, *Karl Mannheim's Sociology of Knowledge* (1978); Henk E.S. Woldring, *Karl Mannheim: The Development of His Thought* (1987); Brian Longhurst, *Karl Mannheim and Knowledge* (1988).

VOLKER MEJA
NICO STEHR

MANSFIELD, Katherine

1883–1923

New Zealand writer

Though Katherine Mansfield (born Kathleen Mansfield Beauchamp) spent most of her adult life in Europe, she clung to memories of her native New Zealand to provide a background for some of her best short stories. Her father, a banker from Wellington, allowed her to study music in London provided she came home after three years. She obeyed him, but was allowed to leave once more for England, where she embarked on a career as a writer. Following an impulsive early marriage in 1909, lasting just twenty-four hours, she met the influential literary critic John Middleton Murry, and the pair began a relationship which endured until her death. Mansfield herself was an unsparing judge of her fellow authors, but made friends with **Virginia Woolf** and **D.H. Lawrence**, stoutly defending the latter's work even when he turned against her. She provided a model for the ruthless character of Gudrun in his *Women In Love*.

With the outbreak of the Great War, Mansfield and Murry, together with Lawrence and his wife Frieda, retreated from London, first to Buckinghamshire and then to Cornwall. Katherine was severely affected by the death of her brother Leslie while serving on the Western Front. Her health, already weakened by untreated gonorrhoea, was now steadily undermined by tuberculosis, for which she sought treatment at sanatoriums in France and Switzerland. Under the influence of the journalist A.R. Orage, whose *New Age* magazine had published several of her stories, Mansfield sought guidance from the popular guru Gurdjieff at his psychic healing centre outside Paris. Her death was doubtless hastened by the spartan nature of the treatment involved.

Mansfield's work shows the strong influence of **Anton Chekhov**, whose writings had begun to appear in English translation during her early years in London, especially in its brilliant awareness of suppressed impulses and its remarkable sensitivity to even the smallest touches of sound, light and colour. In stories such as 'Pictures', the account of an elderly singer's efforts to find work as a film extra, 'The Little Governess', in which an innocent English girl in Munich loses her job after fleeing from a would-be seducer, and 'Je ne parle pas français', where the author describes her affair with the French poet Francis Carco, she displays a rare gift for portraying marginalized or unsympathetic characters.

She was responsible for deepening and extending the technical reach of the short story in English, making a boldly impressionistic use of dialogue, which owes much, in its scrupulous rendering of the pitch and timbre of words and phrases, to her years as a music student. Rather than the communication itself, it is a lack of communication when this is most needed on which Mansfield chooses to dwell. At her best she avoids sentiment, preferring instead to highlight haphazard cruelty, menace, deception and suddenly violent impulses, exploiting all these for their comic as much as their serious potential.

Mansfield's talent flowered early, and her first collection, *In a German Pension* (1911) though she later rejected it, is accomplished and sophisticated. Her longest work, *Prelude* (1918) is a meticulously wrought novella based on her early life in New Zealand. Her influence can most obviously be felt on American women writers such as Flannery O'Connor, **Carson McCullers** and **Eudora Welty**, all of whom, with varying success, reproduced her impressionistic technique and caught a similar sense of lurking evil. While not changing the nature of the short story genre singlehanded, Katherine Mansfield, through her acuteness of focus, vastly expanded its artistic potential as a literary medium.

Further reading

Other works include: *The Garden Party* (1922); *The Dove's Nest* (1923); and *Something Childish* (1924). See: John Middleton Murry, *Katherine Mansfield and Other Literary Studies* (1959); Jeffrey

Meyers, *Katherine Mansfield: A Biography* (1978); Anthony Alpers, *The Life of Katherine Mansfield* (1980); Jane Phillimore, *Katherine Mansfield* (1990); Patrick D. Morrow, *Katherine Mansfield's Fiction* (1993); Mary Burgan, *Illness, Gender, and Writing* (1994); Jan Pilditch (ed.) *The Critical Response to Katherine Mansfield* (1995); Angela Smith, *Katherine Mansfield and Virginia Woolf* (1999) and *Katherine Mansfield: A Literary Life* (2000); Jeffrey Meyers, *Katherine Mansfield: A Darker View* (2002).

JONATHAN KEATES

MAO ZEDONG (MAO TSE-TUNG)

1893–1976

Chinese leader

'Chairman Mao', as he was known during the later stages of his career, was by any measure a world-historic figure. With the exception of Taiwan (then called Formosa), which fell into the hands of his arch-enemy Jiang Jieshi (Chiang Kaishek), and some other, smaller islands, he re-unified a vast nation-empire containing a sixth of humankind that, following the final collapse of the last imperial dynasty, the Qing, in 1912, had endured thirty-seven years of uncertain progress, exacerbated by Japanese occupation. Yet the brighter future that seemed implicit in Mao Zedong's proclamation of a People's Republic in 1949 did not eventuate. Instead, Mao instituted a tyranny that culminated in the notorious, but at the time little understood, Cultural Revolution – launched in 1966, and only 'officially' ended ten years later with his demise. Yet such was Mao's charismatic reputation, both among portions of China's population and among developing nations in Asia, Africa and Latin America, that he was widely perceived as a force for the good. In the aftermath of World War II, when Europe's colonial empires were palpably past their sell-by date, but when the USA was emerging as an interventionist superpower, Mao, who coined the very term 'third world', was the undisputed champion of anti-imperialism, to the extent that his image was cherished as an icon by left-wing students and other radicals, in both Europe and America.

Based on a much firmer knowledge of the quarter-century period of his rule in China, Mao has since been subjected to fierce and unflattering re-appraisal, anecdotally supported by revelations of megalomania, sexual depravity and physical decline contained in *The Private Life of Chairman Mao* (1994), a grotesquely intimate memoir written by Mao's long-serving personal physician, Zhisui Li. While the sheer numbers of those who perished as a result of Mao's ill-conceived policies, running into tens of millions, are sufficient in themselves to bespeak a despot, it is also clear that Mao's impact on China's economy was ruinous. Even so, the concept of Mao as founder of the modern Chinese nation, of Mao the 'great helmsman' in the parlance of the self-propaganda he assiduously promoted, sticks. In the great, 4,000-year sweep of Chinese history, he may even be seen as a traditionalist as much as a revolutionary. Towards the end of his life he increasingly extolled the virtues of Qin Shihuangdi, the 'first' emperor who established the imperial throne in 221 BC on the back of a narrow 'legalist' ideology that, countervailing the paternalist precepts of Confucianism, insisted on the observance of draconian laws. For all its overt debts to **Marx**, **Lenin**, **Stalin** and other communist ideologues, communism as redefined by Mao amounted to a refashioning of an abiding strand in Chinese affairs, its necessity and success, temporary or otherwise, a reflection of the innate difficulties in furnishing an entity as populous, culturally diverse and geographically extensive as China with any sort of centralized government at all; and it has been claimed that Mao's actual achievement was to found a new 'dynasty', based on the one-party state, with the difference that, unlike all previous dynasties, succession is determined not by heredity, but by opaque power-struggles at the apex of a distinctly pyramidal and authoritarian power structure in which cadres, apparatchiks and politburo members have merely replaced the old and equally hierarchical mandarinate.

What is seldom questioned is Mao's formidable political skill, ultimately self-serving though it became. During his rise to supremacy over the nascent Chinese Communist Party (CCP) he repeatedly faced the censure of comrades, but each time toughed it out to consolidate his position.

Born in Shaoshan village in the central province of Hunan, Mao entertained a strong dislike for his father – a 'rich' peasant who profiteered from hoarding grain and whose kind became earmarked for persecution by a government largely moulded by his son a half century later. The family's relative wealth, however, enabled Mao to acquire an education. In 1911 he enrolled at a secondary school in Changsha. Between 1913 and 1918 he attended a teacher training course at Hunan's Fourth Normal School, but although he organized evening classes for workers and contributed to the radical *Xin Qingnian* ('New Youth Magazine'), edited by the future founder of the CCP, Chen Duxiu, it was not until he accepted a post as an assistant to Li Dazhao, the librarian of Beijing University, that Mao found his true political direction.

Under Li's tutelage Mao was introduced to the core tenets of Marxism–Leninism, while also learning about such anarchists as **Proudhon** and **Kropotkin**. As importantly, Li stressed the validity of fomenting a revolutionary spirit among the agrarian classes, and brought Mao to the attention of Chen. Mao was not, however, a founding member of the CCP, which, with the backing of the Soviet Comintern (Communist International), was secretly inaugurated in Shanghai in 1920. By then, Mao had returned to Hunan as a junior school teacher. His commitment to communism was evidenced both by a Marxist study group he set up in Changsha, and by his vociferous support for a boycott of Japanese goods in the wake of the May Fourth Movement of 1919, when Chinese students confronted a Republican government which had acquiesced in Japan's acquisition of German concessions in Shandong province, in accordance with the provisions of the Treaty of Versailles. Only in the following year, 1921, did Mao join the CCP's inner circle, attending its First Congress in Shanghai and becoming Party Secretary for Hunan.

Initially the CCP was dependent on the USSR, to the extent that its policies were directed by Moscow through a succession of political 'agents'. These agents demanded that Chinese communists follow the Russian model by building support among China's urban proletariat, and that they co-operate with the Guomindang, the Chinese Nationalist Party which, under the leadership first of Sun Yat Sen, and from 1925 Jiang Jieshi, endeavoured to restore Chinese unity after the Republic had fallen foul of contending warlords following the death of its first president, Yuan Shikai, in 1916. Such policies did not appeal to Mao, who, although a pragmatist when he had to be, sought a communist state on Chinese terms; and it was because of this, as well as a string of personality clashes, that he frequently fell out with his associates in the years before 1935, when Mao succeeded in stamping his authority on the Party.

From as early as 1923, when he became a Central Committee member, Mao consistently argued that only by mobilizing the peasantry would communism triumph in China. In February 1927 he summarized his views in a 'Report on the Peasant Movement in Hunan', knowing that it would be strongly criticized by the Comintern agent, and in September orchestrated the 'Autumn Harvest Uprising', an attempt to set up a rural soviet in his home province. The failure of this, and of a similar uprising in southern Guangdong, led by Peng Pai, meant that Mao was temporarily excluded from the Party's top echelon. But if Moscow insisted that the CCP co-operate with the Guomindang, the Guomindang, also supported by the USSR, was unminded to co-operate with the CCP, and Jiang was ruthless in liquidating communists in Shanghai and other central cities.

It was against this background that Mao's views began to prevail. A decision was taken to support 'base areas' in the deep countryside. The most significant of these was created by Mao and Zhu De in 1928 in Jinggang, a mountainous region of Jiangxi province, adjacent to Hunan. In effect, Mao and Zhu established a local but autonomous communist government in opposition to Jiang's republican government. Jiang responded by ordering the encirclement of Jianggangshan, in a bid to flush the rebels out. By now, however, the Guomindang had also to contend with growing Japanese militarism – in 1931 Japan, on the slenderest of pretexts, seized Manchuria in the north-east – and it was not until the summer of 1934 that a fifth encirclement campaign looked likely to achieve Jiang's objectives.

Seemingly trapped, Mao and Zhu audaciously led their force of 100,000 ill-equipped men through Guomindang lines in October – the beginning of the Red Army's legendary but also desperate 'Long March' through southern China to Yunnan, and then north to Shaanxi province, where, having lost all but 6,000 of his troops, Mao set up a new base area centred on Yanan. But if the Long March reflected the lowest ebb of the CCP's fortunes, it also made Mao. At a crucial meeting of the communist leadership held at Zunyi (Guizhou province) in February 1935, he persuaded a majority of his associates that the Comintern's strategy was suicidal. Although Mao still faced opposition from Zhang Guotao and other 'Chinese Bolsheviks', henceforth his ascendancy was secure.

In Shaanxi, far from the Guomindang capital at Nanjing, Mao was able to put his theories into practice. Playing his own nationalist card, he also insisted that the communists should take the lead in resisting the Japanese. To this end he extrapolated in full his concept of 'people's war', combining guerrilla tactics with main offences while conducting an unremitting propaganda campaign to win over the populace. By blending in with a well-disposed civilian population, communist guerrillas could operate deep inside enemy lines. It was not until the Allied defeat of Japan in 1945, however, that Mao could realistically contemplate gaining control of all China. For a year, the communists and the Guomindang, now backed by the USA, uneasily shared power, but in June 1946 the inevitable civil war broke out. At first the better armed Guomindang prevailed, but without decisive popular support their cause was stymied. In 1948 the People's Liberation Army (PLA), as the Red Army now called itself, began inflicting defeat on Guomindang forces in open battle. Beijing was taken in January 1949, followed by the capture of Nanjing in April and Shanghai in May. The People's Republic was proclaimed, by Mao himself, in Beijing's Tiananmen Square on 1 October; two months later Jiang fled to Taiwan, to establish a far smaller Chinese republic.

Despite much slimmer resources, it was the Taiwanese, not the communist, republic, that prospered. In mainland China, as elsewhere, the communists' skills were well suited to managing a war, but not peace. The CCP's neo-Stalinist recourse was to institute a totalitarian style of government that, among the totalitarianisms of the twentieth century, ranked as one of the most bloodily repressive. For this, Mao was largely responsible. Using the 'mass-line campaign' as his favoured political instrument, he targeted all the main elements of Chinese society, beginning with capitalists and reactionaries, but extending to elements within the government itself and to Mao's hallowed peasantry.

Initially the People's Republic of China (PRC) reached out to the global socialist movement at large. New laws were introduced granting women access to divorce courts, among other rights, and in December 1949 Mao visited Moscow to express solidarity with Stalin. Thereafter, however, he went determinedly his own way, severing remaining links with the USSR in 1960. As in imperial times, officials were graded according to twenty-four ranks, and by the end of 1950 the first of many purges was in full swing. Not only were former Guomindang followers hunted down, but, as China entered the Korean War against America, so too were 'foreign sympathizers'.

This was followed in 1951 by a 'Five Antis Campaign', aimed against China's 'business class'. Landlords and intellectuals were Mao's next victims, followed by rich peasants. At the same time, the PRC reasserted China's historic hegemony over Tibet, and also the huge western territory of Xinjiang, then mainly inhabited by Uighur and other Muslims. In 1952 the first steps were taken towards 'collectivization' – in effect the abolition of small land-holdings to be replaced by state-run 'co-operative' farms. In 1953 grain markets were closed, and a state monopoly in agricultural produce enforced. Farmers in Guangdong and other southern provinces protested violently, and were violently suppressed. In 1955, during the 'Little Leap Forward', full collectivization was instituted and the last vestiges of private property abolished. In 1956 a system of 'internal passports' was introduced, bringing urban migration and other types of movement under tight government control.

But all this was as nothing compared to what ensued. Some of Mao's Central Committee colleagues, notably Liu Shaoqi and **Deng Xiaoping**, had begun voicing doubts as to the desirability of some of Mao's policies. Mao's response was to launch the 'Hundred Flowers Campaign' of 1957 – on the face of it a gesture at liberalization, since it encouraged intellectuals and others to express their opinions, but in reality a ploy to entice Mao's critics into the open, where they could then be persecuted. At the same time an 'Anti-Rightist Campaign' inaugurated a policy of banishing alleged dissidents from the cities to rural labour camps for 're-education'. Then came the wholly extraordinary 'Great Leap Forward' of 1958, Mao's attempt to drive economic development at such a pace that China would swiftly overtake not only the USSR but also Britain.

By any reckoning the Great Leap Forward was catastrophic. While rural and industrial collectivization was replaced by vast 'people's communes', one instruction was for everybody to increase steel production by melting down everyday metallic objects in 'backyard furnaces'. Another was for the planting of grain seed in a way no rational agriculturalist could conceivably have condoned. As a result an estimated thirty million died of starvation, and Chinese industry sank to its knees. Yet even though Mao himself was among the last to learn of the actual consequences of his initiative – such was the kowtowing that surrounded him that no one until Defence Minister Peng Dehuai in August 1959 dared submit an adverse report – the political fallout was considerable. Although Peng was speedily replaced as Defence Minister by the hardliner Lin Biao, and although Mao launched yet another anti-rightist campaign, purging many middle-ranking cadres, Mao felt it expedient to stand down as head of state, while continuing as Chairman of the Party. By 1962 it was apparent that, on a day-to-day basis at least, Mao was no longer in supreme control.

Liu Shaoqi, the new head of state, and others on the politburo had prevailed. But a Mao so constrained was a Mao at his most lethal. As early as July 1962 he began his counter-offensive. Backed by Lin Biao and the state's security apparatus he launched an attack on 'right revisionists', emphasizing the enduring importance of class struggle. Then he introduced his estranged fourth wife, the malevolent and hypochondriac former Shanghai actress Jiang Qing, on to the public stage. In 1963 he upped the ante by mounting a 'Socialist Education' campaign, with Liu in its sights, while Lin published *Quotations from Chairman Mao*, a slim but hugely effective anthology of Mao's pronouncements that became universally known as 'The Little Red Book'. For the next two years Mao maintained the pressure, adroitly manipulating the *People's Daily* and other media, until a bursting point was reached. Then, using Jiang Qing as his mouthpiece and students as his henchmen, in May 1966 he floated the 'Great Proletarian Cultural Revolution', aimed at the entire class of administrators and professionals.

Within weeks 'Red Guards' – schoolchildren as well as students – ran rampant through the streets of Beijing and other cities, waving copies of the Little Red Book and photographs of Mao. No one, least of all politburo members, was immune from their acrimonious attentions. Teachers, doctors, factory managers and politicians were forced to make abject confessions of their errors in public, during so-called 'struggle sessions'. Massed rallies and 'big character' posters followed. As turbulence spread through China, Liu and Deng were castigated as 'capitalist roadsters'.

This, though, was only the first phase of the Cultural Revolution, which claimed a million lives or more. Although Mao swiftly achieved his personal objectives – the overthrow of Liu (who died in ignominious circumstances in 1969), and the removal of Deng (hounded into internal exile) – the forces he had unleashed threatened to spin out of control after the Red Guards began factionalizing and fighting among themselves. To restore order, in September 1967 Mao authorized the PLA to open fire on radicals 'in self-defence'. The following year 'revolutionary committees' packed with army-men began taking control of schools, hospitals and factories, and increasing numbers of Red Guards were themselves deported to the deep countryside for lengthy spells of re-education, giving rise to the phenomenon of China's 'lost generation'.

The Cultural Revolution – which in essence made a political process based on manufactured class antagonisms itself the goal of political activity – threw other problems Mao's way, in particular the rivalrous ambitions of Lin Biao and Jiang Qing, at the head of her notorious 'Gang of Four'. Both were disgraced, Lin dying in an air-crash while attempting to flee. But by relying on the loyalty of his perennial and popular foreign minister Zhou Enlai, as well as rehabilitating the supremely able Deng, Mao continued to manipulate those around him with apparent ease. Further, in February 1972 he stunned everyone by welcoming President Nixon to Beijing. Designed to infuriate the USSR, Mao's about-turn in Sino-American relations profoundly affected the geopolitical balance at the height of the Cold War.

Mao died on 9 September 1976, following a run of heart attacks. He bequeathed his successors, Hua Guofeng and Deng Xiaoping, an unenviable inheritance. By promoting anarchic dystopia in place of the conventional utopianism of communism, Mao fostered a deep mistrust, as well as a fear, of politics and politicians in China; by regularly deploying such terms as 'left deviationist' and 'right opportunist' against his personal enemies regardless of the substance of such accusations, he consolidated his own power-base only at the cost of debasing political discourse; and by his repeated purges of officialdom, he inhibited the confidence and self-esteem of the new political elite itself. Mao, however, seems to have been impervious of the effect he had. His character was that of a traditional strongman who finally had no sentimental attachment towards anyone or anything other than his own survival. In his polemical writings, directness of purpose and expression yielded some of the best-known maxims of the last century – 'Political power grows out of the barrel of a gun', for instance, or 'A revolution is not a dinner party'. Yet Mao's was also a complex personality, as the calligraphy of such poems as he wrote reveals: an untutored and unkempt hand, but startlingly determined.

Further reading

Other works include: Selected Writings of Mao Tse-tung (1961–77) and are still available from the Foreign Languages Press of Beijing, which also publishes his Poems (1976). Good biographies include Stuart Schram, Mao Tse-tung (1967); Dick Wilson, Mao: The People's Emperor (1979); P. Rule, Mao Zedong (1984); and, especially, Philip Short, Mao: A Life (1999). See also: Edgar Snow, Red Star Over China (1937); Roderick MacFarquar, The Origins of the Cultural Revolution (3 vols, from 1974); Harrison Salisbury, The Long March: The Untold Story (1986); J.K. Fairbank, The Great Chinese Revolution 1966–1982 (1987); Stuart Schram, The Political Thought of Mao Tse-tung (1989); Dick Wilson, China's Revolutionary War (1991); and Jasper Becker, Hungry Ghosts: China's

Secret Famine (1996), exposing the full horror of the Great Leap Forward.

JUSTIN WINTLE

MAPPLETHORPE, Robert

1946–89

US photographer

Robert Mapplethorpe first achieved prominence in the 1980s for his photographic representations of New York's gay subculture, even though the corpus of his work also contained still-lifes, portraits and scenes of everyday life captured by a young man growing up in an exciting urban environment. The candid nature of Mapplethorpe's work, lifestyle and final battle with AIDS have been regarded as emancipatory in communicating the gay experience. Typically he concentrated his artistic interest on the male body as a way of conveying his own arousal at the prohibited, using a formalist approach to capitalize on the provocative aspects of pornography in the then-tawdry society of New York's 42nd Street.

Mapplethorpe's photography duly became the focus of a conservative reaction to the 'illicit content' of much contemporary art, beginning with his 1989 exhibition 'The Perfect Moment', which generated heated controversy in both Washington and Cincinnati, and provoked an on-going debate about government funding of the 'avant-garde'. In Cincinnati the exhibition was forcibly closed. During the ensuing obscenity trial several well-known art curators testified that the classic form of Mapplethorpe's images, and his sheer technique as a photographer, provided a legitimate counterpoint to the obvious raunchiness of his subject-matter. Yet paradoxically this interpretation if anything sanitized and detracted from Mapplethorpe's own perspective, in which sharp focus, close cropping and subtle differentiations of texture were deployed to enhance, not anaesthetize, the content of his pictures, however 'shocking'.

The third in a family of six children, Mapplethorpe grew up in a middle-class district of Queens, near New York City. At sixteen he left home for art school, branching out from the conventions of his upbringing to pursue and vent yearnings for the scandalous and outlandish. Soon after leaving art school he began experimenting with photography, taking Polaroids of himself and others in casual and exotic poses. Among others of this period are self-portraits with his pants down, presaging the exposures of his later, mature work. Then, in the 1970s, he quickly became closely involved with the city's gay underworld, introducing himself to drugs and sadomasochism, and befriending the punk rocker Patti Smith, who served as both muse and sitter. Soon after Mapplethorpe embarked on a romantic liaison with the collector and curator Sam Wagstaff, whose interest in the history of photography expanded Mapplethorpe's visual lexicon and helped determine the compositions in his work during the late 1970s and 1980s.

Yet the excitement and anxiety latent in Mapplethorpe's work ultimately stems from his own engagement in, and fascination with, the sexually forbidden, or socially constructed transgression. He never attempted to disguise his interest in such practices as sadomasochism, but rather sought to capture their provocative qualities with his camera. Many of Mapplethorpe's compositions were conscious reinterpretations of photographs taken by **Man Ray**, who also had an interest in transgressive sexuality, the difference being that, in the later twentieth century, Mapplethorpe's images have found a much broader reception.

As his skills ripened, Mapplethorpe emphasized the maleness and masculine attributes of his homosexual subjects, many of them black men. Yet in 1980–2 he also turned his attention to the female physique, portraiting Lisa Lyon, a white body-builder who had won the first World Women's Body Building Championship. A little predictably, it was this project that initially encouraged the non-gay art world to take a serious interest in Mapplethorpe. Commissions for society portraits followed, and, despite contracting HIV in the first wave of the epidemic, Mapplethorpe survived long enough to attend a retrospective of his work at the Whitney Museum of Modern Art.

Further reading

See: Anne Danto, *Playing with Edge: The Photographic Achievement of Robert Mapplethorpe* (1996) provides a critical analysis of Mapplethorpe's role in contemporary photography. See also Peter F. Spooner, 'The Trials of Robert Mapplethorpe', in Elizabeth C. Childs (ed.) *Suspended License: Censorship in the Visual Arts* (1997); and Richard Meyer, *Outlaw Representation: Censorship and Homosexuality in Twentieth-Century American Art* (2002).

ANNE K. SWARTZ

MARC, Franz

1880–1916

German painter

Marc was one of the leading painters of the German Expressionist movement. 'Expressionism' was a term coined by critics, not by artists, in an attempt to indicate that after a period when the French had led modern painting with their Impressionism, German art had taken the next step. Marc, whose mother was a native of Alsace and who had been influenced, on visits to France, by Impressionist, Post-Impressionist and eventually by Cubist painting, did not subscribe to the nationalism which marked some German artists of the time, not least because his closest artistic contact was the Russian **Kandinsky**, with whom he created Der Blaue Reiter ('The Blue Rider') movement in Munich in 1911, a movement and grouping of artists with an international membership. Kandinsky himself later recalled this second Expressionist movement (after *Die Brücke*), for all those who participated in its exhibitions, in these terms: 'we were two'. French, Russian and Italian Futurist influences there were, but the international flavour of the modern movement had also to co-exist with Marc's awareness of his own national identity. In a

letter of 1915, written from the battle-field, he said:

> I am myself … so wholly German in the old sense, one from the land of German Dreamers, Poets, and Thinkers, the land of Kant and Bach of Schwind [a Romantic painter of whose work he was particularly fond], of Goethe, Hölderlin and **Nietzsche** … [that I wonder uncomfortably] whether the Slavs, especially the Russians, won't soon take over the Spiritual leadership of the world, while Germany's spirit grows worse and worse, involved in business and war matters. But any thought always leads me back to my good little Deer!

Marc's idealist and religious spirit was present in the letter – he had begun a study of philosophy and theology – but the mention of deer leads us to the work for which he has always been best known – as a painter of animals. There were indeed many paintings of deer, some of which he liked to keep in his garden at Sindelsdorf to the south of Munich, but the painting for which he became most famous, and with which he conquered even conventional spirits, was called *Der Turm der blauen Pferde* ('The Tower of Blue Horses') of 1913. The painting has been lost, as have many modern works which were considered by the Nazis to represent what they called *entartete* ('degenerate') art, but photographs show a large painting, vertical in format, where four horses, their heads rising one above another, are set in a landscape whose forms, like those of the horses themselves, bear traces of geometrical simplification in a sub-Cubist manner close to that of Henri Le Fauconnier, one of whose works had been exhibited with the Blaue Reiter group and illustrated in their *Almanac* (1912). Marc's painting was provided with a summit – a rainbow – in neo-Romantic manner.

The Tower is a leading work from Marc's 'middle period', if such a term is applicable to a career which, juvenilia excepted, lasted a bare four years. He had studied at the Munich Academy from 1900 (his own father was a competent landscape painter working in the current tonal manner of Lenbach). His very first paintings were similarly naturalistic. But in 1910 he painted his well-known *Three Red Horses*, followed in 1911 by *The Large Blue Horses*. As can be seen from these titles, naturalism was now abandoned, partly encouraged by the Post-Impressionist works he had seen in Paris and in Munich and furthered by his own belief in the spiritual value of colour. He had no precise and consistent language of colour, nor even the synaesthetic beliefs of Kandinsky, but a belief that art should speak to the soul on an intuitive level. Another aspect of this style is evident in the linear rhythms created both by the horses themselves and in their relationship with their landscape setting. The curvilinear forms seem to owe something to *Jugendstil* (German Art Nouveau) and the holism implied here in morphological terms where horses and setting are seen in unified terms was soon, through the influence of Robert Delaunay, to be supplemented by a colouristic holism. Marc, with his friend the Rhenish painter August Macke, visited Delaunay in Paris in 1912. The Frenchman's 'Orphism' was a 'Pure Painting' (both terms were coined by **Apollinaire**) which dispensed with the object. This art, with Kandinsky's, was enough to encourage Marc and Macke to turn toward a non-objective art. Marc appreciated, too, **Tolstoy's** belief that art should have a purpose, and reconciled this seemingly all too functional belief with his own spirituality by seeing the purpose of art not in social but in ontological terms. After a period of seeking the 'animalization' of painting (which was itself a substitute for the 'impurity' of the human form) this philosophical artist came eventually to find something 'hateful' in all nature and found the abstract form (though not wholly devoid of empathetic implications) to be a purer substitute in both moral and aesthetic terms. Thus in 1914 he painted his *Hot, Playing, Fighting* and *Fragmented Forms*.

This process seems to be summed up in an unintentionally ironically titled drawing (ironic because he was in the artillery) which he made while at the front and titled *Arsenal for a Creation*. Two of his most important works had been painted in 1914. These were *Tirol* and *The Fate of Animals* (*Tierschicksale*), which were both works which could be considered prophetic. *Tirol* was the successor to a painting of 1913 called *Armes Land Tirol* ('The Unhappy Land of Tirol'), a mountain landscape with a graveyard and some skinny horses. *Tirol* itself is far more abstract, and only with reference to its predecessor can a mountain landscape where the light of sunrise and darkness do battle be deduced. No animal is present, but Marc softened these jagged forms by adding as an afterthought a form based on that of a primitive Bavarian woodcarving of the Virgin. Marc had chosen *The Book of Creation* as his subject for a projected series of Bible illustrations, to be undertaken by himself, **Paul Klee**, Alfred Kubin, Erich Heckel of Die Brücke and **Kokoschka**. He was not himself a Catholic, but this Virgin seems to bless the darker side of the landscape. All 'Blue Rider' artists admired primitive art forms, many of which were illustrated in their *Almanac*. Marc himself made some experiments with the Bavarian technique of *Hinterglasmalerei* (painting behind glass). He also made some sculptures of his own, including a *Tiger* which is very powerful and expressive.

The Fate of Animals, which can now be seen in Berne, had an alternative title written on the back by Marc: *Und alles Sein ist flammend Leid* ('All Being is Flaming Suffering'), a quotation from the Vedas. Marc was said by Klee to have considered yet another title: 'The Trees Show Their Rings, the Animals Their Veins.' The effect created is as of a forest fire from which beasts, not least deer, are fleeing. The painting was itself damaged by fire soon after execution and was carefully restored by Paul Klee. Its style is similar to *Tirol* but it is larger and may be considered Marc's masterpiece.

Marc was above all important as a painter whose work quickly became popular and which made 'modernism' accessible to a wide public. He cannot be said to have exerted a strong influence on the specific style of any other artist, but was important as one whose work demonstrated the viability of non-objective values in painting.

Further reading

Other works include: *Briefe 1914–1916 aus dem Felde* (1938) and *August Macke – Franz Marc Briefwechsel* (1964). His 'Aphorisms' can be found in *Franz Marc: Briefe, Aufzeichnungen und Aphorismen* (2 vols, 1920). Alois Schardt's catalogue of the works (1936) is now outdated, but has not been succeeded. See Klaus Lankheit, *Franz Marc* (1950); M. Rosenthal, *Franz Marc* (1989).

BRIAN PETRIE

MARCEAU, Marcel

1923–

French mime artist

The image of mime in the popular imagination is undoubtedly Marceau as 'Bip' in whiteface, hooped shirt, flared trousers and battered hat with red flower. Marceau has toured as Bip for over fifty years and has played in major venues all over the world, giving up to three hundred shows a year. The popularity of Marceau has significantly raised the status of mime as an art form. On the other hand, the notion of mime as silent storytelling that he embodies can be viewed as obscuring the more experimental work of practitioners such as Jacques Copeau (1879–1949), Etienne Decroux (1898–1991) and Jean-Louis Barrault (1910–94).

Marcel Mangel changed his name to Marceau in 1944 when he moved from Limoges to Paris. Earlier that year his father, a kosher butcher, had been killed in Auschwitz and Marcel who, with his brother, had been active in the Resistance, forged a new identity to escape a similar fate. In Paris Marceau enrolled in the school of Charles Dullin (1885–1949) and also studied with Etienne Decroux. Marceau learned the technique of corporal mime from Decroux and this was to serve as the base of his future work. Decroux, however, was disappointed with the use to which Marceau put the technique, feeling

that he was taking mime backwards to the nineteenth century and the work of Deburau, rather than embracing the artistic innovation of the twentieth.

Decroux himself had appeared with Barrault in Carné and Prévert's film *Les Enfants du Paradis* (1945) which is set in the nineteenth century. Decroux and Barrault's skills are used to reconstruct pantomimes based on the *commedia dell'arte* love triangle of Harlequin, Pierrot and Columbine. Barrault's performance as Baptiste Deburau was so successful that he created a stage performance based on the character. In 1946 Marceau joined Barrault's company to play Harlequin alongside Barrault's Pierrot in *Baptiste*. It was while working with Barrault that Marceau created Bip in 1947 and he began performing his own shows. From 1947 to 1964 he performed solo as Bip and as part of a company presenting mimodramas. The solo Bip shows, however, became dominant after 1952 when he began touring outside France.

In 1955 Marceau undertook a two-week run in New York which was phenomenally successful and extended to over six months. During the same period, Bip became known to millions through Marceau's television performances. He has continued to tour to major theatres around the world and perform to full houses ever since.

Marceau's success is not based on a simple attempt to return to the nineteenth-century tradition of mime. It is the synthesis of that tradition with twentieth-century technique and the tradition of silent movie comedy which has enabled him to reach a wide audience. Marceau regards Bip as a brother to **Chaplin's Tramp**, and Deburau's Pierrot. A measure of Marceau's success is that his performances as Bip, like Chaplin's films, continue to appeal to new audiences. Whether Marceau has produced work which will have any lasting significance after his death remains to be seen.

Further reading

See: Thomas Leabhart, *Modern and Post-Modern Mime* (1989); Kathryn Wylie, *Satyric and Heroic*

Mimes: Attitude as the Way of the Mime in Ritual and Beyond (1994); Annette Bercut Lust, *From the Greek Mimes to Marcel Marceau and Beyond: Mimes, Actors, Pierrots and Clowns: A Chronicle of the Many Visages of Mime in the Theatre* (2002). For younger readers: Marcel Marceau, *Bip in a Book* (2001).

FRANC CHAMBERLAIN

MARCONI, Guglielmo

1874–1937

Italian technologist

Marconi was born in Bologna in 1874 and by the end of the century he was famous. A year later, in 1901, his name entered the history books; by 1909 he had won the Nobel Prize. It was a remarkable rise. Marconi subsequently lived to the threshold of the Second World War, an institution rather than a man. He sustained his success: he pushed the technology ahead with nerve and flair; his companies prospered while most of his rivals fell by the wayside. He became rich, fêted, friend of the grand and the powerful.

Marconi was the 'Father of Wireless Telegraphy'. It was Marconi who, against the most weighty scientific opinion of the day, showed first that the 'wireless' could work, second that it could become a reliable system, and third that it could broadcast to the world. Marconi was a single-minded technologist, who worked incessantly to perfect and to develop his wireless system. Marconi's early success was a product of his independence of mind, tenacity, imagination, thoroughness. That he became widely known was partly, no doubt, because his demonstrations *worked*; but also because the press found Marconi's exploits irresistible. The communicators were always interested in developments in communications; they were also interested in this unlikely figure: bi-lingual, Anglo-Italian, well-connected, handsome and a ladies' man. This was a far cry from the typical image of the boorish technologist/unkempt inventor. But Marconi *was* a dedicated technologist: he worked long hours and never shrank from working in conditions like heaving seas, the

cabin awash with seawater, while he kept going determinedly with his transmissions. It was Marconi, more than anyone else, who, by the exercise of imagination and willpower, technical dexterity and flair, practical and commercial judgement, turned the world into an electronic village.

To appreciate Marconi's achievement it is necessary to bear in mind the kind of world into which he was born and in which he grew up. It was a world of new-found communications. Telegraphy was triumphant, with lines criss-crossing Europe and a substantial number of underwater cables linking continents. In 1866 **Brunel** had laid the transatlantic cable, a feat of olympian proportions. Everywhere messages were being carried on *wires* by the agency of this remarkable electricity.

It was in 1887 that **Heinrich Hertz** discovered radio waves or 'Hertzian waves', as they were known at first; but they were little more than a laboratory trick. They were weak, indiscriminate in wavelength, and could only be detected at distances of a few metres. Physicists such as Hertz himself, Oliver Lodge, Bose in India, Righi in Bologna, found them interesting because they confirmed the theoretical predictions of **James Clerk Maxwell**, but the interest was mainly in the phenomenon as a phenomenon, not in what it might be made to do.

Hertz died in 1894 and the young Marconi, then twenty, read an obituary notice about Hertz while holidaying in the Italian Alps. Suddenly the idea came to Marconi that it might be possible to use 'Hertzian waves' to convey messages around the world. He said later: 'In those mountains of Biellese I worked it out in my imagination.'

Suddenly Marconi, whose boyhood had been listless, divided and awkward – bullied at school in Florence, a failure in exams at Leghorn – saw his role in life. He had long been addicted to all things electrical and had infuriated his father with his constant experimenting with scientific toys. Now, however, he had an aim.

Back home at the Villa Grifone he set up his laboratory in the attic. He repeated the basic Hertzian experiments; he devised improvements; he lengthened the range, first to the door of the attic, then down the stairs, then on to the terrace, and finally out into the estate. By chance he discovered the efficacy of combining an aerial with an earth. He tried every permutation of arrangements, always searching for improved efficiency, and always using a minimum of theory. By 1895 his 'range' was over half a mile. He came to England with his talented Anglo-Irish mother to seek resources to go further. On Salisbury Plain his range was four miles, by 1897 nearly nine miles, and in 1899 he sent messages across the Straits of Dover.

Then Marconi staked his reputation and that of his company on sending messages across the Atlantic. It was considered a preposterous idea by the scientific opinion of the day, for the Hertzian waves were like light and would surely travel in straight lines, passing far above Marconi's Newfoundland kite-carried aerials! When, in December 1901, Marconi finally heard the three dots of the morse 'S' faintly audible behind the crackle of transatlantic static, he knew it was the start of a new era. From this beginning it took Marconi several years to perfect his transatlantic service, but he stuck at it and finally got it right.

When Marconi began on the research in 1894 there were three monumental reasons why his work *seemed* to be ill-advised: (1) it was not needed; telegraphy on wires was a proven, reliable, heavily capitalized system; (2) it was hard to see how 'wireless' could be financed; who would be induced to *pay* for information thrown indiscriminately to all and sundry? (3) the range would be very short, at best a hundred miles or so.

Many years later the *Electrician* commented that Marconi had two pieces of striking luck: his talented, well-connected, doting mother, Annie Jameson, and the existence of the ionosphere! It was the ionosphere which bounced his transmissions back to earth and confounded the scientific opposition. It was his mother who kept him going during 1894 and 1895, when he was considered an eccentric fool and the foundations of his triumphs were being laid.

Further reading

See: Address by Marconi to the Institution of Electrical Engineers, *Journal of the Institution of Electrical Engineers*, Vol. 28 (1899); Degna Marconi, *My Father Marconi* (1962); W.P. Jolly, *Marconi* (1972); Gavin Weightman, *Signor Marconi's Magic Box: The Invention that Sparked the Radio Revolution* (2003).

CHRISTOPHER ORMELL

MARCUSE, Herbert
1898–1979
German/US social philosopher

Regarded as the official ideologue of the 1968 'campus revolutions', Herbert Marcuse was born into a prominent and prosperous Berlin Jewish family, and educated at the crack Augusta Gymnasium and at the Universities of Berlin and Freiberg. In 1934, after the establishment of the National Socialist regime in Germany, he took refuge in the USA, becoming a citizen in 1940. There he first joined **Max Horkheimer** and **Theodor Adorno** in the former Frankfurt Institute for Social Research, re-established at Columbia. Further appointments followed at Harvard, Brandeis and – beyond the normal mandatory retiring age – in the University of California at San Diego. In the later war years and for some time after, Marcuse worked for the Office of Intelligence Research, originally the OSS. (Those of his New Left admirers who know that in this capacity he prepared reports for the CIA would presumably think to flatter him by suggesting that he was a saboteur!) An unsuccessful attempt was once made to prevent San Diego giving him another one-year contract, on the grounds that in his vastly popular lectures he was – like Socrates – 'corrupting the youth'.

Marcuse's protracted graduate studies were on Hegel, the results eventually appearing as *Reason and Revolution* (1941). His own philosophy, and his picture of the history of philosophy, have remained always profoundly Hegelian. Nothing much, for instance, is seen to have been done in the Middle Ages; and nothing of value to have been written first in English. There is also the same high love of abstractions. The meaning of these is never spelt out and precisified in terms of concrete particulars, nor is the truth of the propositions in which they are embraced to be tested by reference to crude and stubborn fact. Consider, for instance, a typical Hegelian revelation from *Reason and Revolution*:

> For what does the unity of identity and contradiction mean in the context of social forms and forces? In its ontological terms, it means that the state of negativity is not a distortion of a thing's true essence, but its very essence itself.

A second constant theme is the claim to be in some sense truly Marxist, even if **Marx** himself was not. Thus almost immediately after quoting Marx as saying in *Capital* that 'capitalist production begets, with the inexorability of a law of Nature, its own negation', Marcuse contends: 'it would be a distortion of the entire significance of Marxian theory to argue from the inexorable necessity that governs the development of capitalism to a similar necessity in the matter of transformation to socialism.' Other pretenders to the Marxist name have described Marcuse as a belated Young Hegelian, exposed therefore to the full force of the Founding Fathers' polemic against *The German Ideology*.

In his second book, *Eros and Civilization* (1955), Marcuse comes to terms with **Freud**. Characteristically what appeals is the late Freud of the metaphysical theory rather than the earlier therapist. Equally characteristically Marcuse appears to accept it all, including Thanatos the Death Instinct, without demanding any evidential credentials. Most importantly, perhaps, he attempts to distinguish what has to be repressed for the sake of any civilization at all from the restraints required by a single society.

Third comes the much less read *Soviet Marxism* (1958), and fourth his most popular

and presumably most influential *One-Dimensional Man* (1964). Here he contends that modern society – but mainly, it would seem, those societies normally recognized as most liberal – is intolerably repressive; the one small hope of improvement lying in some revolutionary elite which may, as Rousseau might have said, force the unenlightened to be free. Indeed, the repression alleged is so total that it becomes impossible for Marcuse to account for the publication, much less the reception, of his own book:

> Technical progress, extended to a whole system of domination and co-ordination, creates forms of life (and of power) which appear to reconcile the forces opposing the system and to defeat or refute all protest in the name of the historical prospects of freedom from toil and domination.

It is in the same book that Marcuse develops the bizarre thesis that the business of analytic philosophy is to make people incapable of rational criticism of the social environment: 'logic', in the words of Horkheimer and Adorno, 'has its foundation in the reality of domination'. Since logic of its very nature can forbid only incoherence and self-contradiction, Marcuse is here in effect warring against rationality under the false colours of reason.

In *An Essay on Liberation* (1969), and in his contribution to *A Critique of Pure Tolerance* (1969), Marcuse, under the similarly inept banner of freedom, seeks to pick out those various forces, including the alienated students, which might co-operate to establish the absolutism of a revolutionary elite. The title of his essay, contributed to *A Critique of Pure Tolerance* – 'Repressive Tolerance' – irresistibly recalls slogans issued by the hypertotalitarian Ministry of Truth in **Orwell's** nightmare *1984*.

As the self-stymieing nature of much of Marcuse's work becomes apparent, his future reputation looks increasingly insecure. Leszek Kolakowski, in the definitive *Main Currents of Marxism*, wrote of him: 'There is probably no other philosopher in our day who deserves as completely as Marcuse to be called the "ideologist of obscurantism".'

Further reading

See: Alasdair MacIntyre, *Marcuse* (1970); John Bokina and Timothy J. Lukes (eds) *Marcuse: From the New Left to the Next Left* (1994); Richard Wolin, *Heidegger's Children: Hannah Arendt, Karl Löwith, Hans Jonas and Herbert Marcuse* (2001).

ANTONY FLEW

MARINETTI, Filippo Tommaso

1876–1944

Italian writer

Marinetti was born to a wealthy lawyer living in Egypt. He studied briefly in Paris and made the city his cultural home, soon writing for and editing literary periodicals which attempted to introduce French Symbolist poetry to Italy. His own poetry, of which there was much, was in French until 1912, Symbolist, but with a violent idealist-anarchistic character. In 1909 he published the 'Futurist Manifesto' in *Le Figaro*. It exalted the machines, the violence and the competition of the modern world, and demanded that art abandon conventional subjects and styles, and glorify the present.

The Manifesto was generally interpreted as an iconoclastic tirade in favour of modernism. In fact it went much further, as other manifestos by Marinetti himself and by the painters Boccioni and Carrà and the 'musician' Russolo showed. Futurism wanted art not to *signify* life – least of all 'arty' life – but to *be* life. Conversely, it saw everything in social life as having meaning, as being a language, even food, clothes and gait, and sought to exploit the expressive power of every conceivable medium. War was the perfect aesthetic event.

Marinetti was probably more consciously aware of the impact of what he was proposing than most of the Futurist artists (with the exception of Boccioni). Art was to be part of the competition of modern life rather than an alternative to it. He held '*serate*' – soirées – in theatres where Futurist poetry and music and politics were declaimed. He travelled frenetically, promoting Futurism, organizing exhibitions of painting, paying for the publication of books, and cajoling one artist after another into audacious innovation. By 1914 he was vigorously agitating for Italy's entry into the Great War.

He was a staunch supporter of Fascism – one of the first; indeed, **Mussolini** borrowed much from Futurism – though personally too anarchist to accept corporativism, and too intelligent to stomach the party's imperialist xenophobia. But he never ceased to look after the interests of the Futurist movement, and so tried to keep it in the good graces of the regime.

He made an art of the literary manifesto, bringing to it lyricism, rhetoric and a concise, punchy clarity of diction. He pioneered visual poetry, in which syntax all but disappears, and in which the graphic element of calligraphy and typography played as important a role in the expression as the meaning of the words themselves, mingling writing with drawing and abstract shapes. The influence of these innovations, from **Apollinaire** to the concrete poets and beyond, is incalculable. Marinetti wrote a large number of books which mixed memoir and political and artistic polemic, as well as novels, one of which brought him prosecution for obscenity. His prose style was sharp and simple, but degenerated into empty verbosity later in life. His plays and theoretical writings on the theatre were enormously influential: he proclaimed the abolition of polite, highbrow theatre, which was to be fused with music hall and vaudeville; he destroyed the barrier between stage and audience; he pioneered very short ('synthetic') plays – in one of which only the actors' legs and feet were visible. He wrote abstract aural pieces for radio in the 1930s, and helped make a futurist film.

Marinetti's credit has been low in academic circles because of his fascist associations. Among artists, however, he has had so profound an influence that scarcely any artist in any field can have entirely escaped it. The whole twentieth-century avant-garde owes much of its general audacity and willingness to ignore the past, as well as a number of its detailed innovations, to Marinetti personally and to his Futurist movement. His personal creative works, however, only have real stature for their formal qualities and for their energy. Marinetti does not express profound feelings and thoughts; he can be brash and frivolous. For this reason, though his importance to culture of the last century will grow ever more apparent, his works will always have a limited emotional appeal.

Further reading

Some major works: *Mafarka le futuriste* (1909); *La Ville charnelle* (1908); *Zang Tumb tuuum* (1914); *Les Mots en liberté futuristes* (1919); *L'alcova d'acciaio* (1921). Contained in collections and anthologies are his theatrical writings: *Teatro*, ed. G. Calendoli (1960); and theoretical writings: *Teoria e invenzione futurista*, ed. L. De Maria (1968); *Selected Writings*, ed. R.W. Flint (1972). For his visual poetry, see *Tavole parolibere futuriste*, ed. S. Caruso and L. Martini (1977). See also: Cinzia Sartini Blum, *The Other Modernism: F.T. Marinetti's Futurist Fiction of Power* (1996).

CHRISTOPHER WAGSTAFF

MARLEY, Bob (Robert Nesta)

1945–81

Jamaican musician

Robert Nesta Marley was the archetypal hero, a man from humble beginnings who conquered the world, a man whose legend shows no sign of diminishing in the years since his death.

He was one of the most charismatic musical performers of his time, the first global superstar to emerge from the Third World, but to describe Bob Marley as simply a singer and songwriter who fronted a Jamaican reggae band is to seriously understate his impact. He was a pop culture phenomenon; or, as Judy Mowatt of the I-Threes, his vocal backing group, put it: 'Bob was a musical prophet.'

There was something Messianic about Marley. He has been described as a natural mystic and soul rebel: his work was inspirational and life-changing. In the Third World he's revered as a saviour, in the first world – East and West – he remains an idol.

Marley's strong Rastafarian beliefs were the foundations upon which he built the vision he embodied of 'One World, One Love' – a vision which suffused his music. In the words of Timothy White, author of the biography *Catch a Fire: The Life of Bob Marley* (2000): 'His music was pure rock, in the sense that it was a public expression of a private truth.' His art had, still has, the power to cross all barriers – country, class, language, culture, religion and race. The last Bob Marley and the Wailers tour in 1980 attracted the largest audiences at that time for any musical act in Europe.

Marley was born in Jamaica, into that country's heady racial mix, the son of a middle-aged white father, Captain Norval Marley, and his eighteen-year-old black wife, Cedella. His birthplace was the rural north, not, as many later assumed, the slums of Trenchtown made famous in his song 'No Woman No Cry'. Marley only moved to Kingston as a teenager in the late 1950s, eventually settling in the outlying Trenchtown shanty. He seldom saw his father as he grew up. Norval provided financial support, but constant family pressure kept him away.

Marley's musical ambitions took root in Trenchtown where, with his friend Bunny Livingston, he took his first steps into that world with lessons from famous singer Joe Higgs. It was at one of Higgs' sessions that they hooked up with Peter Tosh in the early 1960s. Bunny, Peter and Bob became the original Wailers, their music tough and urban, taking its cue from the slums.

Cedella, Marley's mother, meanwhile remarried and moved to the United States, sending money for her son to join her. But before he moved in 1966, Marley met and married Rita Anderson. He stayed all of eight months in the USA before returning to his roots. It was at this point that he became increasingly drawn to the Rastafarian faith, as much a militant stand in those days as a blend of both Judaism and Christianity, as Rastas were far from embraced by Jamaican society. By 1967 Marley's music was reflecting his new beliefs. He re-formed the Wailers, signing in 1971 with Chris Blackwell's Island Records, their first rung on the ladder to international fame.

Uncompromising and outspoken, Marley was no stranger to danger in the violent political landscape of 1970s Jamaica. He survived an assassination attempt in 1976 and moved to London to record *Exodus* – the album that put the seal on the band's international status – before returning to his troubled homeland to play the 'One Love' peace concert in front of the prime minister, Michael Manley, and the leader of the opposition.

With lyrics of revolution and revelation, religion and politics resonate passionately throughout Marley's music, but to him there was little distinction. To him it was a way of being and it won him the United Nations' Medal of Peace in 1978. His ninth album, *Survival*, was a statement of pan-African solidarity and precursor to the event that the Wailers considered to be their greatest honour – playing at Zimbabwe's independence celebrations in 1980.

That same year, Marley started his final battle with cancer, first diagnosed three years before in his toe. He'd refused to have the toe amputated, which allowed the cancer to spread, but he was determined not to die. He didn't believe in death. Once he'd accepted that his alternative treatments in Germany had failed, he left for home, where the government had just awarded him the Order of Merit. He never saw Jamaica again – only his body finished the journey.

Bob Marley was thirty-six and the father of nine children when he died in Miami, Florida, on 11 May 1981. He'd dodged the bullets but still his fate was to die young, all in the very best rock tradition.

Further reading

See: Roger Steffens and Leroy Jody Pierson, *Bob Marley and the Wailers: The Definitive Discography*

(2005). See also: Cedella Marley and Gerald Hausman, *56 Thoughts from 56 Hope Road: The Sayings and Psalms of Bob Marley* (2002); Dennis Morris, *Bob Marley: A Rebel Life* (2003); Jeremy Collingwood, *Bob Marley* (2005), Rita Marley and Hettie Jones, *No Woman No Cry: My Life with Bob Marley* (2005). The official Bob Marley website is: http://www.bobmarley.com.

JOAN BIRD

MÁRQUEZ, Gabriel García,

see: GARCÍA MÁRQUEZ, GABRIEL

MARX, Karl Heinrich
1818–83
German historian, economist and revolutionary

Marx was born in Trier on 5 May 1818, the son of a prosperous Jewish lawyer. He studied at the Universities of Bonn and Berlin between 1835 and 1841; in Berlin he associated with the 'Young Hegelians', who constituted the radical wing of Hegel's followers. When the reactionary Friedrich Wilhelm IV came to the Prussian throne in 1840, the government became increasingly hostile to the Young Hegelians, and Marx had to give up all hope of an academic career. Instead, he turned to journalism, and in October 1843 he moved to Paris to take up the editorship of a new journal. His stay in Paris, which lasted until February 1845, was of great importance in his life. It was in Paris that he first met **Friedrich Engels**, who was to become his life-long friend and fellow-worker; it was there, too, that he began a serious criticism of Hegel's philosophy. He was at first influenced in this respect by the German philosopher **Ludwig Feuerbach**, but by 1845 he was criticizing Feuerbach too and was well on the way towards his own distinctive doctrines. Expelled from France in 1845, and later from Belgium and Germany, Marx arrived in London in August 1849. He continued to live in London until his death on 14 March 1883.

Marx's doctrines are of great range and power, and their influence has been enormous. But there have been, and still are, fierce disagreements about the exact nature of the Marxism of Marx. Argument has centred around the problem of whether one is to see his thought as an organic whole, developing in an orderly way, or whether there was a sharp break in his thought. However, there is no reasonable doubt that the main lines of Marx's thought were fixed by 1848, the year in which he and Engels published their *Manifesto of the Communist Party (Manifest der Kommunistischen Partei)*. This is probably their most influential work, and is certainly a masterpiece of polemical literature – compact, wide-ranging and forcibly argued. Though *The Communist Manifesto*, as it is now commonly called, was a joint production, Engels insisted that its basic idea belonged to Marx alone. This basic idea, commonly known as historical materialism, is a thesis about human history, and according to Engels it did for the study of history what **Darwin's** theory had done for the study of organic nature. Very briefly, it asserts the fundamental importance of class struggles, both in the present and in the past, and it claims to explain their nature and inevitability. Section I of *The Communist Manifesto* begins with the assertion, 'The history of all hitherto existing society is the history of class struggles.' This is important both for what it denies and for what it asserts. If you are to understand human history, says Marx, you must not see it as the story of great individuals; you must not even see it simply as the story of states and their conflicts. You must see it as the story of social classes and their struggles with each other. Social classes have changed in the course of time, but in the middle of the nineteenth century the most important classes, Marx argued, were the bourgeoisie and the proletariat. By 'the bourgeoisie' is meant the class of big capitalists, who own the factories and the raw materials which are processed in them. The members of the proletariat, on the other hand, are completely property-less. They do not even own hand-looms or their own small

plots of land, as small-scale manufacturers used to do between the sixteenth and the eighteenth centuries. All that they have is their power to work, and this they sell to the bourgeoisie. These two classes are not merely different from each other, but also have opposite interests. Here we reach the heart of the Marxist position. The struggles between bourgeoisie and proletariat, and the struggles between classes which existed before them, are not a chance affair. They are necessary and, like the existence of the contending classes themselves, they can be explained.

In his explanation, Marx distinguishes between 'productive forces' and 'production relations'. Productive forces include not only tools and machines, but the human beings who make and use them; that is to say, human labour is a productive force. As to relations of production, Marx points out (*Wage Labour and Capital*, 1849) that production is a social matter. When human beings produce things they enter into relations with each other, and only in the context of these social relations does production take place. What is called a 'society' is these relations of production taken as a whole. So far, there have been three main types of society: ancient, feudal and bourgeois. These types of society involve social classes of distinctive sorts – e.g. slaves in ancient society, serfs in feudal society, the proletariat in bourgeois society – so the relations between classes belong to the relations of production. Marx adds that productive forces and production relations, besides being unable to exist in isolation from each other, also influence each other. In *Wage Labour and Capital*, Marx says that production relations 'will naturally vary according to the character of the means of production'. For example, on the introduction of fire-arms – a new instrument of warfare – 'the whole internal organization of the army necessarily changed'. Again, as Marx said in *The Poverty of Philosophy (La Misère de la philosophie*, 1847), an attack on the French socialist **Proudhon**, 'The hand-mill gives you society with the feudal lord; the steam-mill, society with the industrial capitalist.' But production relations can also influence the development of productive forces. For example, the bourgeoisie, in the early stages of its history, helped to develop productive forces, creating (as *The Communist Manifesto* puts it) 'more massive and more colossal productive forces than have all preceding generations together'.

We now reach a very important part of Marx's theory. Corresponding to productive forces of any given sort, Marx thinks, there is a set of production relations that fits those forces. More than this: these fitting production relations will come into existence. Feudalism provides an illustration. At a certain stage in the development of the means of production, feudal property relations ceased to be compatible with the productive forces that had already been developed. In the words of *The Communist Manifesto*: 'They had to be burst asunder; they were burst asunder.' According to Marx, there is a parallel situation in the nineteenth century, but now it is bourgeois society that provides the fetters, in that bourgeois production relations no longer fit the new and powerful forces of production. 'For many a decade past,' says *The Communist Manifesto*, 'the history of industry and commerce is but the history of the revolt of modern productive forces against modern conditions of production, against the property relations that are the conditions for the existence of the bourgeoisie and of its rule.' Marx argues that this revolt will have an inevitable outcome. Just as feudal society was burst asunder, bourgeois society will suffer the same fate.

The detailed defence of this thesis forms an important part of the first volume of Marx's chief work, *Capital* (*Das Kapital*; Vol. 1 was published by Marx in 1867; Vols 2 and 3 were edited by Engels and published in 1885 and 1894). The bulk of this work concerns economics, and its two major principles are the labour theory of value and the theory of surplus value. The latter, according to Engels, was Marx's second great discovery, worthy to be set beside his new conception of history. Marx started from the thesis (which he

derived from Adam Smith and David Ricardo) that labour is the source of all value. He then asked how this can be reconciled with the fact that the workers receive only a part of the value that they create, and have to surrender the rest to the owners of the means of production. In other words, Marx set out to explain the exact nature of what he saw as the exploitation of workers by capitalists, and his theory of surplus value is central to this explanation. So much is clear; but whether Marx succeeded in his aim – whether, as he would claim, the labour theory of value and the theory of surplus value have the status of scientific laws – is far from clear. Certainly, these theories have not had the wide influence enjoyed by Marx's theory of history, and some Marxists go so far as to argue that Marxism can do without the labour theory of value. But the real power of *Capital* lies in the chapters of volume 1 that describe, with burning passion, the rise of capitalism, the misery that it creates, and its future downfall. These culminate in a famous passage, in which the clash between productive forces and production relations is clearly stated:

> The monopoly of capital becomes a fetter upon the mode of production, which has sprung up and flourished along with and under it. Centralization of the means of production and socialization of labour at last reach a point where they become incompatible with their capitalist integument. This integument is burst asunder. The knell of capitalist private property sounds. The expropriators are expropriated.
> (Ch. 24, trans. Moore and Aveling)

To sum up: the relations between hitherto existing social classes – and these are hostile relations, struggles between classes – have to be seen in the light of the development of productive forces, and the way in which this is helped or hindered by the relations of production. But it is also Marx's view that history so far essentially *is* the story of class struggles. In the preface to his *A Contribution to the Critique of Political Economy* (*Zur Kritik der politischen Ökonomie*, 1859) Marx put his point in the form of a metaphor. The passage in question is very condensed, and its precise interpretation is disputed, but Marx's main point is usually taken to be this: that the material productive forces and the relations of production, which together constitute the 'mode of production of material life', form a 'basis', a 'real foundation', on which there arises a 'superstructure' of law, politics, religion, art and philosophy. Marx also asserted that this superstructure is 'determined by' the economic basis. 'It is not,' he says, 'the consciousness of men that determines their existence, but their social existence that determines their consciousness.' So the conflict between the forces of production and the relations of production is of fundamental importance for human history as a whole. Hegel, too, had (in his own way) recognized the importance of conflict within reality, and it may have been this aspect of Hegel's thought which Marx found attractive, and which led him to proclaim himself 'a disciple of that great thinker' (postscript to the second edition of *Capital*, 1873). Hegel, said Marx, had some idea of the true nature of dialectic – i.e. of the basically contradictory nature of reality – but he 'mystified' it by turning the thought process into an independent subject. But there is a rational kernel within the wrappings of mystification, and this can be discovered if one turns Hegel's dialectic the right way up. This seems to mean that we should regard matter (in the shape of the economic basis) as prior to mind, instead of regarding matter as a form of mind, in the way that Hegel did. The extent of Marx's debt to Hegel is hotly disputed. Perhaps the truth is that the way in which Marx presented his views in *Capital* owed something to Hegel's philosophy; but it is unlikely that the *content* of his thought would have been fundamentally different if he had never read a word of Hegel.

Marx's theory of the relations between basis and superstructure, and between the components of the basis itself, is a form of historical determinism. Marx's version of determinism is sometimes called 'the eco-nomic interpretation of history'; here, attention is drawn to the determination of the superstructure by the basis as a whole. Sometimes it is called a 'technological determinism', where the emphasis is on the fundamental role played within the basis by the forces of production. But however it is described, Marx's determinism may seem to involve a paradox. On the one hand, Marx speaks of law, politics, etc. as being determined, i.e. necessitated; on the other, Marxists have always been extremely active politically, and behave as if the outcome of historical development were not a foregone conclusion. The problems of human freedom exercised Engels, but Marx seems to have paid little attention to them. An often-quoted remark from Marx's *The Eighteenth Brumaire of Louis Bonaparte* ('Der achtzehnte Brumaire des Louis Napoleon', 1852), a study of events in France leading up to the seizure of power by Louis Napoleon in 1851, states that 'Men make their own history, but they do not make it just as they please; they do not make it under circumstances chosen by themselves, but under circumstances directly encountered, given and transmitted from the past.' This seems to allow some freedom of action to human beings, but only within certain limits. The same view is presented in the preface to *Capital*, in which Marx says that the discovery of the laws of the movement of society cannot alter the necessary phases of development; it can at best shorten and lessen their birth-pangs. What is certain is that for Marx there can be no question of the proletariat sitting back and letting events take their course; the proletariat's struggle is itself a part of events, a factor in the historical process. Marx emphasizes, too, the practical importance of a comprehension of the nature of historical development. Such a comprehension is not a purely theoretical affair, restricted to a scholar's study; it is itself a factor in the transformation of society. Theory, Marx wrote in an early critique of Hegel (1843), 'becomes a material force as soon as it has gripped the masses'. Marx's term for theory-based revolutionary activity, a union of theory and practice, was 'revolutionary praxis'. The term 'praxis' played an important part in Western Marxism, where it often had a much vaguer sense than that which Marx gave it; for some modern Marxists it seems to mean no more than 'revolutionary activity'.

When he explains the nature of the superstructure in his preface to *The Critique of Political Economy*, Marx makes use of another important concept, that of ideology. He says that law, politics, etc., are so many 'ideological forms' in which men become conscious of the conflict within the basis and fight it out. Just as we do not assess individuals by what they think about themselves, so our judgement of a historical epoch ought not to be based on what it thinks about itself, i.e. on its consciousness of itself. Rather, we should explain this consciousness, which belongs to the superstructure, in the light of conflicts occurring within the economic basis. An ideology, then, is not just a set of ideas; it is not even just a set of false ideas. Rather, it is a set of ideas which mask their true dependence on the economic basis: ideas that involve (to use a phrase employed by Engels) a 'false consciousness'. The ideologist believes, falsely, that his thought is autonomous; he fails to recognize the real forces that impel him.

Marx's thesis about the dependence of the ideological superstructure on the economic basis is a sweeping generalization, the detailed justification of which is beyond the power of any single man. Many Marxists have tried to confirm this thesis in the realms of law, religion, art and philosophy; Marx himself, in his investigations of the dependence of the superstructure on the basis, paid most attention to politics. His account of the nature of the state may serve as an illustration of the character of his arguments, and is also important in its own right. The state, according to Marx, does not exist for the benefit of the community as a whole; it exists to serve a class interest. 'The executive of the modern state,' says *The Communist Manifesto*, 'is but a committee for managing the common affairs of the whole bourgeoisie', and more generally, 'Political power is merely the

organized power of one class for oppressing another.' However, Marx has to qualify this. The theory expounded so far may be called 'instrumentalist', in the sense that it regards the state as just a means by which an exploiting class maintains itself in its dominant position. But Marx had to recognize that this was not always the case. In *The Eighteenth Brumaire of Louis Bonaparte* he described a situation in which there was a balance of social forces, which led to the emergence of a state which was relatively autonomous, in the sense that it was not in the service of any specific class-interest.

Marx's view of the state as a means of class oppression had, as he saw, important implications for the future. With the triumph of the proletariat and the disappearance of the bourgeoisie as a class, there will no longer be a class society, in the sense of a society in which one class opposes another. So the state, as an instrument for the oppression of one class by another, will cease to have a function and will disappear, as a useless part of the body disappears in the course of evolution. As Engels put it, in a famous phrase, 'The state is not "abolished", it withers away.' This does not mean that a future classless society will be without any organs of control. *The Communist Manifesto* says simply that 'the public power will lose its political character', which implies that a public power will still exist. But this power will be exercised by society as a whole and not by one social class over another.

But between the overthrow of the bourgeois state and the establishment of a classless society there will be an interim period. The transition to a classless society, Marx thought, was unlikely to be peaceful. He came to think that a peaceful transition is possible in some countries (England was one); in the main, however, he thought that the overthrow of bourgeois rule would be by means of violent revolution. This being so, there will be a period during which the victorious proletariat and the defeated and resentful bourgeoisie co-exist, and during this period it will be necessary for the proletariat to maintain their dominant position by force. There must be, in other words, what Marx called a 'class dictatorship of the proletariat', as 'the necessary transit point to the abolition of class distinctions generally' (*The Class Struggles in France, Die Klassenkämpfe in Frankreich*, 1850). In his book *The State and Revolution*, written just before his seizure of power in 1917, Lenin laid great emphasis on this part of Marx's political theory. Lenin's 'dictatorship of the proletariat' turned out to be a dictatorship of the Communist Party, and writers on Marxism often point out that Marx and Engels did not have this in mind. According to *The Communist Manifesto*, the Communists are the most advanced section of the working-class parties of each country, but they do not form a separate party. This does not mean that Marx and Engels would have disapproved of **Lenin's** methods; he was operating under conditions that were very different from those envisaged in *The Communist Manifesto*. But they would not have regarded Lenin's idea of a separate, rigidly disciplined Communist Party as necessarily applicable to all epochs and all countries.

It is natural to ask, 'How did Marx envisage the future classless society?' The new society will of course be a communist one, but Marx refuses to speculate about its precise nature. In his view, the elaborate pictures of a new society painted by some socialists and communists, such as Fourier and Robert Owen, are mere Utopias. What is clear is that *The Communist Manifesto* emphasizes, not the abolition of private property as such, but the abolition of *bourgeois* property; it does so because such property is 'the final and most complete expression of the system of producing and appropriating products that is based on class antagonisms'. Earlier, in the so-called *Economic and Philosophic Manuscripts* ('Ökonomisch-philosophische Manuskripte aus dem Jahre 1844', written in Paris in 1844, but not published until 1932), Marx related his ideas about the abolition of private property to what he called 'alienation'. Marx recognizes no fewer than four kinds of alienation in capitalist society. First, the worker is alienated

from his product, in that he sees the product as foreign to him, and indeed as dominating him. Second, the worker is alienated from himself; only when he is not working does he feel truly himself. Third (and more obscurely) the worker is alienated from man's 'species life'. Marx seems to start from the position that labour is fundamental to human beings, i.e. that man is by nature a producer. It follows that, to the extent that the produce of his labour is taken from him by the capitalist, the worker is less of a human being. Finally, in capitalist society man is alienated from man; that is, in a competitive society a man is set against other men. One might expect Marx to say that alienation is produced by private (or, more exactly, bourgeois) property. Curiously, he says that private property is initially the *product* of alienated labour; only later does private property become a cause of alienation. For Marx, the solution to the problem of alienation is communism. But not what he calls 'crude communism' – not, that is, a form of communism which is based on general envy and aims at a levelling-down. Communism of this kind still regards possession as the ultimate end; for Marx, on the other hand, communism is 'the real appropriation of the human essence by and for man'. One may take this to mean that communism is not concerned with what a man has; it is concerned with the fulfilment of his potentialities as a human (and that means as a *social*) being. Communism of this kind, says Marx, is humanism.

Although Marx's theory of alienation had great influence on Western radical thought after the Second World War, Marxists disagreed about its importance in Marx's thought as a whole. It is noteworthy that the term 'alienation' occurs most frequently in works that Marx himself did not publish – in the *Economic and Philosophic Manuscripts* of 1844, and in the so-called *Grundrisse*, a rough draft of *Capital* written in 1857–8. True, Marx always emphasized the miserable lot of the proletariat under capitalism, but the view of alienation that he expounded in 1844 covers much more than that. The dispute has been sharpened by the fact that the Marx of 1844 is often regarded as having a fundamentally different worldview from that of the later Marx. The early Marx, it is argued, saw communism as a moral ideal; the later Marx saw it as a scientific doctrine. Some Marxists see this as introducing a contrast where none exists. Marx, they argue, never drew a sharp distinction between fact and value, and so between the fields of science and morality. If this view of Marx is correct, then the development of his thought from the 1844 manuscripts to the works of his maturity may be regarded as a unified whole. But it cannot yet be said that the problem has been resolved.

Further reading

Although there have been very many editions and translations of the works of Marx and Engels, there is as yet no complete edition. Publication of the complete works in the original languages was begun in Moscow in 1927 but abandoned after 1932; a fresh start was made in 1975 (*Karl Marx/ Friedrich Engels, Gesamtausgabe*, Berlin). In 1975 publication was also begun of a fifty-volume edition in English of *Marx and Engels: Collected Works*. The literature about Marx is enormous. The following books give lucid and critical accounts: Isaiah Berlin, *Karl Marx: His Life and Environment* (1st edn 1939, 4th edn 1978); D. McLellan, *Karl Marx: His Life and Thought* (1973); J. Plamenatz, *Karl Marx's Philosophy of Man* (1975); L. Kolakowski, *Main Currents of Marxism*, Vol. 1, *The Founders* (1978). Of the many defences of Marx's doctrines, one of the most able is G.A. Cohen, *Karl Marx's Theory of History: A Defence* (1978). See also: Terrell Carver (ed.) *The Cambridge Companion to Marx* (1992); Sidney Hook and Christopher Phelps, *From Hegel to Marx: Studies in the Intellectual Development of Karl Marx* (1994); Frank E. Manuel, *A Requiem for Karl Marx* (1995); Terry Eagleton, *Marx* (1999); Francis Wheen, *Karl Marx* (1999).

G.H.R. PARKINSON

MATISSE, Henri

1869–1954

French painter, sculptor, print-maker, illustrator and designer

Henri Matisse was born at Le Cateau Cambrésius in France. As a student he first studied law, then in 1890 turned seriously to painting. For a while he attended classes at the École des Beaux Arts in Paris under the tuition of the Symbolist painter **Gustave Moreau**.

Later Matisse was to use elements from the work of several contemporary artists in order to formulate an original and vibrant style of his own that rapidly became influential as far afield as Moscow and New York. The teachings of Moreau resulted in Matisse taking an imaginative rather than a naturalistic look at the world. At the same time the primitivism of both **Puvis de Chavannes** and of **Gauguin** interested him deeply. Besides these concerns he also appreciated the search for simplicity of structure undertaken by **Cézanne**. In addition Matisse continually endeavoured to increase the brilliance of colour in his painting. For these experiments he found Paul Signac's theories based on **Seurat's** colour perceptions vital.

By 1905 Matisse's art had become sufficiently developed to attract a number of followers including Derain, Vlaminck, **Rouault** and Marquet. The art critic Louis Vauxcelles, when reviewing the Parisian exhibition at the Salon d'Automne in that year, referred to a number of paintings there as those of wild beasts, Les Fauves. This term (Fauvism) remained to designate the work produced by Matisse and his group during the next few years. Their revolutionary style, until the Cubists became more influential, was considered the most avant-garde in Europe.

Besides drawing and painting in the brilliant sunlight of southern France, Matisse visited Spain, Morocco and Italy between 1907 and 1913. These journeys, viewing other cultures and periods besides his own, confirmed for Matisse that rules in art had no existence outside individuals. His aesthetic belief was akin to that of the philosopher **Henri Bergson**. Each work of art should be the result of artistic intuition which is expressed through that work. Matisse's painting and sculpture in fact became an equivalent of his own individual sensibility's response to the visual world. It was not, therefore, a naturalistic representation of objects as seen by the artist.

He practised essentially what was to become known as French Expressionism. This should not be confused with its more pessimistic counterpart, German Expressionism.

Except for one haunting grey war year in 1915, Matisse's constant theme was the joy of life. He felt this as a glorious pantheism, 'a nearly religious feeling' that he had towards man and nature. Mostly naked people, dancing and making music, perhaps relaxing in sunlit landscapes or richly coloured interiors, were his commonest subjects.

Using a dynamically flowing line to control the forms and single colours to give shape a brilliancy, in his mature work Matisse dispensed with tonal variations to suggest the three-dimensionality of an object. This in turn emphasized the flat surface of the canvas and reduced spatial recession.

Matisse's desire to synthesize his imaginative identifications with his subject-matter in the art work led to progressive simplification. In the series of reliefs known as *The Backs* the last one is almost a complete abstraction. The single standing nude female becomes a powerful unity of strength and serenity.

This idea of serenity was important to Matisse. He aimed to avoid depressing subject-matter. In his writings he proposes that his art should be an appeasing influence on tired working people, a mental soother that should 'like a good armchair rest the weary from fatigue'.

In the years immediately before his death, while sick and bedridden Matisse continued to produce his art. By tearing and cutting brightly coloured paper into large shapes he was able to form compositions by giving the pieces to assistants to assemble under his instruction. When attached to walls these shapes seem to float reflectively or energetically in space, reanimating the themes from former years when Matisse painted the murals for the Barnes Foundation at Merion in the USA in the early 1930s, and from 1945 to 1951 decorated the Chapel of the Rosary at Vence not far from his last home. As a superb designer, whether illustrating with etchings **Mallarmé's** poetry and working on a small

scale or producing larger designs for sets to **Diaghilev's** ballet *Le Rossignol*, Matisse, through his unification of the sensual and imaginative, informed his best work with a vibrant lyricism and delightful harmony.

Further reading

Other works include: *Woman with the Hat* (1905); *Joy of Life* (1905–6); *Le Luxe II* (1907–8); *Harmony in Blue* (1908); *Dance* (1909–10); *Lady in Blue* (1937). Book illustration: mainly in the 1940s and mostly of poetry including Baudelaire's *Les Fleurs du Mal* and James Joyce's *Ulysses*. See also: 'Notes d'un peintre' published in *La Grande Revue*, December 1908. About Matisse: A. Barr, *Matisse, His Art and His Public* (1951); W. Liebermann, *Matisse, 50 Years of His Graphic Work* (1956); Hilary Spurling's two-volume biography, *The Unknown Matisse: A Life of Henri Matisse* (1998) and *Matisse the Master* (2005).

PAT TURNER

MATURANA, Humberto R.

1928–

Chilean biologist and philosopher

Maturana studied medicine and biology in Santiago de Chile and in London. He received his PhD at Harvard and worked at the MIT before returning to the University of Santiago in 1960 where he worked in brain and cognition research. In connection with work on colour vision in doves he developed a highly original foundational theory of life and cognition, published in 1970 as *Biology and Cognition*. It was republished ten years later in *Autopoiesis and Cognition: The Realization of the Living* (1980), which he co-authored with Francesco Varela. They also co-authored *The Tree of Knowledge. The Biological Foundations of Human Understanding* (1987) – an attempt to present the autopoietic theory in a systematically complete form.

Early in his career Maturana was convinced he had articulated a major challenge to biology and to the philosophy of knowledge; he could not be so sure of having many listeners. 'When I wrote the essay I decided not to make any concession to existing notions ... even if this seemed to make the text particularly obscure' (1980, xviii). At the heart of his conception is the idea that cognition is a basic operational activity performed by any living being in the process of maintaining its existence in an environment. Exactly this definition holds for scientific observation, once language and method are added. This full circle between scientifically observing life and seeing scientific observation as a form of biological existence makes Maturana's writings exceptional and fascinating. It has established his reputation as one of the founders of radical constructivism, to which he contributed methodological accuracy and philosophical reflection as well as experimental evidence.

Maturana departs from explaining the ontological status of an observing researcher as a living cognitive system. He applies to the observer whatever he or she is prepared to learn about the cognizing organism under study. It follows that the outcome of allegedly objective scientific knowledge can never be anything other than a 'reality' designed by subjective cognition and perception, or 'objectivity in parentheses'. According to Maturana, cognition research has to focus purely on the internal operations of the observed system, instead of observing the system's functional relations to its environment. While conventional functionalistic language speaks of experience as resulting from trial and error, adaptation, learning and control, in Maturana's and Varela's idiom concepts should only refer to the internal circular and recursive operations between perception and cognition. The recursive dynamics generate structural changes and maintain the unity of the living being. Maturana and Varela called this kind of unity production under permanent change 'autopsies' (i.e. self-production). In a condensed and self-referential style characteristic of all his writings Maturana states: 'The circular organization in which the *components* that specify it are those whose synthesis or maintenance it secures in a manner such that the product of their functioning is the same functioning organization that produces them,

is the living organism' (*Biology and Cognition*). Function is restricted here to relate internal structural dynamics to the maintenance of organizational identity – and this applies to the activities of the scientific observer as well.

This approach has several implications. Living systems exist solely in the presence of actually running state changes; they do not have a history or a future. Whatever happens in a system is a life-long loop of recursive dynamics not open to external information but depending on internal interpretations of registered 'irritations'. Cognition is a basic process and co-extensive with the process of life. Communication does not transfer information, and language does not represent reality: rather, they co-ordinate activities between human beings by structural coupling. 'Objectivity' is only accessible as differently constructed *multiversa*.

Taken as a research programme, this paradigm calls for a radical reconstruction of many of the functional terms of biology and cognition such as 'adaptation', 'learning', 'communication' and 'sociality'.

Maturana has been most influential not in biology but in a broad interdisciplinary and cultural discourse on principles of self-organization, which came into prominence in the 1980s and to which various disciplines – cybernetics (**Heinz von Foerster**), thermodynamics (Ilya Prigogine), chemistry/biology (Manfred Eigen), synergetics (Hermann Haken), ecology (C.S. Holling) and chaos theory (Edward Lorenz) contributed. Even if this fascinating merger of ideas did not lead to a completely new worldview, it certainly was most influential in reconsidering the status of science with respect to the 'ontology of the observer' and its embedded 'structural couplings' with society.

Further reading

See: T. Winograd and F. Flores, *Understanding Computers and Cognition* (1986); J. Mingers, *Self-producing Systems: Implications and Applications of Autopsies* (1994).

WOLFGANG KROHN

MAUDIDI, Mawlana Abul Ala

1903–79

Pakistani religious-political leader

Born to Ahmad Hassan – a Sunni lawyer with an ancestry extending back to Qutbuddin Maudud, a renowned leader of the Chishti order of Sufi Islam in the twelfth century – and his wife, in Aurangabad, western India, Abul Ala Maudidi (Mawlana, meaning 'cleric' or 'preacher', being his title) was educated at a local religious school, which combined modern and Islamic education.

When his father died in 1918, he discontinued school and took to journalism to make a living. Two years later he was appointed editor of a weekly magazine published in Jabalpur, central India. In 1921 he moved to Delhi to become editor of *Muslim* (1921–3) and then of *Al Jamiat* ('The Society'), both of them published by the Jamiat-e Ulama-e Hind (Persian: 'Society of Indian Religious-Legal Scholars'). In 1928 he moved to Hyderabad, southern India, where he devoted himself to research and writing.

His self-education – assisted by his proficiency in Arabic, Persian and English – continued while his training as a journalist kept him in touch with current affairs and equipped him with a style that ordinary Muslims found accessible. He advocated combining religious commitment with modern learning and technology.

At twenty-three, he advanced the thesis that Islam was a revolutionary ideology set to destroy the current world social order and reconstruct it from scratch. *Jihad* was a revolutionary struggle, and the ancient conflict between good and evil had become transformed into a conflict between Islam and 'un-Islam', the latter term corresponding to the traditional *jahiliya*, the pre-Islamic age of ignorance, a concept which **Sayyid Muhammad Qutb** would later develop into one of the main pillars of radical Islamist ideology. His essays on the subject, serialized in *Al Jamiat* during 1927–30, were published in a book, entitled *Al Jihad fi al Islam* ('Jihad in Islam').

Later he would argue that Islam was self-sufficient and opposed to both Western and socialist ways of life. Describing the West as morally decadent and corrupt, he concluded that Islam and Western civilization were poles apart in their objectives as well as in their principles of social organization.

In 1933 he was appointed editor of the *Tarjuman al Quran* ('Relevance of the Quran'), a monthly journal which became his main forum. His contribution to Islamic thinking was that he interpreted the terms and ideas in the Sharia (Islamic law), consisting of the Koran and the Hadith (Sayings and Doings of Prophet Muhammad) into modern concepts.

While regarding the government under Prophet Muhammad and the First Four Caliphs as the model, Maudidi gave it a democratic interpretation. He ruled that the leader of an Islamic state today – heading the legislative, judiciary and executive organs – must be elected by the faithful; so must the consultative council. Its members should judge whether or not the leader was following Islamic policies. He had no objection to candidates contesting elections on party tickets, but stipulated that, once elected, they must give up party labels, owe allegiance only to the Islamic state, and vote on issues according to their individual judgement.

He attacked orthodox *ulama* (religious-legal scholars) for confusing the fundamentals of Islam with the details of its application, and diluting Islam by attaching their own rules to the injunctions of the Sharia. He advocated *ijtihad* (interpretative reasoning), but only in accordance with the spirit of the Sharia's commandments.

Maudidi believed that the character of a social order flowed from the top to the bottom, and therefore to change society one had first to change the theoretical thinking of its leaders. So in 1941, when he lived in Pathankot, East Punjab, he founded the Jamiat-e Islami (Persian: 'Islamic Society') to produce a cadre of sincere and disciplined Muslims capable of bringing about the victory of Islam in India.

When British India was partitioned into independent India and Pakistan in 1947, he migrated to Pakistan, where he continued to lead the Jamiat-e Islami. His strident advocacy to turn Pakistan into a fully fledged Islamic state led to his periodic arrests and brief spells in jail. In 1953 he received the death sentence for inciting violence against the heterodox Ahmadiya sect. But, yielding to pressure at home and abroad, the government first commuted it to life imprisonment, and then cancelled it.

When martial law was declared in Pakistan in 1958, all political parties, including Jamiat-e Islami, were banned. In 1959–60 Maudidi toured Saudi Arabia, Jordan (then including the West Bank and East Jerusalem, the site of the Dome of the Rock, the third holiest shrine in Islam), Syria and Egypt to familiarize himself with the places mentioned in the Koran. He was appointed to the Syndicate of the Medina University, Saudi Arabia, established in 1962, a rare honour for a non-Arab.

By early 1970s, Maudidi had emerged as the most important non-Arab Islamic theorist and propagandist in the Sunni world: his numerous books and pamphlets in Urdu had been translated into Arabic, Persian and English. In 1972, he published his master work, *Tahfim al Quran* ('Towards Understanding the Koran'), which had been thirty years in the making.

In poor health, he travelled to Buffalo, New York, where his son worked as a doctor, and died there.

Further reading

Other works include: *Towards Understanding Islam* (1960) and *A Short History of Revivalist Movements in Islam* (1963). See also: Dilip Hiro, *Islamic Fundamentalism* (1989).

DILIP HIRO

MAUPASSANT, Henri René Albert Guy de

1850–93

French short-story writer and novelist

Born near Dieppe, at Fécamp or at the Château de Miromesnil, Guy de Maupassant's native Normandy and his family background both had a determining influence on his development as a writer. The failure of his parents' marriage and their separation when he was eleven created a feeling of instability in the household which was later reflected in the short stories. His mother, Laure, was the sister of Alfred Le Poittevin, the childhood friend of **Flaubert**, who was later to guide Maupassant's first literary efforts. Educated at the seminary of Yvetot and then at the *lycée* in Rouen, he moved to Paris in 1869 to study law and lived briefly with his father. This was soon interrupted by the outbreak of the Franco-Prussian War in 1870.

The years 1873–80 were crucial for Maupassant. His job as an obscure civil servant in Paris and his passion for boating on the Seine provided first-hand material for his narratives. Above all, Flaubert continued to watch over his literary development and brought him into contact with such writers as **Zola**, **Goncourt**, **Turgenev** and **Henry James**. Maupassant was initially associated with the Naturalist movement and was one of six young Naturalists who met at the Trapp restaurant in April 1877 to discuss their admiration for Flaubert, Goncourt and Zola. Three years later he contributed one of his finest short stories, 'Boule de suif', to Zola's Naturalist collection *Les Soirés de Médan*, which enabled him to embark on an independent literary career.

During the following ten years Maupassant produced innumerable stories and novels, balancing a prolific output with an ever increasing enjoyment of the material comforts of life. His literary successes, however, which included 'La Maison Tellier' (1881), 'Mlle Fifi' (1883), 'Miss Harriet' (1884), 'M. Parent' (1885), 'Toine' (1886), 'Le Horla' (1887) and 'L'Inutile Beauté' (1890), could not compensate for the slow disintegration of his mental stability. It was only after 1891 that Maupassant suffered from hallucinations and madness that led to an attempted suicide in 1892 and finally to his premature death the following year in a Paris clinic. Yet, from his early twenties he had been aware that he was suffering from a form of syphilis that attacked the nervous system, and in 1889 he witnessed the death from madness of his younger brother, Hervé, which suggested a hereditary connection. This knowledge and the intellectual energy expended between 1880 and 1890 explains his fascination with stories dealing with morbid mental states such as 'Lui?' and 'Le Horla'.

During the nineteenth century, an expanding reading public and the appearance of short stories in magazines and newspapers led to the increased popularity of short fiction, of which Maupassant was to become the most complete exponent. He wrote over 300 stories which mainly appeared in *Le Gil Blas* and *Le Gaulois*. They reflect the society of the period and deal with objectively observed everyday subjects situated in places familiar to Maupassant, such as Paris, Normandy and the Mediterranean. The subject-matter shows his overriding concern with *l'humble vérité* and underlines his belief that the aesthetic value of literature depends on the artist's ability to penetrate reality. To this end, Maupassant limited his observation to such themes as prostitution ('La Maison Tellier'), the Franco-Prussian War ('Boule de suif'), Norman peasants ('La Ficelle'), struggling civil servants ('La Parure') and, more generally, to themes concerning family relations ('Le Papa de Simon'), money ('Un Million') and affairs of the heart ('Miss Harriet').

Maupassant is a pessimist who portrays the world as contingent and man as the victim of circumstances. Although possessing a sense of humour which reveals a profound humanity, he tends to distance himself ironically from his world and deploys his acute observation to lay bare the foibles of human nature. The rapid tempo of his stories usually moves towards a striking conclusion that conveys a wry picture of an aspect of human experience. The inventive use of the narrator and the oral framework induces a feeling of authenticity, while his style is classical and self-effacing. Maupassant is a great storyteller whose major achievement was to have created a world which appears to mirror reality while at the same time masking the extraordinary artistic selection that makes all this possible.

The relative lack of status of the short story in France probably explains Maupassant's need to prove himself in the novel and why he is more readily appreciated as a short-story writer abroad. His first novel, *A Woman's Life* (*Une vie* 1883, trans. 1965), suffers from the short-story technique. *Bel-Ami* (1885, trans. 1961) is far more successful, in that the shallow psychology of the hero, Duroy, is adequately conveyed through action and the objective technique. *Mont-Oriol* (1887, trans. 1949) has little to recommend it but *Pierre et Jean* (1888, translated as *Pierre and Jean*, 1962) does show that Maupassant could adapt his objective manner to a more penetrating character study. His final novels, (*Fort comme la mort*, 1889, translated as *The Master Passion*, 1949) and *Notre Coeur* (1890, translated as *The Human Heart*, 1929), show a change of direction in which he abandons his earlier techniques and moves towards the psychological novel, made popular by Bourget. Although these novels contain undoubted merit they take Maupassant into areas unsuited to his talents.

The influence of Maupassant on short fiction has been widespread, and his views remain essentially modern; yet his technical orthodoxy and apparent ease of production have often provoked an intellectual reaction, particularly in France, that demotes him to the level of an efficient craftsman who lacks soul. In many ways, Maupassant has become the victim of his artistic sleight of hand, and he leaves us with a picture of society that many secretly recognize but which few care to acknowledge.

Further reading

Other works include: *Oeuvres complètes* (17 vols, 1969–71), to which should be added *Correspondance* (3 vols, 1973). For an excellent edition of the short stories consult *Contes et nouvelles* (2 vols, 1974, 1979). For an English translation see M. Laurie, *The Works* (10 vols, 1923–9). Among numerous editions of the short stories in English, H. Sloman, *Boule de suif and Other Stories* (1946) and *Miss Harriet and Other Stories* (1951) are recommended. See: C. Castella, *Structures romanesques et vision sociale chez Maupassant* (1972); A. Lanoux, *Maupassant le bel-ami* (1967); F. Steegmuller, *Maupassant* (1949); E. Sullivan, *Maupassant the Novelist* (1954) and *Maupassant: The Short Stories* (1962); A. Vial, *Maupassant et l'art du roman* (1954); Paul Perron, *Maupassant: The Semiotics of Text* (1988); Rachel M. Hartig, *Struggling Under the Destructive Glance: Androgyny in the Novels of Guy de Maupassant* (1991); Richard Fusco, *Maupassant and the American Short Story* (1994); Charles J. Stivale, *The Art of Rupture* (1994); Michael Bettencourt, *Guy de Maupassant* (1999).

DAVID BRYANT

MAUSS, Marcel

1872–1950

French sociologist and anthropologist

Mauss has often been called the *alter ego* of the prominent French sociologist, **Émile Durkheim**. He was Durkheim's nephew and, like him, was born in Épinal within a rabbinic family. At the University of Bordeaux he worked under his uncle and did brilliantly in his *agrégation*. He went to Paris and studied ancient languages and then anthropology, though he was never a fieldworker. In 1901 he was made director of studies at the École Pratique des Hautes Études in the history of religions of non-civilized peoples. He was later made joint director of the newly founded Institut d'Ethnologie of the University of Paris in 1925, and was also professor at the Collège de France (1931–9). In 1940 he retired and sadly witnessed the harassment of Jewish colleagues by the Germans, although he himself remained physically unmolested. While possessing great erudition – 'Mauss knows everything,' his students said of him – he never acquired the highest of academic attainments. When he was young he was constantly under pressure to help his uncle and fervently researched ethnology for the *Année sociologique*, edited by Durkheim, which was so influential among French academics.

After 1917 when Durkheim died, Mauss became his literary executor and always looked upon himself as possessing the mantle of his uncle. His efforts to revive the *Année*

sociologique produced limited success. Although he published no book, he exerted through teaching and articles considerable influence over sociologists and anthropologists in the 1920s and 1930s, in particular G. Gurvitch, R. Bastide, G. Bataille, **B. Malinowski**, **A.R. Radcliffe-Brown**, **E.E. Evans-Pritchard**, R. Needham, Mary Douglas, L. Warner and, above all, **Claude Lévi-Strauss**.

Much of Mauss's work up to the time of the First World War was done in collaboration with other Durkheimians, especially H. Hubert, and in the morphological study on the Eskimos (1906) he was assisted by H. Beuchat (translated as *Seasonal Variations of the Eskimo: A Study in Social Morphology*, 1979). In this monograph Mauss demonstrated that social life in its many forms was dependent on a material substratum, but at the same time, it was not the sole determinant of social life. It is impossible for society to maintain a constantly high level of activity and therefore social life passes through stages of activity (or hyperactivity) and recuperation. Two such clear phases exist in Eskimo life. In the summer the Eskimo hunt caribou, live in tents and are dispersed over a wide geographical area. In the winter they are sustained by fish, dwell in long-houses or igloos, and live in high social density. During this period they are subject to continuous religious exaltation (often in the *kashim* or communal house), when myths and legends are recounted, coupled with dancing and magical ceremonies. By contrast, little religious activity occurs in the summer period beyond rites of passage. Rules relating to sex, property and family life also vary with the seasons. Mauss noted that the break between the two phases is not always clear-cut, but the bi-phasal rhythm is of extreme methodological importance.

Biological and technological factors influence social behaviour but so do social factors, and this position is to be seen in Mauss's rejection of 'natural' behaviour. In a concern for dovetailing psychology with sociology, he sought to show that psychology was dependent on or limited by cultural variables. In 'Techniques of the Body' (1935) he demonstrated that virtually no behaviour in sexual, physical or mental spheres is determined in form by innate drives or mental predispositions. Basic human activities have to be learnt and their manner is determined by social norms, which are inevitably relative.

It is generally accepted that Mauss's most influential work was his essay, *The Gift: Forms and Functions of Exchange in Archaic Societies* (1925, trans. 1954), which has turned out to be the forerunner of what is now known as exchange theory. Mauss attempted to derive from ethnographical data and early literature principles whereby a gift has to be repaid. What is given does not consist exclusively of a physical present, of wealth, of real and personal property. It may contain courtesies, entertainment, ritual, women, children, dances, military assistance, the recognition of status. In primitive societies at least, a gift has to be repaid since the recipient stands under an obligation so to do. Failure to respond brings with it social censure. Thus, the elements of the gift-exchange process are related to individuals and groups as much as to the objects themselves; and not only is wealth thereby circulated but so are social relationships. In work, a form of exchange, a man may be said to give something of himself and therefore wages and nothing more are not a satisfactory response. Part of the abhorrence of charity is that the gift is not intended to be repaid. Few if any gifts are spontaneous and disinterested; and generosity is never free from self-interest. Even religious thought is partially based on gift-exchange between an individual and his god. This is an important element in sacrifice – a subject to which in collaboration with Hubert he made a significant contribution. Like Durkheim, Mauss saw that contract is not an amoral social mechanism, but is based on an implied morality: 'Gift-exchange fails to conform to the principles of so-called natural economy or utilitarianism.'

The gift was a perfect example of what Mauss called a total social phenomenon, since it involved legal, economic, moral, religious, aesthetic and other dimensions. He held that it was total social facts rather than institutions that should be the chief subject-matter of sociology. The discipline has to study the concrete and the whole – the facts to be examined are to be total social facts. And Mauss laid perhaps greater emphasis on facts than did Durkheim. Thus, it is necessary to look at entire social systems and to describe their functions. Here one recalls such American functionalists as **Parsons** and Merton. Nevertheless, unlike them, Mauss lays emphasis upon the historical dimension. Lévi-Strauss held that Mauss's approach to sociology, especially the notion of a total social fact, inaugurated a new era for the social sciences. This era Lévi-Strauss himself developed in seeing social systems as interactions between groups which reveal a hidden structure. His interpretation of Mauss has been questioned by Victor Karady.

Although Mauss was trained in philosophy, he was much less philosophical in his writing than Durkheim. Both were influenced by Neo-Kantianism. Mauss was also critical of the alleged extremisms of Durkheim in excluding psychology as part of an explanation of social phenomena, in his near metaphysical concept of society and in his theory of effervescence. In rejecting sociologism, Mauss saw that the task of the social sciences was a study of the entire man and that biology, psychology and sociology could all make contributions within limits. Again, unlike Durkheim, Mauss was openly committed to socialism, evident not least in *The Gift*. Although Mauss said the sociological study of primitive religions was what interested him most, he did not share Durkheim's concern for religion in the present and the future.

Further reading

See: *M. Mauss. Sociologie et anthropologie*, ed. G. Gurvitch, with an introduction by C. Lévi-Strauss (3rd edn, 1966) and *M. Mauss. Oeuvres*, ed. V. Karady (3 vols, 1968–9). Other translations: *Primitive Classification* (1963); *Sacrifice, Its Nature and Function* (1964); *A General Theory of Magic* (1972); *Sociology and Psychology: Essays* (1979). See: Marcel Fournier, *Marcel Mauss: A Biography* (2005).

W.S.F. PICKERING

MAXWELL, James Clerk

1831–79

Scottish physicist

Apart from some periods of ill-health and some friction with his first childhood tutor, Maxwell's background was highly conducive to his progress towards becoming one of the most distinguished physicists of the nineteenth century. His father was laird of a modest Scottish estate and had the means to provide James with the education that suited his needs. During the latter years of his schooling in Edinburgh, the young Maxwell was able to accompany his father to meetings of the Edinburgh Society of Arts and the Royal Society of Edinburgh, both of which were active and thriving. When he was only fifteen, Maxwell made an analysis of the geometry of oval curves that was sufficiently original to be presented to the Royal Society and published in its proceedings. Maxwell received his university education mainly at the University of Cambridge. He was appointed to the Chair of Natural History at the University of Aberdeen in 1856 and moved to a similar position at King's College, London in 1860. For the last eight years of his life Maxwell filled the Chair of Experimental Physics at the University of Cambridge. He superintended the design and construction of the Cavendish Laboratory and directed the early years of its operation.

Maxwell's major achievement was his formulation of electromagnetic field theory, a theory which identified the passage of light with an electromagnetic wave and which was eventually to lead to the production of the first radio waves. By the end of the century this first 'field' theory had led to the undermining of a view widely held in the nineteenth century, namely, that all physical phenomena are mechanical phenomena explicable in terms of Newtonian mechanics.

Maxwell's innovations in electromagnetism stemmed from the researches of Michael Faraday. Faraday pictured what Maxwell came to call electric and magnetic fields in terms of 'lines of force' emanating from the electrically charged bodies and magnets and circling the current-carrying circuits that were their source. Aided by some mechanical analogies of William Thomson's (see **Lord Kelvin**), Maxwell set out to put Faraday's results on a firmer theoretical foundation. In Maxwell's theory magnetic fields corresponded to vortices in the ether and electric fields to some kind of distortion of the ether. The first full version of Maxwell's theory was presented in 'A Dynamic Theory of the Electromagnetic Field' (1864) and was elaborated on in his *Treatise on Electricity and Magnetism* (2 vols, 1873). The feature of the electromagnetic theories of Faraday and Maxwell that makes it appropriate to label them *field* theories is the extent to which they explain electromagnetic phenomena in terms of what goes on in the space surrounding charged bodies, magnets and electric currents. This contrasted with the approach taken by most continental theorists, such as W. Weber and **G. Riemann**, who postulated electric fluids or particles residing in charged bodies and flowing through conducting circuits, at the same time acting upon each other at a distance across empty space.

A spectacular success of the field approach in Maxwell's hands was the formulation of an electromagnetic theory of light. The general equations of Maxwell's theory yielded a wave equation representing transverse waves propagated through space with the velocity of light, and Maxwell was able to identify these with light. Maxwell's successors were able to show on the basis of his theory how radio waves, electromagnetic waves with a longer wavelength than that of visible light, could be produced. The first successfully to realize this possibility in the laboratory was the German physicist **Heinrich Hertz** in 1888.

While Maxwell's theory certainly had its dramatic successes, it also had its weaknesses. One of these was the failure of Maxwell to make at all clear what 'electricity' was. To questions such as 'What is it that resides in electrically charged bodies?' and 'What happens in a wire when a current flows through it?' Maxwell's work offered no clear answer. Clear answers became possible when the Dutch physicist **H.A. Lorentz** reconciled Maxwell's fields with some aspects of the continental 'action–at–a–distance theories.' The result, which had emerged by the final decade of the century, was the electron theory. From the viewpoint of that theory, bodies become charged by acquiring an excess or dearth of electrons while currents through conductors correspond to a flow of electrons. In addition, electrons give rise to fields in the medium surrounding them, the fields corresponding to those of Maxwell's theory.

Lorentz, like Maxwell, understood the electric and magnetic fields to represent mechanical states of an ether. By the beginning of the twentieth century, and particularly in the light of Einstein's theory, it had become clear that electromagnetic fields were elementary entities not reducible to the mechanical states of an ether. The nineteenth-century ideal of reducing all physical phenomena to Newtonian mechanics had collapsed. **Einstein** observed that 'the lion's share of this revolution was Maxwell's'. We thus have the ironical situation that Maxwell embarked on the project of reducing electromagnetic theory to mechanics, and in carrying it out he produced a theory that was to play a major part in undermining that very project.

Maxwell's other major contribution to physics was his work on the kinetic theory of gases, a theory in keeping with the general project of reducing all physical phenomena to Newtonian mechanics. According to the kinetic theory a gas is composed of molecules in random motion, colliding with each other and with the walls of the containing vessel. Prior to Maxwell's work elementary versions of the theory had been put forward, for example by Bernoulli and **Joule**, while Maxwell's contemporary **R. Clausius** had already developed it well beyond its most simple form. As Maxwell realized, the kinetic theory was essentially a statistical one. The aim was to characterize not the motion of each individual molecule, but rather the net effect of the random motions of aggregates of molecules. Maxwell introduced statistical techniques capable of dealing with the random motion of aggregates of molecules and so founded what has since become known as statistical mechanics.

In order to stress the fundamentally statistical character of the theory, Maxwell employed the services of a hypothetical being that has become known as Maxwell's 'demon'. This 'very observant and neat-fingered being' was able to open and close a small frictionless trap door in a partition between two volumes of a gas initially at the same uniform temperature. It is supposed to be so adept at this task that it can open and close the door in such a way that only fast-moving molecules pass one way and only slow-moving molecules pass the other way. By concentrating the faster-moving molecules in one compartment and the slower-moving ones in the other in this way, the demon is able effortlessly to raise the temperature of one compartment with respect to the other. The net result, then, is that heat has been made to flow from a cold to a hot body without the expenditure of work, in violation of the second law of thermodynamics. The fact that this hypothetical occurrence is in conflict with thermodynamics but not with the laws of Newtonian mechanics indicated to Maxwell that the former cannot be simply a species of the latter. The kinetic theory of heat adds a fundamentally statistical component to Newtonian theory so that, in Maxwell's words, 'the second law of thermodynamics has the same degree of truth as the statement that if you throw a tumblerful of water into the sea, you cannot get the same tumblerful of water out again'.

Subsequent to Maxwell's efforts the statistical kinetic theory was further improved, especially by the Austrian **Ludwig Boltzmann**. Some of its deep-seated difficulties could only be removed with the advent of quantum mechanics and the replacement of classical statistics with quantum statistics. In this context, it is interesting to note that, in his very first paper on the kinetic theory, 'Illustrations of the Dynamical Theory of

Gases' (1860), Maxwell noted that the kinetic theory clashed with known results concerning the relation between the principal specific heats of a gas and acknowledged that it 'could not possibly satisfy the known relation'. Since most of the productive development of the theory took place after 1860, we have a nice counter-example to the view that a clash with the facts is a sufficient condition for abandoning a theory. The classical theory never did remove the difficulty highlighted by Maxwell. Only when the theory was replaced by its quantum mechanical successor could specific heats be adequately accounted for.

Maxwell made other contributions to physics that were minor compared with those described above. He was productive in his studies of colour and colour vision, phenomenological thermodynamics and theories of elasticity. He also published a detailed study of possible accounts of the composition of Saturn's rings, a study which first won him general recognition by professional physicists. Maxwell's theoretical work was almost invariably accompanied by extensive experimental work designed to put his theories to the test.

Further reading

Most of Maxwell's scientific papers have been collected in *The Scientific Papers of James Clerk Maxwell*, ed. W.D. Niven (1965). Other works: *Theory of Heat* (1871); *Matter and Motion* (1877); *The Electrical Researches of the Honourable Henry Cavendish, F.R.S.* (1879); *An Elementary Treatise on Electricity* (1881). An early biography is L. Campbell and W. Garnett, *The Life of James Clerk Maxwell* (1882). More recent ones are C.W.F. Everitt, *James Clerk Maxwell: Physicist and Natural Philosopher* (1975) and Basil Mahon, *The Man Who Changed Everything: The Life of James Clerk Maxwell* (2003).

ALAN CHALMERS

McCARTHY, Mary Therese

1912–89
US novelist

After the unhappy childhood in Seattle, Washington, which she describes in *Memories of a Catholic Girlhood* (1957), Mary McCarthy escaped east to Vassar College, where she was deeply influenced by Vassar's simultaneous encouragement and crippling of intellectual seriousness in its women undergraduates. 'Arresting performance in politics, fashion, or art is often taken by the Vassar mind to be synonymous with accomplishment.' This substitution of an outer display of self for the infinitely more difficult struggle to act upon an achieved knowledge became the mark of Mary McCarthy's modern demon, a type most famously realized in Henry Mulcahy, the villain of *Groves of Academe* (1952). By pretending he has been fired for having been a Communist, Mulcahy calls the liberal bluff of ultra-progressive Jocelyn College and gets re-hired. 'He's loyal to himself, objectively, as if he were another person . . . he's foregone his subjectivity and hypostatized himself as an object.'

The popularity of *The Group* (1963) owed much to McCarthy's satiric ventriloquism of a group of Vassar graduates who blatantly lack McCarthy's own intelligence and authority. In all her novels, the promising, intelligent heroines tend to fail, turn into a self-parody or get killed off. Many of McCarthy's sharpest satiric jibes are, however, rewrites of her own past. In *The Group*, up-to-date iconoclastic Kay Strong marries a would-be radical writer immediately after graduation, as McCarthy did. However, while Kay struggles to make Harald appreciate her 'Russel Wright cocktail shaker in the shape of a sky-scraper' and eventually kills herself, McCarthy got work writing for the *New Republic*, the *Nation* and *Partisan Review*, and got divorced in 1936 – rather like Margaret Sargeant, the almost nameless divorcee heroine of the linked stories in McCarthy's brilliant first book, *The Company She Keeps* (1942). Margaret is on her way to Reno when she has a one-night stand, including a humiliating morning after, with 'The Man in the Brooks Brothers Shirt'. At the complacently **Stalinist** magazine *The Liberal*, Margaret is branded a **Trotskyite**, the same fate that befell McCarthy, according to 'My Confession'

(1951), her attack on the witch-hunting of her notorious namesake, Senator Joseph McCarthy.

From 1938 to 1946, McCarthy was married to the critic and man of letters **Edmund Wilson**, whom she divorced to marry Bowden Broadwater. After 1961, when she married diplomat James West, she spent most of her time in Paris, though she became one of the most effective critics of the American involvement in Vietnam. Her fame rests mainly on her satires of liberal intellectuals, particularly in *The Groves of Academe*, now the classic novel of the American liberal arts college, and *A Charmed Life* (1955), her dissection of an intellectual summer colony. McCarthy's readers are held by the attitudes she satirizes, rather than the meagre or arbitrary action. She is less a novelist than an intellectual satirist, like Thomas Love Peacock, or a writer of *contes philosophiques*, like Voltaire.

As a critic, McCarthy regrets the 'snubbing' rejection of the 'novel of ideas' by 'pure' novelists, symbolized for her by Henry James. For McCarthy, as for Tolstoy, the novelist she respects most, the 'idea' at the heart of the novel is actually a moral imperative, a way of being in the world. Yet in McCarthy's world of self-perpetuating oligarchies – the college, the writers' colony, the socially determined 'group', even the aesthetes and liberals trapped in a plane in *Cannibals and Missionaries* (1979) – it is almost impossible to act honestly.

McCarthy felt that the decline of descriptive language had weakened the novel. In past fiction, as in the historic past which she celebrates in *Venice Observed* (1956) and *The Stones of Florence* (1959), the outer appearance yields inner truths: for this reason McCarthy sees aesthetic experiences as part of moral development, like Peter Levi's quixotic admiration for Borromini in *Birds of America* (1971). Yet the loss of a morally reliable world is fodder for McCarthy's satire. As in nineteenth-century fiction, her vindictively accurate catalogues – especially of clothing and décor – hold the key to character, but for McCarthy they ironically display an alienation from nature and the body.

The development of twentieth-century fiction owed little to McCarthy, though her critics were irritated to have to admit that formally unfashionable McCarthy had probably written the most incisive intellectual satire of her generation. It may well be, however, that McCarthy's satire is ultimately not vicious enough. Unlike most satirists, she makes her own moral stance clear; she doesn't share the anarchic energy behind much contemporary 'black comedy'. McCarthy writes in a calm, strongly cadenced prose, more effective in sentence units than in paragraphs or chapters. Her habit of letting her readers know she knows what's right works better in her essays (*On the Contrary*, 1962; *The Writing on the Wall*, 1970) than it does in her fiction. She values honesty, self-knowledge, unselfconscious pursuit of the good, and *aidôs*, the mixture of 'care or ruth' briefly evoked in *The Groves of Academe*. 'The concept doesn't exist for us', so McCarthy mockingly traces the consequences of its loss.

Further reading

See: Elizabeth Niebuhr, 'The Art of Fiction XXVII', *Paris Review*, Vol. 27 (1962); Elizabeth Hardwick, 'Mary McCarthy' in *A View of My Own* (1963); Norman Mailer, 'The Case against McCarthy' in *Cannibals and Christians* (1966); Barbara McKenzie, *Mary McCarthy* (1966); Doris Grumbach, *The Company She Kept* (1967); Irwin Stock, *Mary McCarthy*, University of Minnesota Pamphlets on American Writers No. 72 (1968); C. Gerlderman, *Mary McCarthy* (1988).

HELEN MCNEIL

McEWAN, Ian

1948–

British novelist

Of all the British novelists who came to prominence in the 1970s (and whose promise was sanctified by their appearance on the famous 1983 Granta 'Best of British' list), Ian McEwan is perhaps the only one to have sustained an unremittingly successful career while at the same time transforming public perceptions of the kind of novelist that he is. Initially regarded as a dangerous and transgressive presence, McEwan now draws the kind of critical comment (and the public sales) that suggest he embodies the high seriousness of earlier literary periods.

After reading English Literature at Sussex University, McEwan was one of the first graduates of the University of East Anglia's creative writing course run by Malcolm Bradbury and Angus Wilson. McEwan's early work, including the short-story collections *First Love, Last Rites* (1975) and *In Between the Sheets* (1978), has a willed perversity to it, with a focus on taboo areas such as incest and paedophilia. The culmination of this psychosexual narrative sequence came with *The Comfort of Strangers* (1981) which recounts the involvement of an English man and woman on holiday in Venice with another couple, the extremes of whose sadomasochistic behaviour result in a death. McEwan's style, cool and apparently simple, is in provoking contrast to the somewhat lurid subject-matter.

McEwan's concern with sexual politics found a wider and more fruitful context in the novels and screenplays of the later 1980s and 1990s. Indeed, his interest in politics became literal in what was then his most ambitious novel *A Child in Time* (1987), one of the central characters of which is a government minister. This was a wide-ranging work, touching satirically on the authoritarian tone of the **Thatcher** years but also giving space to ideas drawn from quantum physics (at one point the central character slips back in time and witnesses his parents discussing his own abortion). *A Child in Time* finds its heart in the story of a child's apparent abduction and the reaction of the parents, especially the father, and it was seen as ushering in a warmer, more generous stage in McEwan's writing. *The Innocent* (1990) gave a European dimension to the novelist's work, the 'innocent' of the title being a young and virginal Post Office employee who becomes involved in a surveillance operation in Berlin during the 1950s. The book works very well as a thriller – there are **Hitchcockian** touches of suspense – and the larger sweep of history is suggested by a coda pointing to the fall of the Wall. *Black Dogs* (1992) also contains Berlin sequences and stresses the persistence of the 'black dogs' of fascism in the European landscape.

For *Enduring Love* (1997) and *Amsterdam* (1998) McEwan returned to the present. The former is a story of sexual obsession and stalking, though of a man by a man. McEwan's ability to render bizarre events plausible through meticulous prose is evident not just in the description of the balloon accident which opens the novel but also in the mockscientific documentation at the end. *Amsterdam* is a short work, atypical in some ways, and the book for which McEwan won the 1998 Booker Prize. *Atonement* (2001) is McEwan's most critically acclaimed and commercially successful book to date. Consciously schematic, as McEwan's later work has tended to be, it shows how far he has travelled from the deadpan shock tactics of his early stories. Partly a 1930s country house novel, partly a wartime memoir set at the time of Dunkirk, *Atonement* first shows its central character Briony Tallis as an aspiring thirteen-year-old writer. In the space of a single day and night, she puts away childish things, to disastrous effect. A fatal misidentification and a false accusation of rape haunt her for the rest of her life, and undo her family and her relationship with her sister. The book itself is presented as her reminiscence, the best she can do by way of reparation at the close of her life in 1999. In its recreation of a leisured prewar life, the long opening section recalls L.P. Hartley's *The Go-Between* (1953) and, more generally, **Virginia Woolf**, while the wartime hospital sequences demonstrate that McEwan has lost none of his capacity for unflinching realism. *Atonement* contains many of the elements that are characteristic of the author – perceptions of childhood, loss of innocence, historical sensitivity (particularly as it relates to the sexual climate of an era) – but it contains them in a narrative structure which would have been familiar to any of the classic writers of the last century. It is a measure of how far Ian McEwan has not simply been integrated into the literary mainstream but has come to be one of its dominating figures.

Further reading

McEwan's other work includes the screenplay for *The Ploughman's Lunch* (1988), one of the best English films of its period, three television plays collected in *The Imitation Game* (1981), and *Saturday* (2005). Adam MarsJones's essay 'Venus Envy' (in his collection *Blind Bitter Happiness*, 1997) is an illuminating comparison of McEwan and **Martin Amis**.

PHILIP GOODEN

McLUHAN, Herbert Marshall

1911–80

Canadian culturologist

Born in Alberta, Canada, McLuhan studied at Manitoba University but took his PhD in Thomas Nashe at Cambridge University. He taught in American and Canadian universities (Catholic institutions or branches of them), and worked from his Centre for Culture and Technology, University of Toronto. He became a Catholic in 1937 and this sense of the universe as a purposeful system of incarnate energies impregnates his vision. His main value lies in his exploration of the interfaces set up between traditional genre studies, and his methods lie nearer to those of Alfred Korzybski and **Roland Barthes** than to the separatism of sociology, literary criticism or pure semantics. In fact, his excellent literary criticism repeatedly refers to the cultural and technological context of writing – **Mallarmé** and **Joyce** in relation to newsprint, **Tennyson** to optics, Coleridge to 'radial' thinking, Pope to print technology, and so on. These approaches stem partly from Cambridge attitudes towards literary studies, and partly from the teachings of H.A. Innis, of which he writes in the introduction to a 1964 edition of the latter's *The Bias of*

Communication. Innis belonged to the Chicago University school of the 1920s which included, in its field of teaching and reference **Robert Ezra Park**, **Max Weber**, **John Dewey** and **Thorstein Veblen**. From Park, Innis learned 'how to identify the control mechanisms by which a heterogeneous community yet manages to arrange its affairs with some degree of uniformity', and how technological devices 'have necessarily modified the structure and functions of society'. McLuhan developed these assumptions into a radical investigation of how 'the extensions of man' change both the external and the internal environments (the concept of an internal environment draws on the work of the Canadian experimental psychologist Hans Selye, whose *Stress* and *The Stress of Life* appeared in 1950 and 1956). In 1953 McLuhan founded, with the distinguished anthropologist Edmund S. Carpenter, the journal *Explorations*, a major vehicle for environmental and cultural studies. The selection in *Explorations in Communication* (1960) indicate the distinction of its contributors, who included Northrop Frye, Siegfried Giedion, **Fernand Léger**, David Riesman, Robert Graves and Gilbert Seldes. The semantic category of these studies is indicated in the introduction which speaks of exploring 'the grammars of such languages as print, the newspaper format and television', 'revolutions in the packaging and distribution of ideas and feelings', the 'switch from linear to cluster configuration' in order to understand the 'almost total subliminal universe' of the modern form of 'preliterate man' living within the circuitry of electric media in 'the global village'. The new outlook is 'tribal'. The danger is not merely illiteracy but mediocrity, a society anti-individualistic in its repudiation of the previous print-media culture which still lingers on in a predominantly visual, tactile, oral and aural environment. (Although *Explorations* ended in 1959, an abbreviated version appeared as a supplement to the University of Toronto *Graduate* magazine through the 1970s.)

The warnings implicit in *Explorations* are explicit in *The Mechanical Bride* (1951), a brilliant analysis of advertising and propaganda methods subtitled 'Folklore of Industrial Man' (McLuhan was always concerned to expose contemporary mythology), and designed to show how the media of magazines, newspapers and films control consumption and self-definition in the capitalist state. In fact, the state emerges as a malign work of art (a concept partly derived from Jakob Burckhardt's analysis of Machiavelli). The mechanization of choice moulds human life caught in 'a radical separation between business and society, between action and feeling, office and home, between men and women'. McLuhan believed that these divisions cannot be healed until their fullest extent is perceived. Popular culture, therefore, must be studied to understand the full effect of the media. The historical implications of changes caused by the shift from script to print to electric technology – the major media transition – is documented in *The Gutenberg Galaxy* (1962) from a large variety of texts, selected to elucidate changes towards 'social change which may lead to a genuine increase of human autonomy'. McLuhan's principle is:

> If a technology is not understood either from within or from without a culture, and if it gives new stress or ascendancy to one or another of our senses, the ratio among all our senses is altered ... The result is a break in the ratio among the senses, a kind of loss of identity.

William Blake on the 'perceptive organs' and James Joyce's multilingual *Finnegans Wake*, as a spatial involvement of the whole body–mind system, are presented with a wide range of social, psychological and scientific analysis in 'a mosaic pattern of perception and observation', 'the mode of simultaneous awareness' which is the basis of a culture, its practical and observable 'tribal or collective consciousness'. Media hypnosis is to be restricted by understanding the means and arts of communication. The artist functions primarily in this 'new clairvoyance' of the state's design, a prophetic necessity since 'the new

electric galaxy of events has already moved deeply into the Gutenberg galaxy', causing 'trauma and tension to every living person'.

Understanding Media (1964), which gained McLuhan international fame and a cult status in America, examines the grammars of communication technology, encouraging the student of 'integral patterns' to 'live mythically and in depth' in order to comprehend 'the medium is the message' – that is, how the grammars of environment afford major clues to present and future. 'The machine turned Nature into an art form', and our own 'proliferating technologies have created a whole series of new environments', with the arts functioning as 'anti-environments' or 'counter-environments': 'art as radar acts as "an early alarm system"', 'the function of indispensable perceptual training rather than the role of a privileged diet for the elite'. McLuhan's political and religious attitudes appear in his presentation of 'the revulsion of our times against imposed patterns' and of 'a faith that concerns the ultimate harmony of all beings'. Without social awareness in depth, patterns will be dictated: 'electric technology is within the gates'. One instrument of resistance, which entered the popular jargon of the 1960s, is to recognize 'hot' media – 'low in participation' – from 'cool' or requiring 'completion by the audience', which is therefore actively engaged rather than passively manipulated.

After 1964, McLuhan found himself in demand to analyse, predict and advise. His aphoristic ability to harness slogan or advert methods to penetrating social analysis of surprising sources found favour with the business world (as much as it was suspiciously loathed by the academic fraternity) and his *Dew-Line Newsletter* supplied the information culture controllers needed. In spite of this ambivalence in political action, he continued to function as an early warning system. *The Medium is the Message* (1967, with the designer Quentin Fiore) is a print and picture collage of media criticism composed with considerable wit and humour, a probe (a favourite term of action in his writings) into 'the environment as a processor of information', and therefore as a virulent propaganda system. *War and Peace in the Global Village* (1968, with Fiore) is 'an inventory of some of the current spastic situations that could be eliminated by more feedforward'. At this stage, McLuhan had come to believe that technologies are 'self-amputations' rather than the extensions of the body. 'Mosaic vision' is still necessary to combat 'corporate decision-making for creating a total service environment on this planet'. *Counter Blast* (1969), acknowledging the methods of **Wyndham Lewis's** *Blast* (1914) and incorporating design and typography techniques partly explored in *Explorations 8* (reissued in 1967 with the Joycean subtitle, *Verbi-Voco-Visual Explorations*), probes book, film, videotape, etc. as shapes of our consciousness, and therefore as the form of contemporary myth in which human energies are incarnated (another of his recurrent terms):

> The electronic age is the age of ecology ...
> The Age of Implosion in education spells
> the end of 'subjects' and substitutes instead
> the structural study of the making and
> learning process. Software replaces
> hardware ... In the Age of Information, the
> moving of information is by many times the
> largest business in the world.

Much of the history and theory of these later works is contained in one of McLuhan's most substantial books, *Through the Vanishing Point* (1968, with Harley Parker), a challenge to perception restricted to the 'rear-view mirror' point of view by analysing the history of space design in the arts, including the origins, images and effects of perspective and 'multi-level space' – necessary, since 'civilization is founded upon the isolation and domination of society by the visual sense'. *From Cliché to Archetype* (1970, with Wilfred Watson) is a fascinating discourse on language through such categories as 'Author as Cliché (Book as Probe)', 'Cliché as Breakdown' and 'The One and the Mini'. The range of examples is, once again, extraordinary, and the vivacity of McLuhan's perceptions unmatched. *Culture*

is Our Business (1970) returned to his old obsession, American advertising as mythology – 'a world of festivity and celebration' which indicates 'a flip in American society from hardware to software' and how 'advertising provides the corporate *meaning* for the experience of the private owner ... complex social events and "meanings" minus the experience of the commodities in question'. McLuhan's warning now extended to criticism of the USA's war in Vietnam as part of 'the electric infamy environment'.

Needless to say, his beliefs, techniques and conclusions aroused both controversy and downright hatred. (The best criticism of McLuhan's work remains Sidney Finkelstein's *Sense and Nonsense of McLuhan*, 1968.) But McLuhan himself separated his personal intentions from his emphatic style, particularly in an excellent interview in *Playboy* magazine (No. 64, 1969):

> I'm making explorations ... my books
> constitute the *process* rather than the com-
> pleted product of discovery; my purpose is
> to employ facts as tentative probes, as means
> of insight, of pattern recognition, rather
> than to use them in the traditional and
> sterile sense of classified data, categories,
> containers. I want to map new terrain rather
> than chart old landmarks. But I've never
> presented such explorations as revealed
> truth. As an investigator, I have no fixed
> point of view, no commitment to any
> theory – my own or anyone else's.

Further reading

See: Gerald E. Stearn (ed.) *McLuhan Hot and Cool* (1968); Harry S. Crosby and George R. Bond (eds) *The McLuhan Explosion* (1968); Donald F. Theall, *The Medium is the Rear View Mirror: Understanding McLuhan* (1971); G. Genosko, *McLuhan and Baudrillard: Masters of Implosion* (1999); Paul Levinson, *Digital McLuhan: A Guide to the Information Millennium* (1999); Richard Cavell, *McLuhan in Space: A Cultural Geography* (2002); Janine Marchessault, *Marshall McLuhan* (2004); G. Genosko (ed.) *Marshall McLuhan: Critical Evaluations in Cultural Theory* (3 vols, 2005).

ERIC MOTTRAM

MEAD, Margaret

1901–78

American anthropologist

Born into a New England academic family, Margaret Mead took a BA at Barnard College and higher degrees in anthropology at Columbia University. Here she was greatly influenced by her teachers, **Franz Boas**, the father of modern American anthropology, and Ruth Benedict, whose interest in the relationship between 'culture' and 'personality' was to provide the central scientific preoccupation of Margaret Mead's career.

In 1925 Mead carried out her first field-study, in Samoa, becoming one of the first women to do anthropological field-research and one of the few American anthropologists of her generation to work outside the Americas. She took into the field a problem posed by Boas: whether adolescence was a culturally specific experience, which happened to occur in modern Western societies, or (as the Western folk-view had it) whether adolescence was the symptom of profound biological changes which inevitably manifested themselves in disruptive behaviour. The relaxed, sexually free, responsible Samoan maidens were presented to the American public, in *Coming of Age in Samoa* (1928), as the resolution of that particular argument, and the book became a best-seller.

Her next study, of early childhood in Manus (*Growing Up in New Guinea*, 1931), was less explicitly directed towards the testing of a hypothesis, but her description of how another culture raised its children was directly relevant to educational debates then in progress in the United States – particularly since the Manus employed the free-and-easy techniques in favour in avant-garde European kindergartens. The real problem suggested by the book was left unexplored, namely the contrast between the expressive and indulged Manus infants and the driven adults they were later to become.

The theme of these early works remained the leitmotif of Mead's work. 'Human nature' is plastic; cultural conditioning and environment are more vital than biological factors in determining what kinds of people are found in different societies. Perhaps the most radical version of this argument is to be found in her *Sex and Temperament in Three Primitive Societies* (1935), in which the contrasting male and female types in three New Guinea societies were analysed to show that there is nothing natural or universal about particular 'masculine' or 'feminine' role expectations. Scepticism was aroused at the time by the fortunate coincidence that her fieldwork happened to occur among three societies which formed such a perfect contrast for her purposes, but if the impressionistic descriptions cannot be accepted without reservations, the broad lines of her reports, and the conclusion drawn, have proved reasonably acceptable.

During the Second World War Mead was active in a team which made 'national culture' studies of allies and enemies for the US government, and even after the war she produced significant academic studies, notably her *Continuities in Cultural Evolution* (1964). She also remained for the greater part of her professional life on the staff of the American Museum of Natural History. Nonetheless she increasingly devoted herself to public or popular activities, which she saw as an essential product of her anthropological studies. As she wrote in her autobiography, *Blackberry Winter* (1972): 'I have spent most of my life studying the lives of other peoples, faraway peoples, so that Americans might better understand themselves.' The point of view she propagated was liberal and optimistic, and perhaps characteristically American in its emphasis on cultural malleability, providing a sort of academic blessing for the melting-pot. An intelligent, sophisticated and religious person, she escaped the intellectual vulgarization which her popularizing role might have implied, retaining a sense of the complexity of social issues and an openness to new ideas. *Margaret Mead: The Complete Bibliography 1925–1975* (ed. Joan Gordon, 1976) lists over 1,400 items, bearing witness to a passion for communication which was rewarded by the attention and interest of millions both inside and outside the social sciences.

Further reading

See: Jane Howard. *Margaret Mead: A Life* (1989); Derek Freeman *The Fateful Hoaxing of Margaret Mead: A Historical Analysis of Her Samoan Research* (1999): Hilary Lapsley, *Margaret Mead and Ruth Benedict: The Kinship of Women* (2001); Steven Pinker, *The Blank Slate: The Modern Denial of Human Nature* (2002).

ADAM KUPER

MEDAWAR, (Sir) Peter Brian

1915–87

British immunobiologist

Peter B. Medawar came to England at the age of four. His father was a Brazilian businessman of Lebanese origin and his mother, Edith Muriel Dowling, was British. He was educated at Marlborough College public school, followed by Magdalen College, Oxford University, where he graduated in 1935 with a first-class honours degree in zoology. Even as an undergraduate student Medawar started experiments on cultured embryo cells. After qualifying he joined the pathology department under Professor **Howard Florey**, who later shared the Nobel Prize for discovery of penicillin. Medawar pursued a research career investigating the function of lymphocytes at a time when the significance of these cells was unknown.

During the Second World War Medawar was recruited to investigate skin transplantation in severe wounds and burns of military personnel. He worked at the Burns Unit of the Glasgow Royal Infirmary, studying skin grafts in rabbits and humans. He described accelerated rejection after a second skin graft from the same donor, and suggested that this is an immunologically mediated response ('The Behaviour and Fate of Skin Autografts and Skin Homografts in Rabbits', *Journal of Anatomy*, Vol. 78, 1944). Although initially he thought that antibodies were responsible for graft rejection, when he was unable to find antibodies in the blood of rabbits, and

serum would not transfer the capacity for graft rejection, he discarded this hypothesis. Instead, he adopted cellular immunity as the mechanism of graft rejection, as observed in the tuberculin delayed hypersensitivity reaction (see R.E. Billingham, L. Brent, and P.B. Medawar, 'Quantitative Studies on Tissue Transplantation Immunity. I. The Survival Times of Skin Homografts Exchanged between Members of Different Inbred Strains of Mice', in *Proceedings of the Royal Society, Series B*, Vol. 143, 1954).

Medawar was appointed as Mason Professor of Zoology in 1947, and four years later as Jodrell Professor of Zoology at University College London. At about that time MacFarlane Burnet in Australia hypothesized from the observations of twin cattle chimeras made by Ray Owen that during embryonic life the organism learns to differentiate between 'biological self and nonself'. This hypothesis was tested by Medawar and his collaborators by injecting mouse tissue from a different strain during the perinatal stage of mice when the animals are immunologically immature (see R.E. Billingham, L. Brent and P.B. Medawar, 'Actively Acquired Tolerance of Foreign Cells in Newborn Animals', *Nature*, Vol. 172, 1953). Indeed, the mice would later accept skin grafts from the tissue donor, confirming that tolerance developed and was specific to the donor mouse. This established the immuno-biological basis of transplantation in humans, expressed by Medawar as the 'art of the soluble'. Medawar shared the Nobel Prize in Physiology or Medicine in 1960 with MacFarlane Burnet for his work on skin grafts and prevention of graft rejection by inducing immunological tolerance. His work marked a milestone in the history of biology and was a major influence in the development of the new field of transplant immunity, tolerance, immunobiology and the clinical practice of organ transplantation.

Medawar was appointed in 1962 to the directorship of the National Institute for Medical Research at Mill Hill in London. In addition to scientific administration of a large research institute, he supervised experiments that would prevent graft rejection, among which anti-lymphocyte serum was an important development. In 1969 he became President of the British Association for the Advancement of Science. Unfortunately, at the age of fifty-four he suffered a cerebral haemorrhage, resulting in paralysis of his left arm and leg. He showed great courage and resilience, and with the extraordinary support of his wife he returned to work. Indeed, Peter's wife, Jean née Shinglewood Taylor, whom he met in 1937 in the laboratory in Oxford, was a major influence throughout their married life. Medawar joined the newly created Clinical Research Centre in Northwick Park, London, to study tumour immunology and in 1977 was appointed Professor of Experimental Medicine at the Royal Institution.

Peter Medawar was a brilliant lecturer, showing scholarly erudition and capable of interpreting current ideas within a conceptual framework. He had an impressive style and charisma, and would engage in discussion with infectious enthusiasm. Quite apart from his scientific work in immunobiology, he made important contributions to the education of scientists, described in *Advice to a Young Scientist* (1973). His interests ranged from philosophy and science, to opera and, of course, cricket. Just as with scientific insight, Medawar was a brilliant writer, and his last book – *Memoirs of a Thinking Radish* (1986) – gives an account of his scientific aspirations and career.

Medawar was a major figure of science in the twentieth century. He crossed successfully the boundary of C.P. Snow's 'Two Cultures' between science and art and was awarded virtually every honour known to science: the Nobel Prize, Fellowship of the Royal Society (1949), the Royal Medal (1959), a knighthood (1963), the Copley Medal of the Royal Society (1969), Companion of Honour (1972), Order of Merit (1981) and numerous honorary degrees from universities. Despite his unique status in science, he was a kind, readily accessible and warm human being. When approached to

support a symposium to commemorate the contribution of Peter Gorer to the discovery of the histocompatibility system (MHC) he responded with great enthusiasm, and chaired several meetings in planning and preparation of the International Symposium. This was his last international scientific engagement, which he chaired with great success, despite having suffered by then a second stroke; the proceedings were published as a monograph.

Peter Medawar died in October 1987 at the age of seventy-two, leaving a legacy of scientific achievements that has guided subsequent development of basic and applied science of immunobiology. Indeed, Medawar followed the tradition established by Paul Ehrlich that can be paraphrased, 'from the laboratory to the clinic', which has recently been termed 'translational research'.

Further reading

Other works include: 'A Discussion on Immunological Tolerance', *Proceedings of the Royal Society, London*, Vol. 146 (1956); *The Art of the Soluble* (1967); *Induction and Intuition in Scientific Thought* (1969); the Harvey Lecture of 1956 (*Harvey Lectures*, Vol. 52); and (with Thomas Lehner), *Major Histocompatibility System* (1983). See also: Jean Medawar, *A Very Decent Preference: Life with Peter Medawar* (1990).

THOMAS LEHNER

MELVILLE, Herman

1819–91

US writer

'I love all men who *dive*' – so, in part, runs Melville's reaction on hearing a lecture in Boston in 1849 by **Ralph Waldo Emerson**. It was generous acclaim, for Melville thought Emerson's Transcendentalism largely a fraud, a well-meant but facile credo of optimism and spiritual good cheer which failed to acknowledge the tragic currents in man's condition, his especial vulnerability to pain, war, evil and illusion. But in designating Emerson a 'diver', Melville as aptly might have been speaking of himself. For in nearly all his fiction and poetry, and in his lively correspondence and several reviews, he confirms his own deep probing energies of mind, the writer-diver in search of the elusive, absolute condition of things. This irresistible 'diving' for truth, a life-long, unslackening curiosity which finds expression through the intelligent playfulness and vitality of his style, situates him, with Emerson, **Hawthorne**, **Whitman** and **Thoreau**, at the centre not only of the mid-nineteenth-century 'American Renaissance' but the American literary tradition at large, a restive, major imagination whose powers come best into focus in his whaling epic, *Moby-Dick* (1851), stories like 'Bartleby, The Scrivener' (1853) and 'Benito Cereno' (1855), his 'Ship of Fools' allegory, *The Confidence Man* (1857) and the posthumous novella *Billy Budd* (1888–91). The scale of Melville's 'curiosity' – 'his ontological heroics' as he describes matters in his correspondence – has rarely been better perceived than in the diary entry made in 1856 by Hawthorne, then American Consul in Liverpool, after he and Melville spent an afternoon in discussion on the Southport sands:

> Melville, as he always does, began to reason of Providence and futurity, and of everything that lies beyond human ken ... He can neither believe nor be comfortable in his unbelief; and he is too honest and courageous not to try to do one or the other.

The reputation that once attached to Melville, and which the revival of his critical fortunes, begun in the 1920s, still has not entirely dislodged – that of the compelling but artless teller of sea-stories – has nevertheless given way to a growing awareness of how layered his writing was from the outset. So, at least, from differing angles, fellow-authors like **D.H. Lawrence**, Cesare Pavese, **Albert Camus** and **Charles Olson** have borne impressive witness. Paradoxically for a writer at one time thought only an American-Victorian purveyor of 'adventure', and whose career dissolved into obscurity after *Moby-Dick*, Melville has increasingly been

taken for a prophet of 'modern' consciousness, a wary, sceptical, knowingly ironic voice of resistance to every manner of human ruling illusion. Whether recognized for his arts of narrative, or for the fine ambition of his thought, Melville has justly entered the American literary pantheon. Few of his writings are entirely free of fault, but his essential 'depths', as Hawthorne remarked of *Mardi* (1849), Melville's least gainly book, 'compel a man to swim for his life'.

Melville alleged that his life only 'began' when he wrote his engaging first work, *Typee* (1846). Yet his beginnings were auspicious, if not necessarily for a literary career. He came of two socially eminent American families, the Melvilles of Boston and the Dutch-descended Gansevoorts of Albany, New York. One grandfather, Major Thomas Melvill (sic), took a leading part in the Boston Tea Party; the other, Peter Gansevoort, fought as a general in the War of Independence. This patrician stock was an important source of pride in Melville, the basis of high personal expectations. He grew up, one of eight children, in a busy, well-connected and convivial home, in New York City. In *Redburn* (1849), *Pierre* (1852) and parables like 'Bartleby' and 'The Two Temples' (1854), Melville would reveal himself as a writer of the city as much as the sea. The unexpected bankruptcy, then delirium and death of his father, Allan Melville, an 'Importer of French Goods and Commission Merchant' and a seemingly prosperous member of New York's commercial middle class, in the recession of 1832, brought profound family reverses. For Melville it inflicted a trauma he would try to re-confront in the writing of *Pierre*. In the short run, it made for a series of abrupt personal false starts.

First, in 1834–6, he clerked in an Albany bank, and in the summer of 1835 worked on his uncle's farm at Pittsfield. Fifteen years later, he himself bought a farm in Pittsfield, drafted the early versions of *Moby-Dick* and, following the publication of his essay, 'Hawthorne and his Mosses' (1850), discovered the author of *Mosses from an Old Manse* for his neighbour in nearby Lenox. In 1837, he tried teaching in a country school. The same year he made his writing début in the correspondence columns of a local paper, and then as the author of a two-part Gothic story fragment. In late 1838 he studied engineering in hopes of working on the Lake Erie canal system. In June 1839, he sailed down the Hudson to New York, and secured a place to Liverpool and back as a deckhand on the packetship, *St Lawrence*. His encounters with the brute equations of Victorian sailor and city life he portrays, in some irony, in *Redburn*. Once back in New York, and again jobless, he tried another spell of teaching, and in 1840 took off to Illinois, where he saw and travelled the Mississippi, experience put in store and re-worked in his canny 'metaphysical' satire, *The Confidence Man*.

In near desperation, in January 1841, appropriately the turn of a new year, he sailed out from New Bedford as a whalerman and harpooner aboard the *Acushnet*, the beginning of four years of Polynesian and whaling adventure. His journeys into the South Seas, on the *Acushnet* and two subsequent whalers, took him to a multitude of ports and sailor haunts, and specifically to the Marquesas, Tahiti and Honolulu. Later he would visit ocean outposts like the Galápagos, where he found the inspiration for his cycle of island portraits, 'The Encantadas', as **Darwin** had for his *Origin of Species*. His litany of adventure includes jumping ship and his vaunted 'stay mong the cannibals' (which yielded *Typee*), a spell of detention in the local 'calaboose' and various intervals of beach-combing of which he makes use in *Omoo* (1847), even temporary managership of a bowling-alley, and his eventual return to Boston in 1844 via the Horn and Latin America as an enlisted seaman aboard the frigate *United States*, on which his fifth book, *White-Jacket* (1850), is based. On his reunion with his family, he could look back to these years, life lived dangerously and at full throttle, as a seasoned ex-mariner, the one-time patrician for whom a whaler (as he testifies in *Moby-Dick*) had been his 'Harvard and Yale',

and who knew from the inside the testing, male, enclosed ship-world of the common sailor, and that toughest of forcing-grounds, the Pacific whale-fisheries. It is this dense, energetic personal history, and more, that Melville gives imaginative expression to in the fiction which culminates in *Moby-Dick*.

His early writing, in sequence *Typee*, *Omoo*, *Mardi*, *Redburn* and *White-Jacket*, centres upon a young, usually ingenuous, 'isolato', a quester embarked for adventure, and even outright 'truth', whose eventual incarnation will be Ishmael in *Moby-Dick*. Each narrative, thus, Melville conceives as a journey-out, a remembered diary of events either on land or aboard different types of ship. In *Typee*, Melville's setting is Nuku Hiva in the Marquesas, and a concealed inland 'cannibal' valley to which Tommo, the narrator, and his companion flee, only to become prisoner-guests, two fugitive consciousnesses from the West set down amid the arcana and totemic mysteries of Typee culture. Despite its surfaces as 'adventure', Melville, as he says, 'varnishes' his facts at every turn, playing one ambiguity off against another, and hinting of darker other worlds beneath the affable outward show of the valley. The zest of the telling, and the story's lavish, contrapuntal play of detail, make for an astonishing first effort. *Omoo* continues the saga, Melville's most free-wheeling volume, genuinely light of touch and funny, almost South Seas picaresque. With *Mardi*, he begins as before, another jumping from ship and the promise of Polynesian derring-do. Less than a third along, however, the story changes radically in temper, and for the worse. For into this third narrative, Melville poured an avalanche of recent reading, from Plato and Montaigne, Spenser and the Elizabethans, from the major European Romantics, and even from Victorian books of flower symbolism. The results are painful, a cluttered would-be 'philosophical' travelogue in which Taji, the hero, and his retinue pursue an ethereal albino princess across a mythic archipelago of sixteen islands. *Mardi* with justice can be taken as a dummy-run for *Moby-Dick*, but one which outran Melville's control. Stung by the criticism aroused by *Mardi*, Melville spoke of returning to the 'cakes and ale' world in *Redburn*. Based on the Liverpool journey he made at eighteen, and a subtler effort than he allowed, it tells the rite-of-passage endured by Wellingborough Redburn, youthful confrontations glossed and teased by an older, far wiser head. The stark scenes of sailor DTs, death, malignity in the person of the sailor Jackson, and the observation of Liverpool penury and human suffering and of the plague which breaks out among emigrants in steerage, make for vivid, dramatic narration. In *White-Jacket*, also told as first-person narrative, Melville depicts the hierarchic, man-of-war world of the frigate, a compendious account of American navy custom and life seen from his customary fo'c's'le stance. In the shedding of the narrator's emblematic white coat, as Redburn's before, Melville projects a sea-version of the fall from innocence, the awakening of a deeper, 'ocean' state of knowing.

By the time he published *Moby-Dick*, Melville had married (in 1847) Elizabeth Shaw, daughter of the Chief Justice of Massachusetts; read like a novice possessed the works of Shakespeare; and, having published in *The Literary World* (1850) his admiring account of *Mosses from an Old Manse*, met and began his astonishing correspondence with Nathaniel Hawthorne. His 'whale-book', large, striking in canvas and reach, represents him at full imaginative stretch. Ostensibly the story of the *Pequod*'s search for the definition-eluding white whale, it quickly yields many other levels of quest – for self-meaning, community, 'light', and again, overwhelmingly, 'truth'. Defined one way, then another – by Ahab as evil, by Starbuck as a 'dumb beast', by the Parsee counter-crew as a god, by Queequeg as a hieroglyphic mystery, the whale dominates the narrative, incapable of being 'caught' and fixed by any single meaning. Melville declares the organizing principle of *Moby-Dick* to be 'careful disorderliness', an appropriately flexible mode of narrative able to contain, and actually discipline, the book's

abundance, both the cetology and the epic flights of speculation. Whether read as a simple whale adventure, or metaphysics, or as 'modernist' self-reflexive narration, *Moby-Dick* offers Melville's central legacy, an essential landmark of American literary history.

With *Moby-Dick* behind him, Melville turned his imagination inland, and in *Pierre or The Ambiguities* attempted a portrait of a heroic 'Fool of Truth' ultimately entombed by his endeavour to redeem his father's abandonment of a mysterious, illegitimate daughter, the hero's half-sister. Within its apparent Gothic labyrinths lies a profound drama of sexual feeling, and Melville's own 'inside narrative' of the writer's life. Between 1853, when he tried to secure a consular appointment, and 1857, he turned to the short story, publishing in 1856 his *Piazza Tales*, five pieces (with an introduction) from the fourteen he had issued in *Putnam's Monthly Magazine* and *Harper's New Monthly Magazine*. These stories are now rightly taken to rank among his best efforts. In 'Bartleby' he tells a parable of Wall Street, an account of liberal capitalism's impact on the human spirit redolent of **Kafka**. In 'The Encantadas' he depicts a version of hell, a bleak landscape of island volcanic ruins to complement the saddest and worst of human isolation and loss. In 'Benito Cereno', a story almost **Conradian** in its hints of ineffable corruption, he makes an act of slave-insurrection his occasion, a bleak, violent portrait of the moral blindness slavery requires for its very existence. These, and his other stories of the 1850s, and *Israel Potter* (1855), a satire of American national heroes, prepared the way for his blackest chronicle of illusion, *The Confidence Man*. If literary kin could be claimed for *The Confidence Man*, it would include **Dostoevsky's** *Notes from the Underground*, **Mann's** *Felix Krull* and Kafka's *The Castle*. A Mississippi river story, begun and ended on April Fool's Day aboard the steamer *Fidèle*, it sets about the gullibility and panacea-seeking of latter-day American 'pilgrims' with Swiftian incision. The instrument is an apparent master confidence-man, a 'metaphysical scamp', whose different avatars mock and ensnare the unvigilant. Within its onslaught on different American shibboleths, it contains key clues to Melville's overall theories of fiction (especially chapters XIV, XXXIII and XLIV). Neither the tone, nor the precise direction of Melville's satire, can always easily be pinned down, but his idiom is never less than vigorous, brilliantly alert and inventive.

By 1856, Melville was approaching nervous collapse. He sailed for the Levant as an attempt at recuperation; visited Hawthorne in Liverpool; and in 1857, after his trip to the Holy Land, landed back in America a month after the publication of *The Confidence Man*. In 1858–60 he tried lecturing on the Lyceum circuit; sailed with his brother Tom to San Francisco in 1860; sold the Pittsfield farm in 1862–3 and, dismayingly for a man who had written *Moby-Dick*, in 1866 was obliged to take employment as a minor Customs Inspector in New York, a post he discharged with resigned diligence for nineteen years. His times saw little improvement. His volume of Civil War poems, *Battle-Pieces and Aspects of the War* (1866), and the later *Clarel* (1876), a massive Victorian work of doubt and faith longer than *Paradise Lost*, barely gained a readership. In 1867, his son Malcolm died, a probable suicide, to be followed in 1886 by the second Melville son, Stanwix. Only two further works were published in Melville's lifetime, both privately, the poems in *John Marr and Other Sailors* (1888) and *Timoleon* (1891). The work which first saw light in 1924, however, *Billy Budd*, after a confused textual history, has come to be recognized for Melville's final masterpiece. A fable of 'iniquity' and sacrificial innocence, it explores the triangulation of three 'phenomenal' men, Captain Vere, the master-at-arms John Claggart, and 'welkin-eyed' Billy Budd – hanged for alleged murder aboard a British warship during the Napoleonic Wars and in the wake of the risings at Nore and Spithead. Whether read as Melville's testament of 'acceptance', or 'rebellion', or as more complex dialectical drama, it underscores the enduring, radical strengths of his

art. Melville ended his career as he began, an unyielding 'diver' for truth.

Further reading

See: F.O. Matthiessen, *American Renaissance: Art and Expression in the Age of Emerson and Whitman* (1941); Leon Howard, *Herman Melville: A Biography* (1951); Jay Leyda, *The Melville Log: A Documentary Life of Herman Melville, 1819–91* (2 vols, 1951); Newton Arvin, *Herman Melville* (1957); Charles Olson, *Call Me Ishmael* (1958); Warner Berthoff, *The Example of Melville* (1962); *Melville: A Collection of Critical Essays*, ed. Richard Chase (1962); Edgar A. Dryden, *Melville's Thematics of Form: The Great Art of Telling the Truth* (1968); *Studies in the Novel*, Herman Melville special number, Vol. 1, No. 4 (Winter 1969); *New Perspectives on Melville*, ed. Faith Pullin (1978); Robert S. Levine (ed.) *The Cambridge Companion to Herman Melville* (1998); Hershel Parker, *Herman Melville: A Biography* (2 vols, 2002–5).

A. ROBERT LEE

MENDEL, Gregor

1822–84

Austrian botanist, founder of genetics

As the son of a peasant in the Silesian village of Heinzendorf (Hynčice), Mendel showed promise at the village school and was selected for academic studies in Leipnik and Troppau. When he left the *Gymnasium* at Troppau in 1839 he entered the Philosophy Institute at Olmütz. There financial worries and overwork dogged his progress so that it was with relief that he entered the Augustinian Monastery at Brünn (Brno) in 1843. This was the centre of intellectual life in the area. Several of the monks taught in the local schools, as did Mendel from 1849 until he became abbot of the monastery nineteen years later.

In addition to his work as teacher and cleric Mendel was an active member of the Natural Science Society (Naturforschende Verein in Brünn), he was on the central board of the local agricultural society (K.K. Mährisch-schlesischen Gesellschaft zur Beförderung des Ackerbaues, der Natur – und Landeskunde), and he was known locally as a plant breeder, apiculturist and meteorologist.

Despite Mendel's academic ability and excellence as a teacher he twice failed to pass the teachers' examination in the natural sciences. The time which he spent at Vienna University (1851–3) preparing for re-examination proved invaluable for his subsequent researches into plant hybridization, although it did not lead to success in the teachers' exam. Mendel's hybridization experiments – with the edible pea – lasted from 1856 to 1863. His study of the Hawk-weed (*Hieracium*) was completed in 1871 by which time his duties as abbot took almost all his time. These latter years were marked by controversy over the new ecclesiastical tax on monastery property which Mendel obstinately refused to pay. His funeral in 1884 was a major event in Brünn, but it was another sixteen years before his researches in plant hybridization became generally known and identified as the foundation stone of the modern conception of heredity.

When Mendel studied science at Vienna University the subject of the fixity of species was under discussion. The adherents of *Naturphilosophie* had pictured life as developing progressively under the direction of an inherent, non-material agency of 'world soul'. Species therefore had been changed or transmuted, albeit gradually. The old dogma of the constancy of species had already come under attack in the eighteenth century and Linnaeus had weakened his hard line on the subject when he suggested that many species had originated from the hybridization of a few original types, the generic forms. This claim was greeted with scepticism. It was pointed out that hybrids were frequently sterile, and when they yielded progeny these tended to 'revert' to one or other of the originating species. Debate over this 'hybridization theory' of the origin of species, however, continued and prizes for essays on the subject were offered by the Dutch Academy of Sciences in 1830 and the Paris Academy in 1860.

Mendel recognized that the debate over the hybridization theory would only be settled when a systematic and extensive series of experiments had been carried out in which the transmission of each differing trait united in the hybrid had been followed through successive generations in a large population of its offspring. Between 1856 and 1863 Mendel raised some 28,000 plants, involving crosses between varieties differing in one, two and three hereditary traits.

In all cases where the parents differed in one trait, such as seed shape – round or wrinkled – the seeds produced by the resulting hybrids were either round or wrinkled, never intermediate between the two forms. Moreover, the proportion of round to wrinkled seeds approximated to the ratio 3:1. This proved to be the case for all the seven traits he studied. Further studies revealed that the round seeds were of two types, one breeding true, the other yielding both round and wrinkled seeds. The latter were twice as numerous as the former, so the ratio of 3:1 was really 1:2:1, the middle term representing the hybrid forms, the first and last terms the true-breeding forms.

With his training in mathematics Mendel realized that the 1:2:1 ratio corresponded with the terms of the binomial series: $(A + a^2 = A^2 + 2Aa + a^2)$. Mendel pictured the two letters in the binomial as representing the two contrasted forms brought together in the hybrid. The fact that the offspring yielded by sexual reproduction mirrored the binomial expansion in their statistical relations suggested to Mendel that sexual reproduction involved a process equivalent to the multiplication of the terms A and a. Evidently the forms A and a became separate from each other, then they united in all possible combinations with equal frequency. Since each fertilized egg cell was produced by the fertilization of one female germ cell by one pollen grain, it must be in the formation of these cells and grains that the separation of types A and a occurred. These gametes were hence either of type A or type a and their union in fertilization gave the forms A, Aa and a.

Mendel went on to show that where more than one pair of contrasted characters was involved, the hereditary transmission of each was independent of the other. Thus in the case of two pairs of contrasted characters brought together in a hybrid the offspring showed all possible combinations between the two pairs. These combinatorial forms corresponded in their relative frequencies with the terms in the expansion of *two* binomial series. When dominance was involved the resulting ratio was 9:3:3:1.

These statistical regularities, which have become known as Mendelian ratios, were Mendel's empirical discovery. The explanatory hypothesis which he advanced to account for them is generally known as germinal or Mendelian segregation. Today these achievements tend to be regarded in terms of the light which they have thrown upon the nature of inheritance, a subject which lacked a sound theoretical foundation until Mendel's work became generally known. For Mendel, the significance of his work lay in a different direction. He had set out to throw some light upon the hybridization theory of the origin of species and the conflicting reports of plant hybridists thereon, and it was to their work that he devoted the concluding section of his paper. He urged that the unit of analysis was not the species but the hereditary characters. The results obtained by hybridists therefore depended upon the number of such characters which differed in the originating forms. According to the binomial theorem, if this number was n then the number of different types of hybrid offspring would be $3n$. If n was 7 the reappearance of either of the originating types would be likely to occur only once in 16,000 hybrid offspring, whereas if n was 1 the expected frequency would be 1 in 4. That previous hybridists using different species arrived at different results was hardly surprising. Nor was it a matter for surprise that hybrids showed a wide range of variability, for this again was a function of the number of differing characters crossed. There was no need to postulate the existence of species or of characters with varying degrees of constancy. It sufficed to distinguish hybrids in which germinal segregation occurred, whose

progeny followed the example of the edible pea, and those in which it did not occur, where permanent hybrids were formed which represented new combinations of characters from the originating species.

Although Mendel's papers were referred to a number of times in the nineteenth century their importance was not recognized. Thus the standard bibliographical review of W.O. Focke merely noted Mendel's numerous hybridization experiments and added somewhat sceptically that Mendel 'believed he had found constant numerical ratios between the hybrid types'. When in 1900 three botanists, Hugo de Vries, Erich von Tschermak and Carl Correns, rediscovered Mendelian ratios and read Mendel's paper the Mendelian theory was finally launched. Six years later the term 'genetics' was introduced for the subject whose theoretical foundation had been furnished by Mendel.

Further reading

The best biography of Mendel is still that of Hugo Iltis, *Life of Mendel* (trans. E. and C. Paul, 1932; reprinted 1966). A translation of Mendel's paper and associated documents will be found in C. Stern and R. Sherwood, *The Origin of Genetics: A Mendel Sourcebook* (1966). For a discussion of the context of Mendel's research see R.C. Olby, *Origins of Mendelism* (1966).

ROBERT OLBY

MENDELEYEV, Dmitry Ivanovich
1834–1907
Russian chemist

Mendeleyev was born in Tobolsk, in Siberia, where his father was a teacher. He was the fourteenth and last child of the family. When he was sixteen his mother took him to St Petersburg to be trained as a teacher; he did very well, but quarrelled with bureaucrats and was posted to the Crimea. In 1856 he returned to St Petersburg and took his master's degree in chemistry, supporting the views of Charles Gerhardt who saw molecules as units rather than polar arrangements of diverse atoms, and who classified them into series which he called 'types'. In 1857 he became a *privatdocent* in the University of St Petersburg; and in 1859 he was sent for two years to Germany and France to study chemistry. He attended the Karlsruhe Conference, one of the first major international gatherings of scientists, called in 1860 to try to reach agreement on chemical formulae and atomic weights. In 1861 he became Professor of Chemistry in the St Petersburg Technological Institute, and retained throughout his life an interest in applied chemistry and in industry generally. In 1867 he was in addition made Professor of General Chemistry at the University of St Petersburg. He was a founder of the Russian Chemical Society in 1868.

Chemistry seemed in the 1860s a mass of facts and recipes without clear organizing principles. Students seemed to need to memorize great quantities of data, and the Karlsruhe Conference had only recently produced some agreement about even elementary questions such as whether water was HO or H_2O. Mendeleyev, on being appointed to the Chair of General Chemistry, determined to write a textbook which would bring order into the treatment of the various chemical elements. He was fond of playing Patience, and the arranging of cards into sequences may have helped him in his great triumph of classifying the elements into families. He was not the first to do this, but his was the version which prevailed because he took into account the full range of chemical properties and not just the atomic weight, and because he predicted the existence of certain elements which were indeed soon afterwards isolated.

There were some sixty elements known in the 1860s, and classifying them might have seemed easier than arranging the countless species of insects; but it did not prove so. Some elements like chlorine, bromine and iodine clearly formed a family, but to establish an overall pattern proved very difficult. Following the Karlsruhe Conference, there was agreement on atomic weights; and various attempts were made, notably by J.A.R.

Newlands in Britain, to arrange elements in order of increasing atomic weight but in rows of columns so that similar elements would come in a line. Newlands hit upon a 'law of octaves' according to which every eighth element was similar, but this did not work for all the elements; sometimes two had to be put into the same square, and the result looked forced and artificial.

Mendeleyev in 1868 hit upon his more general 'periodic law', according to which when elements are placed in order of atomic weight then similar elements recur at regular intervals. In order to fit the elements in, Mendeleyev had to leave some gaps; to 'correct' some atomic weights, notably that of cerium; and to put iodine and tellurium out of order. These seemed like devices to make facts fit a theory, and when Mendeleyev published his law and the 'periodic table' based upon it in 1869, it was not received with enthusiasm. In 1871 he published his textbook, *Principles of Chemistry* (*Osnovy Khimii*, trans. 1891), which ultimately became a classic, translated into many languages, and which was based upon his classification; but it was not until after 1875 that the fundamental importance of the periodic table was evident to all. In that year Lecoq de Boisbaudrom, who knew nothing of Mendeleyev's work, isolated a new element which he called gallium; this turned out to be what Mendeleyev had predicted as eka–aluminium, detailing its properties with great accuracy because he knew those of neighbouring elements in the periodic table. Contemporaries were astonished when they found that the theorist had known more about the element than the practical chemist who discovered it; and from then on the table began to assume the prominent place which it occupies in chemistry lecture-theatres.

In 1877 William Crookes drew attention to Mendeleyev's work in a long article on 'The Chemistry of the Future', and later published an English translation of Mendeleyev's long paper. Mendeleyev rapidly acquired a high reputation abroad, and was elected into foreign academies and awarded medals by them. At home, he became a Corresponding Member of the Academy of Sciences, but he was never elected to full membership. His first marriage had ended in divorce, and his remarriage was a social stigma; he was still prone to disputes with officials and quarrels with the Germans then prominent in Russian science. In 1890 he delivered a student petition to the Ministry of Education; the result was that his resignation was demanded. He had powerful friends as well as enemies, and gave up academic life to enter the Civil Service where he spent his latter years at the Ministry of Finance and the Board of Weights and Measures. He kept up with theoretical chemistry, but his own great contribution had been made; at the end of his life he was doubtful about radioactivity and electrons, because he believed in unchanging elements which could be classified once and for all. There is an irony here, because **Ernest Rutherford's** atomic model, with its nucleus surrounded by electrons in quantized orbits, turned out to explain how the elements can be arranged in the periodic table. Mendeleyev's work thus not only brought order into chemistry, but proved to be one of the routes leading towards a theory of matter acceptable to both chemists and physicists.

Further reading

Other works include: *Principles of Chemistry* (1871), which appeared in English translation in 1897, with later editions. On his work, see J.W. van Spronsen, *The Periodic System of Chemical Elements* (1969); and for a biography and bibliography, B.M. Kedrov, 'Mendeleyev', in C.C. Gillispie (ed.) *Dictionary of Scientific Biography*, Vol. IX (1974).

D.M. KNIGHT

MERLEAU-PONTY, Maurice

1908–61

French philosopher

Merleau-Ponty was born in Rochefort-sur-mer. After completing his secondary education, he studied philosophy at the École Normale Supérieure in Paris, achieving the *agrégation* in 1930. From 1931 to 1944 he taught philosophy, with a brief spell in the army from 1939 to 1940. In 1945, he was appointed to a post at the Université de Lyon, where he became professor in 1948. In 1949, he returned to Paris to take up the chair of Child Psychology and Pedagogy at the Sorbonne, and in 1952 was elected to a chair at the Collège de France. His first books, *The Structure of Behaviour* (*La Structure du comportement*, 1942, trans. 1963) and the *Phenomenology of Perception* (*Phénoménologie de la perception*, 1945, trans. 1962), were the product of work in philosophy and psychology on which he had been engaged throughout the 1930s. At that time, the intellectual atmosphere in France was receiving a new stimulus from the work of the German philosophers **Hegel**, Husserl and **Heidegger**, which challenged the dominant trend of French academic philosophy. Although all three were to shape Merleau-Ponty's thought, the phenomenology of Husserl was to prove particularly influential. Merleau-Ponty spent some time before the war consulting Husserl's unpublished manuscripts at the Husserl Archives in Louvain, and considered himself to be a phenomenologist, following in the footsteps of Husserl. He has been criticized for misinterpreting or misrepresenting Husserl, but it is clear that he felt he was being faithful to Husserl's most fundamental intentions. Seeking a method which would enable him to avoid the philosophical difficulties of both rationalism and empiricism and, more specifically, the problems raised by dualism, he stressed the need to return to our original experience of the world, to investigate the genesis of that understanding of the world which we normally take for granted, and to take as the central theme of philosophy the construction of sense and meaning and the constitution of knowledge. His work has been described as a philosophy of ambiguity because of his interest in indeterminate categories of experience, such as the 'probable' or the 'ambiguous'; his interest in categories or concepts which do not have too precise a meaning is part of his critical attitude towards the claims of rationalism.

Although Merleau-Ponty's reputation in France has suffered as a result of the trend away from phenomenology in the direction of structuralism, he is acknowledged as a major exponent of phenomenology. With the translation of his major works, his influence is slowly beginning to make itself felt outside France. His work has proved of interest to many non-philosophers as well, notably in the field of aesthetics. Another aspect of his thought to attract considerable attention has been his analysis of the role of the body and its significance for philosophical reflection.

In 1945, after the Liberation, he collaborated with **Sartre** and a number of other intellectuals in the founding of the review *Les Temps modernes*. He is sometimes thought of as an Existentialist, but in fact there were significant philosophical and political differences between himself and Sartre, and his association with the review came to an end in 1952. The disagreement became public in 1955 with the publication of his book *Adventures of the Dialectic* (*Les Aventures de la dialectique*, trans. 1973) which included a lengthy critique of Sartre. While he had been sympathetic to **Marxism** in the 1940s, Merleau-Ponty now became increasingly disillusioned and moved definitively away from the intellectual left wing. At the time of his death he had returned to philosophy and was making notes for a work (posthumously published in 1964 under the title *Le Visible et l'invisible*, translated as *The Visible and the Invisible*, 1968) which is more Heideggerian than Husserlian in inspiration.

Further reading

Other works include: *Humanism and Terror* (*Humanisme et terreur*, 1947, trans. 1969); *Sense and Non-Sense* (*Sens et non-sens*, 1948, trans. 1964); *In Praise of Philosophy* (*Éloge de la philosophie*, 1953, trans. 1963); *Signs* (*Signes*, 1960, trans. 1964); *The Prose of the World* (*La Prose du monde*, 1969, trans. 1974). Translation of collected essays and articles: *The Primacy of Perception and Other Essays* (1964); *Phenomenology, Language and Sociology* (1974). See also: Colin Smith, *Contemporary French Philosophy* (1964); Albert Rabil Jr, *Merleau-Ponty: Existentialist of the Social World* (1967); M. Langer, *Merleau-Ponty's Phenomenology of Perception* (1989); E. Matthews, *The Philosophy of Merleau-Ponty* (2002).

MARGARET WHITFORD

MESSIAEN, Olivier Eugene Prosper Charles

1908–92
French composer

One of the most gifted French composers of any age, Messiaen attended the Paris Conservatoire from 1919 to 1930, where his teachers included Paul Dukas (composition), Marcel Dupré (organ) and Maurice Emmanuel (history of music). In 1931 he took up the post of organist at the Église de la Sainte Trinité in Paris, a position he held for life. Together with Andre Jolivet and others he formed the group 'La Jeune France' in 1936. This was dedicated to restoring a sense of seriousness to French music, then dominated by the anti-romantic aesthetic of the composers of 'Les Six'. During the war he was interned by the Germans in Stalag VIII, where he performed for the first time his apocalyptic *Quatuor pour la fin du temps* (1941) before the entire assembly of prisoners in icy conditions. Upon his release, he resumed teaching duties in Paris, becoming in 1947 Professor of Analysis, Aesthetics and Rhythm at the Conservatoire. His radical experiments with musical language in the early 1950s attracted some of the outstanding young composers of the day to his classes, including **Pierre Boulez** and **Karlheinz Stockhausen**. After the death of his first wife in 1959, he married his former pupil Yvonne Loriod for whom he had written many of his piano works. In 1966 he became Professor of Composition at the Conservatoire and travelled and taught extensively throughout the world.

Any discussion of Messiaen's music must take as its starting point his artistic personality,

which offers an intensely private and individual response to the traditional concerns of
Christianity, nature and human love. The
astonishing power and commitment of his
work derived in some measure from his
unquestioning acceptance of the diverse
influences of his childhood, while its attraction resides in the integration of a radical
reappraisal of the elements of musical language with an aesthetic that derived unashamedly from **Richard Wagner** and the
French Symbolists.

Many of these features are present in the
early works of the late 1920s and 1930s. If the
titles of the piano *Préludes* (1928) reflect an
obvious **Debussyism** (*Les Sons impalpables du
rêve*, *Un reflet dans le vent*, and so on), their
forms by contrast are constructivist. The same
is also true of the subsequent organ pieces
that stand in the line of **César Franck** and
Jehan Alain and show a characteristic commitment to sacred subjects: *Le Banquet céleste*
(1928), *L'Ascension* (1933) (which also exists
in an orchestral version), *La Nativité du
Seigneur* (1935) and *Les Corps glorieux* (1939).
In the 1940s this line was extended by *Visions
de l'amen* (1943, for two pianos), *Vingt regards
sur l'enfant Jésus* (1944, for piano), and *Trois
petites liturgies de la Présence Divine* (1944, for
women's choir and orchestra). That these
pieces mainly comprise short descriptive
movements points to a life-long preference
for episodic forms, with simple but sharp
internal contrasts, rather than for the integrated, developing forms of the Austro-German tradition. The imaginative stimulus to
using even sacred texts in this way, Messiaen
suggested, arose out of his childhood delight
in the fantastic elements in Shakespeare
(Ariel, Puck); in manhood he created com-
parably fantastic tableaux illustrative of the
'truths' of Catholic dogma, whose range
embraces the extremes of peace and violence,
reverence and penitence.

In the 1930s, he had also composed two
song cycles for Wagnerian voice to his own
surrealistic texts (he derived his literary bent
from his mother, a writer). These celebrated
his marriage (*Poèmes pour Mi*, 1936) and the

birth of a child (*Chants de terre et de ciel*, 1938).
In the 1940s he pursued the themes of secular
love in three works devoted to the Tristan
and Isolde myth: *Harawi* (1945, for voice
and piano), *Turangalilâ-Symphony* (1948, for
orchestra), and *Cinq rechants* (1949, for twelve
solo voices). These works represent the summation of the first part of his life. In the
Symphony especially, the remarkable new
eroticism is projected on the one hand
through a glittering rhythmic brilliance, and
on the other hand through a spaciousness in
repose that had already been adumbrated by
the timeless contemplations of the early organ
music.

In all these works, there had been technical
innovations: still working within a tonal framework, he had devised a number of pitch
modes ('of limited transposition') characterized by internal symmetries that he used in
various combinations; in response to the dis-
association of pitch and rhythmic functions in
The Rite of Spring of **Igor Stravinsky**, he
approached purely rhythmic thought from
several standpoints: he derived small cells
from a Hindu treatise (*Sharngadeva*),
employed Greek rhythms based on conventional ideas of the poetic foot, used prime
numbers to determine large proportions, and
built multi-levelled rhythmic structures out
of canons and ostinati. Increasingly he came
to prefer the 'free, unequal durations' he
found in nature to what he considered to be
the artificial metric regularity of traditional
music. These concerns came to a head in a
number of experimental, and highly influential, keyboard pieces: the *Modes de valeurs et
d'intensités*, *Neumes rythmiques* and *Canté-
jodjayâ* of 1949; the *Île de feu I et II* of 1950;
and the *Livre d'orgue* of 1951. These works, in
part or in whole, reflected the obsessive contemporary desire for a high degree of ordering in all the simply identifiable musical
dimensions – a desire to a certain extent fostered by post-war analyses of the music of
Anton Webern. In pitch terms, although
Messiaen used the twelve-tone scale modally
more often than serially, he here developed
mechanistic permutational patterns in a spirit

he viewed as redolent of the Middle Ages. In rhythmic terms, he measured note-lengths as additions of durational values which he then permutated according to 'interversion' procedures. Comparable methods were applied to dynamic values and to different modes of articulation. Although twelve-tone, these means embodied nothing of the 'organic' processes found in the music of **Arnold Schoenberg** and his school, and, indeed, were crude to a degree. Nevertheless, they undoubtedly ushered in a new phase of European music, and their fruits are, to a certain extent, still with us today.

Immediately after these works, however, there was a dramatic change. For personal reasons he turned to a contemplation of nature – something he knew well from his boyhood in Grenoble – in which he saw, if not a solace, then certainly a refuge from the world. His principal concern was to transcribe the melodies, rhythms and timbres of birdsongs for conventional instruments, and to intersperse the results with musical passages descriptive of the birds' natural habitats. In this he considered he was extending the nature music of Wagner and **Claude Debussy**. While there had been elements of birdsong in his earlier works, three pieces were now entirely given over to it: the *Réveil des oiseaux* (1953, for piano and orchestra), which like the later *Chronochromie* (1960, for orchestra) includes an elaborate dawn chorus; *Oiseaux exotiques* (1956, for piano and orchestra), a fantasy combining birdsongs from all over the world; and *Catalogue d'oiseaux* (1956–8, for piano) a richly imaginative inventory in seven volumes.

The works after 1960 showed once again a profusion of concerns: there was the consolidation of nature imagery (*La Fauvette des jardins*, 1970, for piano, and *Des canyons aux étoiles*, 1971, for orchestra); a return to sacred subjects (*Couleurs de la Cité Céleste*, 1963, for piano and small orchestra, *Et expecto resurrectionem mortuorum*, 1964, for orchestra, *La Transfiguration de notre Seigneur Jésus Christ*, 1963–9, for choir, seven soloists and orchestra, and *Méditations sur le mystère de la Sainte Trinité*, 1969, for organ); and an extension of his interest in exotica (*Sept Haikai*, 1962, for piano and orchestra, which includes an imitation of Sho, the Japanese mouth organ). Here, Messiaen's life-long concern with musical colour achieved a new prominence, especially in the selection and juxtaposition of chords and textures. The sonorities were more brittle and relied particularly on the 'mysterious' resonances of greatly expanded percussion sections. All these features achieved their greatest synthesis in his only opera, *St-François d'Assise* (1975–83) a work of huge proportions written for the Paris Opera that reinterpreted in sacred terms the awe and terror of the Kantian sublime. The late works broke new territory by diversifying his ensembles: *Un vitrail et des oiseaux* (1986) and *La Ville d'En-haut* (1987) were for piano, brass, wind and percussion; *Concert à quatre* (1990–1) was for piano, flute, oboe, cello and orchestra; and *Piece pour piano et quatuor à cordes* (1991) was for piano and string quartet. His last work *Éclairs sur l'au dela*, like *Un sourire* (1989), was for orchestra alone and astonished audiences at its first posthumous performance for its poignant mastery.

While the elements of the Messiaen legacy are in themselves clear enough – and none has been more influential than his concern with the formation of musical language, as testified by his idiosyncratic writings *Technique de mon langage musical* ('Technique of My Musical Language', 1942) and *Traité de rhythme, de couleur, et d'ornithologie* (1949–92) – it is the power of his innate gifts that has proved persuasive: even those whose aesthetic and musical attitudes are quite other than his have acknowledged him as a modern legend.

Further reading

Most of Messiaen's works are published by either Durand or Leduc (Paris). See: Robert Sherlaw Johnson, *Messiaen* (1975); Claude Samuel, *Conversations with Olivier Messiaen* (1976 and 1994); Paul Griffiths, *Olivier Messiaen and the Music of Our Time* (1985); and Peter Hill, *The Messiaen Companion* (1995).

CHRISTOPHER WINTLE

MIES VAN DER ROHE, Ludwig

1886–1969

German/US architect

Mies van der Rohe and **Le Corbusier** are the most important architects of what has been called the Heroic period of modern architecture, the period between the two world wars when the theories and style of the new architecture were first demonstrated. The double challenge that the architects of this time took upon themselves was to derive a form of building which could exploit the new manufacturing technology, which could make use of machine-produced parts, and more importantly create an undecorated architecture, an intention first suggested by **Adolf Loos's** essay 'Decoration and Crime' published in 1908. Through this latter ambition the pioneer architects identified themselves with the urgency of modernism, the desire to break once and for all with the irrelevancies and encumbrances of the past. Although recent reassessment has often been directed towards finding parallels between the works of this period and the more distant past, notably the comparison by Colin Rowe of the villas of Le Corbusier and Palladio, and although a more detailed analysis of Mies might show an unbroken line from the German neoclassicism of Schinkel, received through Behrens with whom he worked at a formative time, the spirit of the early modern movement was obsessively, to borrow Moholy-Nagy's phrase, the New Vision.

In his later work, Le Corbusier displayed a huge and varied talent, whereas Mies held to the same aims – the desire for clarity and purity, expressed through a strict rectilinear geometry and careful detailing – throughout his long career. These qualities were characteristics of all his mature works, from first to last, and this consistency of effort and inspiration explains why his influence is so pervasive, and why he can be considered above all others as the father of steel and glass architecture. The prophetic nature of his abilities can be judged by the models of the glass tower blocks, done between 1919 and 1921.

Mies's mature style found its first clear expression in the design of the German Pavilion for the 1929 International Exhibition in Barcelona. In this small one-storey building can be found the essence of what was to inform the rest of his life's work, demonstrated with complete authority. The characteristics of the style were the building placed upon a pedestal, the use of opulent materials, treated as pure clear-cut rectilinear horizontal and vertical surfaces, spaces within and without treated as overlapping and interlocking, transparent external walls, and a separation of the structure from the walls, using non-load bearing partitions around a regular placing of loadbearing columns, allowing for a free composition of the plan. This approach allowed him to compose the plan unrestricted by the demands of support and gravity, as a painter might compose an abstract painting. The similarity between the plan of the Barcelona Pavilion and the contemporaneous Dutch de Stijl school is notable. It has been pointed out elsewhere that this freedom of the plan was achieved at the cost of a much more rigid, stratified section than is usual with traditional loadbearing wall buildings.

For the Pavilion, Mies designed a chair, a stool and a glass-topped table, examples of which were carefully placed within the buildings to further structure and enhance the clear geometrical organization of the space. The deep transparency of the building conveys a sense of space that flows through and beyond the Pavilion, as if this were some local organization within a universal continuous system, which was capable of consistently organizing the placing of furniture and the relationship of one building to another. Thus from this one building he was able to realize a total vision that would allow him confidently to tackle any scale of work, from the layout of a large campus to the design of other exquisite single transparent pavilions.

Apart from the few pieces of furniture, the Barcelona Pavilion only contained a statue by

Georg Kolbe placed on a pedestal in a pool. As with all his best work, the beauty of the composition is best appreciated when empty, devoid of the random casualness of everyday life.

The ideal of continuous space which he was to serve in later buildings, notably in Crown Hall on the Illinois Institute of Technology (IIT) campus, by stopping the internal partitions short of the ceiling, allows for no clear demarcation of one space from another, and explains why clearly defined doors and isolated windows, the ancient items that mark one space from another, and inside from outside, are an anathema to Mies.

His career divided between the work in Germany, which he left in 1937, and the work of the rest of his life in America. Apart from the Barcelona Pavilion his major achievements include the organization of the Weissenhof exhibition in 1927 at which the major architects of the new style, including Le Corbusier, **Walter Gropius**, J.J.P. Oud and Hans Scharoun, at his invitation contributed buildings to a master plan by Mies, producing a unique assemblage of seminal buildings of the Modern Movement; the Turgendhat house in Brno, Czechoslovakia, in 1930; and the model house for the 1931 Berlin Building Exhibition. These latter two buildings were adaptations of the style of the Barcelona Pavilion to the requirements of a dwelling.

In 1930 he was appointed director of the famous design school, the Bauhaus, on Gropius's recommendation, and remained so until, by his own decision, the school was closed in 1933. His cool courage at this time in the face of considerable harassment by the Fascists was unwavering. He left for America in 1937.

Soon after arriving he was appointed Director of Architecture at what was to become the Illinois Institute of Technology, consequently coming to live in Chicago, the city where he was to remain for the rest of his life, and which was to come to contain the greatest concentration of his buildings. In the 1940s and 1950s there developed a deep empathy between his work and the work of the native American architects.

In his inaugural address at IIT he gave a rare and illuminating insight into his philosophy. Education, he asserted, consisted of leading the student from materials, through function, to creative work. He then, with great passion, expounded the virtues and beauty of primitive building methods. In this was an echo of neo-classicism, of the belief that the Greek temples were a refined development from the first primitive hut, from Adam's first house in Paradise.

He was a man of few public utterances, unlike Le Corbusier who was to the end a tireless polemicist. His two most famous typically sparse statements were 'less is more' and 'God is in the details'. These two, however, when read against his buildings, are as revealing as all the volumes produced by Le Corbusier.

There is an interesting divergence in the work in America of the two newly resident pioneer architects and past directors of the Bauhaus, Mies and Gropius. Gropius after the Second World War, working with Konrad Wasehumann, undertook to develop a system for mass-producing housing, called the General Panel house. Mies started at about the same time the design of a house for a close friend, Dr Edith Farnsworth. The house was to take six years to reach completion. Two more opposed uses of the new techniques and materials of building would be difficult to imagine. In retrospect the seeds of difference are evident in the work done by the pioneers of pre-war Europe, but the early enthusiasm still allows the work to be read as a concerted effort. Mies's differences with much of other Modernist orthodoxy began to become clearer in the post-war period. The early edict that form follows function he gently and firmly inverted, stating that as the function of building was liable to change during its lifetime, then the only permanent quality is beauty. This problem of the subservience of the function to the beauty of the building he resolved in many of his schemes by dropping the necessarily enclosed offices and rooms beneath the pedestal, upon which he then placed the familiar beautiful transparent uncluttered pavilion. This he did with the design for the Bacardi Company in Santiago, which was not built, and with his final building, the National Art Gallery in Berlin. Similarly, truth to materials with Mies became love of materials; thus it was love and not truth that informed how he was to treat particular parts of his buildings.

The site for the Farnsworth House was wooded and rural. He produced his most refined example of the steel and glass transparent structure placed upon a pedestal, albeit the latter was a cantilevered slab. As an object to be looked at and from, the house is the clearest expression of a beautifully made object which relates through its transparency the architecture and its setting. The building allowed him to realize the quality suggested by the drawings for the unbuilt Resor House of 1938, which was his first commission in America. The comment still applies that the beauty depends to a large degree on a sense of emptiness. Once marked by occupancy the nature of transparency becomes something quite different from an agent of an open continuous system. When occupied it is more likely to provoke extremes of privatization in at least two ways: first, not having a dark depth into which to withdraw, to avoid the eyes that see all too well, the window walls are liable to be obscured with total curtaining, or as an alternative one needs to own or at least to control the landscape into which the structure is placed.

The designs for court houses that he experimented with throughout his life were less than urban solutions to this paradox.

In 1940 Mies undertook his largest commission, the overall design of the IIT campus in south Chicago and the design of the individual buildings. This was to be the best opportunity to express the idea of a universal building, of the subservience of function to the form. The buildings were designed with the same skeletal steel structure holding to the same set of dimensions into which the variety of uses, chapel, offices, design studios, were then fitted. The overall plan can be seen as an abstract composition, as with the Barcelona plan, but it lacked the dynamics of interpenetration of the earlier plan, seeming to move towards a more regular, symmetrical organization. Many have seen a spirit of Renaissance planning in the final plan, but it might be that it falls rather uneasily between the continuous, interlocking spaces of the earlier work, and the Renaissance genius of place, the concern for focus and forming of particular spaces.

His work included several tower blocks, some for flats, some for offices, and although they are all distinguished by an unequalled clarity of resolution, they are rather more expected than his glass and steel pavilions. Probably the most famous tower is the Seagram Building in Park Avenue, New York, completed in 1958. The building was set back from the line of the avenue, allowing for the setting out of a plaza, the building and the plaza being related by a clear symmetry. The plaza undoubtedly provided an open public space, but more importantly it acted as a pedestal, a device that allowed the finely detailed, symmetrical tower to be viewed, at the cost of breaking the line and identity of the avenue.

His influence as an educator was enormous, his most faithful and successful ex-students being perhaps Skidmore Owings and Merrill.

The final building was the National Gallery in Berlin, completed after his death in 1969. Thus Mies's mature work is begun and finished by two steel and glass pavilions, placed on pedestals, both commissioned by a German government. Their dissimilarities show a move from asymmetry to symmetry and paradoxically, because of his life-long neoclassical interest in universal solutions, a lessening of concern for context. Their similarities and the consistency of his life's work are striking, and a monument to his unwavering genius.

Further reading

See: Peter Blake, *Mies van der Rohe* (1966); Philip Johnson, *Mies van der Rohe* (1953); F. Schultze,

Mies van der Rohe: A Critical Biography (1986); E.S. Hochman (ed.) *Architects of Fortune: Mies van der Rohe and the Third Reich* (1989).

FREDERICK SCOTT

MILL, John Stuart

1806–73

British thinker and essayist

Mill is a giant among modern thinkers. Nearly all subsequent political philosophers, economists, sociologists and writers on culture and society have started from Mill, whether following, amending or reacting against him. Any student can be taught to find contradictions in parts of him, but no thinker has surpassed him when taken as a whole. For a long time he was thought of as the very model of a fully systematic thinker (or at least an acceptable one: Bentham with feelings). But studies of his whole output, made possible by the reprinting of his scattered major essays, reveal a more complex, contradictory but stimulating thinker than the 'saint of rationalism', 'the prince of utilitarians' or the 'king of the philosophic radicals'. He always strove for conclusions relevant to policy or personal conduct, but finally the red thread running all through his life and works appears as a dedication to free-thinking or to the character-forming process of thinking freely itself: the 'free-spirit' outlasts the 'social-engineer'.

His father was James Mill, a disciple and friend of Jeremy Bentham who, although employed by the East India Company, taught John Stuart himself, in the early mornings and evenings, using the Benthamite principle of didactically associating 'the good' with pleasure and evil with pain. He began Greek at three and by six was reading the great Latin authors. Walking with his father he was questioned ceaselessly on what he had read and prepared during the day. By fifteen, after massive doses of economics, history and philosophy, he was ready to be introduced to Bentham's works themselves: almost at once he understood them as a unifying principle to

be applied to all political, social and moral life, the great 'Felicific Calculus', always to calculate the 'greatest happiness of the greatest number' according to 'our two sovereign masters, Pleasure and Pain'. As he wrote in his *Autobiography* (1873): 'I now had opinions; a creed, a doctrine, a philosophy; in one of the best senses of the word, a religion.' Rarely can a child, except in a strictly religious household (like his father's Calvinistic, Scottish youth), have been brought up so seriously, so ideologically, so solitary and so joyless. At seventeen he became a corresponding clerk with the East India Company, but very soon articles began to flow forth promoting the Benthamite cause, and he was active in forming discussion groups and debating societies with other talented young men, all advocates of reform and, in varying degrees, disciples or admirers of Bentham and James Mill.

In 1825 he performed an awesomely complex and taxing editorial labour for Bentham, reducing to one coherent book three early and varying manuscript versions of his great *Rationale of Judicial Evidence*. The following year he fell into a depression and became obsessed with the pointlessness of activity and the meaninglessness of life. Reading by chance a literary passage about the death of his father, tears flowed, natural feelings or sensibility began to return or to grow and he found that the poetry of Wordsworth and the ideas of Coleridge spoke to him, whom previously he had had to read as bad examples of the Benthamite 'fallacy of the feelings'. Articles at this time showed not repudiation but a subtle and cautious modification of the utilitarian doctrine: there were true *higher* pleasures, such as poetry; ultimately it was better/happier to be 'Socrates unhappy than a pig happy'.

In 1829 Macaulay made a savage attack in the *Edinburgh Review* on James Mill's *Essay on Government*, and when John Stuart came to help his father compose a reply for the *Westminster Review* he dispassionately discovered that, apart from the tone, he was much in agreement with Macaulay: the sum total of self-interest did not add up to the general good or the social interest; good government did not always need an identity of interest between rulers and ruled, one could occasionally know what was best for other people; and the idea of model institutions derived from pure reason needed tempering to custom, culture, different levels of understanding and the relativity of circumstances. But only after Bentham's death in 1832 and the trauma of his father's death in 1835 did he openly attack the limitations of Benthamism in his famous essays on Bentham and on Coleridge which keep him still read by (in our far more culturally fragmented times) students of literature as well as by political philosophers. Mill did not abandon reason and the spirit of the French *philosophes*: rather, he argued that Bentham and his father were wrong to look for a single principle from which rules of legislation and personal conduct could be deduced: there were many such principles of society compelling respect and understanding, and they all had to be adapted to circumstances sociologically and compromised together politically. For a period Mill became so unassertive, so unlike the young Benthamite missionary, that some people thought that he was turning Wordsworthian or Coleridgean Tory; and the myopic Carlyle actually believed that Mill was becoming his disciple, simply because he listened and high-mindedly strove to find some truth in all that sage's early blather. But he read Comte, Saint-Simon and **Tocqueville** as well.

Tocqueville was especially congenial to Mill. His *Autobiography* admits that it was reading Tocqueville that made Mill understand that even democracy needs 'a necessary protection against its degenerating into the only despotism of which, in the modern world, there is real danger – the absolute rule of the head of the executive over a congregation of isolated individuals, all equal but all slaves'. Yet Saint-Simon's speculations on co-operativism and Comte's on necessary cultural stages of society also remained with him.

Amid so much mental change, small wonder that he found in this period 'a perfect friendship'; rather, he fell desperately in love in 1830 with a married woman with three children. Harriet Taylor was the wife of a prosperous, radical merchant and her mind was forceful, bold, energetic but rather vain and mediocre. To Mill she was a perfected human type. In his *Autobiography* Mill wrote that 'it was years ... before my acquaintance with her became at all intimate and confident'. He painted a picture of a high-minded Platonic friendship, a spiritual love which **George Bernard Shaw** was to take as a dramatic model and which some have seen as the forerunner of that alleged 'sacerdotal celibacy' that some of the first generation of married dons at Oxford professed to practise. But it was untrue. Whether or not there was actual sexual intercourse, their letters reveal that the twenty years before her husband's death were full of the most painful and romantic storm and stress, of which her tolerant husband quickly tired, setting her up on her own where Mill was free to visit her, indeed to take her and her children on holiday together while all the time pretending to live at home with his sisters.

His *A System of Logic* (1843) was his first book and the last uninfluenced by Harriet. It dominated British philosophy in the nineteenth century and Book 6, on the method of the social sciences, is of lasting value. While his insistence on inductive method is now generally rejected, as in **Karl Popper's** argument that science begins with hypotheses to be tested and refuted, not with observations made from a *tabula rasa* mind, Mill himself is surpassingly rich in fertile hypotheses, whether or not he thought they were derived from pure reason (deduction) or pure observation (induction). His *Principles of Political Economy* followed in 1853 and he claimed that the 'qualified socialism' of the last chapter on 'The Probable Futurity of the Working Classes' was 'entirely due to her'. Scholars once thought that these were the pietistic words of a besotted lover, but correspondence between them shows this to be all too true: his scepticism was swept away by her idealism and bullying, at the expense of flagrant contradictions in the text. It was the least successful of his major works. Apart from Harriet's socialism, he went back to what his father had taught him in the 1820s, ignoring twenty years of subsequent economic theory.

There is now no reason to doubt that *On Liberty* (1859) was a truly collaborative work, written together after his retirement from the East India Company. But this greatest work was fortunately on a theme on which they had both always basically agreed. He was to speak of the young Benthamites as having had 'an almost unbounded confidence in the efficacy of two things: representative government, and complete freedom of discussion'; only the young Benthamites would not have even appeared to value eccentricity for its own sake, or for example to conformists, but only if it led to the truth. And the essay does contain some criteria for limitations on liberty, which Mill inserted but which Harriet mercifully glossed over, not greatly stressed, but then a famous writer has some right to assume that people knew where he stood already: that there can be *utilitarian* grounds of public order for limiting individualism, but never absolute moral grounds. 'You may not do this because it is not convenient to most of us' at least leaves more in place than the absolute prohibition, 'That is wrong.'

If he enjoyed his great public fame, it must have been somewhat marred by Harriet's quarrelling with nearly all his celebrated friends during their seven years of marriage before she died unexpectedly in Avignon in 1859. Mill moved there with her daughter Helen, bought a house and installed in it the entire furniture and fittings of the hotel room in which she had died. The rationalist shared the Victorian cult of the dead. But gradually his old ways resumed: friendships and publications, and even three years in the House of Commons as Radical Liberal member for Westminster, though unsuccessful in re-election because of his support on principle for the atheist Bradlaugh, a man he disliked personally. *Considerations on Representative Government* appeared in 1861, a subtle discussion of the relationship of the idea of democracy

to types of institutions and circumstances. Democracy was universally possible, but only with universal compulsory education and, moreover, its forms would vary greatly. So strong was national feeling, for instance, that he doubted if representative government was possible in a multi-national state (a view that Lord **Acton** regarded as 'uncivilized'). So an historical relativism had come to temper the old rationalism, and the idea of an open, educated, cultivated and rational elite (open to all eventually, but eventually) tempered the old Millite utilitarians of each actual opinion counting as one. He even advocated, somewhat tentatively, that while each person should have a vote, votes should be weighted according to education. But he noted that the politicians were indeed interested in a property, not an educational franchise. So proportional representation became his last piece of Benthamite institutional advocacy.

The last years were extraordinarily fruitful. The year 1861 saw his final attempt, still intellectually impressive, to synthesize Bentham and Wordsworth, in *Utilitarianism*. During the American Civil War he attacked pro-Southern writers strongly and influentially. In 1871 came *The Subjection of Women*, an emancipatory tract in which, if Harriet's influence is obvious, he was also returning to his first serious criticisms of Bentham and his father, both of whom were somewhat half-hearted in their acceptance of women as equally mankind. He came to terms with his own intellectual development in his *Autobiography*, published in 1873 soon after his death. Though austere and solely concerned with the intellect, it is impressive and moving. Only a few pages were removed by Helen Taylor (now recovered). His last words were: 'You know that I have done my work.' An unseemly public controversy broke out as to whether such a great man who was a sceptic should or could be buried at Westminster Abbey. The wily **Gladstone** hedged on the issue. But Mill had insisted on being interred alongside Harriet at Avignon. His bust appeared in secularist and Unitarian meeting houses until very recently, and every free-thinking intellectual until 1914 had his portrait on the study wall.

Further reading

See: *Collected Works of J.S. Mill*, ed. J.M. Robson *et al.* (33 vols, 1963–91). A good modern selection from both the political and cultural essays is *Essays on Politics and Culture* ed. Gertrude Himmelfarb (1962). See also: F.A. Hayek, *John Stuart Mill and Harriet Taylor* (1951); Michael St John Packe, *The Life of John Stuart Mill* (1954): Joseph Hamburger, *Intellectuals in Politics: John Stuart Mill and the Philosophic Radicals* (1965); A. Ryan, *J.S. Mill* (1974); C.L. Ten, *Mill On Liberty* (1980) and S. Collini, D. Winch and J. Burrow, *The Noble Science of Politics* (1983).

BERNARD CRICK

MILLER, Arthur

1915–2005

US playwright

After **Eugene O'Neill**, Arthur Miller is the most talented and significant playwright America has produced. His theories of drama are provocative; his plays rich and varied.

Miller was the son of a prosperous manufacturer hit hard by the Depression; and one of the ironically creative results of that terrible period in American history was the compassion that it bred in Arthur Miller ('The icebox was empty and the man was sitting there with his mouth open', *The Price*, 1968). It made him realize how adverse circumstances could diminish man's self-respect and dignity; it made him especially critical of men who by their own acts diminished themselves and other people; it made him cherish those individuals who sought above all to preserve their integrity. 'I am Willy Loman,' says the hero of *Death of a Salesman* (1949); 'Give me my name,' says John Proctor in *The Crucible*, 1953. The Depression contributed importantly to Miller's sense that the duty of the dramatist is to deal with the moral problems of the day. As a democrat and American he feels that he has a contribution to make to both the theory and practice of the drama. 'The Common man is as apt a subject for tragedy in its highest sense as kings were,' he has written, and has gone on to define tragedy as 'the consequence of a man's total compulsion to evaluate himself justly' (*Tragedy and the Common Man*, 1949). His 'Introduction' to *Collected Plays* (1957), his essays 'On Social Plays' (1955) and on 'The Family in Modern Drama' (1956) are of profound merit and illuminate the reading and viewing of his plays.

His first successful play, *All My Sons* (1947), was a reproach to the capitalist ethic which led manufacturer Joe Keller to market faulty aircraft parts and thus cause the death of a number of pilots, including one of his sons; his second and greatest play, *Death of a Salesman*, lovingly chronicled the last days of Willy Loman, an insignificant man in terms of his career, but a significant human being who fights to the last against unsympathetic employers, an unhelpful wife, self-centred sons and his own weakness in order to salvage something worthwhile from his life. Willy Loman is, to Arthur Miller, a tragic hero. But Miller's plays are not merely about human potential and its abuse; they are about families. Miller is a moralist who believes that self-realization can only come through helping others; man is a social and caring animal and must show himself as such in his most immediate context, the family unit. But while Miller believes in man's potential for good and happiness he also finds evil and misery wherever he looks. The Lomans live together yet barely understand each other; the great love in the family of immigrant Italians proves a jealous and destructive emotion (*A View from the Bridge*, 1955). Even in the play in which the protagonists are able to articulate precisely how they felt about each other as children, adolescents and adults – *The Price* – there is no real coming together of the brothers Victor and Walter Franz. The play begins with the Victrola playing Gallagher and Shean; it ends with the sound of the laughing record. Miller seems finally to despair of answering the questions he has asked in play after play. 'How may a man make of the outside world a home?' ('The Family in Modern

Drama') and how may a man make a nominal home a real one? *The Creation of the World and Other Business* (1973) indicates his despair – it depicts God as an inept old man, dependent on Satan for breathing life into creation.

Miller is often compared with **Ibsen** – he adapted *An Enemy of the People* (1950) – and there is something of Ibsen's fatalism in Miller's *The Crucible*, which used the seventeenth-century Salem witch trials to point out the true nature of McCarthyism and implied the continuity of evil and persecution. Two plays which deal with the Second World War, *Incident at Vichy* (1965) and *After the Fall* (1964), also sound a note of pessimism as the protagonists attempt to evade the responsibility for chaos which is truly theirs. Rare indeed is Leduc in *Vichy*, who admits: 'Each man has his Jew: it is the other', and John Proctor in *The Crucible*, who manages finally to be true to himself, his family, his society and his God.

Sensitivity, humour, an effective use of Jewish grammatical inversion – 'Attention, attention must be paid' to Willy Loman – a strong sense of dramatic confrontation and an ability to exploit such scenes to the full characterize Miller's work as a playwright. If nothing is too commonplace to be tragic, nothing is too private to publish, as is evident in the self-critical portrait Miller painted of his relationship with his second wife, Marilyn Monroe, in *After the Fall*. His novel *Focus* (1945), about a non-Jew who looks Jewish and feels he discharges a moral debt by pretending to be Jewish, and his short story/screenplay *The Misfits* (1961) suggest that Miller could have been effective as a novelist, had he so chosen. But he is committed to 'the fated mission of the drama', for 'within the dramatic form [lies] the ultimate possibility of raising the truth-consciousness of mankind to a level of such intensity as to transform those who observe it' ('The Family in Modern Drama').

Further reading

Other works include: *Playing for Time* (1981); *Danger: Memory!* (1987); *The Ride Down Mount*

Morgan (1991); *The Last Yankee* (1992) and *Mr Peter's Connections* (1998). See: Dennis Welland, *Arthur Miller* (1961); Edward Murray, *Structure, Character and Theme in the Plays of Arthur Miller* (1966); Leonard Moss, *Arthur Miller* (1967); Robert Martin (ed.) *The Theatre Essays of Arthur Miller* (1978); N. Carson, *Arthur Miller* (1982).

ANN MASSA

MILLER, Henry
1891–1980
US novelist

Born and brought up in New York City of German immigrant parents, Miller never completed his college education at City College, New York, but married unhappily and drifted from one job to another before deciding to be a writer. Moving to Paris in 1930 provided a breakthrough and the books he wrote there formed the basis for his reputation. Attacked by **Kate Millett** and other feminists as a chauvinistic egotist, exalting his sexual prowess at the expense of women degraded to mere sex objects, his novels, in fact, are fictional autobiography and record his own spiritual growth and the struggles and trials of those around him.

Tropic of Cancer (1934) is an account of his life in Paris, and is a combination of a Bohemian idyll of the rootless, penniless artist existing outside, and over against, bourgeois conventionality, and a **Whitmanesque** hymn to the power of unfettered experience to liberate the artist into a prophet and visionary for a potentially perfect humanity. Sexuality becomes the means of revealing both our collective, cultural heritage with its often pernicious demands, guilts and shames, and the essence of the individual's accommodation to reality. The fact that desire is created by another and the response to one's own feelings means that here is a way of grasping the intersubjectivity of our experience.

In his next two novels, *Black Spring* (1938) and *Tropic of Capricorn* (1939), Miller continued to use the events of his own life in Paris and New York as metaphors for the human comedy. In order to reach the possibility of love, be believes we must pass through the 'Land of Fuck' in order to emerge from our privacy, self-importance and narcissism, to encounter and accept others, to risk losing our pride and complacency and to go beyond our 'ego-hood'. Without such openness and risk-taking, sex is merely destructive or sterile, as many of Miller's characters demonstrate.

Reflecting on the earlier stages of his life, Miller continued his personal odyssey in the *Rosy Crucifixion* trilogy: *Sexus* (1945), *Plexus* (1949) and *Nexus* (1960), but with a lessening of intensity, probably related to his growing certainty of the truth of his views and his determination to preach them in such volumes of essays as *The World of Sex* (1940), *The Wisdom of the Heart* (1941) and *Stand Still like the Hummingbird* (1962).

His criticism of America and the modern world, its conformity, repression, violence and insanity, expressed through the championing of artists and eccentrics, as in *The Air-Conditioned Nightmare* (1945), has created for him a wide following, and many writers from **Huxley**, **Orwell** and **Durrell** to **Mailer** and the Beat poets have paid tribute to his liberation of explicit sexual material for use in the novel, and his honesty in exploring the fantasy-rich chaos underlying the surface normality of the West.

Further reading

Other works include: *The Colossus of Maroussi* (1941); essays: *The Cosmological Eye* (1939); *Sunday after the War* (1944); *Big Sur and the Oranges of Hieronymus Bosch* (1957); *Books in My Life* (1952); and *The Nightmare Notebook* (1975). Letters: *Lawrence Durrell and Henry Miller* (1963); *Letters to Anaïs Nin* (1965). See also: Alfred Perles, *My Friend, Henry Miller* (1956); Jory Martin, *Always Merry and Bright* (1978); Robert Ferguson, *Henry Miller: A Life* (1991); Mary V. Dearborn, *The Happiest Man Alive: A Biography of Henry Miller* (1991); Erica Jong, *The Devil at Large* (1993)..Critical studies: Sydney Omarr, *Henry Miller: His World of Urania* (1960); William A. Gordon, *The Mind and Art of Henry Miller* (1967).

DAVID CORKER

MILLET, Jean François

1814–75

French painter

Born into a prosperous peasant family near Cherbourg, Millet studied in Paris under Delaroche. His early work consists mostly of portraits, interspersed with erotic scenes, executed in a florid late-Rococo manner. His first wife's death in 1844, after only three years of marriage, may have helped trigger the reconsideration from which his mature art emerged; these years also coincided with political and social disturbance. In 1849 he moved to the village of Barbizon near Fontainebleau, where landscape artists like **Corot**, Diaz and Theodore Rousseau also worked. Throughout the 1850s a succession of large paintings on peasant themes brought him controversy, and eventually, in his final years, immense popular success.

Millet's essential contribution is to have created an enduring iconography of labour, sufficiently ambiguous to have fertilized a wide variety of later artists, and to have stood for many different creeds at different times. Its genesis remains mysterious; his figures owe something to his study of Brueghel, and also to **Daumier**. Initially interpreted as protests against the plight of the peasant, Millet's chief works would become by the 1890s schoolroom texts for the dignity of labour. *The Sower* (1850) was the first of these archetypal images and exists in several variations; as **Van Gogh** realized when making his own version, it carries unavoidable overtones of parable.

It is this aspect of Millet which the anarchist **Pissarro** found unsympathetic – 'He was just a shade too biblical' – and his own use of Millet's *Peasant Ploughing* as a cover for **Kropotkin's** 'The New Age' underlines this ambiguity; was Millet speaking of present ills or, rather, in praise of some timeless Golden Age? *The Angelus* (1855–7) shows two peasants working overtime in the fields; when they hear the sacred note, the woman bows devoutly, while the man dumbly, or perhaps sullenly, watches. Here as elsewhere the low viewpoint is important in creating monumentality; in Millet's own words: 'It is astonishing toward the approach of night, how grand everything on the plain appears, especially when we see figures thrown up against the sky. Then they look like giants.' Millet was too much a symbolist to be a radical; here the male figure could easily be retailored to become **Puvis de Chavannes's** *Pauvre pêcheur*, rapt in mystical acceptance of his lot.

The figures in *The Gleaners* (1857) are life-size, and in its magnificent rhythmic interval it remains Millet's formal masterpiece, epitomizing also his characteristic use of primary colours, softened by rounded modelling. Yet the contrast between the groaning harvest wagon behind, and the back-breaking labour of the foreground could be more telling; and it might be argued Millet's classic harmony dulls the edge of his protest (in contrast to the rougher music of his contemporary, **le Courbet**). The only work where Millet's radical sympathies emerge unclouded is the terrifying *Man with a Hoe* (1860) whose apocalyptic implications were immediately recognized.

All his life Millet was a peerless draughtsman, in pastel or in black crayon, and the vigorous studies of individual labourers have worn better than the more rhetorical 'machines'. His visionary landscapes are the masterpieces of the 1860s: *November*, the plough abandoned in the desolate crow-haunted field (an image widely known through Van Gogh's version); or *Spring*, from the *Four Seasons* (1865–73), where, amid astonishing light effects, winter is cast out by a rainbow and flowers burst from the glistening grass.

The unfinished *Brushwood Gatherers*, with its funereal bowed procession, can be viewed at Cardiff alongside another late masterpiece, the *Peasant Family*. 'Such works,' wrote **Sickert** in 1912, 'are the ultimate works of art. There is only one way to paint and here it is.' Yet Millet's last and possibly greatest painting stands apart: the bizarre scene, recollected from childhood, of *Boys Clubbing Birds to Death by Torchlight* (1874). The lunging puppet figures, silhouetted against jagged bird-broken aureoles, seem like dancers in some primeval ritual; the resonance is of man's gratuitous and somnambulistic cruelty.

Millet's reputation has fluctuated more than any comparable master. *The Angelus*, originally purchased for 1,000 francs, was fetching 300,000 by the 1880s, and 800,000 ten years later. But over-exposure blurred the originality of his Epic Naturalism; many twentieth-century critics have re-echoed Delacroix's early judgement: 'deep but pretentious feeling'. In France, Millet's influence extended through **Degas's** pastels and **Seurat's** twilight drawings, to Pissarro and **Gauguin**, and to Van Gogh, who above all understood that 'in Millet everything is at once both reality and symbol', and whose art is unimaginable without that example.

Further reading

See: Robert L. Herbert, *Millet* (Arts Council Catalogue, 1976); Rosalyn Bacou, *Millet: One Hundred Drawings* (1975); Julia M. Ady, *Jean François Millet: His Life and Letters* (1986).

TIMOTHY HYMAN

MILLETT, Kate (Katherine Murray)

1934–

US feminist

Born in St Paul, Minnesota into an Irish Catholic family, Kate Millett was the daughter of an insurance saleswoman and a contractor who left the family when she was fourteen. She went to parochial school in St Paul, and then just across the Mississippi River to the University of Minnesota in Minneapolis as an undergraduate. She subsequently attended St Hilda's College, Oxford, and Columbia University for her PhD. Her PhD dissertation, much to her surprise, became the best-selling feminist treatise *Sexual Politics* (1970). The book established her as the premier theorist for the newly rising women's movement and for a time put her at the forefront of public attention in the radical, liberationist and lesbian faction of 1970s American feminism.

Before this Kate Millett was successful as a sculptor, exhibiting in the Judson Gallery in Greenwich Village and in the Miniami Gallery in Tokyo. From 1961 to 1963 she was resident in Japan, where she met her future husband, the Japanese sculptor Fumio Yoshimura. Subsequently they shared a Bowery loft apartment, the bisexual Millett saying of their relationship that they were 'friends and lovers'. They were divorced in 1985.

In contrast to Millett, the other leading early 1970s American feminist theorist, **Betty Friedan**, essentially advocated economic independence and social and political leadership for women, a reformist position. Far more sweeping in what she advocated, Millett articulated a theory of patriarchy and conceptualized the gender and sexual oppression of women in terms that demanded a sex role revolution with radical changes of personal and family lifestyles.

The clash between these two women was also the dividing line between two approaches to the movement and was epitomized in their differing attitudes towards lesbianism. Having identified sexuality per se as the root of masculinist domination of women, Millett consistently sought to affirm lesbianism as part of her programme for the recognition of woman's freedom of sexual expression in general. Friedan, on the other hand, had opposed affirming lesbianism – at least up until the 1977 Houston National Women's Conference. There she announced: 'I've had trouble with this issue. But we must help women who are lesbians in their own civil rights.' Friedan's and the Convention's acceptance of lesbian practice as one of their public policy proposals was seen by most commentators as a vindication of Millett's position.

Intellectually important, *Sexual Politics* was an instant best-seller. Its central ideas are that all power relationships are rooted in gender, that men belong to a 'caste of virility' and

exercise what they, women and society, as well, believe to be a birthright power over women in every arena of human life. Patriarchy (male power) is the dominant mode of Western culture, and women are the victims of submission to it in the family, religion, politics, technology, education, economics and psychology. 'Patriarchy,' Millett says, 'decrees that the status of both child and mother is primarily or ultimately dependent on the male.'

Patriarchy also sets woman against woman ('whore and matron/career woman and housewife') in the confines of seeking status and security through men. Women, Millett says, are separated and subordinated by men's control of institutions, production and access to information. While men invent and manufacture technologically advanced machines, women are not allowed to have the power of knowledge of their design and production, though they may be allowed to operate them. The central institution of male hegemony, however, is the nuclear family. The significant symbol for it is sexual intercourse with the man 'taking' the woman. This leads Millett to document, in a somewhat scattered way, what has come to be called sexism. She provides its historical context, together with four literary examples: the works of **D.H. Lawrence**, **Henry Miller** and **Norman Mailer** exhibiting sexual politics, and **Jean Genet** through his male homosexual queen illustrating an empathetic possibility with the oppression of women.

While *Sexual Politics* was Millett's most widely read book, she sought to move beyond the theory expressed there towards understanding its implications. *Three Lives* (1971) is a film that candidly reveals the actual lives of three women told in their own voices. An equivalent technique informs *The Prostitution Papers* (1971), a book that is divided into four voices, or chapters: two prostitutes, a woman lawyer who specializes in defending prostitutes, and the author's. While Millett did not invent the vocal reproductive form, her use of it is particularly intense, allowing her subjects to pour out the life and observation of prostitution without any apparent editorial interference. In *Flying* (1974) the mode is extended into her own autobiography. Abolishing privacy, a scrupulous transparency is implied as, in a succession of self-revealing details, she describes her relations with lesbian lovers and the subsequent creativity generated through relationships. *Sita* (1977), styled by one critic as a 'ticker-tape account', is even more explicit in its picture of the demise of a love affair, to the point where even her admirers wondered in print whether the public wants to know quite so many moments in the life of Kate Millett.

In 1971, with proceeds from her book sales, Millett bought fields and buildings near Poughkeepsie, New York, and established Women's Art Colony Farm, a place to provide space and community for women writers and artists. This project has continued more than three decades.

By the end of the 1970s, not having been very interested in organizing and promoting for feminism, and not being very effective in public appearances, Millett saw her influence diminish and interest in her work wane. She continued to produce as a visual artist and she continued to write, though her later work got little attention, and *Sexual Politics* was out of print by 1995. Her later books include *The Loony Bin Trip* (1990), an attack on psychiatry and the mental health system after her personal experience with mental health treatment; *The Politics of Cruelty* (1994), a study of state-sanctioned torture in many countries; *A.D.: A Memoir* (1995), an account of her beloved Aunt Dorothy's negativism about Millett's lesbianism and thus their alienation; and *Mother Millett* (2001), a memoir around her mother's dying.

In 2000, a university press re-issued *Sexual Politics* and some of Millett's other writings, paying tribute to the 'groundbreaking nature of her writing, art, and activism'.

Further reading

A feminist scholarly volume, *Women's Autobiography: Essays in Criticism*, edited by Estelle Jeli-nek (1980) contains two essays about Millett's work: Suzanne Juhasz, 'Towards a Theory of Feminist Autobiography: Kate Millett's *Flying* and *Sita* and Maxine Hong Kingston's *The Woman Warrior*'; and Annette Kolodny, 'This Lady's Not for Spurning: Kate Millett and the Critics'.

GAYLE GRAHAM YATES

MIRÓ, Jóan
1893–1983
Spanish painter

Jóan Miró was born in Barcelona. Though his father was a prosperous goldsmith in that town Miró's antecedents were farmers and the landscape and peasant traditions of rural Catalonia were an important part of his early artistic and emotional life. In his late teens he studied at the local art school and in 1919, fully committed to being a painter, he made his way to Paris.

After a relatively short time there he made contact with the leading personalities of French art and almost immediately found himself at the centre of the Surrealist movement. By 1922 he had met, through André Masson, the poet Louis Aragon and the 'pope of Surrealism', **André Breton**, and later, in 1927, he became a close neighbour of the painters **Max Ernst**, **Hans Arp** and **René Magritte**. But despite this ideological barrage Miró, who returned to his native countryside every summer, retained a measure of independence. In works like *Self Portrait* (bought by **Picasso**) and *The Farm* (bought by **Hemingway**) he continued to preserve the identities of well-loved domestic objects realistically intact inside a decorative Cubist structure, but with *The Ploughed Field* (1923–4) reality becomes more scrambled until in *Harlequin's Carnival* (1925–5) human figures, animals, plants, etc., were completely replaced by clusters of new symbols, so laying the foundation of his particular personal style. Between 1925 and 1927 he experimented with the sources of creativity by working spontaneously in self-induced states of hallucination and impaired consciousness producing paintings, like *The Birth of the World* (1925), which departed further and further from the appearance of the common sense world.

He married in 1929 and from then on, with the exception of an unsettled period during the Spanish Civil War and the 1939–45 conflict, he worked in Paris and Spain in a relatively consistent style over a wide variety of media. His paintings have been exhibited worldwide, especially in America where he had his first one-man show in New York as early as 1930, and his vast output also includes designs for the theatre (for Massine and **Diaghilev**), sculpture, ceramics and murals, notably in the Guggenheim Museum, for Harvard University and in 1957 for the UNICEF building in Paris.

Though linked historically with the Surrealists, and though he himself distrusted the term 'abstract', his particular use of signs and symbols is an important contribution to the development of non-figurative painting. While other pioneers more inclined to theory, like **Kandinsky** or **Mondrian**, compared non-representational art to music or mathematics, Miró, no doubt prompted by his interest in poetry and involvement with the mainly literary preoccupations of the Surrealists, instinctively chose the equally fruitful analogy of poetic language. But he also placed as much stress on the essentially visual aspects of painting such as colour, line, composition, etc., which the academic, illustrative artists such as Magritte or **Dalí** tended to neglect.

He cultivated this attitude to form from the start and the works in his first one-man exhibition of 1919 show that he was fully conversant with the latest pictorial advances made by **Matisse** and Picasso and had learned to use bright colour, simplifications and perspective distortions. But this sophistication was not complete. In his landscapes and still-lifes, depictions of vegetables, animals, fruit, foliage and utensils were highly detailed and unschematic and this almost naive particularization carried through into the hieroglyphs which populate the later works. The groups of symbols in *Catalan Landscape* (1923–4), for instance, can be given precise collective and individual interpretations. When placed against lushly painted backgrounds, suggesting interiors or landscapes, they conjure a typically strange non-naturalistic world, entered by the imagination rather than the senses, from which the laws of physical anatomy and gravity are missing. But they are not anarchic daubs. They are formally sound and they relate to a valid if fugitive variety of human experience.

It is precisely in this combination of opposites, combining freedom and control, an excess of form with an excess of content, introspective depth with an original system of public signs which accounts for Miró's continuing reputation. His influence in the 1940s is understandable. The Abstract Expressionists, particularly **Pollock**, **Gorky**, and **Rothko**, derived forms directly from Miró's earlier work, but it is a more unexpected tribute to the balance he achieved that he was just as admired in the 1960s when ideas of meaning, expression and psychology were out of favour.

Further reading

See: Clement Greenberg, *Joan Miró* (1949); Jacques Dupin, *Joan Miró; Life and Work* (1962); Roland Penrose, *Miró* (1970); C. Lanchner, *Joan Miró* (1993).

DAVID SWEET

MISHIMA YUKIO (HIRAOKA KIMITAKE)

1925–70

Japanese writer

Mishima Yukio is the most versatile, and some consider the best, modern Japanese writer. He committed suicide by *harakiri* after calling on Japan's Self-Defence Forces to rise up against the values of the country's post-war democracy. Some right-wing nationalists regard him as their hero, but in his lifetime politics mattered less to him than the desire to 'conquer the world' by his pen.

Mishima Yukio is the pen-name of Hiraoka Kimitake. In his childhood he was much influenced by his grandmother, a strong-willed and aristocratic woman who kept him apart from other children. The dark romanticism of his imagination is already obvious in his early poems and stories. 'A Forest in Full Bloom' ('Hanazakari no Mori', 1944), his first published story, was written at the age of sixteen. Set in a romantic past, it identifies the author as having a privileged destiny. Its theme is the longing for an absolute ideal of beauty, and the consummation of that longing in death.

The war made a deep impression on Mishima. He later described the period 1944–5 as 'a rare time when my own personal nihilism and the nihilism of the age and the society corresponded perfectly'. He was rejected as unfit for active military service, but exulted in the idea of a glorious death on the battlefield. He found himself completely at odds with the left-wing, egalitarian mood of the post-war years in Japan.

He graduated in law from Tokyo University and was a civil servant for a short time. In 1949 his first major work, *Confessions of a Mask* (*Kamen no kokuhaku*, 1949, trans. 1958), was acclaimed by the critics as a masterpiece. It is an autobiographical novel which describes the author's discovery of his own latent homosexuality, and the 'masquerade of reality' he constructs in order to come to terms with the world outside. The book displays a strong streak of narcissism, and explores a private world of sado-masochistic images – especially that of St Sebastian pierced with arrows – to which Mishima often returned in his later writings.

Over the next twenty-one years Mishima produced an astounding quantity of poetry, drama, essays and fiction, including forty novels and eighteen plays. *Forbidden Colours* (*Kinjiki*, part I 1951, part II 1953, trans. 1968) depicts the mentality and milieu of homosexuals in Tokyo. *The Sound of Waves* (*Shiosai*, 1954, trans. 1956) – the only straightforward love story Mishima ever wrote – brought him great popular success. Many people regard *The Temple of the Golden Pavilion* (*Kinkakuji*, 1956, trans. 1959) as his

best novel. It is about a young Zen Buddhist monk perversely obsessed with the beauty of the temple (one of Japan's finest architectural treasures) who finally burns it to the ground. Its theme is characteristic: the sense of an insurmountable barrier between the self and others (the young monk here suffers from a ridiculous stutter) which is only assuaged by an act of wilful destruction. But Mishima also observed contemporary Japanese society with a keen eye. *After the Banquet* (*Utage no Ato*, 1960, trans. 1963), for example, is a vivid satire on the world of politics and patronage.

In 1966 Mishima produced the first part of *The Sea of Fertility*, the tetralogy which he intended to be his crowning achievement. The four successive novels, *Spring Snow* (*Haru no yuki*, 1966, trans. 1972), *Runaway Horses* (*Honma*, 1968, trans. 1973), *The Temple of Dawn* (*Akatsuki no tera*, 1969, trans. 1973) and *The Decay of the Angel* (*Tennin gosui*, 1970, trans. 1974), embrace the whole sweep of Japan's twentieth-century history up until the time of their composition. The central figures in each book are connected by a cycle of reincarnation. But in the final book the awaited sign fails to appear to confirm the thread of destiny, and the whole logic of the narrative is put in question. Mishima wrote this conclusion after making detailed plans for his own death, and it is a clear statement of his lifelong obsession with the impossible quest for some transcendent truth.

Mishima Yukio had an extraordinary zest for life, and thirst for every kind of human experience. In his late twenties he began a rigorous programme of bodybuilding and martial arts, including *kendo* (swordsmanship) and karate. This played an essential part in his personal philosophy of the 'unity of thought and action', a concept with its antecedents in Zen. It also gave him the stamina to keep up a regular routine of writing through every night. At the age of thirty-three Mishima had an arranged marriage, which was successful. He later became the father of two children.

His romantic concern with the role of the Emperor and with *bushido*, the way of the warrior, recurs often in his writing. In 1965 he acted the central role in a film version of his own short story, 'Patriotism', about a young officer who commits *harakiri* at the time of the abortive military uprising in 1936. In 1968 Mishima founded the Shield Society, a 'private army' of one hundred unarmed youths who trained with the Self-Defence Forces. Four of the group's members were with him at the military headquarters in Tokyo where he made his appeal for a return to pre-war nationalist ideals, and one of them died with him.

Mishima's suicide profoundly affected the Japanese people, but had no direct political consequences. His action was widely condemned within Japan, and it prejudiced some critics' assessment of his literary achievement. There is an artificial and morbid strain in some of his work. But he portrayed Japanese life and society in a multitude of aspects with skill and assurance. He used his sure command of classical language and tradition to effect in his modern *Noh* plays and throughout his novels. The novels are untypical of much Japanese fiction in being consistently well structured, and this makes them accessible to Western readers. **Kawabata Yasunari** described Mishima as 'a writer with the kind of exceptional talent which appears only once every two or three hundred years in Japan's history'.

Further reading

Other works include: *Thirst for Love* (*Ai no kawaki*, 1950, trans. 1969); *The Sailor Who Fell from Grace with the Sea* (*Gogo no Eiko*, 1963, trans. 1966). His plays include: *Five Modern Noh Plays* (*Kindai Nogakushu*, 1956, trans. 1957); *Madame de Sade* (*Sado koshaku fujin*, 1965, trans. 1968); 'My Friend Hitler' (*Waga tomo Hittora*, 1968). See also: Henry Scott Stokes, *The Life and Death of Yukio Mishima* (1975); and John Nathan, *Mishima, A Biography* (1974); Marguerite Yourcenar, *Mishima*, trans. A. Manguel (1986); Roy Starrs, *Deadly Dialectics: Sex, Violence and Nihilism in the World of Yukio Mishima* (1994).

WILLIAM HORSLEY

MIZOGUCHI KENJI

1898–1956

Japanese film director

Kenji Mizoguchi was born on 16 May 1898 and died on 24 August 1956. During his lifetime, the cinema went from its infancy as a curious hybrid of vaudeville and mechanical peep show to the quintessential storytelling form in a technological age. In 1898, Japanese culture, still rooted in the social and religious hierarchies nurtured by generations of chosen isolation, regarded itself superior to other Asian societies, and the decadent West as well. By the time of Mizoguchi's death from leukaemia, Japan had suffered the humiliation of World War II, forcing a re-examination of her social and political assumptions, including the brutal system of class and gender roles that set the context for his thirty-four year career as a filmmaker.

Though born into a family of the samurai class, Mizoguchi's early life in Tokyo was splintered by his father's financial failure, which impoverished his family and triggered a series of events that shaped Mizoguchi's attitudes towards family and, especially, women. His sister was given up for adoption and later sold as a geisha. Young Kenji's schooling was interrupted and he was sent away to apprentice as a pharmacist. When he returned home his father refused to send him back to school and he began work designing patterns for kimonos, a job his sister found for him, beginning a dependency on her emotionally and financially. At the age of seventeen he entered the Aiobashi Institute to study painting; here he began his immersion in the Japanese literature of the day, as well as the works of **Maupassant**, **Zola**, **Dostoyevsky** and **Tolstoy**. Through acquaintance with a young actor, Mizoguchi got a job as a set decorator at Nikkatsu Studios, then the premiere film studio in Japan. With the onset of a strike in 1922, he was given his first opportunity to direct, at the age of twenty-four. *The Resurrection of Love*, now lost, demonstrated early his gift for innovation.

Of the approximately eighty feature films Mizoguchi directed between 1922 and 1956 (the records are inconclusive), only thirty are extant.

After the great Tokyo earthquake of 1923, he was moved to Nikkatsu's Kyoto studio where his 'perfectionist' tendencies in working with scriptwriters and set designers began to manifest themselves. In 1925 he was attacked by a jealous prostitute with whom he was living, and suffered razor slashes on his back; this event seems to have focused his concern on the plight of women and, perhaps, led to his famous ambivalence in portraying women as either suffering victims of the social structure or desperate rebels defying convention.

The upheaval of the Great Depression and Japan's rising militarism sharpened Mizoguchi's social conscience and led to his direction, in the early 1930s, of a series of successful but controversial 'tendency films' (*keiko eiga*), influenced heavily by **Marxist** ideology. During this period, he began to experiment with his now-famous *mise-en-scène* technique of 'one shot – one scene' which came to full maturity in the post-war years. **Josef von Sternberg's** luminous images and fluid camera moves were a lasting influence, as were the pre-war films of **John Ford** and William Wyler. Also characteristic of his mature style (which he shared with **Akira Kurosawa**) was his insistence on historically realistic, detailed sets – a demand, Mizoguchi argued, that enabled his actors to perform with a heightened sense of authenticity. To avoid the draft and keep working during World War II, Mizoguchi claimed he was forced to direct four propaganda films, including the competent, but dull, samurai film *The Loyal Forty-Seven Ronin of the Genroku Era* (1941–2). Following the war, and subject to the Allied censors, he was granted permission to work in the banned genre of the 'period film' (*jidai-geki*), resulting in *Utamaro and His Five Women* (1946), and opening the door to his final decade and greatest cinematic achievements.

With the triumph of Kurosawa's *Rashomon* at the Venice Film Festival in 1951, Mizoguchi followed by winning the Silver Lion in 1952 for *The Life of Oharu*, in 1953 for *Ugetsu Monogatari*, and again in 1954 for *Sansho dayu*. This recognition brought him belated international acclaim and the devotion of French New Wave directors **Jean-Luc Godard**, Jacques Rivette and **Eric Rohmer**, as well as the critics of the influential *Cahier du Cinema*. In these three masterpieces, Mizoguchi's great themes find their culmination: the bitter logic of moral and social descent in *Oharu*, the transcendence of death by love in *Ugetsu*, and the will-to-power redeemed by sacrifice in *Sansho*: with women in all their incarnations at the centre. These three films represent a mature genius whose mastery of camera, performance and filmic structure stand at the summit of cinematic achievement, and yield a heartbreaking beauty and grace that, as his cameraman Kazuo Myiagawa said, 'unroll seamlessly, like a scroll'.

Like Shakespeare's *The Tempest,* or the late string quartets of Beethoven, Mizoguchi's final films are at once a summation and transcendence of the struggles that defined his personal life and the cultural life of Japan. The tension between sacred tradition and arrogant modernity, his longing for the ideal of the cohesive family, the redemption of love by sacrifice, and the rejection of worldly desire found their purest expressions in these late works. Though some critics have lamented the lack of moral consistency across his career, including his political confusions and shifting attitudes towards women, in the final analysis, Mizoguchi created films, as Gilbert Adair has remarked, 'for whose sake cinema exists'.

Further reading

A thorough exploration of the relationship of Mizoguchi's life and work can be found in Audie Bock's *Japanese Film Directors* (1978); a feminist perspective in Joan Mellen, *The Waves at Genji's Door – Japan through Its Cinema* (1976); a general view of his place in Japanese film in Donald Richie, *Japanese Cinema: Film Style and National Character,* (1971). Recent assessments include Andrew Dudley and Carole Cavanaugh's monograph *Sansho Dayu*

(2000) and Alexander Jacoby's excellent Internet survey at *Senses of Cinema*, Great Directors: A Critical Database (2002), http://www.sensesofcinema.com/contents/directors/02/mizoguchi.html.

STERLING VAN WAGENEN

MODIGLIANI, Amedeo

1884–1920

Italian artist

Modigliani was born in Livorno, Italy. In 1898 after a severe attack of typhus he was forced to abandon his academic studies in classics. From this point in his life his health was always bad, with a tendency to tuberculosis from which he eventually died; it was this affliction which helped to earn him the title of '*peintre maudit*'. As he showed great promise as a painter his parents sent him to study under Guglielmo Micheli, a pupil of the Macchiaoli painter Giovanni Fattori.

After a serious relapse in 1900 Modigliani travelled throughout Italy attending briefly courses at the academies in Rome, Florence and Venice. During this period he was particularly influenced by the new developments of the Sezession and Art Nouveau artists. It was above all the sculpture of Elie Nadelman which, along with his reading of **Ruskin** on the Italian Primitives and **D'Annunzio's** ideas on aestheticism, led to Modigliani's first elegant attempts at carving in stone. From the beginning of his career his main concern was with the expressive possibilities that might be found in the human face and figure.

In 1906, dissatisfied with the parochial nature of contemporary Italian art, Modigliani moved to Paris where, financed by his mother, he entered the Académie Colarossi and began to work seriously as both painter and sculptor. He quickly befriended leading avant-garde painters like Vlaminck, **Utrillo** and **Picasso** and critics like André Salmon. His poor health and nervous disposition led him at this time to excesses of narcotics and alcohol which contributed as much to the linear tensions and dissonant colours of his art as to his untimely death.

In 1908 Modigliani showed five works at the Salon des Indépendants. The most important in terms of his future development was probably *Le Juive* of 1907 which shows a range of influences encompassing those of **Cézanne**, **Gauguin**, Picasso and **Matisse**. His sculpture of this period shows the influence of African tribal art as well as that of his close acquaintance **Brancusi**. Both media interacted upon one another positively, and from 1910 to 1913 Modigliani's sculpture noticeably shows how far his interests in either were complementary. He attempted to discover formal values by largely disregarding naturalistic modelling and instead developing a synthetic resolution of planes. In this he was of course in step with the experiments of other Parisian artists. To this community of interest he brought a sinuous and rhythmic framework of line bounding his planes and bringing unity to the whole. In his painting these concerns are seen in the use of colour constructively rather than mimetically. Zones of colour bounded by a free and varied line create a simple harmony reminiscent of African and other primitive styles. Before 1914 one of the greatest influences on his work was the large Cézanne exhibition at the Galérie Bernheim. In particular he admired Cézanne's *Young Man with Red Waistcoat*, which first showed him how far the painter can use his subject to expressively distort a human image in the service of a lyrical vision. By 1914 both his painting and his sculpture can be said to have reached their maturity and the rest of his brief career was dedicated to the perfection and refinement of this personal style. The *Portrait of Paul Guillaume* (1916) is a typical example of his work at its best. The tendency to expressive distortion coupled with the peculiar mixture of refinement and primitiveness, in some respects a formula initiated by **Degas**, are resolved in a remote almost hieratic image. Despite Guillaume's casual pose and the picture's disregard for a smooth finish, the final image is one of mask-like detachment and even emptiness.

The physical facts of Modigliani's life in Paris during the war and until his death in 1920, described very evocatively in his daughter's critical biography of 1959, are of illness and poverty. He cared little for money, and even during the harsh years of the war he was to be found selling his drawings in cafés for trifling sums. This lifestyle and dedication to art were virtually lost after the war and Modigliani's personal reputation rests partly on his aristocratic disdain for worldly success and his image of doomed martyr. It should perhaps be mentioned that for some time after his death he received very little acclaim in his native country.

In many respects the varied critical response to Modigliani's work reflects the stylistic uncertainties typical of all early twentieth-century art. His drawing, usually executed swiftly and with little pentimenti, has received praise as psychologically astute and formally terse and subtle. On the other hand critics as diverse as **Wyndham Lewis** and Anthony Blunt have accused his work of being expressively shallow and inventively weak. These are ultimately questions the spectator must decide for himself by comparing his oeuvre with those of other figurative artists of the period struggling with the possibilities offered by recent experimentation in pictorial expression. There can be no doubt, however, that the later series of nudes, often depicting his mistress Jeanne Hebuterne (e.g. *Reclining Nude*, 1919), represent a unique and powerful contribution to the work of the Paris School. This power stems from a severity of line and richness of colour-matching which directly express his haughty, elegant and possibly nostalgic personality. He exerted virtually no influence on his contemporaries but, in the same way as **Rouault**, showed those working in Paris how an expressionist tendency could enrich purely formal interests. He was not an intellectual nor a didactic artist and his work never veered towards neoclassicism or urbane cubism as did that of so many of his colleagues in Paris after 1914.

Further reading

Other works include: *Note e ricordi* (1945). See: J.T. Soby, *Modigliani* (1951); F. Russoli, *Modigliani*

(1958, trans. 1959); J. Modigliani, *Modigliani: Man and Myth* (*Modigliani senza leggenda*, 1959, trans. 1959); W. Schmalenbach, *Modigliani* (1990).

RICHARD HUMPHREYS

MOMMSEN, Theodor

1817–1903

German historian of Rome

Mommsen was born on 30 November 1817 at Garding in Schleswig, a duchy which has produced German-speaking scholars in profusion. He was the son of a poor pastor, educated at the University of Kiel between 1838 and 1843, where he took a degree in law. His most influential teacher and friend was Otto Jahn, musician, philologist and archaeologist, who was dedicated to the idea of a systematic collection of Roman inscriptions. Mommsen's first work was on the Roman associations and tribes, but the three years from 1844 which he spent on a travelling fellowship from the Danish government in Italy were decisive in extending his classical interests beyond the Roman *urbs* to the provinces. He produced pioneering studies of Oscan and the lower Italian dialects of the pre-Roman period, and was encouraged by the Italian scholar Borgesi to make a start on the inscriptions of Samnium and the kingdom of Naples. The Berlin Academy had called on Jahn to start a project on Roman inscriptions similar to that of August Boeckh's *Corpus Inscriptionum Graecarum*. Jahn in his turn went to Mommsen for help, but he rejected the conditions laid down for the work by the Academy; the Academy did not come round to his topographical scheme for inscriptions until the publication of his *Inscriptiones Regni Neapolitani Latinae* in 1852, when he was invited to take charge of the *Corpus Inscriptionum Latinarum*, which was to be the *magnum opus* of a prolific scholarly career.

On his return from Italy, Mommsen had been caught up in the liberal and national politics of 1848, becoming editor of the *Schleswig-Holsteinisch Zeitung*, the organ of the provisional government of the duchy.

The defeat of his cause in 1848 impelled his removal to a professorship of Roman law at Leipzig, where he taught alongside Jahn and Moritz Haupt. But the political arm of reaction reached them all, and the three professors lost their posts in 1851. In 1852 Mommsen became Professor of Roman Law at Zurich, and in 1854 moved on to Breslau, his last staging-post before he made his home in Berlin. The Berlin Academy had summoned him as a member, and he was made Professor of Ancient History there. Publishers who had heard him lecture had already commissioned Mommsen to write a *History of Rome* (*Römische Geschichte*, trans. 1862–75), which appeared in four volumes from 1854 to 1856, taking the story up to the dictatorship of Caesar. This first complete survey of republican history was an instantaneous success in Germany, and rapidly won over scholars and general readers alike in England France, and Italy. Its main advantages were its decisive tone and its energetic dramatization of the crisis of the republic in contemporary terms. Cicero emerged as an ineffectual liberal windbag, Caesar by contrast as a statesman with a realistic grasp of the imperatives of the moment. Mommsen was accused of a hero-worshipping Caesarism, but he always stressed that his interpretation rested on the political collapse of the republic's institutions rather than a glorification of empire. Caesar gave the quietus to the factious oligarchy of the republic, but Mommsen believed that the loss of free self-determination for the majority of the citizens outweighed all the benefits of imperial rule.

In 1858 Mommsen became editor of the *Corpus Inscriptionum Latinarum*, and the appearance of its volumes from 1868 steadily revolutionized the study of Roman history. Mommsen took within its scope all the inscriptions on stone, wood, metal or terracotta produced in the Roman provinces, and insisted on each being examined personally if possible. Apart from the first volume of the inscriptions of the republic, the remainder were arranged geographically and threw a new light on the Romans outside the city.

Mommsen's own fifth volume of his *Roman History*, which appeared in 1885, was the first of a new generation of historical treatments which could do full justice to the Roman provinces (*Provinces of the Roman Empire from Caesar to Diocletian*). Of the sixteen volumes of the *Corpus Inscriptionum Latinarum* in folio, Mommsen was personally responsible for fourteen out of the forty-one parts into which they were divided. But alongside his historical work on inscriptions, he furthered his initial interest in Roman law. From 1870 to 1888 appeared the three volumes of the *Römisches Staatsrecht*, the first systematic treatment of Roman constitutional law. It was built up of a series of monographs on the different institutions, and it remains to this day the foundation stone of all studies of the subject. Mommsen's strength was his ability to bring together the widely scattered source materials, and work them up into a systematic structure; the evolution of institutions over time, and the external influences upon them, played necessarily a smaller role. One of the most significant historical insights to which it gave rise, despite these handicaps, was into the role of the Senate as a continuing source of *auctoritas* under the principate. A dyarchy persisted, in Mommsen's view, until the reign of Diocletian, when principate finally became empire. Mommsen was also the author of the standard work on Roman criminal law, his *Römisches Stafrecht* (1895). If this were not enough for one man, as secretary of the Berlin Academy from 1874 to 1895, Mommsen played an important part in sponsoring work in the new fields of prosopography, systematic archaeology and papyrology. He had already published an important contribution to the study of Roman coinage, and in later life went on to edit several early medieval texts for the *Monumenta Germaniae Historica*.

Mommsen's role in maintaining Germany's lead in studies of ancient history after Niebuhr and Boeckh cannot be overestimated. As a teacher his lecturing technique was not impressive, but he compelled attention by his scholarship, dedication and energy. Even beyond his own sphere of ancient history,

Mommsen was legendary as the type of Germanic scholar, regarded with awe and veneration. The range of his scholarly output and its sheer quantity staggered the contemporary imagination, as it should stagger ours. A century after his death, the most substantial of his works still provides a starting point for study of the social, legal and economic history of the Romans.

Further reading

A full list of Mommsen's books and articles, 1,513 titles in chronological order, is found in K. Zangemeister and E. Jacobs, *Theodor Mommsen als Schriftsteller. Ein Verzeichnis seiner Schriften* (1905). A very good selection appears in Mommsen's eight-volume *Gesammelte Schriften* (1905–13). See: Albert Wucher, *Theodor Mommsen, Geschichtschreibung und Politik* (1956); and L. Wickert, *Theodor Mommsen, Eine Biographie* (3 vols, 1959–80).

PETER JONES

MONDRIAN, Piet

1872–1944

Dutch artist

Piet Mondrian, born in the small country town of Amersfoort into a strictly Calvinist family, became an early painter of Pure Abstraction. Of all the Abstract painters he might be considered the most widely influential and significant. In the early 1880s he studied at the Amsterdam Academy following a traditional Dutch landscape style of dark, almost monochromatic forms against light skies. An awareness of the work of the Dutch Symbolists added to Mondrian's painting the violently twisted and decorative line of Art Nouveau. By 1907–8 he had rejected dark tones for the brilliant colours of the Fauves and fine lines for the broad brush-work of the Post-Impressionists. In *The Red Mill* (1910–11) there is considerable simplicity of shape coupled with strong strokes of vivid red.

During 1909 Mondrian became absorbed in Theosophy, the quasi-religious movement that held the central notion that a great 'New Spiritual Epoch' was at hand. During this era the metaphysical realities which in the past had only been available to a few privileged souls in the form of sacred mysteries would be appreciated by increasing numbers of people as their sensibilities became more refined. Like **Kandinsky**, Mondrian believed that the artist, as seer, could through his art help produce this new state of being.

In 1911 Mondrian arrived in Paris and from a welter of artistic influences meeting in this foremost centre of the art world he chose Cubism as the most relevant. For him the unemotional scaffolding of Analytical Cubism structure pointed the way to increasing simplification of form. The famous tree and also church series were then carried out, whereby Mondrian severely reduced and gradually abstracted the linear structure of both organic and architectural subjects.

After meeting a fellow Theosophist, Dr M.H.J. Schoenmaekers, in 1915 Mondrian formed an artistic group in Holland with his compatriot Theo von Doesberg. Much influenced by Schoenmaekers's neo-Platonic ideas on the relationship of beauty and mathematical proportion they produced a magazine called *De Stijl* and wrote the theory of Neo-Plasticism. This proposed that art had to hold an equal balance between two oppositions, the artist's desire for 'direct creation of universal beauty' and 'the aesthetic expression' of himself. These polarizations they saw as objective and subjective, the one that thinks and the one that experiences, and they wished to marry the two. Ultimately for Mondrian this form resolved itself into the basic opposition of vertical and horizontal, made more dynamic by the use of pure primary colours in solid blocks.

During the 1920s and 1930s, living in an all-white studio in Paris, Mondrian worked simultaneously over long periods on a number of canvases, intuiting the correct balance for his grid forms and colours. The steady progression of this period was from a work such as *Composition Grey Red Yellow and Blue* of around 1920 to *Composition Red Yellow and Blue* of 1937–42. The former is composed of large rectangles of the four colours interlocking and separated only by a narrow line. The latter replaces grey with a white ground that sparkles between the now important and heavier black line grid. Only four rectangles of colour exist in the work. The greater restraint at the same time gives an increased dynamic intensity of contrast.

At the request of **Ben Nicholson**, who visited him in Paris, Mondrian went to England in 1938, and then moved to New York in 1940. Fascinated by the rhythms of urban life, of American jazz and the incessant energies of the 'Big City', he painted his celebratory and perhaps most dynamic work, *Broadway Boogie Woogie* (1942–3). In it the now small multiple blocks of bright colour seem to chase each other down the tracks of the grids and pre-empt with their dazzling colour and tonal oppositions the Op Art movement of the 1960s.

Further reading

See: Essays: *Plastic Art and Pure Plastic Art 1937 and Other Essays* (1945) and *Circle*, ed. B. Nicholson and N. Gabo (1937). See also: Michael Seuphor, *Mondrian* (1957); Frank Elgar, *Mondrian* (trans. 1968); H.L.C. Jaffé, *Mondrian* (1970); J. Joosten and R. Welsh, *Piet Mondrian: A Catalogue Raisonné* (1996).

PAT TURNER

MONET, Claude

1840–1926
French artist

The most important member of the Impressionist group, Monet was born in Paris, the son of a wholesale grocer. At the age of five he moved with his family to Le Havre and lived there until adult. A physically strong and self-willed boy, Monet deeply loved the sea and its shore in all its moods: fierce, stormy or gentle and limpid. No doubt this continuing early fascination provided the basis for much of his art.

He was fortunate to have met in Le Havre, by the age of eighteen, the painter Boudin, among the first to realize that painting carried out in the open air in front of the depicted subject contained an immediacy and vitality lacking in studio work. Boudin's paintings have a delightful freshness and, although more than sketches, retain something of the sensuous excitement to be found in such preliminary work. Monet wrote later that after he had tried Boudin's method he continued to paint *en plein air*. 'It was as if a veil had suddenly been torn from my eyes. I understood. I grasped what painting was capable of.'

While enduring a short term in the army Monet worked with the Dutchman Jongkind, a more dramatic painter than Boudin but one who also worked out of doors. By 1862 the young Monet was in Paris, shortly to study at Gleyre's studio and to see **Manet's** exhibition at the Galerie Martinet, Salon des Refusés. Manet's paintings at this time were not acceptable to the official jury members. Monet was greatly impressed by Manet's work but was soon to diverge from the older man's view of painting, over the question of shadows.

In France during the nineteenth century a number of people were investigating the optical laws of vision and of colour. Chevreul had published *The Principles of Harmony and Contrast of Colours, and Their Application to the Arts* in 1839. This book made clear the theory of negative after-images whereby a colour becomes surrounded faintly after a moment or two by its complement or opposite. This negative effect modifies the surrounding colour so that green which has a patch of yellow in its centre will appear slightly brown because of the mauve after-image superimposed upon it by the eye. Colour complements or oppositions of primary to secondary colours had been known before the nineteenth century. However, Chevreul also discovered that two small areas of colour close together will, when seen at a distance, merge and produce a neutralizing effect. Later the Post-Impressionists realized that, by contrast, when the two complements are used in larger areas, they intensify each other.

The difference between the Impressionism of Monet and Manet lay largely in the treatment of shadows. Manet claimed that to paint sunlight there had to be a sudden change and strong contrast from light and dark. It is as though he imagined not only the artist's eye moving to survey sunshine and shade but the whole person walking into it and being surrounded by sudden shade. Monet took a more objective, distanced and less dramatic view so that the eye could move back and forth, comparing and becoming aware of the effects of refraction and reflection within both light and shade. He sought not the oppositions but the similarities, thus unifying his painting.

When first exhibited, Impressionism seemed strange to the public. Not only was the work produced in the open air, it dealt with contemporary subject-matter rather than historical myths or events, which were the usual province of the painter until **Courbet** broke with that tradition. He met Monet in 1865 when the younger man was already rapidly moving towards the finest period of Impressionism, that of the 1870s.

By 1869 Monet, his friends **Renoir, Pissarro** and Bazille were producing highly accomplished works in the new style and seeking a means of exhibiting them. A typical work of this period by Monet was *La Grenouillère* of 1869. It depicted his great love, water, a bathing and boating area of the River Seine on the outskirts of Paris. Manet and Monet painted a similar view of the same place and the comparison is instructive. Monet's version shows a small island connected by wooden planking to the river bank and to the bathing station. On it people sit or stand. A few bathers, chest-deep in water, look across to the far bank of the river where a mass of variegated yellow greens suggest a line of trees in sunlight. In the foreground the trees are painted in blue greens for they, like the people and boats, are all in the shade. The painting of the water is the most striking effect. Strong short strokes of various colours form the shadow side of lively curving ripples and almost pure white the crests. The work is brilliantly alight and alive, and compared with Renoir's softer version of the same year is crisply and sharply seen. Manet's *River at Argenteuil* (1874) differentiates little between the greens in the foreground and on the far bank. Distance is emphasized by the controlled use of black bonnet ribbons near to, slightly less dark boats in the middle distance and a grey structure even further away.

It was *Impression: Sunrise* of 1872, produced while Monet was in England during the German attack upon Paris, that gave the Impressionist movement its name. The fogs of nineteenth-century industrial London afforded Monet great delight. They had the effect of both unifying the view and dissolving the forms of buildings and structures so that he is left with a mass of reflecting and refracting colour. The Thames was a major source for subject-matter during these visits.

One work of 1878 by Monet, called *Rue Montorgeuil Decked Out with Flags*, foreshadows **Jackson Pollock's** *Blue Poles* of 1953. The New York Abstract Expressionists of the gestural kind, such as Pollock, have admitted a great debt to Monet. Certainly the Monet scene, with tricolours by the hundred fluttering in the quick morning air above an enormous crowd winding down the street, is almost an abstraction of large and small strokes which express an immense hedonistic pleasure in being alive and part of the day's activities. However much Monet attempted to be no more than 'an eye', his sturdy temperament makes itself felt, sometimes with extreme sensitivity as in the painting of his dying and beloved wife Camille.

Gradually he came to realize along with many of his contemporaries, both writers and artists, that 'realism' as it was often termed was not in itself sufficient for great art. For Monet this meant a greater search for colour structure. He rejected **Seurat's** Pointillisme of the 1880s because of its deliberate slow technique and static hieratic effect upon form. Monet, used to painting 'fleeting moments of time', understood movement and change.

He once more became interested in choosing an object and painting it several times under different lighting conditions. In 1891 he produced the *Haystacks* series and the *Poplar on the Epte* variations which he himself prized greatly. The Tate Gallery version shows a dramatic curve and counter-curve of dancing tree tops, from top right-hand corner of the work to bottom left-hand. The wide swinging brush strokes of leaf clusters follow the curve across the row of parallel thin trunks which are set against a brilliant blue sky with swirling small white clouds. It is a painting produced with confidence and panache.

Then follows the exquisite *Rouen Cathedral* series while Monet is building his water gardens at Giverny. The result of this endeavour are the glorious views of these gardens with bridge and water-lilies, works known as the *Nymphéas*.

In 1908, after an illness, Monet visited Venice for the first time and while staying with a friend in a house on the Grand Canal painted views of that city, rising above and reflected in the waterways. The paintings are quieter in mood although intense but unified in colour.

Among his last works are the water-lily decorations (1916–23) in the Musée de l'orangerie, a small palace in Paris. Here, 'subject, sensation and pictorial object have all become identical'. By that Monet means that the picture is an equivalent sensation for that which the eye experiences; an eye, however, constantly on the move but rejecting an entirely intellectual or imaginative appraisal of the visual world.

Further reading

Other works include: *Westminster Bridge* (1871); *Gare St-Lazare* (1877). See: Daniel Wildenstein, *Monet* (biography and catalogue raisonné, 3 vols, 1974–9); Joel Isaacson, *Claude Monet* (1978); John House, *Monet* (1981).

PAT TURNER

MONNET, Omer Marie Gabriel Jean

1888–1979

French businessman and European statesman

Jean Monnet was a man of action rather than an intellectual, but his tenacious commitment to a few basic ideas about economics and politics powerfully helped to create the European Union as we know it today, and to change the way in which Europeans think about the nation-state.

Born in Cognac in 1888, Monnet left school at sixteen to join the family firm as a trader in brandy, and travelled extensively, particularly in Europe and North America. When war came in 1914, his outstanding dynamism and resourcefulness qualified him for a series of senior posts in the Allied planning system, and he ended the war as France's representative in the Allied Military Transport Executive. He then spent three years in Geneva as the first Deputy Secretary-General of the League of Nations. His high-level inside experience of the League, and his close observation of its later failings, convinced him that a weak and inter-governmental organization, hampered by national rights of veto, was not the right answer to big international problems.

From 1922 Monnet developed a new career as an international banker, and became a millionaire by the age of forty. At the outbreak of war in 1939 he was appointed chairman of the Anglo-French Co-ordinating Committee for economic mobilization. In June 1940, in London, he launched a plan, endorsed by **Churchill** and **de Gaulle**, for the merger of France and the United Kingdom in a Franco-British Union. This ambitious project, swept aside by the rapid military defeat of France, was to find an echo in Monnet's post-war designs for the unification of Europe. He spent most of the war in Washington, in a high-level post with the British Supply Council, and in 1944 was briefly a minister in France's provisional government. In 1946 he was appointed head of the National Commissariat for the Plan, where he developed the 'Monnet Plan', a comprehensive design for national reconstruction. The plan's success was due in part to American aid provided under the Marshall Plan of 1947 and managed by the Organization for European Economic Co-operation (OEEC), founded in 1948, with both of which Monnet was actively involved.

Soon, however, he was criticizing the limitations of the inter-governmental OEEC as he had earlier criticized those of the League of Nations, and in 1950 he was to launch his most imaginative and innovative contribution to international institution-building. As the Cold War developed, Western Europe faced strong Soviet pressure, and also the dilemma of how to contain and channel the reviving power of Germany. Even though divided into two republics, East and West, Germany still had the economic potential to destabilize Europe, unless its industrial strength were kept under some form of control. It was Monnet who produced a revolutionary solution to the twin problems of reviving Europe's economic capacity and curbing political conflicts between its major states. In May 1950 Robert Schuman, France's Foreign Minister, made a dramatic proposal inspired by Monnet, which was to mark a turning-point in the history of Europe's unification. The Schuman Plan provided for the pooling of Europe's coal and steel industries (and thus the war-making capacities of hitherto rival nation-states), and for their collective management by a radically new set of institutions. These were to consist of a Council representing the governments of the Coal and Steel Community's member-states and an Assembly drawn from their parliaments, and in addition the highly original feature of a High Authority (later to be renamed Commission), a supranational body empowered to enforce the terms of the founding treaty, and to impose penalties on states or companies that failed to comply with them.

The European Coal and Steel Community (ECSC), originally consisting of six countries, began its operations in 1952, and Jean Monnet, its main creator, was a natural choice to become the first President of the High Authority. In his three years at the ECSC's headquarters in Luxembourg, Monnet presided over substantial progress towards the creation of a single European market for coal and steel. By 1954–5, however, despite this success, another of Monnet's projects, the plan to incorporate West Germany's planned military strength in a European Defence Community or European Army, had come to grief when the French parliament refused to ratify it in August 1954. This was a setback for the general aim of Europe's political unification, and Monnet's response was to resign from his post in Luxemburg and to set up a new high-level pressure-group, the Action Committee for the United States of Europe.

This powerful network, in which Monnet brought together most of Europe's political leaders, was influential in bringing about the 1957 Rome Treaty establishing the European Economic Community (the direct predecessor of today's European Union), and in working successfully for Britain's membership of it in 1973. Monnet also ensured that the ECSC was complemented not only by the broadly conceived Economic Community but also by a special European Atomic Energy Community (Euratom), also established in 1957. He continued to campaign for closer European unity until his death in 1979. In 1975 the European Council of heads of government (a newly created element of Europe's institutional structure, itself partly due to a personal initiative by Monnet) recognized his achievements by electing him an 'Honorary Citizen of Europe', the only person to receive this honour. The title reflects his uniquely important and lasting contribution to the shaping of today's European Union.

Further reading

See: Monnet's *Memoirs* appeared in an English translation (by his long-standing collaborator Richard Mayne) in 1978. The standard biography is *Jean Monnet. The First Statesman of Interdependence* by François Duchene (1994). A more critical assessment is to be found in *The European Rescue of the Nation-State* by Alan Milward (1994).

ROGER MORGAN

MONTAGNIER, Luc B. *see*: GALLO, ROBERT C. AND MONTAGNIER, LUC B.

MONTY PYTHON

(Graham CHAPMAN 1941–89,
John CLEESE 1939–, Terry GILLIAM 1940–,
Eric IDLE 1943–, Terry JONES 1942–
and Michael PALIN 1943–)
(Mostly) British writers, actors, directors
and comedians

The BBC television show *Monty Python's Flying Circus*, which ran in four series between 1969 and 1974, was the comic voice of the generation that did its growing up in the two decades after the Second World War. It was largely the creation of five writer-performers who had emerged in the mid-1960s from the thriving, competitive world of English undergraduate revue. Graham Chapman, John Cleese and Eric Idle had been at Cambridge (they had overlapped, but were not exact contemporaries), Terry Jones and Michael Palin at Oxford. The symmetry is inconsiderately spoiled by Terry Gilliam who is American, and who also differs from the others in possessing a talent that is not primarily verbal; he is a cartoonist and animator who subsequently blossomed into a notable movie-director.

It was Gilliam who created the animated logo – a giant foot, crunching down down, crushing everything in its path – which started every Monty Python programme and defined the tone of the whole enterprise: savage whimsy. The shows themselves weren't *that* savage, but that they certainly had an appetite for destruction. They were also subversive, without taking on any named satirical targets, and unflinchingly literate. In all this, they suggested a graduate version of the Marx Brothers, probably the greatest force in twentieth-century comedy (who themselves derived, whether they knew it or not, from **Lewis Carroll**, the greatest ever). But more immediate influences, from the two British generations immediately preceding the Pythons', were the 1950s BBC radio series *The Goon Show*, whose non-stop anarchic humour communicated a distrust of all authority without actually saying so, and

Beyond the Fringe, the Oxbridge graduate revue that made wonderful jokes, in public, about people and things that had previously been thought untouchable. Idle, seeing it as a teenager, 'had never laughed so hard in my life', and he spoke for most of his contemporaries.

Beyond the Fringe sparked off the British 'satire boom' – basically, saying rude things on television about politicians – and the Pythons, before they became the Pythons, came in on the tail-end of it; some of them wrote material for David Frost (who in those days was still a comedian, or just about). There was a feeling, even then, that that had been done; and when it came to Monty Python, the group stopped doing it. They were interested in a more poetic kind of comedy: Peter Cook, in *Beyond the Fringe*, had impersonated Harold Macmillan: John Cleese created the Minister of Silly Walks, who seems at least as real and whose ministry, once its peculiar premises are accepted, seems a text-book example of the workings of bureaucracy.

The six Pythons broke down into a series of smaller writing-groups who would then meet and pool their ideas with, at least in the earlier years, remarkable amicability. They changed the structure of the TV comedy show; they weren't sitcom, they were sketch-comedy but with a difference. Accepting that the hardest thing to write is a punch-line they let each item merely blend into the next, as incongruously as possible, and as unexpectedly. (Nobody ever expects the Spanish Inquisition.) Or they would simply call a halt and change the subject. The Ministry of Silly Walks shows this process at its most refined. It begins as an absurd film-clip, apparently there for its own sake, then reveals its true and logical nature. Later in the same show it makes a momentary, and killingly funny, reappearance. The effect, a crucial element in the show's enduring cult status, is that of a self-contained comic universe.

If there was an individual comic genius in the group, it was Cleese. His capacity for suggesting upstanding (approximately six foot three) English middle-class respectability with madness in its heart is encapsulated in the two legendary numbers in which he plays an outraged consumer, opposite Palin's imperturbably disobliging shopkeeper: the Dead Parrot Sketch ('this is an ex-parrot!') and the Cheese Sketch. (Cleese's family name would have been Cheese if his father hadn't changed it, which is intriguing if irrelevant.) He wasn't in the last of the TV series, and it shows.

The sextet reunited, however, for a series of movies: *And Now For Something Completely Different* (1971), highlights from the TV shows with enhanced production values: *Monty Python and the Holy Grail* (1974), about King Arthur; *Monty Python's Life of Brian* (1979), about Christianity; and *Monty Python's The Meaning of Life* (1983), about everything. Of these, *Brian* is regarded by the team themselves, and by most others, as their masterpiece. It is not, they insist, a satire on Jesus (of whom they all became fans) but on the things done in his name – and in those of all other beliefs, religious and political. Chapman gives a sublime performance as the accident-and-crucifixion-prone Brian. He was always the group's straight man. Though he was in fact gay. He also differed from the others in being an alcoholic. And, now, dead.

The five survivors have all had successful subsequent careers. Cleese, though he always claimed comedy was only a part-time interest for him, has nevertheless achieved the most in the genre. His TV series *Fawlty Towers* (1975, 1979) raised situation comedy to the level of classic farce and allowed Cleese, as a manic hotelier, to perfect the art of being victim and bully at the same time; the film *A Fish Called Wanda* (1988) went some way to re-kindling the spirit of Britain's post-war Ealing comedies. Idle, who has always been the most concerned with keeping the Python name alive (or, as he might cheerfully admit, exploiting it) and is also the most musical of the bunch, co-wrote and co-composed *Spamelot* (2004), a hugely successful Broadway adaptation of the Holy Grail movie.

Further reading

See: The Pythons with Bob McCabe, *The Pythons' Autobiography* (2003).

ROBERT CUSHMAN

MOORE, George Edward
1873–1958
English philosopher

G.E. Moore was born in London into a comfortable middle-class family, and was educated at Dulwich and Trinity College, Cambridge, where he completed the Moral Science Tripos in 1896. Two years later he was elected to a six-year fellowship at Trinity. When his fellowship expired in 1904, Moore was saved by a private income from the urgency of seeking another position, but he returned to Cambridge to lecture in 1911, and became Professor of Mental Philosophy and Logic in 1925. Moore died in the university city where he had spent so much of his quiet and uneventful life.

Moore's name is often coupled with that of his friend and colleague at Trinity, **Bertrand Russell**, and the two men probably deserve to be called the co-founders of the modern analytic tradition in philosophy. While Russell's *Principia Mathematica* was a towering landmark in the history of Logic, Moore's *Principia Ethica* (1903) has probably been even more influential in the sphere of moral philosophy. The book swiftly achieved an enormous reputation, particularly among the Bloomsbury Group (**Keynes** called it 'better than Plato'); and its effect on theoretical ethics endures even today.

On the book's title page is a quotation from Bishop Butler: 'Everything is what it is and not another thing'; and Moore applies this apparent truism with devastating force to the concept of goodness, the subject of the work. Moore's startling claim is that all the many attempts throughout the history of philosophy to analyse or define goodness are doomed to failure, since goodness is indefinable: '*Good*, if we mean by it that quality which we assert to belong to a thing, when we say that the thing is good, is incapable of definition' (Chapter 1, paragraph 10). The attempt to define goodness in terms of something else Moore called the 'naturalistic fallacy'; goodness, he claims, is *sui generis*; it is a purely ethical quality which cannot be equated with any 'natural', non-ethical property (e.g. the property of being pleasurable). According to Moore, Jeremy Bentham and **J.S. Mill**, the chief exponents of the dominant utilitarian tradition in Ethics, are guilty of just this fallacy, by equating 'good' with some such property as 'being conducive to the general happiness'. Both Moore's specific criticism of Bentham and Mill and his general onslaught against 'naturalistic' accounts of goodness have been immensely influential. The debate on whether ethical naturalism is necessarily fallacious or can somehow be salvaged from Moore's strictures is still not concluded.

If the utilitarian, and other 'naturalistic' definitions of 'good' are to be rejected, how does Moore answer the fundamental question of Ethics, 'What is good?' His solution is that goodness is a simple, unique, unanalysable property which just has to be recognized intuitively: no reason can be given why something is good in itself. This account gave a powerful impetus to the Intuitionist approach to Ethics which flourished during the inter-war years (though for Moore himself the role of intuition was strictly limited: he insisted that the rightness or wrongness of particular acts was a matter for careful calculation).

There is also a more general dimension to the influence of *Principia Ethica*. From the beginning, Moore makes it clear that his enterprise is not a piece of arcane theorizing about the 'nature of goodness', but a painstaking and precise investigation of 'the predicate *good*'. This characteristic stance, which appears increasingly in the essays and articles Moore published later in his career (e.g. the famous 'Is Existence a Predicate?', 1936), is what makes it appropriate to call Moore a

founder of the 'analytic tradition': precise linguistic analysis becomes the chief weapon and distinctive activity of philosophy. The main area in which Moore exercised his formidable analytic powers was not specialized or technical philosophical jargon, but rather ordinary language; and nowhere does this emerge more clearly than in his paper 'A Defence of Common Sense' (1923). Here Moore presents powerful arguments to show that some of our ordinary beliefs (e.g. in the existence of an external world) are so certain and deeply entrenched that any philosophical attempt to undermine them must be self-defeating.

The position taken here by Moore is often seen as influencing the development, much later, of the so-called 'Ordinary Language' school (cf. **J.L. Austin**) of philosophy. Whether this counts to Moore's credit is debatable; for the exaggerated reverence accorded by some ordinary language philosophers to everyday speech led rapidly to a dreary and barren conception of philosophical enquiry. In fairness to Moore, however, he himself never argued that our ordinary beliefs and expressions must necessarily be the sole repositories of truth. The issue, in any case, is a minor one when set against the greatness of Moore's philosophical achievement. The pioneering contribution he made to linguistic analysis in general, and ethical analysis in particular, firmly secures him his place as one of the architects of twentieth-century philosophy.

Further reading

See: *Ethics* (1912). Moore's *Philosophical Papers* (published posthumously 1959) include 'A Defence of Common Sense' and 'Is Existence a Predicate?' Useful introductions to Moore's work may be found in G. Warnock, *English Philosophy since 1900*, and M. Warnock, *Ethics since 1900*. Standard critical works are: A.J. Ayer, *Russell and Moore: The Analytic Heritage* (1971); and A.R. White, *G.E. Moore* (1958). See also: Thomas Baldwin, *G.E. Moore* (1990).

JOHN COTTINGHAM

MOORE, (Sir) Henry

1898–1986

English sculptor

The most celebrated British sculptor of the twentieth century underwent an orthodox training at Leeds School of Art and then at the Royal College of Art in London. But from an early stage his sources of inspiration were extra-curricular. Roger Fry's *Vision and Design* led him to Paris to experience the work of **Cézanne**; and at the British Museum he was deeply impressed by the sculpture of 'primitive' civilizations in pre-Columbian America, the Near East and Archaic Greece. It became clear to him, as he wrote in 1941, that 'the realistic ideal of physical beauty in art ... was only a digression from the main world tradition of sculpture, while, for instance, our equally European Romanesque and Early Gothic are in the main line'. But a tour of Italy ensured that the Renaissance tradition also left its mark on Moore's work – as many of his Reclining Figures testify.

Moore's sculpture of the 1920s and 1930s is extremely diverse. Passing references to **Picasso** and **Hans Arp** are to be found, and to Mexican and African statuary; Moore's experiments with various media culminated in the late 1930s in a series of 'stringed figures', in which parallel threads of string or wire are set against the flowing curves of the sculptured mass. Several of his 'heads' and 'helmets' carry a surrealist flavour, and in 1936 Moore was a contributor to the International Surrealist Exhibition. But he never saw himself as a Surrealist; and although he was closely associated with **Ben Nicholson** and **Barbara Hepworth** in the same decade, Moore did not campaign on behalf of any specific attitude or theory. He was, however, always an articulate analyst of his own work, and in 1937 he seems to have seen his role clearly. **Brancusi** has made us shape-conscious, he wrote, by his simple, polished forms, which cast off the superficial excrescences that had overgrown European sculpture since the Middle Ages. But this 'one-cylindered'

approach might no longer be necessary: 'We can now begin to open out, to relate and combine together several forms of varied sizes, sections and directions into one organic whole.' Moore's figures followed this course with mounting boldness, splitting into two, three or four components. Bronze became his favourite medium, and he undertook an increasing number of large sculptures for exterior locations, where they might become an element of city architecture or (preferably) of natural landscape. Some of Moore's later works are so 'open' that the spectator is able, and indeed encouraged, to walk through them.

Moore advised that 'the sensitive observer must learn to feel shape simply as shape'; many of his own designs have been furnished by the uncomplicated forms of bones and pebbles. But it is the human figure which, above all, has occupied Moore's imagination. As an official War Artist he depicted groups of men and women huddled in air-raid shelters, their faceless immobility suggesting an eternal capacity to endure. In both sculpture and drawing he developed the subtle potentialities of forms to suggest emotional states or qualities, in particular those of maternal or sexual attraction, which animate Moore's 'archetypal' themes of the reclining woman and the mother with child. The power of his *Sheep Piece* (1971–2) lies not only in the physical conformation of the two massive structures, but also in the psychological overtones of warmth and protectiveness which their relationship suggests.

Moore's international reputation was established after the Second World War through major exhibitions in New York, Venice, São Paulo, Toronto, Florence and Zürich. His eightieth birthday was marked in London by an exhibition in Kensington Gardens, largely of recent work, which displayed an undiminished grandeur and vitality.

Further reading

Other works include: *Henry Moore On Sculpture* (1966), ed. Philip James. See: Herbert Read, *Henry*

Moore: A Study of His Life and Work (1965); John Russell, *Henry Moore* (1973); Alan G. Wilkinson, *The Drawings of Henry Moore* (Tate Gallery catalogue, 1977); David Finn, *Henry Moore: Sculpture and Environment* (1977); *Henry Moore 2: Sculpture and Drawings* (4 vols, 1957–77), eds David Sylvester and Alan Bowness; W. Packer, *Henry Moore* (1985); R. Berthoud, *Henry Moore* (1987).

PATRICK CONNER

MOORE, Marianne Craig

1887–1972

US poet

For her last two decades, Marianne Moore was considered 'the greatest living woman poet' in America, a neat little niche which has, on the whole, constrained the understanding of her poetic accomplishment. Sometimes considered eccentric, limited, 'whimsical' (i.e. what one might assume a woman poet to be), Moore has also been placed, wrongly, as a disciple of the Imagist movement. In fact, her deliberate complex poems develop far older traditions of emblem poetry and moral wit, formed according to her own version of modernism: collage-like overlays of the ordinary, the bizarre, and the quoted fragment which are expressed by a syllabic but strongly cadenced metre organized into stanzaic units of sense.

Marianne Moore lived a relatively quiet life, devoted to her mother and brother. After childhood in Carlisle, Pennsylvania, Moore moved to New Jersey and then (with her mother) to New York, where her almost sixty-year 'sojourn in the whale' ended with her being treasured as a kind of cosmopolitan regional poet. At Bryn Mawr College, Moore majored in biology (1905–9), which may partly account for the moral value her poetry puts on precise natural description. At Bryn Mawr, Moore's strong ethical sense was certainly sharpened by the blue-stocking's proud intellectual isolation. In her 'serial' poem 'Marriage', Moore rejected the institution which required 'all one's criminal ingenuity/to avoid!' 'Eve: beautiful woman' is 'the central flaw' in the 'crystal-fine experiment'

of pure Adamic existence, too powerful for Moore: 'each fresh wave of consciousness/is poison'.

Many of Moore's early poems, which appeared from 1915 in the little magazines *Poetry*, the *Egoist* and *Others*, assume both an inner enemy in the poem's object of satire and an outer enemy in a hostile or absent audience. Although Moore's poetry never needs recourse to *persona* to veil the writer's presence in the poem, it displaces her articulate anger by coolly addressing emblematic animals or modes of behaviour. 'You crush all the particles down/into close conformity,' she writes in 'To a Steamroller' (1915), attacking the materialist's destructive attempts to achieve 'impersonal judgement'. In the much-anthologized 'Poetry' her audience's philistinism is taken for granted. 'I, too, dislike it,' she begins, and then pretends to be 'Reading it ... with a perfect contempt for it' until she discovers its capacity for the 'genuine'.

With the publication of *Poems* (1921) and *Observations* (1924) Moore established herself as an important American poet, a position confirmed by the *Selected Poems* of 1935. Scofield Thayer, editor of the long-established arts magazine the *Dial*, accepted many of Moore's poems and reviews, and from 1925 to 1929, when the magazine ceased publication, Moore did most of the *Dial*'s editing and wrote many articles for it. As an editor Moore intelligently publicized the modern movement, even if her tendency to tinker with work and censor it gave offence to **James Joyce** and **Hart Crane**, among others. In her perceptive 1931 essay on **Pound's** *Draft of XXX Cantos* Moore took Pound to task for not distinguishing 'between Calvin the theologian and Calvin the man of letters'. Moore defended Calvin because, like the Prophets, Blake, Sir Thomas Browne or the natural historians and Elizabethan explorers she prefers to quote, his writing forms a traditional Protestant version of experience which Moore, uniquely of the modernists, was prepared to accept and use.

If Pound's Imagist poetic was a flight from abstraction, Moore's poetry used the material world as a means to describe abstractions. She was interested in exotic or mythical animals as borderline cases of the real, not escapes from it. 'The Jerboa', 'The Plumed Basilisk', 'The Frigate Pelican', 'Sea Unicorns and Land Unicorns', 'The Pangolin', 'The Arctic Ox' all tend towards essence because our habit hasn't blunted their 'natural' capacity for imposed meaning. 'The Jerboa', subtitled 'Too Much', with his 'shining silver house/of sand' is an emblem of humility, almost Blakean in its radiance.

The Romantic and modern terror at the gap between subject and object does not exist in Moore's poetry, where everything is already related. The mind's meditative play merges with the object, a deliberate wit which is expressed formally by Moore's stanzas. The first stanza is 'expedient' following the necessity of the subject, the rest turn the arbitrary pattern of the first into an order, the same within each poem, different from poem to poem. Moore's playing upon a curiously malleable 'real' recalls **Wallace Stevens**, who wrote admiringly that for Moore 'Reality is not the thing, but the aspect of the thing.' At first reading, Moore's poem 'He "Digesteth Harde Yron"' has an extraordinarily factual appearance. But it is, after all, an abstraction.' Xenophon's 'camel-sparrow', who, Lyly asserted, ate iron, 'was and is/a symbol of justice', according to historian Bernard Laufer, not merely a stupid bird. Moore assembles her emblem through facets which compact into a kind of quiddity or *gestalt* without ever stabilizing visually.

> he
> whose comic duckling head on its
> great neck revolves with compass-needle
>   nervousness
> when he stands guard.

'He' is equidistant from the encyclopaedia ostrich and the meaning he dramatizes, a meaning which shifts from justice to the heroic solicitude in the course of Moore's interlocked stanzas. For a parallel to this imputed natural value one must look back in American poetry to Edward Taylor's 'Upon a

Spider Catching a Fly' or forward to **Elizabeth Bishop's** 'The Man-Moth'. Moore was not, however, a puritan. She takes too much pleasure in assigning her meanings, and she doesn't believe in original sin. In 'In the Days of Prismatic Color' Eve's gift is rather to make obliqueness ambivalent so that now 'Truth is no Apollo/Belvedere, no formal thing', however much one may long for that inaccurate ideal.

After the Second World War Moore felt more sure of her audience, and permitted her ethical views direct expression. In 'The Arctic Ox (or Goat)', the title poem of a 1964 collection, one quotation suffices. The poem ends with hortatory wit: if we can't use the wool which the musk ox generously produces, 'I think that we deserve to freeze.' From 1945 to 1953 Moore translated the *Fables* of La Fontaine. Since Moore undertook translating long after her style was fixed, and she paraphrases rather than imitates, the *Fables* are interesting mainly as Moore's homage to a kindred spirit (though she is actually more like Molière). Moore's *Collected Poems* (1951) and her mistitled *Complete Poems* (1967, 1968) edit and omit many important earlier poems. 'Omissions are not accidents,' says Moore's one-line Preface to the *Complete Poems*. In the end Moore's belief in values such as 'Humility, Concentration, and Gusto' (the title of a 1948 lecture) and her hard-won power to show 'Feeling and Precision' operating together to reveal truth seemed certainties so alien to her society that it became easier to simply call her eccentric. Perhaps now her readers will find it easier to accept a modernism which isn't based upon despair.

Further reading

See: Jean Garrigue, *Marianne Moore* (a University of Minnesota pamphlet, 1965); Charles Tomlinson (ed.) *Marianne Moore* (1969); Laurence Stapleton, *Marianne Moore: The Poet's Advance* (1978); Joseph Parisi (ed.) *Marianne Moore: The Art of a Modernist* (1990); Charles Molesworth, *Marianne Moore: A Literary Life* (1991); Jeanne Heuving, *Omissions are Not Accidents: Gender in the Art of Marianne Moore*

(1992); E. Gregory, *The Critical Response to Marianne Moore* (1993); Cristanne Miller, *Marianne Moore: Questions of Authority* (1995); Elisabeth W. Joyce, *Cultural Critique and Abstraction: Marianne Moore and the Avant-Garde* (1999).

HELEN MCNEIL

MOREAU, Gustave

1826–98

French artist and teacher

Before attending the École des Beaux Arts in Paris from 1846 to 1850 the young Moreau studied painting in Italy. His knowledge of classical artists, of Greek myths and legends, remained the core of subject-matter for almost all his own art. However this interest in historical subject-matter was synthesized with a number of other influences both from within and from outside art so that his work became highly original.

At the end of his college training Moreau met the painter Chassériau who became a close friend. This artist's style was based largely on that of Delacroix, and with his example in mind Moreau's work became more exotic. Later, stylistically, his painting has similarities with the more decorative aspects of the 'Decadence' and the 'Art for Art's Sake' movements. Included in these developments were considerations of neo-Platonic ideas. Gautier, one of Chassériau's group of friends, wrote in 1856:

> We believe in the autonomy of Art. Art for us is not the means but the end. Any artist who has in view anything but the beautiful is not an artist in our eyes; we have never been able to understand the separation of idea and form.

The cult of the beautiful was anti the Romantic 'sublime'. It sought sophisticated love and eroticism rather than natural storm and terror. It was a different type of subjectivity. In addition to his love of the beautiful, Moreau was contending with strong religious feelings, which led to the concept of the ideal and towards mysticism:

> I believe only in Him. I don't believe either in that which I touch or that which I see. I believe only in that which I don't see and that which I sense. My brain, my reason, seem to me ephemeral and of doubtful reality. My inner sentiment alone seems to me eternal and incontestably certain.

These transcendent concerns are linked to Moreau's relationship with his mother, who was a musician with a strong mind, both adored and feared by her only son. The subjective side of his art drew strongly upon his subconscious neurotic conflicts with her and these, coupled with a vivid imagination and an excessively critical spirit, produced an art of considerable passion, wherein love, eroticism and death are symbolized by the legendary characters and objects of his subject-matter.

Woman came from sensual nature, in Moreau's view. She was the inscrutable mindless force with which man had to battle in order to achieve his spiritual superiority, epitomized by the heroic artist. The first important painting in his oeuvre is *Oedipus and the Sphinx* (1864). In this work the beautiful young man approaches the half-animal, dominating female, to ascertain the source of her inscrutability. Exhibited at the Paris Salon that year it was highly acclaimed and Moreau adulated by society, even to the extent of an invitation to Court.

Later work by the artist, however, becomes more obviously sadistic, and *Prometheus* (1869), depicting an older man, alive but bound while his flesh is viciously attacked by a predatory bird, was severely criticized. Female images also at times turned treacherous or vicious although retaining their sexual beauty.

One of these images is the Christian *Salome* (1876) who turns into the *femme fatale* so attractive to the 'Decadents'. In Moreau's series of works on the subject Salome is standing, half-commanding, half-afraid, before a vision of the bloody head of John the Baptist, which hovers in a vast dimly lit building, more suggestive of Buddhist than

Judaic origins. Moreau's most exquisite version of his theme is celebrated by **Huysmans**, an art critic and controversial author of the period. In his book *À Rebours* the dandy hero, Des Esseintes, adoringly owns the same Salome painting. No doubt Moreau's thought with regard to exoticism is exceedingly close to that of **Flaubert**, whose book *Salaambo* also contains a Salome theme, and to the 'Spleen' poems of **Baudelaire**.

One of the concepts in art that affected Moreau deeply and endeared him to the Symbolist movement of the 1800s was that of a 'beautiful inertia'. If Delacroix was dynamic, rhythmic, fluent in his art, as in *Sardanapulas*, also a subject of rape and sadism, then Moreau was equally dramatic but with a strong sense of the hieratic, so that a scene, such as that in the *Suitors*, begun in 1852, left then finished towards the end of his life, where all the suitors for Penelope's hand are dying violent deaths upon the return of Odysseus, is transfixed into a state of dream-like timelessness and the horror of the moment obtains for ever.

Throughout his life Moreau's technique varied considerably. Not only did he make jewel-like sketches in watercolour which are pure abstractions of extreme beauty and markedly innovatory, but he also produced finished oil paintings that range from smooth purely tonal works to thickly encrusted surfaces containing brilliant colour. He says in his notes:

> Just as a dream is situated in a suitably coloured atmosphere, so a concept, when it becomes a composition, needs to move in a fittingly coloured setting. There is obviously one particular colour attributed to some part of the picture which becomes a key and governs the other parts.

For Moreau, colour has a symbolic as well as a structuring role in the work. He continues:

> All the figures, their arrangement in relation to one another, the landscape or interior, which serves them as a background or horizon, their clothes, everything about them in fact, must serve to illuminate the general idea and wear its original colour, its livery so to speak.

He is involved with the central 'general idea' in art which again brings him into the Symbolist aesthetic with its key concept of 'the Idea'.

It is possible that Wagnerian theory also affected Moreau. **Wagner's** *Gesamtkunstwerk* concept of an art which embraces all the other arts is akin to that which gives the operatic qualities to Moreau's works. The architectural settings are magnificent yet convey little sense of an exact period, therefore the characters can act symbolically and universally and in an excessive manner. Through extremes of sensuality they can be immortalized by their deaths and transcend the earthly flesh. So it is that purity in the form of an expressionless woman can rise on the blood of martyrs. She is the *Mystic Flower* (1890) growing in a rocky canyon from the heart of a lily and raising to heaven a flaming cross over the horde of dead or dying saints.

Perhaps the most beautiful paintings by Moreau are the watercolours forming the illustrations to the fables of La Fontaine. An artist such as Moreau who had spent long hours studying plants and animals from life would find these subjects most acceptable. One such illustration called *The Peacock Complaining to Juno* allows Moreau to indulge in his favourite pose for a woman. Juno's long lissom body follows an arabesque so that she leans to the left with arms outstretched to the right and head turned sharply again to the left so that it is in profile. She thus forms an undulating diagonal across the page, floating in a perfect sky over a jewelled bay with a star above and a gorgeously vivid emerald, blue and gold peacock at her knees. Partially naked, she is Helen, Galatea, Semele – all Moreau's beautiful and innocent heroines in one.

The nearest work in terms of beauty in oils is Moreau's late large-scale oil of *Jupiter and Semele* in 1895. The paint is so thick it becomes almost a relief sculpture and the god fills the canvas with his presence which is felt as powerful and all-embracing; Semele, small and delicate, lies across his knee.

After the death of his mother in 1884 Moreau made a journey to Belgium and Holland to study the mystical realism of the early Flemish primitives. He was then elected to the Académie des Beaux Arts in 1888 and three years later asked to take up teaching at the École des Beaux Arts where he had himself once studied. As a teacher he was much liked and admired by his pupils, many of whom later achieved considerable fame. Perhaps his most important is Matisse. Although Matisse's work while a student with Moreau in no way reflect his master's, he was encouraged to experiment with technique, to study widely and to develop his own personal sense of direction so that his endeavours could attain increasing strength and originality. At times akin to the Englishman **Burne-Jones**, particularly of *King Cophetua and the Beggar Maid*, Moreau's real inheritors are the North European Symbolists such as Khnopff, **Klimt** and **Böcklin**.

Further reading

See: J. Paladilhe and J. Pierre, *Gustave Moreau* (1972); P.-L. Mathieu, *Gustave Moreau* (trans. 1977). Catalogue raisonné of finished works, J. Rewald, *Redon, Moreau, Bresdin* (1962); G. Lacambre, *Gustave Moreau: Between Epic and Dream* (1999).

PAT TURNER

MORGAN, Lewis Henry

1818–81

US ethnologist

'Morgan created the science of Anthropology,' said his biographer, Carl Resek. Some historians would dispute this, but during the 1860s and 1870s he was praised by such famous American historians as Henry Schoolcraft, **Henry Adams**, Francis Parkman, and many prominent British and continental intellectuals, among them **Karl Marx**

and **Friedrich Engels**, who modified some of their own theories after reading Morgan's major work, *Ancient Society* (1877). After becoming enshrined in Marxist eschatology, Morgan's works became subject to remarkably polarized interpretations. Yet he was really only a bourgeois lawyer, financially successful enough to retire in early middle age and devote himself to his ethnological researches on the American Indians – and certainly no kind of socialist.

L.H. Morgan was born near Aurora, New York, graduated from Union College, and practised law in Rochester. In his spare time, he undertook to present to the US government and the public his scientific descriptions of the customs of the neighbouring Seneca Iroquois Indians. In 1858, during a business trip to Marquette, Michigan, Morgan became interested in the Ojibwa Indians there who, although belonging to a language family different from the Iroquois, had a mode of designating kinsmen that was identical to that of the Iroquois and very different from that of Europeans. This was a system which Morgan called 'classificatory' because father's brothers were also called 'father' by an individual ('Ego') and mother's sisters also were 'mother' and the children were all 'brother' and 'sister' to Ego, and their children all became 'son' and 'daughter'. The European terminology, which seemed to Morgan to be more accurately genealogical, he therefore called the 'descriptive system'. When he discovered that still other American Indians, without apparent exception, also used the classificatory system, Morgan felt that he had found a means to trace the provenance of the Indians, perhaps to Asia. After much correspondence with missionaries and colonial officials in remote parts of the world, Morgan found that the Tamil, the Dravidian-speaking people of south India, had a kinship system identical to that of the Iroquois. But he did not allow this discovery to end his researches. The enormous bulk of data on the world's kinship systems that he had acquired over the years was eventually published as *Systems of Consanguinity and Affinity of the Human Family* (1870).

Later Morgan published his *Ancient Society*, which contained his final thoughts on the grand evolution of human society. Essentially, Morgan was a monogenesist in the theological argument against polygenesism (the theory of separate origins of the human races), and against the 'degradation theory' of man's fall from grace. In short, he argued for a theory of evolutionary mental–moral human progress from a lowly origin in savagery to barbarism and finally to civilization. This progress was charted by Morgan in terms of 'inventions and discoveries', the 'idea' of government, the 'idea' of the family, and finally the 'idea' of property. But he paid only lip service to the material inventions and discoveries; by far the dominant concern of the book is with the growth of institutions through ideas, and in particular the development of moral ideas that led humanity from original sexual promiscuity through a stage of 'group marriage' (which accounted for the surviving 'classificatory' kinship systems in the primitive world); and from lack of government to 'democratical' institutions; and from primitive 'communism' in property to a brief immoral stage of feudalistic entailed hereditary estates, towards a society which would 'rise to mastery over property, and define the relations of the state to the property it protects'.

It was this message about property, and how it created the hated principle of aristocracy and privilege, that so impressed Marx and Engels. After the death of Marx, Engels published his own version of their joint appreciation of Morgan as *The Origin of the Family, Private Property and the State* (*Der Ursprung der Familie, des Privatigenthums und des Staates*, 1884).

Morgan's theory of primitive kinship systems was severely criticized in his own time by the Scottish ethnologist John C. McLennan, who considered classificatory kinship terminologies to be not of genealogical relevance at all, but as designating social status in general and therefore not directly related to such imaginary historical reconstructions as 'group marriage'.

Except among Marxists, Morgan's work hung fire until the advent of academic cultural anthropology in the USA in the twentieth century under the leadership of Franz Boas, an anti-evolutionist. Morgan was criticized thereafter by foremost students of **Boas**, A.L. Kroeber and particularly by Robert Lowie in his *Primitive Society* (1920). Finally, American, British and French ethnologists seem to have found little of intellectual value in Morgan, and little to be said favourably of any other theories of cultural or social evolution.

More recently, the American ethnologist Leslie A. White, in several works, has attempted to revitalize Morgan and cultural evolutionism, and the British social anthropologist leader, Meyer Fortes, has published a favourable appraisal of Morgan's scientific 'structuralism' in his *Kinship and the Social Order* (1969). In the USSR and other communist nations and among Marxists elsewhere, ethnologists have remained loyal to the spirit, if not always the letter, of Morgan's works. It is indeed a remarkable episode in the intellectual-scientific history of Western thought that such totally opposite interpretations should exist about a man who would have remained rather insignificant to us today but for the notice he received from Engels and Marx.

Further reading

Other works include: *League of the Ho-de-no-sau-nee, or Iroquois* (1851) and *Houses and House Life of the American Aborigines* (1881). Morgan's main biography is Carl Resek, *Lewis Henry Morgan: American Scholar* (1960). See also Bernhard J. Stern, *Lewis Henry Morgan, Social Evolutionist* (1931), and Leslie A. White, *Pioneers in American Anthropology: The Bandelier–Morgan Letters, 1873–1883* (1940). The major criticisms of Morgan are by Lowie, as cited above and also in his *History of Ethnological Theory* (1937). McLennan's criticisms are best found in his collection of articles, *Studies in Ancient History* (1886). See also: Thomas R. Trautman, *Lewis Henry Morgan and the Invention of Kinship* (1992).

ELMAN SERVICE

MORRIS, Robert

1931–

US artist

Along with **Donald Judd**, Sol Lewitt and **Carl Andre**, Morris is considered primarily to be a Minimal sculptor producing roughly human-sized works which stand on the floor, hang from the ceiling or project from a wall.

Born in Kansas City, Morris studied engineering, then worked in film and theatre while, in his studio in San Francisco, producing paintings strongly influenced by Abstract Expressionism. In New York in 1961 he made his first two sculptures. These resulted from his direct consciousness of space, movement and time, derived from his performance work and in relation to this knowledge of construction. One of these sculptures was *Box with the Sound of its Own Making*, a nine-inch wooden box which completely enclosed a tape loop recording of the noises produced during the making of the box. This work encapsulates much of Morris's artistic thought. The insistence upon forcing the viewer's awareness on to basic artistic processes of making is a device to remove him from art conventions controlled by taste and expression. At the same time the non-referential character of the work concentrates the spectator's attention upon the physical character of the art object and the viewer's own physical relationship with it.

Morris's sculpture is simple and geometric in form except where the materials are soft and draped, as they are in his felt pieces of 1967–70. The form takes up space in the environment. In addition, the volume of space surrounding the work and bounded by the walls of the room is considered as an integral part of the work. Viewer, sculpture and environment are in a tripartite physical relationship mutually presenting similarities and differences.

The sound of Morris's making, which is inherent in all his works, even the silent ones, suggests the man trapped in the box, determined by the event in which he is involved,

by its existence, the process and the duration. There is, however, for the audience a differentiation of human determination from work to work. In some the viewer is controlled by the sculpture, as he is if he walks through Morris's long grey narrowing tunnel; in others the involvement means doing something to the work such as rolling it. Viewer and object in relationship are both partially determined by the other but the human has a degree of choice, for example as to the pace of movement, which gives him his humanity over and above that of being an object.

These simple works paradoxically because of their restraint focus consciousness on physical human processes which are in fact extremely complex and at times mysterious. Morris's insistence on the physical contains links with phenomenological philosophy which gives primacy to sense experience as the source of knowledge and attempts to bracket out already held values in order to consider the world anew. In his sculpture by exploring the lack of freedom of the individual because of his involvement with objects, as well as the spectrum of choices for action produced by objects, Morris causes his audiences to realize more fully the overabundance of objects in a consumer society.

Further reading

Other works include: *I-Box* (1962); Untitled 1967/8 (fibreglass suspended from ceiling); Untitled 1968 (nine open identical aluminium boxes equally spaced); *Continuous Project Continued Daily* (1969). An important series of articles by Morris appeared in *Art Forum* from 1968. See also two exhibition catalogues, of the Whitney Museum (1970) and the Tate Gallery (1971).

PAT TURNER

MORRIS, William

1834–96

English writer and designer

As poet, translator, painter, designer, craftsman, socialist, Morris has rightly been described as a pivotal figure of his age. A rebel against his own time, he was yet deeply of his time, deeply Victorian, and this is only one of the many fertile paradoxes that make his manifold activity so fascinating.

Morris was born into a wealthy bourgeois family (enriched by speculation in copper) which ensured him a handsome private income. In 1853 he went up to Oxford and formed a lasting friendship with the future painter **Burne-Jones**. Their High Church zeal was soon ousted by literature (**Tennyson's** Arthurian legends, medieval chronicles and romances), then, after a visit to the gothic cathedrals of France and Belgium, by art and architecture. Deeply impressed by Carlyle and **Ruskin** – especially the latter's *Stones of Venice*, in which gothic architecture is presented as the supreme example of creative joy in labour under a harmonious, pre-commercial social order – they conceived the ideal of a quasi-medieval fraternity, only then to discover the existence of the nascent Pre-Raphaelite Brotherhood. In 1856 Morris began work for the architect G.E. Street, but was seduced away from architecture to painting by **D.G. Rossetti**. In 1858 a first volume of verse, *The Defence of Guenevere*, was published. Morris's artistic interests extended further into the field of practical designing and in 1861 he founded the 'Firm' (Morris, Marshall, Faulkner & Co., later to become Morris & Co.) which, with help from Burne-Jones and others, would produce fine quality stained-glass, furniture, wallpaper, chintzes, tiles, carpets and tapestries, and in which Morris, with Philip Webb, was to take a major designing role.

The year 1867 saw a first long epic poem, *The Life and Death of Jason*, followed in 1868 by the first volume of the massive *Earthly Paradise*. A period of pessimism – due in part to the failure of his marriage with the Pre-Raphaelite beauty Jane Burden – was countered by the discovery of Norse literature: Morris found its vigorous stoicism a good corrective to 'the maundering side of medievalism'. Not only did he publish 'translations' of Icelandic sagas but also his own

Sigurd the Volsung (1876), probably his most effective epic.

In 1877 Morris, enraged by examples of inept restoration, founded 'Anti-Scrape' (Society for the Protection of Ancient Buildings); subsequently he was to help found the Art Workers' Guild and, through his lectures on the 'lesser arts' in the 1870s and 1880s, to inspire not only the Arts and Crafts movement but the socialist movement as well. For Morris was drawn increasingly into political activity as a necessary extension of his ethical-aesthetic vision. Disillusioned by the opportunism of the Liberals, he joined the Democratic Federation in 1883 but left the following year to found the Socialist League, dedicated to safeguarding the pure principles of socialism. He was to give generously of his income and his energy to the movement. Active in street demonstrations, he also edited the periodical *Commonweal* and published in 1885, after his *Chants for Socialists*, the political poem *The Pilgrims of Hope*. The year 1886 saw the historical prose romance *The Dream of John Ball*, based on the peasant revolt of 1381, while 1888 saw the collection of lectures *Signs of Change*. The romance *The House of the Wolfings* (1888), like *The Roots of the Mountains* (1889), portrays struggles against tyranny in the fifth century, while the important utopian romance *News from Nowhere* (1890) embodies much of Morris's nostalgia, aspiration and vision in the dream of a harmonious, post-revolutionary but curiously neo-medieval England of the twenty-first century. That same year, Morris's Hammersmith Branch split off from the Socialist League, which had become dominated by anarchists. His final years were as creative as ever: in 1891 he founded the Kelmscott Press, to resurrect the art of fine printing, and subsequently published the unhistorical romances *The Wood beyond the World* (1894), *The Well at the World's End* (1896) and, posthumously, *The Water of the Wondrous Isle* and *The Sundering Flood* (1897).

If at first one is struck by the variety of Morris's activities, in the end it is the deeply felt moral unity beneath them that ensures his stature. A true Victorian rebel against commercial and industrial civilization in the lineage of Carlyle and Ruskin, he had a keener historical understanding than either. It is said that he sought to reconcile Ruskin and **Marx**: certainly his vision begins with architecture and the vital question of the nature of work, and is completed and enriched by the insight into commercialism and the historical process he derived from his reading of *Capital*. This saved him from the repressive work-ethic of Carlyle and the equally repressive neo-feudal authoritarianism of Ruskin's late writings. His understanding is best expressed in the lectures on art and society: 'The Art of the People', 'How We Live and How We Might Live', 'The Aims of Art', 'A Factory as it Might Be', etc. Always he returns to his ideal of art 'made by the people and for the people, a joy to the maker and the user' – something that can never be achieved in an inorganic society founded on competition and the search for profit.

Examining Morris's achievement in the individual spheres of his work, we realize that his greatness lies in no particular field *per se*: in each there are contradictions and inadequacies, though also evidence of his influence on succeeding generations. The activities of the Firm offer clear examples of paradox, not least that of a capitalist (albeit paternalistic) enterprise run by an ardent socialist. Morris's own designs, notably for wallpaper and textiles, have kept an astonishing freshness, but the fact remains that his gift was especially for repeating patterns which demanded of the printer a monotonous handwork remote from his ideal of joyous, creative labour. Ironically, these patterns are admirably suited to machine-production, whereas in theory Morris wanted to give precedence to handicrafts over industrial methods. While in his writings he railed against the division of labour, the Firm practised it, often separating designer and 'hand'. His ideal was 'simplicity of life begetting simplicity of taste', but he and his collaborators were, willy-nilly, under the influence of Victorian taste, and the

Firm's interiors were rich and elaborate (though a development towards lightness and relative simplicity is apparent in later work).

Little of what the Firm practised was wholly original – the architect and designer Augustus Pugin had preceded them in many fields, and the medieval revival was very much a feature of the age – but the overriding concern was for quality of design and execution. Throughout, the enemy is clear: 'It is a shoddy age. Shoddy is king. From the statesman to the shoemaker, all is shoddy.' But this gives rise to another paradox: quality of this order was expensive, and for all Morris's democratic principles, his products were available only to the privileged few.

While he never designed a building, his influence on the approach to architecture and planning is real through his writings. He was a pioneer of environmentalism in his insistence on the need to clean the land of pollution, his concern for a more organic environment safeguarding the ideal of community. On industrial architecture and the whole concept of the workplace he had much of lasting importance to say, arguing the need for garden factories combining, in an ethical fusion vital for Morris, daily work with culture and education.

If Morris painted little, finding he had no gift for human figures (his genius in the visual arts was above all for the stylization of natural forms, their transformation into pattern), on the other hand he wrote at enormous length, and his poetry suffers from this prolixity. His verse lies firmly within the Romantic tradition, and is severely limited by it, even though as a thinker and activist he was able to step beyond Romanticism. This is especially apparent in late committed verse, *Chants for Socialists* and *The Pilgrims of Hope*, where the Romantic diction can conflict with the revolutionary subject-matter. His own literary tastes were inflexibly Romantic, and despite the blood and guts in some of his epics, his mode is not the realist one that dominated literature in the second half of the century. His first verse was promising:

The Defence of Guenevere expresses, through the medieval subject, a sense of loss and nostalgia captured in the hesitant, flexible rhythm. This Keats-like quality will later give way to the monotony of rhythmic competence; already in *The Earthly Paradise* the pessimistic nostalgia is diluted in verbiage. More positive in tone, *Sigurd* wields greater force with its stoic theme of steadfast courage in the face of eternal recurrence. The prose romances are also frequently hampered by ornamental archaic diction, the final ones being especially self-indulgent and largely forgotten, though an age that enthuses over Tolkien may well discover a taste for them. However, the best of the romances, *John Ball* and *News from Nowhere*, appear as something more than escapism into remote past or imagined future; for they embody a tension between reality and dream, thanks to the presence within the work of a narrator-dreamer who, belonging to the modern world, can movingly contrast with its inadequacies his vision of apocalyptic change or of the perfect community. Thus a work like *News* is not merely a charming fantasy but a deeply committed work which forces recognition of Morris's political importance generally. Though acknowledging that his work was 'the embodiment of dreams in one form or another', he was anxious that the new socialist theories should not be 'left adrift on the barren shore of Utopianism'. Yet he had little talent for politicking, and the intransigence of the Socialist League tended to cut it off from the 'wearisome shilly-shally of parliamentary politics'. He feared and denounced the tendency for socialism to sink into compromise and palliatory reform, offensive to his total ethical vision. Only in his final years, uncompromisingly styling himself a communist, did he come to accept the educative value of local struggles, while always insisting that these should be catalysts for total change. **Engels** scorned Morris, yet in the end this is a judgement on Engels' own narrow, deterministic outlook. A socialism that can comprehend Morris – in all his variety and all his unity – is more open and human than one

that cannot. If vision is now recognized as 'the education of desire' then not only his best work in particular, but above all the example of the man's thought and activity as a whole, have almost unequalled force in this respect.

Further reading

See: N. Kelvin (ed.) *The Collected Letters of William Morris* (4 vols, 1984–96). See also: E.P. Thompson, *William Morris: Romantic to Revolutionary* (1967); P. Henderson, *William Morris: His Life, Work and Friends* (1967); P. Thompson, *The Life and Work of William Morris* (1967); R. Watkinson, *William Morris as Designer* (1967); J. Lindsay, *William Morris* (1975); I. Bradley, *William Morris and His World* (1978); F. MacCarthy, *William Morris* (1994).

DAVID MEAKIN

MORRISON, Toni
1931–
US novelist

Few if any writers have dramatized and penetrated the Afro-American experience on a larger scale or more consistently than Toni Morrison. However, while her early books were sometimes dismissed as 'village literature', and regarded as suitable only for black female readers, she has with growing fame and skill reached a secure position as a novelist representing not merely a race or sex, but a nation. Interestingly, Morrison's first novels are sometimes re-interpreted in the light of her present image. Today she is routinely compared to **William Faulkner** and, because of her lyrical style, to **Virginia Woolf**. Unlike many American authors, Morrison emphasizes questions of social class, apart from gender and racial issues.

Born as Chloe Anthony Wofford (according to herself) or Chloe Ardelia Wofford (according to recent scholarship), she belonged to a respectable working-class family. Among her childhood interests were literature and classical ballet, and her first ambition was to become a ballerina. Morrison went to Howard University where she studied English, and later to Cornell, obtaining an MFA.

She taught at both universities, then married the Jamaican architect Harold Morrison, by whom she had two sons.

Toni Morrison worked in New York for Random House, the publishing company, divorced her husband, and wrote her first novel, *The Bluest Eye* (1971). This is a disturbing story about a girl whose self-respect and very existence are destroyed by racism. In 1973, *Sula* followed; it depicts two parallel lives, those of an Afro-American young woman who simply marries and has children, and another who leaves her home town, studying and roaming the United States freely. These heroines may be interpreted as aspects of, or possibilities for, the same person. *Song of Solomon* (1977) centres on a middle-class man who explores his roots among rural Afro-Americans, and thus achieves self-knowledge. Black politics during the post-war years play a significant part in the novel, which gained Morrison a National Book Critics Award.

In *Tar Baby* (1981), a couple of white protagonists are introduced; the rest of the cast are black. Set in a Caribbean island, the narrative can partly be read as an allegory of colonialism. There are some suitable allusions here to Shakespeare's *The Tempest*. A mother kills her baby girl, rather than allow her to be turned into a slave, in *Beloved* (1987), a colourful but gruesome novel about the legacy of slavery. *Jazz* (1992) presents love as well as murder in the 1920s against a Harlem backdrop. Formally, the story is said to illustrate a jam session.

Morrison's later books include *Paradise* (1997), with a modern kind of witch-hunt, and *Love* (2003), where many aspects of love, and a black Aphrodite, figure. The highly original *Playing in the Dark: Whiteness and the Literary Imagination* (1992) is a critical study of 'Africanism', seen as a threatening dark presence, and physical whiteness (not necessarily of anyone's skin), another menace, in fiction by white Americans.

In addition, Morrison has written many children's books, a play called *Dreaming Emmett* (premiered 1986), a song cycle, *Honey and Me* (with André Previn, 1992) and the opera libretto *Margaret Garner* (2003).

On her enormous canvas where history, folklore and dreams intersect, Morrison employs magical realism resembling that of **Gabriel García Márquez** and **Salman Rushdie**. There is no questioning her popularity and moral seriousness. But some critics feel that she should be called successful rather than great, and that she is not more than a middlebrow writer who has benefited from being politically correct in several ways. She has also been criticized for relying overmuch on violence and other crude or obvious plot devices.

During her career, Morrison has been 'first' in a number of contexts. She is the first writer to have received both the Nobel Prize for Literature (1993) and a Pulitzer Prize (for *Beloved*). And she was the first Afro-American Nobel laureate, and the first black woman to hold a named chair – that of Robert F. Goheen, Princeton – at an Ivy League university.

Further reading

See: Marc C Conner (ed.) *The Aesthetics of Toni Morrison: Speaking the Unspeakable* (2000); and Missy Dehn Kubitschek, *Toni Morrison: A Critical Companion* (1998).

SUSANNA ROXMAN

MOSCA, Gaetano
1858–1941
Italian political writer

Mosca was for a while a civil servant, taught constitutional law and history of political doctrines in Palermo, Turin and Rome, was a Liberal-Conservative member of parliament, 1908–18, under-secretary for the colonies, 1914–16, and, in 1918, was made a senator for life. He also wrote for newspapers but gradually gave this up towards the end of the 1920s when the Fascists were depriving the press of independence. Although he began as a critic of democratic ideology and institutions, in his later years he came to regard parliamentary government as the least defective. Nonetheless, he made only one speech against **Mussolini**, and remained silent thereafter while retaining his seat in the senate. He never wrote anything either for or against the Fascists, although he did insert incidental remarks on the virtues of representative government into his book and articles on the history of political ideas, which were his only products during the Fascist era.

Mosca's first book (*Teorica dei Governi*, 'Theory of Government', 1887) was a kind of survey of world history and of the contemporary scene, the aim of which was to show that all states had or have a ruling class. Though in a more attenuated form than **Vilfredo Pareto**, he accepts the view of **Marx** and **Engels** about the ubiquity of divisions and conflicts between the classes but rejects their idea that these might be eliminated: a ruling class may be overthrown but will only be replaced by another. This is more or less the same idea as Pareto's theory of circulation of elites. There was a long dispute between them about priority, but it seems that they arrived at very similar conclusions independently and more or less simultaneously. Mosca objected to the term 'elite' on the ground that it implies excellence or superiority: in reality many ruling classes were thoroughly incompetent or wicked. They agree that the fate of the nations depends above all on the quality of their ruling classes, but Pareto thinks that this quality depends on the selection of (presumably genetically determined) psychological types whereas Mosca gives greater weight to moral information.

Mosca looks at political systems as oscillating in two dimensions between two sets of polar alternatives which he called principles: one concerns the composition of the ruling class and the other the manner of governing. The composition of the ruling class may be based on inheritance (that is, 'the aristocratic principle' in his terminology) or on the open entry for talented individuals from the lower classes, which he calls 'the democratic principle'. The rulers may be inclined and

obliged by the constitution to heed the wishes of the ruled or they may disregard and overrule them. In Mosca's terminology the first type of government is based on the liberal principle, while the second is based on the authoritarian principle. It must be noted that what he calls 'the liberal principle' is what most people nowadays would call 'the democratic principle'. Following Aristotle and Polybius, Mosca thinks that the best political system is a mixed one where none of the said principles is pushed to the extreme. However, they spoke only of a golden mean between democracy, oligarchy and monarchy – which Mosca reinterprets as a balance between the liberal and authoritarian principles. In addition, he extends the idea of balance to the composition of the ruling class. A hereditary closure of the ruling class produces ossification but a certain degree of closure may be beneficial, because it dampens the intensity of the struggle for power and permits a transmission of traditions and skills which may have considerable value.

Another crucial point in Mosca's view of history and politics is his widening of Montesquieu's theory of the division of power between the independent legislative, executive and judicial authority as a condition of freedom. Mosca finds it too legalistic and likely to remain or become a mere piece of paper unless it rests upon a division of social forces. He does not define 'social forces' but from the examples he gives we can see that he is thinking of social classes as well as institutions such as the church, the bureaucracy or the army. Even more important than the division indicated by Montesquieu is the division between the political, economic and spiritual powers. On the basis of this theory Mosca made a remarkable prediction in 1902 (in the article 'Inchiesta sul Socialismo', reprinted in *Cio che la Storia Potrebbe Insegnare*, 'What History Could Teach Us') of the results of an application of the Marxist doctrine. Assuming that it would entail a fusion between the political, economic and spiritual powers, he was able to forecast the main features of **Stalinism**.

Mosca was largely uninterested in methodology and philosophy. He simply believed that by studying history and observing people we can discover regularities in social processes; and that this knowledge would enable us to explain many phenomena and understand what was possible and desirable. He arrives at his generalizations by rough and ready induction without attempting any systematic confrontation of the thesis with data. Thus he never discusses the tricky question of the boundaries of the ruling class (or 'the political class' in his terminology) although he talks about it all the time. Nonetheless, his main work, *Elementi de Scienza Politica* ('Elements of Political Science', Vol. I, 1895, rev. 1923; Vol. II, 1923), remains a comprehensive treatise on politics, remarkable for its subtlety and originality, and the range of problems addressed. For example, Mosca was the first writer to study civil–military relations from a comparative viewpoint. One of the many illuminating rule-of-thumb generalizations which he puts forth is his 'law of the alloy', according to which an ideology or doctrine can become a political force only if it appeals to the noble and the base motives at the same time.

Mosca can be described as either a realist or a pessimist. He believed that oppression and strife were the rule, while a higher civilization was very fragile. Extreme democracy and authoritarianism appeared to him as equally dangerous. Although he called himself a liberal, he thought that 'freedom' was a chimerical notion and that the only attainable ideal was 'juridical defence', by which he meant the rule of law and the checks on arbitrary exercise of power. His practical preoccupations remain topical: he thought that the greatest dangers to the liberal political system stemmed from the growth of the power of the bureaucracy and of the unions – especially of the unions of public employees.

Further reading

Other works include: *Elementi de Scienza Politica*, which were reprinted in 1939 with a few additional footnotes by the author. *Teorica dei Governi* (an astoundingly erudite book for an author who was only twenty-five), together with various shorter works and the short reflections published posthumously, are reprinted in *Cio Che la Storia Potrebbe Insegnare* (1958). Other articles from journals are reprinted in *Partiti e Sindicati Nella Crisi del Regime Parlamentare* ('Parties and Trade Unions in the Crises of Parliamentary Rule', 1949). Articles from newspapers are reprinted in *Il Tramonto dello Stato Liberale* ('The Decline of the Liberal State', 1971), each with a useful introduction by Antonio Lombardo. *The Ruling Class* (1939) is a slightly abridged and rearranged translation of *Elementi* with a scholarly introduction by Arthur Livingstone. Mosca's last book was *Storia delle Dottrine Politiche* ('History of Political Doctrines', 1933) based on his yearly lectures on history of political institutions and ideas at the University of Rome. See also: James H. Meisel, *Myth of the Ruling Class: Gaetano Mosca and the Elite* (1958).

STANISLAV ANDRESKI

MUHAMMAD, Elijah

1897–1975

US racial and religious leader

Born into a large, impoverished family on a tenant farm in Georgia, Elijah Poole was the son of former slaves. After receiving only a minimum of schooling, he left home at sixteen and worked at a variety of unskilled jobs. In 1919 Poole married Clara Evans and in 1923 joined the tide of black migration from the South. He moved to Detroit where he worked for a time at an automobile plant, and, like his father, also did some Baptist preaching. In 1930 Poole met Wallace D. Fard, a mysterious clothing pedlar who claimed to come from Mecca with the mission of awakening the Black Nation to their true and unique greatness within Islam. Under the influence of Fard, usually referred to as 'the Prophet', Elijah Poole's life took on focus and purpose. He was given the name Elijah Karriem, and when he soon became the Prophet's chief assistant, his name was changed to Elijah Muhammad in order to denote his higher status.

When Fard disappeared in 1933, he left some 8,000 black followers (mostly in

Detroit) organized as the Nation of Islam. Elijah Muhammad was Fard's logical successor, and he also assumed the mantle of 'Prophet'. Muhammad organized additional 'temples' of followers in Chicago, Milwaukee and Washington DC, but factional disputes and numerous attempts by outside groups to infiltrate the Nation hindered its growth. By 1942, in fact, membership had declined to less than 1,000. During these years of struggle, however, Muhammad had refined a programme of theological and moral precepts which would become the basis for a mass movement among black Americans in the years after the Second World War. He saw himself as part of the long tradition of black nationalism in the USA and declared that he intended to finish up 'what those before started'. Maintaining that Allah, in the person of Prophet Fard, had explained to him the true story of creation and assured him of the ultimate victory of the coloured peoples of the world, Elijah Muhammad told his black followers that they had been cheated and oppressed by the devil (represented by all whites). Muhammad explained, however, that black Americans had been chosen by Allah to redeem the promise of victory for other oppressed peoples. Before becoming capable of fulfilling this special redemptive role, black Americans were told that they must adhere to a rigid discipline of social and psychological reform. Elijah Muhammad viewed the poverty and degradation of the black masses as the result of persecution by the white devil, but he insisted that they could be saved only by themselves. On the one hand, he elaborated a complex regimen of behaviour partly influenced by orthodox Islam, and yet on the other hand, he borrowed heavily from the values of white middle-class America. Cleanliness, modesty, fidelity, thrift and self-denial were the cornerstones of Elijah Muhammad's social teachings.

The teachings of Elijah Muhammad struck an increasingly responsive chord during the 1950s and 1960s. As the civil rights campaigns grew in momentum, black Americans steadily gained in self-confidence and at the same time gave vent to a growing sense of group indignation at their oppressions. Elijah Muhammad's strategy during these years was to achieve a higher profile for his followers and his message. His most prominent minister was Malcolm X, a former convict of keen intelligence and powerful personality. Largely through the work of **Malcolm X**, membership grew and considerable public attention descended upon Muhammad's Nation of Islam. His followers came to be known popularly as 'Black Muslims', and both whites and black civil rights leaders voiced fears of Muhammad's influence. Muslims were denounced as black racists and apostles of hate. And yet they grew in public stature throughout the 1960s, benefiting from the publicity attendant to the conversion of heavyweight boxing champion Muhammad Ali (Cassius Clay) and surviving a damaging split when Malcolm X left the sect (and subsequently was assassinated a year later) in 1964. As membership grew, so did the financial resources of the organization and the personal power of Elijah Muhammad. The Muslims opened a variety of small businesses and built up a multi-million dollar headquarters in Chicago, complete with elegant homes for Muhammad and the families of most of his eight children.

As the heat of the 1960s passed and as Elijah Muhammad's reputation increased, he became less strident in his denunciation of whites. Membership stabilized and the urgency of the movement declined. Nevertheless, at the time of Elijah Muhammad's death in 1975 there were over seventy-six mosques in the US and an estimated 200,000 members. At Elijah Muhammad's direction, his son, Wallace Muhammad, became the new leader of the Nation of Islam.

Further reading

See: C. Eric Lincoln, *The Black Muslims in America* (1961); E.U. Essien-Udom, *Black Nationalism: A Search for an Identity in America* (1962); and Louis Lomax, *When the Word is Given* (1964); Chris Nickson, *An Original Man: Elijah Muhammad*

(1997); Karl Evanzz, *The Messenger: The Rise and Fall of Elijah Muhammad* (1999).

LESTER C. LAMON

MUNCH, Edvard

1863–1944

Norwegian painter

The naturalistic description of appearances in painting reached its culmination in Impressionism. Munch was a leading figure in transcending this, creating an art of the archetypal and symbolic. Born in provincial Norway, he became, through his assimilation of French art and especially that of **Gauguin**, one of Europe's principal artists at the turn of the century. The undulating lines of contemporary Art Nouveau, normally essentially decorative, provided him with a vehicle for profound psychological revelations. His principal themes were sex, love, loneliness, illness and death.

Many of his paintings originated in emotionally painful memories, for example his earliest masterpiece *The Sick Child* (1885–6) recalling the death of a sister. The intensity of this painting was largely achieved through prolonged scratching away of layers of paint, the novelty of which method caused contemporaries to condemn it as 'unfinished'. The pain of loss is accompanied by the pain of isolation, as in *The Death Chamber* (*c.* 1894–5), where members of the bereaved family stand stiffly, each wrapped in his own incommunicable thoughts. In Munch's work, individuals are isolated not only from each other but also from nature, including their own nature, which becomes a threatening 'other'. Nature, furthermore, is symbolically equated with Woman. Munch was profoundly mistrustful of sexual love, sensing union with a woman as a kind of death, as can be seen most obviously in *The Vampire* (1894), but also in his many versions of *The Kiss*. This was not simply misogyny – see, for example, his sympathetic treatment of a young girl's anxiety in *Puberty* (1894) – but something much deeper: the fear of the destruction of the creative ego through its (desperately desired) union with natural forces. The flowing lines in many of his landscapes are the same as those of the hair in his ambivalently sexual *Madonna* (1893–4). In *The Scream* (1893), probably his most famous painting, the form of the screaming creature in the foreground is echoed in the forms of the landscape beyond and the swirling blood-red sky above: anxiety is raised to a cosmic level.

Despite his emphasis, however, on the more painful aspects of life, Munch was aiming at a broad synthesis of all fundamental aspects of human experience, balancing the dark against the light. In 1902 he exhibited, under the title of *The Frieze of Life*, a series of pictures which between them were intended to show 'life in all its fulness, its variety, its joys and its sorrows'. Close parallels exist between his art and the drama of Strindberg, of whom he painted several portraits, and Ibsen, for whose *Ghosts* he designed the décor in **Max Reinhardt's** 1906 production. Like them, he raised contemporary themes, acutely observed, to a more universal plane, infused with a partly tragic, partly mystical vision.

In 1908–9, Munch underwent a nervous breakdown. With certain notable exceptions, his work after that date seldom achieved the dramatic intensity of his early work nor was it any longer revolutionary in art historical terms. He had already, however, by then had the profoundest influence on European art, having become famous in Germany during the 1890s, somewhat helped by a fortunate art-world scandal. Technically, his paintings and graphic work, especially his woodcuts, directly influenced such German Expressionists as **Nolde** and **Kirchner**. But in a deeper sense, too, it could be claimed that he was the single most important spiritual precursor of Expressionism. He combined the traditional mysticism and anxiety of Northern art with a specifically modern awareness of the predicament of the individual cut adrift from the restrictions, and the securities, of a socially sanctioned system of values.

Further reading

See: J.P. Hodin, *Edvard Munch: Norway's Genius* (1945); Hannah B. Muller, *Edvard Munch: A Bibliography* (1951); Otto Benesch, *Edvard Munch* (1960); Werner Timm, *The Graphic Art of Edvard Munch* (1969); Reinhold Heller, *Edvard Munch's 'The Scream'* (1972); John Boulton Smith, *Munch* (1977); Ketil Bjornstad, *The Story of Edvard Munch* (2005); Sue Prideaux, *Edvard Munch: Behind the Scream* (2005).

GRAY WATSON

MURRAY, (Sir) James

1837–1915

British lexicographer

Sir James Murray was the founding father of scientific lexicography. He established the principles and set in motion the prodigious labours that produced *The Oxford English Dictionary* (1884–1928) over fifty years. He did not live to see it completed, but more than half of it was produced under his personal editorship. The *Dictionary* is still the only comprehensive historical dictionary in the world; and many of the principles and methods invented by Murray are still followed by his epigoni.

Murray was the son of the village tailor of Denholm, near Hawick, in the Borders. He was a precocious boy, fascinated by the local dialects and all varieties of language. He left school when he was fourteen, and took casual jobs on neighbouring farms while continuing to educate himself. He was appointed an assistant master at Hawick United School, and became the Border Aristotle in pursuit of antiquities, phonetics and languages. He moved to London and took a job as a bank clerk in a vain attempt to save the health of his first wife.

He continued his studies in his spare time until he must have been the most learned bank clerk in history. Incredibly, in view of his lack of academic qualifications, he was invited to read papers to the Philological Society; he edited a volume for the Early English Text Society; and he published a treatise on the *Dialect of the Southern Counties of Scotland* (1873). He established his reputation as a professional philologist by his article on the English language in the *Encyclopaedia Britannica*.

To make more time for study he returned to schoolmastering, this time at Mill Hill. While there he was appointed editor of *The Oxford English Dictionary* in 1879. It was agreed that the work should take ten years. In fact it took fifty. Murray built a scriptorium at Mill Hill, which served as a model for the corrugated-iron shed he built in his back garden up the Banbury Road when he removed, slip and slippage, to Oxford. From these improbable cottage-industry erections, with a few assistants, mainly some of his eleven children with Anglo-Saxon names, he devised the great engine of research that published the greatest dictionary of modern times.

The idea of a completely new English dictionary was conceived and the collection of materials started in 1857. The purpose was to produce for the first time a dictionary that showed the history of words and families of words, and to record the changes of form and sense that words had historically passed through. The original title was *A New English Dictionary on Historical Principles*. Its first editors were Herbert Coleridge and Dr F.J. Furnivall, but their work consisted only of collection of illustrative quotations and other materials.

When Murray took over, that disorganized enthusiast Dr Furnivall sent him some ton and three-quarters of materials that had accumulated under his roof. Murray organized the material and procured much more; he maintained the enthusiasm of more than 800 voluntary readers; and he set in motion the preparation of material for the press and its publication.

In addition to the innovation of tracing the history of words from their earliest appearance, the dictionary illustrated each change with dated quotations. It listed and defined all recorded English words from the seventh century to the twentieth. It gave etymologies and pronunciations for the first time determined professionally by modern scholarship. The *Dictionary* contains 414,825 headwords. There are 1,827,306 quotations to illustrate them. The apparently simple little word 'set', for example, was given more than twenty-two large pages of three columns each.

Although he was personally responsible for only half of the *Dictionary* (A–D, H–K, O, P, T) Murray was its chief creator, trained his successors, and laid down the plan and the scope. The first fascicle or section, *A–Ant*, was published in 1884; the other fascicles followed in majestic procession until *Wh–Wo* was the last published in 1928.

The labours were much greater than anyone had calculated. The remuneration was mean. Academic and national recognition came shamefully late: until Murray proved otherwise, lexicographers had been considered artisans, not scholars. The process that Murray invented of recording the history of a language in its words continues with *Supplements to The Oxford English Dictionary* and other historical dictionaries in other languages.

Further reading

See: Frederick James Furnivall, *A Volume of Personal Record* (1911); Lady Mildred Murray, *The Making of a Civil Servant, Sir Oswyn Murray* (1940); K.M. Elizabeth Murray, *Caught in the Web of Words* (1977); Simon Winchester, *The Surgeon of Crowthorne: A Tale of Murder, Madness and the Love of Words* (1998) and *The Meaning of Everything: The Story of the Oxford English Dictionary* (2003).

PHILIP HOWARD

MUSIL, Robert

1880–1942

Austrian novelist

Robert Musil was born in Klagenfurt into a family of civil servants, academics and officers. His father, a civil service engineer and university professor, was ennobled in 1917, shortly before the fall of the Hapsburg monarchy. Musil's career shows both his attachment to conservative family traditions and his efforts to break free from encirclement by stifling authority and family expectations. He was sent to a military academy to be trained as an officer, but left to study mechanical engineering in Brünn and in 1902 he became an instructor at the technical university of Stuttgart (Germany). He developed a remarkable breadth of talent spanning the sciences and arts. In 1903 he took up philosophy and experimental psychology, as well as mathematics and physics at Berlin University, where he gained a doctoral degree in 1908 with a dissertation on the positivist philosopher **Ernst Mach**, whose theory of cognition strongly influenced Musil's perception of the crisis of individuality in the age of mass society. He stayed in Berlin until 1910, when he returned to Austria to work first as a librarian and then as editor of a literary-political magazine (*Die Neue Rundschau*). He became an officer in the First World War, edited a newspaper for soldiers, worked in the press service of the Austrian ministry for foreign affairs and then as a civil servant in the war ministry. From 1923 onwards he lived as a freelance writer, constantly plagued by financial worries. In 1938, after the incorporation of Austria into the German Reich, he emigrated to Switzerland where he died in intellectual and social isolation.

Musil's first novel, *Young Törless* (*Die Verwirrungen des Zöglings Törless*, 1906, trans. 1955), is a sensitive fictional transposition of the author's experiences as a student at the senior army cadet school at Weisskirchen. In retrospect, i.e. after the rise and fall of fascism in central and southern Europe, this novel came to be seen as a subtle portrayal of the psychological predeterminations of fascist character traits slumbering beneath the smooth façade of conservative bourgeois respectability, correctness and patriotism, a reading which Musil himself supported. Influenced by **Dostoevsky**, **Nietzsche** and Mach, Musil rejected the naturalist mode of writing. He is therefore not interested in giving a faithful account of a boarding-school milieu pervaded by the sergeant-major mentality of the masters and the parade-ground command tone of their language. Musil's primary concern is with Törless's mind and his reflection of experience. For Törless reality is at one time a rationally ordered, causally connected set of alien and distinct entities, which at other times lose their distinctness, form a diffuse merger and assume a close and intimate familiarity. At such times Törless feels drawn into a kind of mystical union with people and objects, his identity dissolving in a contradictory complexity of de-individualizing emotions. Musil's description of Törless is clearly influenced by Mach's theory of cognition which conceives man as a disjointed ensemble of experiential moments, capable of a multiplicity of moral and amoral stances. Within the experiments in group dynamics, led by his fellow student cadets, Beineberg and Reiting, with Basini as their chief victim, Törless is a participant observer, identifying both with the persecutors and with the victim. He becomes involved in a plot of blackmail, devious manipulation, cynical subjugation and dictatorial exploitation in which the victim responds with subaltern submission and servility. The interpersonal relations among the cadets in Young Törless do indeed reveal traits of the 'authoritarian personality' (see **Adorno**) and a type of group dynamics, complete with aspects of mass psychology, which became all too familiar in the subsequent age of fascist dictatorships. Törless, far from opposing the callous schemes of the ringleaders in the plot, uses it to explore the confusions and uncertainties of his own morality, of the borderlines between the rational and the irrational. He finally has to leave the institution because he raises uncanny questions about the irrationality of the apparently rational which are felt to threaten the condescending paternalism and the positivist categories of truth operated by the schoolmasters. The tale about boys in their period of puberty becomes a visionary narrative about the seductions of authoritarian society and positivist rationality at the turn of the century, with the conservative intellectual fascinated by irrationalism, mass

manipulation and cold connivance in experiments in human enslavement.

Musil's subsequent development can be plotted in a number of essays ('Politisches Bekenntnis eines jungen Mannes', 1913; 'Geist und Erfahrung', 1921; 'Die Nation als Ideal und Wirklichkeit', 1921; 'Das hilflose Europa', 1922; 'Der deutsche Mensch als Symptom', 1923), short stories and novellas (e.g. 'Drei Frauen' and the stories edited in 1936 under the title Nachlass zu Lebzeiten) and plays (Die Schwärmer, 1921, and Vinzenz und die Freundin bedeutender Manner, 1923). All these works may be regarded as preliminary studies to one of the most voluminous and complex novels of the twentieth century: The Man without Qualities (Der Mann ohne Eigenschaften, 3 vols, the first portion of which was published in 1931, the second in 1933, the rest posthumously in 1943 and 1952, trans. 1953–60). This major work, an intricately wrought pattern of fiction and thought, of powerful similes and philosophical abstraction, of detailed character portrayal and sweetly tentative sententiousness, has remained a giant torso.

The setting is 'Kakania', a country whose name was fashioned by Musil from the two k's in the official designation of Austria before the First World War, when it was 'kaiserly-kingly'. That Austria is not only a crucible of nations and races, of currents of thought traditional and modern, feudal and bourgeois, it is also used as a paradigm to describe and reflect the fundamental shifts in the socio-political fabric and in mental attitudes which occurred in twentieth-century European society as it grew out of and took over from that of the nineteenth century. In other words, the novel is an attempt to trace a world in transition, a world of traditional values and institutions, of aristocratic and popular culture pervaded by feudal stratification and order being undermined and exploded by the mathematical spirit of capitalist technology and profiteering rationality, by the cash nexus as the quantifying leveller of all qualities and the foundation of a democracy of clashing egoisms. Qualities of character once considered the inalienable hallmarks of personality formation, the distinctness of individuality, the uniqueness of personal demeanour are revealed as clichéd stances, as conformist practices following the shibboleths of a bygone age. They now serve as ready-made costumes which society has on offer in a variety of measurements, all calculated to make the individual useful and usable within the macro-social mechanism of a struggle of all against all and of the martial hegemony of states and superstates.

This is the scenario in which Ulrich, Musil's protagonist and alter ego, strikes his pose as a 'man without qualities', that is one who has an abundance of qualities but is committed to none of them. He is alienated by a society in a state of anomie, with its legal and moral consensus eroded, about to sweep away the feudal veneer of the old order to reveal the bleak pattern of a lacerated social cohesion being reforged by the relentless forces of global technology and technocracy. Ulrich is out of tune with the old aristocratic conservatism, but loves its idealist commitment to high culture. He is equally out of tune with the profiteering spirit of finance capital, which negates cultural values, but he admires its energy in reshaping nature and society. Unable to take sides, disgusted by the limitation of the real, he seeks refuge in a realm of pure spirit, of the infinity of the possible, in a utopian idyll where he can merge in mystical union with a kindred soul (his sister Agathe).

As a bourgeois in well-heeled retirement at the comparatively young age of thirty-two, Ulrich experiences society and politics as a comic and fatal charade, as a world provoking cynicism, satire and withdrawal. Yet Musil is too complex and intellectually sophisticated to allow Ulrich's escape into a utopian idyll to appear as a simple reaffirmation of pure mysticism and irrationality. The journey into the idyll of pure thought, pure feeling is part of Musil's pathology of the critical bourgeois intellectual's position in the history of contemporary society. This history is seen as one of warring ideologies hell-bent on dressing up the world of economic necessity as a realm of ideas, and economic prosperity as freedom and happiness. In *The Man without Qualities* Musil is attempting to restate the need for a world transcending material necessity. While large sections of humanity are still far from affluent, this kind of concern remains the privilege of a class living in luxury. But Ulrich's groping for a utopia of the possible is not so much a denial of the necessity for modern technology to become universally accessible; but more a protest against the reduction of man to conformism with programmes of social convention and mass-produced images. If the novel is agonizingly left fragmentary, then so are the issues of contemporary history which it reflects.

Further reading

Musil's collected works are available in a critical edition, ed. Adolf Frise (9 vols, 1978). See also *Tagebücher* (2 vols, 1976). About Musil: Karl Dinklage (ed.) *Robert Musil. Leben, Werk, Wirkung* (1960); Burton Pike, *Robert Musil: An Introduction to His Work* (1962, trans. 1972); Wilfried Berghahn, *Robert Musil* (1963, trans. 1978). See also *Musil Forum*, a bi-annual journal (from 1975); Hannah Hickman, *Robert Musil and the Culture of Vienna* (1984); Steffan Jonsson, *Robert Musil and the History of Modern Identity* (2001).

WILFRIED VAN DER WILL

MUSSOLINI, Benito

1883–1945

Italian politician

Benito Mussolini was born in the Romagna and he was executed by Italian partisans on 23 April 1945. He was a qualified schoolteacher (his subject was French) but from an early stage he made his living as a journalist and propagandist. At this time he was a Socialist and after periods in exile in Switzerland and Austria he became editor of *Avanti!*, the Socialist journal. He became alienated from Socialism due to his demand that Italy participate in the First World War. In the aftermath of Italy's defeat at Caporetto in 1917 and the disintegration of Italian political life that ensued, Mussolini decided to form his own political party.

His supporters were revolutionary war veterans and determined anti-Bolsheviks who formed groups which amalgamated in March 1919 to constitute the Fascist Party. By October 1922 their *Duce* had managed to become prime minister. His meteoric rise was partly the result of the crises of previous years but mostly because he threatened to seize power unless given it legally. And, indeed, his Fascist squads were ready to fight their way to the capital, which allowed his coup to be named 'the March on Rome'.

Mussolini was certain that his success in politics would depend on his possessing total control of Italian affairs. He not only sanctioned the assassination of the Socialist leader Matteotti in order to intimidate all opposition, but he ruthlessly imposed his own policies. By 1925 he was able to pronounce himself Italian dictator and to hold eight other ministries besides. In 1929 he came to an agreement with the Roman Catholic Church which ensured that it would not criticize his misdeeds.

The source of Mussolini's power was not traditional and it gave the world something new to think about. It was based on a readiness to use violence combined with a skilful charismatic approach, a combination of warlord and populist. He took personal responsibility for Italy's fortunes and, when the symbolic trains ran on time, he could also reap the credit. His followers, of whom many were non-Italian, saw him as the man who could transform backwardness through progress, a notion that could, however, only be fostered through dynamic foreign policies. Despite Fascist claims that Mussolini was 'always right', domestic successes were few.

After an early excursion into Greek waters, Mussolini decided in 1935 to colonize Ethiopia. He rejoiced in the gravest acts of barbarism which included the burning alive of a generation of intellectuals and other prisoners. The highpoint of his foreign ambitions came at Munich in 1938 where he,

and one of his admirers, **Adolf Hitler**, could prove that they were able to dictate to the great democracies as well as to their own people. Italian participation in the Second World War, which was part of this demonstration, failed nevertheless to produce anything but a series of humiliating disasters. Mussolini naturally suffered from this and when the Allies invaded Sicily he was overthrown. Following the Nazi invasion of Italy, however, he was freed in order to found the new Fascist Republic of Salo.

Mussolini's ideas were far cleverer than Hitler's although they lacked the Nazi leader's distinctiveness. Mussolini was more conventional, too, since the problems he identified were the traditional ones of Europe. Hitler's, on the other hand, tended to be ones which most people saw as specifically German. It was, as a consequence, easier for non-Italians to sympathize with Mussolini. He was, for example, always concerned to find the correct place for organized labour in society, even in Salo, something that Hitler tended to think unproblematical. Similarly it comes as no surprise to find that until 1938 the appeal of the Nazis' racial politics escaped the *Duce* although he later keenly assisted in the extermination of the Jews of Europe.

The intellectual background of Italian Fascism may readily be sought in a reaction against the dominant ideologies of the era, liberalism, Socialism and, perhaps, Catholicism. Action was more important than doctrine or debate. Fascism's relation to nationalism, however, was something that caused difficulties. In seeking a new aggressive form of nationalism, which was not defined like Nazism in racial terms, Mussolini's growing reliance on Hitler led to his own patriotism being doubted. And as Hitler's armies began to suffer defeat, even the Fascists of Italy began to question the wisdom of being sacrificed for Germany. Mussolini's political ideas depended on dynamism. Contraction and failure destroyed the fiction he had managed to purvey. It is, even so, a remarkable fact that twenty-two years of Fascist rule in Italy were ended only by the

Allies' invasion and not by any widespread anti-Fascist revolt among the Italian people.

Further reading

Other works include: *My Autobiography* (1928); *The Political and Social Doctrine of Fascism* (1949). About Mussolini: G. Ciano, *Diaries 1939–43* (1946); Edward Tannenbaum, *Fascism in Italy 1922–45* (1973); Dennis Mack Smith, *Mussolini's Roman Empire* (1978); Richard Lamb, *Mussolini and the British* (1997); R.J.B. Bosworth, *Mussolini* (2002); Nicholas Farrell, *Mussolini* (2004); Ray Mosely, *Mussolini: The Last 600 Days of Il Duce* (2004).

ANTHONY GLEES

MUSSORGSKY, Modest Petrovich

1839–81

Russian composer

The most original composer of the 'Mighty Handful' was educated privately and then at the Cadet School of the Guards in St Petersburg. He served in the Preobrazhensky Regiment of Guards and was later employed in the civil service. His interests shifted from the traditional pursuits of Guards officers to some of the most advanced ideas of the time. He claimed to have been drawn to music through folk art rather than art music, and despised the rules and conventions of the latter. In 1857 he encountered for the first time **Balakirev**, Stasov and Dargomyzhsky. The first-named attempted to guide him along his customary musical path, Stasov eventually became a life-long friend, and Dargomyzhsky pioneered some of the ideas and techniques which Mussorgsky later embodied in his own compositions. From 1863 or so his music begins to show his deep interest in folk art and his attachment to truth rather than beauty as an artistic ideal. His projected opera *The Marriage* (1868) is the laboratory in which he experimented with modelling vocal lines on the inflections of (Russian) speech, an idea recently tried out in Dargomyzhsky's *The Stone Guest*. His avoidance of grandiose cosmopolitan subjects, his concentration on various aspects of Russian life, treated realis-

tically, and his taste for caricature draw him close to the utilitarian ideas of the time and to the group of painters known as the 'Itinerants'. But his talent for vivid representation through highly unorthodox musical devices put his works beyond the comprehension of the majority of his contemporaries, even of many musicians sympathetically disposed to him. In his case bouts of alcoholism compounded the inability, characteristic of many Russian composers of this period, to bring projected compositions to completion, and his works were much altered after his death in the name of turning them into performable material.

Ever an enemy of routine and convention, Mussorgsky did not really try to make a successful career as a composer by the lights of the time. Particularly in its first version (1868–9), but to some extent also in the second (1871–2, performed in 1874), the opera *Boris Godunov* was not tailored for immediate success. Its very subject made it liable to censorship troubles. It was deficient in opportunities for the expected vocal display and ballet, and it was short of love interest and comedy. Yet it is a masterly work, in its own terms, in which Mussorgsky's gift for characterization is brought to bear on the psychological development of Boris himself, and in which the stark and sombre music magnificently reflects and communicates the events and atmosphere of the time. The 'time of troubles' in the early seventeenth century which preceded the beginning of the Romanov dynasty's rule provided the composer with a serious subject from the Russian past which gave him scope for musical depiction of a wide variety of characters, including nobles, peasants, clergy, Polish aristocrats and Jesuits. His knowledge of Russian folk music determined the character of the greatest part of the Russian scenes. **Rimsky-Korsakov's** version, which for long kept out Mussorgsky's original, has smoothed out and made 'grammatical' what in the original was more striking and novel, while its orchestration has often substituted conventional tinsel for what the composer had coloured with greater discrimination and sensitivity.

With *Khovanshchina*, on which Mussorgsky worked from 1872 until his death, it is more defensible to use Rimsky-Korsakov's version of 1883, given the incomplete and rather unsatisfactory state in which the composer left it. Once more the subject is a troubled period of Russian history – the 1680s, when the Princes Khovansky tried to overthrow the ruling Romanovs. The former personify the old feudal class and the latter more modern ideas. An important part is played by Old Believers, who remained faithful to details or Orthodox ritual after these had been changed by Patriarch Nikon in 1653. It is probable that Mussorgsky intended to close the opera (in good *grand opéra* style) with their mass suicide by fire. The precise course of the action was not worked out in advance, and the plot is sprawling and over-elaborate. Like *Boris*, it is concerned not so much with the interaction of individuals as with the unfolding of a national tragedy. There is much fine music in it.

Still less was written of *Sorochintsy Fair* on which the composer worked between 1874 and his death. This opera, based on a short story by **Gogol**, was more humorous in tone but still allowed Mussorgsky to use his gift for graphic characterization. He was handicapped, however, by his failure to work out a scheme to begin with and by an inadequate immersion in the Ukrainian language and background of the proposed opera. *Pictures from an Exhibition* (1874) is a series of short piano pieces, each 'representing' a work by the artist Victor Hartmann, linked by a 'walking' theme ('Promenade'). Each is a brilliant miniature which seizes on some aspect of the picture's content and translates it into sound.

Mussorgsky's particular talent for characterization is made clear in his nearly fifty songs, plus three cycles. The vast range over which this talent extended, together with the development of the composer's style and technique, is also shown in the songs. 'Where Are You, Little Star?' (1857) has strong references to the modes, harmony, cadences and ornamentation of folk song. *Kalistrat*

(1864), *The Peasant Lullaby* (1865), *Hopak* (1866) and *Eryomushka's Lullaby* (1868, dedicated 'to the great teacher of musical truth, A.S. Dargomyzhsky') follow on from it in still more rigorous style. *Gathering Mushrooms* (1867) and the first song of the *Nursery* cycle (1868–72) exemplify the composer's attempts to capture speech inflections while using a single note-value (the crotchet) for the vocal part. The cycle shows his ability to penetrate the thought processes of a child, and his readiness to encapsulate them in musical language of unprecedented empiricism.

In *Svetik Savishna* (1866) Mussorgsky depicts an unhappy idiot declaring his love for a girl while acknowledging that his condition deprives him of everything including love. The music is 'realistic' in the sense that it most cleverly reflects the manner of voice and gesture of the scene; from such songs we might well deduce that the composer was a mimic of considerable talent. *The Seminarist* (1866) shows a student learning Latin nouns and indulging simultaneously in amorous reflections. *The Classicist* (1867) is a lampoon of a critic who had attacked the 'modernism' of Rimsky-Korsakov's *Sadko*. A subjective lyrical vein and a more conventional handling of musical figures are revealed in the cycle *Sunless* (1874). The bold graphic quality of many other songs is here replaced by a degree of stylization. The *Songs and Dances of Death* (1875–77) sum up the most important features of Mussorgsky's songs. Vivid yet structured, inventive yet disciplined, speech-inflected yet generating lyrical melody – this cycle is one of the composer's best works. Each song shows the intervention of death in an area of human life – taking a sick child from its mother, serenading a sick girl, dancing with a drunken peasant, and on the battlefield – and treats each subject like a miniature *scena*.

When he had characters and dramatic situations to stimulate him, Mussorgsky could respond with music of wonderful truth and imagination. Song and opera offered greatest scope, and it is in these forms that Mussorgsky's splendid marriage of music with drama succeeded most consistently. His influence was felt most strongly after his lifetime – by **Debussy**, **Stravinsky**, **Prokofiev** and **Shostakovich**.

Further reading

See: Jay Leyda and Sergei Bertensson, *The Mussorgsky Reader* (1974); M.D. Calvocoressi (com-pleted and revised by Gerald Abraham), *Mussorgsky* (1974); A. Orlova (ed.) *Remembering Mussorgsky* (1991); R. Taruskin, *Mussorgsky: Eight Essays and an Epilogue* (1992); Carl Emerson, *The Life of Mussorgsky* (1999); David Brown, *Mussorgsky* (2004).

STUART CAMPBELL

N

NABOKOV, Vladimir Vladimirovich

1899–1977

Russian/US novelist

Nabokov was a writer (primarily a novelist) who wrote in two languages (Russian and English), had two literary careers (as an émigré under the pen-name of Sirin and as a major American author), and whose art is preoccupied with worlds within and beyond other worlds. Born in St Petersburg, the son of a well-known liberal politician, he left Russia with his family after the Revolution of 1917. After taking a degree in French and Russian at Cambridge, he settled in Berlin, where he became a prominent and distinguished member of the Russian émigré literary world (the name Sirin is an obscure homage to the Russian publishing house which brought out Andrey Bely's modernistic novel *Petersburg*, much admired by Nabokov). His first novel, *Mashenka*, was published in Russian in 1926 and translated into German two years later (translated into English as *Mary*, 1970). Its theme of exile, loss and erotic yearning, as well as its comic and parodistic elements, and its self-conscious illusionism, foreshadow later and greater works, especially those which hold up distorting mirrors to a distorted reality, like *Despair* (1936/66), *Invitation to a Beheading* (1935/60), and *Bend Sinister* (1947). The erotic strain in *Mashenka* foreshadows *Lolita* (1955), while the element of fictitious biography is developed in *Glory* (1932/71) and *The Defence* (1930/64) as well as two novels which, with *Lolita*, may be considered his crowning achievement, *The Gift* (1937/63) and *Pale Fire* (1962), the former a sophisticated revaluation (by means of parody) of the Russian literary tradition, the other a novel lying hidden among the references and cross-references of a misleadingly erudite commentary to a limpid and lengthy pastiche poem in the manner of **Robert Frost** (with more than a dash of **Wallace Stevens**). The writings and rewritings of biography/autobiography, doubtless an artistic transformation of personal insecurity, also lie behind Nabokov's first novel in English, *The Real Life of Sebastian Knight* (1941).

Nabokov, who married in 1925 and had one son, Dimitri, in 1934, continued to live and work in Berlin, where his father had been assassinated by right-wing extremists in 1922, until history (a nightmare from which, like **Joyce's** Stephen Dedalus, he could not awake) forced him to move to Paris, and thence, in 1939, to the USA. His peregrinations are recorded, very subjectively, in his 'real' autobiography, *Speak, Memory*, but his full bitterness at the horrific turn of historic events is evoked (always by way of parody and mockery, never direct commentary) in *Invitation to a Beheading*, a Kafkaesque work uninfluenced by **Kafka**, and *Bend Sinister*, a kind of carnivalesque *1984* in which European totalitarianism is grotesquely garbed in the banalities of American comic strip. In America, in addition to a fairly obscure academic career, Nabokov enjoyed some small repute as a lepidopterist, until his life was transformed by the overnight notoriety of a novel which 'respectable' publishers would not handle, *Lolita*, now recognizably one of the seminal works of twentieth-century American fiction. Suddenly the émigré academic (not unlike his own creation, *Pnin*, 1957) became a best-seller. He moved with his wife to Montreux in Switzerland, and continued to live there in a hotel until his death, publishing regularly.

Lolita has been considered variously as a story of true love and as forming part of the 'literature of exhaustion', and there is no doubt that part of its fascination lies in its power of appealing at different levels. The love of the obscure émigré, Humbert Humbert, for the nymphet Lolita (both household words since Nabokov) is both text and pre-text in a symbolic journey in the American tradition (and loaded with Americana past and present): part flight, part quest, where innocent desire plays a deadly game with retributive lust, the latter being embodied in the character of one Clare Quilty, C.Q. the pursuer, the avenging angel or the devil in disguise. Quilty is (like Emerald in *Pale Fire*) simply, on another level, the novelist playing chess with his protagonist, or the mechanism of 'plot' with its ineluctable ending. On the moral plane, he is an emanation of Humbert's guilty conscience, and when Humbert kills him in a mock-Hollywood shoot-up, Humbert is a lost soul. 'Decadent' as the subject-matter of *Lolita* may be, the centre of attention in the novel is not morbid psychology but the creative potentialities of language itself: Nabokov's wit plays over a wide range of narrative modes and devices, exploring in particular the tensions of memory and desire, the quasi-erotic longing for a symbolic order.

The exceptional awareness of the limits of literary conventions, born of Nabokov's peculiarly 'extraterritorial' (to use George Steiner's term) situation, has led critics to emphasize his kinship with such writers as **Borges**, **Robbe–Grillet** and **Pynchon**, at the expense of his Russianness and the direct relationship of his art to such writers as Pushkin and **Chekhov** via Bely. Nevertheless,

just as Nabokov influenced American fiction, so it influenced him: his work became more labyrinthine and mannerist, while remaining beneath the surface profoundly personal, even plangent. The crazed commentator of *Pale Fire* is a sadomasochistic double of the scholarly Nabokov, who edited and translated – very brilliantly – Pushkin's *Eugene Onegin* (1964); the family chronicle of *Ada* (1969), strikingly combining motifs from American and Russian culture, is a kaleidoscope of statelessness as well as an exercise in translation; while the strangely brief *Transparent Things* (1972) and *Look at the Harlequins* (1974) are respectively the fictionalized epilogue and the index-cum-bibliography to Nabokov's life's work, as if death might coincide, by a higher authorial logic, with 'the end' on the page. Although occasionally hinting at new stylistic departures, these late works are nostalgic and solipsistic, suggesting that the mandarin stance Nabokov assiduously cultivated in his later years preyed, in the end, on his talent.

Further reading

Critical studies of Nabokov include: Page Stegner, *Escape into Aesthetics* (1966); L.S. Dembo (ed.) *Nabokov: The Man and His Works* (1967); Andrew Field, *Nabokov: His Life in Art* (1967); Karl Proffer, *Keys to Lolita* (1968); Julian Moynahan, *Vladimir Nabokov* (1971); Alfred Appel, *Nabokov's Dark Cinema* (1974); John O. Stark, *The Literature of Exhaustion* (1974); H. Grabes, *Fictitious Biographies* (1977); G.M. Hyde, *Vladimir Nabokov: America's Russian Novelist* (1977); Vladimir E. Alexandrov (ed.) *The Garland Companion to Vladimir Nabokov* (1995); Kurt Johnson and Stephen Coates, *Nabokov's Blues: The Scientific Odyssey of a Literary Genius* (2001); Jane Grayson, *Nabokov's World* (2 vols, 2001); Stanley P. Baldwin, *Vladimir Nabokov: His Life and Works* (2004); Julian W. Connolly (ed.) *The Cambridge Companion to Nabokov* (2005).

G.M. HYDE

NADER, Ralph

1934–

US social reformer

Ralph Nader represents the consumer movement in the United States and a form of social activism reaching far beyond consumer affairs. With the publication in 1966 of his book, *Unsafe at Any Speed*, attacking the safety record of the General Motors' automobile, Corvair, Nader first came to wide public attention. Subsequent revelations of General Motors' surveillance of Nader helped launch his public career as a social critic and activist.

During the late 1960s and early 1970s, Nader and his assistants conducted a number of highly visible investigations of government agencies. These carefully documented studies of the failure of government agencies to protect the health, safety and economic well-being of the people provided the impetus for administrative and legislative reform. Relying heavily upon student volunteers and media exposure, Nader became, without public office or official position, one of the most politically influential persons in the United States.

While continuing the investigation of government and business, Nader in the mid-1970s turned increasingly to more permanent organizations. These groups, specializing in litigation before the courts, lobbying before Congress or continuous examination of particular industries or government agencies, became the foundation of Nader's activities.

In 1980 Nader was appointed director of the Public Citizen Foundation, and in 1996 was nominated by the American Green Party as its candidate in the US presidential elections.

The range of Nader's interests has been broad, ranging from meat and poultry inspection and automobile safety to nuclear energy. Through all of Nader's activities, however, run two themes: that power must be accountable and that individual citizens have the responsibility to ensure that accountability.

Nader's activities emphasized a number of principles to render accountable large concentrations of power. First, where possible, Nader has sought to break up concentrations of power. He championed the consumer cooperative movement and the rigorous enforcement of laws designed to limit the size of

business enterprises. In part his long opposition to nuclear energy rests not only on safety concerns but also upon its centralizing effect upon social organization.

Second, Nader has sought to control the exercise of power by both business and government. In areas affecting public health and safety Nader has been a consistent advocate of effective government regulation. The Coal Mine Health and Safety Act, the National Highway Traffic Safety Act, the Occupational Health and Safety Act, the Meat and Poultry Inspection Act represent only some of Nader's successful legislative activities. Nader has worked for more open government. An early supporter of strengthened open government laws such as the United States Freedom of Information Act, Nader through his organizations has become one of the most effective protectors of citizen access to government information. These reforms sought to enable those affected by decisions to understand and influence those decisions.

Third, Nader has stressed the personal responsibility of those persons who work in large organizations. On the principle that evil is committed by persons and not organizations, Nader has pursued reform of the federal civil service to make government officials personally accountable for their decisions. In some areas, Nader has established the precedent that a civil servant may be subject to discipline on the basis of a citizen complaint to a body independent of the civil servant's agency. Nader has also successfully provided protection through legislation to government employees who expose corruption, wrongdoing, waste or inefficiency within government agencies and has sought to provide similar protections for employees of private industry.

Perhaps what makes Nader most unique is the tradition of individual citizen activism he has nurtured. Nader believes in the responsibility of the individual. Crucial to all reform is the ability of citizens to gain access to information regarding government and business, to participate in decisions, and to hold accountable those who exercise power over them. The responsibility of each citizen is to participate in public affairs. It is this vision of individual responsibility and of the role of the individual in social change that may be Nader's most significant legacy.

Further reading

Other books by Nader include *The Menace of Atomic Energy* (1977); *Who's Poisoning America?* (1980); *Winning the Insurance Game* (1990).

ROBERT G. VAUGHN
(REVISED AND UPDATED BY THE EDITOR)

NAGEL, Ernest

1901–85

US philosopher

Ernest Nagel was born at Nove Mesto, Czechoslovakia, moved to the United States in 1911, and was naturalized in 1919. He attended City College, New York, and obtained an MA in Mathematics and a PhD in Philosophy at Columbia University where he spent his academic career as Professor of Philosophy.

Nagel was most renowned as a teacher and expositor. These gifts were evident in his *An Introduction to Logic* (1934), written with his former teacher, M.R. Cohen, which is a lucid, lively, traditionally oriented introduction to logic. Its greatest merit is its extensive introduction to scientific method which made it a standard text for many years. In *Godel's Proof* (1958), written with J.R. Newman, Nagel succeeds in conveying the content and significance of **Godel's** important theorems in a manner which made them accessible to non-logicians. It remains the best elementary exposition of Godel's results.

Nagel, a naturalist and logical empiricist, displays in his work the influence of **Dewey**, **Peirce**, **Russell** and the Vienna Circle (especially **Schlick**) whose meetings he attended briefly. His *The Structure of Science* (1961) is a refined and rich account of the scientific enterprise from that perspective. A central theme in this work is the unity of science; the methods of all sciences are essentially those of the physical sciences. Particular attention is given to explanation which for Nagel, as for the logical positivists, is deductive in form. For instance, in giving a causal explanation of the occurrence of an event at some time in a system, one derives a statement asserting the occurrence of that event from statements specifying the state of the system at an earlier time and the laws governing the system. Explanations in biology in which the behaviour of a system is explained by citing goals or purposes of the system appear at first glance not to be deductive in form. According to Nagel these explanations can be translated into causal explanations of the deductive type. This general line of argument is extended more controversially to all social sciences; social sciences are capable in principle of discovering general laws which can be used in deductive explanations and in so far as satisfactory explanations have been produced, they are deductive in form. While, according to Nagel, there are more practical difficulties in gathering the requisite data and in achieving value neutrality in the social sciences than in the physical sciences, progress in the former is to be attained by emulating the latter.

The doctrine of the unity of science is a consequence of Nagel's naturalism which he characterizes as the general assumption that spatio-temporally located material bodies are the only agents of causal change. All events, including mental events, are to be explained by reference to such bodies. There can, therefore, be no immaterial spirits. The limited ontology of naturalism generates difficulties in accounting for the ground of the truth of logical and mathematical statements. Nagel explored these in his *Logic Without Metaphysics* (1956). For instance, the naturalist is committed to rejecting the thesis that arithmetical statements are truths about a realm of non-empirical objects, the numbers. Nagel objects to the view of Mill that such statements are contingent generalizations about physical objects on the grounds that true arithmetical statements are necessarily true. He articulates, somewhat vaguely, the view that mathematical and logical statements are to be understood through the role they play in inquiry and discourse. Their necessity is said to arise in virtue of their exclusive authority in any system of discourse.

Further reading

Other works include: *The Logic of Measurement* (1930); *Principles of Probability* (1939); *Sovereign Reason* (1954); *Teleology Revisited* (1979). See also *Philosophy, Science and Method: In Honour of Ernest Nagel* (1969); M. Ruse, *The Philosophy of Biology Today* (1988).

W.H. NEWTON-SMITH

NAIPAUL, (Sir) Vidiadhar Surajprasad

1932–

Trinidadian/British writer

A prolific novelist, essayist and travel writer of Indian descent, V.S. Naipaul has attracted critical admiration and antagonism in almost equal measure. Written after he first came to England from Trinidad in 1950, his early fiction, *The Mystic Masseur* (1957), *The Suffrage of Elvira* (1958) and *Miguel Street* (1959), mingles warm comedy, farce and satire in its representation of urban and rural Trinidadians and their aspirations during the 1940s. *A House for Mr Biswas* (1961) portrayed with humour and pathos the childhood and struggle for independence from a feudal Indian culture of its protagonist (based on Naipaul's father). These early works suggest the influence of **Dickens** in their characterization and keen ear for dialogue. In 1962 he published his first travel book, *The Middle Passage*, a record of his return journey to Trinidad, and to Guyana and other Caribbean islands, in which he angered Caribbean writers and readers by his declaration that 'nothing was ever created in the Caribbean'. In return, Barbadian novelist George Lamming accused Naipaul of producing nothing but 'castrated satire', and the Guyanan novelist Wilson Harris condemned Naipaul's adherence to

the form and techniques of the European realist novel of manners. Two years later, a travel book about India, *An Area of Darkness*, brought outcries from Indian readers who rejected his sweeping characterization of Indians as fatalistic and backward-looking.

On his award of the Nobel Prize for Literature in 2001, Naipaul spoke of the importance of his travel writing in giving him a larger view of the world and an understanding of the lasting consequences of empire. Here he also implicitly acknowledges the influence of **Conrad** as another exiled writer whose characters observe and reflect upon 'outposts of the empire' and 'areas of darkness'. Travel writing also allowed him to move on to a new kind of fiction, *The Mimic Men* (1966). A bleak and devastating depiction of those who had been uprooted from their ancestral homelands and remain unable to find a sustained commitment to the communities they find themselves in, either in the Caribbean or in England, this novel, Naipaul claimed in his Nobel speech, remains an accurate analysis of the general condition of 'colonial schizophrenia', a book 'about how the powerless lie about themselves, and lie to themselves, since it is their only resource'. But it is also, like later works such as *Enigma of Arrival* (1987), *A Way in the World* (1994), *Half a Life* (2001) and *Magic Seeds* (2004), about memory, self-discovery and the process of writing.

Naipaul continued as a prolific and often controversial writer during the 1970s and 1980s, publishing four works of fiction and seven collections of travel writing. He was awarded the Booker Prize in 1971 for *In a Free State*, a sequence of short stories and novellas dealing with displaced characters and set in London, the Caribbean, India, Africa and Washington. His accounts of the murders perpetrated by the Trinidadian black power militant Michael X, Mobutu's Congo, travels in Argentina, and a return visit to India were first published in *The New York Review of Books* before being revised and republished in book form. The material on Michael X and the Congo is also fictionalized in the novels

Guerrillas (1975), which includes both *Jane Eyre* and *Wuthering Heights* as subtexts, and *A Bend in the River* (1979), which can be read as a contemporary version of Conrad's *Heart of Darkness*. Naipaul's portrayal of the Congo and of Africans brought fierce attacks from African writers such as **Chinua Achebe** for his pessimism and what was read as a condescending and dismissive characterization of Africans. Other critics have been dismayed by what they see as a deep-seated misogyny in his fiction.

In the United Kingdom and North America, however, Naipaul's fiction and travel writing has received considerable acclaim. He is praised for the clarity, subtlety and flexibility of his prose, the precision of detail, the calmly reflective and authoritative tone, his analysis of the intricate interweaving of private desires and historical forces, the wide range of cultures and geographies he has dealt with, his innovations in blending the genres of essay, novel and travel writing. He received an honorary DLitt from Cambridge in 1983, the T.S. Eliot Award for creative writing in 1986, a knighthood in 1990, and in 1993 the David Cohen British Literature Prize in recognition of a 'lifetime's achievement by a living author'. At the same time, Naipaul's recent comments on Islam and support for the more fundamentalist Hindu politics in India have dismayed even some of his admirers in the West.

Further reading

Other writings include: *The Loss of Eldorado: A History* (1969); *The Overcrowded Baracoon and Other Articles* (1972); *India: A Wounded Civilization* (1977); *The Return of Eva Peron, with the Killings in Trinidad* (1980); *A Congo Diary* (1980); *Among the Believers: An Islamic Journey* (1981); *Finding the Centre: Two Narratives* (1984); *A Turn in the South* (1989); *India: A Million Mutinies Now* (1990); and *Beyond Belief: Islamic Excursions among the Converted Peoples* (1998). *Mr Stone and the Knights Companion* (1963) is a novel set in England; *A Flag on the Island* (1967) a collection of early shorter fiction. See: Bruce King, *V.S. Naipaul* (1990); Rob Nixon, *London Calling: V.S. Naipaul, Travel Writer and Postcolonial Mandarin* (1992); Dennis Walder,

'V.S. Naipaul and the Postcolonial Order', in his *Recasting the World* (1993); Judith Levy, *Naipaul: Displacement and Autobiography* (1995); Feroza Jussawalla, *Conversations with V.S. Naipaul* (1996).

LYN INNES

NASSER, Gamal Abdel
1918–70
Egyptian statesman

Effectively ruler of Egypt from 1952 until his death from a heart attack, 'Colonel' Nasser, as he was unsentimentally known to his British adversaries, for a while bestrode the Middle East, promoting a secularist fusion of anti-imperialism, anti-Zionism, pan-Arabism and socialism. Yet his ambitions far outran his achievements, and although still revered by some Egyptians, his reputation elsewhere in the Arab world and indeed Islam is dogged by controversy, not least because of his determined hostility toward the Islamist Muslim Brotherhood.

He was born in Alexandria, the son of a postmaster. Throughout his life he stressed his *fellahin* (broadly 'peasant') background and connections, as well as his Arab blood, neither of which claims was wholly authenticated. At the time Egypt was to all intents and purposes still a British protectorate, although some democratic institutions and the existence of an Egyptian throne lent a semblance of autonomy. As a youngster, Nasser was fiercely nationalistic, attending his first anti-British demonstration at the age of eleven. In 1937, the year after an Anglo-Egyptian treaty had paved the way for Egypt to acquire an army of its own, he enrolled at a military academy. Inside the army, Nasser co-ordinated a secretive group of cadet officers, later known as the Free Officers, committed to the cause of Egyptian independence, and whose members included Nasser's eventual successor, Anwar Sadat, as well as Mohammed Neguib.

In 1948 Nasser fought in the Palestine War against the Israelis, and it was during that time that he began plotting the overthrow of

King Farouk. The conspiracy came to fruition in the summer of 1952 when, following an anti-British upheaval at the beginning of the year, the Free Officers staged a coup that led to the proclamation of a republic in June 1953. Nasser, however, preferred for the time being to remain in the background, and it was Neguib who initially became both president and prime minister. But when Neguib began urging his colleagues on the Revolutionary Command Council to restore civilian rule, Nasser moved against him. Neguib was removed from a power he had never really exercised in November 1954, and Nasser became Egypt's titular ruler

Behind Neguib's ouster was a murky episode that involved a failed assassination attempt against Nasser as he was making a speech by a member of the Muslim Brotherhood, an extremist or at any rate puritanical indigenous body dating back to the early 1920s. One of the declared pretexts for getting rid of Neguib was that he was sympathetic to the Brotherhood, which Nasser had long despised, most probably because it presented a credible threat to his own political aspirations. Rumours spread that the assassination attempt had been engineered by Nasser himself. Notwithstanding, his elevation to overt top-dog status was swiftly followed by a purge of Brotherhood members, some of whom were executed, while others were incarcerated. Among the latter was **Sayyid Qutb**, the most gifted ideologue of Islamic fundamentalism during this period, eventually awarded the death penalty by Nasser in 1966.

Nasser's determination to exclude the Brotherhood from Egypt's political and social life had severe and violent long-term consequences: the country became less, not more, united. In the short term, the Brotherhood, as well as other oppositional forces, made Nasser's hold on power precarious. But thanks to the Suez crisis of 1956, sparked by Nasser's nationalization of the Anglo-French Suez Canal Company, he was able to consolidate his standing not only in Egypt, but throughout the Arab world.

The British and the French, joined by Israel, went immediately on the offensive, but their invasion of Egypt came to a sudden halt when the two superpowers – the USA and USSR – decided to oppose the occupation of Suez by Anglo-French forces, albeit for very different strategic reasons. The humiliation of the former colonial power especially enabled Nasser to present himself, however fortuitously, as a champion of anti-imperialism, and for ten years his reputation was unrivalled in the Middle East. In 1967, however, he came resoundingly unstuck during the Six Day War. Forming an alliance with Syria and Jordan, and supported by some Palestinian guerrillas as well as Saudi Arabia, Yemen and Libya, he prepared an all-out attack on Israel, intending to obliterate the Jewish state; but in a devastating pre-emptive strike masterminded by Defence Secretary Moshe Dayan and his chief-of-staff Yitzhak Rabin, and made possible by state-of-the-art American weaponry, Israel crushed its enemies, seizing the Sinai Desert and Gaza Strip, the West Bank and Jerusalem, and the Golan Heights in the process.

For Islam, this was the darkest week in the entire twentieth century, and fuelled a critical shift towards fundamentalism, the consequences of which have continued into the twenty-first century. Outside Egypt Nasser was widely discredited, although inside, strongly supported by the ever-faithful *fellahin*, he managed to retain power until his death three years later.

Along the way Nasser had done real damage to the Egyptian economy by stifling private enterprise and instituting wide-ranging 'socialist reforms' that finally satisfied nobody. Instead, under his dictatorial aegis, Egypt became an impoverished police state. Even the Aswan Dam, reckoned among his principal achievements despite the fact that it had been conceived before his accession to power, failed to deliver any benefits to the Egyptian people until long after his departure. Although, briefly, he presided over a United Arab Republic that bound Egypt, Syria and the Yemen together between 1958 and 1961, his dreams of a revived single Arab nation were antithetical to Saudi and Gulf States interests. Nor did two other visions, set out in his idiosyncratic book *Philosophy of the Revolution* as early as 1954, fare any better. He failed to make Egypt the arbiter of African affairs north of old Rhodesia (modern Zimbabwe), and even more he failed in his ultimate ambition, which was to unite the whole of Islam under his own temporal stewardship. Yet his scent lingers on. Just as Nasser was influenced by the two foremost examples of modern secularist Muslim rulers who preceded him – Egypt's own Mohammad Ali (d. 1849) and Turkey's Mustafa Kemal (**Atatürk**) – so he has been emulated by latterday Muslim secularists (among them Saddam Hussein). And it was this, Nasser's commitment to non-theocratic government, that makes even his sternest critics outside Islam cautious of altogether disavowing his memory.

Further reading

See: Robert St John, *The Boss* (1961); Raymond William Baker, *Egypt's Uncertain Revolution under Nasser* (1978); Michael Haag, *The Rough Guide History of Egypt* (2003); Said K. Aburish, *Nasser: The Last Arab* (2004); Sam Witte, *Gamal Abdel Nasser* (2004).

JUSTIN WINTLE

NEEDHAM, Joseph

1900–95

Anglo-Scottish biochemist, historian and sinologist

As **Arthur Waley** worked indefatigably to bring the riches of oriental literature to the attention of Western readers through his translations of Chinese and Japanese classics, so Joseph Needham, in his monumental and posthumously ongoing *Science and Civilisation in China*, mounted a sustained campaign to destroy a widely held assumption that 'science' is a Western preserve. In so doing, he adumbrated an 'ecumenical' theory of

world civilization which, while being broadly evolutionist, addressed such issues as the volume and reciprocity of technological transfer between civilizations – India and Islam as well as China and the West – as well as the apparent reasons for success and failure in scientific advancement at specific times in specific places. Never content merely to document the mechanical and theoretical achievements of non-European cultures, especially China's, he sought to demonstrate how social, economic and, particularly, religious and ideological variables can act as either local enhancers or local inhibitors in the fulfilment of what he conceived as a truly global undertaking: a final (though still far distant) rapprochement between humankind's spirituality and its thirst for manipulating the physical world in which it finds itself embedded.

Such a protean, inclusive vision of history only coalesced when Needham was well into his middle age and had already made a name for himself as a biochemist. Born in London, he was the only child of bickering Scottish parents. From Oundle School he progressed to Gonville and Caius College, Cambridge University, where he took a first degree in medicine, then, in 1925, a doctorate in biochemistry. Specializing in embryology and morphogenesis, he published scores of papers, leading to the publication of *Chemical Embryology* (3 vols, 1931) and *Biology and Morphogenesis* (1941). Excellence and productivity in his chosen field secured him a fellowship at Caius, and, much later, the college mastership, from 1966 to 1976. But although Needham continued to teach biochemistry until 1966, from early on in his career he sought to promote the history of science as a discrete discipline.

Like many intellectuals of his generation Needham was drawn towards **Marxism**, although at Cambridge he also contemplated a religious life, for several years attending the Oratory of the Good Shepherd, an Anglo-Catholic brotherhood. But the event that finally determined his future course was the arrival in Cambridge of three biochemistry students from Nationalist China in 1936, among them Lu Gwei-djen, who helped Needham learn to read and write Chinese, and whom he eventually married in 1989, following the death of his first wife, Dorothy Moyle. Fired by a passion for China, Needham secured for himself the directorship of the wartime Anglo-Chinese Science Co-operation Office, based in Chonqing, between 1942 and 1946. There he met the historian Wang Ling, later to become the most important of Needham's many research collaborators.

After the war Needham headed up the Natural Science division of the newly created UNESCO, before returning to Cambridge in 1948 to begin work on *Science and Civilisation in China*. Although from the outset this project was conceived on the grand scale – Needham soon mapped out seven volumes, the first being published in 1954 – it expanded beyond even his expectations, and was unfinished at his death, though work on it continues under the auspices of the Needham Research Institute, founded in 1989.

Until Needham began publishing his findings, it was acknowledged by some that a handful of key inventions, among them printing, gunpowder and the magnetic compass, may have originated in China. Not only did *Science and Civilisation* confirm such speculation, but added vastly to the number of historic Chinese inventions and discoveries, among them (in chronological sequence) the iron ploughshare (sixth century BCE), sunspots, cast iron, the double-action piston, the kite, the collar-harness, the rotary fan, the seed drill, steel, circulation of the blood, the parachute, endocrinology, the armillary ring, deep drilling for salt and gas, the belt-drive, the wheelbarrow, sliding callipers, decimal fractions, the square-pallet chain pump, the suspension bridge, the stern rudder, the seismograph, tear gas, the fishing reel, the metal stirrup, porcelain, the umbrella, chess, the paddle boat, solar wind, the segmental bridge, the mechanical clock, playing cards, immunology and, in the tenth century, phosphorescent paint.

To provide detailed, scholarly accounts of each of these and many other developments, *Science and Civilisation* is divided up by field. Thus Volume V, running to thirteen parts and itself published as three separate volumes, is subtitled 'Chemistry and Chemical Technology'. Each volume too, while always bearing the stamp of Needham's approach and authority, benefits from the collaboration of other researchers. But if the net effect is to provide overwhelming evidence that, during the Sui, Tang and Song dynasties certainly (589–1279), China was unquestionably the most advanced civilization anywhere, at least in material terms, the very success of Needham's advocacy posited a fundamental problem, often referred to as 'Needham's Grand Question': if the Chinese were so spectacularly good at 'science', then why did it befall Europe, for so long so backward, to achieve the breakthroughs needed for 'modern science'?

Needham recognized this dilemma from the outset, and the scope of his response, informing the entire project, is what makes *Science and Civilisation* a landmark investigation. Volumes I and II specifically set out to describe the myriad circumstances in which Chinese science both flourished and stagnated. If he recommends that the close-to-nature, anti-authoritarian, experimental, holistic character of Daoism was the most consistent driving force, he also allows Confucianism's promotion of scholarly learning a place, while examining such other traditional Chinese philosophies as Legalism and Mohism. Equally, he elaborates China's trading relations with other parts of Eurasia, as well as its own internal social and productive requirements. Brilliantly, he demonstrates how an advanced hydraulics emerged out of China's need to manage its water resources to keep both people and empire alive. What inhibited further advances was the period of Mongol rule (1289–1368), followed by the distinctly conservative Ming Dynasty (1368–1644).

Although Needham is at pains to point up the contiguities of science as practised in different parts of the Eurasian landmass over a stretch of time far exceeding the twelve centuries of Edward Gibbon's *Decline and Fall of the Roman Empire* (1766–88), he acknowledges the qualitative difference of European science as it began emerging in the sixteenth and seventeenth centuries. Essentially, in Needham's view, the new European science was mathematically axiomatic in a Euclidean way, and it was this, combined with an ultimately religious belief in immutable laws of nature the unity of which is supposedly guaranteed by God, that gave it its radical edge.

Needham's account of the success of European (later American) science in the modern period is generally considered less persuasive than his account of Chinese science. He undervalued both the questioning fomentation of the European Reformation and the role played by such centralizing scientific bodies as the Royal Society, and perhaps allowed too little room for the unpredictability of individual genius. Yet his larger thesis – that 'science' is a human universal – remains intact, borne out by an increasing incidence of discovery and invention outside the magic circle of Euro-American laboratories.

Notwithstanding his unrivalled achievements as a historian and promoter of Western respect for Chinese ingenuity, Needham has not been without his critics, quite apart from contentious issues surrounding his Grand Question. Chinese science owed more to an influx of such primary technologies as weaving, the wheel and probably bronze-making via the central Asian 'steppe corridor' from the Black Sea region in the late Neolithic Age than Needham seems prepared to concede, and the structure of *Science and Civilisation in China* reflects Western, not indigenous, scientific categories. Conversely, a rose-tinted attitude towards Marxism ('the only possible moral theology'), and towards **Joseph Stalin** as well as **Mao Zedong**, sometimes cast Needham in a too determinedly anti-Western light. Unwisely, in 1954 he supported unfounded Chinese claims that the USA had used biological weapons during the Korean War. As a consequence he was blacklisted by the US State Department, though this did not deter him from protesting America's actual use of chemical weapons during the Vietnam War in the following decade.

Further reading

To date thirteen volumes of *Science and Civilisation in China* (from 1954) have been published. Robert Temple, *The Genius of China: 3000 Years of Science, Discovery and Invention* (1986) furnishes a somewhat slapdash but authorized resumé of Needham's findings. Other books by Needham include: *Chinese Science* (with Dorothy Moyle, 1945); *The Grand Titration: Science and Society in East and West* (1969); *Science in Traditional China* (1982). Needham's biography has yet to be written, but, for an overview of his philosophy, see Maurice Cowling, 'Joseph Needham & the History of Chinese Science', in *The New Criterion* Vol. 11, No. 6 (February 1993).

JUSTIN WINTLE

NERUDA, Pablo (Neftalí REYES)
1904–73
Chilean poet

Parral, central Chile, where Neruda was born, and Temuco where he was brought up by his train-guard father (his mother died early on), is the source of much of his basic imagery – a wet, misty, forested area (rain, river, sea – all natural elements). He adopted the pseudonym Neruda (from a nineteenth-century Czech writer) for fear of ridicule from his 'humble' companions. Neruda always saw himself as a natural, born poet. He linked poetry with the vitalistic elements and natural energies, although the myth of facility and spontaneity has camouflaged the careful craftsman behind the exuberant images. From the start Neruda assumed the role of bard.

Neruda was a very successful poet. His second book, *Twenty Love Poems* (*Veinte poemas de amor y una canción desesperada*, 1924), became one of the best-known collections in Spanish. These poems deal with Neruda's move from his provincial roots to the capital

Santiago in terms of two contrasting love affairs in a dense and moody language based on symbols and images taken from nature. The poet's *persona* is that of a melancholic anarchist at odds with the world.

But popularity was a trap and Neruda sought a diplomatic post (rather than train as a schoolteacher) to enrich his experience. From 1927 to 1943 he lived outside Chile, in the Far East (Rangoon, Colombo, Java), Spain and Mexico. This was the central (and best?) phase collected in the three volumes of his *Residence on Earth* (*Residencia en la tierra*, 1925–47). The first two *Residencias* (1925–35) are magnificent crisis poems dealing with Neruda's confusion and loneliness as a foreigner 'abandoned' abroad in terms of the breakdown of his literary and Romantic *persona*.

The borrowed surrealistic devices are moulded into his vision in hermetic poems working out shifting and obsessive emotional knots almost as therapy. But it was the Spanish Civil War, and his friend **Lorca's** murder, that shocked Neruda out of his private spiritual anguish. His *Spain in My Heart* (*España en el corazón*, 1937) reflects this change of responsibility in a more conscious, controlled poetry, based on anger, indignation. His years in Spain confirmed his reputation as one of the foremost poets of his age.

Neruda was not converted to **Marxism** but found in it an answer to his own dark emotions: it was an ordering and granting of purpose to his life. Neruda's best political poems barely differ from his earlier ones with the same luxuriant, sensual language, a 'daylight' poetry of visual, tactile things. The year 1943 was crucial in the development of Neruda's Latin American consciousness: from a visit to Machu-picchu (the Inca fort) he began elaborating his dream of writing an epic combining his commitment to his *pueblo* (people) with a poetic re-vision of Latin American history. Paralleling this, in 1945 he was elected senator and began a long career in politics that ended with being a presidential nominee (1970, standing down for his friend Allende). Political persecution and exile (1947) pushed him to complete the *Canto general* (1950), a poetical, political history of his continent. He aimed to create a new sense of identity based on his belief in his role and identity with his land and people where the poet interprets the silent masses. In 1951, with **Picasso**, he won the **Lenin** Peace Prize.

This change towards an earthy simplicity – a constant in his poetry – led to his *Elemental Odes* (*Odas elementales*, 1954) celebrating tomatoes and fallen chestnuts and so forth. From here to his death Neruda was to combine all his phases, using long or short lines with a Protean freedom; the best books being: *Estravagario* (1958); *Memorial de Isla Negra* (1964); the posthumous *La rosa separada* (1973) and *El mar y las campanas* (1973).

Through this diversity Neruda remained a Romantic poet, the *registro sensible* (sensitive register); his best poems are always personal (great erotic and nature poems). Neruda exploited the sensuality of words, the body of the world. He was an amazingly popular public reader and he enjoyed this prestige. He moved through many relationships and places, but his best biography is his poetry (see Monegal). In his personal response to experience Neruda avoided introspection, self-analysis, philosophizing in favour of a poetry of love for the world, objects, women and physical sensations.

From 1970 to 1973 Neruda was Allende's ambassador in Paris. In 1971 he won the Nobel Prize for Literature. He died soon after his friend Allende fell. As a sensitive witness to his age, Neruda condensed in his work the history of Chile and of his continent; what unites his work and makes it Nerudian are the basic responses to nature and the self learned in Parral and childhood, the need to establish a poetic identity with his own working-class roots and his craftsmanship. Neruda was a poet who sought a responsible social function that fused his personal anguish (the misery of being isolated and unloved) with the need to forge a new myth (based on solidarity) as a way to deal with the individual's death. He was both innovative, modern and anachronistic, prolonging the Romantic/symbolist tradition.

Further reading

Other works include: *Obras completas* (1999), and his *Memoirs* (1978). Good biographies are Volodia Teitelboim, *Neruda: An Intimate Biography* (1991) and Adam Feinstein, *Pablo Neruda. A Passion for Life* (2004). A good anthology is Robert Pring-Mill, *Pablo Neruda. A Basic Anthology* (1975). Good criticism: René de Costa, *The Poetry of Pablo Neruda* (1979); John Felstiner, *Translating Neruda: The Way to Macchu Picchu* (1980); Manuel Durán and Margery Safir, *Earth Tones: The Poetry of Pablo Neruda* (1981); and Christopher Perriam, *The Late Poetry of Pablo Neruda* (1989).

JASON WILSON

NEWMAN, John Henry (Cardinal)

1801–90

English churchman and theologian

Born in London, the son of a banker, Newman spent his childhood and adolescence there, and he was schooled privately in Ealing, where he demonstrated remarkable intellectual gifts, with a strong predilection for the Greek classics and the Greek New Testament. In 1816 he underwent a singularly profound experience of Christian 'conversion' which dominated the future course of his life and career, although the exact content of this conversion has for long been a matter of speculation and disagreement within Newman scholarship, some contending that it was more or less a conventional 'Evangelical-Protestant' experience (based upon study of the Scriptures), others suggesting that it was more 'Catholic' and doctrinal in content and orientation.

In 1817 Newman went up to Trinity College, Oxford, where, because of an infirm disposition and mental strain brought on by overwork, he was awarded a poor degree towards the end of 1820. Despite this, he won a fellowship at Oriel by examination the following year. It was at this time that Newman, the raw Evangelical, came under the

theological influence of Richard Whately, later to be Archbishop of Dublin, and the High Churchman Edward Hawkins (1787–1863), later provost of Oriel. Although both men were later critical of the Tractarians, in the 1820s they did much to steer Newman towards a more 'Anglo-Catholic' direction, Edward Bouverie Pusey, after 1841 to be the acknowledged leader of the Oxford Movement. Newman also received an impetus towards a more metaphysical type of theology by reading Bishop Butler's *Analogy of Religion*.

Newman was ordained to the diaconate in 1824, at about the time when he finally decided that he was called to live a celibate life, and when he was considering missionary service abroad. But he accepted an invitation from Whately, the new principal of St Alban's Hall, to become its vice-principal, and he was ordained priest in May 1825. In the following year, Newman was appointed a tutor at Oriel, at about the same time when two new fellows were elected to Oriel: Robert Isaac Wilberforce and Richard Hurrell Froude, who soon became an intimate friend.

With John Keble, who had been a fellow and tutor of Oriel from 1817 to 1823, the brilliant group which included Newman, Froude, Wilberforce, Pusey, Isaac Williams, William Palmer, J.B. Mozley and H.J. Rose (1795–1838), may be considered responsible for the so-called 'Oxford Movement' which aimed at a Catholic revival, in doctrine and practice, within the Church of England. The group became increasingly critical of the contemporary state of the Church of England, and in the year 1832–3 Newman and Froude made a tour of Mediterranean countries, which made Froude wax lyrical about the glories of Catholic Christendom; in his view the Church of England had well-nigh lost such glories through sinful and lukewarm apathy. The Oxford Movement may be said to have begun with the conference on church reform at Hadleigh Rectory (where Rose was the incumbent) on 25 July 1833, eleven days after Keble preached his famous 'assize sermon' before the University of Oxford. The sermon *began* as a protest against the attempt of the civil legislature, in the teeth of ecclesiastical opposition, to suppress ten Irish bishoprics, but it quickly developed into something else – the declaration that the entire nation was in 'apostasy', allowing, because of its profound and insidious apathy (clothed in the disguise of 'tolerance') to the supernatural life of grace enshrined within the Christian Church, a secular, even profane, civil authority to interfere in the affairs of a body which Christ had committed to his apostles and their successors alone. Keble's sentiments were enthusiastically shared by his colleagues, including Newman, who had since 1828 been vicar of St Mary's, the university church in Oxford. The most obvious consequence of these events was the beginning of the publication of the 'Tracts for the Times' and the formation of an Association of Friends of the Church. The scene was now set for a bitter conflict, with Newman and his sympathizers on the one side and their civil and ecclesiastical opponents on the other.

Newman had already begun a life of scholarship inspired by the writings of the early Fathers of the Church, reflected in *The Arians of the Fourth Century* (1833) and in his multi-volumed *Parochial and Plain Sermons* (1834–42). And this patristic orientation and inspiration is plain in the very first tract of the series, which came from Newman's pen, 'Thoughts on the Ministerial Commission Respectfully Addressed to the Clergy'. In this, one of the twenty-four tracts for which he was responsible, Newman argued that the episcopate and the priesthood cannot derive from a civil state, but from a commission of Christ alone, who set apart his apostles in a peculiar sense and gave them authority to hand down their powers and gifts through an 'apostolic succession', which has been preserved, miraculously, in the Church of England. Such a society, the Body of Christ (no less), is independent of and invulnerable to the degradations of a godless civil society. Throughout his own tracts Newman loyally defended what came to be known as the *via*

media anglicana – the principle that the Church of England occupies the middle ground between the extremes of 'Romanism' on the one hand and 'Dissent' (Reformed Protestantism) on the other. But, on the whole, the authors of the tracts (Newman included) set before themselves the aim of pushing the Church of England in the direction of Catholicism as represented by Rome – hence the stress of the Tractarians on the doctrine of the Real Presence of Christ in the Eucharist, on priestly celibacy, the veneration of the saints, monastic asceticism, fasting, confession, baptismal regeneration, the apostolic succession, the minutiae of the liturgy, and the like.

It is not easy to characterize the spirit which motivated the Tractarians: certainly, the Oxford Movement was an ideologically conservative reaction against the liberalism, toleration and rationalism unleashed in Europe by the 1789 Revolution in France and a philosophical reaction against the utilitarianism of Bentham; equally it was a protest, in the name of metaphysical and supranaturalistic religion, against the alleged reductionistic naturalism and empiricism which were seen as the inevitable consequence of the *Aufklärung* in Germany; doubtlessly, it was an understandable protest against the lethargy and over-comfortable moderation of many in the post-Enlightenment Church. Importantly, it was an unmistakable aspect of the European Romantic Revival pitted over against the severe, classical, quasi-mathematical spirit of the Age of Reason, an aspect which found expression in the nineteenth-century preoccupation with the Middle Ages, in speculations concerning angels and the doctrine of transubstantiation, and in the Gothic revival in architecture.

About Newman, though, there was something which separated him from most of his fellow Tractarians, who shrank from pursuing their theological inquiries or indulging in liturgical or devotional practices to that point which would carry them out of the Church of England or detach them permanently from the basic principle of the *via media*. Newman had a pitiless logicality, an inability to do other than follow the truth (as he saw it) wheresoever it would lead him, even if this meant abandoning the church he had been born into. In 1837 he published his *Lectures on the Prophetical Office of the Church* and in 1838 his *Lectures on Justification*, both of them still subtle defences of the *via media*. But from around 1839, it is clear, he began to change his mind. Until then he believed that the Church of England approximated more or less to the true Church of Christ in its possession of holiness, catholicity and antiquity, and that it was still in essential unity with it. But the Protestantism and 'insularity' firmly embedded in the *via media* worried him intensely and created in him the unshakable suspicion that the Church of England might not at all share in those ancient and unmistakable marks of the true Church of God which were clearly displayed for all to behold in the Church of Rome. The outcome was the publication in 1840 of the notorious Tract No. 90, whose object was to demonstrate the compatibility of the Thirty-nine Articles of the Church of England with the post-Tridentine theology of the Roman Church, but whose consequence was the harsh accusation flung at Newman that in his subtle playing with familiar words he was clearly a deceitful trickster. The argument that in condemning the Romish doctrine of Purgatory the framers of the Thirty-nine Articles did not intend to reject *the* doctrine of Purgatory, or in rejecting 'the sacrifices of masses' sixteenth-century Anglican Protestants did not intend to repudiate '*the* sacrifice of the Mass', proved to be the last straw for an outraged ecclesiastical establishment, and the teaching of Tract No. 90 was condemned out of hand by the university authorities at Oxford in 1841.

What probably lay behind the writing of Tract No. 90 was Newman's reading in 1839 of an article in the *Dublin Review* by Monsignor (later Cardinal) Wiseman, Superior of the English College in Rome, in which Wiseman compared the position of the Anglican communion to that of the heretical Donatist sect in the fourth century. At that very moment Newman happened to be studying the history of the heretical Monophysite sect in the fifth century, and he was struck by the parallel between Anglicanism's relation to Rome in the modern world and that of Monophysitism's relationship to Rome fourteen hundred years earlier; his conclusion was that if the Monophysites were heretics and schismatics, then so were the Anglicans.

Such reflections inevitably set Newman on course for a submission to Rome. In 1842 he moved from Oxford to Littlemore; in 1843 he resigned the living of St Mary's. In 1845 he was received, as he later put it, 'into the Church of Christ' by Friar Dominic Barberi, a Passionist. By June 1847 Newman had been (conditionally) ordained priest by Cardinal Fransoni in St John Lateran in Rome.

By 1849 Newman had founded the oratory at Birmingham, which became, except for the four abortive years 1854–8 trying to found a Catholic university in Ireland, his home until his death. Conversion did not, however, bring Newman peace and serenity. He continued be assailed by doubts and worries, and was frequently attacked by both Anglicans and Catholics. In 1845, almost contemporaneous with his reception into Rome, Newman published *An Essay on the Development of Christian Doctrine*, partly in order to explain his own imminent assent to Roman dogma. This was a subtle work of great erudition and brilliance. In it Newman argued that everything taught by contemporary Catholicism can be traced right back to the Early Church and indeed to the Apostolic Church. It did not endear Newman to his Protestant contemporaries, but nor did it win over every Catholic heart. Some traditionalist Roman Catholics regarded the *Essay* as tainted by Protestant apologetic rationalism which its author had brought with him to Rome. There is abundant evidence that the freshly converted Newman did not quite understand the mentalities of his new co-religionists, and that this misunderstanding simply generated more suspicion of him in high ecclesiastical quarters. A case in point was Newman's attempt to found a Catholic university for the education of the laity in Dublin. Newman simply did not, because he could not, comprehend that the Roman Catholic hierarchy did not want a laity which was university educated.

In January 1864 the Anglican divine **Charles Kingsley**, reviewing J.A. Froude's *History of England* in *Macmillan's Magazine*, remarked:

> Truth, for its own sake, had never been a virtue with the Roman clergy. Father Newman informs us that it need not, and on the whole ought not to be; that cunning is the weapon which heaven has given to the Saints.

Newman responded with *Apologia Pro Vita Sua* (1864), one of the great autobiographies in the English language, which takes the form of a history of the Oxford Movement and of Newman's part in it, and lays bare the motives which led Newman and his colleagues to write and act as they did. It is an intensely moving work, rich in pathos, and filled with spiritual honesty and insight. Its closing passage is said to have moved even **George Eliot** to tears, and the *Apologia* as a whole led the sceptical **Lytton Strachey** to remark that 'Kingsley could no more understand Newman than a subaltern in a line regiment can understand a Brahmin of Benares'.

In the period leading up to the promulgation of papal infallibility in 1870, the fact that Newman was an 'Inopportunist' brought him into conflict both with the ultramontane Cardinal Manning and Pius IX's powerful personal secretary, Monsignor Talbot. They were both hostile to Newman's expressed fears about the pope's temporal claims, his desire to see the laity of the Catholic Church consulted in matters of doctrine, and his ambition for Catholics to seek entrance to the universities, especially Oxford.

The year 1870 also saw the publication of Newman's most profoundly intellectual work, his *Essay in Aid of a Grammar of Assent*,

which is devoted roughly to the areas of metaphysics and epistemology, with special reference to man's knowledge of God. Its argument is remarkable in its differences from the metaphysical proofs found in the schoolmen of the Middle Ages, and the classical theistic demonstrations we find in the English rationalists of the seventeenth and eighteenth centuries. Newman gives a prominent place to conscience and the facts of moral experience in the starting-point of his argument, and he reserves a unique place for the will as a motive for knowing the divine existence. Finally, the argument is made to turn upon man's possession and use of his 'illative sense' which, in the words of one of his distinguished interpreters, 'signifies the capacity of our intellect to undertake an informal inference in order to discern a unified pattern of evidence in a group of independent but converging arguments' (James Collins, *God in Modern Philosophy*, 1960).

Newman's last years were marked by a partial rehabilitation in Roman and Anglican circles. In 1877 he was elected to an honorary fellowship by his old Oxford college, Trinity. In 1879, due partly to the happy intervention in Rome of prominent and influential members of the English Catholic aristocracy, he was created a Cardinal Deacon by **Leo XIII**. He died in his ninetieth year, one of the most famous and influential Englishmen of the nineteenth century.

Newman's influence was, and continues be, felt across denominational boundaries. Catholic Anglicans remain grateful to him for beginning a movement which did so much to enrich and revive the life, teaching, worship and witness of the modern Church of England. In certain Roman Catholic circles, he is hailed as the great nineteenth-century prophet, anticipator and luminary of the twentieth-century Second Vatican Council. On account of his scholarship, his contributions to spirituality (he was the author of *The Dream of Gerontius*, 1865), his long life of Christian witness and faithful endurance under affliction, there has existed for some time a considerable movement whose aim is his canonization. Equally there have been liberal theologians, especially those who are well informed of German developments, who conclude that there was something impoverishingly defective and philosophically narrow in his life-long 'anti-liberal' convictions and antipathies; that if modern religious thought has consisted largely in rich and varied epistemological and logical responses to forces, difficulties and challenges released by the Enlightenment, the overall thrust of Newman and his sympathizers was to push Christian theology into excessively 'churchy', supranaturalistic, antiquarian and dogmatically authoritarian channels.

Further reading

Other works include *The Idea of a University* (1852); *Certain Difficulties Felt by Anglicans in Catholic Teaching* (1876). See: Sir Samuel Hall, *A Short History of the Oxford Movement* (1906); Wilfrid Ward, *The Life of John Henry Cardinal Newman* (1927); G.C. Faber, *Oxford Apostles* (1933); Louis Bouyer, *Newman: His Life and Spirituality* (1958); James C. Livingston, *Modern Christian Thought* (1971); Roderick Strange, *Newman and the Gospel of Christ* (1981); Ian Ker, *John Henry Newman: A Biography* (1989); Michael Ffinch, *Cardinal Newman* (1991); Frank Turner, *John Henry Newman: The Challenge to Evangelical Religion* (2002).

JAMES RICHMOND

NICHOLSON, Ben

1894–1982

English artist

Born into a family of extravert artists, Ben Nicholson studied for a brief period at the Slade School of Art, but then moved rapidly away from the mainstream of Edwardian painting. During the 1920s, during which he worked closely with his first wife Winifred Dacre, his still-lifes became increasingly more schematic, employing the pared-down profile of a bottle, a glass or a guitar, and sometimes scraps of newspaper or lettering. He travelled frequently on the Continent, where he was inspired by the work of **Cézanne**, **Picasso** and **Braque**, and in the following decade by **Mondrian**.

In the mid-1930s Nicholson's work became abstract to a more radical and controversial degree. He experimented with rarefied colour and, significantly, with carved surfaces; in 1934 his first white reliefs were exhibited in London. In the same year he married the sculptor **Barbara Hepworth**. Well aware of the close relationship of his own painting to other forms of art, he became in the mid-1930s an active member of 'Unit One', a group of British painters, architects and sculptors which spread the concept of a 'modern movement' in Britain. With **Naum Gabo** and the architect Leslie Martin, moreover, he edited *Circle – International Survey of Constructive Art* (1937); among the contributors were Mondrian and **Le Corbusier**, and *Circle* firmly identified the work of Ben and Winifred Nicholson, **Henry Moore** and Hepworth with the School of Paris and with an 'international modern' style.

Nicholson's art was not restricted to austere geometrical forms; he remained fascinated by the outlines of household utensils, the coastal curves and rooftops of Cornwall (where he lived during the 1940s and most of the 1950s), and the contours of the lakes and hills of Switzerland. In his view abstraction represented not a withdrawal of the artist from 'reality', but a means of bringing art back into everyday life, and a liberation of form and colour. The constant features of his work are delicacy, precision and a readiness to explore new textures and configurations. Towards the end of the 1950s he began to increase the scale of his productions, a development which led in the 1960s to his 'relief projects' for free-standing walls. Nicholson enjoyed international recognition from the 1950s; a major retrospective exhibition of his work toured the United States in 1978–9.

Further reading

The artist's statements and reminiscences are collected in *Ben Nicholson*, a *Studio International* special issue, ed. Maurice de Saumarez (1969). Exhibition catalogues: Tate Gallery (1969); and *Ben Nicholson: Fifty Years of His Art* (Albright-Knox Art Gallery, Buffalo, NY, 1978). See also Herbert Read, *Ben Nicholson, Paintings, Reliefs, Drawings* (Vol. I, 1948; Vol. II, 1956), and *Ben Nicholson, Drawings, Paintings and Reliefs 1911–68* (1969); J. Lewison, *Ben Nicholson* (1991).

PATRICK CONNER

NIEBUHR, Reinhold

1892–1971

US theologian and social moralist

Niebuhr was ordained to the ministry of the American Evangelical Church in 1914 and from 1915 to 1928 he was minister of the Bethel Evangelical Church in industrial Detroit, an experience which was strongly to colour his thinking and activities for the remainder of his life and career. On the one hand, he viewed at close quarters the impersonalism, self-interest, callousness and cupidity of American business and industrial life; on the other, he experienced with dismay the hopeless inadequacy to deal with this of the mild and moralistic idealism of contemporary American theology, especially that determined by the utopian and progressivist Social Gospel, which had been heavily influenced by turn-of-the-century European liberal Protestantism.

Called to be Professor of Applied Christianity in Union Theological Seminary in New York City in 1928, he became one of the most important figures within American Protestantism in the following forty years. It was widely alleged that Niebuhr was heavily influenced early in his career by the new neo-orthodox theology associated with **Barth** and Emil Brunner, and there is truth in this allegation. Certainly, much of his effort was directed from the beginning towards resuscitating the Christian doctrine of sin, and of original sin, and it is perhaps unfair that Niebuhr's work has been interpreted almost exclusively as devoted to this topic, for there is much in it besides. He taught that the essence of sin is pride, the

pride of man in his human accomplishments which is for ever in danger of being absolutized. This sin is to be characterized as *original*, for there is nothing in the human dimension which is untouched by it – industrial advance, creative culture, the impressive products of religion. In his earlier days Niebuhr was impressed and influenced by **Marxism**, and his sharpest words seemed to be reserved for American big business and the products of 'the American Dream', built as these were on what he regarded as an excessive American adulation for and pursuit of individualistic, capitalistic freedom, unrestrained and unhampered by state control and interference. But as his thought developed, he became increasingly critical also of the pretensions of (left-wing) revolutionaries, who were tempted by their pride to absolutize *their* achievements in a godless direction. Also, his profound researches on the Christian doctrines of sin and grace impelled him to judge that the Marxist analysis of the human predicament, as grounded in economic and social factors alone, was superficial and unacceptable. In other words, his increasingly theo-centric theology reflected his disillusionment with merely human panaceas.

Influenced as he was by the Barthian protest in Europe, and although firm parallels can be drawn between Barth's work and his own, certain clear divergences developed as Niebuhr's thought developed. He became extremely critical of the marked 'churchy' tone of Barthian neo-orthodoxy, and came to deplore the tendency of such theology to be inward-looking, designed to alter and determine the thought of those within the Christian community, to the detriment of going out into the world with the intention of engaging and challenging and changing the thought of those in factory, board-room and market-place. And indeed, Niebuhr himself was no mere academic theoretician, but during his career actively involved himself in political, social and international affairs, both off and on academic campuses. Again, it is vital to recall that his heavy stress on sin was but the other side of the coin of *human freedom*, for which he had a high respect. Indeed, sin is a *misuse* of freedom; man sins *in* freedom. This view made him very critical of Barth's tendency so to exalt the sovereignty and freedom of God that man's dignified and responsible freedom is undercut. Third, Niebuhr was (unlike the Barthians) anything but a Christian exclusivist; he spoke of a 'hidden Christ' operating in the human dimension as a whole, and never denied the possibility of grace to those who live and strive outside the Christian circle. Accordingly, he spoke of those 'indeterminate possibilities' which belong to humankind as such, striving for human betterment and a more just society. It is unfortunate that this aspect of Niebuhr's optimism is not better known than it is, in order at least to offset the unjust stereotype of him as a thinker whose principal topic was human sinfulness and limitation.

Possibly the phrase which most readily springs to mind at the mention of Niebuhr's name is 'Christian realism', a theme which further distinguishes him from neo-orthodox Barthians. For Niebuhr taught that Christians must not shrink from going out into the world in order to engage in social and political predicaments of great complexity and even danger. But if they do, they must avoid political and ethical naivety like the plague. They must not fail to recognize that social reality is an area of power, and that therefore there may be occasions when power must be balanced with power. For these reasons, Niebuhr himself did not hesitate to attack the pacifists of the 1930s. He deplored their naive and quietistic refusal to dirty their hands with 'militarism', because they did not see that a power-movement like German National Socialism could, in the circumstances, only be countered and destroyed by superior power. Likewise, in the context of American political life, he did not on occasion shrink from advocating the use of power within the state in order that the weak and defenceless be defended and justice upheld. Although he personally abhorred violence, his Christian realism led to a refusal to absolutize pacifist forms of non-resistance.

Although Niebuhr objected to being called a 'theologian', and although he has been stereotyped as a social moralist and political activist, it would be gravely mistaken to interpret his thought outside of that Christian faith which insists that the moral ambiguities of history cannot be finally eliminated in space and time, and that the consummation of world affairs is only to be looked for in the final judgement and reconciliation of God.

Further reading

Other works include: *Does Civilization Need Religion?* (1928); *Moral Man and Immoral Society* (1932); *The Nature and Destiny of Man* (2 vols, 1941–43); *Christian Realism and Political Problems* (1954). See: C.W. Kegley and R.W. Bretall, *Reinhold Niebuhr, Social and Political Thought* (1956); G. Harland, *The Thought of Reinhold Niebuhr* (1960); John C. Bennett, 'Reinhold Niebuhr', in A.W. and E. Hastings (eds) *Theologians of Our Time* (1966); Richard Wightman Fox, *Reinhold Niebuhr: A Biography* (1996).

JAMES RICHMOND

NIEMEYER, Oscar

1907–

Brazilian architect

In 1930 Niemeyer began his architectural studies at the National School of Fine Art in Rio de Janeiro, and in 1934 joined the office of the influential Lucio Costa who at that time was responsible for much of the restoration of Brazil's historic buildings. Costa, who tried to dissuade Niemeyer because of the limited amount of work he could offer such a promising young man, became one of the two major influences in his life. The other was the important European **Le Corbusier**, who paid a brief visit to Brazil in 1929 and returned for a spell of three months in 1936 to work on his plans for the campus of the University of Rio de Janeiro and a new building for the Ministry of Education. Niemeyer worked directly under Le Corbusier and as a result of this fruitful and exciting experience produced his designs for the Athletic Centre in Rio and the Aeronautical Training Centre at São José dos Campos. Like Le Corbusier he saw architecture as a fine art and continued to associate with painters and sculptors, believing that a successful environment can only be achieved if all those concerned with the total design are closely involved with the project right from the start, and like Le Corbusier in this respect he was something of an elitist.

In 1939 he built the Brazilian Pavilion for the New York World Fair in conjunction with Lucio Costa, with whom he was later to be associated on a far grander scale in his most dramatic contribution to modern design at Brasilia.

The dominant style in Brazilian architectural history is the extremely flamboyant and richly decorative Portuguese Baroque which came to a full colonial flowering in a country which offered an equally rich and exotic natural environment for its undoubted excesses. A somewhat mundane functionalism followed, but after the Second World War Brazil became one of the leading countries in the development of the ideas of the Congrès Internationaux d'Architecture Moderne (CIAM) culminating in 1957 with the concept of Brasilia.

Brasilia was conceived as a bureaucratically controlled city of superblocks and functional zoning. Luca Costa drew up the Utopian plans and Niemeyer was appointed Architectural Adviser to Nova Cap, the organization instituted to create the brave new capital. Later he was made Chief Architect.

Though we may have second thoughts as to the wisdom of the scheme, bearing in mind the bleak living conditions of the majority of Brazilians at the time and bearing in mind that Brazilian political systems are far from stable, it can be argued in Niemeyer's defence that he did see the project as an architectural challenge, and did approach each individual building with care and attention to functional rightness.

He designed the Hotel in 1958 and later the same year the President's Palace. He built the Law Courts and the Cathedral and the whole scheme was based on a policy of rapid urbanization. Despite the urgency, Niemeyer's forms have a grace and refinement and his solutions to the varying problems set by the diverse requirements are novel and wholly satisfying. The result is a kind of super-modern Baroque reduced to a crisp geometric formal arrangement which well answers the needs required of it.

Niemeyer's first really personal contribution to modern architecture was the Church of St Francis which he built at Pampulha outside Belo Horizonte in 1942 and, though not without its critics, it has a rightness and simplicity of form well suited to its modest scale.

The house he built for himself outside Rio de Janeiro in 1953 reflects his understanding of Le Corbusier's civilized thoughts on how to live well, and it seems that it is at this scale that Niemeyer is at his best, and not in the vast impersonal scale of Brasilia. Like Le Corbusier he has often been tempted to overreach himself. Yet, during a career lasting seventy years, Niemeyer has consistently surprised with his inventiveness, too often confined to sketches of unrealized projects.

Further reading

See: Oscar Niemeyer, *The Curves of Time: Memoirs* (2000); and *The Work of Oscar Niemeyer*, Foreword by Lucio Costa (1950); Charles Jencks, *Modern Movements in Architecture* (1973); David Kendrick Underwood, *Oscar Niemeyer and the Architecture of Brazil* (1994).

NIETZSCHE, Friedrich

1844–1900

German philosopher

Nietzsche was born in 1844 in Saxony, then a part of Prussia. His life-long intellectual war with Christianity was tied to his having come from a male line of Lutheran pastors and his father having died when Nietzsche was only four, a traumatic event for the young boy, who thereafter grew up in a household of women. At the extraordinarily young age of twenty-four Nietzsche was appointed to the

Chair of Classical Philology in Basel, a position he held for ten years until failing health forced his resignation. From the age of twenty-seven his life was to be a persistent struggle with torturing migraine, stomach complaints and various other illnesses. Commentators have related his poor health to syphilis, which he may have caught as a university student. The one strong influence on Nietzsche's thought had both an intellectual and a personal side. For most of the Basel years he was a close friend of **Richard Wagner**, to the point that he virtually became a member of the family. Through Wagner he was also influenced at this time by **Schopenhauer's** work.

From 1879 when he left Basel, Nietzsche spent ten years travelling alone, from single room to single room, from Genoa to Sils Mania to Turin, living out of one suitcase, reading little, rarely meeting friends and then briefly, his notebooks his only steady companions. No philosopher has ever lived in such intimate contact with his work – these years saw him write most of his important work, above all *The Gay Science* (*Die Fröhliche Wissenschaft,* 1882, trans. 1974), *Thus Spake Zarathustra* (*Also Sprach Zarathustra,* 1883–5, trans. 1954), *Beyond Good and Evil* (*Jenseits von Gut und Böse,* 1886, trans. 1968) and *The Genealogy of Morals* (*Zur Genealogie der Moral,* 1887, trans. 1968). In Turin in 1889, after running across a square to protect a horse that was being cruelly whipped, Nietzsche collapsed into madness. He lived until 1900 in an increasingly catatonic state, mainly in the care of his mother.

Nietzsche's importance is predominantly in two spheres, as a theorist of culture and as a psychologist. His theory of culture is put most profoundly in his first book, *Die Geburt der Tragödie* (1872, translated as *The Birth of Tragedy*, 1968). He argues that culture is in essence *mythos* – the classical Greek conception exemplified in its tragedies, in which the 'Dionysian' forces of power-mania, lust and sadism, which underpin human existence, are balanced by an ordering and rational 'Apollonian' principle, which in turn provides

individuals with beautiful illusions that give meaning to their lives. The great destroyer of culture was Socrates, who attacked the tragic perspective as barbaric, replacing it with a rationalist optimism that has dominated the West ever since. Nietzsche identifies Socrates with the view that through thinking we can become both better and happier people – in effect, that reason can reform being. For Nietzsche this is the great turning point in the history of the West, and the death of culture.

Nietzsche is the first psychologist in the sense that we who live after Freud now use that term. He was the first man to go intensively and across a broad frontier into the question of motives, of why people do what they do. There are thousands of Nietzsche's aphorisms that explore the complicated relations between impulses and desires, fantasies and rationalizations – and how they influence what we do. Typical of the content and style of his aphorisms is: '"I have done that," says my memory. "I cannot have done that," says my pride, and remains inexorable. Eventually, memory yields.'

The focus of Nietzsche's psychologizing is over morality. His starting point is the query as to whether morality itself does not present the greatest danger to human society. Perhaps what has hitherto been praised as 'good' is 'a seduction, a poison, a narcotic, through which the present was possibly living at the expense of the future'. According to Nietzsche's history of morality there was originally an aristocratic age in which the terms 'good' and 'bad' were employed to describe noble, high-spirited, self-affirming action, and alternatively that which was plebeian, uninspired and utilitarian. Only late in human history did the relationship of the noble to the common become moralized. Simultaneously the egoist–altruist dichotomy took possession of human consciousness. The early product of, and in turn catalyst for, this transition was the priest; with him emerged the reactive type, he who, in the absence of spontaneous passions to direct his actions, applies his intellect to create a network of moral, religious and metaphysical rules to guide his conduct. The reactive emotions – pity, compassion and humility – are endowed with supreme virtue; altruism is established as the moral yardstick for social interaction. Finally, a second type of reactive emotion – vengeance, envy and resentment – takes root at a deeper level, and erodes the remaining capacities for impulsive, expressive action: 'the slave revolt in morals begins by "resentment" turning creative and giving birth to values.'

Nietzsche maintains that it was in a desperate attempt to avoid pain, to evade the cruelty and hostility of his neighbour, that man was driven to sharpen his wits, to extend his memory – to think. But this same struggle to reduce tension also gave birth to morality; thereby it provided community with its most powerful nexus, its most resilient self-preserving bond. Nietzsche is led finally to differentiate the universe of human action into two broad classes: the one aristocratic, powerful, hedonistically vital, later egoistic, creative, irreligious, and asocial; the other structured and rationalized according to a strict moral code, Christian, utilitarian, reactive emotionally, and community-centred.

However, the history of morality is not simply a malign one. European culture, and with it the highest achievements of civilization, have been nurtured in the same soil, that of the slave's attempt to master his hostile environment: the priest with his evil introduced the seeds out of which the individual grew 'interesting', 'complex' and 'deep'. The quality of a philosopher's thought, for instance, is directly related to the levels of instinctual repression under whose burden he struggles. Ultimately Nietzsche does not criticize the slave morality itself, but a society in which the priest has gained too much power, where the creative forces of the master are in danger of becoming completely repressed. It is this advance of the naive conception that morality and social constraint, and the instinctual renunciation that they enforce, are fully ameliorable that prepares the way for Freud's insights into the psychological nature and necessities of civilization.

Nietzsche's life-long wrestling with the problem of morality drove him ultimately to choose the beautiful rather than the good. Thus it is that his central socio-historical concern is with *Kultur;* thus it is that he scorns ethical commitment to individual happiness and social melioration; and thus it is that he singles out the politically optimistic philosophies of liberalism and socialism as mutilating human reality through their ideals. Nietzsche's qualms about humanist ethics stem from his fatalist conviction that the human individual does not have the power, by means of conscious choice or application, to improve the quality of his or her life. 'Quality' is an aesthetic concept, and the 'beautiful', whether in the form of a human creation or of an exemplary individual, is supra-historical – it can neither be predicted nor prepared for. Man is more than an animal only in finding expression for the beautiful. Additionally, it is significant merely that he may recognize and praise that beauty which moves him. The ugliness of the ideological and the political lies in their legitimating the pursuit of the trivial: they have no rapport with the essence of beauty, nor with its elusive origins.

In terms of the status of philosophy and knowledge Nietzsche was a sceptic. He argues that philosophers have placed an unwarranted trust in concepts, they have absurdly overestimated consciousness. He poses the question again and again of whether the whole of conscious life is not a reflected image, of whether thought and belief bear any relation to active life other than that of providing it with an *ex post* signature.

This querying of *homo sapiens*' cardinal assumption about himself intensifies **Hegel's** reflection that the owl of Minerva takes flight at dusk, that the time for philosophy is when the action is over. Nietzsche's sounding of knowledge is potentially far more radical, and self-annihilating, than **Marx's** contention that hitherto philosophy had failed to change the world. Nietzsche, in addition, questions the very assumptions of our thinking, calling the principle of causality at best a useful fiction.

Nietzsche identifies philosophy as being like tragedy, one of the high arts of living. At its best, philosophy is the means used by one type of exceptional individual to represent himself, to tell his tale with the uncompromising honesty which renders it hauntingly beautiful. The reflective process is in this case vindicated:

> Gradually it has become clear to me what every great philosophy so far has been: namely, the personal confession of its author and a kind of involuntary and unconscious memoir; also that the moral (or immoral) intentions in every philosophy constituted the real germ of life from which the whole plant had grown.

Nietzsche implies that the search for knowledge conducted on any other basis, for example that of positivist science, is not fundamentally serious.

Nietzsche called himself the philosopher with a hammer. His psychology and his scepticism fuse in his model for philosophy, or thinking. All modern individuals are infected with slave morality, and as a result bad conscience and half-heartedness. Zarathustra mimics the modern decadent: 'One has one's little pleasure for the day and one's little pleasure for the night: but one has a regard for health. "We have invented happiness," say the last men, and they blink.' The slave morality's leading symptom is idealism, the fact that humans need to tell themselves what they *ought* to do, and whom they *ought* to be. Nietzsche sets up his philosophy as a method of self-criticism, of individuals putting their own ideals into question. 'Self-overcoming' is the first task of thinking. Nietzsche describes himself as taking a tuning fork to the ideals of the time, including his own, and tapping them to hear how hollow they sound.

Nietzsche is famous for his proclaiming the 'death of God'. He meant to command and to warn, for once God is truly removed there are no moral markers left to tell humans what to do. Only those with an undertow of driving, Dionysiac instincts will survive, if there are such people left. With characteristic ambivalence Nietzsche places nihilism as the cardinal modern disease, and at the same time advocates a mode of thinking guaranteed to make humans less confident in their moral attachments.

The Anglo-Saxon world in particular has often condemned Nietzsche as one of the founders of Nazi ideology. In fact, Nietzsche loathed anti-Semites and the Nazi movement itself would have appalled him. Nevertheless there are parts of his political philosophy, and his ideal of the 'superman', that have affinities with the later ideas of Nazism. But essentially Nietzsche was an unpolitical man: as Thomas Mann suggested, his political views are the fantasies of an inexperienced child, anticipating rather than creating fascist ideology.

It is more important to recognize, in conclusion, that much of Nietzsche's own life, like his politics, was disturbed. To take him at his own instruction, to judge the work in terms of the man, should make us wary of his philosophy, and perhaps turn to his great French precursor, La Rochefoucauld, a sane and engagingly urbane character who produced a similar psychology, and also in the form of maxims. However, that would be to deny the brilliance of Nietzsche's insights, the uncanny accuracy and pungency of much of his prophecy, and especially his theory of culture; all of which makes him one of the handful of great thinkers of the nineteenth century. Freud several times said of Nietzsche that he had a more penetrating knowledge of himself than any other man who ever lived or was ever likely to live.

Further reading

Other works include: *Unzeitgemässe Betrachtungen* (4 vols 1873–6, translated as *Thoughts Out of Season*, 2 vols 1909); *Menschliches Allzumenschliches* (1878, translated as *Human All-Too-Human*, 1911); *Götzendammerung* (1889, translated as *Twilight of the Idols*, 1968); *Der Antichrist* (1895, translated as *The Antichrist*, 1968); *Nietzsche Contra Wagner* (1895, trans. 1954); *Ecce Homo* (1908, trans. 1968). See: Arthur C. Danto, *Nietzsche as Philosopher* (1965); Karl Jaspers, *Nietzsche* (1965); Walter Kaufman, *Nietzsche: Philosopher, Psychologist, Antichrist* (1968);

Alex McIntyre, *The Sovereignty of Joy: Nietzsche's Vision of Grand Politics* (1997); Thomas Heilke, *Nietzsche's Tragic Regime* (1998); Rüdinger Safranski, *Nietzsche: A Philosophical Biography* (2002).

JOHN CARROLL

NIGHTINGALE, Florence

1820–1910

English founder of modern nursing

The second daughter of a wealthy and cultivated country squire, Florence Nightingale was educated at home by her father. She studied classical and modern languages, history and philosophy. Florence proved an excellent scholar but early on grew restless in the confines on the drawing-room. When she was not yet seventeen she wrote that God had called her to his service.

She was twenty-four when she decided that nursing was to be her vocation but the shocked disapproval of her family prevented her from entering a hospital. Instead she prepared herself by studying official publications on public health and hospitals. She also visited hospitals in England and on the continent whenever she could. In 1851 she trained for four months as a nurse at the Kaiserswerth Institution for Deaconesses in Germany.

In 1853 she took up her first post as superintendent of an institution for sick gentlewomen in distressed circumstances in London, successfully reorganizing the administration and accounts of the establishment.

In March the following year England and France declared war on Russia. By the autumn the British public had grown indignant at the appalling suffering of the casualties in the Crimea publicized by *The Times*. A call for Englishwomen to nurse the troops was made in the newspaper.

Florence Nightingale's letter volunteering her services crossed with an invitation from Sidney Herbert, the Secretary at War, asking her to introduce female nurses into hospitals in the British army. She was appointed officially as 'Superintendent of the Female Nursing Establishment of the English General Hospitals in Turkey'.

In November 1854 Miss Nightingale and her party of thirty-eight nurses arrived at the huge barracks hospital at Scutari on the shores of the Bosphorus. She found the converted Turkish barracks verminous and filthy, desperately short of medical supplies, food, clothing, bedding and furniture. At first the doctors, furious at the 'unwise indulgence' of allowing women to nurse soldiers, ignored Miss Nightingale and the supplies that she had brought with her.

A few days after her party arrived, hundreds of fresh casualties from the battle of Inkerman were brought into a hospital totally unprepared to receive them. There were no operating tables, bandages, pillows or blankets. The army method for supplying the hospital was confused and antiquated and it broke down completely under the strain of overcrowding. The only person with money and the authority to spend it was Florence Nightingale. She had about £30,000, through funds raised by *The Times* and public money, and became, in effect, purveyor to the hospital.

The first requisition she made was for 200 scrubbing brushes. Sanitation was non-existent. The privies were overflowing, the water-pipes blocked up and dysentery cases were dying at the rate of one in two.

Through her organizational ability and iron will she cut through the army's red tape. Extra diet kitchens were set up, wards were cleaned, repaired and equipped, sewers were flushed and walls lime-washed. By the spring of 1855 the mortality rate had dropped dramatically and Miss Nightingale had established an orderly, hygienic base hospital.

Army officials still obstructed her, but she had saved the lives of hundreds of the troops and they adored her. She alone on the British side emerged from the Crimean War with a high reputation.

The government offered a man-of-war to take her home in state after the war but she slipped back into England incognito. On her return she campaigned for army reform, determined that the costly chaos of the Crimea should never recur. On her insistence and with the support of **Queen Victoria**, a Royal Commission on the Health of the Army was set up, with Florence Nightingale approving the selection of the commissioners and advising them at every turn. Her long and detailed evidence was held to be conclusive. As a result, the diet and living conditions of the soldier were improved in peace and war and the design, administration and equipment of military hospitals were reformed. Careful statistical records of illness and disease were also kept.

The Indian Mutiny of 1857 drew her attention to army conditions in India and she painstakingly collated a record of the health of the troops in every Indian army station although she had never visited India. Successive viceroys consulted her on questions of public health and through her intervention a sanitary department was set up in the India Office.

Her influence spread to civilian hospitals where preventive medicine was no less necessary to reverse the high mortality rate. After her book *Notes on Hospitals* was published in 1859 she was constantly asked for her advice on hospital construction. In 1860 she opened the Nightingale Training School for Nurses at St Thomas's Hospital, with the proceeds of a fund raised in her honour. She was organizer and patron of the school, which was designed to produce nurses of a high calibre, capable of training others. She was also instrumental in establishing a school for midwives and for reforming conditions and nursing in the workhouses in the course of a long and extraordinarily industrious life.

Yet she lived as an invalid and a recluse after her return from the Crimea, without any official position, directing operations from her sofa where ministers of state, doctors and civil servants called daily.

She exploited her 'illness' in order to devote herself to work and she drove her collaborators beyond their endurance. Yet she was ruthless with herself too and she detested the sentimental image of 'the Lady with the Lamp' so cherished by the public. In 1907, when she was nearly ninety, she was the first woman to receive the Order of Merit. Her personal influence raised the status of nursing from a menial occupation to an honourable profession and improved the standard of public health in Britain and abroad.

Further reading

Florence Nightingale's other writings include: *Notes on Matters Affecting the Health, Efficiency and Hospital Administration of the British Army* (1858); *Notes on Nursing* (1860); *Observations on the Evidence contained in the Stational Reports submitted to the Royal Commission on the Sanitary State of India* (1863). The standard biography is Cecil Woodham-Smith, *Florence Nightingale* (1950). See also Lytton Strachey's debunking essay in *Eminent Victorians* (1918); E. Huxley, *Florence Nightingale* (1976); S. Dengler, *Florence Nightingale* (1988).

JUNE ROSE

NOBEL, Alfred Bernhard

1833–96

Swedish industrialist and philanthropist

Nobel was brought up in Stockholm and, from 1842, St Petersburg where his father, a failed architect, moved in 1837 after being declared bankrupt in Sweden. He was tutored privately and before joining his father's munitions business in 1853 travelled widely in Europe and the United States. A further bankruptcy in 1859 forced the family back to Sweden.

Success appeared to have come to Nobel's father at last when, in 1862, he seemed to have worked out a reasonably secure method for the large-scale production of nitroglycerine. This powerful explosive was discovered by the Italian chemist A. Sobrero in 1846 by nitrating glycerine but, despite the attempts of several chemists to develop its commercial potential, it had proved far too unstable to handle in any quantity. In 1864 the family factory, starkly called Nitroglycerin Inc., was opened at Heleneborg outside Stockholm. Hardly had production begun when a serious explosion destroyed much of the factory and killed Nobel's brother Emil. Clearly much more needed to be done.

It was Alfred Nobel three years later who made the crucial step permitting the full commercial development of the new explosive. He mixed the oily nitroglycerine with an inert earth known as kieselguhr able to absorb some three to four times its own weight. Exploded by the mercury fulminate detonator developed by Nobel in 1863 the new explosive, known as dynamite, became one of the great forces of change, allowing feats of construction to be executed which would not have been even considered earlier in the century.

Dynamite, patented by 1867 in Sweden, America and Britain, used throughout the world by the civil engineer rather than the military, was the basis for Nobel's vast fortune. A further advance was made in 1875 when he developed blasting gelatine. More powerful, less sensitive to shock and with greater resistance to moisture, the new explosive opened up additional markets, including the safe-cracker, under the more familiar name of gelignite.

Despite his fortune Nobel's life was far from idyllic. His offer of marriage to his secretary Bertha Kinsky was rejected and in later life he suffered from angina. He wrote of himself: 'When at the age of 54 one is left so alone in this world, and a paid servant is the only person who has so far showed one the most kindness, then come heavy thoughts, heavier than most people imagine.' There were also business disputes and legal battles in his later years which added to his general gloom.

In his will Nobel left most of his fortune of 33 million kroner to set up a fund, the income of which would be used to award annually five prizes. Specifically, prizes were to be awarded in the fields of physics, chemistry, and medicine and physiology for 'the most important discoveries or inventions made during the previous year', in literature for 'the most outstanding work ... of idealistic tendency' and the peace prize for 'the best work for fraternity among nations'.

The prizes were first awarded in 1901 and have since continued, despite several minor crises of confidence, to hold an unchallenged esteem in both the popular imagination and the world of learning. The conjunction of peace prize and explosives manufacturer added precisely the right degree of paradox to guarantee its uniqueness.

Further reading

Nobel wrote one book, *On Modern Blasting Agents* (1875). See also: E. Bergengren, *A. Nobel, the Man and His Work* (1962); and H. Schück and R. Sohlman, *The Life of A. Nobel* (1929). Details of the Nobel Foundation and its operations can be found in *Nobel, the Man and the Prizes* (1962), edited by the Foundation itself, and sociological aspects of the prizes are dealt with in H. Zuckermann, *Scientific Elite* (1977).

DEREK GJERTSEN

NOLAN, (Sir) Sidney Robert

1917–92

Australian artist

The oldest of the four children of a tram driver and parttime publican and bookmaker, Sidney Nolan was born in the Melbourne suburb of Carlton and led a typically sport-mad Australian working-class youth. Lean and muscular until his last days, he was a passionate swimmer, diver and cyclist and, although enrolled as a student at the National Gallery of Victoria Art School for evening classes, he devoted the bulk of his intellectual energies to reading. As a result he was a formidable autodidact and his wide and omnivorous reading influenced his choice of subject-matter and his sometimes almost literary narrative style. He also, throughout his life, wrote poetry, sometimes solely for its own sake, sometimes to complement particular visual works.

His oeuvre was essentially figurative, tinged with the *fauxnaif* quality of a **Douanier**

Rousseau but never less than sophisticated, realistic without ever being academic and, above all, a maker of powerful images which once seen were never forgotten.

An encounter with an artloving solicitor in Melbourne, John Reed, and his wife, Sunday, led to an easing of his poverty (a youthful marriage and a child and a need to work at a hamburger stand, etc.). His juvenilia included an abstract *Head of Rimbaud* exhibited in 1939 at the inaugural exhibition of the Victoria Contemporary Art Society and, in Sydney, the décor for Serge Lifar's ballet *Icarus*, which was the first of many distinguished stage designs for opera and ballet throughout his life. He also painted vivid scenes of beach life at St Kilda on the coast near Melbourne.

But it was with the Reeds that his work flowered, despite his service in the wartime Australian army in the Wimmera. During the period 1944–7 he not only depicted the wheatlands of the Wimmera with bright colours and interestingly skewed perspectives, but also managed a *ménage à trois* with the Reeds, deserted from the army but avoided prosecution, and produced the work for which he is still most celebrated.

A series of paintings devoted to the life, crimes and misadventures (ending in being hanged in Melbourne Gaol) of the nineteenth-century Victorian bush ranger, bank robber and outlaw Ned Kelly brought Nolan instant recognition. His classic image of Kelly in his rectangular iron armour and on horseback became an icon for the Australian spirit of independent, freethinking bloody-mindedness and even figured in the Sydney Olympic Games of 2000.

Nolan also created images for the greatest Australian literary hoax, the 'poems' of Ern Malley, (invented by two bored wartime soldiers), but the Kelly paintings, the boldest and most 'modern' Australian art seen to date, were seminal in his oeuvre and in the making of his reputation.

They were also significant for Nolan in that they were his first exploration of a specific theme and henceforth his major works were largely thematic in conception. He went on painting Kelly pictures until his death, when he was experimenting with spray painting, a technique he had first toyed with as a teenage worker in a hat factory. Other themes which produced notable imagery included the catastrophic journey of the explorers Burke and Wills in their pursuit of the South–North crossing of the Australian continent, Leda and the Swan (based in part upon **W.B. Yeats's** sonnet), the shipwreck of Mrs Fraser and her adventures with the escaped convict Bracefell, and the military fiasco at Gallipoli during the First World War when ANZAC soldiers fought heroically but suffered terrible losses.

Given this subject-matter it is impossible not to notice that Nolan's best work taps into the Australian worship of failure which, in his interpretations, is biased firmly towards the Japanese view of the nobility of failure.

Nolan's encounter with the Reeds was catalytic and gave him a base in Australia. But it was his meeting with Sir Kenneth Clark, who visited his studio in Sydney, to which he had moved with John Reed's sister Cynthia, which brought him eventually to England. It was the patronage of Clark, a kingmaker in British art circles, and his retrospective exhibition at the Whitechapel Gallery in 1957, which brought him more or less instant fame and prosperity in England and subsequent exhibitions in Europe and America.

Apart from his semimythical transformations of legendary Australian figures, he was also an obsessive painter, in all media, of landscape, animals and the flora and fauna of Australia which he celebrated in *Snake* which, with *Shark* and *Paradise Garden*, constituted a vast work, collectively entitled *Oceania*, consisting of several thousand small paintings in oil on paper mounted in hundreds of panels and of considerable architectonic grandeur.

In his later years he mingled with royalty, became a Royal Academician, was decorated with the Order of Merit and knighted and, after the death of Cynthia, married and lived quietly with Mary Perceval, the sister of his life-long friend and rival for the title of most distinguished Australian painter of the twentieth century, Arthur Boyd. His style was always his own and unique. He showed hardly any influences in his own work and influenced no other painters. He was, in all senses, a true original.

Further reading

See: Kenneth Clark, Colin McInnes and Bryan Robertson, *Sidney Nolan* (1961); Jane Clark, *Sidney Nolan: Landscapes and Legends* (1987); T.G. Rosenthal, *Sidney Nolan* (2002)

T.G. ROSENTHAL

NOLDE, Emil

1867–1956

German painter

Born into a German peasant family in an area then Danish and now Polish, Emil Hansen (he took the name of his village, Nolde, only in 1902) was trained as a wood carver in Flensburg; then, after periods in Munich and Berlin, he taught technical drawing for six years in St Gall. At the age of thirty-one he committed himself to painting, studying in Munich, in Paris at the Académie Julian, and in Copenhagen, where he met his wife. From 1900 he divided his time between the island of Alsen and Berlin. His work gradually evolved from the heightened Impressionism characteristic of Sezession art, and in 1906 he found himself lionized by **Kirchner** and the wild and rebellious young artists of Die Brücke in Dresden. In 1910 he quarrelled bitterly and publicly with the Sezession president, Max Liebermann. But meanwhile, in 1909, he had completed his first fully mature work, *The Last Supper*, and this was soon followed by a nine-part altarpiece, *The Life of Christ* (both are now at the Nolde Foundation at Sëebull). In 1913–14 he took part in a government expedition to the South Seas, which confirmed him in his primitivistic tendencies.

His character as a painter was now formed, and he developed little over the next twenty years, gradually withdrawing to the house he built near the North Sea. His splendidly immediate watercolours, of flowers and dramatic skies, date mostly from this period. In 1920 Nolde had joined the Nazi party, attracted by its nationalist and racial tenets, but in 1937 he was singled out for special condemnation in the Degenerate Art campaign. 'All the ideals of my life,' he wrote in 1942, 'are turned into disgust.' Isolated in his house at Sëebull, the old man believed he had actually been forbidden to paint, but embarked secretly on a series of tiny watercolours, self-exploratory and automatist in character, the *Ungemalte Bilder* or 'Unpainted Pictures', which many regard as his testament. After the war he was one of the few great survivors left in West Germany, and – perhaps undeservedly – enjoyed a martyr's homage.

Nolde's contribution to twentieth-century art lies above all in his uniquely powerful colour, and in his creation of perhaps the only fully convincing religious paintings of his times. 'Expressionism' was a label he always rejected, but in some respects his art epitomizes all that we mean by it; an art that appeals to the guts rather than the intellect, and where intensity is sought above all other values. Its primitivism was authentic, but it also comes out of a complex historical synthesis; in the 1900s he met **Munch** and Ensor, looked at Grünewald and medieval art, read **Nietzsche**, and linked all this to his experience in Paris of **Daumier**, **Van Gogh** and **Gauguin**.

The 1909 *Last Supper* owes much to Rembrandt's *Conspiracy* but goes further towards the primitive; the mask-like heads are his inheritance from Ensor, but here they no longer embody hypocrisy. In Nolde the mask regains the meaning it had in the Dionysiac theatre – the god that speaks through man at moments of extreme emotion – and *Excited People* (1913, Sëebull) seems almost an illustration to Nietzschean ideas. Nolde always opposed himself to the element of negation in the modernist aesthetic (and implicit in Cubism): 'Instead of disintegration I sought after cohesion, instead of the break-up of forms I wanted concentration, and in place of taste and technique I searched for deepened expression, broad planes, and healthy strong colours.' He also spoke of an art made up of 'magically illuminated areas of planes', and in *Christ Among the Children* (1910) we watch the sequence of a blue Christ turning away from the sombre apostles, to become identified with the yellow abandoned rhythms of the children. Often Nolde borders on vulgarity, but his magnificently frank sensuality – as in the *Candle Dancers* (1912) – gives him a full-bloodedness rare in our time. In describing him as 'a demon of the lower depths' his contemporary Paul **Klee** was contrasting him with his own more butterfly-like sensibility, yet at the same time affirming his value. 'Metaphysical or unworldly abstractionists often forget that Nolde exists. I do not.'

Further reading

See: the Nolde Foundation at Sëebull, who also publish his writings and other material; and Peter Selz, *Emil Nolde* (1963); Werner Haftmann, *Emil Nolde* (1959); M. Urban, *Emil Nolde: Catalogue Raisonné of the Oil Paintings* (2 vols, 1987–90); P. Vergo and S. Lunn, *Emil Norde* (exhibition catalogue, 1995).

TIMOTHY HYMAN

NOZICK, Robert

1938–2002

US social philosopher

Born in Brooklyn, educated at schools in New York City and in the universities of Columbia and Princeton, Robert Nozick held a Fulbright Scholarship in Oxford before his first appointment at Harvard in 1965. His *Anarchy, State and Utopia* (1974) won a National Book Award in 1975, and was widely hailed as heralding the emergence of a brilliant new philosophical superstar.

Although its flow is sometimes interrupted by indulgences in superfluous symbolism, the verbal parts are consistently fresh, luminous and vital. The book is perhaps best described

as a general offensive against the prevailing tendencies towards a state-imposed uniformity of condition; tendencies epitomized and, hopefully, rationalized in the main life's work of Nozick's respected older colleague **John Rawls**. In *A Theory of Justice* Rawls assumed: that all the wealth produced or to be produced in any society must be available for distribution, free of any legitimate prior claims, at the absolute discretion of the sovereign collective; and that all individual talents, and the fruits of their exercise, are to be regarded as collective assets. Curiously Rawls neither recognized these assumptions as totally socialist, nor considered them reasonably questionable.

Nozick, by contrast, argues for a conservative alternative: that everyone has a right to keep both whatever he has, unless it has been unjustly gained, and whatever he may in the future by the free exercise of his own talents and energies acquire. In a typically radical argument Nozick asks us to consider a situation in which half a population is born two-eyed and the other half eyeless. Suppose that eye transplant operations were possible. Would justice require that the state take all the second eyes by force for transplanting into the sockets of the eyeless? But now if we allow that everyone has a basic right to their bodily parts, how can we possibly maintain that everything produced by the exercise of any of those parts must be treated as a collective asset, as public property? With the same vigorously swinging libertarian radicalism Nozick also argues: that income taxes are morally equivalent to forced labour; that the position of a citizen subject to, and supposedly part of, an unlimited Rousseauian democracy can be no better than that of a slave; that the protagonists of a Rawlsian, or any other, programme of approved distribution will have to forbid all capitalist acts, even between consenting adults; and – just by the way – that in the USA today everyone ought to be a vegetarian.

As a Harvard professor, Nozick produced a string of further works, some more strictly philosophical than others, but all of them characterized by a provocative curiosity that drew on an increasingly wide range of source materials; but it is for *Anarchy, State and Utopia* that he is most widely remembered.

Further reading

Nozick's other works include: *Philosophical Explanations* (1981): *The Examined Life* (1989); *The Nature of Rationality* (1993); *Socratic Puzzles* (1997); and *Invariances* (2001).

ANTONY FLEW

NUSSBAUM, Martha Craven

1947–

US philosopher

Noted for her richly illuminating readings of Western and especially classical literature, Martha Nussbaum has been a distinctive and important voice in contemporary moral philosophy. Against the increasing academic tendency to retreat into the safety of narrowly specialized disciplines, she has opened up new possibilities for the mutual enrichment of the philosophical and the literary domains. She was trained in classical philology at Harvard, and her first major work was a critical edition and translation of Aristotle's *Motion of Animals* (1978). There followed *The Fragility of Goodness*, published to great critical acclaim in 1986, which remains her most influential work.

The book is an exploration of the relation between luck and ethics: it unravels a dominant preoccupation of ancient Greek ethical thought – that the good life for human beings is crucially dependent on factors outside our control. Through detailed analyses of the works of the great tragedians (including Aeschylus' *Agamemnon*, Sophocles' *Antigone* and Euripides' *Hecuba*), intertwined with philosophical examination of the ethical theories of Plato and Aristotle, Nussbaum offers a compelling account of the precariousness of the human condition: 'we need to be born with adequate capacities, to live a fostering natural and social circumstances, to stay clear

of abrupt catastrophe, and to develop confirming associations with other human beings'; yet all these needs and achievements are hostages to contingency or vulnerable to potential loss. A classic philosophical response is to advance an ideal of ethical self-sufficiency (found in some of Plato's writings, and much later deployed, in a different guise, in Kant's notion of a domain of moral value immune to the assaults of luck). But the 'aspiration to make the goodness of a good human life safe from luck through the controlling power of reason' cannot be achieved without a cost, as Nussbaum argues in her subtle account of the various ways in which Plato's and Aristotle's theories of the good life struggle with the problem of human vulnerability – the 'fragility' of her title.

The overall vision to emerge from the book is a sombre one: 'that an event that simply happens to me may, without my consent, alter my life; that it is equally problematic to entrust one's good to friends, lovers or country, and to try to have a good life without them' are 'not just the materials of tragedy but everyday facts of lived practical reason'. A secondary theme explored in *Fragility* concerns the internal as opposed to external risks to our attainment of the good – the frequent power of our own appetites, feelings and emotions to upset the settled deliverances of reason on how we should live. These issues are taken up in Nussbaum's subsequent collections of essays, *Love's Knowledge* (1990) and *The Therapy of Desire* (1994), the latter providing a critical examination of the ancient Stoic account of the danger of the emotions and their need for philosophical control. In *Love's Knowledge*, whose range extends beyond the classical world to **Proust**, **Henry James**, **Beckett** and others, Nussbaum provides a powerful defence of the role of the feelings not merely as human impulses that need to be accommodated in any plausible philosophical recipe for well-being, but as themselves constitutive of a certain kind of understanding. Here as in all her writings, Nussbaum shows how much our moral awareness can be developed not via abstract analysis alone, but through the particular examples and the specific forms of expression found in the great dramatists and novelists and poets.

In her latter career Nussbaum has applied herself to a variety of political and social issues, including problems of inequality, for example in *Sex and Social Justice* (1998). But her more lasting influence on moral philosophy is likely to be her conception of the subject as one which engages with our grasp of the human condition on all levels, emotional as well as intellectual, literary as well as narrowly philosophical. In writing with such insight and honesty about the nature of the good for humankind, she not only illuminates, but exemplifies, that commitment, fraught with risk, that is at the heart of the moral enterprise.

Further reading

Other works include: *The Therapy of Desire* (1994); (ed.) *The Poetics of Therapy* (1990); *Upheavals of Thought: The Intelligence of the Emotions* (2001). See also: D. Statman (ed.) *Moral Luck* (1993); G.W. Harris, *Dignity and Vulnerability* (1997).

JOHN COTTINGHAM

O

OATES, Joyce Carol

1938–

US author

Given the hundred or more titles of fiction, poetry, drama, anthology work, essays and discursive writing, and whose span runs from the stories of *By the North Gate* (1963) through to her working personal credo and *compte rendu, The Faith of a Writer: Life, Craft, Art* (2003), it can little surprise that Joyce Carol Oates immediately stirs cavils. Is this not a writer in over-drive, at risk of being thought a one-woman paper mill? Has she not long ago traded quality for quantity?

However best regarded, the author raised in rural upstate New York, which she pointedly names Eden County in several of her novels, and to a family marked by the Depression and with its own history of traumatic death, cannot be thought other than singular. Educated at Syracuse and Wisconsin Universities, with professorships to follow in Detroit and Windsor, Canada, for three decades she has led the amiable, if busy, life of writer-in-residence at Princeton University where she continues to edit the *Ontario Review: A North American Journal of the Arts* which she and her husband, Raymond Smith, co-founded in 1974. In art as in life she has been nothing if not one of American literature's genuine distance-runners.

A genuinely sustained craftsmanship, moreover, underwrites her stories of an America off-tilt, shadowed in violence and psychological blight, and whether to be met with in family, suburbia, the professions, gangs, guns or drugs. She has made an especial forte of exploring damage in the lives of adolescents and women. New Gothic has been one kind of shorthand for her writing, Oates's intricately observed America of township and country the equivalent of **Faulkner's** Yoknapatawpha or Flannery O'Connor's Georgia. But talk of Gothic serves only to an extent.

An extraordinary range of interests and command of detail mark out her work, be it the pathology of murder in *Expensive People* (1968), family collapse in *Wonderland* (1971), case law as against moral law in *Do With Me What You Will* (1973), the power-play of evangelism with its anticipation of the Jim Jones massacre in Jonestown, Guyana, in *Son of the Morning* (1978), dynastic revenge in *Angel of Light* (1981), or America as staging-ground of gender contests and claims with dips into vampirism, mysticism and the nineteenth century in her strategically feminist trilogy *Bellefleur* (1980), *A Broadsmoor Romance* (1982) and *Mysteries of Winterthurn* (1984). Women's friendship, intense, affirming and unmediated by male intrusion or gaze, lies at the centre of *Solstice* (1985). Boxing, an interest from childhood as borne out in her friendship with Mike Tyson and the reportage of *On Boxing* (1987), plays a role also in the **Jamesian** chronicle of generational time-and-change she creates in *You Must Remember This* (1987). Race as America's perennial haunting, its historical secret sharer, lies at the heart of the 1950s black–white love affair of *Because it is Bitter and Because it is My Heart* (1990).

Few of her writings have quite shown the finesse of *Black Water* (1992) as drawn from the Senator Edward Kennedy–Mary Jo Kopechne scandal, a woman's violent drowning reconstructed as both visionary nightmare and identity lost inside the totemism of media and politics. Later fiction reworks the Jeffrey Dahmer case, for all its macabre sexuality a deliberately de-theatricalizing story of cannibalism and lobotomy, in *Zombie* (1995); rape and its ambient middle-class family repercussion in her best-selling *We Were the Mulvaneys* (1996); and Marilyn Monroe as America's ultimate, near transcendent icon of the beauty-myth, and what it refracts about the culture-at-large, in her epic fiction of fact *Blonde* (2002).

Most of Oates's best strengths, her grasp of character psychology and setting, the control of rhythm and viewpoint, are to be found in her short stories. Few work to keener or more representative effect than 'Where Are You Going, Where Have You Been?' which Oates based on the so-called Pied Piper murders in Tucson, Arizona. The encounter of pretty, boy-struck Ellie, fifteen years of age, with the chill, beguiling Arnold Friend, their back-and-forth talk, and the denouement of her teenager's final sexual sacrifice to save her family from murder even as he dawdles over her with talk of 'My sweet little blue-eyed girl', depends upon a surest gathering pace. It bears the winning hallmarks of the craft she calls for in her writer's manual and autobiographical essay-collection *(Woman) Writer: Occasions and Opportunities* (1988).

Further reading

See: Greg Johnson, *Understanding Joyce Carol Oates* (1987), *Joyce Carol Oates: A Study of the Short Fiction* (1994) and *Invisible Writer: A Biography of Joyce Carol Oates* (1998); Linda W. Wagner (ed.) *Critical Essays on Joyce Carol Oates* (1979); Ellen G. Friedman, *Joyce Carol Oates* (1980); Eileen Teper Bender, *Artist in Residence* (1987); Nancy Ann Watanabe, *Love Eclipsed: Joyce Carol Oates's Faustian Moral Vision* (1988); Lee Milazzo (ed.) *Conversations with Joyce Carol Oates* (1989); Joanne V. Creighton, *Joyce Carol Oates: Novels of The Middle Years* (1992); Brenda Daly, *Lavish Self-Divisions: The Novels of Joyce Carol Oates* (1996).

A. ROBERT LEE

O'CASEY, Sean

1884–1964

Irish playwright

Born into the Dublin working class at a time when conditions in the city were perhaps the most barbarous in Europe, O'Casey might seem on first reflection to be a classic proletarian artist. However, both his background and his career are more complex than any such formulation.

O'Casey's family had roots in both the Catholic masses and in the tiny Protestant minority. Brought up in an atmosphere of missionary Protestantism and poverty, he quickly turned his back on all religious affiliations. His plays, however, not only reflect sectarian tensions (e.g. *The Plough and the Stars,* 1926), but their language utilizes the rhythms and images of Victorian hymnology and pious rhetoric – usually to bitterly ironic effect. The occasional satires directly at sectarian folly in the early plays grow, none too painlessly, into the theme of *The Bishop's Bonfire* (1955).

Educated on the Bible, Shakespeare and visits to Dublin's conventional Victorian theatre – Dion Boucicault and music hall for the most part – it was O'Casey's lot to find on his entry to the theatre in the Abbey an admirably independent company but one dominated by self-consciously aristocratic ambitions. O'Casey's relationship with **W.B. Yeats** was never easy, and the latter's rejection of *The Silver Tassie* (1928) virtually sent O'Casey into English exile. His relationship with Lady Gregory, on the other hand, was deeply felt on both sides, and assisted his maturing as a writer.

O'Casey's politics evidence a further area of uneasy dislocation. A left-winger from the outset, he regarded the 1916 rebellion as a bourgeois adventure in nationalism; the antagonism which greeted *The Plough and the Stars* in part stems from the Irish public's inability to assess its political origins, and in part reveals their resentment of O'Casey's personal detachment. In the 1930s he constantly announced himself to be an orthodox communist, though his exile in England lends an air of unreality to many of his later pronouncements.

The plays are usually seen as falling into two groups. The first – *The Shadow of a Gunman (1923)*, *Juno and the Paycock* (1924) and *The Plough and the Stars* – are ostensibly naturalistic dramas of working-class life during the Irish troubles; the Shakespeare of *Henry IV Part One* is a powerful influence here. *The Silver Tassie* is a transitional work employing expressionist techniques in Act 2 depicting the Great War. From the 1930s onwards there is a greater concentration on formal organization together with a more determined political purpose. *The Star Turns Red* (1940) is important here. The late plays have a caustic celebratory quality, as in the near-unstageable but brilliant *Cock a Doodle Dandy* (1949).

O'Casey's reputation has slowly fallen. His language, in its gutsy lushness, appears sentimental, while his political concerns can appear remote. He is nevertheless a natural man of the theatre, whose appetite for life often allowed him to swallow some rather undercooked moments in dramatic construction. His six volumes of autobiographies (1939–56, collected in *Mirror in My House*, 1956), written in the third person, shed much light on Irish conditions and attitudes. In an age where literature has overshadowed theatre, and where the seminar room dominates both, O'Casey's talents require a sympathetic hearing.

Further reading

Other works include: *Within the Gates* (1934); *Red Roses for Me* (1946); and *Behind the Green Curtains* (1961). See: David Krause, *Sean O'Casey: The Man and His Work* (1962); R. Ayling and M.J. Durkan, *Sean O'Casey: A Bibliography* (1978); C. Desmond Greaves, *Sean O'Casey, Politics and Art* (1979); Heinz Kosok, *O'Casey the Dramatist* (1985); E.H. Mikhail, *Sean O'Casey and His Critics: An Annotated Bibliography* (1985); Bernice Schrank, *Sean O'Casey: A Research and Production Sourcebook* (1996).

W.J. MCCORMACK

ODETS, Clifford
1906–63
US dramatist, screenwriter and director

Clifford Odets was born into a wealthy, middle-class, Jewish family which moved from Philadelphia to the Bronx when he was aged six. Leaving school at fifteen, he acted with several small theatre companies, becoming a founder-member of the influential Group Theatre, set up in 1931 by Harold Clurman, Cheryl Crawford and Lee Strasberg to revitalize the social meaning of drama, using and exploiting **Stanislavskyan** techniques. A poor actor, Odets turned to writing, and *Waiting for Lefty* was first performed in 1935. He was by then a member of the Communist Party, and his commitment to left-wing politics is nowhere more in evidence. A 'proletarian morality tale', *Lefty* is radical in both content and dramatic method. Set at a highly charged union meeting, where a proposed strike is under discussion, actors planted in the audience make it a part of the action, and the theatrical performance a truly group experience. Like **Brecht**, Odets used a number of 'alienation' techniques to present a series of flashbacks within the framework of the strike meeting. But while Brecht's plays of the 1930s are often coldly analytical, *Lefty* appeals to raw emotions. In his production notes Odets advised: 'Do not hesitate to use music wherever possible. It is very valuable in emotionally stirring an audience.' These techniques also indicate the longstanding influence of the cinema on Odets's theatrical work.

Lefty, and plays like *Till the Day I Die* (1935), dealing with the struggle of the German Communists, led to Odets being labelled a proletarian writer. But he was more often concerned with the spiritual decay of the middle classes, notably in *Awake and Sing!* (1935). This has resulted in frequent comparisons with **Chekhov**, with whom he shared an ear for dialogue and an ability to portray that peculiar kind of self-absorption which leads to self-destruction. Clearest examples of this are *Golden Boy* (1937), *The Big Knife* (1949) and *The Country Girl* (1950; retitled *Winter Journey* in Britain).

Odets was soon courted by Hollywood, and wrote his first screenplay; *The General Dies at Dawn,* in 1936. He continued to write for Group Theatre, but after the company folded in 1941, his stage-work became increasingly sporadic and less overtly political. (Odets's testimony before the House Committee on Un-American Activities in 1952 lost him many admirers.) His plays became more obviously personal; concerned with the tortured individual rather than class conflicts. The earlier, ideologically committed pieces are often criticized for their naivety, but they have a passion and an integrity which is lacking in much of the later work. The central character in *The Big Knife* gives up a promising career in boxing to become a successful Hollywood actor, selling his soul to the studio; the play ends with his suicide. Odets repeatedly returned to this theme of lost opportunities and forsaken principles, and it is easily related to his own transition from committed playwright to, ultimately, screen-writer on an **Elvis Presley** pot-boiler.

The major achievement of Odets's later work is its vivid characterization; this is particularly true of *The Country Girl*, his most frequently revived play. But Odets's most important contribution to twentieth-century drama remains the Group Theatre productions, and especially *Waiting for Lefty*. He here brought something new, in form and content, to the American stage, and was a major influence on the development of a political theatre in Britain in the late 1930s.

Further reading

Other works include: *Paradise Lost* (1935); *Rocket to the Moon* (1938); *The Silent Partner* (1938); *Night Music* (1940); *Clash by Night* (1941); *The Russian People* (an adaptation, 1942); and *The Flowering Peach* (1954). His screenplays include: *None but the Lonely Heart* (1944); *Deadline at Dawn* (1946); and adaptations of his own plays. In 1960 he also directed *The Story on Page One*. About Odets: R. Baird Shuman, *Clifford Odets* (1962); E. Murray, *Clifford Odets* (1968); William W. Demastes, *Clifford Odets: A Research and Production Sourcebook* (1991); Harold Cantor (ed.) *Clifford Odets: Playwright-Poet* (2000); Christopher J. Herr, *Clifford Odets and American Political Theatre* (2003). See also Harold Clurman, *The Fervent Years* (1945).

PAUL NICHOLLS

ŌE KENZABURŌ

1935–

Japanese author

When Ōe Kenzaburō was awarded the Nobel Prize for Literature in 1994, the accompanying citation referred specifically to the 'poetic force' that the author deploys in his literature to 'create an imagined world where life and myth condense to form a disturbing picture of the human predicament today'. The comment is incisive: Ōe's oeuvre, while always challenging and often shocking, retains a focus on the difficult moral questions of the day, as it attempts to question the evolving meaning of being Japanese, initially as the nation sought to come to terms with defeat, nuclear devastation and the need for rapid economic regeneration and, thereafter, with the search for spiritual direction among Japan's disaffected youth.

Born in a small mountain village in Shikoku, the smallest and most rural of Japan's four main islands, Ōe's literary considerations of the human condition can be seen as premised on his own experience of life on the periphery; indeed, some of his most memorable protagonists are themselves marginal figures attempting to make sense of the dictates of mainstream society. For Ōe, moreover, this divide was brought into sharper focus, first by his experience of primary school education under the relentless scrutiny of Japan's military authorities and subsequently by his decision to relocate to Tokyo to study French literature.

The majority of Ōe's early protagonists are typical post-war males. Secular individuals, torn between personal desires and an awareness of wider responsibilities to society, many find themselves confronted by a series of seemingly impossible choices over which they struggle to exercise their own free will. Here, too, echoes of Ōe's own personal experience are never far beneath the surface, leading several critics to portray Ōe as a natural successor to the pre-war generation of *shishōsetsuka* ('I-novelists'). The comparison may be expedient, but it masks a complexity in the relationship between author and his creations – and a sharply ideological intent – not identified with the traditional 'I-novel'.

The autobiographical element is particularly prominent in Ōe's early work, with 'Prize Stock' ('Shiiku', 1958, trans. 1981), the early story for which Ōe was awarded the prestigious Akutagawa Prize for fiction, a prime example. Here, the unremarkable life of a small Shikoku village is disturbed by the arrival of an African-American soldier captured during the intense fighting towards the end of the war. Initially, the villagers 'adopt' the soldier, whom they come to see as a 'beautiful animal'; and when the order comes from above that he is to be killed, a scuffle ensues in which the father of the young protagonist succeeds in severing his son's hand along with the soldier's head. The allegory is rich, as the broken relationship that ensues between father and son is equated with the loss of the father figure, the Emperor, following renunciation of the latter's divine status after defeat in the war.

Another issue introduced here and pursued in more detail in Ōe's subsequent writing is that of mainstream society's inhuman treatment of the disempowered – and this theme lies at the heart of the three works, written during the 1960s, with which Ōe secured his

international reputation. The first, *A Personal Matter* (*Kojinteki na taiken*, 1964, trans. 1968), was penned in the aftermath of the birth, with a severe brain hernia, of Ōe's son, Hikari. Reduced to desperation at the sight of his son, the protagonist, Bird, initially seeks solace in the sexual embrace of a former girlfriend, and the two contemplate abandoning the baby to the whims of a neighbourhood quack doctor and escaping to Africa. Eventually, however, Bird is obliged to confront reality – and the responsibilities of fatherhood – and, although the ending has been much criticized for its incongruity with the savagery that has preceded it, the work helped secure Ōe's reputation as a masterful portrayer of the human psychological drama. Shortly after publication of this work, Ōe, already a noted activist for several left-wing causes, made a trip to Hiroshima where his interviews with several *hibakusha* (A-bomb victims) resulted in *Hiroshima Notes* (*Hiroshima nōto*, 1965, trans. 1982), his second work dealing with those struggling on the margins. Before long, however, these enquiries led Ōe to a consideration of Japan's often awkward political position *vis-à-vis* the outside world – and the result was *The Silent Cry* (*Man'en gannen no futtobōru*, 1967, trans. 1974), a lengthy novel which, in its depiction of Takashi attempting to foment a revolution in a rural Shikoku village in order to reinstate a premodern Japanese sense of community, evokes the arrival of Commodore Perry in Yokohama Bay a century earlier as well as the US–Japan Security Treaty riots of the 1960s. Here as elsewhere, however, the more Ōe explores the tensions and contradictions between centre and periphery, the more he discerns there, not so much a straight inequality, but rather a genuinely symbiotic relationship.

In 1970, Ōe was as stunned as the rest of Japan by the death by ritual disembowelling of his literary nemesis **Mishima Yukio**, and in the years that followed he proceeded to write a series of novels, epitomised by *The Day He Himself Shall Wipe My Tears Away* (*Waga namida o nuguitamau hi*, 1972, trans.

1977) in which he sought to critique what he saw as the latter's romanticized, single-minded fanaticism towards the emperor system. At the same time, in works such as *The Game of Contemporaneity* (*Dōjidai geemu*, 1979), he frequently resorted to inspiration from the folklore and legends of his native Shikoku as an antidote to the pernicious influence of the myths that Mishima and others had sought to weave around the imperial institution.

In all of this, there is an increasingly spiritual tenor to Ōe's more 'mature' writing, this being particularly evident in *The Burning Green Tree* (*Moeagaru midori no ki*, 1993–5), the work often cited as his 'lifework' and which best betrays the oft-cited influence on his work of the likes of **Norman Mailer** and Flannery O'Connor, as well as **Yeats** and **Dante**. Here, Ōe's life-long social focus leads to an exploration, through the image of the 'church of the green tree', of the frustration evidenced by a segment of Japanese youth at the lack of an obvious viable future, their lack of clear purpose resulting in the contemporary boom in the 'new, new' religions. Ōe's concern here is with the messianic and often apocalyptic messages spawned by these cults, the decision of those involved to embrace destruction subtly contrasted with the quiet yet desperate optimism he had earlier encountered in the *hibakusha*.

Following receipt of the Nobel Prize in 1994, Ōe vowed to renounce literature. It was not long, however, before he returned to his tried and trusted vocation, his 1999 novel, *Somersault* (*Chūgaeri*, trans. 2003), offering novel treatment of many of his earlier concerns.

Further reading

After Ōe received the Nobel Prize, there was a boom in translations of his work into a number of languages. Most of his major work is now available in translation. For critical discussion of Ōe's work, see Susan Napier, *Escape from the Wasteland: Romanticism and Realism in the Fiction of Mishima Yukio and Ōe Kenzaburō*, 1991; and Michiko

Wilson, *The Marginal World of Ōe Kenzaburō: A Study in Themes and Techniques*, 1986.

MARK WILLIAMS

OFFENBACH, Jacques (Jacob)
1819–80
French composer

At the age of fourteen Offenbach left his home town of Cologne and went to Paris to pursue his musical studies and make a career. His father rightly took the view that France offered better prospects to a musician of Jewish extraction than did Germany in the illiberal days of the first half of the nineteenth century. All places at the Conservatoire were normally reserved for French pupils, but Cherubini was so impressed by Offenbach's promise as a cellist that he stretched the regulations and admitted him. Within a year, however, the lad parted company with his teachers and began making a precarious living as a soloist and orchestral player. He rapidly gained a reputation as a virtuoso, sometimes performing his own compositions. Far more important in the development of his interest in music for the stage was the experience he gained in the orchestra pit, first at the Ambigu Comique, then at the Opéra Comique. He was also fortunate to serve as musical director of the Comédie-Française for five years from 1850, despite the frustrations of working in a theatre that persisted in treating music as a mere adjunct to the spoken word in drama.

In 1855, the year of the great International Exhibition in Paris, Offenbach decided to make a bid for independence. So far he had had scant success in interesting theatre managers in his operettas. Now, with crowds of tourists expected and every prospect of a brilliant season, he judged the time had come to found a company of his own to perform his works. With financial backing from Henri de Villemessant, founder of *Le Figaro*, he leased a tiny theatre in the Champs-Elysées. Under the name Les Bouffes-Parisiens, the new company was an immediate success. In the autumn, when the exhibition closed, Offenbach looked for more central premises, and the company moved into the Théâtre des Jeunes-Élèves in the fashionable Passage Choiseul. Police regulations at the time stipulated that no more than four characters should appear in productions in the minor Parisian theatres, and Offenbach's operettas from this period are marred by this unnatural limitation. Generally they are in a single act, three separate works making up an evening's entertainment. The plots are simple and either hackneyed or the working out of just one fresh idea. Light in tone, sometimes sentimental or else spiced with a certain topicality, these operettas were extremely popular in their day. Some of the credit is due to the librettists, Henri Meilhac (1831–97) and Ludovic Halévy (1834–1908). But Offenbach was the driving force behind Les Bouffes-Parisiens, and it was his gift for catchy tunes and bright orchestration that gave life to these trifles.

Orpheus in the Underworld (*Orphée aux enfers*) was first performed in 1858. It was in two acts, and this longer form allowed Offenbach to develop his delight in uproarious travesty and irreverent parody, sparing neither Homer nor Gluck. Six years later, Offenbach surpassed this triumph with *Fair Helen* (*La Belle Hélène*). In 1866 he transformed a hoary horror story into farce in *Bluebeard* (*Barbe-bleue*). That same year he also pretended to treat contemporary life in the French capital in *La Vie parisienne*, only to show a succession of hilarious escapades. *La Grande-Duchesse de Gerolstein* (1867) is set in a petty German state, complete with minuscule army and haughty aristocrats. The basic attitude, however, remains the same, as the Grand Duchess pursues her amours with reckless abandon, like the inhabitants of Offenbach's Olympus. Many critics emphasize satiric qualities in these operettas, seeing in them sharp criticism of the hollow vanity of the Second Empire with its parvenu aristocracy and thinly veneered immorality. But it could be more useful to think rather of festive comedy, in which, for a short while, the jester is at liberty to make mock of all that is held sacred.

Napoleon III dealt harshly with any subversive force yet he enjoyed the operettas, while Offenbach, who acquired French citizenship thanks to the emperor's intervention when his application for naturalization was under consideration, became something of an establishment figure. Cheeky, irreverent, always ready to see the funny side of everybody who took himself seriously, an inveterate parodist of everything that was pretentious, Offenbach was too joyous to be a satirist. In his great creative phase, Offenbach owed much to the artistes he employed, especially the ever-popular Hortense Schneider, and Meilhac and Halévy continued to supply him with deftly constructed (if poorly worded) librettos. But these operettas would not be remembered today were it not for Offenbach's gifts as a melodist and orchestrator.

Offenbach's success waned with the collapse of the Second Empire, though he went on writing for the theatre, providing, for instance, incidental music for **Sardou's** spectacular melodrama *Hatred* (*La Haine*) in 1874. He died in 1880 before completing *The Tales of Hoffmann* (*Les Contes d'Hoffmann*); it is a fine score by an accomplished musician and reveals a more profound vein than the operettas.

Further reading

Offenbach's own account of a moderately successful visit to America in 1873 has been translated by Lander MacClintock under the title *Orpheus in America* (1958). See: Alexander Faris, *Jacques Offenbach* (1980); J. Harding, *Jacques Offenbach* (1980); J.-C. Yon, *Jacques Offenbach* (2000). In French, A. Decaux, *Offenbach, roi du Second Empire* (1958); and Jacques Brindejont-Offenbach, *Offenbach, mon grandpère* (1940); See also: Gervase Hughes, *Composers of Operetta* (1962).

C.N. SMITH

OLDENBURG, Claes

1929–

US artist

'Everything I do is completely original – I made it up when I was a little kid.' Born in

Stockholm, Oldenburg was brought up in Chicago from 1936. Slightly an outsider, he created an imaginary island, Neubern, a coherent parallel reality worked out in minute detail, which contained the germs of most of his later work.

After interdisciplinary studies at Yale, he worked as a crime reporter while attending night classes at the Art Institute of Chicago. Arriving in New York in 1956, it was the life of the slums that inspired his exhibition/environment *The Street* (1960). Next year he set up *The Store*, in which were exhibited parodies of clothes, food and other objects, for example *Blue Shirt, Striped Tie* and *Slice of Yellow Pie* (both 1961). The splashed paintwork on this pseudo-merchandise was a recognition of Abstract Expressionism, then the dominant style in avant-garde painting. But Oldenburg's involvement with vulgar, everyday reality was in deliberate opposition to abstract art's hermeticism. Inspired by Kaprow's idea that **Pollock's** actions were more significant than the finished product, he staged several Happenings at The Store and later elsewhere.

An important exponent of Happenings, Oldenburg became, with **Warhol,** one of the principal figures of American Pop Art. Invited to exhibit uptown, he continued to make parodies of consumer goods, but glossier and more commercial-looking than before, and without the splashes. He played with textures, creating a hard, geometrical *Bedroom Ensemble* (1963) and, by contrast, 'soft machines', for example the *Soft Typewriter* (1963) and *Soft Dormeyer Mixer* (1965). He also played with scale, as in the *Floorburger (Giant Hamburger)* (1962) and *Giant Pool Balls* (1967). The interest in scale led on to designs for colossal monuments, of which to begin with very few were executed. Unrealized proposals from the 1960s include a *Teddy Bear* (1965), at least the size of the surrounding buildings, for Central Park, New York, and a *Ball* (1967) for the River Thames, London, like a vast lavatory cistern, rising and falling with the tide. The first large-scale project that was realized was *Lipstick (Ascending)*

on Caterpillar Tracks (1969–74) for Yale University, a symbol of love rising from death made in the context of the Vietnam War.

Since 1976 Oldenburg has collaborated with Coosje van Bruggen, whom he married in 1977. They have concentrated on making sculptures for specific outdoor urban sites in which familiar objects are vastly magnified, simultaneously parodying and extending the monumental tradition. These include: *Clothespin* (1976) for Philadelphia; *Flashlight* (1981) for Las Vegas; *Dropped Bowl with Scattered Slices and Peels* (1990) for Miami; *Inverted Collar and Tie* (1994) for Frankfurt-am-Main; *Saw, Sawing* (1996) for Tokyo; and *Cupid's Span* (2002), a vast bow and arrow, for San Francisco. Sometimes the sculptures interact with a building, as in *Knife Slicing through Wall* (1986) in Los Angeles, and *Dropped Cone* (2001), a massive inverted ice cream cone on top of a building in Cologne. The work most fully integrated with architecture is *Binoculars* (1991) which forms the central segment of a building designed by **Frank Gehry** in Venice, California. These works constitute a major contribution to public art.

Oldenburg has always wanted to be fully involved with the real world, to touch and be touched. The tactility in his work is therapeutic both for himself and for society, especially American society. As an immigrant, he was fascinated by everything typically American and in his creative-destructive alter ego, Ray Gun, he semi-ironically fused himself with American maleness. He continues to celebrate the democratic aspiration to freedom but, through his humour, undermines the repressions of a culture both puritanical and phallic, proposing instead a more complete, childlike, tactile freedom, related to **Freud's** concept of 'polymorphous perversity'. Satirical and mystical, realistic and fantastic, personal and public, Oldenburg's complex art aims at a synthesis completely human.

Further reading

Other works include: *Injun and Other Histories* (1966), *Notes* (1968) and *Raw Notes* (1973). The classic text on his early work is Barbara Rose, *Claes Oldenburg* (1970). *Claes Oldenburg: An Anthology* (1995), published by the Solomon R. Guggenheim Museum, with texts by Oldenburg and others, is very useful, as is Germano Celant (ed.) *Claes Oldenburg, Coosje van Bruggen* (1999). See also: Richard Morphet, *Claes Oldenburg and Van Bruggen* (2002).

GRAY WATSON

OMAR, Mullah Muhammad

1959–

Afghan religious-political leader

Born in the Hotak tribe of the Ghilzai branch of ethnic Pushtuns to a landless peasant in Nodeh village, Muhammad Omar (Mullah, meaning 'cleric' or 'preacher', being his title) studied at a religious school in nearby Kandahar, the traditional capital of southern Afghanistan. In the early 1980s, he settled in Singesar as the local mullah and opened a religious school there. He engaged in guerrilla actions against the Soviet-backed **Marxist** government in Kabul, which escalated in the mid-1980s. By the time Moscow withdrew its forces from Afghanistan in 1989, Omar had suffered injuries four times, one of which blinded him in the right eye.

He stayed out of the internecine violence among the victorious Afghan Mujahedin, which erupted after the overthrow of the leftist Muhammad Najibullah's regime in 1992. Frustrated by civil war, Pakistan's Inter-Services Intelligence (ISI) sponsored the formation of a new Afghan party – consisting primarily of current or former students of religious schools, mostly based in Pakistan, where they had grown up in refugee camps – called the Taliban, plural of *talib*, one who pursues religious learning.

Soon after Omar's election as the Taliban leader in spring 1994, Singesar's residents complained against a commander of the nearby military camp who had raped two teenage girls. Leading a band of local Taliban, Omar attacked the camp, freed the girls, seized arms and ammunition, and hanged the commander. His fame grew. In July he formalized the founding of the Taliban militia by adopting a black turban as their uniform and a white flag as their emblem.

Three months later, Omar captured a garrison near the Pakistani border and seized 18,000 Kalashnikov rifles, dozens of artillery guns, ammunition and many military vehicles. He then captured Kandahar, and armed the 12,000-strong Taliban militia with MiG-21s fighter jets and scores of tanks and armoured vehicles.

After disarming civilians and irregular militias, Omar imposed his version of the Sharia (Islamic law), an amalgam of an extremist interpretation of the Hanbali school of Sunni Islam and its puritanical Wahhabi subsect. He required women to wear the head-to-toe shrouds, *burqas*, and men to don long shirts, loose trousers and turbans, and grow bushy beards. He shut down all girls' schools and forbade women from working outside the home. His blanket ban on music and television resulted in the destruction of audio- and video-tapes as well as television sets. The reason for prohibiting music, singing and dancing was that they aroused lust and led to fornication, thus undermining marital fidelity and the stable family structure, the foundations of a truly Islamic social order.

He also prohibited chess, football and kite-flying as well as keeping birds as pets. To prevent idolatry, he ordered the tearing up of all pictures and portraits, and prohibited photography. He outlawed gambling and charging interest on loans. He prescribed compulsory prayer, and banned all transport during prayer times. These edicts were enforced by the Department of Propagating Virtue and Preventing Vice.

The Taliban captured province after province, often by bribing local warlords with the funds supplied initially by Pakistan's ISI and later by the Saudi intelligence agency, and opening up roads, which lowered food prices and gained them instant popularity. By disarming all irregular militias, punishing corrupt officials and warlords, and restoring law and order, the Taliban expanded their popular base among a war-weary people.

On the eve of the Afghan New Year, 21 March 1996, about 1,200 Sunni clerics and tribal leaders from all over Afghanistan, except the north, gathered in Kandahar to deliberate on the future of the Taliban and Omar. On 4 April, they decided to accept him as their Emir al Mumineen ('Commander of the Faithful').

The speed with which the Taliban captured Kabul in September dazed not just them and their domestic enemies but also Afghanistan's neighbouring states, except Pakistan. Omar appointed a six-man consultative council, headed by Mullah Muhammad Rabbani, who acted as prime minister. In that capacity, Rabbani held talks with **Osama bin Laden**, then based in Jalalabad, and offered him protection after he had recognized Omar as the Commander of the Faithful.

Omar extended to Kabul the social-religious edicts he had earlier applied to Kandahar and other provinces. By disarming civilians and non-Taliban militias, the new regime brought peace and tranquillity to Kabul where some 50,000 people had died in the four-year civil conflict. This consideration weighed so heavily that many non-Taliban politicians, including Hamid Karzai (elected president of Afghanistan in the democratic elections of October 2004), backed the Taliban.

Following the bombing of the US embassies in Nairobi and Dar es Salaam on 7 August 1998, resulting in 227 deaths, Washington held bin Laden responsible for the deadly blasts, and called on the Taliban regime to hand him over. Omar refused.

In July 2000, when Omar controlled 95 per cent of Afghanistan, he banned poppy cultivation, and enforced the ban strictly. In December, the United Nations Security Council declared the Taliban-controlled Afghanistan as the world centre of terrorism, and demanded bin Laden's extradition within a month. Omar refused to comply, and UN sanctions went into effect.

When US President George W. Bush demanded bin Laden's extradition for his involvement in the 11 September 2001 attacks on New York and Washington, Omar replied that bin Laden had no pilots and there were no facilities for training pilots in Afghanistan.

Following the US-led bombing campaign that began on 7 October, 2001, the Taliban militia fled Kabul on 12–13 November. Kandahar fell on 7 December. Omar was seen fleeing on a motor cycle in the dark. Since then he has issued taped messages, attacking the Americans and Karzai's pro-Western government. Operating underground in southern Afghanistan, he has since then reorganized Taliban remnants.

Further reading

See: Peter Marsden, *The Taliban: War, Religion and the New Order in Afghanistan* (1998); Ahmed Rashid, *Taliban: Islam, Oil and the New Great Game in Central Asia* (2000); Dilip Hiro, *War Without End: The Rise of Islamist Terrorism and Global Response* (2002); Neamatollah Nojumi, *The Rise of the Taliban in Afghanistan: Mass Mobilization, Civil War, and the Future of the Region* (2002); See: Jason Burke, *Al-Qaeda: Casting a Shadow of Terror* (2003).

DILIP HIRO

O'NEILL, Eugene Gladstone

1888–1953

US dramatist

To all intents and purposes modern American drama began with Eugene O'Neill. The son of a famous actor father, he began writing in a tuberculosis sanatorium where he spent six months in 1912. His first produced play, *Bound East for Cardiff*, staged by the Provincetown Players in the Wharf Theatre in 1916, marked a sharp break with a theatre which for the most part had simply exchanged the melodrama of action for a melodrama of character, in replacing the sentimentalities of nineteenth-century popular art with a naturalism which O'Neill rejected as the mere 'holding of the family Kodak up to ill-nature'. He wished to transcend 'the banality of surfaces' and in his early sea plays he offered tone poems, lyric portraits of marginal characters straining to make sense of a life whose dominant mood was one of loss and whose central need was for a sense of belonging.

In part this sense of alienation was a product of social divisiveness, a division between the classes, which he dramatized in *The Hairy Ape* (1922), and between races, which he presented in *All God's Chillun* (1924). But this merely concealed a more fundamental sense of abandonment.

Accused of pessimism, he insisted that he was concerned with the tragic spirit, for 'to me, the tragic alone has that significant beauty which is truth. It is the meaning of life − and the hope.' And tragedy, for him, emerged essentially from the gulf between human aspirations and their consistently denied fulfilment − transcendence deriving from the greatness of the dream and the persistence with which it is pursued. But the same gulf which could generate tragedy could equally create a fierce undertow of absurdity, and in fact it is this rather than any sense of tragic transcendence which really typifies his work.

For the transfiguring Apollonian vision, the dream designed to aestheticize life and give it the shape which in reality it lacked, devolved all too often into simple self-deception. More often than not his plays are not about a glorious struggle against fate, an heroic pursuit of the unattainable. They are concerned with the desperate illusions which are the acknowledgement of defeat. It is difficult, indeed, to think of any of his plays which adequately expressed this potential. In *Beyond the Horizon* (1920) the visions are wilfully abandoned, as fate intervenes to deflect the aspiring mind into simple irony. *The Emperor Jones* (1920) is an account of the collapse of illusion and character alike. *Anna Christie* (1921) pitches wilful sentimentalities against determinism. Yank, in *The Hairy Ape*, is ironically transfigured but his vision is hopelessly naive and self-destructive in a way which has very little to do with the tragic. Even *Desire Under the Elms* (1924) and *Mourning Becomes Electra* (1931) offer psycho-pathology in the place of tragic fatalism.

But his talent lay elsewhere. He was a determined experimenter. In *The Emperor Jones*, for example, he mobilized the *mise-en-scène*, making it an active element in a play which concerned itself with the deconstruction of character and language. Brilliantly original, it dramatized a personal and racial reversion to archetype. In *The Great God Brown* (1926) he used masks to dramatize the public and private selves of his characters and in *Strange Interlude* (1928) breathed life into the dramatic aside, seeing this as an apt symbol of the conscious and unconscious self.

Few of his plays were without flaws. His enthusiasms were seldom less than total, whether it be for such devices as those identified above or for the work and ideas of Schopenhauer, **Nietzsche**, **Strindberg**, **Freud** and **Jung**. Their mark is clear on his work. Too often, indeed, character became a function of idea and subject deferred to method. But he was a writer of genuine originality and energy. His range was phenomenal and in his last plays, plays written as he wrestled with disease, he created some of the most powerful works of modern drama.

The Iceman Cometh (1939) is set in Harry Hope's New York bar. In many ways we are apparently offered an absurdist vision. A group of individuals are suspended in a timeless void, cut off from past and future. Their vulnerability, the irony of their situation, seems simply exacerbated by action. Thus they pass the time sitting motionless, using drink to deny the consciousness which is the source of their pain. Virtually all of them are betrayers. They have failed the causes which they have served, the people they have loved, the world which in their youth they had perceived as opportunity but which now they regard as a lost cause. Their drunkenness, their retreat into self, into unreality, is a protection against knowledge of that imperfection. And yet there is a crucial connection between their imperfection and the compassion which is equally generated by despair and which becomes a primary value.

The Iceman Cometh was, O'Neill suggested, a denial of any other experience of faith in his work and it was so primarily through his acceptance of that progression identified by **Albert Camus** when he asserted that 'The end of the movement of absurdity, of rebellion, etc. ... is compassion ... that is to say, in the last analysis, love.' Certainly his dedication to his greatest play, *Long Day's Journey into Night* (1939–41), speaks of a 'faith in love' inspired by his marriage to Carlotta, which enables him to face his dead in a play written 'with deep pity and understanding and forgiveness'. It is a play which re-creates his own painful family experiences. Set in 1912, the year of his own attempted suicide, it is an attempt to understand himself and those to whom he was irrevocably tied by fate and by love. It is the finest and most powerful play to have come out of America.

Further reading

See *The Plays of Eugene O'Neill* (3 vols, 1951). The principal biographies are by Arthur and Barbara Gelb (1974) and by Louis Sheaffer (1968). See also: Stephen Black, *Eugene O'Neill: Beyond Mourning and Tragedy* (1999); Travis Bogard, *Contour in Time: The Plays of Eugene O'Neill* (revised edn, 1988); Michael Mannheim (ed.) *The Cambridge Companion to O'Neill* (1998).

C.W.E. BIGSBY

ONO, Yoko

1933–

Japanese artist

While Yoko Ono is known throughout the world as John Lennon's widow (The **Beatles**), she is to be regarded as an artist in her own right, working in a number of different media, including performance art. As the most celebrated Japanese woman of her era, who has deliberately and successfully broken with the traditions and customs that conventionally constrict the Japanese female, she has, too, made a startling contribution to feminism, albeit through implicit rather than explicit means. Her advocacy of peace, on the other hand, is explicit, and has been fully articulated through her work.

Ono was born in Tokyo, the oldest of three children. After surviving World War II and the bombing of the Japanese capital, she moved with her family to New York State. Studying music in New York City, and writing her first compositions, she mingled freely with avant-garde composers, soon marrying Toshi Ichiyanagi. Already, though, she was turning her mind to art, and her downtown apartment on Chambers Street became something of a *salon*. Inevitably, perhaps, she was drawn to, and became associated with, the Fluxus art group **(George Maciunas)**, encouraging her to further widen the means of her own creative expression, which now for the first time included early versions of some of the 'performances' which later gained her notoriety.

The fun-loving but haphazard aesthetics of Fluxus, together with its connection to the American composer **John Cage**, and its commitment to beneficial social change, struck deep chords with Ono. In 1961 she exhibited a series of 'instruction paintings' at the AG Gallery, part-owned by Maciunas. These consisted of proto-minimalist canvases that bore sometimes ironic injunctions to the viewer on their use, and established Ono's artistic credentials. To underscore that the instructions embodied ideas and did not function as aesthetic or graphic representations, she insisted that they were typed. Later, after the AG Gallery had closed and Fluxus had become internationalized, she removed the artwork from the paintings, and presented the instructions as objects, thus overturning the traditional relationship between object and commentary.

Shortly after Ono divorced Ichiyanagi and briefly returned to Japan, marrying Tony Cox, a musician and film producer by whom she had a daughter, Kyoko, in 1963. In 1964 she returned to New York, rejoined Fluxus, and redoubled her productivity, adding poetry-writing to the lengthening list of her accomplishments. In 1966 she visited London to attend a symposium for the 'Destruction of Art', and there performed for the first time

Cut Piece. In this Ono, still a young woman, knelt on the stage as members of the audience were invited to remove pieces of her clothing with pairs of scissors. Thirty-eight years later, and approaching seventy, she returned to London for a repeat performance, consciously substituting her known iconic status for a lost youth.

The original performance of *Cut Piece* resulted in Ono being invited to mount an exhibition of her work at London's Indica Gallery, and it was at the preview of this show that she met an admiring John Lennon, seven years her junior.

In 1969 Ono and Lennon married, following a second divorce. A mutual interest in each other's work led to collaboration in recordings, performances and events. Famously they spent their honeymoon in a hotel room in New York, staging a 'Bed-In for Peace' attended by the press and media, partly in protest against the Vietnam War, but also against the proliferation of nuclear weapons during the Cold War.

Ono's conceptual activities fed Lennon's desire to make a more conceptual kind of music, and her influence is present in much of his later solo work. Together they released new albums, made films and generally confounded their respective audiences, along the way forming the Plastic Ono Band. Conversely, their close relationship, viewed by outsiders as cloying, was held responsible by an ungenerous public for the break-up of the Beatles, with Ono being obliged to bear the brunt of media censure.

Fans of the 'Fab Four' never forgave her, even though in the 1970s Lennon produced much of his best work. Resilient by nature, Ono too continued with her own work, publishing a book, *Grapefruit*, in 1970, and releasing her own solo album, *Approximately Infinite Universe*, in 1972. Press and media attention did, however, get to them both, and in part explained a temporary separation. But in 1975 Ono gave birth to a son, Sean Lennon, and the couple were 'together' until Lennon's murder outside their home in New York in December 1980.

Ono had now to contend with her husband's followers, as well as her own grief. Steadfast in her values, she has, ever since, adroitly managed Lennon's legacy while sometimes exhibiting new works of her own, turning her apparent isolation into an ambiguous art object in itself.

Further reading

Other works include: *Yes Yoko Ono* (2000) is a comprehensive catalogue of Yoko Ono's output published in conjunction with a major retrospective of her work mounted by the Japan Society of New York in the same year. See also Barbara Haskell, *Yoko Ono: Arias and Objects* (1991).

ANNE K. SWARTZ

OPHÜLS, Max

1902–57

German film director

Max Ophüls was born as Max Oppenheimer in Saarbrücken, Germany. A stage actor and producer in the 1920s, he began his career in film in 1930 as an assistant and dialogue director for Anatole Litvak The comedy short *Dann schon lieber Lebertan* (1931) was his first directorial effort. He gained attention with *The Bartered Bride* (1932), but it was *Liebelei* (1932), with its bittersweet tone and expressive lighting and fluid camera movements, that fully revealed his artistic signature as a film director.

A Jew, Ophüls emigrated to France when **Hitler** came to power and became a French citizen five years later. In France, he made *Divine* (1935); *La Tendre Ennemie* (1936); *Yoshiwara* (1937); *Werther* (1938), a romantic comedy version of Goethe's classic; *Sans lendemain* (1939), a remake of John Stahl's 1933 Hollywood melodrama *Only Yesterday*; and *De Mayerling à Sarajevo* (1940), released just before the German occupation. In the years leading up to the Second World War, the cosmopolitan Ophüls also made *La Signora di tutti* (1934) – perhaps his greatest film of the period – in Italy and *Komedie om geld* (1936) in the Netherlands. After the fall of France, he worked briefly in Switzerland on *École des femmes*, an adaptation of Molière, a project that had to be abandoned when Louis Jouvet quit after a few weeks of shooting.

In 1941, Ophüls arrived in the United States. He lived in Hollywood until he returned to Europe in 1950, but it was not until after the end of the war that he was given an opportunity to direct an American film. Douglas Fairbanks, Jr – the film's producer and screenwriter, as well as its swashbuckling star – asked Ophüls to direct *The Exile* (1947), a sweeping, romantic costume picture dramatizing the restoration of the exiled Charles II to the throne of England.

More typical of Ophüls's oeuvre is the second film he made in the United States, *Letter from an Unknown Woman* (1948), adapted by Howard Koch (and, uncredited, Ophüls himself) from the **Stefan Zweig** novella and produced by John Houseman. In Hollywood immediately after the end of the Second World War, there was a spate of films – the most famous is William Wyler's *The Best Years of Our Lives* – that were made by independent production companies and had an affinity, philosophically, with humanistic films then being made in post-war Italy and Japan. In the course of the production of *Letter from an Unknown Woman*, however, the political climate in Hollywood changed. So did the economic climate, which was no longer friendly to independent production. For Ophüls, the handwriting was on the wall. He was to make only two more Hollywood films (*Caught*, 1949, and *The Reckless Moment*, 1949, both powerful but relatively low-budget film noirs) before leaving America for good. And, in order to complete *Letter from an Unknown Woman*, he was forced to make artistic compromises. Arguably, however, some of these compromises – especially the ending; he was forced to have Stefan remember Lisa, although poetically too late – actually strengthen the film by bringing it into closer alignment with the perfectionist morality of the greatest Hollywood melodramas

(*Blonde Venus*, *Stella Dallas*, *Gaslight* and *Now, Voyager*, for example), and thus making *Letter from an Unknown Woman* a great *American* film as well as a great expression of Ophüls's distinctly European sensibility.

Back in France, Ophüls made the bittersweet sexual comedies *La Ronde* (1950), *Le Plaisir* (1951) and *Madame de . . .* (1953), and the ironic *Lola Montes* (1955), which many consider his artistic masterpiece. These films brought his elaborate, fluid camera movements to new heights of sublimity, and achieved his deepest, most exquisite expressions of romantic nostalgia, for love lost and betrayed.

It has been said that when Ophüls died in 1957, of rheumatic heart disease, all the camera dollies and cranes in the world snapped to attention to pay their respects to the director who gave camera movement its finest moments in the history of cinema.

Further reading

See: Alan Williams, *Max Ophüls and the Cinema of Desire* (1980); Susan White, *The Cinema of Max Ophüls: Magisterial Vision and the Figure of Woman* (1995); Virginia Wright Wexman (ed.) *Letter from an Unknown Woman* (1986). Lutz Bacher, *Max Ophüls in the Hollywood Studios* (1996) is a detailed account of the production of Ophüls's American films.

WILLIAM ROTHMAN

OPPENHEIMER, J. Robert

1904–67

US nuclear physicist

While the development and first use of the nuclear bomb was a collaborative effort between America's political administration, its military and a large group of scientists, it is J. Robert Oppenheimer who must for ever bear the stigma of being its principal architect. Whether or not he quoted a verse from the Baghavad Ghita – 'I am become death, the destroyer of worlds' – after his atom bomb was successfully tested in New Mexico is doubted: he may just have said 'It worked!'

But no other words could have been more appropriate. Science, the handmaiden of warfare throughout history, had finally revealed its potential to ruin just about everything; and the man best placed to prevent the bomb's deployment preferred instead to watch the deadliest of research programmes reach fruition.

It is perhaps an irony that Oppenheimer came of Jewish German stock, in an era when the Jewish people suffered the Nazi Holocaust. His father was a wealthy New York textile merchant, his mother a painter. As a child and as a student he was exceptionally clever, graduating *summa cum laude* in chemistry at Harvard University. Immediately his attention turned to theoretical physics, and he packed off to England, where, aged just twenty-two, he gained a doctorate at Cambridge University's Cavendish Institute, under the supervision of **J.J. Thomson** and the influence of **Ernest Rutherford**.

He next attended the University of Göttingen, in Germany, to study quantum theory under Max Born, with whom he developed the 'Born–Oppenheimer approximation', which distinguished nuclear from electron motion. Returning to America in 1927 he temporarily became a staff member at Harvard before joining the California Institute of Technology (Caltech), a department of the University of California at Berkeley. There he remained nineteen years.

Something of a scientific gadfly, he broadened his interests to include, as well as nuclear physics, spectroscopy and astrophysics – he was among the first, if not *the* first, to posit the existence of black holes in deep space. At Berkeley, Oppenheimer became intimate with Ernest O. Lawrence, who had established the Radiation Laboratory that was already attracting the attention of the US army, and which provided a link to Washington. As early as 1939 President **F.D. Roosevelt** created the Uranium Committee specifically to investigate ways of utilizing nuclear physics for military purposes. Out of

these circumstances was born the Manhattan Project, tasked with fast-tracking the production of a nuclear bomb, headed up by General Leslie R. Groves – who also oversaw the building of the Pentagon – with Oppenheimer as its science director.

Oppenheimer assembled a team of frontline scientists, whose members eventually included, *inter alia*, Hans Berthe, Enrico Fermi, Edward Teller, Victor Weisskopf and Robert R. Wilson. At first research was carried out at various academic departments across America, but for the sake of expediency, and also security, a secret centre was built at Los Alamos in New Mexico.

Impetus for the Manhattan Project came from intelligence reports that **Hitler's** Germany was pursuing the same goal. The first nuclear bomb, nicknamed 'Trinity' by Oppenheimer, was exploded at Alamohardo on 16 July 1945, almost two months after Germany had finally capitulated, and in the knowledge that the German nuclear programme was stillborn. Less than a month later, on 5 August, a uranium bomb ('Little Boy') was dropped on Hiroshima. On 8 August a second, plutonium bomb ('Fat Boy') was dropped on Nagasaki, almost directly above the largest Christian community in Japan. All told, as a result of both the immediate blasts and long-term radiation sickness, several hundred thousand non-combatants died.

During the lead-up to these deployments fierce arguments had raged at Los Alamos: would a nuclear explosion ignite the whole of Earth's atmosphere? would it not be better simply to intimidate Japan by dropping the bombs away from civilian centres? On both counts, as project leader, Oppenheimer argued passionately in favour of the actual outcome.

Oppenheimer showed some, but not overwhelming, remorse for what he had achieved. After the Pacific War ended, he became chief consultant to the Atomic Energy Commission, set up to regulate the further use and development of nuclear technology, and thereby hoping to stop the

USSR from acquiring a nuclear capability. For a while he opposed production of the greatly more destructive hydrogen bomb, but in 1951 political pressure made him acquiesce, particularly after Russia acquired the capability it sought and the nuclear arms race had become a reality. In Oppenheimer's own words, the hydrogen bomb was 'technically so sweet'.

By then Oppenheimer had moved to Princeton University. There was, however, a fly in his ointment. In the 1930s Oppenheimer's circle had included several communists, and although he never joined the party himself, it was thought he had been a sympathizer. In 1953 he fell victim to Senator Joe McCarthy's anti-communist witch-hunt. Although he was not arraigned before the infamous Un-American Activities Committee, President Eisenhower revoked his security clearance, and Oppenheimer, while remaining academically employed, took no further part in military research.

Still in his middle age, Oppenheimer became increasingly reclusive, spending much of his time on a beach in the Virgin Islands. A partial rehabilitation came in 1963, when **J.F. Kennedy** bestowed upon him the Enrico Fermi Award for his contribution to theoretical physics. Four years later he died of cancer of the throat.

As a man, Oppenheimer was unstable. Given to depressions, he once attempted to strangle a friend – Francis Ferguson – in Paris. But like many depressives, he had a crusading energy; and like many crusaders, he was unable to take a rounded view of the likely consequences of what he did.

Further reading

See: Peter Goodchild, *J. Robert Oppenheimer: Shatterer of Worlds* (1981); Ken Bird and Martin J. Sherwin, *American Prometheus: The Triumph and Tragedy of J. Robert Oppenheimer* (2005); David C. Cassidy, *J. Robert Oppenheimer and the American Century* (2005). See also: John Hersey, *Hiroshima* (1946).

JUSTIN WINTLE

ORTEGA y GASSET, José

1883–1955

Spanish philosopher and essayist

Ortega studied philosophy at Madrid University and from 1905 to 1907 in Leipzig, Berlin and Marburg. He was appointed professor of metaphysics in Madrid in 1910, a post he occupied until 1936, drawing large audiences with his eloquent and dramatic accounts of philosophy. In 1902 he began a steady flow of articles, reviews and books which continued almost throughout his life and constitutes the eleven volumes of his *Complete Works*. In 1923 he founded the *Revista de Occidente*, Spain's leading cultural and philosophical periodical. He left the country during the Civil War, but returned in 1945 to continue his writing and teaching amidst the asphyxiating anti-intellectualism of **Franco's** Spain, viewed with hostility by Catholic fanatics and with suspicion by the authorities.

He is remembered in Spain primarily as an elitist social theorist and as a critic of philosophical rationalism. Like many Spanish intellectuals, he commented freely on a vast range of topics – history, art, literature, music, painting, sociology, women, sport, education, psychology – and soon acquired a gigantic intellectual standing among the semi-educated reading public of the day who were awed by what more exacting readers are inclined to dismiss as his dilettantism, rhetoric and frequent theoretical vulgarities. In his early sociopolitical works, *Invertebrate Spain* (1921, *España invertebrada*, trans. 1937), *The Dehumanization of Art* (1925, *La deshumanización del arte*, trans. 1956), and *The Revolt of the Masses* (1929, *La rebelión de las masas*, trans. 1932), all heavily influenced by German right-wing theories, he argued that culture and civilization are intrinsically opposed to democracy. The modern age is unique in its rejection of the elitist concept of society. Instead of obediently receiving his values, models and goals from an aristocracy of 'superior' men, the 'mass man' is now presuming to impose his own values of conformism, intolerance and vulgarity as ruling social principles. Ortega's most famous work in this vein is his short essay *The Dehumanization of Art* which is a provocative defence of modern art, literature and music on the grounds that it is anti-egalitarian and undemocratic. Ortega claims that the intention of 'difficult' artists like **Mallarmé, Stravinsky, Picasso, Joyce** or **Pirandello** is deliberately to humiliate and exclude the masses from cultural life which is always an elite activity. 'Mass men', Ortega claims, are always 'realists' in art and literature, since they appreciate the arts only to the extent that the latter reflect their everyday existence. In *The Revolt of the Masses* he strikes a contemporary note by appealing for European unity in defence of a common Western culture against the barbarism of socialists and similar mediocrities.

Ortega is extremely thin on detail. Nowhere does he explain how the elite will be chosen (he merely claims it is an elite of 'excellence', not money) and virtually his only definition of the superior man is the utterly circular argument that he freely wills his own goals while the masses passively obey norms 'set by others'. However, his hatred of mass politics and tastes is at the heart of his copiously developed critique of rationalism. In such books as *The Modern Theme* (*El tema de nuestro tiempo*, 1923, trans. 1931, which includes 'The Decline of Revolutions'), *History as System* (*Historia como sistema*, 1935, trans. 1961), 'Ideas and Beliefs' (*Ideas y creencias*, 1940), he argues the need to 'subject reason to life'. Utopian rationalism (i.e. 'thought abstracted from the abundant and splendid stream of life') is typical of the revolutionary's tendency to develop the critical faculty at the expense of the 'biological' continuity of life. We must learn to reason 'historically', i.e. to confine our intellectualizing to the limits set by the time and place we live in: 'We must seek out our circumstances ... in their limitation and specificity ... the reabsorption of circumstance is the real destiny of man ... I am myself and my circumstances' – a statement

which has been hailed as a great Spanish contribution to existentialism.

Such arguments might be taken as a straightforward defence of historicism: the world and human consciousness evolve at a set rate and rationalism should not attempt to alter the outcome. Nevertheless, Ortega did not identify himself with the conservative or ultra-right political movements of his day. He always considered himself a liberal, and viewed Nazism and militarism with the same patrician contempt as socialism and other 'mass' manifestations. This liberal, individualist thrust in his thought exonerates him from the charge of reaction and fascism, but lays him open to the accusation of confusion and inconsistency. Just as the 'superior' man is self-willing, so must we all 'possess a set of convictions about the world which must be truly ours' (*Man and Crisis, En Torno a Galileo*, 1933, trans. 1959), for 'it is false to talk of human nature ... man must not only make himself but is free by compulsion' (*History as System*). Thus man must apparently think for himself and seek personal authenticity, but such thinking should not run against the prevailing ideological currents of his day, or, as Ortega puts it, he must be 'abreast of his times' (*a la altura de los tiempos*). This may be a useful appeal for the modernization of Spanish thought, but it sounds very much like the subjection of human reason to the dictates of fashion.

Ortega is now out of favour in Spain, his thought having once been favourably viewed by the founders of the Fascist Party; not has he had many supporters outside Spain. But *The Dehumanization of Art* remains a provocative explanation of modernism which continues to stimulate readers.

Further reading

Ortega's complete works, in eleven volumes, have been published by *Revista de Occidente* (1946–69). See P. Garagorri, *Introdución a Ortega* (1970); Andrew Dobson, *An Introduction to the Politics and Philosophy of José Ortega y Gasset* (1989).

JOHN BUTT

ORTON, Joe

1933–67

English playwright

Joe Orton was the first modern English playwright to transfer the clown's phallic fun from the stage to the page. A prankster, Orton wanted to goose his audience and take it for a tumble. His unique style of wit and stage mayhem tested the values of English society and often scandalized it. 'I know that my voice is better than anyone else,' he once wrote to his agent. 'It is vulgar and offensive to middle-class susceptibilities.' Always the outsider (a working–class lad who was both an unrepentant homosexual and a former prisoner who had done time for comically defacing public library books), Orton's anger was never co-opted by his meteoric success. Instead, it made his laughter more dangerous. 'Cleanse my heart,' Orton wrote in an unpublished novel during the ten years of his literary apprenticeship. 'Teach me to rage correctly.' On stage, he found the proper outlet for his hostility. He reinvented the farce genre to marry terror and elation.

Orton was born John Orton in Leicester. He was the first of four children. His mother was a factory worker and char. His father was a gardener. Asthmatic and underprivileged as a child, Orton didn't pass his eleven–plus, and by the time he was fourteen this quintessential master of modern English could neither spell nor speak properly. He conceived the idea of being an actor and going to RADA, even before he'd had an amateur role. But he persevered; and in 1951 he was accepted. While at RADA, where he did well, Orton met Kenneth Halliwell who was, at twenty-five, eight years older and much more sophisticated. Halliwell, who killed Orton with a hammer in 1967 and then took his own life, became Orton's mentor. They lived together, and, after brief stints in repertory, set out to become writers. The writing was Halliwell's idea. Their novels, with such titles as *The Mechanical Womb* and *The Last Days of Sodom*, were comic novels in the **Firbankian** mode, a writer they both idolized. By 1957,

Orton and Halliwell were writing separately but with equal failure. Orton's frustration, an anger at both his own public invisibility and the inadequacy of his writing, fed fantasies of disruption. He set out his battle plan long before he had the talent to achieve it. 'To be destructive,' he wrote in *The Vision of Gombold Proval* (1961), 'words had to be irrefutable ... if you could lock the enemy into a room somewhere, you could get a kind of seismic disturbance.'

The comic defacements of library books they thought middle-brow were salvoes that misfired. Orton rewrote blurbs on the jacket and collaged covers. In 1962, when they were arrested, Orton and Halliwell finally made the newspapers; but also earned six months in jail. After jail, Orton's laughter finally found its target. 'Being in the nick brought detachment to my writing. I wasn't involved any more.'

Between 1963 when his first play was accepted and 1967 when he died, Orton became a playwright of international reputation. His oeuvre was small but his impact was large. By 1967 the term 'Ortonesque' had worked its way into the English vocabulary, a shorthand adjective for scenes of macabre outrageousness. Orton wrote three first-class full-length plays: *Entertaining Mr Sloane* (1964), *Loot* (1966) and *What the Butler Saw* (1967), as well as four one-act plays. Two films were made from his plays, and *Loot* was voted the *Evening Standard*'s Best Play of 1966. Orton's plays had often scandalized audiences (he fanned the flames by damning himself in print under the pseudonym Edna Welthorpe) but his wit made the outrage scintillating. Orton's laughter bore out **Nietzsche's** dictum that 'He who writes in blood and aphorisms does not want to be read, he wants to be learned by heart.' Orton brought the epigram back to the contemporary stage to illuminate a violent world. 'It's life that defeats the Christian Church, she's always been well-equipped to deal with death' (*The Erpinham Camp*, 1965). 'All classes are criminal today. We live in an age of equality' (*Funeral Games*, 1966). Orton's laughter created a 'panic'. His stage gargoyles tried to frighten their audience into new life.

Unlike **Harold Pinter**, whose work Orton began by imitating and ended by parodying, Orton created images of action, not entropy. 'The whole trouble with Western civilization,' Orton wrote in his diary, 'is the lack of anything worth concealing.' In Orton's world there is no uncertainty and no secrets. Reality is outrageous enough without mystifying it. People say what they mean – but the truth does not help them. 'How dare you involve me in a situation for which no memo has been issued,' says the corrupt Detective Truscott in *Loot*. All Orton's characters speak a language of reason and live a life of chaos.

Orton found a way of extending the boundaries of farce beyond the bedroom; and in his masterpiece, *What the Butler Saw*, he turns the genre itself into vision of life. Orton fed his characters into the fun machine and made them bleed. 'As I understood it, farce originally was very close to tragedy and differed only in the treatment of its themes like rape, bastardy, prostitution,' Orton said. He returned comedy to its aggressive roots, a hard-edged attack on society to show it the flimsiness of reason and the thin carapace of normality. A master craftsman and an instinctive anarch, Orton produced out of his dark fantasies that rarest of theatrical by-products: joy.

Further reading

See: *The Complete Plays* (1977); *Up Against It* (unproduced film script for the Beatles, 1979); *Head to Toe* (novel, 1971). See also John Lahr, *Prick Up Your Ears: The Biography of Joe Orton* (1978); C.W.E. Bigsby, *Joe Orton* (1982); Maurice Chaney, *Joe Orton* (1984); Simon Shepherd, *Because We're Queers: The Life and Crimes of Kenneth Halliwell and Joe Orton* (1988).

JOHN LAHR

ORWELL, George

1903–50

English essayist and novelist

Orwell's real name was Eric Blair and he was born in India, the son of an official in the Opium Service, and was brought to England by his mother at the age of three. He gained a scholarship to St Cyprian's, a fashionable preparatory school where Cyril Connolly was among his contemporaries. His family were of what he called 'the lower-upper middle class', that is the 'upper-middle class without money'. He was crammed for a scholarship to Eton but did little work there, already being something of an odd man out and against the system. His most brilliant contemporaries went on to Cambridge, but he entered the Burma police, a very unprestigious part of the Imperial Civil Service. He endured it for five years but resigned in 1927, having come to hate the social pretentiousness of the British in Burma and their indifference to Burmese culture. All this comes out in his first published novel, some say his best pre-war novel, *Burmese Days* (1935).

Burmese Days is often taken to be socialist because it is anti-imperialist. But between 1927 and 1934 Orwell often called himself, when other young writers asked 'Where do you stand?', simply 'a Tory anarchist'. He was first an individualist who resented one man or one culture imposing its values on another; and though he was familiar with socialist arguments about economic exploitation, he did not fully agree with them until 1935 and 1936. Immediately after his return from Burma he tried to write novels, which have not survived, and published a few essays, poems and book reviews. Searching for material and wondering whether English working men suffered like the Burmans, he began spasmodic but intense spells of living among tramps. He taught some poorly paid jobs in awful private schools and knew poverty. He ran out of money while spending a year and a half writing in Paris, worked as a dishwasher, and lived in a Parisian slum, all of which experience led to his first and characteristic published book, *Down and Out in Paris and London* (1933). Victor Gollancz published it and had great faith in Orwell as a writer, especially as a novelist, though political differences finally led to a rupture. He suggested the theme of *The Road to Wigan*

Pier (1937) to Orwell, who wrote it as a brilliant account of how the unemployed live, adding an eccentric but provocative section announcing both his conversion to socialism and the indifference to freedom of most socialist intellectuals.

He went to Spain to fight, not to write, but *Homage to Catalonia* (1938) resulted. It sold badly at the time but is now seen both as a classic and an honest description of war, and as one of the shrewdest of polemics against the **Stalinist** attempt to dominate both the Spanish Republic and the whole international Left. For a brief period until 1939 he was militantly anti-war, close to pacifism, a member of the Independent Labour Party, often mistakenly called – like his new publisher Frederic Warburg – **Trotskyite**, because they were strongly left-wing, egalitarian and both anti-Labour Party and anti-Communist. Gollancz continued to publish his novels, *A Clergyman's Daughter* (1935), *Keep the Aspidistra Flying* (1936) and *Coming Up for Air* (1939). Only the latter, written in the middle-brow tradition of **Dickens** and **H.G. Wells**, came up to the now extraordinarily high standard of his documentaries and his essays. The war had a great influence on him. He saw the need to defend even a shoddy and hypocritical democracy against Fascism, but thought, as in *The Lion and the Unicorn* (1941), that a socialist revolution was taking place in the ranks of the British army. He rescued patriotism from its identification with nationalism, trying to show that its roots were radical as much as Conservative. Being tubercular, he was not accepted for military service and wasted two years in the BBC's Far Eastern Service before becoming literary editor of *Tribune*, a wholly congenial post with Aneurin Bevan as the editor. He was an 'English Socialist' of the kind of Michael Foot and Bevan: libertarian, egalitarian, but quite untheoretical, almost anti-theoretical. Early in the war he conceived a grand design for a three-volume novel of social analysis and warning which would deal with the decay of the old order, the betrayal of the revolution and what an English totalitarianism

would be like if it ever came to power. This design never came to be, but the pre-war novels have some such connection with his masterpiece *Animal Farm* (1945) and his most famous work, *1984* (1949). *Animal Farm* is a story of the good revolution of the animals betrayed by the (Stalinist) pigs. It is not a parable of the impossibility of revolution; and *1984* is *not* a *prophecy* of what will happen but a satiric warning of what could happen if power is pursued for its own sake – despite some right-wing American critics reading him in a contrary sense. His values remained those of a left-wing socialist until his early death from tuberculosis; only his hope of seeing 'the Republic' emerge in our times declined.

There is so much more in Orwell than his books. Some critics plausibly see his genius as an essayist. 'A Hanging' and 'Shooting an Elephant' are both ambiguously short-story or personal recollections, but both didactic or moral writing of great stature. His *Tribune* 'As I Please' column virtually invented mixed column journalism, polemical and discursive. Rich humour is found in nearly all his essays, as when he would mock the fierce readers of *Tribune* by describing the mating habits of a common toad or the virtues of a sixpenny Woolworth's rose, all of which would form part of the good life, even in the classless society.

He wrote major essays on censorship, plain language, the social beliefs of boys' magazines, and on pornography and violence: he believed passionately in liberty, but also in condemning the bad both morally and aesthetically. Literary criticism would be the less without his seminal essays on Dickens, Swift and in 'Inside the Whale' on the failings of the intellectuals in the 1930s. The *Collected Essays, Journalism and Letters* (4 vols, 1968), edited by his second wife and widow, Sonia Orwell, together with Ian Angus, though not in fact 'complete', for the first time enabled the remarkable range of his essay writing to be appreciated. Unfortunately by 1968 many distinguished critics had committed themselves to positions based on little more than reading his books. Almost certainly he is the greatest English polemical writer since Swift, and a master of simple prose, someone whose style has had more influence than any over his contemporaries: plain, easy, colloquial, yet precise and capable of great variations between the formal, the informal, the leisurely and the excited. He always distinguished between good writers and bad men; he insisted against the Left that **Pound** and **Eliot** were great writers, though he condemned them as moralists. Those who admire Orwell's plain speaking against Communism may need reminding that his values became and remained Socialist through and through.

He wrote well on national character and is rightly seen, for his style, his commonsense philosophy, his simple way of living and love of the countryside, and his somewhat eccentric preoccupations with little things as well as great moral issues, as essentially an English writer. Above all else, he said of himself that he was 'a political writer', with a hatred of 'totalitarianism' and a love of 'democratic Socialism'. But in the phrase 'political writer', the integrity of each word is of equal value.

Further reading

See: Richard Rees, *George Orwell: Fugitive from the Camp of Victory* (1962); George Woodcock, *The Crystal Spirit* (1966); William Steinhoff, *George Orwell and the Origins of 1984* (1975); *George Orwell: The Critical Heritage*, ed. Jeffrey Meyers (1976); Bernard Crick, *George Orwell: A Life* (1980); J.R. Hammond, *A George Orwell Companion* (1982); M. Shelden, *Orwell* (1991); P. Davison, *George Orwell* (1996).

BERNARD CRICK

OWEN, Wilfred
1893–1918
English poet

Brought up in the back streets of Birkenhead and Shrewsbury, where his father was assistant superintendent of the railways, Wilfred Owen first became aware of his poetic calling at the age of ten or eleven. The dominant presence of his childhood was his devout and adoring mother, who hoped he might eventually enter the church. It was as a result of her influence that, having failed to win a scholarship to London University, he accepted an unpaid post as lay assistant to the vicar of Dunsden, Oxfordshire, in return for board, lodging and coaching towards a second attempt at a university scholarship. Fifteen months in the vicarage convinced him that his belief in evangelical religion was less strong than his allegiance to poetry, and he left in 1913 to teach English in France, first at a Berlitz school, and subsequently as a private tutor. For more than a year after the outbreak of war he could not decide whether or not to join up, but in September 1915 returned to England and enlisted in the Artists' Rifles. Plunged into the battle of the Somme in January 1917, he was involved in heavy fighting and in May was found to be suffering from neurasthenia, or shell-shock, and invalided back by stages to Craiglockhart War Hospital, near Edinburgh. There he met Siegfried Sassoon and, largely as a result of the older man's encouragement and practical criticism, abandoned the sub-Keatsian luxuriance of his early style in favour of the disciplined sensuality, the passionate intelligence characteristic of the poems written during the fourteen months that remained to him. Sassoon's influence is discernible in the shock tactics, and especially in the explosive colloquialisms, of such of Owen's first 'war poems' as 'The Dead-Beat' and 'Dulce et Decorum Est', but he soon found his own more meditative and resonant voice.

The ten months following his discharge from Craiglockhart in November 1917 were the most creative of his life. He was based in Scarborough and Ripon and spent a succession of leaves in London, where he was introduced to a wider circle of literary acquaintance that included **Arnold Bennett**, **H.G. Wells**, Robert Ross, Osbert Sitwell and Charles Scott Moncrieff. The last three and certain of Owen's other friends were homosexual, and the extent to which he came to acknowledge and indulge his own latent homosexual tendencies at this time is a matter of speculation. What is certain, however, is that he wrote more eloquently than other poets of the tragedy of young men killed in battle because he felt that tragedy more acutely.

He was being considered for a home posting when Sassoon returned wounded to England, and Owen decided that his duty as a poet lay in taking his friend's place as a witness to the suffering of the troops. He crossed to France in September 1918, was awarded the Military Cross some weeks later, and seven days before the Armistice was killed.

He lived to see only five of his poems in print, but the selections edited by Sassoon (1920) and Edmund Blunden (1931) were a potent influence on the left-wing poets of the 1930s, who hailed him as hero and martyr for his stand against 'the old men' responsible for the conduct of the war, against whose successors they were themselves in revolt. Owen's use of pararhyme (*escaped/scooped, groined/ground*) was widely emulated; the fragmentary Preface to his poems became one of the most famous of literary manifestos; and the compassion, learnt among the poor at Dunsden and expressed in his poems from the Western Front, reached an international audience as the basis of **Benjamin Britten's** *War Requiem* (1962).

Further reading

See: C. Day Lewis (ed.) *The Collected Poems of Wilfred Owen* (1963) and Harold Owen and John Bell (eds) *Wilfred Owen: Collected Letters* (1967). About Owen: D.S.R. Welland, *Wilfred Owen: A Critical Study* (1960, revised 1978); Harold Owen, *Journey from Obscurity* (3 vols, 1963, 1964, 1965); Jon Stallworthy, *Wilfred Owen: A Biography* (1974); Dominic Hibberd, *Wilfred Owen* (1975); M. Williams, *Wilfred Owen* (1993); D. Kerr, *Wilfred Owen's Voices* (1993).

JON STALLWORTHY

OZ, Amos (Amos KLAUSNER)

1939–

Israeli writer

Amos Oz was born Amos Klausner in Jerusalem to parents who had fled Europe and emigrated to Palestine in 1933. Aged fifteen, and just two years after his mother had committed suicide, young Amos left Jerusalem, settled in Kibbutz Hulda (where he adopted the name 'Oz'), completed his secondary education and stayed there for many years. After military service from 1957 to 1960, Oz studied philosophy and literature at the Hebrew University, Jerusalem. As a reserve soldier he fought in the Sinai desert during the 1967 Six Day War, and on the Golan Heights during the October 1973 Yom Kippur War.

His debut as a writer came in 1965 when *Where the Jackals Howl* (*Artzot Ha-Tan* in Hebrew), a collection of stories, was published in Israel and received immediate critical acclaim. The stories focused on the lives of ordinary Israelis and were set against the backdrop of community life in a *kibbutz*, an institution which, like Jerusalem in many of his other stories, Oz regarded as a microcosm of Israeli society. In *Where the Jackals Howl* Oz examined the very issues which would run as a common thread through his other works, namely human nature and the tension between traditional ideals and the needs and problems that ordinary Israelis face in their modern daily life.

My Michael (*Michael Sheli*, 1968) is perhaps Oz's best-known novel, published just a year after the traumatic Six Day War. Set in Jerusalem, it tells the story of a young married woman descending into madness and of the conflicts between the obligations she feels she has and her real needs. Like his other works, *My Michael* is written in an unspectacular, straightforward style, which goes well with the fact that it deals with everyday life – the fate of the individuals, their drives and ambitions, all rooted in Israel's stormy history.

Strongly identified with the Israeli left, Oz has been a leading figure in the Peace-Now movement since 1977, writing extensively on the Israeli–Palestinian–Arab conflict and advocating a compromise and a negotiated division of the disputed occupied territories based on mutual recognition, respect and coexistence. Many of Oz's political pieces appeared in *Under This Blazing Light* (1979), a collection of essays from 1962 to 1978. Oz's views on war and peace were also expressed in *In the Land of Israel* (*Po Ve-Sham Be-Eretz Israel*), a series of essays published in 1983 in which Oz describes a journey he made through Israel during the controversial 1982 Lebanon War. The essays, which originally appeared in the newspaper *Davar* and caused a storm of protest and admiration, combined documentary interviews Oz conducted with various ideological individuals in Israel with his personal observations.

Further reading

Amos Oz's fiction and non-fiction writing has been translated into more than thirty languages. His works in English include *My Michael* (1972); *Elsewhere, Perhaps* (1973); *Touch the Water, Touch the Wind* (1974); the novellas *Unto Death, Crusade* and *Late Love* (1975); *The Hill of Evil Counsel* (1978); *Where the Jackals Howl* (1981); *In the Land of Israel* (1983); *Perfect Peace* (1985); *The Story Begins: Essays on Literature* (1999). Books about Amos Oz and his work (in English) include Mazor Yair, *Somber Lust – The Art of Amos Oz* (2002); Balaban Avraham, *Between God and Beast – An Examination of Amos Oz's Prose* (1993).

AHRON BREGMAN

OZU YASUJIRŌ

1903–63

Japanese film director

Ozu was born in Tokyo, but from the age of ten lived with his mother and brothers at his father's family home in Matsusaka. In 1923 he returned to Tokyo and began working as an assistant cameraman for one of Japan's leading film studios Shōchiku, where he would stay for the rest of his life. In 1926 he became an assistant director to Ōkubo Tadamoto and in 1927 he made his first film, a period drama (*jidaigeki*) scripted by Noda Kōgo, a collaboration that would continue throughout his career.

In the late 1920s, the Shōchiku Tokyo Studios, specializing in contemporary dramas (*gendaigeki*) under the leadership of Kido Shirō, provided an innovative and challenging setting in which Western cinematic techniques and narrative styles were actively studied and adapted to the Japanese setting. Influenced by American directors such as Ernst Lubitsch and **Charles Chaplin**, Ozu's early films, often humorous, drew on themes from Hollywood genres being peopled with gangsters, boxers, students and the ubiquitous Japanese equivalent of the American 'flapper', the 'modern girl'. However, it is his 1932 film *I Was Born But . . .* (*Umarete wa mita keredo*) in which the subtleties of humour and poignant social observations first achieve the narrative pathos that would define Ozu's films for the remainder of his career. Thereafter, confining himself to a minimalist economy of filming techniques which would become his stylistic trademark, he reportedly resisted the introduction of sound, making his first 'talkie' in 1936, *The Only Son* (*Hitori musuko*), five years after Shōchiku released Japan's first sound film, *The Neighbour's Wife and Mine* (*Madamu to nyōbō*). Later he would resist the introduction of colour, making his first colour film in 1958, *Equinox Flower* (*Higanbana*), at the insistence of the studio.

Both *I Was Born But . . .* and *The Only Son* are set in the urban conurbation of Tokyo and depict the influences of social change stemming from modernity and economic recession on the Japanese family unit. During the war period, Ozu returned to the father/son theme of *I Was Born But . . .* and *Passing Fancy* (*Dekigokoro*, 1933) with a poignant study of separation and loss in *There was a Father* (*Chichi ariki*, 1942). One is tempted to make reference to biographical data in linking this theme to Ozu's own experiences of growing up in Matsusaka while his father continued to spend much of his time in Tokyo.

In the post-war era, Ozu continued to document the impact of economic and social change on the Japanese family. His 1953 film *Tokyo Story* (*Tōkyō Monogatari*) continues the theme of the disintegration of the filial ethic that is evident in *The Only Son*. Aged parents visit their adult children in Tokyo only to feel disappointment and disillusionment as they discover that their children have become distanced due to the demands of careers and city life. Ozu continued to develop the theme of the alienated individual in the material world of urban society in his later post-war films. However, this critique increasingly became linked to consumerism as desirable objects – TV sets, refrigerators, golf clubs and train sets – become narrative devices around which minor conflicts develop – *Early Summer* (*Bakushū*, 1951), *Early Spring* (*Sōshun*, 1956), *Good Morning* (aka *Too Much Talk*, *Ohayō*, 1959) and *An Autumn Afternoon* (*Sanma no aji*, 1962).

Ozu's oeuvre of some fifty films spanned from the early days of Japanese cinema to its box office admissions peak in the late 1950s. Through his concentration on essentially one dominant theme, a portrayal of the deterioration of human relationships against the backdrop of the urban *mise-en-scène* of Tokyo's conurbation, Ozu's film oeuvre documents the disintegration of the Neo-Confucian derived ethics of the extended family. Throughout his career Ozu received numerous awards for his films in Japan (in the 1930s alone, three films were listed in the *Kinema Junpō* top ten), but for many years considered the most Japanese of film directors, his films did not receive the international recognition that was their due. However, as the German director Wim Wenders so eloquently explains in his film tribute to Ozu, *Tokyo Ga* (1985), Ozu's films have resonance far beyond the geographical borders of Japan.

> As thoroughly Japanese as they are, these films are at the same time universal. In them I can recognize all families in all countries of the world, as well as my parents, my brothers and myself. For me, never before and never since has cinema been so close to its essence and its purpose, to present an image of man in our century. A usable, true and valid image in which he not only recognizes himself, but from which above all else he may learn about himself.

Further reading

See: Donald Richie, *Ozu* (1974); Noel Burch, *To the Distant Observer* (1979); David Bordwell, *Ozu and the Poetics of Cinema* (1988); David Desser (ed.) *Ozu's 'Tokyo Story'* (1997); Isolde Standish, *A New History of Japanese Cinema: A Century of Narrative Film* (2005).

ISOLDE STANDISH

P

PALMER, Samuel

1805–81

English painter

Palmer's present reputation rests over-whelmingly on the works he produced between 1825 and 1832 at Shoreham, Kent, some of which are among the finest jewels of English landscape painting.

He was born and brought up on the still rural edges of London and Kent. Although his parents were Baptists, Palmer's liking for tradition and ritual led him to join the Church of England. He acquired very early a love for poetry, his favourites being Virgil and Milton, both of whom could endow familiar country scenes with spiritual significance. His older friend John Linnell perceptively steered him away from contemporary landscape painting, which had little to offer him, towards the early Italian, Flemish and German old masters, especially Dürer. In 1824, Linnell introduced him to William Blake, whose ideas on art, poetry and religion were to be crucial to Palmer throughout his life; and it was in the same year that he first visited Shoreham. From 1825 dates a series of works in sepia, including *The Valley Thick with Corn,* which depict nature in all its fecundity and possess an almost hallucinatory intensity. Palmer went to live in Shoreham, which he called the 'Valley of Vision', in 1826 and was joined there by a circle of like-minded friends calling themselves the 'Ancients', who were united by their admiration for Blake.

Palmer's Shoreham paintings combine an accuracy of detail with an extraordinary ima-ginative freedom. The compositions make use of a somewhat flattened, Gothic perspective and a high horizon line, above which a large moon sometimes dominates, as in *Coming from Evening Church* (1830); there is always a 'mystic glimmer behind the hills'. The hills, which are rounded and breast-like, are com-plemented by trees and church spires and, although Palmer would have been shocked by a sexual interpretation of his symbols, it seems to modern eyes that they may well derive part of their power from this source; nevertheless, the erotic charge is doubtless the greater for not being explicit. In typically Romantic fashion, his landscapes usually (but not always) contain at least one person, which aids the viewer's participation in the scene: such is the role of the figure walking through the twilight with his large staff in *Cornfield by Moonlight with the Evening Star* (*c.* 1830). If the contemplative mood of this picture is tinged with melancholy, the same, though less obviously, is true of nearly all Palmer's many depictions of harvest, even though they are first and foremost celebra-tions of God's plenty. For his love of the harvest was linked to his High Church and Tory love of tradition: an appreciation of things that have come to glorious fruition, made more poignant by the knowledge that their passing away is imminent. Although the Shoreham years were the most fulfilled of Palmer's life, he was never even then free from bouts of despair; these had first been brought on by his mother's death when he was thirteen and were later to become worse with the early death of two of his three children. This disposition to a pessimistic view of life fuelled his horror at the unpoetic and secular quality of advancing industrialism; a horror which accounted for his semi-feudal views and his tendency, somewhat corrected later in life, to romanticize the condition of the rural poor, with whom at Shoreham he was on amicable but never intimate terms. No doubt this made it easier for him to paint, as he did, in the pastoral tradition. His paintings, many of which depict shepherds and/or shepherdesses with their flocks or similarly tranquil bucolic scenes, re-create an earthly paradise. But if his aims were not realistic, nor were they idealizing in the manner of Claude. Suffused with emotion and the desire for redemption, Palmer's Shoreham landscapes fulfilled his ambition of revealing the divine behind the natural.

In 1834, partly for financial reasons and partly from personal disappointments, Palmer returned to London. The vision faded. Several tours in the British Isles produced work which was little more than topographical. In 1837 he married Linnell's daughter and toured Italy with her for two years. It is true that in a sense this experience broadened his art but it also diluted it, robbing it of almost everything that had made it special. Financially dependent as he was on his increasingly tyrannical father-in-law, Palmer fell ever more victim to the mediocrity which the Linnells in practice forced on him, even to the extent of living in a vulgarly mock-Tudor villa in Redhill, Surrey, the antithesis of everything in which he believed. His art never recovered to the level of the Shoreham period but he did master a new medium, that of etching, in which in the last years of his life he produced some outstanding work. In 1865, he began a series of etchings illustrating Milton, of which *The Lonely Tower* and *The Bellman* are particularly fine examples. From 1872 he worked on a series of etchings illustrating Virgil, although these were less successful – doubtless because Palmer's genius

and feeling for landscape were firmly anchored in the North European tradition, a fact which he did himself a great disservice by ignoring so often. His influence was not felt until the twentieth century and then, characteristically, it surfaced in the work of two thoroughly English painters: Paul Nash and Graham Sutherland.

Further reading

See: Geoffrey Grigson, *Samuel Palmer: The Visionary Years* (1947); Carlos Peacock, *Samuel Palmer: Shoreham and After* (1968); David Cecil, *Visionary and Dreamer* (1969); James Sellars, *Samuel Palmer* (1974); R. Lister, *Catalogue Raisonné of the Works of Samuel Palmer* (1988).

GRAY WATSON

PAOLOZZI, (Sir) Eduardo
1924–2005
British sculptor, decorative artist and printmaker

Eduardo Paolozzi's mission as an artist is to give permanent expression to the ephemeral and neglected in popular culture in order to enhance the visual experience of modern life. His work is as likely to be found in a shopping mall or an airport as in the Tate Gallery. In scale it ranges from a postage stamp to the monumental bronze sculpture *Newton* in the courtyard of the British Library. Whether decorating Tottenham Court Road underground station with images from the street, making sculptures for the passer-by on the banks of the Rhine in Cologne, or designing stained glass for a cathedral in Edinburgh, Paolozzi brings an internationalism to art which transcends the limitations of the avant-garde by which he was first known.

Born in Edinburgh to Italian parents, trained in London and inspired by living in Paris, he played a major role in the development of pop art in London in the early 1950s. In 1952 he represented Britain at the Venice Biennale, and from 1958 to 1969 exhibited widely in Europe and America and was regularly awarded international prizes for sculpture and prints. Unlike many post-war artists whose modernism became increasingly reductive, Paolozzi adopts an inclusive agenda, by embracing 'low' and 'high' art, philosophy and literature, music and the cinema. He has done much to bridge the 'two cultures' of which C.P. Snow wrote; and the relationship between man and machine is a subject he has made his own. Paolozzi's ironic sculpture of robots and machine intelligence, and his variations on **Duchamp's** readymades, have also influenced younger artists in Britain. The garden shed, bicycle wheel and other odds and ends in the *This is Tomorrow* exhibition of 1956 was the first time such humble everyday things had been seen in a British art gallery. Paolozzi's work is based on collage, a technique that owes much to Dada and Surrealism, some of whose practitioners, including **Arp** and **Giacometti,** Paolozzi knew in Paris. By cutting up images and recombining them, Paolozzi suggests the schizophrenic experience of urban living which he expressed in 1960 as 'the golden ability of the artist to achieve a metamorphosis of quite ordinary things into something wonderful and extraordinary'.

In the 1960s Paolozzi pioneered screenprinting and explored relationships between language and picture-making with twelve prints based on the life of the philosopher **Ludwig Wittgenstein**. Although initially attracted by the glamour of consumerism, on which he passed sardonic comment with some brilliantly coloured screenprints, Paolozzi's love affairs with America waned before the end of the Vietnam War. In 1970 he severed his connections with the USA and concentrated on abstract relief sculpture with a practical function which was incorporated into architecture as in the *Cleish Castle Ceiling* (reinstalled in the Dean Gallery, Edinburgh) and the *Hunterian Art Gallery Doors*, Glasgow University (but now a room divider). This in turn gave way to figurative sculpture which reflected his concern for the waste and pollution that threatens the future of the planet. In the 1980s he began a series of expressionist

heads illustrative of what he perceived as 'the madness of modern life'. His last series of prints was dedicated to the life and work of the great twentieth-century cryptologist **Alan Turing**.

Paolozzi was Her Majesty's Sculptor in Ordinary for Scotland (1986); was Professor of Sculpture at the Munich Academy of Fine Art (1981–91) and recipient of the Goethe Medal (1991). A permanent display of his art, presided over by his two-storey-high figure of *Vulcan*, is in the Dean Gallery, Edinburgh.

Further reading

See: Eduardo Paolozzi, *Writings and Interviews*, ed. Robin Spencer (2000), and *Lost Magic Kingdoms* (exhibition catalogue, 1985). See also: Diane Kirkpatrick, *Eduardo Paolozzi* (1970); Winnfried Konnertz, *Eduardo Paolozzi* (1984); Fiona Pearson, *Eduardo Paolozzi* (1999); Robin Spencer, *Eduardo Paolozzi Recurring Themes* (exhibition catalogue, 1984); Frank Whitford, *Eduardo Paolozzi* (exhibition catalogue, 1971).

ROBIN SPENCER

PARETO, Vilfredo

1848–1923

Italian sociologist and economist

As the son of an Italian aristocrat exiled for Mazzinian sympaties, Pareto spent his earliest years in France. After his family returned home he completed his education at the Polytechnic Institute in Turin, graduating in mathematics and physics. He worked first as a railway engineer and then as manager of an iron-mining concern. Living in Florence, he was drawn into contemporary debates over free trade, which he favoured as a means of promoting the further development of newly unified Italy. His contributions elicited interest from Léon Walras, Professor of Political Economy at the University of Lausanne. To this chair Pareto himself succeeded in 1893. From the turn of the century onwards he lived largely as a recluse, suffering particularly from disillusionment with the inefficiency and corruption that characterized liberal politics in the new Italy. Only with **Mussolini's** accession to power in October 1922 did Pareto re-emerge into public life, accepting appointment as senator within the Fascist regime. By the time of his death in the following August he was already having second thoughts about the wisdom of such association with the Duce.

Pareto's main works as an economist were the *Cours d'économie politique* ('Course of Political Economy', 1896–7) and the *Manuale di economia politica*. ('Manual of Political Economy', 1906). Here his most notable contribution was to lend to the study of such topics as income distribution a more rigorous mathematical foundation than was then usual. This proved symptomatic of a more general positivist aim to make the laws of society come as close as possible, in generality and predictive power, to those which he had studied earlier in physics. Pareto saw that, at least in the abstract, economics dealt with a relatively tidy sphere of broadly logical behaviour devoted to the maximization of material gain. But clearly there were grave difficulties in applying economic theory to the real world, where it came into conflict with a more richly diverse set of motivations, many non-rational in nature. It is for his socio-logical studies of these phenomena that Pareto is best remembered. With **Weber** and **Durkheim** he ranks as a founding father of twentieth-century academic sociology; in particular he contributed important ideas to the psychological dimension of social studies.

In *Les Systèmes socialistes* ('Socialist Systems', 1902) Pareto accepted that class struggles were a reality. But he dissented from the **Marxist** view that proletarian victory would bring them to an end. One elite would merely be replaced by another, claiming to speak in the proletariat's name. Pareto stressed that, because of differential natural ability, some such 'circulation of elites' was inescapable. The few wielding real power could do so only so long as they proved more capable than any competitors at the task of manipulating the rest of society. Such control was most successful when practised by those who understood the nature and scope of non-rational motivation. This was the linkage which Pareto sought to explore in *Mind and Society* (*Trattato di sociologia generale*, 1916–23, trans. 1963). Despite strained vocabulary and turgid prose, this ambitious attempt to construct a general framework of laws about behaviour became Pareto's most renowned work. Its investigation of the interaction between rational and non-rational conduct centred around a model involving a threefold categorization. We must distinguish between 'sentiments' (characteristics of the mind that are permanent but not directly observable), 'residues' (observable actions that relate to such sentiments and take the form of conduct which is, at least partly, non-rational) and 'derivations' (rhetorical structures which rationalize the residues). Pareto suggested that, though all these factors were constantly acting upon one another, sentiments were clearly the strongest of the three. He concluded that the chief element in an elite's retention of power was an ability to exploit derivations as a means of putting a rational veneer upon its authority. Thus he erected the framework for a doctrine of power and propagandist manipulation divorced from any consideration beyond that of oligarchical self-preservation.

In earlier times Pareto's assertions about the inevitability of elite domination would have seemed quite simply platitudinous. But in the twentieth century, so full of rhetoric about egalitarian democratic fulfilment, his ideas have had an altogether more abrasive effect.

Further reading

Other works include: *Fatti e Teorie* ('Facts and Theories', 1920); *Trasformazione della Democrazia* (1921). For an excellent selection and commentary, see S.E. Finer (ed.) *Vilfredo Pareto: Sociological Writings* (1966). See also: G.C. Homans and C.P. Curtis, *An Introduction to Pareto* (1934); T. Parsons, *The Structure of Social Action*, Vol. 1 (1968); J.H. Meisel (ed.) *Pareto and Mosca* (1965); R. Aron, *Main Currents in Sociological Thought*, Vol. 2 (1968); C. Wright Mills, *The Power Elite* (1956); Charles H. Powers, *Vilfredo Pareto* (1987).

MICHAEL BIDDISS

PARKER, Charles Christopher, Jr (Bird)

1920–55

US jazz alto saxophonist, composer

Charlie Parker embodied the popular stereotype of the jazz musician as an inspired, self-destructive genius. From a man whose personal and professional life was a chaos of narcotics, alcohol and abused personal relationships flowed an endless stream of inventive and passionate improvisation performed with astounding virtuosity. Whereas early jazz and swing had been multiracial and intimately linked with light-hearted entertainment, bebop, the music of Parker, was predominantly for black people, played by black people (at first), and it was serious. Although it grew out of swing, it deliberately broke with tradition, and this break was significant for black Americans.

Parker was a self-taught musician who, at the age of nineteen, was playing alto saxophone with the Jay McShann band. He soon dropped out and went to live in New York, taking on casual jobs and sitting in with the bands that played in the clubs of 52nd Street, where the new style of Parker, Dizzy Gillespie (trumpet), Thelonius Monk (piano) and Kenny Clarke (drums) was being worked out. Clarke was moving the accents from the first and third beats of the bar to the second and fourth. Gillespie and Parker were developing the melodic and harmonic aspects of the music, at first independently of each other.

Their music avoided the simple harmonies of earlier jazz, added chords to the sequences of the tunes they played, and filled out major and minor triads with the higher intervals. In their melodic improvisations they tended to make great use of these higher intervals, and of alterations to the standard intervals – the characteristic sound of Bird and Diz has lowered fifths and ninths, often accented at the end of a phrase on the second quaver of the first beat in the bar (the name 'bebop' is in imitation of this). Their phrases were not tailored to the conventional two- and four-bar lengths, and would cross the junctions between the sections of the song that they were playing, making it quite difficult for non-musicians listening to follow the solo. This obscurity was partly offset by the fact that Parker often chose either the chord sequence of *I Got Rhythm* or of the twelve-bar blues – naturally with added harmonies.

Slam Slam's Blues (1945) has Parker and Gillespie standing out from the other, more conventional, swing players for the rhythm, phrasing and harmonic structure of their solos. In 1943 Parker and Gillespie were in the Earl Hines and then the Billy Eckstine big bands, and in 1945 recorded together in sessions that have become classic. Parker's erratic behaviour led to a break with Gillespie (who rarely played with him after that), and **Miles Davis** joined the Parker quintet for a series of recordings for the Savoy and Dial labels.

Three types of Parker solo can be mentioned here: very fast quaver runs, spiced with triplets, syncopation and great variety of accent on *Ko Ko* (1945); blues such as the slowish *Parker's Mood* (1948) where rhythmic variety and melodic agility are combined with intense emotional expression; and ballads (*Embraceable You*, 1947) where Parker embroiders on the melody with flurries of semi- and demi-semiquavers through added passing chords.

Parker's health and constitution began to give way under the strain of heroin, alcohol and disordered living, and his usefulness as a musician suffered when he could not be counted on to turn up for engagements. He went through a number of marriages (the first at the age of fifteen), and was hospitalized. He recorded with strings (*Just Friends*, 1949), toured with various organizations and bands, and played in a justly famous concert in Toronto in 1953. He became more and more down and out, and finally died while watching television in the apartment of a friend.

Parker's unedifying life fuels the legend of the artist sacrificing himself to his art, and that of the black man oppressed by the American system. But the music he played is not a matter of legend. It laid the basis of the language of jazz improvisation for the next twenty years, turned jazz towards the cult of the solo improviser, and offered an example of supreme cultural achievement to two generations of black Americans.

Further reading

Parker's recordings have been reissued on LP records by Savoy, Spotlite, Verve and many other labels. Transcribed solos can be found in *Charlie Parker Omnibook* (1978). See: Robert Reisner, *Bird: The Legend of Charlie Parker* (1962); Ross Russell, *Bird Lives* (1972); Leonard Feather, *Inside Bebop* (1949, republished as *Inside Jazz*, 1977); C. Woideck, *Charlie Parker: His Music and Life* (1997); C. Woideck (ed.) *The Charlie Parker Companion: Six Decades of Commentary* (1998).

CHRISTOPHER WAGSTAFF

PARKMAN, Francis

1823–93

American historian

Born in Boston, Massachusetts, Francis Parkman was descended from a New England family of wealth and social standing. Even as a child, and more obviously as a student at Harvard during the early 1840s, Parkman showed a consuming interest in the geographical explorations made by the earliest American settlers. Throughout his youth he journeyed into areas of wilderness and in 1845 published accounts of his adventures.

By 1846, Parkman seems to have formed a clear plan of his life's work. In April he embarked on his 'Oregon Trail' from St Louis with the twofold aim of studying the Indians and improving his health, which had begun to deteriorate at Harvard. The first aim was successfully achieved: he became intimately acquainted with the conditions of life at the edges of European culture. But his health broke down completely, and during his convalescence he wrote the still popular *Oregon Trail* (1849).

In 1848 he began his *History of the Conspiracy of Pontiac*, the first volume of his monumental work depicting the struggle

between France and England for possession of the continent, eventually to be called *France and England in North America*. Labouring under the immense difficulties of nervous and physical disorders, Parkman completed the book three years later. After the death of his wife and son, he suffered a further nervous crisis in 1858. But in 1865 appeared *Pioneers of France in the New World*, a remarkable achievement of will and determination, which secured his reputation as a historian. Between 1867 and 1877 there followed *The Jesuits in North America, La Salle and the Discovery of the Great West* (1869), *The Old Régime in Canada* (1874) and *Count Frontenac and New France under Louis XIV* (1877). Fearing the approach of a final collapse, Parkman broke the chronological sequence to write its conclusion, which was published in 1884 as *Montcalm and Wolfe* (2 vols). In 1892 he completed the series with *A Half-Century of Conflict* (2 vols). Shortly afterwards he contracted pleurisy and died less than a year later.

It is as both a historian and as a literary artist that Parkman's lasting reputation has been established. As a historian, Parkman combines the subjectively interpretative approach of the nineteenth century with the modern Germanic devotion to precise and scrupulous examination of empirical evidence. His work not only charts the chronological progress of the Anglo-French struggle in America, but portrays too the landscapes in which this conflict was enacted and the psychology of its protagonists. Parkman's unique blending of history and geography, narrative and drama, sustains the dominant theme of his historical writings: the contest between two highly developed civilizations for control of an emerging continent of wilderness and savagery. His imagination is occupied in re-creating the challenge of geographical expansion so that his colonizers and frontiersmen embody the heroic virtues of self-reliance and endurance. Hence, Parkman's writing possesses a quality of grandeur as he celebrates the spirit of conquest.

While Parkman's episodic approach may now seem simplistic, his documentary researches were exhaustive, and he gathered together manuscript material which, in its field, has not been entirely superseded. His research also included a personal familiarity with the conditions and lifestyles of the early explorers. There is much that his work does not take into account, and it inevitably lacks the philosophical sophistication of recent historical writing. Nevertheless, Parkman does undertake some sort of comparison between the social and political organizations of the rival civilizations in order to suggest a fundamental reason for the final outcome.

It is no accident that Parkman responded imaginatively to embodiments of indomitable resolve, for his own task was achieved during a lifetime blighted by severe physical and nervous disorders. Yet the enormous strength of will required to continue his work is belied by the elegant clarity and urbane ease of his prose. At least one writer in the twentieth century has paid tribute to Parkman's literary qualities: Donald Davie's lengthy poem, *A Sequence for Francis Parkman* (1961), draws its inspiration from Parkman's prose and celebrates a man whose intense suffering and resolute determination never obscured his humanity.

Further reading

Collected editions of Parkman's work: *The Works of Francis Parkman* (20 vols, 1897–8) and *Francis Parkman's Works* (12 vols, 1901–3). Biographical studies include C.H. Farnham, *A Life of Francis Parkman* (1900), and H.D. Sedgwick, *Francis Parkman* (1904). Among more recent studies are: R.L. Gale, *Francis Parkman* (1973); D. Levin, *History as Romantic Art* (1959); O. Pease, *Parkman's History: The Historian as Literary Artist* (1953); M. Wade, *Francis Parkman: Heroic Historian* (1942); Charles Haight Farnham, *Life of Francis Parkman* (1982).

ANDREW SWARBRICK

PARSONS, Talcott

1902–79

US sociologist

Against the highly empiricist background of American sociology, Parsons stands out as an 'incurable theorist', to use his own self-characterization. After an undergraduate degree in biology and graduate studies in economics at the London School of Economics, he did a doctorate in sociology at Heidelberg. In 1927 he joined the Harvard economics department and four years later transferred to the newly formed sociology department at Harvard. He stayed there until his retirement in 1973 and served as Department Chairman from 1944 to 1956. A great deal of his influence comes from having taught more than a dozen of the best-known subsequent American sociologists, including Kingsley Davis, Marion Levy and Harold Garfinkel.

The central concern of Parson's first book, *The Structure of Social Action* (1937), is the problem of order – why society is not characterized by a Hobbesian war of all against all. He maintains that a satisfactory solution to this problem is possible only if men are seen as striving to achieve a shared system of ends and guided by common norms. The importance of a shared normative structure, he argues, was converged on by Alfred Marshall, **Pareto, Durkheim** and **Max Weber**. His analysis proved extremely influential, partly because it was the first major English-language exposition of Durkheim and Weber.

Parsons's subsequent work is remarkable for the wide range of substantive issues and theoretical topics covered. His interests have ranged from the Nazis to school classrooms to developing his own conceptions of power and influence. One of his more influential analyses tackles the place of professionals in modern society. It is unsatisfactory, he argues, to characterize businessmen as self-interested and professionals as altruistic, for they both play major roles in the same economy. Instead of seeing them in motivational terms, he argues for classifying them in terms of how they relate to others in their work. This he does in terms of a set of pattern-variables which are neutrality–affectivity, universalism–particularism, specificity–diffuseness and performance–quality. By this approach businessmen and professionals fit together easily, for both are doing the same type of activity in their occupational roles. Both relate to others neutrally (without emotion), universalistically (in terms of objective criteria), for specific purposes and in terms of the performance they expect of the other.

Parsons has developed his own variety of structural-functionalism which focuses on four functional dimensions or problems. As any system in order to survive has to solve four functional problems – adaptation, goal-attainment, integration and latency (pattern maintenance and tension management) – a system can be analysed in terms of these functional dimensions. For a society, the economy focuses on adaptation, the polity on goal-attainment, the stratification system on integration and socializing institutions like the family and school on latency. This classification also provides the basis of Parsons's human action schema. Cultural systems, personality systems and social systems varying in size from two-person groups to societies can all be analysed in terms of the functional dimensions. In his *Societies: Evolutionary and Comparative Perspectives* (1966) and *The System of Modern Societies* (1971) he combines the four functional dimensions with an evolutionary perspective. This provides a view of human history as the gradually evolving differentiation of subsystems of a society each focusing on a particular functional problem.

Many sociologists in the 1940s and 1950s related their research to his ideas and used concepts from his work, for he is the leading non-**Marxist** sociologist of his generation. In the 1960s, his view of society as based on normative consensus and geared to the solution of four functional problems came under increasing attack. Many argued his approach could not deal with change and conflict. Now this reaction is viewed as too simplistic and the ways of dealing with these topics in his framework are still being explored.

Further reading

Other works include: *The Social System* (1951); *Economy and Society*, with N. Smelser (1956);

Sociological Theory and Modern Society (1967); and *The American University*, with G. Platt (1973). Critical evaluations of his ideas can be found in H. Bershady, *Ideology and Social Knowledge* (1973); M. Black (ed.) *The Social Theories of Talcott Parsons* (1961); K. Menzies, *Talcott Parsons and the Social Image of Man* (1977); G. Rocher, *Talcott Parsons and American Sociology* (1975); Bryan S. Turner (ed.) *Parsons Reader* (1999); Uta Gerhardt, *Talcott Parsons: An Intellectual Biography* (2002).

K.S. MENZIES

PASK, Andrew Gordon Speedie
1928–96
English cybernetician and educator

If cybernetics is, like mathematics, a general discipline that has application and meaning in many other disciplines – as its originators insisted – then Gordon Pask was its multidisciplinary practitioner, whose interests and areas of exploration led him to work in a variety of fields. In essence Pask was a generalist, and (wearing his educationalist's hat) he produced an interpretation of learning styles to demonstrate this.

Pask's career had three strands. The most obvious, at least to those who met him, was the theatrical. To see him lecture, even to meet him in the street, was to experience performance. His wedding present to his wife, Elizabeth Poole, was a moribund theatre. He worked with the impresario and theatrical director Joan Littlewood, specially on **Cedric Price's** designs for a Fun Palace, and with a number of those associated with Littlewood. His interest in the theatre was expressed in lyrics he wrote, and in never-dimmed ambitions to produce musicals. However, his enduring reputation rests on his work as a teacher, and his contributions to cybernetics: the field that emerged in the late 1940s concerned with control and communication, specially involving the circularity introduced in error regulation by feedback and its concomitant, circular causality. Cybernetics was described in **Norbert Wiener's** eponymous book (1948) as 'communication and control in the animal and the machine', or, in the terms of the Josiah Macy Jr Foundation meetings on Cybernetics (1946–52) as concerned with 'circular causal and feedback mechanisms'.

Pask was a builder of machines. The actuality of the machine pervades his thought. His cybernetics began as it continued: with interaction. An early machine, *Musicolour* (built with his life-long business partner and collaborator, Robin McKinnon-Wood, in their independent research venture, System Research) was an active – rather than responsive – participant in the making of improvised music. Long before the term was devalued by the computer industry, Pask produced machines that interacted with their users in such a manner that something surprising, coming from neither machine nor user but through what each brought to the interaction, might happen. These machines were self-adaptive: from the early 1950s Pask made machines that could rewrite their data and/or program in response to the situations they faced.

Pask's method for introducing interaction became the 'conversation'. Few human activities are more interactive: an evening's conversation moves along unexpected and unpredictable trajectories in which new ideas/insights pop up as all contribute from their (different) positions. Conversation is also the means by which we reduce 'errors' between our understandings and those of others, asking for explanations and restatements, in order to make 'corrections'.

His initial use of the conversation was to test learning by students inhabiting the learning environments he experimented with, starting about 1970. He had been interested in the learning exhibited by cybernetic machines and their users, as demonstrated in his self-adaptive machines, and is commonly credited as the father of computer-aided learning (a field he came to abhor because of the superficial and crude trivialization it suffered). He soon realized that conversation implied consequences, in keeping with **von Foerster's** second-order cybernetics, but also already apparent in his own work. This

directed his work to the epistemological examination of learnables. He started with a mapping of the relationships between knowables ('Entailment Meshes'). Thence he developed a syntax for these meshes, extending into questions of learning – what may be learnt, individual difference in learning content (understanding) and style, ways of learning, and so on. In later life, he attempted to generalize this work, known as Conversation Theory, into a less temporarily limited Interaction of Actors Theory.

Pask was not interested in education as a mechanic. As a teacher, he lived his interest. There were two streams to his teaching. He supervised doctoral students at a number of universities around the world, in a way which was both challenging and supportive (his main positions were at Brunel University in the UK, Concordia University in Canada, Old Dominion University in the USA, and the University of Amsterdam in the Netherlands). A number of his students have distinguished themselves. These include: Ricardo Uribe and Paul Pangaro; in computing, Bernard Scott and Oeter Medina-Maartins; in social science Pablo Navarro, Jan-Gerrit Schuurman and Harrie van Haaster; and, in cybernetics, Ranulph Glanville. He had a profound and lasting influence on Nicholas Negroponte and the Architecture Machine Group at MIT, which later became the original Media Lab.

Pask also had a leaning for the arts: for instance, he created a 'Colloquy of Mobiles' that interacted with each other and visitors to the Cybernetic Serendipity Exhibition in London in 1968. He lectured in art schools. But most of all he had a long-term relationship with the Architectural Association School (London) from the mid-1960s to his death, where he explored his interest in the wider meaning of architecture and influenced architects from contemporaries such as Price and the **Archigram** group, through doctoral students to generations of architects deeply touched by his insights, person and interpretation of cybernetics in architecture, of whom the most immediate include John

Hamilton Frazer, Ysak Haytman and Stephen Gage.

His work as the founder of what became educational technology was recognized when he was appointed professor in that subject at the inception of the Open University. His life and achievements were in all respects singular. He held the only DSc from Downing College Cambridge. He was a real world engineer who found himself surprised that his discoveries invited him to explore epistemology.

The third, and by twenty years the youngest, son of Percy and Mary Pask, he was a sickly child who was not expected to survive. During his long and lonely childhood, often in a sick bed, he invented his friends and a whole world for them to inhabit, with which he could converse and explore. These friends stayed with him all his life, and were the reason he always left small piles of food on the side of his plate 'for the fairies'.

Further reading

See Gordon Pask, *An Approach to Cybernetics* (1961); Gordon Pask and Susan Cullan, *Microman: Computers and the Evolution of Consciousness* (1982).

RANULPH GLANVILLE

PASOLINI, Pier Paolo

1922–75

Italian filmmaker, writer

The brutal murder of Pier Paolo Pasolini on a piece of waste ground on the outskirts of Rome on 2 November 1975 brought to a hideous end the most spectacular artistic career in Italy since the Second World War. Known outside Italy mainly as a filmmaker, Pasolini was also a novelist, poet, essayist and journalist and a public figure of some notoriety. His early novels – *Ragazzi di vita* (1955) and *Una vita violenta* (1959) – established him as a linguistic innovator. His poetry – *Le ceneri di Gramsci* (1957), *La religione del mio tempo* (1961) – managed to combine public content with a highly distinctive speaking voice, in sharp contrast to the prevailing poetic tradition

in which a largely private content was expressed from a somewhat impersonal stance.

He began his film career as a scriptwriter for a number of generally undistinguished films about the Roman underworld. The first film he directed himself, *Accattone* (1961), also had an underworld and subproletarian setting (as indeed do his novels), but its treatment was very remote from the kind of 'low-life picturesque' favoured by his contemporaries. With *The Gospel According to Matthew* (1964) he took a further step away from the debased heritage of neo-realism, but laid himself open to a different misconstruction – this time as 'Catholic-Marxist'. In fact he was neither (though he was both religious and politically left-wing) and the appellation only makes sense to the extent that Catholicism and **Marxism** are the two great rival orthodoxies in Italy whose influence it is impossible to escape. Pasolini, however, was a heretic in relation to both, constantly and self-consciously at odds with every form of either Marxist or Catholic orthodoxy. His political heterodoxy was most clearly revealed in 1968, when he published a poem 'Dear Students, I Hate You', which was instantly read as an attack on student radicalism and a defence of the riot police. It re-emerged around 1973 when he took up position against the campaign to liberalize the abortion law. It was also in the course of this debate that Pasolini 'came out' on the question of his own homosexuality. Meanwhile, his religiosity became increasingly pagan. While never losing his respect for what he called the '*sacrale*' (sacredness), he came to locate this sacredness further and further away from the world of organized religion, particularly as organized by the Vatican and Christian Democracy. What he did retain, however, was a sentimental attachment to the religion of the poor, to be defended against lay intellectuals and prelates alike.

Pasolini's later films, beginning with *Oedipus Rex* (1967), are distinguished by an overt fascination with primitivism and by an underlying structure through which he sets out to affirm values antithetical to those of modern capitalist society. The values he opposes are those of technology, capitalism, patriarchy, heterosexual monogamy, conformity and repression. Against those negative but all too real features of the modern world Pasolini sets up various imaginary alternatives. Most of his films are set in the past – in the Middle Ages or in prehistory. When set in the present – as with *Theorem* (1968) or *Salò* (1975) – they show bourgeois society as a network of corruption and repression from which only a few innocents can escape. In all the films there is a search for lost innocence, which is always regressive, coupled with a recognition that recovery of this innocence is difficult if not impossible. Knowledge always comes too late, and takes the form of a knowledge of being already guilty.

Stylistically, these films are chiefly remarkable for the role they ascribe to the image. Whereas most films consist of a series of shots whose meaning is established either through contrast or continuity with other shots composing the narrative, in Pasolini's films narrative continuity is weak and each shot stands on its own, evocative of a meaning which is not always decipherable in narrative terms. The result is to enhance the imaginary character of the films, since not only is the intellectual content predicated on a negation of contemporary reality, but the presentation of it is hallucinatory and dream-like. Whereas in his essays Pasolini is explicit in his denunciation of the modern world, but unable to envisage any realistic alternative, the films do offer an alternative – but only to the extent that the world they portray is avowedly imaginary. That this imaginary journey might bring one closer to a psychic 'real' that ordinary reality denies is a dialectical possibility not to be dismissed.

Further reading

Other works include: *Uccellacci e uccelli* (1966); *The Decameron* (1970); *The Arabian Nights* (1974). Books include: a volume of essays, *Empirismo eretico* (1972); a collection of journalism, *Scritti corsari* (1975); and his last work *La Divina Mimesi* (1975). See: Oswald Stack, *Pasolini on Pasolini* (1969); P. Willemen (ed.) *Pier Paolo Pasolini* (1977); Enzo Siciliano, *Vita di Pasolini* (1978); Naomi Greene, *Pier Paolo Pasolini: Cinema as Heresy* (1990); Patrick Rumble and Bart Testa (eds) *Pier Paolo Pasolini: Contemporary Perspectives* (1995); Robert S.C. Gordon, *Pasolini: Forms of Subjectivity* (1996).

GEOFFREY NOWELL-SMITH

PASTERNAK, Boris Leonidovich
1890–1960
Russian poet and novelist

Boris Pasternak grew up in a highly cultivated Moscow environment; his father Leonid was an important painter and his mother a former concert pianist. Much influenced by **Scriabin**, Pasternak at first wanted to become a composer; it was only in 1912, after some months as a philosophy student in Germany, that he committed himself to poetry. After the Revolution he remained in Russia, and in 1922 published his best-known book of poems, *My Sister Life* (*Sestra moya – zhizn*, 1922). This was followed soon afterwards by *Themes and Variations* (*Temy i variatsii*, 1923). In the 1920s Pasternak occupied a somewhat isolated position in the Soviet literary world; he was a poet of great prestige, but many regarded him as at best a lukewarm friend to the new regime. Various writings of this period show his attempt to come to terms with the Revolution, both long poems such as *Lofty Malady* (*Vysokaya bolezn*, 1924) and *Lieutenant Schmidt* (1926–7) and the volume of lyric poetry *Second Birth* (*Vtoroe rozhdenie*, 1932), which also reflects the break-up of his first marriage and his love for the woman who was to become his second wife.

From early on Pasternak had also been writing prose and he came to place more and more emphasis on it as a means of doing justice to his own experience and that of his country. In 1931 he published the autobiographical *Safe Conduct* (*Okhrannaya gramota*) and in the 1930s he began work on his novel

Dr Zhivago. This was the great work of his last two decades, though he also produced several remarkable sequences of verse and a large number of memorable translations, in particular of Shakespeare. *Dr Zhivago* was rejected by the journal *Novy Mir* in 1956, but at the end of the following year it was published in Italy and in 1958 Pasternak was awarded the Nobel Prize for Literature. This gave rise to a violent campaign of denunciation in the Soviet Union; Pasternak was expelled from the Writers' Union and forced to decline the prize in order to remain in his native country. Greatly shaken by this experience, he died near Moscow in 1960.

For most non-Russian readers, Pasternak is above all the author of *Dr Zhivago*, and this is as he would have wanted it. For many Russian readers, however, his finest work is to be found in his early collections, particularly *My Sister Life*. In the pre-Revolutionary period he had been associated with the Futurist movement and his early poems show a verbal inventiveness (and sometimes obscurity) which matches that of Mayakovsky. But Pasternak was not interested in verbal experiment for its own sake. His conception of poetry was essentially expressive; in his words, 'focused upon a reality that has been displaced by feeling, art is a record of this displacement'. In his poems figures of speech, sound orchestration and rhythm all serve to render the vivid feeling of life. One of the dominant themes is renewal or transfiguration, often conveyed through images of weather, wind, rain and storm. The starting point is personal experience – *My Sister Life* is constructed round a love affair – but Pasternak characteristically brings together the great and the small, the universe and the detail. He later interpreted the excited consciousness of *My Sister Life* as reflecting the heightened vitality of the year of revolutions, though it is worth noting that the poems which compose it were written between February and October 1917.

My Sister Life brought Pasternak an outstanding reputation, but he later turned against the 'frills and fancies' of his early

verse, aiming for what he once described as an 'unheard-of simplicity'. This is opposed rather to official jargon than to obscure poetry; what he was interested in was a realistic art that would 'contain' the world (**Chekhov** and **Chopin** were models), and this did not necessarily involve writing poems of banal accessibility. Even so, his late poems are certainly easier for the average reader. At their best (and above all in the poems which make up the final chapter of *Dr Zhivago*) they show the same concern for life as the early work, together with an increased emphasis on ethical and historical questions. All of this is well seen in one of Pasternak's most famous poems, 'Hamlet'. At times, however, and particularly in his last collection *When the Weather Clears* (*Kogda razgulyaetsa*, 1956–9), there is something of a decline into banality.

Dr Zhivago (trans. Max Hayward and Manya Harari, 1958), although hailed by some Western reviewers as a novel in the **Tolstoyan** tradition, is very much a poet's novel, a highly personal view of the destiny of modern Russia as experienced by a young doctor-poet to whom Pasternak attributes some of his own best poems. Many of the themes of the early collections are present in the novel, together with their author's intense awareness of the life of the world. The book is permeated by a symbolism which is accentuated by the poems of the final chapter; it expresses Pasternak's faith in traditional ethical and religious values and his hope for a future in which the best features of the Revolution (seen here largely in negative terms) and of the old intellectual tradition would be reconciled. One may feel that the novelist is too close to his hero and does not always avoid a certain sentimental idealizing, but it can hardly be denied that *Dr Zhivago* is a major novel of the last century. At the same time, it should not be allowed to overshadow the marvellous achievement of the early poems.

Further reading

Other works, including *Dr Zhivago*, are in the three-volume Russian edition by G.P. Struve and

B.A. Filippov (1961). Other translations include: *Fifty Poems* (trans. Lydia Pasternak Slater, 1963); *Poems* (trans. E.M. Kayden, 1959); *The Poetry of Boris Pasternak* (trans. G. Reavey, 1959); *Collected Prose*, ed. C. Barnes (1977). On Pasternak see: H. Gifford, *Pasternak* (1977); D. Davie and A. Livingstone (eds) *Pasternak: Modern Judgments* (1969); V. Erlich (ed.) *Pasternak: A Collection of Critical Essays* (1978); Christopher Barnes, *Boris Pasternak: A Literary Biography* (2 vols, 1989–2004).

PETER FRANCE

PASTEUR, Louis

1822–95

French chemist and microbiologist

As one of the greatest scientists of the nineteenth century Pasteur provides a striking example of social promotion from provincial obscurity to the rank of a national hero on the basis of a career in scientific research. The son of a tanner from the Franche-Comté region of France, Louis was born in Dole but spent most of his young life in nearby Arbois. In 1838 his father was persuaded to send him to M. Barbet's school in Paris with the intention that he should go on to the École Normale. Unfortunately the young Pasteur did not settle and was returned to Arbois. Although he continued his education at Arbois and Besançon he was forced eventually to return to M. Barbet's school before he passed to the École Normale. His three years there as a student (1843–6) and two as *préparateur* in chemistry were followed by two provincial professorships in chemistry, first at Strasbourg (1849–52), then at Lille (1854–7), where he was also dean of the faculty of sciences. Despite the undoubted success of his work in Lille University, when the call came to return to the École Normale he accepted. Apart from the seven years he spent as Professor of Chemistry at the Sorbonne Pasteur remained at the École Normale until he became director of the new Institut Pasteur in 1888.

In his life Pasteur exemplified the industrious, upright and independent qualities which marked his family. An admirer of authority and leadership, his political inclinations were towards the Second Empire of Louis Napoleon. He was intensely patriotic and so keenly did he feel the defeat of France in 1871 that he returned the honorary degree conferred on him by the University of Bonn, requesting that his name be effaced from the archives of the medical faculty. It was during the Franco-Prussian War that Pasteur took up the subject of brewing with the intention of laying the foundation for an improved French product that would rival and supersede the beers of Germany so popular in Paris cafés.

Like Galileo, Pasteur was combative and self-confident. Despite the pleading of his elders he could never refrain from responding to criticism, and opponents were demolished without mercy. One such victim challenged him to a duel. Another, the famous **Robert Koch**, was forced to concede ground. If Pasteur's claims were questioned he would issue a challenge, as he did to the Turin Veterinary School over the effectiveness of his anthrax vaccine, to Charles Bastian over spontaneous generation, and to Justus von Liebig on acetic acid fermentation. Added to his qualities as debater and experimentalist Pasteur was an excellent organizer and he attracted support for his researches which by French standards was exceptional. For the Pasteur Institut alone two million francs were collected.

Pasteur first made his reputation in the field of crystallography. It was known that substances with different crystal forms affected polarized light differently. Some rotated the plane of polarization to the right, others to the left, and yet others were optically inactive. Against this general rule two substances which had the same chemical composition and allegedly the same crystalline form – tartaric acid and paratartaric or racemic acid – affected light differently. The former rotated the plane of polarization to the right while the latter was optically inactive. Pasteur studied the tartrates and paratartrates and revealed the presence of facets on certain corners of the crystals which rendered them asymmetric and hemihedral. All the crystals of the tartrates showed the same hemihedra, but those of the paratartrates were either symmetrical or, as in the sodium-ammonium salt, of two kinds – right-handed and left-handed hemihedra. Their separate solutions affected light differently, one rotating the plane of polarization to the right, the other to the left. Together, as in the paratartrate, the solution was optically inactive. Pasteur advanced his law of hemihedral correlation with much boldness; only later under the pressure of exceptions did he place more emphasis upon the relation between optical activity and molecular structure rather than with crystal structure.

This very simple and striking work constituted a major foundation to the growing subject of stereochemistry. To Pasteur it seemed rather to open a route to the experimental study of another great problem – that of life itself – for he was convinced that all optically active organic compounds were the products of living organisms and could not be synthesized in the laboratory. Only in living things were the requisite asymmetric forces at work which would yield such asymmetric molecules. Needless to say, his own attempts to stimulate such forces in the laboratory were fruitless.

Pasteur's move to the industrial town of Lille brought him into contact with the manufacturers of alcohol from beetroot by fermentation. Another product of fermentation, amyl alcohol, which must have been available in the town, was of special interest to Pasteur because of its optical activity. Clearly for Pasteur its synthesis required the presence of living organisms, and since it was a product of fermentation it was natural that Pasteur should side with those who claimed that fermentation was a vital process rather than a mere chemical process as the chemists Liebig and Berzelius maintained. Pasteur realized that fermentation was no simple chemical disintegration but a complex process in which a variety of products resulted. In addition to alcohol these included glycerin, succinic acid, amyl alcohol and lactic acid. Just as his predecessors had shown the invariable presence of yeast wherever alcoholic fermentation occurred so Pasteur demonstrated the presence of a fine grey deposit of another yeast-like substance where lactic fermentation took place.

From these and succeeding studies Pasteur was able to correlate a whole range of different fermentations with different micro-organisms. The simple chemical theory was not designed to cope with such diversity. Moreover it required the presence of organic nitrogenous matter in the process of disintegration, for this was held to be the agent of fermentation. In 1858 Pasteur succeeded in bringing about fermentation in the absence of organic nitrogen, thus destroying the central feature of the chemical theory. He concluded that the different fermentations were due to the activity of different micro-organisms. Their germs were present in ordinary air and water; they contaminated the surfaces of vessels, corks, hands, etc. Depending upon the environment, one or another of these micro-organisms would reproduce in the medium – grape juice, malt, beet sugar – bringing about its particular type of fermentation. Some, like the butyric ferment, could only live in the absence of oxygen; others, like yeast, could exist with or without oxygen; yet others, like the *Mycoderma asceti*, required oxygen for its fermentation to yield vinegar.

In 1860 a prize was offered for experiments on the subject of spontaneous generation. Pasteur decided to compete. All his experiments, some very ingenious, were designed to show that such generation of living organisms only occurs in a sterile organic medium if it becomes contaminated with microscopic germs from outside. As in the study of fermentation, so in this study he constructed his programme upon his faith in the existence of microscopic germs. Believing that their distribution would vary according to location and altitude he broke and resealed a series of flasks containing a sterile medium at his laboratory and in the vaults of the Observatory, then at the foot of the Jura and at 2,000 metres on the Mer de Glace. Only one of the twenty flasks at 2,000 metres showed microbial growth. In 1862 Pasteur was awarded the prize.

Meanwhile, Felix Pouchet, whose experiments with spontaneous generation of hay infusions had caused the revival of interest in the subject, decided to expose such infusions at an even greater height than Pasteur. With Nicolas Jolet and Charles Musset he exposed eight flasks at 3,000 metres in the Pyrenees, all of which showed spontaneous generation. In 1864 the Académie set up a commission to decide between Pasteur and Pouchet. In the event Pouchet withdrew from the contest, leaving the field to Pasteur. Thirteen years later Charles Bastian also decided not to repeat his experiments on spontaneous generation before the commission set up to judge between him and Pasteur. Both these opponents of Pasteur had demonstrated spontaneous generation in sterile conditions because, unknown to them, the hay infusions they employed contained bacterial spores resistant to boiling. Had they persisted in their challenge the two commissions would have been forced to accept their results.

The implications of the germ theory of fermentation for surgery were appreciated by **Joseph Lister** whose introduction of antisepsis was made in the 1860s. The suggestion that contagious diseases were, like fermentation, due to microbes gained support only slowly. In his first study of animal diseases – the *pébrine* and *flacherie* of silkworms – Pasteur proved curiously resistant to the microbial or germ theory. By 1867 his attitude had changed. He went on to contribute to the microbiology of anthrax, fowl cholera, swine erysipelas, and rabies. His greatest achievement was to show that weakened or 'attenuated' forms of these diseases could be produced by serial culture which, like Jenner's cowpox vaccinations, rarely caused the disease, but conferred resistance to the virulent strain, thus protecting or immunizing the host. Pasteur gave dramatic demonstration of the effectiveness of his vaccines in the case of anthrax at Pouilly-le-Fort in 1881 and in the case of rabies when he vaccinated Joseph Meister in 1885. In the ensuing decade some

20,000 people bitten by rabid animals were given the vaccine and less than 0.5 per cent died. These achievements established the germ theory decisively in medicine as the basis for treatment of contagious diseases.

It had required three attempts before Pasteur was elected to the mineralogy section of the Académie in 1862, six years after the Royal Society had awarded him the Rumford Medal. In the 1880s honours were heaped upon him. His death was a national event marked by a state funeral at Notre Dame.

Further reading

All Pasteur's publications and a large part of his correspondence have been published in *Oeuvres de Pasteur* (7 vols, 1922–39) and *Correspondance* (4 vols, 1940–51). See René Vallery-Radot, *The Life of Pasteur* (trans. 1928), although the treatment of his later scientific career is hagiographic; and R. Dubois, *Louis Pasteur* (1986). The best scientific rather than historical analysis of Pasteur's work is Emile Duclaux, *Pasteur: The History of a Mind* (trans. 1920).

ROBERT OLBY

PATER, Walter Horatio

1839–94

English writer

Walter Pater was born in Stepney, London. His father was a surgeon in a predominantly slumland area. After his death in 1842 the family moved to Enfield. In 1853 Walter went to King's School, Canterbury, and in 1858 entered Queen's College, Oxford, as an exhibitioner in classics. He attended **Matthew Arnold's** lectures and received private tuition from the influential classicist **Benjamin Jowett**. His earliest interests had been poetry and religion, and as a boy he had determined to become a priest. At Oxford, however, he became sceptical of church dogma and retained only an aesthetic interest in the liturgy. Amidst a general atmosphere of theological uncertainty he turned increasingly to painting and literature as objects of spiritual devotion. In part this reflects an interest in Hegelian philosophy and Arnold's concept of culture, and in part a temperamental predisposition to satisfy the desires of a reclusive and intuitive sensibility. Both Arnold's 'Hellenism' and the Oxford Hegelians had seen a conscious certainty of the 'self' as attainable through an intense concentration on one's own impressions, in response to the disruptive flux scientific thought had made an apparently dangerous fact of existence. Such a dedication to the imagination and sensibility was, furthermore, a healthy balancing factor against the unduly pragmatic and provincial cast of Victorian morality. With these abstract interests Pater combined a quite radical interest in modern French authors like Gautier, **Flaubert** and **Baudelaire**, a passion for Renaissance painting and a rather obsessive concern with mortality.

In 1864 Pater was elected a fellow of Brasenose College, Oxford, and quickly developed a close friendship with a pupil, C.L. Shadwell, with whom he travelled in Italy in 1865. Pater was suspected of being a homosexual throughout his adult life, but although his name was twice mentioned during Oscar **Wilde's** trial in 1895, no firm proof of his sexual tendencies was ever discovered. His other friends at Oxford included the 'scandalous' Simeon Solomon, a painter later convicted for his homosexuality, and the poet **Swinburne**. During the late 1860s Pater became something of a cult figure among undergraduates for his supposedly immoral and 'pagan' opinions and at this time published a number of articles including important pieces on Coleridge and Winckelmann. In both these men Pater found sympathetic figures, dedicated to the pursuit of the highest aesthetic experience and also both clergy *manqués*. It was in 1873, however, that he first attained widespread notoriety with the publication of his *Studies in the History of the Renaissance*. This was a collection of not especially scholarly essays on, among others, Pico della Mirandola, Du Bellay and Leonardo da Vinci. In the latter's *Mona Lisa* Pater finds the mysteries of history in a single image.

'The picture summed up a thousand experiences ... and ... all modes of thought and life.' In his essay on Botticelli he rediscovered a great Italian painter. It was in Pater's 'Conclusion' to the *Renaissance* that his ideas were fully expressed. Each individual mind is a 'narrow chamber' receiving fleeting impressions and its main activity must be to attain sharp and eager observation. 'To burn always with this gem-like flame, to maintain this ecstasy, is success in life. Failure is to form habits; for habit is relative to a stereotyped world.' Pater renounced the claims of abstract philosophy or fixed morality and thereby shocked the orthodox opinions of most of his academic colleagues.

> Of this wisdom, the poetic passion, the desire of beauty, the love of art for art's sake has most; for art comes to you professing frankly to give nothing but the highest quality to your moments as they pass, and simply for those moments' sake.

This almost existential sense of passing instants of awareness was seen as a direct threat to notions of an after-life posited in an idealized future and perhaps more dangerously, as an exhortation to discover an excess of natural and not-so-natural physical pleasures. On more than one occasion the Bishop of Oxford used Pater's text to warn his congregation of the dangers of the new pagan sensibility arising in an age of uncertainty.

Pater published nothing more, in fact, until 1885 when his imaginary portrait of *Marius the Epicurean* appeared, telling the story of a Roman in the times of Marcus Aurelius who moves from paganism to Christianity. When Flavian, Marius's early friend, is killed off by disease and Cornelius, the Christian, wins his affection, Pater symbolically recounts his gradual withdrawal to his desire as a young man to find a more substantial philosophy than that he actually propounded in the *Renaissance*.

After the publication of *Appreciations* in 1889 Pater became a national celebrity and won the admiration of men like Wilde, Lionel Johnson, Arthur Symons and **Aubrey**

Beardsley. He was flattered by the attention of these rising stars but embarrassed by his reputation as a sort of demonic and anglicized Baudelaire. (He had repressed the 'Conclusion' in the second edition of the *Renaissance* to avoid further accusations of being a corrupter of youth.) As a close examination of his writings on art, literature, history and ideas shows, the reduction of his thought to a purely 'sensationalist' bias is inaccurate and distorts his full idea of 'style' which he presented in an essay of the same title in 1888. In this piece he asserts that it is finally the matter that determines whether a work of art is of significance or otherwise and not merely the form. Thus 'true and noble' ideas are the hallmarks of the great geniuses like Dante and Goethe. The artist must search for concrete expression of ideas which further the cause of peace and humanity as well as startling the mind to heightened apprehensions of beauty in the present. In his essay on Wordsworth, Pater declared, 'That the end of life is not action but contemplation – being as distinct from *doing* – a certain disposition of the mind: is, in some shape or other, the principle of all the higher morality.'

Pater's thought stands somewhere between Arnold's, which emphasizes the need for strict canons of taste and ascertainable standards in art, and Wilde's, which largely saw the artist's and critic's task as presenting subjective impressions only. Pater touches on all the vexing intellectual issues that concerned the later Victorians and is alert to subtleties of culture and morality as well as to those of his own passing appetites and perceptions. It is his prose style which has perhaps withstood best the test of time, fittingly, with its beautifully wrought images and cadences and its capacity to inspire the closest scrutiny of the individual work. This, naturally, has tended to place him firmly in the camp of the aesthetes and decadents and has obscured the real complexity of his outlook and personality.

Further reading

See: A. Ward, *The Idea in Nature* (1966); Iain Fletcher, *Walter Pater* (1971); S. Wright, *A Bibliography of the Writings of W. Pater* (1975); M. Levey, *The Case of Walter Pater* (1978); *W. Pater: The Critical Heritage*, ed. R.M. Seiler (1980); and R.H. Seiler, *Walter Pater* (1987).

RICHARD HUMPHREYS

PAVLOV, Ivan Petrovich
1849–1936
Russian physiologist

As the eldest of the ten children of the family of Pyotr Dmitrievich, a member of the lowest priesthood in the provincial town of Ryazan, Pavlov knew poverty and unremitting toil. Following in his father's footsteps he entered the theological seminary in Ryazan where contact with scientific and philosophical literature kindled in him an enthusiasm for science. George Lewes's *The Physiology of Everyday Life* (Russian translation 1861) and I.M. Sechenov's *Refleksy golovonogo mozga* (1863) left a deep impression upon him. These authors who expounded the empiricist stance and experimental method in physiology, and championed mechanism and objectives as against vitalism and subjectivism, found a ready disciple in Pavlov. The popular writings of the radical intellectual, Dmitri Pisarev – his conviction of the progressive character of natural science – and especially his enthusiastic account of **Darwin** also influenced the young Pavlov.

Although no revolutionary activist Pavlov had hopes for the ameliorating impact of science upon society. Leaving the Ryazan seminary before completion of his studies he enrolled in the natural science section of the faculty of physics and mathematics at St Petersburg University. By 1874 he had made physiology his major subject. The next year M.I. Afanasiev and he were awarded a gold medal for their study of the enervation of the pancreas. Physiology was but a young science in Pavlov's student days; those who had fought for its status as an experimental science belonged to the nineteenth century. Russia, though considered backward in relation to other European countries, had a galaxy of outstanding scientists in St Petersburg, the physiologists I.M. Sechenov and E.F. Cyon, the clinician S.P. Botkin, and the chemists **Mendeleyev** and Butlerov. Sechenov had founded Russia's first school of physiology at St Petersburg before he resigned his post there in 1870. In 1890 Pavlov wisely chose to stay in St Petersburg and accept the Chair of Pharmacology offered him by the Military-Medical Academy rather than go to the new University of Tomsk in Siberia. He remained in or near St Petersburg for the rest of his life.

Pavlov's researches can be divided into three phases: his study of blood circulation between 1874 and 1888, his research into the physiology of digestion from 1879 to 1902 for which he was awarded the Nobel Prize in Physiology and Medicine in 1904, and his investigations into the conditioned reflex and higher nervous activity from 1902 to the end of his life. All this work was marked by a conscious concern over method. When he moved on to the higher mental processes, thus entering the field of psychology and psychiatry, he remained true to his physiological upbringing and relied upon the objective methods of that science. Like a later generation of behaviourists in America, Pavlov described in his Nobel lecture how he and his co-workers tried to discipline their thought and speech 'in order to completely ignore the mental state of the animal'. Unlike the behaviourists, however, they 'desired to remain physiologists instead of becoming psychologists'. All three phases of Pavlov's work were also marked by recognition of the leading part played by the central nervous system in all physiological processes. This was Botkin's doctrine of 'nervism'. It was a recognition of the integration of physiological processes by the centripetal nerves and of the action of the *whole* organism in relation to its surrounding environment. This relation was subtle and adaptive, and to investigate it successfully called for great care in surgical treatment so that the animal remained healthy and normal. Both in his studies of physiological and of psychical secretion he developed chronic as opposed to acute surgical treatment which left the animal functioning normally and with a reasonable life expectancy. Some of the greatest achievements of nineteenth-century physiology were in the field of digestion. Beginning with the studies of an open-stomach wound described by William Beaumont in 1833, physiologists used surgery to produce a duct or 'fistula' from the digestive glands to the exterior. Glandular secretion could then be studied. Unfortunately such fistulas tended to close up, or the normal pattern of secretion disappeared; often the animal died soon after the operation. After a period of study under Rudolf Heidenhain, hitherto the most successful practitioner of the fistula, Pavlov and his co-workers overcame these problems by modifications of technique and skilful surgery. Pavlov described these problems and his solutions to them in his famous *Lectures on the Work of the Principal Digestive Glands* (*Lektsii o rabote glavnukh pishchevaritelnykn zhelez*), publication of which in 1897 brought their author international recognition.

Pavlov's studies of the digestive glands had impressed him with the remarkable powers of adaptation of the organism to changes in its diet. On a carbohydrate diet the intestinal digestive juices were weak in proteolytic enzymes but strong in such enzymes for a protein-rich diet. Likewise, a dry diet stimulated a copious secretion of saliva, a moist diet only a slight secretion. Also striking was the power of the stomach to start secretion after the animal had been 'sham-fed', i.e. food from the mouth was diverted by surgical modification from the stomach. Evidently it was not the direct contact with food that caused gastric secretion but a more remote 'signalling' system. Likewise salivary secretion was stimulated by the sight or smell of food before the food made contact with the lining of the mouth. Pavlov referred to this production as 'appetite juice' or 'psychical secretion'. In his address to the International Congress of Medicine in Madrid in 1903 Pavlov recalled how he and his co-workers 'had honestly endeavoured to explain our results by fancying the subjective condition of the animal. But nothing came of it except unsuccessful controversies.' Rejecting subjective explanations, Pavlov turned instead to the physiological theory of the reflex. The result, he told his audience, was the opening of 'a second immense part of the physiology of the nervous system'. The first part had concerned the relations within the organism, the second concerned its relations with the surrounding world.

In that there was a definite stimulus or signal and a response, psychic secretion did not differ from physiological secretion. The difference lay in the distance of the stimulus and the 'unessential' even accidental property of the stimulus. In a physiological reflex the property of the stimulus was 'essential', i.e. intimately connected with the physiological role of the glandular secretion. Furthermore, he noted a striking contrast between the constancy or *unconditioned* nature of physiological secretion and the inconstancy and apparent capriciousness of psychic secretion. The latter he therefore called a *conditioned* reflex. Its performance was conditional upon its association with the stimulus to the unconditioned reflex. The more frequently this association was made the stronger the conditioned reflex became. It was in his Madrid lecture that Pavlov described his efforts to discover the laws governing conditioned reflexes based upon the experiments on the dog carried out by his co-worker, F. Tolochinov. To the English-speaking world he gave a more developed version of the subject in his **Thomas Huxley lecture** in London in 1906. Not until the translation of his *Lectures on Conditioned Reflexes* in 1929 by his American co-worker, W. Horsley Gantt, however, did the riches of the Pavlovian experimental programme become fully appreciated in the Western world.

In the first phase of these studies Pavlov had used 'natural' conditioned reflexes – those formed by the 'natural association' between, for example, the sight of food and eating it. Later work concentrated on 'unnatural' conditioned reflexes, such as the sound of a bell before presenting food. Such reflexes

could be rendered exact, were easily controlled and varied, and they opened up a vast field for research. Both types of conditioned reflex showed law-like behaviour. Repeated without the unconditioned stimulus – e.g. food – the conditioned stimulus evoked progressively less response until it was completely extinguished. Left unstimulated for a few hours the animal's conditioned response was spontaneously restored. Restoration was also achieved by presentation of the conditioned stimulus with the unconditioned stimulus. Such a procedure could be repeated to reinforce it, but coupling the unconditioned stimulus with another signal inhibited the original conditioned response. It was the temporary nature of these reflexes which allowed the organism to be delicately adapted to its changing environment.

Further studies showed that the power to make conditioned reflexes was associated with the cerebral hemispheres, and stimuli could only be effective if the centre in the cerebral cortex to which the sense organ in question was connected remained intact. Pavlov looked upon these centres and their associated sense organs as 'analysers'. They acted as a signalling system since they gave the animal signals for its needs. The number of potentially significant signals for food were legion, but with repeated presentation of a given stimulus with food the conditioning became more narrowly limited to this signal. This was possible because the analysers decomposed the mass of signals from the animal's surroundings. In 1932 Pavlov suggested that in addition to this first signal system there was in man a second signal system which generalized and analysed the multitude of signals from the first system. The most important signals for this second system were those from the kinaesthetic stimulations of the speech organs; its functions were abstraction and speech. It marked 'the very last attainment in the evolutionary process'.

In the earlier phase of his study of conditioned reflexes Pavlov was distinctly hostile to psychologists. When he became familiar with the work of Thorndike and later with those of the early behaviourists he modified his position, but he criticized E.R. Guthrie and K. Lashley. To the school of Gestalt psychology he was vehemently opposed. Köhler especially he viewed as a serious threat to objective research, and in one of his 'Wednesday' meetings he declared 'We are at war with him. This is a serious struggle against psychologists.' Pavlov was not a crude materialist but he believed in the need for objective methods and denigrated what he considered were the subjective methods of psychology. Yet he looked forward to a time when 'the physiological and the psychological, the objective and the subjective will really merge, when the painful contradiction between our mind and our body ... will either *actually* be solved or [will] disappear in a natural way'.

The theory of the conditioned reflex had a considerable impact upon psychology. In the nineteenth century the reflex had been a prominent element in **Herbert Spencer's** psychology and it was the dominant element in I.M. Sechenov's treatment of higher mental processes, but it was the incorporation of the *conditioned* reflex into behaviourist literature around 1915 that introduced it to the mainstream of twentieth-century psychology. Many of the numerous instincts attributed to animals in the literature of comparative psychology were then banished and their place taken by conditioned reflexes. Shorn of the special surgical difficulties associated with Pavlov's fistula technique, conditioning experiments became a major feature of behaviourist research.

Further reading

The best collection of extracts from Pavlov's writing is *I.P. Pavlov: Selected Works*, ed. K.S. Koshtoyants, trans. from Russian by S. Belsky (1955); his best-known work is the *Lectures on Conditioned Reflexes* (2 vols, 1928 and 1941). There are many biographies, the most readily available of which is E.A. Asratyan, *Ivan Petrovitch Pavlov, Work* (1953, latest edn 1979). See also: Jeffrey A. Gray, *Pavlov* (1979).

ROBERT OLBY

PAZ, Octavio

1914–98
Mexican poet and critic

A poet and critic of astonishing range and insight, Octavio Paz was a modernist on the world stage – but always a Mexican in dialogue with his own traditions. In a key early essay of 1942 – 'Poetry of Solitude and Poetry of Communion' ('Poesía de soledad y poesía de comunión') – Paz defined the conflict at the heart of the modern experience. The aspiration to transform the world led, in his view, to repeated experiences of authoritarianism; the modern world offered the instruments of change, then betrayed the promise of freedom. Yet it was still possible to create a community, to imagine that transformation of the self – and to realize it in and as poetry.

In 1936, Paz was present in the early months of the Spanish civil war; but his relationship with the socialist left was brief. The political idealism expressed in early poems like 'They Shall Not Pass' ('No pasarán') did not survive Paz's encounter with **Stalinism** and his subsequent rapid disillusionment. In fact Paz suppressed that poem in his later collections. In the years that followed Paz embarked on a journey into poetry itself – as he put it, from revolution to revelation. It was a journey from silence to a word that could reconcile difference in a new kind of harmony – an erotic encounter, very often, in a poetic space somewhere outside history, reborn among the ruins of the past. Paz's poem 'Hymn among Ruins' ('Himno entre ruinas', 1948) employs the characteristic dualist form of many of his works – the parallel development of two realities moving towards destruction and solitude on the one hand, and to utopian harmony on the other. That same movement shapes one of his most famous poems, 'Sunstone' ('Piedra de sol', 1957), the triumphant colophon to his collection *Liberty on Parole* (*Libertad bajo palabra*), published in 1960. The poem is in some ways autobiographical, and affirms that 'the world changes/if two people, wild and interwoven/

fall on to grass ... a total time where nothing happens/except its own happy passing' ('*el mundo cambia/si dos, vertiginosos y enlazados/ caen sobre la yerba ... tiempo total donde no pasa nada/sino su propio transcurrir dichoso*').

Paz returns to this restless movement of the word in his introduction to the collective anthology of Mexican poets *Poetry in Movement* (*Poesía en movimiento*, 1966), which expresses Paz's growing interest in the Orient in its translation of his enduring dialectical preoccupations into the metaphor of *yin* and *yang*. It echoed a series of new works which corresponded to Paz's move to the Far East as a diplomat – and ultimately as Mexico's ambassador to India. *The Eastern Slope* (*Ladera este*, 1969) and *White* (*Blanco*, 1967) reflect a growing interest in Buddhism and eastern religion more generally, perhaps because Paz's explicit aspiration to find the word that could change the nature of man, that 'presence born of absence', resonated so clearly in those bodies of thought.

A prolific essayist, Paz seems to have been engaged in two very different kinds of cumulative meditation. His critical approaches to poetry locate his own work, and that of his contemporaries, in a continuing exploration of poetry's transgressive and transforming function. At the same time, he sustained an often contentious debate with the history of his own country. *The Labyrinth of Solitude* (*El laberinto de la soledad*), first published in 1950 and frequently revised thereafter, meditated upon the self-imposed isolation of Mexicans. His critique of the Mexican state as an embodiment of that denial of universality reached a high pitch of intensity with his *Postscript* (*Posdata*, 1970), written as a final addendum to *The Labyrinth of Solitude* in the wake of the massacre of student demonstrators by the Mexican state in October 1968 in Mexico City's Tlatelolco Square. His resignation from his post in protest at the massacre underlined both his consistency as a critic of the corrupt and authoritarian Mexican state and his stature as an independent political figure. Yet there was throughout his life an apparent disjuncture

between the radicalism of his literary project and the deeply conservative political positions he adopted. As editor of the influential journal *Vuelta* he became a leading advocate of neo-liberal strategies whose insistence on economic freedom seemed to sit uneasily with an advocacy of civil liberties in the Mexico of the final decades of the century.

The award of the Nobel Prize for Literature in 1990 was a fitting acknowledgment for a poet and critic who had linked Latin America to the flows and counterflows of poetry across the world. This was a poet who cherished the independence of the 'moral legislator of mankind'. Yet his political radicalism located him firmly on the ideological right. The contradiction remained unresolved – the presentness of the economic imperative continued to sit uneasily with the endless transformations which his poetry both promised and enacted for more than two generations.

Further reading

See: *Selected Poems*, trans. Muriel Rukeyser (1963); *Selected Poems*, ed. Charles Tomlinson (1979); *Poemas (1935–1975)* (1979); *Lo mejor de Octavio Paz. El fuego de cada día* (1989); *The Labyrinth of Solitude*, trans. Lysander Kemp (1957, originally published as *El laberinto de la soledad*, 1950); *Children of the Mire: Poetry from Romanticism to the Avant-Garde*, trans. Rachel Phillips (1974, originally published as *Los hijos del limo: del romanticismo a la vanguardia*, 1974); *Alternating Current*, trans. Helen Lane (1973, originally published as *Corriente alterna*, 1967); and *Convergences: Selected Essays on Art and Literature*, trans. Helen Lane (1987). Also see: John M. Fein, *Toward Octavio Paz: A Reading of His Major Poems, 1957–1976* (1986); Rachel Phillips, *The Poetic Modes of Octavio Paz* (1972); Jose Quiroga, *Understanding Octavio Paz* (1999); Jason Wilson, *Octavio Paz: A Study of His Poetics* (1979).

MIKE GONZALEZ

PEAKE, Mervyn Laurence

1911–68

English novelist and artist

Mervyn Peake was born the son of a missionary doctor in Kulin, China. He attended

Tianjin Grammar School and, on his family's return to England, Eltham College in Kent; subsequently he trained at the Croydon School of Art, and 1929–33 at the Royal Academy Schools. For much of his life he practised as a painter and illustrator, as well as writing poetry and plays, but his reputation as a major figure is based on the three 'Titus' novels: *Titus Groan* (1946), *Gormenghast* (1950) and *Titus Alone* (1959; revised edition edited by Langdon Jones, 1970).

Peake is the most accomplished Fantastic Realist in modern English literature, having more stylistically in common with **Dickens** than with any of his British contemporaries. The world of Gormenghast and its inhabitants is the exaggerated one of dreams and nightmares. Where Dickens was eccentric, Peake is entirely grotesque. His only rival in scale is **Tolkien** whose work, if better known to the public, lacks the inexhaustible invention and depth of Peake's. Perhaps his nearest contemporary parallels were not writers at all but the Fantastic Realist painters of Vienna: Fuchs, Brauer, Hutter. Like theirs, his work is surreal in its conceptions and yet rendered with a meticulous technique and a concern for detail that is almost pathological in its intensity. It induces in the reader to an exceptional degree that 'subtle attitude of awed listening' which was H.P. Lovecraft's test for success in fantasy. Peake's own outlook he described in a radio talk, 1947:

> As I see it, or as I want to see it, the marvels of the visible world are not things in themselves but revelations to stir the imagination – to conduct us to amazing climates of the mind, which climates it is for the artist to translate into paint or into words ... whether he can assimilate and build from it an original work of art depends largely on how deeply he is obsessed by his work.

The books are concerned with growth and the search for liberation in the early life of Titus Groan, the seventy-seventh earl, with whose birth in the ancient precincts of Gormenghast Castle the novel opens. The narrative of the first two novels is long and complex. The third and much shorter volume was not properly finished because of the progress of the author's Parkinson's Disease. Nonetheless, *Titus Alone* in its revised version is an extraordinary book. After the incestuous density of its predecessors, the space and speed of the third is one of fiction's great dislocating events. The mind, coffered into the elaborate chambers of Gormenghast, is suddenly reeling across phantasmagorical landscapes and through settlements which belong if anywhere to the future. This transposition from the archaic to the futuristic, without passing through a reality in any way contiguous to our own, confirms the autonomy of Peake's creation and heightens the sense of wonder. If it is possible to put Gormenghast into a frame of mind reminiscent of the late eighteenth century's preoccupation with the Middle Ages (for this reason Peake is sometimes referred to as a gothic novelist), this is no longer tenable once the author's own mind begins to panic. Peake's illness has introduced an urgent rhythm that is quite unexpected. The trilogy is thereby turned into more than a brilliantly contrived otherworld. It has become the strangest kind of autobiography and an emotionally powerful work of art.

Peake is a virtuoso prose writer in the baroque style. His syntax is never experimental but his use of words is muscular and flamboyant, his images are outlandish and transferred to the reader with a lurid three-dimensional tactility. This power of incision is the consequence of a technically spectacular writer being perfectly focused upon his vision and therefore having the capacity to trace it in all its paralogical ramifications. One only has to read the work of an imitator such as **John Barth** to be reminded of how exceptional Peake's performance is. Since Peake, the novels of **García Márquez** have come closest to giving an equivalent sensual enchantment and imaginative satisfaction of the intellect. Although a writer of short stories, **Borges** too has much in common with him. Peake's acclaim was posthumous and he is still considered a maverick, even intellectually suspect figure, something which two recent biographies, an ambitious BBC adaptation and an opera have failed to correct. But there is a case to be made for Peake as the characteristic English genius of that strange, murky, broken decade the 1940s, a view bolstered by the growing reputation of his pictures. His work thrived in the abnormal, heightened sensibility of war and is often said to have been deeply coloured by his being the first graphic artist admitted to the opening of the Belsen concentration camp.

Further reading

Other works include: *Mr Pye* (1953); *Boy in Darkness* (a novella in *Sometime, Never*, 1956); *Selected Poems* (1972); *Writings and Drawings of Mervyn Peake* (1974); *Peake's Progress*, ed. Maeve Gilmore (1979). See also: Maeve Gilmore, *A World Away: A Memoir of Mervyn Peake* (1970); John Batchelor, *Mervyn Peake: A Biographical and Critical Exploration* (1974); John Watney, *Mervyn Peake* (1976); Malcolm Yorke, *Mervyn Peake: A Life* (2000); G. Peter Winnington, *Vast Alchemies: The Life and Work of Mervyn Peake* (2000).

DUNCAN FALLOWELL

PEI, Ieoh Ming

1917–

American architect

When the Eiffel Tower was finished, in 1889, the Parisian monument by **Gustave Eiffel** almost instantly became the symbol of France, appearing for decades afterwards on countless postcards, travel posters and book covers. Exactly a century later, in 1989, the venerable cast-iron tower was abruptly pushed aside as a French icon by the crystalline glass-and-steel pyramid designed by I.M. Pei for the Louvre Museum.

For the culturally elitist French to select a Chinese-born American architect to remake the symbolic heart of their national culture was a tribute to an extraordinary individual.

Pei was born in Canton, China, in 1917, the son of a prosperous banker. After moving to Shanghai, the family spent vacations at a garden villa in Suzhou, where the young Pei developed a keen sense of landscape design. In 1935, like many Chinese of his social class, Pei travelled to the United States, to study architecture at the University of Pennsylvania. He dropped out when he despaired of competing with his fellow students' skills as draftsmen. He then enrolled at the Massachusetts Institute of Technology in engineering. From there, he went on to Harvard's Graduate School of design, where he pursued architecture under the pioneering European Modernists **Walter Gropius** and Marcel Breuer, developing a life-long fascination with abstract geometry.

Surprisingly for an architect with his training, Pei in 1948 went to work as an in-house architect for William Zeckendorf, a flamboyant New York City real-estate magnate. But the move proved to be a canny one, because Pei acquired a firm grounding in the realities of business, real-estate development and construction technology.

As the Zeckendorf empire began to falter, in the 1950s, Pei struck out on his own, establishing I.M. Pei & Associates, and designing a succession of buildings, the most striking of which was the muscular National Center for Atmospheric Research, in Boulder, Colorado, begun in 1961. That building so impressed Jacqueline Kennedy, the widow of the assassinated president, **John F. Kennedy**, that she selected the little-known Pei in 1964 as architect for the John F. Kennedy Library, eventually built in Boston, Massachusetts.

Although the firm was staggered in 1973 by failing windows at its John Hancock Tower in Boston, Pei rebounded with a series of small art museums that led to his selection by the philanthropist Paul Mellon as architect of the East Building of the National Gallery of Art. The Gallery, finished in 1978, was widely praised for its geometric power, but criticized by some for subsuming the art on display to the architecture that contained it.

Nevertheless, other prestigious commissions quickly followed, most notably the seventy-storey Bank of China tower in Hong Kong.

But the most important by far was at the invitation of François Mitterrand, the president of France, for the Louvre Museum in Paris. Although the starkly geometric glass pyramid that served as the museum's new main entrance attracted the most public attention (some of it outraged), the reorganization of the former palace into a rationally functioning art museum made Pei's achievement a landmark of both design and urban planning.

The 'Louvre effect' stimulated invitations from Luxembourg and Germany to do two more museums, but they were compromised by political disputes and bureaucratic infighting. These disappointments were redeemed, however, by the invitation to design the Miho art museum, near Kyoto, Japan. This assignment, completed in 1997, combined all of Pei's strongest interests − in art, in landscape design, and in East Asian culture. And its success confirmed what had contributed most to all of Pei's best works − a close personal relationship with a wealthy client, in this case the matriarch of a religious denomination who was intimately familiar with the Chinese classical texts that had informed the growth of Japanese high culture.

Even at an age when most architects are long retired, Pei, having stepped away from a full-time role in his firm (now Pei Cobb Freed & Partners), has continued to work and to evolve as a designer, doing a tiny garden 'folie' for a wealthy English family and an Islamic art museum in Doha, Qatar. His most recent project is something of a sentimental journey, designing (in collaboration with his sons) a town plan and a history museum for his childhood retreat of Suzhou.

While Pei has been faulted for an excessively corporate approach to design, this can be seen partly as a practical response to the realities of American architecture in the twentieth century. 'I am not a revolutionary,' he has said, 'but an evolutionary.' In any case, the buildings that his highly successful firm has done in the commercial realm have allowed Pei himself to integrate Chinese, European and American traditions in a remarkable number of the world's most admired works of the art of architecture.

Further reading

See: Carter Wiseman, *I.M. Pei, A Profile in American Architecture* (2001); Carter Wiseman, *Twentieth-Century American Architecture: The Buildings and Their Makers* (2000); Bruno Suner, *Ieoh Ming Pei* (1988); Michael Cannell, *I.M. Pei, Mandarin of Modernism* (1995).

CARTER WISEMAN

PEIRCE, Charles Sanders

1839–1914
US philosopher and logician

One of the most original and versatile thinkers America has produced, C.S. Peirce was born in Cambridge, Massachusetts, the son of the leading American mathematician of his times, Benjamin Peirce, Perkins Professor of Mathematics and Astronomy at Harvard University. After reading mathematics, physics and chemistry at Harvard, he joined the US Coast Survey in 1861. He made significant contributions not only to the survey but also to the theory and techniques of measurement in physics. Resigning his post in 1891, he retired to the seclusion of a farm near Milford, Pennsylvania, where, in poverty, he pursued his research in philosophy and logic. Twice married, he had no children.

Deeply influenced by Kant as an undergraduate, Peirce sought to create a systematic philosophy closely in tune with the methods of modern science. To this end he proposed a theory of meaning which he called 'pragmatism', according to which the cognitive meaning of a concept lies solely in its conceivable bearing on the conduct of life. Our idea of an object consists entirely in our conception of those effects of it which have a conceivable bearing on our action. Since observable effects have the most conspicuous influence on our actions, these must play the most prominent role in our idea of the object. In calling a substance 'hard', for example, what we mean is that it will not easily be scratched by many other substances. This theory was first proposed in the article 'How to Make Our Ideas Clear' (*Popular Science Monthly*, January 1878). It was taken up and elaborated by **William James**, whose version of it Peirce rejected on the grounds that it was too phenomenalist and subjectivist.

Pragmatism was the main tool with which Peirce constructed his theory of knowledge. He argued that just as our ideas concern those characteristics of things which bear upon action, so our beliefs constitute rules or habits of acting, for what we believe partly determines how we act. Belief is preferable to doubt, for, unlike doubt, it generally makes for appropriate action. It is the purpose of inquiry to secure stable beliefs and remove doubt. Science provides the best method of inquiry, for its method is the best means for fixing belief. All other methods, such as intuition and authority, produce beliefs which readily fall prey to doubt. No scientific belief, however, is certain, and any may be mistaken, for science consists in reasoning on the basis of experience, and the experience can never attain absolute exactness or universality. Nevertheless the scientific method provides a definite means for settling doubt whenever it arises. Moreover, as the method is pursued indefinitely, the beliefs it leads to become more and more fixed. But why should we value fixed beliefs? Because, Peirce replies, absolute fixity is indistinguishable from truth: the truth is what would be believed ultimately if the scientific method were pursued *in infinitum*. As science progresses, it approximates asymptotically towards the whole truth; but at any finite time it is never certain.

The essential point of this doctrine, which Peirce called 'fallibilism', is that although scientific method is fallible, it is self-correcting. Science proposes explanatory hypotheses which are tested by observing whether or not their empirical consequences occur. For example, a general hypothesis of the form 'The proportion of *A*s that are *B* is x/y' is tested by observing what proportion of *A*s are

B among a numerous random sample of *A*s. If the observed proportion differs from that hypothesized, then the hypothesis can be corrected by further sampling, which is bound to lead to a closer and closer approximation to the correct ratio. This is the method of induction. Its validity, Peirce argued, does not depend upon a metaphysical principle of the uniformity of nature; it depends solely on the fact that if pursued indefinitely, its results will necessarily approximate to the facts. Consequently, the rationality of science presupposes a commitment to a co-operative, never-ending quest.

In his metaphysics Peirce was a realist in one sense, for he rejected the idealist view that to be is to be perceived, holding instead that reality is what exists independently of what any individual mind thinks or perceives. Following Duns Scotus, he held that properties (universals), laws (universal facts) and possibilities are real – a view he called 'scholastic realism'. The hardness of a diamond, for example, is a real potentiality – an ability to resist scratching – which may never be realized: a diamond that never has been, or ever will be, scratched is nonetheless hard. Peirce classified real entities into three fundamental categories: under 'firstness' come properties and possibilities; under 'secondness' come things and actualities; and under 'thirdness' come thoughts and laws.

In another sense Peirce was not a realist, but rather an 'objective idealist', for he held that reality, as what corresponds to true beliefs, is the object of the beliefs at which scientific inquiry, pursued *in infinitum*, would ultimately settle. A concept of reality as wholly independent of thought is meaningless from the pragmatist point of view. Peirce's objective idealism bears a certain similarity to Kant's transcendental idealism.

Peirce's most substantive metaphysical thesis – 'synechism' – is that there are real continuities, such as space, time, matter and consciousness. These are continuous in the sense that between any two distinct parts, or successive intervals, of them there is a third part or interval. He regarded this as an explanatory and heuristic hypothesis that gave coherence and direction to scientific inquiry. Synechism implies fallibilism: since absolutely exact values of continuous quantities can never be observed, laws of nature can never be absolutely exact; hence our knowledge always swims, as it were, 'in a continuum of uncertainty and indeterminacy'. Laws of nature, moreover, are not absolutely strict or deterministic, but probabilistic, for there are chance departures from them. They express the general propensities or habits of things. This hypothesis – 'tychism' – he thought was required to explain the growing diversification of the universe. Strict law can explain the regularity in the universe; only absolute chance can account for its variety. The very laws of nature are evolving, from a chaos of irregularity in the infinitely distant past towards a harmony of absolute regularity in the infinitely far-off future. Yet there will always be, at any finite time in the future, chance aberrations from strict law. There is a corresponding evolution of mind into matter: 'Matter is effete mind, inveterate habits becoming physical laws.'

A logician of extraordinary originality, Peirce largely founded the theory of relations and the theory of signs, discovered quantification theory (independently of **Frege**) and the truth-value method of proving logical theorems, as well as making important contributions to Boolean algebra (see **Boole**) and set theory.

Although he had a great influence on William James and **John Dewey** and later American thinkers such as **Willard Van Orman Quine**, he received little recognition during his lifetime, largely because his philosophical writings were published in diverse journals and because he never held a permanent academic position, though he gave some lectures on logic at Harvard and Johns Hopkins. Besides, his thinking was very avant-garde: ideas like fallibilism and indeterminacy had little appeal to an age whose faith in classical physics was at its highest pitch; they had to await more propitious times, when they were re-introduced

by thinkers such as Popper and Heisenberg respectively.

Further reading

See: *The Collected Papers of Charles Sanders Peirce*, ed. C. Harshorne, P. Weiss and A.W. Burks (8 vols, 1931–58). Useful collections are *Philosophical Writings of Peirce*, ed. Justus Buchler (1955), and *Charles S. Peirce: The Essential Writings*, ed. Edward C. Moore (1972). See also: M. Fisch, *Peirce, Semiotic and Pragmatism* (1986); J. Brent, *Charles Sanders Peirce: A Life* (1993).

D.R. MURDOCH

PENDERECKI, Krzysztof

1933–

Polish composer

An astonishing stylistic volte-face a third of the way through Krzysztof Penderecki's output to date – severe even by the protean norms of twentieth-century compositional practice – indicates one of the reasons why he is the most fascinating Polish composer of his generation. For there are two Pendereckis to consider, both of whom have connected to impressively large audiences beyond the contemporary art music ghetto. One is the young Polish firebrand whose hyper-expressionistic 'sonorism' scores of the 1960s marked him out as one of the avant-garde's most original voices, and whose music subsequently became known to millions through its use on film soundtracks. The other is a doyen of the more traditionally-minded wing of the classical music establishment, a purveyor of grand symphonies and oratorios in possession of a neo-romantic musical voice that did not so much turn its back on the earlier Penderecki's achievements as perform a backward somersault into its late nineteenth-century idiom.

Penderecki emerged as a force on the Polish music scene in 1959 when, following studies at the Music Academy in Kraków (1954–8), he won all three top prizes at a national competition. This was a timely emergence for an ambitious and creatively audacious composer. In the late 1950s, the post-**Stalinist** new wave of Polish art music was seeking to process the flux of the international avant-garde. No one responded to this challenge with more panache and verve than Penderecki, who moved swiftly, via neo-classical and modernist models, to the creation of a stunningly novel soundworld. One of those triple award-winning pieces, *Emanacje* ('Emanations', 1958), which features two string orchestras tuned a semitone apart, inaugurated a swiftly expanding body of triumphs including *Tren* for fifty-two strings ('Threnody to the Victims of Hiroshima', 1960), *Polymorphia* for forty-eight string instruments (1961), which is arguably his finest essay in sound, and the electrifyingly sensuous *Capriccio* for violin and orchestra (1967). Rightly lauded for his bold approach to timbre, texture and musical time, Penderecki's sonoristic scores pushed back the frontiers of instrumental and notational technique in the service of a more primal force: forthright musical drama. Having pared modernism down to bands of evolving sonority and intensity, Penderecki was able to create scores so direct in their gestural and affective immediacy that he seemed simultaneously to sculpt his audience's emotional experience – hence at least some of his music's efficacy on horror movie soundtracks including William Friedkin's *The Exorcist* (1973) and **Stanley Kubrick's** *The Shining* (1980).

It was Penderecki's *St Luke Passion* (1963–6), however, which catapulted him to international success; and, when 15,000 people attended a performance in the courtyard of Kraków's Wawel Castle, the oratorio also became a national icon, bringing religion (a symbol of Polish resistance to oppression) to the centre of his country's musical life. Harnessing his flair for drama to the Passion story, the oratorio's singular musical impact rests on its potent fusion of sonorism, serialism and – crucially – refracted traditional resources (Polish religious songs, the B.A.C.H. motive). This stylistic continuum enabled Penderecki to move between the extremes of allusions to J.S. Bach and sonorism's obliteration of pitch and pulse. Later, Penderecki went on to make statements of a more consciously political nature, such as the *Polish Requiem* (1980–4, expanded 1993), parts of which commemorate tragedies suffered by Poles, and *Seven Gates of Jerusalem* (1996), which commemorates the 3,000th anniversary of Jerusalem's founding while addressing, through Christian allegory, the conflicts encompassed by that city's walls.

The expanded palette of the *Passion*, as well as providing a blueprint for Penderecki's operas – including the deliciously profane *Devils of Loudon* (1969) and rumbustious *Ubu Rex* ('King Ubu', 1990–1) – can also be connected to Penderecki's change of style in the mid 1970s. His Violin Concerto No. 1 (1976–7) and Symphony No. 2 (1979–80) cemented the dominant features of the new Penderecki. Increasingly tonal harmony, clearer-cut melodies, simpler rhythmic patterns and generic forms all returned to be deployed within a gestural language deeply indebted to late romanticism, and prone to veering into darkly turbulent emotional territory. A string of symphonies, concertos and choral works followed, and at their best – as in the serene *Adagio* at the centre of Symphony No. 3 (1988–95), the blazing climax of Symphony No. 5 (1992), or the desolate close of Violin Concerto No. 2 (1992–5) – this is music of impressive scope and power. Some recent works, moreover, have revealed a brightening of Penderecki's occasionally oppressive atmospheres to admit more delicate and even playful music, as in the delightful Quartet for clarinet and strings (1993). Penderecki has made some bold pronouncements concerning these later works. He has described his recent symphonies, for example, as arks designed to protect all that was important, from his current perspective, in the tradition of art music during the twentieth century. Yet although they would not be permitted to board this ark of neo-romantic values, Penderecki's earlier modernist scores may ultimately mark his most significant cultural contributions.

Further reading

Recordings of all Penderecki's major works, often conducted with accomplishment by the composer himself, are readily available on CD. Wolfram Schwinger's *Krzysztof Penderecki: His Life and Work* (1989) is a useful survey up to the *Polish Requiem*, while Penderecki's own *Labyrinth of Time: Five Addresses for the End of the Millennium* (1998) can be consulted regarding his later aesthetics.

NICK REYLAND

PÉREZ GALDÓS, Benito

1843–1920

Spanish novelist and dramatist

The most important single Spanish writer between the Romantics and the Generation of 1898. After abandoning his law studies in the University of Madrid, he devoted his life exclusively to writing, except for brief forays into politics on the Liberal-Progressive side, and to extensive travel both in Spain and abroad. He remained a bachelor, but was far from being a celibate. Elected to the Spanish Academy in 1889, he was a candidate for the Nobel Prize in 1912.

He was essentially a realist writer; Balzac and **Dickens** (whose *Pickwick Papers* he translated, from the French, in 1868) were his acknowledged masters. Before 1870, when he published his first (historical) novel, *La Fontana de Oro* ('The Fountain of Gold'), Spanish fiction had been in a phase of decline. The Revolution of 1868 and the loosening of censorship produced a recovery. Until 1875 Galdós continued to produce historical novels, including a first set of *Episodios nacionales*, exploring systematically Spain's past since 1807 with the basic intention of tracing the living forces, social and political, which were still at work in his own day. He went on producing historical *Episodios* (which were excellent money-spinners) until well into the twentieth century, discreetly advocating political moderation and civic responsibility. Eventually they ran into thirty-four volumes. But disillusion with his own middle class and its betrayal of the ideals of 1868 in the end led him to disenchantment and to sympathy with the Republican-Socialist opposition.

Already in 1876, after the restoration of the Bourbons to the throne had begun to offset the achievements of 1868, Galdós had turned to contemporary Spain with one of his most famous works, *Doña Perfecta*, a head-on attack against religious fanaticism, followed by *Gloria* (1876–7) and *La familia de León Roch* (1878) in similar vein. These are novels of dramatic conflict rather than psychological studies, but their heavy emphasis on theme does not preclude an adequately balanced presentation of the clash of traditionalist and progressive outlooks. In 1881, with *La desheredada* ('The Disinherited'), the central phase of Galdós's fictional work opened. Leaning slightly more towards naturalism, with its emphasis on the uglier aspects of social and psychological reality and on hereditary and environmental determinism, Galdós now abandoned fictional settings for his novels and emerged as the classic novelist of nineteenth-century Madrid. Emphasis on social mobility replaces a static vision of a closed society, characterization becomes less ideological and more subtly ambiguous, dialogue becomes more realistic. Galdós's interest in the religious question now merges into deeper and more widely perceptive social criticism and satire. In *El amigo Manso* (1882), *El doctor Centeno* (1883), *Torment* (*Tormento*, 1884, trans. 1952), *The Spendthrifts* (*La de Bringas*, 1884, trans. 1951), and *Lo prohibido* ('The Forbidden', 1884–5), Galdós uses Balzac's techniques of reappearing characters and the interlacing of national events with private life-stories to depict a Spain which is hollow, squalid, devoid of ideals, peopled by fools, rogues and mediocrities, and dominated by self-deception, hypocrisy, immorality, administrative inefficiency and the cult of appearances.

The year 1886–7 brought plenitude and Galdós's masterpiece *Fortunata and Jacinta*, (*Fortunata y Jacinta*, trans. 1973). The chronicle of two family groups in Madrid, its story concerns the illicit relationship between the middle-class Juanito Santa Cruz and his working-class mistress Fortunata, together with their respective legal marriages. The inner theme is the struggle between natural instinct and social conventions. Both marriages, though sanctified by the church, are unsuitable and sterile; the liaison is fulfilling and produces children. At the end, for almost the only time in Galdós's major works, harmony and equilibrium triumph as Fortunata is vicariously accepted into the bourgeois family of her lover when she gives up her child to the childless Jacinta, Juanito's wife. Although technically the novel belongs to **Henry James's** category of 'loose, baggy monsters', we recognize in it one of the lasting achievements of nineteenth-century realism.

With *Miau* (*Miau,* 1888, trans. 1963) Galdós entered his final phase, in which he began to move away from realism towards the exploration of abnormal states of mind and behaviour, though no longer as in *Lo prohibido* in a specifically social perspective. The note of spiritual preoccupation, never far from Galdós's mind, begins to sound strongly once more, but not as in his early aggressive novels of thesis. Thus God appears as a speaking voice in *Miau*, the story of the suicide of a redundant civil servant. *La incógnita* ('The Unknown', 1888–9) and *Realidad* ('Reality', 1889) explore the loneliness of ethical superiority in a rotting, bourgeois society. *Angel Guerra* ('Angel War' 1890–1) and a series of four novels published between 1889 and 1895 whose central figure is Torquemada, a grasping moneylender, develop the bifurcation between social and spiritual reality already prominent in *Miau*. Finally in *Nazarín* (1895), which has been successfully filmed by Buñuel, *Halma* (1895) and *Misericordia* (1897), Galdós studies varieties of saintliness. Benina in *Misericordia* is Galdós's most memorable heroine, a supreme example of practical Christian charity, though founded on small-scale fraud. In the same ironic way both Christ and the mad Don Quixote serve as models for the creation of Nazarín. Galdós's last major novel, *El abuelo* ('The Grandfather', 1904), proposes the theme of

tradition and renewal which links Galdós to the Generation of 1898.

The great speed at which Galdós wrote did not preclude skilful construction and considerable technical originality. A number of the earlier novels especially show great dramatic ability combined with a fine sense of narrative tempo and economy of method. Later, in *El amigo Manso* for example, Galdós was able to portend some of the techniques of Unamuno in the twentieth century and to blend observation, humour and fantasy in a strikingly innovatory way. But his fondness for symbolic names, novelesque contrivances and proliferation of characters are of his time.

As a dramatist Galdós produced more than twenty original plays and adaptations of his novels. These were staged chiefly in two periods: 1892–6 and 1901–5. They included four striking successes: *La de San Quintín* (1894), *Doña Perfecta* (1896), *Electra* (1901) and *El abuelo* (1904). *Electra*, once more on the theme of misguided religious zeal, was the greatest theatrical sensation of its time in Spain, sold 20,000 copies in a matter of days and was a major factor in bringing about the fall of the government. In general Galdós's plays represent an isolated attempt to revitalize Spanish drama, which was dominated by debased post-Romantic theatricality. But Galdós did not possess the technical skill to achieve his aims consistently, his audiences were unready to accept his innovations of form and content, and he failed to create a lasting movement.

Galdós's influence was enormous. Later novelists in Spain, such as Baroja and Pérez de Ayala, confessed it eloquently. In Latin America it is clearly visible in novelists up to and including **Carlos Fuentes** and in some pre-Second World War dramatists. Frequent cheap re-editions of his major novels attest their popularity, and critical interest has been so great that a journal, *Anales Galdosianos*, has been devoted exclusively to his work.

Further reading

W.T. Pattison, *Benito Pérez Galdós* (1975), is a handy general study. More specific and critical are:

S.H. Eoff, *The Novels of Pérez Galdós* (1954); and the critical guides to *Miau* by E. Rodgers (1978) and to *Fortunata y Jacinta* by G. Ribbans (1977); B.J. Dendle, *Galdós: The Mature Thought* (1980)

D.L. SHAW

PETRIE, (Sir) William Matthew Flinders

1853–1942

English archaeologist and Egyptologist

The individual style of Petrie's work owed much to youthful isolation. The only child of an energetic middle-class professional family, he was brought up largely in the company of adults, and given very little formal education. Earnest self-improvement took its place. He collected Greek coins, studied his mother's collection of minerals, and taught himself mathematics and surveying. As a young man he took to making long, solitary walking trips in the south of England, surveying earthworks and stone circles, intending to publish the results in a series of volumes. One on Stonehenge rapidly appeared, as did a precocious treatise on the whole subject of ancient metrology. These works display an obsession with measurements and numbers, and led, through a family interest, to his undertaking a private survey of the Giza Pyramids in Egypt, with great and lasting success. It was during this visit that he developed an urge to excavate, partly as a reaction to the rapid destruction of ancient sites which he witnessed, and partly from an emerging ambition: to establish with precision the full spectrum of changes in ancient fashions so that artefacts from any point within ancient Egyptian history could be dated to within a few reigns. These twin motives remained to guide Petrie through a long career as an archaeologist, and go far in explaining the pattern of his work. Thenceforth he managed an almost annual expedition to Egypt or to Palestine, apart from the years of the First World War, which he used as an opportunity for preparing catalogue volumes of the extensive collections he built up at University College, London. In the early years he worked partly with private backing and partly on behalf of the Egypt Exploration Fund, with which body his relations were often strained.

The exploration of ancient Egypt had already witnessed a number of meticulous surveys of standing ruins, but excavation was crude and undisciplined. Petrie's principal innovation was a concern for pottery and other small finds, even when broken, which he saw as an essential part of the full picture of Egyptian civilization which he wished to build up. His first major success was in the discovery and excavation of the Greek colony of Naukratis in the western Nile Delta, made in 1884–5. In addition to rescuing an outline plan from a site already badly plundered, he provided a schematic section to illustrate the vertical distribution of finds at one part of the site, and illustrated in his report a mass of pottery and fragmentary artefacts. In 1890 he carried out a single season of excavation in Palestine on the mound of Tell el-Hesy (Eglon or Lachish). Again, by means of schematic vertical recording of finds and study and publication of selection of pottery, he established an outline history of the site, and with it an archaeological framework for Palestine from pre-biblical to Roman times. Many of his later excavations were on cemeteries in Egypt, and at Nagada in 1895 he cleared with some care the largest predynastic (Neolithic) cemetery ever to be found in Egypt. From the results he constructed a relative chronology of the predynastic period which stands as an important early application of statistical methods to archaeology. Five years later, at Abydos, by sifting carefully the debris from a recent French excavation, he was able to salvage a coherent record of the tombs of Egypt's earliest kings, those of the First Dynasty (*c.* 3000 BC).

Petrie's worthy scientific motives, however, were becoming the means for expressing a pronounced restlessness. Most years had to see a new site started, and in retrospect it is clear that many of his excavations were only limited soundings, though a flair for locating the most productive areas gave him constant success. By hard work and a practised shorthand form of publication he managed to maintain a flow of excavation memoirs such as few, if any, other archaeologists have ever achieved. They are often characterized by a kind of instant scholarship made possible by a retentive memory, yet frequently highly selective in its scope, and unresponsive to current scholarship. This characteristic enabled him, at the same time, to range with confidence over a wide field of subjects: the formation of the alphabet, prehistoric hill figures of England, the growth of the Gospels, to name but a few.

A useful division in Petrie's long career can be made at 1905. He had, since 1892, been Professor of Egyptology at University College, London, and had collected a number of honorary degrees. Now came a manual on excavation, *Methods and Aims in Archaeology*, his thirty-third book. At the same time his intolerant attitude towards colleagues who did not share his dedication to archaeology as a serious, full-time pursuit led him to break, for the second time, with the Egypt Exploration Fund. As a support for his future work he set up a rival organization, the British School of Archaeology in Egypt, based at University College. This enabled him to continue fieldwork in Egypt and, after 1926, in Palestine. But the style of his work remained in the same mould as that of his early days, sometimes with less attention to detail.

As a nineteenth-century figure Petrie has the heroic stature of the largely unaided outsider who became an innovator and moulder of attitudes in a new discipline. His contribution to Egyptology by virtue of the quantity of material found and published is considerable and lasting. But to the modern archaeologist, who may prefer to see as the founding figure of his subject the leisurely and painstaking figure of General **Pitt Rivers**, Petrie commands only passing attention. The great flaw in Petrie's approach lay in the disparity between the scale of the work attempted and the amount of archaeological skill available. On any dig one archaeologist can cope with only a very restricted area of ground. For Petrie, with limited resources, results which satisfied appetites whetted by half a century of treasure-hunting in Egypt required the directing of enormous energy not just at the skilled tasks of recording, but at controlling a labour force of Egyptian peasants. Petrie's writings have much to say on this topic. The terrible lure of quick and arresting results caught Petrie, as it has continued to catch others, in the trap of trying to apply a scientifically objective eye to a way and to a scale of digging which is inherently crude.

Further reading

A comprehensive bibliography of Petrie, comprising 1,024 items, is in the *Journal of Near Eastern Studies*, Vol. 31 (1972), pp. 356–79; *Seventy Years in Archaeology* (1931) is his autobiography. See also W.R. Dawson and E.P. Uphill, *Who Was Who in Egyptology* (2nd edn, 1972); Margaret S. Drower, *Flinders Petrie* (1985).

BARRY J. KEMP

PIAGET, Jean

1896–1980

Swiss psychologist, philosopher and biologist

Jean Piaget was born in Neuchâtel, Switzerland. His father was a Professor of Medieval Literature and one of his grandparents was English. He was a precocious youngster. Between seven and ten he interested himself in the study of birds, fossils and natural history. By fifteen he had become an authority on molluscs and had published a number of articles on this topic. On their strength he was offered a post as curator of the important mollusc collection at the Natural History Museum at Geneva. One can imagine the consternation of the Museum director when he found he was only dealing with a schoolboy.

At the University of Neuchâtel he took his doctor's degree in zoology. He next studied psychology in Zürich, read **Freud** and attended **Jung's** lectures. A year later in 1919 he left for Paris where he spent two further years studying abnormal psychology, logic and the philosophy of science at the Sorbonne. Piaget did some work in elementary schools in Paris where he engaged children in conversations modelled on psychoanalytical questioning, with the aim of discovering something about the thought processes underlying their answers. Piaget was then appointed Director of Studies at the Institut J.-J. Rousseau, Geneva (1921); Assistant Director (1929); Co-Director (1932). His other appointments include: Professor of Philosophy, University of Neuchâtel (1925); Professor of the History of Scientific Thought, University of Geneva (1929); Professor of Experimental Psychology and Director of the Psychological Laboratory, Geneva (1940); Professor of Child Psychology at the Sorbonne and Director of the Centre International d'Epistémologie Génétique, Geneva (1955). He was at one time associated with UNESCO as its Assistant Director General.

Piaget's main contribution to knowledge was to open up to experimental investigation the whole subject of concept formation. As a result of suggestive questioning and making the subject handle concrete materials such as building blocks and toys, he showed how the child learned to employ simple classifications and serial ordering, upon which the more complex hypothetico-deductive reasoning of the adolescent and adult is based. His experiments dealt with such topics as logic, mathematics, space, time, chance, morality, play and language. His work is of interest from a number of different points of view. From that of the psychologist, a knowledge of the normal process of concept formation in the individual is likely to help in the understanding of the thought of the abnormal adult. In the educational field it is of considerable importance to realize at what levels it is possible to acquire certain abstract concepts. Much of our teaching may be thwarted if we teach certain subjects before the child is ripe for

them. From the point of view of the philosopher of science, the origin of concepts which have been so widely used in science is clearly important. Piaget has shown that the space, time and causality of physics are adult conceptions, and that the conceptual apparatus by means of which the child orders the world around him is of a much more naive variety than had previously been suspected.

Apart from attempting to provide a philosophical foundation for his empirical findings, to which study he gave the name of *genetic epistemology*, he also developed a sociological theory based on the notion of social exchange between individuals. His work in moral psychology suggests that at least in our society there exist in the child two levels of morality. At an early stage the child follows the voice of authority, while at adolescence equity and justice begin to play a dominant role. In the biological field, Piaget has carried out studies concerned with evolutionary adaptation. One may mention his work on a specific kind of snail inhabiting the Alpine lakes, in which he showed that the shape of their shells was related to the harshness of their environment. He attempted to explain this phenomenon by constructing an evolutionary theory, which he took as a *tertium quid* between Lamarckianism and Neo-Darwinianism.

Piaget wrote over fifty books and numerous articles. This led to some repetition and to a certain looseness and prolixity of expression in his writings. He has been criticized by psychologists for being too philosophical and by philosophers for being too psychological. Perhaps this is the fate of any creative thinker whose work straddles different disciplines. It would, however, be difficult to deny Piaget a place among the great thinkers of the last century. He carried out a Copernican revolution in our study of child thought, and showed how adult thought has its roots in it.

Further reading

Other works include: *The Language and Thought of the Child* (1924); *Judgment and Reasoning in the Child* (1924); *The Child's Conception of Causality*

(1927); *The Moral Judgment of the Child* (1932); *The Child's Concept of Number* (with Alice Szeminska, 1952); *The Origin of Intelligence in the Child* (1953); *The Child's Construction of Reality* (1955); *The Child's Conception of Space* (with Bärbel Inhelder, 1956); *Play, Dream and Imitation in Childhood* (1962); *The Mechanisms of Perception* (1969); *The Child's Conception of Time* (1969); *Biology and Knowledge* (1971); *Structuralism* (1971); *Insights and Illusions of Philosophy* (1972); *The Principles of Genetic Epistemology* (1972). See also Howard E. Gruber and J. Jacques Vonèche (eds) *The Essential Piaget* (1977). About Piaget: Margaret Boden, *Piaget* (1979); Peter Bryant, *Perception and Understanding in Young Children* (1974); J.H. Flavell, *The Developmental Psychology of Piaget* (1963); H.G. Furth, *Piaget and Knowledge* (1969); T. Mischel (ed.) *Cognitive Development and Epistemology* (1971); Brian Rotman, *Jean Piaget: Psychologist of the Real* (1977); James Russell, *The Acquisition of Knowledge* (1978); Fernando Vidal, *Piaget Before Piaget* (1994); Margaret Boden, *Piaget* (1995).

WOLFE MAYS

PICASSO, Pablo (Ruiz y)

1881–1973

Spanish/French artist

Pablo Picasso was born into a comfortable middle-class family in Málaga, Spain, in 1881. His father was a curator of a museum and teacher of painting. From an early age Picasso had shown remarkable talent which his father made every effort to foster. By 1895 the family had moved to Barcelona where Picasso's professional life began, centred around the café of El Quatre Gats. It was in Barcelona that Picasso saw Symbolist works including those of the Englishman **Edward Burne-Jones**, whose sad-eyed processions carried the same inward melancholy as the Continental zSymbolists. Picasso's own Symbolist 'Blue' period with its subject-matter of old age, poverty and lonely clowns maintained this mood of psychological depression, but in its contemporaneity of subject-matter came closer to the poetry of **Jules Laforgue**.

In 1900 Picasso left Spain for the first time, visited France and decided in 1904 to settle in Paris. From then on he holidayed frequently in his native land until 1934, when he became a permanent exile. France then became his second mother country and promoted his talent to such an extent that he became a living legend as the greatest twentieth-century artistic genius of the Western world, comparable with such masters as Velázquez and **Manet**, both of whom influenced him deeply.

It is perhaps useful to consider the vast oeuvre of Picasso in phases. The early 'Blue' period gave way to a happier 'Pink' period in Paris, while Picasso was living with Fernande Olivier. It was, for this restless man, a brief time of relative tranquillity when his work reflected a classic serenity. This was soon to be shattered.

During 1906 and 1907 Picasso painted the awkward and primitive *Demoiselles D'Avignon*, undoubtedly one of the key works of the first half of the twentieth century, when he was only twenty-five years of age. This painting set in motion the movement that later became known as Cubism, without which it is doubtful whether Pure Abstraction such as that of **Mondrian** and **Malevich** would have occurred when and in the way that it did.

Picasso's concern with primitivism as a way of seeing afresh, of connecting again with the vital creative forces of artistic endeavour that he felt had been lost to the Renaissance tradition produced the *Demoiselles*, a bold and dramatically direct statement. Five figures of nude women squat or stand showing progressive distortions and flattenings of form from left to right of the work. Space is diminished and colour limited. Picasso had become aware of African tribal carvings and early Iberian sculpture in the Trocadéro Museum in Paris. He had also seen much of the work of **Gauguin** with its primitive South Sea island subjects. He well knew also **Cézanne's** painting with its floating colour orchestrations of the structure of space and object. Both these artists had shown regularly at Paris exhibitions in the years immediately preceding 1907.

Georges Braque was introduced to Picasso at this time, saw the *Demoiselles* and understood its revolutionary significance. He himself had studied Cézanne thoroughly. Together the two painters went on 'roped together like rock climbers' to work out Cubist form which had as its central tenet the breaking of single-point perspective. Both Braque and Picasso felt that perspective had become 'a stranglehold on art', stultifying it with irrelevant rules. It was possible to remember an object from another view while seeing it in front of the eyes. Perception became multidimensional if you included existing concepts. They realized that this could form a new reality for art.

During the early analytical stage of Cubism from 1907 until 1912, objects were painted as though viewed from many angles. Simple, often rectangular, hence the name Cubist, facets of these various views were then painted flat, overlapping and parallel to the picture surface, emphasizing that surface and shutting out distance. Bright colour was abandoned to avoid an emotional impact and to focus on the restructuring of space–object relationships. Only later did rich and at times brittle colour appear during the synthetic Cubist period (1912–15). At this time also decorative patterns were used and actual paper cut-outs or pieces of objects stuck on to the canvas surface to form *papier collé* or collage. This latter technique was in part to emphasize the flatness or two-dimensionality of the canvas and therefore the autonomy of the work of art as an object in its own right, denying its role as an illusion of natural appearances. However, it was also to make concrete for the viewer the reality the artist was dealing with. Both Picasso and Braque had felt around 1912 that their myriads of small facets had become too abstract. For this reason they also added words or parts of words to the paintings – labels for the objects, in fact.

The First World War separated the two artists, for Braque, as a Frenchman, had to enlist. They did not see each other again. During the war Picasso met **Diaghilev**, master of the Ballets Russes, and worked on sets for the ballet *Parade*. He also loved and married one of the dancers, Olga. As a result of his marriage he produced many portraits and statuesque half-figures of full and fruitful women and children. These take on once more a Classical figurative appearance, at times parodying that style. A return to Classical form was common throughout Europe after the war in many of the arts. However, in Picasso's case it was not long lasting; Dada and Surrealist ideas provided more exciting material to work with.

André Breton, the poet leader of the Surrealist movement, knew Picasso and admired his work. Picasso in turn took an interest in Breton's writings and the Surrealist journal he edited called *La Révolution surréaliste*. The year 1925 saw the first large Surrealist exhibition and it was also the date of Picasso's painting *The Three Dancers* with both Surrealist and Expressionist influences. In it Picasso utilizes again, as he had done for a year or two previously, Cubist flattening of form and lack of depth in space. Three figures, with a fourth death's head, entwine in a primitive dance of conflicting passions. The Surrealist element in the work which gives the left-hand figure its violent contortions derives from **Freudian** concerns with the erotic. The woman, both symbolically and expressively sexual, is linked with the man and the death's head on the right. Between the two and across the linked hands is a cruciform figure suggesting pain and suffering. Picasso had taken the traditional archetypal theme of love and death and added to it several personal significances connected not only with his own marital difficulties but also with the past love affair of a friend who had committed suicide.

Throughout the 1930s Picasso's work carried this double level of interpretation, the universal and the particular, with much use of visual metaphor. A hand could also look like a bird's wing and so suggest the qualities of touch as well as of vision. There is no doubt that Picasso was very physical in his approach to his art. He enjoyed sculpting and was strongly aware of volumetric form. It was this very acute consciousness that made him more especially able to visualize forms as expressive shapes.

At the time of the Spanish Civil War in 1936 Picasso had acquired facility with a great range of expressive subject-matter and formal devices. His experiments with themes of young maidens carried off by bulls or horses, of man desiring and woman enticing, of crucifixion and fear, meant that for the greatest theme of his life, *Guernica*, he had a vivid repertoire on which to draw.

The war itself was a shock to Europe. For the first time the political far left confronted and fought fascism. The outrage of bombing one of Spain's small and defenceless towns with no warning meant a deepening of Picasso's commitment to communism and the total absorption of his dynamic personality in the theme of war. Again the archetypal themes of weeping women, of animals and savagely torn bodies were given a new and personal significance by Picasso's physical and emotional identification with his subject-matter.

The forms in *Guernica* and other works of the period became sharply jagged, hard in colour and texture, twisted and wrenched apart with the tensions of pain and grief. Yet at the same time a classically rhythmic structure underlies the drawing and composition. The twentieth-century element remains as the degree of distortion set in Cubist space.

Faced soon with the isolation, deprivation and hardship of Paris during the Second World War, Picasso sculpted and painted with whatever materials he could assemble. The works were bleak, gaunt and at times fragile. The *Charnel House* of 1944 competes with *Guernica* as a great visual document of protest against human suffering.

After the war, the joyous release gave rise to works of warmth, wit and invention. Picasso's sculptural interests turned more to pottery, which he carried out at Vallauris in the Mediterranean South. By Françoise Gilot he produced more children, and life was perhaps supremely zestful. However, although great themes were not lacking, a more literal look at war as in the painting *Massacre in Korea* of 1951 did not produce works to compare with *Guernica*.

The creativity of this period that commands the greatest respect is more personal and self-revealing. Drawings of old age and youth where Picasso sees himself as less than heroically hiding behind a mask to gaze on the beauty of his young beloved move the viewer at the deepest levels.

Intermittently also, Picasso explored, after the war, paintings of earlier artists. Variations on Velázquez's *Las Meninas* are works of a high order in their own right. As interpretations of the enclosed social milieu of court life and its infantas they must frequently have reminded Picasso of his own. He had from youth been encouraged as a prince among painters. During his mature life the world press followed him as routinely as any member of royalty.

In many senses for Picasso, as for **Matisse**, intuition and expression were one, but as a Spaniard he responded most strongly to themes of the greatest dramatic content, which meant ultimately to tragedy.

Further reading

See: Christian Zervos, *Pablo Picasso* (catalogue raisonné, 23 vols, 1932–71); Alfred H. Barr (ed.) *Picasso: Fifty Years of His Art* (1946); H. Jaffé, *Picasso* (1964); J. Berger, *Picasso: Success and Failure* (1965); John Golding, *Cubism* (1965); J. Crespinelle, *Picasso and His Women* (trans. 1969); Timothy Hilton, *Picasso* (1975); J. Richardson, *A Life of Picasso* (2 vols, 1991–6).

PAT TURNER

PINTER, Harold

1930–

English dramatist

A surprise but wholly justified winner of the 2005 Nobel Prize for Literature, Harold Pinter grew up in Jewish Hackney, East London. After wartime evacuation he attended Hackney Downs Grammar School, then the Royal Academy of Dramatic Art for two disenchanting terms. In 1948–9 Pinter twice stood trial for refusing National Service and was fined as a conscientious objector. *Poetry London* published two poems (1950). After a spell at the Central School of Speech and Drama Pinter began his acting career in earnest by touring Ireland with Anew McMaster's repertory company. Between 1951 and 1957 he acted, wrote poetry, married (one son), did odd jobs, and wrote an unpublished novel, *The Dwarfs*. Since 1957, though occasionally acting and frequently directing, Pinter has written for all media, including celebrated screenplays for **Joseph Losey**, and published a *Proust Screenplay* (1978), later reworked as a less than convincing stage play, *Remembrance of Things Past* (2000).

Nearly all Pinter's plays remove a wall from a domestic interior and reveal existences in process. Truth of character relationship is uncertain, unverifiable and remains unexplored by dramatic exposition. Evasion of communication exacerbates the menace of intruders – agents or victims of psychological and physical domination and dispossession. Pinter's foremost stylistic is obtrusive idiomatic naturalism heightened, almost expressionistically, by an hallucinatory atmosphere which is duplicated by patterns of structural augmentation evoking alternate laughter and apprehensive silence in the audience. The plays are powerful emotional experiences not intellectual blueprints of modern thought. Comedy is a means not an end. The complicity of laughter qualifies the audience's final recognition of a state of being: the failure or betrayal of friendship and love.

In the first plays, *The Room* (1957), *The Dumb Waiter* (1957), *The Birthday Party* (1958) and *A Slight Ache* (1959), a mundane setting is entered by something bizarre which brings blindness, betrayal and death. An incapacitated and alien bearer of identity, a blind Negro, enters the room of an elderly housewife's subservient existence with a silently dominating husband who eventually kicks the Negro to death, precipitating his wife's blindness. The two men waiting argumentatively beside the dumb-waiter of a café basement for instructions are neither workmen nor lodgers but hired gunmen. The order is that one kill the other. The birthday party is given by two strangers for the seedy bullying lodger of a seaside boarding house. Hysteria and final breakdown follow celebration and the strangers abduct the lodger. A slight ache anticipates the blindness that occurs with the admission of a voiceless tramp matchseller to a seemingly complacent middle-class household. In all, physical disability symbolizes moral deficiency.

The year 1960 saw the first performance of four plays. *A Night Out* studies naturalistically the shifting pattern of domination from mother to son, son to prostitute, the son failing to grasp the one possibility of friendship in an otherwise jeering world. *The Caretaker* is Pinter's masterpiece of intuitive psychological insight into three damaged lives: a tramp, an ex-mental patient and his brother, warped by 'normality'. The need for mutual 'caretaking' is betrayed by alternating self-assertion, aggression, domination and rejection. In spite of critical insistence on allegorical interpretation (fostered by the symbolism of the earlier plays), the exhausting realism of *The Caretaker* established Pinter's popular reputation. *The Dwarfs*, a strained reworking from the earlier novel, are creatures of a paranoid imagination breaking down at the betrayal of friendships. In *Night School* and, later, *Tea Party* (1965), Pinter saw the danger of capitulating to mannerism which, he felt, would amount to betrayal of his characters.

A developed sense of dramatic form produced two virtuoso pieces, *The Collection* (1961) and *The Lover* (1963), concerned, respectively, with verification of the truth or otherwise of an adulterous betrayal, and the almost algebraic inversion of a pattern of erotic domination. It was as if Pinter were practising for a large-scale formal assault on the mind and senses which is *The Homecoming* (1965), a modern *King Lear*. Shakespeare explores a pagan world bereft of Christ's grace, Pinter a womanless family abandoned to animality and suburban barbarism, unredeemed by human love, tainted and tainting all.

The script of *The Basement* (1967) dates back to 1963 and both characters and structure belong to the earlier period. Sexual rivalry as an expression of combative egoism leads to a circular pattern of intrusion, betrayal and expropriation. In 1969 Pinter turned startlingly to the extremes of Beckettian austerity and attenuation in *Landscape* and *Silence*. But with *Old Times* (1971) and *No Man's Land* (1975) it could be seen that the primary concern was with double betrayal, by fallibility and disclosure, of memory, that both appropriates and rejects – in thought, image or embodied intruder, the past marooning the present, leaving Pinter's characters stranded by time as well as in place.

Betrayal (1978), focuses through retrospective time sequence on the illusory nature of assumed mutuality in love and friendship. Love can only be betrayed if it is real. The origin of all betrayals lies in fostering initial illusion. The characters are incapable of consummating true betrayal. Beneath the patterned, desultory surface there is the intensity of the later Shakespeare sonnets.

With *One for the Road* (1984), *Mountain Language* (1988) and *The New World Order* (1991), Pinter's theatre veered towards the overtly, even uncomfortably, political, torture and other human rights concerns representing a newfound subject-matter. *Celebration* (2000) – a portrait of aimless, ageing yuppies dining out in an upmarket restaurant that encroaches on the perimeters of **John Osborne**-land – is notable as a species of self-parody, the emptiness of its characters' lives echoing, and mirrored by, the final emptiness of the play itself. Pinter, coming up for seventy, seems in this work to have lost his touch for original ambiguity, but still makes theatre out of it. The faintly **Ibsenesque** *Moonlight* (1993) is judged by some the last authentic Pinter play: its central bedridden character, surrounded by his family, twists between a lingering appetite for control and a besetting sense of powerlessness.

Increasingly Pinter has publicly protested his political concerns, seldom missing an opportunity to express his hostility towards, particularly, US foreign policy. To the delight of the London press, in 1985 Pinter famously stormed out of a reception given to honour his fellow playwright **Arthur Miller** at the American Embassy. His private life too has come under scrutiny, following his divorce from the actress Vivien Merchant in favour of Lord Longford's daughter Lady Antonia Fraser, in 1977. His plays, particularly the earlier, are often discussed in terms of Theatre of the Absurd, Black Comedy, or Comedy of Menace. Acknowledged admiration for **Kafka** and **Beckett** might appear to support this, but the most powerful and least discussed artistic influences are the multifarious traditions of comedy absorbed through years of acting. Pinter's style and power have been copied, but rarely followed, the young **Joe Orton** being a conspicuous example.

Further reading

Other works include: *Revue Sketches* in *A Slight Ache and Other Plays* (1961); *Night* (1969); *Five Screenplays* (1971); *Monologue* (1973); *Poems and Prose* (1978); *The Hothouse* (written 1958, first performed 1980); *A Kind of Alaska* (1982); *Ashes to Ashes* (1996); *Conference* (2002). See also: J.R. Brown, *Theatre Language* (1972); Martin Esslin, *Pinter. A Study of His Plays* (3rd edn, 1977); Harold Bloom (ed.) *Harold Pinter* (1987); Michael Billington, *The Life and Works of Harold Pinter* (1996). Pinter's official website–http://www.haroldpinter.org–is eminently visitable.

RONALD KNOWLES
(REVISED AND UPDATED BY THE EDITOR)

PIRANDELLO, Luigi

1867–1936

Italian poet, short-story writer, novelist and dramatist

The Sicilian Pirandello was educated at the Universities of Rome and Bonn, where he wrote a doctoral thesis on his native dialect. That he wrote verse (*Mal giocondo*, 1889; *Pasqua di Gea*, 1891) was more an indication of the prestige of poetry than a recognition of his true gifts. In Rome in 1893, Pirandello was induced by a fellow Sicilian, Luigi Capuana, to write prose. His first novel, *The Outcast* (*L'esclusa*, 1908, written in 1894, trans. 1925), deals with a woman wrongly suspected of adultery, cast off by her husband, and forced by social pressures to become what she was thought to be. The themes of Pirandello's early fiction are the contrast between appearance and reality, form and life, the tragedies of a society which values appearance and formality. Until 1910–12, Pirandello wrote novels and short stories – sketches of peasant and middle-class life, coloured by his conviction that external reality is unknowable and that we are irremediably alone. He is capable of humour, as in *The Jar* (*La giara*, short story 1909, play 1925, trans. 1928), but for the most part his laughter is either sardonic or compassionate, as he explains in the essay *L'umorismo* (1908).

Although in his first fiction Pirandello seemed the natural heir of the Sicilian naturalists, **Verga** and Capuana, he soon turned to the exploration of ideas. The first full formulation of his attitude to life comes in the novel *The Late Mattia Pascal* (*Il fu Mattia Pascal*, 1904, trans. 1923). The phrase 'relativity of personality' is often used to describe his belief that personality is a subjective phenomenon. Deriving from Alfred Binet and **Henri Bergson**, Pirandello's attitude is philosophically unsound, but expressed with lucidity and emotional conviction.

His ear for the spoken language led him naturally to cast his tales in dramatic form, with lively dialogue. He wrote his first play, *The Vice* (*La morsa*, trans. 1928) in 1908, and he was several times invited to write for the theatre. In 1916, he wrote nine plays in a year, of which the best known is *Right You Are, If You Think So!* (*Così è, se vi pare!*, 1918, trans. 1960). In this group of plays, the ideas at stake are recognizably Pirandellian, but his techniques are conventional. Contacts with avant-garde theatre groups between 1915 and 1920 helped him to clarify his ideas. He learned from Craig the importance of harmonizing all elements on the stage, and

from Bragaglia the use of lighting to clarify the action. From 1920 onwards, his stage directions became much more detailed and precise, his sets less realistic, often illustrating symbolically the different levels of reality at which the action takes place.

Pirandello's 'total theatre' has its origin in the story *A Character in Distress* (*Tragedia di un personaggio*, 1911, trans. 1938), which led to the play *Six Characters in Search of an Author* (*Sei personaggi in cerca d'autore*, 1921, trans. 1923). This is often regarded as the first in a 'trilogy' which is crucial for our understanding of his contribution to the theatre, the others being *Each in His Own Way* (*Ciascuno a suo modo*, 1924, trans. 1924) and *Tonight We Improvise* (*Questa sera si recita a soggetto*, 1930, trans. 1932). He stresses that the theatre is illusion, but that it is superior to life since it has, or rather, *is* form, 'form that moves', and so has a stability missing in life, which is all flux. His plays therefore have a polemical thrust and are not concerned with pointing to an alternative set of values other than in the realm of abstract ideas. His situations are contrived, so exceptional that they can never constitute the basis of another norm. As Raymond Williams writes: 'It is, really, a mystification of demystification, since the experience ... depends on a theatrical special case.' *Henry IV* (*Enrico IV*, 1922, trans. 1923) remains Pirandello's most performed play, because it is the most imbued with deep feeling. Henry's tragedy is that the mask of madness, which he has consciously chosen to wear, is at the end of the play forced on him by the pressures of emotions outside his control. In his depiction of the loss of identity and the reduction of personality to a social role, Pirandello achieved his greatest success.

Further reading

Other works include: the novel *The Old and the Young* (*I vecchi e i giovani*, 1913, trans. 1928); and the plays *Naked* (*Vestire gli ignudi*, 1923, trans. 1924) and *The Man with a Flower in His Mouth* (*L'uomo dal fiore in bocca*, 1926, trans. 1928). See: G. Giudice, *Luigi Pirandello* (1963); A.L. De Castris, *Storia di Pirandello* (1966); R. Williams, *Modern*

Tragedy (1966); John Louis DiGaetani (ed.) *A Companion to Pirandello Studies* (1991).

BRIAN MOLONEY

PISSARRO, Camille

1831–1903

French painter

A prolific though essentially modest painter, Pissarro is remembered for his close friendships with **Claude Monet** and **Paul Cézanne** and for his lasting commitment to the aims of French Impressionism. Initially influenced by Corot and the painters of Barbizon, he exhibited regularly at the Paris Salon though was considered sufficiently progressive to be the only artist to show his work in all eight Impressionist exhibitions from 1874 to 1886. The admiration for Corot was readily acknowledged and the early work has all the clarity of detail that we associate with the painter of orderly landscapes set under clear southern skies. But the Impressionists were more concerned with the systematic study of particular effects of light and the absolute necessity for working out of doors face to face with the motif to ensure the authenticity of their vision. Here Corot was of little help, and a less precise method was needed. The robust palette-knife of **Courbet** was a possible answer and Pissarro had much sympathy for the older man's Socialist principles, but it was the fruitful working relationship with Claude Monet whom he met at the Académie Suisse in 1859 that helped to mould the style of his middle years. The two men worked together and evolved a less exacting technique better suited to capturing the fleeting effects of sudden movement, though as late as 1865 Pissarro still exhibited at the Salon as a 'pupil of Corot'. In 1870 both men were in London avoiding the threat and disruptions of the Franco-Prussian War and there is little doubt that they were impressed by the works of the English landscape painters, in particular the vivid atmospheric effects and seemingly spontaneous compositions of J.M.W. Turner, though there is no evidence that they were able to see the countless watercolour sketches we now see as his most 'impressionist' works.

Less impressed by the damp mist and London fog, Pissarro moved to the outer suburbs and the paintings made there have a delicacy and deftness of touch quite unlike anything he had painted in France. The friendship with Paul Cézanne dates from 1861 and the two men worked closely together. Pissarro encouraged Cézanne to move away from the turgid, melodramatic and often erotic subject-matter of his early years and he began to produce works in the Impressionist manner. In turn Pissarro's work shows a firmer grasp of pictorial structure in which the angled brush-strokes reflect the surface of the canvas as much as any specific natural phenomena. Both men relished the opportunity to work directly from nature and to be strictly objective in their vision. For a time Pissarro flirted with the optical-mixtures of **Seurat**, but soon returned to his now settled descriptive style in which what he saw as the truth of the matter was the essence of his art. Ironically, like Monet his eyesight failed and towards the very end of his life he was forced indoors; the paintings seen from the studio window inevitably have an unwanted distance that weakens the normally perceptive way of seeing. There is a sad *Self Portrait* (Tate Gallery, London) painted in 1903, the year of his death, which sums up his life-long achievement. The near blind man sits with his back to the window from which he has been working; the face with the thin spectacles is little more than a delicate impression and the beard a lightly applied multi-coloured mixture of small brush-strokes. In sharp contrast the silhouetted dark hat and coat show an awareness of the need for controlled formal organization. Pale sunlight filters into the room from the street outside. It is a small picture of no great importance. Pissarro left no masterpieces but his contribution to the more revolutionary art of his friends and his simple uncomplicated eye enable us to see clearly why he was so well loved by those who changed the course of nineteenth-century art.

Further reading

Other works include: *Letters to His Son* (trans. 1943). See also: L.R. Pissarro and L. Venturi, *Camille Pissarro. son art, son oeuvre* (12 vols 1939); John Rewald, *The History of Impressionism* (1961); John Rewald, *Camille Pissarro* (1963); C. Lloyd, *Camille Pissarro* (1981); A. Thorold (ed.) *The Letters of Lucien to Camille Pissarro* (1993).

JOHN FURSE

PITT RIVERS, Augustus Lane Fox

1827–1900

British archaeologist

Augustus Lane Fox, as he was known until 1880, was born into an upper-class military family. Although he became a professional soldier, serving with distinction in the Crimean War and ultimately attaining the rank of major-general, army life does not seem to have been altogether congenial to him. Most of his military career was spent in non-combatant roles and he was especially concerned with the development of the modern rifle. He became a collector of fire-arms and other weapons from every part of the world and this stimulated his interest both in primitive peoples and in the history of weaponry. He believed that the key to the history of weaponry, and other artefacts, lay in their *typology* – a term he was the first to use in its modern archaeological sense. He became convinced that there was a precise analogy between the way types of artefact developed in complexity and **Darwinian** evolution. Accordingly, the progress of human societies, as revealed by their material culture, was to be investigated in just the same way as the phenomena of the natural world.

Lane Fox's vision of a science of the 'evolution of culture' was set out forcibly in a lecture under that name delivered to the Royal Institution in 1875. This lecture rejected outright the idealistic and Romantic view that the human mind and spirit will always resist scientific inquiry: history could not claim exemption from the logic of evolution, whose understanding constituted the highest form of knowledge. 'Human ideas', he argued,

> as represented by the products of human industry, are capable of classification into genera, species and varieties in the same manner as the products of the animal and vegetable kingdoms, and in their development from the homogeneous to the heterogeneous they obey the same laws ... History is but another name for evolution.

A society was successful to the extent that it was a vehicle of those ideas that proved 'fittest' and hence survived in the long term. For Lane Fox this was proved by the progress of technology, whose products were seen as symbols of the human mind.

Lane Fox's fortunes were transfigured in 1880 when he inherited the vast estates of his distant relative, Lord Rivers, at Cranborne Chase in Wiltshire. As Pitt Rivers, he now dedicated himself to the twin tasks of promoting evolutionary concepts in the popular mind and the scientific investigation of archaeological sites. He was a forerunner of many twentieth-century aristocrats in opening up his estates to the masses and erecting a public museum and zoo. His motives, however, were not commercial (entry was free), but purely instructive. For several years he served as the first Inspector of Ancient Monuments under the act introduced in Parliament by his son-in-law, Sir John Lubbock, and travelled to all parts of Britain. Most of his excavations, however, were undertaken on unspectacular sites within his own grounds. He learnt something from Canon Greenwell, the excavator of Yorkshire barrows, but his techniques were really the product of his own systematic experimentation. Under his hands excavation was transformed into a science, as exacting in its way as clinical dissection. Technically his methods fell only a little short of those followed in the best excavations at the present day.

Pitt Rivers's apocalyptic evolutionism, though an ascendant faith in his time, now seems overblown and inapposite. His typological studies still have some value, but his most lasting contribution to the sum of human knowledge was his demonstration that archaeology could not attempt to be a substitute history: it has its own special kind of data. He taught that archaeology's most valuable documents were the evidences for the lives of ordinary people: the commonplace objects of everyday existence were richer in meaning than the rare 'art' pieces. In this, as in his excavation methods, Pitt Rivers stands out as a pioneer of modern archaeology, in contrast to his contemporaries, like Schliemann and even **Sir Arthur Evans**. The Pitt Rivers Museum in Oxford was formed around nucleus collections made by Pitt Rivers and the whole is arranged according to his typological principles.

Further reading

M.V. Thompson, *General Pitt Rivers* (1977) is the only biography. This contains a reprint of the 1875 lecture, *On the Evolution of Culture*. For Pitt Rivers's archaeological achievement see Glyn Daniel, *One Hundred and Fifty Years of Archaeology* (1975).

C.F. HAWKE-SMITH

PLANCK, Max Karl

1858–1947

German physicist

Max Planck was born in Kiel where his father was Professor of Constitutional Law. Educated at the Maximilian-Gymnasium in Munich, he studied mathematics and physics at the Universities of Munich and Berlin, obtaining his doctorate in physics from Munich in 1879 for a thesis on the second law of thermodynamics. He then taught physics at Munich until he was appointed to a special chair in mathematical physics at Kiel in 1885. In 1889 he moved to a professorship at Berlin made vacant by the death of Gustav Kirchhoff. He was president of the Kaiser-Wilhelm Institut (1930–5) which after the Second World War was renamed the Max-Planck Institut.

In his early years Planck made significant contributions to physics, particularly to the understanding of heat and physical chemistry. His work at the time received little attention. Between 1894 and 1900 Planck worked on thermodynamics, statistical mechanics and electro-magnetic theory. By applying his work in these areas in novel ways to the problem of black-body radiation, Planck was led in 1900 to the discovery of the quantum, a discovery which was to revolutionize physics. A black-body (approximated by a piece of soot) is a perfect absorber of radiation which when heated emits all types of radiation. At the end of the last century no law had been discovered which would correctly predict the distribution of radiation given off by a black-body. The Rayleigh–Jeans law (1900) worked for high but not for low temperature. Wilhelm Wien's formula (1883), on the other hand, gave correct predictions for low but not high temperatures. Planck, who at a previous stage had had doubts about the atomic theory of matter, now assumed that for his purposes the radiating matter could be thought of as composed of discrete vibrating electrons. Prior to Planck it had been assumed that energy was given off continuously by radiating electrons. Working on the entirely novel assumption that the energy was in fact given off in discrete bundles, Planck arrived at his radiation law which correctly predicts the distribution of radiation from a black-body for all temperatures. In Planck's theory the energy E of an electron vibrating with frequency ν is given by the equation: $E = nh\nu$, with h a constant now known as Planck's constant whose value he calculated to be 6.55 @ 10–27 erg-seconds. The discrete, quantized character of energy is revealed through the fact that n can only take as values 0, 1, 2, ... For this work Planck was awarded the Nobel Prize in 1919.

Planck was subsequently exercised by the problem of reconciling the emission of radiation in discrete bundles with the application to the radiation once emitted of **Maxwell's** field equations, which appeared to require treating it as continuous. It was left to **Einstein** to show how to extend the quantum treatment to all radiation. The discovery of other areas requiring a quantum approach led to the development of quantum mechanics by **Schrödinger** and **Heisenberg**. The crucial role played in that theory by Planck's constant led to the realization that it is one of the most fundamental of all physical constants. Planck's work was crucial to the discovery of quantum mechanics which represents the most fundamental transformations in physics since Newton.

Planck was cultured, musically talented and politically conservative. He wrote extensively on the state of physics and on the philosophy of science, vigorously attacking the early positivists who regarded physical objects as complexes of sensations. Planck was a realist, holding it to be a cardinal principle of science that there is a real external world existing independently of our cognition which is not directly knowable and which is governed by immutable laws, to be discovered, not created, by the scientist. A firm believer in causality, he sought to refute the indeterministic construal of quantum mechanics by attempting unconvincingly to distinguish between what he called the 'world picture of physics' and the 'sense world'. The world picture of physics was, he held, rigorously deterministic. Any indeterminism indicated by quantum mechanics reflected only uncertainly in the correlation of items from these two worlds. His determinism did not extend to human action, for he maintained that the individual ego acting in its own living present is not subject to causation. A religious man, who held that there was no real opposition between science and religion, he argued for the existence of God by appeal to a version of the argument by design. Notwithstanding his strong belief in the success and importance of physics, he had a somewhat cynical view of institutionalized science deriving from his feelings early in his career that certain vested interests had stood in the way of the recognition of his work. Writing in his *Scientific Autobiography* (1949), he remarked that new truths triumph not by convincing opponents

and making them see the light but rather because the opponents eventually die.

Further reading

Other works include: *Treatise on Thermodynamics* (*Vorlesungen über Thermodynamik*, 1897); *Theory of Heat Radiation* (*Vorlesungen über die Theorie der Wärmestrahlung* 1923); *Introduction to Theoretical Physics* (1932); *Where is Science Going?* (1933); *The Philosophy of Physics* (1936); *The Universe in the Light of Modern Physics* (1937). See: J.L. Heilbron, *The Dilemmas of an Upright Man: Max Planck and the Fortunes of German Science* (1986).

W.H. NEWTON-SMITH

PLATH, Sylvia
1932–63
US poet

Sylvia Plath's suicide launched a tragic myth which was largely validated by the dramatic, intensely imaged and highly personal poems of her posthumous *Ariel* (1965). Today, Plath's life and writings are still often seen through the distorting glass of opinions about the myth of poet as female victim and rebel. In the women's movement, Plath has functioned both as an image of heroic development towards a female poetic and as a contemporary avatar of a much older type, the suicide-prone Romantic poet, sensitive to the point of madness, persecuted by family and society. While such uses of Plath involve misreadings of her total accomplishment, the ways in which a writer can be used inevitably become part of that writer's historic role. And Plath is one of the few recent poets to have had an undoubted social, as well as literary, impact.

Part of the 'personal' reading of Plath has a genuine basis in her text. One need not agree with A. Alvarez's aesthetic of death in *The Savage God* (1971) – where he argues that suicide and attempted suicide are, for the writer, existential investigations of extremes – in order to feel that Plath's phenomenal development during her short career owed much to the energies released when she began to incorporate covert, then overt, allusions to her private life in her poetry. Like many mythologized poets (Shelley, Byron, Heine) Plath made inner biographical incident and subjective images of herself into part of the poetic armoury with which she faced her audience. In *Ariel* and in some earlier poems, Plath represented herself and threats to herself through a few repeated images: moon, egg, blank-faced corpse, sack of blood. She used several *personae*: the mummy ('All the Dead Dears'), the Jew ('Daddy'), the ritual victim ('The Bee Meeting'), the resurrected corpse ('Lady Lazarus'), the cold nihilist ('Lesbos'). Often, as in 'Tulips', the speaker is assaulted by the physical world, from which she longs to escape ('Fever 103°', 'In Plaster'). Plath's masks are convincing, their dilemmas passionately expressed, but ultimately they are fictions, more about a way of seeing than about the 'real' person seeing it. Plath began and ended as a metaphoric poet, and her literary life was highly professional.

In 'Daddy', probably her most famous poem, Plath moves from mute grief at her lost father (Otto Plath had died when Plath was eight) to rejection of Oedipal obsession with both father and husband. In this poem Plath's story fragments do seem to play a partly extraliterary role in creating sympathy for the author, while the mythic images carry the thematic burden of an archetypal truth.

> If I've killed one man, I've killed two—
> The vampire who said he was you
> And drank my blood for a year,
> Seven years, if you want to know.

The apparently casual revision of 'a year' to 'seven' has been left in the finished text to signal that the mythic vampire is Plath's real husband, English poet **Ted Hughes**, whom she had known for seven years. At first the 'daddy' addressed by the poem is an archetypal patriarch, 'Marble-heavy, a bag full of God,/Ghastly statue.' But he also comes from Germany, like Plath's father, and he is seen 'at the blackboard' like Plath's father, an entomologist who researched into the habits of bees. The poem's pressure towards a psychological resolution forces the private event over into myth, where, as myth, it can be encompassed, if not solved. Plath's father is described as a fascist, Plath as 'a bit of a Jew', biographically incorrect remarks which express the larger truth that 'Every woman loves a fascist', and woman will remain enslaved until the concept of the all-powerful 'daddy', whether father or husband, has been violently rejected: 'Daddy, daddy, you bastard, I'm through.'

Plath's first volume of poems, *The Colossus* (1960), was an impersonal, highly crafted collection of poems whose interpretable ambiguities located it firmly in the era influenced by the criticism of **T.S. Eliot** and William Empson. Plath had obviously been reading the metaphysical poets and Jacobean dramatists, as well as **W.B. Yeats** and **Emily Dickinson**. She further enlarged her vocabulary by writing with a thesaurus at hand. The *Colossus* poems are written in tightly imaged, short lines and precise stanzas. Plath's small characteristic body of images was already present: the colours white, black and blood-red. There is a threatening, even Gothic, outer world, as in 'Hardcastle Crags', and lurking, insinuating death, as in 'Two Views of a Cadaver Room'. The poet, when present, is almost bewitched by 'The Disquieting Muses' 'with heads like darning eggs' brought down on her from the cradle by her witch-like mother: 'And this is the kingdom you bore me to,/Mother, mother.'

When *The Colossus* was published, Plath had already settled in England with Hughes. In the early years of their marriage, they worked closely together, and some of Hughes's interests are reflected in Plath's use of primitivist animal imagery. Even when she was an undergraduate at Smith College in Massachusetts, Plath had deliberately taken on influences. At first she wanted to become a short-story writer like Frank O'Connor: 'I will imitate until I can feel, I'm using what he can teach.' In the apprentice pieces subsequently collected in *Johnny Panic and the Bible of Dreams* (1977), Plath aimed for the impersonal writerly craft of the 1950s. As she wrote in her diary, 'I justified the mess I made of life by saying I'd give it order, form, beauty, writing about it. The highly formed writing would then reciprocally "give me life" (and prestige to life).'

While Plath's drive for success has dismayed critics who like their tragedy pure, it meant that she strove to understand other writers in order to extend her own range. When Plath read the poetry of **Theodore Roethke** in the late 1950s, she adapted his use of **Jungian** archetypal image to re-work painful personal loss into poetic knowledge; Roethke's influence is almost palpable in poems like 'Maenad', 'Dark House' and 'The Beast' and in the theme of the lost father. In the summer of 1959 Plath and poet **Anne Sexton** visited **Robert Lowell's** poetry seminar at Harvard. Plath was deeply impressed by the 'confessional' mode of Lowell's *Life Studies*, even if her own poems do not seek to give the impression of the 'real' poet to the extent that Lowell's do. Also, Plath, unlike Lowell, read history primarily as myth. Once some – but not all – of the poems written between *The Colossus* and *Ariel* had been collected in *Crossing the Water* (1971) and some others written during the period of *Ariel* appeared in *Winter Trees* (1971), it was clear that Plath arrived at the rage and recognition of *Ariel* through poems like 'I Am Vertical', which embraces the temptations of death and release from the body:

> And I shall be useful when I lie down
> > finally:
> Then the trees may touch me for once,
> > and the flowers
> have time for me.

Other poems focus on specifically womanly compulsions, expressing loathing and identification: 'Heavy Women', 'The Zoo-Keeper's Wife' and 'Three Women: A Monologue for Three Voices' (1968), a 1962 BBC broadcast.

The Bell Jar (1963), Plath's autobiographical novel, begins the story of Esther Greenwood's breakdown and attempted suicide as a satiric novel of adolescence. Esther, like Plath, has won a literary prize and goes off to New York to be exploited by the women's magazine which has awarded it. Through her episodic adventures, Esther realizes that the radical hostility between men and women can't be got rid of by throwing up, taking a purifying bath, writing a scathing letter, briefly adopting a false identity, or even cynically getting herself deflowered. Destined, as a woman, for the life in the kitchen which was the 'feminine mystique' of the 1950s, Esther feels she can't write unless she has the mysterious 'experience' denied her by the banality of her aspirations. Esther stops writing, sleeping and washing: 'I could see day after day after day glaring ahead of me like a white, broad, infinitely desolate avenue.' She takes sleeping pills and crawls underground to die. Rescued (like Plath) after her suicide attempt, Esther spends months in a mental institution (quite wittily described). Helped by a friendly woman doctor, Esther sees the 'bell jar' of schizophrenic isolation rise, and she returns to the outside world. She now realizes, among other rejections, that she hates the overbearing mother whom she always tried to please. Although it lacks the metaphoric power of the poems in *Ariel*, *The Bell Jar* is an important novel, since it links its heroine's breakdown to the contradictory social demands of the age, and it does so with a lucid appreciation of complexity.

Further reading

Other works include: *Collected Poems*, ed. Ted Hughes (1982). See also: Charles Newman (ed.) *The Art of Sylvia Plath: A Symposium* (1970); Margaret D. Uroff, *Sylvia Plath and Ted Hughes* (1979); Judith Kroll, *Chapters in a Mythology: The Poetry of Sylvia Plath* (1976); Gary Lane (ed.) *Sylvia Plath: New Views on the Poetry* (1978); A. Stevenson, *Bitter Fame* (1989); Ronald Hayman, *The Death and Life of Sylvia Plath* (1991); Jacqueline Rose, *The Haunting of Sylvia Plath* (1991); Janet Malcolm, *The Silent Woman* (1994); Erica Wagner,

Ariel's Gift (2000); Jo Gill (ed.) *The Cambridge Companion to Sylvia Plath* (2006).

HELEN MCNEIL

POINCARÉ, Henri

1854–1912

French mathematician

In Henri Poincaré France produced a mathematical giant who subsequently became a philosophical and literary giant. This is not a common transition, and one must turn to **Bertrand Russell** and **Alfred North Whitehead** for figures of similar power and breadth in recent times. But there is a difference between the two Englishmen and the Frenchman they admired: Poincaré began as a creative mathematician of astonishing originality and punch, whereas the Englishmen were primarily mathematical logicians and systematizers in their early years.

Poincaré is often called the 'Father' or 'Founder' of the mathematical science of topology. One can hardly expect exact scientific accuracy in such a claim: it is, rather, an expression of the way in which he saw, as a whole and as a potential unity, a mass of questions which, before his day, had been dealt with under various heads. Poincaré was to topology as Gilbert was to magnetism: the man whose name is indelibly linked with the new knowledge, because it was he (Poincaré) who saw its interconnectedness, its significance as an attempt to answer a small set of fundamentally similar questions.

Poincaré was born in Nancy in 1854. His father was Professor of Medicine at the university, his mother a warm, intelligent, cultivated woman, who set about educating her precocious, but frail, son at home – at least until he was able to enter the local *lycée*. Henri's progress at the Nancy *lycée* left his contemporaries standing, but there was one Achilles heel – Poincaré was poorly co-ordinated and, as a result of this, could never draw to the standard expected of an outstandingly clever boy. When he subsequently sat the examination for the École Polytechnique his mark for drawing was actually zero! (In spite of this the examiners made an exception and let him in.)

The École Polytechnique led to the School of Mines and, in 1879 at the age of twenty-five, Poincaré received his doctorate in mathematical science at the University of Paris. After two years on the faculty at Caen, he moved to Paris in 1881, first to be Maître de Conférences, and later (in 1886) to be Professor of Mathematical Physics and Probability.

From the time when he received his doctorate onwards Poincaré maintained a prodigious output of books and papers. During his life he published nearly 500 memoirs on mathematical topics, more than thirty books on mathematical physics and astronomy, and six books on more general themes.

Poincaré's recognition of the importance of topology is all of a piece with his poor drawing skill, because a poorly drawn but complete figure and a well-drawn figure have this in common: they are topologically equal. Topology is concerned only with the question whether two points p and q are joined by a continuous line or curve, not with the shape of the curve nor straightness of the line. Later popularizers have called topology 'rubber sheet geometry' because it is about those properties of spatial relationships which remain intact when the figures, drawn on a rubber sheet, are pulled around, i.e. deformed, but not cut or torn.

Poincaré's work on topology, entitled *Analysis situ*, was published in 1895. With this event mathematicians began to recognize the existence of a major new research area – a comparatively rare event in the history of mathematics. The new science could be applied to many things besides plane figures: to space as a whole (general relativity), to tangles (knot theory), and to spatial permutation (combinatorial topology). Yet none of these applications has quite justified the feeling of intellectual pregnancy associated with topology for more than eighty years. Throughout this period it has captured the interest of many of the most creative research mathematicians and has been widely seen as the modern branch of mathematics *par excellence*. There is a direct link with Thom's later 'Catastrophe Theory'. But the subject has yet to generate the kind of substantial body of intellectually important applications which it has seemed to promise. The prime target for such applications must be the biological topic of morphology, but the breakthrough to a neat, intellectually elegant treatment of this area still eludes us.

Poincaré's greatest technical achievement in mathematics was his theory of automorphic functions. These were functions which remained unchanged when one changed their 'arguments' in certain ways. (The argument of a function is the variable to which one applies the function: for example '*x*' is the argument of the function log (*x*).) The simplest elementary example of an automorphic function is sin (q), which obviously remains unchanged when one adds 360 to its 'argument' q – having turned through a complete circle, one is left pointing in the same direction. It was this theory (of automorphic functions) which led Poincaré to non-Euclidean geometry and topology, to new ways of solving differential equations, and to the solution of other technical problems in mathematics. Poincaré also did important work on the classical 'three body problem', leading to the new methods of 'asymptotic expansions' and 'integral invariants'. Poincaré did not solve the problem – which is about the mutual effects of three or more bodies attracting each other gravitationally in space – but he did make enough progress to qualify for the prize given by the king of Sweden for work in this area.

In astronomy Poincaré showed that a rotating gravitational fluid mass subject to the influence of a steady torque would gradually become pear shaped and would finally throw off a moon.

In philosophy of science Poincaré's name is associated with a view often described as 'conventionality'. He pointed out, for example, that it is possible to describe space using non-Euclidean geometries, so that there is a certain degree of conventionality in our normal use of the Euclidean concept of space to describe the world around us. Nevertheless, there is a reason for adopting one convention rather than another, namely that the Euclidean point of view is 'simpler', 'more convenient' or 'advantageous'. 'Geometry,' he says in *Science and Method* (*Science et Méthode*, 1908, trans. 1914), 'is not true, it is advantageous.' Poincaré applied this view of conceptual frameworks to other examples, such as time, rotation and the laws of mechanics.

The nineteenth century produced a crop of individuals of astonishing intellectual power whose influence came to fruition after 1900: men like **Babbage**, **Mendel**, **Peirce** and Karl Pearson. Even in this select company Poincaré stands out. It is a triumph of mind over matter that Poincaré, who was physically myopic, developed intellectually into a figure exceptionally long-, and exceptionally broad-, sighted. But unlike the thinkers mentioned above, he was not neglected in his day. He won almost every honour, prize, medal or fellowship for which he was eligible. His books were widely read. He wrote to be understood, and he was understood.

Further reading

Other works include: *Oeuvres de Henri Poincaré*, Académie des Sciences de Paris (10 vols, 1916–54); *The Foundations of Science*, trans. G.B. Halsted (1913); *Dernières Pensées* (1913), trans. *Mathematics and Science: Last Essays* (1963). See: E.T. Bell, *Men of Mathematics* (1937), Ch. 28. An interesting obituary notice may be found in *Proceedings of the Royal Society*, Series A, Vol. 91 (1915), pp. 5–16

CHRISTOPHER ORMELL

POIRET, Paul

1879–1944

French couturier

Born in Paris, the young Poiret showed great aptitude for painting, drawing, costume design and the performing arts. In an effort to divert these interests his father, a draper, refused to send him to university, apprenticing him instead to an umbrella-maker. But, with scraps of silk from the workshop, Poiret constructed miniature costumes, and was soon selling sketches of these to the fashion establishments he visited in the course of delivering umbrellas. At seventeen, his father finally relenting, he went to work for Jacques Doucet, then the leading designer in Paris. At the Maison Doucet Poiret designed the most famous theatrical costume of the century – the white suit worn by Sarah Bernhardt as the Prince Imperial in *L'Aiglon*.

In 1903 Poiret opened his own salon. The Fauve of fashion, he startled the public with a bright new spectrum of colours. Filling his windows with artistic arrangements of foliage, fabrics and frivolities appropriate to the season as a backdrop to his designs, he invented modern window display. More important perhaps, in those early days of the feminist movement, was his contribution to the modern fashion revolution. His designs – slender, supple tunics tied gently beneath the bust and descending in a simple sheath to the floor, reminiscent of classic Greek and oriental draperies – liberated women from the huge hats, billowing skirts and stiff corsets of the Belle Époque.

To popularize his new fashion look, which prefigured **Bakst**, **Diaghilev** and the Ballets Russes, Poiret commissioned two illustrated books, *Les Robes de Paul Poiret racontées par Paul Iribe* (1908) and *Les Choses de Paul Poiret vues par Georges Lepape* (1911). These established the modern style and tradition of fashion illustration. In 1911 he also established the Martine School of Decorative Arts, in the belief that barriers between fashion and the applied arts should not exist. Under his direction the School created a total design environment, or 'complete lifestyle': curtains, draperies, wall panels and papers, screens, porcelain, tapestries, rugs, embroideries, bedclothes, furniture fabrics and the furniture itself were all linked by the same design motifs and colour themes. The *style Martine*, developed by girls with no formal artistic straining, was a striking and original blend of naivety, naturalism and sophistication similar to, but in no way derivative of, the work of **Henri Rousseau** and **Matisse**.

Poiret was also responsible for creating 'designer fabrics' as we know them today. The fabrics which he commissioned from the painter Raoul Dufy revolutionized the French textile industry, and resulted in the first production of printed satins, velvets and linens. In addition his interest in perfumes led him to create modern promotional packaging. Replacing then prevalent light floral scents with his own more exotic blends, his preparations, sold under the *Rosine* label, were presented in boxes with nightgowns, matching handkerchiefs or luxurious drawstring bags. The perfumes were followed by *Rosine* soaps, toilet-waters and *eaux de cologne*, with a range of day, evening and stage make-up.

A passable actor and director, Poiret was renowned as a patron of the arts and a collector. He delighted in devising elaborate entertainments, among them the 'Bal de la Mille et Deuxième Nuit' (1911), which symbolized the extravagance, exuberance and elegance of his heyday. But his facility for business was no match for his talent: through a series of financial misadventures he was forced to give up his practice in 1929. Poiret 'le Magnifique' died in poverty, his last years clouded by Parkinson's disease.

Further reading

Other works include: *My First Fifty Years* (*En habillant l'Époque*, 1930, trans. 1931); *Revenez-y* (1932). See also: Palmer White, *Poiret* (1973); *Catalogue de l'exposition 'Poiret le Magnifique'* (Musée Jacquemart-André, 1974).

KAORI O'CONNOR

POL POT (SALOTH SAR)

1925–98

Cambodian leader

From 1962, Pol Pot secretly ran the Cambodian communist underground, which the country's ruler Prince Norodom Sihanouk dubbed the 'Khmers Rouges' (Cambodian Reds). Pol Pot's Communist Party of Kampuchea

(CPK) seized power in 1975 and established the regime of Democratic Kampuchea (DK), which ruled Cambodia until 1979. As CPK General Secretary and Prime Minister of DK, Pol Pot oversaw four years of genocide and other crimes against humanity, and war crimes against neighbouring Vietnam and Thailand. In all, 1.7 million Cambodians and ethnic minorities perished, more than a fifth of the country's population.

Pol Pot's deleterious contribution to international culture was to fashion a unique ideological amalgam of communism and racism. His regime simultaneously annihilated urban classes, considering them traitors contaminated by foreign influences and by ethnic groups, which it stereotyped as suspect social classes. These disingenuous campaigns allowed Pol Pot and the other CPK leaders to pose as Cambodian nationalist heroes. Rewriting the CPK's own history reinforced that claim.

Pol Pot began it all much earlier with little lies about his age and his name. He was born Saloth Sar, in a village in Kompong Thom province, on 19 May 1925. Sar's father, Phen Saloth, was a rich Khmer peasant owning 12 hectares of farmland. Sar's sister was a royal consort in the capital, Phnom Penh; his brother Suong was a palace protocol officer. At age nine, the family sent Sar to join them at the palace. Understating his age by three years helped place Sar for a year in the leading royal Buddhist monastery, followed by six years in an elite Catholic school. Sar's upbringing was strict, removed from the Khmer vernacular, rural culture. Apart from Cambodia's French colonial rulers, only a minority of Phnom Penh's inhabitants were Khmer. Most were Chinese traders and Vietnamese workers, later to become victims of the genocide.

At age twenty-three, still claiming to be three years younger, Sar received a scholarship to study radio-electricity in Paris. Inspired by anti-colonial nationalism, he joined the French Communist Party, expressing his new political views under a racial *nom de plume*: the 'Original Cambodian' (*khmaer da'em*). He

failed his course three years in a row. He met Khieu Ponnary, the first Cambodian woman to get the Baccalauréat. Back home in Phnom Penh in 1956, the couple chose Bastille Day for their wedding. On their marriage certificate, Sar again lied about his age, claiming to be twenty-eight, instead of thirty-one.

Yet Sar took good advantage of his real age. It gave him seniority as the oldest member of the new cohort of younger Khmer communists, mostly with elite backgrounds and French training. During the 1960s, this radical group displaced the relatively moderate Buddhist monks and peasants who had founded the party under Vietnamese guidance during the 1945–54 war of independence. Sar and his younger, more anti-Vietnamese, urban-educated circle rose to dominate Cambodian communist ranks, secretly working more closely with Hanoi's rival, the Chinese Communist Party. They excised their veteran predecessors from the CPK's official history by moving the date of the Party's 'First Congress' from 1951 to 1960.

The 'Original Khmer' trusted few of the grass-roots, more pragmatic, veteran Khmer communists trained by the Vietnamese. Having fought for Cambodia's independence, they placed too much value on the neutral foreign policy of Sihanouk's regime. Taking to the jungle, in 1967 Sar launched a new insurgency to overthrow the Prince. Sar saw war and secrecy as 'the basis of the revolution'. He adopted the code-name 'Pol', and after victory, from 1976, he used the name Pol Pot.

He never publicly admitted he was Saloth Sar. A 1977 official biography gave his year of birth as 1925. Yet it falsely claimed 'Pol Pot' had been a farmer, omitting his childhood in Phnom Penh and his four years in France. Few Cambodians knew who Pol Pot was. One DK official even described him as a former rubber plantation worker. Asked in 1978, 'Who are you, comrade Pol Pot?' he mentioned having studied in France while adding new lies: that he had spent six years in a pagoda and two years as a Buddhist monk. Running the secretive ruling party, Pol Pot even came to be referred to in its documents as 'the Organization' (*angkar*) itself – a shadowy impersonal autocracy that made speeches, had a home address, watched movies, and was sometimes termed 'busy working'. He had no children. His wife Ponnary went mad.

Sar's brother Suong did not know who was running the country either. In late 1978, Suong saw a poster of 'Pol Pot' displayed in a communal mess hall. He gasped. It was his younger brother. Terrified, he kept quiet about what he knew, and survived. Two months later, Phnom Penh fell to a Vietnamese invasion, and the Khmer Rouge remnants fled to the Thai border.

Their anti-Vietnamese cause attracted US support for the Khmer Rouge, but Pol Pot's genocidal record became an embarrassment to both. In 1985 he told the truth about his age to justify a new lie that he had just retired from politics, hoping it would win the Khmer Rouge new support. Pol Pot now claimed to have reached DK's official retiring age of sixty. Few believed the Khmer Rouge had ever adopted a 'retiring age'. His marriage certificate suggested he was only fifty-seven anyway. Yet that document had been just another lie.

The pattern persisted. Pol Pot did not step down, but continued to run the Khmer Rouge from the shadows. In a secret speech in Thailand in 1988, he blamed most of his former regime's killings on 'Vietnamese agents'. As for DK's 1975–6 massacres of defeated pro-US leaders and troops, he insisted: 'This strata of the imperialists had to be totally destroyed.' Pol Pot's army continued to wage war from the Thai border until broken by defections and mutinies in 1996–8. He died in the jungle on 15 April 1998.

He never faced trial for his crimes. From 1979 to 1993, the United Nations, at the insistence of China and the USA, legitimized Pol Pot's anti-Vietnamese cause and supported his exiled Khmer Rouge as Cambodia's representatives. In 1999, the UN proposed establishing an international tribunal to judge his surviving accomplices for genocide and crimes against humanity. Cambodia and the UN agreed in 2003 to set up a special court. In 2005, against Washington's opposition, the UN faced difficulty raising the tribunal's $60 million budget. The 'Original Khmer' still poisons modern culture.

Further reading

See: Ben Kiernan, *The Pol Pot Regime* (2002) and *How Pol Pot Came to Power* (2004); Nic Dunlop, *The Lost Executioner* (2005). See also: Pin Yathay, *Stay Alive My Son* (1987); Chanrithy Him, *When Broken Glass Floats* (2000); Loung Ung, *First They Killed My Father* (2000); Robert Gellately and Ben Kiernan (eds) *The Specter of Genocide: Mass Murder in Historical Perspective* (2003).

BEN KIERNAN

POLANSKI, Roman
1933–
Polish film director

For a man whose mother died in Auschwitz and whose wife was murdered, Roman Polanski makes films less graphically violent than might be supposed. He does, however, take a pointedly absurd view of the world which cruelly and implacably separates its subjects into survivors and victims. Polanski's films are essentially heartless – perfect metaphors for the cool but troubled 1960s and early 1970s – kept buoyant by a strong curiosity and wry, bizarre humour.

Polanski was born in Paris to Polish parents who returned to Cracow when he was three. There he fended for himself from an early age after his parents were arrested by the Germans. Films, Polanski has admitted, were an escape. He began acting at the age of fourteen and appeared in the films of **Andrej Wajda**, notably *A Generation* and *Innocent Sorcerers*. After art school Polanski attended the Lodz Film School where his short film *Two Men and a Wardrobe* (1958) attracted considerable attention. This fifteen-minute exercise drew far more from the Polish avant-garde, particularly the Theatre of the Absurd, than from the dominant tradition of social realism. Polanski's first feature, *Knife in the Water* (1962), was also made in Poland, after a sojourn in Paris. This cool tale about a *ménage à trois* aboard a yacht develops the jaundiced view of human behaviour apparent in the short film and it introduces the intruder figure that was to become central to many of the later films. At the time *Knife in the Water* was read as about the conflict between the Polish bourgeoisie and rebellious youth, although it now looks more like the product of a fundamentally more conservative and pessimistic universal philosophy.

Polanski's next feature was made two years later at the invitation of a Polish producer working in England. Ostensibly a horror film made for a company specializing mostly in sex products, *Repulsion* (1965) in fact remains one of Polanski's most disturbing films for its treatment of a young woman's sexual obsession and mental disintegration. The presiding influence was **Luis Buñuel**, a debt acknowledged in the credits' reference to *Un chien andalou*. The fissures of Catherine Deneuve's cracking-up gain concrete form through the use of surreal images, particularly those inside her oppressive, crumbling London mansion block whose very walls split open in the end and turn against her.

Polanski's commercial astuteness enabled him to find financial backers eager for cultural prestige: Hugh Hefner of *Playboy* magazine financed *Macbeth* (1971). *Rosemary's Baby* (1968) – the first Hollywood film by a director from behind the Iron Curtain – which turned the occult into a subject for major rather than second features, was produced by William Castle, who made his reputation in low-budget exploitation films.

In a sense, Polanski's recurring explorations of sexual tensions, linked to a visceral rather than intellectual surrealism, have made the director attractive to commercial backers.

Money for Polanski's second film in England, an earlier project called *Cul-de-Sac* (1966), was forthcoming after the success of *Repulsion*. The result was a public and critical failure that nevertheless remains Polanski's personal favourite. The themes of intrusion and sexual humiliation find a broader base than before in a black comedy and satire strongly influenced by **Beckett** and **Pinter**, and reinforced by the use of Jack MacGowran and Donald Pleasence, both known foremost as actors for the respective playwrights. Polanski's next film, *Dance of the Vampires* (1967), affectionately parodied horror films and in it Polanski played a bumbling assistant that echoed his role in an earlier short film about a master–servant relationship, *Le Gros et le maigre* (1963). Sharon Tate, his wife, played one of the leading parts in *Dance of the Vampires*. She was murdered later in Los Angeles by the followers of Charles Manson. Polanski's next film, based on Shakespeare's *Macbeth*, was his bloodiest and also continued the diabolic, supernatural theme of the hugely successful *Rosemary's Baby*; it has been noticed that the only birth in the Polanski canon brings forth the child of Satan.

Polanski's style was given its freest rein in *What?* (1972), a droll and inconsequential piece of humour in which an American innocent abroad finds herself in the middle of a comedy of sex and embarrassment. Polanski again appears in the film, clearly delighted to observe such strange behaviour in rich summer villas. The wry, throwaway humour (which teases at the edges of much of his work) is the same kind that in *Chinatown* (1974) put an unglamorous bandage on the nose of its hero.

Restricted settings, like the villa in *What?*, are made much of by Polanski, who favours long takes and frugal editing to allow the cast as much space as possible and to enhance the atmosphere of the geography. Castles in *Cul-de-Sac* and *Macbeth*, apartments in *Repulsion*, *Rosemary's Baby* and *The Tenant* (1976) are all treated in an expressionistic fashion. The urban paranoia of the last three is also central to *Chinatown*, one of his least personal but most successful works. The script by Robert Towne was the first that Polanski did not have a hand in but its themes of complicity and urban corruption make it central to Polanski's cinema.

From the mid-1970s Polanski worked in France after fleeing America following a sex scandal that involved the rape of a thirteen-year old girl – a crime he acknowledged. Whether the personal pressures in his life took their toll is hard to say. *The Tenant* (1976) was a disappointing small-scale return to the territory of *Repulsion*. Polanski's leaving America forced him to give up the direction of *Hurricane*. His next large-scale project was his screen adaptation of **Thomas Hardy's** *Tess* (1979), but this was not universally applauded. During the 1980s he made only two films, *Pirates* (1986) and *Frantic* (1988), neither of which enhanced his reputation. But if critics and his admirers thought Polanski was played out, they were wrong. He rediscovered some of his form at least in the 1990s, with *Bitter Moon* (1992), *Death and the Maiden* (1994) and *The Ninth Gate*, before stunning everyone with *The Pianist* (2002), a semi-autobiographical, profoundly lyrical, though characteristically disturbing, evocation of the Holocaust in his native Poland that won Polanski both an Academy Award for direction, and the *Palme d'Or* at Cannes.

Further reading

Other works include: *Oliver Twist* (2005). See: Ivan Butler, *The Cinema of Roman Polanski* (1970); Thomas Kiernan, *Repulsion: The Life and Times of Roman Polanski* (1981); Roman Polanski, *Roman* (1984); Pierre-Andre Boutang (ed.) *Polanski par Polanski: textes et documents* (1986); John Parker, *Polanski* (1993).

CHRIS PETIT (REVISED AND UPDATED BY THE EDITOR)

POLLOCK, Jackson

1912–56

US painter

After the Second World War the centre of avant-garde painting switched from Paris to New York, where a revolutionary new movement, later to be called Abstract Expressionism, emerged. The principal artists of this New York School were Pollock, **de Kooning** and **Rothko**. It was Pollock who, in de Kooning's words, 'broke the ice'. It was also Pollock who probably departed the furthest – certainly further than de Kooning – from all European antecedents.

Born in Cody, Wyoming, Pollock studied in New York under the Regionalist painter Thomas Hart Benton. The old masters who interested him most were those who stressed vigorous movement; his favourite moderns were **Picasso** and **Miró**. He became interested in **Jung** and it was to a Jungian psychotherapist that he turned for help with his alcoholism. In the 1940s, in search of a personal yet universal mythology, he painted a series of pictures filled with references to archaic symbols, including *Guardians of the Secret* and *Pasiphaë* (both 1943). Deciding that these were too literal, and partly inspired by Surrealist automatism, he sought to convey the workings of his unconscious more directly through abstract marks, transforming the canvas into an 'all-over' field of energy. In 1947, he began placing the canvas on the floor and throwing or dripping paint on to it, while moving around it. The act of painting became like a ritualistic dance, involving his whole body. Complete trance-like concentration and a total psychic involvement with the picture, as it developed its 'independent life', was essential. When successful, the dense web of swirling lines conveyed a sense of liberated energy and perfectly controlled yet spontaneous movement, as in free-form jazz, which Pollock loved. The 'all-over' quality suggested an endless time–space flux. Physically very large, violent yet (increasingly) lyrical, Pollock's dripped paintings constitute his 'heroic' phase. Among the first were *Gothic* and *Full Fathom Five* (both 1947). Some, like *One* and *Autumn Rhythm* (both 1950), evoke the mood of the natural environment, specifically that of Long Island, while remaining totally abstract. Using such paints as Duco, Dev-o-Lac and (silver) aluminium, Pollock produced extraordinary colour harmonies. Nevertheless, he was a draughtsman even more than a colourist and it was the linear element which predominated.

In 1951–2 he restricted himself to black and white; at the same time, strongly figurative motives reappeared. The following year, he painted what many consider his masterpiece, the massive *Blue Poles*. The dark blue poles of the title act as markers of rhythm in a frenzied field of bright, artificial colour, providing the work with its special strength and authority.

Pollock's influence on subsequent art has been immense, though in two essentially contradictory directions. Some, believing his work represents a new beginning in painting, have tackled some of the formal, pictorial problems it raises. For others, his 'action painting' has signalled the end of painting as such, pointing rather to the artist as performer or shaman. Pollock's status as a culture-hero makes it difficult to distinguish what is inherent in his paintings from what is reflected back into them from the legends woven around him. Perhaps the distinction is anyhow a false one. Pollock himself sometimes wondered, not whether he was making good paintings, but whether he was making 'paintings' at all. The ambiguity of his influence may result from the ambiguity, and hence the richness, of his life's work.

Further reading

See: Bryan Robertson, *Jackson Pollock* (1960); Francis V. O'Connor, *Jackson Pollock* (1967); I. Tomassoni, *Jackson Pollock* (1968); Bernice Rose, *Jackson Pollock: Works on Paper* (1969); Alberto Busignani, *Pollock* (1971); C.L. Wysuph, *Jackson Pollock: Psychoanalytic Drawings* (1971); B.H. Friedman, *Jackson Pollock: Energy Made Visible* (1973); S. Naifeh and G.H. Smith, *Jackson Pollock: An American Saga* (1990).

GRAY WATSON

POPPER, (Sir) Karl Raimund

1902–94

Austrian/British philosopher

Karl Popper was born in Vienna, the son of a well-to-do lawyer. Both Popper's parents were Jewish, but were baptized in the Lutheran Church before he was born. Popper's late teens coincided with the upheaval following the First World War and the collapse of the Austrian Empire. At this time Popper was strongly influenced by socialist thought; for a short time he became a Marxist, but was soon disenchanted. His wide-ranging interests while he was a student at the University of Vienna included philosophy, psychology, music and science; after taking his PhD in 1928 he qualified as a secondary-school teacher in mathematics and physics. In the later 1920s he became involved in the internationally renowned Vienna Circle of philosophers, and he received encouragement from some of its members, notably Herbert Feigl. From the beginning, however, Popper was highly critical of the group's central doctrines, and many of these criticisms appeared in his masterpiece *The Logic of Scientific Discovery* (*Logik der Forschung*, 1934). A year before **Hitler** marched into Austria, Popper left Vienna with his wife, and took up a position at the University of New Zealand in Christchurch. Here he perfected his English, and in 1945 published the work which won him recognition in the English-speaking world, the two-volume *The Open Society and Its Enemies* (5th edn 1966). In 1946 he took up residence in England. He taught at the London School of Economics, and was made Professor of Logic and Scientific Method in 1949. He was knighted in 1972, and continued to be philosophically productive, his *Objective Knowledge* appearing in 1972.

The Logic of Scientific Discovery is a powerfully original contribution to our understanding of scientific method. When Popper wrote this book the prevailing account of empirical science was that it used 'inductive methods' – that is, inferences from particular observations and experiments to universal laws. Yet ever since Hume such inductive procedures had faced a serious problem: how can observation of a finite number of particular instances logically justify the scientist's confident belief in general laws which are supposed to hold good for all time? Popper's revolutionary suggestion was that the problem of induction was irrelevant to scientific knowledge. How scientists arrived at their theories was a matter for psychology, not logic. What was important was the *testing* of a scientific theory once proposed. And here Popper argued that strictly logical, deductive reasoning is applicable: scientific theories cannot logically be guaranteed to be true, but they are logically capable of being proven *false*. And it is this – the principle of falsification – that is the essence of the logic of science. Science thus works by a process of *Conjectures and Refutations* (the title of a later book – revised 1972 – in which Popper amplified his position). A scientific theory has the status of a tentative hypothesis which is then matched against observations; if the observations actually made are inconsistent with those predicted by the theory, then the theory is refuted and the way is open for a new conjecture.

One remarkable feature of Popper's book is that, at a time when the verificationism of the Logical Positivists was the ruling doctrine, he had already grasped the fundamental weakness that was to lead to its ultimate downfall (i.e. its inability to specify a logic for the verification of scientific law). In place of verifiability Popper's slogan was falsifiability, though, unlike the Positivists, Popper never offered his principle as a criterion of meaningfulness. Instead he suggested it as a principle of demarcation, which separated genuine science from pseudo-science. The mark of a true scientific theorist was the willingness to 'stick one's neck out': theories which did not take the risk of empirical falsification were not entitled to claim scientific status.

It would be hard to overestimate Popper's influence on the methodology of science. It is probably correct to say that the bulk of scientists practising today would accept the Popperian model of the status of scientific theories. On the philosophical front, two problems with Popper's approach are worth noting. First, it is not at all clear that the problem of induction can be disposed of as neatly as Popper supposed. Second, the work of **Thomas Kuhn** has demonstrated the

extent to which entrenched scientific theories are immunized against the possibility of falsification. But even Popper's strongest critics would admit that the contemporary scene in the philosophy of science would be unrecognizable without the foundations which he laid.

There is a close link between Popper's seminal work on scientific methodology and the important contribution to political theory and sociology which he went on to produce. The scientific attitude, as defined by Popper, was one of 'critical rationalism' – the preparedness to submit one's ideas to criticism and modification. This approach, Popper proceeded to argue, was applicable not just in science, but throughout social life, and was the hallmark of what he called the 'open society'. The open society is a highly individualistic one, characterized by free critical thinking; it is a society where individuals are confronted with responsibility for their personal decisions. The closed society, by contrast, embodies the 'organic' view of the state: it is in effect a throw-back to 'tribalism', where the identity of individuals is submerged within a harmonious whole. This distinction leads to the main thesis of *The Open Society and its Enemies*: totalitarianism, with its closed society, is not, in essence, a new movement, but is a form of reactionary primitivism – an attempt to resist the increasing expansion of the critical powers of individual man.

Popper's targets, the theorists of the closed society, are Plato, Hegel and **Marx**. His attack on Plato upset many scholars, but Popper was undoubtedly correct in arguing that the concept of justice in Plato's *Republic* is a collectivist one in which individuality is subordinated to the good of the state. Popper's most violent strictures are reserved for Hegel for his totalitarian glorification of the state, his 'bombastic and hysterical Platonism'. The triumph of Popper's book, however, is his systematic and devastating attack on all aspects of Marxist theory. In particular, Popper attacks Marx as an economic 'historicist'. The argument ties up with the companion work to *The Open Society, The Poverty of Historicism* (1957); historicism is there defined as

> an approach to the social sciences which assumes that historical prediction is their principal aim, and which assumes that this aim is attainable by discovering the 'rhythms' or the 'patterns', the 'laws' or the 'trends' that underlie the evolution of history.

Popper's position is that even in the natural sciences complete deterministic prediction is impossible; and his arguments against the possibility of determinism in the social sphere provide a powerful challenge to any sociological theory with serious predictive aspirations.

In his later book, *Objective Knowledge* (1972), Popper returned to his fundamental preoccupation – the development of human knowledge. Popper now saw his earlier notion of science proceeding by a constant process of conjecture and refutation as a special case of evolution by natural selection: the continuous production of tentative conjectures and 'the constant building up of selective pressures on these conjectures [by criticizing them]'. The evolution of knowledge is, in effect, a continuation of the 'problem-solving' activities in which all organisms are engaged. In developing this position, Popper introduced an important conceptual category which he labels 'World 3'. Most philosophers have habitually distinguished between the objective world of physical things and the subjective world of human experience; to these two categories (which he labels Worlds 1 and 2 respectively) Popper now adds a third, independent world of philosophical and scientific knowledge, of 'problems, theories and critical arguments'. This world, though the product of human activity, has a real and autonomous existence whose repercussions on us are as great or greater than those of our physical environment. Popper has made great claims for the explanatory power of this notion of a man-made yet autonomous Third World. In particular, he has proposed that the thorny problem of the emergence of self-consciousness can be solved by analysing it in terms of

an interaction between the self and the objects of World 3. Though this is certainly a fascinating approach, it has yet to be satisfactorily developed; and it is not at present clear whether it will turn out to be as philosophically fruitful as Popper confidently predicts.

If his later ideas met with some scepticism among the philosophical establishment, this was nothing new to Popper, who had always been something of a rebel. In his early career he was a lone critic of the orthodoxy of the Logical Positivists; in later life he consistently condemned the dominant 'linguistic' approach to philosophy as a retreat from the 'great problems' into trivial scholasticism. Whatever the truth of this judgement, there can be no doubt about Popper's own extraordinary contribution to the 'great problems'. To categorize or neatly label this contribution is impossible, for Popper's thought ranges so widely and illuminates so many different aspects of philosophy. He was one of the truly original and creative thinkers of his century.

Further reading

Other works include: *Unended Quest* (1976, originally *Autobiography of Karl Popper*, 1974); see also: Thomas Kuhn, *The Structure of Scientific Revolutions* (1962); I. Lakatos and A. Musgrove (eds) *Criticism and the Growth of Knowledge* (1970); R. Bambrough (ed.) *Plato, Popper and Society* (1967); Brian Magee, *Popper* (1973); Malachi Hacohen, *Karl Popper: The Formative Years, 1902–1945* (2000).

JOHN COTTINGHAM

PORTER, Cole

1891–1964

US popular composer

Of America's 'golden age' songwriters, Cole Porter is the one most fondly remembered for his particular creations – for his songs' wit, warmth, sophistication and currency as 'standards'. Because of their jazz-age titles, love-wise lyrics and harmonic breadth, 'Anything Goes', 'I've Got You Under My Skin', 'Night and Day', 'Just One of Those Things', 'At Long Last Love', 'Always True to You in

My Fashion' and many other numbers have become particularly associated with black artists such as Ella Fitzgerald and led at least one reference book to state, erroneously, that Porter was African American. In his own day Harold Arlen was more concretely associated with black culture; Porter's view of the matter was that, born a white millionaire Protestant from Indiana, the secret of his success was that he learnt to write 'Jewish', apparently meaning that he exploited minor-key harmonies (though rarely through to the end of a song). Like **Kern** and **Gershwin**, Porter wrote the vast majority of his songs for stage entertainments (musical comedies and revues) or for musical films, and as with them, it is the songs, not the musicals, that have survived, with very few canonical exceptions, basically *Anything Goes* (1934), *Kiss Me, Kate* (1948) and perhaps *High Society* (film, 1956) and *Silk Stockings* (1955).

Anything Goes is a routine, indeed rather old-fashioned shipboard farce, but *Kiss Me, Kate*, with its multiple layers of diegesis and its incorporation of the core of Shakespeare's *The Taming of the Shrew*, was the perfect vehicle for Porter's verbal innuendo (he always wrote his own lyrics), encyclopaedic smartness (he excelled at 'list' songs) and sidelong view of love, though the music ranges curiously between antique pastiche, Broadway pizzazz and operetta romanticism. Beyond this, high society, if not the silk stockings, was exactly Porter's milieu. The image of the elderly gay man, in constant pain since a riding accident in 1937 (one leg had eventually to be amputated), predeceased by his beautiful wife, Linda, dining with his butler because he could not conceive of foregoing either the company or the formal elegance, lends his artistry a legendary dimension lacking in his contemporaries. It had always been understood that, after his Yale education, Porter would excel as a connoisseur, *bon vivant* and musical dilettante, and going to live in Paris with Linda in the 1920s seemed for a while to confirm the traditional expectation of talent and the good life cancelling each other out; but it was

Porter's hard-working, determined effort to learn the Broadway and then the Hollywood trade that caused the steady, much admired rise in his reputation until the accident, after which it was expected that he would revert at most to the occasional purveying of amusement. (*Kiss Me, Kate*'s triumph came as a glorious surprise.)

At the same time the songs are undoubtedly party pieces, and it is their mixed revelation and concealment of the sexual truth that continues to bind them to the man. (Porter recorded some of them, including 'Anything Goes' with any number of encore verses, in his deadpan piano style and clipped sardonic voice, in obvious parallel to **Noël Coward** as a musical *raconteur*.) He had trouble with the censor, and 'Kate the Great' still sounds daring today. Given the law, it was an honestly chosen lifestyle for a sociable, wealthy man; Linda valued the protection, Cole fell for many a younger man and took it as far as he could without jeopardizing his marriage. The result was a lifelong bittersweet stand-off with love that he knew would find its fulfilment in the songs. In 'Begin the Beguine' he lengthened the Tin Pan Alley song's frame and enlarged its emotional scope magnificently; in 'Ev'ry Time We Say Goodbye', the most unlettered listener can feel their heart stop at the sad 'change from major to minor' which Porter's genius effortlessly conveyed.

Further reading

Cole Porter on Broadway (1987) is a useful song anthology; there are others. *Anything Goes* and *Kiss Me, Kate* are available complete in piano/vocal score. Robert Kimball has edited *The Lyrics of Cole Porter* (1983). The definitive biography is William McBrien: *Cole Porter* (1998); see also Charles Schwartz: *Cole Porter* (1978).

STEPHEN BANFIELD

POULENC, Francis

1899–1963

French composer

Poulenc's early career was determined not so much by his formal studies with Charles

Koechlin (which took place in 1921–4, after he established himself as a composer) as by his association with **Jean Cocteau** and with fellow-members of the group known as Les Six. Poulenc came to the attention of this circle in 1917 with his precocious and absurd *Rapsodie nègre* for voice and chamber ensemble, a work showing those qualities of cool wit and sophistication which were to mark much of his output. He followed Cocteau's demands for economy and crispness in many of the works which immediately followed the *Rapsodie*, but the musical influence of **Satie** was gradually superseded by that of **Stravinsky**: the early wind sonatas, for two clarinets (1918), clarinet and bassoon (1922) and brass trio (1922), show this quite clearly. Inevitably his talent was noticed by **Diaghilev**, for whom he wrote *Les Biches* (1923), a suave and seductive picture of high society life.

Les Biches proved Poulenc's almost Stravinskyan ability to take alien kinds of music, whether from history or from the dance band, and make them his own. He applied this skill with capricious delight in many of his subsequent larger works, creating in his *Concert champêtre* for harpsichord and orchestra (1927–8), for instance, a knowing backwards glance at eighteenth-century elegance. The Concerto in G minor for organ, strings and timpani (1938) looks back through **Liszt** to Bach, and to a grand rhetoric which is nonchalantly coupled with music of café-style triviality. More exuberant pastiches are to be found in the Concerto for two pianos and orchestra (1932) and in the Piano Concerto (1949), which is rather rare among Poulenc's post-war works in its outgoing vivacity.

His cultivation of a more serious manner can be dated to 1936, in which year he returned to a devout Catholicism. A simple inward piety is expressed in the sacred pieces which followed, including the *Litanies à la Vierge Noire* for women's or children's voices and organ (1936), the Mass in G major for unaccompanied choir (1937) and various motets, while the larger religious works for soprano, choir and orchestra, a *Stabat mater*

(1950) and a *Gloria* (1959), are in a colourful and dramatic style which shows Poulenc's continuing debt to Stravinsky. He did not, however, follow that master in taking up serialism, but instead pursued his own very French style, tuneful and diatonic, bringing it to a peak of refinement in his late sonatas for flute (1956), clarinet (1962) and oboe (1962).

Poulenc's later works also include three operas of very different character: *Les Mamelles de Tirésias* (1944), a typically witty setting of **Apollinaire's** play; *Dialogues des Carmélites* (1953–5), where the convent location of Bernanos's libretto gave him the opportunity for an operatic exposure of his religious manner; and *La Voix humaine* (1958), a soprano monologue of fleeting mood set to words by Cocteau. The last of these in particular shows the sensitivity to language which made Poulenc the most versatile and distinguished contributor to the repertory of French song since **Fauré**. Specially noteworthy are his song cycles to poems by **Apollinaire** (*Le Bestiaire*, 1919; *Banalités*, 1940; *Calligrammes*, 1948), **Eluard** (*Tel Jour, telle nuit*, 1936–7; *Le Fraîcheur et le feu*, 1950; *Le Travail du peintre*, 1956), Cocteau (*Cocardes*, 1919) and Carême (*La Courte paille*, 1960). Many of these were written for the baritone Pierre Bernac, with whom from 1935 he appeared often in recitals.

Further reading

Other works include: *Aubade* for piano and small orchestra (1929); *Suite française* for ten instruments or piano (1935); *Sextet* for piano and wind (1932–9); *Les Animaux modèles*, ballet (1940); Violin Sonata (1942–3, revised 1949); *Figure humaine* for chorus (1943); *L'Histoire de Babar* for narrator and piano (1940–5); *Sinfonietta* (1947); Cello Sonata (1948); Sonata for two pianos (1952–3); many solo piano pieces. Writings: *Emmanuel Chabrier* (1961); *Moi et mes amis* (1963); *Correspondance, 1915–1963*, ed. Hélène de Wendel (1967); *Journal de mes mélodies* (1964). About Poulenc: Henri Hell, *Francis Poulenc* (1958, trans. 1959); Jean Roy, *Francis Poulenc* (1964); Wilfred Mellers, *Francis Poulenc* (1995); B. Ivry, *Francis Poulenc* (1996); S. Buckland and M. Chimènes (eds) *Francis Poulenc: Music, Art and Literature* (1999).

PAUL GRIFFITHS

POUND, Ezra Loomis

1885–1972

US poet

Born in Idaho, in the American north-west, of Quaker parents, Ezra Pound moved east as a child when his father became an assayer at the US Mint in Philadelphia. He studied at Hamilton College, the University of Pennsylvania, where he met **William Carlos Williams** and the imagist poet Hilda Doolittle. A year of postgraduate study in Romance languages led to a small scholarship to travel and study in Europe. In Italy he published his first book of verse, *A Lume Spento*, in 1908. In England from 1909, he taught a course at the Regent Street Polytechnic which he turned into a collection of lively and original essays on *The Spirit of Romance* (1910; revised 1953), but his life in London is now better remembered for his spirited involvement in contemporary literary movements. Together with F.S. Flint, he promulgated the aesthetics of imagism, that crucial reaction against the metaphysical speculation and heavily declarative syntax of Victorian public verse. Advocating 'direct treatment of the "thing", whether subjective or objective', the pure imagist poet described objects or emotions in non-literary language, leaving explicit analysis, where necessary, to the reader.

While in London, Pound also promoted individual careers. Though **W.B. Yeats's** generous testimony to Pound's helpful advice probably overstates the effect the young American could have had on his late work, there is no doubt that Pound arranged for the publication of **Joyce's** *Portrait of the Artist as a Young Man* and some of **Eliot's** early short poems, and Pound's midwifery at the delivery of *The Waste Land* is a matter of record.

His own poems written during this period, published in various collections like *Exultations* (1909), *Canzoni* (1911) and *Ripostes* (1912), show an increasing economy of expression, and they also reflect his interest in classical and medieval subjects. It may be because the theory of imagism discourages the presence of 'subjects' that he began to turn increasingly to translation, a device by which an author can transmit ideas without overt editorial comment. Pound's version of poems by the Chinese Li Bo (Li Po), taken from Japanese transliterations and English prose translations by Ernest Fenollosa, was published as *Cathay* in 1915. Like his translation of the Old English *The Seafarer* (published in *Ripostes*) and his 'Homage to Sextus Propertius' (in *Quia Pauper Amavi*, 1919), *Cathay* contained a number of mistakes – some intentional, some inspired, and others just wrong – yet the effect of these works is of astonishing insights into the sensibilities of three entirely different cultures.

As Pound began to have more and more to say – about the war and its causes in the economics of Europe and America – imagism began to look increasingly mannered and miniaturist to him. It was at this point that he began work on a much more ambitious project for his poetry. Originally conceived as a **Browningesque** dramatic monologue about the ironies of attempting to educate America in the European past, the first three *Cantos* (published in *Quia Pauper Amavi*) were later revised so as to give prominence to a reworking, in 'Seafarer' metre, of what Pound took to be the oldest kernel of the Odyssey story, the epic hero's visit to the underworld. Just as Odysseus had to beat back the beguiling shades of his comrades and relations (including his own mother) so as to get, from Teiresias, the facts he needed to pilot himself and his crew back to Ithaca, so Pound had to raid the past selectively in order to guide his culture back 'home' to the integral society from which he thought it had departed. The *Cantos*, which finally comprised well over a hundred separate, though related, poems, were to occupy him for the rest of his long life.

Despairing of the revolution in taste and politics which he had once hoped to further in England, Pound left London in 1920. Together with his English wife, the artist Dorothy Shakespear, he lived for a while in Paris before settling in Rapallo, Italy, four years later. His departure from the city in which his chief interests had been formed, and his poetry much firmed, was signalled in *Hugh Selwyn Mauberley* (1920), for many critics still his most admired work. An allusive, multi-faceted satire on English life and letters, *Mauberley* is also a kind of exorcism, like Eliot's 'Prufrock' and **Wallace Stevens's** 'The Comedian as the Letter C', of an aspect of the author as dilettante that he felt he had outgrown.

In Italy Pound formed an alliance with the American violinist Olga Rudge. Their daughter, Mary, born in 1925, was fostered by a peasant family in the Tyrol. But Dorothy also remained in Rapallo, and their son, Omar, was born there in 1926. By 1930 Pound had completed the first thirty *Cantos*, and he continued to produce essays on literature and economics, incorporating his ideas and discoveries into *Cantos* XXXI to LXXI. His attraction to Italian fascism, as his short book *Jefferson and/or Mussolini* (1935) makes clear, was based on his analogy between the remaking of the Italian economy under **Mussolini** and the work of Jefferson, Madison and Martin Van Buren in establishing the American Republic. His infamous broadcasts from Rome under the sponsorship of the fascist regime began in 1940 and continued until after the United States was at war with Italy. As he saw it, Pound never attacked the basic American principles of government, but supported the Constitution against its perversion by more recent American administrations. In 1943 he was indicted for treason by a Washington, DC, grand jury, and in 1945, near the end of the European war, was imprisoned in a US Army 'disciplinary training centre' north of Pisa. Returned to the United States later that year to stand trial, he was found to be 'suffering from a paranoid state' and unfit to advise counsel. He was subsequently committed to St Elizabeth's Hospital, outside Washington, for treatment.

In St Elizabeth's he continued to read and write, completing his translations from Confucius first made into Italian (finally published in English as *The Unwobbling Pivot and The Great Digest*, 1947) and *Cantos* LXXIV–LXXXIV, begun in Pisa. The *Pisan Cantos* (1948) are thought, even by critics normally hostile to Pound, to be especially sensitive evocations of his mental state as he reflected on his public and private life in his captivity. For them he was awarded, amidst considerable controversy, the prestigious American Bollingen Prize for poetry in 1949. In 1956 he completed and published the next ten *Cantos* as *Section: Rock Drill*. In 1958 his indictment for treason was quashed, and he was released from St Elizabeth's to join his daughter Mary and her husband in Italy. In 1959 *Cantos* XCVI–CIX appeared as *Thrones*, and ten years later, *Drafts and Fragments of Cantos C–CXVII*. He died in 1972.

Ezra Pound's life and work invite the adjective 'modern' not least in their perennial difficulty. Though most of his translations and shorter poems have found an uneasy place in contemporary critical esteem, the *Cantos* have been slow to be accommodated in the school and university courses that now govern the sense of a 'tradition' in English and American literature. This must be due in part to their wide range of reference to Greek, Latin, Provençal, early American and Chinese history, as well as his recollections (mainly in the *Pisan Cantos* and later) to the author's many friends and antagonists, both illustrious and obscure. Again, the *Cantos* do not tell a story, or pause – except occasionally – for moments of lyric repose, but dive restlessly into various versions of the past to find whole chunks of letters, laws, books on economics, and (more rarely) works of literature, with which to confront the wayward present. Though these documents are sometimes cited with inviting economy and almost always 'rhymed' with great subtlety, readers accustomed to the self-sufficient literary object, the 'words on the page', have been deterred by the pressure outwards into non-literary materials beyond the poet's aesthetic frame. One answer to this problem is that Pound was always more of a translator and a maker of syllabi than he was a poet in the conventional sense of the term, and that a major satisfaction of the *Cantos* is predicated in a subsequent reading of the documents towards which they gesture. But the reader is not expected to have got there before the poet, and the guilt or pique apparently felt by some critics at not having anticipated Pound's cultural 'set' is probably misplaced.

Not just the form, but also the contents of the *Cantos*, have given offence. Regular readers of poetry can accept the denunciation of usury in the much-anthologized *Canto XLV* as being in some general sense against nature, but Pound's more specific and contemporary advocacy, elsewhere in the *Cantos*, of the state control of credit has been criticized as too cranky, or at any rate too unliterary, a subject for poetry. Cranky it certainly was not; the economic theories of Douglas, Gesell, Alexander Del Mar and Christopher Hollis, whatever their differences, had in common a search for alternatives to monetarism, an attempt to put money back into the community and to get unemployed men and facilities back to work, without committing the taxpayer to ever-increasing charges for interest. Whether Pound managed to make poetry out of the topic depends partly on the success with which he worked it in with other themes. In the *Cantos*, at least, it was always part of his larger subject, or what might be called his one idea: that every contrivance of the human imagination, from a metaphor to a political system, may be either derived from, or imposed upon, nature. Telling the difference is the one essential discrimination, the necessary moral discipline. This idea did not originate with Pound, but it connects his earliest imagism with the most specific topics in the *Cantos*. 'Banker's Credit' is suspect, therefore, because it does not reflect the 'natural' wealth of a country's material and human resources.

But Pound's anti-semitism remains beyond accommodation. Though restricted largely to his broadcasts and other polemical pieces, and though derived ultimately from the rhetoric of the American Populists, whose economics Pound shared, his use of Jews as a shorthand for usurers showed a failure of sympathy and foresight that cannot be brushed aside by his admirers. It is hard to deny, furthermore, that elements of the paranoia and hectic self-righteousness that have accompanied the more serious forms of anti-semitism are present in Pound's work, even when he is not treating of the economy.

Ultimately Pound's reputation must rest on his life's work, the *Cantos*. He finally came to see them as a failure, because though begun as an epic on the model of *The Divine Comedy* they never get their hero (in this case, the poet himself) home to Paradise at the end. But the *Cantos* are a classic 'made new': an address to the times adducing ancient sources of a better future. In this respect they resemble millennial projections, and should put the reader in mind of that other great, unfinished apocalypse, *Piers Plowman*. Both poems keep interrupting their progress towards the empyrean to cite contemporary abuses, especially by those institutions (for Langland the monasteries, for Pound the banks) considered by the authors to be most capable of reforming the fallen society, and therefore most culpable in failing to do so. The *Cantos* are a great synthesis, a great excursion in an open field of reference.

Further reading

Other works include: *Cantos* (except nos LXXII and LXXIII) see *The Cantos of Ezra Pound* (1972). See: *Selected Poems* (1975); and *Ezra Pound, Selected Prose 1909–1965*, ed. William Cookson (1973). The standard biography is Noel Stock, *The Life of Ezra Pound* (1970). See also: Hugh Kenner, *The Poetry of Ezra Pound* (1971); *Paideuma*, a journal devoted to Pound studies (quarterly, from the University of Maine at Orono); John Tytell, *Ezra Pound: The Solitary Volcano* (1987); Ira B. Nadel, *The Cambridge Companion to Ezra Pound* (1999) and *Ezra Pound: A Literary Life* (2004); Demetres P. Tryphonopoulos and Stephen J. Adams (eds) *The Ezra Pound Encyclopedia* (2005).

STEPHEN FENDER

POWELL, Anthony

1905–2000

English novelist

Anthony Powell was educated at Eton and Balliol College, Oxford. Before and after World War II, during which he served in the Intelligence Corps and as a Liaison Officer, he worked in publishing and literary journalism. Powell's early work, such as *From a View to a Death* (1933), was often compared to **Evelyn Waugh's**. His most substantial literary achievement was *A Dance to the Music of Time*, twelve novels published between 1951 and 1975, a sequence which is both a social and a personal history. All have the same narrator, Nick Jenkins, whose outward life generally seems to parallel Powell's own. The limitations of a single standpoint are overcome by making Jenkins a willing listener, or at least a tolerant one, to others' stories. The limited social world in which he moves – upper- and middle-class England (except for military service) – also makes credible Jenkins's ability to follow the careers and fortunes of many of the several hundred characters who appear in the novels.

Another kind of unity is provided by Powell's leisurely, speculative style which orders the often eccentric actions and speech of his figures. The first novel, *A Question of Upbringing* (1951), opens with a scene which evokes for Jenkins a Poussin picture where people move 'hand in hand in intricate measure: stepping slowly, methodically, sometimes a trifle awkwardly, in evolutions that take recognizable shape'. The last novel, *Hearing Secret Harmonies* (1975), closes with a passing reference to that same scene. In between is an extraordinary feat of recollection, thousands of pages long. The arrangement of events is usually chronological although Powell allows excursions into earlier periods, as at the beginning of *The Kindly Ones* (1962) when Jenkins recalls his childhood near Aldershot (his father was a soldier) on the eve of World War I.

Powell tends to refer to public or historic events only when they impinge on his characters' lives or, as in the final three books which cover as great a spread of time as the first nine, to establish a sense of period. His people are generally inward-looking. The war, covered by the trilogy *The Valley of Bones* (1964), *The Soldier's Art* (1966) and *The Military Philosophers* (1968), is seen sometimes as a masquerade, sometimes as a dull if grotesque bureaucratic exercise in which the enemy goes almost unmentioned. The incursions of death, for instance during the air-raid in *The Soldier's Art*, are the more effective for being understated.

Jenkins's social world expands during the first half of the sequence and contracts through mortality in the second. Most of the new figures introduced during the six final novels – Pamela Flitton ('It was Death she liked'), the novelist X. Trapnel (based on Julian McLaren-Ross) – have a macabre aspect. The individual characters are rarely types, although Powell uses some of them as yardsticks for generalization: the industrialist Sir Magnus Donners exemplifies the mysterious banality of power, the painter Barnby is used as a mouthpiece for comments about womanizing.

Besides the frequent reappearances of such characters and the narrator's well-disposed curiosity about them, another link between the novels is provided by Jenkins's preoccupation with art. The chief antithesis among many in the sequence is between the will to power and the intrinsically less energetic drive to create. The embodiment of the latter is the storyteller; the former is most amply suggested by Widmerpool, who moves jerkily from business success to high military rank to politics to a peerage. An ogrish figure to the reader and also a cult one, Widmerpool's pretensions are undermined by sexual humiliation. On a solitary run at school he is the first character named in the sequence. Member of a sinister 1960s commune in the final novel, he collapses and dies on another run and his death closes the account.

All that is retrieved from the closing débâcle is a **Modigliani** drawing, salvaged 'a little crumpled' from a bonfire of Widmerpool's effects by Bithel, one of the most pathetically comic figures in *The Music of Time*. The ordering of social confusion through art and the partial survival of that art, mediated through Nick Jenkins the novelist, are Powell's final aims.

Between 1976 and 1982 Powell produced several volumes of memoirs under the collective title of *To Keep the Ball Rolling*, which are interesting in their own right but also valuable as background to *The Music of Time*.

Further reading

Other works include: *The Music of Time: A Buyer's Market* (1952); *The Acceptance World* (1955); *At Lady Molly's* (1957); *Casanova's Chinese Restaurant* (1960); *Books Do Furnish a Room* (1971); and *Temporary Kings* (1973). See also: James Tucker, *The Novels of Anthony Powell* (1976); and Michael Barber, *Anthony Powell: A Life* (2004).

PHILIP GOODEN

PRESLEY, Elvis Aaron

1935–77

US popular singer

Although the invention of rock 'n' roll is generally accredited to Bill Haley, it was Elvis Presley who transformed a new musical vogue into a social phenomenon. The son of a poor farm worker from South Tupelo, Mississippi, Presley's dangerous good looks and wonderfully expressive voice made him the first and most charismatic icon in the post-war development of an independent youth culture based on music.

In 1954 he recorded for Sun Records, Memphis, a song called 'That's All Right Mama'. Though not a national success at the time, it defines the sources of rock 'n' roll: a white country singer records a black song and for the first time, instead of eliminating black emotion and physicality, retains them in a new synthesis of country music and the blues. Colonel Tom Parker became Presley's manager soon after, and in 1955 they signed a contract with RCA Records. Most of his classic rock 'n' roll numbers were recorded the following

year: 'Heartbreak Hotel', 'Blue Suede Shoes', 'Tutti Frutti', 'Lawdy Miss Clawdy', 'Shake Rattle and Roll', 'Hound Dog', etc. Presley's impact, conveyed by his records and stage appearances with their swaggering content of sex and insubordination, was amplified through films, and hysteria climaxed in 1957 with the film *Jailhouse Rock*, which many cinema managers banned when it became associated with teenage rioting.

At the end of 1957 Presley was drafted into the army and when he returned to civilian life it was without anarchic overtones. Hereafter he was simply the world's most famous pop singer. Only at his death, the victim of obesity and drugs, did he again touch the deepest emotions of the public.

Presley was not a composer, he did not direct his own career, and his only articulation was in performance. At its height his music was blamed for the rise of 'juvenile delinquency', a period catch-phrase which referred only to the negative aspect of a spectacular outburst of energy among young people. Positively, he was the inspirational figurehead in the origination of a new cultural group, with its own financial resources, between the traditional categories of childhood and adulthood – that of youth.

Further reading

Alan Harbinson, *The Life and Death of Elvis Presley* (1977).

DUNCAN FALLOWELL

PRICE, Cedric John

1934–2003

English architect

Demonstrating his concept of 'anticipatory architecture', Cedric Price placed architecture in an entirely new perspective, generating models for a future architecture as yet unrealized. The astonishing range and output of projects served to explore his generic ideas about new ways of making environments responsive to the needs and desires of their users and became the fundamental archetypes of a new deal for users – or a new 'menu' for the consumers of architecture in Price's terminology.

Born in Staffordshire, Price was to become the most provocative questioner of the architectural profession and its assumptions, rejecting traditional architectural conventions and values and challenging the social, functional and aesthetic norms. Price was extremely highly regarded and acknowledged by the leading architectural thinkers of the time, but remained an enigma to the rest of the 'sleepy profession'. At a time when architects were beginning to acquire a social conscience, Price went much further and centred his thinking on social and ethical concerns of which architecture might, almost incidentally, be a by-product. He continually challenged the preconceptions of the profession and society about the limits and social usefulness of architecture, in the process generating an astounding variety of provocative and inspirational ideas. Working always through the medium of testable propositions, his projects and ideas are extraordinarily powerful and challenging, but also delivered with a sense of mischief, fun and pure delight.

Having studied architecture at Cambridge University (1952–5) and then at the independent Architectural Association School in London (1955–7), he worked briefly for Fry, Drew and Partners and Erno Goldfinger before setting up his own practice in 1960. The catalogue of projects from his small practice is immense in quantity as well as in the quality of their thinking, but most of all was a staggering ability to 'think the unimaginable'. His projects are recognized as the seminal architectural propositions of the twentieth century.

The impresario Joan Littlewood came to Price with a project to replace the formalism of theatre and amusement facilities and reincorporate them into the everyday life of the city, a brief which resulted in the proposition to create a Fun Palace – a concept of a flexible and indeterminate space which reverberated through two generations, inspiring

Piano and **Rogers'** Pompidou Centre in Paris, and being the topic of an entire conference in Berlin in 2004 which reaffirmed the visionary nature of the project. Price's concept was not a static monument, but an ever-changing environment responding to the appetites of its users. There was no façade or even formal enclosure, but cranes redeploying a kit of parts as needed and all under cybernetic control (consultant **Gordon Pask**). A different configuration is shown in every drawing, the conventional labels such as Elevation being replaced with titles such as 'Selection', 'Assembly', 'Movement' and 'Control', and the whole proposition is only grasped from a helicopter view at night with the roof retracted. Writing in the *New Statesman* in 1964, **Reyner Banham** started a public debate about the social potential of architecture by comparing the traditional frozen monumentality of the then recently completed Crystal Palace sports centre with the flexibility and new set of choices in proposed Price's Fun Palace.

Price quickly followed his radical thinking about reconfigurable places of entertainment by rethinking higher education with the Potteries Thinkbelt proposal (1963–6). At a time when new universities were still being constructed following the monastic model, Price proposed a new form of university organization which was mobile and dispersed, utilizing an abandoned rail network in the derelict potteries and mining areas of north Staffordshire. The university was conceived as a reconfigurable network of mobile classrooms and laboratories, a thinkbelt following the existing rail line. Provocatively, Price described higher education as a major industrial undertaking integrated into the community rather than a service for the elite.

Price moved on to tackle the office environment. The Generator project (1976) for the Gilman Paper Corporation located in a forest in Florida was described by Price as 'A forest facility … a place to work, create, think and stare.' Architecture is used as an aid to the extension of the users' own interests, a series of structures, fittings and components that respond to the appetites they themselves may generate: a 'menu' of items for individual and group demands of space, control, containment and delight. However the Generator moves further than previous projects by offering a clear programme of how and why change is to be effected and what the variation in resulting environments might be like. It poses the notion of an intelligent building that learns from its own experience. The Generator is a field of reconfigurable units, a mobile crane permanently on site and a completely worked-out strategy for self-organization. Price's cybernetics consultants suggested that the site and the elements on it should have a life and intelligence of their own, and the programme would start to generate unsolicited plans, improvements and modifications in response to users' comments, records of activities, or even by building in a boredom concept so that the site starts to make proposals about changes of itself if no changes are made. Inevitably dubbed by the press as the world's first intelligent building, it was the logical conclusion of Price's thinking about interactive buildings since the Fun Palace – the new ideas included embedded intelligence in the form of a microprocessor into the reconfigurable elements of the building, and having organizational software learning from experience during use.

There followed a galaxy of spectacular projects which moved his thinking into urban environments internationally with projects such as Magnet, which proposed a series of temporary constructions for London and Tokyo that would be redeployed as magnets to attract regeneration. The ideas were rich and varied continuing the 'questioning of indisputable premises'.

Price's vast output of projects and ideas was hugely influential but largely unbuilt. However, what he did manage to construct provides insights into how his thinking might have been realized on a large scale. For example the Aviary for London Zoo 1961 (in collaboration with Lord Snowdon and Frank Newby) was designed on the tensegrity principles of **Buckminster Fuller** (with whom he also collaborated on a number of projects) which generate highly efficient minimal structures with maximum transparency and clear flying space for the birds and exemplifies his interest in lightweight ephemeral structures. The Inter-Action Trust Community Centre in Kentish Town in 1971 gave Price the opportunity to realize on a small scale some parts of the Fun Palace concept, embracing at least flexibility, and impermanence to the extent of opposing the listing of the Centre for cultural preservation and insisting on demolition. Apart from the Pompidou Centre, his ideas found their way through to other mainstream architectural designs; even the London Eye, erected to celebrate the new millennium in 2000, was originally proposed by Price in his 1984 plans for the South Bank commissioned by the then Greater London Council. His feasibility studies and proposals for British Rail for Stratford East and the Thames Gateway are now to be realized for the London Olympic Games of 2012.

Espousing no arbitrary formal allegiances, Price's process of problem-questioning thrust his projects far beyond the bounds and methods of existing architecture 'Architecture should have little to do with problem-solving – rather it should create desirable conditions and opportunities hitherto thought impossible.' Projects where functions and spaces continuously move about are understood by some to be the architectural equivalent of the preoccupations of **John Cage**, or are dismissed as formless or as being more like a permanent construction site; for others they embodied anonymous design. But certainly the work was provocative and distanced itself from the formal preoccupations of shape-making that obsesses architecture and industrial design.

Formally recognized with awards such as the prestigious Kiesler Prize (previously awarded to **Frank Gehry**), Price's influence and status rest on the radical nature of his propositions, assisted by their wide publication, and his influence on several generations of students as a visiting critic and occasional tutor mostly at the Architectural Association in London. His acknowledged professional influence was extensive and ranges from **Archigram**, then **Norman Foster**, **Richard Rogers**, through to the younger generation of **Ken Yeang**, Will Allsop and Rem Koolhaus.

Further reading

Price's drawings and papers are mostly archived in the Canadian Centre for Architecture, Montreal, the Museum of Modern Art, New York or in private collections. Exhibitions included the Architectural Association (1984) and the Design Museum, London (2005); Cedric Price, *Works II* (1984), *The Square Book* (2003) and *Re: CP* (2003); Royston Landau, *New Directions in British Architecture* (1968); Neil Spiller (ed.) *Cyber–Reader* (2002), which includes the Generator project; Reyner Banham, *A Critic Writes* (1996); and Samantha Hardingham, *Cedric Price OPERA* (2003).

JOHN HAMILTON FRAZER

PROKOFIEV, Sergei Sergeievich

1891–1953

Russian composer and pianist

Born in the village of Sontsovka, the son of an agricultural engineer who managed a large estate in the Ukrainian steppe, Prokofiev was musically precocious to an unusual degree. By 1902, when he received his first formal tuition in music from the composer Rheinhold Glière, he was already the composer of two operas and numerous short piano pieces. On Alexander Glazunov's advice, he entered the St Petersburg Conservatory in 1904, where he spent a stormy and unhappy ten years. At a time of increasing political tension, the Conservatory provided a less than ideal environment for the unruly student, and his classes with **Rimsky-Korsakov**, Lyadov, Winkler and Cherepnin made less impact on his development than his contact with progressive artistic groups in St Petersburg – the 'World of Art' and the Evenings of Contemporary Music. At the height of the

Scriabin cult, and in the heyday of the literary Symbolists, he was encouraged to evolve a novel style of his own, and some of his most iconoclastic and aggressive music dates from the immediately pre-war years – works like the First and Second Piano Concertos (1912 and 1913), and the piano *Sarcasms* (1912–14). The highly charged Romanticism of late Scriabin and early **Richard Strauss** also influenced him for a time, and by contrast with his piano music, his early songs, symphonic poems and the opera *Maddalena* (1911–13) are intense and strongly atmospheric works.

His career as a St Petersburg *enfant terrible* took a new turn in the summer of 1914, when, on a trip to London, he attended the season of **Diaghilev's** Ballets Russes, the heady glamour of which he found irresistible. For the first and perhaps the only time in his career, he found the direct influence of another composer inescapable: the impact of **Stravinsky's** ballets, in particular *The Rite of Spring*, is evident in many of his large works of the following years, from the ballet *The Buffoon* (1915) to the Second Symphony (1925). The occasion also marked the beginning of Prokofiev's own involvement with the Ballets Russes, which was to last until Diaghilev's death in 1929.

The first of Prokofiev's works to gain international recognition, the 'Classical' Symphony – deliberately close to Haydn in style, but with 'something new' as well – was written in the summer of 1917, as political events in Russia were reaching a crisis. With the Revolution and the ensuing civil war, it seemed to Prokofiev that his own country might, for the foreseeable future, have graver concerns than for new music. In May 1918 he left for the United States, where his reception was initially encouraging: the music of Stravinsky and the performances of Rachmaninov had set an artistic fashion for all things Russian. He was soon disillusioned, however, by both the commercialism of concert promoters and the basic conservatism of audiences, and it was increasingly in Western Europe, particularly in Paris, that he found a more receptive audience for his music. Yet it was in these artistically and financially difficult first years abroad that some of his most characteristic and popular works were written. The music for *The Buffoon*, revised in 1920, the Third Piano Concerto (1921), the opera *Love of Three Oranges* (1919), and the Fifth Piano Sonata (1923, rev. 1953) are flights of energetic fancy, clear, incisive, and often humorous; Prokofiev's music was never more dynamic nor more whimsically imaginative.

By the end of the 1920s, the time of the opera *The Fiery Angel* (1923, rev. 1926–7) and the ballet *The Prodigal Son* (1929), Prokofiev was at the height of his composing career in the West. As a pianist, too, he was in demand throughout Europe and in North and South America. But in 1929, with the death of Diaghilev and his spirit of artistic adventure, and with the repercussions of the Wall Street collapse in Europe, the market for new music received a severe blow. Between 1932 and 1936 he received only two commissions – the Sonata for Two Violins (1932) and the Second Violin Concerto (1935) – from Western Europe. Over the same period he received seven Soviet commissions, including those for *Lieutenant Kije* (orchestral suite, 1934), *Romeo and Juliet* (ballet, 1936), and *Peter and the Wolf* (symphonic tale, 1936) – three of his best-known and finest scores. He had renewed contact with the Soviet Union during a concert tour in 1927. After some years of apparent indecision he returned there permanently in the spring of 1936.

Prokofiev's first Soviet works – works in which he was very conscious of the need for a much wider popular appeal – are the result not merely of a process of simplification in his idiom; his musical style underwent a change of emphasis. The Romanticism of his youth, never entirely absent from his works, re-emerged: in his Second Violin Concerto, *Romeo and Juliet* and *Alexander Nevsky* (cantata, 1939) it takes the form of a more serene lyricism and textural warmth. The earlier whimsy with which he juxtaposed dynamic

ideas was resolved in the clarity and breadth of his later musical structures: his later symphonies and sonatas have a typically Russian 'epic' feel to them. The sardonic humour of *Love of Three Oranges* was replaced by the elegant wit of *The Duenna* (opera, 1940–1) and *Cinderella* (ballet, 1944) – though, sadly, after *Cinderella*, in the face of the Second World War and the Communist Party's strictures on the arts which both preceded and followed it, Prokofiev's music was rarely frivolous in content. The characteristic works of his later years – the Fifth and Seventh Symphonies (1944 and 1952), the operas *Semyon Kotko* (1939) and *War and Peace* (1943, rev. 1946–52), the music for **Eisenstein's** *Ivan the Terrible* (1944–8) – are 'heroic' and traditional works, serious in intent.

After 1938 Prokofiev's contact with Western Europe ceased; he gave no further concerts abroad. In 1941 he suffered the first of a series of heart attacks. His last concert appearance, as the conductor of his Fifth Symphony, was in 1945. After a bad fall that year his health deteriorated. His prodigious rate of composition slowed down in his last years, and he died of a brain haemorrhage on 5 March 1953, the same day as **Stalin** died.

The scope of Prokofiev's career, and the contradictions it embodies, are in most respects a product of the times in which he lived. Cut off from the roots of his own Russian traditions by the Revolution in 1917, he had to attempt to rediscover them in 1936, but by then he was a product of the sophisticated 1920s in the West. Yet, as a Russian, and because of his uncompromising personality, he had found it difficult to meet the West on its own musical ground, and in any case his efforts were pre-empted by Stravinsky. Outside Russia, his music, and especially the dynamic nature of his earlier piano music, has become a familiar element in contemporary concert programmes, but his overall influence has been indirect. His return to Russia had a significant impact on the course of Soviet music, however, and the flavour of Prokofiev's melodies, rhythms and turns of cadence characterized much of the music of Khachaturyan, Kabalevsky and even **Shostakovich** in the 1940s and 1950s.

Further reading

Other works include: operas: *The Gambler* (1917, rev. 1927–8); *The Story of a Real Man* (1948); ballets: *Le Pas d'Acier* (1926); *The Tale of a Stone Flower* (1948–53); symphonies: No. 3 (1928); No. 4 (1930); No. 6 (1947); concertos: for piano: No. 4 for left hand only (1931); No. 5 (1932); for violin: No. 1 (1917); Sinfonia Concerto for Cello and Orchestra (1950–52); *Cantata for the Twentieth Anniversary of the October Revolution* (1937); and nine sonatas for piano (1909–47). See: *Sergei Prokofiev: Autobiography, Articles, Reminiscences*, ed. S. Shlifstein (1956, trans. 1960); *Prokofiev by Prokofiev* (1979); Israel V. Nestyev, *Prokofiev* (trans. 1961); Victor Seroff, *Prokofiev: A Soviet Tragedy* (1968); Claude Samuel, *Prokofiev* (trans. 1971); H. Robinson, *Sergei Prokofiev: A Biography* (1987); O. Prokofiev (trans. and ed.) *Sergei Prokofiev: Soviet Diary 1927 and Other Writings* (1991).

RITA MCALISTER

PROUDHON, Pierre-Joseph

1809–65

French socialist and anarchist

Proudhon was born at Besançon in the Franche-Comté, his father a notably honest brewer who refused to make a profit, so that the family was raised in poverty. Proudhon attended the Collège de Besançon, but was primarily self-educated at the town's public library. Later a forceful polemicist – he is best known for the phrases 'property is theft' and 'God is evil' – Proudhon established anarchism as a major force in French, and later European, political life, primarily through a critique of authority. His books are usually a disorganized but exhilarating combination of angry polemics, philosophical reasoning and political analysis, dealing with a multitude of subjects. He remained strongly attached to his peasant origins, though his work mainly influenced the new urban working class then becoming established in France. His origins may account for the unexpected survival of a strand of anti-feminism in his thought.

He was apprenticed as a printer, and his earliest contact with radical thought occurred in 1829 when he supervised the printing of *Le Nouveau Monde industriel et sociétaire* ('The New Industrial and Co-operative World') by Charles Fourier; Fourier's proposals for co-operatives were an early influence, later rejected. Proudhon's most important early work was *What is Property?* (*Qu'est-ce que la propriété?*, 1840, trans. 1969), which attacks the injustices caused by property, but does not deny the need for possessions. In 1843 his contact with the Lyons Mutualists, a secret society of working men, led to an interest in the question of association. This developed into a theory of organization, later called 'Mutualism', in which members of small units worked together, and credit was to be reformed through a People's Bank.

From the revolution of 1848 onwards Proudhon's thought developed in direct response to political events. During the Second Republic he wrote for or edited four Paris newspapers between April 1848 and October 1850. These were *Le Représentant du peuple* (1848), *Le Peuple* (1848–9), *La Voix du peuple* (1849–50), and the short-lived *Le Peuple de 1850* (1850). His intention was to provide the ideas which he believed the revolution lacked. Proudhon's journalism is remarkable for its perceptive critiques of events; he also correctly anticipated that Louis-Napoleon Bonaparte would become president of the republic and later emperor. He attracted considerable support among the Parisian working class after other socialists were discredited or imprisoned, but in accordance with his theories firmly refused to head a party or political group. His attacks on Louis-Napoleon led to his imprisonment in 1849, though under conditions which allowed him to continue as editor and author.

Proudhon's *Confessions d'un révolutionnaire* ('Confessions of a Revolutionary', 1849) is indispensable for an understanding of the events of 1848, but the major theoretical work to emerge from this period is the *General Idea of the Revolution in the Nineteenth Century* (*Idée générale de la révolution au XIXe siècle*, 1851, trans. 1923). Proudhon had been elected to the National Assembly in 1848, but found himself cut off from events and from the people he represented; further, the extended franchise had led to the election of a reactionary assembly and a bourgeois president. The *General Idea* therefore criticizes representative democracy, objecting that even when the people are supposedly sovereign, actual political authority is exercised by only a small number of people. Arguing for individual liberty, Proudhon proposes a network of contracts between individuals: 'The producer deals with the consumer, the member with his society, the farmer with his township, the township with the province, the province with the State.' In this way the citizen and the state were to be equalized.

In 1854 he survived an attack of cholera which caused him increasing ill-health as well as difficulty in writing, until his death in 1865. A scurrilous attack by a Roman Catholic priest provoked the composition of his greatest work, *De la justice dans la révolution et dans l'Église*, ('Justice in the Revolution and in the Church', 1858), described by George Woodcock as 'one of the noblest works of social thought of the nineteenth century'. Justice is put forward as a moral concept based on a recognition of human dignity. It is the basis of the relations between people, and consequently of their social and economic relations. Men most naturally co-operate in work, and groups of working men would form the basis of the revolutionary movement. Proudhon's arguments, here as elsewhere, proceed by identifying related opposites or antinomies, setting them in conflict and proposing the establishment between them of a dynamic equilibrium. This dynamism would ensure the vitality of any society applying such ideas. *Principle of Federation* (*Du principe fédératif*, 1863, trans. 1980) sets out clearly Proudhon's mature federalist theory of the relations between individuals, larger groups and states.

Proudhon's debate with **Marx** had important consequences for the development of nineteenth-century revolutionary politics.

Proudhon's identification of Marx's latent authoritarianism ('Do not let us become the leaders of a new intolerance ... Let us accumulate and encourage protest [against our own ideas]' in a letter of 1846 ended direct relations between the two men. In response to Proudhon's *System of Economic Contradictions* (*Système des contradictions économiques, ou philosophie de la misère*, 1846, trans. 1972), Marx wrote his attack *The Poverty of Philosophy* (*Misère de la philosophie*, 1847, trans. 1936). In 1864 the International Working Men's Association (the First International) was founded, in which Proudhon's followers were Marx's most powerful opponents.

Proudhon's primary influence was upon the libertarian socialist movement in nineteenth-century France, which was opposed to the authoritarian Marxist tradition which eventually triumphed because of its greater relevance to industrial societies. In the anarchist tradition **Mikhail Bakunin** and **Petr Kropotkin** most effectively continued Proudhon's ideas, particularly his federalism; though Bakunin, unlike Proudhon, believed in the necessity of violent revolution. In the 1870s Proudhon's ideas spread through Pi y Margall to Spain; and through **Alexander Herzen** and **Leo Tolstoy** to Russia. He influenced **Georges Sorel** and in England **Wyndham Lewis**. Proudhon was less influential on the anarcho-syndicalist movement at the turn of the century, and in recent decades his direct influence has been almost nonexistent; but spontaneous revolts, such as that in Paris in 1968, are anticipated in his writings as an appropriate form of revolutionary activity.

Further reading

Other works include: *Oeuvres complètes*, ed. C. Bouglé and H. Moysset (19 vols, 1923–59). Not completed. *Correspondence* (14 vols, 1875); *Carnets* ('Diaries'), ed. P. Haubtmann (from 1960). Other works: *De la capacité politique des classes ouvrières* (1865); *La Guerre et la paix* (1970); *La Pornocratie, ou les femmes dans les temps modernes* (1865). Selections in English: *Selected Writings*, ed. S. Edwards (1969). See: Edward Hyams, *Pierre-Joseph Proudhon:*

His Revolutionary Life, Mind and Works (1979). See also: Robert L. Hoffman, *Revolutionary Justice: The Social and Political Theory of P.J. Proudhon* (1972); J. Hampden Jackson, *Marx, Proudhon and European Socialism* (1958); Henri de Lubac, *Proudhon et le Christianisme* (1945; trans. *The Un-Marxian Socialist: A Study of Proudhon*, 1948); Alan Ritter, *The Political Thought of Pierre-Joseph Proudhon* (1969).

ALAN MUNTON

PROUST, Marcel

1871–1922
French novelist

Marcel Proust was born into an upper-middle-class family of strong scientific and artistic interests that marked both the subject-matter of his future writing and the metaphors through which he was to convey his picture of the mind. His father was an eminent physician, conversant with French psychology of the day, and his mother, with whom he had the more intense relationship, a cultured and witty woman. The letters exchanged between mother and son show the ambivalent intimacy that may have been responsible for his susceptible and unhappy adult relationships, which were homosexual.

Of contemporary influences, that which most affected him during his education at the Lycée Condorcet and the École des Sciences Politiques (where he took degrees in law and philosophy) was perhaps Henri **Bergson's**, but to speak of this one only would be an absurdly narrow assessment of a catholic taste that had absorbed not only the finest writings of the nineteenth century in France and England but the classics of world literature, music and painting. Both direct references and metaphors in his writing show what he owed to **Baudelaire**, Nerval, **George Eliot**; to the Bible, and the Italian Renaissance; to French medieval epic, and to hundreds of other works of art. As one critic says, 'he sucked so much nourishment into his own great plant that his successors had to grow roots in other ground' (J. Cocking; see bibliography).

There has been a widely held picture of the young Proust as a dilettante: this in spite of the publication of a collection of short stories, 'portraits' and poems in his twenties (*Les Plaisirs et les jours, Pleasures and Regrets*, 1896, trans. 1950); the translation and annotation of some **Ruskin** in his thirties; and the discovery in the 1950s of an early unfinished novel, *Jean Santeuil* (1952, trans. 1955). Nevertheless, it is still true that, although Proust was clearly brilliant, he published nothing of major artistic importance until *Remembrance of Things Past* (the inept English title for *À la recherche du temps perdu*, 1913–27, trans. 1922–31). His previous sketches, and longer essays or fiction, show that he already had all his themes, many of his characters, a gift for imagery, and wit; but he was still groping towards a structure for these, and still often lacked complete stylistic control. It does seem that he may have had a sudden inspiration, round about 1909, comparable to that he describes for the hero of his novel, even if it was only how to use insights long held. The result was *Remembrance of Things Past*, the greatest twentieth-century French novel, and considered by some to be the greatest twentieth-century European novel.

Its influence has been huge: its unprecedentedly bold use of a subjective first-person narrator, its stress on the relativity of perception, its radical departures from linear chronology, and its ostentatious patterning by image, association and coincidence have profoundly marked the novel both inside and outside France. Even French novelists of the 1930s and 1940s like **Malraux** and **Sartre**, seeming to depart from Proust with novels exploring political decisions and the biological solidarity of the human species, still show their debt to Proust's psychological perceptions and his methods of creating fluid or volte-face character. Later, the French *nouveau roman* took up the lessons of *Remembrance of Things Past*, and wove them into a game more elaborate than anything since **Gide's** *The Counterfeiters* (which is, incidentally, often wrongly credited with many of Proust's narrative innovations).

And in general, modern preoccupations with the interpretation of chaotic material, or with the meaning of language, had already reached perhaps their most adult expression and their most satisfactory explanation in *Remembrance of Things Past*.

Proust's novel is not an easy one; Roger Shattuck claims that it is the least read of the modern classics, and it is true that to read it with enjoyment, one must discard all habits of short-cutting. One of Proust's earliest critics, Léon Pierre-Quint, recommended that readers should start with twenty pages a day for the first week, then, slowly working up, increase this by five pages a day. Yet, like all great novels, it is its peculiar balance between simplicity and complexity that makes *Remembrance of Things Past* rewarding. The plot, for instance, can be seen as a bare and satisfying one – an odyssey of kinds. The nameless narrator, whom critics usually call Marcel, grows up longing to be a great artist, and filled with attractive but illusory notions about travel, the aristocracy, and love. He superficially fulfils his worldly ambitions, going to places he had wanted to visit, achieving outstanding social successes, and entering close relationships with three of the women he desires; but he finds that none of these experiences brings him the excitements he had hoped for, and that love can be agonizing. Above all, though his evaluation of art deepens and brings him a certain wisdom, he cannot, himself, create. Finally – in the last 200 pages of the total 3,000 – he reaches a nadir of discouragement. Nature no longer moves him; he cannot even believe in art. Then – an ending presented as quasi-miraculous – a series of physical sensations brings back to him a flood of involuntary memories, which make him both realize the richness of his own life, and, by suggesting to him the continuity of his personality – which he had mainly experienced as disparate and contradictory – give him the faith to create his work of art: a book about his life. He is approaching death, but, after this illumination, he retreats from the world with a new appreciation of ecstasy and sadness to write his work with what strength he still has.

Within this uncluttered framework, Proust plays dazzling variations on certain conceptions of time, personality, love and art – some his own, some clearly in a nineteenth-century lineage, some coinciding startlingly with those of other great contemporary thinkers whom he could not have read, like **Freud**. Those suggestions of Proust's which have disturbed the largest number of critics are the ones about love. Proust illustrates over hundreds of pages his own assertions that love is almost always unreciprocal and that we attribute to the loved one qualities and faults which issue merely from our own imaginations. We fall in love less with the beauty, kindness or intelligence of the beloved than as a result of our belief that he or she represents a world into which we wish to penetrate but from which we feel excluded. These ideas are stated baldly in *Remembrance of Things Past*, but it is still surprising that they should have seemed so controversial, since most of them had already been mooted, in one form or another, by Mme de la Fayette, Racine, Constant, Stendhal and Flaubert. Other insights of Proust's have been greeted with equally strong reactions; for instance, the fact that a large number of his characters prove bisexual has not made critics realize how heterosexually biased the novel had been before him, but has, instead, provoked numerous accusations of partiality on Proust's part and affirmations of the critics' own orthodox sexuality.

More acceptable has been Proust's depiction of the power of involuntary memory, which he shows as able to break down habit – the great blunter of perception – and to restore our freshest impressions of years ago, both sensory responses and intimate hopes and fears of the time. And, although few critics have tackled his style in detail, all accord him the praise of being an outstanding prose stylist. Proust is a master of the short, maxim-like sentence, and of the deliberately dissonant repetition, but he is more famous for the long sinuous sentences that re-create the multilayered quality of both physical sensations and inner associations; for the metaphors and similes which have the gift of seeming simultaneously an accurate commentary and joyously extravagant; and for his handling of the generalizations about human nature that appear on almost every page, and that are couched in physical and figurative terms that make them more integrated with the fictional narrative than in many other great novels.

What, finally, also makes *Remembrance of Things Past* a work of genius is its comedy. The same early critic who recommended a gradually increasing daily quota of Proust was honest enough to admit that it was only on his second reading that he realized how amusing the novel was; the first time he was too overwhelmed by the prose-poetry and the generalizations to notice the entertainment. Proust has at his command an unusually wide range of comic talents: he is able to write, with equal success, in a vein of relaxed whimsy or one of burlesque caricature. He follows the nineteenth-century movement away from divisions of genre, rarely strictly separating darker topics from amusing ones, and often, at the gravest moments, slipping in some light-hearted aside; he also takes much further than did Flaubert, Balzac or Stendhal the exploitation of tics of speech for comic effect. There is, too, a less frequently commented-on tradition of French literature into which Proust falls: the earthy one. He treats gross subjects with such delicate irony that many commentators have been able to overlook them, and to judge the work over-refined, or 'art for art's sake'; in fact, there are physically farcical episodes, scatological diatribes, and much play on love of food. Among Proust's finest comic passages are literary parody, deliberately bathetic combinations of phrases, and embroidery on an already comic reference after an interval of pages or even chapters; and one of his most frequent sources of comedy is snobbery, which he sees everywhere: in love and even in sadism (the sadist is trying to penetrate into the circle of the glamorously wicked).

Proust's novel has been said to be rarefied, masturbatory, merely toying with political issues – this in spite of a profound thoughtfulness in its treatment of the Dreyfus Affair and anti-semitism, the First World War, the possibilities of class-mobility, and the mutual fascinations whereby the aristocracy and working classes maintain each other in rigid stereotypes. Devoted Proustians would, however, doubtless maintain that the greatest reward of reading him is the changes he effects in one's own perception of sense-impressions.

Further reading

Other works include: *By Way of Sainte-Beuve* (*Contre Sainte-Beuve*, 1954, trans. 1958). Publication of Proust's complete *Correspondance*, ed. Philip Kolb, began in 1970. See: G.D. Painter, *Marcel Proust: A Biography* (2 vols, 1959 and 1965). See also: Samuel Beckett, *Proust* (1931); J. Cocking, *Proust* (1956); G. Poulet, *L'Espace proustien* (1963); V. Graham, *The Imagery of Proust* (1966); G. Brée, *The World of Marcel Proust* (1967); J.H.P. Richard, *Proust et le monde sensible* (1974); R. Shattuck, *Proust* (1974); M. Bowie, *Proust, Jealousy, Knowledge* (1978); T. Kilmartin, *A Reader's Guide to Remembrance of Things Past* (1983); Richard Sprinker, *History and Ideology in Proust* (1994); Jean-Yves Tadie, *Marcel Proust: A Biography*, trans. Euan Cameron (2000); Richard Bales (ed.) *The Cambridge Companion to Proust* (2001).

ALISON FINCH

PUCCINI, Giacomo

1858–1924

Italian composer

Puccini was born into a family whose musical tradition stretched back several generations and included composers of sacred as well as secular music. His early training in Lucca was primarily as a church musician, but in 1876 a performance of **Verdi's** *Aida* persuaded him to pursue an operatic career. He moved to Milan to study composition with Amilcare Ponchielli, and it was there, in 1884, that his first opera, *Le villi*, was produced. *Edgar* (1889), his next work, was less successful with the public, but *Manon Lescaut* (1893) brought him an international reputation, in spite of inevitable comparisons with Jules Massenet's opera of the same title.

This success was consolidated with the next three works, all of which remain firmly in the operatic repertoire. *La Bohème* (1896) depicts a tragic love affair against the background of bohemian artistic life in Paris; the sentimentality of the plot and its blending of comic and serious elements have led many to consider it the opera in which subject-matter is most convincingly matched with Puccini's particular musico-dramatic gifts. However, *Tosca* (1900) marked a sharp change in direction. The violence and cruelty of the plot did not prevent Puccini from including several lyrical scenes, but it did perhaps encourage him to experiment with various 'modernistic' musical devices, in particular with harmony based on the whole-tone scale. *Madama Butterfly* (1904) again attempted to break new ground, this time with an exotic, oriental setting and, at least on the surface, a more refined orchestral sonority.

After *Butterfly* the pace of Puccini's creative output slowed considerably. From his published letters it seems that the major problem was that of finding suitable operatic subjects. As we can see from the last three operas discussed, he clearly disliked repeating himself in his choice of dramatic setting, presumably because the background of a work produced the initial stimulus towards composition. In every respect the comparison with Verdi's relatively unproductive period (from *Aida* to *Otello*) is striking and relevant, and can tell us much about the composers' creative processes. The breakthrough finally occurred when Puccini discovered a story set in the Californian gold-rush of 1849. *La fanciulla del West* (1910) was, in the violence and austerity of its plot, somewhat akin to *Tosca*, but it noticeably lacked the earlier opera's sections of sustained lyricism and perhaps for this reason has tended to be less popular with the opera-going public.

La rondine (1917) has been even less frequently revived, but the next work, *Il trittico*

(1918), showed many interesting innovations. Three contrasting one-act operas make up the evening: a sinister melodrama (*Il tabarro*); a sentimental tragedy, entirely for female voices (*Suor Angelica*); and a pure comic opera, set in thirteenth-century Florence (*Gianni Schicchi*). Though rarely seen as a complete evening, these operas (particularly the first and third) are important documents in the development of Puccini's musical personality. The new orchestral refinements of *Il tabarro* show that the composer was less indifferent to the music of his more radical contemporaries, **Debussy** in particular, than is sometimes suggested (we might also remember that he was an attentive listener at one of the earliest performances of **Schoenberg's** *Pierrot Lunaire*). On the other hand, *Gianni Schicchi* places in the clearest possible context Puccini's debt to Verdi, and to that composer's last opera, *Falstaff*, in particular.

Puccini's final work, *Turandot* (first performed 1926), represented yet another change in dramatic direction. The fairy-tale atmosphere of the plot, and its bold mixture of various dramatic genres, initially struck the composer as a source of limitless possibilities, as a chance to supersede all his previous work; but ultimately the complicated dramatic structure created severe problems of musical continuity, and the work remained unfinished at the composer's death. It is performed today in a completed version by Franco Alfano.

In spite (perhaps, in some circles, because) of Puccini's vast popular success, he has sometimes been the target of academic/critical abuse, on both the dramatic and the musical level. Joseph Kerman, for example, described the musical texture of *Tosca* as 'consistently, throughout, of café-music banality', and eventually identifies the 'failure, or, more correctly, the triviality of [Puccini's] attempt to invent genuine musical drama'. More recently a less jaundiced view has prevailed, even though it is conceded that his mature musical language (from *La Bohème* onwards) changed little, and was only marginally affected by contemporary developments. Puccini was above all a master of the theatrical situation – his operas can be assessed realistically only in the opera house itself. There the almost fanatical precision with which he judged the pace of the drama always seems to justify itself magnificently, and even in some cases to transcend the limitations of his musical language.

Further reading

Other works include: religious music and a few choral, orchestral and chamber works, the vast majority of them written during the 1880s. Source writings: *Epistolario*, ed. Giuseppe Adami (1928, trans. Ena Makin, *Letters of Giacomo Puccini*, 1931); and *Carteggi Pucciniani*, ed. Eugenio Gara (1958). Mosco Carner, *Puccini: A Critical Biography* (2nd edn, 1974), covers all the works in detail and includes a full biography. See: M. Girardi, *Puccini: His International Art* (2000); Mary Jane Phillips-Matz, *Puccini: A Biography* (2002); Julian Budden, *Puccini: His Life and Works* (2005).

ROGER PARKER

PUDOVKIN, Vsevolod Illarionovich

1893–1953

Russian film director

Born into a family of peasant extraction in Penza, Pudovkin studied physics and chemistry at the University of Moscow. Mobilized during the First World War, he joined the Russian artillery and, after being wounded in 1915, spent three years in a POW camp before escaping. On his return to Moscow he worked as an industrial chemist until 1920. Then, at the age of twenty-seven, inspired by **D.W. Griffith's** *Intolerance*, he enrolled at the State Cinema School where he worked under Vladimir Gardin before moving to join the workshop of Lev Kuleshov, six years his junior. In this period Pudovkin took part in the writing, direction, acting and set-design for a number of films, notably Kuleshov's *The Extraordinary Adventures of Mr West in the Land of the Bolsheviks* (1924) and *Death Ray* (1925).

In 1925 Pudovkin joined Mezhrabpom-Russ to direct a popularizing account of **Pavlov**, *Mechanics of the Brain*, and a short comedy, *Chess Fever* (1926). These led at once to his first internationally famous work, *Mother* (1926), an adaptation of **Gorky's** novel commemorating the political enlightenment of a revolutionary's mother during the unsuccessful revolution of 1905. Like other Soviet directors, Pudovkin produced probably his best, and certainly his most celebrated, work by 1930. Just as *Mother* parallels **Eisenstein's** *Battleship Potemkin* (1925) in its return to 1905, so Pudovkin's *The End of St Petersburg* (1927) complements Eisenstein's *October* (1927) in its account of the successful revolution of 1917. *Storm over Asia* (1928), his last major film of the silent era, told the story of a Mongolian hunter in his struggles against the British Occupation Forces during the Civil War. At the end of the 1920s Pudovkin returned to acting, taking the starring role in Otsep's *A Living Corpse*, as well as parts in Kuleshov's *The Gay Canary* and Kozintsev's and Trauberg's *The New Babylon* (all 1929).

The 1930s were a depressed period for Pudovkin, as for other Soviet directors. After the failure of *Life is Very Good* (1930), unsuccessfully revised as *The Story of a Simple Case* (1932), Pudovkin completed *Deserter* (1933), on the struggles within German Communism, a film exemplifying the call for the experimental use of sound, particularly sound-image counterpoint, announced in Pudovkin's, Eisenstein's and Alexandrov's 1928 manifesto. The year in which he received the Order of Lenin, 1925, also saw the death of his established scenarist, Nathan Zharki, in a road accident which also injured Pudovkin. Illness subsequently kept him away from the studios, maintaining his involvement at the level of theoretical work and teaching at the Higher Cinema Institute. In the later 1930s Pudovkin's talents were channelled into the genre of patriotic historical dramas produced by the Soviet propaganda machine to combat the rise of Fascism. *Victory* (1938) deals with a popular revolt against the Polish occupation of Moscow in the seventeenth century; *Minin and Pojarsky* (1939) celebrates the partnership between the

Novgorod butcher and the Moscow prince which liberated the homeland from the Poles in 1612.

Pudovkin entered the 1940s by co-directing, with documentarist Esther Schub, the anniversary feature *Twenty Years of Cinema* (1940) before returning to historical drama with *Suvorov* (1940), a study of the later years of the eighteenth-century general of the same name. His wartime work consisted of newsreel and documentary work, together with a version of the great popular patriotic theatrical success of the day, Simonov's story of the partisans, *In the Name of the Fatherland*. Pudovkin did not long survive the post-war freeze. *Admiral Nakhimov* (1946), devoted to the memory of the Commander of the Black Sea Squadron in the Crimean War, was severely criticized (along with Eisenstein's *Ivan the Terrible*, Part 2) by the Central Committee of the Party, and released the following year in a revised version. This was followed by *Zhukovsky* (1950), a simplified biography of the nineteenth-century aerodynamicist, a collaboration with Yutkevitch on the reworking of Ptouchko's drama of homecoming from war, *Three Returns* (1948), and the rural love story *The Return of Vasily Bortnikov* (1953). Pudovkin died of a heart attack, on the Baltic, in the same year.

Pudovkin's influence stems from his trilogy of crises of conscience – *Mother*, *The End of St Petersburg*, and *Storm over Asia* – and from his theoretical treatises *Film Technique* (1926) and *Film Acting* (1934). Certainly, Pudovkin cannot easily be assimilated to the highly associative and disjunctive montage aesthetic explored by Eisenstein and **Vertov**, a distinction encapsulated by Eisenstein when he described Pudovkin's use of editing as being designed to provide 'linkage', his own to cause 'collision'. Instead we have, in Georges Sadoul's words, a series of 'romanesque films marked by an approach at once lyrical, psychological, and social, showing the evolution of characters who are individualistic yet selected for their value as social types'.

Further reading

See: *Izbrannyiye Statyi* ('Selected Texts', 1955); *Film Technique and Film Acting* (1958); Barthélémy Amengual, *V.I. Poudovkine* (1968); Luda and Jean Schnitzer, *Vsevolod Poudovkine* (1966); Jay Leyda, *Kino: A History of the Russian and Soviet Film* (2nd edn, 1973); Amy Sargeant, *Vsevolod Pudovkin: Classic Films of the Soviet Avant-garde* (2001).

PHILIP DRUMMOND

PUTNAM, Hilary

1926–

US philosopher

Hilary Putnam is a US philosopher with wide-ranging interests in epistemology, cognitive psychology, philosophy of science, language, logic and mathematics. Putnam is unusual in his willingness constantly to revisit his own earlier arguments and – very often – to come up with doubts, misgivings or objections which he takes to require a more-or-less drastic change of approach. The best-known example is the series of shifts in Putnam's thinking as regards the question of scientific realism: that is, the issue as to whether or not we are rationally justified in maintaining the existence of an objective, mind-independent world together with its various objects, properties, structures, causal dispositions, and so forth. Some of Putnam's earliest (and most influential) essays defended just such a strong realist view. This involved certain modal concepts, i.e. concepts of necessity and possibility, such that (for instance) it is a necessary truth in our physical world and all other worlds physically congruent with ours that *water* should possess the molecular structure H_2O or *gold* the atomic number 79. So – in Putnam's famous thought-experiment – if a space-traveller from Earth landed on the planet Twin-Earth and happily exclaimed 'Lots of water around here!' she would be right if all that watery-looking stuff was indeed H_2O but wrong if it happened to display just the same manifest properties but (unbeknownst to her) had the molecular constitution XYZ.

Putnam rings some ingenious changes on this theme so as to bring out his realist point that 'meanings just ain't in the head', i.e. that what fixes the reference of natural-kind terms and hence the truth-value of statements containing them is *not* their meaning as conceived by this or that speaker but rather their picking out objects or substances of just the specified kind. This he takes to have significant implications for philosophy of science and the issue as to just what constitutes the truth or falsehood of our scientific theories. With respect to physical properties like molecular or subatomic structure it is a matter of *a posteriori* necessity that 'water = H_2O': that is to say, a truth which had to be discovered through some process of empirical investigation but which nonetheless holds necessarily if that investigation was on the right track. Thus 'water' referred to H_2O even when nobody had the least idea about its molecular constitution, just as 'gold' properly referred to gold even when nobody knew about atomic numbers and descriptions fastened on manifest attributes like 'yellow', 'ductile' or (at a later stage of scientific advance) 'soluble in dilute nitric acid'. Indeed, it referred to the same sort of stuff – the identical natural kind – right back to the time when 'expert' opinion tended to confuse gold with iron pyrites ('fool's gold') on account of the latter's superficially similar appearance and physical properties.

Putnam later backed away from this position under pressure of various (as he thought them) decisive counter-arguments. He now took the view that his earlier standpoint of 'metaphysical' (objectivist) realism was one that placed truth beyond the utmost reach of humanly attainable knowledge. Much better, Putnam thought, to give up that inherently self-defeating (and scepticism-inducing) idea in favour of a framework-relativist conception of knowledge or warranted belief. Such an outlook could be saved from wholesale relativism by invoking some limit-point notion such as 'idealized rational acceptability', truth 'at the end of enquiry', or that upon which our investigations are destined to converge when all the evidence is in and subject to assessment under optimal conditions of evaluative grasp. This seems to Putnam the only hope of heading off the kinds of epistemological doubt that have plagued philosophy from Descartes to the present. Otherwise there will always be room for the sceptic to claim that we can *either* have objective (recognition-transcendent) truth *or* knowledge within the bounds of present-best human cognitive grasp but surely not both.

Opinions differ as to whether Putnam's middle-ground approach manages to head off the sceptical challenge while retaining its realist credentials or whether it amounts to just a kind of figleaf pseudo-realism. At the same time he has changed tack on issues in cognitive psychology, from the functionalist position that mental processes can be specified entirely in terms of computations on various (physical but not necessarily organic, perhaps silicon-based) sorts of 'hardware' to an approach that accords far less weight to such science-led concepts of explanatory worth. Here again there is much debate as to just how far Putnam has gone in a contrary direction: that is, towards an outlook that endorses the priority of human meanings, intentions or beliefs over the claims of a reductionist or physicalist approach. Still it should be clear to any reader of Putnam's later work that this tendency has always been countered by a sense of the need for philosophers to square their views with current thinking in the physical sciences. Hence his keen awareness of the problems thrown up for any 'metaphysical'-realist approach by developments such as non-Euclidean geometry, quantum mechanics and the paradoxes of classical set-theory. Few thinkers in recent times have managed to keep such an open mind on such a range of complex philosophical topics while never letting go of the desire for clearer, more adequate explanations.

Further reading

Hilary Putnam's works include: *Mind, Language and Reality* (1975); *Mathematics, Matter and Method*

(1975); *Reason, Truth and History* (1981); *Realism and Reason* (1983); *Pragmatism: An Open Question* (1995); *Realism with a Human Face* (1990); *Words and Life*, ed. James Conant (1994); *The Threefold Cord: Mind, Body, and World* (1999); *The Collapse of the Fact/Value Dichotomy, and Other Essays* (2003). See: George Boolos (ed.) *Meaning and Method: Essays in Honour of Hilary Putnam* (1990); Peter Clark and Bob Hale (eds) *Reading Putnam* (1994); Christopher Norris, *Hilary Putnam: Realism, Reason, and the Uses of Uncertainty* (2002).

CHRISTOPHER NORRIS

PUVIS DE CHAVANNES, Pierre

1824–98

French artist

Puvis de Chavannes appears to have been a man of sanguine temperament, simple tastes and liked by almost everyone. No other painter of the period seems to have avoided the strife and confusions of the art world in mid-nineteenth-century France as well as Puvis. Serenely he designed and carried out large-scale decorations which after exhibition at the official salons were then placed in the major public buildings for which they were intended in cities throughout France. It seems likely that Puvis avoided conflict mainly because his paintings were not easel paintings and commissioned for the most part by the state. Consequently he was not competing in the same field for recognition as the Realists and Naturalists, who were at times critical of his work.

Born in Lyons, son of a civil engineer, Puvis was sent to study law in Paris but transferred his attentions to the ateliers of art. Having twice visited Italy he was taught first by Henry Scheffer, briefly by Delacroix, and finally settled to study with Couture, himself a pupil of Ingres. Here Puvis found an education more in tune with his inclinations for his studies were of classicism and it was the Italian old masters whom he admired most, in particular the grace and delicacy of Piero della Francesca, and later the idealism of the French Poussin.

His first Salon appearance was of a religious subject, a *Pietà* of 1850, in which a group comprising three figures crouch, mourning in an imaginary landscape. This liking for nature, idealized and made beautiful, provides a perfect setting for the saints and allegorical figures which Puvis used to portray all the virtues of both the Bible and Ancient Greece. Puvis made it the source for a kind of primitive Golden Age in which groups of figures are for the most part shown as children of nature, thus making architecture an unimportant part of the designs. For the most part where architecture does appear it takes the form of rough shelters or screens and only occasionally a simple building from the early Renaissance.

In 1865 Puvis received a commission from Amiens, in 1869 from Marseilles, then Poitiers in 1874. By 1880 his reputation was established and attacks by such supporters of Realism as Castagnary ceased. Impressionism itself was now the target for adverse comment and taste in art was moving towards a more imaginative literary as well as painterly style, that of Symbolism. It was here that Puvis found his greatest support.

Besides mural decorations the artist had produced and regularly exhibited a number of smaller easel paintings. Among these were the famous *The Poor Fisherman* (1881), the *Prodigal Son* (c. 1879) and *Hope* (c. \1871), all symbolic figures projecting delicate nuances of mood and painted in a simple manner. They convey a dream-like quality that endeared Puvis to all the Symbolists, poets such as **Mallarmé** and **Rimbaud**, as well as painters like **Gauguin** and his followers, the Nabis.

Porcelain (1891), a later painting and part of Puvis's decoration for the gallery at Rouen, is of two women in Victorian dress and unusual in that it relinquishes the classical for the contemporary. The two women carry a dish and an urn along a path between decorative flower beds which border simple square buildings. The tipping forward of the straight pathway so that it appears flattened on to the surface of the canvas at right angles to a transverse path echoes the severity of the buildings. This reduction and flattening of form contrasts with the fluent shapes of the women and the decorative plant forms. In subject–matter, composition and style, the work is markedly similar to Maurice Denis's treble portrait of Mademoiselle Yvonne Lerolle (1896–7). Equally, when viewing the section entitled *Pottery* one is irresistibly reminded of **Holman Hunt's** early sagas such as *A Converted British Family, Sheltering a Christian Priest from the Persecution of the Druids* (1899–50). Indeed, Puvis's development seems strongly to parallel that of the Pre-Raphaelites in some respects. The influence of early Italian Quattrocento art, the symbolism, the simplicity of form synthesized with flower decoration, the increasing richness of colour are all factors. However, the insistence upon 'truth to appearances' in Pre-Raphaelite thought is contrary to Puvis's idealizing search for essential beauty.

He was to write that 'Simplicity means an untrammelled idea, the simplest conception will be found to be the most beautiful', and again 'It is necessary to cut away from nature everything that is ineffective and accidental, everything that for the moment is without force.' Perhaps Puvis's two most famous decorative series are those for the Panthéon in Paris, depicting the life of Sainte Geneviève, started in 1876 and finished the year of his death, and those for the Hôtel de Ville in Paris, entitled *Summer* and *Winter* (1890 and 1893).

Finally, it is of interest to compare Puvis de Chavannes's work with that of **Gustave Moreau**. Both artists were working at the same period; both were concerned with classical and Christian mythology; both idealized and generalized. However, whereas Puvis reduced his forms in such a way that they begin to look forward to expressive abstraction, Moreau complicated his and made addition upon addition to his surface. Further, where Moreau's art is violent and often sadistic, Puvis's is gentle and mildly melancholic. It can be said that of the two styles, Puvis's, in its primitivism, its reduction

of form and intensification of mood, must have been the more progressive art for its time.

Further reading

See: André Michel *Puvis de Chavannes: A Biographical and Critical Study* (trans. 1912); René Jean, *Puvis de Chavannes* (2nd edn, 1933); Brian Petrie, *Puvis de Chavannes* (1981); Russell T. Clement (ed.) *Four French Symbolists: A Sourcebook on Pierre Puvis de Chavannes, Gustave Moreau, Odilon Redon and Maurice Denis* (1996); B. Petrie, *Puvis de Chavannes* (1997); Jennifer L. Shaw, *Dream States: Puvis de Chavannes, Modernism and the Fantasy of France* (2002).

PAT TURNER

PYNCHON, Thomas

1937–

US novelist

Born in Long Island, New York, Pynchon attended the engineering department at Cornell University, but did not graduate, instead joining the US Navy. He returned to Cornell in 1957, to complete a degree in English in 1959. Controversy surrounds whether or not he was a student of **Vladimir Nabokov** there. Although following graduation he almost immediately set about writing fiction, he joined the Boeing Corporation as an engineering assistant in 1960, drafting technical papers some of which related to nuclear arms projects, before the critical and commercial success of his first novel, *V* (1963) enabled him to set aside regular employment. Since then he has published only four further novels, but these have kept Pynchon's reputation as one of America's foremost, and arguably most interesting, novelists alive. Famously, like Nabokov, and even more like **J.D. Salinger**, he has eschewed contact with the media, telling CNN in a rare interview in 1997, 'My belief is that "recluse" is a code word generated by journalists … meaning, "doesn't like to talk to reporters".' Like **Stephen Hawking**, he has become a character in the long-running *The Simpsons* television cartoon series. That he has survived and prospered as an iconic writer secluded from the public gaze, however, is down to the undoubted quality of his work. A new Pynchon novel is always a literary event of the first magnitude.

V creates a world constituted by a bewildering variety of groups and individuals, all searching for truths to live by and emerging with an utterly fantastic variety of lifestyles; these range from the systematic sexual exploitation and extermination of an African people to the exaltation of plastic surgery or dentistry to the status of a religion. Of the central characters, Benny Profane sees himself as a *schlemiel*, at the mercy of the material world, and hence excused effort or involvement, while Stencil, searching for 'V', the object of his grandfather's quest, which is simultaneously a place, a person and a truth, treats himself as a character in a work of fiction, and hence refers to himself in the third person. References to 'V' abound in the book, but their very multiplicity undermines the quest as a whole, especially when their common element emerges as a desire to fuse with the mineral world, to become inert, stable and immortal.

Pynchon's second novel, *The Crying of Lot 49* (1966), which won a National Book Award but was denied a Pulitzer Prize when the Pulitzer committee overruled the jurors' unanimous decision in its favour, takes the heroine Oedipa Maas into a twilight zone between paranoia and the revelation of an alternative postal communication system, Trystero, which seems to offer a way of transcending alienation and of genuinely being in touch with others across space and time. The more information she gains, however, the more the plot thickens in a baroque fashion, and the closer it gets to an obsessive and insane need for there to be a parallel realm of meaning and truth to the obvious everyday world. In *Gravity's Rainbow* (1973), however, this quotidian reality has been entirely swallowed up in the nightmare of the Second World War. The hero of the book is Tyrone Slothrop who, subjected to Pavlovian conditioning in childhood, finds himself sexually aroused by the future firing of a V2 rocket, and drawn to its place of impact. This inversion of causal sequence finds many echoes in the book and picks up the earlier themes of erotic submission to the world of matter and technology. Instead of 'gravity's rainbow', a natural parabola of excitation and release, of life and death, science seeks a continuous increase of energy and power, abetted by the multinational companies which profit by war. War is the logical outcome as the greatest possible centralization of power, squandering of energy, growth of knowledge and mobilization of individuals' energy through the eroticization of violence and submission by sado-masochistic conditioning.

Around the time *Gravity's Rainbow* was published, the elusive Thomas Pynchon (sometimes dubbed 'the Greta Garbo of American Letters') was alleged to have settled in California. At any rate, his fourth novel, *Vineland*, is best described as a Californian extravaganza with serious undertones. Its central relationship, between an FBI agent and a feminist filmmaker, is used to explore as well as satirize tensions between authority and liberalism. The style and mood of the book, however, is persistently governed, or contaminated, by a welter of allusions to *Star Trek* and other Hollywood enterprises. Drugs are present, as is a subset of characters called 'Thanatoids', who, hovering somewhere between life and death, represent latter-day Transcendentalism.

At some point in the mid-1990s Pynchon returned to New York, where he married his literary agent Melanie Jackson. His fifth, and to date most recent, novel, *Mason & Dixon*, appeared in 1997. As the title suggests, it canvasses the fortunes of the cartographers Charles Mason and Jeremiah Dixon, who between them devised the eponymous Mason–Dixon Line, that divided the northern and southern states in the pre-Independence period. Insofar as Pynchon ever makes a didactic point, his message here is that manmade frontiers and boundaries are always bad news, whatever the context. On its surface

Mason & Dixon adopts the spirit, if not always the form, of an eighteenth-century picaresque novel, but as always with Pynchon there is too much going on beneath the surface for genre classification to be of much help. Wry jokes abound: for example, an observation that sitting beneath trees may be conducive of enlightenment – Pynchon cites not only Newton and the Buddha, but also Adam and Eve. But collectively, as forests, trees are forbidding, and the novel is shot through with a lingering sense of unease as its protagonists investigate what was then 'virgin' territory.

Critics have responded variously to *Mason & Dixon*, some seeing it as the latest in a series of masterpieces, others condemning it as unwieldy and unfocused. Most, however, would perhaps agree that there is about Pynchon an enduring quality of indeterminability, which has given him at least the reputation of America's premier postmodern author. His is an entropic vision in which the accumulation and dissemination of information and the geometrical increase in usable and used energy create a condition where there is no central organizing agency or truth. This is (or can be read as) a moral insight into the ways we have brought upon ourselves by seeking to be the victims or passive objects of forces we identify as being outside ourselves. In Pynchon, however, our inner neuroses and paranoia create the history we ostensibly seek to avoid.

Further reading

Other works include: *Slow Learner*, a collection of early short stories (1984). See: George Levine and David Laverenz (eds) *Mindful Pleasures: Essays on Thomas Pynchon,* (1976); T.H. Schaub, *Pynchon: The Voice of Ambiguity* (1981); Robert D. Newman. *Understanding Thomas Pynchon* (1986); Steven Weisenburger, *A Gravity's Rainbow Companion: Sources and Contexts for Pynchon's Novel* (1988); Deborah L. Madsen, *The Postmodernist Allegories of Thomas Pynchon* (1991).

DAVID CORKER
(REVISED AND UPDATED BY THE EDITOR)

Q

QADAFI *see:* GADAFFI, MUAMMAR AL-

QUENEAU, Raymond

1903–76

French writer

Born in Le Havre, Queneau studied philosophy at the Sorbonne from 1920 to 1925. He participated in the Surrealist movement between 1924 and 1929, but thereafter, while still remaining close to contemporary intellectual developments, he generally avoided doctrines and schools. With *Le Chiendent* (*The Bark-Tree*, 1933, trans. 1968), his first novel and possibly his best, he reached literary maturity. Here the formative influences – **Joyce**, **Flaubert**, Hegel, silent cinema, comic strips – are perfectly harmonized, and the primary – and recurrent – themes of illusion and reality, time, history, perception and identity and the quest for knowledge are elaborated in Queneau's favourite setting of suburban Paris. More novels followed, some autobiographically based, as well as a number of important essays and critical articles, most now republished in *Le Voyage en Grèce* ('The Journey to Greece', 1973), and several translations. In 1938 Queneau began his long association with the Paris publishing house of Gallimard; he became secretary-general in 1941 and, in 1945, director of Gallimard's *Encyclopédie de la Pléiade*. After the war he further developed his range of activities, producing poetry,

short stories, more novels, songs (for Zizi Jeanmaire) and film scripts (for **Buñuel** and René Clément) and exhibiting his paintings. His literary reputation grew with the popularity of *Exercices de style* (*Exercises in Style*, 1947, trans. 1958) – ninety-nine stylistic variations on one simple anecdote – and after his election to the Académie Goncourt in 1951; it was further consolidated in 1959 by the commercial success of *Zazie dans le métro* (*Zazie*, trans. 1960), the comic adventures of an anarchic child unleashed on the adult world. In 1960 he joined the Ouvroir de Littérature Potentielle, an experimental group which enabled him to combine literary work with his life-long fascination with mathematics.

While he acknowledged the arbitrariness and inevitable imperfection of language, Queneau was ever preoccupied with enriching the possibilities of literary discourse – annexing the syntax and vocabulary of spoken French, borrowing from other languages, adding his own inventions. His treatment of the French language does, however, fall short of the revolution implied in the polemics of *Bâtons, chiffres et lettres* ('Strokes, Figures and Letters', 1950). Queneau sought to break down barriers not merely between linguistic codes but also between literary kinds: he claimed to see no essential differences between the novel and poetry, and in much of his work in both genres he applied the formal rigour whose absence he had eventually found intolerable in Surrealist writing. The assimilation of the culture of the past, through simple quotation and more complex patterns of allusion, and his adaptation of devices from other artistic genres, notably film, theatre and music, are also essential features of his technique. But his achievement extends beyond the merely technical, for he succeeded in creating a complete imaginative universe – one in which the problems of existence are examined with a discretion and a humour which challenge received ideas and never allow of definitive solutions. Queneau himself is perhaps best approached with similar open-mindedness for he resists any simple categorization. Just as he belongs to no school, so he engenders none (despite his influence on Boris Vian and the *nouveau roman*); and the various attempts made to isolate individual aspects of his work fail, by definition, to do justice to this writer's rich variety.

Further reading

Other works include: *Pierrot mon ami* (*Pierrot*, 1942, trans. 1950); *Le Dimanche de la vie* (*The Sunday of Life*, 1952, trans. 1976); and *Les Fleurs bleues* (*Between Blue and Blue*, 1965, trans. 1967), all novels; *L'Instant fatal* (*The Fatal Moment*, 1948); *Chêne et chien* ('Oak and Dog', 1937); and *Le Chien à la mandoline* (*The Dog with the Mandolin*, 1965), verse. On Queneau: Jean Queval, *Raymond Queneau* (1971); Jacques Guicharnaud, *Raymond Queneau* (1965). See also Martin Esslin's essay 'Raymond Queneau, b. 1903' in John Cruickshank (ed.) *The Novelist as Philosopher* (1962); S. Shorley, *Queneau's Fiction* (1985); J.A. Hale, *The Lyric Encyclopaedia of Raymond Queneau* (1989); M. Velguth, *The Representation of Women in the Autobiographical Fiction of Raymond Queneau* (1990); Constantin Toloudis, *Rewriting Greece: Queneau and the Agony of Presence* (1995); Jordan Stump, *Naming and Unnaming: On Raymond Queneau* (1998).

CHRIS SHORLEY

QUINE, Willard Van Orman

1908–2000

US philosopher

'To be is to be the value of a variable' ('On What There Is') is one of those aphoristic quotations which haunt philosophy examination papers, and it epitomizes Quine's philosophy. Questions of ontology, ontological commitment and reference are never far from the centre of attention in his writings and his thought on such questions is coloured by viewing philosophical problems through the spectacles of formal logic.

Quine spent most of his academic life at Harvard University, where he was Edgar Pierce Professor of Philosophy. Born in Akron, Ohio, he graduated from Oberlin College in 1930, having majored in mathematics. He went on to write a doctoral thesis on logic under **A.N. Whitehead** at Harvard, and taught there from 1936. Before this he visited Vienna and studied mathematical logic at Warsaw and Prague. In Prague he met **Rudolf Carnap**, who had a formative influence on his philosophy, although this influence was tempered by the other sources to which Quine traces his philosophical ancestry, namely the American pragmatists **John Dewey** and **Charles Saunders Peirce**. In 1985 he published his autobiography *The Time of My Life*.

Epistemology, which Quine conceives as concern with the foundations of science, would be a label that could be attached to all of his philosophy even though this appears to fall into two distinct categories: formal studies in logic and the foundations of mathematics, on the one hand, and works on language, the philosophy of mind and the philosophy of logic, on the other. The motivation behind **Russell** and Whitehead's studies in the foundations of mathematics was epistemological. A reduction of mathematics to logic would both explain and justify the privileged status accorded to mathematical theorems by showing them to be of the same character as self-evident logical truths. The work of **Cantor** and **Dedekind** on the nature of numbers had already shown that numbers can be defined in terms of sets, or collections of objects, but Russell's paradox indicates that some care is needed to formulate a contradiction-free theory of sets. The final step in reducing number theory to logic would thus be to show that logic can provide a theory of sets. Quine contributed to this programme, developing his own system (New Foundations) of set theory. This system has perplexed philosophers and mathematicians since its conception in that the considerations motivating its construction are largely pragmatic – it is designed to avoid Russell's paradox while preserving as much as possible of **Frege's** original system, so eliminating the complications introduced in *Principia Mathematica* (see Russell). Quine's system does not rest on prior intuitions as to what sets exist, and in consequence is not readily compared with the other systems of set theory now commonly used by mathematicians. Indeed, many unsuccessful attempts have been made to prove New Foundations inconsistent.

Just because of the unobviousness of its postulates, New Foundations cannot claim to be successful as an epistemological underpinning for mathematics. Conceptual clarification is gained by the reduction of mathematics to set theory, but epistemological guarantees are not supplied. In a later work, *Set Theory and its Logic* (1963), Quine sets out in detail the view that logic stops where ontological commitments begin and that ontological commitments begin in mathematics just where sets have to be admitted as the values of variables open to quantification. He pays such attention to this issue because of his broader philosophical commitment to extensionalism.

In the minds of Russell and other logical empiricists, this reductive programme in mathematics was paralleled by a programme for giving natural science an epistemological foundation in sense experience. This programme was most nearly completed by Carnap in his *Logische Aufbau der Welt*. Initially attracted by the project of the *Aufbau*, Quine soon, with Carnap, realized that it could not be completed; the sentences of scientific theories cannot be translated into sentences about sense data. His reaction to the failure of these two reductive programmes was, however, much more radical than Carnap's.

In his famous 'Two Dogmas of Empiricism' (*Philosophical Review*, 1951), Quine attacked the conception which underwrites the reductive programmes – the idea that each meaningful sentence must either have its own, determinate empirical content, or be true in virtue of the meanings of the words it contains. In his view the Vienna Circle did not take the verification theory of meaning seriously enough. Combining Peirce's claim that the meaning of a sentence turns purely on what would count as evidence for its truth with **Duhem's** view that theoretical sentences have their evidence not as single sentences, but only as parts of theories, the conclusion should be that a theory as a whole (or even the totality of beliefs generally held by a community) is the unit of empirical significance. The resulting picture, which many have found seductive, is of a system of beliefs as a field of force on which experience impinges at the periphery to effect distortions of the field, modifying not just individual beliefs but also the interconnections between beliefs, i.e. modifying the structure of the whole field. Some beliefs, those near the periphery, are more susceptible to modification in the light of experience than others, those nearer the centre, but this is only a matter of degree; there is no distinction in kind between mathematical statements, lying near the centre, and statements about trees which lie near the periphery. Empirical content attaches only to the whole system of beliefs, and how it is distributed over the sentences expressing individual beliefs is not a question admitting a unique answer. This leads to the view that theory (the inner part of the field) is underdetermined by data (the periphery), a topic which has subsequently received much attention from philosophers of science.

The consequences of Quine's denial that one can talk of *the* empirical content of a sentence are far reaching and their development occupies the bulk of Quine's subsequent philosophy. He sees two direct consequences: (1) there is no uniquely correct way of translating one language into another, since any translation preserving the empirical content of the whole is 'correct' (the thesis of the indeterminacy of translation); (2) the want of a plausible alternative lends support to Dewey's naturalistic approach to language and epistemology. For Dewey, meaning is primarily a property of behaviour; there can be no likeness or distinctness of meaning beyond what is implicit in people's dispositions to overt behaviour. Pursuit of this approach gives rise to the idea of radical translation.

The hypothetical radical translator is a field linguist, who is also a convinced behaviourist psychologist of the **B.F. Skinner** variety and so sees language acquisition as the acquisition of dispositions to specific verbal responses on receipt of certain physical stimuli. He is confronted with a tribe of natives who have had no contact with the outside world and is to attempt a translation of their language. He starts correlating utterances with situations, guessing at what gestures signify assent and dissent. He then tries to establish, for some of these utterances, the conditions under which assent and dissent occur, so establishing their 'stimulus meaning' (the physical stimuli which trigger assent and dissent responses). This provides him with data on which to construct his 'analytical hypotheses' as to the logical structure of the native utterances and hence to propose a theoretical picture of their language. It is this idea which has been taken up by one of Quine's associates, Donald Davidson, who claims that reflection on radical translation is the route to insight on the nature of language.

In 1998 Quine delivered his last paper 'Three Networks: Similarity, Implication and Membership' to the Twentieth World Congress of Philosophy in Boston.

Further reading

The system New Foundations appeared originally in 'New Foundations for Mathematical Logic', *American Mathematical Monthly*, Vol. 44 (1937); an extended version is contained in the collection *From a Logical Point of View* (1953), which also contains 'Two Dogmas of Empiricism' and 'On What There Is'. Other works include: *Word and Object* (1960); *Ontological Relativity and Other Essays* (1969); *Philosophy of Logic* (1970); *The Roots of Reference* (1971); *The Pursuit of Truth* (1990); *The Logic of Sequences* (1990) and *From Stimulus to Science* (1995). Detailed responses to *Word and Object* are contained in D. Davidson and J. Hintikka (eds) *Words and Objections: Essays on the Work of W.V. Quine* (1969), A representative selection of Quine's work is contained in *Quintessence* (2004).

MARY TILES

QUTB, Sayyid Muhammad

1906–66

Egyptian Islamist

Born into a poor, but notable, family near Asyut in Lower Egypt, Sayyid Muhammad Qutb trained as a teacher in Cairo. Deeply interested in literature, he had literary ambitions. He joined the ministry of education as a teacher and graduated to a school inspector.

His writing covered not only essays and literary criticism but also fiction, all of which bore the stamp of his fluency in Arabic. An early autobiographical novel conveyed his disenchantment with romantic love, which was so intense that he remained a bachelor all his life.

Since Cairo was the headquarters of the League of Arab States, which declared war on the newly established Israel on 15 May 1948, Qutb could not remain immune from the political events of the region. Later that year, the ministry of education sent him to Colorado State College, Greenly, in the United States for further studies. He stayed in America for three years. The experience left him disillusioned with the US in particular and the West in general, and made him turn to his Islamic roots and Islam.

In *America as I Saw It*, his account of his travels in that country, serialized in a journal of the Muslim Brotherhood, the leading political-religious party in Egypt, he conveyed his loathing for the gross materialism, racism, sexual licentiousness and depravity, and widespread backing for Zionism, that he witnessed in the United States, and cited his personal experiences to illustrate his statements. He then expanded his thesis to include the rest of the Western world, and concluded that decadent Western civilization was following the path of ancient Rome in decline. Using Islamic terminology, he asserted that the West was turning into a *jahiliya* ('ignorant') society.

Later, in *Islam and the Problem of Civilization*, Qutb would pose a series of rhetorical questions, 'What is to be done about America and the West, given their overwhelming danger to humanity? Should we not issue a sentence of death? Is this not the verdict most appropriate to the nature of the crime?' Decades later, such views would be expressed by **Osama bin Laden** and his intellectual mentor, **Ayman Zawahiri**.

On his return to Egypt in 1951, the education ministry found his anti-American views so objectionable that it forced him to resign. Freed from the restrictions of the civil service, he became a religious and political activist. He joined the Muslim Brotherhood, and quickly established himself as one of its most eminent members.

Following the ban on the Muslim Brotherhood in 1954, Qutb was arrested and held in a concentration camp. Here he wrote his classic, *Maalim fi al Tariq* (Arabic: 'Signposts on the Road', or simply 'Signposts'), which is the primer for radical Islamists worldwide. It was smuggled out, and published in 1964, the year Qutb along with other Brotherhood detainees was released.

In *Maalim fi al Tariq* Qutb divided social systems into two categories: the Order of Islam and the Order of Jahiliya, which was decadent and ignorant, the type which had existed in Arabia before Prophet Muhammad had received the Word of God, when men revered not God but other men disguised as deities. He argued that the regime of Egyptian President **Abdul Gamal Nasser** was a modern version of *jahiliya*. This earned him the approval and respect of young Brothers and the opprobrium of the political and religious establishment.

The militant members of the (still clandestine) Muslim Brotherhood drafted Qutb into the leadership. They wanted him to avenge the persecution of the Brotherhood in the mid 1950s. By inclination a thinker, he wished to avoid violence. But when his radical followers pressed for a *jihad* to be waged against the social order he had himself labelled *jahiliya* because of its betrayal of Islamic precepts, Qutb could find no way out.

During his trial in 1966 he did not contest the charge of sedition, and instead tried to explain his position ideologically, arguing that the bonds of ideology and belief were sturdier than those of patriotism based upon region, and false distinctions among Muslims on a regional basis was an expression of the Crusading and Zionist imperialism, which had to be eradicated. In his view, *watan* (homeland) was not a land but the community of believers, *umma*.

He argued that once the Brothers had declared someone to be *jahil* (ignorant/infidel), they had the right to attack his person or property, a right granted in Islam, and that if, in the course of performing this religious duty of waging a jihad against unbelievers, a Brother found himself on the path of sedition, so be it. The responsibility for creating such a situation lay with those who through their policies had created such circumstances.

Qutb's subsequent execution turned him into a martyr in the eyes of his followers. This gained his thesis a wider acceptance in the Arab and Muslim world, infused the mainstream of Muslim thought, and helped change the age-old habits of lethargy and passivity.

Further reading

Qutb's books include an exegesis of the Koran, *Fi Zilal al-Koran* ('In the Shadow of the Koran'), being published in nine volumes (1954). English translations of his work include *Islam: The Religion of the Future* (1977); *Milestones* 1991; *Sayyid Qutb and Islamic Activism: A Translation and Critical Analysis of Social Justice in Islam* (trans. William E. Shepard, 1996); and *Social Justice in Islam* (trans. John Hardie, 2000). See also: Dilip Hiro, *War Without End: The Rise of Islamist Terrorism and Global Response* (2002)

DILIP HIRO

R

RACHMANINOV, Sergei

1873–1943
Russian composer and pianist

Born into the lesser Russian nobility at a time when the family fortunes were waning, Rachmaninov had an insecure home life, though his musical ability was recognized and encouraged from an early age. A continuation of these reduced circumstances caused the family to split up and move to a much humbler home in St Petersburg. This emotional turmoil, together with the loss of his younger sister, did much to fashion the composer's life-long feelings of emotional insecurity and fear of death shielded by a rather subdued temperament. In 1882 he attended the local conservatoire where he received piano lessons together with a general education. Lack of self-motivation promoted a move to the Moscow Conservatoire, where tuition under the pedagogue and disciplinarian Nikolai Zverev caused him to show immediate improvement by way of a concentrated work programme involving a study of the classics and the virtuoso piano tradition of **Liszt** and contemporaries. Living in at the Zverev household, he was to meet the foremost musicians of his day including the pianist Anton Rubinstein, the composers Arensky and Taniev who were soon to become his teachers and above all **Tchaikovsky**, whom he idolized.

By 1890 Rachmaninov had sketched his First Piano Concerto and was also promoting other compositions via many public concerts.

His graduation exercise, the opera *Aleko* from Pushkin, won him the conservatoire's Great Gold Medal in 1893 and the approval of Tchaikovsky, though a later performance at the Bolshoi Ballet was only moderately successful. By 1895 he had completed the First Symphony but a disastrous première under the baton of the popular Glazunov plunged him into the depths of despair: he withdrew the work and sought the help of a psychiatrist. Under this successful treatment he produced the famous Second Piano Concerto (1901) and its companion piece, the Second Suite for Two Pianos (1901) which has become equally popular. His marriage to his cousin in 1902 brought great stability into his life and soon afterwards he released his first book of Piano Preludes, Op. 23 (1903) and another Pushkin opera entitled *The Miserly Knight* (1905).

During the early years of the twentieth century he took up various conducting posts, starting at the Bolshoi Opera where his own works were premièred, though he soon moved to Dresden where he began the beautifully lyrical Second Symphony (1906). At this time he also wrote one of his most haunting works, the symphonic poem *The Isle of the Dead* (1909) based on a Symbolist painting by **Böcklin**. The same year an offer to tour America resulted in the exceedingly difficult Third Piano Concerto which won him new audiences for both his piano playing and his conducting of Russian music. On his return to Europe he once more sought emotional security and purchased a large estate called 'Ivanovka' where he could work in seclusion. Indeed, this was one of Rachmaninov's most fertile composing periods for he was to pen the choral *Liturgy of St Chrysostom* (1910) and two more sets of piano pieces, the Preludes, Op. 32 and the *Études Tableaux*, Op. 33. The continuation of some conducting work did not prevent him occasionally from going abroad and it was on a trip to Rome in 1913 that he wrote his choral symphony *The Bells*, though the outbreak of war led to the cancellation of its projected performance in England.

The crisis of world events and the fact that Rachmaninov was a member of the landed gentry put him in a precarious position. Accordingly he decided to leave Russia on the pretext of a concert tour of Scandinavia. Now finding himself an exile, he emigrated to the USA, setting up home in San Francisco in 1919 and signing important contracts with recording companies. Throughout the 1920s he travelled extensively around Europe, though very few compositions were produced during this period. The poor reception of the Fourth Piano Concerto (1926), which was criticized for its lack of melodic interest, once more plunged him into a depressive state. As a result he moved first to Paris and then to Lucerne, where he wrote the highly inventive *Rhapsody on a Theme of Paganini* (1934), to be followed by the Third Symphony (1935). The final decade of Rachmaninov's life brought him international success not only because of his extensive concert tours but also because of a collaboration with the Philadelphia Orchestra which recorded most of his major works under the baton of Eugene Ormandy. These performances, together with those of solo repertoire, are both superb documents of creative insight and remarkably modern in interpretation. Already the strain of such a busy lifestyle was beginning to take its toll, though the composer, after rejecting many requests for film scores, did produce his last and probably most nostalgic Russian work, the *Three Symphonic Dances* (1940). Indeed, these are the summation of a whole life's

work and incorporate all the influences on his mature style while adding yet a new dimension of chamber scoring to the often ethereal textures of the piece. By 1942 Rachmaninov was already very ill with cancer and, after the cancellation of an important concert tour, he died the following year at the age of sixty-nine.

Rachmaninov is generally thought of as a composer in the late Romantic tradition who followed in the footsteps of Tchaikovsky. Though this is true, unlike his predecessor's, most of his compositions were conceived in terms of keyboard figuration, whether in the songs, where the vocal lines are often woven within the piano counterpoint, or in the orchestral works which were initially sketched at the piano. Like Tchaikovsky his output contains a strong vein of lyricism, melancholy tone and rhapsodic expansiveness of a kind rarely seen in the more nationalist works of **Borodin** and **Rimsky-Korsakov**. The orchestral scoring is more weighty than that of his contemporaries, being influenced by the fuller textures of **Brahms** and the German school. To this Rachmaninov adds thematic material which is exclusively Russian with melodies reminiscent of Orthodox chant and modal folk song often gravitating around one note. An early interest in Symbolist art with its dream and death imagery pervades many of his pieces: this obsession often takes the shape of the 'Dies Irae' which is hinted at in the symphonic slow movements and in the *Isle of the Dead*.

Throughout his busy life as pianist, composer and conductor there was the inevitable conflict caused by an inability to fulfil all his ambitions at once. The failure of his early works may explain why he experimented little over forty creative years. Having lost all his possessions as an exile, he was often faced with financial problems which drove him on to the concert platform all too frequently, though his recitals always met with great success especially when he played popular transcriptions of his own songs and instrumental compositions by Bach, Mendelssohn and Fritz Kreisler. Such appearances invariably detracted from the appreciation of his larger orchestral and choral compositions, as did the wholesale plagiarism of his Romantic style by Hollywood film composers. Fortunately the recent revival of interest in large-scale symphonic writing, the availability once more of Rachmaninov's expert recordings and the unbiased assessment of his music by a younger generation have shown that his performances were remarkably up to date in conception, and ensured his place in musical history as the finest pianist of his day and a composer whose music is expertly crafted and full of emotional sincerity.

Further reading

See: V.I. Seroff, *Rachmaninov* (1951); S. Bertensson and J. Leyda, *Sergei Rachmaninov: A Lifetime in Music* (1965); R. Threlfall, *Sergei Rachmaninov* (1973); P. Piggott, *Rachmaninov's Orchestral Music* (1974); G. Norris, *Rachmaninov* (1976); P. Piggott, *Rachmaninov* (1978); B. Martyn, *Rachmaninoff: Composer, Pianist, Conductor* (1999).

MICHAEL ALEXANDER

RADCLIFFE-BROWN, Alfred Reginald

1881–1955

English anthropologist

Brought up in genteel poverty in Birmingham, where he attended the King Edward's School, A.R. Brown (later Radcliffe-Brown) was sent to Cambridge by an elder brother. He read moral sciences, taking a first, and went on to be **W.H. Rivers's** first pupil in anthropology. He carried out field-studies in the Andaman Islands (1906–8) and Australia (1910–12), but in contrast to his famous anthropological contemporaries **Boas** and **Malinowski**, his central contribution was to be theoretical rather than ethnographic. Shortly after completing an initial ethnological account of the Andamanese, Radcliffe-Brown was converted to Durkheim's view of the sociological enterprise, and parallel with **Durkheim's** nephew **Mauss** he devoted his life to the application of Durkheimian sociology to the findings of modern ethnography.

His *The Andaman Islanders* (1922) is largely concerned with demonstrating that ceremony and ritual are to be understood as ways of maintaining the sentiments on which socially required behaviour depends. The actual Andaman ethnographic materials cited were taken largely from the reports of an earlier observer. Similarly, his Australian studies relied heavily on the ethnographic reports of others, but brought to these a powerful analytic mind, rigorously defining the synchronic relations among institutions. His essays on Australian social organization remain central texts in the debate on these complex systems.

In 1921 Radcliffe-Brown was appointed to a foundation chair in social anthropology in Cape Town, subsequently holding chairs in the discipline in Sydney, Chicago, and from 1937 until his retirement in 1946, in Oxford. In these universities he was the central figure in the establishment of what amounted to a new discipline, so marked was the break with the ethnological tradition. Much of Radcliffe-Brown's writings in the latter part of his career consists of essays and lectures aiming at a definition and defence of the new science. Consequently a certain repetitiveness and contentiousness is often apparent, and the more specific essays and analyses have lasted best. In particular, Radcliffe-Brown's development of his views on kinship have proved important. He insisted on the systematic nature of kinship organization, the parts of the systems to be understood in their interrelationships.

While the Durkheimian influence was central, Radcliffe-Brown remained an evolutionist in the tradition of **Herbert Spencer**. Societies were like organisms, and could be studied by the methods of the natural sciences. Like organisms, they evolved in the direction of increasing diversity and complexity. 'Culture' was a product of a set of social relations. Social relations, social structure, provided the primary reality with which an anthropologist dealt. The anthropologist's aim was to uncover the normal form of such a system of relationships, and by comparison with similar sets to establish general laws of social relationships. An enduring value of this formulation is that it clears the decks for a rigorous study of the internal relationships characterizing a set of social facts, reducing the temptation to make a precipitate escape into psychological, biological or historical reductionism. Because he insisted that the parts of such systems of social relations contributed to the maintenance of the system as a whole, Radcliffe-Brown was often called a functionalist. This led to a confusion with Malinowski's ideas, which he deplored, but even among some who called themselves functionalists he went out of fashion because of his positivist insistence that systems of social relations can be directly observed, that their forms can be established empirically. Still a controversial figure, it is difficult to think of another theoretical writer to set beside him in twentieth century British sociology and social anthropology.

Further reading

Other works include: *The Social Anthropology of Radcliffe-Brown*, ed. Adam Kuper (1977), is the most extensive collection of Radcliffe-Brown's shorter studies and essays, while *A Natural Science of Society* (1957) is a series of posthumously published lectures. See also Adam Kuper, *Anthropologists and Anthropology* (1975).

ADAM KUPER

RAHNER, Karl, SJ

1904–84

German Roman Catholic theologian

Karl Rahner was a magisterial Catholic theologian of almost indescribable significance. It has been said that he stood to fundamental Christian theology as **Einstein** stood to mathematical physics. His influence overflowed German-speaking countries into European, American, Australasian and other geographical cultures. He thereby earned the title of global theologian, whose influence on non-Catholic churches has also been unparalleled. He was a genuinely ecumenical theologian.

Rahner was born at Freiburg-im-Breisgau. He followed his eminent brother Hugo into the novitiate of the Society of Jesus at Feldkirch in Austria in 1922. After studies in Holland (1929–33), he was ordained to the Catholic priesthood. A decision – momentous for his future work – was then made to send him to the University of Freiburg, where the existentialist **Martin Heidegger** was a professor of philosophy. Researching a doctorate under the supervision of the neo-scholastic Martin Honecker, Rahner was an assiduous attender at Heidegger's seminars. His interpretation of Aquinas's epistemology was judged by Honecker to be excessively Heideggerian (i.e. too anthropocentric) and Honecker withdrew his support as *Doktorvater*, thus preventing Rahner from being awarded his degree.

This failure had great portent for Rahner's future. His thesis was published as *Spirit in World* (*Geist in Welt*, 1939). He went to Innsbruck Jesuit Faculty where he wrote a doctoral dissertation in the field of patristics. During World War II he worked in several centres, and was appointed to a chair at Innsbruck in 1949. In 1963 he moved to the philosophical faculty at Munich, but found his post and its syllabus excessively restrictive, so in 1967 he accepted a chair in the Catholic faculty in Münster, from which he retired in 1971.

It is difficult to place Rahner precisely within the spectrum of the various parties in European and American Catholicism. The liberals regarded him as an immovable traditionalist, a champion of the Marian dogmas and blistering opponent of **Hans Küng's** reformist view of Papal Infallibility, and as an abstract thinker whose language and terminology are 'impenetrable'. Conversely, traditionalists were suspicious of the 'Heideggerian' existentialist and anthropological trends which Rahner 'imported' into Catholic thought. It was therefore natural that he was regarded with some suspicion by traditionalists during the papacies of Pius XII and Paul VI, who regarded Innsbruck as a suitable 'exile' for him. These assessments were somewhat reversed by 'good' Pope **John XXIII**, who appointed Rahner one of the commissioners in the preparations for the Second Vatican Council.

Perhaps Rahner may be best judged to have attempted significantly to humanize Catholicism by gently easing it away from what had become a somewhat arid neo-scholastic orthodoxy. This he did by considering the central question of nature's relation to grace, which led once more to the humanizing of the Christian world-picture which he constructed. In essays contained in *Theological Investigations* (*Schriften zur Theologie*, 23 volumes, 1961–92) and elsewhere he identifies the average view of the relationship, which he calls *extrinsicism*, which had been current, he believed, in Catholic circles for 'the last few centuries'. In this view, grace appears as a mere superstructure imposed upon nature by God's decree. Nature does acknowledge a supernatural order as a highest good, but does not see why it should waste time on it, separate as it is from consciousness and experience.

One problem is that this view supposes that natural man knows what his nature is and how far it extends. Nature and grace are two superimposed layers which do not interact with each other. For the average view is that grace (i.e. supernature) is knowable by the imparting of verbal, prepositional Revelation alone, which reaches natural man by God's proclamation alone. Man is disturbed by it; he resents it, for he regards it as foreign, alien to his nature. Rahner considered the roots of modern anti-religious secularism and asks whether this extrinsicist view has not helped to contribute to modern naturalism and secularism.

Rahner believed that it was time to re-open the nature–grace debate. One impulse for doing so derived from the modern dialogue between Roman Catholicism and Reformed theology. One modern tradition of this (and here it is impossible not to think that Rahner had in mind the system of **Karl Barth** and his school) is to be found in the Reformed churches of the Western world.

Rahner believes that Western thought has become existential and dynamic (as contrasted with ontic and static). Rahner wants to say that man, in his experiential nature, encounters grace in his everyday life, thinking and striving, rather than simply by an external imperative proceeding from a God who lies quite beyond his concrete life, striving and interest.

In rather more philosophical language, grace is *a priori*, imparted to man in his divine creation as a so-called natural being (i.e. belonging solely to the realm of nature). It follows that there is no such being as raw, purely natural man, bereft of grace. Man is a mysterious being who experiences himself daily as both nature and grace. Man possesses the *potentia obedientalis*, which enables him to receive the Christian message, for he has by his creation the potentiality, the desire, the longing for it in his natural life.

Rahner spoke much of man's experience, exhorting his readers to ask how man in his natural, everyday experience encounters grace. Yet how does Rahner's highly theoretical analysis achieve verification and realization in man's natural life? Rahner answers this question in a number of startling passages, contained in his *Theological Investigations*. One in particular deserves and invites examination and meditation. Nature realizes its saturation by grace in

> the experience of infinite longings, of unquenchable discontent, of the torment of the insufficiency of everything attainable, of the radical protest against death; in the experience of being confronted with an absolute love precisely where it is lethally incomprehensible and seems to be silent and aloof, the experience of a radical guilt and of a still abiding hope etc. These elements are in fact tributary to that divine force which impels the created spirit – by grace – to an absolute fulfilment. Hence in them grace is experienced and the natural being of man.

Many have found passages such as this illuminate brightly Rahner's vision of the relation of divine grace to natural man.

It is views such as these which have made Rahner a truly ecumenical theologian. Scholars have identified in them a startling affinity not only with Kierkegaard in the nineteenth century, but also with the phenomenological work of Heidegger, placing him in empathy with the **Bultmann–Tillich** stream of fundamental theology. It follows from this that his views would conflict violently with those of the Barthian neo-orthodox fundamental Protestant theology. It is also clear why Rahner has been credited with pioneering the term 'anonymous Christians'. Rahner taught that we might plausibly judge that grace influenced the philosophers, sometimes referred to as 'pagan thinkers' – we think here of the church's deep respect for and preoccupation with the works of Plato and Aristotle. But it is worth remembering that Rahner's views here can also be traced firmly to ancient classical Scriptural doctrines such as man's creation in the image of God, and the *analogia entis* between God and man.

Further reading

See: Karl Rahner, *Foundations of Christian Faith: An Introduction to the Idea of Christianity* (1978); Karl Rahner and Herbert Vorgrimler, *Concise Theological Dictionary* (1965). See also Louis Roberts, *The Achievement of Karl Rahner* (1967).

JAMES RICHMOND

RAUSCHENBERG, Robert

1925–

US artist

Rauschenberg's art does not operate within fixed parameters. Heterogeneous and open-ended, it straddles boundaries both between different domains of art and between these and the outside world. The categories into which it is sometimes put, proto-Pop, neo-Dada, junk, etc., merely characterize it by certain of its aspects and do little justice to its richness and complexity.

Born and educated in Texas, Rauschenberg studied painting in Kansas and Paris before enrolling at Black Mountain College, North Carolina, under **Albers**, primarily for the discipline which Albers offered. On leaving, Rauschenberg produced a series of White Paintings, which he described as 'hypersensitive', registering as they did the colours and shadows of passers-by: these have been compared with **Cage's** – slightly later – silent piece *4′33″*. Then came a series of Black Paintings with strongly textured surfaces. There are close parallels between these monochrome works and those of **Yves Klein**.

In 1953 Rauschenberg turned to red, which for him was the most difficult colour. The climax of the red series was *Charlene* (1954), in which appear photographs, newsprint, fabrics, a flattened parcel and even a functional light bulb, along with the paint. This led directly to his Combine Paintings and Free-standing Combines, operating somewhere between painting and sculpture. If the physical substantiality of paint was already stressed in the monochrome works, in the Combines it is just one substance among several others. As Rauschenberg put it: 'A pair of socks is not less suitable to make a painting with than wood, nails, turpentine, oil and fabric.' Each component of his extended 'palette' brings with it associations specific to its background. Paint brings the tradition of painting and most specifically (since it is usually splashed on) that of **de Kooning**; photographs, when included, conjure up various associations depending on their subject-matter, as well as suggesting a pin-up board; while the other objects, usually categorized as junk, far from being reduced simply to elements within a formal composition, are given a new lease of life and new meanings by being placed in this non-utilitarian context. Particularly successful Combine Paintings are *Bed* (1955), containing a real pillow, sheet and patchwork quilt, the sinister *Canyon* (1959), containing a flattened oil drum and stuffed eagle, and *Trophy I* (1959), dedicated to the dancer **Merce Cunningham**, with whose troupe Rauschenberg, like Cage, was closely associated.

The most striking Free-standing Combine is probably *Monogram* (1959), whose main motif is a stuffed angora goat encircled by a rubber tyre.

In 1959–60, Rauschenberg turned to the illustration of a specific text with his complex and powerfully evocative *Thirty-Four Drawings for Dante's Inferno*. During the 1960s his paintings mainly consisted of silkscreened images, a notable example being *Estate* (1963). In these, as in his Combines, Rauschenberg creates a specifically urban poetry, largely from the detritus of technological, industrial civilization. An involvement with technology's active side came in 1966 when he co-founded EAT (Experiments in Art and Technology), evidence of his refusal to accept the confines of a specialist profession. His performance pieces of the 1960s also involved him in collaboration with others. Throughout the 1980s and 1990s he continued experimenting, especially in collage and new ways of transferring photographic images. From 1986 to 1985 he created several series of paintings on metal: the 'Shiners' series (1986–93) were almost mirror-like; less extremely reflective were the 'Night Shades' series, combining photographic imagery with gestural marks on aluminium surfaces which both absorbed and reflected light in a highly poetic way. A big retrospective of his work was held at the Guggenheim, New York, in 1997 and travelled to Houston and around Europe in 1998. Since then, Rauschenberg has undertaken a number of high-profile public projects as well as continuing working in the relative seclusion of his home in Florida, where a number of younger artists have come to be his assistants.

The triumph of Abstract Expressionism in avant-garde art circles had, by the mid-1950s, led to an impasse. Rauschenberg's art was, with that of **Jasper Johns**, the principal means by which this was overcome. By abandoning art's ivory-tower isolation and proposing all aspects of the modern world as in principle equally worthy of artistic attention, Rauschenberg not only paved the way for Pop Art but, more widely, helped create an inclusive, outward-looking aesthetic to which a great deal of subsequent art is deeply indebted.

Further reading

A classic study of Rauschenberg is Andrew Forge, *Robert Rauschenberg* (1969). See also: Sam Hunter, *Robert Rauschenberg*, (2000); Robert Saltonstall Mattison, *Robert Rauschenberg: Breaking Boundaries* (2003); Branden W. Joseph, *Robert Rauschenberg and the Neo-Avant-Garde* (2003); Mary Lynn Kotz, *Rauschenberg/Art and Life* (2004).

GRAY WATSON

RAVEL, Joseph Maurice
1875–1937
French composer

Of mixed Swiss-Basque parentage, Ravel was born in the Basque region of France but grew up in Paris. In 1889 he entered the Paris Conservatoire, where he remained until 1904, studying composition with **Fauré** and others. During this period he came to know **Satie**, whose influence is to be felt in his earliest published work, the *Meneut antique* for piano (1895). He was also one of the 'apaches', a group of self-styled outlaw artists which also included the poet Tristan Klingsor and the pianist Ricardo Viñes: Klingsor supplied the text for one of his great vocal works, *Shéhérazade* for soprano and orchestra (1903), and Viñes gave the first performance of most of his earlier piano works, including the *Pavane pour une infante défunte* (1899, orchestrated 1910) and *Jeux d'eau* (1901).

Between 1901 and 1905 Ravel entered the competition for the Prix de Rome four times; the failure of the judges to award him the prize, despite the fact that he was already a mature and proven composer, caused a public scandal. There was also heated debate at this time about his debt to **Debussy** and Debussy's to him. Undoubtedly *Shéhérazade* owes something to the composer of *Pelléas et Mélisande*, though the work has a languid opulence which is quite foreign to Debussy's style; equally, the similarities between *Jeux* *d'eau* and some of Debussy's more brilliant preludes can be attributed to a shared appreciation of **Liszt** rather than to direct imitation.

In any event, Ravel was swiftly drawing away from the ambit of the older composer. In 1907 he produced two major Spanish works, the orchestral *Rapsodie espagnole* and the one-act comic opera *L'Heure espagnole*, which, while contributing to a favoured genre among French composers, strike a quite individual note. The composer's distinctive quirky gaiety is to the fore, and for all their gusto the scores show too his high regard for technical precision, for an exact matching of means to effect and for the creation of perfect musical objects. He was to return to the Spanish motif again at the end of his career in the orchestral *Boléro* (1928) and in *Don Quichotte à Dulcinée* (1932), a set of three songs for voice and piano or orchestra.

Spain was not the only country Ravel visited in his music. He was often stimulated by the prospect of applying his skills to conventional musical genres: the Viennese waltz in *Valses nobles et sentimentales* for piano (1911, orchestrated 1912) and in the dark orchestral fantasy *La Valse* (1919–20), the Baroque suite in *La Tombeau de Couperin* for piano (1917, orchestrated 1919), gypsy violin-playing in *Tzigane* for violin and piano or orchestra (1924) and jazz in the Piano Concerto in G major (1931). By using such disguises he was able to distance himself from his creation, and this tendency led him gradually to abandon the harmonic lushness and the rich colour washes of his earlier output. His ballet or 'choreographic symphony' *Daphnis et Chloé* (1909–11), commissioned by **Diaghilev**, marked the end of his impressionist period, a sustained wander through the idyllic Grecian landscape that Debussy had discovered in his *Prélude à 'L'après-midi d'un faune'*.

Daphnis was followed by a number of works in which Ravel appears to have been testing new possibilities, composing more slowly and circumspectly than hitherto. In the *Trois Poèmes de Stéphane Mallarmé* (1913), a refined and rarefied score for soprano and nonet, he reacted, though at some distance,

to the experience of *Pierrot Lunaire*: there are tinges of atonality, and the instrumentation is modelled on **Schoenberg's**. The Piano Trio of 1914 has middle movements more exactingly patterned on a Malayan verse form (the pantoum) and on the passacaglia, presaging the full-blown neo-classicism of *Le Tombeau de Couperin*. Then, in his Sonata for violin and cello (1920–2), Ravel produced an acerbic response to the bitonality and the neoclassical imitations of **Stravinsky**.

Contemporary with this last work was the best known of Ravel's orchestrations, his version of **Mussorgsky's** *Pictures from an Exhibition*. He was a masterly orchestrator, developing his technique from that of **Rimsky-Korsakov** and creating scores of crystal clarity in which every detail tells. Apart from the Mussorgsky, he also orchestrated music by Debussy, Satie, Schumann and others as well as a great many of his own piano compositions. His scoring suggests a willingness to take pains with the tiniest detail, a fascination with perfecting musical objects which is also apparent in the substance of many of his works: *Boléro*, based on the continued redecoration of one idea, is only the most blatant example.

Another facet of this concern with the small is exposed in those works in which Ravel entered the world of childhood with penetrating insight, notably *Ma Mère l'oye* for piano duet (1908, orchestrated 1911), based on Pérrault's fairy-tales, and the opera *L'Enfant et les sortilèges* (1920–5) to a libretto by Colette in which a child is hounded by the animals and household objects he has abused.

Ravel never married, nor did he accept any official position. He appeared only rarely as a pianist or conductor: he had originally intended the G major concerto for himself, but did not in the event play it (the contemporary left-hand concerto, a searching shadow of its exuberant companion, was composed specially for Paul Wittgenstein). **Vaughan Williams** was one of his private composition pupils; those influenced by his music make up a larger group, embracing Milhaud, Roussel, **Poulenc** and even **Boulez**.

Further reading

Other works include: String Quartet in F (1902–3); Sonatine for piano (1905); *Miroirs* for piano (1905); Introduction and Allegro for harp and sextet (1906); *Cinq Mélodies populaires grecques* for voice and piano (1904–6); *Histoires naturelles* for voice and piano (1906); *Gaspard de la nuit* for piano (1908); *Deux Mélodies hébraïques* for voice and piano or orchestra (1914); *Trois Chansons* for chorus (1915); *Chants populaires* for voice and piano (1910–17); *Ronsard à son âme* for voice and piano or orchestra (1924); *Chansons madécasses* for voice and trio (1925–7); Violin Sonata (1923–7). About Ravel: Vladimir Jankélévitch, *Ravel* (1959); Rollo H. Myers, *Ravel* (1960); H.H. Stuckenschmidt, *Maurice Ravel* (1968); Arbie Orenstein, *Ravel* (1975); Roger Nichols, *Ravel* (1977); A. Orenstein (ed.) *A Ravel Reader* (1990); D. Mawer (ed.) *The Cambridge Companion to Ravel* (2000).

PAUL GRIFFITHS

RAWLS, John Bordley

1921–2002

US philosopher and university teacher

John Rawls was born in Baltimore, Maryland, on 21 February 1921. He entered Princeton University in 1939 as an undergraduate. There he was first introduced to political philosophy by Norman Malcolm, a student of **Ludwig Wittgenstein**. Rawls wrote his senior thesis on the 'problem of evil'. Upon graduating in January 1943, he joined the US army as a private in the Infantry and saw active combat service in the Pacific (1943–6). He then returned to Princeton in 1946 to begin postgraduate studies in philosophy, receiving his PhD degree in 1951. In 1952–3 Rawls had a Fulbright Scholarship to Oxford University, where he was affiliated with Christ Church College. At Oxford Rawls attended, and was especially influenced by, lectures by H.L.A. Hart on the philosophy of law and a seminar on social and moral theory jointly taught by Isaiah **Berlin** and Stuart Hampshire.

From the time Rawls received his PhD degree a period of persistent tension, marked by the spectre of nuclear war, had begun between the NATO nations and the Soviet bloc. This 'cold war', as it was called, lasted until the demise of the Soviet Union in the early 1990s. In short, from the time Rawls became an adult until his retirement (in 1991) from his longtime university chair at Harvard, an ongoing and demanding challenge – physical as well as intellectual – threatened liberal political institutions. The theoretical side of this challenge was advanced by Fascism/ Nazism, on the one hand, and by **Marxism**, on the other. Though these theoretical challenges were significantly different from one another, they had certain points of agreement: they concurred in a deep contempt of parliamentary government and an intolerance for political controversy (disdaining the idea of a 'loyal opposition' or any acceptable difference of opinion from the official line); and they had no commitment to and no respect for the idea of the rights of individuals, human or constitutional.

These challenges are the wellspring of Rawls's political thinking. He believed that they were not being effectively met by utilitarianism, the dominant political and moral theory in the Anglo-American world at the time he began his reflections. In the preface to the 1999 revised edition of his *Theory of Justice* (originally published in 1971), Rawls says that he 'wanted to work out a conception of justice that provides a reasonably systematic alternative to utilitarianism'.

Where did Rawls turn for the materials for this 'alternative to utilitarianism'? To three sources mainly: to the social contract tradition, as found in the writings of Locke and Rousseau and especially Kant; to the notion of liberalism as set forth most notably in **J.S. Mill's** *On Liberty*; and to the practice and theory of democratic politics.

In the thirty or so years since the original publication of *Theory of Justice*, the dominant philosophical theorist of justice in the last thirty years of the twentieth century, certainly in the English-speaking world and in much of Western Europe, has been John Rawls. The heart of *Theory of Justice* is Rawls's idea that two principles are central to political liberalism – the principle of equal basic rights and liberties and a principle of economic justice, which stresses equality of opportunity, reciprocal benefit, and egalitarianism. What is distinctive about Rawls's arguments for these principles is that he represents them as taking place ultimately in an ideal arena for decision-making, which he calls the 'original position'. The features of the original position (in particular, the so-called veil of ignorance and the requirements of publicity and unanimity) taken together provide a setting for structuring the competition between potential governing principles (for example, the Rawlsian two principles versus various forms of utilitarianism) in a fair and objective way and then for determining a preference, if possible, for one of the candidate principles of justice over the others.

In time, Rawls came to have some dissatisfaction with this approach and he began to reconfigure his basic theory in new and interesting directions. He loosened things up in two distinct ways. First, he moved the focus away from his own two principles and towards a family of liberal principles (which included his two principles as one possible option). And second, he developed a background theory of justifying this family of principles that did not require people to come to any sort of unanimous foundational agreement. In short, people didn't have to hold one and the same basic moral theory or profess one and the same religion in order for the family of liberal principles to be conclusively justified; rather, the issue of justification could be approached from a number of different angles, and this would work out all right, he argued, if a sufficient overlapping consensus developed over time. Rawls thought that this new theory (which he developed in his second book, *Political Liberalism*, 1993, revised edition 1996) solved the main problem he had seen in his own earlier theory of justice. It did so by taking account of the fact that in a free and open society there is very likely going to be an irreducible and continuing pluralism of ultimate moral and religious beliefs.

In a third book, *The Law of Peoples* (1999), Rawls then took this new theory (which he called political liberalism) and tried to outline a constructive place for it in the international order that has emerged since the Second World War. This order is, like the international orders that have come before it, a world of disparate peoples and of incommensurable values; but it also exhibits much more *worldwide* economic and even political integration than has ever been the case before. One notable example of this is the widespread human rights culture that has emerged since the UN's *Universal Declaration of Human Rights* (1948). The law of peoples, about which this third book is written, includes the traditional international relations view of states, that they have independence, sovereign status, territorial integrity and formal equality with other states (the old Westphalian system, in short), but adds to it certain conditions or constraints on that traditional view. All these constraints derive from the post-World War II settlement; the most important of them are the prohibition on waging war except in self-defence (or in collective defence), the idea that human rights are to be respected (and even enforced by international action in the case of grave violations), and the claim that nations have a duty to provide economic and development aid to burdened societies.

Further reading

Other works include: *John Rawls: Collected Papers*, ed. Samuel Freeman (1999); Barbara Herman (ed.) *Lectures on the History of Moral Philosophy* (2000): and *Justice as Fairness: A Restatement*, ed. Erin Kelly (2001) – based on a lecture set of 1989 of his political philosophy lectures at Harvard, as revised by Rawls in the early 1990s. See also: *The Philosophy of John Rawls*, ed. Henry S. Richardson and Paul J. Weithman (5 vols, 1999); *John Rawls*, ed. Chandran Kukathas (4 vols, 2003); *The Cambridge Companion to Rawls* (2003); *Rawls's Law of Peoples*, ed. Rex Martin and David Reidy (2006).

REX MARTIN

RAY, Man

1890–1976

US artist

Man Ray probably did more than anyone else to integrate the traditions of photography and avant-garde painting. Growing up in New York, where his family had moved from Philadelphia when he was seven, he first encountered modern art in the gallery of the photographer Stieglitz. In 1913 came the Armory Show, where **Duchamp's** *Nude Descending a Staircase* enjoyed a *succès de scandale*. Ray's sensibility was in many ways very close to that of Duchamp, and when they met soon afterwards they became life-long friends. Like Duchamp's, Ray's oeuvre is unified not by a consistent stylistic development but rather by a witty and enquiring intelligence. Like Duchamp, too, Ray was quick to appreciate the central cultural importance of the machine and to incorporate it, with highly ambiguous connotations, into his painting. A work of 1920 includes cogwheels interlocking so tightly that they are unable to turn, and the word 'Dancer' which can also be read 'Danger'. Duchamp and Ray were the leading figures in the short-lived New York Dada movement, and in 1921 Ray followed Duchamp back to Paris, where he was introduced to the circle of writers and intellectuals who, believing that Dada was now outliving its usefulness, were evolving the doctrines of Surrealism. Ray created several powerfully sinister Surrealist objects, including *Gift* (1921), a flat-iron to which is attached a row of tin-tacks, and *Indestructible Object*, originally called *Object to be Destroyed* (1923), a metronome to which was clipped a photograph of an eye. He collaborated with the Surrealist poet **Paul Eluard** to produce a book of love poetry, *Facile* (1935), in which his photographs were integrated with Eluard's verse in a visually superb combination.

Photography brought Ray into the most fashionable circles in France, somewhat in contrast to his more revolutionary Surrealist connections. His film *The Mystery of the Château of Dice* (1926) was made during a house-party at the home of the Vicomte de Noailles, whose distinguished guests provided the cast. Ray produced fashion photography of the highest order as well as portraits of many of the leading artistic and cultural figures of the age. Perhaps his most original contributions in the photographic field were the inventions of new technical processes, arrived at in suitably Dada style by chance accidents. Most famous of these was the 'Rayograph', produced by placing objects directly on to sensitized paper, thus obviating even the need for a camera. He also exploited the phenomenon of 'solarization', some of his most remarkable solarized photographs being published in his album *The Age of Light* (1934).

In 1940 Ray escaped from occupied France and went to live in Hollywood, almost immediately meeting his bride-to-be, Juliet. In 1951 he returned with her to Paris, his spiritual home. With his love of girls and fast cars and his ability to mix in widely differing circles, Ray was gifted with exceptional charm as well as talent and originality. Despite several excursions into the sinister, the principal quality in his work is a commitment to freedom, individuality and happiness.

Further reading

Other works include: *Électricité: 10 Rayographes* (1931); *La Photographie n'est pas l'Art* (1937); *Man Ray* (1944); *Revolving Doors* (1972). His other films were: *The Return to Reason* (1923); *Emak Bakia* (1926); *L'Étoile de mer* (1928). On Ray: Louis Aragon, Jean Arp *et al.*, *Man Ray: Sixty Years of Liberties* (1971); Roland Penrose, *Man Ray* (1975); Arturo Schwarz, *Man Ray* (1977); M. Foresta (ed.) *Perpetual Motif: The Art of Man Ray* (1988).

GRAY WATSON

RAY, Satyajit

1921–92

Indian film director

The most distinguished filmmaker to emerge from India, Satyajit Ray is also the one who most successfully bridged the gulf between Eastern and Western cinemas. Coming from a cultured middle-class background, Ray completed his studies of music and the arts at Santineketan, to whose founder he devoted the documentary *Rabindranath Tagore* (1961). With a keen critical interest in film (Hollywood, **Jean Renoir**, the Italian neo-realists) but no prior professional experience, he embarked in the mid-1950s on what was to become one of the cinema's major trilogies: *The Song of the Road* (1955), *The Unvanquished* (1956) and *The World of Apu* (1959). Working in a minority language, Bengali, and in face of the indifference of the bulk of the Indian film industry, Ray succeeded in part thanks to the international acclaim which greeted his work from the very beginning.

Subsequently his subjects, mostly taken from existing Bengali stories, have ranged widely. *The Music Room* (1958) and *The Goddess* (1960) were both depictions of an upper-class society in decline, brought down by pride and superstition. The early 1960s saw several delicate studies of the difficulties faced by Indian women in rural and urban societies: *Two Daughters* (adapted from **Tagore** stories, 1961), *The Big City* (1963) and *Charulata* (1964). *Days and Nights in the Forest* (1970), a brilliantly realized portrayal of four young town dwellers out of their depths in the country just outside Calcutta, opened a fresh decade of achievement, marked by a number of films on the irreconcilable tensions created by the decline of traditional values in Calcutta: *The Adversary* (1970), *Company Ltd* (1971) and *The Middleman* (1975). Though Ray used colour as early as *Kanchanjungha*, made in 1962, most of his work has been photographed in black and white, with the camera in the hands of only two photographers, Subrata Mitra and Soumendu Roy, but colour was used for two recent oblique studies of the impact of world events on Indian rural societies, *Distant Thunder* (1973) on the famine caused by the Second World War and *The Chess Players* (1977), which depicts the annexation by the British of an Indian state. This latter film is a

departure too in being made in Urdu for the mass Hindi market.

Ray was a complete film author, responsible for the direction, script and (after 1961) the music of all his films, and working closely with a constant team of actors and technicians whom he trained himself. Though he remains essentially true to his Indian, or more precisely Bengali, origins, Ray can also be seen as the greatest heir to the humanist tradition of Western filmmaking which uses a basically realistic film style and finds its European peak in the work of Renoir and the neo-realists. Though he described himself as a commercial director, Ray's work derives from a moral impulse. His statement in 1958 that 'working in Bengali, we are obliged morally and artistically to make films that have their roots in the soil of our province' set out a programme to which he remained faithful.

In 1992, the year of his death, Satyajit Ray received the Lifetime Achievement Award from the American Academy of Motion Picture Arts and Sciences.

Further reading

Other works include: *The Philosopher's Stone* (1957); *Expedition* (1962); *The Coward and the Holy Man* (1965); *The Hero* (1966); *The Zoo* (1967); *The Adventures of Goopy and Bagha* (1968); *The Inner Eye* (documentary, 1974); *Golden Fortress* (1974); *Bala* (documentary, 1976); *The Home and the World* (1984); *An Enemy of the People* (1989); *The Stranger* (1991). See: Satyajit Ray, *Our Films, Their Films* (1976); see also Marie Seton, *Portrait of a Director – Satyajit Ray* (1971); Robin Wood, *The Apu Trilogy* (1972); Surabji Banerjee, *Satyajit Ray: Beyond the Frame* (1996); Darius Cooper, *The Cinema of Satyajit Ray* (1999).

ROY ARMES
(REVISED AND UPDATED BY THE EDITOR)

REDON, Odilon

1840–1916

French artist

Redon belonged to the generation of the Impressionists and shared many of their attitudes and experiences. Like them, he explored the expressive force of texture and colour in an individualistic style that was independent of state institutions and of conservative orthodoxy in the arts. But he differed radically from the Impressionists in his understanding of the basic aim of art. He called them 'parasites of the object' and reproached them for neglecting what he considered to be the true subject of art: nature transformed by the imagination. He became a leading figure in French Symbolism, regarded during his lifetime and since as the **Mallarmé** of painting.

Redon's early opposition to both conservative art and progressive Impressionism isolated him from groupings of artists until Decadents and Symbolists became a coherent force in Paris in the 1880s and 1890s. The teaching establishments of the Second Empire were anathema to him; when young he failed as a student of architecture and as a pupil of the academic painter Gérôme in Paris. He turned for guidance to individualist artists who were developing aspects of Romanticism towards new possibilities, such as Corot and Fromentin, and was profoundly influenced by Delacroix. He also turned away from Paris, usually the goal of the aspiring painter, to the provincial context of his home region around Bordeaux, where a small group of mentors provided him with help and advice. The minor painter Stanislas Gorin discussed with him the implications of Romantic art. The botanist Armand Clavaud introduced him to contemporary literature, including **Baudelaire**, and made him familiar with the mysterious aspects of plant life. The etcher and lithographer Rodolphe Bresdin was an encouraging example to him there, both of the isolated artist and of one who transformed nature through fantasy; Redon shared with Bresdin a life-long passion for the engravings of Rembrandt and Dürer. The Bordeaux region, above all, offered Redon the physical setting that he came to regard as an essential source of his art: Peyrelebade, the family estate in the bleak and lonely Médoc where Redon spent his childhood.

Throughout his life, Redon would divide his time between Paris and the Bordeaux region, the public and private poles of his existence. One of the few events of his life, remarkable for its lack of incident, was the enforced sale of Peyrelebade in 1897.

Until about 1870, Redon produced works that were exploratory and often derivative. After the Franco-Prussian War, he began to produce mature works in quantity, chiefly charcoal drawings that he called his *Noirs* ('Blacks'). The medium of charcoal suited him first because of the richness of its textures, and second because restriction to black and white takes the spectator away from objective perceptions towards subjective experiences. In these *Noirs* temporal and spatial dimensions become ambiguous or unidentifiable. Landscapes are deliberately imprecise or are inhabited by disconcerting and bizarre figures. These figures suggest areas of subject-matter but deny particularization. They sometimes relate to legends or myths, such as Orpheus or Faust, but in an opaque and plurivalent manner that cannot be reduced to a scenario or allegory. Hybrid creatures are formed by the conjunction of normally unassociated details of the perceived world, such as a smiling spider (*L'Araignée souriante*, 1881), and chimerical beasts of Antiquity, such as Pegasus, are given a new significance. Animal and plant forms fuse. Disembodied floating heads form striking geometric structures. Redon referred to this sombre domain as 'the dark world of the indeterminate'. Its purpose was to express indefinite but intense states of mind, generally pessimistic in tone. The strength of its imagery stems from its relationship with observed nature, as Redon himself pointed out: 'All my originality therefore consists of making unreal beings live humanly according to the laws of the real, by putting, as far as possible, the logic of the visible at the service of the invisible.'

The small scale and originality of such works made effective exhibiting of them difficult, and they remained virtually unknown until Decadents and Symbolists in Paris after

1880 saw in them all that they aspired to in art. Even then, it was writers rather than fellow painters who praised Redon. He was seized upon by the literary avant-garde, becoming the friend and ally of **Huysmans**, Mallarmé and others. This success was prompted partly by two exhibitions Redon held in Paris in 1881 and 1882, but far more by his adoption of lithography at the very time that Symbolism was becoming a force in Paris. Lithographs, unlike drawings, could be disseminated in quantity, and Redon added to this advantage a technical virtuosity that made lithography more than the equal of charcoal. Between 1879 and 1899 Redon published twelve lithograph albums that spearheaded his reputation in France and abroad. Although still neglected by the public at large, he became influential among writers and artists in Paris and in Brussels, and contributed to the foundation of the Société des Artistes Indépendants in Paris in 1884. The literary orientation of his career in turn influenced his own style, notably in lithograph albums that bore literary titles and captions, as in À Edgar Poe (1882) or were inspired by literary texts, as in the three albums (1888, 1889 and 1896) based upon descriptive passages from **Flaubert's** Tentation de Saint Antoine. Some critics have seen this literary dimension as a weakness of Redon's style, but interaction between images and words was a feature of a general interpenetration of art forms that, stimulated partly by **Wagner**, was a rich aspect of French Symbolism. Like other Symbolists, Redon was attracted by the notion of the unity of the arts, and constantly compared the effect of his works to that of music. Like **Gauguin**, he was a skilful writer. Towards the end of his life, he began to collect his writings into a book that was published posthumously as À soi-même ('To Oneself', 1922).

Throughout these years Redon had used colour, but only for studies and occasional works. From 1890 onwards, he began to give colour a more central place in his output (e.g. Les Yeux clos, Closed Eyes, 1890) and some ten years later he abandoned black and white altogether. Charcoal gave way to pastel; oil, watercolour and gouache were all adapted to his use of suggestive texture. Some changes in subject-matter occurred; nightmarish scenes were succeeded by sumptuously lyrical flower pictures and large-scale decorative works, such as his murals (1910–11) at Fontfroide Abbey in southern France. Serenity and optimism replaced pessimism. This slow and complex change was occasioned partly by personal circumstances, such as the birth of his son Arï in 1889, and the sale of Peyrelebade in 1897, a physical break with a primary source of the Noirs. But it was also part of a change of artistic climate in France, involving the demise of Symbolism and the emergence of Fauvism. Redon knew and was admired by **Bonnard**, **Matisse**, van Dongen and other young colourists. His colour works contributed to new developments in French painting until the advent of Cubism.

Since his death, Redon's late colour pictures have been more admired than his Noirs and have even been considered to be quite different in style from them. This view fails to perceive the underlying unity that binds all these works together. Despite a shift of emphasis in later years from dark nightmare to light flowers, all Redon's works are concerned with a relationship between nature and the mind, between observation and imagination, between experience and meditation. The Noirs take their cue, directly or indirectly, from nature; the late flower pictures suggest states of mind. Although he was not concerned with ideas, Redon is making assumptions about the functioning of the human mind that belong to nineteenth-century idealist philosophy. This separates him from the Surrealists, to whom he is sometimes compared, as well as from Impressionism.

Redon's form of art has never won wide understanding from the public; today his achievements are often ignored or distorted. But young artists at the turn of the century, including **Marcel Duchamp** as well as the Nabis and the Fauves, unhesitatingly saw in him both an original style and a liberating force, comparable in importance to them to the art of **Cézanne**.

Further reading

See: André Mellerio, *Odilon Redon* (1913, reprinted 1968). See also Alfred Werner, *The Graphic Works of Odilon Redon* (1969). The chief studies of Redon are: André Mellerio, *Odilon Redon, peintre, dessinateur et graveur* (1923); Sven Sandström, *Le Monde imaginaire d'Odilon Redon* (1955); Roseline Bacou, *Odilon Redon* (1956); Klaus Berger, *Odilon Redon, Phantasie und Farbe* (1964, translated as *Odilon Redon, Fantasy and Colour*, no date); Jean Cassou, *Odilon Redon* (1972); and Richard Hobbs, *Odilon Redon* (1977); D.W. Druick, *Odilon Redon* (1994).

RICHARD HOBBS

REICH, Steve

1936–

American composer

Steve Reich has been a pioneering figure in developing the mechanical repetitive music which became known as minimalism. Precursors in this loose group of American composers were La Monte Young and Terry Riley, but by 1965 Reich had started to create unique repetitive compositions on tape with different tracks moving in and out of synchronization. His fascination with process contributed to a new kind of music which soon challenged mainstream modernism, absorbed non-Western influences and resembled rock groups in its use of electronics and composer-performer direction. But Reich had roots in bebop, Bach and **Stravinsky** and in 1998 said: 'The reason I wanted to devote my life to music was because I'd heard those musics.' He recognized this as an emotional engagement.

Reich was born in New York in 1936 but travelled regularly between divorced parents there and in California. He read philosophy at Cornell University, with a thesis on **Wittgenstein**, then went to Juilliard and Mills College, California, where he studied with Darius Milhaud and **Luciano Berio**.

In San Francisco he wrote *It's Gonna Rain*, based on recordings of speech patterns manipulated to move gradually out of phase. It was a crucial discovery, followed up when he returned to New York with *Come Out to Show Them*. Reich had performed with Terry Riley's group but set up his own ensemble in 1966, initially with three players but later expanded to eighteen. He then applied phase techniques to instruments in *Piano Phase*, *Violin Phase* and *Four Organs*.

In 1970 Reich spent five weeks studying drumming with a master of the Ewe tribe in Ghana. When he was asked how this visit affected his music he replied: 'Confirmation. It confirmed my intuition that acoustic instruments and voices could be used to produce music that was genuinely richer in sound than that produced by electronic instruments, as well as confirming my natural inclination towards percussion.' He later studied Balinese Gamelan on the west coast. On his return from Africa he wrote *Drumming* for an enlarged ensemble; in the original version it lasted an hour and a half. By now he was gaining attention with recordings and performances in orchestral concerts under prominent conductors such as **Pierre Boulez** and Michael Tilson Thomas.

Reich had initially confined his works to his own group but by the mid-1970s he had found a music publisher, his *Writings about Music* had appeared and he was receiving international commissions. A particular landmark was *Tehillim* (1981) for voices and instruments through which Reich, dissatisfied with yoga and Buddhist meditation, returned to his Jewish origins. These became of increasing importance as he studied Hebrew and went to Israel to listen to different types of cantillation. The result was a celebratory religious work in the tradition of Stravinsky's *Symphony of Psalms*. Extended pieces such as *Music for 18 Musicians* (1976) and *Music for a Large Ensemble* (1978) led Reich towards the full symphony orchestra for the first time in *The Desert Music* (1984), with a text by **William Carlos Williams**.

After further orchestral works such as *Three Movements* (1986) and *The Four Sections*

(1987) Reich went back to smaller forces and some of his work took a more serious turn. *Different Trains* (1988) uses voices from interviews about contrasted train journeys set against a string quartet and tape recordings of train sounds. The journeys relate back to the coast-to-coast treks Reich made in his youth but also, in a more sinister way, to the trains which took Jews to the concentration camps under Hitler. The work is a homage to those who died.

In the early 1990s Reich began working with video images in collaboration with his wife Beryl Korot to produce *The Cave* (1993), with the visual aspect and the sound closely integrated. This gave Reich the opportunity to work with performers such as Paul Hillier who were experienced in early music. *Proverb* (1995) was written for his Theatre of Voices and the text took Reich back to his student study of Ludwig Wittgenstein, whom he has called 'an enormously provocative genius'.

Reich initially represented minimalism in its purest form delivered by his own group under his own direction. His mesmeric repetitions tending towards trance-like states now seem to symbolize the 1960s, but they led him into wider concerns and provided an example for younger composers. After some misunderstanding his work has now fed back into the mainstream and has helped to find a new audience for serious music.

Further reading

See: S. Reich, *Writings on Music 1965–2000*, ed. P. Hiller (2002); D.J. Hoek, *Steve Reich: A Bio-Bibliography* (2002); K. Potter, *Four Musical Minimalists: La Monte Young, Terry Riley, Steve Reich, Philip Glass* (2000); *Minimalists*, K. R. Schwarz (1996); *Talking Music*, ed. W. Duckworth (1995).

PETER DICKINSON

REICH, Wilhelm

1897–1957

Austro-US psychoanalyst

Wilhelm Reich, psychoanalyst, Marxist and prophet of the sexual revolution, was the elder son of a prosperous Jewish, but unreligious, farmer. Born in Galicia and brought up in Bukowina, he was an Austrian citizen, even though these two provinces ceased to be part of Austria after the collapse of the Hapsburg empire in 1918. When he was fourteen his mother committed suicide; his father died three years later. In 1916 he joined the Austrian army, seeing active service in Italy. At the end of the war Reich went to Vienna, an impoverished twenty-one-year-old war veteran, both his parents dead and his childhood home, which he never revisited, cut from him by the new frontiers drawn by the Treaty of Versailles. After a brief flirtation with the law Reich became a medical student and, aged only twenty-two, a practising psychologist and member of the Vienna Psychoanalytical Society. In 1927 he published the first version of his most famous book, *The Function of the Orgasm*, sought psychoanalytical treatment with **Freud**, who refused, and spent some months in a sanatorium for the tuberculous. In 1928 he joined the Austrian Communist Party, and was a co-founder of the Socialist Society for Sex Consultation and Sexological Research, which aimed to make sexual and psychological counselling available to the working classes. In 1929 his *Dialectical Materialism and Psychoanalysis* was published in Moscow, and in 1930 he moved to Berlin, which in view of his Austrian citizenship was not such a foolhardy act as it sounds. There he again founded an association working for the sexual liberation of the masses.

Although by no means the only psychoanalyst concerned to reconcile Freud and **Marx**, nor the only Marxist to be interested in Freud, Reich's political activities got him into trouble with both camps. In 1933 he was expelled from the German Communist Party, which thought he was diverting into sexual-hygiene campaigns energies that were, in view of the rise of **Hitler**, urgently required for direct political action, and in 1934 he was dropped by the International Psychoanalytical Association, which hoped, vainly as it turned out, to weather the storm of fascism by remaining academic and apolitical. In the same year Reich published *The Mass Psychology of Fascism* in Denmark and *Character Analysis* in Vienna, and emigrated, first to Denmark, then to Norway, and finally, in 1938, to the United States, where he remained until his death in 1957 of a heart disease in the psychiatric wing of the Lewisburg Penitentiary, where he was serving a two-year sentence for contempt of court: he had refused to admit the competence of the courts to adjudicate on matters of scientific fact and, in particular, on whether the 'orgone accumulators' he had invented really were capable of curing physical and mental illnesses. The line of thought which led him to make such a claim is accepted by his disciples as evidence that he was, as he himself thought, a persecuted saviour of mankind who had successfully broken out of the 'intellectual framework of . . . the civilization of the last 5,000 years', but is regarded by the more sceptical as evidence that from 1934 onwards Reich was a crank and perhaps a little mad.

The year 1934 is in any case the turning point in Reich's life and thought. His writings before that were, and still are, taken seriously by those most competent to judge them. His view, expressed in *The Function of the Orgasm*, that damning up of libido is the fundamental cause of all neurosis and that, given the ubiquity of neurosis, full orgastic capacity is a rarity, has become almost a commonplace among psychoanalysts, as has also the idea, expressed in *Character Analysis*, that the aim of psychoanalytical treatment is to challenge and dissolve the character armour which neurotics construct to repress their native spontaneity. Similarly, his idea that the cause of sexual repression is the bourgeois authoritarian family, in which the fathers repress the sexual spontaneity of their wives and children, and that the masses only accept social repression because they are sexually repressed endured in Marxist circles. But there is something crude, unscholarly, provincial and ranting about even his earlier writings which is an embarrassment to those who are sympathetically disposed to them. Indeed, Reich himself came to feel that his writings on orgasm were liable to misconstruction and vulgarization and to fear that they would be used to unleash 'a free-for-all fucking epidemic'. The 1960s slogan 'Make love, not war' was a posthumous tribute to his ideas to which he would have given only qualified blessing.

After 1934, however, Reich's ideas took the turn which isolated him from both his Freudian and his Marxist roots, and led him into territory where only a few have been able to follow him. After a short period in which he sought to dissolve character armour by physical means, assuming, surely correctly, that character is reflected in posture and muscle tone and that compelling patients to relax would facilitate release of whatever had been repressed, he embarked on a search for the physical basis of libido and persuaded himself that he had found it. There was, he claimed, a substance, orgone energy, which was 'visible, measurable and applicable' and 'universally present and demonstrable visually, thermically, electroscopically and by means of Geiger-Müller counters'. The activities of this substance were responsible, he declared, not only for sexual excitement and discharge but also for everything that the religious designate as love. By discovering it Reich had, he believed, broken down all boundaries between science and religion and taken a step forward in human consciousness comparable to that taken by Jesus Christ, who was in Reich's opinion the archetypal genital character. Furthermore, this orgone energy could be stored in accumulators or 'orgone boxes' and used to cure physical and mental illnesses. No one else has ever succeeded in seeing orgone energy, and in 1954 the US Federal Food and Drug Administration sued Reich for renting a fraudulent therapeutic device, thereby initiating the train of events which ended with his death in the psychiatric wing of a prison, but nonetheless= 'legally sane and competent' – an ironic end to the life of a man who was both a victim and a hero of the catastrophes of our times.

Further reading

Other works include *Character Analysis* (1949); *The Function of Orgasm* (1942); *The Sexual Revolution* (4th revised edn, 1969); *Selected Writings*, ed. Mary Boyd Higgins (1960). *The Encyclopedia of Philosophy* gives a full bibliography. About Reich: Paul A. Robinson, *The Freudian Left* (1969); Ilse Ollendorf Reich, *Wilhelm Reich: A Personal Biography* (1969); Charles Rycroft, *Reich* (1971); Leo Raditsa, *Some Sense about Reich* (1978); Myron Sharif, *Fury on Earth: A Biography of Wilhelm Reich* (1994); Robert S. Corrington, *Wilhelm Reich: Psychoanalyst and Radical Naturalist* (2003).

CHARLES RYCROFT

REINHARDT, Ad

1913–67

US painter

In 1935 Reinhardt graduated from Columbia University, where he had studied with Meyer Schapiro, and simultaneously attended the American Artists School (with Carl Holty and Frances Criss) and the National Academy of Design (with Karl Anderson). Holty encouraged him to join the American Abstract Artists group and he did so in 1937. In the same year he joined the Artists Union and was hired by Burgoyne Diller on the Federal Art Project as an 'Artist, Class 1, Grade 4' in the Easel Division.

After he had hovered indecisively between different styles, in the early 1940s an individual manner prevailed. It was a hard-won victory; for Reinhardt cerebration ranked as highly as 'pure' feeling, and any change in stance had to be justified and defended intellectually. He joked about the distinction between his late 1930s 'late-classical-mannerist-post-cubist, geometric abstractions' and his post-1940 'rococo-semi-surrealist fragmentation' and 'all - over - baroque - geometric - expressionist patterns'. But Reinhardt's jokes were always serious, as his cartoons demonstrate. He was aligning himself with non-gestural New York painting in a quest for a serene, stable, cool art inspired by studies of Chinese and Japanese culture and Islamic decoration, with Alfred Salmony at the New York Institute of the Fine Arts (1945–51). His 1940s paintings, lately reconsidered by critics, have been compared to Oriental scrolls or Persian carpets, achieving an effect of deliquescence, a loss of spatial bearings. He called his late 1940s work 'archaic colour-brick-brushwork impressionism and black-and-white constructivist calligraphies'. Styles followed thick and fast until in 1953 the first of the 'early-classical, hieratic, red, blue, black monochrome square crossbeam symmetries' was created. His reputation rests on these pictures and the theories which support them.

The most mysterious of his works are the black-on-black paintings of 1960 to 1966, symmetrical in format with a horizontal band bisecting a vertical of equal size, both trisecting the sides of the canvas, painted in extremely close-toned colours. His political vigilance and artistic militancy had been concentrated into a one-man campaign for purity. 'Fine art can only be defined as exclusive, negative, absolute and timeless,' he wrote in 1957, and though he saw his late works as a critique of the religiosity creeping into the thought of the masters of Abstract Expressionism, the strings of negatives by which art is defined in his essays indicate a mystical approach akin to Zen or St John of the Cross's 'Dark Night of the Soul'. Reinhardt's influence was on a younger generation of artists working on 'minimal' structures. Regarded as an entire career, however, his achievement may finally prove closer in quality to that of **Rothko** or Newman than he himself would have accepted. In his lifetime Reinhardt was attacked fiercely. Even supporters lost faith when he agreed to a retrospective exhibition at the Jewish Museum in New York. There are more pressing problems than those of art politics, however. Reinhardt's nihilism and the sheer presence of the paintings remain at loggerheads. The last word remains with the artist: 'I'm just making the last paintings which any artist can make.'

Further reading

Art as Art, ed. Barbara Rose (1975), is a selection of Reinhardt's writings. See: Lucy Lippard, *Ad*

Reinhardt: Paintings, a catalogue for the Jewish Museum exhibition (1967); *Ad Reinhardt: Art Comics and Satires* (Truman Gallery catalogue, 1976); Thomas Hess, *The Art Comics and Satires of Ad Reinhardt* (1975); L. Lippard, *Ad Reinhardt* (1981).

STUART MORGAN

REINHARDT, Max

1873–1943

Austrian/German theatre producer and director

Max Reinhardt was foremost among the theatrical innovators who, at the turn of the twentieth century, created the concept of the director as the principal artistic force in the theatre. Born near Vienna as the son of a Jewish merchant – his original family name was Goldmann – Reinhardt was already, as a boy, deeply imbued with the enthusiasm for the theatre which plays so large a part in the life of Vienna, a city in which the spirit of an old tradition of *commedia dell'arte* and flamboyantly spectacular baroque machine opera was still alive and in which a splendid national theatre, the *Burgtheater*, provided excellent performances of the classics at nominal prices.

At the age of nineteen Reinhardt obtained his first engagement as a character actor (while still in his teens he particularly excelled in old men's parts). Otto Brahm, the director of the Berlin Deutsches Theater, the cradle of German naturalism, brought him to Berlin in 1894, when he was twenty-one. For seven years he was a leading member of the company of that most famous of German theatres, but became gradually dissatisfied with the lack of colour, the excessive emphasis on the sordid side of life, inherent in the naturalistic style prevalent there. To escape from the depressing monotony and greyness of this work he induced a number of his fellow-actors to join him in a group which gave late-night cabaret performances and soon attained fame under the title *Schall und Rauch* ('Sound and Smoke'). This group developed into a full-scale company which also presented full-length plays, the Kleines Theater (1902), under Reinhardt's leadership. Here he began to cultivate a post-naturalistic repertoire, based on neo-romantics like **Wilde**, Hofmannsthal and Schnitzler, as well as the early expressionism of **Strindberg** and **Wedekind**. So successful was this work that in 1905 Reinhardt was offered the directorship of the Deutsches Theater as successor to Brahm.

Reinhardt's approach was basically theatrical. For him the actor was the centre of the dramatic experience and the stage a place of magic. The rapid development of technology had given him the chance of achieving hitherto undreamt-of effects on the stage through the use of hydraulics, revolving platforms and, above all, electric lighting which could be dimmed and faded at will and thus make the director a veritable painter in light. Reinhardt was one of the first theatrical practitioners to realize the full potential of this new technology: he abandoned painted backdrops and went in for solidly built, three-dimensional scenery, which, when revolved, could make the audience actually see the characters on the stage moving from indoors to outdoors, or walking through the narrow streets of Venice, crossing bridges over canals, while the sun was rising or going down. To achieve these effects Reinhardt evolved the concept of the director as the presiding intelligence over a whole team of artists and technicians, the guiding spirit who conceives the basic plan of the play: its total meaning, its prevailing colour scheme, its spatial dimensionality, the mood of its lighting, and then initiates and co-ordinates the work of the specialists – the set and costume designers, the lighting engineer, the musical director, the creator of masks and properties and other artists and technicians. But, above all, in Reinhardt's new concept, the director was the guiding spirit and co-ordinator of the actors whom he had to mould into a coherent whole, where the work of each enhances that of all the others. Reinhardt's work with actors was immensely inspiring and spectacularly successful. Having himself been a superb actor, he could show each of his actors how he could best use his own potential.

In the Deutsches Theater Reinhardt at first concentrated on the classical repertoire which he imbued with the full force of his new stage magic. Among his first major successes were productions of Shakespeare's *A Midsummer Night's Dream*, *The Winter's Tale*, *Romeo and Juliet*, *Twelfth Night*, Kleist's *Kaethchen von Heilbronn* and Schiller's *Brigands*.

But Reinhardt's ambitions went beyond the traditional proscenium arch theatre; he wanted to create a complex of theatres to meet all possible stylistic demands: an intimate theatre for plays requiring the subtlest psychological nuance; and, at the other end of the spectrum, a large open arena holding thousands of spectators to accommodate performances requiring large crowds of extras. The first step towards realizing this programme was the building of a small theatre adjoining the Deutsches Theater, the Kammerspiele (Chamber Theatre), which was opened in 1906. Here the stage was barely raised above the level of the auditorium so that the four hundred spectators could get the feeling of being in the same room with the characters in plays by **Ibsen** and Strindberg. To realize the second part of his plan Reinhardt began to convert a big circus building in Berlin, the Zirkus Schumann, into an immense theatre with an open arena stage, the Grosses Schauspielhaus (Large Spectacle House), which, after many delays caused by the First World War, was finally opened in November 1919.

In the meantime, however, Reinhardt had broken out of the conventional theatre building altogether. To exploit the full and at that time still sensationally novel impact of the new theatrical magic, he created a series of spectacles which almost totally dispensed with speech and largely relied on visual imagery alone. These were his famous *Pantomimen* (mime plays, rather than pantomimes in the English sense of the word), of which the most spectacular, which established him as a world celebrity, was *The Miracle*, staged in December 1911 at Olympia, the great London exhibition centre. He transformed the vast hall into the interior of a Gothic cathedral, where thousands of spectators could see the fortunes of a medieval nun, who leaves her convent for a life of sensual love only to find, on her repentant return many years later, that the Madonna herself has taken her place there to spare her shame and punishment. So successful was this spectacle that Reinhardt was asked to re-stage it in Vienna (1912), Berlin (1914) and New York and other major American cities (1924).

After the First World War Reinhardt wanted to return to his native Austria. In 1920 he staged, on the cathedral square of Salzburg (where he had spent one of his early seasons as a young actor) Hofmannsthal's adaptation of the old English morality play *Everyman*. This production marked a further stage in Reinhardt's movement away from the traditional theatre space: here he used the backdrop of the façade of the baroque church, as well as the whole town itself; the voices calling for Everyman in the hour of his death came from all the church spires of the city and even from the distant castle high on the hill above it, and as night fell and Everyman went to his death, all the church bells of Salzburg began to toll. This production not only became a classic which was repeated annually for several decades, but it also initiated the first of the great international music and drama festivals, which have since then become so important an annual feature throughout the world. Reinhardt was, without doubt, the creator of this concept, the inventor of the modern festival idea.

Throughout the 1920s and early 1930s Reinhardt presided over a vast theatrical empire in Berlin, Vienna (where he had acquired the Theater in der Josefstadt) and Salzburg, where he resided as a grand seigneur in a castle built by one of the archbishops of the city, Leopoldskron. In addition he staged spectacular open-air productions in places as diverse as a square in Venice, the garden of an Oxford college or the Boboli Gardens in Florence.

After **Hitler** came to power in Germany, Reinhardt had to leave Berlin and, while continuing to run his theatrical enterprises in Austria, spent an increasing amount of time in the United States. He opened a theatre academy in Hollywood and directed a film version of *A Midsummer Night's Dream* for Warner Brothers, in which he showed his brilliance with actors by making James Cagney as Bottom and Mickey Rooney as Puck give the best performances of their lives (1935).

After Hitler's occupation of Austria in 1938 Reinhardt moved to the United States. He repeatedly tried to achieve a success on Broadway, but failed in each instance.

Further reading

Other works include: *Schriften* (1974). There is a Max Reinhardt research centre (Max Reinhardt Forschungsstaette) in Salzburg and a Reinhardt Archive at the New York State University at Binghamton, New York. See: M. Jacobs and J. Warren (eds) *Max Reinhardt: The Oxford Symposium* (1986); J.L. Styan, *Max Reinhardt* (1982).

RENAN, Joseph-Ernest

1823–92

French philologist, critic and historian of religions

Renan might have fitted comfortably into the twenty-first century, with celebrity status and a guaranteed, though controversial, position as a tele-don. Today, beyond those with a specialist interest, few are aware of his importance or even of his existence. In the 1950s, a normally educated Frenchman would certainly have known his name, and would have been able to quote titles of two of his works, usually *L'Avenir de la science* and *Souvenirs d'enfance et de jeunesse*. It did not follow that either had been read.

There is much folklore surrounding Renan's origins. Because he was a late addition to the family – fourteen years younger

than his brother, Alain, twelve years younger than Henriette – he has been described as an unwanted child, the result of his father's alcohol-fuelled urge. Drink is also given as the reason for the father's drowning at sea, although neither theory prevented Renan, in his later years, from seeing the Breton love of alcohol in nostalgic rose-tinted terms. Indeed, the accompanying combination of melancholy and poetry, moderated by the Gascon gaiety he claimed to have inherited from his mother, are what he sees as his own defining characteristics.

It is a matter of fact that he rose from modest beginnings to a situation of distinction within the French establishment of the time. His education began in the École ecclésiatique in his home town, Tréguier. The regime was one of standard orthodoxy; if the pupils were to go anywhere, it would be into the church, and that precluded knowledge of anything later than the seventeenth century. His success at school was closely followed by his sister, who having moved to Paris to make her living as a teacher was alive to the possibilities that might exist for her younger brother in the capital.

Henriette made use of her contacts to get him a scholarship into the Saint-Nicolas-du-Chardonnet seminary, run by Dupanloup, later to become bishop of Orléans. By bringing together the fee-paying sons of the well-to-do and bright scholarship boys, he created a climate in which the teaching provided by the church came into inevitable contact with the modern world. Renan's later claim that discussion was almost exclusively to do with contemporary literature may have been an exaggeration; that influence was certainly present. As, more importantly, were the areas of study not directly related to the formation of village priests, or to giving an educational gloss to the sons of well-connected Paris families.

Biblical exegesis, to which Renan was introduced by Le Hir, a fellow Breton, led him inevitably to German philologists of the eighteenth century, a period that the church was in general anxious to avoid. The revelation for Renan was that, when the Bible was studied using philological – or 'scientific' – techniques, rather than through church dogma, it took on a very different appearance. The Vulgate, upon which the dogma was based, too often presented an image that was at odds with the texts of which it claimed to be the translation. For Renan, the effects were far-reaching.

It is arguable that, in any event, his faith was never rock-solid. In May 1845, in a 'psychological essay' that he hoped would help him to resolve the problems in what he saw as the weaknesses of the theological teaching he had received, he called upon Jesus to give him a yes or no answer to his questions. He then adds: 'At this point, I went to the chapel to pray to Jesus, and he said nothing to me.' A few months later, he had left the church and launched into a career in the outside world.

Renan has often been called a 'Positivist' as though he were a follower of August Comte, for whose work he in fact had little regard. When he applies the word 'positive' to his own work, he uses it in a scientific sense, deriving both from a rational and philological approach to the study of ancient texts and from the methods he learnt from the natural sciences thanks to his chemist friend, Marcellin Berthelot. It is a technique that led to early success. In 1847, he won the Volney Prize for a study of semitic languages; the following year, the Académie des Inscriptions et Belles Lettres (to which he would be elected in 1856) awarded him a further prize for a study of Greek in the East during the Middle Ages. While working on his doctoral thesis, completed in 1852, he contributed numerous articles to periodicals.

In 1862, he took up a chair at the Collège de France and created a public scandal by referring to Jesus as an 'incomparable man' – rather than as the Son of God. The notoriety that followed was both positive and negative. He was attacked in an enormous number of publications by believers, and his tenure of his chair was suspended. He would not return to the Collège de France until the end of the Second Empire. The result was that he was now free to carry out his research and to publish without the constraints of other employment. The publication of his *Vie de Jésus* in 1863 (translated into English as *The Life of Jesus* a year later) was followed by a 'popular' edition, shorn of the more scholarly elements. The integrity of both works has since been critically scrutinized, the first by Jean Pommier, who questions Renan's intellectual honesty in deriving much of his material from sources that he does not acknowledge (in particular **David Strauss**, who had published a life of Jesus in German). For his part, Georges Pholien, comparing the 'scholarly' and the 'popular' editions of Renan's work, points out that the second is not merely a simplified version of the first, but rather a product resembling a novel, in which is projected the image of an idealized Jesus – corresponding to what Renan would like him to be as well as to the way in which he would perhaps like to be seen himself.

These severe evaluations date from the 1970s and 1980s, long after the extraordinary publishing success of both works from the 1860s on. Renan may have been out of a job but he was not short of money and, over the next twenty years, produced the eight volumes that make up his *History of the Origins of Christianity*. These were followed, between 1887 and 1893, by what might be seen as a prequel: the five volumes of his *History of the People of Israel*. Taken together, the two enormous undertakings represent three of the ten volumes that make up the 'definitive' edition of Renan's work, published by his grand-daughter, Henriette Psichari, from 1947 to 1961.

In other words, the production of these major works did not prevent him from pursuing many other activities. Throughout his career, he produced much work of great diversity: extended book reviews which gave him the opportunity to reflect upon the subject dealt with, articles on questions to do with history, the intellectual life of the time, metaphysics, politics (he was an unsuccessful candidate in elections in 1869 and 1878). The end of the Second Empire and the defeat of France by the Germans in 1870 lead to reflections on what he saw as the causes of that disaster (*La Réforme intellectuelle et morale*, 1871), as well as to speculation on the future of the human race (*Dialogues et fragments philosophiques*, 1876, translated into English as *Philosophical Dialogues and Fragments*, 1883). The setting up of the 'democratic' Third Republic in 1875 was not looked upon with particular favour by the elitist establishment figure that he had become, although he learnt to live with it – and indeed to prosper: he was by now a member of the Académie Française and, having been reinstated in his chair at the Collège de France, became its *Administrateur* (Director), a position he occupied until his death.

Nevertheless, it is in this period that he adopted an attitude of ironical detachment, while at the same time taking refuge in works like his *Souvenirs d'enfance et de jeunesse* (*Recollections of My Youth*), which went through twenty-three printings between 1883 and 1897. Here he offered a self-indulgent portrait of himself, characterized by wisdom and benign understanding of others. During his summer holidays, separated from his library, he turned to works of the imagination, as in his 'Philosophical Dialogues' (*Dialogues philosophiques*, 1876) or his *Drames philosophiques* (1888). And then, in 1890, he published *L'Avenir de la science, pensées de 1848* (*The Future of Science, Ideas of 1848*, 1891), the work of a young man, as he put it, suffering from 'acute encephalitis'. He had sensibly followed the advice not to publish this excitable volume at the start of his career, but regularly pillaged it for source material he could use in other pieces. Now, near the end of his life, he felt it appropriate to put his youthful work before the public.

L'Avenir de la science is like all of his subsequent writing in that it demonstrates the facility with which words flowed from his pen. It is different in being more affirmative; later, partly no doubt because of his education

within the church, he tended to avoid advancing his opinions in too assertive a manner. A well-placed 'but', even when he was putting forward potentially controversial views, showed that he admitted the possibility of other options, and so frustrated his critics: they felt that they could never nail him down. Amongst those critics were those who never forgave him for leaving the church and, in their opinion, adopting a hostile stance with regard to that institution. Others saw him as ambitious and anxious to curry favour with those high up in the social hierarchy – see, for example, the references to him in the Goncourt brothers' diaries.

Renan was nevertheless much read, largely because the views he expressed were shared by many contemporaries. In that sense, what he presented as a body of 'scientific' work was often a popularization of the mainstream thinking of this time, whether on the subject of religion, or of the current state of France, or indeed of science in a century that saw progress as one of its dominant characteristics. In many ways Renan now seems dated, especially since the controversies that surrounded him have lost their edge. Even so, many of the problems that exercised him remain relevant to our own time.

Further reading

Other works include: *Œuvres complètes* (10 vols, 1947–61); E. Renan and M. Berthelot, *Correspondance, 1847–1892* (1898); *Essai psychologique sur Jésus-Christ* (1923); *Travaux de jeunesse, 1843– 1844* (1931); *Voyages. Italie (1849) – Norvège (1870)* [no date]. See also: Gaston Strauss, *La Politique de Renan* (1909); Jean Pommier, *La Pensée religieuse de Renan* (1925); Jean Pommier, *La Jeunesse cléricale d'Ernest Renan: Saint-Sulpice* (1933); Henriette Psichari, *Renan et la guerre de 70* (1947); Harold Wardman, *Ernest Renan: A Critical Biography* (1964); Keith Gore, *L'Idée de progrès dans la pensée de Renan* (1970); Henri Gouhier, *Renan: auteur dramatique* (1972); Jean Pommier, *La 'Vie de Jésus' et ses mystères* (1973); Georges Pholien, *Les Deux 'Vie de Jésus' de Renan* (1983); Jean Balcou, *Renan et la Bretagne* (1992); David Lee, *Ernest Renan: In the Shadow of Faith* (1996).

KEITH GORE

RENOIR, Jean

1894–1979

French film director

The most influential of all French film directors, Jean Renoir was the second son of
the Impressionist painter **Pierre-Auguste
Renoir**, whose impact on him was crucial
(see his book of memoirs, *Renoir, My Father*,
1962). Throughout his life Jean Renoir
remained open to the influence of landscape,
outside events and the personalities of others,
and many of his films are examples of true
collaborative effort. For years he was uncertain about his career, serving as a cavalry
officer and pilot in the First World War and
working for years in ceramics. Only at the
age of thirty did he turn to filmmaking,
inspired principally by Erich von Stroheim's
Foolish Wives. His first films were made for
his own production company, with his wife
as star. From his very first film, *La Fille de
l'eau* (1924), the characteristic themes of
landscape and love, and an intermixing of
varied styles, were apparent. His major silent
film, an adaptation of **Zola's** *Nana* (1926),
was commercially unsuccessful and his later
silent films were commercial ventures.

In the 1930s, which were the years of his
greatest successes, he achieved notable impact
with *La Chienne* (1931) and *Boudu sauvé des
eaux* (1932), both starring the anarchic
Michel Simon. *Toni* (1935) was a major
departure. Shot on location with little-
known players, it shows a deepening social
concern and in many ways anticipates post-
war Italian neo-realism. In 1936, with Jacques Prévert, he made *Le Crime de Monsieur
Lange*, in which the social optimism of the
Popular Front is most apparent, and subsequently took his political commitment a stage
further by making *La Vie est à nous* (1936) for
the French Communist Party. But Renoir
was not a man to be confined within one
style or ideological approach and his work far
transcends the limitation of the cinematic
'poetic realism' of the period. Subsequent
films include a delicately observed adaptation
from **Maupassant**, *Une Partie de campagne*

(1936); a passionate denunciation of war, the
highly successful *La Grande Illusion* (1937); a
patriotic epic, *La Marseillaise* (1938); and a
further adaptation of Zola, *La Bête humaine*
(1938). His masterpiece is *La Règle du jeu*
(1939) which, beneath surface frivolity,
shows a disintegrating society on its way to
self-destruction.

Renoir spent the 1940s in exile in Hollywood where he made several notable films,
among them *The Southerner* (1945), despite
the alien atmosphere of the studios. After a
visit to India to make *The River* (1950), he
returned to Europe to direct a number of
colourful meditations on art and life, among
them *Le Carrosse d'or* (1953) and *French Can-
can* (1955). In his later years he explored new
methods of production and his last film, *Le
Petit Théâtre de Jean Renoir* (1970) was shot for
television.

The impact of Renoir's work and personality has been enormous. Apart from the
inspiration given by his great series of works
in the 1930s, he has personally influenced a
large number of young filmmakers at a crucial moment of their careers: **Luchino Visconti** in the late 1930s, **Satyajit Ray** while
in India in 1950, and above all the group of
would-be filmmakers gathered around André
Bazin and the magazine *Cahiers du cinéma* in
the late 1950s – **Truffaut**, **Godard**, Rivette,
Rohmer among them.

Further reading

Other works are: *Sur un air de charleston* (1927); *La
Petite Marchande d'allumettes* (1928); *Marquitta*
(1927); *Tire au flanc* (1928); *Le Tournoi dans la cité*
(1929); *Le Bled* (1929); *On purge bébé* (1931); *La
Nuit du carrefour* (1932); *Chotard et cie* (1933);
Madame Bovary (1934); *Swamp Water* (1941); *This
Land is Mine* (1943); *The Diary of a Chambermaid*
(1946); *The Woman on the Beach* (1948); *Elena et les
hommes* (1956); *Le Testament du Docteur Cordelier*
(1961); *Le Déjeuner sur l'herbe* (1959); *Le Caporal
épinglé* (1962). Books by Renoir, as well as his
book on his father, are: *The Notebooks of Captain
Georges* (a novel, 1966), and *My Life and My Films*
(1974). See also: André Bazin, *Jean Renoir* (1974);
Leo Braudy, *Jean Renoir – The World of His Films*
(1972); Raymond Durgnat, *Jean Renoir* (1975);
Christopher Faulkner, *The Social Cinema of Jean*

Renoir (1992); Martin O'Shaughnessy, *Jean Renoir* (2000); Bert Cardullo, *Jean Renoir: Interviews* (2005).

ROY ARMES

RENOIR, Pierre-Auguste

1841–1919

French painter

Although he is always chiefly regarded as one of the leaders of the Impressionist group, Renoir's career extends into the twentieth century, well beyond the Impressionist years, and his art embraces other styles and other subjects than the sunlit landscapes with which Impressionism is often associated. After the initial years of struggle and hardship, he achieved success at the Salon and found himself sought after by society as a portraitist. His output was enormous, and the greater proportion of his work dates from the last thirty years of his life, when, his reputation established, he devoted himself above all to his family, painting countless pictures of his wife, his sons, his servants and the models that posed for him at his country house near Cagnes.

However, there are consistent strands which link together his life's work. Renoir was not an intellectual painter and he was not an eager revolutionary. He was little concerned with theories of perception and of the analysis of light, and was gratified by public recognition when it came. Even while participating in the Impressionist group exhibitions, he continued to submit works to the Salon, and of all the Impressionists he had most success in official circles. He was the first of the major artists of the group to grow disillusioned with its aims and return to a more traditional idiom, and unlike **Monet** and **Pissarro** he had no interest in politics or social concerns. All this is reflected in his work, in the sustained note of charm and gaiety that permeates it. Renoir was always attracted by people, and even his landscapes are seldom without a strong human element. As an unrepentant hedonist, he gave free expression to the pleasure he found in beautiful women and pretty children. He wanted no further pretence for a picture than a lovely face or a seductive figure. When his master, the academic painter Gleyre, remarked to him 'one does not paint for amusement', Renoir is said to have replied, 'If it didn't amuse me, I wouldn't paint', words which neatly sum up his approach to painting.

It would be wrong, though, to think of Renoir as a mere dabbler, a kitten playing with coloured wool, as **Degas** spoke of him. His origins were working class. He was born in Limoges, the son of a tailor, and in Paris, where he came as a child, he was trained as a porcelain painter. His ambition was to be an artist, and he graduated to it through painting china, fans and decorative blinds. But through this arduous apprenticeship he developed a strong belief in the importance of craftsmanship, and a sense of pride in something well done. Throughout his life he applied himself to painting in long and regular sessions, like an artisan rigorously carrying out his obligations.

In 1862 Renoir enrolled at the École des Beaux Arts and took tuition at the studio of Gleyre, where he befriended Monet, Bazille and **Sisley**, his fellow pupils. It was in their company that he began to study landscape painting, working in the open in the forest of Fontainebleau, and with them he shared an admiration for **Courbet** and Corot. It is the influence of Courbet above all that dominates his early works, such as *At the Inn of Mother Anthony, Marlotte* (1866), *Lise* (1867), *Diana* (1867) and *Alfred Sisley and His Wife* (1868). These pictures are firmly modelled, sombre in colouring and show Renoir striving towards an official manner. He had some success, exhibiting at the Salon in 1864, 1865, 1868, 1869 and 1870, but only at the expense of suppressing his own personality. Diaz had advised him to use more colour, and the effect of his advice shows in his more private work. He formed a strong friendship with Monet, and the two of them painted together at the popular bathing and boating place of La Grenouillère on the Seine near

Bougival, in the summer of 1869. Renoir's paintings of the scene are light in tone and abound with life. His experience as a porcelain painter reveals itself in the high-keyed colour and delicate touch. He painted alongside Monet, but the difference in their characters already shows, in Monet's concentration on effects of light and in Renoir's delight in the holidaymakers. People are given peremptory treatment by Monet; Renoir focuses his attention on them, so that their light-hearted mood permeates the pictures. As described by **Maupassant** some years later, La Grenouillère was a vulgar and sordid place, but, as one of the bourgeoisie, Renoir shares in the frivolity and his paintings have more the air of an eighteenth-century *fête galante* than a nineteenth-century resort. As a porcelain painter, Renoir had copied Watteau and Boucher, and it is their spirit which infuses his scenes of modern life.

The Franco-Prussian War of 1870, in which he fought, interrupted Renoir's artistic development, but back in Paris afterwards he worked again with Sisley, and in search of inspiration undertook some free imitations of Delacroix – costume pieces with models posing as Algerians. But he was at last finding his own idiom, and the decade of the 1870s saw some of his finest productions. He maintained the light tone of the La Grenouillère pictures and applied it to a series of paintings which are modern in subject and personal in feeling – that is, they express his sense of pleasure in the sights and experiences of modern life. Amongst the earliest and most famous is *La Loge*, which he exhibited in 1874 at the first Impressionist exhibition, a picture which is charming and richly evocative of the spirit of the time. It is also more technically accomplished than anything Renoir had yet painted – subtle in colour, confident in its modelling, and yet using softly merged paintwork to give the effect of life captured in a fleeting impression. He also strove to capture the light and atmosphere of the open air. Not such a fervent apostle of *plein air* as Monet, he confined himself to subjects he loved: couples, women and children

enjoying themselves in the sunshine. He could see no point in painting snow scenes or unpopulated landscapes. *The Swing* (1876) is typical of this genre. The filtering of light through trees and the colouring of the shadows are brilliantly caught, but their effect is above all to add charm to the image of the woman at a swing in the alley of a garden, a subject that might be taken from Fragonard – as indeed might the subject of one of Renoir's chief works of the 1870s, *The Ball at the Moulin de la Galette* (1876). **Manet** had treated a similar theme in his *Concert in the Tuileries Gardens* in 1860, and thereby opened the door to paintings of modern-day entertainments, light-hearted pictures without story or moral. But Renoir's fondness for his theme makes his treatment more *galante*, in an eighteenth-century sense, than Manet's. Although the dancers are only the artists and shop-girls of Montmartre, in Renoir's eyes they are elegant and beautiful. It means that he misses the more profound aspects of the life he depicts, that note of tragi-comedy that Manet hints at in his café scenes. Renoir's people are always charming, rarely interesting or moving. But the sincerity of his vision does mean that his charm is authentic, and in the nineteenth century this is a rare commodity. His women and children are robust, healthy and endowed with a well-being which is as deep and refreshing as Renoir's own.

In spite of this, Renoir, like the other Impressionists, had difficulty in selling his works and was attacked by the more conservative elements of the press. Albert Wolff, the critic of the *Figaro* and one of the fiercest opponents of Impressionism, wrote of his *Torso of a Woman in the Sun* (1876), 'Try to explain to M. Renoir that the body of a woman is not a mass of decomposing flesh, with the green and purple spots that denote the entire purification of a corpse.' Like his friends, Renoir sold works to Père Martin and Père Tanguy for small sums, and the dealer Paul Durand-Ruel courageously bought his pictures knowing he had little chance of selling them. But gradually Renoir built up a small circle of patrons, amongst them a civil servant, Victor Chocquet (who shared with him a passionate admiration for Delacroix and whom Renoir introduced to **Cézanne**), and Georges Charpentier, the publisher, and his wife. Chocquet was a highly sensitive man (as can be seen in Renoir's touching portrait of him in the Reinhart Collection, Winterthur) and greatly appreciated Renoir's painterly art, but it was the Charpentiers who 'made' the artist. At Madame Charpentier's *Salon* he became known to visitors and intellectuals, and his large portrait of her with her daughters was a great success at the Salon of 1879.

The commissions he received from the Charpentiers released Renoir from financial constraint and for the first time in his life he was able to travel. In 1880 he visited Algiers and in 1881, after his marriage, he travelled in Italy where he discovered Raphael and the Roman frescoes at Pompeii. His Italian experience coincided with a developing discontentment with his own work and the methods of Impressionism. He confessed that he did not know how to paint, and set out to introduce greater structure and discipline into his work. There is a new clarity in his pictures of couples dancing (1883), and *The Umbrellas*, which was painted over a period of years and completed around 1884, clearly shows the change in style. The women and children on the right are painted in his earlier 'soft' manner; the girl on the left and the umbrellas in a new, linear style. Renoir stayed at l'Estaque with Cézanne too at this time and may well have derived something of this austere manner – his *manière aigre* – from the Provençal painter. The pictures of this period are more laboriously worked-up than hitherto, consciously assembled in the studio, and sometimes, like the *Grandes Baigneuses* of 1885, they are based on traditional prototypes. Renoir borrowed the composition for this work from a bas-relief at Versailles by the sculptor Girardon. The painting itself is linear and sculptural, and the colour (little more than tinting) no longer conveys the light and atmosphere of the open air.

Renoir was temperamentally unsuited to such a chaste and academic approach, and by 1890 he had reverted again to soft contours, merging colour and swelling forms. But the work of his last years is far from the naturalism of early Impressionism. His figures and landscapes are robust, warmly coloured and simply modelled, an evocation of physical well-being, an imagined golden age. The onset of arthritis caused him from about 1902 to move south to Cagnes, and there he centred his attentions increasingly on his family, his wife, his sons Pierre, Jean and Claude, and their servant Gabrielle, all of whom regularly appear in his paintings. In Cagnes the family lived prosperously. Renoir had many commissions for portraits, bathers and decorative panels, and the dealers Durand-Ruel and, from 1894, Vollard had no difficulty placing his work. Success was accompanied by official acclaim. In 1896 six of his works, included in the Caillebotte bequest, were finally hung in the Luxembourg Museum and in 1900 he was awarded the Legion of Honour. Only the outbreak of war in 1914, when the two eldest sons were called to the front, disturbed the calm tenor of life at Cagnes, and Renoir died there in 1919, finally crippled by arthritis. But he continued to paint up to his death, in a wheelchair with brushes strapped to his hand. And he also directed an assistant to model sculptures, the three-dimensional counterparts of his painted figures. The last paintings are broad in treatment, lacking in all detail, yet rich in colour and of extraordinary amplitude, with no less a sense of the pleasure of life than the great Impressionist pictures of forty years earlier.

Further reading

See: *Catalogue raisonné de l'oeuvre peint*, ed. François Daulte (4 vols from 1971); John Rewald, *Renoir: Drawings* (1946). See also: Albert C. Barnes and Violette de Mazia, *The Art of Renoir* (1935); Jean Renoir, *Renoir, My Father* (trans. 1962); William Gaunt, *Renoir* (1962); Lawrence Hanson, *Renoir: The Man, the Painter and His World* (1968); Parker Taylor, *Renoir* (1969); B.E. White, *Renoir: His*

Life, Art and Letters (1984); A. Distel and J. House, *Renoir* (exhibition catalogue, 1985).

MICHAEL WILSON

RESNAIS, Alain

1922–

French film director

A delicate child, Alain Resnais was educated at home by his mother, developing a lifelong love of literature and music. Subsequently he studied first acting and then film editing at the IDHEC (French Film School). While still in his teens he made a number of short amateur films and, later, two feature-length dramas (now lost) and a number of studies of painters, all in 16 mm format. The success of one of the latter led directly to the beginning of his professional career, with three documentaries on *Van Gogh* (1948), *Gauguin* (1950) and **Picasso's** *Guernica* (1950). In the next nine years, while planning a breakthrough into feature filmmaking, he was commissioned to direct five documentaries on a wide variety of subjects: colonization (*Les Statues meurent aussi*, 1950–3), the Nazi concentration camps (*Nuit et brouillard*, 1955), the French National Library (*Toute la mémoire du monde*, 1956), industrial safety (*Le Mystère de l'atelier 15*, 1957) and the manufacture of polystyrene (*Le Chant du styrène*, 1958). With these unlikely subjects he developed the techniques which he would use in his early features: a disregard for the synchronization of image and sound and instead a separation and new fusion of the elements of image, music and text (the latter often by a well-known literary figure, such as **Paul Eluard** or **Raymond Queneau**).

Resnais's début as a feature filmmaker came in 1959 with *Hiroshima mon amour*, from a script by **Marguerite Duras**. In the 1960s he followed this same pattern of work on four further features, collaborating with **Alain Robbe-Grillet** on *L'Année dernière à Marienbad* (1961), Jean Cayrol on *Muriel* (1963), Jorge Semprun on *La Guerre est finie* (1966), and Jacques Sternberg on *Je t'aime, je*

t'aime (1968). All five films are marked by the use of novel formal structures: the interplay of past and present in *Hiroshima*, the refusal of chronology in *Marienbad*, and its opposite, the strict chronology of *Muriel*, the flash forward shots of anticipation in *La Guerre est finie* and the almost aleatory interweaving of levels of time and reality in *Je t'aime*. When he resumed his directing career in 1974, with *Stavisky* (from a script by Semprun) and then, in 1977, with *Providence* (shot in English from a text by David Mercer), the same technical assurance was apparent, but also a certain shallowness beneath the immaculate surface. Subsequently his work has alternated between attempts to recapture his position as an artist of the avant-garde, and more commercial ventures.

Resnais's reputation, based on his work between 1955 and 1963, is secure, but he remains a paradoxical figure, ten years older than the New Wave directors with whom his name was once erroneously linked: a one-time amateur filmmaker whose work denies improvisatory freedom; an intellectual filmmaker whose stated preferences are for **Hitchcock**, the comic strips and pulp fiction serials; a creator of revolutionary filmic structures whose working methods seem to cry out for the controlled atmosphere of the traditional studio. His direct impact is undeniable – all four of his first writers went on to direct features – and elsewhere in modern cinema one finds a more diffuse influence as powerful but hidden as the mainsprings of his own creative imagination.

Further reading

Other works include: *My American Uncle* (1980); *La Vie est un roman* (1983); *Mélo* (1986); *Gershwin* (1992); *Smoking* (1993); *No Smoking* (1993) and *Pas sur la bouche* (2003). See: Roy Armes, *The Cinema of Alain Resnais* (1968); John Ward, *Alain Resnais, or the Theme of Time* (1968); James Monaco, *Alain Resnais* (1978).

ROY ARMES
(REVISED AND UPDATED BY THE EDITOR)

REUTER, (Baron) Paul Julius von

1816–99

German/British journalist and businessman

Paul Julius Reuter was the father of modern news. Without Reuter's commercialism the telegraph wire might never have become the newswire, a powerful tool that moved the world on from third-hand information relayed after days or weeks to an era of 24-hour breaking news that defines today's news culture.

Reuter was born in the north German town of Kassel in 1816 under the name Israel Beer, the son of local rabbi and shopkeeper Samuel Levi Josephat. Reuter was soon to move on to train as a bank clerk in the university town of Göttingen, where in 1833 he met the German physicist and mathematician **Carl Friedrich Gauss**. In 1840 Reuter moved to Berlin and married Ida Maria Magnus, the daughter of an influential banker.

In 1845 Reuter visited London for the first time, using the name Joseph Josephat, and on 16 November was baptized Paul Julius Reuter at St George's Lutheran Chapel in London's Whitechapel district. A week later he had married Ida and within two years had bought into the respected German publishing house Stargardt.

Reuter's career as publisher was cut short in 1848, Prussia's year of bourgeois revolution, as Reuter & Stargardt's publication of revolutionary tracts attracted the attention of the absolutist state's police. Reuter fled to Paris were he worked for a time as a translator in the news office of Charles Havas.

By the time Reuter had set up his first news bureau in the city, the telegraph was already establishing itself as a tool for government communications. In 1849 Reuter's native Prussia opened the Berlin–Aachen telegraph line and was quickly followed by France, which set up a line between Paris and Brussels the following year.

Reuter, who had long been aware of the telegraph's potential having witnessed early experiments conducted by Gauss, spotted a gap in the market and used carrier pigeons to carry telegraph messages between his Paris office and a new office in Aachen, enabling for the first time the free uninterrupted flow of news between the French and Prussian capitals.

Reuter then took the idea of uninterrupted news flow to London as the first cross-channel telegraph link was completed between Dover and Calais. In 1851 Reuter closed a deal with the London Stock Exchange to supply traders and businessmen with opening and closing prices for both the Parisian and London markets, and quickly expanded his service to cover Amsterdam, Berlin, Vienna and Athens.

But the full impact of Reuter's telegraph wire and network of journalists only became apparent on New Year's Day 1859. A Reuter's correspondent's report of Napoleon III's words to the Austrian ambassador spoken at about 1 p.m. were quickly transmitted and reproduced just two hours later in a third edition of *The Times*. The French king's indication of a cooling of relations between the two countries and of a subsequent inflammatory speech to the French parliament were both read by readers in London the same day.

Reuter continued to go to extraordinary lengths to ensure his network had timely news, arranging for transatlantic steamers to toss canisters of information to Reuter's employees in Ireland on their way to Britain. In 1865 this strategy helped Reuter's to get news of President Lincoln's assassination two weeks earlier than its European competition.

By the time of his death in Nice in 1899, Reuter had established the basis of the international news network that was to become the respected company that now bears his name. But he had also wrought an irreversible change on business and political culture, by making information an invaluable commodity in itself through timely and accurate news gathering.

Further reading

See: Harry McNicol, *Six Men of Business: Roths-child, Reuter, Rhodes, Cadbury, Carnegie, Rockefeller* (1944); Donald Read, *The Power of News: The History of Reuters* (1999).

TOM WILLIAMS

RICHARDSON, Henry Hobson

1838–86

US architect

There is only one idea of America: it is that of the New World, that of not a Utopia, but of a Paradise. The American Constitution is a programme for realizing this. Her heroes are those that have this idea central in their being; her traitors are those who attempt to emulate the values and styles of the Old World. Thus it may often appear that the most cultured are the most philistine. The condition only becomes apparent at times of cultural crisis. The true American artist retains his nation's vision through a primitive quality in his work, and this he finds by descent.

Henry Hobson Richardson was born in 1838 on a plantation in Louisiana, of English ancestry, studied at Harvard, and received his architectural training at the École des Beaux Arts in Paris, the second American ever to do so, during the Civil War years, which delayed his return. He arrived back in New York in 1865 at the second beginning of the American Nation after the end of the Civil War, marrying his fiancée Julia Gordon Hayden from Cambridge, Massachusetts, and settling in Staten Island, the island on which were landing the waves of immigrants from the Old World.

The war effectively finished the reign of the Neoclassical 'colonial' style of architecture over American buildings. On his return, Richardson found two contesting and essentially illusory styles dominating, one with English and one with French origins: the styles of **Ruskinesque Gothic** and of the Deuxième Empire. They were, however, the mirror of his own experience, of his Beaux Arts training and of his travels and interest in England.

He established his practice with buildings in both styles, building, to begin with, two churches from 1866 to 1869 which, except for a certain wildness about the openings, would appear unremarkable in an English Victorian suburb. In 1869 he completed the Western Railway Offices at Springfield, which from above the ground floor was an equally unremarkable exercise in the Neo-Renaissance style. The lower level, however, was handled with signs of a startling vigour, the symmetrical composition formed using roughly hewn stone, more primitive than any European rustication. The dichotomy of style reached a crisis with the building of the Worcester High School in 1871, a hugely unsuccessful attempt to work in the flux between the Classic and the Gothic. He attempted to resolve the difficulty of his task and of his path to an authentic American architecture in two important church commissions, built within sight of one another in Boston, by reversion to a working of a round-arched Romanesque style. This style had been propounded earlier as appropriate for the emergent Great Society, intuitively, perhaps attempting to avoid **de Tocqueville's** censure, to sustain civilization between barbarism and the decadence that great wealth and freedom constantly offer.

The first building, the Brattle Square Church of 1872, shows a newfound ease of composition using simpler, more elemental forms and openings, particularly in the design of the tower. Between this and the second church, he worked on a large lunatic asylum in Buffalo, which had an increasing assurance at elevating Beaux Arts rational planning into an early Gothic form.

Trinity Church, built as a result of his winning a limited competition, is often considered one of his masterworks, but is better seen as a summation of his achievements up to that time. The plan has a wonderful rigorous resolution which was a tribute to his Beaux Arts training, and the massing as shown in the competition drawings was as picturesque as any English Gothicist, and greater than anything he would attempt again. As is typical of the artist's progress, he learnt here not what he would have expected, which would have been some attitude to prevalent styles, but that the architecture could be changed and fully realized during the building, that the form might have a will to be independent of the drawings. This deeply absorbed illumination was crucial to his emergence.

The tower of Trinity Church as shown in the drawings caused many dissatisfactions and difficulties in the building. The story goes that he was sent a photograph of the cathedral at Salamanca and handed it to his assistant, Stanford White, who brilliantly adapted the form of the Romanesque tower for the new church. In the task of adapting the half-finished building he began a close lifelong association with his builders, the Norcross brothers. From this time onwards he increasingly distrusted drawings, except in the solving of the plan, and increasingly worked with a southern engagement, his fine mind in a powerful body competing to shape his creations as they emerged from the Arcadian earth. It has been said that often neither his assistant, clients, builders, and perhaps not he himself, could see what he was driving at until the building was finished. He required, consequently, a considerable indulgence from all parties, and, being adored, he was allowed this on enough of his major projects.

Richardson came to believe that the architect's primary responsibility was, if he saw how to improve a building, to change it even as it approached completion. Such an approach necessarily depended upon a soundness of the plan.

Building Trinity prompted him to move home to be near it. He rented a house near Boston in a landscape of rolling hills, punctuated with rock outcrops, carefully landscaped in an untamed romantic manner, thinly populated by the cultured, rich and influential. From these surroundings he was to draw out his most important clients, collaborators and friends. The most important was F.L. Olmsted, who lived within, for such large men, a stone's throw of the Richardson house; he was an established landscape designer of great vision, a man who thought in terms of whole regions, deeply concerned as he was, after Rousseau and **Thoreau**, for democratic man's place in nature. Brookline, as the estate where they lived is called, was described then, and could be now, as containing the most impressive pieces of real estate in an area of rare loveliness.

Olmsted collaborated on many projects, but more importantly he by proxy provided Richardson with the theoretical basis for his work that the architect himself never wished to articulate but which is the essential of all great architecture, and with the image of a social programme that at least all architecture since the eighteenth century has needed.

Richardson's maturity of work and life, the two symbiotically linked, began with his move to Brookline. Adjoining the house he added studios (within which he grew an intimacy with his assistants that was essential to his art) and his library (being a great lover of books and of much else).

Fittingly, many of his finest buildings are libraries. In particular the Crane library of 1883 at Quincy, Massachusetts, and the Ames Memorial library at North Easton of 1879 are both convincing examples of his mature work, of how he made the Romanesque style strange and new. Although nearly literal in many of their details, in their massing, in the organization and form of the openings, doors and windows and in the wild surface of the stone, they are completely American and his own. However massive and simple the form, in the savage treatment of the surface and the originality of the composition, the buildings have an urgent freedom about them, as if the Romanesque style had been received from books found in a cave or washed up on the shore in this other Eden.

The entrances to both libraries were huge, engulfing arches of pure geometry and rough stone. This motif he was to work repeatedly in other buildings, reaching its most elemental in the Ames Memorial Gatehouse. As

Warren Chalk has said, this motif was to recur, and will recur again, in the work of all the finest American architects after him. Although he made an important contribution to what was to be called by Vincent Scully the 'shingle style' with the Stoughton House of 1883 in Cambridge, Massachusetts, quintessentially his material was stone. The question remains: if the shingle style can only make large private houses, if this is the true American style, is this then the adequate and appropriate programme?

Richardson built many of his finest works for Harvard University, notably the Austin Hall Law School, completed in 1883. His most impressive assemblage is the Allegheny County Court House and Jail of 1884 and his most charming small buildings are the commuter railway stations on the Boston and Albany Railway.

During the 1880s, the decade of his greatest successes and declining health, he undoubtedly undertook too many commissions, and the varied quality of many of the works that carry his name bears witness to this. Of all his achievements, in the end he drew pride from the Pittsburgh Court House and the Marshall Field building in Chicago, of 1887. The Field building was to be a large commercial building, what was then a new programme in a new city, with new pressures of space and money, and as such a crucial test for his art. Considered by many to be his opus, the building is in many ways away from the body of his other best work, at an extreme of his favoured methods of working. The façade, for instance, was obviously resolved through drawing. It cannot be said that in this engagement between the new programmes and an ancient art a complete harmony was achieved. The conflict was between the pressure of the utilitarian volume within the building and the use of stone for the walls. The depth of the plan required extensive daylighting, and the increasing height of such buildings depended upon a sophistication of structure that only metal could fulfil, all of which served to stretch and dilute the power of his beloved rock.

Richardson was a difficult architect to follow. His two most brilliant ex-assistants, White and McKim, working in partnership, in reaction emulated the Beaux Arts style in their most important works, and he remains today, like his contemporary Frank Furness, peculiarly undigested by American architectural thought and practice. In the grotesque refinements of the European Modern movement practised by many current American architects, purged of social relevance, there is no inheritance. The question remains: apart from the large private house and the office block, what is the appropriate programme that will revive a true American architecture, to which Richardson first gave expression?

Further reading

See: Henry-Russell Hitchcock, *The Architecture of H.H. Richardson and His Times* (1966); M.G. Van Rensselaer, *Henry Hobson Richardson* (1969); James F. O'Gorman, *H.H. Richardson and His Office* (1974); Jeffrey Karl Ochsner (ed.), *H.H. Richardson: Complete Architectural Works* (1982); Maureen Meister (ed.), *H.H. Richardson: The Architect, His Peers and Their Era* (1999); Kenneth A. Breisch, *Henry Hobson Richardson and the Small Public Library in America: A Study in Typology* (2003).

FREDERICK SCOTT

RIEFENSTAHL, Leni (Helene Bertha Amalie)

1902–2003

German film director and photographer

Born in Berlin, Leni Riefenstahl was the daughter of a rich plumbing and heating engineer. Against her father's wishes she decided at an early age to be a dancer, and was trained at the Berlin Russian Ballet School. After touring Europe for three years in various companies, she rejected **Max Reinhardt's** plans for her in order to take part in Arnold Fanck's film *The Holy Mountain* (*Die heilige Berg*, 1925), one of many 'mountain films' attracting large audiences in Germany throughout the 1920s and 1930s.

Over the next few years she appeared in a number of similar ventures, including the highly successful *Storms over Mont Blanc* (*Stürme über dem Mont Blanc*, 1930), experience which not only developed her considerable acting ability but also exposed her to the complexities of location photography. It was against this background that, with the help of Bela Balazs, she directed her first film, *The Blue Light* (*Das blaue Licht*, 1932), which she also produced, wrote and starred in. This won the Gold Medal at the Venice Film Festival, immediately establishing Riefenstahl as a remarkably talented woman in a male-dominated industry. She was idolized in Germany, and the Nazis quickly recognized a compatibility between her style and theirs: **Hitler** himself commissioned Riefenstahl to make *Sieg des Glaubens* ('Victory of Belief', 1933), a short documentary of the Nürnberg party congress brilliantly capturing the spirit of the Nazi movement and the near deification of its leader. This was the decisive stage of her career: protected by her friendship with Hitler even from the interference of Goebbels, she enjoyed a unique advantage over other chroniclers of the Reich; but when the Reich itself collapsed, her career went with it. Although she repudiated everything to do with Nazism in 1952, she was unable to resume life as a director, and only completed one film in the years that followed the war, *Tiefland* (1954), a project begun in 1940 but abandoned then due to one of her recurrent breakdowns in health. Her natural talent, however, was not to be daunted. She re-emerged at the end of the 1960s as a photographer, producing two acclaimed studies of remote African tribal life, *The Last of the Nuba* (1969) and *The People of Kau* (1976). At the age of seventy-five she began deep-sea diving and underwater photography, which led to the equally remarkable *Coral Gardens* (1978). Surviving a helicopter crash at the age of ninety-eight, she celebrated her own centenary with the completion of her last film, *Impressionen unter Wasser* ('Underwater Impressions').

Whatever their politics, Riefenstahl's films represent a rare cinematic achievement. *Triumph of the Will* (*Triumph des Willens*, 1935) is a record of the 1934 Nürnberg party congress. From the first sight of Hitler's plane emerging from the clouds, to the pace of the triumphal drive through Nürnberg, to the Führer's appearance in one long shot amongst the rows of immaculate uniformed soldiers, walking among so many beetles to pay homage to the dead in the gigantic stadium, her genius here lies in her ability to create a mounting tension surrounding an event the outcome of which is never in doubt. This was followed by *Day of Freedom* (*Tag der Freiheit*, 1935), about the Wehrmacht, intended to redress the fancied slight of their exclusion from *Triumph of the Will*. Her masterpiece, however, was *Olympia* (*Olympische Spiele*, 1936), an epic documentary of the Munich Games in two parts, recording athletes and sports as an evocation of human physical beauty at rest or in motion. The first part, the lyrical *Festival of the Nationals* (*Fest der Völker*), includes a mystical, languid eurhythmic display expressing the sensual aspects of physical exercise, followed by a sequence on contemporary Berlin and, inevitably, Hitler, juxtaposed with footage on Greece filmed by Willy Zielke. Part Two, *Festival of Beauty* (*Fest der Schönheit*), depicts the Olympic Village, and the main events. Apart from its brilliant photography and accompanying score by Herbert Windt, the film was a feat of organization. Riefenstahl employed thirty cameramen in special pits, on rails and hoists, often with equipment that had been specifically manufactured for her requirements. It took six months just to train the photographers of the diving sequences. But the work owes its coherence to the eighteen months' solitary editing by Riefenstahl once the Games were over, reducing 400,000 metres of film to 6,151. Of the many awards given to *Olympia*, perhaps the least expected were the diploma and Gold Medal presented to Riefenstahl by the Olympic Committee in 1948, the time when she was suffering most heavily for her Nazi associations.

Olympia was followed by *Berchtesgaden über Salzberg* ('Berchtesgarden near Salzburg', 1938), a short documentary on Hitler's mountain retreat, and in 1944 a terse, gloomy portrait of the sculptor Arno Breker.

Further reading

See: *The Sieve of Time* (1993) is Riefenstahl's autobiography. See also: Glenn B. Infield, *Leni Riefenstahl: The Fallen Film Goddess* (1976); David Stewart Hull, *Film in the Third Reich* (1969).

MICHAEL PICK

RIEFF, Philip

1922–

US sociologist

As a theorist of culture, Philip Rieff belongs to the deeper mainstream in the modern West that takes **Nietzsche's** 'death of God' and its nihilistic consequences as the central problem of its civilization. **Max Weber** had given this tradition a particular sociological flavour by embedding it in the dependency of the rise of capitalism on the Protestant ethic; and the nineteenth-century effects of the lapsing of Protestant faith, leading to a routine, over-rationalized world, profanely emptied of meaning. Rieff continues this line by engaging it with a close critique of **Freud**, whom he takes to be the central theorist of the twentieth century. His work develops through three stages, each identified with a key book.

First, there is Rieff the exegete. His first major book – *Freud: The Mind of the Moralist* (1959) – brought him international recognition. It provides intricate detailed readings of Freud's major themes and categories. It is distinguished from the vast secondary literature on Freud by its sophistication and penetration, and its cultural overview of psychoanalysis.

Second, there is Rieff the moralist and culture critic. He remains best known for the phrase with which he titled his second major book – *The Triumph of the Therapeutic* (1965). Here he develops an argument that had

begun in the final chapter of Freud, titled 'The Emergence of Psychological Man'. He begins to build the theory of culture which will prove the central preoccupation of his later work.

Culture is interdicts – a central body of commanding 'Thou shalt nots'. They are contravened at the individual's peril. Every society depends on orders of authority – from parents to teachers, priests to rulers – whose fundamental responsibility is to maintain the interdicts, and by means of guilt-inducing repressions. Interdicts are softened by remissions, excusing reasons stipulated for special circumstances in which it is permitted to disobey. Cultures go into decline when the interdicts are not defended by the elites, and the remissions take over.

This is the condition of the modern West, where it is increasingly forbidden to forbid, and the trend is towards everything being permitted. In place of the traditional response to feeling bad: 'Pull yourself together!' which assumes that individual character is responsible for its own malaise, the modern reflex is remissive. The therapist replaces the priest as the society's central authority figure.

Third, there is Rieff the prophet of cultural despair. Rieff saw a main part of his mission as teacher – teachers are the custodians of culture. He believed that learning was only possible in a methodical, painstaking process with small groups of students, carefully working through canonical texts. He himself taught mainly at the University of Pennsylvania, where he was professor of sociology from 1961 until retirement in 1993. His book *Fellow Teachers* first appeared in 1972 in the form of what turned out to be an influential long interview in the journal *Salmagundi*. This work is a highly charged, polemical analysis of the cultural revolution of the 1960s. Unsystematic, aphoristic in the style of Nietzsche, it is a brilliant, subtly Byzantine collage demanding microscopic focus in reading.

> For my fellow teachers, in remembrance, I rededicate the highest aims of education,

indistinct from worship as these are bound to become so high up. Our highest aims are twofold: (1) to know that God forbids; (2) to know what God forbids. From these two nodes of knowing, equal and irreducible in culture, every liberty – to do and think whatever is not forbidden – derives.

Rieff's *revision* of an Old Testament theory of culture finds its fullest exposition in three late essays. In keeping with his view that culture works indirectly, these are oblique fragments – an Epilogue to the second edition of *Freud* (1979); a Preface to the second edition of *Fellow Teachers* (1985); and an essay, 'By What Authority?'

Increasingly, St Augustine's notion of a 'second death' comes to the fore – that the soul may die before the body. Rieff reads the modern West as plunging into a spiritless void, in which bodies live on narcissistically pursuing their profane pleasures. Once the therapist has taken over, then culture is denied. In therapy, all guilts are to be erased as sicknesses; all interdicts are to be read as impediments to wellbeing. Given that it is culture that maintains the vertical which connects individuals to the divine, they are flattened to the horizontal – the plane of the corpse.

The Rieff legacy will not be marked with fanfares and celebrity intellectual status – he would not want it that way. However, at the core of the discipline of sociology is the issue of culture – of the role it plays in giving meaning and direction to individual and collective life, and the pathologies that strike when it declines, from anomie and disenchantment to crises of meaning. One might claim the same for the humanities at large. Given this, Rieff is arguably the most important social theorist since the discipline's founding fathers, **Durkheim** and **Weber**.

Further reading

Other works include: a collection of essays and lectures edited by one of his students, Jonathan B. Imber, under the title, *The Feeling Intellect* (1990).

JOHN CARROLL

RIEMANN, Georg Friedrich Bernhard

1826–66

German mathematician

Bernhard Riemann was born in 1826, the second of six children of a Lutheran pastor. He lived only to the age of thirty-nine, and his life was composed largely of poverty and family tragedy. His mother and a sister died early on of consumption, which disease later accounted for the lives of two more sisters and a brother. In addition his father long opposed Bernhard's mathematical vocation, intending him for the ministry. And yet by every account his exceptional mathematical talent exhibited itself from the earliest age. At ten he was far ahead of his first teacher, Schulz, himself a reasonable mathematician. At fourteen, Riemann attended the Lyceum, a gymnasium in Hanover, where he stayed with his grandmother. When she died two years later, he returned to his home town, Quickborn, and attended another gymnasium in nearby Luneburg. There he read Legendre's *Théorie des Nombres* in six days and it was this early reading which probably led to his interest in prime numbers and so eventually to the conceptualization of the 'Riemann Hypothesis'.

In 1846 Riemann was enrolled at the University of Göttingen, but soon moved to the mathematically more stimulating University of Berlin. He returned in 1849 to Göttingen to prepare for his doctorate. In 1851 he submitted his thesis, which was warmly praised by the elderly Carl Fiederich Gauss. Staying at Göttingen, he was admitted as a *privatdozent* in 1854, and appointed professor extraordinarius in 1857. It was not until he became a full professor in 1859, however, that he gained adequate remuneration, by which time his reputation as Gauss's true successor had already begun to spread. Now honoured and fêted by learned societies in Berlin, London and Paris, Riemann was not long to enjoy his success. A month after his marriage to Elise Koch in 1862 he contracted pleurisy, which in turn led to tuberculosis. Despite travels in Italy and

Switzerland there was no lasting remission, and he died in 1866 at Selasca on Lake Maggiore.

If his health had been stronger, Riemann might have surpassed Gauss to become the nineteenth century's leading mathematician. As it is, he is justly famous for his work in non-Euclidean geometry, taking on from where Lobachevsky and János Bolyai had left off. He discovered the second great branch of non-Euclidean geometry ('elliptic geometry') which still retains many Euclidean features. He also discovered more general varieties, thus providing the basic material for Einstein's General Theory of Relativity, given to the world fifty years after Riemann's death.

Euclid had maintained, in his celebrated Fifth Postulate, that when we are given a line L and a point p, not belonging to L, there is one and only one line through p which never meets L however far it is produced. Lobachevsky showed that one could consistently postulate more than one such line, and that this immediately entailed that there would be an infinite number of such lines. Riemann realized that there was another case: there might be no such line through p. And it was by replacing the Fifth Postulate of Euclid with the postulate that no such line existed – together with some other, minor changes – that he was led to form a system of elliptic geometry. This was not so spectacular a discovery as that of Lobachevsky and Bolyai, because the principle had already been established that non-Euclidean geometries were possible; but it led Riemann to general forms of geometry which turned out to be even more significant in the long run.

The key to these new geometries was Riemann's analysis of three fundamental concepts: distance, curvature and manifold. Taking the last first, Riemann discovered that one could get a kind of abstract 'space' by forming sets of co-ordinates of any respectable mathematical kind, including things like imaginary numbers or elements of Galois fields. Riemann then showed how these abstract co-ordinates could be used to define

a kind of 'distance', or *metric* in modern terminology. Finally, he showed that it was possible to define the degree of curvature of the 'space' under consideration without any reference to another space enclosing it. This final point is of immense significance, as it allowed physicists to postulate that physical space was 'curved' without committing them to assert the existence of an unknowable containing space within which it was curved. In principle he showed how one could determine the 'curvature' of space entirely by means of measurements made within that space; and this meant it was possible to talk about the curvature of space without resorting to metaphysics. That Riemann was fully conscious of the direction in which his work was moving is manifest from his comment at the end of the famous paper of 1854, in which he developed the theory: 'This leads us into the domain of another science, that of physics, into which the object of this work does not allow us to go today.'

Riemann is known to students of mathematics as the author of a variety of integration, of several functions, of 'Riemann surfaces' and of the celebrated 'Riemann Hypothesis', which is still an unsolved problem. Like Gauss, he is a mathematician's mathematician. But unlike Gauss he was much less prepared to undertake mammoth feats of symbolic manipulation. Rather, he achieved his results by searching premathematical thought, by careful selection of question, and careful selection of method. The revolution in the core concepts of mathematics that earlier in the century had emerged from the work of Gauss, Lobachevsky and Galois found its flowering in Riemann, who was the first complete master of the modern style. Of those who followed, perhaps only **Poincaré** could match the depth and profundity of Riemann's thought.

Further reading

The *Collected Works*, ed. H. Weber with the assistance of R. Dedekind (1876), were first translated in 1953. See: H. Freudenthal, 'Riemann', in *The*

Dictionary of Scientific Biography (Vol. XI, 1975); E.T. Bell, 'Anima Candida', in *Men of Mathematics* (1937, 1953).

CHRISTOPHER ORMELL

RILEY, Bridget Louise

1931–

English artist

Famed for her contributions to Op Art ('optical art'), Bridget Riley was born in London. She attended Cheltenham Ladies' College, Goldsmiths College and then the Royal College of Art (1952–5), after which she practised as a commercial artist. In 1962, however, she announced her future intentions with a one-woman exhibition in the capital. While her earlier paintings were mostly of figurative images, an intense study of **Georges Seurat's** excessively rational approach to colour theory, begun in 1958, and an abiding interest in **Van Gogh's** non-descriptive use of colour led Riley into making art emancipated from any kind of naturalistic agenda. In particular she moved quickly into geometric abstraction, and it was this that became her signature style. Using black and white, and more rarely colour, she created patterns that seemed to vibrate and resonate on the flat surface of a canvas, stimulating an array of visual effects through seemingly minimum means.

Riley's breakthrough followed a personal crisis in 1961, as a result of which she distanced herself from her mentor, Maurice de Sausmarez. For a while working strictly in monochromes, over the next ten years she produced most of the works for which she is most celebrated – including the 'wool mark' for the British garment industry. Her pieces of this period explore almost infinite permutations of curvilinear geometric forms, generating striking optical displays that were entirely new and unexpected in art. Typically such works have simple titles – *Static*, for example, or *Suspension*, or *Straight Curve* – which belie the actual complexity of the visual experience achieved.

The boldness of Riley's art, as well as its originality, led to swift celebrity. In 1965 an exhibition of her work at Richard Feigenbaum's gallery sold out before it opened, and the artist benefited further from her inclusion in 'The Responsive Eye', an exhibition of Op Art mounted at New York's Museum of Modern Art in the same year. Even greater success followed in 1968, when Riley won the Grand Prize at the Venice Biennale – the first woman, and also the first English painter, to win the most coveted of awards in the art world. By then she was already being widely imitated, her idiom influencing fashion and interior design especially.

Prior to the Venice Biennale, Riley had expanded her palette to include variations of grey, although immediately afterwards she returned to using saturated colours, before, in the 1970s, experimenting with colour relationships, often using white to bleed or diminish the intensity of particular colours. She continued, however, to explore stripe and wave forms, a visit to Egypt in 1980–1 and exposure to its ancient monuments kindling in her an interest in vertical bands.

In the latter stages of her career Riley has often dealt with shapes in wave patterns. Among her principal later works are the decor of the Royal Liverpool Hospital (1983), and she has been accorded retrospectives at both the Hayward and Tate galleries in London (1992 and 1994). Although her paintings are dismissed by some as little more than perception studies or colour experiments, her use of nineteenth-century divisionist techniques is just one of the features of her art that indicate a more profound engagement with the visual forms of technology. It may also be said that many of her paintings do present some or other sort of inexplicable emotional experience, even though, like some other contemporary artists, Riley has used assistants to execute her ideas in larger scale, deploying the traditions of the workshop to her own ends. Equally, the way in which Riley's work can lend itself to the instantaneity of the mass media has sometimes masked its less obvious subtleties.

Further reading

See: Bridget Riley, *Dialogues on Art*, ed. Richard Kudielka (1995); Lynne Cooke, *Bridget Riley* (2001) and Paul Moorhouse, *Bridget Riley* (2003).

ANNE K. SWARTZ

RILKE, Rainer Maria

1875–1926

Austrian poet

Born, like **Kafka**, into the German-speaking minority in Prague, Rilke suffered in his early years from enforced oscillation between extremes; from the smothering influence of his posturing, religiose mother to the rigours of a Prussian-style military academy; from the aridity of two terms at a business school in Linz to the adoption, back in Prague, of a pose of *fin-de-siècle* aestheticism. His studies, which, being subjugated to his early efflorescence as a writer, were somewhat perfunctory, took him from the universities of Prague to Munich and thence to Berlin. In Munich he had met and fallen under the influence of the remarkable Russian intellectual Lou Andreas-Salomé (who had been loved by **Nietzsche** and was later to become one of the early pupils of **Freud**). In 1899 and 1900 Rilke, who became for a while her lover, accompanied her on two journeys to Russia. On his return he joined an artists' colony in Worpswede in north Germany, where he met and married the sculptress Clara Westhoff, a pupil of Rodin. But the claims of marriage, or indeed of any demanding emotional relationship, were always, for Rilke, irreconcilable with his poetic vocation, and the couple, after the birth of a daughter, agreed to separate. Soon afterwards, in August 1902, Rilke moved to Paris.

Throughout his life, Rilke was a restless traveller and a detailed biography would therefore have to consist in large part of a conscientious account of his itineraries. Three places, however, may be singled out as the significant *loci* of his life: Russia, Paris and the Canton Valais of Switzerland. In later life Rilke himself was to point to the contrasting influences on his own sensibility of Russia and Paris. From the former he gained a sense of the inexorable and intransigent vastness of experience. In *Das Stundenbuch* ('The Book of Hours', 1899–1903, published 1905), the work most directly influenced by the Russian journeys, a humble Russian monk addresses to God utterances which can only ironically be described as prayers: for God here, far from representing the God of Christianity (which Rilke had vehemently repudiated in his Tuscan Diary of 1898), is a figure of fluctuating significance, sometimes creator, sometimes created by the speaker, now entreated, now despised, the origin and the goal of ceaseless proliferations of metaphor. The *Stundenbuch* is an abundant and a fluent work, but in its very fluency Rilke saw signs of danger: Paris, and in particular the example of Rodin, was to provide the necessary antidote. *Das Buch der Bilder* ('The Book of Images', 1902) and, more radically, *Neue Gedichte* ('New Poems', published 1907 and 1908) are concerned essentially with the tension between perception and experience: but experience not, as in the *Stundenbuch*, on a cosmic scale, but in the form of isolated minutiae, objects or beings whose elusive significance both attracts and challenges the poet's 'shaping spirit'. The element of challenge is more intensely dramatized in the novel *The Notebook of Malte Laurids Brigge* (*Die Aufzeichnungen des Malte Laurids Brigge*, 1910, trans. 1930). The eponymous hero of this work, a young Danish poet living in Paris, is possessed of (and by) an acute and painful power of empathy; immediate perceptions, childhood memories and recollections from history and myth crowd in upon him, but Malte's sensibility is too passive for him to be able to master creatively the overwhelming multiplicity of experience. Ironically then, *Malte Laurids Brigge* is a work of art constructed out of the agonies of artistic insufficiency.

The claims of experience *vis-à-vis* the individual consciousness: this, essentially, is the theme of Rilke's two major cycles, *Duino*

Elegies (*Duineser Elegien*, trans. 1939) and *Sonnets to Orpheus* (*Die Sonette an Orpheus*, trans. 1936), both completed in Muzot in the Canton Valais of Switzerland in 1922. The *Elegies*, begun at Duino, a castle on the Adriatic, in 1912, took Rilke ten years to complete and were regarded by him as his major achievement, They are a series of ten poetic meditations on a number of inter-related problems, the chief of which is that of the creative sensibility (and, by extension, the human sensibility as a whole) in a transient world; its awareness, in the light of inevitable death, of the disparate and fragmentary nature of human achievement and the imperma-nence of love; its consciousness of, but inability to emulate, figures which, through their all-consuming singleness of aim, achieve a kind of existential integrity – the hero, the saint, the child, the animal. Chief of these figures, and the poet's ultimate point of reference, are the terrible and unapproachable Angels, beings of infinite beauty and cosmic energy, whose sublime indifference to man is an implicit rejection of him. The *Elegies* move from lamentation over man's alienation to a triumphant climax in which the trans-formatory powers of man are celebrated: his ability to overcome alienation by translating outer experience into *Weltinnenraum* (world-inner-space), a realm of inner sensibility in which time, and hence transience, is over-come by being transformed into space – the infinite space of the creative imagination which can overcome even death. Orpheus, the tutelary deity of the *Sonnets*, is the singer-god who, in gentler, more conciliatory form, possesses the undivided consciousness of the Elegiac Angels and in particular their ability to move unconcernedly between the realms of the living and the dead. Polarities are reconciled not in any static synthesis, but rather in a sort of mobility of spirit which can comprehend and even emulate the fluid and the fixed, productive dynamism and significant stasis:

Zu der stillen Erde sag: ich rinne.
Zu dem raschen Wasser sprich: ich bin.

(Say to the still earth: I flow/Say to the rapid water: I am.)

Rilke's work, it is perhaps fair to say, is important not so much for any particular *Weltanschauung* which may be extracted from it as for the unmistakable tone and range of utterance. Although Rilke was the most cos-mopolitan of German-speaking poets (his later work contains several cycles of poems in French) and although he assimilated influ-ences from many sources, these hetero-geneous elements are transmuted by an intensely individual poetic voice. It is a voice which has not pleased all his readers and he has been blamed by some critics for such faults as over-preciosity or a somewhat ethe-real brand of sentimentality. But Rilke's range is considerably wider than his detrac-tors admit, and extends from the most subtly delicate lyricism to the most piercing angula-rities of Modernism. Rilke is a master at dis-solving the fixed forms of the external world and reshaping them into new ones; at infus-ing everyday objects with new and vivid sig-nificance; at finding verbal correlatives for the most elusive and evanescent emotions. His poetic sensibility was at once extraordinarily fine and intensely ambitious; or, to put it another way, he had on the one hand the artist's desire for form and, on the other, an acute and anxious awareness of a vastness of experience which no formal impulse could subjugate. It is his expression of the tension between these extremes and his total dedica-tion to its resolution that places Rilke firmly in the mainstream of modern poetry.

Further reading

Other works include: *Sämtliche Werke*, ed. Ernst Zinn (6 vols, 1955–66). Other translations include: *Selected Works, Vol. I: Prose*, trans. G. Craig Hous-ton (1954); *Vol. II: Poetry*, trans. J.B. Leishman (1960); *Selected Letters of Rainer Maria Rilke 1902–1926*, trans. R.F.C. Hull (1947). See also: E.M. Butler, *Rainer Maria Rilke* (1941); H.E. Holthusen, *Rainer Maria Rilke: A Study of His Later Poetry*, trans. J.P. Stern (1952); Frank Wood, *Rainer Maria Rilke: The Ring of Forms* (1958); H.F. Peters, *Rainer Maria Rilke: Masks and the Man* (1960); E.C.

Mason, *Rilke* (1963); Patricia Brodsky, *Rainer Maria Rilke* (1988); D. Kleinbard, *The Beginning of Terror: A Psychological Study of R.M. Rilke's Life and Work* (1993).

CORBET STEWART

RIMBAUD, Arthur

1854–91

French poet

At a superficial level Rimbaud has attracted worldwide attention as a quasi-mythical figure, the archetypal rebel, the poet prodigy who abandoned poetry at the age of twenty, and eventually became a trader in Abyssinia. More significantly for modern culture, his actual work places him at the source of modernism, exercising its influence up to the present day.

Born in 1854 in Charleville in the Ardennes, he had, by the age of fifteen, gone through the stages first of pastiche and then of parody of poets such as **Hugo**, Leconte de Lisle and Banville, and was writing poetry which though still traditional in form was already intensely personal. Characteristically it swings between the two poles of idealism and revolt, the idealism taking the form of a passionate desire for freedom and adventure, for a oneness of body and soul, and a sublimation of eroticism into an ecstatic communion with nature: the revolt is against all constraints, in particular those of bourgeois society and religious hypocrisy. God and Napoleon III also come in for their fair share of opprobrium; but the intense disgust seems to apply to all the limitations of the human condition generally.

The best-known poems of this period are 'Dormeur du Val', 'Ma Bohème', 'Premières Communions', 'Les Assis'. He was also at this time developing ideas which have their sources in the social illuminism of earlier nineteenth-century thinkers like de Maistre and Fourier, and which unite a belief in social revolution and possibilities of a new fraternity with a mystical desire to fuse with the one dynamic, spiritual force uniforming the

universe. Rimbaud's practical hopes for social change were dashed after a brief disillusioning experience of the actuality of revolution in Paris just before the tragic experience of the Commune, and with characteristic intransigence and ambition he then turned all his energies to his vocation as poet and *voyant*. The aim was nothing less than to '*changer la vie*' (the phrase that, taken out of its context, has done more than anything to make him typify the revolutionary stance). The task of the poet as *voyant* is to attain, to 'see' the spiritual unknown, and then to express his visions in a form which will inculcate in his fellows a new sense of harmony and splendour and lead them forward to social progress. The means of attaining these visions of the unknown were to be found through the famous '*dérèglement de tous les sens*', the abuse of the body through alcohol, fasting, drugs, perversions of all kinds, in order to extend consciousness, even if these experiments might lead the *voyant* to the point of death.

These theories, first expressed in May 1871 in two short letters to a schoolteacher and to a schoolfriend, were put into practice in the deservedly famous 'Le Bateau ivre' where the dazzling imagery, the powerful rhythms, the poignant intensity of tone go some way to justifying the pretensions of the ambitious young *voyant*. This was the poem with which he hoped to take Paris by storm. With admirable generosity a group of writers headed by **Verlaine** had invited him to join them there, but Rimbaud's scandalous behaviour and in particular his passionate affair with the recently married Verlaine, eventually tried even the patience of those who admired his genius and he was sent back to the Ardennes in the summer of 1872. There he produced a fascinating, still enigmatic collection of poems, *Derniers vers*, very much under the influence of Verlaine. Indeed, these delicate, tenuous poems, expressing in simple folk melodies not only his tortured love but also the extreme states of mystical experience engendered by the physical deprivations which were leading him close to madness and even death, can also be read as part of a dialogue perhaps unique in literature, a *réplique* and already a critique of Verlaine and his *Romances sans paroles*.

In September the anguish turned to euphoria as Verlaine decided to leave his wife and go with Rimbaud first to Belgium and then to London. It was there during the winter of 1872–3 that Rimbaud began to write his extraordinary collection of prose-poems: *Les Illuminations*, which best show his revolutionary attempts to translate his visions of the 'unknown' into a form which will be organic and no longer preordained. True to their title these visions, whether of the unknown or of a childish, primitive world of fantasy and wish-fulfilment, are brilliant, dynamic, theatrical, as vivid and sometimes as frightening as hallucinations. They manage to create a total imaginary universe, with its own mythology, its own new god-like beings, its landscape and its fabulous new towns which may have something to do with London but more with Rimbaud's own New Jerusalem. Rimbaud's avowed aim as poet-voyant had been to find a language which would appeal to all the senses so as to attract the reader into his vision magnetically. Through the associative powers of the imagery, the dense musical patterns, and the hypnotic rhythms, these brilliant, breathless fragments indeed show an innovatory use of language which has been immensely fertile in its influence on the development of French poetry.

The affair with Verlaine ended abruptly and tragically. In the summer of 1873 Verlaine left Rimbaud, who, however, followed him to Brussels. Tried beyond his endurance, he actually shot at Rimbaud, wounding him slightly. The ensuing case against Verlaine was influenced by the revelation about his homosexuality and he was sentenced to three years in prison. The effect on Rimbaud was traumatic. In the autumn he completed a short prose work, *Une Saison en enfer*, which, although written out of the personal hell of a guilt-ridden and unhappy passion as well as the failure of an over-ambitious aesthetic, has also wider significance in the way in which it works through the idea of hell itself as fostered by Christianity towards a new and still ill-defined humanism, inspired by the characteristic ideas of fraternity (as opposed to dependence on a debilitating sexual passion), of a new and proud love (as opposed to Christian charity and guilt due to original sin) and a transcendence of the age-old dualism between the flesh and the spirit. Each short prose piece condenses in highly dramatic and often ironical form a stage in this rapid evolution. The progress is via a dialectic; the pull of the past, of superstition and human weakness, relived through brief, bright images, works against the visionary fragments of an impossible idealism in order to produce a third, more realistic stance, that of the sane, the independent, the possible. It is a unique work: in highly condensed form an exemplar of a whole spiritual crisis in Western society.

Rimbaud had claimed that his fate depended on this book. It was in fact not published until much later. Whether this marked the end of his literary endeavour, or whether he continued to add to the *Illuminations* during the following year when he came back to England with Germain Nouveau, became a subject of critical discussion for many years. Certainly from 1875, that is at the age of twenty-one, he showed no further sign of interest in a literary career and embarked on a quite different life of travel and adventures, eventually setting up in 1880 as a trader in Harrar, Abyssinia. He died of cancer in a hospital in Marseilles in 1891. It was due finally to Verlaine that most of the *Illuminations* were published for the first time in *La Vogue*, in 1886.

The ambivalence implicit in his life and work has continued in the nature of his influence. The topicality of problems raised by his '*dérèglement de tous les sens*' is too obvious to be stressed. **Claudel** is said to have been converted to Christianity after reading Rimbaud. The Surrealists used his '*changer la vie*' as their device for revolution and yet could not forgive him for having sold out. However, it is through them, and their recognition that he had found a language fit to explore and express the urges and desires of the unconscious, that his influence has been fostered. Few living French poets would deny if not a positive influence at least a deep admiration.

Further reading

Other works include: *Oeuvres complètes* (1972). For poetry in translation see: *A Season in Hell, The Illuminations*, by Enid Rhodes Peschel (1973); *Complete Works*, by Paul Schmidt (1967). The most useful critical works in English are: Wallace Fowlie, *Rimbaud* (1965); C.A. Hackett, *Rimbaud; A Critical Introduction* (1981); N. Osmond, introduction and notes to his edition of *The Illuminations* (1979). The best biographical work in English remains Enid Starkie, *Rimbaud* (1949).

MARGARET DAVIES

RIMSKY-KORSAKOV, Nikolay Andreyevich

1844–1908

Russian composer

It was into an aristocratic family with a tradition of service to the state that the composer was born. His earliest years were spent in the provinces where folk music and the gorgeous ritual of a nearby monastery made a profound impression on him. The Corps of Naval Cadets in St Petersburg provided his education from 1856 to 1862, and the musical life of that city introduced him to a wider musical world. Until 1873 he served in the navy, both aboard ship and ashore; as with many such appointments in the Russian public service, duties were not at all onerous. In 1871 he was appointed to a professorship at the St Petersburg Conservatoire, where he remained on the staff (with a brief interruption, for political reasons, in 1905) until his death. He was also at various times inspector of Naval Bands, director of the Free School of Music, and assistant musical director in the Imperial Chapel. His career encompassed teaching, conducting, editing or completing the works of others (including Dargomyzhsky, **Borodin** and **Mussorgsky**),

authorship and folk-song collecting as well as composition.

The single most important event in his musical development occurred when he met **Balakirev** in 1861. He thus was introduced to the circle of dilettante musicians drawn 'as if by magnetism' by the power of Balakirev's personality. He exchanged ideas with like-minded young composers (Borodin, Cui, Mussorgsky) and under Balakirev's tutelage the compositional activity of all of them was given direction and purpose. Their mentor persuaded his disciples to undertake works on a scale they would never have attempted without him, and thus they progressed from talented dabblers to serious composers. With his Conservatoire appointment, however, Rimsky-Korsakov felt an obligation to study systematically the elements of music ('practical composition and instrumentation' initially) which he was employed to teach, and he went on, by self-instruction, to acquire a greater mastery of the technical aspects of music than any of these associates ever possessed. In completing or preparing for publication the works of Mussorgsky, he at times substituted more conventional treatment for the boldly original ideas of the composer; this is notoriously the case with *Boris Godunov*. Though now regretted, Rimsky-Korsakov's work did begin to acquaint the public with that and other masterpieces.

Rimsky-Korsakov began to compose with the example of Glinka before him. Mendelssohn, Schumann, **Berlioz** and especially Liszt also served as models, but the composer was primarily animated by the idea of writing Russian music. In the subject-matter of his operas and orchestral music, Russian material predominates. History and folklore supply the majority of subjects, sometimes viewed through the works of Russian writers. His treatment inclines to the objective, avoids emotional excess and eschews the extremes of experiment of, for instance, Mussorgsky. He regarded opera as 'primarily a musical phenomenon', and had no sympathy with **Wagner's** ideas about musical drama. He completed fifteen operas, and some of these are his most important works.

His orchestral music is noteworthy for the brilliance of its orchestration. Acquaintance with much of it reveals a restricted melodic invention and a paucity of constructional resource. The finest works are *Sheherazade* and the *Russian Easter Festival Overture* (both 1888). The influence of the composer's orchestration may be felt not only in the work of his Russian pupils, who include Lyadov, Glazunov, **Stravinsky** and **Proko-fiev**, but also in orchestral music by **Debussy**, **Ravel** and other composers.

Serious historical topics and fantastic tales involving the supernatural are the main areas for operatic subjects. Convincing characters are conspicuous by their rarity, and the composer is happier with a ritualistic enactment of historical events or imaginary, fairy-tale figures. The real world of his own time never impinges, unless *The Golden Cockerel* (1906–7) is viewed as a burlesque of the Russo-Japanese War of 1904 and Russian government; this is a debatable interpretation, though there was no doubt at the time that the opera was near the bone. The musical representation of good and evil, or 'real' and fantastic is achieved in this opera (as in many other works) by the use of diatonic music for the former and chromatic music for the latter; this distinction, familiar from Weber's *Der Freischütz*, is exploited in Glinka's *Ruslan* and later in Stravinsky's *The Firebird*. Rimsky-Korsakov takes it further by contriving fresh arrangements of notes in non-diatonic scale patterns.

The outstanding example of an opera using folk motives is *The Snow Maiden* (1880–1). This incorporates elements from folk wedding celebrations and the Shrovetide festival, and is full of folk-like melodies and instrumental effects. The method of treating brief tunes of narrow melodic range, relying on ostinatos and pedals, is distinctive. *The Maid of Pskov* (1868–72, 1876–7 and 1891–2) is perhaps the best example of a historical opera by this composer. It deals with Ivan the Terrible's campaign of 1570, in which the inhabitants of Pskov are menaced by the same cruel treatment the tsar has just meted out to Novgorod. This fate is prevented by the tsar's discovery in Pskov of one who is his own daughter. Her lover, though, wishes to kill the tsar and rescue the 'maid of Pskov' from him. She is accidentally killed in the ensuing fight.

Further reading

Other works include: Symphony No. 2 (*Antar*, 1868, 1875, 1897); *Musical Picture – Sadko* (1869, rev. 1892); *Capriccio espagnol* (1887). Operas: *May Night* (1878–9); *Christmas Eve* (1894–5); *Sadko* (1894–6); *The Tsar's Bride* (1898–9); *The Tale of Tsar Saltan* (1899–1900); *The Legend of the Invisible City of Kitezh and the Maid Fevroniya* (1903–5). *Forty Folksongs*, a collection compiled in 1875; *Collection of 100 Russian Folksongs*, compiled in 1875–6. Rimsky-Korsakov's *Chronicle of My Musical Life* is available in a translation by J.A. Joffe (1942); his *Principles of Orchestration*, ed. M.O. Shteynberg, has also been published in English (2nd edn, 1964). See: Gerald Abraham, *Rimsky-Korsakov – A Short Biography* (1945); S.A. Griffiths, *A Critical Study of the Music of Rimsky-Korsakov* (1989).

STUART CAMPBELL

RIOPELLE, Jean-Paul
1923–2002
French-Canadian artist

Quebec's foremost and most prolific artist was a native of Montreal, where he studied mathematics before switching to the Fine Arts school. At the École du Meuble, he worked under the charismatic teacher and painter Paul-Émile Borduas, who inspired his students to rebel against the entrenched cultural conservatism of mid-century Quebec. Having exhibited as a group in Montreal in 1946, Riopelle and his fellows were to countersign Borduas's provocative manifesto *Refus Global* ('Refusal on All Fronts', 1948), which railed against the repressive influence of the Catholic Church. Known as the Automatistes, they aligned their non-premeditated gestural approach to abstraction with the surrealist notion of psychic automatism. In 1947, Riopelle himself organized an Automatistes show in Paris, where he began to cultivate contacts with an emerging circle of cosmopolitan abstractionists, such as Georges Mathieu, Nicolas de Staël, Zao Wou-Ki and Sam Francis, as well as with the influential critic Georges Duthuit. He also met the surrealists, and participated in their 1947 international exhibition. By now it was clear that the artist from Quebec was intent on performing on a wider stage.

By the end of 1948 Riopelle had settled permanently in Paris and in 1951 contributed to the epoch-making show *Véhémences confrontées* ('Forces in Confrontation') staged by the theorist Michel Tapié, who coined the formula *Art informel* (others spoke of *Tachisme* or *Abstraction lyrique*). *Art informel* ('Art beyond form') was in effect the Paris wing of international Abstract Expressionism. Tapié's show also acknowledged American 'action painters' such as **Willem de Kooning** and **Jackson Pollock**, though Riopelle was keen to distance himself from the New York school.

Through the 1950s, Riopelle produced some of his most exciting work, consumed by a veritable passion for expression without constraint. He would launch violent brushstrokes across a large canvas, squeeze colours directly from the tube, and apply pigment with a palette knife in agitated smears. An all-over composition such as *Vent traversier* ('Cross-wind', 1952) consists of spectacular accretions of luminescent hues, over which pass ultra-thin threads of white or bright yellow paint. The effect is of a vast landscape seen from on high, of multiple jostling facets aspiring to coherence.

In 1957 Riopelle began a long association with Joan Mitchell, herself an abstract painter of note; they lived near Paris, in **Monet's** former home. Riopelle's reputation as the leading Canadian artist was now established, and his career was henceforth punctuated by major commissions, awards and international exhibitions. In 1962 he became the first Canadian painter to win a prize at the Venice Biennale, and in 1963 his native country honoured him with a retrospective mounted in Ottawa, Montreal and Toronto. In 1981 the French initiated a retrospective which subsequently toured to Canada and Mexico. Commissioned for Toronto International Airport, *Point de rencontre* ('Meeting Place', 1963) was a controversial painting measuring over 4 by 5 metres; in 1989 it was donated to the French and now hangs in the Bastille opera-house in Paris.

In 1958 Riopelle had begun to produce bronze sculptures and in 1976 an ambitious installation, *La Joute* ('The Animal Fight'), was set up in the Olympic Park in Montreal: this gathering of multiple animal sculptures was embellished with flames and spurting water, and was later relocated to the city centre at the Place Jean-Paul Riopelle. The artist's zestful versatility also led to work in the media of tapestry, ceramics, lithography, watercolour and collage.

In 1989, Riopelle re-settled in his native Quebec, close to the Saint Lawrence River. Bleak landscapes and wild birds, especially owls and geese, began to mark his canvases, as did the use of aerosol sprays. His last large-scale work was a fresco over 40 metres long, made up of thirty paintings dominated by the bird motif. Entitled *Hommage à Rosa Luxemburg* ('Homage to Rosa Luxemburg', 1992), it was donated by the artist to the Musée du Québec.

In 1994 Riopelle acquired a manor house dramatically sited at the tip of the Isle-aux-Grues, an island in the Saint Lawrence. It was here that he died in 2002. Controversy continued to the end, when the state funeral of this fervent atheist involved a mass in the Montreal Church of the Immaculate Conception.

Further reading

See: Guy Robert, *Riopelle ou la poétique du geste* (1970); Pierre Schneider, *Riopelle. Signes mêlés* (1972); Michel Martin (ed.) *Jean-Paul Riopelle. Peinture 1946–1977* (1981); Jacques Dupin, *L'Espace autrement dit* (1982); Daniel Gagnon, *Riopelle grandeur nature* (1988); Ray Ellenwood,

Egregor. The Montreal Automatist Movement (1992); Jeffrey Spalding *et al.*, *Riopelle* (2002); René Viau, *Jean-Paul Riopelle, la traversée du paysage* (2002).

ROGER CARDINAL

RIVERA, Diego

1886–1957

Mexican painter and muralist

Diego Rivera said that his earliest memory was of his making a drawing. He was only twelve when he entered the Academia de San Carlos, Mexico City, where he took lessons in drawing and learned the laws of perspective. The refined, inventive, and facile drawing-style Rivera developed at the Academia would form the basis of his entire artistic output. Also at San Carlos Rivera was introduced to the Golden Section, which he would use to create a system of interrelated geometrical forms and mathematical ratios that would form the compositional 'skeleton' of his future murals.

In 1911 Rivera settled in Paris, and in 1913 he began to work in the Cubist style. Rivera produced about 200 Cubist works before 1917, when he abandoned this style for figuration. In 1920 he travelled to Italy to study the murals and works on panel of the proto- and early-Renaissance artists Cimabue, Giotto, Paolo Uccello, and Masaccio, among others. His close studies of these artists would be an important influence on his future mural work.

Soon after his return to Mexico in 1921, Rivera began to cover the walls of public buildings with epic murals depicting the history and life of the indigenous population, its customs, hardships and the political and economic issues it confronted. His first mural, *Creation*, encaustic and gold leaf (1922–3), is in the Anfiteatro Bolívar of the Escuela Nacional Preparatoria, Mexico City. This was followed by his decoration in true fresco technique of the stairway and of the loggias in the Courtyards of Labor and of Fiestas in the Secretaría de Educación Pública, Mexico City. In 1924 and 1926–7 he worked on frescoes for the administration building and

chapel of the Universidad Autónoma de Chapingo. Rivera's fresco cycle in the chapel at Chapingo, in which the theme of social revolution parallels that of Nature's evolution, is a masterwork and among the artist's greatest achievements.

In 1929–30 and in 1935 Rivera painted the *History of Mexico* in the stairway of the Palacio Nacional, Mexico City. The composition of this fresco cycle, with its brilliant interrelation of multiple views on single wall panels, has been cited as demonstrating the influence of Cubism as well as the experiments in montage by the filmmakers **Fritz Lang** and **Sergei Eisenstein** (whom Rivera met in Moscow in 1927). In 1930 Rivera left Mexico to fulfil commissions in the United States, after he had completed the frescoes in the Secretaría de Salubridad y Asistencia, Mexico City, and in the loggia of the Palace of Cortés, Cuernavaca.

Although he was born into the middle class, Rivera identified with workers and peasants. He was a member of the Union of Technical Workers, Painters, and Sculptors (Sindicato de Obreros Técnicos, Pintores y Escultores), and he held firmly to a **Marxist** ideology of class struggle and a future workers' utopia – ideas that informed many of his murals. Rivera's murals were financed by the Mexican government and by North American capitalists, and he moved among an international set of artists and intellectuals; however, emotionally and artistically he remained devoted to the working class and Mexico's indigenous culture.

In 1931 Rivera painted the fresco *Allegory of California* for the Luncheon Club of the Pacific Stock Exchange, San Francisco. Later that same year he painted *The Making of a Fresco Showing the Building of a City* for the California School of Fine Arts, now the San Francisco Art Institute, and *Still Life with Blossoming Almond Trees* for the dining room of Mrs. Sigmund Stern, which is now in the foyer of Stern Hall, University of California at Berkeley. In December 1931 the Museum of Modern Art, New York, opened a retrospective exhibition of Rivera's work,

In May 1932 Rivera began work on *Detroit Industry* at the Detroit Institute of Arts. This fresco cycle is a celebration of the city's three principal industries at the time: the automobile, chemicals and pharmaceuticals. In the panels devoted to the making of the automobile, workers move in harmony with the machines, which are both accurately rendered and informed with a majesty that recalls Mexico's monumental pre-Columbian sculptures, an important aesthetic influence on Rivera's art. Rivera celebrated the machine and looked forward to the day when workers' lives would be made easier by it. Yet he had misgivings about the machine's effect on the lives of workers, and the tension between these two states of mind is evident in these frescoes.

In 1933 Rivera began work on *Man at the Crossroads* at the Radio Corporation of America (RCA) Building, Rockefeller Center, New York. While at work on this project the artist decided to incorporate the portrait of **Vladimir Lenin** and refused to eliminate this image at the request of the Rockefeller family. The fresco had been created on a portable base, and because of the deadlock between artist and patron, the Museum of Modern Art agreed to accept it into its collection; however, on the weekend of 10 February 1934, the nearly-completed fresco was destroyed. After painting a series of portable frescoes, *Portrait of America*, for the New Workers School, New York, Rivera returned to Mexico where he created a revised duplication of the RCA fresco in the Palacio de las Bellas Artes, Mexico City. In 1940 Rivera returned to the United States to participate in the Art in Action Project at San Francisco's Golden Gate International Exhibition. The ten moveable frescoes on the theme of Pan-American Unity, which he created for this project, are in the collection of the City College of San Francisco.

Rivera's work profoundly influenced many young North American artists who were participants in the New Deal's cultural-support programmes, such as the Public Works Art Project (1933–4), under whose auspices twenty-six artists decorated the interior of the Coit Tower, San Francisco. Ben Shahn, who assisted Rivera at Rockefeller Center and the New Workers School, later created murals with support from the Treasury Department's Section of Painting and Sculpture (1934–43). During this period, Rivera was an especially strong influence on American artists of African ethnicity. Rivera's example gave these artists the courage to paint the history and customs of African-Americans as well as the social and economic issues that affected their lives. Among these artists are Hale Woodruff, who studied with Rivera in Mexico, Jacob Lawrence, Charles White, Elizabeth Catlett and Charles Alston, who frequently visited Rivera while he was working on the Rockefeller project.

In his later years Rivera created a number of public works in Mexico City. Among the most notable are *Dream of a Sunday Afternoon in the Alameda* (1947–8) in the Hotel del Prado and an underwater fresco on the floor and walls of an open cistern in the Pavilion of the Lerma waterworks (Cárcamo del Río Lerma), 1943–51. In addition Rivera designed for the adjoining water basin a monumental bas-relief mosaic sculpture of the Aztec rain god Tláloc, which is reminiscent of Native American earth sculptures. In 1953 Rivera's mosaic *A Popular History of Mexico* was installed on the façade of the Teatro de los Insurgentes.

The subject of many of Rivera's easel paintings was the folk life of Mexico's indigenous people, but he was also an accomplished portrait painter. He applied his rich and subtle palette in the representation of family, friends, members of fashionable society, as well as portraits of himself; his murals abound with renderings of people he knew.

In 1956, while convalescing from an illness, Rivera painted a series of twenty sunsets, oil and tempera on canvas, at the Acapulco home of his friend Dolores Olmedo. He died a year later, on 24 November 1957, at his home in San Angel, Mexico City.

Further reading

See: Bertram D. Wolfe, *The Fabulous Life of Diego Rivera* (1939). See also: Rámon Favela, *Diego Rivera: The Cubist Years* (1984); Linda Downs, Ellen Sharp *et al.*, *Diego Rivera: A Retrospective* (1986); Valerie Fletcher, *Crosscurrents of Modernism: Four Latin American Pioneers: Diego Rivera, Joaquin Torres-Garcia, Wilfredo Lam, Matta* (1992); Lizetta LeFalle-Collins and Shifra M. Goldman, *In the Spirit of Resistance: African-American Modernists and the Mexican Muralist School (En el espíritu de la resistencia: Los modernistas africanoamericanos y la Escuela Muralista Mexicana*, 1996).

GINA A. GRANGER

RIVERS, William Halse Rivers

1864–1922
English anthropologist

W.H.R. Rivers was born at Luton near Chatham, Kent, the son of a clergyman and the nephew of James Hunt, the flamboyant founder and president of the Anthropological Society of London (1863). He studied at Tonbridge School and entered St Bartholomew's Hospital in 1882, graduating as a doctor in medicine in 1888. After further studies in Jena and Heidelberg he was appointed to a lectureship in Physiological and Experimental Psychology at Cambridge in 1893. In 1898–9, Rivers took part in the Cambridge Expedition to the Torres Strait under the leadership of A.C. Haddon. Further journeys included a visit to the Todas in southern India (1902), and extensive travelling through Melanesia (1908 and 1914). During the First World War he worked as a psychiatrist at Maghull Military Hospital, which specialized in the treatment of shell-shock. When he died unexpectedly of a strangulated hernia he was President-in-Charge of the Royal Anthropological Institute and a Fellow of the Royal Society.

Rivers's most decisive contributions were made in social anthropology, though he never held a university position in that field. He was a shy man with an awkward stammer who allowed his fellowship at St John's (Cambridge) to safeguard him from the meandrous avenues of self-promotion, avenues which led lesser men to greater fame. Even now all but one of his books are out of print. In the available *Kinship and Social Organization* (1914) Rivers described the *genealogical method* for recording kinship material, a method which is still standard practice among anthropologists. Convinced that kinship terminologies provide evidence of former marriage regulations and are strictly correlated to attitudinal systems, he achieved in these matters a level of analytical sophistication rarely attained since: his concern in establishing a genealogy of possible marriage systems has even been confused by later anthropologists with inadequate descriptions of definite marriage systems.

In his Introduction to *The Todas* (1906), and in *Anthropological Research outside America* (1913), Rivers provided the first rigorous theorization for ethnographic fieldwork method. Although, despite his travels, he never personally practised the fieldwork he advocated, his techniques were vindicated by his pupil John Layard and by **Malinowski**, in eastern and northern Melanesia respectively; it is through their works that Rivers's influence, seldom directly credited, has been most effective.

Towards the end of his career Rivers was himself influenced by the German Historical School of Anthropology (of which P.W. Schmidt was the most prominent figure), and by the historical speculations of his friend Sir G. Elliot Smith. This led him to make some first-rate investigations on regressive aspects in culture, in particular the 'disappearance of useful arts' in some societies. But his achievements in this particular domain were again undervalued, this time largely because of the dominant place achieved by the Functionalist School in the years immediately following his death.

A.R. Radcliffe-Brown was Rivers's first student in social anthropology, and there can be no doubt of the last imprint left on the pupil's anthropological style. It was, however, left to other pupils to develop Rivers's proficiency in kinship studies, among them

W.E. Armstrong, Brenda Z. Seligman and John Layard; and while Malinowski was never formally under Rivers's tutelage, it is indicative that Malinowski deliberately chose to match his work with the Cambridge recluse.

Such reputation as Rivers enjoyed during his life came to him also from his studies in neurophysiology and psychology. He provided a controversial distinction between *protopathic* and *epicritic* nerve sensitivity, concepts elaborated in an investigation with and on Henry Head (nervous terminations recovered sensitivity after a nerve had been severed in Head's arm), as well as pioneering work on perception of colour and shape in different societies. He also participated in the then current debate on the group-mind, focusing his attention on the effects of *suggestion*, which he traced in the manifestations of alcoholic intoxication; while *Instinct and the Unconscious* (1920) and *Conflict and Dream* (1923) proposed a neat compromise between **Freud's** metapsychology and Hughlings Jackson's hierarchical theory of the nervous system.

Further reading

Other works include: *The History of Melanesian Society* (2 vols, 1914) and *Psychology and Ethnology* (1926). See also: R. Slobodin, *W.H.R. Rivers* (1978).

PAUL JORION

ROBBE-GRILLET, Alain

1922–

French novelist and filmmaker

There seems little obvious connection between Robbe-Grillet's early life and his subsequent career as the best-known and most radical figure in the group known as the Nouveau Roman. He grew up in Brittany, studied agronomy, and worked as an agricultural scientist in various parts of the world before becoming a full-time writer.

His first novel, *Un Régicide*, was completed in 1949, but was not published until 1978. It was the publication of his second novel, *The Erasers* (*Les Gommes*, 1953), which began his career as a writer of critical notoriety. With a few notable exceptions (such as **Roland Barthes**), critics were appalled first by what they saw as a pointless, detailed description of a dehumanized world, then by the apparent lack of novelistic coherence in his books, and from the late 1960s, by the blatantly sado-erotic aspect of his work. Robbe-Grillet grew up reading **Kafka**, **Rudyard Kipling**, Raymond Roussel and **Queneau** but without realizing that they did not represent the mainstream of conventional fiction, so that his own challenge to traditional forms of the realist novel can to some extent be seen as unwitting or involuntary. However, once he was aware of his subversive position, he continued to emphasize and refine it, and he played a significant role in the development of modern French fiction through his association with his publisher, Jérôme Lindon at the Éditions de Minuit, for whom he worked as editorial adviser for a number of years in the 1950s and 1960s. His creative work was also accompanied by an explicit interest in theoretical questions, and he published numerous essays and interviews on the novel.

In the early years, Robbe-Grillet gained a reputation as the champion of *chosisme*, the flat, meticulous description of the physical world – a tomato slice or the layout of a banana plantation. The implication is that the world can be described but not interpreted. His attacks on plot and character in the early essays (collected in *Towards a New Novel*, *Pour un Nouveau Roman*, 1963) were based on the view that they constitute false interpretative models for fundamentally meaningless experience: life cannot be read as narrative, nor people as characters. The detectives who appear intermittently throughout Robbe-Grillet's work illustrate (sometimes very comically) the impossibility of making sense of the factual evidence they are confronted with. Wallas, the hero of *The Erasers*, becomes so disorientated that he ends up by accidentally committing the crime he has been sent to investigate. The jealous husband whom we are invited to imagine as a possible source of the apparently narratorless *Jealousy* (*La Jalousie*, 1957), is in a similar position to the detective's, for he is tantalized by an inability to interpret appearances with any confidence. There are signs that his wife is having an affair with a friend, but he proves incapable of reading them as straightforward indications of her adultery. Like many of Robbe-Grillet's characters and narrators, he swings between purely factual observation on the one hand and obsessive, unbridled imagination on the other hand.

With the appearance of *In the Labyrinth* (*Dans le labyrinthe*, 1959) it became clear that one can no longer even count on the unambiguous presence of the physical world in Robbe-Grillet's novels. The world represented in these later novels is self-contradictory and inconsistent. Characters change names, plots go round in circles, descriptions of reality prove to be descriptions of paintings or theatrical performances, – or vice versa. The policeman-narrator in *Recollections of the Golden Triangle* (*Souvenirs du triangle d'or,* 1978) simply invents his reports. It is not only impossible to give meaning to the world, but even confidently to represent it. For this reason one can no longer talk of realism in the traditional sense of the word. The real world is one thing, the written world of Robbe-Grillet's novels another. Or so it seems, until Robbe-Grillet goes one step further and suggests that assumptions about the real world are just a set of constructions and myths which happen to be popularly shared. It might be possible to speak of a new kind of realism in Robbe-Grillet's fiction, consisting in the representation of these collective views or the current mythology about the world. The exaggeratedly stereotyped setting and plot of *The House of Assignation* (*La Maison de rendez-vous*, 1965) in a world of prostitution, vice and drug-smuggling in Hong Kong, or those of *Project for a Revolution in New York* (*Projet pour une révolution à New York*, 1970) in a world of revolutionary conspiracy and subway violence, or the mix of gothic fantasy and spy-fiction in *Djinn* (1981), exemplify

very well these new forms of such realism. Robbe-Grillet's realism consists in drawing attention to our contemporary mythology, and not necessarily in distinguishing between reality and invention, making coherent narratives, or avoiding contradictions. The sado-eroticism which invaded the novels with increasing explicitness from *The House of Assignation* onwards, is in one sense simply an extension of this representation of popular mythology and culture. His preoccupation with surface rather than meaning, writing rather than subject-matter, made this engagement with sexual issues problematic and provocative, and in 1974 his film *Glissements progressifs du plaisir* was put on trial in Italy for the offence of outraging public decency – much to Robbe-Grillet's own personal outrage. From then on, his writing began to show signs of a much greater suspicion of his reading public, including the reading public of the *nouveau roman* itself. In 1984 he published the first volume (*Ghosts in the Mirror, Le Miroir qui revient*) of his semi-autobiographical trilogy, in which he sought to confound the supporters of the very principles which he had campaigned to establish, but which by then had become widely accepted within the academic institution. The turn to autobiographical writing was a polemical gesture aimed at keeping the spirit of controversy and invention alive, and in Robbe-Grillet's hands this shows as a mix of frank confession, half-truths, fiction and overt fantasy which was continued over two further volumes, *Angélique ou l'enchantement* (1988) and *Les Derniers Jours de Corinthe* (1994).

In 2001 he published another novel, *Repetition* (*La Reprise*), set in Berlin at the end of the war, but for the latter part of his career Robbe-Grillet devoted himself more to film than to fiction, a medium in which he had less popular prestige than in the field of literature, but which allowed him to continue to explore in cinematic terms many of the same issues and problems found in his novels. His first venture into cinema was his script for a film made in collaboration with **Alain**

Resnais, *Last Year at Marienbad* (*L 'Année dernière à Marienbad*, 1961). This launched him on a career as a filmmaker in his own right, which he began with *L'Immortelle* in 1963, followed by *Trans-Europ-Express* (1966, starring himself and his publisher, Lindon), and various other experimental films with limited distribution, directed by himself. This work also led to the creation of a new genre, the *ciné-roman*, halfway between fiction and film, more than the script and yet not simply the novel of the film. *L'Année dernière à Marienbad* was the first of these, and it was followed by *L'Immortelle*, and others, concluding with *C'est Gradiva qui vous appelle* (2002), whose film counterpart was never made because of lack of funding. His collected interviews on cinema appeared in English under the title *The Erotic Dream Machine* (1992), a title which could also describe a number of his collaborations with visual artists, such as *Dreams of Young Girls* (*Rêves de jeunes filles*, 1971) and *Sisters* (*Les Demoiselles de Hamilton*, 1972), both with photographs by David Hamilton, or *Traces suspectes en surface* (1978) with lithographs by **Robert Rauschenberg**, and *La Belle Captive* (1975) using paintings and illustrations by **René Magritte**. In 1972, **Harrison Birtwhistle** used the text of one of Robbe-Grillet's short pieces collected in *Snapshots* (*Instantanés*) for his piece *La Plage: Eight Arias of Remembrance for Soprano and Five Instruments*.

Robbe-Grillet taught for several years as visiting professor in a number of universities in the USA, and in 2004, he became a somewhat surprising new addition to the broadly establishment Académie Française. He is one of the most eloquent – if provocatively inconsistent – commentators on his own work, and a volume of collected essays, *Le Voyageur* (2003) was published to coincide with his eightieth birthday.

Further reading

Other works include: *The Voyeur* (*Le Voyeur*, 1955) and *Topology of a Phantom City* (*Topologie d'une cité fantôme*, 1976). Further film titles include, *L'Homme qui ment* (1968); and *L'Eden et après*

(1970), *N. a pris les dés* (1971, an anagram version of *L'Eden et après*), *Le Jeu avec le feu* (1975), *La Belle Captive* (1983), *The Blue Villa* (*Un bruit qui rend fou*, 1995). See also: Bruce Morrissette, *Novel and Film: Essays in Two Genres* (1985), Ben Stoltzfus, *Alain Robbe-Grillet: Life, Work, and Criticism* (1987).

ANN JEFFERSON

ROCHE, Martin *see:* HOLABIRD, WILLIAM AND ROCHE, MARTIN

ROCKWELL, Norman

1894–1978

US illustrator and artist

For much of the twentieth century Norman Rockwell was America's best-known, and best-loved, illustrator, most readily associated with *The Saturday Evening Post*, for which, between 1916 and 1963, he painted 321 cover pictures. Far more than any exponent of Pop Art, Rockwell was a genuinely popular artist, at least in the sense of being an artist of the people and for the people, though that did not prevent him becoming a source for Pop Art towards the end of his career.

A New Yorker by birth, Rockwell received his training at the Chase Art School, the National Academy of Design and the Art Students League. From as early as 1912 he sought and received commissions to supply book and magazine illustrations. In 1915 he moved to New Rochelle, New York State, to share a studio with the cartoonist Clyde Forsythe, and it was through Forsythe that his long association with *The Saturday Evening Post* began. Another enduring relationship was with the Boy Scouts of America: for decades he contributed paintings and drawings both to the Scouts' annual calendar, and to its *Boy's Life* magazine.

A dedicated patriot, during the latter stages of World War I Rockwell enlisted with the US Navy, but to his chagrin he did not see active service, being employed as a military artist instead. During World War II his many contributions to government propaganda included four large oils depicting the four 'fundamental' freedoms outlined in a speech made by President **Franklin D. Roosevelt** in 1943: *Freedom from Want, Freedom of Speech, Freedom to Worship* and *Freedom from Fear.* Reproduced as covers for *The Saturday Evening Post*, these were used by the Treasury Department in its campaign to sell war bonds.

The Second World War also inspired another of Rockwell's most celebrated images, *Rosie the Riveter* (1943), even though this was preceded by a similar depiction bearing the legend 'We Can Do It!', contained in a poster by J. Howard Miller. As men left their factory jobs for service overseas, there was a need for women to take their places if production was to be maintained. The female figure created by Rockwell was, like so many of his portraited Americans, earnest, energetic, thrifty, decent and not a little banal. Notwithstanding, the betrousered 'Rosie' endured long afterwards as an emblem of popular feminism.

Although some of his work was destroyed by a fire in his studio in 1944, at his death there were in excess of 2,000 'original' Rockwells extant. While the majority of these related to his work as a commercial illustrator, his reputation was such that other commissions included portraits of Jawaharlal Nehru and **Gamal Abd al-Nasser** as well as Presidents Eisenhower and **Kennedy**, and in 1977 he was awarded the ultra-prestigious Presidential Medal of Freedom. No one else had contributed more to the positive iconography of his country. Among fine art critics he is, and has been, less appreciated, however. Although in the 1960s his covers for *The Saturday Evening Post* and then *Look!* magazine began addressing such social issues as racial segregation and American poverty, in terms of both content and style Rockwell seldom lifted clear of an uncritical though technically accomplished celebration of the values he and millions of his compatriots considered quintessentially American. As well as Boy Scouts the thrice-married Rockwell extolled baseball players. At their best his pictures help explain the impulses behind the

USA's mid-century confidence in its own culture; at their worst they devolve into a species of literalistic optimism that had its counterpart in the Social Realism practised in the USSR. But about himself Rockwell entertained no pretensions. Instinctively at home in the world of weekly print journalism, he seldom thought of himself as anything other than a journeyman loyalist.

Further reading

See: Norman and Tom Rockwell, *Adventures as an Illustrator* (autobiography, 1960); Tom Rockwell, *The Best of Norman Rockwell* (2000). See also: Christopher Finch, *Norman Rockwell's America* (1985) and *Norman Rockwell: 332 Magazine Covers* (1995); Fred Bauer, *Norman Rockwell's Faith in America* (1996); Donald Stoltz, *Norman Rockwell & The Saturday Evening Post: The Later Years* (1997).

SAMANTHA GOAT

RODGERS, Richard

1902–79

US popular composer

Rodgers was the most versatile and durable of the 'big six' songsmiths of America's golden age before and after World War II (the others being **Berlin**, **Gershwin**, **Kern** and **Porter**, with Harold Arlen and Harry Warren vying for sixth place). Like all the others except Porter and Warren, he was Jewish (his father a doctor, his mother a pianist); like Gershwin, he preferred not to write his own lyrics but to work with a stable partner, though after **Hammerstein's** death in 1960 this changed, and earlier, when working with Lorenz Hart, he helped write the show's 'book' in many cases. His career divides neatly into the years with Hart (1920–42), the years with Hammerstein (1943–60), and his last two decades working with a variety of collaborators. His most notable successes belong to the first two periods, though the late shows, including *Do I Hear a Waltz?* (1965) with **Stephen Sondheim** as lyricist, may yet come into their own. His output was prodigious (though Kern's was nearly as large), comprising the scores for thirty stage musicals with Hart, nine with Hammerstein, four in the late period (notably *No Strings*, 1962, for which he supplied his own lyrics), plus a dozen film musicals and a few television assignments including the marathon *Victory at Sea*, 1952. Unlike Kern and Hammerstein, Rodgers and Hart spent a precise, fruitful period (1930–5) at the service of Hollywood before returning decisively to Broadway for their greatest critical successes, *On Your Toes* (1936), *Babes in Arms* (1937), *The Boys from Syracuse* (1938) and *Pal Joey* (1940). The best of their Hollywood musicals is *Love Me Tonight* (1932), directed by Rouben Mamoulian, in which Maurice Chevalier sings 'Mimi' as though the song had always been there, as much a part of Paris as the Eiffel Tower. (For details of Rodgers's work with Hammerstein, see Hammerstein's entry.)

Rodgers's greatness as a melodist – truly a matter, as always in the tonal tradition, of deep emotion conveyed through harmony as well as tune, which is what has made so many of his songs into jazz standards – is unassailable. 'My Funny Valentine' from *Babes in Arms* reconciles the minor-key motivic intensity of **Brahms** or **Mahler** with the need for a show tune to end in the major. 'You'll Never Walk Alone' (*Carousel*) anticipates developments in pop music with its modal harmony; here and elsewhere, as with 'Climb Ev'ry Mountain' (*The Sound of Music*), Rodgers understood better than anyone the American musical's sacralizing potential, inheriting Christian musical functions and language and grafting them on to the aspirations of liberal, secular Americanism. Whether or not this now seems an imperialist project (much more noticeable in his work with Hammerstein, after World War II had engulfed the USA), there is no denying the sublimating power of Rodgers's waltzes ('I'm in Love with a Wonderful Guy', 'This Nearly was Mine', both from *South Pacific*), the tenderness of his love scenes ('If I Loved You' from *Carousel*), the folky *élan* of his gallops and two-steps (*Oklahoma!*'s title song and 'The Surrey with the Fringe on Top', 'Way

Out West' from *Babes in Arms*) and the cheerful cosiness of his domestic vision ('Getting to Know You' from *The King and I*, 'There's a Small Hotel' from *On Your Toes*, 'I Enjoy Being a Girl' from *Flower Drum Song*). The style is always recognizable, with often a last fresh application of romantic vocabulary as in the diminished sevenths of 'Bali Ha'i' (*South Pacific*) and the similar, symbolic dissonance at 'The Hills are Alive with the Sound of Music' from the show of that name.

The man Rodgers was less warm; quite the opposite of Hammerstein, and possibly exploiter of the tragic Hart, who may have been in love with him. Yet alone among the Broadway masters he founded a dynasty, for his daughter Mary Rodgers also composed shows (*Once Upon a Mattress*, 1959) and with her son Adam Guettel (*Floyd Collins*, 1996) perhaps resides the Broadway musical's best hope of a future.

Further reading

Rodgers & Hart: A Musical Anthology (1984) is the standard selection of the earlier songs; most of the Rodgers and Hammerstein musicals are still available complete in piano/vocal score. Essential books are Geoffrey Block, *Richard Rodgers* (2004) and (ed.) *The Richard Rodgers Reader* (2002); Stanley Green, *Rodgers and Hammerstein Fact Book* (1980); William Hyland, *Richard Rodgers* (1988); Ethan Mordden, *Rodgers & Hammerstein* (1992); and Richard Rodgers, *Musical Stages: An Autobiography* (1975).

STEPHEN BANFIELD

RODIN, François-Auguste-René
1840–1917
French sculptor

Rodin's early life was marred by two failures. First, after a period at the 'Petite École' (École Spéciale de Dessin et de Mathématiques) under Horace Lecoq de Boisbaudran, he was refused by the 'Grande École' (École des Beaux Arts). Second, when he submitted a bust to the Paris Salon in 1864 it was rejected. Meanwhile he earned a living by taking various craftsmanly jobs, working for jewellers, stonecutters, architectural decorators and the Sèvres porcelain factory. Only by the early 1880s were financial conditions less straitened. By that time Rodin's sculptural career had begun.

In his first full-length work, *The Age of Bronze* (1876), a gesture of anguish was transformed to one of awakening – not into erotic self-awareness, like Michelangelo's *Bound Slave*, seen six months before on a visit to Italy – but into a realm of pure thought. Accustomed only to Salon suavity, his audience accused him of working from casts of his model, Auguste Neyt. *St John the Baptist Preaching* (1878–80), another full-length bronze, this time of an Italian named Pignatelli, was less stable and coolly modelled. It displayed what Rodin himself called 'progressive development of movement'; the man, speaking as he walked, had been captured in the process of shifting his weight from foot to foot. Physically, it was a study in mobility, emotionally an impression of the way a powerfully felt message could conquer hardship and derision, historically a meditation on transition, announcement, a bridge from one era to another. Both figures have the air of a manifesto; they speak of the blindness of the present and the gigantic effort needed to transcend it. Both have the qualities of all of Rodin's work – a tension between idealization, nobility, a desire to elevate the audience, and a counterbalancing appeal to reality, the hard facts of day-to-day experience. Both figures are taken beyond their merely physical existence by thought, inspiration or faith. One reviewer compared the man in *The Age of Bronze* to a sleepwalker. Indeed, thought has provided the only escape route possible. St John concerns himself with more public issues, yet lacks any evidence whatsoever. Only his fervour can sustain him. One key issue in Rodin's art is the passionate desire to express spiritual values simply by means of physical gesture, to combine the spiritual and aesthetic. Like St John, he descended into an arena of action.

In 1880 the French Government Fine Arts Committee commissioned him to make a door. At his death *The Gates of Hell* remained unfinished. For thirty-seven years he altered over 180 figures which filled the double portal. They became an anthology of his most poignant themes and the faces and gestures he returned to most often in his life. The theme was religious, yet vital to his entire conception was a reading of **Baudelaire's** *Les Fleurs du mal*, which he illustrated. Surmounting the hosts of the damned is not God but simply a man thinking, a miniature version of his *Thinker* (1880). Of the figure he said, 'He is no longer dreamer, he is creator', an indication that once again he wished to challenge the theme of thought as an escape from the world of action. By transferring the whole of Dante into the mind of the artist he was dramatizing the divisions which most concerned him as an artist – between interiority and superficies, spirit and musculature, mind and matter – but also, perhaps, seeking vainly to heal the breach between these oppositions. The Gothic sculptors he so respected recognized no such dichotomies. Between their time and the nineteenth century some **Eliotean** 'dissociation of sensibility' had occurred, or rather some undermining caused by the 'death of God'. Rodin's religious views are obscure and possibly irrelevant. He had, however, been a member of a religious order, taking the name Brother Auguste. In his art he concerned himself with every kind of physical existence, from sanctity to high eroticism. There is an almost dogged desire to run whatever gamut the flesh could offer. Could this have concealed some search for an enabling philosophy?

The Burghers of Calais was commissioned in 1884. Taken from an incident in Froissart's *Chronicles*, it showed the sacrifice of six Calais citizens who had surrendered to Edward III during the Hundred Years' War in exchange for his ceasing an eleven-month siege of their city. One of Rodin's original plans was to fix his six statues one behind the other on the stones of the *place* outside the Calais town hall, so that they would seem to be wending their way towards Edward's camp. 'And the people of Calais of today, almost elbowing them, would have felt more deeply the tradition of solidarity which unites them to the heroes.' That proposal was rejected. Instead, the figures moved in a circle, at differing speeds and with various degrees of visible distress, united in passivity by the concordant diagonal sweep of their procession, most clearly seen from behind. As with *The Gates of Hell*, Rodin researched each of the figures fully before beginning, worked from models and made nude maquettes before clothing his characters. In *The Gates of Hell* Rodin had accepted no programme; he would work, he said, simply from his imagination. In *The Burghers of Calais* he was operating in a definable historical mode. Perhaps the need to establish and authenticate some sense of historical otherness – in Dante, in Froissart – is a familiar result of artistic estrangement in the nineteenth century. Paradoxically, if this can be seen most easily in Rodin's public, monumental pieces, it could be possible to interpret it as the indication of a deeply felt private doubt. **Bernard Shaw** reported that as he watched his own portrait being sculpted, Rodin took it through Byzantine, Mannerist and classical phases before allowing it to congeal into some final likeness. In his description we sense at once the international 'modernist' of the twentieth century, adrift in time and space. If the thinking man at the top of *The Gates of Hell* is Dante, he is also Baudelaire watching Paris being rebuilt, Tiresias or H.C. Earwicker dreaming their respective masterpieces. Are his eyes open or closed? Is he locked into history or is the whole of time his domain?

The easiest way to answer the question is by examining Rodin's greatest achievement, his *Balzac*. Honoré de Balzac had died when Rodin was ten. Working from caricatures, photographs, details remembered by acquaintances, even tailors' records, he reconstructed the figure of the paunchy, gap-toothed writer. Even at the outset it was evident that the research methods of the two men bore striking resemblances; Rodin visited the district where Balzac was born in order to study facial types. After several full-scale experiments in which his subject stood nude, he eventually hit on the idea of radical simplification; the entire body would be covered by the Dominican friar's habit he wore when writing.

> I had to show Balzac in his study, breathless, hair in disorder, eyes lost in a dream, a genius who in his little room reconstructs piece by piece all of society in order to bring it to tumultuous life before his contemporaries and generations to come.

The press pilloried the final version of *Balzac*. And, indeed, the way the great writer had been captured almost invites such treatment; the portrait is a vivid and immediate presence such as every satirist yearns to convey. Yet it is only registered, not pushed to satirical ends. The sheer arrogance of the creative mind unaware of anything except its own imaginative process is an ultimate Romantic solution. Yet for a sculptor the means of conveying the dialogue between the self and the other differs fundamentally from that of the writer. When he made a portrait of Baudelaire Rodin refused to create anything but a head, polished until it shone, eyes glazed, inviting ambiguous responses without providing any keys to unlock them. He defended his decision to dispense entirely with the body. 'With him the head is everything,' he replied. Balzac seems all body, and his body, as critics have since pointed out, is a man-size column reminiscent of a phallus; in his sheer fecundity Balzac has been transformed into an instrument of reproduction. Yet we cannot *see* writers in the act of creation. By some lateral legerdemain the spectator reads 'mind' for 'body', takes assertion for truth, interprets narcissism as genius. Rosalind Krauss, who has pointed out that the mature career of Rodin coincides with that of **Husserl**, has suggested that their attitudes may have a lot in common. The idea that meaning is synchronous with experience, the notion that if self is private and inaccessible then each of us would be two people – one to ourselves and another to others – can be paralleled in

Rodin. Absence of premeditation and fore-knowledge, best and most obviously proposed in an examination of the act of creation, and a total emotional dependence on the external gesture reveal Rodin's religion as a kind of paganism, total truth achieved by a realization that the self is what is manifested to others. 'Truth to materials' in his work takes the form of a record of the procedure by which the goal was accomplished. On the surface is the whole story of the bronze, its handling and casting. Rodin did not devise a solution to the problems raised by all of the dichotomies which beset him. But he did lodge himself securely between the poles of each, and *Balzac* reveals how brilliant a device that was.

After a century of academic dullness in sculpture, Rodin came and, as **Brancusi** said, 'succeeded in transforming everything'. Honoured and abused during his lifetime, he was seldom ignored. Private affairs were publicized, his technical prowess became legendary, and his work was fiercely attacked. A century later he remains an enigma. Rooted in academic models, he persisted in applying mythological and literary titles to his sculpture despite an uncanny grasp of modernist abstraction. Obsessed with the rehabilitation of monumental sculpture, his approach probably hastened its decline. Instrumental in encouraging **Degas** to experiment, he himself drew back from the course he may have advocated. Rodin's use of the fragment alone ensures him a place as a proto-modern. Yet as the Rodin expert Albert Elsen wrote:

Like the biblical Moses, he lived only long enough to look on the Promised Land. Not his death, however, but his steadfast adherence to naturalism and certain of its traditions prevented Rodin from entering into the new territories that were being surveyed and colonized by younger sculptors.

Further reading

See: Albert Elsen, *Rodin's Gates of Hell* (1960) and *Rodin* (1963); *Rodin, Readings on His Life and Work*, ed. A. Elsen (1965); Robert Descharnes and J.F. Chabrun, *Auguste Rodin* (1967); *The Drawings of Rodin*, ed. A. Elsen and K. Varnedoe (1972); A. Elsen, S. McGough and S. Wander (eds) *Rodin and Balzac* (1973); Victoria Thorson, *Rodin Graphics* (1975); Monique Laurent, *The Rodin Museum of Paris* (1977); R. Butler, *The Shape of Genius* (1993).

STUART MORGAN

ROETHKE, Theodore
1908–63
US poet

Born in Saginaw, Michigan, Roethke attended the University of Michigan and the University of Harvard, and subsequently taught English at Lafayette College, Pennsylvania (where he also coached tennis), Pennsylvania State College and Bennington College, Vermont, before becoming Professor of English at the University of Washington from 1948 until his death. He published his first volume of poetry, *Open House*, in 1941, and later books won him numerous awards including the Pulitzer Prize in 1964, the Bollingen Prize in Poetry, and the National Book Award.

Burdened by a fierce sense of inadequacy in the adult world, of an emotional and spiritual insufficiency, Roethke turned for succour and understanding in his early verse – particularly his second volume, *The Lost Son and Other Poems* (1948) – to the world of his childhood, imaging his quest for moral growth and enlightenment in a sensitive response to the mystery of plant life. He in fact remained fixed for inspiration throughout his life on memories of his father's greenhouse, which he called 'my symbol for the whole of life, a womb, a heaven-on-earth'. His major themes are a sense of psychological dislocation and loss of mature identity, a feeling of selflessness and awe before the organic life of flora and fauna, and (in numerous poems) an apprehension of emotional and spiritual transcendence overcoming existential anguish. Although some poems show a certain derivativeness from literary models such as **W.B. Yeats**, perhaps the majority manifest fully compensating qualities of sensory tact and achieved lyricism of an extremely high order. Much of his work is powerfully original, at once frightening in its radical imperatives and illuminating. The sequence entitled 'The Lost Son' evokes the primary forces of life in a spirit both of regressiveness and of courageous emotional enquiry. Scrutinizing the specific vegetal scenes of his boyhood, the poem wins through to a feeling of quiescence by a process of dark querulousness: 'After the dark night,' Roethke himself commented, 'the morning brings with it the suggestion of a renewing light, the coming of "Papa" ... the papa on earth and heaven are blended.' 'Open Letter' and Roethke's other essays collected by Ralph J. Mills (*On the Poet and His Craft: Selected Prose of Theodore Roethke*, 1965) provide succinct and shrewdly self-aware snippets of information about his own poetry and the stages of his writing.

With a similarly deft combination of lyrical power and profound psychological inquisition, *Praise to the End!* (1948) furthers the poet's obsession with what he called 'the dark world'. Shifting from negative moods to tactile assurance, the title poem attains momentary rest in intimate association with natural life: 'sublimation carried to its ultimate end', Roethke wrote in one of his letters (see *Selected Letters of Theodore Roethke*, ed. Ralph J. Mills, 1968).

Roethke's growth in technical accomplishment and the ever deeper exploration of his themes are genuinely all of a piece. From several fine longer sequences and individual poems, 'Meditations of an Old Woman' (*Words for the Wind*, 1958) deserves special mention: the poem impersonates and probes the valedictory thoughts of the character as she wavers through periods of alienation, pain and confusion, before reaching a tender close in which the woman finds herself at peace with Nature, with the onset of death, and with herself.

Roethke's gift is consummately sustained in this last volume, *The Far Field* (1964), which was posthumously published. Among a number of notable poems in the book, the title poem merits its place as the final expression of the poet's sublime art of marrying his intuitions of the fecundity and indeed the mysticism of life with his own lambent style, in the face of the morbid fears and emotional breakdowns from which Roethke found no respite in his personal life. It is not at all surprising that his poetry exercised a compelling appeal for younger poets such as **Sylvia Plath**; her early work collected in *The Colossus* (1960) shows the marked influence of Roethke's work and the colour of his mind.

Further reading

See: *The Collected Poems of Theodore Roethke* (1966); and Karl Malkoff's, *Theodore Roethke: An Introduction to the Poetry* (1966); Rosemary Sullivan, *The Garden Master: Style and Identity in the Poetry of Theodore Roethke* (1975); and Jenijoy La Belle, *The Echoing Wood of Theodore Roethke* (1976); Allan Seager, *The Glass House: The Life of Theodore Roethke* (1991); Jenijoy La Belle, *The Echoing World of Theodore Roethke* (1992).

JOHN HAFFENDEN

ROGERS, Carl Ranson

1902–87

US psychologist

Born in Oak Park, Illinois, Carl Rogers describes his background as one marked by close family ties, a very strict and uncompromising religious and ethical atmosphere and what amounted to a worship of hard work. Having spent two years at Union Theological Seminary, he then spent two further years at the new Institute for Child Guidance where he received an orthodox **Freudian** training prior to taking up a position as child psychologist in the Child Study Department of the Society for the Prevention of Cruelty to Children, in Rochester, New York State; here he spent twelve years during which he published *Clinical Treatment of the Problem Child* (1939) before joining Ohio State University. After five years there, he spent further periods of time at the Universities of Chicago and Wisconsin before becoming a Resident Fellow at the Center for Studies of the Person, La Jolla, California.

Rogers has been called the dean of the Encounter Movement in view of his pioneering work in relation to the development of counselling and reality-oriented psychotherapy. The appearance of *Counselling and Psychotherapy* (1942) and *Client-Centred Therapy: Its Current Practice, Implications and Theory* (1951) quickly laid the foundations of a therapeutic movement which is optimistic in philosophy, anti-elitist in posture and which challenges the rigid orthodoxy of both classical Freudianism and mid-West puritanism. Reacting against the formal therapist–patient scenario, with the therapist endowed with knowledge, technical skills and experience and the patient endowed only with his problems, Rogers re-framed the therapeutic encounter, postulating an equality between 'counsellor' and 'client', discarding much of the complex theory and jargon of psychoanalysis and emphasizing three cardinal qualities in the counsellor. The first, *empathy*, he defined as sensitive listening, an ability to enter the world and the experience of the other person; the second, *genuineness*, is defined as congruence or realness and refers to the lack of façade, professional detachment or distance on the part of the counsellor; while the third quality is *caring*, or prizing, whereby the counsellor possesses unconditional positive regard for the person who is the client. In the encounter, the crucial therapeutic activity is not treatment, interpretation, revelation or advice, but listening. The two basic beliefs that underpin Rogerian psychotherapy are that the person has a basically positive direction or, in the language of Rogers, possesses an instinctual self-actualizing tendency, and experience for the individual is the highest authority. These two beliefs, endorsed throughout the encounter movement, also underpin the remarkable plethora of so-called 'fringe' and unorthodox therapies which flowered after the Second World War in the United States, a development which

explains why Rogers was seen as one of the founders, along with Abraham Maslow and Fritz Perls, of the 'new' psychotherapies.

Most Rogerian work is done within the so-called Encounter group (*Encounter Groups*, 1977), whose optimum size ranges between six and ten members. A counsellor or facilitator encourages participants to express their true and immediate feelings about their own selves and each other and the aim of therapy is the facilitation of 'growth', a key word in this form of psychotherapy. Encounter approaches have been used not merely in psychiatry and clinical psychology but in business, education, probation and penal settings, and even in areas of political and racial conflict. Indeed, Rogers, particularly in his later writings, such as *On Becoming a Person* (1961) and *Carl Rogers on Personal Power* (1978), classifies his theories more in terms of a philosophy of living suitable for people in various walks of life rather than as a therapy for people who are sick and suffering.

Rogerian psychotherapy is an optimistic creed which posits the possibility of self-perfection for all and which rejects the notion of man as a flawed, forked animal battling with conflicting passions and impulses. It has flowered particularly in North America, and it has played a key role in the gradual movement there away from the notion of formal and expensive psychoanalysis for the relatively rich and few to a populist and widely available therapy available to the masses. In so far as Rogers's ideas have been tested, there is some support for his views on the importance of empathy, genuineness and caring, but the aims of client-centred therapy are difficult to evaluate in more specific terms and the applicability of such theories to the treatment of more severely ill psychiatric and other medical patients remains to be established.

As one of the founders of the Association of Humanistic Psychology, Rogers took a profoundly anti-behaviourist stance. His later writings tended towards endorsement of the 'experiential' at the expense of the 'rational' in man. While he disavowed any responsibility for the more extreme movements within the field of encounter and growth, his rejection of expertise in favour of immediacy gave the movement an intellectual respectability. While his own practice stayed close to mainstream group and individual psychotherapy, his followers took encounter ideas and developed them in therapeutic packages which involved marathon groups, gestalt theories, body massage, meditation and such physical activities as dance and jogging.

Further reading

See: C.B. Traux and R.R. Carkhuff, *Toward Effective Counselling in Psychotherapy: Training and Practice* (1967); M.A. Lieberman, I.D. Yalom and M.B. Miles, *Encounter Groups: First Facts* (1973); Brian Thorne, *Carl Rogers* (1992); David Cohen, *Carl Rogers: A Critical Biography* (2000).

ANTHONY W. CLARE

ROGERS (of Riverside), Richard George (Lord)

1933–

British architect

Richard Rogers was born in Florence of British parents. He was educated at the Architectural Association in London and, as a Fulbright Scholar, at Yale University, where he was taught by Paul Rudolf and **Louis Kahn**.

His first job was a house at Creek Vean in Cornwall, for his family. He gave it white walls and large windows, and it still looks modern today. Then, in partnership with Su Rogers and Norman and **Wendy Foster**, a foursome working as Team 4, he designed a factory at Swindon for Reliance Controls Ltd (1967) which made its mark by the visual quality of its structural system, a row of rectangular bays stiffened by tensioned diagonal braces.

He has since then committed himself to the clarity of such structural tours-de-force. The Centre Pompidou in Paris (1971–7, with Renzo Piano) is still the most famous

example of this approach. The south elevation is marked by a clear succession of bays overlaid by diagonal tension cables, in front of which an escalator mounts the facade in one continuous line. This motif has since become the logo for the Centre. The north elevation is further distinguished by the pipes and ducts displayed on the outside.

This display of the mechanisms brings architecture close to the machine, but it also endows it with a sculptural richness. There is an evident influence from the **Archigram group**, some of whom were employed as technicians. But it also expresses Rogers' attitude to architecture: an intellectual movement towards the 'real' sources of functional truth. As Louis Kahn proposed, the services become the essence of the building. Rogers proposes a functionalist architecture that goes beyond Kahn in an attempt to eliminate the arbitrary character of façade-making. Also important is a devotion to the principles of change and indeterminacy in use, of which the prophet was the Archigram guru, **Reyner Banham**.

A more balanced approach is evident in the European Court of Human Rights (1989–94) at Strasbourg. Here the elements into which the complex is broken down are not the service elements as such, but spaces of use; they stand on the ground, more expressive of human habitation, while the building takes its shape from its context on the curve of a river. This increased sensitivity towards the city is also evident in the very elegant project for the Alcazar, in Marseilles (1988), which shows a distinct sensitivity not only to an analytical idea of urban form but also to the sense of civic propriety.

Richard Rogers has been recognized as a master of modern design: he was made a Chevalier de la Légion d'Honneur in 1985, elected to the Royal Academy in 1978, awarded the Royal Gold Medal of the RIBA in 1985, knighted in 1991 and made a peer in 1996. This role enables him to influence in political and practical terms the future of architecture within Britain. He will go down to posterity as the principal author of the

Millennial Dome at Greenwich, where a tent suspended from steel gantries is given the spread and authority of an immense domed space. His designs continue to exploit the cutting edge of architectural technology. Midway through the first decade of the twenty-first century he has many projects ongoing across the world, including in China and the United States.

When invited by the BBC in 1995 to give the Reith Lectures, he chose to build his lectures around the theme of the dense modern city. Although a major pollutant, it can, he believes, be modified scientifically so that it contributes to a sustainable environment, while preserving the social vivacity that makes it vital. We may hope then to see his architecture come to terms with the demands of civic space, for cities evolve through time and are not cultural entities unless they preserve as well as innovate. There *is* a sense of continuity in Rogers' designs: at Pompidou, the structural frame behind the escalators has a classic dignity and grace, and the public place which the building forms with the ancient city of Paris is positive and useful. Its shelving shape pays tribute to one of the greatest civic spaces in the world – the Campo in Siena.

Further reading

See: Richard Rogers, *Architecture – A Modern View* (1990); Kenneth Powell (ed.) *Richard Rogers* (1994).

ROBERT MAXWELL

ROHMER, Eric

1920–

French film director

Before adopting his pseudonym, Jean-Marie Maurice Scherer was a literature teacher, newspaper reporter and novelist. In 1951 Rohmer founded *La Gazette du Cinéma* with **Jean-Luc Godard** and Jacques Rivette. When that journal failed, Rohmer joined André Bazin at *Cahiers du Cinéma*. From 1957 to 1963, he was editor-in-chief of *Cahiers*.

In his *Cahiers* articles, his book on Murnau's *Faust,* and the book on **Hitchcock** co-authored with Claude Chabrol, Rohmer continually returned to the idea that film's basis in photography makes it a medium in which reality plays a special role. Film transforms or transfigures reality, but it is reality in its ambiguity and mystery – life and not its mere semblance – that is projected on the screen. 'I do not say, I show,' Rohmer writes. 'I show people who move and speak. That is all I know how to do; but that is my true subject.'

Rohmer made several short films before *Le Signe du lion* (1959), his first feature. However, it was the six 'Moral Tales' (*La Boulangère de Monceau*, 1963, *La Carrière de Suzanne,* 1963, *La Collecteuneuse,* 1967, *Ma Nuit chez Maud,* 1969, *Le Genou de Claire,* 1970, and *L'Amour l'après-midi,* 1972) that established his artistic identity. Most Rohmer films are contemporary romantic comedies. Set in a milieu of articulate young people free of material concerns that might distract them from their love lives, they revolve around women who follow their own hearts, not books, but also feature male characters who are trained in philosophy and are for ever charting, through books, those women's ways of thinking and living.

Rohmer is in the great French tradition of such dramatists as Corneille, Marivaux and Musset, whose characters likewise enjoy the leisure to converse about their feelings and emotions and display the ability, and the interest in their experience, to explain themselves with intelligence and passion. The difference is that Rohmer's art is film, not theatre or literature. Understanding that the people his films 'show' are not only 'characters' but also the flesh-and-blood actresses and actors who incarnate those characters, he developed an idiosyncratic method of composing his screenplays. He conducts extensive interviews with his actors and especially his actresses – conversations that last for months – that allow him to model his characters so precisely on their 'originals' that they emerge on film with the very breath of life.

With the 'Comedies and Proverbs' (*La Femme de l'aviateur*, 1981; *Le Beau marriage*, 1982; *Pauline à la plage*, 1983; *Les Nuits de la pleine lune*, 1984; *Le Rayon vert*, 1986; *L'Ami de mon amie*, 1987), Rohmer returned to the romantic relationships of contemporary young French men and women.

His 'Tales of the Four Seasons' (*Conte de printemps*, 1990; *Conte d'hiver*, 1992; *Conte d'été*, 1996; *Conte d'automne*, 1998) reveal the director, in his seventies, to be in top form. In *Conte d'hiver*, the female protagonist is taken by her philosopher friend to Shakespeare's *Winter's Tale*. When Leontes expresses astonishment at an art capable of instilling in a statue the very breath of life, who can doubt that in this late work Shakespeare is reflecting on theatre, or that Rohmer, in his late work, is thinking of his own art of film, which promises to bring not words but the *world* to life?

In his eighties, Rohmer is still breaking new ground. *L'Anglaise et le duc* (2001), set during the French Revolution, is a costume drama – as were the two great films sandwiched between the 'Moral Tales' and 'Comedies and Proverbs', *Die Marquise von O …* (1976), his faithful adaptation of the Kleist novella, and the stylized *Perceval* (1978) – that not only addresses political issues with a directness unprecedented in Rohmer's oeuvre, but also employs CGI technology in ways that are startlingly innovative, especially for an octogenarian. *Triple Agent* (2004), set during the Second World War, is, if anything, even more astonishing. Who would have expected Rohmer to make a spy thriller?

Further reading

Other works include: *The Taste for Beauty* (1989); *Six Moral Tales* (1980) and *Hitchcock: The First Forty-Four Films* (with Claude Chabrol, 1979). A useful critical study is C.G. Crisp, *Eric Rohmer, Realist and Moralist* (1988).

WILLIAM ROTHMAN

ROLFE, Frederick William (Baron CORVO)

1860–1913
English novelist

Rolfe was born near St Paul's Cathedral in the City of London into a family of dissenting piano-makers and, according to his brother Herbert, was 'eccentric from early youth'. At the age of fourteen he had his breast tattooed with a cross, and soon after experienced a profound vocation for the priesthood which, thwarted as it was by his own exasperating temperament, was to shadow the rest of his life.

He left school at fifteen and the lack of formal education explains an ostentatious display of learning in his works. While still in his teens he managed to become a schoolmaster, a task at which he excelled since his interest in boys went beyond obligation. But in 1886 he was received into the Roman Catholic Church and had consequently to surrender his post at Grantham Grammar School. The following year he went to study for the priesthood at St Mary's College, Oscott, where he pursued his interest in poetry, painting and photography at the expense of his devotions, and was obliged to leave.

In 1889 under the sponsorship of the Roman Catholic Archbishop of Edinburgh – another surprising contrivance – he entered the Scots College, Rome. Again he caused widespread offence and after six months had to be physically removed from the premises by the college servants. Now began his life of drifting, sponging and wild vituperation.

Rolfe took refuge with an Englishwoman, the Duchess of Sforza-Cesarini, spending the summer at her house in the Alban Hills where he met a young Italian peasant called Toto and confirmed the love for Italy which forms the background to most of his work. He reappeared in England calling himself Baron Corvo, a title he claimed the Duchess had given him, and worked as an itinerant artist, photographer and journalist, propelled round the country by debts and violent rows with friends.

As 'Corvo' he began to contribute his 'Toto' stories to the *Yellow Book* in 1895. This led to two collections, *Stories Toto told Me* (1898) and *In His Own Image* (1901), in which his favourite themes of Catholicism, paganism and pederasty are blended with a dry humour. He continued to employ the pseudonym for his lurid history *Chronicles of the House of Borgia* (1901), and his translation of the *Rubaiyat of Umar Khaiyam* (1903) from the French. But even Rolfe seems eventually to have found the title onerous, because hereafter he prefers to mislead in another way – as 'Fr Rolfe'. Besides, as Baron Corvo, his pathetic pretensions had already been exposed in well-researched detail by a newspaper in Aberdeen (where he had once resided). The author was never ascertained but to the Catholic Church's spiritual humiliation was now added social disgrace, underlined when soon after Rolfe was forced to seek shelter in a Welsh workhouse. These painful experiences fed the strains of paranoia and megalomania in his personality.

In 1899 he took an attic in Hampstead where he worked on his most famous book, *Hadrian the Seventh* (1904), whose opening pages contain a frank and vivid self-portrait. Rolfe was well able to regard himself objectively, but on the whole he preferred a far more romantic, aggressive outlook, often insufferable for others. The book is both strongly autobiographical and a dream of wish-fulfilment, a tragi-comic extravaganza of great beauty and intensity, full of thinly disguised portraits of contemporaries he wished to revile, and at the centre Rolfe as the hero George Rose, scourged by the church which, seeing itself in error, apologizes by asking him to become pope. Self-obsessed, driven inwards by loneliness and poverty, embittered by lack of recognition as an artist, lack of love as a man, Rolfe corrected it all in this baroque climax to nineteenth-century England's love–hate affair with Roman Catholicism. Just as Rolfe was a natural and gifted writer who often referred to the 'loathsome occupation of writing', so he was a devout Catholic who detested the church. *Hadrian* earned him no money but it brought him the admiration of the few, especially of the Catholic convert R.H. Benson, son of the Archbishop of Canterbury. Benson expressed his delight that Rolfe was a 'proper pagan', adding 'All sound Catholics must be that.'

Don Tarquinio, a Kataleptic Phantasmatic Romance was published in 1905, an account in voluptuous language of one crucial day in 1495 in the life of a young Roman aristocrat and outlaw. After this, nothing. Rolfe continued to write, as he put it, 'profusely and with difficulty', but he had pledged so much of his future income against loans that he came to prefer no publication at all than that someone other than himself should gain from it. His energies were bled further by the pointless literary partnerships with nonentities into which he went in search of 'the Divine Friend'. All of them, including one with Benson, disintegrated in acrimony.

In the summer of 1908 Professor R.M. Dawkins took Rolfe on holiday to Venice. He never left it. Despite enormous hardship in which he had to be increasingly grateful for his robust constitution, Rolfe found an emotional refuge there and in return added to its legends. His letters to Charles Masson Fox, published as *The Venice Letters* (ed. Cecil Woolf, 1972), were appeals for money via detailed and exuberant homosexual depictions of lagoon life. Before his death in the Palazzo Marcello from heart failure, Rolfe found a generous patron in the Reverend Justus Serjeant whose allowances briefly enabled Rolfe to indulge his fantasies for the first time. He became a tourist attraction by parading on the waters in an outrageously caparisoned boat, reclining on a leopard skin, and rowed by his boy lovers in livery.

Rolfe's 'Romance of Modern Venice', *The Desire and Pursuit of the Whole*, was not published until 1934, the same year as the book to which he owes his resurrection, A.J.A. Symons's *The Quest for Corvo*. Two other important novels were published posthumously, *Nicholas Crabbe, or The One and the Many* (1958), a picture of London literary life which stands between *Hadrian* and *The Desire* in the autobiographical trilogy wherein Rolfe recast his adult life; and *Don Renato, or An Ideal Content* (1963), the diary of a priest attached to Don Tarquinio's family in the early sixteenth century – Rolfe had suppressed it on the verge of publication in 1909.

In these large fantastic books with their love of richness and careful exaggeration, Rolfe provides an unexpected link between the works of **Charles Dickens** and **Mervyn Peake**. Bitter and crazed though he was, there is something truly heroic in his life, and in his writings a conviction and artistry which endure.

Despite the pedantry and the religiosity, Rolfe is an authentic sensualist, guiltless and spirited. His fascination with surface, his love of language, verbal invention and the tactility of prose, the brilliance of his imagery, express a joy in physical existence whose presiding deity was of the Toto type: direct, beautiful, animal, warm. Rolfe's Catholicism was a wholesome flight to the senses in a world of Victorian inhibition. His love of the Italian Renaissance grew from his vigorous distaste for English puritanism. It was in the tradition of **Pater's** and Symonds's preoccupation with pagan Greece and Rome, but it was sharper, more open and much more modern.

Further reading

See: Donald Weeks, *Corvo* (1971); Miriam J. Benkovitz, *Frederick Rolfe: Baron Corvo* (1977).

DUNCAN FALLOWELL

ROLLING STONES, The

1960s British rock band

Mick Jagger (1943–), Keith Richard (1943–), Brian Jones (1944–69), Charlie Watts (1941–) and Bill Wyman (1941–) formed their musical taste on the growing number of urban black American rhythm and blues players whose work was becoming known in England in the late 1950s. This strident strutting music of heavily rhythmic guitar, harsh harmonica wails and raw vocal style offered intense emotional excitement along with a subversive challenge to white sexual and social conventions. The Rolling Stones' emergence in the 1960s as 'The Greatest Rock 'n' Roll Band in the World' was on the development and exploitation of these roots.

Their early performance repertoire and recordings consisted of material derived directly from artists like Muddy Waters, Bo Diddley, Howlin' Wolf, Jimmy Reed, Slim Harpo and Chuck Berry. This deliberate embracing of transatlantic idiom and myth was recreated and given thrilling freshness through Jagger's extraordinary voice. Early in 1962 he had bitten off the tip of his tongue in a gym mishap, which radically altered his delivery and lent extra lasciviousness to the sexual ambiguities of songs like 'I'm a King Bee' and 'Walking the Dog' (both on *The Rolling Stones*, 1964). In the still highly repressed climate of late-Tory, post-Profumo Britain, the erotic rhythmic assertiveness and unabashed suggestiveness of lyric constituted a threat to the bourgeois citadel. This was augmented by a public posture of cynicism and defiance, carefully orchestrated by Andrew Loog Oldham, the group's manager. Deliberately shunning the **Beatles'** whimsical charm, and refusing the popular music form of consolatory romantic love, the Stones marketed a mood of aggressive anger which caught a genuine feel of the times, despite being initially channelled through rural and urban Negro frustration;

With their fourth and fifth LPs (*Aftermath*, 1966, and *Big Hits* (*High Tide and Green Grass*), 1966), Jagger and Richard largely turned their backs on borrowed material in favour of their own compositions. Songs like 'Satisfaction', 'Paint It Black', 'Get Off of My Cloud' and '19th Nervous Breakdown' relocated the target of a ferocious resentment firmly within experience of drugs and capitalist media neurosis. Elements of nihilism and sado-masochism were central to the group's work in the 1960s, and were to endure in its productions. Another central element was trans-sexualism. Jagger's stage act as a non-musician had always been provocatively athletic, partly from childhood agilities acquired from his physical education instructor father, partly from imitation of James Brown. Through androgynous make-up and gesture, and sexually cajoling voice distortion, he questioned the supposed rigid divide between male and female in a manner broad enough to include self-mockery. Overt transvestism, later to be copied *ad nauseam* in the rock world, was broached with Jerry Schatzberg's publicity photograph for the single 'Have You Seen Your Mother, Baby, Standing in the Shadow?' (1966). Apocalyptic, primeval atmospheres of bacchanalian violence were projected through a version of rhythm and blues deliberately jagged, hard and flashy, with some tracks (such as 'Jumpin' Jack Flash', on *Through the Past Darkly*, 1969) partially recorded on cassette to achieve this effect.

The vast youth following for this symbolic desecration of public order produced hysterical establishment reaction. Systematic harassment of the group by media and police culminated in the arrest of Jagger and Richard, and their sentencing to imprisonment on petty drugs offences. The convictions were quashed on appeal, not without some atypical assistance from a *Times* leader ('Who Breaks a Butterfly on a Wheel?', 1 July 1967), which drew a parallel with the hounding of Stephen Ward in the Profumo affair, and suggested that the case was 'a symbol of the conflict between the sound traditional values of Britain and the new hedonism'. Further cannabis charges against Brian Jones were partially responsible for his leaving the group in 1969 and his apparent suicide that year in the swimming pool of his Sussex house, where A.A. Milne had written *Winnie the Pooh*.

Late 1960s political ferment was superficially reflected in *Beggars Banquet* (1968) with 'Factory Girl', 'Salt of the Earth' and notably with 'Street Fighting Man', taken by many as an invitation to storm the barricades, but in fact proposing rock 'n' roll as a substitute area for revolutionary action. The invitation to ecstatic participation which was a feature of music festivals of the period gave serious

encouragement to a vague diabolism in the group's work. Brian Jones's fascination with the Dionysiac musical rituals of the Moroccan Bou Jeloud (*Joujouka*, 1972) was registered in *Their Satanic Majesties Request* (1967), and developed specifically in 'Sympathy for the Devil' (on *Beggars Banquet*), the number Jagger was singing at the Altamont Speedway, California, in 1969, while below him Hell's Angels bodyguards stabbed to death a young black. This sacrificial death flowed with seeming inevitability from the demand for adulatory homage exerted by gods, devils and stars alike. It nullified the optimism of the Woodstock generation. Lucifer resurfaces in 'Midnight Rambler' (on *Let It Bleed*, 1969), with Jagger incorporating words from the confession of the Boston Strangler. Nevertheless, *Let It Bleed* presents a synthesis of the Stones' musical excellence across a range of rock, blues and country styles.

In the 1970s their politics of delinquency became increasingly dominated by camp theatricality and international drug-culture chic, purveyed through lavishly staged shows and some powerful recordings.

Further reading

Other works include: *The Rolling Stones No. 2* (1965); *Out of Our Heads* (1965); *Between the Buttons* (1967); *Get Yer Ya Yas Out* (1970); *Sticky Fingers* (1971); *Exile on Main Street* (1972); *Goats Head Soup* (1973); *It's Only Rock 'n' Roll* (1974); *Black and Blue* (1976); *Some Girls* (1978); See: David Dalton, *The Rolling Stones* (1972); Roy Carr, *The Rolling Stones* (1976); *The 'Rolling Stone' Rock 'n' Roll Reader*, ed. Ben Fong-Torres (1974); P. Norman, *The Stones* (1984); S. Booth, *The Adventures of the Rolling Stones* (1985); G. Giuliano, *Paint It Black* (1994).

JOHN PORTER

ROOSEVELT, Franklin Delano

1882–1945

US statesman

As president from 1933 to 1945 Roosevelt radically transformed American government in policies, process and politics, while advancing a massive programme of economic reform and leading the nation to victory over totalitarian aggression. These achievements had profound long-run effects on the political order of the United States and of the world at large

Physically paralysed by polio from the age of thirty-nine, his victorious struggle with pain, depression and immobility was a spiritual rebirth, engendering in him sympathy with human frailty, serene self-assurance and a passion, as he said in his famous Inaugural of 1933, for 'action and action now'. Facing a country devastated by the great depression, he launched the New Deal, a programme of government intervention breaking sharply with the 'rugged individualism' of the past. This widening of scope led to a centralization of power in the federal government and in the presidency. FDR not only directed this nationalization of policy and process, but also evoked and masterfully led a electoral coalition which on balance kept the Democratic party in power at all levels for the next generation

In what way were these achievements the work of FDR? One can think of the New Deal as simply a string of the ad hoc reactions of an ambitious pol to group pressures, thereby inferring that he was no statesman but a wheeler-dealer and/or lucky figurehead. In the many and varied programmes of the New Deal, however, one sees certain common purposes which testify to an ideology. This outlook identified two problems which had been emerging in recent decades of industrialization. They were such economic concentration and economic deprivation as to create a severe imbalance of power and wealth between the two extremes, which FDR personalized as the 'economic royalists' and 'the forgotten man'. Accordingly the solutions attempted by the New Deal were directed at redressing this imbalance by programmes of empowerment and entitlement.

In fundamentals Roosevelt did not originate, but inherited this assessment of problems and solutions from the Progressive movement exemplified by President Theodore Roosevelt, his cousin and the idol of his youth, and President Woodrow Wilson, whom he served as assistant secretary of the navy. Progressivism, moreover, was part of a broad political movement in the Western world in the late nineteenth century away from individualism and towards collectivism. In the capitalist democracies this movement gave rise to the welfare state of the twentieth century. Usually, this reaction to the industrial economy also produced a strong socialist party. Not in the United States, however, and Roosevelt reflected this preference when he named his cause 'liberalism'. He thereby introduced this term into common use in American political discourse, proclaimed in effect that his proposals did have an ideology and distinguished it from socialism. This curious adoption of the term, which traditionally had denominated the individualist creed, Roosevelt owes to the example of the radical programme of the Liberal government of 1908–16 founding the welfare state in Britain. When one examines how the New Deal performed a similar role in the United States, the British comparison brings out the distinctively American/Rooseveltian innovations, such as the different ways of institutionalizing the principle of social insurance and the needs of organized labour. The pressures of the industrial order in general and its current collapse in particular could be perceived and confronted in different ways. Those tumultuous times generated a great array of isms. What Roosevelt called 'liberalism' defined the ends and means which his ambition needed if he was to choose among these possibilities.

In foreign affairs Roosevelt's greatest achievement was his leadership of the great victories over the Axis powers. The magnitude of the American effort in preparing for war and in four years of fighting was prodigious. In the Pacific, victory over the Japanese was won virtually alone by the Americans, climaxing in their use of the atom bomb. In the European theatre, although the Russians were almost entirely responsible for the German defeat, the American contribution was indispensable. In these achievements of American power Roosevelt's leadership was to bring a reluctant and isolationist nation to the brink of war and then to direct and invigorate its military and industrial response once it had been attacked. In the conduct of the war, he dealt with its political implications in the company of **Churchill** and **Stalin**. Their decisions were mainly concerned with the international order following the peace whose goals Roosevelt set forth repeatedly as the Four Freedoms of speech, of religion, from want and from fear, 'everywhere in the world'. This new order of peace and justice he sought to realize and safeguard by the establishment, largely under his inspiration, of the United Nations.

What are the long-run impacts of FDR's achievements? In the United States, despite swings in public policy between public choice and market choice, the political culture basically supports the institutions of the welfare state and managed capitalist economy, which were established by Roosevelt, and developed by his like-minded successors. Thanks in some degree to the success of American liberalism, socialism is no longer a serious model elsewhere in the contemporary world. On the other hand, Roosevelt's global vision has suffered severe disappointments. The Russian veto prevented the UN from coping with the great post-war conflict of the Cold War, the American policy of Soviet containment being effected thanks to the North Atlantic Treaty Organization and the nuclear stand-off. One happy survival has been 'the special relationship' between Britain and the United States which emerged during the war and has continued to this day.

Despite the failures of the UN in practice, the principles which Roosevelt intended it to serve have lived on and flourished as the powerful worldwide movement for universal human rights. When one reflects on such statements of purpose as the Four Freedoms 'everywhere in the world', the promise seems utopian and even dangerous. For here is not merely the promise of the negative rights of the old League of Nations to protect member

nations against attack, but also the promise of collective action to enforce within nations the positive rights of democracy and social justice. The echo of Rooseveltian liberalism is unmistakable. But surely the mightiest of the unintended consequences of his achievements has been the emergence of the United States as the superpower. FDR did not foresee this eventuality. But it was a massive side-effect of the enormous economic and military potential achieved and demonstrated by the United States during World War II and the Cold War. As the UN displayed its incapacity, this superpower found itself confronting those grand Rooseveltian commitments to secure human rights universally 'everywhere in the world'.

Further reading

See: James MacGregor Burns, *Roosevelt: The Lion and the Fox* (1956); Arthur M. Schlesinger, Jr, *The Age of Roosevelt* (3 vols, 1957–60); and Frank Freidel, *Franklin D. Roosevelt* (4 vols, 1952–73). The most recent major study is Conrad Black, *Franklin Delano Roosevelt: Soldier of Freedom* (2003.): superficial and grandiose as interpretation, but at 1,280 pages encyclopaedic as a compilation of facts, with a huge bibliography.

SAMUEL H. BEER

ROSSETTI, Christina Georgina
1830–94
English poet

The nineteenth century is full of examples of lives which imitate and fulfil the principles and intentions of art, and among the most interesting of these in terms both of personality and career is that of the subdued and somewhat enigmatic figure of Christina Georgina Rossetti. The innumerable likenesses of her by painters and photographers (notably her brother **Dante Gabriel Rossetti** and that most distinguished of amateurs **Lewis Carroll**) testify to her remarkable ability to represent, better perhaps than a professional model, a prevailing artistic idea of form and intelligence towards which the more thoughtful Victorians could stretch out. As the Virgin in her brother's superb treatment of the Annunciation, *Ecce Ancilla Domini* (though she was merely one among several types studied for the figure), she contributed, not only through her facial features but through a characteristic expression of sombre intuitiveness, to a species of womanhood far removed from the mixture of upholstery and 'accomplishments' which constituted the orthodox mid-century ideal of femininity. Yet she was not, in any declared sense, a feminist, and her life was well characterized by her brother William Michael as 'replete with the spirit of self-postponement'.

Her upbringing and childhood world were as ordinary as being the daughter of a free-thinking Neapolitan *improvvisatore* and an Anglican schoolmistress, whose Italian father had written a successful horror story before committing suicide, would allow. In the atmosphere of the Rossetti household, noisy with 'fleshy good-natured Neapolitans, keen Tuscans, emphatic Romans' and the *enragé* painter friends of her brothers (including Millais and **Holman Hunt**, with whom they banded together as the Pre-Raphaelite group) Christina herself was a shrewd and tranquil presence, partly owing, as contemporaries were aware, to a natural vein of indolence, and partly to a love of solitude and retirement which made many of her acquaintance wonder why she shrank from joining any of the contemplative religious societies which Tractarianism and the reviving interest in Romanism had made popular.

Certainly her concerns were more frankly devotional than those of either William Michael, who substantially supported his family on the earnings of a civil service clerk, or Dante Gabriel, for whom religious subjects were simply the fuel to a tumid visual imagination. Christian faith played a large part in her rejection of two suitors, to both of whom she was nevertheless deeply attached. In deference to her scruples the Catholic painter James Collinson converted to Anglicanism, but a deep pang of conscience sent him back to Catholicism and lost him Christina. Religious issues were again involved in her estrangement from Charles Bagot-Cayley, though she continued to love and esteem him. She seems, indeed, to have meditated entering a convent on various occasions, but the thoughts which finally gave her pause are powerfully conveyed in her poem 'The Convent Threshold'.

Much of her later life had, in any case, those qualities of retirement built into it for which she most craved. It is impossible to view her role as an affectionate daughter and sister and a long-suffering invalid without relating these to her evident desire to distance herself from a world whose more trivial realities meant less and less to her. The preoccupation of the Pre-Raphaelite circle with a romantically envisaged medieval past, linked as this obsession was with ideas which, voiced by **Ruskin** and **Morris**, were to create a marked and enduring strain in modern English liberal culture, found a ready echo in Christina's poetry, some of the very best written in the century's later decades and only recently starting to earn a reappraisal. Her diction is correspondingly touched with moments of High Art quaintness, and like Morris, Jean Ingelow and others of her generation, she is heavily influenced by the form, rhythm and vocabulary of the early English ballads.

The themes of her poems reflect her concern with retirement, not simply from the life around her, but from existence itself. She is arguably the most morbid of all the Victorian poets, in an age which invested death with a unique quality of melodrama. Yet her treatment of dying and burial is calm, reflective and wholly lacking in sentimentality or hysteria. Her imagination is of a type which builds upon the positive aspects of worldly renunciation without gloom or regret, and in certain of her shorter pieces she comes curiously close, both in mood and in the assurance of her technique, to the writers of the seventeenth-century meditative tradition which was being rediscovered in the years immediately before her death in 1894.

Like her brother Dante Gabriel she was an accomplished sonneteer, with a firm grasp of the medium's more flexible and immediate qualities which relates works such as her 'Monna Innominata' (from *A Pageant and Other Poems*, 1881) to Mrs Browning's influential 'Sonnets from the Portuguese' and distinguishes Christina from the jewelled preciosity of some of her male imitators of the 1890s. Of her longer poems the finest are unquestionably the allegorical *Prince's Progress* of 1866 and the almost insidiously subtle *Goblin Market* of 1862, a tale of sin and redemption which, both in overtones and undertones, held a powerful appeal for her contemporaries. Hers is a quiet, authoritative voice, not obviously linked with any literary trend except those she created for herself, and her work, after the inevitable period of rejection, now commands an increasing critical interest.

Further reading

See: William M. Rossetti, *The Family Letters of Christina Georgina Rossetti* (1908); R.W. Crump (ed.) *The Complete Poems of Christina Rossetti* (3 vols 1979–90); A.H. Harrison, *The Letters of Christina Rossetti* (4 vols, from 1990). See also: Margaret Sawtell, *Christina Rossetti: Her Life and Religion* (1955); Lona Mosk Packer, *Christina Rossetti* (1963); Georgina Battiscombe, *Christina Rossetti* (1965); A. Chapman, *The Afterlife of Christina Rossetti* (2000).

JONATHAN KEATES

ROSSETTI, Dante Gabriel (Gabriel Charles Dante ROSSETTI)

1828–82

English painter and poet

More than that of most creative men, Rossetti's was a divided nature. At its simplest this is reflected in his Anglo-Italian background out of which came the translations from Dante (who was always an obsession, hence the transposition of his Christian names, and who was drawn, like most of Rossetti's iconography, from a not wholly imaginary time when the Renaissance overlapped the Middle Ages) and the early Italian poets (1861, revised as *Dante and His Circle*, 1874). At its deepest was an impossible conflict between the spiritual and the sensual which he attempted to overcome by transferring to art much that had previously belonged to religion and to sexual love, hence the charge of fleshliness made in poetry by Robert Buchanan (*The Fleshly School of Poetry*, 1871) and in painting by **Holman Hunt**, who in a letter as early as 1860 said that Rossetti's picture *Bocca Baciata* was 'remarkable for gross sensuality of a revolting kind'. The assertion of the flesh was of course an urgent need in Rossetti's day, although it is typical of his neurosis that he was never comfortable with the nude.

The ambivalence of his origins, aggravated by a patchy education in London (where he was born and where, on the whole, he lived) made Rossetti both pugnacious and socially sensitive. He was a natural leader but his confidence and powers of application were constantly undermined by an excess of self-questioning. He was lazy and brooding, and therefore came to venerate inspiration – always a woman. He was extremely vulnerable to criticism and suffered from periods of persecution mania. He disliked showing in public and stopped doing so as soon as his reputation was made, retaining the copyright of his pictures to prevent their unauthorized exhibition. He was an exaggerated Romantic, not a Decadent, because in him remorse was pitched as high as passion and he vibrated helplessly between these two points of command. The only possibility for blunting this conflict was the horrible descent into melancholy. His work is dominated by the autumnal mode, but never was this mode more vehement.

In the heyday of bohemianism in London and Paris, when the writings of **Ruskin** and **Baudelaire** had revived the romance of the artistic life, Rossetti's was as artistic as any. His was the originating genius of the Pre-Raphaelite movement. He and Elizabeth Siddal (known as 'Guggums') were the classic

Pre-Raphaelite couple, imprisoned by guilt, anxiety and death. She took to veronal, gave birth to a dead child, and within two years of their marriage killed herself. Stricken by a bad conscience, Rossetti buried a manuscript of poems with her. But in 1869, seven years later, at the prompting of Charles Howell who supervised the macabre operation, the manuscript was exhumed and published as *Poems* (1870) – naturally to great acclaim. In that year Rossetti also completed his portrait of Elizabeth, *Beata Beatrix*, perhaps his greatest picture. Yet he was unable to exorcize her – on the contrary, he attempted to make contact through seances. Buchanan's attack precipitated a collapse in 1872 and Rossetti tried to commit suicide by swallowing a bottle of laudanum: his morbidity had been made insufferable by an obsession for **William Morris's** wife, Jane. But the tortured dreamer was also a hard-headed man of business. He derived a large income from the *nouveau riche* magnates of the north of England (*Astarte Syriaca*, his most ambitious portrait of Jane Morris, was commissioned by Clarence Fry for two thousand guineas) and was tough in his dealings with clients. Many of his finest pictures are now to be found in the public galleries of Manchester and Liverpool. Rossetti became addicted to chloral, taken originally for insomnia, and was helped through his last years by Watts-Dunton and finally Hall Caine.

It is understandable that a man for whom art was simply a more vivid form of life should extend his activity into literature and aesthetics generally. His poetry provides a link in the strain of mysticism which passes between Blake and **W.B. Yeats**, although in Rossetti's case this is usually expressed as 'yearning'. But it is the distinctive intensity of his visual imagination which continues to be fascinating, especially in his portraits of women where his sexuality is made ferocious by denial. The Rossetti woman was such an extreme type that she came to be fixed in the popular mind as the Art Woman, to be replaced eventually not by Isadora Duncan but by the attenuated figures of Edith Sitwell

and **Virginia Woolf**. Heavy, fecund, the embodiment of a lust made drowsy with the weight of accumulated delay, but capable, when aroused by the inflictions of sado-masochism, of an overwhelming congress, she is empress-like in scale, but whether one sees her as an Amazon or a cow depends on mood because she is both (Rossetti's menagerie at Tudor House in Chelsea included a Brahmin bull because he said its eyes reminded him of Jane Morris's). These female figures, like Michelangelo's male nudes on the Sistine ceiling, border on the grotesque, even on the comic, but the laughter is uneasy and they remain very powerful presences, unlike anything else in art.

Rossetti liked to play up his English aspect but it was the infusion of his warm Mediterranean blood into the English artistic world which supplied the audacity which the other Pre-Raphaelites required in order to fulfil themselves; because the Pre-Raphaelite movement, even when it thought otherwise, was fundamentally dedicated to a reawakening of the senses in a society dulled by habits of prudery and obligation.

Millais was technically more accomplished, Holman Hunt more moral, and **Burne-Jones** a purer master, but it is the art of Rossetti which expresses fully that crucial moment in nineteenth-century culture when the challenge to decorum is held in a paralysis of tragic passion.

Further reading

See: Max Beerbohm, *Rossetti and His Circle* (1922); Evelyn Waugh, *A Life of Rossetti* (1928); Oswald Doughty, *A Victorian Romantic* (1949); Christopher Wood, *The Pre-Raphaelites* (1981); J. Marsh, *Dante Gabriel Rossetti* (2000).

DUNCAN FALLOWELL

ROSTAND, Edmond

1868–1918

French poet and dramatist

Edmond Rostand was born in Marseilles into a prosperous family on 1 April 1868. He studied, but never practised, law, and devoted most of his life to the theatre. His plays were interpreted by some of the most famous actors and actresses of the day: Coquelin, Sarah Bernhardt (for whom the Duc de Reichstadt in *L'Aiglon*, verse drama, 1900, was written), Lucien Guitry, de Max, and many others. Except in his last two plays he achieved an overwhelming popular success. The last twenty years or so of his life he lived principally in Arnaga, his estate in the South of France. He died in 1918.

Rostand is obviously not today a popular dramatist, nor is he favourably treated by those few critics who bother to mention him at all. Yet *Cyrano de Bergerac* (verse heroic comedy, 1897) is widely read and fairly frequently revived, if only because it provides a spectacular 'vehicle' in Coquelin's old role of Cyrano. The latest of several film versions, with Gerard Depardieu taking the title role in 1990, won both critical claim and large audiences. *L'Aiglon* too is read and acted in France and was revived on British television some years ago, though it is too lachrymose and chauvinistic for modern taste.

The popularity of the plays in their own day largely depended on their defiant patriotism, their colourful, self-indulgent lyricism, their wit and astounding verbal acrobatics and their uninhibited Romantic challenge to the grim Naturalism of European literature of their time. The Dreyfus scandal may also have helped to give French audiences a taste for romantic entertainment, and particularly for such a self-congratulatory image of France as Rostand's plays provided. He himself came out strongly in support of Dreyfus in the controversy, which was at its height when *Cyrano de Bergerac* was produced.

Rostand's greatest debt is clearly to **Victor Hugo's** dramas and dramatic theories about the mixture of the sublime and the grotesque. He follows Hugo in his elaborate plots, his combination of lyricism and melodrama – though in Rostand the lyricism is more strained and the melodrama less portentous heavy-handed. The characters too are for the most part taken from the Romantic stock,

where an unpromising physique is almost a guarantee of a heart of gold, and where boundless if rather simple-minded ambitions are thwarted by the heroes' incapacity for ordinary action. But, whereas Hugo's heroes live in an unambiguous, if improbable, world of virtue and misconduct – Lucrèce Borgia knows she's a bad lot – Rostand's *La Princesse Lointaine* (1895) and *L'Aiglon*, for example, breathe a far more sentimental and decadent air: the moral worlds of these plays are far more ambiguous.

Though *La Princesse Lointaine* suffers from its echoes of *Phèdre* and *Tristan und Isolde* and though Rostand's sensibility makes *L'Aiglon* almost unendurably mawkish, his main virtue is an unerring, if somewhat extravagant, sense of what goes in the theatre. The poetry is too lush, the verbal tricks and clever rhymes become an irritating mannerism, and his habit of endlessly embroidering a verbal effect can be tiring; but he has a wonderful skill in painting a scene, managing intricate crowd conversation and movement, and developing an argument, – qualities that all but triumph over his obvious weaknesses. His dialogue is sparkling and varied. Above all, he has a sense of humour and an eye for the absurd: despite his models, his plays are rarely unintentionally funny. In fact, it is as a writer of comedy that he excels: if *La Princesse Lointaine, La Samaritaine* (biblical verse drama, 1897) and even *L'Aiglon* are for one reason or another virtually unreadable today, there is still life in *Les Romanesques* (verse comedy, 1894) despite the pawkiness of this little Romeo and Juliet-inspired comedy, while the atmospheric and ingenious *La Dernière Nuit de Don Juan* (dramatic poem, posthumous) is in its way masterly, and *Chantecler* (verse play, 1910) though difficult to imagine in the theatre, and again much too long-winded, has moments of real beauty and inspiration.

If Rostand is a flawed dramatist in general, *Cyrano de Bergerac* is a triumph. It has been criticized for being improbable – which it is; psychologically inconsistent – which it is; historically inaccurate, and many uncomplimentary things (all in their way true) besides.

But here in this one play Rostand has created a masterpiece, almost despite himself. His sentimentality, his ingenuity, his verbosity, his skill in the direction of crowd scenes, his outrageous rhymes, even his exaggerated and schematic characterization; above all the sheer energy – the famous *panache* – carry the audience along. The very theatricality of the play saves it from the fate of much Romantic drama: it has the courage of its own artificiality. Whereas Hugo's heroes demand – impossibly – to be taken seriously, Rostand's hero is protected by the irony with which he is presented: he is sublime *because* he is absurd. The play's artificiality and excess allow the spectator to enter imaginatively into a purely theatrical context, where improbability ceases to be an obstacle to our acceptance of the hero. The nineteenth-century Romantic heroes generally fail to convince because we are aware that for all their 'historical' authenticity they belong in the property-box. Cyrano lives only in the imagination: Rostand has invented a folk-hero whom we can accept on much the same terms as we accept Bluebeard or Baron Munchhausen. We can forget that Rostand was at best a derivative minor poet: *Cyrano de Bergerac* may not have the literary quality of Musset's *Lorenzaccio*, but between them they show that Romantic tragedy and heroic comedy should not necessarily be despised.

Further reading

See: *Plays of Edmond Rostand*, trans. Henderson D. Norman (2 vols, 1921); Jean Suberville, *Le Théâtre d'Edmond Rostand* (1919); R. Gerard, *Edmond Rostand* (1935); Hobart Ryland, *The Sources of the Play Cyrano de Bergerac* (1936); Sue Lloyd, *The Man who was Cyrano: A Life of Edmond Rostand* (2003).

JOSEPH BAIN

ROTH, Philip Milton

1933–

US writer

Twenty or more novels on from *Goodbye, Columbus* (1959), with which he made his bow, Philip Roth occupies a simply luminous place not only in the Jewish American literary roster but in America's canon-at-large. Newark-born, educated at Rutgers, Bucknell and the University of Chicago, much resident in Europe, husband until their divorce to the actress Claire Bloom, and editor of an influential East European author-series, he has frequently been enrolled in a kind of Jewish imaginative collective along with **Saul Bellow**, Bernard Malamud, **Norman Mailer** or Cynthia Ozick. Nor have other affinities gone unnoted, whether America's literature of manners from **Henry James** to **John Updike** or Europe's legacy of Gogol, **Kafka** and **Kundera**. But few would deny Roth ever to have been his own man, the fierce, often comic-sardonic spilling of Jewish family secrets, the repertoire of style and irony.

His first book gave the signposts for this daring, whether *Goodbye, Columbus* as the title novella's wonderfully furtive encounter of the lower-class Neil Klugman with the affluent family of Brenda Patimkin as Jewish princess, or an accompanying story like 'The Conversion of the Jews' with the boy Ozzie Freedman's zany, precocious questioning of Rabbi Marvin Binder as to the Jews as Chosen People in an American republic of equals or God's credibility in the face of science. A shared virtuosity marks out other early fiction, whether *Letting Go* (1962), his Jamesian-Jewish anatomy of campus and suburb, *Portnoy's Complaint* (1969), his best-seller of a life literally haunted by masturbatory over authentic value and told, pilloryingly and with coruscating wit, as though from the psychiatrist's couch, *Our Gang* (1971) as his devastating send-up of Nixonism, or *The Great American Novel* (1973) which turns on baseball as obsession, at once pastime and key to American life. It little surprises that firestorms frequently have flared around him for his alleged Jewish betrayals, self-hate or derogation of women, not least among them Sophie Portnoy as Jewish mother.

Roth has also laid his claim to having written two *romans fleuve*. His 'Nathan Zuckerman' series makes a first appearance in

My Life as a Man (1975), sexual adventuring as the mirror of a larger American gender politics. *The Ghost Writer* (1979) offers the finely nuanced New England portrait of generational literary influence and competition with its footfalls in Roth's own relationship to Bernard Malamud. *Zuckerman Unbound* (1981) unravels a chronicle of the glut, screens and false turns attendant upon literary fame. In *The Anatomy Lesson* (1983), Rembrandt's 1632 painting serves as the metaphor of Zuckerman's own medical stasis as a writer. *The Prague Orgy* (1985) uses Zuckerman's notebooks for its take on Yiddish heritage and the writer's life under Soviet rule. *The Counterlife* (1987) best can be thought a parable of art's transforming powers of life over death told as the history of the brothers Nathan and Henry Zuckerman. *Patrimony: A True Story* (1991) invokes painful son and father intimacy, the latter dying of a tumour, as fact–fiction memoir. *I Married a Communist* (1998) explores the play of writerly self and persona within the McCarthy era. With *The Human Stain* (2000) Roth puts the Clinton era under ironic purview, identity politics to latter-day class hierarchy, PC to Viagra. David Kapesh, Comp. Lit. academic and writer, serves as main figure and viewpoint in three novels: *The Breast* (1972), Roth's reflexive American adaptation of Kafka's *The Metamorphosis*; *The Professor of Desire* (1977) as the ongoing sexual-autobiographical diary of the campus as a species of shadow-life; and *The Dying Animal* (2001) with its self-mocking anatomy of male sexual libido and rapacity from professor–student affairs to phone sex.

Roth's energy has little flagged as *American Pastoral* (1997), his Pulitzer-winning novel set in the Vietnam-era of the 1960s and told one more time in the voice of Nathan Zuckerman, bears witness. Its life and times of Seymour Levov, affectionately known on account of his blond hair as The Swede, admired high school athlete and spouse to a former Miss Jersey, and of his daughter Mary and her haunting act of terrorist bombing, serves to challenge the American illusion of itself as benign New World garden. It is not hard to see why he continues to be a source of controversy. But, as he confirms in *Operation Shylock* (1993), *Sabbath Theater* (1995) or *The Facts: A Novelist's Autobiography* (1988), texts given to the writer as double-voiced puppeteer or ventriloquist while themselves full of artful feint, Roth is not to be denied. He remains a contemporary of wily, unflagging invention, if Jewish bad boy then also one of American literature's vital gamesters against life reduced to cliché.

Further reading

See: John McDaniel, *The Fiction of Philip Roth* (1974); Sanford Pinsker, *The Comedy that 'Hoits'* (1975); *A Philip Roth Reader*, ed. Martin Green (1980); *Critical Essays on Philip Roth*, ed. Sanford Pinsker (1982); Hermione Lee, *Philip Roth* (1982); *Philip Roth*, ed. Harold Bloom (1986); Jay Halio, *Philip Roth Revisited* (1992); Alan Cooper, *Philip Roth and the Jews* (1996); Stephen Wade, *Imagination in Transit: The Fiction of Philip Roth* (1996); Steven Milowitz, *Philip Roth Considered: The Concentratory Universe of the American Writer* (2000); Mark Shechner, *Up Society's Ass, Copper: Rereading Philip Roth* (2003).

A. ROBERT LEE

ROTHKO, Mark

1903–70

US artist

There were two principal streams in New York Abstract Expressionism: the gestural painting of **Pollock** and **de Kooning**, and colour-field painting, of which Rothko was probably the foremost representative.

Many of his paintings in the 1930s were of isolated human beings in cities. Early in the 1940s, inspired by Surrealist automatism and by his interest in Classical mythology, he began to paint biomorphic images, as in *The Omen of the Eagle* (1942), where he hoped to evoke 'the spirit of Myth, which is generic to all myths of all times. It involves a pantheism in which man, bird, beast and tree ... merge into a single tragic idea.' The backgrounds of these paintings were thinly washed, suggesting an atmosphere suffused with a magic light. Increasingly, these washed backgrounds ousted the semi-figurative elements, in accordance with his desire to create a general and universal symbolic image. This he finally achieved by 1950, from which time on he consistently used an arrangement of soft-edged rectangles, placed vertically above each other. Nearly all his paintings from then until his death are in this format, the most usual variant being a vertical canvas with two or three horizontal rectangles. Because the image is symmetrical one is not encouraged to see it in relational terms, as one would with **Mondrian**, but on the contrary as holistic, an effect increased by the fact that the rectangles seem to fill the whole canvas. Rothko's paintings are usually extremely large, not because he wished to create a public art but, on the contrary, because he believed that the large scale made them more intimate. As he said: 'To paint a small picture is to place yourself *outside* your experience as a stereopticon view or with a reducing glass. However you paint the large picture, you are *in* it. It isn't something you command.' Rothko's scale is architectural, in that rather than a space being created within the painting, the painting – or group of paintings – modifies the real space of its environment. The mood generated is essentially contemplative and mystical. Although he greatly admired **Matisse**, Rothko's use of colour was never sensuous or hedonistic. Rather, it was a vehicle for transcendence of this world. The paintings made at the very end of his life were entirely grey and black. In 1970 he committed suicide. There is about his art something perhaps passive, certainly tragic and, above all, profoundly moving.

Further reading

See: Diane Waldman, *Mark Rothko* (1978); also the catalogue to his exhibition at the Museum of Modern Art, New York (1961); James E.B. Breslin, *Mark Rothko: A Biography* (1993); Diane Waldman, *Mark Rothko, 1903–1970* (2001).

GRAY WATSON

ROUAULT, Georges

1871–1958

French painter

Rouault was born in Paris of a poor family and received his first tuition in drawing from his grandfather, Alexandre Champdavoine, at the age of ten. At fourteen he became an apprentice in stained-glass decoration with the firm of Tamoni & Hirsch. He trained for five years, during which time he was engaged mostly in the restoration of medieval windows. In 1890 he became a student at the École des Beaux-Arts where, after studying for two years under Élie Delaunay, he entered the studio of the symbolist painter **Gustave Moreau**. He soon became the master's favourite pupil. Moreau's predilection for mystical subject-matter and style stimulated Rouault's already strong preference for religious and hieratic painting. During the 1890s he also came under the influence of the neo-Catholic writer Léon Bloy. Bloy later introduced him to the scholastic philosopher Jacques Maritain, who wrote an essay on Rouault in 1924, by which time he was acquiring an international reputation.

Rouault's first entries for the Prix de Rome, *Samson tournant la meule* (1893) and *Le Christ Mort pleuré par les Saintes Femmes* (1895), were unsuccessful and this led to a psychological crisis at the end of the decade. In 1898 he held the job of curator at the Musée Moreau for a brief period. His first exhibits at the Salon d'Automne between 1903 and 1908, having lost their explicitly religious aspects and discovered some of the recent developments in art, were to associate him in the public's mind with the Fauve painters, such as **Matisse** and Vlaminck, whose work his resembled in fierceness of form and colour, though not in spirit. The series of clowns and whores shown in 1905 caused a particular sensation on account of their almost barbaric portrayal of misery and degradation. In 1910 he received wide acclaim as a result of his first one-man show at the Galérie Druet. His fame was further advanced in 1913 when the major Parisian dealer, Ambrose Vollard, bought the entire contents of his studio. (In fact in 1947, upon the dealer's death, a large number of these canvases were returned to Rouault who burned over 300 of them.) In 1952 he was given a major retrospective in Paris and upon his death six years later he was honoured by a state funeral. During his life he became an important, if often reclusive, representative of the modernist Catholic institution. His output was large and varied and includes oil paintings, gouaches, watercolours, tapestries, enamels and graphics executed with considerable versatility. In 1929 he designed the sets and costumes for **Diaghilev's** ballet *Le Fils prodigue*.

Rouault's art is characterized by two major themes, one formal and the other iconographic. The deep luminosity of his colours, very often sombre reds and blues, and the thick, almost primitive dark lines which enclose and highlight them, reveal an obvious debt to his experience in working on stained-glass. His deep concern for the continuing health of an expressive religious art ran parallel to this adoption of certain modern aspects of style. The colour and line are thus Fauvist in one sense but highly traditional in another. Where his art is not straightforwardly religious in content, it dwells upon the outcasts of society whom **Picasso** had introduced into his work of the 'Blue' period. Clowns, acrobats and prostitutes are portrayed with an expressionist intensity more typical of German and Scandinavian artists than of French ones – although Rouault balanced this content with scathing portraits of the more successful members of society, like advocates and judges, who are antithetically opposed to the potentially redeemed failures. His work has, thus, in its imagery of revealed despair and evil, a kinship with that of the nineteenth-century satirist **Daumier**. His art, very largely drawn out of the literary inspiration of writers like Bloy and Péguy, is a visual equivalent for that area of French literary culture which combines an interest in modern form with essentially conservative intellectual concepts.

Jacques Maritain once described Bloy as 'Job on the dunghill of modern civilization', and this description would no doubt have suited Rouault. Man was, in this apocalyptic version of catholicism, a fallen creature facing a terrifying Old Testament deity. Of his own work Rouault once wrote that it was 'A cry in the night! A stifled sob! A laughter that chokes itself!'

In 1916 Rouault stopped painting and began to work on a series of graphic works, the most important of which were fifty-seven plates collectively entitled *Miserere et guerre*. These were commissioned by Vollard. The original composition was transferred by photomechanical process on to the copper plate which Rouault would then work over with a variety of engraving tools. The luminosity and strength of the finished plates are, as in the oil paintings, founded on deep colours bounded by thick expressive lines. In many respects these works echo the late canvases and prints of Rembrandt, an artist, along with Daumier, who exerted a great influence on Rouault's mature style. This can also be seen in his other major print series of the same period, *Réincarnations du Père Ubu*, *Le Cirque* and *Paysages légendaires*.

In 1929 Rouault began painting again. Although at first he struggled with his old medium he gradually overcame these problems and went on to produce a succession of masterpieces which, during the 1940s, became solely religious in content. In 1938 he was given a major exhibition of his graphic work at the Museum of Modern Art in New York and in 1945 a retrospective by the same gallery which included the large windows he had executed for the church at Assy.

Rouault was in many respects a painter apart in France. The urbanity and intellectualism common to the mainstream of the Paris school were quite at odds with the expressionist conscience he represented. He opposed an enlightenment vision of man perfected and free with his own of man fallen and bestial. His art was explicitly dogmatic and was executed from a traditional stance of the artist as scourge rather than as comforter.

His contemporary, Matisse, using a related pictorial vocabulary, was aiming at an art which would function as a '*calmant cérébral*'. He wished to transcend ethical issues by ignoring or denying the religious sense of the fatality of the self's relationship with the world. He has written, 'We must learn how to discover joy in the sky, in the trees and the flowers. How to draw happiness from ourselves, from a full working day and the light it can cast into the midst around us.' Rouault believed that this missed the religious truth of *la condition humaine*.

Further reading

Other works include: *Souvenirs intimes* (1926) and *Correspondance de Rouault et de Suarès* (1960). See: L. Venturi, *Georges Rouault* (1948); J.T. Soby, *Georges Rouault* (1945); P. Courthion, *Rouault* (1962); F. Hergott and S. Whitfield, *Georges Rouault: The Early Years, 1903–1920* (exhibition catalogue, 1993).

RICHARD HUMPHREYS

ROUSSEAU, Henri ('Le Douanier')

1844–1910

French painter

After a period in the French army, Henri Rousseau worked for some years as a minor official in the Paris toll-gate service, whence the grandiose nickname he later received: 'Le Douanier', the Customs Officer. He was in his forties before he began to paint, but he at once found his idiom and gave up his job to devote himself to art, making a living from occasional private lessons in painting and music. From 1886 onwards he regularly exhibited in Paris at the annual Salon des Indépendants, his intention clearly being to gain recognition as an artist among other artists; this aim he pursued with dignity and total dedication, even though many considered his entries to be a standing joke. His reputation grew as sponsorship came from a succession of writers and artists, whose attitude seems to have evolved from tongue-in-cheek patronage to genuine, somewhat startled

enthusiasm. The poets **Alfred Jarry** and, later, **Guillaume Apollinaire** had their portraits painted by Rousseau; Robert Delaunay became a sincere admirer and friend, while **Picasso** began collecting his pictures in the same spirit as he collected African tribal art – seeing in them a significant formal stimulus and a demonstration of the power of innocent vision. Half figure of fun, half aesthetic innovator, Rousseau was to emerge as both mascot and exemplar for the avant-garde of Fauvism and Cubism; his mixture of naivety and skill fulfilled a necessary myth of spontaneity, of inventive design liberated from academic constraints.

Almost entirely an autodidact, Rousseau kept to a narrow range of favourite subjects: principally portraits, cityscapes and exotic landscapes. The portraits, usually of neighbours and their children, give the clearest indication of his untutored hand: sitters are portrayed as monumental figures with stereotyped features standing woodenly in decorative parkland. Rousseau's cityscapes record picturesque aspects of Paris and environs, often showing bourgeois families out for a Sunday stroll in the public gardens or along the river; they are characterized by the naive artist's affection for the telling detail: the distant Eiffel Tower, an ostentatiously posed fisherman, an airship as if pinned up on the sky. The impression of whimsicality mingled with painstaking literalness modulates into something more compelling when Rousseau turns to imaginary exotic landscapes; it is indeed these which have most contributed to his reputation as a naive who somehow transcends his naivety.

Rousseau's art is certainly 'naive' in the sense that it falls short of the standards of traditional mimesis to which, it appears, he nevertheless diligently sought to conform. His figures look frozen stiff rather than simply immobile; his sense of scale is aberrant, his grasp of perspective faulty. But undismayed by such deficiencies (if indeed he ever recognized them as such), Rousseau was able to compile a repertoire of compensatory virtues. His sharply outlined and flattened figures can have a strange formal seductiveness: a chestnut tree or a standing woman take on an emblematic radiance once placed within a scene. And the meticulous rendering of detail, the insistent patterning of such repeated elements as foliage, the concern for nuances of colouring, the compulsive brushing-in of each last square inch of canvas – these symptoms of over-earnestness, of the naive's desire to produce 'the professional look' at all costs, do end up creating an idiom of intensity which has a coherence and an allurement all of its own.

Rousseau's most powerful effect – a kind of hypnotic translucency of finish – is nowhere more memorably achieved than in the series of paintings of wild beasts in exotic settings. In *The Sleeping Gypsy* (*La Bohémienne endormie*, 1897), a lion is shown nuzzling a sleeping woman beneath a desert moon. The woman, black-skinned and massive, wears a dress patterned in bright multicoloured stripes which echo the design on her pillow and the parallels of the strings on the nearby mandolin. The contrast between this visual dazzlement and the stark simplicity of the surrounding sand, hills and sky creates an effect of visual consternation and a queer mood of suspense. In *The Snake Charmer* (*La Charmeuse de serpents*, 1907), a naked negress plays her flute by the river bank. As snakes sway towards her out of the jungle, she herself remains in shadow, an inexplicable silhouette set against the gleaming water and sky: we discern only two staring eyes within the illegible blackness of her form. The impression is of hidden depths, an enigma equally suggestive of unspoken ferocity and utopian tenderness.

Several jungle paintings exploit the incongruity of setting a lady in splendid town clothes down in the middle of a profusion of tropical vegetation. Such a juxtaposition of the familiar and the extraordinary is a favourite device, and may be seen as translating Rousseau's basic project of offering us windows through which we can perceive the world in an adventurous new way. However, it cannot be claimed that the jungle pictures,

with their rampant beasts of prey, eccentric birds and tropical storms, are at all naturalistic. The animals are frequently derived from such sources as illustrations in popular encyclopaedias; the plants are thought to be largely inspired by Rousseau's visits to the tropical section of the botanical gardens in Paris, the Jardin des Plantes. And whole pictures have been shown to be the result of simplified copying from undistinguished engravings. Yet by a curious reversal, Rousseau's images are at their most compelling to the extent that they are manifestly unrealistic and thus most overtly fantastical. His most sophisticated performances arise from a fine balance between the theatrics of his jungle tableaux, where leaping jaguars and flamboyant orchids appear almost to be snipped out from cardboard, and the sheer resplendence and depth of his colours – he once boasted that he had used twenty-two variants of green in a single canvas – and no less a colourist than Gauguin is said to have envied him his command of black tones.

Elevated by the avant-garde into a kind of cult hero for Modernism, Rousseau has a claim to being seen as a central figure in the development of twentieth-century art. His influence has been traced to Surrealism and the work of De Chirico, and to the current of Magical Realism in Germany and Austria. As a naive, Rousseau also takes his place in the specific history of neo-primitive painting. Promoted in the 1920s by collectors such as Wilhelm Uhde, who placed him with other naives like Séraphine Louis and Camille Bombois, he has since been universally acknowledged as the grand master of naive art in the last century. Meanwhile, seen within a more academically respectable perspective, his work has been considered worthy of representation in the Louvre and the National Gallery in London.

How then should Rousseau finally be evaluated? It has to be said quite bluntly that some of his pictures reveal the untutored hand at its worst; they are downright incompetent and lack any saving grace in terms of impetuous colouring or artless design. Again, several paintings have that fussy prettiness which is one of the less stimulating characteristics of naive art. But above these loom the true masterpieces, from *A Carnival Evening* (*Un soir de carnaval c.* 1886) to *The Dream* (*Le Rêve* 1910), a series of works which remain marvellously authoritative and consistently appealing. These are paintings whose subject-matter may be palpably ridiculous or else merely trivial, yet whose technical execution lifts everything on to an entirely fresh expressive plane. In them, Rousseau is able to transcend all the ready-made categories and to assert his originality as the creator of an inimitable personal style.

Further reading

See: Ronald Alley, *Portrait of a Primitive: The Art of Henri Rousseau* (1978); Adolphe Basler, *Henri Rousseau* (1927); Roger Shattuck, *The Banquet Years* (1969); Wilhelm Uhde, *Henri Rousseau* (1921); Dora Vallier, *Henri Rousseau* (1961); Roger Shattuck, *Henri Rousseau* (1986); Gotz Adriani, *Henri Rousseau* (2001).

ROGER CARDINAL

RUSHDIE, Salman

1947–

British/Indian novelist

Son of a Cambridge-educated Indian businessman, Salman Rushdie was born into a Muslim family in Bombay in the year of India's independence. He was sent to England to be educated at Rugby School, which he disliked, and while he was there his family moved to the Islamic state of Pakistan. By now Rushdie had been a Muslim in Hindu India, an Indian in Pakistan, and an Asian at an English public school.

Rushdie worked as an advertising copywriter after graduating from Cambridge, and was responsible for the cream slogan 'Naughty but Nice'. During this time he published his first novel, *Grimus* (1975), which featured an American Indian searching for the meaning of life, but he only became well known in 1981 with his magic realist epic *Midnight's Children*. Comparable in scope to the work of **Gabriel García Márquez**, this was a humorous, allegorical, and ultimately critical novel that followed the recent history of India through the life of its narrator and one thousand other children born in the hour after the declaration of India's Independence. It won the Booker Prize and was acclaimed both in Britain and India, although it caused offence to Indira Gandhi; she won a libel suit against Rushdie shortly before being assassinated.

Rushdie then turned his attention to Pakistan in *Shame* (1983), a harsher, less humorous and far less affectionate book which was almost immediately banned in Pakistan. When General Zia-ul-Haq ('Old Razor Guts' in the book) died in a plane bomb in August 1988, Rushdie commented 'Dead dictators are my speciality . . . all the political figures most featured in my writing . . . have now come to sticky ends . . . This is a service I can perform, perhaps. A sort of literary contract.'

Rushdie's tendency to put noses out of joint escalated to an unforeseen level in September 1988, with the publication of *The Satanic Verses*. Still concerned with postcolonial history, as well as the nature of narrative and belief, *The Satanic Verses* dealt with Islam and included a number of 'in-jokes', hardly noticed by most Westerners, such as giving the names of Mohammed's wives to prostitutes.

Many Muslims felt this calculated irreverence was an act of treachery and apostasy, and the insiderish aspect only increased the offence. In February 1989 the **Ayatollah Khomeini**, Iran's religious leader, pronounced a *fatwa* not just on Rushdie but on all those who knowingly had anything to do with the book's production: 'I call on all zealous Muslims to execute them quickly.' A million dollar bounty was offered, later increased to 2.5 million.

The *fatwa* was of questionable legality under Islamic law, but neither Rushdie's life nor his significance would be the same again. There were a number of deaths, including that of his Japanese translator, and Rushdie went into protracted hiding, protected by the British police. His virtual confinement continued for several years, during which his second marriage, to the American writer Marianne Wiggins, cracked under the strain, and he reviewed *The Oxford Guide to Card Games* for the *Times Literary Supplement.*

Rushdie was now fully established as a *cause célèbre*, although he remained controversial in Britain: some commentators felt it was ironic that the British state (which Rushdie had earlier spoken of in the same breath as apartheid South Africa and Nazi Germany) should bear the considerable cost of protecting him. After a meeting with Islamic scholars in Christmas 1990, Rushdie affirmed the Oneness of God and the genuineness of the Prophet Mohammed's revelation, leading to his essay 'Why I Have Embraced Islam.' In 1996, however, he described this as a 'depressed and despairing moment . . . a very foolish attempt at appeasing the opposition,' adding 'I have no problem with other people's religious beliefs. I just don't happen to have any.'

Rushdie was reported to have hopes of a Nobel Prize, which has not yet materialized – **Martin Amis** claimed 'Salman even knows the names of the cats and dogs belonging to the Nobel Prize judges' – but in 1993 *Midnight's Children* was awarded the Booker of Bookers. In 1994 he published a collection of short stories *East, West*, exploring the interface and interpenetration of the title, and in 1995 another major novel, *The Moor's Last Sigh*, the multi-cultural and miscegenated family history of a Jewish Indian descended from a Muslim Sultan. The book's depiction of a Hindu fundamentalist caused it to be temporarily banned in India.

Aside from their magic realism, a genre associated with post-colonial writing, Rushdie's fictions are remarkable for their supple, polyphonic, pun-packed linguistic verve, and the teeming multiplicity of their plots and inventions: reviewers variously acclaimed one book as 'several of the best novels he has ever written' (Robert Irwin) and complained that another had 'too much too muchness'

(Michael Gorra). This multi-faceted abundance can itself be read as a post-colonial refusal to be categorized or forced to choose.

As well as declaring himself a citizen of Sarajevo, Rushdie was elected first Head of the International Writers' Parliament in 1994. The *fatwa* – perhaps the major landmark of the showdown between liberal globalization and Islamic fundamentalism before 9/11 – was lifted in 1998, but the literary merits and demerits of Rushdie's work have been all but overshadowed by his status as an icon of free speech.

Further reading

Other works include: *The Jaguar Smile* (1987), a partisan account of his time in Nicaragua; *Haroun and the Sea of Stories* (1990), ostensibly for children; *The Ground Beneath Her Feet* (1999), which led to a stage appearance with the rock band U2; and *Fury* (2000), a product of his later life in New York. His essays have been collected in *Imaginary Homelands* (1991), predominantly about post-colonial issues, and the more journalistic collection *Step Across This Line* (2002), which also contains his 2002 Tanner Lectures on Human Values as its title piece.

PHIL BAKER

RUSKIN, John

1819–1900

English writer on art and critic of society

John Ruskin was the only man of his century whose writings on painting and architecture were widely read outside specialist circles; and the extent of his influence in artistic matters has never been matched. He achieved this pre-eminence, however, without publicizing the trivial or immediately appealing aspects of art. On the contrary, he subjected his readers to a stern re-examination of the fundamental principles of art, and its connections with human personality and social behaviour.

The only child of a wealthy sherry importer, John Ruskin was educated privately in south London, but the seclusion of his childhood was relieved by annual tours with his parents, in Britain and abroad. By the age of twenty he had published scholarly essays on geographical phenomena, and a book-length series of articles entitled *The Poetry of Architecture*. At Oxford University he gained a reputation as a skilful watercolourist and amateur geologist. In 1843, as 'A Graduate of Oxford', he published the first volume of *Modern Painters*, boldly proclaiming 'the superiority of the modern painters to the old ones', and eulogizing above all the art of J.M.W. Turner. Ruskin was scathing in his analysis of many of the established masters of seventeenth-century painting, but won respect nevertheless for his acute observation of nature and for his lyrical evocations of Turner's art.

In 1845, on a momentous visit to Italy, Ruskin 'discovered' the work of the fourteenth- and fifteenth-century artists of Pisa, Florence and Venice. It was these artists, together with Tintoretto, who were the heroes of the second volume of *Modern Painters* (1846). Ruskin commended the sense of calm devotion which he discerned in the painting of the early Italian masters, contrasting this quality with the insipidity and self-absorption which he found in the work of Raphael and his successors of the 'High Renaissance'. These sentiments were largely shared by a group of young British artists, led by **William Holman Hunt**, John Millais and **Dante Gabriel Rossetti**, who formed the Pre-Raphaelite Brotherhood in 1848; and when in 1851 the Pre-Raphaelites were fiercely criticized, Ruskin defended them in the columns of *The Times*, and initiated a revival of their fortunes.

By this time Ruskin was preoccupied with architecture. In *Seven Lamps of Architecture* (1849) and *The Stones of Venice* (1851–3), he drew the attention of the public to the merits of pre-Renaissance Italian architecture, and thereby broadened the scope of the Gothic Revival in Britain; substantial evidence of his persuasive powers can still be seen in the Anglo-Venetian capitals and arches of many an English suburb – as Ruskin himself

observed, and regretted, in later life. These books also exerted a more fundamental influence on Victorian attitudes to architecture. *Seven Lamps* put forward, a little clumsily, the notion of architecture as a manifestation of such moral qualities as 'truth', 'life' and 'sacrifice'. Then *The Stones of Venice*, Ruskin's *tour de force*, fully exemplified his conception that a work of art reflects the personality of its creator – and in the case of architecture, a collective personality or age-spirit, whose growth, health and decay could be traced even in the smallest details of architectural decoration.

Ruskin espoused architecture, however, at the expense of his wife, who left him in 1854. Their marriage, which in six years had not been consummated, was annulled, and she married Millais in the following year. Meanwhile Ruskin began to patronize Rossetti, and his writing proved an inspiration to **William Morris** and **Edward Burne-Jones**, whose enthusiasm carried Pre-Raphaelite principles into many branches of the decorative arts. They inherited from Ruskin a hostility to classical and Renaissance culture which extended to the arts and design of their own time. Ruskin and his followers believed that the nineteenth century was still afflicted by a demand for mass-production and standardization which had been initiated in the sixteenth century or even earlier. They opposed themselves to mechanized production, meaningless ornament and anonymous architecture of cast iron and plate glass – all symbolized in the Great Exhibition and Crystal Palace of 1851.

Towards the end of the 1850s Ruskin's message was significantly redirected. As he lost his faith in the Protestant Christianity of his youth, he became less confident in the correlation of artistic merit with purity of soul, and found a new respect for the 'magnificent animality' of Titian, Giorgione and Veronese. He taught drawing at the Working Men's College, and became concerned increasingly with the economic and social aspects of art. In his Manchester lectures of 1857, on 'The Political Economy of Art' (republished as *A Joy for Ever*), he emerged as an articulate opponent of capitalism and the ideology of laissez-faire. The pursuit of profit, he maintained, condemned the working man to an inhuman existence of mindless routine. Proclaiming that the principle of co-operation was superior to that of competition, he called for a return to the guild system of craftsmanship, the manufacture of articles of lasting value, and a steady wage guaranteed by a strong, paternal government.

These proposals were unacceptable to many of Ruskin's contemporaries; the fury aroused by a series of articles written by Ruskin for the *Cornhill Magazine*, attacking the libertarian principles of Ricardo and **J.S. Mill**, prompted its editor, Thackeray, to cut short the series. But in the succeeding decades these articles, reprinted as *Unto this Last*, reached a wide audience; such diverse figures as **Tolstoy, Mahatma Gandhi** and the early leaders of the British Labour movement acknowledged the powerful influence of *Unto this Last* on their own philosophy.

Conversely, those works of Ruskin's which were most popular at the time of publication – *Sesame and Lilies* (1864) and *The Ethics of the Dust* (1866) – have appealed much less to subsequent generations. These offered advice to young men and women on their proper roles in life, with (in the second work) elaborate geological and botanical allegories. Ruskin continued to revel in controversy, however, lecturing to the cadets of Woolwich Academy on the glories of war, and advising the citizens of Bradford to decorate their new town hall with pendant purses in honour of their presiding deity, the 'Goddess of Getting-on' (*The Crown of Wild Olive*, 1866).

The last decades of his life were occupied with short-lived philanthropic ventures, unrequited love for young girls, lectures delivered as Slade Professor of Fine Art at Oxford University, and debilitating bouts of mental illness, whose effects are often evident in his monthly publication commenced in 1871, *Fors Clavigera*. In these 'Letters to the Workmen and Labourers of Great Britain' he pronounced erratically on art, literature, mythology and political economy. In an early issue he launched 'The St George's Guild', a form of rural commune financed principally by himself, on which there were to be 'no steam engines ... no untended creatures ... no liberty'. The Guild gained few Companions, but much of its museum still survives.

In a later issue of *Fors* **Ruskin** criticized a painting by **Whistler**, *Nocturne in Black and Gold: The Falling Rocket*: 'I never expected to hear a coxcomb ask two hundred guineas for flinging a pot of paint in the public's face.' Whistler sued for libel, won a farthing's damages without costs, and was bankrupted. Ruskin was perhaps seen as the moral victor, but in retrospect this celebrated lawsuit of 1878 has come to symbolize the clash between the traditional but outmoded values of figurative art and the daring innovations of the modern movement – an ironic reversal of roles in the case of Ruskin, once the champion of the avant-garde.

Ruskin spent most of his final fifteen years as an invalid at Brantwood, near Coniston, but managed to produce one last major work: his unfinished autobiography *Praeterita*, which, although unreliable in matters of fact, is as compellingly lucid as any of the works of his prime.

Further reading

See: *The Works of John Ruskin*, ed. E.T. Cook and A. Wedderburn (39 vols, 1903–12), whose massive index volume is the single most valuable aid to the study of Ruskin. Many volumes of Ruskin's letters and diaries have been published subsequently, notably *The Diaries of John Ruskin*, ed. Joan Evans and John H. Whitehouse (3 vols, 1956–9): these are listed in *Ruskin: A Bibliography 1900–1974*, ed. H. Kirk Beetz (1977). Recent studies include: Quentin Bell, *Ruskin* (1963); Robert Hewison, *John Ruskin: The Argument of the Eye* (1976); John D. Unrau, *Looking at Architecture with Ruskin* (1978); Patrick Conner, *Savage Ruskin* (1979); Joan Abse, *John Ruskin: The Passionate Moralist* (1980); John Dixon Hunt, *The Wider Sea: A Life of John Ruskin* (1982); D. Birch, *Ruskin's Myths* (1988); Timothy Hilton, *John Ruskin: The Early Years* (1985) and *John Ruskin: The Later Years*

(2000). Ruskin's artistic output is examined in Paul Walton, *The Drawings of John Ruskin* (1972).

PATRICK CONNER

RUSSELL, Bertrand Arthur William (Earl)

1872–1970

British philosopher

Russell was born into an aristocratic family; his grandfather, Lord John Russell, had twice been prime minister. When he was orphaned at the age of three, the will of his free-thinking parents was set aside with the result that he and his older brother (upon whose death in 1931 he succeeded to the earldom) were given a strict and puritanical upbringing by their paternal grandmother. When Russell entered Cambridge in 1890, he had been, apart from a period spent preparing for scholarship examinations, educated entirely at home by governesses and tutors. He entered Cambridge with a passionate interest in mathematics which he claimed (*Autobiography*, Vol. I, 1967) had been at one time all that prevented a suicidal outcome to his adolescent loneliness and despair.

Russell sought in mathematics the certainty and perfection of object he had lost when he abandoned his early religious beliefs, and was gradually disillusioned by the teaching at Cambridge, where, 'The "proofs" that were offered of mathematical theorems were an insult to the logical intelligence' (*My Philosophical Development*, 1959). His final undergraduate year was devoted entirely to philosophy and he absorbed the prevailing Hegelian idealism of the time. Study of the *Greater Logic*, however, led Russell to the conclusion that 'all [Hegel] says about mathematics is muddle-headed nonsense' (P.A. Schilpp (ed.) *The Philosophy of Bertrand Russell*, 1944) and in 1898 he was ripe to follow his friend **G.E. Moore** in revolt against idealism.

Moore persuaded Russell in the name of common sense to accept the existence of fact independent of experience, while Russell reinforced the rebellion by exposing the logical nerve of the argument by which the English Hegelian, F.H. Bradley, had sought to establish the impossibility of knowledge of anything which did not involve knowledge of everything. Russell saw in Bradley's argument the same mistake about relations which he previously discerned in Leibniz (in *A Critical Exposition of the Philosophy of Leibniz*, 1900), the belief that every relation requires foundation in the intrinsic properties of the objects related; these intrinsic properties turn out on deeper investigation to be properties of the whole which the objects compose. The critique of Bradley provided the foundation for the subsequent development of Russell's techniques of analysis: understanding of a complex can be achieved by an account of how its simple parts form a whole.

While the revolt against idealism was mounted in the name of common sense, there remained much in Russell's thinking not sanctioned by common sense. Maintaining that for a word to mean something it must stand for some kind of object, Russell was led to a belief that numerals, predicate-expressions, even the definite article must stand for non-material entities of some kind. This crude Platonism was eroded over the following decades by the successive development of logical techniques which enabled Russell to distinguish between the apparent logical form of a sentence and the true form of the proposition it expressed. The principle, that for something to be meaningful it must stand for something, could then be applied only to the true logical form.

The soil in which these techniques germinated was the philosophy of mathematics. In 1900 Russell attended a conference in Paris where he encountered the work of the Italian mathematician, Giuseppe Peano. Impressed by the rigour, and aided by the advances, in Peano's work, Russell wrote a treatise (*The Principles of Mathematics*, 1903) which, while heavy with Platonic commitment, was able to eliminate numbers as metaphysical entities in favour of similarity classes, i.e. of classes all members of which can be placed in one–one correspondence with each other. This was the first step in what became a highly influential programme (see **Carnap**) for 'logical construction', the principle of which emerged in 1918 under the slogan, 'Whenever possible logical constructions are to be substituted for inferences to unknown entities' (*Mysticism and Logic*, 1917).

Because he regarded *class* as a logical notion, the *Principles* was Russell's first defence of the 'logicist thesis': 'that all pure mathematics follows from purely logical premises and uses only concepts definable in logical terms' (*My Philosophical Development*). Russell soon discovered he had been anticipated by sixteen years in the work of the German mathematician **Gottlob Frege**, but it was Russell who uncovered a problem with the notion of class which threatened the logicist programme for mathematics. Known as 'Russell's Paradox', it points out that the class of all classes not belonging to themselves can neither belong nor fail to belong to itself. The paradox turned out to be one of a family of similar difficulties and could not be ignored. Frege was eventually led to abandon logicism, but Russell pressed on.

Between 1900 and 1910, Russell collaborated with his friend and former teacher at Cambridge, **A.N. Whitehead**, on an improved presentation of the logicist position, the three-volume *Principia Mathematica* (1913). During this period Russell was frustrated by his inability to find a satisfactory solution to the problems surrounding his paradox. Progress on another front suggested a way of eliminating classes in the same spirit as numbers had been eliminated. The progress consisted in a logical representation of sentences involving definite descriptions. Known since as 'Russell's theory of descriptions', it obviated the problems caused by descriptive expressions which purport to refer to what in fact does not exist. However, to apply a similar idea to classes in such a way as to avoid all the paradoxes ('the ramified theory of types') invalidated vital parts of mathematics and Russell was forced to resort to what many regarded as an *ad hoc* principle, the axiom of reducibility.

Principia and its problems stimulated important mathematical and philosophical work in the three decades after its publication. Among the philosophical work was that of Russell's pupil, **Ludwig Wittgenstein**, who acknowledged, in his *Tractatus*, the importance of the distinction between apparent and true logical form which had emerged with the theory of descriptions. Wittgenstein's principles of 'atomicity' and 'extension' in turn clarified further for Russell the aim and nature of analysis. Between them these principles suggest the world consists of 'atomic facts' which can be described by propositions, the truth of each of which is independent of every other atomic proposition and from which one can infer all other true propositions.

Wittgenstein's development of this idea avoided confronting questions about how human beings know or could know the world so conceived. Russell's development was alive to such epistemological questions from the start. Even before he had assimilated the influence of Wittgenstein, the theory of descriptions had suggested the outline of a sophisticated version of Hume's empiricism. Russell founded his empiricism on the principle, 'Every proposition which we can understand must be composed wholly of constituents with which we are acquainted' (*Mysticism and Logic*) and developed some of Whitehead's techniques for eliminating, by means of logical constructions, such theoretical ideas in science as points, instants and particles, with which we could not claim acquaintance (*Our Knowledge of the External World*, 1914).

Logical atomism required a purification of the notion of acquaintance. Russell wanted the constituents of atomic propositions to be known by acquaintance, but for the propositions to retain their logical independence this acquaintance had to be based on pure experience without taint of inference. To claim to be acquainted with a particular man involves inferences based on more immediate sensory experience, hence men and other material objects are notions requiring elimination by means of logical constructions. Russell even attempted (in *The Analysis of Mind*, 1921) to replace the knowing subject by a construction. He was the first to acknowledge the limitations in his analyses and the shortcomings of his logical constructions. In his last major philosophic work (*Human Knowledge, Its Scope and Limits*, 1948), he explored the extent to which what we accept as knowledge can be founded on the data of immediate experience by means of non-deductive inference.

It is difficult to gauge Russell's influence. Important though *Principia* was, it did not set the style of subsequent mathematical foundations. Mathematicians concurred with the view expressed by **Gödel** in 1944 that compared to Frege the logical precision of *Principia* represented 'a considerable step backward'. In philosophy the influence of Russell's epistemological theories has waned with growing doubts about the intelligibility of the immediate personal experience which Russell required for the foundation of knowledge. Where Russell's influence is still strong, it is probably so complete and pervasive it is hard to detect. Russell set new goals and problems for philosophic inquiry and demonstrated a new way of pursuing them. Anglo-American philosophy nowadays pays much lip service to the name of Frege, but the conduct of analytical philosophy remains a most sincere, if often unconscious, tribute to Russell.

Part of the explanation for the pervasiveness of Russell's influence lies in his skill as a popularizer and in the charm and accessibility of many of his important works. Addressing an audience of philosophers in 1966, **Quine** testified, 'I think many of us were drawn to our profession by Russell's books.' Russell's influence, moreover, extended well beyond academic philosophy. Involved directly in many social and political issues he wrote passionately about most of them. His pamphleteering on behalf of pacifism and against conscription during 1914–18 earned him at first a fine, then loss of his Cambridge lectureship, refusal of a passport, and finally six months in prison. His pacifism cost him many friends on the right, but he was not afraid to alienate his friends on the left when, after a visit to Russia, he published a prophetic attack on the communist regime in *The Practice and Theory of Bolshevism* (1920). He stood unsuccessfully for parliament as a women's suffrage candidate in 1907 and again as a Labour candidate in 1923. Interest in the education of his children led him to establish with his second wife (he was married four times) a progressive school, Beacon Hill. He lectured extensively in the United States, both on tour and in university posts. His unconventional ideas, particularly about sexual morality (see *Marriage and Morals*, 1926), led to a civil lawsuit in 1940 which successfully blocked his appointment at City College, New York.

He was awarded the Order of Merit in 1949 and the Nobel Prize for Literature in 1950. During the last fifteen years of his life, he tried to impress upon the world the threat to human survival posed by nuclear arms. He helped found the Campaign for Nuclear Disarmament in 1958 and was sent to prison for a second time (two months reduced to seven days) in 1961 for civil disobedience activity with the Committee of 100.

Further reading

Other works include: *The Problems of Philosophy* (1912); *An Introduction to Mathematical Philosophy* (1919); *The Analysis of Matter* (1927); *An Inquiry into Meaning and Truth* (1940); *A History of Western Philosophy* (1945). Collections of Russell's articles and essays: *Philosophical Essays* (1910); *Logic and Knowledge*, ed. Robert C. Marsh (1956); *Basic Writing of Bertrand Russell, 1903–1959*, ed. R.E. Egner and L.E. Dennon (1961); *Essays in Analysis*, ed. Douglas Lackey (1973). For Russell's life, see his three-volume *Autobiography* (1967–9) and R.W. Clark, *The Life of Bertrand Russell* (1975). Critical studies: F.P. Ramsey, *The Foundations of Mathematics* (1931); D.F. Pears, *Bertrand Russell and the British Tradition in Philosophy* (1967); A.J. Ayer, *Russell and Moore: The Analytical Heritage* (1971); N. Griffin (ed.) *The Cambridge Companion to Bertrand Russell* (2003).

J.E. TILES

RUSTIN, Bayard

1912–87

US rights activist

Bayard Rustin, co-ordinator of the historic 1963 March on Washington, and leading black American strategist and organizer in both the civil rights and war resistance movements, was frequently sidelined during his lifetime, and remained, at least until the turn of the present century, relatively unknown. The principal reason for this is that he was openly gay in a society which ostracized and criminalized its gay and lesbian community and continues to regard it with suspicion or outright hostility.

The FBI made no such miscalculation about his significance. From the early 1940s onwards it kept him under repeated surveillance. Rustin himself loved to recount an incident which occurred during a visit to an antique shop in New York, when he asked its blind proprietor if he could inspect a carpet on display more closely. 'Certainly, Mr Rustin,' the man replied. When the astonished Rustin asked him how he knew his name, the man explained that as a former FBI operative he recognized his voice from their phone taps.

Rustin was born in West Chester, Pennsylvania, to a young single woman and brought up by his Quaker grandparents. After studying at Wilberforce University, Ohio, and Cheyney State Teachers College, he moved in 1937 to New York where he completed his studies at City College, paying his way by singing with the Josh White quartet. In 1938 he became an organizer for the Young Communist League, but left the organization in 1941 when it abandoned its anti-war stance following **Hitler's** invasion of Russia. But it was his association during that period with Rev Abraham Johannes Muste, 'A.J.', of the Christian pacifist Fellowship of Reconciliation (FOR), and with the black trade union leader A. Philip Randolph that was to have an enduring influence on his life and work.

A.J., a labour organizer in the 1920s and 1930s, brought a revolutionary vision and organizing experience to FOR when he became its Executive Director in 1940 and began to recruit to its staff young activists inspired by socialist and **Gandhian** ideals and practice. Rustin joined it in 1941, as did another young black American and future civil rights leader, James Farmer. In 1942, FOR launched the Congress of Racial Equality (CORE) which pioneered nonviolent direct action against racial injustice, including sit-ins at lunch-counters and restaurants, prefiguring the mass student sit-ins from 1960 onwards co-ordinated by the Student Nonviolent Coordinating Committee (SNCC).

In January 1944, Rustin was sentenced to three years' imprisonment for refusing to comply with the draft. There he and other conscientious objectors organized strikes and demonstrations against racial discrimination within the prison system. On his release in June 1946, he resumed work for the FOR and in 1947 was one of a mixed black and white group of twelve volunteers who undertook a joint FOR/CORE-sponsored 'Journey of Reconciliation' through the Southern states to test whether the Supreme Court ruling of the previous year outlawing segregation on inter-state transport was being implemented. This was the model for the more famous CORE Freedom Rides of the early 1960s. Rustin was among those arrested in North Carolina and eventually served twenty-two days on a chain gang. A series of articles he wrote on his release for the *New York Post* describing the scandalous conditions on the chain gang led to its abolition in North Carolina.

In 1948 he embarked on the first of a succession of tours and lectures in Europe, India and Africa. However, his arrest and conviction in Pasadena, California, in 1953 on a morals charge for a homosexual encounter with two men was a serious blow to his position and continued to be used against him by political rivals and enemies alike for the rest of his career, notoriously by Senator Strom Thurmond shortly before the March on Washington in a vain attempt to sabotage it.

After the Pasadena incident, Rustin left the FOR staff and worked for the secular pacifist organization, War Resisters League. During the Montgomery Bus Boycott of 1955–6, he provided invaluable advice to **Martin Luther King** on organizing the campaign and played a key role in the establishment of the Southern Christian Leadership Council (SCLC). He was equally active during this period with the US and international anti-war movement and was one of the main speakers at the start of the first Aldermaston March against Britain's nuclear weapons at Easter 1958. The following year he joined a transnational team in Ghana which attempted to drive through the Sahara to the French atomic bomb test site in Algeria. But it was the March on Washington, his and Randolph's brainchild, that marked the peak of his achievement, and provided him with his fifteen minutes of fame when the two men appeared on the front cover of *Life* magazine.

Rustin's intellectual ability paralleled his organizational flair. He was a powerful speaker and persuasive writer, not afraid to take unpopular positions. He opposed black separatism and publicly debated the issue with **Malcolm X** in 1960 and subsequently with Stokely Carmichael. In an essay entitled 'From Protest to Politics' in 1964 he argued that as the movement shifted away from an exclusive emphasis on ending discrimination to tackle the related problems of jobs, housing, poverty and so forth, street protest was becoming less important; it was time to form alliances and engage in more mainstream politics. In his case, this meant working with the trade unions through the A Philip Randolph Institute, established in 1965 with the backing of the AFL-CIO, and in some kind of working alliance with the Democratic Party.

That this would involve compromise, he was well aware. As he put it in one interview: 'In protest, there must never be any compromise. In politics there is always compromise.' Vietnam was the toughest issue, since forthright opposition to the war might jeopardize relations with the Johnson Administration

and the Democratic Party. Rustin signed a Declaration of Conscience against the war, but he stood aside from the anti-war protests and was critical of those in the civil rights movement who switched their energies to it. On this and other issues, notably his call in 1970 for Washington to supply jets to Israel, he found himself at odds with younger activists and with many of his former colleagues.

However, in the last years of his life, he re-engaged with the anti-war movement. In 1985 he attended the Triennial Conference of War Resisters International in India where he was visibly moved by the account by two South African resisters of the End Conscription Campaign whose members refused military service so long as the repression in the black townships continued, and he immediately offered to organize a lecture tour for the two young men in the US. It was the kind of campaign that resonated with his deepest convictions, asserting the individual right of conscience while at the same time contributing to the broader struggle for black – and human – emancipation.

Further reading

See: Devon W. Carbado and Donald Weise (eds) *Time on Two Crosses: The Collected Writings of Bayard Rustin* (2003). See also: Taylor Branch, *Parting of the Waters: America in the King Years, 1954–63* (1989); Jervis Anderson, *Bayard Rustin: Troubles I've Seen* (1997); D. Levine, *Bayard Rustin and the Civil Rights Movement* (2000); John D'Emilio, *Lost Prophet: The Life and Times of Bayard Rustin* (2003). N. Kates and B. Singer, *Brother Outsider: The Life of Bayard Rustin* (2003) is a film documentary with a transcript available from http://www.pbs.org/pov/utils/pressroom2002/brotheroutsider/brotheroutsider_transcript.doc.

MICHAEL RANDLE

RUTHERFORD, Ernest

1871–1937

New Zealand/British physicist

Most Nobel Prize-winning scientists are remembered for a single contribution. Rutherford, in keeping with the great enthusiasm and energy he brought to his work, is known for at least three major advances of modern physics.

Born and educated in New Zealand, with notable encouragement at Canterbury College, he sought further training in **J.J. Thomson's** Cavendish Laboratory, at Cambridge University, in order to escape the colony's limited opportunities. His arrival, in 1895, came shortly before the discovery of X-rays and radio-activity, and he soon became the dominant figure in the latter field, even more so than Henri Becquerel or Pierre and **Marie Curie**.

Rutherford early detected that the radiation from uranium was not uniform, and labelled the weakly penetrating rays 'alpha' and those able to pass through thin sheets of foil 'beta'. (The far more penetrating gamma radiation was discovered by Paul Villard in 1900.) He next examined thorium, which also was known to be radioactive, and found a gaseous emission which he called 'emanation'. The emanation itself rendered everything it touched radioactive, and Rutherford recognized that an 'active deposit' was being laid down. This active deposit, in turn, changed into a series of other radioactive products, each with a characteristic period or 'half-life', and for those capable of determination, specific chemical properties.

The source of the enormous quantities of energy emitted in these reactions and the mechanism of the phenomenon itself were major puzzles early in this century; their solution helped overturn the Victorian attitude that the edifice of scientific knowledge was largely complete. In 1902–3, Rutherford and a chemical colleague, Frederick Soddy, advanced an iconoclastic interpretation of radioactivity. Alchemy had long been exorcized from 'scientific chemistry', but these young men in effect reintroduced transmutation. Radioactivity, they maintained, was a spontaneous disintegration of an unstable atom into another atom, which might itself be unstable, with the simultaneous emission of radiation. It was primarily for this work that Rutherford was awarded the Nobel Prize

(in chemistry!) in 1908. But the transistory nature of many radioactive bodies presented a problem, for could substances which were not permanent be considered elements? And if they were elements, could so many fit into the limited number of boxes of the periodic table of elements? These were resolved in the affirmative a decade later by Soddy and Kasimir Fajans.

Rutherford subsequently devoted ever more attention to the alpha rays. Betas had been identified as electrons by Becquerel in 1900, and by 1903 Rutherford had shown alphas to be particles, but confirmation that they were charged helium atoms eluded him until 1908. In his experiments he had noticed that alphas often were deflected from their paths, a fact he considered impressive in view of their great velocities and relatively large mass. More precise measurements under his sponsorship led him to challenge the prevailing picture of the atom as a sphere of positive electrification, with negative electrons embedded here and there in it. To account for the large-angle deflections suffered by some alphas when striking atoms in a target, Rutherford proposed that the atom's mass was concentrated in a sphere at least ten thousand times smaller than hitherto accepted, and the electrons were seen as orbiting this core. The 'nuclear model of the atom' proved extremely valuable when **Niels Bohr** added quantum conditions to the orbits and was able to explain much data that had been collected. Not only was the atom no longer considered stable and uniform throughout, but it was now irrevocably tied to the modern concepts of quantum physics.

Of Rutherford's three major contributions, the transformation theory was in radioactivity, the nuclear model may be placed in atomic physics since it gave a new structure to the atom, and the last was in nuclear physics: indeed, it was the origin of this subject. The alpha particle, as indicated above, was known to be an energetic particle ejected from many radioactive elements. Why not, Rutherford reasoned, use it as a projectile to disrupt nuclei and learn something about their structure, much as he already had used it to investigate atomic structure? In experiments begun during the First World War and published in 1919, he bombarded nitrogen with alphas, caused a rearrangement of the nuclear constituents, and produced oxygen and protons. Thus his 1902–3 work on radioactivity with Soddy had involved spontaneous, or uncontrollable, nuclear transformations, while the 1919 research showed that nuclear changes could deliberately be made to occur, although the means were 'natural', i.e. the projectiles came from naturally decaying radioelements. This set the stage for deliberate transformations by artificial means, namely the accelerating machines that began to proliferate in the 1930s, as more copious beams of more energetic projectiles were needed to bombard the heavier elements. The first successful machine transmutation was achieved, appropriately enough, in Rutherford's laboratory by John Cockcroft and E.T.S. Walton, in 1932, and a spin-off benefit of their work was the earliest confirmation of **Albert Einstein's** famous $E = mc^2$ equation of 1905, stating the equivalence of mass and energy.

Rutherford held professorships at McGill University, Manchester University and Cambridge University, where he succeeded his old teacher J.J. Thomson. He was also active in numerous professional organizations, serving for example as president of both the Royal Society and the British Association for the Advancement of Science. Many honours came to him, including the Order of Merit, knighthood, being raised to the peerage as Baron Rutherford of Nelson, the Copley and Rumford Medals of the Royal Society, and several honorary degrees. He was widely regarded as the greatest experimental physicist since Michael Faraday. But, like Faraday, he has strong claims to theoretical advances as well, for though his work was not highly mathematical, his contributions clearly consist of not just experimental discoveries but ideas and interpretations.

Rutherford was notable also as a highly successful laboratory director, training a generation of physicists to fill many of the chairs in the British Commonwealth, and imparting superior research skills that earned these students the highest honours in science. In this connection, he was a key figure in the transition from 'little science' to 'Big Science', the evolution from a sealing-wax and string economy of science to a science characterized by large apparatus, research teams and generous funding. Although he died before nuclear fission was discovered, Rutherford stands firmly as a major link in the scientific chain leading to nuclear weapons and nuclear reactors. Indeed, many of his students worked on the applications of nuclear energy which their 'Prof' did so much to reveal.

Further reading

Other works include: *The Collected Papers of Lord Rutherford of Nelson* (3 vols, 1962, 1963, 1965). A bibliography of all his books and almost everything written about him appears following his entry by Lawrence Badash in the *Dictionary of Scientific Biography*, Vol. 12 (1975). See also: A.S. Eve, *Rutherford* (1939); E.N. da C. Andrade, *Rutherford and the Nature of the Atom* (1964); Norman Feather, *Lord Rutherford* (1940, revised 1973); Peter Kelman, *Ernest Rutherford: Architect of the Atom* (1994); John L. Heilbron, *Ernest Rutherford and the Explosion of Atoms* (2003).

LAWRENCE BADASH

RYLE, Gilbert

1900–76

English philosopher

Ryle was educated at Brighton College and Queen's College, Oxford, where he took firsts in Mods, Greats and PPE. At the age of twenty-four he became a lecturer at Christ Church, and was to remain an Oxford don all his life. In 1945 he was appointed Waynflete Professor of Metaphysics at the university, and from 1947 to 1971 he edited the important philosophical journal *Mind*. During the post-war expansion of university education, Ryle's academic prestige was in many ways unrivalled, and he exercised a unique influence on the way philosophy was taught and practised in Britain.

Ryle produced many influential articles, but his most famous philosophical contribution is his book *The Concept of Mind* (1949). This exemplifies Ryle's unique philosophical style – witty, discursive and, depending on your taste, delightfully or irksomely rich in examples ('By feelings I refer to the sorts of things which people often describe as thrills, twinges, pangs, throbs, wrenches, itches, prickings, chills, glows, loads, qualms, hankerings, curdlings, sinkings, tensions, gnawings and shocks'). The book's purpose is to demolish a widely prevailing account of the human mind which Ryle dubs 'Descartes's myth':

> What has physical existence is composed of matter . . . what has mental existence consists of consciousness . . . There is thus a total opposition between mind and matter . . . Such in outline is the Official Theory. I shall often refer to it with deliberate abusiveness as the dogma of the ghost in the machine.

To construe the mind as a mysterious ghostly entity distinct from the body is, according to Ryle, a kind of logical error – a 'category mistake'. Mental states, claims Ryle, are not occult private events occurring in the 'mind', but are simply dispositions to behave in a certain way: 'To talk of someone's mind is . . . to talk of the person's abilities, liabilities and inclinations to do certain sorts of things.'

Ryle's position here can be seen as a sophisticated philosophical articulation of the behaviourist approach to psychology which was dominant for much of the twentieth century. But as an account of mental phenomena, it conspicuously fails to do justice to the undeniable existence within each of us of thoughts and feelings which are often not manifested in any overt behaviour. In spite of this difficulty, to which Ryle was never to offer a satisfactory answer, his book has had a pervasive and continuing influence, which has more to do with method than content. For *The Concept of Mind* articulates a particular view of philosophy: the job of the philosopher is seen not as theory-construction or system-building, but as the task of clarifying concepts ('determining their logical geography', as Ryle put it) and removing conceptual confusion. Ryle is thus entitled to be seen, along with **Austin** and, in his later period, **Wittgenstein**, as a prime exponent of the method of conceptual analysis which to this day dominates so much of the philosophy of the English-speaking tradition.

Further reading

See: *Dilemmas* (a collection of essays, 1954); *Plato's Progress* (1966); *Collected Papers: Critical Essays and Collected Essays 1929–68* (1998). About Ryle: Oscar Wood (ed.) *Ryle* (1970): William E.R. Lyons, *Gilbert Ryle: An Introduction to His Philosophy* (1986).

JOHN COTTINGHAM

S

SAID, Edward Wadie

1935–2003

Palestinian writer and critic

Edward W. Said was born in Jerusalem into a Christian Arab family and was educated at St George's, the Eton of Mandate Palestine. When the Saids moved to Egypt and settled in Cairo, young Edward attended Victoria College, a Britishrun school. Aged sixteen, he was sent for further education at Mount Hermon, a private school in Massachusetts, where he blossomed academically, finding the American attitude to learning more imaginative and stimulating than the British approach in Cairo. After a degree at Princeton Said embarked on a PhD at Harvard graduate school where he also won the Bowdoin Prize for the best scholarly dissertation written by a student – it was on **Joseph Conrad**. In 1963, he was appointed Assistant Professor of Comparative Literature at Columbia University, New York where he later became a full Professor. In the ensuing years he also served as a Visiting Professor at Harvard, Yale, John Hopkins and Toronto Universities.

Said's writings, some of them translated into twentysix languages, included many books and covered a range of subjects. Books such as *Joseph Conrad and the Fiction of Autobiography* (1966) and *The World, the Text, and the Critic* (1983) established Said as one of the world's leading literary theorists. But it was his 1978 study, *Orientalism*, which became his most influential and original intellectual

contribution. In *Orientalism*, which is a historical examination of attitudes to the Middle East, Said wrote of how the West has stereotyped and degraded the Arab world over the centuries. Using a wide variety of texts, from eighteenthcentury travellers' journals to Victorian treatises on Islam, Said shows how these had reinforced negative stereotypes of Arabs as ignorant, lazy and untrustworthy. At the same time, the 'Orient' was seen as exotic and alluring, inviting the rule of European colonial powers.

With *Orientalism*, Said single-handedly launched what later became known as Post Colonial Studies. The book also had a strong impact in enabling academics from non-Western lands to take advantage of the mood of political correctness *Orientalism* helped to engender by associating themselves with 'narratives of oppression', creating successful careers out of representing the non Western 'other'. Said's *Orientalism* helped transform the way people looked at the Arabs, Islam and the Middle East, but it also drew much criticism and its author was attacked by literary critics, especially in England, for forcing his facts to fit into a predetermined thesis and for distorting the views of such English writers as Jane Austen.

Said was not an armchair intellectual who only theorized about the ideology of imperialism. He became one of its most articulate public opponents. It was the 1967 Middle East war between Israel and the Arabs which shocked Said to the core and stirred him to political activism as his own identity as a

Palestinian, suppressed for so many years, became evident. In the 1970s, Said became the most prominent voice in the USA to defend the Palestinian struggle for justice and self determination and to point at the fact that the Israeli–Palestinian conflict was a battle between a state, namely Israel with its 'colonial army' attacking 'a colonized population'.

Said's literary creativity also shifted to focus on Palestinian issues and in a stream of articles, opinion pieces and books, notably in *The Question of Palestine* (1979), he argued the Palestinian case with clarity and forcefulness. In his final years, however, he took a conscious decision to withdraw from political controversy and channel his energies into music: he was an accomplished pianist who gave occasional public recitals.

Further reading

Other works include: two collections of literary essays, *Beginnings: Intention and Method* (1975) and *The World, the Text and the Critic* (1983); an elegiac work entitled *After the Last Sky: Palestinian Lives* (1986); a contemporary reprise of the theme of *Orientalism* in *Covering Islam* (1981); *Musical Elaborations* (1991); *Culture and Imperialism* (1993); *The Politics of Dispossession* (1994); *Representations of the Intellectual* (1994); *Peace and Its Discontents* (1995); and *Out of Place* (1999), Said's memoirs. See also: Paul A. Bove (ed.) *Edward Said and the Work of the Critic: Speaking Truth to Power* (2000); Bill Ashcroft, Pal Ahluwalia and D.P.S. Ahluwalia (eds) *Edward Said* (2001).

AHRON BREGMAN

SAIGŌ TAKAMORI

1828–77

Japanese hero, rebel and government member

Saigō was born to a minor official in the Satsuma fief, which was in the far south of Japan and had long cherished a spirit of independence and reluctant subservience to central government authority. He was reportedly blessed with an enormous frame and an amiable disposition and these factors helped him acquire a certain prominence within the fief, where he was associated with the anti-government side in the years leading up to the Meiji Restoration of 1868. Under the patronage of the *daimyo* of the fief he took part in a number of delicate political intrigues in the capital and elsewhere, but upon the latter's death in 1858 Saigō was caught up in a purge of anti-government elements and spent some five years in internal exile. It was also at this time that he made an abortive suicide attempt: his failure seems to have nurtured in him something of a death-wish and it may well have exerted the influence on his future conduct it is often supposed to have done.

Once he had been released from his place of exile, he threw himself once again into anti-government activities and was instrumental in organizing the coalition of southern fiefs whose concerted action sealed the fate of the Tokugawa government and ushered in the Meiji Restoration, whereby power was nominally restored to the emperor after centuries of military rule. Saigō also played a leading role in some of the military operations accompanying the Restoration, but was noted for his attempts to minimize the bloodshed. He was subsequently offered high honours by the new government in recognition of his services, but he declined them, although he did in 1871 yield to requests that he join the government: he was made a counsellor of state, thereby participating in the governance of Japan, and the following year he was given command of all the armed forces in the land. However, he was soon disturbed by the indulgence of his colleagues in the trappings and personal perquisites of office, all of which he disdained, and by the pace of the centralization and Westernization being carried out by the government to which he belonged.

During 1872–3 many members of the government were overseas on the Iwakura mission to Europe and America, which reminded Japanese government leaders forcefully of Japan's relative backwardness and the fragility of her international position. Saigō, however, stayed at home and became embroiled in a diplomatic dispute with Korea. Japanese efforts in 1872 to have Korea open its doors to trade had been rebuffed and the emperor's dignity had been impugned. Saigō and others were in favour of a punitive mission and Saigō proposed that he be sent to Korea as an ambassador, fully expecting that he would be killed there, in which event an invasion would be justified. Among his motives for favouring an invasion was the desire to provide opportunities for the Samurai class, which by then had been dispossessed by the Meiji government and which in Saigō's opinion had been shamefully treated. However, the returned members of the Iwakura mission were convinced that the priorities were to develop Japan's economic and military strength and not to indulge in costly overseas adventures that might arouse the antagonism of the European powers, and they managed to scotch Saigō's plan. Saigō thereupon left the government, as did a number of his supporters, and withdrew to Satsuma where he poured his resources into educational establishments specializing in agriculture, the military arts and moral training. And he refused several offers from his former government colleagues, who wished him to return to their circles.

In 1874 and subsequent years there were a number of minor rebellions of former Samurai in various parts of the country. The leaders of some of these had been associated with Saigō, so the government became anxious about a possible uprising in Satsuma and attempted to move arms and ammunition by boat from the largest city in the province to a safer location. However, as soon as they heard of the attempt, some of Saigō's younger followers launched an attack, thereby forestalling the move as well as translating hostility into open rebellion. Saigō was aware that he could not hope to be successful against the forces the government had at its disposal but nevertheless he took up leadership of the rebellion and declared that his quarrel was not with the emperor but with his malicious and wrong-headed advisers, a formula that has often been resorted to in

Japanese history. The army ranged against Saigō and his adherents was vastly superior in both numbers and supplies. The campaign lasted seven months and cost many casualties, but the new army of peasant conscripts proved itself in combat against Saigō's Samurai army and thus put an end to the military supremacy of the Samurai. When the end was near Saigō disembowelled himself, and most of his followers did the same or were killed.

In spite of the rebellion and his official disgrace, Saigō has remained a popular and respected figure. In 1890 he was posthumously pardoned and restored to his former ranks. He had been one of the key figures in the Restoration movement and one of the Meiji leaders, but his political influence was never great and the reasons for his lasting popularity must be sought elsewhere. Thus Saigō could easily be seen as the representative of all those who were feeling left behind by the rapid changes Japan was going through. He was one of the few government members who had never visited the West, his tastes were simple in the extreme and untouched by the tide of Westernization, and he remained attached to his provincial origins in the midst of the Tokyo-centred world of Meiji Japan. So he could be and was admired both by nationalists, for his defence of traditional Japanese values, and by radicals, for the anti-Establishment strand in his life.

Further reading

See: I. Morris, *The Nobility of Failure* (1975); and H. Borton, *Japan's Modern Century* (2nd edn, 1970).

PETER KORNICKI

SAINT-SAËNS, Charles Camille

1835–1921

French composer

From his earliest years Camille Saint-Saëns demonstrated an astonishing facility as both composer and performer. For about eighty years he composed prolifically, and his enormous output encompasses all the nineteenth-century categories of music. Besides all this, he left a great deal of writing about music, expressing clear and strongly held views on all aspects of his art. In composition his very facility worked against him: it all came so easily and rapidly that there seemed to be little time for self-criticism and discernment of musical quality. In consequence, only a small number of his works have withstood the test of time. He believed that a composer produces music 'as naturally as an apple-tree produces apples'. Like **Stravinsky**, he set little store by inspiration and the expression of emotion in his composing; the important things were clarity of style, purity of line, satisfying form. Steeped in the Viennese models of sonatas, symphonies and concertos, and strongly influenced by Mozart, Bach, Mendelssohn and Schumann, Saint-Saëns pursued an art of assimilation, basically conservative, in which Austrian, German and French traditions were blended. But there were many other ingredients – the French dance forms of the seventeenth century, Spanish influences, oriental colouring – all was grist to the Saint-Saëns mill. The result is a kind of stylelessness, or rather a multitude of styles, in his works, with many saving graces – a spontaneous lyrical gift, a colourful imagination, a sense of humour and much good humour; and always an infallible craftsmanship.

Saint-Saëns started learning the piano from his great-aunt when he was two and a half years old; and his first piano piece was written at the age of three. Eventually, he entered the Paris Conservatoire when he was thirteen; and at sixteen, his *Ode à Sainte-Cécile* (for voices and orchestra) won a prize awarded by the Société de Sainte-Cécile in Paris, and it was given a performance. He was only twenty-two when he obtained the important appointment of organist of the Madeleine. **Liszt**, who became a close and lasting friend, was a strong influence in his development. Saint-Saëns began to write symphonies. For four years he taught music at the École Niedermeyer – his only teaching

appointment – and among his pupils were Messager and **Fauré** (another lasting friendship). Meanwhile, he had acquired a formidable reputation as a pianist and organist.

All fields, in fact, were there to be conquered. The five piano concertos, which extend over a period of about thirty years, were a showcase for Saint-Saëns to appear in the Lisztian combination of composer and virtuoso-pianist, which he did with enormous success. The second, fourth and fifth retain a popularity today – especially the fourth, in C minor, which is one of the composer's most unified and satisfying works. The fifth is known as the 'Egyptian' Concerto because it was composed in Luxor in 1895 and makes use of some oriental flavouring.

Saint-Saëns was indeed an inveterate traveller – in Europe, Africa, Indo-China, South America and the USA – sometimes as soloist, sometimes as conductor. And he frequently visited England, where he was always warmly received – the first time in 1871, when he gave some organ recitals at London's Albert Hall. Cambridge University made him an honorary Doctor of Music in 1893.

With Romain Bussini, in 1871, Saint-Saëns founded the Société Nationale de Musique. Its motto, *Ars gallica*, emphasized its purpose, which was the encouragement and performance of new French music – particularly orchestral and other instrumental music. Important works by **Franck**, d'Indy, Chausson, Fauré and others were first heard under the Societé's auspices, and some extremely interesting symphonic poems by Saint-Saëns himself. It might be thought that with his views on 'pure' music, anything resembling a descriptive 'programme' would have been anathema to him. But his stipulation was that it should always be justifiable in itself as music, whatever the initial conception may have been. To this category belong Saint-Saëns's *Le Rouet d'Omphale, Phaëton* and *Danse macabre* – all of which are still heard today – and, of course, *Le Carnaval des Animaux*. The last-named was written as a private joke, caricaturing music by many other composers – and his own *Danse macabre*. The composer disliked the *Carnaval* and forbade performances of it during his lifetime; it is now, ironically, his most popular work.

Of the symphonies of Saint-Saëns, the one most frequently heard today is No. 3, the so-called 'Organ' Symphony (because of its important part for organ). Dedicated to the memory of Liszt, this was first performed in 1886 in London, at a concert of the (now Royal) Philharmonic Society.

Although Saint-Saëns devoted a good deal of his energy to writing music for the theatre, his immense gifts did not include the ability to portray drama and character really convincingly through music. It is significant that his most successful opera, *Samson et Dalila*, dating from the 1870s, was originally conceived as an oratorio; and the work in its final form is a series of tableaux rather than a developing musical drama.

In musical terms the range and variety of Saint-Saëns's output is enormous. Besides operas and other stage works, symphonies, concertos and concert-pieces for various instruments, overtures, symphonic poems, the list of his chamber music is formidable; likewise, there is a large amount of vocal music, with and without orchestra, and innumerable solo songs with piano. Curiously, for a renowned keyboard exponent, the solo piano and organ compositions are the least interesting side of his output. Saint-Saëns was a man of wide culture, and in his literary works he vividly expresses the viewpoint of one who believes in 'art for art's sake' – very different from the widely held nineteenth-century Romantic viewpoint. His work as a whole, with its clarity, wit and craftsmanship, provided a powerful example and stimulus to many other French composers, including Fauré and **Ravel**.

Further reading

See: *École buissonnière* (1913); and Arthur Hervey, *Saint-Saëns* (1921); James Harding, *Saint-Saëns and His Circle* (1965); R. Smith, *Saint-Saëns and the*

Organ (1992); Brian Rees, *Saint-Saëns* (1999); Timothy Flynn, *Camille Saint-Saëns: A Guide to Research* (2003).

DAVID COX

SALINGER, Jerome David

1919–

US writer

J.D. Salinger was born in New York City of a Jewish father and Christian mother. He graduated from Valley Forge Military Academy, then studied at New York University and Ursinus College. He never received a degree but did attend Whit Burnett's short-story writing class at Columbia. During the Second World War he took part in the D-Day landings and five campaigns. His war experiences may have had a marked effect upon his attitude towards man, as he has chosen to live in seclusion with his family in New Hampshire, granting only one interview and avoiding all contact with the public. This lifestyle, combined with lengthy gaps between appearances in print, has given Salinger an aura of mystery.

He has been one of the most popular American authors and remains an important fiction writer of the post-war period. His major work is the novel of adolescent rebellion, *The Catcher in the Rye* (1951). Holden Caulfield, the protagonist, is a twentieth-century alienated youth trying to find what he considers honesty in a materialistic and superficial post-war America. Speaking in an adolescent vernacular with a strongly black humorous tinge, he finds that the word 'phony' describes most of what he sees. One can find in this novel the major themes of Salinger's best work: the inability of man to live without love; the need for acceptance of people's shortcomings, this acceptance possibly proving to be a sign of wisdom; and the importance of children, who can provide the key to a return to emotional stability.

The movement towards emotional stability and a reintegration with human society also occurs in Salinger's best short story, 'For

Esmé – with Love and Squalor' (1950). Through the influence of two children the protagonist is able to achieve a sense of peace with himself despite the horrors of war. Esmé in particular permits Sergeant X to overcome the squalor of his situation. This 'squalor' would be explored again the following year in terms of twentieth-century society in *Catcher*.

Peace is not, however, granted to Seymour ('See-more'), the poet-sage of the Glass family, whose suicide is described in 'A Perfect Day for Bananafish' (1948). Chronicling the Glass family has become Salinger's primary literary effort, and a number of the stories collected in *Nine Stories* (1953) contain various family members. Salinger's interest in Zen Buddhism is reflected in Seymour's influence upon various of the younger Glasses, who have been both aided and hindered in their development by Seymour's stress upon universal love, looking beyond externals to what lies beneath, and intense introspection. Seymour's suicide has not lessened the validity of his teachings for the younger Glasses and, one suspects, for Salinger himself.

The style in later works concerning the Glass family like 'Franny' (1955), 'Zooey' (1957), 'Raise High the Roofbeam, Carpenters' (1955), and 'Seymour: An Introduction' (1959) is, with the exception of 'Franny', verbose, lacking in focus and, unlike *Catcher*, not particularly humorous. Salinger places a heavy hand upon the narrative, which mars the effectiveness of the tales. There is a self-indulgence in 'Zooey', 'Roofbeam', and 'Seymour' which tends to blunt appreciation of Salinger's ideas.

Between 1963 and 1997, when he published *Hapworth*, a novella, Salinger fell silent, claiming in a rare interview that publication represents a 'terrible invasion of my privacy'. Instead he has preferred the life of a recluse in rural New Hampshire. An assurance that he has always continued to write, however, promises a revival of his cult standing among American readers.

Further reading

Other collections of Salinger's work include: *Franny and Zooey* (1961); *Raise High the Roofbeam,* *Carpenters; and Seymour: An Introduction* (1963). See also: Frederick L. Gwynn and Joseph L. Blotner, *The Fiction of J.D. Salinger* (1958); William F. Belcher and James W. Lee (eds) *J.D. Salinger and the Critics* (1962); Warren French, *J.D. Salinger* (1963); Malcolm M. Marsden (ed.) *If You Really Want to Know: A Catcher Casebook* (1963); Ian Hamilton, *In Search of J.D. Salinger* (1988).

E.A. ABRAMSON

SANDBURG, Carl
1878–1967
US writer

Carl Sandburg was more than a writer; he was an institution. As a novelist, a biographer, a dramatist, a writer of children's stories, a folk singer and a collector of folk songs, he celebrated, throughout his long life, the men, ideas, ways and speech of the Middle West where he was born. His birthplace was Galesburg, Illinois, and he came of a family of Swedish immigrants. When he was thirteen, he left school to work as a labourer and, for the next seven years travelled in Kansas, Nebraska and Colorado. In 1898, he went back to Galesburg with the trade of house-painter, enlisted in the Sixth Illinois Infantry and was sent to the Spanish-American War. After eight months' service, however, he returned once more to Galesburg, and, between the ages of twenty and twenty-four, worked his way through the local college. In 1902, he left again on his wanderings, ending up in 1910 in Milwaukee as secretary to the mayor.

In the meantime he had married the sister of Steichen the photographer and published a pamphlet with the title *In Restless Ecstasy* (1904). In 1913, at the age of thirty-five, he moved to Chicago and began a career as a journalist and poet. As a result of the publication of 'Chicago' and other poems in the newly founded magazine *Poetry*, he was awarded a literary prize (1914). More solid success, however, came with the appearance of *Chicago Poems* (1916), capped by *Cornhuskers* (1918). At the end of the war he went to Stockholm as a foreign correspondent, but returned to join the Chicago *Daily News* as an editorial writer. After the publication of *Smoke and Steel* (1920), Sandburg began to tour the country as a lecturer and folk singer. Another book of poems, *Slabs of the Sunburnt West*, came out in 1922, and, in the same year, a children's book, *Rootabaga Stories*.

In 1926, Sandburg brought out the first two volumes of his monumental biography of Lincoln, *Abraham Lincoln: The Prairie Years*, and, in 1927, *The American Songbag*, a collection of folk songs. In 1928 he published *Good Morning, America* and was Phi Beta Kappa poet at Harvard. His biography, *Mary Lincoln: Wife and Widow*, was published in 1932, and a year later he retired from the *Chicago Daily News* to work full-time on his biography of **Lincoln**. He was then fifty-four. If he had retired from journalism, however, he had not retired from professional life. In 1936, in the middle of the Depression years, after a period as lecturer at the University of Hawaii, he brought out his most ambitious and perhaps his best book of poems, *The People, Yes* (1936). *Abraham Lincoln: The War Years* (4 vols) appeared on the eve of the Second World War, after which time Sandburg published a novel, *Remembrance Rock* (1948), and an autobiography, *Always the Young Strangers* (1953). In his old age Sandburg was still giving lectures and singing folk songs in his own highly individual way all over America.

Sandburg is often compared with **Whitman**, but the resemblance – except in some of the early poems like 'Chicago' – is scarcely more than superficial. Whitman was far more of a 'literary' man than Sandburg. He may have talked about going among the people but his composition was of the study. Not the rhythms of speech or folk song, but the rhythms of the Bible were Whitman's interest. The antithesis and parallelism in Whitman's verse are based on literary example; the free rhythms of Sandburg spring direct from talk and verbal storytelling. To this degree, he is an heir of **Mark Twain** and the 'tall-tale' tellers of the West. Indeed, many modern tall-tales may be found in *The People, Yes*. The faith that Sandburg had in Lincoln as the

greatest representative of the democratic spirit of America comes from the folk faith in Lincoln that he encountered in his early prairie wanderings. Finally, where Whitman used the egocentric 'I' as a symbolic device, and, like other questioners and askers of his time, probed his own soul in relation to the universe, Sandburg was a political and social recorder. This, however, is no mean feat. As a representative of the spirit of the Middle West and of his time, Sandburg is unique.

Further reading

See: Harry Golden, *Carl Sandburg* (1961); Richard Crowder, *Carl Sandburg* (1963); Gay Wilson Allen, *Carl Sandburg* (1972); Lucas Longo, *Carl Sandburg: Poet and Historian* (1972); North Callahan, *Carl Sandburg: His Life and Works* (1989).

GEOFFREY MOORE

SANTAYANA, George

1863–1952

Spanish/US philosopher and critic

Born in Madrid of Spanish parents. Santayana was taken by his mother to Boston at the age of eight. He was educated at Harvard, a pupil of **William James** and Josiah Royce, and he himself taught philosophy there until 1911 when he resigned his professorship. He lived first in England, which he had visited in 1896, and then briefly in France before in the 1920s settling permanently to a life of strenuous contemplation in Rome, the city where, in the words of his splendid autobiography *Persons and Places* (3 vols, 1944–53), 'nature and art were most beautiful, and mankind least distorted from their complete character'. In his last years he was cared for by the sisters of a Catholic nursing home.

The Sense of Beauty (1896), Santayana's first book apart from a volume of verse published two years earlier, adopts a naturalistic approach to aesthetics and argues that the object of beauty is in effect endowed with the observer's reaction to it; beauty may be defined as 'pleasure objectified'. The sub-title of *The Life of Reason* (5 vols, 1905–6), the major work of this early period, was 'The Phases of Human Progress'. Here Santayana again presents a naturalistic interpretation of consciousness and analyses the role of reason in human life and the extent to which consciousness is capable of ordering disparate impulses into a harmonious whole. As in *Interpretations of Poetry and Religion* (1900), he views the religious impulse as essentially a poetic truth, so that religion may be described as 'poetry intervening in life', a point of view unfairly summarized in the quip that for Santayana there is no God and Mary is his mother.

His philosophical writings in the 1920s and 1930s both reinforce and refine these earlier statements. *Scepticism and Animal Faith* (1923) acts as an introduction to the arguments advanced in *The Realms of Being* (4 vols, 1927–40) where Santayana attempts to combine his radical scepticism with a theory of universal 'essences', modes of being which do not exist but which are nevertheless real. Belief in the realm of matter, which is anterior to the other realms of essence, truth and spirit, depends upon an act of 'animal faith', an instinctive belief, since matter may be apprehended only through its exemplification of essences.

It has sometimes been claimed that Santayana was neither an American nor a philosopher. He never adopted American nationality yet he spent forty years in that country and announced: 'It is as an American writer that I must be counted, if I am counted at all.' In his identification of the 'genteel tradition' in American life and thought Santayana was probably unfair to some of the Transcendentalists whose doctrines, together with those of Calvinism, he regarded as the sources of much that was antipathetic to him in American life. The phrase passed into common usage and was taken up by later and even more iconoclastic critics. In *The Last Puritan: A Memoir in the Form of a Novel* (1936) Santayana examines in fictional form the effects of this tradition in the 'absolutist conscience' of his hero Oliver Alden. Philosophical stances are embodied in some of the characters but the book is first and foremost an eminently readable novel which depicts a tradition in decay with a wry and ironic compassion.

The fact that Santayana in his work combined philosophical and literary activities has to some extent ensured that he has not received the attention he deserves either as a philosopher or as a critic. His special gift was for metaphor rather than for linguistic analysis, and his avoidance of the specialized concerns which have occupied philosophy during this century caused him to be viewed as the last humanist. While it is true that his entire writing, in poetry, fiction, essay and philosophy, may be interpreted as an extended meditation upon the human condition, his epistemology and ontology have slowly begun to receive serious attention.

Further reading

Other works include: *Three Philosophical Poets: Lucretius, Dante, and Goethe* (1910); *Character and Opinion in the United States* (1920); *Soliloquies in England and Later Soliloquies* (1922); *Dialogues in Limbo* (1926, rev. 1948); *Dominations and Powers* (1951). See also: James Ballowe (ed.) *George Santayana's America* (1967); Douglas Wilson (ed.) *The Genteel Tradition* (1967); R. C. Lyon (ed.) *Santayana on America* (1968); Daniel Cory (ed.) *The Letters of George Santayana* (1955). About Santayana: Paul A. Schilpp (ed.) *The Philosophy of George Santayana* (1940); Daniel Cory, *Santayana: The Later Years. A Portrait with Letters* (1963); Newton P. Stallknecht, *George Santayana* (1971); Timothy L.S. Sprigge, *Santayana: An Examination of His Philosophy* (1974); Lois Hughson, *Thresholds of Reality: George Santayana and Modernist Poetics* (1977); H.S. Levinson, *Santayana, Pragmatism and the Spiritual Life* (1992); Noel O'Sullivan, *Santayana* (1993).

HOWELL DANIELS

SAPIR, Edward

1884–1939

US anthropological linguist

Undoubtedly among the most brilliant and original contributors to the discipline, Sapir came somewhat fortuitously to linguistics. Transplanted to the US from his native Lauenburg (Pomerania) at the age of five, he won a scholarship to Columbia, graduated with distinction in 1904, and immediately embarked on a master's degree which seemed to point him firmly to a career as a Germanist. Still at Columbia, he met and came under the influence of the distinguished anthropologist **Franz Boas**, who had pioneered work on the cultures and languages of the American Indians. Fired by Boas's erudition and the richness of his concept of linguistic structure, Sapir changed completely the direction of his research, first leaving to do fieldwork among the Wishram Indians of Washington State and then undertaking a grammatical analysis of the Takelma language, for which he gained his doctorate in 1909. Within a few years, seizing the opportunities offered by an initially nomadic professional career (Berkeley 1907–8, Pennsylvania 1908–10, Ottawa 1910–25), he had widened his knowledge to include Yana, Paiute, Nootka and several of the Athabaskan group of languages. His first major appointment was as Chief of the Division of Anthropology in the Geological Survey of the Canadian National Museum; from there, he went to a chair in Chicago (1925–31) where he carried out some of his best-known work on the Navaho and Hupa, and finally to Yale where he became mentor to a glittering group of research students, among them Mary Haas, Morris Swadesh and **Benjamin Lee Whorf**. He died at Yale, after a series of heart attacks.

Sapir was a prolific and far-ranging writer, although by no means all his output reached print: at his death he left a mass of *inedita*, only a small part of which has been published, and sketches for a major work on the *Psychology of Culture*. *Language* (1921) was his only book. Otherwise, Sapir's professional writings consist of crisp accounts of the phonology and grammar of Amerindian languages, monograph collections of texts, anthropological studies and a handful of articles of wider theoretical import. He also composed poetry and wrote on music and literary criticism and, towards the end of his life, on Talmudic scholarship.

When Sapir began his fieldwork with the Wishram, foundations for the study of Amerindian languages had been laid by several cultural anthropologists – principally Boas – but extant linguistic material had been assembled less for its own sake than as part of a wider investigation of culture. It was fragmentary and gave little idea of relationships. Sapir aimed to redress the balance. He focused clearly on language, while retaining the research methods of an anthropologist (intensive work with an informant followed by a period 'in the field'), and developed as the need arose new techniques of linguistic analysis. He refined traditional concepts of typology and classification, applying his ideas not only to Amerindian languages but also to problems in the Indo-European and Semitic groups, notably the position of Tocharian.

Among linguists and non-specialists alike, Sapir is best remembered for his work on the interdependence of language and thought. Though sceptical about any deterministic relation of language and culture, his fieldwork convinced him that: 'Language and our thought-grooves are inextricably interrelated, are, in a sense, one and the same' (*Language*). He gave strong encouragement and material assistance to Whorf, who had arrived independently at similar ideas, whence the now almost universal label 'Sapir–Whorf hypothesis'. In its strongest form (one to which neither scholar would probably have subscribed) it claims that linguistic structure so conditions thought patterns as to *determine* perception of the outside world. In a weaker version – that language predisposes a particular world view – the theory now has many adherents and an impressive body of supporting evidence, though its interpretation remains inevitably controversial. In more narrowly linguistic circles, Sapir is quoted for his 'psychological' view of the phoneme (he believed that native speakers have an intuitive awareness of the pertinent sound-units of their language as much as of words), and for his theory of linguistic 'drift', an attempt to see, beyond the 'mechanistic' concept of language, change as a series of blind sound laws, a much longer-term coherence and directionality in the evolution.

Important as these technical questions are, Sapir's influence has been much more fundamental and pervasive – it amounts almost to an attitude of mind in linguistic research; for the mentalism/mechanism debate was essentially a struggle of the titans, Sapir versus Leonard Bloomfield (1887–1949). If Bloomfield gained the ascendant from the 1930s to the late 1950s, linguistics subsequently returned to an orientation much more in tune with that of Sapir.

Further reading

Other works include: *Selected Writings of Edward Sapir in Language, Culture and Personality*, ed. D.G. Mandelbaum (1949); *Navaho Texts*, ed. Harry Hoijer (1942); *Phonology and Morphology of the Navaho Language*, ed. Harry Hoijer (1967). The best critical appreciation of Sapir in the context of twentieth-century American linguistics is that of Georges Mounin, in *La Linguistique du XXe siècle* (1972). See also J.M. Penn, *Linguistic Relativity versus Innate Ideas* (1972); Regna Darnell, *Edward Sapir: Linguist, Anthropologist, Humanist* (1992); E.F.K. Koerner (ed.) *Edward Sapir: Critical Assessments of Leading Linguists* (2006).

JOHN N. GREEN

SARDOU, Victorien

1831–1908

French playwright

A prolific and successful writer, Sardou is identified by posterity with the formula of the 'well-made play' which he inherited from Eugène Scribe (1791–1861), who dominated the popular theatre in France from the 1820s to his death. The well-made play (whose plot is constructed according to a tight logic, not according to the looser, less predictable dictates of character; character being subordinated to plot, and plot conceived in terms of preparation, crisis and dénouement, with a series of contrived climaxes to create suspense) perfectly suited the *comédie-vaudeville*

of the middle of the nineteenth century. However, when the same mechanical construction, turning characters into puppets controlled by chance, was applied (by Sardou and others) to more serious social dramas and problem plays, the limitations of the formula became very evident. Sardou, who frequently wrote for Sarah Bernhardt, to whom the success of many of his plays in Paris was due, was also much played in the London theatres from the 1860s to the end of the century, and **Bernard Shaw** became his most forceful critic. Shaw coined the term 'Sardoodledom' to devalue the empty craftsmanship of melodramas like *Fedora* (1882); and his scornful denunciation of Sardou's contrivances ('the two Sardovian servants ... their pretended function being to expound the plot, their real one to bore the audience sufficiently to make the principals doubly welcome when they arrive') and coincidences ('the postal arrangements, the telegraphic arrangements, the police arrangements, the names and addresses, the hours and seasons, the tables of consanguinity, the railway and shipping timetables, the arrivals and departures, the whole welter of Bradshaw and Baedeker, Court Guide and Post Office Directory ... make up an entertainment too Bedlamite for many with settled wits to preconceive') makes very amusing reading. In fact Sardou had a remarkably wide range. The genres in which he achieved his best-known successes – those of social drama or melodrama (*La Famille Benoiton,* 1865; *Rabagas,* 1872) or historical melodrama (*Madame Sans-gene,* 1893; *La Tosca,* 1887, which was adapted by Giacosa and Illica in the libretto for **Puccini's** opera) – show his dramaturgy at its most mechanical and least inspired; and he was capable of writing both with a lighter touch and in a more genuinely serious vein. For instance, the widespread public interest in the projected divorce legislation (passed in 1883) gave rise to two very different plays on this topical subject: in *Divorçons* (1880) Sardou adopted the manner of the vaudeville, producing a lively farce in the style of Labiche or **Feydeau** (in which the proliferation of coincidences is of course an asset), whereas in *Daniel Rochat* (1880) a clash of attitudes towards marriage produces a serious, even a moving, study in credible terms of the relationship of a young couple. One hallmark of a Sardou play, whether on a modern or a historical subject, was a punctilious attention to detailed realism-of-setting, an inheritance from the *couleur locale* which had so preoccupied Dumas *père,* for instance, in his historical dramas, just as much as from the realist theatre of the Second Empire. In Sardou's case, there is a tendency for such stage 'business' at times to conceal a certain absence of more weighty or more memorable qualities. Not invariably, by any means: the subject of *Thermidor* (1891), for instance, was capable of provoking a near-riot in the Comédie-Française by left-wing students objecting to Sardou's condemnation of Robespierre and the Terror; the banning of the play by the Minister of the Interior was upheld by Clemenceau after a stormy Cabinet meeting.

Despite his great success in his lifetime both on Parisian stages and abroad, Sardou is largely forgotten except by the specialist. Like Scribe before him, he was the servant of the theatrical public, ready to exploit whatever dramatic form seemed assured of popular success. He lacked the higher ambition to guide and direct public taste, and was largely content to follow it.

Further reading

See: *Théâtre complet* (15 vols, 1934–61); R. Doumic, *De Scribe à Ibsen* (1912); J.A. Hart, *Sardou and the Sardou Plays* (1913).

W.D. HOWARTH

SARGENT, John Singer

1856–1925

US painter

Sargent always retained his American nationality, although he was born in Florence and trailed all over Europe as a child by his peripatetic parents, studied art in Paris and spent most of his career in London. The mentor of his early life as an artist was the fashionable Parisian portraitist Charles-Émile-Auguste Carolus-Duran, whose studio he entered in 1874 at the age of eighteen. The cornerstones of Carolus-Duran's teaching were bold brushwork, modelling by means of strong tonal contrasts and painting *au premier coup*, without preparatory sketches or underpainting. Keenly observant and gifted with extraordinary manual dexterity, Sargent became a star pupil. He left to set up his own studio in 1879. In the same year he visited Madrid and in 1880 Haarlem, where his education in the painterly manner was filled out by a study of Velasquez and Frans Hals. Sargent had a life-long fascination with travel and the exotic, and the most important of his early subject-pictures, *El Jaleo* (1882), was inspired by a flamboyant Andalusian dance he witnessed in Spain.

The influence of Carolus-Duran, Velasquez and Hals was augmented in the later 1880s by that of the French Impressionist painters. Curiously, it was not in France that Sargent painted his first pictures to show an assimilation of Impressionism, but England, during summer visits to the Cotswold villages of Broadway and Fladbury. Indebted above all to **Monet**, whom he knew and visited at least once at Giverny, Sargent began to show a new delight in broken brushwork, bright colour and transient effects of light. Nowhere is this more in evidence than in the masterpiece of this part of his career, *Carnation, Lily, Lily, Rose* (1885–6), a study of the two daughters of his artist friend Frederick Barnard lighting Chinese lanterns in a garden at twilight; and yet, with its relatively careful drawing, wistful mood and latent symbolism, *Carnation, Lily, Lily, Rose* stops short of the extreme objectivity and dissolution of form to which Impressionist ideas led Monet. Impressionism extended Sargent's range as a painter but, perhaps because the human figure was always his first interest, it never wholly claimed him. The most Impressionist works of his mature career were to be the oil and watercolour landscape sketches he made in large numbers, and purely for his own pleasure, on his long summer holidays abroad.

In 1886, still smarting from the ridicule levelled at his portrait of the society beauty *Madame Gautreau* when it was shown at the Paris Salon of 1884, and having found a circle of artistic friends in England far warmer and more sympathetic than anyone he knew in France (they included **Henry James** and **Edmund Gosse** as well as the painters Frederick Barnard and Alfred Parsons), Sargent decided to move to London; he lived in Tite Street, Chelsea, for the rest of his life. *Madame Gautreau* had been the culmination of an impressive series of portraits painted in Paris and Sargent had hoped it would establish his reputation specifically as a portraitist. In London his reputation in this field grew with almost startling ease and rapidity. By 1894, when he was elected an Associate of the Royal Academy (he became a full Academician in 1897), he was more or less universally recognized as the leading portraitist in England; and he only gave up this position at his own wish, virtually abandoning his practice around 1907 except for quick head-and-shoulders sketches in charcoal. Dubbed by **Rodin** 'the Van Dyck of our times', he enjoyed the patronage of both aristocracy and *nouveaux riches*, investing such sitters as the Duke and Duchess of Marlborough with the appropriate pomp and superiority but clearly more at home with the family of Asher Wertheimer, a Bond Street art dealer of unashamed affluence, whom he painted in a series of portraits, most of which are now at the Tate Gallery.

Sargent's technique, always the most fascinating aspect of his work, becomes ever more dashing in his London portraits, ever more that of the supremely confident virtuoso; brushwork which at the proper distance denotes some accessory or part of a dress becomes quite meaningless, though often ravishingly beautiful as a purely abstract design, when seen close to. Sitters were struck by his way of charging at the canvas from a distance, armed with a loaded brush and muttering strange oaths, rapidly painting in an area and then retiring to contemplate the result. At his best, Sargent shows just as much flair for overall design as for brushwork, taking idiosyncratic viewpoints, inventing brilliantly original poses and, in the case of portraits including more than one sitter, groupings that suggest complex psychological relationships. He was a worthy heir to the great tradition of portraiture in Britain stretching back to Van Dyck via Reynolds, Gainsborough and Lawrence – a tradition that had languished for most of the Victorian period and has languished ever since.

In the work on a monumental scale that Sargent carried on from 1890 onwards in the form of his murals in the Public Library and the Museum of Fine Arts in Boston, he is hardly recognizable as the same artist. Tackling an elaborate symbolical programme describing the development of religious thought from paganism to Christianity in the first, and various classical themes in the second, he replaces painterly bravura with a rather routine decorative style derived largely from Italian Renaissance models. More successful than any of the murals is the large-scale figure composition entitled simply *Gassed* 1918–19), which Sargent painted to a commission from the War Artists Committee. The feeling of authenticity about *Gassed* is undeniably powerful, but set against the work of younger war artists such as Paul Nash, its realism looks just as undeniably antediluvian.

For much of the twentieth century Sargent's reputation suffered from the tendency of art history to pass over artists who are not of the avant-garde, from the too easy equation of facility with superficiality and, perhaps most of all, from the fact that his work is so closely bound up with wealth and class. Latterly the balance has begun to be righted in recent years, largely by Richard Ormond's book *John Singer Sargent* (1970) and the exhibition *John Singer Sargent and the Edwardian Age* held at Lotherton Hall in Leeds, the National Portrait Gallery in London and the Detroit

Institute of Arts in 1979 (catalogue by James Lomax and Richard Ormond).

Further reading

See: S. Olson, *John Singer Sargent: His Portrait* (1986)

MALCOLM WARNER

SARRAUTE, Nathalie

1900–99

French novelist, playwright, autobiographer

Nathalie Sarraute was one of the great prose writers of twentieth-century France, best known first for her association with the experimental fiction of the *nouveau roman*, and later, with the appearance of *Enfance (Childhood)*, as a distinctive voice in the emergence of a new kind of autobiography in the 1980s.

Born in Russia of Russian-Jewish parents who divorced when she was two, she grew up in a multi-lingual, cosmopolitan world, principally between St Petersburg and Paris where she settled with her father, whose links with revolutionary groups had forced him into exile. She had a largely French school-education. After obtaining a degree in English at the Sorbonne, she spent a year at Oxford University, and another at Berlin University before returning to the Faculté de Droit in Paris to study law. She practised law for a number of years, though with little enthusiasm, and devoted herself increasingly to writing. She married a fellow law student Raymond Sarraute in 1925 and had three daughters between 1927 and 1933. As a married woman, she was initially required by French law to have the written consent of her husband for the publication of her work.

During the 1930s her earliest literary efforts took the form of short prose pieces for which the inspiration was pan-European, namely **Proust**, **Rilke**, **Virginia Woolf** and **Katherine Mansfield**. After being turned down by a number of prestigious publishers, they eventually appeared in 1939 under the title *Tropismes* published by Robert Denoël (also the publisher of **Céline**). This term, *tropismes*, sums up what lies at the heart of all her preoccupations, namely the responses of people to each other in the form of semi-conscious sensations on the borders of consciousness, and which escape conventional forms of linguistic expression. She continued to write under the German Occupation, during which she officially divorced her husband so that his ability to practise as a lawyer would not be compromised because of his marriage to a Jewish wife. She was eventually obliged to go into hiding and posed under a pseudonym as schoolteacher and aunt to her own children.

It was only after the war that she started to become established as a writer. A meeting with **Sartre** in 1945 led to an association with *Les Temps modernes* in which extracts of her first two novels and a number of important critical essays were published between 1946 and 1953. Sartre wrote a preface to her first novel, *Portrait of a Man Unknown* (*Portrait d'un inconnu*, 1948) and helped to find a publisher for it. But despite some similarities with certain features of Sartre's novel *La Nausée*, there was no deeper common cause between Sarraute and the broad project of Existentialism. A second novel, *Martereau*, appeared in 1953. Her essays attacking the continuation of traditional forms of fiction and proposing new lines of development were published in book form (as *L'Ere du soupçon*, 'The Age of Suspicion') in 1956 and attracted the attention of **Alain Robbe-Grillet** who shared her mpatience with current novelistic conventions. It was this collaboration which consolidated the existence of the *nouveau roman*, a term coined in 1957 and used to describe the work of Sarraute, Robbe-Grillet, Butor, Claude Simon and a number of others. Sarraute's earlier novels are now read as part of this movement. Others followed: *The Planetarium* (*Le Planétarium*, 1959), *The Golden Fruits* (*Les Fruits d'or*, 1963) which established Nathalie Sarraute as a major literary figure by winning her the Prix International de

Littérature, *Between Life and Death* (*Entre la vie et la mort*, 1968), *Do You Hear Them?* (*Vous les entendez?*, 1972) and *Fools Say* (*Disent les imbéciles*, 1976).

Although the polemical essays attacking character and plot in particular assured her of a central place in the *nouveau roman*, Nathalie Sarraute seems to have found her association with her fellow-writers in this group increasingly uncomfortable during the 1960s because of their shift of emphasis from the portrayal of new areas of reality, to the idea of language as the sole reality. She always regarded the representation of psychic experience as the central feature of her work, and her own particular view of it is summed up in her term 'tropisms'. The anonymous characters in her novels, whatever their overt social position, preoccupations and behaviour, are all ultimately subject to the 'tropism', to the 'terrible desire to establish contact' (a phrase borrowed from Katherine Mansfield), a longing for contact with the other and a concomitant fear of vulnerability or rejection. The underlying action of her novels consists in a ceaseless mutual probing and testing between the characters, which goes on behind the pretext or mask of purely social behaviour: buying a chair, telling anecdotes, discussing a book or admiring a piece of sculpture.

Although passion and desire in these novels are as intense and as extreme as in **Dostoevsky** always a seminal point of reference), Sarraute's is a world of talk. All contact, betrayal or violence takes place behind and by means of talk whose potentially destructive effects are adumbrated through what she calls a 'sous-conversation' of imagery, rather than through conventional psychological analysis. This emphasis on dialogue in the novel has a parallel which Sarraute herself drew with the works of two English novelists, **Henry Green** and **Ivy Compton-Burnett**, though neither could be regarded as direct influences on her fiction.

During the 1960s Sarraute embarked on a new, parallel career as a dramatist. In response to a commission from Süddeutscher Rundfunk,

she wrote the first of a series of plays for radio, beginning with *The Lie* (*Le Mensonge*, first broadcast in 1964) and *Silence* (*Le Silence*, broadcast in France and Germany in 1966). These were subsequently performed in stage versions, notably by Jean-Louis Barrault, who put on a double-bill in the Odéon theatre in 1967, and this experience led ultimately to the writing of two plays directly for the stage, *She is There* (*Elle est là*, 1978) and *For a Yes or a No* (*Pour un oui ou pour un non*, 1982). A film version of this last play with Jean-Louis Trintignant was made by Jacques Doillon in 1988. The dramatic tension in Sarraute's dialogues was what made this transition to theatre possible, and the result was a quite distinctive dramatic idiom which has become an established part of the modern repertoire in France.

Never entirely happy with either the scale or the conventions of the novel, Nathalie Sarraute reverted increasingly to the short prose-text as the basic building block of her work from the 1980s onwards. *The Use of Speech* (*L'Usage de la parole*, 1980) consists of a series of unrelated texts, each of which worries away at the implications of a remembered utterance. This fragmentary structure is used also in the autobiographical *Childhood* (*Enfance*, 1983) which takes words from the author's past as the focus of each free-standing episode and is narrated in the form of a dialogue between the author and her alter ego. *Enfance* established Sarraute definitively as a writer on her own terms, rather than as an exponent of the *nouveau roman*. It also helped to inaugurate an era of experimental autobiography (with other examples from Marguerite Duras, **Alain Robbe-Grillet**) and is the most widely read of her writings. This fragmentary form was used in the last two of Sarraute's works, first in *Ici* ('Here', 1995), and, two years before her death, in *Open* (*Ouvrez*, 1997), where words themselves become the protagonists of each episode.

Most of the action she portrays could be summed up as 'how to do things with words', and those things are often presented as extreme and cruel. This is because, for

Sarraute, words are weapons used every day in 'innumerable small crimes', and always remain open to infinite speculation about the intent behind them. The role of Sarraute's writing is to articulate the imaginings of her characters about these 'crimes' in often comically grotesque translations of their semi-conscious responses, creating a parallel reality to the ordinary forms of everyday existence. She had a sharp ear for the rhythms of speech and her written prose vividly conveys the inflections of the spoken word. Although she is one of the major women writers in twentieth-century French literature, she resisted all attempts to place her work in the camps of *écriture féminine* or feminist theory, insisting that writing is produced in an anonymous place inside the self where gender does not apply.

Further reading

See: Valerie Minogue, *Nathalie Sarraute and the War of the Words* (1981) and Ann Jefferson, *Nathalie Sarraute, Fiction and Theory: Questions of Difference (2000)*.

ANN JEFFERSON

SARTRE, Jean-Paul

1905–80

French philosopher, novelist, playwright, essayist, left-wing militant

A traditional French educational background prepared Sartre well for a characteristic middle-class career. After the *lycée*, he went to the École Normale Supérieure, where he studied philosophy. He failed his first attempt at the *agrégation* completely, but tried it again the following year (1929) and came out first in that competitive examination. From this point, the road ahead was clear for a successful future as a teacher, first in a *lycée* and then in the university. And, indeed, following his military service, he was appointed to a teaching post in Le Havre in 1931; his teaching career subsequently took him to Laon, and then to Paris, where it eventually

came to an end in 1944: his period of notoriety had begun.

We may believe Sartre when, in his autobiography, *Words* (*Les Mots*, 1963, trans. 1964), he tells us that he began writing in his earliest years. His first published text dates from 1923, when he was still only seventeen, but it was not until 1936, with the publication of two pieces of work, that he gave some solid indication of his future development. The first, *Imagination: A Psychological Critique* (*L'Imagination*, 1936, trans. 1962), is a revised version of a study of theories of the imagination from the time of Descartes on, first undertaken as a student in 1926, and includes an account of **Husserl's** views, with which Sartre had come into contact in the year 1933–4, when he had lived and studied in Berlin. The second text, *The Transcendence of the Ego: An Existentialist Theory of Consciousness* (*La Transcendance de l'Ego: esquisse d'une description phénoménologique*, 1936, trans. 1957), together with an article published in 1939 under the title 'Intentionality: A Fundamental Idea of Husserl's Phenomenology' ('Une idée fondamentale de la phénoménologie de Husserl: l'intentionnalité', trans. 1970), was written during his stay in Berlin. All three are of importance, not only as evidence of Sartre's early interest in the imagination and his dissatisfaction with deterministic views of individual psychology, but also as a reminder that, contrary to what seems often to be believed, his philosophical existence did not begin only in 1943, with the publication of *Being and Nothingness: An Essay in Phenomenological Ontology* (*L'Être et le néant, essai de phénoménologie ontologique*, 1943, trans. 1956).

Indeed, the importance of Sartre's intellectual activity during the 1930s cannot be exaggerated. Publication dates give a false sense of chronology: the fact of the matter is that a whole series of works was being elaborated concurrently in the pre-war years: apart from those already mentioned, Sartre was also working on his *Sketch for a Theory of the Emotions* (*Esquisse d'une théorie des émotions*, 1936, trans. 1962, and *The Emotions, Outline of a Theory*, 1948), the stories collected in 1939 under the title *Le Mur* (1939, trans. as *Intimacy and Other Stories*, 1949, and *The Wall and Other Stories*, 1948), *The Diary of Antoine Roquentin* (*La Nausée*, 1938, trans. 1949, and as *Nausea*, 1949), in progress since 1931, *Psychology of the Imagination* (*L'Imaginaire, psychologie phénoménologique de l'imagination*, 1940, trans. 1949), the second part of *Imagination*. *Being and Nothingness* itself was the result of his philosophical reflections since the encounter with the thought of Husserl in 1933, and began to take form in 1939. By the time it appeared in print, it was already in one sense a work attached to Sartre's past rather than to his present: the notion of commitment, which began to assume importance for him in 1940, had brought about a change of emphasis in his thinking.

A change of emphasis, but not a revolution, in that his literary, aesthetic and moral preoccupations remained strong, continuing to produce tension with that part of him which aspired towards a direct involvement in the affairs of the day. *The Diary of Antoine Roquentin*, quite apart from its considerable qualities as a novel, provides clear evidence why this should be so. To the extent that the starting-point for Roquentin's diary is an anxiety to do with the nature of being and existence, the novel clearly has metaphysical resonances; Roquentin perceives the problem, however, largely in terms of his immediate environment. The awareness of his own contingency through the insistence with which the material world forces itself upon his attention is linked to the absence of relationships between him and his fellow-men. This has the advantage of making it possible for him to view the inhabitants of Bouville from a privileged, detached standpoint, and to take a highly critical view of their behaviour and of the 'values' by which they live. On the other hand, his observation of them as manifestations, among others, of the phenomenon of Existence, does nothing to relieve his anxiety: he can be no less contingent than they. It is not, therefore, surprising that he should seek an escape from an obsession with his contingency in a direction that removes him even further from other men: a work of literature, independent of the material world, having its being in the non-real universe of the imaginary, will both distance him from his fellows and place him in a situation superior to them.

The procedure is consistent with Sartre's views on the imagination and the imaginary, but it is Sartrean in other respects as well. Roquentin shares Sartre's romantic view of the privileged situation of the artist, as well as the notion that salvation may be achieved through the production of works of art: and it may well be that this one idea, more than any other, for a long while prevented Sartre from understanding that commitment implies necessarily the abandoning of any kind of individual privilege. In addition, Roquentin illustrates the curious link between Sartre's aesthetic and moral views which will be evident in many of his characters. The work of art is absolute and non-contingent because it is imaginary; but it is the product of the imagination of the artist, who is relative and contingent. It may therefore be a source of salvation for the artist, as Roquentin sees, in that he, as a contingent existent, must transcend himself in the act of creating the non-contingent art-object. As Roquentin equally clearly sees, however, such a form of salvation may apply only to the past; it is neither a justification for the future self (which does not exist), nor a guide for living.

Others are not so clear-sighted: they, too, will seek to create an image – an image of themselves, which will therefore exist *outside* them, but which at the same time will *be* them, and with which they will attempt to coincide. The most obvious examples are those bourgeois in *The Diary of Antoine Roquentin* who actually pay painters to fix the image on canvas, in what Sartre elsewhere calls '*portraits officiels*', whose function is to 'defend man against himself'. The attempt is understandable: our existence is not justified, we have no prior definition, we create ourselves through our acts, and can be known as a complete entity only when the series of acts is complete – namely, at death. The resulting anguish is what may lead us to anticipate that moment by the creation of a self-image which, since we shall see it as definitive, will at the same time dictate our future conduct. The procedure is characteristic of the 'bad faith' (*mauvaise foi*) displayed by so many of Sartre's characters, attempting to persuade themselves that they have succeeded in the impossible task of bringing about a coincidence between the real and the ideal.

The theme is exploited throughout a large part of Sartre's career – most notably in his theatre, always concerned with action (an ambiguous term, in that the 'action' we see in a play is imaginary, and so unreal), and with his characters' attempts to escape the consequences of the need to act. The fact should not surprise us: the evidence of the autobiography is that, despite his efforts in other directions, Sartre himself remained attached to his role as a writer at least until the 1950s.

In the meantime, his growing reputation placed him in the forefront of French intellectual life, and made him a figure of international consequence. Along with a group of more or less like-minded intellectuals and artists (among them **Simone de Beauvoir**, with whom he had enjoyed a close relationship since 1929, and who would continue to participate closely in his varied activities), he had emerged as a significant force in the first post-war generation. The Existentialist vogue of the years immediately following the liberation of Paris, combined with his own intense activity, meant that his name was constantly before the public. It was not simply a matter of publishing novels or writing plays, but also of taking part in a great debate about the nature of Existentialism, attacked on the left as a manifestation of a bourgeois culture in the process of decomposition, and on the right as a form of mental illness. Sartre was, of course, more concerned about the attacks from the left than about the reactions of the right, and many of the articles he produced for his monthly revue, *Les Temps modernes*, which began publication in October 1945, were an attempt to present his views on

contemporary issues as well as on his situation as a writer (see, for example, his *Présentation* in the first number, in which he defines his editorial line and gives his views on committed literature).

His controversial position in public life led inevitably to tension between himself and those around him. As early as June 1946, **Raymond Aron** left *Les Temps modernes*; a few months later a quarrel with **Camus** kept them apart for a year. The final break with Aron (along with **Arthur Koestler**) came at the end of 1947, and with Camus in 1952. At the same time, he was involved in the ideological differences of the post-war world, and in 1948 was a leading figure in the creation of a new – but not long-lived – political party, the Rassemblement Démocratique Révolutionnaire (RDR). The 1950s, corresponding with the point at which he finally realized that the fact of being a writer gave him no particularly privileged position, see him more and more heavily engaged in the affairs of the day, the more so in that the Algerian war emerged as a conflict which demanded commitment. The list of the events on which he took a stand between that time and his death is very long – whether by writing, interview, public declaration or direct participation. He made pronouncements on major political and international issues, stood up for what he saw as oppressed minorities, gave his moral or material backing to struggling or harassed left-wing publications. Eventually his activity was severely restricted by the deterioration of his eyesight to a state of near-blindness.

Even before the onset of physical infirmity, however, it was clear to Sartre himself that he had never been, and was not, the kind of intellectual he would wish to be in the contemporary world – a man ready and able to put his gifts at the service of the people instead of using them as a means of perpetuating a bourgeois culture. It is true that, in this respect, he was not necessarily his own best friend. During the 1950s, he published his study of **Jean Genet**, as well as three plays; the 1960s saw the appearance of his autobiography, his adaptation of the *Trojan*

Women, and a number of studies of painters; his three large volumes on **Flaubert** followed in 1971–2. All of this work is of a kind one might well expect from an intellectual of Sartre's background. And, indeed, the same might be said of his *Critique de la raison dialectique* ('Critique of Dialectical Reason', 1960), intended as a bridge-building operation between Existentialism and **Marxism**, but given relatively little attention, partly, no doubt, because many have been daunted by its 750 closely printed pages.

It is not, of course, the case that such work prevented Sartre from continuing on his more obviously political course; on the contrary, as his bibliography makes clear. Nevertheless, it is a fact that, by the age of fifty, he had become a victim of his own reputation: whatever his own wishes in the matter, his public image was already firmly fixed. The problem is well illustrated by the award to him, in 1964, of the Nobel Prize for Literature. Sartre wished to refuse the prize, both because he believed that the writer should not allow himself to be transformed into an institution, and because he had no desire for the bourgeois respectability bestowed by the Swedish Academy. But he discovered that potential recipients are not consulted as to whether or not they are prepared to accept the prize; what is more, they may not refuse it. Despite his resistance, Sartre *is* the Nobel prizewinner for 1964.

For a man who worked so energetically and so productively, Sartre left a surprising amount of work incomplete. Apart from some fragments, the Ethics promised at the end of *Being and Nothingness* did not see the light of day; the same is true of the final volume of his *Roads to Freedom* (*Les Chemins de la liberté*, 3 vols, Paris 1945–9, trans. 1947–50). The second part of the *Critique de la raison dialectique* was not written, and the fourth and final volume of the study of Flaubert was abandoned. This is not necessarily evidence of failure, but rather of the fact that changing circumstances may, for example, deprive long-term projects of their *raison d'être*. Failures there were, though, most notably in

the area of bridge-building between Existentialism and Marxism: for the Sartre of the 1940s and 1950s, such an operation was unrealizable both because of the resistances of Communist orthodoxy and Party suspicion of the bourgeois intellectual, and because of his own inability to free himself from many of the middle-class, liberal, idealist and romantic assumptions of his earlier years. After 1968 – too late – he saw that the intellectual should put himself at the disposal of the proletariat whose interests he wishes to promote, while avoiding the imposition of his own categories or habits of thought. Nevertheless, his achievement was considerable – as an intellectual influence on the post-1945 generation, and, curiously, as a moral example whose honesty and self-questioning were, in time, recognized even by those who were his enemies.

Further reading

Other works include: Plays – *The Flies* (*Les Mouches*, 1943, trans. 1946); *No Exit* (*Huis clos*, 1945, trans. 1946); *The Victors* (*Morts sans sépulture*, 1946, trans. 1949, as *Men Without Shadows* in UK); *The Respectful Prostitute* (*La Putain respecteuse*, 1946, trans. 1949); *Dirty Hands* (*Les Mains sales*, 1948, trans. 1949, as *Crime Passionnel* in UK); *Lucifer and the Lord* (*Le Diable et le bon Dieu*, 1951, trans. 1953, as *The Devil and the Good Lord* in USA, 1960); *Kean* (1956, trans. 1956); *Loser Wins* (*Les Séquestrés d'Altona*, 1959, trans. 1960, as *The Condemned of Altona* in USA, 1961); 'Existential Psychoanalysis' – *Baudelaire* (1947, trans. 1950); *Saint Genet, Actor and Martyr* (*Saint Genet, comédien et martyr*, 1952, trans. 1953); *L'Idiot de la famille: Gustave Flaubert de 1821 à 1857* ('The Idiot of the Family: Gustave Flaubert 1821–57', 3 vols, 1971–2). The most important of Sartre's periodical and occasional writings are collected in *Situations* (10 vols, Paris 1947–76). See also: *Un théâtre de situation* (1973), ed. M. Contat and M. Rybalka, who also produced the indispensable *The Writings of Jean-Paul Sartre: A Bibliographical Life* (*Les Ecrits de Sartre: chronologie, bibliographie commentée*, 1970, trans. 2 vols, 1974). On Sartre: Francis Jeanson, *Le Problème moral et la pensée de Sartre* (1947, rev. 1965) and *Sartre par lui-même* (1954); R. Laing and D. Cooper, *Reason and Violence: A Decade of Sartre's Philosophy 1950–60* (1964); A. Manser, *Sartre, a Philosophic Study* (1966); I. Murdoch, *Sartre: Romantic Rationalist* (1953); A.C. Solal, *Sartre* (1988).

KEITH GORE

SATIE, Erik

1866–1925

French composer

Recognized to be one of the major influences on experimental music in the twentieth century, Satie was born in the Normandy port of Honfleur of part-Scottish ancestry and brought up in a sheltered environment coloured by the friendship of an eccentric seafaring uncle. He received his first musical training from the local organist, a pupil of the Niedermeyer school of church music, and as a result developed a life-long interest in plain-song and the ritual of the Catholic Church. After an unsuccessful stay at the Paris Conservatoire he took up the life of a bohemian and was employed as second pianist at the famous 'Chat Noir' cabaret in Montmartre where he was exposed to the influences of the music-hall song and the infectious rhythms of the American cakewalk and early ragtime. Already writing short piano pieces in a rather austere modal style (*Sarabandes*, 1887, and *Gymnopédies*, 1888) he was to become involved with the mystic sect of the Rosicrucians headed by Sâr Peladan who asked him to contribute pieces of incidental music for the 'Rose-Croix' productions (*Upsud*, *Le Fils de l'étoiles*, *Messe des pauvres*, 1892–5). His mentor's increasing interest in the music and aesthetic of **Wagner** compelled him to dissociate himself from the sect and Paris life as a whole. Instead he took lodgings in the shabby southern suburb of Arceuil-Cachan where he remained for the rest of his life. Satie's tendency towards introversion and moodiness deprived him of many worth while friendships; however, his early meeting with **Debussy** caused him to cement a life-long relationship which, though fraught with constant misunderstandings on Satie's part, was to prove a major contribution to the musical output of both composers.

At the turn of the century French musical life was dominated by the influence of Wagner and **César Franck**, with the result that leading composers of this period like D'Indy, Debussy and Dukas were writing romantic orchestral and operatic works of massive proportions; Satie, in contrast, had only produced a handful of café songs and piano miniatures while enduring a life of total self-sufficiency and utter poverty. A decision at the age of forty to improve his own musical education by enrolling for a three-year course in counterpoint at the Schola Cantorum run by D'Indy showed him to be a man of continuing intellectual curiosity and humility. On gaining his diploma in 1908 he felt disillusioned by the fact that his new works were contrived and lacked the intuitive simplicity of his earlier ones: as a result he composed very little until the appearance of the suite for orchestra or piano entitled *En Habit de cheval* (1911). Despite this personal crisis, performances of his music were becoming more regular, and with the encouragement of his friends and teachers he was spurred on to write and publish more works. The piano suite *Sports et divertissements* (1914) is indicative of his mature style with its twenty thumbnail sketches of recreational pursuits painstakingly drawn in the most expert musical calligraphy and smattered with examples of the composer's laconic scenic descriptions.

The coming of the Great War, coupled with the onslaught of Cubism and Dada on the sensibilities of the Parisian artistic milieu, occasioned a meeting between the composer and **Jean Cocteau**. This, together with a commission in 1916 from **Diaghilev**, resulted in the first Cubist 'Ballet Realiste' called *Parade* with choreography by Massine and sets designed by **Picasso**. At last Erik Satie's reputation as France's foremost avant-garde composer was established and during the remaining years of his life he was to produce two further experimental ballets as well as *Socrate*, a symphonic drama for orchestra and voices (1919), which represented a return to the classical proportions and economy of means and expression in his first piano compositions.

Satie's contribution lies not only in his development of musical statements which are unique in construction, but also in his inspired aesthetic sense which endeavours to extend the listener's realm of aural perception. Most of his mature works are short and convey an elongated time sense using modal harmonies, repeated rhythmic patterns, aphoristic melodic shapes and a minimum of dynamic variation. Major composers who have openly acknowledged their debt to Satie number **Ravel**, Debussy, **Stravinsky** and some members of 'Les Six' who continued to write collaborative works for Diaghilev after his death. In the US **Aaron Copland** and Virgil Thomson cited the ballet *Relâche* (1924) with its special film score for René Char's 'Entracte Cinématographique' as a seminal influence in their own works; **Varèse** compares some of the Rosicrucian music to early experiments in electronic music and 'process composers' such as **Steve Reich** and Terry Riley have derived inspiration from Satie's use of a minimum of melodic material. In the post-war period Satie's greatest influence was in the works of **John Cage** and contemporaries, where the concept of 'Musique d'Ameublement' (Wallpaper Music) has formed a basis for their mixed-media events and 'Happenings'.

Further reading

See: Pierre-Daniel Templier, *Erik Satie* (1932, trans. 1969); Rollo Myers, *Erik Satie* (1948); Roger Shattuck, *The Banquet Years* (rev. edn 1968); James Harding, *Erik Satie* (1971) and *The Ox on the Roof* (1976); S.M. Whiting, *Satie the Bohemian: From Cabaret to Concert Hall* (1999).

MICHAEL ALEXANDER

SAUSSURE, Mongin-Ferdinand de

1857–1913

Swiss linguist

By virtue of one book, *Course in General Linguistics* (*Cours de linguistique générale*, 1916, trans. 1959), edited posthumously from students' lecture-notes, Saussure is commonly acknowledged as the father of modern linguistics and of the 'structuralist' movement.

Ferdinand de Saussure was the son of a prominent Genevese Huguenot family which had emigrated from Lorraine during the French wars of religion in the late sixteenth century. Ferdinand displayed a bent for language study in childhood and, after a false start reading science at Geneva University, went to study philology at Leipzig and Berlin. At twenty-one Saussure published his *Mémoire sur le système primitif des voyelles dans les langues indo-européennes* ('Memoir on the Original System of Vowels in the Indo-European Languages'), a monograph which has been described as 'the most splendid work of comparative philology ever written'; its chief theoretical conclusion, propounded by Saussure purely on the basis of logical analysis, was corroborated almost fifty years later from archaeological evidence.

Saussure lectured at the École Pratique des Hautes Études, Paris, from 1881 to 1891, before returning to a chair at Geneva, where he remained until his death. His life was uneventful; after publishing his doctoral dissertation in 1881 he wrote only some short notes and reviews, and his publications, like the bulk of his teaching, were concerned exclusively with the established discipline of Indo-European philology. Saussure resisted requests to expound his ideas on the theoretical foundations of linguistics, and finally lectured on the subject only because a colleague teaching general linguistics happened to retire in the middle of a session.

Saussure's *Course* can be seen as part of a shift from the nineteenth-century emphasis on the historical approach as the key to understanding cultural phenomena to the twentieth-century emphasis on the sociological approach. For the ordinary (non-scholarly) speaker, Saussure said, his language has no history; if we wish to describe a language as a vehicle of communication, we need to explain not how its various components came to have their present form but how they relate to one another as a system now. Saussure called this kind of non-historical description 'synchronic' as opposed to 'diachronic'. In a synchronic '*état de langue*', what matter are not the individual components but the system of relationships between them. To understand the 'value' of the English word *sheep* we need to know that it contrasts with another word *mutton*; French *mouton* enters into no such contrast, so the 'value' of *mouton* is rather different from the 'value' of *sheep*. The units of sound called 'phonemes' are likewise defined by their contrasts with other phonemes. Saussure compares language to chess, in which the past history of a game is irrelevant to the situation reached at a given point, and the potential of any piece depends crucially on its relationships with other pieces, but not on its intrinsic properties: we could agree to replace the white queen by a lump of chalk without affecting the state of play.

It is oddly difficult to say how far Saussure has influenced subsequent thought. The idea that what matter in a system of meanings are the contrasts between elements rather than the elements themselves is axiomatic in contemporary linguistics; but this idea was already implicit in the work of **Franz Boas**, independently of Saussure. The related notion that the realms of thought and speech-sound are devoid of inherent structure, being articulated only by various languages which bring them into different arbitrary relationships with one another, was abandoned by later linguists such as **Roman Jakobson** (without this rejection being presented explicitly as a repudiation of Saussure). Saussure's **Durkheimian** view of language-structure as inhering in society as an organism, rather than in its individual members, has been largely ignored by subsequent linguists (and the relationship between Saussure's and Durkheim's thought has itself become a controversial question). Finally, recent work on language variation and change has suggested that Saussure's sharp distinction between synchrony and diachrony cannot be maintained, and that (contrary to Saussure's assumption) language changes may themselves be systematic in nature.

Within linguistics, Saussure became something of a cult figure whom many regard as a master but few read closely enough to appreciate how little they agree with him. Saussure's lasting influence has been primarily on the 'structuralist' movement, represented, for example, by **Claude Lévi-Strauss**, which takes its paradigm of enquiry from linguistics but applies it chiefly to other subjects.

Further reading

See: E.F.K. Koerner, *Ferdinand de Saussure* (1973); Jonathan Culler, *Saussure* (1976).

GEOFFREY SAMPSON

SCHENKER, Heinrich
1868–1935
Austrian music theorist

In the twenty-first century we might expect the dust around Heinrich Schenker to have settled. His biography is clear: he studied in Vienna with **Anton Bruckner**, and remained there for the rest of his life. He established an undisputed reputation as a critic, editor, piano accompanist, player of chamber music and private music teacher, and attracted to his cause some of the outstanding musicians of his day. His writings on music theory and analysis are now available in meticulously edited modern editions; they have been the subject of intense scrutiny; they have spawned several worthy efforts to distil their essence into a teaching and listening 'method'; they feature widely in music curricula; and they continue to attract the interest of composers and performers around the world. Yet the dust still swirls. Why?

There are two main arguments. The first is *ad hominem*. How, it is asked, could an eminent Jewish theorist promote a radically conservative, anti-modernist, 'élitist' agenda, pour such scorn on his opponents and admire the National Socialists (albeit in their early days)? After all, he despised the French, loathed the British, and would only admit Chopin and Scarlatti as honorary Germans. At a time when historians were reclaiming great tracts of early music, how could he confine himself mainly to the German instrumental masterpieces of the Bach-to-**Brahms** era, something he did in *Der Tonwille* (1921–4), *Das Meisterwerk in der Musik* (1925–30) and in earlier monographs on Beethoven's symphonies and sonatas? Was he not a reactionary chauvinist, *tout court*?

The second argument is historical. Again it is asked, although Schenker devised an approach that related 'free composition' (*Der freie Satz*, 1935) to a 'strict' background of harmony (*Harmonielehre*, 1906) and counterpoint (*Kontrapunkt*, 1910 and 1922), not forgetting ornamentation, articulation and dynamics, and although he rooted his work in 150 years of tradition (emanating from the eighteenth-century composer-theorists J.J. Fux and C.P.E. Bach) and through the Vienna *Photogramm-Archiv für Musikalische Meisterhandschriften* (founded in 1927) revolutionized editorial practice by sweeping away the whims of performers in favour of composers' autographs (notably in his editions of Beethoven sonatas), had he not also introduced a covert agenda of his own? True, he analysed movements in terms of their 'large line' as **Wagner** had done. But why he did posit the 'unutterably mystical' presence of a deep line, the '*Ursatz*' (a dynamic large-scale cadence perceptible only in small-scale pieces), when history offered no evidence for such a thing? Did not the synthesis by which he reconstructed pieces of music from hidden depths to visible surface point to the organicist metaphysics of his own age (as in his *Fünf Urlinie-tafeln*, 1935)? In his lust to show the relation of part to whole, had he not privileged the centripetal over the centrifugal, the strict forms over the loose ones (the fantasia and ballad) with their progressive tonalities? Had he not reduced the complex issues of modality to that of the single tonic major-minor system, dispensing with relative minor and modulation in favour of a bland 'monotonality'? Surely there is nothing for it but to replace his historical understanding with a more flexible one of our own?

Many of these arguments have won the day without annihilating their opponent. Critics recognize that Schenker clearly understood the mosaic-like construction of Wagner's music dramas; the musical world has endorsed his misgivings about **Schoenberg's** twelve-note 'system'; the classical concert repertory clings to the works he championed; and scholars have used his precepts to explore music from the early Renaissance to that of the present day. More still, his account of at least local tonal procedures rooted in 'linear progressions' holds good even though their origins now seem to lie in the Franco-Italian tradition; his description of tonal layers has won the interest of transformational linguistics; his notion of buried motifs remains revolutionary; his startling set of symbols for 'tonal coherence' have been universally adopted; and his unique approach to integrating line, harmony and key has been successfully integrated with new initiatives that emphasize rhetoric, genre and affect. That is to say, the notion that his 'Ideas' are timeless is rapidly gaining currency.

However, the most fruitful difference of views was with Arnold Schoenberg. Traditionally, Schoenberg believed composers should work with concrete and well-characterized phrases and forms to reveal the *individual* 'Idea' of a work; Schenker believed they should transfigure commonplaces that belong to the *collective* resource of music ('always the same, but always in a different way'). Analysts today would see the triumph of the Bach–Brahms era as holding these (and other) demands in balance. But at a time when modern ('spectral') composers eschew the 'concrete' in favour of working from the raw elements of sound, they may also find Schenker's insistence on 'abstraction' startlingly, if unexpectedly prophetic.

Further reading

See: *The New Grove Dictionary of Music and Musicians*, sixth edition, ed. Stanley Sadie (1980, revised 2000); and Heinrich Schenker's *Five Graphic Music Analyses*, ed. Felix Salzer (1969); Oswald Jonas, *Introduction to the Theory of Heinrich Schenker* (1934, trans. John Rothgeb, 1982).

CHRISTOPHER WINTLE

SCHLICK, Moritz

1882–1936

Austrian philosopher

Moritz Schlick was born in Berlin of prosperous parents. He studied at the University of Berlin where he did research in physics under **Max Planck**, obtaining his doctorate in 1904 for a thesis on the reflection of light in a non-homogeneous medium. After teaching at the University of Rostock from 1911 to 1917 he was appointed Professor at the University of Kiel in 1921 and moved as Professor to the University of Vienna in 1922. He remained there until his death in 1936 when, on his way to lecture at the university, he was fatally wounded by a deranged student making his second attempt on Schlick's life.

Schlick's background in science played a major role in his philosophical activities. He was one of the first philosophers to understand the physical content and philosophical significance of **Einstein's** Special and General Theories of Relativity. His early work, *Space and Time in Contemporary Physics* (*Raum und Zeit in der gegenwärtigen Physik,* 1917), provided a lucid non-technical introduction to relativity theory in which the verificationism characteristic of his mature philosophical position can be discerned. He argued that Einstein's work provided decisive reasons for rejecting the Kantian enterprise of attempting to discover synthetic truths about the structure of space and time through *a priori* investigations. In his *General Theory of Knowledge* (*Allgemeine Erkenntnislehre,* 1918) he broadens his Kantian critique, arguing that in no sphere of knowledge are there *synthetic a priori* judgements. At this stage Schlick held that there was a genuine controversy between realism and idealism which could be resolved philosophically in favour of what he called critical realism. The critical realist does not seek a certain base for knowledge in the Cartesian tradition but rather takes the individual sciences to provide knowledge of reality and limits himself to weeding out contradictions in science and to understanding the

significance of scientific achievements. Schlick attempted to resolve the traditional mind–body problem through identifying brain process with mental processes. In this work, as in his latter writings, the influence of Hume, **Mach**, Poincaré, **Russell** and Hilbert are evident.

Hans Hahn (mathematician), Phillip Frank (physicist) and Otto Neurath (economist), who had been meeting informally to discuss the philosophy of science, were responsible for Schlick's appointment in Vienna. Schlick became the leader of this group holding a weekly seminar, whose participants included (besides the above) Friedrich Waismann, Herbert Feigl, **Kurt Gödel** and **Rudolf Carnap**. The group, known as the Vienna Circle, developed and propagated Logical Positivism. Schlick's influence derives from his own work after coming to Vienna and through his organization of the Vienna Circle, which met regularly until his death.

Stimulated by these meetings and by his reading of **Wittgenstein's** *Tractatus Logico-Philosophicus,* which arguably he misinterpreted, Schlick re-examined his philosophical position. He ceased to see philosophy as a means for acquiring knowledge. Philosophy became the activity of revealing the meaning of propositions. With the exception of analytic statements which are true in virtue of their meaning and say nothing about the world, the meaning of empirical assertions is to be displayed by showing what would verify their truth. This doctrine was enshrined in his notorious verification principle (the central tenet of logical positivism) that the meaning of a sentence is the method of its verification. Henceforth metaphysics as traditionally conceived was to be dismissed. Logical analysis of the meaning of an assertion of a metaphysician would reveal three possibilities. The assertion might be analytically true and hence it would say nothing about the world. It might be a verifiable and hence meaningful empirical assertion, the investigation of the truth of which would be a matter for science. Or, more likely, it would be a meaningless concatenation of signs. Returning to the realist–idealist controversy, Schlick now argued that this represents a pseudo-problem, for the assertion of the realist that there is a transcendental reality and the denial of that assertion by the idealist are both meaningless in virtue of being unverifiable. Schlick applied his style of analysis to a wide range of concepts. For instance, he sought to remove metaphysical elements from the conception of causality by reducing causality to a matter of mere regularity in a manner reminiscent of Hume. He also discussed concepts specific to individual sciences, arguing against vitalism in biology and displaying the variation in the sense in which the concept of space is used in different sciences.

Unlike other members of the Circle, Schlick took the scope of science to include ethics, and in his lively and provocative *Problems of Ethics* (*Fragen der Ethik*, 1930) argued that theoretical ethics is a factual science whose cardinal principle is the empirical law that men act so as to maximize their own pleasure. To say that an act is good is to say that society holds the act to be pleasure-increasing. Thus, the determination of the good is a factual matter. For one sensitive as Schlick was to the importance of ascertaining the meaning of expressions, his analysis of ethical concepts is surprisingly crude.

Schlick was instrumental to the development and propagation of the doctrines of Logical Positivism. Often caricatured and generally rejected, the school as such has waned as much through a growing realization of the simplistic character of their conception of science as through an awareness of the philosophical problems in the verification principle. The logical positivists aspired to have philosophy take science seriously; to maintain the highest standards of rigour and clarity; to concern itself with meaning. Its influence can be seen in these continuing trends in contemporary philosophy.

Further reading

All Schlick's papers published between 1909 and his death are among those included in *Philosophical Papers,* vols I and II (1979); these volumes also include biographical sketches and a bibliography. See: Brian McGuinness (ed.) *Moritz Schlick* (1986); Sahotra Sarkar (ed.) *Logical Empiricism at Its Peak: Schlick, Carnap, and Neurath* (1996).

W.H. NEWTON-SMITH

SCHLIEMANN, Heinrich
1822–90
German archaeologist

Schliemann, the son of a clergyman, was compelled to break off his formal education at the age of fourteen to serve a five-year apprenticeship as a grocer. At the end of this he set out from Germany to make his fortune in Venezuela but was shipwrecked just off the Dutch coast. He abandoned his South American scheme and took a job as a clerk in Holland, in his spare time learning several languages, including Russian. In 1846 he was sent to St Petersburg as the agent of an export firm and soon began trading on his own account, exploiting the circumstances of the Crimean War to win huge profits handling chemicals. The next twelve years were devoted to expanding his business and at the end of that period Schliemann had amassed a vast fortune. He then wound up his business so that he could spend the rest of his life realizing a childhood ambition – the excavation of the ruins of Homeric Greece.

At this period the world of classical learning was divided between those who regarded the *Iliad* and the *Odyssey* as pure fiction, and those who believed that they contained a kernel of historical truth. In general the German school was hostile to historical interpretation, whose greatest support came from amateur classical scholars in England, like **Gladstone**. Schliemann, however, seems originally to have taken the extreme view that the Homeric poems could be read straightforwardly as historical documents. It was by acting on the detailed geographical evidence provided by the poems – the subject of his doctoral dissertation in 1869 – that he located Troy where he did.

The site, at Hissarlik in western Anatolia, was a huge artificial mound or 'tell', which Schliemann tackled by cutting a wide trench across from north to south. The results of the first three seasons, in which he was assisted by his young Greek wife, were disappointing. His technical competence was far in arrears of his enthusiasm: he did not appreciate the complex stratigraphy of the site, which reflected the collapse of successive settlements of clay brick dwellings over a period of some 2,000 years. The later layers, including those belonging to the city now believed to have been Homeric Troy (Troy VI), were simply hacked away with the object of reaching solid stone walls. The sort of success Schliemann was looking for came in 1873 with the discovery of fortress walls and above all a mass of gold, silver and copper vessels and weapons. These are now assigned to a city of the Early Bronze Age (Troy II) c. 2300 BC. At the time these finds were greeted by the scholarly world mainly with amused scepticism.

Schliemann had then to break off his Trojan enterprise because of the offence he had caused by smuggling out the entire Trojan 'treasure', one half of which had been promised to the Turks. He turned his attention in 1874 to the Homeric cities of Greece itself, and here his successes were more immediate and sensational. Great quantities of gold, silver and bronze items were unearthed from a series of cist burials, known as the Shaft Graves. The best known of these is the beaten gold mask that Schliemann christened the 'head of Agamemnon'. These excavations were the subject of enormous fascination to the European public at all levels, though many scholars refused to believe that they belonged to the Homeric age, preferring to attribute them to the medieval Dark Ages.

When Schliemann returned to Hissarlik in 1879, and again in 1882–3 and 1889–90, he was assisted by experts in classical archaeology. Techniques were improving rapidly, and the fruits of these years have considerably more scientific value. In the intervening years he dug at Orchomenos, Tiryns and Ithaka. All these excavations were promptly and comprehensively written up and published.

Perhaps only a Schliemann with the amateur scholar's naivety and the self-made millionaire's assurance and initiative could have accomplished so much in the space of two decades. The popular mind was excited by the sheer brilliance of the treasures he had unearthed. This had an impact far in excess of any other archaeological discoveries before, and perhaps since. He did not only prove (though not in the way he imagined) the historical foundation of the Homeric poems; he also proved that the past is recoverable by techniques other than the study of the written word. It was archaeology's first public triumph.

Further reading

See: Leo Denel, *Memoirs of Heinrich Schliemann* (1978) is based on Schliemann's own writings. The standard biography of Schliemann is by Emil Ludwig (1931); a more recent popular biography is Robert Payne, *The Gold of Troy* (1959). See: C. Schuchhardt, *Schliemann's Discoveries of the Ancient World* (1891, reprinted 1979); C.W. Ceram, *The World of Archaeology* (1966); Glyn Daniel, *One Hundred and Fifty Years of Archaeology* (1975); David Traill, *Schliemann of Troy: Treasure and Deceit* (1995); Caroline Moorehead, *Lost and Found: The 9,000 Treasures of Troy: Heinrich Schliemann and the Gold That Got Away* (1996).

C.F. HAWKE-SMITH

SCHNITTKE, Alfred

1934–98

Soviet composer

Alfred Schnittke was born in the Autonomous Soviet Republic of Volga Germans, to a Jewish father from Frankfurt am Main and a Volga German mother, whose origins were Roman Catholic. This decidedly un-Russian background had powerful significance for the composer, who was fond of quoting **Mahler's** comment (itself a reference to Chamisso) that he was 'thrice homeless'. In 1946 Schnittke's family moved for two years to Vienna. The resulting contact with Austro-German culture was again significant, granting familiarity with a tradition inaccessible in the Soviet Union.

In 1953 (the year of **Stalin's** death) Schnittke enrolled at the Moscow Conservatory, studying with Yevgeny Golubev and Nikolay Rakov. Although access to their work was still restricted, it was at this period he began to discover **Schoenberg**, **Berg**, **Webern** and **Stravinsky** (still derided as a traitor). For his graduation in 1958, Schnittke produced an oratorio, *Nagasaki*, which was criticized for 'modernism'. Nonetheless, he was accepted on the postgraduate programme, completing in 1961, after which he entered the Composers' Union and began teaching at the Moscow Conservatory where he remained until 1971. In 1962 the Bolshoy Theatre commissioned an opera (never performed) which caused official disapproval and the composer's exclusion from public musical life for the next twenty-five years. In the same year Schnittke wrote his first film score; the cinema remained his means of earning a living for most of the rest of his life (he scored sixty-six movies).

In common with many of his age-group, Schnittke was affected by visits by Western musicians such as Glenn Gould (1957) and Luigi Nono (1963), bringing glimpses of outlooks regarded with hostility by Soviet officialdom. He was involved in the so-called 'underground' or 'non-official' artistic world that included colleagues like Edison Denisov, Sofia Gubaidulina, Arvo Pärt, Valentin Silvestrov and Andrey Volkonsky, as well as like-minded painters, writers and journalists. In this environment he emerged as a leader and an ideologue, especially as he began a second career as a combative critic (a collection of his essays is available in English).

Schnittke's mature music divides neatly into three periods which mirror not only his artistic journey but the changes convulsing Soviet culture in his lifetime.

During the 1960s, he grappled to overcome the enforced cultural isolation of the USSR and was fascinated by various Western modernisms, including the Second Viennese and Darmstadt Schools (especially **Stockhausen**,

Berio and Nono), **Ives**, **Ligeti** and later Bernd Alois Zimmermann and the American Minimalists. Attempts to reconcile such diversity with the Soviet heritage of **Shostakovich** and **Prokofiev** produced works of High Modernist purity like *Pianissimo* for orchestra (1968) and the *Concerto for Oboe, Harp and Strings* (1971), but mostly drove him towards neo-Schoenbergian expressionism, as in his String Quartet No. 1 (1966) and Violin Sonata No. 2 ('Quasi una sonata', 1969).

Grappling with irreconcilable influences was by no means a feature only of Soviet music of the period, but in the USSR such undertakings carried heightened significance and the threat of conflict with the authorities. The strain of this led Schnittke to an imaginative eruption in perhaps his most important piece, Symphony No. 1 (composed over several years but completed in 1972).

In this hour-long work, all the elements of Schnittke's world co-exist in a musical Tower of Babel. The models of Berio, Zimmermann and Ives are important, but the dramatic impulse is Schnittke's own. Contradictory fragments are held together by a tightly constructed (and serially based) musical scaffolding that is largely inaudible as Schnittke pours over it a whole inventory of technical and rhetorical devices. In the first movement, fragments of the musical past collide in a post-Mahlerian wasteland. The second movement is a collage of fragments of the composer's own film scores, in every style from mock-Baroque to Big Band and Soviet Mass Song. The third addresses the confessional slow movement of Beethoven, **Bruckner** and Mahler, while the finale mocks and undermines everything before, simultaneously aspiring to Shostakovichian tragedy.

Most remarkable is the complexity of this piece's tone of voice, and the great difficulty for the listener of knowing how to 'take' it. It was this aspect especially that launched the composer over the next few years on an exploration of the symphony's consequences, producing a torrent of pieces including Symphonies 2–5, 'concerti grossi', concertos for violin, viola, cello and other instruments (mostly written for his close friends among performers of his generation like Oleg Kagan, Natalya Gutman, Gidon Kremer and Yuri Bashmet), as well as chamber music. One quality of this period of Schnittke's output that has provoked critical distaste was his highly self-conscious reliance on kitsch.

The last part of Schnittke's life was marked by failing health. The result was a turn towards intimacy and religious contemplation, and a retreat from garishness into an asceticism that in works like symphonies 6 (1992) and 7 (1993) reaches impressive intensity. These late works are difficult to bring off in performance, but, at their finest, display integrity and, to use an unfashionable word, originality.

In 1990, Schnittke moved to Hamburg, Germany, where he died in 1998.

Further reading

See: Alexander Ivashkin, *Alfred Schnittke* (1996); *A Schnittke Reader*, ed. Alexander Ivashkin (2002); Alexander Ivashkin, *Besedy s Al'fredom Shnitke* ('Conversations with Alfred Schnittke', 1994); D.I. Shul'gin, *Gody neizvestnosti Al'freda Shnittke* ('The Unknown Years of Alfred Schnittke', 1993); and continuing publications from the Schnittke Centre in Moscow.

GERARD MCBURNEY

SCHOENBERG, Arnold Franz Walter

1874–1951

Austrian composer

It is reported that during army service in the First World War, Arnold Schoenberg was asked by an officer if he was that controversial composer of the same name, to which he replied, 'Somebody had to be, and nobody else wanted the job, so I took it on myself.' The answer neatly sums up his sense of the inevitability of his creative mission, and the belief that his personal wishes had little to do with it: he was in many ways an unwilling revolutionary, driven by the need for continual clarification of his emotional and artistic concerns.

The son of a free-thinking Jewish shoemaker, Schoenberg was born in Vienna and began composing at the age of nine. He was virtually self-taught, beyond some lessons from the slightly older Alexander von Zemlinsky; his real training derived from the practical experience of playing classical chamber music, conducting workers' choirs, and making hack arrangements and orchestrations of other composers' works. By the turn of the century he had already composed two major pieces, the string sextet *Verklärte Nacht* and the vast romantic cantata *Gurrelieder*. After an unhappy period as musical director of a cabaret in Berlin (1901–2) he returned to Vienna, where he gained the support of **Mahler** and began teaching composition privately – his earliest pupils included **Alban Berg** and **Anton von Webern**. In 1908 a personal and artistic crisis turned Schoenberg's music sharply in the direction of extreme *Angst*-ridden subjectivity, made possible by an equally sudden and extreme transformation of its language. In such works as the *Five Pieces for Orchestra* (Op. 16, 1909) and the monodrama *Erwartung* (Op. 17, not performed until 1924) he drew near to the aesthetic ideals of the Expressionist painters, and began himself to paint in intervals when he felt composition impossible.

Failure to secure either adequate means of living or an audience for his music in Vienna led him to move back to Berlin in 1911 – via Munich, where he established contact with **Kandinsky** and became associated with the Blaue Reiter group. In Berlin he was befriended by **Busoni**, acquired more pupils and gained performances from London to St Petersburg, but this good fortune was cut short by the outbreak of war. He served for a time in the Austrian infantry, and in the immediate post-war years addressed himself to the problem of picking up the cultural pieces in a shattered and inflation-torn Vienna. His Verein für musikalische Privataufführungen (Society for Private Musical Performances, 1918–22) drew its performing talent from Schoenberg's ever-widening circle of pupils and admirers, presented a wide range of contemporary music in thoroughly rehearsed and repeated performances, and became the model for many later and larger Modern Music organizations in Europe and America. This activity coincided with a creative blockage, only cleared as Schoenberg developed the 'method of composition with twelve notes related only to one another' which first made its appearance in the *Serenade* (Op. 24) and piano pieces (Opp. 23, 25) composed 1921–3.

In 1925 Schoenberg returned to Berlin for the third time, as director of the Composition Masterclass at the Prussian Academy of Arts, in succession to Busoni. This period of comparative eminence (he once described it as 'the time when everybody made believe he understood **Einstein's** theories and Schoenberg's music') saw the production of such large-scale works as the *Variations for Orchestra* (Op. 31, 1926–8) and the opera *Moses und Aron* (1930–2) but came to an end with the rise of Nazism: in 1933, he was dismissed from his post as part of **Hitler's** campaign to 'break the Jewish stranglehold on Western Music'. In the same year he emigrated to the USA. After a short period teaching in New York and Boston, he moved to California and taught first at the University of Southern California (1935–6) and then at the University of California in Los Angeles (1936–44). Compelled to resign from the latter post on a tiny pension at the age of seventy, Schoenberg spent his last years teaching, writing and composing, frequently in precarious health. He died in Brentwood Park, Hollywood: it is said that his last words were 'Harmony! Harmony! Harmony!'

By temperament a romantic, but intellectually committed to classical ideals of structural proportion and consistency, Schoenberg in many respects resembled his first musical hero, **Brahms**. His creative path was guided by instinct first, only secondarily by the desire for a rational explanation of what instinct had produced. His earliest characteristic music synthesized and built upon the achievements of Brahms and **Wagner**, from whom he derived two distinct but interdependent

concepts: that of 'the unity of musical space', whereby the constituent elements of a composition – melody, accompaniment, harmony, rhythm – should be intimately related expressions of the same idea in different dimensions; and the principle of 'developing variation', which tended ever away from exact repetition of ideas towards their perpetual transformation as a major structural impulse. The dazzlingly quick mind and passionate urge for maximum communication which he brought to the development of these two concepts makes such a fundamentally traditional score as the String Quartet No. 1 (Op. 7, 1905) already daunting in the sheer volume of musical information which the listener must assimilate.

The emotionally and intellectually supercharged style of this and other works of the early 1900s exploded after 1908 into the music of Schoenberg's 'Expressionist' phase, where he strove to represent extreme states of mind and feeling more or less directly, without any intervening decorum of form. His ideal, he said, was a music 'without architecture, without structure. Only an everchanging, unbroken succession of colours, rhythms and moods.' The works of this period are accordingly characterized by an unprecedented degree of harmonic ambiguity, asymmetry of melody and phraselengths, wide and dissonant melodic intervals, abrupt contrasts in register, texture, stasis and dynamism. All twelve notes of the chromatic scale occur with extreme frequency and consequently the harmonic language shifts away from any kind of diatonic hierarchy towards a state of total chromaticism – an 'emancipation of dissonance' which does not, however, prevent the covert and allusive operation of tonal functions and so belies the popular misnomer, 'atonality', which posterity has happily foisted on it.

In fact, Schoenberg was concerned almost at once to reintroduce principles of 'architecture' into his music, aware that the supremely intuitive, quasi-improvisational achievement of *Erwartung* was by definition unrepeatable, and that his linguistic revolution had for the moment put traditional means of large-scale organization beyond his grasp. Most of his works for the next decade were vocal, the text helping to determine the progress of the form. At the same time he began to concentrate on intensive development of the constituent tones of principal thematic ideas, and cultivated a wide range of canonic and other 'ancient' contrapuntal devices to provide structural backbone. All these tendencies are found in *Pierrot Lunaire* (Op. 21, 1912) for instrumental ensemble and *Sprechstimme* (half-sung recitation), an ironic cycle of rondel-settings with elements of Expressionist cabaret which has remained one of his best-known scores; and they reached a new intensity, and an impasse, in the unfinished oratorio *Die Jakobsleiter* (*Jacob's Ladder*, 1917–22), a fragment of a gigantic project that brought his musical, philosophical and religious dilemmas into sharp focus.

To employ a psychological metaphor: the 'Expressionist' works had brought a host of previously inadmissible musical 'traumas' into the open, harbingers of chaos and disruption which nineteenth-century tradition and theory had rigorously suppressed. Schoenberg's struggle was to accept and assimilate these 'negative' forces into the existing scheme of musical discourse, to objectify them in an enlarged musical language which he could consciously apply in further works. His solution was the development of the 'twelve-note method'. A fixed series of all the notes of the chromatic scale, derived from the initial melodic and harmonic ideas for a piece, becomes the kernel, the essence, the germinating cell of that piece's unique tonal properties. The series is developed continually through transposition, inversion, retrograde motion, in whole or in part, in melodic lines and in chords, to provide an inexhaustible and self-consistent source of invention which Schoenberg then deploys on the largest scale through a revivification of classical forms. The works of the 1920s, such as the Wind Quintet (Op. 26, 1924) and String Quartet No. 3 (Op. 30, 1927), are imbued with an almost neo-classical spirit while retaining

something of the raw immediacy of the Expressionist vision.

In the 1930s Schoenberg continued to refine and develop the method, enlarging its melodic vocabulary and relaxing some of his original 'rules' for twelve-note composition to effect an accommodation with an intermittent sense of traditional tonality. He even composed some diatonically based works of his own, averring that there was 'still a lot of good music to be written in C major'. Tonal and serial resources enriched each other in the 1940s in a series of works where the old Expressionist urgency is recaptured within a sure structural control: the String Trio (Op. 45, 1946) and the 'ghetto' cantata *A Survivor from Warsaw* (Op. 46, 1947) are the peak of this development. His last works were vocal, to his own texts: he left unfinished the first of a series of *Modern Psalms* dealing with the predicament of Man (principally, but not exclusively, Jewish Man) in the Atomic Age.

During his lifetime and for twenty years after it, Schoenberg's music was generally more talked about than listened to. But his influence has been immense. Not only was he the mentor, inspirer and incarnate artistic conscience of three generations of pupils, many of whom (e.g. Berg, Webern, Wellesz, **Eisler**, Gerhard, Skalkottas, **Cage**) became important figures in their own right; but his compositional methods were adopted and extended by many others. Perhaps none of them has been driven to forge the twelve-note method out of his own experience by a similarly compelling need: but the basic techniques of the method are so fruitfully simple, so easily adapted to multifarious ends, that it became the cornerstone of succeeding innovations, and an integral part of the twentieth century's musical thought. Unfortunately, it also engendered in many quarters a stress on technique and abstract formal criteria at the expense of music's expressive content, the 'idea', the 'representation of a *vision*' which for Schoenberg was music's paramount *raison d'être*. Only toward the end of the century was the balance begun redressed, in the study of his own works, away from what he called 'how it is done' towards 'what it *is!*'

Schoenberg was a pithy and ironic writer whose pungent style was influenced by his friend **Karl Kraus**. In addition to the texts and libretti of many of his works he wrote poetry, a play, some stories and a vast number of essays and aphorisms on musical and other topics, as well as several pedagogical works. The most celebrated of these last, *Theory of Harmony* (*Harmonielehre*, 1911, rev. 1922, trans. 1978), is an idiosyncratic but often massively illuminating study of traditional harmonic principles up to the threshold of his own radical departure from them. The paradox is characteristic. He may yet be seen, not as modern music's *monstre sacré*, the composer audiences most like to hate, but as the last great custodian of the ethical (as opposed to aesthetic) values of musical Romanticism.

Further reading

Other works include: operas – *Die glückliche Hand* (1913); *Von heute auf Morgen* (1929); *Kol Nidre*, for chorus and orchestra (1938); *Das Buch der hängenden Gärten* (song cycle, 1908–9); *Ode to Napoleon*, for reciter and piano quintet (1942); *Pelleas und Melisande* (symphonic poem, 1902–3); two Chamber Symphonies (1906 and 1938); *Suite in G* for strings (1934); *Theme and Variations* for wind band (1943); concertos for Piano (1942), Violin (1935–6), Cello (1932–3), and String Quartet (1933); five String Quartets (1897, 1905, 1908, 1927, 1936); *Phantasy* for violin and piano (1949). Writings: *Style and Idea* (1950, rev. 1975); *Selected Letters* (1964), ed. E. Stein. See: J. Rufer, *The Works of Arnold Schoenberg* (trans. 1962); C. Rosen, *Schoenberg* (1975); M. MacDonald, *Schoenberg* (1976); H. H. Stuckenschmidt, *Schoenberg: His Life, World and Work* (trans. 1977); W. Frisch (ed.) *Schoenberg and His World* (1999); Allen Shawn, *Arnold Schoenberg's Journey* (2002).

MALCOLM MACDONALD

SCHRÖDINGER, Erwin

1887–1961

Austrian physicist

Educated in Vienna, Schrödinger succeeded, shortly after his war service, to the chair, earlier held by **Einstein**, at Zürich. He was already expert in the frontiers of relativity theory, statistical mechanics and the old quantum theory, but his great discovery, the invention of wave mechanics, came five years later, late in 1925, when he was thirty-seven. He subsequently taught at Berlin, Oxford and Graz, and spent the last seventeen years of his career at the Dublin Institute for Advanced Studies.

Under the influence of his earlier teacher Franz Exner, of a life-long preoccupation with the problem of reconciling free will and determinism, and of a famous 1924 paper by **Niels Bohr** and others, Schrödinger had first toyed with the idea of solving the problems of the old quantum theory by turning energy-momentum conservation into a purely statistical law. But the experimental results came out against this and Schrödinger turned instead to the ideas which had recently been proposed by Louis de Broglie. De Broglie had conceived electrons as classical particles with which waves were, nevertheless, somehow associated and which allowed periodic particle motions only when they interfered with themselves constructively rather than destructively. Surprisingly, this rather makeshift theory of de Broglie's had yielded the correct relativistic energy levels of the hydrogen atom.

Schrödinger's idea was to construct a fully consistent wave theory of electrons, which would yield the successes of de Broglie's theory and which would stand in the identical relation to Newtonian particle mechanics that wave optics (and ultimately **Maxwell's** equations for the electromagnetic field) stood to Newton's particle theory of light. The theory, wave mechanics, which Schrödinger obtained more or less by a process of trial and error, with various wave equations guessed by analogy, failed to fulfil all Schrödinger's intentions, but nevertheless became the theory which physicists still believe, but with a different interpretation. For the problem of recovering particle-like behaviour from the new theory proved much more refractory than Schrödinger had anticipated. Schrödinger's equation did not allow localized particle-like wave packets to remain localized, and to treat several particles by his equation he had to consider waves in an abstract higher dimensional space rather than in ordinary physical space. Max Born then proposed that Schrödinger's waves be reinterpreted as merely statistical descriptions of the behaviour of particles. But it was later realized (though only rigorously proved some forty years later) that a mere statistical ignorance interpretation of the Schrödinger wave-function is mathematically untenable. Therefore it became standard theoretical practice, which remains with us today, to treat Schrödinger's waves as physically real up to the point at which the system interacts with a measuring apparatus, and as expressing our statistical ignorance immediately after that interaction. Schrödinger was one of the first to point out the inconsistency of this procedure, through his famous cat paradox, in which a cat ends up in a state in which, according to the theory, it is neither dead nor alive and only becomes definitely the one or the other when we ourselves examine it. The difficulty is that the mathematical theory we have inherited from Schrödinger is deterministic, whereas the interpretation we now graft on to it is indeterministic: the conflict between these two aspects has never been satisfactorily resolved, but the theory works.

It was soon discovered by Schrödinger himself that an apparently rival quantum theory, **Heisenberg's** matrix mechanics, which had been invented shortly before Schrödinger's wave mechanics, was in fact mathematically equivalent, at a deep level, to Schrödinger's own theory. Heisenberg's approach proved to give a profounder insight into what had to be done to the theory of light in order to generate the particle properties of photons. Schrödinger's idea had been simply to couple his equation with Maxwell's equations in order to provide a unified classical continuum theory of light and matter. Though such a theory gave a beautifully visualizable classical account of the emission and absorption of radiation by atoms (and attempts were made

to revive this theory under the name of 'neo-classical radiation theory') it has never proved possible to account successfully for the particle properties of both matter and radiation within such a view. The orthodox modern theory of radiation is quite different, and owes more to Heisenberg and Dirac than to Schrödinger.

Schrödinger continued in later life to draw attention to the unsatisfactory character of the quantum theory of which he had been the joint inventor. In other work he helped to clarify the foundations of general relativity and of thermodynamics and statistical mechanics. His 1944 book *What is Life?* was a brilliant popular exposition of the state of molecular biology and its relations to the law of entropy increase. In an epilogue Schrödinger defended the mystical view that our minds are part of the mind of the deity, as one possible way to reconcile the inexorability of God's laws with human freedom.

Further reading

Other works include: *Science and the Human Temperament* (1935); *Science and Humanism* (1951); *Nature and the Greeks* (1954); *Mind and Matter* (1958); *My View of the World* (1964); See also: L. Wessels, 'Schrödinger's Route to Wave Mechanics', *Studies in History and Philosophy of Science* (1979); W.T. Scott, *Erwin Schrödinger: An Introduction to His Writings* (1967); Schrödinger, *Papers on Wave Mechanics* (1928); A. d'Abro, *The Rise of the New Physics* (1951); Walter J. Moore, *Schrödinger: Life and Thought* (1989); Michel Bitbol, *Schrödinger's Philosophy of Quantum Mechanics* (1996).

JON DORLING

SCORSESE, Martin

1942–

US director, actor, film historian and cultural preservationist

A prolific cinéaste and a passionate cinephile, and author of a number of films which are now regarded as classics of the American cinema, Scorsese is widely acknowledged as one of the greatest filmmakers of the latter half of the twentieth century, if not of the entire history of cinema. His highly personal, distinctively styled and brilliantly crafted films have brought him the acclaim of film critics and historians worldwide and his working methods have also earned him the universal respect of actors and fellow directors. After receiving numerous prizes and international awards for his films, in 2002 he was honoured with the Directors' Guild of America Lifetime Achievement Award which placed him in the company of legendary directors like **John Ford** and **Alfred Hitchcock**. Notwithstanding his reputation and the high regard in which he is held, however, and despite being nominated five times, he has yet to receive the ultimate accolade of an Academy Award for Best Director.

Scorsese's love affair with the cinema began at a very early age. The second child of Sicilian migrants who had settled in New York's Lower East Side, Scorsese began suffering from asthma at the age of three. Unable to take part in the usual physical activities of children he spent most of his time at the movies or watching films on television. His Italian Catholic background also instilled a strong religious vocation in him, prompting him to enter a seminary at the end of high school with the intention of becoming a priest. A year later he abandoned his religious vocation in order to study film at New York University. However a sense of spiritual guilt and religious aspirations continued to haunt him thereafter, and although he would soon become famous for his gritty, street-wise studies of urban violence and social alienation, a certain religious dimension would continue to permeate his films. The realistically depicted male aggression and violent braggadocio in his first major film, *Mean Streets* (1973), for example, also carry symbolic connotations of expiation and penance in an attempt to achieve some form of spiritual redemption and sainthood. As the voice-over which opens *Mean Streets* declares: 'You don't make up for your sins in the church. You make up for them on the streets.'

It was undoubtedly Scorsese's continuing obsession with this paradoxically redemptive violence which led the now-notorious director of such parables of male aggression and urban psychosis as *Taxi Driver* (1976) and *Raging Bull* (1980) to make *The Last Temptation of Christ* (1988). Adapted from **Nikos Kazantzakis'** theological-existential novel, it had been a project dear to Scorsese's heart since he had read the book in the early 1970s. Although the release of the film generated enormous controversy and opposition, especially from Christian fundamentalist groups who thought it blasphemous, the film was in fact something of a pious devotion, and making it under dire circumstances in the Moroccan desert allowed Scorsese to finally square accounts with his Catholic roots. It seems significant that the distinctive religious overtones of the early 'street' films come to be absent from post-*Temptation* gangster films like *Goodfellas* (1990) and *Casino* (1995). While the theme of self-sacrifice certainly reappears in *Bringing Out the Dead* (1999), the protagonists' mission to save the human flotsam and jetsam of New York's mean streets in that film – in direct contrast with the avenging angel of *Taxi Driver* who would attempt to wash them away in a apocalyptic bloodbath – is decidedly secular and social rather than religious. And perhaps it was also this successful settling of accounts with his Italian-Catholic background that finally freed Scorsese to engage with the non-violence of Buddhism in *Kundun* (1997), a remarkably moving adaptation of the autobiography of the 14th **Dalai Lama**. He would nevertheless return to the violence of the urban jungle of Manhattan in grand style with his *Gangs of New York* (2002), a technically awe-inspiring but essentially entertaining historical epic of urban warfare shot entirely, however, in the studios of Cinecittà.

Influenced by both classic American Hollywood cinema (including its less respectable traditions of the crime film and film noir) and by the more experimental European auteur cinema – particularly **Fellini** – Scorsese brought to every one of his films a rich and audacious polyphonic style which sought to exploit all the possibilities of the camera for expressive ends. This exciting visual style, which doesn't hesitate to mix documentary realism with stylized expressionism, is complemented in all the films by a brilliant orchestration of sound and music to create a pulsating soundtrack which has itself become part of the Scorsese signature.

The other distinctive trait of Scorsese's filmmaking has been a longstanding collaboration over a number of films with scriptwriter Paul Shrader and actor Robert De Niro. The unique combination of the talents of all three was undoubtedly responsible for the artistic success of what are arguably Scorsese's greatest films, *Taxi Driver* and *Raging Bull*.

While Scorsese's fame will always rest solidly on the extraordinary artistry of his films, his contribution to modern culture has ranged much more widely than that of any other contemporary film maker. Drawing on his own extensive first-hand knowledge of the history of cinema he has increasingly taken on the role of film historian and popularizer: in 1994 he responded to a request from the BFI to make *A Personal Journey through American Cinema with Martin Scorsese*, providing a selective but instructive overview of American cinema from its earliest days. A few years later with the six-hour *My Voyage to Italy* (1999–2002) Scorsese made a similar pedagogic journey through his favourite Italian films, highlighting the inspiration he had drawn from the work of directors such as **Rossellini**, **De Sica** and **Visconti**. Since 1980 Scorsese has also been a passionate campaigner for more attention and effort to be devoted to film conservation. At the same time he has initiated and guided a number of group projects to conserve cultural memory such as the PBS Blues project, which brought together seven major directors to each make a one-hour documentary on a major aspect of Blues music. The most exciting venture to date, however, is *No Direction Home* (2005), a four-hour television documentary on **Bob Dylan's** early career.

Further reading

Other films include: *Boxcar Bertha (1972)*, *Alice Doesn't Live Here Anymore* (1974), *Italianamerican* (documentary, 1974), *New York, New York* (1977), *The Last Waltz* (rock music documentary, 1978), *The King of Comedy* (1983), *After Hours* (1985), *The Color of Money* (1986), *Cape Fear* (1991), *Age of Innocence* (1993), *The Aviator* (2004). Recommended reading: Michael Bliss, *The Word Made Flesh: Catholicism and Conflict in the Films of Martin Scorsese* (1995); *Martin Scorsese: Interviews*, edited Peter Brunette (1999); Ben Nyce, *Scorsese Up Close: A Study of the Films* (2004); Maria Miliora, *The Scorsese Psyche on Screen* (2004).

GINO MOLITERNO

SCOTT, George Gilbert

1811–78

British architect

The son of a clergyman, Gilbert Scott was born into a household without any special claims to artistry. His grandfather was the noted theologian Thomas Scott (1747–1821). Scott's professional life as an architect began twenty-four years later when, in 1835, he formed a partnership (lasting until 1846) with W.B. Moffatt, following his apprenticeship in several architects' offices, including those of Sir John Smirke and Henry Roberts. His first works were mainly workhouses and asylums, and Reading Gaol (1842–4, where **Oscar Wilde** was later imprisoned), but he rapidly progressed to ecclesiastical architecture under the influence of Pugin and the assertions of the *Ecclesiologist* magazine. Indeed, it was ecclesiastical work that provided most of Scott's (eventually enormous) office's livelihood, the acceptable basis for his style, and his first major foreign commission – Hamburg's Nikolaikirche. This he won in competition in 1844 (although it was not completed until 1860); the design was specially commended for its appropriate style, reflecting Scott's belief, expressed in his 1857 book *Remarks on Secular and Domestic Architecture*, in, above all, the Gothic of northern Italy, the Low Countries and Germany. Several large-scale church commissions followed, including

St John's Cathedral, Newfoundland (1847–8), St John's College Chapel, Cambridge (1836–72), and the Episcopalian Cathedral, Edinburgh (1874–9).

Scott's ecclesiastical work also extended to considerable restoration work, of which Ely (begun 1847) and Lichfield (begun 1857) Cathedrals are notable examples – but which were particularly disliked by **Ruskin** – together with Hereford, Salisbury, Ripon and Westminster Abbey. By restoration the Victorians did not mean what we mean by conservation today. The Victorian Gothicists actually believed their medieval originals to be defective – the result of an incomplete understanding and too slow working methods – and they felt it their duty to correct the consequent flaws in the originals. Hence the feeling often engendered today that their restoration work is insensitive, inappropriate, even gross. Scott, through his restoration work, was nevertheless jointly responsible for the founding of the Society for the Protection of Ancient Buildings.

Established as the major star in the Gothic firmament, following Pugin's early death (1852), promoting a style seen as truly (and ironically, in view of his book's concerns) British and symbolic of a national revival, Scott in 1856 entered the two competitions for the Foreign and Home Offices in Whitehall – the first ever competitions for offices – with designs in the stipulated Gothic style. In spite of winning neither, he was eventually commissioned to create both in a unified Government Office design: a typical outcome of the wheeling and dealing, compromise and lobbying that characterized the immensely important competitions of the time. However, Palmerston, after his election as prime minister, insisted on a change in style to a sixteenth-century interpretation of the Byzantine. Scott compromised and agreed to change style rather than lose a large and significant commission, to the annoyance of his former apprentices, such as the eventual winner of the Law Courts competition, G.E. Street, who came to believe they and not Scott were sporting the true Gothic banner.

Thus it came about that political dictates concerning style caused the two outstanding governmental buildings of the mid-Victorian era to be built by architects in the 'wrong' style: Scott's classical Government Offices and Barry's Gothic Palace of Westminster.

Scott built many other secular buildings in Gothic. Of these, the Albert Memorial (1863–72) is interesting as both a social document (public testament to **Albert**, focus of a Victorian urban development, and demonstrative of the Victorians' evaluation of great forms and figures of the past) and in reflecting Scott's own interpretation of Victorian architecture. The architects represented on its famous frieze of worthies are Cockerell, Barry, Pugin and (in the background) Scott himself. The idea for the memorial is, however, strongly influenced by two unrepresented architects, Thomas Worthington (the Albert Memorial in Manchester, 1862–7) and Meikle Kemp (the Scott Memorial, 1840–4, in Edinburgh).

Probably Scott's greatest secular achievement is the Midland Grand Hotel at St Pancras (1868–74). Here, on an awkward London site, he erected the most splendid of London's railway hotels, complete with vast galleries, staircases and the celebrated dining-room. The building sweeps round and up to the elevated height of the platforms behind. The elevation is crowned by a clock tower clearly based on Barry's and Pugin's Big Ben clock tower at the Palace of Westminster. But perhaps more remarkable than the building itself is the contrast between the hotel and the station behind, covered by its wonderful single span arch (W.H. Barlow and R.M. Ordish, 1863–5). Here the difference in attitude to architecture and engineering and their uses becomes absolutely apparent: architecture reflecting in the decoration of the various styles the pomp and self-esteem of the age, fronting the real, wealth-creating achievements of the engineers.

Scott's office produced, in his working life, over a thousand designs – an enormous output – including several housing estates and country houses. Like Barry and also Alfred

Waterhouse he founded a family architectural dynasty, and like Barry he was outstripped by the stylistic developments of his time (a development in stylism of which **Thomas Hardy**, himself trained as an architect, writes so scathingly in 'A Laodicean') – Barry by the supremacy of Gothic, Scott by changing understandings of that same Gothic. Nevertheless he was held in continuing respect, being knighted in 1872 and becoming an early president of the Royal Institute of British Architects (1873–5), whose Gold Medal he also won.

Further reading

See: *Personal and Professional Recollections by the late Sir George Gilbert Scott, R.A.*, ed. and with new material by Gavin Stamp (1995). See also: J. Summerson, *Victorian Architecture in England: Four Studies in Evaluation* (1970); R. Dixon and S. Muthesius, *Victorian Architecture* (1978); David Cole, *The Work of Sir Gilbert Scott* (1980).

RANULPH GLANVILLE

SCOTT, Ridley

1939–

British film director and producer

Ridley Scott's background as a student at London's Royal College of Art and then as an acclaimed director of television commercials is a good pointer to the character of his films: superbly mounted in their look and design, sweeping and energetic in tempo, lavishly calculated in their effects. The jobbing nature of advertising work – although Scott long ago reached the stage where he chose only the most prestigious projects – also informs his curiously eclectic film output. Where is he most at home? Everywhere and nowhere might be the answer. His films encompass the discovery of the New World (1492: *Conquest of Paradise*, 1992); an account of obsessive adversaries set during the Napoleonic period which was derived from a **Joseph Conrad** story (*The Duellists*, 1977); a couple of efficient contemporary police thrillers (*Someone to Watch Over Me*, 1987,

and *Black Rain*, 1989) as well as the proto-feminist road movie *Thelma and Louise* (1991). When the Roman epic *Gladiator* (2000), the Crusade-oriented *Kingdom of Heaven* (2005) and the dystopic scifi classics *Alien* (1979) and *Blade Runner* (1982) are added to the mix, it becomes apparent that in terms of range Ridley Scott can only be compared with **Stanley Kubrick**, who also travelled from the Roman era (*Spartacus*, 1960) to the near future (*2001*, 1968). And there is besides in Scott's work something of Kubrick's obsessive interest in surface and a corresponding sense of the littleness of the human presence.

Scott's mainstream masterpiece is *Alien*. The story of the crew of a workaday spacecraft, one of whom is the unwitting host to a parasitic monster, it is a highly worked conflation of the haunted house thriller, space odyssey and horror film. Yet Scott both transcends and subverts the formulas. For an audience accustomed to the galactic cosiness of Steven **Spielberg** or the highjinks of George Lucas – respective directors of the hugely successful *Close Encounters of the Third Kind* (1977) and *Star Wars* (also 1977) – Scott's vision of the future was bracingly bleak, even shocking. The spaceship is a vast and nearderelict floating warehouse while the crew, bitching about their pay and conditions, are immune to the glamour of the stars. The creature is progressively revealed in glimpses through masterly direction and cutting. The single survivor, and ultimate nemesis of the monster, is a woman known only as Ripley (played by Sigourney Weaver). It's worth noting that Scott has a habit of foregrounding strong, independent women, even to a point of absurdity as in *G.I. Jane* (1997) where Demi Moore's attempt to outmacho her fellow marines seems to be the sole purpose of the picture. This latter film, together with *Black Hawk Down* (2001), also shows Scott's preoccupation with the ethos of the military.

Blade Runner was a comparative failure on its first release, although it was quickly reassessed and is the subject of continued interest and analysis. Adapted from a story by the idiosyncratic writer **Philip K. Dick**, the film is set in a grimly futuristic Los Angeles. As in *Alien*, Scott uses narrative devices from another genre, in this case the privateeye thrillers of **Raymond Chandler**. Deckard (played by Harrison Ford) is employed to hunt down and destroy rogue androids or replicants, and the story conforms to the traditional pattern of clues, deductions and violent confrontations. But the most impressive and influential feature of *Blade Runner* is its look and texture. The city, seemingly more eastern than western, is permanently veiled by rain and crowded with impassive inhabitants. Paradoxically the 'robots', where it's possible to distinguish them from humans, are the most sympathetic characters. All of this, together with the high-tech squalor of the interior scenes and the suggestion of control by shadowy corporations, makes for a cogent vision of the future.

Further reading

Ridley Scott's subsequent projects, like *Gladiator* or *Hannibal* (2001), show a continued reluctance to stick within a single genre. *Gladiator* was played straight, a return to the sword and sandal Hollywood spectacle of the 1950s and 1960s, with twenty-first century effects but an old-fashioned attitude to heroism. By contrast, *Hannibal*, a knowing sequel to Jonathan Demme's *Silence of The Lambs* (1991), was watchable enough but overly dependent on nudging, visceral shocks, the kind of effect which Scott deployed with greater subtlety in *Alien*.

PHILIP GOODEN

SCRIABIN, Aleksandr Nikolayevich

1872–1915

Russian pianist and composer

Scriabin (also Skryabin, Scirabine, Skrjabin) came from an aristocratic Moscow family and was brought up not by his parents but by doting female relatives who may be responsible

for his highly fastidious and egocentric behaviour in later years. His musical gifts were nourished by Konyus, Zverev and Taneyev, and in 1888 he entered the Moscow Conservatoire where **Rachmaninov** was a fellow-pupil. He was soon launched on a career as a pianist and his early compositions, heavily influenced by the music of Chopin, appeared in rapid succession in the 1890s from the houses of Jurgenson and Belyayev, the latter of whom extended his bountiful patronage to Scriabin, sending him on a European tour in 1895–6 and providing financial support.

From about 1902 until his early death in 1915 Scriabin displayed an increasing preoccupation with philosophical and mystical ideas, and at the same time his musical style developed so startlingly that he was soon heralded, along with **Schoenberg** and **Richard Strauss**, as one of the most advanced composers of his time. After the abandonment of his marriage he travelled widely in Europe and America, only returning to Russia for any extended period in the last few years.

His compositions are almost exclusively for the piano and for orchestra. He had no feeling for vocal music and gave up plans for a 'philosophical opera'. The ten piano sonatas and the five large orchestral works span his brief career, with numerous smaller piano pieces – mostly entitled 'prelude' or 'poem' – and some early orchestral pieces to complete his output. The charming manner of the early preludes and mazurkas (the titles betray their debt to Chopin) was replaced first by a more massive, **Lisztian** style, then by a dynamic, sensuous style derived from extended chromatic harmony and decorated with poetic titles and instructions. The first two symphonies were untitled, but the third was the *Divine Poem* of 1902–4, for large orchestra, which explored areas of voluptuous and dramatic ecstasy new to symphonic thought. The *Poem of Ecstasy* (1905–8) took this process considerably further with a feverish concentration of lush orchestral sound in a single movement. Scriabin published a long poem to accompany the music, revealing his obsession with the dream-like, semi-mystical images that filled his notebooks at this time. Originally drawn to **Nietzsche**, he transferred his obsessive devotions to theosophy and the teaching of Madame Blavatsky, with a growing conviction that he himself was the god-like centre of the cosmos, dominating all things with his creativity. This egomania lies behind his last orchestral work, *Prometheus, Poem of Fire* (1908–10), which, despite this background, is a work of supreme originality and craftsmanship composed in an advanced post-tonal style Scriabin had both invented and perfected in a very short period. It introduced a 'colour-organ' to give an extra dimension to the music.

His gradual emancipation from tonal mannerisms is more clearly traced in the piano music. He relished the sonorous, non-functional identity of chords, as did **Debussy**, and built up extensions of dominant sevenths over little or no rhythmic pulse, creating a languid, timeless sound-world. The last five sonatas (1911–13) form an astonishing group of exploratory works, each in one movement, each individually characterized in harmonic colour and form. The very last pieces, of 1914, took him even further into atonal territory.

Scriabin's best work, of all periods, is highly concentrated, imaginative in technique and carefully balanced in structure. The dazzling progress from early to late music may be attributed to his unswerving consciousness of his own genius, backed up by a characteristically Russian obsession with an idea, pursued beyond what to more moderate minds would seem reasonable limits. After 1920 his reputation quickly subsided and his excesses were easily decried. In recent years his music has been reappraised and is now more fairly classed among the most cogent and progressive of its time.

Further reading

See: Faubion Bowers, *Scriabin* (2 vols, Tokyo, 1969), provides a very full biography drawn from Russian sources, especially his letters. The most searching exploration of Scriabin's ideas and their infusion in his music is found in Manfred Kelkel, *Alexandre Scriabine* (Paris, 1978), and there are numerous analytical studies of the music by, for example: C.C. von Gleich, *Die sinfonischen Werke von Alexander Skrjabin* (1963); V. Dernova, *Garmoniya Skryabina* (1968); Hanns Steger, *Der Weg der Klaviersonaten bei Alexander Skryabin* (1972); Dietrich Mast, *Struktur und Form bei Alexander N. Skrjabin* (1981). A general introduction to the music is found in Hugh Macdonald, *Skryabin* (1978). See also: J. Barker, *The Music of Alexander Scriabin* (1986); Boris de Schloezer, *Scriabin: Artist and Music* (1987).

HUGH MACDONALD

SEARLE, John

1932–

US philosopher

The overwhelming trend among Anglo-American analytic philosophers of the twentieth and early twenty-first centuries has been towards an increasing specialization in narrower and narrower domains of expertise, domains circumscribed by their own conferences, journals and labyrinths of technical jargon. John Searle bucks this trend. Eschewing needless technicality, his overarching goal is to articulate the ways in which a range of human phenomena that are often thought to be recalcitrant to any science-friendly or science-compatible viewpoint – phenomena such as consciousness, language, freedom, rationality and social reality – fit together as ultimately unified and unmysterious parts of the natural world. The vast scope of this project places Searle squarely in the venerable philosophical tradition of grand system builders.

If Searle had a slogan it might arguably be 'face the facts'. This signals his opposition to, and his impatience with, philosophical positions that deny the existence of a mind-independent reality and/or the idea that truth is about arriving at propositions that correspond to that reality. The facts in question might be those of science or of reflected-upon common sense, but the message is the same: if your theory compels you to say something that fails to fit the facts, then so much the worse for your theory.

Searle's first major work was his 1969 book *Speech Acts: An Essay in the Philosophy of Language*. Here he provides a general theoretical framework for speech acts (communicative uses of language involving acts such as giving commands, asking questions or making promises). The key idea is that when I say something like 'I promise to wash the dishes' my utterance counts as an act of promising because in making that utterance I am thereby subjecting myself to a set of institutionally embedded constitutive rules that defines that type of act. This enables Searle to address one of the hardy perennials of modern philosophy – whether or not one can ever derive a normative statement (about what one ought to do) from a purely descriptive statement (about what is the case). Searle's answer is 'yes'. Roughly, one can derive the normative statement 'Mike ought to wash the dishes' from the descriptive statement 'Mike uttered the words "I promise to wash the dishes"' because, through the relevant constitutive rules and institutional facts, the concept of promising is linked logically to the concept of obligation, so in making the utterance in question I thereby pick up the corresponding duty. The issue of whether or not this kind of analysis can be extended to solve the specific problem of deriving a *morally loaded* ought from a purely descriptive statement has been questioned, although Searle himself may never have intended the analysis to carry quite that amount of philosophical weight.

Perhaps Searle's most famous contribution beyond philosophy is his Chinese Room argument (*Minds, Brains and Programs*, 1980; *Minds, Brains and Science*, 1984). Some researchers in the field of artificial intelligence claim that a computer could literally have a mind (understand, think, be conscious ...) solely in virtue of running an appropriate programme. Searle has responded with a thought experiment. Take a mono-lingual English speaker and lock her in a room. Give her a rule book in English that tells her how to manipulate a bunch of (to her) strange symbols that she can recognize only by their formal properties (e.g. their shapes). Now imagine that we pass into the room a sequence of symbols. Our room-trapped subject looks up that sequence in her rule book and then passes out another set of symbols, as determined by the appropriate rule. Unbeknownst to her, the symbols are Chinese characters. Chinese speakers outside the room interpret the first sequence of symbols as a particular question, and the second sequence as a sensible reply to that question. The question Searle asks is this: does our subject understand Chinese? The answer, it seems, is 'no'. But then in her purely formal symbol-manipulating activity, she is the equivalent of a computer's central processing unit, and the rule book she follows is the equivalent of its program. So since merely performing formal symbol manipulations does not give our subject an understanding of Chinese, it cannot give a computer an understanding of Chinese. And this conclusion goes for mental states in general. QED. The Chinese Room provoked, and continues to provoke, varied and sometimes hostile responses, perhaps the most heroic of which is that while the person-in-the-room does not understand Chinese, the complete person-room-rule-book system does. In the face of such responses Searle has remained resolutely defiant.

To be clear, Searle does not deny that brains cause minds. So what is his account of how this happens? More specifically, since, for Searle, consciousness is the pivotal psychological phenomenon, how is it that brains cause consciousness? In *The Rediscovery of the Mind* (1992), and later in *The Mystery of Consciousness* (1997), he argues that consciousness is a higher-order property of the brain in the same way that solidity is a higher-order property of certain systems of molecules. And that, Searle maintains, wraps things up for the traditional philosophical problem of how minds and bodies are related. That problem turns out to be no more than a consequence of bad thinking about thinking.

In this brief piece we have had to bypass much of Searle's work (e.g. on intentionality, on freedom and on rationality and action; see bibliography below). However, let's finish with a comforting sense of returning to where we began. In *The Construction of Social Reality* (1995), Searle starts with his view that there is a reality that exists independent of our representations of it. The fundamental character of that reality is that the world is composed entirely of physical particles in fields of force. It's at this level of description that we find what he calls 'the basic facts'. He then gives an account of the ontology of social reality (the human-relative facts of money, property, marriage, government, cricket, and so on). Here Searle extends the account of constitutive rules and institutional facts that first appeared in *Speech Acts*. And he argues that the institutional facts are dependent on the basic facts. This claim of dependency has, of course, angered a good few thinkers. Why, critics such as Mary Midgley have asked, should the features of the world described by physics be treated as more fundamental than other features? But Searle is characteristically robust: although you can have physical particles without a society, you can't have a society without physical particles. As Searle himself might have put it: face the facts.

Further reading

John Searle's main books are mentioned above, apart from *Expression and Meaning: Studies in the Theory of Speech Acts* (1979), *Intentionality: An Essay in the Philosophy of Mind* (1983), *Mind, Language and Society: Philosophy in the Real World* (1998), *Rationality in Action* (2001), *Consciousness and Language* (2002), and *Mind: A Brief Introduction* (2005). For critical discussion, see, for example: Ernest Lepore and Robert van Gulick (eds) *John Searle and His Critics* (1991); John Preston and Mark Bishop (eds) *Views into the Chinese Room: New Essays on Searle and Artificial Intelligence* (2002); Barry Smith (ed.) *John Searle* (2003).

MICHAEL WHEELER

SEBALD, Winfried Georg

1944–2001

German writer

W.G. Sebald was born in 1944 at Wertach in the south of Germany, close to the Austrian Tyrol. His father was in the army. The family prospered under the Third Reich and was silenced by its defeat. Sebald graduated in German from Freiburg University in 1965. In 1966 he 'decided for various reasons' (as he wrote in *The Emigrants*) to move to England. It is typical that he should give no more detail about what was the most significant fact in his professional and artistic life. However, the Auschwitz trials were going on in Frankfurt at the time and this probably focused his discomfort in his homeland.

In 1967 he married and the couple had a daughter, but this aspect of his life does not feature in his art which is that of the lonely wanderer, shy, voyeuristic and obsessional. After three years as an assistant lecturer in German at Manchester University he flirted briefly with the idea of being a schoolmaster in Switzerland, but returned to England in 1970 to a post at the University of East Anglia where he spent the rest of his life. In 1987 he became its Professor of European Literature and in 1989 the first director of the British Centre for Literary Translation.

Though he has published academic nonfiction, his reputation rests on four novels: *Vertigo* (*Schwindel, Gefühle*, 1990), *The Emigrants* (*Die Ausgewanderten*, 1992), *The Rings of Saturn* (*Die Ringe des Saturn*, 1995) and *Austerlitz* (*Austerlitz*, 2001). They were published in Germany according to the dates given, but later and out of sequence elsewhere. They are perhaps the most pensive of the numerous works by various authors which have sought to make sense of Germany's tragedy in the twentieth century. In the end he only confirms the conundrum of the relationship between civilization and barbarism, vigour and decay; in *The Rings of Saturn* (subtitled 'An English Pilgrimage' in the German edition) he views it through the prism of Britain's imperial greatness.

The above titles are called novels because they are challenging works of literary creativity, but Sebald himself was uneasy with the ascription and in German used the word *Erzählung*, meaning 'narrative'. They might almost as easily be called essays or meditations insofar as they fuse autobiography, travel, art and history in a seamless forward movement. The amount of invention or fantasy is never clear, but it is always Sebald's intention to convince us that what we are reading is actually true. *Austerlitz* is more like a novel than the others and has in consequence a greater sense of contrivance, seeming less open to the elements.

The inventor of this hybrid form is Sacheverell Sitwell in *Southern Baroque Art* (1924) and developed in his subsequent, weird prose rhapsodies, though it harks back to de Nerval, De Quincey and even Rousseau (*Les Rêveries du Promeneur solitaire*), while Sebald's moods of elegiac melancholy, lush nostalgia, gameplaying and lurking paranoia link him to **Rilke**, **Proust**, **Borges** and **Kafka**.

Association is very much part of his method and yet the effect is wholly original. First, this is because of presentation. He made a weak but graceful beginning in *After Nature* (*Nach der Natur*, 1988) in which the prose is printed as lines of poetry, a mannerism he did not repeat. A novel by Sebald doesn't look like anyone else's. Facing pages of solid text are frequent, with no dialogue or paragraph indentations. The page is rendered less forbidding to the modern eye by extra space between the lines and by black-and-white photographs, often of banal or incidental subjects such as a bus ticket or restaurant bill whose function is to act as evidence of actuality. That the photographs are printed within the body of the text renders them murky, which increases the sense of mystery they are ostensibly there to dispel. They are sometimes fakes.

The second aspect of originality is in the writing itself, done in a high yet languid style of the pre-computer, indeed the pre-television age. The texts are relatively short but have the aura of full-length works because their prose unrolls with few breaks. The sentences are very long in an age which commands them to be short; seductive and intimate, moving like tentacles of exploration through the deeps of memory and imagination; and they seem to emerge from a great hush, always in a cello tone, and ask to be taken slowly. The text is literally eccentric since it develops as a fractal does, by repeatedly moving off centre.

Lastly the content. A boundary-leaping postmodernist he may be, but there is no sex, no humour, no identifiable authorial presence. Writing in the first person, he tells us exactly where he is but never who he is: a ghost among ghosts. Quite often we discover *how* he is, and mostly he isn't very well. Panic attacks, terror of flying, nervous breakdown, insomnia, stomach trouble, allergies, claustrophobia all point to a temperament repelled by modern life and which found the remote spaciousness of East Anglia therapeutic. This pathos is often moving, occasionally ridiculous.

One of Sebald's great charms is that he has never been lost to popularity. Reading him has a private beauty associated more with poetry, obscure black-and-white films, forgotten artists in old albums. His achievement is to revive the highest ambitions for prose at a time when it is everywhere being degraded by the mass market. Like Luis Cernuda and Elias Canetti when they lived in Britain, Sebald was largely ignored by the British literary establishment until his death in a car crash at the age of fifty-seven (cf. **Camus**) gave him mythic status. The English translations by Michael Hulse are particularly fine.

Further reading

See: 'A Symposium on W.G. Sebald', *The Threepenny Review* (Spring 2002).

DUNCAN FALLOWELL

SEN, Amartya

1933–

Indian economist

The Nobel Prize-winning economist Professor Amartya Sen has achieved international renown for his pioneering work on a framework for economic analysis that focuses on individual substantive freedom rather than income and growth. Sen's distinctive blend of economic insight and ethical reflection has challenged orthodoxies and resulted in the development of important new paradigms and approaches in theoretical and empirical economics and in a range of related fields across the social sciences (including development, social policy, gender studies, political theory, philosophy and human rights). His work has expanded knowledge about critical world problems including inequality, poverty and starvation and has had a major international impact beyond academia by driving forward international debates and influencing the policies of key international organizations.

Sen was born in Santiniketan (West Bengal). His father taught chemistry at Dhaka University and he received much of his education at the school founded by the poet and writer **Rabindranath Tagore**. While being immersed in Indian intellectual life from an early age, Sen was not disengaged from the wider world. Formative experiences helped to shape his passionate commitment to making economic analysis relevant to the problems that people confront and the situations in which they live. The communal violence of the 1940s heightened Sen's awareness of diversity and difference and raised a critical question that he would pursue at the theoretical level for more than five decades: how to reconcile commitments to universal human values and substantive equity with respect for pluralism and tolerance. Early observations of the impact of entrenched inequality and gender discrimination, and of the phenomena of poverty, hunger and starvation, were also important influences. Memories of the Bengal famine of 1943 would motivate and inform later projects and helped to clarify a critical theme in Sen's work – that the socioeconomic processes by which individuals and groups fulfil their basic needs should be subjected to critical scrutiny, taking account of both the adequacy of people's opportunities, and the influences and constraints on their choices.

As an undergraduate in 1950s Calcutta, Indian philosophical and cultural traditions as well as **Marxist** thought (especially the focus on the nature of value, 'commodity fetishism' and the perspective of human need) must have fuelled the development of this idea. The debates of the day at Trinity College, Cambridge (England), where Sen completed a doctoral thesis in 1959, were another important influence. However, it was not in **Keynsian**, neoclassical or Marxist economics, but in the emergent field of social choice, that Sen's inclinations and skills found early application. Focusing on the relationship between individual values and collective decision-making, this mathematically exacting branch of welfare economics addresses a critical foundational question: given important differences between people (including differences in tastes, interests and judgements), is it possible to aggregate 'individual preferences' into a procedure for collective choice that is both theoretically robust and morally defendable? Kenneth Arrow's groundbreaking work had set the stage with its underlying message of pessimism. In *Collective Choice and Social Welfare* (1970), Sen set out to restore the possibility of social choice by addressing the informational basis of Arrow's 'Impossibility Theorem' and exploring the ways in which alternative assumptions about interpersonal comparability can influence the search for a 'reasonable' rule for collective decisions. Early emphasis on the importance of freedoms and rights was reflected in the key article 'The Impossibility of a Paretian Liberal' (1970).

These contributions in the field of social choice were followed by proposals for the measurement of poverty and inequality and by innovative analyses of the nature and causes of deprivation, hunger and starvation. *On Economic Inequality* (1973) provided a systematic analysis of the measurement of income distribution, while empirical examinations of 'excess mortality' in parts of Asia and North Africa (the phenomenon of

'Missing Women') highlighted gender discrimination and the neglect of female health and nutrition. The influential study *Poverty and Famines: An Essay on Entitlement and Deprivation* (1981) focused on the socioeconomic processes underlying hunger and starvation and helped to shift the focus of international food security policy away from aggregate food supply and towards the differential ability of individuals, groups and classes to acquire sufficient food in practice (the 'entitlement approach'). The idea that competitive market outcomes and processes of growth and development can generate very different results for individuals and groups is pivotal to Sen's work. Important empirical insights on this issue were reported in *Hunger and Public Action* (1989, with Jean Drèze). These include the finding that income and growth can be poor predictors of the quality of life and that public action and institutional conditions (including democracy and the protection of human rights) can be of critical importance in securing the fulfilment of basic needs.

The search for a more adequate metric of individual advantage is a central theme that integrates Sen's work in economics and philosophy. Sen has emphasized the limitations of traditional 'incomebased' and 'utilitybased' frameworks (including the 'Fundamental Theorems of Welfare Economics' and the criterion of 'Pareto Optimality') from the perspectives of inequality, poverty, freedoms and rights. Later contributions, including the Dewey Lectures on 'Wellbeing, Agency and Freedom' (1984), *On Economic Inequality after a Quarter of a Century* (1997, with James Foster) and *Development as Freedom* (1999), have highlighted the idea that evaluative exercises concerning basic human interests should focus on individual substantive freedoms (such as the ability to avoid premature mortality, to be adequately nourished and to have access to basic health and education) rather than alternative informational focuses (such as income, growth, utility, liberty and 'primary goods'). The 'capability approach' provides an alternative 'informational focus' to both

libertarianism and utilitarianism and underpins influential proposals for assessing economic processes and arrangements as well as Sen's important and innovative contributions to ethical debates about equality, freedom and human rights. The far-reaching international impact of this idea is reflected in the emergence of new paradigms and approaches across the social sciences and beyond academia (e.g. in the UN's 'Human Development Index').

Sen's career has taken him through a series of prestigious appointments at leading universities including Cambridge, the Delhi School of Economics, the London School of Economics, Oxford and Harvard. He has published prolifically, edited leading journals, presided over important societies and organizations, and received countless awards and accolades. The far-reaching influence of Sen's work on international organizations including the United Nations Development Programme, the Food and Agricultural Programme and the World Bank is widely acknowledged. He was awarded the Nobel Prize in 1998 for his contributions to welfare economics.

Further reading

Other works include: *Choice, Welfare and Measurement* (1982), *Resources, Values and Development* (1984); *On Ethics and Economics* (1987); *Markets and Freedoms: Achievements and Limitations of the Market Mechanism in Promoting Individual Freedoms* (1993); *Consequential Evaluation and Practical Reason* (2000); and *Rationality and Freedom* (2002).

POLLY VIZARD

SENGHOR, Léopold Sédar
1906–2001
Senegalese poet and politician

One of the founding fathers of the literary and philosophical discourse of Negritude, Léopold Sédar Senghor was a leading figure in the development of black francophone African literature and as a political theorist and statesman played an instrumental role in the decolonization process and the emergence of Senegalese independence. As an ethnic Serer and devout Christian in a predominantly Wolof and Muslim society, Senghor was the product of a dual cultural heritage: African by birth and European by assimilation. Drawn to the French language and tradition, he earned critical recognition as a poet of meditation and reconciliation, merging sensuality and celebration of the black experience with romantic lyricism and elements of modernism. An eloquent and persuasive voice in the African struggle for self-determination and liberation, Senghor was elected the first president of Senegal in 1960 and governed for nearly two decades before retiring to private life in Verson, France.

Born in the coastal village of Joal in the Sine-Saloum region of Senegal, Senghor attended Catholic mission school in Ngazobil and completed his secondary education in the capital city of Dakar. Awarded a partial scholarship from the Federation of French West Africa, he went to Paris in 1928, where he continued his studies at the Lycée Louis-le-Grand and at the Sorbonne, becoming the first African *agrégé*, the highest distinction in the French educational system. Immersing himself in the diasporic African and West Indian intellectual community, Senghor joined with writers such as Aimé Césaire of Martinique, Léon-Gontran Damas of French Guiana, and his compatriots Birago Diop and Ousmane Socé Diop to reassess the inadequacies of colonialism and to formulate the principles of Negritude, which signified a revalorization of black culture as well as the affirmation and assertion of black identity. Conscripted into the French army during World War II, Senghor spent two years as a German prisoner of war. After his release, he returned to Paris and resumed a career in teaching while establishing his reputation as a writer, politician and advocate for Pan-African nationalism.

Senghor published his first collection of poetry in 1945, entitled *Chants d'ombre* ('Shadow Songs'), and in the following year

was elected as one of two deputies from Senegal to the French National Assembly. Published in 1948, his second collection of poems, *Hosties noires* ('Black Hosts' or 'Black Victims'), appeared in the same year as his influential *Anthologie de la nouvelle poésie nègre et malgache de langue française* ('Anthology of New Black and Malagasy Poetry in the French Language'), with a preface written by **Jean-Paul Sartre**, which included writers from the West Indies, Madagascar and French Africa. Later collections of his poetry include *Ethiopiques* ('Ethiopics'), published in 1956; *Nocturnes*, published in 1961 and translated into English under the same title in 1969, which received the Grand Prix International de Poésie, given by the Society of Poets and Artists of France; *Lettres d'hivernage* ('Letters in the Season of Hivernage'); and *Elégies majeures* ('Major Elegies'), published in 1972 and 1979 respectively. His collected poetry was published in 1990 as *Oeuvre poétique* ('Poetical Work') and translated into English in the following year as *The Collected Poetry*. From 1964 to 1993, he published his selected non-fiction in five volumes under the general title of *Liberté* ('Liberty') and in 1988 published a memoir, *Ce que je crois: negritude, francité et civilization de l'universel* ('That Which I Believe: Negritude, Frenchness, and Universal Civilization').

Originating in the mid-1930s as a form of ideological expression, the concept of Negritude evolved in the post-war era with a multitude of interpretations generating widespread debate as well as controversy; for Senghor, Negritude assumed a political dimension that envisioned a reawakening of black consciousness and a rebirth of the African personality. Among the most astute and respected post-independence African leaders, Senghor was not without criticism during his presidency for imposing policies that compromised social and economic reform and for restrictive measures that established authoritarian rule. Diligent in his efforts to promote unity and solidarity in Africa and the Third World, he left office voluntarily at the end of 1980; in 1984

Senghor was inducted into the Académie Française, the first African to receive the honour in the history of the institution.

Further reading

Other works include: *Nationhood and the African Road to Socialism* (*Nation et voie africaine du socialisme*, 1962, revised and enlarged as *On African Socialism*, 1964); *Selected Poems* (1964); *Prose and Poetry* (1965); *Selected Poems of Léopold Sédar Senghor* (1977); *Poems of a Black Orpheus* (1981). The major biographical and critical treatment published in English is Janet G. Vaillant, *Black, French, and African: A Life of Léopold Sédar Senghor* (1990). See also: S. Okechukwu Mezu, *The Poetry of Léopold Sédar Senghor* (1973) and Janice S. Spleth ed., *Critical Perspectives on Léopold Sédar Senghor* (1993).

STEVEN SERAFIN

SEURAT, Georges Pierre

1859–91

French painter

Georges Seurat was born in Paris, the youngest child of a bailiff. He was a pupil of Henri Lehmann, a disciple of Ingres, at the École des Beaux Arts, 1878–9. He studied antique sculpture, the Renaissance masters and the drawing of Ingres. While on military service at Brest, 1879–80, he began to paint landscapes. On his return to Paris he became interested in urban social subject-matter and began to develop the distinctive drawing style for which he is famous, using soft *conté* crayon on heavily textured paper. These studies with their monumental forms devoid of hard outline were prototypes for his painted figures. While working at drawing and painting Seurat read the works of Charles Blanc and Michel-Eugène Chevreul on colour contrast and harmony and Hermann von Helmholtz on physiological optics. His painting style during this period was close to that of Barbizon and Impressionist artists. In the autumn of 1884 he showed his celebrated large canvas *Une baignade à Asnières* (1883–4), which had been refused by the Salon, at the first exhibition of the Société des Artistes

Indépendants, which he had founded with Signac, **Redon** and other radical artists. In 1886 he exhibited the other very large canvas for which he is renowned, *La Grande Jatte* (1883–5), at the last Impressionist exhibition. This was his first major attempt at what became known as 'pointillism' or 'neo-Impressionism'. A number of Symbolist writers and critics, like Felix Fenéon and Gustave Kahn, rallied round Seurat and also Paul Signac, in defence of their art and theories. Painters like Cross, Angrand, Lucien Pissarro and Luce became 'neo-Impressionists' and **Van Gogh**, who met Seurat this year, incorporated some of the latter's ideas into his own work. Seurat died quite suddenly of infectious angina in 1891. He produced seven large canvases, sixty small ones, 160 very small wood panel studies and nearly 500 drawings.

Seurat's art, developed in a little over ten years, grew from a number of 'scientific researches' into physiological optics, colour theory and the affective qualities of colours, lines and forms, as well as from a scrupulous technique and a great deal of study of earlier masters. His earliest researches into the simultaneous contrast of colours, based on a reading of Blanc and Chevreul and a study of Delacroix's use of colour, led to *Une baignade*, on which he worked for over a year and which he reworked in 1887. Seurat made thirteen preparatory oil sketches and numerous drawings for this work which, with its elemental composition, its monumental figures and banal industrial suburb for background, seems to be a secular reworking of Piero della Francesca's art. It certainly bears a relationship to the work of Seurat's Symbolist contemporary **Puvis de Chavannes**. Although the work is based on firmly moulded forms and a geometrical composition, the first traces of the pointillist technique can be discerned in the grass in the foreground. All the hues have a luminosity and intensity which derives from the use of pure and largely unmixed colours.

It was *La Grande Jatte*, showing Parisians relaxing on a Sunday afternoon, which was the first extreme example of pointillism and fully reveals the influence of scientific ideas on his work. All the colour is applied in small dots and strokes which, at a certain distance, are 'optically mixed' by the spectator's eye. Around the edge of this and future canvases is a thin border or 'false frame', which contrasts with adjacent colours. The figures are still and hieratic, as if seen in an atmospheric frieze, and the first traces of an elegant 'art nouveau' line can be traced in some of the forms. As with most of Seurat's major works, *La Grande Jatte* was carefully composed over a long period from a large number of studies. After 1886, under the influence of the scientist and aesthetician Charles Henry, Seurat's work often deals with movement and he developed in his last years a complex linear style which was meant directly to affect the beholder's emotions by its formal arrangement. The emotional tones of pictures like *Le Chahut* (1889–90) and *Le Cirque* (1890–1) show the considerable impact of Henry's ideas concerning the relationships obtained between linear directions by measuring their angles with a *Rapporteur esthétique*, a sort of aesthete's protractor.

Seurat's own formulation of these theories was made in a letter to a friend, the writer Maurice Beaubourg, in August 1890, in which he stated, 'Art is Harmony. Harmony is the analogy of contrary and similar qualities in tone, colour and line, considered with reference to a Dominant and under the influence of a scheme of lighting in cheerful, calm or sad combinations.' These ideas had a major impact on later Symbolist and abstractionist theories of art and, in revising the tenets of Impressionism, led to the creation of more conceptual and schematic art forms than either Impressionism or traditional varieties of realism had offered. The Italian 'Divisionists', in particular Boccioni and Balla, were to develop these ideas into Futurism. Similar experiments in Germany by **Kandinsky** and **Klee** were to lay some of the foundations of a formally non-objective art. Like **Degas** and **Cézanne**, Seurat tried to reinvent the classical elements of structure

and overall design in painting without sacrificing the mainly scientific advances that had been made since the advent of Impressionism. Seurat, in his scientific studies and researches, revived the image of the artist-philosopher in the tradition of Poussin and, before him, Leonardo.

Further reading

See: H. Dorra and J. Rewald, *Seurat* (Paris, 1960); *Seurat's Drawings*, ed. R.L. Herbert (1963); W.I. Homer, *Seurat and the Science of Painting* (1964); J. Russell, *Seurat* (1965); J. Arguelles, *Charles Henry and the Formation of a Psychological Aesthetic* (1972); R. Thomson, *Seurat* (1985).

RICHARD HUMPHREYS

SHAH, Idries
1924–96
Afghan writer

Sayed Idries Shah was born at Simla in India, into a family directly descended from Mohammed, and from many of the great Sufi masters of Central Asia, notably Afghanistan, the family home. Having studied the Moslem heritage in the company of Sufis, Shah wrote many books based on their teaching, and he is generally recognized as a leading disseminator of Eastern wisdom in the West. Between *The Sufis* (1964) and *Learning How to Learn* (1978) his collections of mostly ancient parables and anecdotes had a huge circulation throughout the world. Those who studied with him were recommended to familiarize themselves with these entertaining but oddly pointed stories, as a result of which the student was expected to lose his complacent satisfaction with much that had previously been taken for granted.

Retaining a strong sense of spiritual values, Shah's concern was to reveal the essentials which underlie all cultures, the hidden factors responsible for the behaviour of individuals, alone and in relationship with others in different environments and circumstances; and the links between these factors. While it is difficult to summarize an enterprise that does not, like most contemporary didactic Western teaching, summarize itself, certain themes recur. In particular Shah discounted the attention given in the West to the appearances and superficialities of culture – often reflecting what is merely habit or fashion – and suggested such attention would be more appropriately applied to the study of the springs of culture, to the unconscious and mixed motives of people, and to the even more mysterious motivations of groups of people. Again, he disagreed with the practice of piecemeal cultural analysis, maintaining that a culture, like an individual, is indivisible, and cannot therefore be studied objectively if some aspects of it are deliberately excluded, or others disproportionately promoted. To do this obscures overall patterns. For example, Shah observed how, both on personal and on community levels, immediate disasters prove in the long term to be blessings, and vice versa, yet the available evidence for this has had little impact on reactions to events as they occur.

Through his own wide experience, as a reader and as a traveller, through his books, and through the Institute for Cultural Research, which he established in London in 1966, Shah endeavoured to create the conditions for the objective study he advocates. His exact status remains indefinable. Disclaiming the identity of a guru, and disclaiming any intention to found a cult or a sect, he also rejected the academic cap. An Eastern Orientalist, he was perhaps best seen as an embodiment of the tradition in which the contemplative and intuitive aspects of the mind are regarded as being most productive when working together.

Further reading

Shah's many other books include: *Caravan of Dreams* (1968); *The Way of the Sufi* (1968); *Tales of the Dervishes* (1967); *Thinkers of the East* (1971); *Wisdom of the Idiots* (1970); *The Magic Monastery* (1972); *The Dermis Probe* (1970); *The Exploits of the Incomparable Mulla Nasrudin* (1966); *The Pleasantries of the Incredible Mulla Nasrudin* (1968); *The Subtleties*

of the Inimitable Mulla Nasrudin (1973); *Reflections* (1983); *Special Illumination: The Sufi Use of Humour* (1983); *The Book of the Book* (1986). See also *Letters and Lectures of Idries Shah* (1981).

MICHAEL RUBINSTEIN

SHAW, George Bernard
1856–1950
Irish writer

'I am a typical Irishman,' Shaw told **G.K. Chesterton**, 'my family came from Yorkshire.' He was born in Dublin on 26 July 1856, the third and last child of George Carr Shaw, a redundant Civil Servant turned grain merchant, and his wife Lucinda Elizabeth, a lapsed Protestant who tampered with the occult. They were an unattractive couple and they achieved a miserable marriage that began in Synge Street – 'an awful little kennel', Shaw later described it. They did not physically ill-treat their son: they ignored him. If he had failed to come home from one of the genteel day schools to which he was sent, he did not think that either of them would have noticed.

Mrs Shaw despised her husband, who was a failed teetotaller, and she seems to have felt that their son was tainted by a similar ineffectualness. She looked down on all men: except one, 'a mesmeric conductor and daringly original teacher of Music' called George John Vandeleur Lee. The impact of this man on the Shaw household was revolutionary. Having discovered Mrs Shaw to be a fine mezzo-soprano, he trained her voice, made her the right-hand woman of his Amateur Musical Society and invited the Shaws to share both his smart house in Dublin and his seaside cottage at Dalkey. He banished family prayers, reduced Mr Shaw to nullity and filled the house with music. The ménage-à-trois was all the more remarkable in the strict caste society of Ireland since Lee was Catholic and the Shaws Protestant. But in 1873, in rather dubious circumstances, Lee suddenly left Dublin for London. A fortnight later, on her twenty-first wedding anniversary,

Mrs Shaw followed him. Though she was to bring both her daughters to live with her, she left 'Sonny' (as he had been called) in lodging with her husband. It was then, turning deprivation to advantage, that Shaw taught himself music from textbooks and the piano. After leaving school in 1871 he had become a junior clerk in 'a highly exclusive gentlemanly estate office', Uniacke Townshend & Co. Early in 1876 he resigned and, one of his sisters having died, went to take her room in his mother's home in London.

These first twenty years in Ireland had left Shaw bereft of all passions except two: the passion of laughter and a passion for reform. His early experiences were to control to an extraordinary degree the range and tone of his work. The art of paradox, which turned tragedy on its head and fulfilled a moral obligation to optimism, became his 'criticism of life'. Believing that he had inherited from his father the tendency to an obsession, he transferred it from drink to work, making himself, as he said, into a writing-machine. For professional purposes he dropped the name George (so uncomfortably shared by Lee and his father) and created a public being, G.B.S., a 'pantomime ostrich' which was modelled on the example of Lee whom he depicted as a phenomenon too impersonal to attract affection, but whose mercurial personality had won him the admiration, so much sought after by Sonny, of Mrs Shaw.

Shaw's progress in London at setting himself up as 'a professional man of genius' was dismayingly slow, and over the first nine years he calculated that he had earned less than ten pounds. 'I did not throw myself into the struggle for life: I threw my mother into it. I was not a staff to my father's old age: I hung on to his coat tails.' In this period he wrote five novels that were rejected by every publisher, though four of them eventually achieved publication in socialist magazines.

In 1884 Shaw joined the Fabian Society which, up to the First World War, often by means of permeating the Tories and Liberals with its socialist ideas, chiefly expressed the opinions of Shaw and **Sidney Webb**.

The Fabian Society became Shaw's new family and his socialist reforms a means of changing society so that no child should have to go through the sort of upbringing he had endured. Believing himself to be unlovable, he made out of Collectivism a weapon against individualist romantic propaganda. Shaw's socialism was composed of the abolition of private property plus the introduction of equality of income. To this, as a refinement to democracy, aimed at achieving efficiency and real adult suffrage, he proposed adding the Coupled Vote – every valid vote going to a man-and-woman. Shaw's socialism, which invades many of his plays and much of his journalism, found its outlet in numerous Fabian Tracts (of which he made a selection in *Essays in Fabian Socialism*), in *The Intelligent Woman's Guide to Socialism and Capitalism* (1928) and *Everybody's Political What's What* (1944). Shaw also spent a great deal of time speaking at street corners and working on committees, but eventually concluded that **William Morris** was right and that it had not been practical for socialists to enter the circus of party politics. Shaw believed that the Labour Party, so far from being a force for socialism against capitalism, was a trade union party dedicated to fighting the employer's federations in a new class war. A measure of his disenchantment with British politics may be seen from his enthusiasm for Soviet Russia, which he visited in 1931 and advertised on his return as an experimental Fabian colony.

Shaw was known as a journalist and critic long before he became famous as a playwright. His art reviews in *Our Corner and the World* (1885–9), though mainly anonymous, made him well known among his colleagues; while his celebrated musical criticism, first as 'Corno di Bassetto' in the *Star* (1888–90) and then as 'G.B.S.' in the *World* (1890–4), extended his fame. From 1895 to 1898 he contributed theatre criticism to the Saturday Review, making outrageous use of Shakespeare (whose politics, he claimed, 'would hardly impress the Thames Conservancy Board') to promote his campaign for a revolution on the late-Victorian stage. According to his successor

Max Beerbohm, he had become 'the most brilliant and remarkable journalist in London'.

But most critics agreed that he would have made a 'better Bishop than a playwright'. Almost all of them acknowledged that he could produce entertaining prose extravaganzas (*Arms and the Man, You Never Can Tell*), but they were based not on human emotions but piles of bluebooks, tracts, social statistics (*Widowers' Houses, Mrs. Warren's Profession*). Sometimes these compositions, amalgams of lecture and farce, the critics conceded, were almost as good as plays.

Success did not finally come until, during the Vedrenne-Barker management at the Court Theatre, the special furniture hired for a royal command performance of *John Bull's Other Island* on 11 March 1905 crashed beneath the king, who was laughing too hard, and flung Shaw's reputation high into the air. Despite his efforts to do so ('I am not in the popular entertainment business'), Shaw never fully recovered his unpopularity. *Fanny's First Play* ran for 622 performances in London (1912–13), and the number of revivals of *Pygmalion* (1913) and *Saint Joan* (1923) established him as a box-office success throughout the world.

But under the sparkle and to one side of the sermonizing lay an ingenious Shavian theme. He believed that he had inherited from his parents incompatible qualities that he must reconcile within himself. In *The Quintessence of Ibsenism* (1891) he had stressed the importance of efficiency over aspiration, but in later writings such as *Candida* (1894) and *The Perfect Wagnerite* (1898) he tried to expand this pragmatism so that it might serve not just a social but a religious purpose. From this process emerged his concept of the Life Force which is not a symbol of power but a unit of synthesis.

With this new religion came new drama in which, as a series of parables, Shaw rewrote past history and tried to navigate a course for the future. The synthesis of *Man and Superman* (1903) was a fantasy, and when in *John Bull's Other Island* (1904) and *Major Barbara* (1905) he tried to apply it to actual life he found that he could not reconcile all the separated elements. Like a conjuror with too many objects revolving in the air, he had to dispense with something and, in *Back to Methuselah* (1924), it was the body that he eliminated.

In later years Shaw lusted after a non-physical consummation – 'all life and no matter' – between earth and heaven. That man would have to change out of all recognition or be superseded by another species did not cause him to despair, for he had increasingly turned his attention away from the individual and the body as a vehicle of emotion. At times, like Ellie Dunn at the end of *Heartbreak House* (1919), he appears 'radiant at the prospect' of the human species being scrapped, and the Life Force taking another mate.

Shaw did not stop short at rewriting the past: he re-enacted it. Many of his affairs with women were three-cornered, often with the wife of some socialist friend. Shaw flirted, but never made love to anyone's wife. He acted his own version of Lee in other people's households – a sort of Sunday husband. In these relationships he was seeking a second childhood in which he received all the attention he had been denied. His liaisons became part of his theatrical life, the excitement producing an ejaculation of words from which plays were born. In 1898 he married Charlotte Payne Townshend, 'my green-eyed millionairess', who came from the same family as the Dublin estate agents. At Charlotte's request it was a *mariage blanc*. In their fashion they loved each other and when Charlotte died in 1943 Shaw was grief-stricken. Her death had been a great loss to him, he admitted; then at the last moment he turned it into a Shavian joke – 'a great financial loss'.

Further reading

See: the Standard Edition in thirty-six volumes published by Constable (1931–51); *Bernard Shaw and Mrs Patrick Campbell: Their Correspondence*, ed. Alan Dent (1952); *Ellen Terry and Bernard Shaw – A Correspondence*, ed. Christopher St John (1931); *Collected Plays* and their *Prefaces* in seven volumes (1970–4) and *Collected Letters* ed. Dan H. Laurence

(4 vols 1965–88). Among the many biographies, Michael Holroyd, *Bernard Shaw* (5 vols 1988–92) is perhaps definitive, while those by St John Ervine (1956) and Hesketh Pearson (1942, revised 1961) are also recommended. Critical and other studies include: Eric Bentley, *Shaw* (1946, revised 1957); Martin Meisel, *Shaw and the Nineteenth Century Theatre* (1963); J.M. Wisenthal, *The Marriage of Contraries* (1974); Alfred Turco Jr, *Shaw's Moral Vision* (1976); *The Genius of Shaw*, ed. Michael Holroyd (1979); and C. Innes (ed.) *The Cambridge Companion to George Bernard Shaw* (1998).

MICHAEL HOLROYD

SHAW, Richard Norman

1831–1912

Anglo-Scottish architect

Norman Shaw is one of the most important domestic architects of the late **Victorian** period. Works most associated with his name are those designed in the Old English styles and that of the Queen Anne revival, and yet his manner and sources remained diverse, sometimes looking to vernacular cottages in Sussex, at other times to the Scottish baronial (New Scotland Yard). He was, in part, responsible for the move away from the severity of High Victorian Gothic designs to a more 'homely' and habitable style, today seen vulgarized in the semi-detached suburban house.

Born in Edinburgh, he came to London when young and began his architectural apprenticeship in 1849 under William Burn. In 1856 he was articled to Salvin, in whose office he met W.E. Nesfield with whom he formed a partnership from 1863 to 1866. Though each worked independently a cross-influence of styles was inevitable. It was working in G.E. Street's office, as principal assistant, following Phillip Webb, that was the most decisive influence during his training. It was there, so he said, that he learnt everything he knew about architecture. Street's influence can be seen most especially in Shaw's High Victorian church architecture such as Holy Trinity, Bingley, Yorkshire (1866–7).

At this period Shaw was considering a career in ecclesiastical architecture – a field that had been so securely occupied by A.W. Pugin, W. Butterfield and Street. It is this interest which is shown in his first publication, *Architectural Sketches from the Continent* (1858). The one hundred lithographs consist mainly of Gothic cathedrals and monuments, after sketches he had made while touring Italy, France and Germany in 1854–6, a tour made possible by his winning the Royal Academy Travelling Scholarship award in 1854.

It was not until 1862, on a visit to Sussex with Nesfield, that Shaw shifted his interests from church designs towards domestic, an area where there seemed greater opportunity for commissions. His sketches of that date show an interest in vernacular buildings, an example of one such being Sedlescomb, East Sussex, of c. 1611, and this research was important for the development of Shaw's Old English style, a term loosely covering borrowings from the Gothic and Tudor periods.

Shaw's first significant commission was the extending of a Georgian house at Willesley for John Calcott Horsely RA. Shaw imposes an irregularity on the existing eighteenth-century house which is not altogether successful, and much of the rustic decoration is amateurish. Yet the inclusion of a medieval hall was to become a regular feature of his large country houses, a characteristic that was later taken up by Baillie Scott.

Glen Andred (1868), Leyswood (1870) and Hillside (1870–1) are the major works in the Old English style, and in their imposing settings they appear as descendants of the aesthetic of the picturesque movement.

The 'fortress-like' Leyswood, one of Shaw's most influential buildings, both in England and America, announced the vocabulary of his mature Old English style, in its use of tile hanging, half-timbering, lofty gables and massive ribbed chimney stacks. The clarity of the blocks and firmness of the individual detail show an assurance in part indebted to Street, that escapes nostalgic references and muddled planning of so many Victorian houses.

In the towns where Old English was felt to be inappropriate it was the Queen Anne style that caught on, taking the place of Italianate stuccoed façades. Nesfield had already experimented with this style in his Kew Lodge (1867), but it was Shaw who was responsible for its popularity. The label, again inappropriate, refers to takings from English and Dutch red-brick architecture of the seventeenth and eighteenth centuries with some French and Flemish details.

In 1872, a year after he started his London career, he was commissioned to build Lowther Lodge, a town 'country' house near Hyde Park, using as a model the seventeenth-century Kew Palace. Queen Anne elements introduced here become more prominent in other works of this decade, such as New Zealand Chambers (1871–3), Swan House (1875–7), the Albert Hall Mansions, and the many houses he designed in Cadogan Square, Queen's Gate and along the Chelsea Embankment.

In later years Shaw increasingly turned towards the classical style, the two most ambitious projects being Bryanston (1889–94) and his additions to Chesters (1891–3), the latter in a free classical style with a baroque vocabulary that he later employed in the Piccadilly Hotel (1905–8).

Shaw's achievement lies in his revolutionary contribution to country house design. His influence, continued through his pupils Lethaby, Prior and Newton, was not only felt in England but, through publications, contributed to the development of the 'Shingle' style in America.

Further reading

Other works include: Cragside (enlargement of shooting lodge into a country house, 1869–86); Convent of Sisters of Bethany, Bournemouth (1873–5 and 1878–80); 196 Queen's Gate, London (1874–6); Cheyne House (1875–7); Clock House, Chelsea Embankment (1878–80); All Saints' Church, Compton, Leek (1884–7). See: Andrew Saint, *Richard Norman Shaw* (1976); Robert Bartlett Harmon, *English Elegance in the Domestic Architecture of Richard Norman Shaw: A Selected Bibliography* (1982).

CALAN LEWIS

SHOLOKHOV, Mikhail Aleksandrovich

1905–84
Russian novelist

Mikhail Sholokhov's novel *And Quiet Flows the Don* (*Tikhiy Don*) has been unique in the acclaim which it has received from public and critics in both the Soviet Union and the West. Grigory, the main hero of the novel, is a figure with whom many can feel sympathy; however little a contemporary reader might seem to have in common with a Cossack struggling through the horrors of the Russian civil war, he presents with anguished sharpness the bitter choice confronting those who were attracted by the ideal of Communism and at the same time repelled by the barbarity and ruthlessness of Bolshevik practice.

In 1925 Sholokhov embarked on the formidable task of explaining the role of the Cossacks in the revolution. The Russians traditionally regarded them as willing servants of the tsars in suppressing any stirrings of dissent, but in 1917 the Cossacks refused to side with the right-wing parties. Fear that they might lose their prosperous landholdings made them reluctant to identify completely with the Red cause and Grigory found himself involved in a hopeless rebellion against Soviet power in the central Don area. All the complex political dilemmas of the Cossacks are reflected in his wavering and heart-searching. Sholokhov has given a remarkably accurate account of the war, which he witnessed in his homeland, and has placed his hero at the centre of conflicts of class and local allegiances which threaten to destroy his personality.

Although *Tikhiy Don* depicts faithfully the shattering of the old Cossack traditions in the years from 1912 to 1922, the work rests its main reputation on its success as imaginative fiction. In contrast to those who were brutalized by the endless carnage Grigory becomes increasingly sensitive and noble, but his development seems valid thanks to Sholokhov's abundant use of concrete detail. He is shown throughout the novel in ever-changing relationships with all too human members of his village and his openly declared attachment with Aksin'ya breaks even the free conventions of Cossack society The author found great difficulty in finishing the novel, but eventually in 1940 published the last part in which Grigory is driven to final surrender to Bolshevik power. By this time Sholokhov had been given official recognition as a leading Soviet writer and did not suffer for his refusal to provide a trite ending at a time when literature was expected to serve as an arm of propaganda for official optimism. Instead, the more orthodox critics tried to explain that the tragedy of Grigory must be set against the triumph of the new era which was dawning. Oceans of ink have been spent on this classic Soviet novel; with the less artificial climate which came in after **Stalin's** death there has been general recognition that as a reaction away from the 'anti-psychologism' of the early 1920s Sholokhov was returning to the traditions of the nineteenth century on which he had principally been nurtured after leaving school at the age of thirteen – and that Grigory's downfall followed the classical recipe for a tragic hero who is destroyed not by his weaknesses but by his positive qualities.

None of Sholokhov's other works can approach *Tikhiy Don* for literary merit, though *Virgin Soil Upturned* (*Podnyataya tselina*) has been successful with Soviet readers, and the first part in particular contains some striking scenes on the collectivization of agriculture. As a young man Sholokhov had considerable difficulty in getting his work published without heavy cutting and distortion – and indeed the 1953 edition of *Tikhiy Don* was shamelessly bowdlerized throughout. Rumours were started that he had plagiarized the novel and these have been persistently revived, though no hard evidence ever seems to have been produced to support them.

Sholokhov did not feel kindly disposed towards many members of the Moscow intelligentsia and lived the greater part of his life at Vyoshenskaya on the middle course of the Don near the village where he was born. Showered with honours by the state and the recipient of the Nobel Prize for Literature in 1965, he generally took a hard line against any dissident voices in literature and furthered the cause of conservative careerists aspiring to positions of power in the literary hierarchy. Most Russians acknowledge his achievement as the leading writer on the civil war, though many would attack his role in public life.

Further reading

Other works include: *Tikhiy Don* in four 'books', was published over twelve years, from 1928 to 1940. It was translated in two volumes, *And Quiet Flows the Don* (1934) and *The Don Flows Home to the Sea* (1940); but an English translation of the entire text, *And Quiet Flows the Don*, has been issued in Moscow (1960). *Podnyataya tselina* (1932–60) has been similarly dismembered into *Virgin Soil Upturned* (1959) and *Harvest on the Don* (1961). Sholokhov's other work includes *Tales from the Don* (*Donskiye rasskazy*, 1926, trans. 1961). See: D.H. Stewart, *Mikhail Sholokhov – A Critical Introduction* (1967); L. Yakimenko, *Sholokhov: A Critical Appreciation* (trans. 1973); and A.B. Murphy, M. Duncan, V. Swoboda and V.P. Butt, 'A Commentary on *Tikhiy Don*', *New Zealand Slavonic Review* (1975).

A.B. MURPHY

SHOSTAKOVICH, Dmitri Dmitrievich
1906–75
Russian composer

Shostakovich was born in St Petersburg and took piano lessons from the age of nine. It soon became clear that he had exceptional talent and in 1919 he was enrolled at the Conservatoire in that city (by this time renamed Petrograd). He was obliged to support his family by playing for silent films but nevertheless completed his course with a First Symphony (1925) so well received that it immediately became part of the repertoire, first in Russia and then abroad, a position it has maintained to the present.

It revealed the composer as open to much of the exploratory music being written in the West at the time – **Hindemith's** and **Berg's** in particular – as well as reflecting the conflicting Russian traditions: symphonic in the manner of **Tchaikovsky** and more Russophile after the example of the Five, the famous nineteenth-century group of composers, among whom **Rimsky-Korsakov** had been prominent. The latter's son-in-law, M. Steinberg, had been Shostakovich's composition teacher.

Shostakovich graduated as a pianist as well as composer and after leaving the Conservatoire won a prize at a recital contest in Warsaw and gave concerts throughout Russia. Composition remained of paramount importance to him, however, although he continued to give recitals, principally involving his own music, throughout his career.

In the late 1920s Shostakovich's musical modernism continued in the Second and Third Symphony, the ballets *The Golden Age* (1930) and *The Bolt* (1931), and the operas *The Nose* (1930) and *Lady Macbeth of Mtensk* (1934). Two current tendencies were present in Soviet music at the time – the 'proletarian' which insisted that music should be widely comprehensible and the 'modernistic' which asserted that revolution in art should accompany revolution in society. Both tendencies had their associations and both were wound up in the early 1930s as the ideas of Socialist Realism were formulated.

Shostakovich inclined towards the modernistic tendency but there are clear signs of stylistic crisis in his Fourth Symphony (withdrawn during rehearsal in 1936). An unwieldy and discursive structure supports a language that is not fully coherent and this problem, together with an article 'Chaos instead of Music', which appeared in *Pravda* in 1936 concerning his opera *Lady Macbeth of Mtensk*, forced on him a retrenchment and reconsideration.

Starting with the Fifth Symphony (1937) his style becomes clearer and more traditional but equally more personal. Long-range tonal organization deriving from classical practice is allied with a detailed concentration on motif usually expressed in traditional forms. He turned to chamber music at this time,

beginning his series of string quartets and producing two definitive works in piano chamber music – the Piano Quintet (1940) and the Piano Trio (1944). Both won **Stalin** Prizes as did the Seventh Symphony (1941), the *Leningrad*, composed and premiered under conditions of great privation during the German siege of that city. This work became the musical symbol of the Russian resistance when performed in concerts in the USA and unoccupied Europe.

At the end of the war Shostakovich failed to produce a victory symphony: instead his Ninth, perhaps from fear of comparison with Beethoven's, was a *jeu d'esprit* that revealed nothing of the horrors of the previous years. This failure possibly contributed towards a government intervention in music in 1948 as the state's duty to have concern for all aspects of cultural life was reasserted. Between then and 1953 Shostakovich produced two types of work – the public, e.g. film scores, which won him Stalin Prizes and the title People's Artist, and the private, including the First Violin Concerto (1948) and the song cycle *From Jewish Folk Poetry*. Neither of the latter was released until 1953; at the same time the Tenth Symphony was performed.

Although still within a traditional idiom, these works reveal a widening of the language and a willingness to experiment a little with structure, and with the success of these pieces Shostakovich's final period was set. He turned increasingly towards the more personal medium of the string quartet and produced many fine works in this genre: Nos 7 and 8 (both from 1960), 12 (1968) and 13 (1970) and 15 (1974) are particularly remarkable pieces. Those dating from the late 1960s reveal an interest in twelve-note technique (cf. **Schoenberg**), always used within a diatonic context as a deepening of the expressive power of the music.

More public music from this period utilized the virtuosity of Russian performers, e.g. Oistrakh in the two Violin Concertos (the Second dating from 1967), and Rostropovitch in two Cello Concertos (1958 and 1967), or, alternatively, involved text in an exposition of the composer's increasing obsession with death.

In their various ways the Thirteenth and Fourteenth Symphonies (1962 and 1969) and *Suite to Poems by Michelangelo* (1974) make explicit a despair left implicit in the brooding chamber music of the time and, although honours continued to be showered on him both at home and abroad, the music of his last works is largely powerfully depressive, the more so for being contained within clearly defined structures.

In the context of European music Shostakovich was a conservative, like **Britten**, whose music he admired. But Schoenberg had said there was much good music still to be written in C major and Shostakovich undoubtedly contributed much to this quantity. In the field of Russian music he was the first internationally acclaimed musical talent o emerge from the Soviet Union and was its most prominent representative throughout his career. Because of the interventionist nature of its government his career may also function as a touchstone for relationships between music and society: a relationship that, in Shostakovich's case, was not always of the happiest.

Further reading

Other works include: two Piano Concertos (1933 and 1957); *24 Preludes and Fugues* for piano (1951); and the choral work *The Execution of Stepan Razin* (1964). See: D. Rabinovich, *Dmitri Shostakovich* (1959); N. Kay, *Shostakovich* (1971); R. Blokker with R. Dearling, *The Music of Shostakovich* (1979); *Testimony: The Memoirs of Shostakovich*, ed. S. Volkov (1979); Christopher Norris (ed.) *Shostakovich* (1982); Eric Roseberry, *Shostakovich: His Life and Times* (1982); and I. MacDonald, *The New Shostakovich* (1992). See also: Boris Schwarz, *Music and Musical Life in Soviet Russia 1917–70* (1972).

MALCOLM BARRY

SIBELIUS, Jean

1865–1957
Finnish composer

Jean Sibelius is Finland's greatest composer and a master of the symphony. His music

bears witness to an all-consuming love of the nordic landscape and a preoccupation with its mythology, and more particularly, the repository of myth enshrined in the Finnish national epic, the *Kalevala*. Born in Hämeenlinna in Finland, he was christened Johan Julius Christian but subsequently Gallicized it, on discovering a set of visiting cards used by a sea-faring uncle who had adopted this form of the name. He showed an early talent for the violin and little interest in the law studies to which his family had set him. After some years in Helsinki as a pupil of Martin Wegelius, with whom he studied composition, he went abroad to Berlin in 1889 and the following year to Vienna, where he became a pupil of Goldmark. Up to this time his output comprised chamber music as opportunities to compose for the orchestra had been few. Helsinki did not possess a permanent symphony orchestra until 1888.

The *Kullervo Symphony*, an ambitious seventy-minute, five-movement work for soloists, male chorus and orchestra, put him on the map in 1892, and together with *En Saga* (1893), *Karelia* (1893) and the *Four Legends* (1895) established him as the leading figure in Finnish music. His popularity abroad began to grow a decade later with such works as *Finlandia* (1900) and *Valse triste* (1903). The 1890s show him developing as a nationalist composer, working within the Romantic musical tradition and responding positively to the influence of **Tchaikovsky**. His student works also show the influence of the Viennese classics and, of course, **Grieg**. After the Second Symphony (1902) and the Violin Concerto (1903, revised 1905), he moved away from the climate of post-Romanticism towards a more austere and classical language. His instinctive feeling for the Viennese classics strengthened, and works such as *Pohjola's Daughter* (1906) and the Third Symphony (1904–7) show a classicism at variance with the spirit of their time. In 1907 **Mahler** visited Helsinki and their oft-quoted exchange on the nature of the symphony reveals the difference of emphasis in their approach to the form. Sibelius said he admired 'its severity and style, and the profound logic that created an inner connection between all the motifs', to which Mahler replied, 'No, for me the symphony must be like the world: it must embrace everything.'

Championed by conductors, such as his countryman Robert Kajanus, Hans Richter, Sir Henry Wood and others, as well as such important critics as Rosa Newmarch and Ernest Newman, Sibelius's music gradually won acceptance both in England and America. In 1899 he had acquired the German publisher, Breitkopf and Härtel, and made numerous visits to both Germany and Italy. **Busoni** was among the figures who championed his music; he conducted both the Second Symphony and *Pohjola's Daughter* in Berlin. In 1909 Sibelius was operated on for a throat tumour, which may account for the greater austerity and depth of his Fourth Symphony (1911), as well as the greater seriousness and concentration of such scores as *The Bard* and *Luonnotar*.

With the outbreak of the First World War in 1914 he was cut off from his German royalties. He composed during this period a large number of light instrumental pieces in the hope of repeating the great success of *Valse triste*, the rights to which he had sold on derisory terms. From the war years comes the Fifth Symphony (1915), which he twice revised and which reached its definitive form only in 1919. The voyage from the climate of Slav romanticism that had fostered the First Symphony (1899) into the wholly isolated and profoundly original world of the Sixth (1923) and Seventh (1924), at a time when the mainstream of music was moving in other directions, was one of courageous spiritual discovery. Like all great artists, Sibelius's approach to the symphony is never the same. From the vantage point of the Fourth, it would be impossible to foretell the shape and character of the Fifth. Likewise, the Sixth is a wholly unpredictable phenomenon when viewed from the achievement of its predecessor, and in terms of the musical climate of the 1920s. There is no set of prescriptive rules for any Sibelius symphony: each differs from the other and from the genre as a whole. The Seventh's one movement is completely original in form, subtle in its handling of tempi, individual in its treatment of key and wholly organic in growth.

Tapiola (1926), in which his lifework culminated, united the symphonic process with his life-long preoccupation with nature and myth. The sheer stature of the seven symphonies overshadowed Sibelius's achievement in the field of the tone-poem. This genre occupied him throughout his creative life and his contribution to its literature is no less important than that of **Liszt** and **Richard Strauss**. Incidental music for the stage also constitutes an important part of his output and culminated in the ambitious and imaginative score he composed for the 1926 production of *The Tempest*. This saw the end of his creative career, though it is almost certain that an Eighth Symphony was composed and subsequently destroyed. After the 1920s, Sibelius gave up conducting and travelling and retired to the isolation of his home in Järvenpää, some miles outside Helsinki.

Further reading

See: Cecil Gray, *Sibelius: The Symphonies* (1931); Gerald Abraham (ed.) *Sibelius: A Symposium* (1947); Robert Layton, *Sibelius* (1965) and *Sibelius and His World* (1970); Erik Tawaststjerna, *Sibelius* (5 vols, 1968, abridged to 3 vols and translated by Robert Layton, 1976–97). See also F. Blum, *Jean Sibelius: An International Bibliography on the Occasion of the Centennial Celebration* (1965); G.D. Goss (ed.) *The Sibelius Symposium* (1996); T.L. Jackson and V. Murtomäki (eds) *Sibelius Studies* (2000).

ROBERT LAYTON

SICKERT, Walter Richard

1860–1942

English artist

Walter Sickert was born in Munich on 31 May 1860, of Danish descent. Both his father and his grandfather had been distinguished painters, and his mother, who was English, had been on the stage. The family settled in England in 1868 and, after attending various schools in London, Sickert himself went into the theatre in 1877, playing in numerous companies including that of Henry Irving, an experience he made much of in later life. In 1881 he enrolled at the Slade but left soon afterwards to become a studio assistant to **Whistler**, whom he had first met in 1879. He was strongly influenced by the older artist, and through him became acquainted with many of the leading figures in the London and Paris avant-garde, meeting **Degas** in 1883, who was to become the major single influence on his later work and beliefs.

Like Whistler, Sickert fused elements of both British and French art in his own painting, but he looked to very different examples in both cultures, preferring the British illustrative tradition of Cruikshank, Rowlandson and Charles Keene, and the starker, more painterly realism of Degas and the Nabis. This led to an inevitable break with Whistler, who was unable to tolerate evidence of independence among his immediate acolytes. In the 1890s Sickert was generally associated with the *Yellow Book* circle in London, contributing illustrations to the magazine in 1894 and 1895. He was also a prime mover in the establishment of the London Impressionist group, a secessionary breakaway group from the increasingly conservative New English Art Club, writing the catalogue preface for the group's first exhibition in 1889. Having been divorced by his first wife in 1899, he spent several years living and working in Europe, spending long periods in Dieppe, Paris and Venice. He returned to London in 1905 at the age of forty-five, convinced that a younger generation of painters would be more receptive to his own strong missionary sense of what constituted the correct modern tradition. To this end he formed the Fitzroy Street Group in 1907, with a number of painters who had recently left the Slade, including Harold Gilman and Spencer Gore. This was in a sense another

attempt to capture the lead of the British avant-garde, which he had failed to do in 1889, but it was also the first of many groups which Sickert formed as informal alliances over the next twenty years, meeting regularly 'at home' in order to discuss painting and to sell directly to clients from the artist's studio.

The most celebrated of these groups was the Camden Town Group, which was founded in 1911 in response to the tremendous success of Roger Fry's Post-Impressionist exhibitions. The bulk of Sickert's followers joined forces with those of Fry to form the London Group in 1914, following the premature death of Spencer Gore, but Sickert remained outside this group in protest at the presence of such figures as **Jacob Epstein** and **Wyndham Lewis**. It is characteristic of Sickert that he resigned from the Royal Academy in 1935 to protest at the then president's refusal to sign an appeal for the preservation of Epstein's sculptures on the BMA building in the Strand. He continued to work prolifically, and to exhibit regularly in London and Paris, moving from London to Thanet in Kent in 1934, and finally to Bathampton in 1938, where he died four years later, the grand old man of British painting. He was survived by his third wife, the artist Thérèse Lessore, until her death in 1945.

In 1900 Sickert was almost exactly halfway through his life. His career cannot, however, simply be divided in two. As a young painter and etcher he had been completely overwhelmed by the presence of Whistler, just as he was later to become overwhelmed by Degas. His own prickly, eccentric and somewhat autocratic personality comprised a bulwark of mannerisms which he slowly accreted in self-defence against his tendency to hero-worship. In a similar way he had to dig very deeply into his own social and cultural roots in order to establish his uniquely complex identity as a painter. Hence the highly personal iconography of much of his work, and his constant references to working-class life and popular culture in such titles as *Off to the Pub, What Shall We Do for the Rent?*, and so on, as well as his ironic use of classical titles. Sickert was possessed by his sense of the history of painting and believed, like Roger Fry, that it was up to him to guarantee the survival of a particular kind of artistic cultural practice. Hence his rejection of Whistler, whose technique of lowering all tonal values in a lacquer-like manner seemed increasingly incompatible with the qualities of direct painting in careful stages from drawings which he most admired in certain British and French traditions. Indeed, it might be said that he tended to apply the lessons of 'La Peinture' to the example of British draughtsmanship.

At the same time it should be noted that Sickert's best work invariably proceeded from his own psychological conflicts and complexity. Highly reticent about his private life, he poured his fantasies and obsessions into his subject-matter – claustrophobic images of sexual tension and domestic stress, as well as random memories of popular prints, places, music-hall scenes and so on, which he returned to again and again, with a rare trust in the intrinsic value of whatever he personally found fascinating. But Sickert's lasting achievement lay in his ability to match such highly varied themes with painting techniques approximating to their significance, ranging from the extraordinarily violent painting of many early nudes and interiors to the subtle *contre-jour* effects of his Camden Town Group period and the raw surface qualities of his later work, most of which derived from photographs or Victorian graphic sources. Sickert almost always worked by a process of indirection in order to control his responses to the actual motif, just as he preferred to leave a considerable period of time, often many years, between the initial blocking in of a canvas and its eventual completion. Unlike most of his contemporaries, he never settled into a formulaic relation between subject-matter and style. Hence the range and alertness of his work, right up to old age. He was also a considerable critic, and the posthumous collection of his writings, *A Free House! or The Artist as Craftsman* (1947), edited by Sir Oswald Sitwell, remains one of the handful of necessary books of twentieth-century art theory.

Further reading

See: *Sickert* (1973). The standard biography remains Robert Emmons, *The Life and Opinions of Walter Richard Sickert* (1941). See also: Marjorie Lilly, *Sickert: The Painter and His Circle* (1971); Simon Watney, *English Post-Impressionism* (1980); R. Shone, *Sickert* (1988).

SIMON WATNEY

SIMMEL, Georg
1858–1918
German philosopher and sociologist

Born in the very heart of Berlin, Simmel stayed in that thriving commercial and cultural centre until 1914. Quite an urbane 'Berliner' – and 'The Metropolis and Mental Life' ('Die Grosstädte und das Geistesleben', 1903) is perhaps the most genial essay on modern urban culture ever written – Simmel became a symbol of intellectual modernity in a milieu stifled by Wilhelmian pomp, Prussian bureaucracy and professorial rigidities, yet pulsating with intellectual and political counter-currents. Through prolific writings, virtuoso lecturing and cultivated salons hosted with his wife Gertrud, herself an accomplished philosophical writer, Simmel became a magnet for Berlin's intellectual elite in the two decades preceding the First World War.

Simmel's parents stemmed from the Jewish community of Wroclaw (Breslau). Before they married and moved to Berlin his mother converted to Protestantism, and his father, while travelling in Paris on business, to Catholicism. Georg, the youngest of seven offspring, was baptized in his mother's faith. Often described as Jewish in intellectual style and physical mannerisms, Simmel rarely expressed any affinity with his ancestral traditions, though he did once confess to the Jewish philosopher **Martin Buber**, 'We really are a remarkable people.' Despite his Protestant affiliation, expressed anti-Semitism was a factor in keeping him from a regular academic post for nearly all of his career.

The academic establishment also frowned on Simmel's apparent dilettantism. A person of wide-ranging aesthetic as well as philosophic interests, Simmel studied piano and violin and wrote on the history of music, befriended Germany's leading poets **Rainer Maria Rilke** and Stefan George, corresponded with the French sculptor **Auguste Rodin**, and published memorable essays on the theatre and on Michelangelo and Rembrandt. His scholarly work was often reproached for its 'aestheticism'.

When Simmel was sixteen his father died; his guardian, the musical publisher Julius Friedländer who founded the famed 'Edition Peters', bequeathed him fortune enough to live comfortably despite the fragility of his academic status. The combination of religious and academic marginality with independent means fortified Simmel's disposition to pursue work noted for its individuality and earned him the reputation of a 'brilliant gadfly'.

After studying history, psychology, anthropology and philosophy at the University of Berlin, where his mentors included such luminaries as **Mommsen**, Treitschke, Droysen, Grimm, Lazarus and Bastian, Simmel established himself as a philosopher with a dissertation on Kant (1881) and a few years later began to offer courses on ethics, epistemology and aesthetics as an unsalaried lecturer at his alma mater. His two major early works were *The Problems of the Philosophy of History* (*Die Probleme der Geschichtsphilosophie*, 1892, revised 1905 and 1907, trans. 1977) and *Einleitung in die Moralwissenschaft* ('Introduction to the Science of Ethics', 2 vols, 1892–3). Both works reflect his longstanding concern to adapt the formulations of Kant to the problems of contemporary philosophy. His *Kant: Sechzehn Vorlesungen* ('Lectures on Kant', 1904) remains a fresh and distinctive interpretation of that philosopher; characteristically, he observed that the book was 'not only one by Simmel about Kant, but also by Kant about Simmel'.

Simmel's most profound work was *The Philosophy of Money* (*Philosophie des Geldes*, 1900, enlarged 1907, trans. 1978). It begins with a tightly argued formulation of a 'relativistic' metaphysics and epistemology, and goes on to develop a speculative interpretation of the effects of a money economy on modern culture. These effects include an accentuation of man's capacity for rational calculation and an enormous expansion of the domain of human freedom, and at the same time a pervasive moral deracination and the manufacture of cultural products which are alienated from the absorptive capacities of human consumers. In his later years, under the impact of **Bergson**, but with renewed interest in Goethe, Schopenhauer and **Nietzsche** as well, his chief project was to articulate a philosophy of life. In *Lebensanschauung: Vier Metaphysische Kapitel* ('View of Life: Four Metaphysical Chapters', 1918; Chapter 1 trans. in D.N. Levine, 1971) he argued that an essential characteristic of human life is the propensity both to create novel forms and then to attack those forms as obstructions to the life process, and that death should be regarded not as the termination of life but as an integral dimension of life itself.

In Germany Simmel was known chiefly as a neo-Kantian, a philosopher of culture or a philosopher of life, and as such his influence on the major German thinkers of his century – including **Ernst Cassirer**, **Edmund Husserl**, **Max Weber**, Max Scheler, Alfred Schutz, Albert Schweitzer, Ernst Bloch, **Georg Lukács** and **Max Horkheimer** – has been amply documented. Outside Germany, however, he was and is known chiefly for his work as a seminal sociologist, indeed one of the pantheon of founding fathers of modern sociology along with **Émile Durkheim** and **Max Weber**.

Simmel began to lecture on sociological topics in 1887 and published his first sociological monograph, *Über soziale Differenzierung* ('On Social Differentiation'), in 1890. In that work and again in 'Das Problem der Soziologie' ('The Problem of Sociology', 1894) Simmel staked out a programme for sociology he would follow the rest of his life: one which conceived sociology as an abstract discipline devoted to analysing the diverse forms of social interaction, forms such as exchange, conflict, super- and subordination, secrecy and honour. For this view of the field he is often labelled a 'formal sociologist'. His major work in this vein was published in *Soziologie: Untersuchungen über die Formen der Vergesellschaftung* ('Sociology: Studies of the Forms of Association', 1908), a work which continues to stimulate sociological investigators. Especially well known are its discussion of the ways social conflict produces group cohesion, its analysis of the effect of group size on modes of interaction, and its depiction of social types like 'the stranger', 'the poor', 'the mediator' and 'the renegade'. Its most striking features include the attempt to apply the Kantian notion of *a priori* categories to the domain of social interaction, and the direction of sociological attention to the phenomenology of everyday interaction. Simmel's delineation of what persons experience in sociable gatherings, when exchanging letters, or in relationships coloured by jealousy or gratitude has helped inspire scholars to create what is known now as the 'sociology of everyday life'.

Simmel's sociological writings won him immediate attention in other countries and were promptly translated into several foreign languages. His impact was greatest in the United States, thanks largely to the efforts of sociologists Albion Small and **Robert Park** at the University of Chicago. He was also a major influence on German sociology in the 1920s.

Despite this record of achievement and the constant support of leading German academics like Weber, Rickert and Husserl, Simmel was consistently denied a regular appointment in the German university system. Only in 1914, four years before his death, did one materialize at the University of Strasbourg. He lectured there for but one semester when the outbreak of war closed down the lecture halls. The war fired his German nationalism: Simmel lapsed into uncharacteristic sentimentality about its

energizing potential and publicly abetted the German war effort. Yet the civilized philosopher in him was not wholly subdued. In the *Berliner Tageblatt* of 7 March 1915 he dared to publish a luminous article on 'The Idea of Europe', in which he scorned 'the blindness and criminal frivolity of a handful of Europeans' for sparking off a war which entailed 'the suicidal destruction of existing European values', and tried to discern some way in which the idea of Europe might yet survive as a 'locus of spiritual values which the contemporary cultured man reveres'.

Further reading

Other works include: *Kant and Goethe* (1906); *The Sociology of Religion* (*Die Religion*, 1906, trans. 1959); *Schopenhauer und Nietzsche* (1907); *Hauptprobleme der Philosophie* (1910); *Philosophische Kultur* (1911); *Goethe* (1913); *Fundamental Problems of Sociology* (*Grundfragen der Soziologie*, 1917, trans. 1950); *Der Krieg und die geistigen Entscheidungen* (1917); *Zur Philosophie der Kunst* (1922). Anthologies: K.H. Wolff, *The Sociology of Georg Simmel* (1950); D.N. Levine, *Georg Simmel on Individuality and Social Forms* (1971); P. Lawrence, *Georg Simmel: Sociologist and European* (1976). On Simmel: N. Spykman, *The Social Theory of Georg Simmel* (1925); R. Weingartner, *Experience and Culture: The Philosophy of Georg Simmel* (1962); D.N. Levine, E.B. Carter and E.M. Gorman, 'Simmel's Influence on American Sociology', *American Journal of Sociology*, Vol. 81 (January and March 1976); L. Coser, 'Georg Simmel', in *Masters of Sociological Thought* (1977); David Frisby, *Georg Simmel* (1984), *Simmel and Since: Essays on Georg Simmel's Social Theory* (1992), and *Sociological Impressionism: A Reassessment of Georg Simmel's Social Theory* (1992); Ralph M. Leck, *Georg Simmel and the Avant-Garde Society* (2000).

DONALD N. LEVINE

SINGER, Isaac Bashevis

1904–91

Polish/American novelist and short-story writer

Although Isaac Bashevis Singer has been called the last and greatest writer in Yiddish, most of his readers have been anglophone, and all his books were sooner or later translated into English. It was a process in which he actively took part, and he regarded these translations as 'second originals'.

Singer was born in Leoncyn, Poland; his sister Esther Singer (Kreitman) and brother Israel Yoshua Singer also became novelists. It was partly thanks to the Singer siblings that Yiddish fiction came of age. Much of Isaac's work is set in Poland among Jews before the Second World War. He said that he wanted to preserve the memory of a lifestyle which, because of secularization, assimilation and the Holocaust, had disappeared.

His father, a Hasidic rabbi, was a naïve, deeply religious man who didn't wish Isaac to study Polish, for the reason that the Messiah might appear any day and he would probably speak Hebrew. The mother was more intellectual, as was her own father, an orthodox rabbi. Isaac was reared on legends about Hasidic saints, but read the Kabbala and Spinoza as well. Among Isaac's favourite novelists were **Balzac**, Blixen, **Dickens**, **Dostoyevsky**, **Gogol**, **Thomas Mann** and **Tolstoy**. After two years at a rabbinical seminary in Warsaw, Singer worked in that city as a proofreader and translator. And he broke with Jewish orthodoxy, a decision that caused him considerable inner agony.

In all his work Singer would draw on his early years, but especially in the autobiographical novels *In My Father's Court* (1966), *A Little Boy in Search of God: Mysticism in a Personal Light* (1976), *A Young Man in Search of Love* (1978) and *Lost in America* (1981). Because of growing Polish antisemitism, Israel and Isaac emigrated to the USA (1934 and 1935, respectively). Isaac became a contributor to the *Jewish Daily Forward*, and married Alma Haimann; the couple had one son. Israel's premature death was a terrible shock to Isaac.

Fame didn't come to him until after the Second World War. It helped Singer that fiction about Jewish life had attained a certain dignity after the Holocaust. He had already promised himself never to write about people without passions, and never to create in cold blood.

In Singer's fiction there is a tension between belief in free will and a grim determinism. He asserted that God equals free will, while Satan stands for anything 'determined', unfree. Singer's characters tend to be the slaves of their own emotions, and unable to make free choices. There is a streak of mysticism in Singer as well, who defined a 'mystic' as 'a person who constantly feels surprised'.

His masterpiece is the trilogy *The Family Moskat* (1950), *The Manor* (1967) and *The Estate* (1969). These novels have reminded many of Mann, and their narrative mode is traditionally realistic. They are mostly set in Poland; the eponymous manor represents that country during the period of industrialization. Singer's enormous cast includes Gentiles as well as Jews. One of the themes is the struggle between orthodoxy and secularization. A claustrophobic feeling of predestined destruction characterizes *The Family Moskat*, which ends in 1939 when the Germans start bombing Warsaw.

Most critics have neglected Singer's prose style. One example of his carefully crafted imagery is *The Manor*, where it always seems to be winter. People skate or travel by sleigh. Snowflakes are dry as salt, and snow lies bunched up like cats on the branches of trees.

Other novels by Singer focus on individuals who are tempted or confronted by evil. *Satan in Goray* (1955) describes Messianism and mass hysteria in seventeenth-century Poland. Also *The Slave* (1962) presents Polish Jewry during that epoch. Jacob, the protagonist, may stand for the wandering, suffering Jew. *The Magician of Lublin* (1960) can be read as an allegory of the artist's life and development. There are allegorical elements also in *Shosha* (1978). The title figure, a girl who refuses to grow up, represents goodness and innocence. Singer sympathized with the plight of women in patriarchal societies. In 'Yentl the Yeshiva Boy' (*The Spinoza of Market Street and Other Stories*, 1961), a gifted Jewish girl disguises herself as a boy in order to become a scholar. The story was recast as a successful play (produced 1974, New York),

and turned into a musical film, *Yentl* (1983), starring Barbra Streisand.

Singer's 'Zeitl and Rickel' (*The Séance and Other Stories*, 1968) is about a lesbian love affair in a small town.

His short stories, whether for adults or children, often use motifs from Jewish folklore, and have been compared to **Chagall's** paintings, with their naivism, supernatural details and stained-glass colours.

Singer received the Nobel Prize for Literature in 1978. In the USA he was the recipient of two National Endowment for the Arts grants and two National Book Awards.

Further reading

Other works include: *Enemies: A Love Story* (1972) and *Reaches of Heaven* (1980). See also:Grace Farrell (Lee), *From Exile to Redemption: The Fiction of Isaac Bashevis Singer* (1987); and Janet Hadda, *Isaac Bashevis Singer* (1997) – a biography.

SUSANNA ROXMAN

SIRK, Douglas

1900–87

Danish/German/US film director

It was only in the 1970s that the genius of Douglas Sirk was recognized. Even in his last years at Universal, when films like *All That Heaven Allows* (1955) and *Imitation of Life* (1959) were huge commercial successes, his mastery was ignored. His work, however, is important not only in itself as the richest body of melodrama to emerge from Hollywood, but also in terms of the complex aesthetic and stylistic questions it raises.

Sirk himself is the locus of many contradictions. Of all the German émigré population in Hollywood, Sirk was arguably the one most fascinated and stimulated by American culture. Yet he brought to Hollywood a breathtaking knowledge of European avant-garde theatre of the 1920s, painting, poetry and music.

Claus Detlef Sierck was born in Hamburg of Danish parents. After spending his early childhood in Skagen, he returned to Hamburg. His university education was wide-reaching: law in Munich, philosophy in Jena, and finally art history in Hamburg, where he studied under Erwin Panovsky. His mastery of lighting, composition and set-design undoubtedly owes much to this period. Another important formative experience was in Munich in 1919, when he witnessed the short-lived Bavarian Soviet, the only revolution to be masterminded and led by poets and intellectuals.

He entered the theatre in 1920, as a second-line *dramaturg* at the Deutsches Schauspielhaus, Hamburg. From 1923 to 1929, he was artistic director at the Schauspielhaus, Bremen, followed by seven years as *Direktor* at the Altes Theater, Leipzig. He proved an extremely gifted theatrical director, already demonstrating his ability to transform and to transcend awkward material. His knowledge of the structure of classical drama stemming from his productions of Molière, Shakespeare, Büchner and others, was to prove invaluable in enabling him to shape the intractable material with which he was confronted in Hollywood.

In 1934, his production of Shakespeare's *Twelfth Night* at the Berlin Volksbühne led to an invitation to join UFA, the leading German film studio. In spite of his left-wing reputation and the political controversy surrounding his period at Leipzig, Sierck was allowed considerable freedom at UFA. In his early films there (like *April, April*, 1935), he immediately displayed his extraordinary ability to transform recalcitrant material into something substantial and outstanding. His second feature, *Das Mädchen vom Moorhof* (1935), already filmed by Victor Sjöström, revealed many of what were to become Sirkian trademarks: the use of mirror shots, the dismantling of suspense and the theme of the exposure of hypocrisy.

His decision to make *Schlussakkord* (1936) was a landmark in his career, for in choosing an atrociously mawkish story on which he would make a full-blooded assault, he was breaking away from literary values to pursue the purely cinematic. He also made other major melodramas in Germany in 1937: *Zu Neuen Ufern*, which transformed Swedish actress Zarah Leander into a star, and *La Habanera*. In these tough, anti-colonialist films, he showed a mastery of the medium that was to be apparent in his later Hollywood masterpieces, *Written on the Wind* (1956) and *The Tarnished Angels* (1957).

In December 1937, Douglas Sirk (as he became known) left Germany for Hollywood, via Paris and Holland. After a difficult period at Columbia under the idiosyncratic Harry Cohn, and a happier period alfalfa farming, he signed with Universal in 1950. As 'house director', he had little control over the choice of projects, but could at least restructure material, shoot and edit as he wished. Only when maverick producer Albert Zugsmith spent a brief period at Universal was Sirk able to pursue two projects of his own choice: *The Tarnished Angels*, an adaptation of **William Faulkner's** novel of the Depression, *Pylon*, and *Written on the Wind*. To understand Sirk, it is instructive to compare these two masterpieces with the films he made with producer Ross Hunter, like *All That Heaven Allows* and *Imitation of Life*. All four are brilliant films, yet in those produced by Hunter, Sirk somehow triumphs over the material: in those produced by Zugsmith, he has the freedom to express his personal vision of America. Ross Hunter imposed on Sirk 'happy endings' which were at variance with Sirk's leanings towards themes of despair and disintegration, and which result in irony. In *The Tarnished Angels* and *Written on the Wind*, Sirk could follow through his vision of men and women driven to extremes in a society on the point of collapse. Both films deal with breakdown and with failure. In the latter, images of infirmity, of alcoholism, of sexual frustration and of fear of sterility abound. Throughout his work, images of illness recur, with individual illness representing social breakdown. Problems of vision also predominate, as characters suffer from blindness, or fail to see themselves, or others, clearly. Sirk's use of mirrors throughout

his films also underlines this theme, suggestive too of the surfaces within which the characters are trapped.

Sirk believed that criticism and comment in art should be distanced, and that melodrama was the ideal genre at that particular historical conjecture to express his views on American society. He respected the rules of the genre, and used it to expose mercilessly the hypocrisy and deceit of Eisenhowerian America. His films shatter the complacency of American society in the 1950s, revealing the possibility of imminent collapse.

He was arguably the greatest stylist in Hollywood in the 1950s. In *Imitation of Life*, his last Hollywood film and one of Universal's most successful films commercially, he again succeeded in transcending a dreadful story through brilliant use of lighting, composition, camerawork and music. Sirk left Hollywood in 1958, leaving *Imitation of Life* as his farewell gesture. He returned to Europe, directing theatre in Germany, and teaching film at the Munich Film School. The influence of his work on a new generation of directors, ranging from **Rainer Werner Fassbinder** to Bernardo **Bertolucci**, became increasingly evident during the 1970s.

Further reading

See: Jon Halliday, *Sirk on Sirk* (1971); B. Klinger, *Melodrama and Meaning: History, Culture and the Films of Douglas Sirk* (1994); Jon Halliday (ed.) *Sirk on Sirk* (1997).

LINDA MILES

SISLEY, Alfred

1839–99

French painter

Alone among the major Impressionist painters, Sisley's fame and popularity, in his own lifetime and since, have been eclipsed by the movement of which he was a part. In spite of the freshness of his work, he has not been esteemed as he deserved, and he remains overshadowed by **Manet**, **Renoir** and **Pissarro**.

Sisley was born in Paris of wealthy English parents, and except for brief visits to England and Wales lived and worked all his life in France, chiefly in the countryside around Paris. As a youth he was sent to London for four years (1857–61) to learn the language and prepare for a career in commerce. He returned to France, however, intent on becoming a painter, and in 1862 entered the studio of Gleyre at the École des Beaux Arts where he befriended **Monet**, Renoir and Bazille. In 1863 they worked together in the open, at Chailly near Fontainebleau, and in the following years Sisley continued to paint with Renoir in the region. He had some success at the Salon but in 1870 fled France, and war, for London. The Franco-Prussian War brought financial ruin to his father, and what had been for Sisley a diverting occupation became an earnest struggle. In the succeeding years he endured extreme poverty, and even when his friends began to find buyers for their works and to become more popular, Sisley's paintings sold, if at all, for derisive sums.

Early in the 1870s Sisley habitually worked in those places around Paris that Impressionism has made famous – Louveciennes, Argenteuil, Marly, Bougival and Pontoise – and in 1874 he spent the summer in London with one of the rare patrons of the Impressionists, the singer Faure, painting at Hampton Court. In 1877 he moved to Sèvres, working at Meudon and Saint-Cloud, then in 1879 to Moret, and in 1882 to Moret-sur-Loing where he finally settled.

Sisley exhibited five landscapes at the first Impressionist Exhibition in 1874 and contributed to three of the subsequent shows (1876, 1877 and 1882). In 1883 Durand-Ruel gave him a one-man show, which had little success, and Sisley remained neglected until only a few weeks before his death, when a series of articles by Gustave Geffroy stimulated interest in his work.

It is hard to understand why Sisley should have been ignored, since his work has an obvious charm, and does not in either style or subject-matter openly challenge convention to the extent of Monet's, for example. He was almost exclusively a painter of landscape, and the influence of **Courbet**, **Corot** and Daubigny is not hard to discern. His predilection for secluded rural scenery and the villages and the country towns of the Île de France bind him strongly to the earlier *plein air* painters, and throughout his life he, alone among the Impressionists, continued to treat the same subjects – river banks, country lanes, orchards, kitchen gardens – in a direct, uncomplicated manner. Sisley was a quiet, retiring man, and his character is reflected in his pictures, which invariably show peaceful corners of the countryside, with only the occasional passer-by. It is probably this reticence, the lack of variation in his themes, and the absence of large canvases and boisterous figure-subjects, that account for his neglect.

The quiet tenor of Sisley's paintings is deceptive. On to a basis of careful observation inherited from Corot, Sisley, from about 1870, grafted a clear, light-toned palette and a vigorous technique of quick, broken touches of colour, gleaned from Monet. Such paintings as *The Foot-Bridge at Argenteuil* (1872), *View of the Sèvres Road* (1873) and *Louveciennes, Hilltops at Marly* (1873), all in the Musée du Jeu de Paume, Paris, display a freedom and a sureness of touch unparalleled by any but Monet. With extraordinary speed, Sisley grasped the basic tenets of Impressionism as discovered by Monet on the eve of the Franco-Prussian War. His shadows are richly coloured, his surfaces vibrate with broken lines, and, above all, his skies and waters are limpid and luminous. His colour is never muddy, never false, and the quick, sure touches of liquid paint which make up his pictures always convey light, air and space with breathtaking freshness. Although he is relegated, mistakenly, to the second rank, Sisley's paintings in the 1870s epitomize Impressionism. With tenacity and, as his pictures prove, penetrating vision, Sisley explored every effect of light through all times of day and all seasons. There are snow scenes, like *Snow at Louveciennes* (1878), views of flooding, where the water reflects dazzling winter sunlight

(*Boat in the Flood at Port-Marly*, 1876), autumnal scenes of mist in cottage gardens (*Fog*, 1874), and countless summer land-scapes. Among a simple repertoire of rural themes Sisley seems for ever to find untried viewpoints, fresh and arresting effects of light, and new insights into nature. His inventive-ness, while disguised by the simplicity of his themes, is apparent in his constant avoidance of hackneyed and formulaic effects.

In continuing up to his death with the same range of subjects Sisley was regrettably unable to maintain the inspired freshness of his early work. His technique grew looser and his observation less sharp. With the acuteness of his vision dimmed, his pictures lose interest. Nevertheless, while he was unable to halt this decline, he retained the luminosity and sensitivity of touch which are the hallmarks of his work.

Further reading

See: George Besson, *Sisley* (1946); François Daulte, *Sisley: Landscapes* (1963). See also: John Rewald, *History of Impressionism* (rev. edn. 1961); R. Shone, *Sisley* (1992).

MICHAEL WILSON

SKINNER, Burrhus Frederic

1904–90

US psychologist

The high priest of behaviourism – a now-outmoded but once vigorously challenging ideology in its application to human affairs – B.F. Skinner was born in Susquehanna, Pennsylvania, and educated at Hamilton College, New York, and at Harvard Uni-versity. There he became a fellow in 1931, and Edgar Pierce Professor of Psychology from 1947 to 1975. His *Behaviour of Organisms* appeared in 1938, and *Science and Human Behaviour* in 1953. His most famous book, however, was, and remains, the utopian novel *Walden Two* (1948), while the definitive statement of his philosophical and scientific outlook is *Beyond Freedom and Dignity* (1971).

Most of Skinner's work as an experimental psychologist was concerned with behaviour modification in animals. The following is a typical example:

> We study the height at which a pigeon's head is normally held, and select some line on the height scale which is reached only infrequently. Keeping our eye on the scale we begin to open the food tray very quickly whenever the head rises above the line. The result is invariable: we observe an immediate change in the frequency with which the head crosses the line.
>
> (*Science and Human Behaviour*)

In this standard Skinnerian experiment, the food is termed the *reinforcer*; presenting the food whenever the desired response is pro-duced is called *reinforcement*; the resulting change in the frequency with which the head is lifted is the process of *operant conditioning*.

Skinner's meticulous and painstaking research showed how such procedures can be extended to produce remarkably complex behavioural responses. But Skinner's impor-tance lay not in his experimental results, impressive though they were, nor in the theory of conditioned response (which was first systematized by Sechenov and **Pavlov**), but in his insistence that it is proper, and indeed desirable, to apply the methods and procedures of behavioural psychology to the human domain. Skinner pioneered such ideas as the teaching machine and programmed learning; his inventions included mechanical baby-tenders, and the 'Skinner box' – a con-trolled environment for monitoring beha-vioural changes. Yet even this, for Skinner, was merely a beginning. While other beha-vioural psychologists adopted the techniques of conditioning to effect cures of specific mental disorders (cf. **J.B. Watson**), Skinner sought, via the same means, to recondition society itself. 'What would you do,' asks the hero of *Walden Two*, 'if you found yourself in possession of an effective science of beha-viour? Suppose you found it possible to control the behaviour of men as you wished. What would you do?' Skinner's answer, made explicit in *Walden Two*, is that he would design a new society – a society in which stability, harmony and satisfaction would be, in the literal sense, behaviourally engineered.

The methods which Skinner advocated for this end were much simpler than the eugenics and hypnotherapy envisaged in **Aldous Huxley's** *Brave New World*. Skinner's 'technology of behaviour' relied largely on reinforcement, especially 'positive' rather than 'negative' reinforcement (in plain English, a system of rewards, rather than coercion or punishment).

> We can achieve a sort of control under which the controlled, though they are following a code much more scrupulously than was ever the case under the old system, now *feel free*. That's the source of the tremendous power of positive reinforcement.

The vision of a controlled society was hardly unfamiliar. What was disturbing was Skinner's enthusiasm for it. It needs to be asked, in particular, what place remains, in Skinner's scheme of things, for individual freedom and responsibility. Skinner's answer was quite uncompromising. In *Beyond Freedom and Dignity* he proposed that we should abandon completely the notion of 'autonomous man' – the free, responsible agent who is the author of his actions.

> As a science of behaviour adopts the strategy of physics and biology, the autonomous agent to which behaviour has traditionally been attributed is replaced by the environment – the environment in which the species evolved and in which the behaviour of the individual is shaped and maintained.

Autonomous man is simply 'a device used to explain what we cannot explain any other way. His abolition has been long overdue.'

To support his case, Skinner defended a radical form of philosophical behaviourism. Good science, claimed Skinner, has no place for appeal to internal mental states. To explain someone's conduct by reference to an inner feeling is as unhelpful as the ancient view that a falling body accelerates because it feels more jubilant as it finds itself nearer home. 'Young people refuse to get jobs not because they feel alienated, but because of defective social environments.'

Of the many criticisms that might be levelled against Skinner's approach, two are of particular relevance. First, the rejection of explanations appealing to inner mental states is too glib. Attributing jubilation to stones is unhelpful precisely because it is *anthropomorphic*: we are ascribing to stones person-like properties which they do not in fact possess. Yet this hardly shows that it is inappropriate to invoke such properties when we come to deal with an *anthropos*, a person; people, as we all know from direct personal experience, quite simply *do* possess feelings.

Second, and more generally, Skinner's version of a 'scientific' approach to society was flawed by a fundamental contradiction. Freedom and autonomy, he claimed, are a sham; all human behaviour is environmentally determined. Yet on the other hand, we are told that 'the intentional design of a culture and control of human behaviour is essential' (*Beyond Freedom and Dignity*). Intentional design and control *by whom?* Clearly, in Skinner's scheme of things there are, after all, autonomous agents – the behavioural technocrats and planners. These god-like creatures apparently stand outside the deterministic nexus that binds the rest of us: they take free and rational decisions about how our culture is to be designed. The upshot is that Skinner's insistence on a planned society presupposes the existence – at least for a minority – of the very autonomy that his deterministic behaviourism ruled out.

Despite its contradictions and lack of philosophical sophistication, Skinner's message exercised a firm hold over many of his contemporaries – though not **Noam Chomsky**, who in 1959 attacked his claims for the efficacy of 'reinforcement' in the context of linguistic behaviour. Perhaps just because it was so facile, the once celebrated slogan from *Walden Two* – 'When a science of behaviour has been achieved, there's no alternative to a planned society' – struck a chord with those who, in a post-war climate, sought simple solutions to enduring problems without thinking through the possible consequences.

In time Skinner's ideas were widely rejected, especially within liberal individualistic communities of the sort inspired by **Henry David Thoreau's** original *Walden*. It is admittedly true that all governments necessarily practice 'social engineering' to some degree, whatever name they care to give it, but Skinner's cardinal error may just have been that he overstated his case; for unless people are in some measure susceptible to inducements, it is difficult to conceive how any society can be managed, or manage itself.

Further reading

See: Tibor R. Machan, *The Pseudo-science of B.F. Skinner* (1974); John A. Weigel, *B.F. Skinner* (1977); A. Charles Catania and Stevan Hamad (eds) *The Selection of Behaviourism: The Operant Behaviourism of B.F. Skinner* (1988); James T. Todd and Edward K. Morris (eds) *Modern Perspectives on B.F. Skinner and Contemporary Behaviourism* (1995).

JOHN COTTINGHAM

SMETANA, Bedich

1824–84

Bohemian (Czech) composer

Smetana was born in Litomyčl in eastern Bohemia, then part of the Austro-Hungarian Empire, but unlike other musicians from the Austrian provinces he spent most of his working life on home territory. Not only that, he associated himself with the nationalist cause and is justly regarded as the founder of a specifically Czech music. In 1848 he even took part in the unsuccessful rising in Prague, where he had been living since 1843, working as a private teacher and eventually setting up his own music school (it was also during this time that he struck up a friendship with **Liszt**).

For several years from 1856 he was away from Bohemia, first taking a conducting post at Göteborg in Sweden, then touring as a concert pianist, and it was during this period that he composed his first notable works, three symphonic poems based on Liszt's model: *Richard III* (1857), *Wallenstein's Camp* (1859–60) and *Hakon Jarl* (1861). Then in 1863 he returned to Prague and spent the rest of his life there. And now his nationalist feelings began to gain expression in his music, first and most freshly in his opera *Prodaná nevečtá* (*The Bartered Bride*, 1864, revised 1870). Smetana had been brought up German-speaking and he had difficulty in setting Czech words, but despite this he contrived to create a score which, while using few actual folk melodies, appealed strongly to national instincts in its alternately joyous and sentimental portrayal of the Bohemian peasantry.

He followed up his success with a more serious opera, *Dalibor* (1867), which, however, was criticized for its Wagnerism, though in fact Smetana's technique here still owes much more to Liszt than to **Wagner**. Then came *Libuče* (1868–72), not so much an opera as a festival pageant, ending with a prophecy of the Czechs' glorious future. Its première was delayed until it could be used to inaugurate the National Theatre in Prague in 1881, by which time Smetana had composed three more operas: *Dvě vdovy* (*The Two Widows*, 1873–74), *Hubička* (*The Kiss*, 1875) and *Tajemstvi* (*The Secret*, 1877). When *Libuče* was produced it proved a great success, and Smetana was encouraged to finish another opera, *Čertova Stěna* (*The Devil's Wall*, 1879–82). This, however, was a failure, and he made only slow progress on his last, unfinished opera, *Viola* (begun 1881), based on *Twelfth Night*.

Throughout the last ten years of his life Smetana was totally deaf, and yet it is to this period that many of his finest works belong, including not only the operas mentioned above but also his two string quartets and his cycle of symphonic poems *Má vlast* (*My Country*). This is a set of six separate works, composed between 1874 and 1879, and suggestive of various aspects of Bohemia's history and landscape:

*Vyčehrad (*The High Citadel*)*, Vltava *(the river, better known by its German name of Moldau)*, Šárka *(leader of the Bohemian Amazons)*, Z českych luhů a hájů *(From Bohemia's Fields and Woods)*, Tabor *(the Hussite stronghold)*, and Bláník *(a mountain, the Hussite Valhalla)*.

If *Má vlast* was Smetana's finest tribute to his country, in the quartets he looked into himself, both of them having the title *Z mého života (From My Life)*, though this is now normally reserved for the first, in E minor (1876). Here he looks back on a youth of love, art and dancing, and then, in the fourth movement, turns to his joy in creating national music, a joy destroyed by the piercing high E that was constantly in his ears as deafness approached. The second quartet, in D minor (1883), continues the auto-biography, containing, as he said, 'the whirl-pool of music in a man who has lost his hearing'. Smetana's example, in combining illustrative content with classical chamber-musical form, was not lost on later composers, including **Tchaikovsky** and **Schoenberg**, while his discovery of a Czech musical idiom, particularly in *The Bartered Bride* and *Má vlast*, was a vital stimulus to musicians in his own country.

Further reading

See: Brian Large, *Smetana* (1970); John Clapham, *Smetana* (1972); Anton Neumayr, *Music and Medicine: Chopin, Smetana, Tchaikovsky, Mahler* (1997)

PAUL GRIFFITHS

SMITH, David Roland

1906–65

US sculptor

Smith's art training consisted of a year at Ohio University, two weeks at Notre Dame University and about five years as a painting student at the Art Students' League in New York under John Sloan and Jan Matulka, 'the guy I'd rather give more credit than anyone else'. Other formative influences were a vacation spent on a Studebaker plant at South Bend, Indiana, an evening class in poetry in Washington DC and, around 1930, meetings with the informal 'group' of artist friends of John D. Graham (Stuart Davis, **Wilhelm de Kooning**, Jean Xceron and Arshile Gorky). From 1935 to 1936 he travelled to Greece, the USSR, London and Paris with his first wife Dorothy Dehner.

As a man, Smith was stubborn, passionate, vulnerable and boundlessly ambitious. As an artist, he spent thirty years refining techniques for drawing in welded steel. Beginning with coral constructions made in the Virgin Islands in 1931, Smith moved slowly from painting to sculpture, evolving hybrids from early modern forms, yet retaining a concern with figuration. His output includes incidental virtuoso performances such as the *Medals for Dishonor*, a group of satirical anti-war plaques shown in 1940, or the nearly unbelievable production of twenty-six large sculptures in thirty days in 1962 at Spoleto, Italy. Yet the main pressure is from uncertain experiments with Constructivism through an assured command of Surrealist imagery in the 1940s to the abstract, Cubist language of the late 1950s and 1960s.

Critics have stressed Smith's formal concerns at the expense of personal identity. Throughout his career he dramatized his relationships and states of mind. Works such as *Pillar of Sunday*, a comment on his mother's Methodist beliefs, *Home of the Welder*, a complex domestic scene, and *Becca*, dedicated to one of his daughters, speak of celebration and dread of women. Both of Smith's marriages ended in divorce. Drawings return obsessively to images of women courting and defying destructive masculine forces. The battle of the sexes – 'who shall have the mastery', in Chaucer's terms – is fundamental to Smith's thinking. 'I only make girl sculptures,' he told Frank O'Hara in a TV interview, 'I don't make boy sculptures at all.' Nevertheless, Smith thrived on male companionship. *Blackburn – Song of an Irish Blacksmith*, a tribute to a workmate, is a rhapsody on male values and routines.

Apparent shifts of intention between early and late Smith sculptures can be resolved in various ways. One metaphor is outstanding. Smith's father had been an inventor. Smith himself collected antique cannons and dreamed of a 'sculpture train', a mobile exhibition of his work to be drawn through the towns of America. His love–hate relationship with modern techniques and artefacts was the overriding 'influence' on Smith, greater even than Cubism. Disciples demonstrate exactly the paradox of factory worker versus blacksmith – Alain Kirili emphasizing the latter, Antony Caro and his St Martin's 'school' the former. There is a point in American art history when extravert 1930s politics undergoes a sea-change. With the evolution of the New York School in the early 1940s, artistic decision-making may or may not have inherited the role which 'public' activities had previously occupied. In Smith's case his entire career can be regarded as a struggle for hard-won freedom, his early political fervour by no means diminished, but rather enhanced by the unprecedented clarity and expressive power of the late *Zigs* and *Cubi*.

Further reading

See: Rosalind Krauss, *Terminal Iron Works* (1971); Garnett McCoy (ed.) *David Smith* (1973); Paul Cummings, *David Smith: The Drawings* (Whitney Museum of American Art, 1979); K. Wilkin, *David Smith* (1984).

STUART MORGAN

SMITH, William Robertson

1846–94

British biblical and Semitic scholar, editor, librarian

W. Robertson Smith was one of the most famous Semitic scholars of the nineteenth century, whose influence extended far beyond biblical and Arabic studies to affect the foundation of the sociological study of religion and later anthropological research in the social organization of pre-literate peoples.

In addition, Smith edited the great ninth edition of the *Encyclopaedia Britannica* which popularized the scholarly breakthroughs of that period. He also served as chief librarian of the University of Cambridge during its modernization.

Smith was educated at home, mainly due to ill-health. His father, a minister in the Free Church of Scotland, provided an extraordinarily intensive education allowing Smith to enter Aberdeen University on a scholarship at the age of fifteen, where he distinguished himself in physics, mathematics, languages and religious studies. Graduating from Aberdeen (1865), Smith entered New College, University of Edinburgh, which he left the year he was ordained (1870) to take up a chair in Hebrew and Old Testament studies at the Free Church College at Aberdeen. Earlier (1868, 1869) he studied intermittently at Bonn and Göttingen, where he absorbed the new biblical criticisms pioneered by German and Dutch scholars.

At Aberdeen Smith began contributing essays on biblical topics to the new *Encyclopaedia Britannica* which he presented in terms of the new criticism. These incited violent criticism from the conservative Free Church, culminating in a much publicized trial and dismissal from his post (1880). The case consumed nearly five years during which Smith toured the Near East, lectured in his defence and published further encyclopaedia essays which only exacerbated his difficulties. In defence of his position he published *The Old Testament and the Jewish Church* (1881) and *The Prophets of Israel* (1882). After his dismissal, he was made a co-editor of the *Encyclopaedia Britannica* and soon became chief editor, eventually writing over two hundred entries. In this capacity he exerted immense influence on popular understanding of modern biblical studies. In 1883 Smith was appointed reader in Arabic at the University of Cambridge (Trinity College) and in 1885 became a fellow of Christ's College, where he remained until his death. In 1885 he published *Kinship and Marriage in Early Arabia*. In 1888 he was fêted by international scholars assembled at Cambridge to celebrate the completion of the *Encyclopaedia*. In 1888–9 Smith delivered the Burnett lectures at the University of Aberdeen, covering the very topics that had led to his earlier disgrace in that city. These were published as *Lectures on the Religion of the Semites* (1889), his most influential work. That same year Smith was appointed to the Chair of Arabic at Cambridge. By then Smith was seriously ill; apparently always tubercular, he died prematurely, in large part due to overwork. A collection of his most important essays was published posthumously (*Lectures and Essays of William Robertson Smith*, ed. J.S. Black and G. Chrystal, 1912).

Unlike most biblical scholars Smith made repeated visits to the Near East to improve his spoken Arabic and to gain a better feel for the region. He toured the remoter areas of the Arabian peninsula and visited Fayum oasis with **Sir Richard Burton** (1879).

Smith believed that the Bible could best be understood within the context of the society in which it was written. Consequently he argued that apparent discrepancies in it were in large part due to the differences in understanding and needs which various writers held on account of the varying social conditions when they wrote. Each addressed himself to his own time. This was grounded both in a form of social relativism in which meaning and values reflected particular social situations and, given the nature of Christian belief, in a more universalistic, evolutionary scheme whereby primitive Old Testament belief slowly culminated in Christianity. The first set of ideas led Smith to develop a sociology of religion where beliefs reflected society, while the second led to a developmental analysis which sought to isolate essential or core ideas from which more elaborate and 'higher' beliefs and conditions evolved. Smith's study of early Arab kinship was an attempt to grasp the most basic aspects of Semitic society, thereby paving the way for understanding its primal beliefs. Such an approach became discredited, but this study provided anthropologists with the first clear analysis of how pre-literate societies could be

politically organized through kinship, feud and warfare without formal institutions of government.

Smith's study of religion emphasizes social action (ritual) over belief (myth), centring his work on the study of sacrifice which he saw as a commensal rather than a piacular rite. This view is now in decline among biblical scholars but in different forms profoundly influenced important social thinkers such as **Durkheim** and **Freud**. Durkheim's *Elementary Forms of the Religious Life* was deeply influenced by Smith's communal theory of ritual. A less fortunate but influential aspect of Smith's work was his promotion of his friend J.F. McLennan's theories about the origin of religion in totemic beliefs, culminating in Smith's relating biblical sacrifice to totemic propitiation. Not only was this approach taken up by Durkheim but it was widely elaborated in Freud's *Totem and Taboo*. To support these theories Smith encouraged his student, **Sir James Frazer**, to write *Totemism* (1887) which led in turn to *The Golden Bough* (1890).

Despite inevitable inaccuracies when measured against subsequent scholarly findings, many of Smith's arguments remain vigorous and are permanently reflected in the fact that no scholar would now attempt meaningful analysis of religious beliefs outside the context of the social fabric in which these were produced and developed.

Further reading

See: J.S. Black and G. Chrystal's, *The Life of William Robertson Smith* (1912). The basic evaluation of his work and definitive bibliography of his publications and those of his critics is T.O. Beidelman, *W. Robertson Smith and the Sociological Study of Religion* (1974); and William Johnstone (ed.) *William Robertson Smith: Essays in Reassessment* (1995).

T.O. BEIDELMAN

SOLZHENITSYN, Aleksandr Isayevich

1918–

Russian writer

Solzhenitsyn was born in Kislovodsk. His father, a serving artillery officer, was accidentally killed six months beforehand. In 1924 his mother, a shorthand typist, moved to Rostov-on-Don where he received his first schooling. On leaving school in 1936 he hoped to be a writer but was obliged instead to take a degree course in mathematics and physics at Rostov University, although this was supplemented by a two-year correspondence course in literature. He married N.A. Reshetovskaya in 1940 and was appointed a physics teacher at Morozovka in the Rostov region. Called up in October 1940, he was commissioned as an artillery officer the following year, fought at Kursk in 1943 and participated in the advance towards Germany. In February 1945, during the battle for Koenigsberg, he was arrested for having made disrespectful references to **Stalin** in private correspondence and was returned to Moscow for investigation and sentencing to eight years' imprisonment followed by 'perpetual exile'. In July 1946 he was transferred from parquet-laying work in a block of flats on Lenin Prospekt to the 'Sharashka' at Marfino, north of Sheremet'yevo airport (Mavrino of *The First Circle*, *V kruge pervom*, 1968), where his scientific training was used to promote research into listening devices. He was later transferred to a Siberian labour camp, the setting of his first published work *One Day in the Life of Ivan Denisovich* (*Odin den' Ivana Denisovicha*, 1962), from which he was released in 1953. The first thing he learned on his release was news of Stalin's death. Serious recurrence of cancer obliged him to enter the Tashkent clinic that forms the setting for *Cancer Ward* (*Rakovy korpus*, 1969) where he eventually recovered. He was not released from 'perpetual exile' until 1956 and then chose to live in Torfoprodukt, near Vladimir, the scene of *Matryona's Place* (*Matryonin dvor*, 1963). Divorced by Reshetovskaya after his sentencing, it was at this time that they remarried and settled in Ryazan, where his literary fame and notoriety began.

The publication of *One Day in the Life of Ivan Denisovich* in Tvardovsky's journal *Novy Mir* in 1962 became a political event of the first magnitude. This masterpiece of twentieth-century prison literature was the first work published in the Soviet Union to give an explicit picture of life in Stalin's slave-labour camps. Although he became famous almost overnight and was publicly praised by Nikita Khrushchev, his increasingly outspoken criticism of Stalinism and the Soviet establishment soon proved too much for the authorities and by 1966 he had ceased to find official outlets for his work. His plays and novels were all refused publication, notwithstanding his frequent appeals to the Union of Soviet Writers, and had to be published abroad. When he was awarded the Nobel Prize for Literature in 1970 a campaign of vilification was launched against him, his *August 1914* (*Avgust 14-ogo*, 1971) was banned and his role as spokesman of Soviet dissidence began gradually to assume as great an importance as his role as a writer.

This reputation received endorsement with his decision to release for publication abroad in 1973 Parts I and II of *The Gulag Archipelago* (*Arkhipelag gulag*), his carefully documented exposure of the Soviet slave-labour system. The attacks on him and his associates increased in ferocity until, in February 1974, he was arrested, interrogated, stripped of his citizenship and summarily exiled to the West. He took up residence in Zurich, where he was joined by his second wife (formerly Natalya Svetlova) and their three sons. He later moved to an extensive estate in Vermont in the United States to live a reclusive life punctuated by occasional public appearances for interviews or speeches. Of the latter the most noteworthy was the speech delivered at Harvard on the award of an honorary Doctor of Letters in June 1978, when he denounced the West for its neglect of Christian responsibilities and its spiritual bankruptcy, or on the receipt of the Templeton Prize in London in 1983 when the religious emphasis in his thinking was especially marked.

His eighteen-year residence in the United States was spent mostly in the composition of 'knots' II, III and IV of *The Red Wheel* (*Krasnoe koleso*) and the third part of *The Gulag Archipelago* devoted to experiences of surviving the slave-labour system. Throughout the period of exile he remained convinced that he would eventually return to Russia, but to a Russia, in his view, modelled on neo-Slavophile principles and a socio-political form of subsidiarity reminiscent of the Swiss system. Hopefully, when the moment came for his return in 1994 after his citizenship had been restored in 1990, his message of a rebuilt Russia would have gone before him. Though his was a triumphant slow progress across Siberia from Magadan to Moscow by train, filmed for TV by the BBC, his welcome home was ultimately as characteristically lukewarm as that given to most prophets. He settled on an estate to the north of Moscow where, on the abandonment of his TV show and other public commitments, he lived as reclusively as before, his most significant achievement at this time being the establishment of a generous literary prize.

Solzhenitsyn's literary reputation can be justifiably set within the tradition of Russian denunciatory literature that had its beginnings in the eighteenth century and the critical realism of much nineteenth-century writing. Denunciation and prophecy were never far apart in his work, with an increasing tendency for the publicistic element to overwhelm the literary. The harsh but memorable portrayal of the prisoners in *One Day* and *The First Circle*, the profound, often symbolic, analysis of the institutional forms and attitudes that gave rise to such gulag worlds, and the compressed power of his writing made his first works into outstanding examples of a literature combining denunciation of the Soviet system with universal literary values. His studies of the sickness pervading Soviet society in such brilliant pictures of enclosed, intimately observed worlds as those of *Cancer Ward* or his little masterpiece *Matryona's Place* demonstrated his remarkable authority as a writer whose range of critical assessment and philosophical awareness was matched by an equivalent understanding of the depths of emotion and commitment involved in human relationships. With the appearance of *August 1914*

doubts about his imaginative power and ability to handle panoramic events on a scale matching **Leo Tolstoy's** were largely justified. The ensuing 'knots' of the tetralogy *The Red Wheel* comprising his longest work – *October 1916* (pub. 2 vols, 1984; trans. 1989), *Mart semnadtsatogo* (2 vols, 1986–8), *Aprel' semnadtsatogo* (1991) – were as much faction as fiction, designed to show a Russian readership the complex evolution of events, day by day and hour by hour, that led to the February Revolution of 1917 and **Lenin's** return from abroad. The crushing pressure exerted on the reader by *The Red Wheel's* ponderously detailed manner doubtless suggested realistically enough the slow, inevitable revolving of the wheel of history towards October.

Solzhenitsyn's birthright was the October Revolution and the Soviet Union that sprang from it. Even if he outlived it, his reputation must be largely confined to it. His commitment to Christianity derived from the bitterest personal experience, but his dislike of the Communist system, like his criticism of the West, transcended both the personal and the local in its insistence on sincere, if vaguely universal concepts of justice and responsibility that have their source in the human conscience. His most memorable pronouncements have concerned the writer's freedom of conscience, as, for example, his assertion that

> A writer's tasks … concern the secrets of the human heart and conscience, of the conflict between life and death, the overcoming of spiritual sorrow and those laws extending throughout all humanity which were born in the immemorial depths of the millennia and will cease only when the sun is extinguished.

or a writer is both 'a humble apprentice beneath God's heaven' and 'a great writer is, so to speak, a second government. That is why no regime has ever loved its great writers, only its minor ones.' Solzhenitsyn, with his denunciatory exposure of the worst evils of the Soviet system, his readiness to denounce materialism, whether consumerist or ideological, his advocacy of spiritual values and his pleas for justice and freedom in his literary and publicistic work, must remain among the most significant moral authorities of the twentieth century.

Further reading

Other works include: *For the Good of the Cause* (1964); *Short Stories and Prose Poems* (1970); 'One Word of Truth Shall Outweigh the Whole World', The Nobel Speech (1972); *From under the Rubble, Lenin in Zurich*(1975); *The Oak and the Calf* (1980); *Invisible Allies* (1995). See: G. Lukacs, *Solzhenitsyn* (1970); L. Labedz, *Solzhenitsyn – A Documentary Record* (1973); M. Scammell, *Solzhenitsyn: A Biography* (1984). J. Pearce, *Solzhenitsyn: A Soul in Exile* (1999); Harold Bloom (ed.) *Aleksandr Solzhenitsyn: Modern Critical Views* (2001).

RICHARD FREEBORN

SONDHEIM, Stephen

1930–

US musical theatre composer

Sondheim has spent his entire creative life living in Manhattan and writing musicals, or rather writing the music and lyrics for musicals, for the Broadway stage. This is a restrictive craft, one might think, essentially that of a songwriter, for unlike his teacher **Oscar Hammerstein II**, Sondheim leaves the 'book' – the spoken portion of a libretto – to others, which has not prevented the resulting musical plays being treated as though they were his, even when entire scenes play without music. His collaborators on the script have included Burt Shevelove (*A Funny Thing Happened on the Way to the Forum*, 1962; *The Frogs*, 1974, with Larry Gelbart); George Furth (*Company*, 1970; *Merrily We Roll Along*, 1981), James Goldman (*Evening Primrose*, for television, 1966; *Follies*, 1971), Hugh Wheeler (*A Little Night Music*, 1973; *Sweeney Todd*, 1979), John Weidman (*Pacific Overtures*, 1976; *Assassins*, 1991; *Bounce*, 2003) and James Lapine (*Sunday in the Park with George*, 1983; *Into the Woods*, 1987; *Passion*, 1994). As

well as *Anyone Can Whistle* (1964), Arthur Laurents authored *West Side Story* (1957), *Gypsy* (1959) and *Do I Hear a Waltz?* (1965), the three shows for which Sondheim was asked to supply lyrics but not the music, which was by **Leonard Bernstein**, Jule Styne and **Richard Rodgers** respectively. An early show, *Saturday Night* (1954), was completed but not produced until 1997. The above titles furnish the Sondheim canon, augmented by occasional film songs (*Dick Tracy*, 1990) and one (non-musical) film score, *Stavisky* (1973). In show output Sondheim has outdistanced all the post-war Broadway masters including Rodgers and Hammerstein (though Lloyd Webber, born on the same day seventeen years later, is fast creeping up on him). He has stuck to the game, often saying that the only way to overcome your critics is to outlive them.

At first Sondheim was seen as difficult and modernist. The episodic construction of *Company*, with its ambivalent ending, and the nervous breakdown in mid-song at the end of *Follies* (though this also happens in *Gypsy*), gave rise to much talk about 'concept musicals', their metaphoric packages deconstructing contemporary America in these two shows, as also its past in *Pacific Overtures* and *Assassins*; structural ideas are similarly part of the experience in *Merrily We Roll Along*, whose chronology runs backwards, *Sunday in the Park with George*, its second act set a hundred years after the first, and *Into the Woods*, which combines four fairy tales and places their 'happily ever after' only halfway through the narrative. But Bernstein's musical language in *West Side Story* was more aggressive and challenging than Sondheim's has ever been, and in the long run he is more likely to be viewed as the last classical master of the American musical in succession to **Kern**, **Gershwin**, **Porter**, Rodgers and their lesser contemporaries. Just as *Saturday Night* revealed his early melodiousness, *Bounce* (his last musical?) reinstates it, while his most musically affecting songs in between speak the common emotional language of tonality – 'What Can You Lose?' (*Dick Tracy*) a good example. Nevertheless, **Stravinsky** and musical minimalism had as far-reaching an effect on *Sweeney Todd* and *Sunday* as **Debussy** and **Rachmaninov** on 'Send in the Clowns' (*A Little Night Music*), Sondheim's best-known song. **Ravel** has been the most steadfast of his musical influences; those from pop music decidedly lacking (which separates Sondheim from Lloyd Webber), though jazzy pastiche occurs.

Sondheim the dramatist has accomplished the anatomy of twentieth-century manners, foibles and psychic *angst* with the devastating wit, logical cleverness and fundamental sympathy (though he was long judged cold) of an Ayckbourn, a Neil Simon, perhaps an **Albee** when it comes to the downward trajectory. Lyrics accomplish this, and somehow so does the music; once again it hardly seems possible that he does not write the plays. **Stoppard** parallels the work he makes words do: 'Meanwhile' (its music too) structures a song and a philosophy in 'The Miller's Son' (*A Little Night Music*); 'Going, Going, Gone' cadences a melody, a metaphor, a relationship, an entire musical (*Merrily We Roll Along*); 'Today I Woke Too Weak to Walk' (*Forum*) takes algebra to explain its full network of melopoetic meanings. Sondheim's mind is extraordinary, its other outlets including published puzzles, two murder mysteries, and a town house full of artefacts that inspired Anthony Shaffer's *Sleuth*. Yet more important than this cleverness, his characters' monologues and their prickly or glowing harmonies have spoken to an era grasping at some epigrammatic beauty in the welter of urban postmodernity. Gays responded most; but the cultural resonances are far wider, with a Shakespearean richness in *Into the Woods* and *Sweeney Todd*.

Further reading

The complete piano/vocal scores of all the musicals, expensive but obtainable, are supplemented by a four-volume song anthology, *All Sondheim*. Most of the shows' playscripts are published with introductions. The essential book is Craig Zadan: *Sondheim & Co* (various editions); see also Stephen Banfield: *Sondheim's Broadway Musicals* (1993); Meryle Secrest: *Stephen Sondheim* (1998); and Mark Eden Horowitz: *Sondheim on Music* (2003).

STEPHEN BANFIELD

SOREL, Georges

1847–1922
French social thinker

The first forty years or so of Sorel's life gave little forewarning of the excited confusion that was to characterize much of his new career as writer over the subsequent three decades, during which time he expressed with passionate vigour a series of ideas that would call into question every conventional scheme of political labelling and allegiance. Born at Cherbourg into the family of an unsuccessful businessman, he trained in Paris at the École Polytechnique where he excelled at mathematics and qualified as an engineer. He then pursued this profession until 1892, making very respectable progress within the government department of roads and bridges. At that point, fortified with a modest legacy from his mother, he simply resigned. Three years earlier he had brought out in Paris his first two works, the *Contribution à l'étude profane de la Bible* ('Contribution to the Secular Study of the Bible') and *Le Procès de Socrate* ('The Trial of Socrates'). Now he was determined to devote his full attention to further study and publication in the broad field of social and political affairs. The rest of his career seemed devoted to shocking a bourgeoisie whose notions of respectability still influenced his own private life, even to the point where he would not legitimize his 'marriage' with a servant-girl whose humble status made her unacceptable to his relations.

Much of Sorel's writing appeared first in newspapers and journals, and usually constituted a response to some problem of the moment. The lasting repute that he eventually won rested more on the penetrative power of particular insights than on any possible claim to systematic theoretical coherence, and the record of his own volatile political loyalties serves to confirm the untidiness in his thinking. During the mid-1890s Sorel put aside his earlier faith in the value of liberal conservatism and moved into a phase of full Marxist enthusiasm. This coincided with a period of similar sentiment on the part of the idealist philosopher **Benedetto Croce**, and for a time the two were closely associated in spreading the communist message among an Italian public. Dissatisfaction with the deterministic scientism of **Friedrich Engels** and Karl Kautsky soon drove Sorel from the camp of the self-styled 'orthodox' − a departure illuminated by a work of 1902 published at Palermo, the *Saggi di critica del marxismo* ('Critical Essays on Marxism'). Even so, there was no cessation of his sympathetic engagement with issues raised by **Marx** himself, such as the nature and significance of class warfare. By the end of the 1890s Sorel was moving towards the reformist social-democratic position defended by Eduard Bernstein and the 'revisionists'. Though he counted himself among the supporters of Captain Dreyfus, Sorel was so deeply disgusted by the manner in which other sympathizers − most notably Jean Jaurès − had exploited the great affair for immediate political advantage that he never returned again to any advocacy of parliamentary democracy. His interests now shifted in the direction of revolutionary syndicalism which, especially in France and Italy, linked anarchist inspirations with the organizational potential of the trade unions. He believed for a time that this at last offered to the proletariat an opportunity of implementing the creative tasks which now fell upon it as the one morally uncompromised class within contemporary society.

By 1910 Sorel was again changing his ground, having become disillusioned by the way in which even the anarchosyndicalists were showing compromising reformist tendencies. Increasingly indebted to Henri **Bergson's** vitalist philosophy, he was now enthusing over the nationalistic mysticism represented by the rhetoric of *la terre et les morts* ('the soil and the dead') found in **Maurice Barrès** and the Action Française. The French war-effort of 1914–18 appalled him, however, in so far as it was characterized as a defence of liberal-democratic values. After the Great War he felt able not only to praise the new Bolshevik regime but also to show sympathy for the nascent Italian Fascist movement which then attained power shortly after his death. While **Lenin** ignored him, **Mussolini** showed that he was in greater need of intellectual fig-leaves. Thus the Duce declared: 'I owe much to Georges Sorel. This master of syndicalism by his rough theories of revolutionary tactics has contributed most to form the discipline, energy, and power of the Fascist cohorts.'

Even our mere summary of Sorel's career indicates that here was a mind refusing to be constrained by customary categories and labels. But beneath the swirl of inconsistency there did flow certain steadier currents. In particular, Sorelian thought was marked by three more constant themes: a revolt against the bourgeois world's acquisitiveness and its search for passive contentment, a dialogue with Marx's legacy, and an exploration of the realms of creative violent energy.

These features were at their clearest during Sorel's phase of association with French syndicalism. His immediate influence on the movement was small. But its journal, *Le Mouvement Socialiste*, provided an organ for the essays making up his best-known works, *The Illusions of Progress* (*Les Illusions du progrès*, trans. 1969) and the *Reflections on Violence* (*Réflexions sur la violence*, trans. 1916), both published as books in Paris in 1908. Especially in the latter study, Sorel made his own major contribution to that 'revolt against positivism' which Stuart Hughes (in *Consciousness and Society: The Reorientation of European Social Thought, 1890–1930*, 1959) has encouraged us to regard as the pivotal characteristic of cultural and intellectual history at this epoch. The *Reflections* advocated the deflation of rationalistic presumptuousness, not least among socialists themselves, and treated Bergson's *élan vital*, or 'life force', as a conception in concordance with Sorel's own belief that human fulfilment depended upon an energetic creativity which had to be appreciated emotionally rather than scientifically. The bourgeois world could be overthrown only by a form of socialism founded not upon scientism but upon 'social poetry' – by a Marxism less concerned with the material than with the moral order and thus by a creed which had converted itself into an elite-inspired 'myth'. The efficacy of myth as an instrument of social change was not to be correlated with the extent of its accuracy as a representation of reality. Its ability to generate activity and thereby to mould the future was related, rather, to its capacity for mobilizing the will and channelling the emotions. At the time of the *Reflections*, Sorel believed that the anarcho-syndicalist weapon of a totally uncompromising general strike provided the most promising basis for a myth of this kind. Labour would there be withdrawn not in order to improve conditions within a corrupt system but in order utterly to shatter the system itself – and, above all, its dehumanizing attitude towards workers as mere objects of profit.

Even when he went on to embrace mystical nationalism, Sorel was consistent in searching still for whatever would foster an epic state of mind as precondition for social, and indeed moral, regeneration. 'Violence,' he declared, 'is an intellectual doctrine, the will of powerful minds who know what they are doing.' Sorel, like the anarchist **Peter Kropotkin**, wished to distinguish between this liberating violence and the repression stemming from the employment of mere force. Nonetheless, we can easily see what hostages he left to fortune, especially in its Fascist version. In the final analysis, he must be included within the ranks of those whose achievement was more impressive in its negative than in its positive aspects. Yet, like his contemporary **Friedrich Nietzsche**, he cannot be dismissed simply on that account. Most particularly, Sorel remains worthy of attention because his corrosive criticism and his concern with the non-rational springs of human action touched upon so many of the major points of agenda confronting those writers, such as **Émile Durkheim**, **Max Weber**, and **Vilfredo Pareto**, who were at the same epoch engaged, in a less eccentric and untidy manner, upon establishing the foundations for academic social science as we now know it.

Further reading

Other works include: *Introduction à l'économie moderne* (*Introduction to the Modern Economy*, 1903); *La Décomposition du marxisme* (*The Decomposition of Marxism*, 1908); and *La Révolution dreyfusienne* (*The Dreyfusard Revolution*, 1909). See also: J.H. Meisel, *The Genesis of Georges Sorel* (1951); Richard D. Humphrey, *Georges Sorel, Prophet with Honour: A Study in Anti-Intellectualism* (1951); Irving L. Horowitz, *Radicalism and the Revolt against Reason: The Social Theories of Georges Sorel* (1961); Isaiah Berlin, 'George Sorel', in *Against the Current: Essays in the History of Ideas* (1979): John Jack Joseph Roth, *The Cult of Violence: Sorel and the Sorelians* (1980); L. Stanley, *Sociology of Virtue: The Political and Social Theories of Georges Sorel* (1981); James Hans Meisel, *The Genesis of Georges Sorel* (1982).

MICHAEL BIDDISS

SOUTINE, Chaim

1894–1943
Russian painter

Born in a Jewish ghetto in the small village of Smilivitchi near Minsk in Russian Lithuania, Soutine's early life was one of extreme poverty and, even after his arrival in Paris in 1913 where he studied at the École des Beaux Arts, he continued to live in the most wretched circumstances. He also drank heavily. His studies, though important, were not the major influence on his work. This is to be found in the art galleries of France and Holland where his lasting admiration for the great realists – in particular Rembrandt, Chardin and **Courbet** – was formed. Strangely, the seemingly obvious affinity for **Van Gogh** was vehemently denied. Ironically this liking for the past was partly responsible for the undoubted decline in quality after his discovery by the American art collector Alfred C. Barnes in 1923. Barnes bought a large number of paintings and Soutine's way of life changed literally overnight. He couldn't cope. He became increasingly ashamed of the early work and went to great lengths to destroy as much of it as he could lay his hands on. Quite simply he felt it to be far too crude and uncontrolled to compare in any way with what he saw as the real art of the museums. He particularly disliked the series of landscapes painted at Ceret in Provence between 1919 and 1922, which in retrospect seem to be by far the most meaningful works of his entire oeuvre. Full of impulsive, often exaggerated gesture, the paint surges across the surface of the canvas drawing immediate attention to the underlying energy of the subject. The picture-plane is of prime importance and the brush strokes themselves as essential to our understanding of the pictorial space as the motif itself. Here we can clearly see the impact Soutine was to have on the later American Abstract Expressionists and in particular on **Wilhelm de Kooning**.

The choice of subject–matter was unremarkable, though the series of still-lifes worked between 1922 and 1926, which include the Rembrandt pastiches of the carcasses of beef, show a morbid liking for the dead animal which hints at an almost primitive sympathy for a way of life which was becoming increasingly foreign to him. Soutine undoubtedly lost his way and certainly lost the richly expressive urgency of the early years, but in so doing drew attention to the fundamental truth of his vision.

Further reading

See: M. Wheeler, *Soutine* (Museum of Modern Art, New York 1950); *Chaim Soutine*, exhibition catalogue with introduction by David Sylvester (Arts Council, London, 1963); Maurice Tuchman and Cologne Galerie Gmurzynska (eds) *The Impact of Chaim Soutine (1893–1943): De Kooning, Pollock, Dubuffet, Bacon* (2002).

JOHN FURSE

SOYINKA, Wole

1934–

Nigerian writer

Soyinka enjoys a high profile as a writer, intellectual and international celebrity. He made an early mark as a dramatist, and throughout his career has commented trenchantly on international issues and, more directly, on the situation in his native Nigeria through his plays. While primarily a dramatist, he has long expressed himself in a wide variety of forms, and is well known as a poet, novelist, critic, polemicist, satirist and social reformer. Expressed almost entirely in English, his vision combines an intense individualism with a profound commitment to human rights. Volatile and combative, he is quick to detect conspiracies and is drawn to independent, sometimes precipitate, action or speech. In recent years, some observers have detected signs of 'mellowing', but he remains vigorously engaged, particularly in Nigeria where he is still more of a Young Turk than an elder statesman.

Born to parents from the Ijebu and Egba communities in Yoruba-speaking Nigeria, Soyinka has written about growing up in a well-connected Christian African household. His early years were spent largely in the western Nigerian educational and commercial town of Abeokuta, but he made important visits to Ijebu Isara where he came into contact with a community that was comparatively unaffected by European influences. The book that brought the personalities and widening horizons of his childhood world to a large readership, *Aké* (1981), has been followed by an imaginative reconstruction of the challenges faced by his father's generation of Nigerians (*Isarà, a Voyage Around 'Essay'*, 1989), and by a 'factional', third-person account of his own young manhood, *Ibadan, the 'Penkelemes' Years* (1994). The ability of Yoruba communities to accommodate diverse elements and the failure of local leadership in the post-independence period emerge repeatedly in these writings. Soyinka consistently emphasizes positive elements in

Yoruba culture, and attacks the synthetic and homogenous in much that is imported. A sceptical humanist, he lambastes the divisiveness introduced into the world he knew by militant, proselytizing fundamentalist mono-theists, and insists on respect for indigenous *orisha* worship. He has long since rejected the Christianity of his parents and found within the Yoruba pantheon an inspirational patron deity, Ogun.

Soyinka received a privileged British-style education in federal government institutions. In 1952, he entered University College, Ibadan, where he did the first two years of a general arts degree before moving to the University of Leeds to complete an honours degree in English. From this period of vigorous intellectual and creative challenges, Soyinka retains a respect for a broad Socialist agenda, a suspicion of 'vulgar Marxism', and an intimate acquaintance with a wide range of European and American writers. His political education in England included encountering racist attitudes, and protesting against the invasion of Suez and of Hungary. As his creative responses to plays by writers from Euripides to **Genet** reveal, he belongs to a generation fascinated by ideas of cultural coincidence, and determined to explore African, or in this instance Yoruba, sources of inspiration.

While he was still in Britain, two of Soyinka's plays, *The Lion and the Jewel* and *The Swamp Dwellers*, were presented at the Arts Theatre, University College, Ibadan (1958). Both showed a determination to combine European dialogue drama with the performance conventions of his native land. They also reflect his anxiety to contribute to debates about the choices facing a nation at independence, especially a poor nation pos-sessed, as it soon transpired, of sizeable oil reserves.

The early plays' success opened doors for Soyinka in London, where he gained valuable experience attached to the Royal Court Theatre. He shares with his contemporaries there (e.g. **Howard Brenton**) a vision of the theatre as a place for serious comment on major social issues. At the beginning of 1960, however, Soyinka took up an academic fel-lowship in Nigeria, where he was supported by the Rockefeller Foundation. During the next two years, he made progress towards realizing his dream of creating a Nigerian National Theatre by founding the 1960 Masks; but by accepting an American fellowship, and by making a second home in the USA in the 1990s, he aroused suspicions that he was promoting pro-Western interests, for all that his criticism of some aspects of the American way of life has been vociferous, notably in *Golden Accord* (1992) and *1994* (1996). In these dramas Soyinka addressed the confession culture and cult of political correctness that particularly nauseated him.

Soyinka's versatility as a playwright, and his determination to use local resources, is shown in the play he directed when Nigeria became independent (October 1960), *A Dance of the Forests*. A sprawling text, it was in some respects 'overtaken' by his brilliant, com-pressed, evocative and often neglected ritual drama, *The Strong Breed* (1963). During the early 1960s, as the hopes raised by indepen-dence wilted, Soyinka began using the theatre to expose villainy and ridicule. His output has always been marked by the personalization of issues, and this can be seen in the songs and revue sketches brought together in *Before the Blackout* (*c.* 1972), and to a lesser extent in his more diffuse major plays from the mid-1960s, *The Road* and *Kongi's Harvest*.

Long used to operating as a literary critic, Soyinka early on detected the fundamental racism in **Leopold Senghor's** 'Negritude', and, from quips in the early 1960s to lyrics put in the mouth of Boky/Bokassa (*Opera Wonyosi*, 1977), challenged it. Later essays collected in *Burden of Memory, the Muse of Forgiveness* (1999) continued to keep 'the philosophy' at a distance while showing a more nuanced awareness of its historical context.

Following a London triumph at the Commonwealth Arts Festival (1965), Soyinka hurled himself into the increasingly violent political conflicts erupting in western

Nigeria. To protest the 'hijacking' of an election, the intellectual/activist held up a radio station in Ibadan (November 1965) and then went into hiding. After a trial that was given front-page coverage in the Nigerian press, Soyinka was acquitted on a technicality and carried shoulder-high from the court. The hold-up has been seen variously as a 'rag stunt', a brave political intervention by a concerned democrat, part of an anarchist plot, and a rehearsal for a *coup d'état*. The 'lone gunman' has since spoken of seeking 'the clarity of action', but in this instance his action caused considerable confusion. While supporters describe him as bold, others regard him as foolhardy; dramatic actions that some see as progressive, others dismiss as irrelevant gestures.

Soyinka's individualist activism was again apparent in 1966 when, as the country slid towards civil war, he stepped into the political arena through characteristically intemperate and almost certainly counter-productive words, and by making contact with secessionist 'Biafrans'. He was detained without trial for more than two years, an experience that informs *Madmen and Specialists* (play, published, 1971), *Shuttle in the Crypt* (poems, 1972) and *The Man Died* (prison notes, 1972). For the duration of the war, the imprisoned writer became for many the incarcerated conscience of the nation, though once again his intervention confused as much as clarified. The experience of extended solitary confinement seems to have thrown Soyinka back on the classics of Western literature, and edged his vision towards the nihilistic.

During the early 1970s, Soyinka was a fellow at Churchill College, Cambridge, where, continuing his interaction with classical texts, he prepared a version of *The Bacchae of Euripides*. That Africa occupied an important part of his consciousness is shown by the series of influential lectures subsequently published as *Myth, Literature and the African World* (1976). Experience of institutionalized racism over the arrangements to deliver the lectures encouraged Soyinka to dramatize an episode from Nigeria's colonial history under the title *Death and the King's Horseman*, a play has been widely anthologized and has come to occupy a significant place within post-colonial studies programmes.

After Cambridge, Soyinka moved to Accra, Ghana, where he took over the editorship of *Transition*, and turned it into *Chi'Indaba*, a campaigning publication. He used the magazine's pages to engage in a literary controversy with the lightweight authors of *Toward the Decolonization of African Literature*, who had accused him of being alienated from Yoruba traditions and of imitating 'Euro-Modernist' poets. On this occasion Soyinka dealt brusquely with his critics, but there is little evidence of any thoroughgoing engagement with more recent critical thinking. It is significant that, while some of his works have been used as illustrations by those concerned with post-colonialism, his essays are rarely analysed in such discussions.

After Murtala Mohammed replaced Yakubu Gowon as head of state, Soyinka returned to Nigeria (1976) and took up a professorship at the University of Ile-Ife, where he became involved in university politics at a time of mounting tension on campuses, manifested by (among other symptoms) the emergence of murderous cults, mischievously said by Soyinka's opponents to be modelled on a fraternity, the Pyrates, that he had co-founded during the 1950s. Soyinka also came in for censure from a left-wing Ibadan-Ife group. While dismissing these prescriptive **Marxist** critics as 'leftocrats', he responded to them creatively by adapting **Brecht's** *Three-Penny Opera* as *Opera Wonyosi* (premiered 1977), and through a series of sketches written for a guerrilla theatre troupe he started (*Before the Blowout*). The desire to communicate with a mass audience apparent in such works has drawn Soyinka into various other ventures over the years. These have included the release of a record, *Unlimited Liability Company* (1983), and the making of a film, *Blues for the Prodigal*, replete with *vox pop* interviews. Simultaneously Soyinka expended huge resources of time and energy endeavouring to make Nigeria's notoriously dangerous roads safer.

Although since being awarded the Nobel Prize for Literature in 1986 Soyinka has continued to see himself principally as a playwright, his international activities have overshadowed recent, and generally undistinguished, dramatic writing. His later output includes: *Beatification of Area Boy*, premiered at Leeds in 1995; *Travel Club and the Boy Soldier* (1997); *Document of Identity* (BBC, 1997); *King Baabu* (2001); *Rain of Stones* (BBC, 2002); and *Oyedipo at Kholoni* (after Sophocles, 2002). A volume of poetry, *Samarkand and Other Markets I Have Known*, appeared in 2002, and there have been numerous newspaper articles, keynote addresses and lectures, some of which have been published in a series entitled *Interventions*. In 2004, Soyinka delivered the Reith Lectures for the BBC on the threats to peace posed by fundamentalist religious groups and the United States.

King Baabu, the most substantial of the more recent plays, reflects the campaign against Nigerian military dictator Sani Abacha that Soyinka waged during the 1990s. Indeed, the playwright campaigned to such effect that Abacha had him declared a traitor. That someone who has devoted so much creative endeavour to national affairs should be so stigmatized is profoundly ironic.

Further reading

See: Gerald Moore, *Wole Soyinka* (1971); E.D. Jones, *Wole Soyinka* (1973); Derek Wright, *Wole Soyinka Revisited* (1993); Biodun Jeyifo (ed.) *Perspectives on Wole Soyinka: Freedom and Complexity* (2001); Biodun Jeyifo, *Wole Soyinka: Politics, Poetics and Post-colonialism* (2003); Martin Banham (with Judith Greenfield and Chuck Mike), *African Theatre: Wole Soyinka* (2005).

JAMES GIBBS

SPENCER, Herbert

1820–1903

English philosopher

Outside the fields of the natural sciences and technology on one side and artistic literature on the other, Herbert Spencer appears as the dominant intellectual figure of the English-speaking world of the later part of the nineteenth century. In particular his concept of evolution presided the nascent studies of sociology and anthropology, and permeated the view of the world held by educated Europeans and Americans. The later success of this concept was due to **Darwin** and **Wallace**, but it was Spencer who gave it currency. Darwin gave a causal explanation of the processes through which species are modified and eventually transformed, whereas Spencer's concept of evolution (which means 'unfolding') suggests a pre-determined goal or plan guiding the general trend. Spencer believed that there was a universal movement from the simple to the complex, the criterion of complexity being differentiation of the parts and their integration, that is mutual dependence.

There is some overlap between him and Darwin, according to whom the more complex organisms have come into existence by gradual modifications of the simpler and, therefore, appeared later in time. But Darwin does not say that the simple organisms are likely to disappear, and postulates no all-embracing trend throughout the animate nature, whereas Spencer sees it not only there and in the socio-cultural realm, which he calls 'superorganic', but in inanimate nature as well. His 'evolution' could be described as a cosmic anti-entropic trend. Although he tries to underpin it with references to astronomy, physics and chemistry, his diagnosis goes far beyond what could have been inferred from these sciences. It is even less tenable now, as modern physics postulates entropy – that is, the tendency towards an equal distribution of energy throughout the universe – and sees a movement in the contrary direction as possible only in restricted parts of the universe. As a cosmological principle, however, entropy is perhaps even less tenable than Spencer's evolution, because how can anything be undergoing a process of dispersion without having previously undergone a process of concentration?

Although he did not believe in a personalized God, and explained the origins of religion in terms of dream experiences, Spencer can be classified as a deist on the ground that he believed he knew the fundamental principle presiding over all the changes in the universe. There is some contradiction between his definition of God as 'the Great Unknown' and his claim to know the ultimate goal of the cosmos. The infusion of this metaphysical element enabled Spencer to build a system of ethics on the tacit assumption that since evolution – that is, the trend from the simple to the complex – is universal, it must be good, from which follows that whatever promotes this trend is good, while whatever impedes it is bad. Almost needless to say, this involves a jump over David Hume's barrier between what is the case and what ought to be the case. It may be worth noting that if we tried to make an analogous jump and build a system of ethics on the physics of today, then the principle of entropy would lead us to advocacy of nihilistic destructiveness.

Spencer was influenced by Auguste Comte but disapproved of his scheme for a new society and wanted to improve upon his theories. They were the only authors in modern times who imitated Aristotle in covering all branches of knowledge, although Spencer only briefly refers to mathematics, physics and chemistry in his *The First Principles* (1862), while Comte devotes the first half of his six-volume *Cours de la philosophie positive* to an exposition of their most general ideas. Spencer, however, deals at greater length with biology where his master key is more useful. Nevertheless, though admired for the remarkable breadth of his knowledge by the few who have read *The Principles of Biology* (2 vols, 1864 and 1867), Spencer is not regarded as important by the historians of biology. *The Principles of Psychology* (1855; 2nd edn, 2 vols, 1870 and 1872) also had little influence on the development of its field. Perhaps it was too early for such a book to be written, as neither systematic or clinical observation nor experimentation had yet begun, and so there was no knowledge,

going beyond introspection and common sense, to be synthesized.

Undoubtedly the most permanent legacy of Spencer lies in sociology and anthropology, which were dominated by 'evolutionism' until the early twentieth century. What made it possible was the better fit between Spencer's concept of evolution and the facts in these fields, and the bridge which it provided between these and Darwinian biology. In the realm of the superorganic, the more complex forms have displaced the less complex which (unlike the micro-organisms) are disappearing. We can see here, to use another of Spencer's terms, a general 'advance of organization'. Dealing with social evolution he not only diagnoses correctly a general trend but also offers a convincing explanation: in the struggle for survival between groups the larger and more highly organized invariably win when the difference on these scores is big enough. A large state can never be defeated by small tribes of hunters, whereas a mammal can be killed by bacteria and is powerless against insects. Spencer's celebrated expression 'survival of the fittest' is circular in biology, where fitness is measured by survival, but in sociology it can be interpreted as meaning that the more highly organized groups tend to survive. **Marx's** Law of Industrial Concentration can be subsumed under this evolutionary principle.

The primeval form of struggle for survival is war, and Spencer correctly sees in it a prime agent of social evolution which, through conquests and alliances for defence, has led to the emergence of large polities where a more advanced differentiation and integration of parts is possible.

In *The Principles of Sociology* (3 vols, 1876–96), Spencer deals in turn with various institutions – religious beliefs, the family, ceremonies, professions, economic (or, as he calls them, industrial) and political organizations – showing the origins of the more recent and complex forms in the simpler. His treatment is of the most lasting value where his master key fits best – that is, where the process of differentiation and integration can be discerned most clearly – which is in the political and economic structures. Best of all is his treatment of the political and military institutions on the level of the transition from tribes to states, because here we can see in its purest form the mechanism which he regards as the cause of evolution: namely, the struggle for survival and the elimination of the simpler formations by the more complex. His treatment of the family, religion and art is less illuminating, because in these spheres no clear trend from the simple to the complex can be ascertained, and it is not clear what the struggle for survival means in this context. Indeed, the structures of kinship are much simpler in ours than in the primitive societies. Although there are more words in the languages of contemporary nations (which, however, does not mean that the average individual knows more words), the grammatical structures of languages spoken by minute tribes can be very complex. Furthermore, it is impossible to reconstruct the stages in the evolution of language between the simple simian forms and the (structurally more or less equally complex) known human languages. Nor can we know what were the prehistoric forms of the family or religion. Evolutionism fell into disrepute largely because of its exponents' concern with the latter domains where they could not go beyond completely unverifiable conjectures.

Although Spencer coined the term 'comparative sociology', he did not practise comparative analysis of the kind which we can find in **Durkheim's** *Le Suicide*, or in Otto Hintze's essay on the conditions of emergence of representative governments, where they try to unravel causal links with the aid of comparisons which approximately fit methods of induction. Spencer compares mainly to classify or illustrate the stages of evolution, giving an astounding number of examples from all epochs and parts of the globe but going into none of them in great detail: in contrast, for example, to T.H. Buckle who compares only four countries of Europe but employs a mass of factual data to unravel the constellations of forces which

have propelled these countries in different directions. Spencer's evolutionary classification of societies is just as good (if not better) than any other which has been proposed, but classifying must be a dead end unless it is supplemented by studies of causation. While some of Spencer's propositions do assert causal links, he is only interested in the most general factors of evolution: he explains, for instance, polygyny as an adaptation to warfare which has a great survival value on the tribal level, but (in contrast to, for example, John Mackinnon Robertson) he says nothing which would help us to understand why evolution occurred faster in one place or era than another: why, for example, science developed in Europe rather than India or why the industrial revolution occurred in Britain rather than Spain.

The other part of Spencer's heritage is known as 'organicism', the essence of which is the focus on analogies between organisms and societies and searches for homologous structures and functions. Thus, for instance, trade and transportation are likened to the circulation of the blood, and the nervous system to the administrative machinery of the state. This approach was a valuable step towards a full appreciation of the enormous complexity of social differentiation, integration and self-regulation. However, especially in the hands of Spencer's less subtle followers, it soon degenerated into an unfruitful game of listing superficial analogies. Although he followed Spencer very closely in his first major book, *De la division de travail social* (1893), Emile Durkheim initiated a new departure by insisting on more detailed study of facts of social life and a deeper analysis of social causation. Later, A.R. Radcliffe-Brown, who was a keen student of Spencer and Durkheim, transmitted the concern with the concepts of structure, function and their integration to the 'functionalist school' of anthropology, of which he was a co-founder. The functionalists abandoned all interest in evolution and (with the exception of Radcliffe-Brown) in comparative analysis, concentrating on intensive studies of individual primitive societies, which was the very opposite of Spencer's classificatory schemes. But they took from Spencer the idea of mutual interdependence of structures and functions, and ordered the data of their field work from this viewpoint, often discovering connections undreamt of by Spencer.

More recently, Spencer's idea that all self-regulating systems have common character-istics has been revived in the new form of general systems theory, although it is possible that its exponents did not get their inspiration from Spencer, as they never mention him. Nonetheless, he was their forerunner. Any-one who has read Spencer and reads J.G. Miller's *Living Systems* (1978) will see that it is pure Spencerianism brought up to date.

Until the rise of machine industry, political (and especially military) structures were much more complex than the industrial; and they grew in complexity through the raw struggle for survival. After the industrial revolution the growth in complexity occurred mainly in economic institutions. Commercial competi-tion can be regarded as the new propellant of evolution which brings forth ever larger and more complex entities, while the smaller and weaker are eliminated. Spencer hovered on the brink of such an interpretation, which would have brought him to **Marx's** Law of Industrial Concentration. Such a conclusion, however, would have clashed with his com-mitment to fundamentalist liberalism, which he never abandoned despite its incompat-ibility with organicism, more consistent with authoritarian collectivism because the growth of complexity of organisms is accompanied by an increase in the control of all parts of the body by the brain. Consequently, the idea of survival of the fittest was only used (especially by his followers) to justify the position of individual victors in commercial competi-tion. This use – known as Social Darwinism – was based on confusing social with biological success, the only measure of which is the number of offspring who survive and repro-duce. Unlike Comte and Marx, who con-demned the societies in which they lived and entertained visions of a better order, Spencer

was a mildly reformist conservative who saw in the Victorian liberal order – which only needed to be purged of the remnants of militarism, Toryism and bureaucracy – the end product of evolution. This view was connected with the idea which he got from Saint-Simon that militarism (or, as he puts it, militancy) was being displaced by indus-trialism: that is, an orientation towards peaceful production instead of war. Indus-trialism, according to this view, also entailed a transition from coercion to co-operation. Since he paid so much attention to the role of war as the motor of evolution, and believed that this motor was due to stop, it is not perhaps surprising that he could not envisage evolution going far beyond the Britain of his time.

Despite its inconsistency with his socio-logical theory, Spencer's advocacy of ultra liberalism brought him widespread respect, usually given to able apologists of the domi-nant social forces. Though widely applauded, his eloquent tirades against governmental regulation had little relevance to the ills of the Victorian Britain which (together with the United States of that era) was the most unbureaucratic large-scale society which ever existed. In contrast, Marx – bitter enemy of ill-treatment of the sellers of labour by the owners of capital – died almost in obscurity. With the decline of the businessman and the rise of the bureaucrat, Spencer was pushed into the shade, while Marx – whose theories condemn the capitalist and exonerate the bureaucrat – was posthumously brought into the limelight, just as the ills against which he thundered lost their acuteness while those which Spencer attacked acquired gravity which they did not have when he was writing.

In his life and character, Spencer typifies the greatness and the oddities of Victorian Britain. An abstemious and puritanical hypo-chondriac, he put all his energies into intel-lectual endeavour. An amateur belonging to no university, he was free from the academic routine and ritual and the temptations and pressures of petty politics. Having been taught by relatives in a highly individual manner, he was never subjected to scholastic standardization. He did, however, have to submit to the discipline of work because, as a son of a private tutor, he had to earn his living early and qualified as an engineer on the railways at the age of seventeen. He made a couple of minor mechanical inventions but soon began to be involved in reformist and political activities, and to write for provincial periodicals, At twenty-eight he became a sub-editor on *The Economist*, moved to London and entered into contacts with the intellectual circles. Some years later he received an inheritance which gave him the means to devote himself to scholarly pursuits provided he did not have a family to support. He chose not to marry. With extraordinary persistence he went on with his project of a synthetic philosophy which he completed with *The Principles of Ethics* (2 vols, 1879 and 1893) when he was seventy-six. Always eccentric, in his later years he often put plugs into his ears in order not to have to listen to others' nonsense.

Further reading

Other works include: *Social Statics or the Conditions essential to Human Happiness specified, and the First of them Developed* (1850); *Education: Intellectual, Moral and Physical* (1861); *The Study of Sociology* (1873); *Descriptive Sociology* (1874 – compiled by others on principles laid down by Spencer, and continued after his death); *The Man versus the State* (1884); *An Autobiography* (1904). See also: *Structure, Function and Evolution*, ed. S.L. Andreski (1971); Y.D.Y. Peel, *Herbert Spencer, Evolution of a Sociologist* (1971); R. Richards, *Darwin and the Emergence of Evolutionary Theories of Mind and Behaviour* (1987).

STANISLAV ANDRESKI

SPENCER, (Sir) Stanley

1881–1959
English artist

Stanley Spencer was one of the most eccentric artistic characters of the last century. Born in the small Berkshire town of Cookham, he studied at the Slade School of Art in London and was known to his roistering, Bohemian fellow students as 'Cookham' because of his habit of invariably going back there daily on the 5.08 train from Paddington.

Barely five feet tall, with a workhouse pudding basin haircut and a disastrous marital life, much recorded in his paintings and in an excellent play by Pam Gems called *Stanley*, he could, even when knighted, frequently be seen wheeling his painting gear around in a ramshackle perambulator.

He served, modestly and heroically, as a medical orderly in the Macedonian campaign in World War I; this gave rise to some notable war paintings which still dominate the permanent collection at the Imperial War Museum. In World War II he was an official war artist and painted remarkable large canvasses of the Port Glasgow Docks and factories. His other most notable war paintings are to be found in the frescoes he did for the Sandham Memorial Chapel at Burghclere in Hampshire, a private commission by the sister and brotherinlaw of an army officer who also served in Macedonia but died there. When he secured the commission, being a great admirer of the Arena Chapel in Padua, he exclaimed, 'What ho, Giotto.'

Spencer, doubtless because of the complexity and failure of his marital life, devoted much energy to erotic drawings and paintings, and at one stage the awful antiavant-garde President of the Royal Academy, Sir Alfred Munnings, tried unsuccessfully to get Spencer prosecuted by the Director of Public Prosecutions. His erotic masterpiece, known as the *Leg of Mutton* painting, is a bleak vision of sexual frustration.

Spencer once observed to his brother Gilbert, also a successful – although much more conventional – painter, that 'art is ninety per cent living'. This is doubtless why so much of his work is so personal in its imagery and why his student nickname of Cookham turned out to be so prophetic.

Apart from his war paintings and his highly charged pictures of wives and mistresses, his most notable pictures – and those for which he is most recognized – are his religious subjects, nearly all of which are set in an entirely recognizable Cookham high street and land-scape. Spencer's daughter said that 'He was extremely sacramental', and religion was his second most cherished obsession after sex. Any broad description of his Cookham-fixated religious paintings could make him sound like a naïve artist, but this he was certainly was not. The almost architectonic skill of his vast compositions – *Resurrection, Cookham* of 1924–7 is 274 cm by 549 cm – is that of a highly sophisticated artist. As for the idea of placing Christ or various saints in a con-temporary Berkshire countryside, he was simply following the practice of Renaissance artists who placed their holy men and women on the hillsides of Umbria or the campagna of Tuscany. (When Spencer went off to Mace-donia and war he carried in his pockets little books of reproductions of paintings by Masaccio and Fra Angelico as well as Giotto.)

Not all his Cookham paintings are religious epics like *Resurrection* or *Christ's Entry into Jerusalem*. There are affectionate versions of the local regatta and even an immaculate and charming vision of a garage. Anything human interested him, although the religious and the erotic remained not only his most absorbing interests but also inspired his finest pictures. And while the *Leg of Mutton* painting is an agonized rendering of sexual dysfunction, the marvellous *On the Tiger Rug* is a joyous cele-bration of his affair with Daphne Charlton and presumably its title is meant to recall the doggerel: 'Would you like to sin/With Elinor Glyn/On a tiger skin?'

Spencer was one of England's finest pain-ters of the first half of the last century. He had no followers, had no influence because his style and his subject-matter were so personal, eccen-tric and idiosyncratic; but he is indispensable to the understanding of English art.

Further reading

See: Fiona MacCarthy, *Stanley Spencer: An English Vision* (1998); Maurice Collis, *Stanley Spencer (A Biography)* (1962); Keith Bell, *Stanley Spencer: A Complete Catalogue of the Paintings* (1993).

T.G. ROSENTHAL

SPENGLER, Oswald

1880–1936

German historian

Spengler came from a middle-class north German family of moderate means. After a brief period as a secondary school teacher in Hamburg (his specialities were mathematics and natural science), he left the profession for ever, settling in Munich and living modestly on the income from an inheritance and the proceeds of articles and reviews. The subjects of his doctoral thesis (Heraclitus) and of his qualifying thesis for the teaching profession ('The Development of the Organ of Sight in the Chief Stages of Animal Life') were an unlikely prelude to historical activity, but they are consistent with the speculative cast of his writing and with its constant exploitation of biology as a source of metaphor. Neither in practice nor temperamentally was he ever part of the German historical establishment, and ill-health was probably merely a con-tributory factor in his refusal of chairs of his-tory at Göttingen and Leipzig after *The Decline of the West* had made him a public figure.

The Decline of the West (*Der Untergang des Abendlandes*), on which Spengler's reputation is based, appeared in two volumes, *Form and Actuality* (*Gestalt und Wirklichkeit*, 1918, trans. 1926) and *Perspectives of World-History* (*Wel-thistorische Perspektiven*, 1922, trans. 1928). Its success in Germany (in particular the success of its first volume) owed much to an under-standable but not strictly warranted confusion in readers' minds between Germany's military defeat and the more far-reaching and gradual decline evoked by Spengler. Although in the 1920s Spengler was to address himself specifically, if with limited success, to the German political situation, what he offers in *The Decline* is both a philo-sophy of history and, as a corollary, a prediction of the future course of Western civilization as a whole. Spengler's view of history is cyclical and organic, and has little room for causality: cultures move through the 'age-phases of the individual man'; plant-like, they realize the possibilities contained within them and, having fulfilled themselves, die. Spengler particularly stresses the specificity of cultures (concerning himself chiefly with the two he describes as Classical and as Western or 'Faustian'), which express their individual 'soul' in a succession of forms (economic, social, artistic) and remain impenetrable to other cultures – an extreme development of the historicist idea of individuality. Yet it is a paradox of the work that Spengler's whole method is a comparative one which asserts parallelisms between separate cultures in spite of their discontinuity: Democritus and Leibniz, Archimedes and **Helmholtz** are thus, to use Spengler's term, 'contemporaries', appearing at the same stage in Classical and Western culture respectively.

The dominant tone of *The Decline* is elegiac, both because Western culture is presented as potentially absent (already well engaged in its final phase, it will pass through the tyranny of Caesarism before it subsides for ever) and because Spengler's attitude towards cultures which have *already* disappeared affirms their inaccessibility while striving to overcome it imaginatively (in this respect there are some surprising similarities with **Lévi-Strauss's** *Tristes Tropiques*). Spengler pursues this paradoxical ambition by the ingenious detection of symbolic correspondences *within* cultures (which allows him to intuit them as comprehensible totalities), by the use of biological analogy to characterize *all* cultures, by the deployment of parallels ('homologies') *between* cultures, and, more generally, by the setting of these cultures against the permanence of an indifferent cosmic back-drop which establishes them as ephemeral if significant incidents in a common pathos.

The ethical relativism professed by Spengler and the importance he attributes to the state place *The Decline* within the historicist tradition, but, drawing freely upon **Nietzsche** (with Goethe, an important influence), he also smuggles an aristocratic ethic into history. This preference no doubt lay behind his subsequent hostility to **Hitler** (a 'heroic tenor' rather than a 'hero') and

National Socialism, to which the nationalism, the opposition to parliamentary democracy and the corporate conception of the state evidenced in his political writing might otherwise have been expected to draw him.

Spengler's reputation never regained its high point of the early 1920s and his conception of history, which was never an orthodoxy, is now largely discredited, but *The Decline* can still provide intellectual excitement (see, for example, his chapter, 'The Meaning of Numbers') and, in its solemnly resonant celebration of transience, moments of aesthetic pleasure.

Further reading

Other works include: *Man and Technics: A Contribution to a Philosophy of Life (Der Mensch und die Technik: Beitrag zu einer Philosophie des Lebens*, 1931, trans. 1932); *The Hour of Decision: Germany and World-Historical Evolution (Jahre der Entscheidung: Deutschland und die weltgeschichtliche Entwicklung*, 1933, trans. 1934); *Politische Schriften* (1932). On Spengler see: H. Stuart Hughes, *Oswald Spengler: A Critical Estimate* (1952); R.G. Collingwood, Oswald Spengler and the Theory of Historical Cycles', *Antiquity: A Quarterly Review of Archaeology*, Vol. I (September 1927); Theodor W. Adorno, 'Spengler nach dem Untergang', *Der Monat* (May 1950); Klaus P. Fischer, *History and Prophecy: Oswald Spengler and the Decline of the West* (1989); H. Stuart Hughes, *Oswald Spengler: A Critical Estimate* (1991); John Farrenkopf, *Prophet of Decline: Spengler on World History and Politics* (2001).

ROGER S. HUSS

SPIELBERG, Steven
1946–
American film maker

Born in Cincinnati, Ohio, raised in Scottsdale and Phoenix, Arizona, Steven Spielberg is now synonymous with Hollywood, the place and its metonymic associations, the film industry and film culture. At twelve years old he filmed an eight-minute Western; at fourteen he made a forty-minute war film; at sixteen he finished a feature-length science fiction movie. By the end of high school, he was working, as an office assistant, on the lot at Universal Studios. Though he was not accepted to film school, his short film *Amblin'* (1968) won a festival prize and got him another job at Universal, this time directing television dramas, including a *Columbo* mystery (1971) and a memorable episode of *Rod Serling's Night Gallery* (1970) starring Joan Crawford.

His first important film was the TV movie *Duel* (1971), which merited an international theatrical release. The story of a traveller harassed by an anonymous monolith, in this case a long-haul truck, would create a paradigm for the narrative structure of many of Spielberg's later films. In his first feature, *The Sugarland Express* (1974), an overwhelming force of police follow an escaped convict, his wife, and their hostage as the couple seek to reclaim their child. The monolith in *Jaws* (1975), of course, is the shark, the prototype for the dinosaurs of *Jurassic Park* (1993) and *The Lost World: Jurassic Park* (1997). With these films Spielberg also created an industrial model of turning best-selling adventure-thriller novels into blockbuster summer movies. *Raiders of the Lost Ark* (1981) and its second sequel, *Indiana Jones and the Last Crusade* (1989), exploit a monolithic evil of historical proportions, the Nazi party, its ideology and military power. War itself is the immeasurable, terrible adversary to be survived in *Empire of the Sun* (1987) and *Saving Private Ryan* (1998). And in *E.T. the Extra-Terrestrial* (1982) and *Minority Report* (2002) it is our own government and its unsympathetic, self-sustaining institutions that threaten the individual. A lone driver or adventurer, a small group of ordinary people, an abandoned child or alien – the protagonists of Spielberg's signature films are recognizable types (even the child-like E.T.) given mythic responsibilities, to find the intrepid soul within and prevail against unthinking, uncaring, seemingly unlimited enmity.

Several of Spielberg's most serious works complicate the paradigm. In *Amistad* (1997) government is challenged to repudiate the institution of slavery. His most complex work, *Schindler's List* (1993), analyses evil, investigating the psychology of Nazism and the vicissitudes and emotional toll of heroism. Commentators often note the recurring themes of family and fatherhood in most of Spielberg's work, from *The Sugarland Express* to *Catch Me If You Can* (2002). Steven Spielberg is the oldest of four children, has fathered four and adopted two, was distraught at his parents' divorce, and is divorced himself (and remarried to actress Kate Capshaw). In Spielberg films, fatherless families and failed, troubled husbands abound, like those in *Close Encounters of the Third Kind* (1977), *The Color Purple* (1985, from Alice Walker's Pulitzer-Prize novel) and *Artificial Intelligence: AI* (2001, taken over from **Stanley Kubrick**). Every kind of father figure and shade of fatherly behaviour, from the ideal (*Indiana Jones and the Temple of Doom*, 1984; *Saving Private Ryan*) to the demonic (*Jaws, Minority Report*) to the clash of both (*Hook*, 1991; *Jurassic Park, Schindler's List*), appear in Spielberg's filmography, and taken in total create an impressive exploration of the theme.

Spielberg's phenomenal popular success as a director – *E.T.* in the early 1980s and *Jurassic Park* in the early 1990s were both the largest grossing films ever – led to unrivalled power as a producer. In 1982 he formed Amblin Entertainment, a production company that created, among other projects, *Poltergeist* (1982), *Back to the Future* (1985), *Men in Black* (1997) and a number of his own most famous films. Amblin produced animated feature films and cartoon shorts and shows, and Spielberg was an executive producer on television series, such as *ER*, and mini-series, like *Band of Brothers* (2001). The Academy of Motion Picture Arts and Sciences awarded Spielberg the Irving G. Thalberg Memorial Award, an Oscar, in 1986 for producing a body of high-quality creative work in cinema. In 1994 he was one of the three founders of DreamWorks SKG, the first new fully functioning movie studio created in Hollywood in over seven decades. And after several nominations he won Academy Awards for Best Director for his work on *Schindler's List* and *Saving Private Ryan*. He has become a monolithic institution himself, a name above the title, but with such philanthropic projects as the Shoah Visual History Foundation, which records the testimony of Holocaust survivors and witnesses, he seeks to redress, to the extent that he can, the patterns of conflict and struggle throughout history and human psychology that his films record.

Further reading

See: Douglas Brode, *The Films of Steven Spielberg* (1995); Joseph McBride, *Steven Spielberg* (1997).

DENNIS PAOLI

SPOCK, Benjamin McLane

1903–98

US paediatrician and author

Son of a corporation lawyer, Benjamin Spock grew up in a puritanical but devoted New England family. After graduating from Yale, he went on to study at Yale Medical School and qualified as a doctor in 1929 at the College of Physicians and Surgeons, Columbia University. He served residencies in paediatrics and psychiatry, and as part of his psychiatric training underwent five years in psychoanalysis. Between 1933 and 1947 Spock practised paediatrics in New York City during which period he also taught paediatrics at Cornell Medical College and acted as Consultant in Paediatric Psychiatry to New York City Health Department.

After a period of wartime service in the US Naval Reserve as a lieutenant commander, Spock moved to Minnesota to join the staff of the Mayo Clinic and later became Associate Professor of Psychiatry with the Mayo Foundation, University of Minnesota. From there he became Professor of Child Development at the University of Pittsburgh (1951–55), and occupied the same post at Western Reserve University from 1955 until he retired in 1967.

It was during this period of service in the Naval Reserve that Spock wrote the bulk of what was to become his major work. First published as *The Commonsense Book of Baby and Child Care* (1946) and later simply as *Baby and Child Care*, the book known to two generations of parents as 'Dr Spock' has achieved worldwide sales running into the tens of millions.

Keynote of *Baby and Child Care* was reassurance – 'Trust yourself … Don't be afraid to trust your own common sense.' It was unique in offering to the ordinary parent a detailed guide to the child's physical, social and emotional development and well-being, couched in non-technical terms. Its appeal was further strengthened by Spock's highly distinctive conversational approach, a style he perfected when reading the manuscript aloud to his wife Jane, who also collaborated on research and the enormously detailed index.

Before the appearance of *Baby and Child Care*, childcare experts had tended towards the inflexible and prescriptive, especially in the areas of feeding and toilet training. *Baby and Child Care* succeeded in popularizing the growing feeling among psychoanalysts, educators and paediatricians that greater understanding and flexibility were essential in the care of young children.

In subsequent editions Spock made it clear that this had indeed been his intention but also expressed concern at the swing towards a child-centred culture and the over-permissiveness which he felt typified American child-rearing through the 1950s and 1960s. In the 1979 edition Spock attempts to eliminate the sexist bias of which he has been accused by feminists; for the first time the child is referred to as 'she' and he acknowledges the changes in parental roles – 'Now I recognize that the father's responsibility is as great as the mother's.'

A member of SANE (Committee for a Sane Nuclear Policy) from 1962, Spock became increasingly involved in the American peace movement until in 1968 he, with other opponents of American involvement in Vietnam, was tried for conspiring to 'counsel, aid and abet' violations of the conscription law. He was found guilty but later acquitted, and continued to be active in the peace movement. His later writings reflected an increasing concern with the wider problems of society. *Decent and Indecent – Our Personal and Political Behaviour* (1969) is dedicated to 'the young people, black and white, who are being clubbed, jailed and even killed for showing us the way to justice'.

Further reading

Other works include: *A Baby's First Year* (with J. Reinhart and W. Miller, 1954); *Feeding Your Baby and Child* (with M. Lowenberg, 1955); *Caring for Your Disabled Child* (with M. Lerringo, 1965); *Dr Spock on Vietnam* (with Mitchell Zimmerman, 1968); *A Better World for Our Children* (1994). See Jessica Mitford, *The Trial of Dr Spock* (1969); Lynn Z. Bloom, *Doctor Spock: Biography of a Conservative Radical* (1972).

HELEN WAITES

STALIN, Joseph

1879–1953

Russian political leader

Joseph Vissarionovich Dzhugashvili – Stalin – was born at Gori in Tiflis province. A Georgian by nationality, he was the son of a shoemaker. In 1893 Stalin completed his studies at the ecclesiastical school in Gori. He entered the Tiflis Orthodox Seminary, which at that time was a hotbed of revolutionary ideas – populist, nationalist as well as Marxist. In 1897 Stalin became involved in Marxist circles there. In 1898 he officially joined the Tiflis Russian Social Democratic and Labour Party organization. Until his first arrest in March 1902 he was active in revolutionary politics. Over the next few years, but like thousands of the same generation, he was to be imprisoned and deported several times. Despite the mythology surrounding Stalin's early political years, it is clear that his overall role was only minor and his influence mainly provincial. He spoke no foreign languages. Unlike other Russian Marxists he had no experience of the European labour movement. As a Marxist theoretician he was irrelevant. He was above all an organization man whose roots were entirely Russian. It was for this reason alone that **Lenin** valued him. Stalin's one claim to early intellectual credibility, *Marxism and the National and Colonial Question* (1913, trans. 1936), was even written under Lenin's direction.

After the February Revolution in 1917, Stalin returned to Petrograd. For a short period and with Kamenev and Muranov, he led the Bolshevik Party. He declared himself in favour of lending critical support to the Provisional Government and of a Bolshevik–Menshevik unification. For fifteen days he opposed Lenin's 'April Theses' which called for a revolutionary transfer of power to the newly formed Soviets. His role during the October Revolution was marginal. The view, again fostered by Stalin in power, that he was Lenin's right-hand man and closest collaborator during the uprising is a complete distortion. Ironically, this description fits **Trotsky** far better.

During the Civil War Stalin, like many Bolsheviks, had military tasks thrust upon him. In this period his conflict with Trotsky, the main organizer of the Red Army, began to assume serious proportions. His ill will towards military 'specialists' of any kind and his refusal to obey orders during the Polish campaign were first shots in a long battle. In these conflicts Lenin consistently supported Trotsky.

Stalin's real role, however, was at the centre of the Party machine. With Sverdlov he kept the Party running during the repression of the Bolsheviks in July and August 1917; he was co-director of *Pravda*; one of the seven members of the Politburo, which was set up in October to prepare the insurrection but never met; and he was Commissar for Nationalities. He was one of the four members of the 'small cabinet' of the Central Committee set up after October (Lenin, Trotsky, Sverdlov, Stalin). In 1919 Stalin was appointed Commissar for the Peasants' and Workers' Inspectorate (Rabkrin) and made one of the five established members of the first Politburo (Kamenev, Krestinsky, Lenin, Stalin, Trotsky); in April 1920 he became a member of the Orgburo. In April 1922 he was appointed as the Party's General Secretary. In the space of five years his organizational capacity and personal ambition at the centre of the merging party bureaucracy had led to an unbelievable accumulation of administrative posts.

In 1922 Lenin fell ill. In the course of the same year Stalin began to oppose Lenin on several fronts – on the foreign trade monopoly; on the Constitution of the USSR; on the Georgian nationality question; and on Lenin's increasing opposition to Stalin's power. In his Testament in 1922–3 Lenin finally called for Stalin's removal. Lenin's last heart attack in January 1923 probably saved Stalin.

With Lenin incapacitated (he died in January 1924), the oppositional tendencies divided and with his own control over the machine, Stalin's rise to power was assured. The receding prospects of world revolution, the political and social exhaustion inside Russia after the Civil War, and the general demoralization which pervaded the Party, all worked in Stalin's favour. The Left Opposition led by Trotsky, whatever the correctness of their views, were doomed to defeat. History was rapidly turning against a revolutionary programme.

Stalin's general strategy corresponded with the needs and aspirations of the growing Party bureaucracy. Socialism in one country, the campaign against egalitarianism, forced industrialization and collectivization and the whole conservative-nationalist retrenchment of the 1930s all related to their interests. The purges and destruction of the Old Bolshevik Party between 1936 and 1939 led to their final consolidation as a group.

Stalin's policy after 1929 was dictated by two considerations. One, was to ensure his own position and the second was rapid economic growth at any cost. The logic of this inevitably led to increasing repression, economic wastage and the extension of the forced labour camp system. Industrialization

was thus purchased at enormous social and political cost.

The Second World War at first threw Stalin into disarray. It is clear that the Pact with **Hitler** (1939–41) had lulled the USSR into a false sense of security. Furthermore, the purges of the Red Army in 1937 had left the country dangerously exposed. All of these weaknesses were rapidly revealed in the early months of the war. However, Nazi racist savagery, the enormous sacrifice made by the Soviet people, and Allied military aid, finally helped turn the course of the war. Stalin, who had, in large part, prepared the ground for early Soviet setbacks, received much of the subsequent personal acclaim.

The post-war years saw no relief for the Soviet people. Sacrifice was still the order of the day. Repression in all spheres of life intensified – estimates of the total number of victims of Stalin's purges, policies and persecutions run as high as 17,000,000. The Cold War was functional for Stalin in so far as it provided the necessary justification for his harsh internal policies and his personal power. He died on 5 March 1953, revered, feared, but not loved; the USSR a world power, but clearly at variance with the socialist ideal.

Further reading

See: Boris Souvarine, *Stalin: A Critical Study of Bolshevism* (1939); Leon Trotsky, *Stalin: An Appraisal of the Man and His Influence* (2nd edn, 1946); Isaac Deutscher, *Stalin: A Political Biography* (2nd edn, 1966); Robert Conquest, *The Great Terror* (1968); Leonard Schapiro, *The Communist Party of the Soviet Union* (2nd edn, 1970); Robert Conquest, *Stalin: Breaker of Nations* (1991); Robert Service, *Stalin* (2004).

MICHAEL COX

STANISLAVSKY, Konstantin (Konstantin Sergeyevich ALEXEYEV)

1863–1938

Russian theatre director and actor

Stanislavsky was the stage-name of the son of a wealthy Moscow industrialist. He was, from an early age, fascinated by the theatre, and although, upon completion of his formal education, he joined the family business, Stanislavsky devoted much of his energy to amateur acting and directing. In 1888 he founded the Society of Art and Literature. In 1897 he met Vladimir Nemirovich-Danchenko, a successful playwright and teacher, and found they shared a profound disillusion with the state of contemporary Russian theatre. Out of their meeting came the establishment, in 1898, of the Moscow Art Theatre. The 'realism' of this new company made it an immediate success, with major productions of **Gorky**, **Maeterlink**, Shakespeare and, most important of all, **Chekhov**. From 1906 they frequently toured abroad. Although taking much of the directing upon himself, Stanislavsky also continued his own career as a performer, becoming one of Russia's leading actors, and the consummate interpreter of Chekhov. But Stanislavsky himself became increasingly dissatisfied with his own performances, and in 1906 attempted, for the first time, an analysis of acting techniques. From this he developed, over a period of years, a system of training actors which became known as the 'Stanislavskyan Method'.

Following the October Revolution, Stanislavsky continued to live and work in the USSR, making a major tour of Western Europe and the United States in 1922–4. During the 1920s he came in for considerable criticism at home, where he was accused of catering for bourgeois tastes. But, although producing several revolutionary dramas, he refused to give in to pressure, and was, during the 1930s, welcomed into the fold of official 'socialist realism'. In fact, the situation developed in which the methods of the bourgeois Stanislavsky were supported in opposition to those of the Marxist **Bertolt Brecht**. Stanislavsky spent his last years writing, and died in the city of his birth.

The essence of Stanislavsky's system is a rejection of the 'theatrical' in favour of the 'creative'. He recognized that much acting, including his own, was merely imitative, a series of stage-tricks slavishly repeated. In the work of a great actor, on the other hand, he saw an 'inner-truth', a sincerity which made a performance a 'reality' both for the actor and his audience. He wrote that, 'Nothing should take place ... on the stage without having first gone through the filter of the artistic feeling for truth.' Acting, instead of being a conscious 'trick', should become a habit, a natural process. If someone 'acts' a role, rather than 'experiencing' it, his performance is a lie, and therefore, in Stanislavsky's terms, non-creative. He found that through total relaxation, attained by intensive physical and psychological exercises, it was possible to 'summon up' a performance at will, but always as a new experience, rather than a mechanical process. He called this the recreation of 'the life of the human spirit'.

It is a popular misconception that Stanislavsky's system demands that an actor be 'taken-over' by his part. On the contrary, it calls for a high degree of control, over voice, physical movement and the emotions. Stanislavsky often quoted the Italian actor Tommaso Salvini (1828–1916): 'An actor lives, weeps and laughs on the stage, and while weeping or laughing, he observes his laughter and tears.' It is impossible to overestimate the effect of Stanislavsky's ideas on the subsequent training of actors, especially in the United States, where Lee Strasberg, at the Actors Studio in New York, changed the whole face of American acting with his own idiosyncratic interpretation of 'the Method'.

Further reading

See: *My Life in Art* (1924, his only book to be published in the USSR during his lifetime); *An Actor Prepares* (1936); *Building a Character* (1949); and *Creating a Role* (1961). See also: David Magarshack, *Stanislavsky: A Life* (1950) and *Stanislavsky on the Art of the Stage* (1950); R. Williams, *Drama in Performance* (1954); S. Moore, *The Stanislavski System* (1965); Jean Benedetti, *Stanislavski: A Biography* (1988); Sharon M. Carnicke, *Stanislavsky in Focus* (1998).

PAUL NICHOLLS

STANLEY, Henry Morton

1841–1904

British/US journalist and explorer

When Henry Morton Stanley encountered **David Livingstone** on the shores of Lake Tanganyika in 1872 the age of African exploration's innocence was over. Stanley was the product of a new world, greedier, more pragmatic, less romantic than that from which Livingstone sprang. It was hard on Stanley that the more perfectly he embodied the new order and the more scrupulously he lived up to its standards, the more society felt it imperative that it should be seen to reject its creation.

By the time he met Livingstone, at the age of thirty, he had escaped from the Welsh workhouse in which he received what formal education he possessed, crossed the Atlantic as a deckhand, run a store in the backlands of Arkansas, fought for the Southern cause in the American Civil War, turned his coat to escape from a prisoner-of-war camp, served aboard several merchant ships and with the American navy, escaped death at the hands of Turkish bandits, and made himself the *New York Herald*'s ace reporter. His first assignment was to cover General Sherman's Peace Commission, whose function was to persuade Indians to go quietly to reservations, leaving the way free for the railroad, an exercise which foreshadowed much of Stanley's subsequent work in Africa. His second was to follow the British army to Abyssinia, where, giving early evidence of his administrative genius, he contrived to get his report of the fall of Magdala back to the *Herald* several days before even the Foreign Secretary had been informed it had taken place.

Stanley set about his African expeditions with ruthless efficiency. He did what he was asked, whether it was to contact Livingstone, locate the sources of the Nile, rescue Emin Pasha or lay the foundations of a Congo Free State. He was extravagant with money and, more seriously, with men, but he always got results. Over and over again he was to be naively surprised at the unpopularity he won for doing what he thought was wanted.

His finding of Livingstone made him a celebrity, but there was unspoken feeling in English scientific and aristocratic circles that in making the saintly doctor the subject of a sensational newspaper story he had defiled the whole high-minded business of African exploration and missionary work. He was even accused of forging the letters he brought back from Livingstone.

When, five years later, he returned from the astonishingly successful voyage of discovery during which he finally sorted out, in truly horrific conditions, the whole question of the sources of the Nile and Congo and followed the latter right across Africa, he was met again with apathy. He called the Western nations to establish commerce, Christianity and civilization in the vast area he had opened up. The statesmen of Europe were embarrassed by his blunt invitation to colonize. From 1880 he served King Leopold of the Belgians in the Congo but his ostensible employer was the Association Internationale Africaine, a philanthropic front for Belgium's imperial ambitions. Between 1880 and 1884 he established a chain of trading stations in the inhospitable jungle. His ability to get roads built through unpromising terrain earned him the name Bula Matari, the Breaker of Rocks. He negotiated 450 separate treaties with tribal chiefs, thus making possible the creation of a unified Congo Free State. It was an astonishing achievement, but Leopold was as unappreciative as posterity, which still remembers Stanley chiefly for the pomposity with which he greeted Livingstone.

In 1887 Stanley led a mission to rescue Emin Pasha, a German-born Muslim who, as one of General Gordon's lieutenants, had been cut off in equatorial Africa after the fall of Khartoum. The journey was successful but traumatic. Stanley returned, for once, to an enthusiastic welcome. But the rapture wore off once the cost of the expedition had been counted. Stanley was a tough leader. To maintain discipline he once hanged two of his porters. When he encountered hostile tribes he bought them off where he could and where he could not he fought his way through their territory. In 1875, in a brutal and foolish act of vengeance, he fired on the inhabitants of Bumbiri, an island in Lake Victoria. His record with his own men was poor. Of the 356 men who accompanied him on his first Congo expedition 241 were to die en route, including all three of his white companions. For Emin Pasha's rescue he divided his party into two. He led the advance party, of whom 173 out of 384 reached Lake Albert. When, having contacted Emin, he returned to discover the fate of the rear column he found only 60 out of 271 left alive.

Men who ventured into uncharted jungle with the inadequate medicines of the time were exposing themselves to grave physical risk. Those who attempted to settle an already inhabited land would eventually fall foul of the natives. Geographical expeditions involving several hundred people, the majority of whom felt no personal loyalty to their leader or ideological commitment to his aims, could only be kept moving by dint of stern discipline. These unpalatable truths distressed Victorian Britain.

After the Berlin Conference of 1884 Britain, France, Germany, Belgium and Holland set about dividing up Africa, but the imperialists liked to have as their predecessors martyrs and chivalric warriors. Stanley, the shy and often boorish boy from the workhouse, who once embarrassed Leopold by openly admitting that the French and Belgians, ostensibly joint benefactors of the Africans, were in competition in the Congo basin, antagonized the colonial masters by showing them the truth about themselves. After a short and undistinguished career as an MP he retired from public life. His last wish, to be buried in Westminster Abbey next to Livingstone, was not granted.

Further reading

See: *How I Found Livingstone* (1872); *The Autobiography of Sir Henry Morton Stanley*, ed. D. Stanley (1909); R. Hall, *Stanley: An Adventurer Explored* (1974); John Bierman, *Dark Safari: The Life Behind the Legend of Henry Morton Stanley* (1990); Frank McLynn and Charles Whiting, *Stanley: The Making of an African Explorer* (2001)

LUCY HUGHES-HALLETT

STANTON, Elizabeth Cady

1815–1902
US feminist

The woman honoured as the principal thinker of nineteenth-century feminism should properly be the woman who took the word 'obey' out of her own marriage service in 1840 and asked her correspondents to address her mail to her in her own name by 1848 rather than to 'Mrs Henry B. Stanton' and thus obscure her identity in that of her husband. Elizabeth Cady Stanton's intelligence and theoretical far-sightedness combined with the activism she and her partner in the women's rights struggle in America, **Susan B. Anthony**, shared to give justly the two of them credit as the central co-founders of American feminism.

Stanton's personality was gracious and relaxed, warm and endearing; Anthony's was resolute and driving. Stanton was beautiful; Anthony was plain. Anthony was a splendid organizer; Stanton a better theorist and rhetorician. Stanton was an anxious public speaker; Anthony quick on her feet with words. Anthony was single; Stanton, married and the mother of seven children. After their fateful meeting in 1851, they formed one of the best fitting and mutually beneficial political partnerships and friendships in American history. In their lifetimes Stanton was more popular than Anthony, though Anthony has subsequently been given more credit for the work towards which each made her contribution.

Stanton was born in Johnstown, New York, to Margaret Livingston Cady and Daniel Cady. Daniel Cady was a successful lawyer, legislator and eventually a New York supreme court judge. Elizabeth's childhood biography yields three crucial shaping events for her feminist future. She was distressed as a child around her father's law offices when she saw examples of the deprivation of women under the law of their property and their children. At the time of her only brother's death, when she was eleven years old, her father said to her in his grief, 'Oh, my daughter, I wish you were a boy!' She resolved to prove to him that a daughter was just as valuable, a resolve that she was to make abundantly clear to the world and future generations, but there is no evidence her father (or her husband) learned this from her. She was also restrained as a child by her family's Calvinistic Presbyterian religion, a restraint against which she made radical rebellion years later.

In 1840 she married Henry Stanton, a well-known abolitionist ten years older than she. They left at once from their wedding for London where Henry was to be a delegate to the World's Anti-Slavery Convention. At that convention, there was a protest about the refusal to seat women delegates and Elizabeth joined the dissent and spent many hours with the Philadelphia Quaker minister, Lucretia Mott, with whom she vowed to hold a women's rights convention when they returned to America.

Between 1840 and 1848, the Stantons lived in Johnstown where Henry studied law with Elizabeth's father and Elizabeth had the first of their children. They then moved to Boston and had a lively life among Boston's liberals where Elizabeth was active in pressing legislators for a married women's property bill. Then they moved to Seneca Falls in western New York where Henry was to practise law. Small Seneca Falls was dull compared to Boston, and Elizabeth resented the restrictions of her five children and household responsibility. In 1848 Lucretia Mott visited the locality, and the two women, joined by Jane Hunt, Mary McClintock and Martha C. Wright, called the first women's rights convention to be held in America. The Seneca Falls Convention of 1848 was held in the Wesleyan Chapel and was presided over by Mott's husband, James Mott (Henry Stanton was out of town, probably deliberately). Elizabeth presented the women's 'Declaration of Sentiments', a document of profound historic importance.

The 'Declaration of Sentiments' was patterned after the American Declaration of Independence. Insisting that 'men and women are created equal', the declaration decried legal, moral and educational neglect and abuse of women and called for the vote for women the first time in a public proclamation in America. It was a rallying document for women for decades.

The Seneca Falls Convention, the long campaign for women's rights and woman suffrage, its documentation in the first three of the six-volume *History of Woman Suffrage* (1882, 1882, 1886) and *The Woman's Bible* were Elizabeth Cady Stanton's dominant contributions to history. The suffrage campaign she shared particularly with Susan B. Anthony.

The two women set up women's rights conventions together, travelled to make speeches together, wrote and organized petitions together, established the newspaper the *Revolution* in 1868 and ran it for a year and a half, and organized the National Woman Suffrage Association in 1869 over which Stanton presided for twenty-one years. Suffrage was their overriding theme. Though they had other goals, they did believe at times that the gaining of the vote would be the completion of women's equal rights with men. Anthony believed this more than Stanton, writing to Stanton on her last birthday in 1902:

We little believed when we began this contest, optimistic with the hope and buoyancy of youth, that half a century later we would be compelled to leave the finish of the battle to another generation of women. But our hearts are filled with joy to know that they enter upon this task equipped with a college education, business experience, the right to speak in public – all of which were denied to women fifty years ago. They have practically all but one point to gain – the suffrage: we had all.

Stanton's open-mindedness increased and she became more radicalized as she grew older. While her children were young, she clearly resented the care they took, though she grew mellow about joyful motherhood in her elder years. She wrote with great pride about the naturalness of her own physical child-bearing and wrote advocating healthy child-bearing in a natural way in her later life, as well as recommending general good health for women that included wearing sensible clothing and doing exercise such as bicycling.

She and her husband were never close, he not being supportive of her work, but they remained together throughout his life. Still, she was impassioned in her arguments for the right to divorce for women, suggesting something from her own experience fed the intensity of her arguments. Her radicalism was most evident in a late project of her life, undertaken in 1895, *The Woman's Bible*, an interpretation of Scripture and religious thought that she and some other women published. The aftermath of its publication was an enormous controversy, and she lost some of her popularity in the women's movement as well as in the public at that time.

In 1898, her husband having been dead twelve years, she published her memoirs, *Eighty Years and More*. She died four years before Susan B. Anthony and eighteen years before the passage of the woman's suffrage amendment to the American Constitution.

Further reading

See: *Elizabeth Cady Stanton as Revealed in Her Letters, Diary, and Reminiscences*, ed. Theodore Stanton and Harriot Stanton Blatch (2 vols, 1922); Alma Lutz, *Created Equal: A Biography of Elizabeth Cady Stanton* (1940); Eleanor Flexner, *Century of Struggle* (1968); Alice S. Rossi (ed.) *The Feminist Papers* (1973); Paul and Mari Jo Buhle (eds) *The Concise History of Woman Suffrage* (1978); Lois W. Banner, *Elizabeth Cady Stanton: A Radical for Women's Rights* (1980); Zillah Eisenstein, *The Radical Future of Liberal Feminism* (1981); Geoffrey C. Ward and Ken Burns, *Not for Ourselves Alone: The Story of Elizabeth Cady Stanton and Susan B. Anthony* (1999); Judith Wellman, *Road to Seneca Falls: Elizabeth Cady Stanton and the First Woman's Rights* (2004).

GAYLE GRAHAM YATES

STEIN, Gertrude
1874–1946
US writer

Born in Allegheny, Pennsylvania, and brought up in Vienna, Paris and California, Gertrude Stein's background combined European culture with an interest in contemporary American theories of education. Later, while at Radcliffe College, she attended Harvard lectures and read psychology under **William James**. During a brief career as a medical student she studied brain anatomy at Johns Hopkins University, publishing two articles in *Psychological Review*, in 1896 and 1898.

She was first to recognize the aesthetic implications of James's pragmatism. Observation based upon inductively gathered data was to stimulate her interest in things being 'the same but different'. James taught her to exclude nothing in the search for evidence, but also to simplify by discerning patterns. After she became a writer she believed that her repetitious speech in 'word portraits' would reveal the 'bottom nature' of people.

By 1902 she felt that medicine was 'not interesting' and joined her brother Leo in Paris. They settled at 27 rue de Fleurus, which became a clearing house for modernism for nearly thirty years. Many friends, among them Sherwood Anderson and **Hemingway**, would also be writers in exile who, as she would put it in *transition* in 1928, found America very Victorian and, like one's parents' home, a comfortable place to grow up in but not a good place to work. The years between 1907 and 1910 (before Leo was replaced by Alice Toklas) were formative for Gertrude, who tended to sit silently while Leo held forth about aesthetics, **Freudian** psychoanalysis or his own painting. She was, however, busy observing people, thinking about language, pictures, the nature of time and being.

In 1905 at the Salon d'Automne Gertrude and Leo had bought Matisse's painting *Woman with a Hat*. Thereafter their controversial art collection grew, as did their group of friends, which included, besides **Matisse** himself, **Braque** and the young **Picasso**, who painted Gertrude's portrait in 1905–6. During sittings she composed parts of *The Making of Americans* (not published until 1925), a long 'history' in which she attempted to describe every known human type.

By 1914 she had accomplished what she considered to be a major literary innovation. Cubism, as developed between 1908 and 1912 by Braque and Picasso, inspired Stein's 'composition' of objects, not in space but in time. She abandoned the traditional chronological story sequence and instead incorporated her knowledge of James's philosophy with Cubist attitudes and with **Bergson's** notion of *durée*, denying the traditional view of an objective static world and re-creating it perceptually as a world in continuous flux. 'In composition,' she said, 'one thing is as important as another thing.'

Through analysis of dream life Freud had discovered the continuous present tense of the unconscious; Stein sought to elucidate the continuous present tense of conscious experience through art. In a 1934 lecture she stated: 'The business of art ... is to live in the actual present, that is the complete actual present, and to completely express that complete actual present.' The continuous present tense, in which the structure or compositional mode corresponds to the structure of dynamic events, was her attempt to suspend time within a narrative form by demonstrating all aspects of her subject, just as **Cézanne** and the Cubists presented the aspects of a mass from many perspectives at once in their paintings. During many experiments between 1903 (in *Q.E.D.*, later published as *Things as They Are*) and 1914 (in the prose 'still lifes' of *Tender Buttons*) Stein produced *Three Lives* (1909), of which the most important is 'Melanctha'. Here her theory of 'immediate history' and an interest in American syntax lead to her 'direct description'. She wanted to write 'the thing itself' and exploit values of words other than their accepted denotative meanings. 'A noun is the name of anything,

why after a thing is named write about it?' she said in 'Poetry and Grammar', another lecture. In her efforts to join art to life she also sought a distinction between cause and effect. As she wrote of herself in *The Autobiography of Alice B. Toklas* (in fact a self-study, told 'through' Miss Toklas, who had become Gertrude's companion), 'She knows that beauty, music, decoration, the result of emotion should never be the cause ... of emotion ... They should consist of an exact reproduction of either an outer or an inner reality.'

When she was fifty-six, Stein decided that she and Miss Toklas must become publishers. *Lucy Church Amiably* (1930) initiated Plain Editions. A good example of her 'landscapes', almost nothing happens in this novel 'that looks like an engraving' and reproduced her delight in the countryside near her home at Belignin. Other Plain Editions included *How to Write* (1931), and the prose portraits *Matisse, Picasso and Gertrude Stein* (1933). But it was not until the publication of *The Autobiography of Alice B. Toklas* that she gained some of *la gloire* and the sales she craved. Following a successful lecture tour in America, Bennett Cerf of Random House offered to take over all the unsold Plain Editions stock and publish one book of Gertrude Stein's a year. Her reputation was further enhanced by the successful production of her friend Virgil Thomson's opera *Four Saints in Three Acts*, in 1934, for which Stein had written the libretto in 1927. The performance, in Hartford, Connecticut, was followed by a second American lecture tour. But the triumph was shortlived. In 1935 *transition* – whose editor Eugene Jolas had valued Stein, along with her innovative opposite **James Joyce**, as the symbolic figure of his 'Revolution of the Word' – issued *The Testimony Against Gertrude Stein*, in refutation of *The Autobiography*. Its contributors, who included many of her former friends, said that she had no understanding of the times. Thus Braque claimed she misunderstood Cubism, seeing it 'in terms of personalities'; Matisse that she represented the epoch without taste and without relation to reality; **Tristan Tzara** that she was a megalomaniac.

Since then Stein's work has evinced more ridicule and antagonism than appreciation. Many critics cannot accept her gargantuan egotism ('Think of the Bible and Homer, think of Shakespeare and think of me') which blinds them to her moral and physical courage, particularly during the two world wars. Her frequently tedious repetition and apparent naivety often discourage perception of her ability to integrate subject and technique. The search for 'meaning' prevents many readers from experiencing Gertrude Stein's real contribution to Modernist literature: her concern to reveal all reality through the sounds and rhythms of language and her joyful immersion in the present.

Further reading

Other works include: *Portrait of Mabel Dodge* (1912); *Geography and Plays* (1922); *A Book Concluding with As a Wife Has a Cow* (1926); *Lectures in America* (1935); *Paris France* (1940); *What Are Masterpieces?* (1940); *Brewsie and Willie* (1946). See also: Robert Bartlett Haas (ed.) *A Primer for the Gradual Understanding of Gertrude Stein* (3 vols, 1971–4). About Stein: Elizabeth Sprigge, *Gertrude Stein: Her Life and Works* (1957); Robert Bridgman, *Gertrude Stein in Pieces* (1970); Janet Hobhouse, *Everybody Who Was Anybody* (1975); Bruce Kellner (ed.) *A Gertrude Stein Companion* (1988); Brenda Wineapple, *Sister Brother: Gertrude and Leo Stein* (1996); Cameron Northouse, *The Critical Response to Gertrude Stein* (2000); Dana Cairns Watson, *Gertrude Stein and the Essence of What Happens* (2004); Sarah Bay-Cheng, *Mama Dada: Gertrude Stein's Avant-garde Theater* (2004).

ALISON ARMSTRONG

STEINBECK, John Ernst

1902–68

US novelist

John Steinbeck has always been popular with both European and American readers. As a serious novelist, however, he seems to have been more highly regarded outside his own country. Whereas the French included him in their honourable roll of '*les cinq grands*' modern American novelists, it is almost *de rigueur* for American critics to dismiss his achievement with some such adjective as 'sentimental' or 'primitive'. It is true that there is more than a streak of sentimentality in Steinbeck, and that his work, in general, showed a falling-off after *The Grapes of Wrath* (1939). He wrote some good things after that, however, and the sharpness of American critical comment makes one suspect an animus which has more to do with the sociology of his novels than with their literary merit.

There is a tendency, in other words, to criticize Steinbeck's treatment of social issues for being oversimplified and his characters for being grotesques. On both counts, the allegations are not without some justification. It is doubtful, however, whether it is valid criticism of a novel to say that *paisanos* never in real life lived like the characters of *Tortilla Flat* (1935), nor Oklahoma dirt-farmers like the Joads. The criterion is surely whether, given the terms within which he is working, the novelist's work as a whole has life and substance, and presents a convincing picture of human existence.

Steinbeck's best work – which is probably to be found in his short stories – does carry this kind of conviction. *The Red Pony* (1949) has that peculiar mixture of sympathy and savagery, an awareness of life's fundamentals, which all Steinbeck's best work has. When he attempts the larger canvas, however, his vision tends to become warped by the very sympathy which makes his shorter work so satisfying. This is true of *In Dubious Battle* (1936) and *The Grapes of Wrath* where fierce loyalties forced him nearer to propaganda than is healthy for a novelist. In quite another type of novel, *Of Mice and Men* (1937), not only the type of character chosen but also the manner in which the (simple-minded) protagonist is treated is more simple (and sentimental) than the highest standards require. Similarly, the near-whimsicality of *Tortilla Flat* turns into the gamey indulgence of *Cannery Row* (1945), without touching that norm of human conduct which, if Steinbeck only knew it, was his *forte*. Yet another attempt, *East of Eden* (1952) was too large, too rambling and too melodramatic for success, although, as one is always forced to recognize with Steinbeck's work, it is full of excellent things.

The quality of the *farouche* in Steinbeck spills over into his writings. Unlike **Hemingway**, he cannot seem to keep it in check for the sake of artistic perfection. Technically, there is some similarity between the two writers. Both, by selecting the minutiae of a given situation, render its inner emotion through a series of apparently objective notations. So far as their pre-occupations are concerned, however, they seem to be working on different co-ordinates. Hemingway was always a conscious artist. Steinbeck comes near to achieving that kind of perfection only when, by a happy accident, his feeling for a simple human situation fuses with his talent for selecting significant detail. It is this quality which he so triumphantly achieves in *The Red Pony* and which could perhaps be called, after the French, 'poetic realism'. Here Steinbeck's 'primitivism' is subordinated to his humanity.

The so-called 'primitivism' of Steinbeck's view of life has been referred to his back-ground. Born in 1902 in Salinas, California, he knew at first hand both the richness of nature and the poverty of man in 'The Long Valley'. From 1919 to 1925 he went to Stanford University, supporting himself by working as a labourer and 'sampling' courses that interested him. In 1925 he worked his way to New York on a cattle boat, as others had worked their way to Europe. Having written pieces for university magazines, his purpose was to make his living as a writer. After a short time as a reporter, however, he went back to California, and worked at whatever jobs he could get while writing his early novels.

The first to appear was *Cup of Gold*, an account, in fictional form, of the life of the buccaneer, Sir Henry Morgan. His early stories, all based on a Californian valley, were published in 1932 under the title of *The Pastures of Heaven*, a title taken from the Spanish and chosen with some ironical intention. *To a God Unknown*, in the following year, foreshadowed that feeling for the land, its nature and its rhythms, which was to be so strong a motif in Steinbeck's later work. During the twenty-seven years from *Tortilla Flat* to the award of the Nobel Prize in 1962, Steinbeck was a highly controversial figure, never lacking courage to attack the problems of the moment nor to present the joys and tribulations of people about whom only an act of self-abnegation would force the average novelist to write.

Steinbeck was always fascinated by biology. One remembers the land-turtle crawling across the Western highway at the beginning of *The Grapes of Wrath* and the comment that this implies on the 'Okies' who are to make their pilgrimage to California. Men may or may not have souls, he seems to be saying; this is something which cannot be measured or tested. What one *can* perceive, however, is that they are as subject to natural laws as the animals. This biological interest in human existence no doubt accounts for whatever simplification of human motive critics have found in Steinbeck's work. Yet despite this he never, as a narrower author might, gives the impression of being clinical, precisely because of the love and care he has for the simple people about whom he writes. He has an unembarrassed ability to speak out. He does not try to be clever or sophisticated. At his best he strikes a note of affirmation and this, coupled with his talent for selective detail, makes some of his characters and scenes stay in the mind long after the precise details of the novel or story have faded. Whether or not that makes him a great novelist is another matter. What is indis-putable, however, is that he was a highly talented and serious one.

Further reading

See: E.W. Tedlock Jr and C.V. Wicker, *Steinbeck and His Critics: A Record of Twenty-Five Years* (1957); Peter Lisca, *The Wide World of John Steinbeck*

(1958); Warren French, *John Steinbeck* (1961); F.W. Watt, *Steinbeck* (1962); P. McCarthy, *John Steinbeck* (1980); John H. Timmerman, *John Steinbeck's Fiction* (1986); Jay Parini, *John Steinbeck* (1994); John Steinbeck IV and Nancy Steinbeck, *The Other Side of Eden: Life with John Steinbeck* (2000).

GEOFFREY MOORE

STELLA, Frank Philip
1936–
US painter

Born in Malden, Massachusetts, Stella attended Phillips Academy, Andover, where he studied under Patrick Morgan and met **Carl Andre** and Hollis Frampton. In 1954 he entered Princeton, where he was taught by William Seitz and Stephen Greene. Fellow students were Walter Darby Bannard and Michael Fried. After leaving Princeton Stella worked as a house painter before beginning his Black series. In these his great influence was **Jasper Johns**, whose one-man exhibition at the Castelli Gallery Stella saw in 1958. 'The thing that struck me,' he said, 'was the way he stuck to the motif.' In this, his first major series of twenty-three paintings (Winter 1958–February 1960), he opted for neutral stability rather than emotional flux. Using dollar-a-gallon commercial black enamel he painted even, unruled symmetrical 'stripes' which followed the shape of the canvas and left 'pinstripes' of white showing between them. In a lecture at the Pratt Institute in 1960 Stella spoke of finding a new solution to problems of balancing the parts in a painting. Lean, sombre, hypnotic, his Black series adapted the all-over technique of **Pollock**. Abstract Expressionism had foundered in the late 1950s. The shift in sensibility effected by Stella – paralleled in sculpture by Andre and **Donald Judd** and in film by Hollis Frampton – was towards symmetry, reticence and iconicity. In the Black paintings, as Stella himself explained, he 'forced illusionistic space out of the painting at a constant rate of using a regulation pattern'. In the Aluminum series which followed Stella found a radical

solution to the problem of space 'left over' between the modular bands; the space was simply cut away, following a suggestion of Darby Bannard.

Stella was investigating the viability of shape, in Michael Fried's phrase. In his *Three American Painters* catalogue of 1966 Fried continued, 'I mean its power to hold, to stamp itself out, and IN – as verisimilitude and narrative and symbolism used to impress themselves – compelling conviction. Stella's undertaking in these paintings is therapeutic: to restore shape to health.' Fried, like other formalist critics of the time, was quick to take up Stella's cause, using as an appropriate critical tool a dogmatically applied version of Clement Greenberg's argument that modernist painting would thrive only by purification and separation from the other arts. That purification and separation, he believed, would only take place when painting acknowledged its limitations. That a canvas *was* a flat canvas, sculpted into a given shape, that that shape could interact with the shapes depicted within the canvas ... Stella's approach seemed a proper, logical, even dutiful extension of Greenberg. One of his triumphs as an artist, however, has been to outpace his critics, to provide them with the unexpected and, like any great artist, to renew criticism and adumbrate new critical forms by means of his work. Operating in series, Stella has explored squares, mazes and concentricity, perimeters and polygons and notched Vs. The series are carefully named and defined in William Rubin's monograph.

In 1966 Stella's progress was complicated by the introduction of irregular configurations. From now on his path would parallel that of Ellsworth Kelly and Kenneth Noland, and the main issue of his painting would be the juxtaposition of uninflected areas of colour. With the Protractor series in 1967, Stella returned to scholarly interests from his Princeton days – Arabic design and Hiberno–Saxon illustration. In these huge, almost architectural, paintings the eye is sent hurrying around curved contours in such a joyous, even luxurious way that it is impossible to ignore the strong emotional impact of Stella's art, which formalist critics seemed intent on forgetting. With the *Polish Village* series (1970–3) painted wooden reliefs were notched and superimposed, while the *Brazilian* series (1974–5) was made in aluminium and steel. The *Exotic Bird* series which began in 1976 took the scribbly application of colour and the buffing effects a stage further, fixing 'found' shapes like drawing curves over the loose surface. Loose, relaxed, humorous, they signalled another departure in a distinguished, self-conscious career, both inside and outside the avant-garde.

In the final decades of the century, Stella increasingly undertook public commissions, providing architecture as well as art works for Miami, New York and, especially, other American cities.

Further reading

See: William Rubin, *Frank Stella* (New York, Museum of Modern Art, 1970); Brenda Richardson, *Frank Stella: The Black Paintings* (Baltimore Museum of Art, 1976); Philip Leider, *Stella since 1970* (Fort Worth Art Museum, 1978); J. Golding, 'Frank Stella's Working Space', in *Visions of the Modern* (1994).

STUART MORGAN

STEVENS, Wallace

1879–1955

US poet

Now ranked with **Eliot**, **Pound** and **W.B. Yeats** as one of the outstanding English language poets of the twentieth century, it is only since his death that Wallace Stevens's technical mastery and seriousness have gradually assured him a reputation. There were perhaps two main reasons for this: first, his peculiar difficulty, arising from a conjunction of simple declarative grammar with extreme allusiveness of style; and, second, the unfashionableness of his poetic manner. In an age which demanded the bareness of later Yeats and the acerbity of early Eliot, Stevens's highly polished surfaces were impenetrable to all but the most persevering of readers. In particular some critics claimed that his poetry lacked 'the urgency of human passion'. However, just as over the years most readers of poetry have grown familiar with Eliot's elliptical style, his personal references and highly subjective choice of literary allusions, so they have acclimatized themselves to Stevens. He is, in some respects, indeed easier for the 'unliterary' person – that ideal intelligent reader for whom even Eliot craved – since his difficulties are intrinsic and do not depend on reference to a body of literature which may or may not be known. Stevens's chief fault is a tendency towards whimsicality and aestheticism, but he is no more a mere player with words than Eliot is a mere paster-together of quotations. A meditative poet of the highest order, Stevens masked his seriousness with flippancy and bravura – mannerisms that were part of his literary *persona*.

Stevens was born in Reading, Pennsylvania, the son of Garret Barckalow Stevens and Mary Catherine Zeller Stevens. The Zeller family was Dutch and, according to Stevens's own account, went to America for religious reasons. After studying law at Harvard, where he was attracted to the teaching of **Santayana**, Stevens attended the New York University Law School. During the period between 1904, when he was admitted to the Bar, and 1916, when he became a member of the Hartford Accident and Indemnity Company, he practised both law and poetry in New York. He was associated with a Greenwich Village group of whom the leader was Alfred Kreymborg, and his poems were published in small magazines, among them Harriet Monroe's *Poetry*. It was not until he was forty-four that *Harmonium*, his first book, appeared. A second edition, revised and enlarged, was published in 1931, followed in 1935 by *Ideas of Order*. *Owl's Clover*, which he excluded from his *Collected Poems* (1954), came out in 1936, and was followed by *The Man with the Blue Guitar* (1937), *Parts of a World* and *Notes Toward a Supreme Fiction* (both 1942). *Esthétique du Mal* (1945), *Transport to Summer* (1947), *A Primitive Like an Orb* (1948), *Auroras of Autumn* (1950) complete the poetic canon, although since his death in 1955 Samuel French Morse has published plays and poems, either unprinted in book form or allowed to go out of print, in *Opus Posthumous* (1957). This book also contains Stevens's aphoristic 'Adagia' and other prose complementary to *The Necessary Angel: Essays on Reality and the Imagination* (1951).

A corporation lawyer in Hartford for nearly forty years of his life, Stevens negotiated the world of business with that mixture of diffidence and authority which is also part of the success of his poems. Behind what at first sight might seem like a charming example of Connecticut rococo, there stands the solidity of a Dutch barn, a toughness of mind scarcely equalled among poets of our time.

The surely savoured ambivalence of his situation reveals itself in the title of his first book. And the titles of the poems: 'Le Monocle de Mon Oncle', 'The Paltry Nude Starts on a Spring Voyage', 'The Worms at Heaven's Gate', 'Tea at the Palaz of Hoon' – what are we to make of them? Some have acute, if oblique, relevance; others are comments on the irony of the human situation as Stevens saw it. Stevens's poetic manner varies from the extravagant rhetoric of 'The Comedian as the Letter C' to the subtle sobriety of 'Esthétique du Mal'. Two main themes run through the bulk of his poetry: first, the matter of belief in the modern world, and second, the philosophical problem of appearance and reality. The 'belief poems' are central. From 'Sunday Morning' to 'Notes Toward a Supreme Fiction', Stevens was engaged by the problem of the religious man in a world whose religion he cannot accept. The woman in 'Sunday Morning' asks why she should 'give her bounty to the dead'. She feels that the things of this world are all that we know, in contrast to the myths of an afterlife which men in their hunger have fabricated for themselves. And yet, even despite her acceptance that 'divinity' must

live within herself, she still feels the need for some 'imperishable bliss'. The answer that Stevens gives is a stoical one: that 'Death is the mother of beauty'. The awful fact of death, the knowledge that it is really the end of existence, and that there is nothing beyond, enables us to savour the bittersweetness of the human situation. Stevens mocks the vision of paradise which we have created after our own image. There was a man called Jesus, but his tomb is no 'porch of spirits', only a grave. We are alone on this earth. No benign spirit watches over us. We have the world in our time, and that should be enough.

But it is not enough. If the reasoner is religious by nature, as Stevens was, age and maturity will yearly increase the necessity for belief in someone or something greater than man. Stevens found it in poetry, the 'supreme fiction'. As he said in a memorandum to Henry Church in 1940:

> The major poetic idea in the work is and always has been the idea of God. One of the visible movements of the modern imagination is the movement away from the idea of God. The poetry that created the idea of God will either adapt it to our different intelligence, or create a substitute for it, or make it unnecessary.

'Notes Toward a Supreme Fiction' deals with the basic philosophical and spiritual imperatives towards which Stevens had steadily been moving all his life. The imagination, in its attempt to abstract truth, brings up the idea of man, 'major man' – not the exceptional man, but the best in every man. Change, which we deplore as bringing death and destruction, is the source of vital freshness in life and its many forms. The flow of reality is that which brings us our moments of perfection, of happiness and love. The 'order' that Stevens seeks must be flexible, organic, partaking of the freshness of transformation. We must celebrate the world by a constant and amazed delight in the unexpectedness of each moment, a more difficult rigour than to follow ceremony in the form of traditional beliefs. This is the poet's way, and every man can be a poet, not necessarily by writing poems but by living with sensibility and wholeness.

'Notes Toward a Supreme Fiction' comprises an aggregate of ideas and feelings, expressed with such mutational amplitude, with such controlled jugglery of parenthetical impressions, that half a dozen lines of simultaneous commentary would be needed to do it justice. Yet, being supplied, they would, of course, do no justice at all, for it is the essence of Stevens's art that 'poetry is the subject of the poem' and that it 'must defeat the intelligence almost successfully'. Consistently, and with great courage, Stevens tackled what he saw to be the main problem of our time. Because he did it in poetry, and poetry which is very difficult, his art has not been sufficiently recognized. But by doing it this way, which was the only way he could – for he was a poet and not a philosopher – he could in a sense take his speculation further. His poetry begins where most other poetry leaves us, in a state of heightened awareness. Through the aesthetic experience he explored the possibility of a new epistemology, pushing the boundaries of poetic communication to a new limit. There is only one other modern American poet who is comparable with him in seriousness and range, and that is T.S. Eliot.

Further reading

See: Frank Kermode, *Wallace Stevens* 1960; Ashley Brown and Robert Haller, *The Achievement of Wallace Stevens* (1962); Marie Boroff, *Wallace Stevens, A Collection of Critical Essays* (1963); R.H. Pearce and J.H. Miller, *The Act of the Mind* (1965); Helen Vendler, *On Extended Wings* (1969); A. Walton Litz, *Introspective Voyager* (1972); Tony Sharpe, *Wallace Stevens: A Literary Life* (1999); Lee M. Jenkins, *Wallace Stevens: Rage for Order* (1999); Tim Morris, *Wallace Stevens: Poetry and Criticism* (2005).

GEOFFREY MOORE

STEVENSON, Robert Louis
(Robert Lewis Balfour STEVENSON)
1850–94
Scottish novelist, essayist, poet, dramatist and short-story writer

It is the fate of many artists to be remembered for the wrong reasons. Such is the case with Robert Louis Stevenson. Two of his novels – *Treasure Island* (1883) and *Kidnapped* (1886) – have been among the most widely read in the English language, and as a result Stevenson has come to be classed alongside Henty and Ballantyne as a writer of 'boys' stories'. It tends to be forgotten that his talents were highly praised by, among others, **Henry James**, and that Stevenson was considered, in his day, to be 'a man of letters'. Born in Edinburgh, he was the son of Margaret Balfour and Thomas Stevenson, and heir to a famous family of engineers. As a child Stevenson suffered from chest complaints, and during long periods of confinement developed a deep love for literature. At the age of fifteen he wrote an imaginative account of the Pentland Rising of 1666, which his father published privately. When illness allowed, Stevenson attended a number of schools, including Edinburgh Academy. He then entered Edinburgh University to read engineering but was an indifferent student, devoting his energies instead to writing. When he was twenty he told his father that he had no intention of becoming an engineer, and wished to be a writer. Thomas Stevenson reluctantly accepted the first point, but not the second; writing was not the profession of a gentleman, and he insisted that his son read law. This he did, but with no more application than he had previously studied engineering. Stevenson was called to the Bar in 1875, but was by then becoming estranged from his father.

Stevenson was a regular visitor to France, and in 1876, at Fontainebleau, he met Fanny Osbourne, an American eleven years older than himself who was separated from her husband. They fell in love, to the horror of his father, and in 1879 Stevenson followed her to America, arriving in California penniless and ill but with the material for several books. They married early in 1880, and their honeymoon formed the basis of *The Silverado Squatters* (1883). Following a letter from his father, Stevenson, his wife and two stepchildren returned to Scotland, where he was reconciled with his family.

Stevenson had by now developed tuberculosis, but in spite of this began work on *Treasure Island* in 1881. The following year he visited the Highlands, and wrote some of his finest short stories, including 'Thrawn Janet'. But he also experienced several lung haemorrhages, and was forced to move with Fanny to the south of France. They then set up residence in Bournemouth, where Stevenson wrote *Kidnapped* and *The Strange Case of Dr Jekyll and Mr Hyde* (1886). However, the British climate proved intolerable to him, and in 1887 he sailed with his family to America. In 1888 he chartered a ship for an excursion to the South Seas. Wandering from island to island, Stevenson became fascinated by the local inhabitants and their environment, and his books on the region are remarkable pieces of journalism. He finally settled with his wife on the island of Samoa, where he died, without warning, of a cerebral haemorrhage.

Stevenson applied his literary talents in a variety of ways. His essays, particularly those in *Virginibus Pueresque* (1881), are stylish, though rarely profound, and with a tendency towards melancholy. He privately published a number of plays, and his *Child's Garden of Verses* (1885) contains some of the finest poetry ever written specifically for young children. But it is undoubtedly as a novelist that Stevenson merits his place in literary history. He had an austere Calvinist upbringing, and this fact has been used to explain the moral ambiguity which pervades much of his fiction. It is certainly true that Predestination – the belief that all who have not been marked for Redemption at birth are eternally damned – held a fascination for him, and that several of his novels seem intent

on disproving the doctrine. In *Jekyll and Hyde* 'good' and 'evil' are revealed as facets of a single personality. Elsewhere, Stevenson refused automatically to couple heroic actions with conventional moral goodness. In *The Master of Ballantrae* (1889), the ruthless Master is nevertheless allowed a kind of heroism, while his unexceptional brother is shown to be morally degenerate under pressure. Perhaps the archetypal hero-villain is Long John Silver, the complex and charismatic central figure of *Treasure Island*. Squire Trelawny and his fellow treasure-hunters are presented by Stevenson as little better than Silver, and ultimately they survive more by luck than by virtue of any superior morality.

Stevenson was only forty-four when he died, and the novel left unfinished at his death would clearly have marked a turning-point in his career. *The Weir of Hermiston* (1895), although only a fragment, is Stevenson's finest achievement in the art of story-telling, at which he always excelled. Opposed to literary 'realism', he was nonetheless able to create a convincing world within each of his novels, through a concentration upon the development of character and action, against the background of a carefully observed landscape. *The Weir of Hermiston* is colourful and exciting, every word apparently chosen for a specific effect, and Stevenson utilizes Scottish dialect with consummate skill. Compared to the previous generation of English novelists, Stevenson's was a minor talent, perhaps. But academic snobbery continues to undervalue his work and its simple narrative form.

Further reading

Other works include: *An Inland Voyage* (1878); *Travels with a Donkey* (1879); *New Arabian Nights* (1882); *Prince Otto* (1885); *The Wrong Box* (1889; written with his stepson, Lloyd Osbourne); *Across the Plains* (1892); *Catriona* (1893; US title: *David Balfour*); *The Ebb-Tide* (1894); *St Ives* (1896; unfinished). The best biographies are: D. Daiches, *Robert Louis Stevenson* (1947); and J.C. Furnas, *Voyage to Windward* (1951). See also: D. Daiches,

Stevenson and the Art of Fiction (1951); Robert Louis Stevenson: The Critical Heritage, ed. Paul Maixner (1981); T. Hubbard, Seeking Mr Hyde: Studies in R.L. Stevenson, Symbolism, Myth and the Pre-Modern (1995).

PAUL NICHOLLS

STOCKHAUSEN, Karlheinz

1928–

German composer

It is not often that the trajectory of Western music, or any other art, has been decisively shaped by an orphaned farmhand. Yet that is exactly the situation in which the seventeen-year-old Karlheinz Stockhausen found himself at the end of the Second World War. Somehow, after a couple of years, he managed to enrol in a music education course at the conservatory (Musikhochschule) in Cologne. In August 1951 he went to the Summer Courses for New Music in Darmstadt, where he heard a recording of a radical, highly abstract new piano piece by **Olivier Messiaen**: Mode de valeurs et d'intensités. It was a classic epiphany: hearing this 'fantastic star-music' dispelled any residual post-war malaise: this was the path Stockhausen wanted to follow, and within a few months he was studying with Messiaen in Paris.

However, he didn't remain a 'follower' for long. Immediately after the Darmstadt experience, he had written Kreuzspiel ('Crossplay'), a piece whose rigorous numerical organization of every notated dimension – the pitches, length and loudness of notes, and even their timbre – made it, in retrospect, an early classic of so-called integral serialism. Such music constituted a conscious tabula rasa: it sought to sweep away everything that smacked of traditions (even the most recent ones) and start again from degree zero, but with a fanatical emphasis on the absolute conceptual unity of musical materials, and the need to recreate these materials 'uniquely' for each new work. When Stockhausen says that as a young composer he felt he had **Schoenberg** peering over one shoulder, and

Stravinsky over the other, this had nothing to do with style, but everything to do with standards. His responsibility to the past was to surge beyond it: like **Rilke's** angels, he would 'obey by overstepping'.

Did Stockhausen's orphan status, coupled with his unquestionable genius, leave him ideally placed to head up this tabula rasa? Maybe so: at any rate, after returning to Cologne in 1953, for at least the next decade Stockhausen set the tone for the European avant-garde. Each new work opened up new perspectives, not only for himself, but for all the young composers around him. Within the newly evolving world of electronic music, it was he who set the standard – not just technically, but aesthetically: works like Gesang der Jünglinge ('Song of the Youths', 1956) and Kontakte ('Contacts', 1960) were unrivalled then, and in many respects remain so half a century later. But it wasn't just a matter of electronics: in his instrumental music there was an exploration of everything from the utmost control – as in Gruppen ('Groups') for three orchestras (1957), where each orchestral group plays highly complex music in a different tempo – to works in which the interpreter can significantly shape not only momentary detail, but even the overall form.

This was a time of stark polarities: of instrumental music versus electronic music, pitch versus noise, and European structuralism versus the seemingly anarchic freedom espoused by **John Cage** and his 'New York School'. Here, Stockhausen's genius lay not least in his capacity to posit seeming contradictions as opposite ends of a continuum, and to create aesthetically astounding works (such as Kontakte) that moved effortlessly through this continuum. But by the start of the 1960s, fuelled by what the composer now, somewhat regretfully, calls 'utopian idealism', he was becoming increasingly fascinated by the idea of composition as a collaborative endeavour, to which he would contribute a structural framework and certain transformational processes, but leave their realization in 'real time' to his interpreters. A forerunner of this was *Plus Minus* (1963), a fascinating attempt – requiring careful realization – to formulate the creative act as a kind of genetic process where, in certain extreme situations, linear evolution leads to extinction or radical mutation.

In the short term this piece (which remains one of Stockhausen's most fascinating conceptions) was just too idealistic. In the following years there were three significant areas of exploration: one was live electronics, which brought sound transformations previously only available in the studio into the arena of live performance (the first examples are *Mixtur* and *Mikrophonie I*, both from 1964) and another was the expansion of new music's time scale to re-embrace works of epic proportions, such as *Hymnen* ('Anthems', 1967) and *Momente* (1965–72), both lasting a couple of hours. But perhaps the most striking and controversial strand in Stockhausen's work of the late 1960s was the series of 'process compositions' – for example *Prozession* (1967) and *Kurzwellen* ('Short-waves', 1968) – written for Stockhausen's own hand-picked ensemble, where the scores were reduced to sequences of signs indicating how virtually any musical materials could be spontaneously transformed. The question of authorship implicit here became even more acute in the 'intuitive music' of *Aus den sieben Tagen* ('From the Seven Days', 1968), which comprises texts with instructions such as 'Play a vibration in the rhythm of the universe'. A priori, this may seem frankly absurd, but as the studio recordings from Darmstadt in 1969 show, it could give rise to a unique form of music-making, unthinkable without Stockhausen's involvement.

Yet if Stockhausen's open-form explorations of the late 1960s were controversial, the about-face signalled by *Mantra* (1970) for two electronically modified pianos proved even more so. It wasn't just a matter of returning to a very exactly structured music in which the central material had an almost 'retro' thematic content, but also of emphasizing a spiritual content that had always been implicit in his work but that most commentators had chosen to overlook. After the 1973 Parisian premiere of *Inori* ('Adorations'), a 70-minute work for praying mime and orchestra, Maurice Fleuret wrote, 'In drawing close to his God, Stockhausen is withdrawing from us.' And at least in a broad sense, it was true. Not only was he acutely aware of the spiritual gap that separated him from most of his more **Marxist**-orientated composer-contemporaries, but he had lost interest in being the avant-garde's figurehead. He had his own path to pursue: a music which sought to pave the way for a higher consciousness not necessarily defined by terrestrial models.

It is extraordinary to see how rapidly, especially in the early 1970s, former idolization turned to vilification, especially in Germany. It's as if, after the failures of 1960s idealism, people needed someone to hate and mock. The 'resentment against new music' that **Theodor Adorno** had invoked long before in relation to Schoenberg and his school now focused on Stockhausen, even – and in fact, especially – from within the ranks of the avant-garde. Former adherents, few of whom had achieved even a fraction of what Stockhausen had achieved, lost no opportunity to turn on him.

It was in this antagonistic context that Stockhausen embarked on a project that inevitably conjured up the name of **Wagner**. In 1977 he announced that the next twenty-five years of his life would be devoted to the composition of seven operas entitled *LICHT – the Seven Days of the Week*, and in fact this is (fairly) exactly what happened: the cycle was completed in 2003. The outcome – almost thirty hours of music, bound together by a 'Super-formula' that defines both macro- and micro-form – is perhaps the most extraordinary project in the history of Western music. Not least because of its overtly sacred orientation, it was initially the subject of trenchant criticism. Yet now, increasingly, its sheer musical substance is forcing a re-evaluation. Moreover, as the bland relativism implicit in postmodernist theorizing comes to seem ever more 'anti-aesthetic', Stockhausen's highly distinctive work provides an increasingly compelling counter-force.

Having completed *LICHT* ('LIGHT'), Stockhausen embarked on a new cycle of works entitled *KLANG* ('Sound', from 2004). Here, the 'Super-formula' concept of the past twenty-five years has been swept aside. Even in his seventies, Stockhausen is constantly looking for new options.

Further reading

Other works include: *Zeitmaße* ('Time Measures', 1956) for wind quintet; *Carré* (1960) for four choirs and orchestra; *Trans* (1971) for orchestra; and *Sirius* (1975) for four soloists and electronic music. Stockhausen's own writings to 1991 are published in ten volumes of *Texte* ('Texts'). The main biography to date is Michael Kurtz, *Stockhausen: A Biography* (1992); the best English-language introduction to the music is Robin Maconie's somewhat idiosyncratic *The Works of Karlheinz Stockhausen* (2nd edn, 1990). Though over thirty years old, Jonathan Cott's book of interviews, *Stockhausen – Conversations with the Composer* (1973), can also be recommended. The Stockhausen entry in *The New Grove Dictionary of Music and Musicians* (2nd edn, 2001) includes a particularly comprehensive work list and bibliography.

RICHARD TOOP

STOPES, Marie Carmichael

1880–1958

Scottish pioneer of birth control clinics, palaeobotanist

Marie Stopes was born in Edinburgh to Charlotte Carmichael and Henry Stopes. Her mother was an enthusiast of the Rational Dress Society and the first woman in Scotland to take a university certificate. Her father was a brewer whose major interest in life was archaeology. Between them they taught their daughter nothing positive about human sexuality. Marie Stopes was to become one of the most famous women of her time as a result of her passionate belief that the human race would improve through the selective use of birth control.

After an inauspicious academic start with no formal education until twelve, Stopes won a science scholarship and at the age of nineteen enrolled in the science faculty at University College, London. After two years of study she won her degree in botany and geology and gained the Gilchrist Scholarship which took her to Munich to study the cellular structure of ovules and ova of cycad specimens. It was here that her long and platonic relationship with an assistant professor included her first kiss, which she described as 'quite horrid'. In Munich she won a doctorate after the university rules had been changed on her behalf. In 1904 she became the first woman on the scientific staff of Manchester University. She won a DSc in London in 1905, becoming the youngest Doctor of Science in Britain.

Stopes married a Canadian geneticist Dr R.R. Gates in 1911 and, still a virgin, left him in 1914. Since lawyers seemed unable to advise her on her marital plight, characteristically she undertook the task of reading all the books on sex in three languages in the British Museum. In 1917 the marriage was annulled on grounds of non-consummation.

Although her reputation as a fossil botanist was unrivalled it was unlikely that this would provide the fame of which she had dreamt since her earlier years. The path to fame was started by the publication in 1918 of her book *Married Love*. In this Stopes sought to tell the world what she had discovered from her hours in the British Museum – that it was possible to combine a happy marriage with perfect sexual experience at the same time as avoiding unwanted pregnancies. Stopes was at the time thirty-eight, a virgin and unmarried.

In 1918 she married H.V. Roe, a wealthy manufacturer and aviator. Her dream of establishing birth control clinics was cemented by his financial position. In 1920 she opened the Mothers' Clinic for Constructive Birth Control in Holloway – the first birth control clinic in the British Empire. She favoured the use of trained nurses in her clinic, feeling that women would respond to them more readily than to doctors.

There was intense rivalry and disagreement among the various pioneering birth control campaigners – a situation which increased in bitterness for the rest of Stopes's life. The Malthusian League was a major early rival. Their clinic in Walworth, south London, favoured the Dutch cap while Stopes invented her own cervical cap which she trade-marked the Pro-race cap.

As well as rivalries within the movement Stopes, editing her own periodical the *Birth Control News*, was constantly involved in and continued to arouse intense public and religious debate. As part of this, in 1922 she issued a writ for libel against a Dr Halliday Sutherland, who as a Catholic medical doctor contended that birth control education was nothing but a cruel experiment on the poor who were unable to resist. Sutherland's appeal went to the House of Lords, where he was supported by a vote of four to one. Fame together with public sympathy and admiration belonged to Stopes. The Catholic Church became her bitter enemy. The result of the happenings of all these years took their toll. Stopes became increasingly idiosyncratic and difficult to deal with. In 1924 she fulfilled another dream and gave birth to a much-wanted child, whose birth announcement *The Times* refused to print. Over the following years she continued her fight for birth control and applied herself increasingly to her literary interests by writing poetry, plays and more books. Despite her insistence that she would live to 120, one of the century's most extraordinary women died in 1958 alone and unloved.

Her dream of free contraceptive advice for all who ask has become a reality in Britain, as part of the care offered by the NHS. The clinic which she founded and ran until her death continues to operate.

Further reading

Other books include: *Ancient Plants* (1910); *Love Letters of a Japanese* (1911); *Wise Parenthood* (1918); *A Letter to Working Mothers; On How to Have Healthy Children and Avoid Weakening Pregnancies* (1919); *Radiant Motherhood* (1920); *The First Five Thousand* (1925); *Mother England* (1929); *Love Songs for Young Lovers* (1939); *Joy and Verity* (1952). See also: H.V. Stopes-Roe, with Ian Scott, *Marie Stopes and Birth Control* (1974); R. Hall, *Marie Stopes* (1977); June Rose, *Marie Stopes and the Sexual Revolution* (1993).

JANICE BUMSTEAD

STOPPARD, (Sir) Tom

1937–

British playwright

Tom Stoppard was a theatre critic before he was a dramatist, and it may have been this experience of watching things from out front that led him to declare, at a fairly early stage in his second career, that the audience owes the playwright absolutely *nothing*. He also said, equally sensibly, that the theatre ought to be in the hands of people who understand show business. This is also a playwright who has said that he would rather have written *The House at Pooh Corner* than the complete works of Bertolt **Brecht**, and who counts among his formative influences the memory of a line from *The Goon Show*: 'And then the monsoons came. And they couldn't have come at a worse time, right in the middle of the rainy season.' This is a playwright to love.

He has confessed to being driven by a consuming fear of being boring. To avoid this he has often filled his plays with contrasting elements: at one moment, metaphysical discussion, at another song-and-dance. Two of his major early plays, *Jumpers* (1972) and *Travesties* (1974), end with popular tunes ('Sentimental Journey' and 'My Blue Heaven' respectively) and their success may well have something to do with the fact that they sent their audiences home humming. Other playwrights have attempted to use music in the same way, but their efforts have usually come across as forced and programmatic. With Stoppard they seem spontaneous outgrowths of the exuberant dialogue and construction, which in turn are an expression of the writer's humanity. Other playwrights may treat of the human condition, social or metaphysical, with more obvious earnestness. He is almost alone in making the audience feel, through the actual texture of his work, that the condition is really worth bothering about – or, in plainer terms, that life might actually be worth living.

Stoppard used to divide his plays, in interviews, into 'nuts-and-bolts comedies' and seriously intended works. But this is misleading; the differences are more of scale than of kind. The obsessively neat patterning and verbal leap-frogging of *The Real Inspector Hound* (1968) parallel those in *Rosencrantz and Guildenstern are Dead* (1967 – the play that established him), *Jumpers* and *Travesties*. The long-running farce *Dirty Linen* (1976) may be slight but it deals with personal responsibility in public situations, as do the overtly political *Professional Foul* (television, 1976), *Every Good Boy Deserves Favour* (music by André Previn, 1977) and *Night and Day* (1978).

EGBDF deals with the persecution of dissidents in Soviet Russia, *Professional Foul* with state terror in Stoppard's native Czechoslovakia (which he left at the age of two). These plays prompted their first critics to welcome (or deplore) Stoppard's increasing 'seriousness'. But there is nothing in them that could not have been foreseen from *Jumpers,* the best comedy written in English since 1945. The play, which of all his work best achieves his stated aim of effecting a perfect marriage between play-of-ideas and madcap farce, is among other things a protest against intellectual bullying; and the introduction of a pugnacious (and electorally victorious) Radical-Liberal Party, represented on stage by a trendy and omnicompetent University Vice-Chancellor, is a clear indication of the ease with which this can extend to physical bullying. The nicest (though still dangerously self-absorbed) character on stage is the Professor of Ethics, trying to justify his belief in a moral force which he chooses, rather to his own embarrassment, to call God. In declaring that morality goes deeper than politics, and crucially influences it, Stoppard wrote a political play that made most others of the species look dangerously naive. *Travesties*, formally less satisfying, takes the argument a step further by examining the motives that make men into politicians, or for that matter artists: to each his own ego-trip. The play lines up **Joyce**, **Lenin**, the **Dadaist Tristan Tzara**; if the author's sympathies are obviously with the first, the artist, rather than with the two disparate (and highly plausible) philistines, this rarely upsets the comic balance.

Presiding over the whole, remembering it and usually getting it wrong, is the minor consular official Henry Carr, one of Stoppard's immortal onlooker figures (like Rosencrantz, Guildenstern, George of *Jumpers*, the theatre critics of *Inspector Hound* and the timid Moon of the 1966 novel *Lord Malquist and Mr Moon*). These culminate perhaps in the suaver academic philosopher of *Professional Foul* who is finally – perhaps marking a decisive breakthrough in Stoppard's work – nudged into action. He takes it by making exquisite and scrupulous use of the enemy's moral weapons, showing that Stoppard's symmetrical sense, of which an outward sign is his passion for puns, was as safe and as satisfying as ever.

The same critics who saluted Stoppard's new-found 'seriousness' also hailed the comparative naturalism of *Night and Day*, whose preoccupations included journalism and adultery. *The Real Thing* (1982) offered further comfort to those who wanted him to write the same kind of plays as everybody else, while dismaying those who would have preferred him to go on being himself. A fine revival in 1999, with far greater sexual presence, reassured both sides, revealing that he had in fact written a witty, painful and very personal play about love.

He seems to have dropped the distinction between serious plays and nuts-and-bolts assignments; his later works divide more into originals and adaptations. The latter category has been the likelier to release the funster in him, as in *On the Razzle* (1981, after Nestroy), in which virtually every line is a joke, and *Rough Crossing* (1984, after Molnar), which has a hilarious first act and a second which loses its audience by trying to make them follow a purposely incomprehensible plot. Curiously, he makes much the same mistake in the original and far more ambitious *Hapgood* (1988) which alienates its audience not with its discussion of quantum physics but with its hopelessly frustrating spy-story.

Among the adaptations must be included his many filmscripts including the excellent *The Russia House* (1990, from **John Le Carré**) and maybe the Oscar-winning *Shakespeare in Love* (1998) which seems to be a re-working of a script by Marc Norman (the two share credit) but which bears Stoppard's mark in almost every line. At any rate, it's an enchanting picture, crammed with characteristically telling anachronisms ('Their business is show,' cries a Puritan preacher, before being swept with the crowd into the first performance of *Romeo and Juliet*) and intoxicating as a love-letter to the theatre, whose 'natural condition' is definitively characterized as 'one of unsurmountable obstacles on the road to imminent disaster . . . strangely enough it all turns out well'.

Back in the real theatre Stoppard reached mature twin peaks with *Arcadia* (1993) and *The Invention of Love* (1997). The former, juxtaposing nineteenth-century with modern action in the same country-house room, may be his most seamless structural achievement, both formally and intellectually; the latter may be his most moving, culminating in the cry of **A.E. Housman** – poet, scholar and unfulfilled homosexual – to his life-long beloved: 'I would have died for you if I'd only had the luck.' It also has some of his sharpest jokes: 'I don't suppose I'll have time to meet everyone,' says Housman the classicist, on Charon's boat to the underworld: 'Oh yes, you will,' says his conductor. His most recent play *The Coast of Utopia* (2002) has probably to be called his most ambitious; it's an uneven trilogy tracing the progress of the great generation of Russian idealists through the turbulent middle of the nineteenth century. The protagonist, Alexander Herzen,

is told, 'You could be Minister of Paradox, with special responsibility for Irony,' which would be a fine office for Stoppard himself. He remains the wittiest and most humane of contemporary playwrights. Stoppard's literary and intellectual concerns have naturally made him a favourite subject for academic criticism, most of which reads like something that might be parodied in one of his plays. Few of the commentators (Jim Hunter is a notable exception) convey any sense of how his plays work in the theatre or of how blessedly funny they are.

Further reading

Other works include: *Enter a Free Man* (1968); *If You're Glad I'll be Frank* (radio, 1966); *Albert's Bridge* (radio, 1967); *After Magritte* (1970); *Dogg's Our Pet* (1971); *Artist Descending a Staircase* (radio, 1972); *New-Found-Land* (1976); *Dogg's Hamlet* and *Cahoot's Macbeth* (1979): *In the Native State* (radio, 1991); *Indian Ink* (1995) See: Tom Stoppard, *Conversations with Stoppard* (1995). See also: Ronald Hayman, *Tom Stoppard* (1977); Jim Hunter, *Tom Stoppard's Plays* (1982); Tim Brassell, *Stoppard: An Assessment* (1985); Michael Billington, *Stoppard the Playwright* (1987); Neil Sammells, *Tom Stoppard: The Artist as Critic* (1988); Anthony Jenkins, *The Theatre of Tom Stoppard* (1989); Jim Hunter, *Tom Stoppard* (2000); Katherine E. Kelly (ed.) *The Cambridge Companion to Tom Stoppard* (2001).

ROBERT CUSHMAN

STOWE, Harriet Beecher

1811–96

US author and reformer

The absence of credible historical evidence for believing that **Abraham Lincoln** did in fact attribute the outbreak of the American Civil War to Mrs Stowe's *Uncle Tom's Cabin* (1851–2) makes her no less remarkable a nineteenth-century phenomenon. She became, on the basis of her story of Uncle Tom, Little Eva and Simon Legree, a figure of international myth, an antislavery colossus in the mould of William Wilberforce or William Lloyd Garrison, who enjoyed a trans-Atlantic reputation unequalled by any other American woman of her time. Although, then as now, her name is identified with the cause of abolition, a dutiful, unerring New England voice of reform, she was not actually a straightforward abolitionist, however malign she thought slavery. Nor, paradoxically given the notoriety it achieved, was *Uncle Tom's Cabin* her best work, or even a major work when measured against the American writing which appeared in the same decade, like **Emerson's** essays, the 'hidden' poems of **Emily Dickinson**, *The Scarlet Letter* (1850), *Moby-Dick* (1851), *Walden* (1854) and *Leaves of Grass* (1855). Nevertheless, it was with *Uncle Tom's Cabin* that she caught the conscience of the Western world, a landmark Christian indictment of slavery which was at once subtler than its fervent admirers wholly acknowledged yet a weaker literary performance than its reputation suggests.

Behind the Mrs Stowe of received myth, the reductive picture of her as simply a righteous crusader, as behind *Uncle Tom's Cabin* itself, resides a more complex, more tentative and hence more interesting, personality. She was born into stern Calvinist stock in Connecticut, where she was raised in the shadow of her male siblings and stepmother, having lost her own mother at five in 1816, where the talk was frequently of sin, damnation and the hallelujahs of redemption, and which was unabashedly male-dominated and directed. Her father was no less than Lyman Beecher, a true Calvinist believer and apostle of the teachings of the eighteenth-century fundamentalist Jonathan Edwards and as acclaimed and unbending an orthodox Congregationalist as any in New England. Her brother, Henry Ward Beecher, similarly won a massive following as the leading pulpit orator of the day. In 1836, after a girlhood in which she struggled to reconcile this ancestral Calvinism with the belief in a gentler Jesus of love and reconciliation (she eventually became an Episcopalian), she married another celebrated minister, Calvin Stowe, who, though a traditional New England protestant divine, did encourage her literary inclinations.

Despite this difficult unbringing and an immediate family of her own, seven children in all which included twins, a long stint in provincial, plague-torn Cincinnati (1832–50) – she lost a child to cholera in 1849 – and her frequently admitted sense of household weariness and harassment, she consolidated the career which eventually yielded nearly thirty full-length volumes and a vast miscellany of pamphlets and essays.

In 1850, she returned to New England when Calvin Stowe was appointed to the faculty at Bowdoin College, Maine, then to a professorship at Andover Theological Seminary in Massachusetts in 1852. In 1853, 1856 and 1859, riding the crest of her success with *Uncle Tom's Cabin*, she made three rapturous visits to England and Europe, welcomed by **Queen Victoria** and others, but also courting English disaffection by her intrusion into the controversy over Lord Byron (in *Lady Byron Vindicated*, 1870, and earlier magazine pieces she alleged that Byron committed incest). She lost her eldest son in a drowning accident in 1857, for which she sought consolation in spiritualism. Another son, Frederick, was badly wounded in the Civil War. In 1868 she bought and wintered at a converted mansion in Florida, about which she wrote *Palmetto Leaves* (1873) and where she continued her work on behalf of Negro Americans. In 1873, she acquired a house in Hartford, Connecticut, close to **Mark Twain's** home, a return to family roots. By her later years she had declined into a slightly senile, anachronistic presence, manifesting the mild eccentricity which had always threatened. If, to the public gaze, a figure of great apparent public success, she also lived a life beset with inner conflicts, the struggle of a talented Victorian-American and New England woman to achieve an identity of her own making.

The inspiration of *Uncle Tom's Cabin*, her second book, came while she was at prayer in Brunswick, Maine, in the form of a vision of an aged, white-haired slave being flogged, and from the Fugitive Slave Bill of 1850. Published first as a serial in 1851–2, in *The*

National Era, then as a novel in its own right, it immediately became a stupendous best-seller and caused controversy and outrage everywhere, not least in Kentucky and the Southern slave states where Mrs Stowe had done meticulous research. Acclaim was frequent, from fellow reformers and from writers like **Tolstoy**, Heine, George Sand and Macaulay. In America it aroused especially fierce debate about abolition, miscegenation, the truth of its portraiture, and the claims and counter-claims of Yankee and Southerner. Within its plantation and river plot-line, *Uncle Tom's Cabin* brings into play a formidable variety of ingredients – slavery not only as racial but sexual exploitation, the Victorian cult of the child (Eva and Topsy), the complicity of both Northerner and Southerner in slave-holding (Legree is a Yankee), the gory reality of floggings, slave-sales, the break-up of families, and the intricate layers of caste within both black and white slave culture. In Uncle Tom himself, the novel's antislavery readers saw a saintly Christian martyr, even though to a later age his name is synonymous with fawning racial subservice, a label of contempt. *Uncle Tom's Cabin* can be inept and mawkish, yet as **Edmund Wilson** testifies, also simply 'startling' in its understanding of the whole edifice of slave ownership. It continues to impress, not only because of the energetic fullness with which the novel's world is given, but because of the deep fund of historic moral outrage behind it and which Mrs Stowe shared with every reform-minded Victorian. For doubters who thought her story too lurid, all exaggeration and melodrama, and for the slave-holding lobby which reviled her, Mrs Stowe corroborated the detail of her indictments with *A Key to Uncle Tom's Cabin* (1853), in which she offered case-histories and documentation like that of Father Josiah Hendon, an ex-slave, to whose story she wrote a preface in 1858. In this respect her novel usefully compares with other great ex-slave narratives like **Frederick Douglass's** *Narrative* (1845) or **Booker T. Washington's** *Up from Slavery* (1901). Whether **James Baldwin** is right in

judging Mrs Stowe 'not so much a novelist as an impassioned pamphleteer', she assuredly had at least part of the measure of her achievement when she spoke of *Uncle Tom's Cabin* as 'incendiary', an attack on the 'peculiar institution' of slavery for which her Puritan heritage of Christian conscience and mission had given her a singularly appropriate preparation.

In serving as her centrepiece, *Uncle Tom's Cabin* has had the effect of eclipsing her other literary work, both the lesser efforts and her deserving novels of New England life. Among the occasional books should be included *The Mayflower, Or, Sketches of Scenes and Character among the Descendants of the Pilgrims* (1843), an encomium to Puritan history; *Sunny Memories of Foreign Lands* (1854), based on her European visits; her three autobiographical and family reminiscences, *Our Charley and What to Do with Him* (1858), *My Wife and I* (1871) and *We and Our Neighbours* (1875); *Religious Poems* (1867), a useful guide to the nature of Mrs Stowe's Christianity; and the local and children's writing she did under the pen name of Christopher Crowfield. The best of her other fiction undoubtedly requires mention: *Dred: A Tale of the Great Dismal Swamp* (1856), a tale of slave escape and religious fanaticism which argues the moral deterioration brought on by slavery, and her sequence of New England novels: *The Minister's Wooing* (1859), a slightly arch adventure and love story set in late eighteenth-century Rhode Island which makes use of an abundance of regional detail; *The Pearl of Orr's Island* (1862), a moral tale of marital duty given an Atlantic seaboard context; *Oldtown Folks* (1869), Mrs Stowe's most impressive novel which offers her shrewd, knowledgeable analysis of New England social custom and the legacy of Calvinism; *Sam Lawson's Oldtown Fireside Stories* (1872), fifteen local-colour sketches reprinted from the *Atlantic Monthly*; and *Poganuc People* (1878), a deeply autobiographical fiction based on her early, and not wholly enchanted, childhood in the Beecher household. None of Mrs Stowe's novels is without flaw. She frequently veers into melodrama. Her style never completely frees itself of awkwardness. But she is both better and worse than her legend has allowed and she deserves to be read as the historic begetter not only of *Uncle Tom's Cabin* but of a considerable literary oeuvre, a complex, interesting nineteenth-century literary woman and Christian New Englander.

Further reading

See: Constance M. Rourke, *Trumpets of Jubilee* (1921); Charles H. Foster, *The Rungless Ladder: Harriet Beecher Stowe and New England Puritanism* (1954); Edmund Wilson, *Patriotic Gore* (1962); John R Adams, *Harriet Beecher Stowe* (1963); Edward Waggenknecht, *Harriet Beecher Stowe: The Known and The Unknown* (1965); Alice C. Crozier, *The Novels of Harriet Beecher Stowe* (1970); John R. Adams, *Harriet Beecher Stowe* (1989); Joan D. Hedrick, *Harriet Beecher Stowe: A Life* (1994); Jean Fritz, *Harriet Beecher Stowe and the Beecher Preachers* (1994); Norma Johnston, *Harriet: The Life and World of Harriet Beecher Stowe* (1994).

A. ROBERT LEE

STRACHEY, Giles Lytton

1880–1932

English biographer and essayist

After an oppressive childhood in London, much undermined by ill-health, and an unhappy year at Liverpool University, Lytton Strachey went up to Trinity College, Cambridge, in 1899. Cambridge altered the whole tenor of his life. As a member of a secret society known as the 'Apostles', he was brought into contact with older men such as Desmond MacCarthy, **G.E. Moore** and **Bertrand Russell** and, among his contemporaries, **Maynard Keynes** and **Leonard Woolf**. Extracting from Moore's *Principia Ethica* the equation that personal relationships plus aesthetic sensibility equalled the good life, Strachey took the nineteenth-century cult of homosexuality and turned it into a weapon of twentieth-century revolt. As a member of the Bloomsbury Group that developed in London from the Cambridge

Apostles and included **E.M. Forster**, **Roger Fry** and **Virginia Woolf**, he proclaimed a fierce antagonism to the dogmas of Christianity and the worldly religion of success.

It was not until 1918, when his polemic *Eminent Victorians* was published, that he became well known. The war (in which he had been a conscientious objector) acted as a catalyst in the writing of these four biographical essays, altering Strachey's original concept of the book so that its theme became the ironic sifting of those Victorian pretensions that seemed to have led civilization into a holocaust. Its impact was tremendous. The world was weary of big guns and big phrases, and Strachey's witty polemic was specially appealing to the jaded palate of the younger generation. His four subjects were treated with the acuteness of caricature. In 'Cardinal Manning' he attacked the church; in 'Dr Arnold' he ridiculed the tribal deity of the public schools; in 'The End of General Gordon' his target was imperialism and power politics; and in 'Florence Nightingale' he exposed the false basis of that humanitarianism with which the Victorian Age had salved its conscience.

Three years later he produced his classic life of *Queen Victoria* which was to become a model for future biographers. From the anarchism of *Eminent Victorians* he reverted to his natural romanticism and produced a perfectly constructed biography that playfully enhanced the legend of the little old lady on the throne − a whimsical, teasing, half-admiring, half-mocking view that found in **Victoria** a quaintly impressive symbol of a quaintly impressive age. With his Mandarin style, so exactly suited to anecdote, he gave us by means of carefully plotted chapter-stories a life of miraculous compactness that was a work, not of polemics, but of art.

Then, in 1928, came his last biography *Elizabeth and Essex*, subtitled 'A Tragic History'. This story of the love-affair between Queen Elizabeth and the Earl of Essex was quite unlike Strachey's previous books. An experiment in biographical technique, it was constructed along the lines of a five-act Elizabethan play. Wherever possible,

Strachey treats his readers as onlookers, and the visual scenes are neatly framed by entrances and exits. The other great influence on him was that of **Freud** whose theories concerning father–daughter relationships he used to describe Elizabeth's underlying attitude to Essex's death. Between the lines of the book may be read something of Strachey's own homosexual love-affair with the handsome Old Etonian Roger Senhouse. He imagined Elizabeth's feeling for Essex as being similar to his own for Senhouse. Though the book was frowned upon by academic historians, this dual involvement gave it an extraordinary tension and design.

Strachey's battles as a polemicist are mostly won, but his influence persists as the man who revolutionized modern biography. In his private life, he set an example of forbearance in human relationships. For the last sixteen years of his life he lived with the painter Dora Carrington and her husband Ralph Partridge in a *ménage-à-trois* that involved other men and women whose amatory gyrations produced a tragi-comedy of intensely felt emotions.

On 21 January 1932 Strachey died from cancer of the stomach. 'If this is dying,' he said just before the end, 'then I don't think much of it.'

Further reading

Strachey's first book was a volume of literary criticism, *Landmarks in French Literature* (1912); in 1948, as part of his Collected Works, most of his essays were regrouped by James Strachey and published as *Biographical Essays* and *Literary Essays*. A selection of all these essays, with some hitherto uncollected additions, entitled *The Shorter Strachey*, ed. Michael Holroyd and Paul Levy, appeared in his centenary year 1980. A pornographic *jeu d'esprit*, *Ermyntrude and Esmerelda*, came out in 1968; in 1971 his autobiographical writings were edited by Michael Holroyd in a volume called *Lytton Strachey by Himself*, and the following year there appeared *The Really Interesting Question and Other Papers*, ed. Paul Levy, that contained some of his Apostles' speeches. About Strachey: Michael Holroyd, *Lytton Strachey, A Critical Biography* (1968, revised 1971); J. Ferns, *Lytton Strachey* (1988).

MICHAEL HOLROYD

STRAUSS, David Friedrich

1808–74

German theologian and New Testament critic

Born in Ludwigsburg, Strauss was a member (1821–5) of the brilliant group of students who sat at the feet of F.C. Baur at Blaubeuren theological seminary. He continued his studies under Baur at Tübingen when the latter received a chair there in 1826, and also attended the classes of the two biblical 'supernaturalists' Steudel and Bengel. His admiration for the work of Schleiermacher and Hegel attracted him to Berlin from 1831 to 1832, although Hegel died shortly after Strauss's arrival there. From 1832 to 1835 he was a *Repetent* (occasional lecturer) at the Stift (theological seminary) at Tübingen, although suspicion of this theological position obliged him to teach mainly in the area of philosophy, which he did from an unambiguously Hegelian standpoint. The appearance in 1835 of his first and greatest work *The Life of Jesus Critically Examined* (*Das Leben Jesu Kritisch Bearbeitet*, trans. 1892), it has been said, simultaneously procured for Strauss not only fame but academic and ecclesiastical ruin, in that he was immediately dismissed from his teaching post at the Stift by Steudel, its president. Until around 1840 repeated attempts by Strauss to rehabilitate himself with his opponents failed, and the successful attempt to procure for him the Chair of Dogmatics at Zürich came to nothing, since conservative opposition to his position prevented him ever from occupying the chair, whose stipend he was thereafter paid in the form of a pension. His two-volumed *Christliche Glaubenslehre* ('Christian Faith', 2 vols, 1840–41) is a hostile account of the development of Christian doctrine down to his own day, and finally ruined any residual chance of reconciliation with the academic and ecclesiastical establishment. The remainder of Strauss's life was negative and sad: he involved himself in journalism and biography (writing on Ulrich von Hutten and H.S. Reimarus); he contracted an unhappy marriage (with Agnese

Schebest, the opera singer); he became embittered and cynical. His popular version of the life of Jesus (1864) did not affect his reputation one way or the other. His final book *The Old Faith and the New* (*Der alte und der neue Glaube*, 1872, trans. 1873) was notable for its rejection, on the grounds of Hegelianism and of the fashionable materialistic metaphysics of the day, of personal human immortality. On his death in 1874, Strauss was buried, on the explicit conditions laid down in his will of 1864, without any religious rites whatever.

Of all the possible descriptions of Strauss's theological position, that of 'radical' (or 'left-wing') Hegelianism does not wildly or unjustly distort it. In approaching the Gospel accounts of Jesus's life, Strauss importantly identified an impasse between two traditional, but mutually exclusive and incompatible positions: first, a 'naturalism' (rooted in the scepticism of the *Aufklärung*) that affirmed, dogmatically and *a priori*, the impossibility of the Gospel stories of the miraculous and the supernatural, and arguing that absolutely natural (i.e. scientifically intelligible) explanations must be sought for all such; and second, a 'supernaturalism' (as defended by his academic superior Steudel) which affirmed, according to Strauss, just as dogmatically and *a priori*, that, since at the heart of the Gospel narratives we find the coming into of flesh of none less than the Son of God, we have no logical right to make predictions (or to form hypotheses) about the worldly consequences of this *vis-à-vis* the everyday causal structure of experience, so that scepticism about allegations of miraculous and supernatural events in the Gospels is not only inappropriate but intellectually arrogant, approximating to blasphemy.

The persistence of such an impasse meant for Strauss a dead end for biblical studies, and it was towards resolving this impasse that his historico-critical research may be said to have been directed. He did so by positing his celebrated theory that the problematic elements in the life of Jesus (miraculous, supernatural, apocalyptic,

cosmic) should be classified and treated as 'myth' (German, *Mythus*, *Mythos*). He was aware that he was not the first modern scholar to do so, and that the term had been used by Eichhorn, Gabler (both Old Testament scholars), Hegel, Semler, de Wette and Paulus. But he was dissatisfied with their piecemeal and partial application of the category; much attention had been directed to the myth of the Creation, or to the Birth and Resurrection narratives in the New Testament, and Hegel had been much preoccupied with the myth of the Fall in Genesis 3. Strauss now proposed the scientific and consistent application of the category to the Gospel materials as a whole.

At the heart of Strauss's theory (as expounded and applied in the opening section of his *magnum opus*, *Das Leben Jesu*) lies the incalculably important distinction between 'idea' and 'fact' (or, as we might now say, 'significance' and 'history'), and his interpretation of the relationship between the two. The key to understanding Strauss's book is his conviction that the 'idea', in Hegelian terms, is incomparably the more significant of the two, and possessed ontological, temporal and significative priority over historical 'fact' or 'facts'. Indeed, it is 'ideas', 'interpretative motifs' which form or determine so-called 'historical' factual complexes or patterns. Also close to the heart of his theory is his important analysis of historical religious community as essentially a 'myth-making' entity. If we combine these two notions of Strauss, we see that his fundamental thesis is that before, long before, the historical advent of Jesus, the religious community of Israel had been generating a considerable corpus of Messianic-soteriological-eschatological ideas in its 'corporate mind', with which in due season it crowned the historical person of Jesus of Nazareth. But the 'ideas' pre-date and indeed determine and constitute the so-called historical fact. Not that Strauss denied that there is a certain, if rather indeterminate, substratum of fact in the Jesus story: that Jesus was a Galilean who was baptized by John and indeed preached in Galilee; that he threw down the gauntlet to much contemporary Jewish belief and practice, an act which led to his trial and judicial crucifixion shortly after AD 30. But interwoven into this rather meagre historical outline is much that is, as sheer factual history, problematically unacceptable: the Virgin Birth narratives, the supernatural motifs of the baptism, the temptations, the miracles, the transfiguration, highly specific predictions by Jesus of his death, resurrection and second coming, and finally, the resurrection and ascension themselves. These latter must be interpreted in terms of ideas, expectations and motifs already existing in the corporate consciousness of the community as applicable to the 'Coming One'. An excellent example of what Strauss means by 'pure' myth is the transfiguration story (Mark 9: 2–8; cf. Matthew 17: 1–8, and Luke 9: 28–36): in the foreground are portrayed enduring religious 'ideas'; the high and holy mountain, the glistening white clothing of the messianic figure, the supernatural appearance of Moses and Elijah as representing the Law and the Prophets, the 'cloud of the presence', the heavenly voice and the rest; the character and historical concreteness of Jesus fade into relative insignificance. (Apart from 'pure' myth, Strauss conceded the existence of 'historical' myths, whose existence may have been generated by some historical event or other in the career of Jesus, although the precise nature of such events is now quite inaccessible to us.)

Of truly outstanding importance in Strauss's book is the set of criteria he offers by which myth may be readily identified – the irreconcilability of certain Gospel narratives with universally acknowledged laws of science, of natural succession, of human psychology (for the knowledge of which Strauss was clearly indebted to the critical philosophy of the *Aufklärung*). Of possibly equal importance is Strauss's breaking down of the Gospel narrative into 'blocks' and his demonstration of historical inconsistencies between them, work which contributed valuably to the modern science of 'synoptic' criticism. Myth may also be recognized by *form* (e.g. poetry)

and *content* (e.g. Jewish legend, genealogy and prediction).

Now that the ecclesiastical and academic dust that was thrown up by the case of the 'alienated theologian' has long settled, it is possible to reach a balanced and judicious estimate of Strauss's significance and work. On the positive side, mention has already been made of his contribution to synoptic criticism; in the famous words of Albert Schweitzer, Strauss's subdivision of the Gospel materials 'marked out the ground which is now occupied by modern critical research', and ensured his place as a pioneer in this science. Again, he broke new ground in the study of biblical myth and stimulated much modern research in this area, and his research could be said to provide an important link between the theological scholars of the *Aufklärung* and the important twentieth-century 'demythologizing' proposals of **Rudolf Bultmann** (there is more Strauss in Bultmann than is generally realized).

However, on the negative side, two large and grave questions still loom large over Strauss's work. First, was not Strauss's unmistakable Hegelianism, with its stress on eternally valid but ahistorical 'ideas' developing and achieving configurations within the corporate consciousness of the religious community (Mind or *Geist* achieving self-consciousness in the human spirit) not every bit as dogmatically *a priori* as the dogmatic rationalism or supernaturalism which Strauss strove so valiantly to overcome? Did not Strauss approach Scripture with a pre-formed set of hermeneutical and philosophical presuppositions which determined well in advance what Scripture was allowed to say?

Second, and possibly more importantly, there is one huge question that Strauss did not and, on his restrictive philosophical presuppositions, could not, answer. Given that there was, in the religious consciousness of Israel, a considerable corpus of Messianic, apocalyptic and eschatological motifs and expectations, why were these heaped upon such a vague, nebulous and insubstantial character as Strauss's Jesus? According to **Karl**

Barth, Strauss's Jesus was 'shrouded in a veil of myth', and according to H.R. Mackintosh Strauss's view was that the primitive Christian community 'wove a wreath of adoration round the Master's head by worshipping fancy'. But why *this* man, rather than some other? What was there about *this* particular *historical* man that invited such treatment from his followers, who founded upon *his* person and work a worldwide church? Strauss's inability to give plausible answers to such questions explains partly at least the excessively harsh and unforgiving treatment meted out to him by the establishment of his day. But his work, by focusing critical attention upon such questions and answers, contributed vastly to historico-critical research into the life of Jesus during the following century.

Further reading

See: D.F. Strauss, *The Life of Jesus Critically Examined*, edited with a long introduction by Peter C. Hodgson (1973); Van A. Harvey, 'The Alienated Theologian', *McCormick Quarterly*, Vol. 23 (May 1970), pp. 234–65; Karl Barth, *Protestant Theology in the Nineteenth Century* (1972); Claude Welch, *Protestant Thought in the Nineteenth Century*, Vol. I, 1799–1870 (1972); Otto Pfleiderer, *The Development of Theology in Germany since Kant* (1890); James C. Livingston, *Modern Christian Thought: From the Enlightenment to Vatican II* (1971); William Madges, *The Core of Christian Faith: D.F. Strauss and His Catholic Critics* (1987).

JAMES RICHMOND

STRAUSS, Johann

1825–99

Austrian composer

Johann Strauss was the most celebrated member of a distinguished Viennese family of musicians who made their names directing and composing for their own dance orchestras. His father, the elder Johann Strauss (1804–49), had begun the family tradition, gaining acclaim during the second quarter of the nineteenth century not only in Vienna but also on extensive tours that included Britain in **Queen Victoria's** coronation season. Though nowadays remembered for his *Radetzky March* (1848), it was largely through the elder Strauss that the waltz became established not only as the principal attraction of elegant society balls but also as music worth playing and hearing for its own sake.

The father opposed his sons following in his footsteps, so that the younger Johann was at first intended for a banking career. However, with his mother's encouragement he had taken violin lessons from a member of his father's orchestra and subsequently studied theory with Joseph Drechsler (1782–1852). In October 1844 he made his début with his own small orchestra at a *soirée dansante* and soon began to establish himself as his father's most serious rival – a rivalry heightened when the two supported opposing factions in the Revolution of 1848.

After the father's death the younger Johann continued to extend the family reputation both in Vienna and further afield – eventually inheriting from his father the accolade of 'Waltz King'. In 1863 he was appointed to the official position of Music Director of the Court Balls. With the demand for his services increasing, he was fortunate to be able to enlist the services of his brothers Josef (1827–70) and Eduard (1835–1916). Now the orchestra could be split, to enable it to fulfil simultaneous engagements during Vienna's Carnival time (January/February) or to enable one portion to remain in Vienna while another went on tour. Johann himself conducted summer concerts at Pavlovsk in Russia annually from 1856 to 1865 and visited Paris and London in 1867 and Boston and New York in 1872.

By 1870, however, Strauss was increasingly recoiling from incessant public adulation. Simultaneously Viennese impresarios, alarmed at the dominance of the Viennese musical theatre by the imported works of **Offenbach**, sought to enlist Strauss's services. He accepted, resigned his position as Music Director of the Court Balls and, with

Josef now dead, left the direction of the family orchestra to Eduard. He continued to compose operettas for the rest of his life, while contriving to continue to provide new material for the ballroom by adapting themes from his operettas, as well as composing the occasional dance for special occasions. In the late 1880s his attention turned to the composition of a genuine opera, but the resulting *Ritter Pázmán* (Vienna Court Opera, 1 January 1892) enjoyed no more than a *succés d'estime*.

Besides his fifteen operettas, one opera and one ballet, Strauss's compositions number some 170 waltzes, 150 polkas, 30 polka-mazurkas, over 70 quadrilles and nearly 50 marches. His finest waltzes mostly date from the 1860s: *Accelerationen* ('Accelerations', 1860), *Morgenblätter* ('Morning Papers', 1864), *An der schönen blauen Donau* ('By the Beautiful Blue Danube', 1867), *Künsterleben* ('Artist's Life', 1867), *Geschichten aus dem Wienerwald* ('Tales from the Vienna Woods', 1868) and *Wein, Weib und Gesang* ('Wine, Woman and Song', 1869). Later examples include *Wiener Blut* ('Vienna Blood', 1873), *Rosen aus dem Süden* ('Roses from the South', 1880), the coloratura soprano showpiece *Frühlingsstimmen* ('Voices of Spring', 1883) and the *Kaiser-Walzer* ('Emperor Waltz', 1889). His most famous polkas include the *Annen-Polka* ('Anna Polka', 1852), the *Tritsch-Tratsch-Polka* ('Chit-Chat Polka', 1858), *Unter Donner und Blitz* ('In Thunder and Lightning', 1868) and the *Pizzicato Polka* (1869) composed jointly with Josef.

In assessing the stature of Johann Strauss's dance music one should not isolate his name from that of his brother Josef. Certainly Johann produced the more immediately striking and therefore more widely popular melodies. Josef, however, was perhaps the more cultivated musician, adding an extra sense of tenderness or emotional tension that leads many to consider his the greater talent. Between them, at any rate, they produced dance music unequalled by any of their many rivals, music which reflects the glamour and brilliance of the Habsburg monarchy at its height and which transcends the constraints

of dance rhythms as never before or since. To the regular beat of the polka they added a unique range of picturesque invention, while always using with discretion the special effects that were often added to give a piece individuality. It was, however, in the rhythm of the waltz that they had the finest vehicle for their talents.

The standard pattern of the waltz had already been established in the works of the elder Strauss, with a sequence of simple waltz themes preceded by an introductory section and rounded off by a coda recapitulating the main themes. His sons developed the structure by building up the introductions into miniature tone poems, lengthening the span of the waltz melodies and extending their range of expression. None of their imitators ever approached their consistent freshness of invention, their ability to build upon a striking main theme and renew attention throughout, or the utterly natural way in which they integrated the various contrasted waltz sections. The refined shading of their orchestration has always been especially admired.

For the composition of operettas Strauss was far less well suited. He never became a good judge of a libretto and never acquired a taste for setting lyrics to music. Some of the best music came when, in possession of no more than an outline of the action, he built up an appropriately atmospheric sequence of melodies to which words were then fitted by his lyricist Richard Genée (1825–95). It was his prodigious melodic invention that enabled him to overcome his natural shortcomings and create the distinctive Viennese operetta based on the waltz – a form successfully developed in the twentieth century by such composers as Franz Lehár (1870–1948). Of Strauss's fifteen operettas three are acknowledged masterpieces, each with its own distinctive style – the sparkling *Die Fledermaus* ('The Bat', 1874), the graceful *Eine Nacht in Venedig* ('A Night in Venice', 1883) and the more solid *Der Zigeunerbaron* ('The Gipsy Baron', 1885).

In his time Strauss used the popularity of his orchestra to introduce new music to a wider public – introducing themes from **Wagner's** *Tristan und Isolde* to Vienna for the first time and giving the première of an early **Tchaikovsky** composition in Pavlovsk. In return he enjoyed the admiration of many of the greatest musicians, including **Brahms** who was a close personal friend. In our own time, too, his music continues to be performed around the world by the greatest orchestras, opera companies, conductors and singers to a degree enjoyed by no other composer of music for the ballroom and popular musical theatre.

Further reading

See: *Johann Strauss: Weltgeschichte im Walzertakt* (1975). Biographies in English include Joseph Wechsberg, *The Waltz Emperors* (1973), but the best assessment is the article (including list of works and bibliography) by Mosco Carner and Max Schönherr in *The New Grove Dictionary of Music and Musicians* (1980).

ANDREW LAMB

STRAUSS, Leo
1899–1973
German/American political philosopher

Leo Strauss was a Jew who left his native Germany in 1932, eventually settling in the United States where he had a distinguished academic career mostly at the New School for Social Research and the University of Chicago. He was primarily a historian of political philosophy – he did not write a single book dedicated to the expression of his own philosophical or political views. But his historical discoveries were such that they had far-reaching philosophical-theological-political consequences. Accordingly, he has become at once one of the most admired and hated figures in the Academy.

The twentieth-century thinker closest to Strauss in intention, if not in the content of thought, was **Edmund Husserl**. Both thinkers were concerned with 'the crisis of European sciences' or 'the crisis of the West'.

But what distinguishes Strauss and Husserl from their contemporaries is that this crisis did not lead them to despair (**Spengler**), to wilful affirmation of the scientific outlook in the face of formidable objections (**Weber**), or to the abandonment of the scientific outlook in favour of a non-theoretical outlook (**Heidegger**). Instead, they attempted to replace a discredited philosophy with an adequate philosophy, a philosophy that could rightly claim to be a rigorous science or a philosophy that could redress its theoretical difficulties by means of moral-political reflections.

What distinguishes Strauss from Husserl is that he was from the beginning much more interested in God and politics and their claim on man – indeed, most of the writings of the young Strauss were dedicated to theological and political questions. He was also deeply impressed with Heidegger's criticism of Husserl, a feature of which is Heidegger's argument that man's primary grasp of the world is not theoretical. Accordingly, Strauss attempted to fulfil Husserl's theoretical intention by acknowledging the primacy of the claims of practice. This path of defending theory in the court of practice (morality and religious law) was opened to him by his rediscovery of the true nature of Platonic political philosophy, which he partly learned from such students of the classics as Farabi, Averroes and Maimonides (see below, *Philosophie und Gesetz*).

But before he could be confident of this defence of theory, he had to confront the contention that knowledge of theoretical and practical matters is impossible because all human thought is historically relative, a contention that was articulated most intelligently by Martin Heidegger. Since this contention was partly based on an analysis of the limits of human thought and partly on an interpretation of the history of human thought (because the analysis was not sufficient to establish the truth of the contention), and since Heidegger's interpretation of that history was in fact guided by the contention that it was meant to support, Strauss focused much of his energy in 1940s and 1950s on historical investigations that did not take for granted the truth of historicism.

We limit ourselves to two important historical discoveries made by Strauss. First, Strauss rediscovered exotericism, the practice of philosophic writers of concealing their true thoughts from the vast majority of their readers while revealing them by various indications to the few potential philosophers among their readers. These philosophers who were living in illiberal societies chose to write in this way out of fear of persecution, a sense of social responsibility and their belief that one does not educate one's readers by spoonfeeding them. Now, this rediscovery is exhilarating in general because it helps one see that there is much in old philosophic books that one had not even imagined, but it also makes the thesis of historicism less strong because it suggests that many statements of the philosophers which seemed merely the expressions of the ideas of their society were in fact conscious accommodations to those ideas.

Second, in the last hundred years it has become common to regard Western philosophic thought as an evolving and continuous tradition, a view that leads to the impression that our current situation is humanity in its maturity. Accordingly, we are apt to identify the perplexity of man in late modernity with insight into the true situation of man. Strauss in contrast has argued that there is a radical difference between ancient and modern philosophy, of which the founders of modern philosophy were fully conscious. Strauss focused his attention on modern political philosophy (Machiavelli, Hobbes, Spinoza and Locke), because he argued that modern philosophy, the modern attempt to settle the question of nature, was necessarily accompanied by a political project, by a deliberate attempt to establish an utterly new kind of society, and that contemporary doubts about philosophy (and the existence of natural limits) were connected with doubts about the new society. Accordingly, Strauss's historical investigations re-open the old but forgotten quarrel between the ancients and the

moderns. This quarrel has a bearing on the claims of historical relativism, for if the decision made by modern political philosophers turns out to have been irrational, doubts about modern ideas or modern society would not be a sufficient basis for rejecting reason as one's guide.

Today, Strauss is perhaps more known for being one of the intellectual sources of neoconservatism than for the historical-philosophical accomplishments briefly sketched above. Although we cannot identify Strauss with the politics of some of his admirers – he had admirers from both the left (**R.H. Tawney**) and the right (Willmoore Kendall) – his investigations do have political implications. His critical examination of the foundations of modern society is certainly a challenge to the liberal hope that a well-constructed society can dispense with religion, with character formation and with the use of moral language (the language of good and evil) in politics. Just as liberal relativism has made it questionable for its adherents to engage in policies that do not have the support of world community, Strauss's critique of relativism or his defence of natural right has made it possible to believe that modern liberal democracy is more in accordance with natural right than its contemporary alternatives, and thus it deserves to be defended. And his appreciation of classical political philosophy paves the way for the possibility of a new (at least new to us) kind of conservatism – one which is not hostile to reason, which recognizes the dignity of political life, and which does not forget the moral ambiguity of unrestrained commerce. But perhaps the most important political lesson he learned from his historical investigations is the realization that the problems of human life cannot be solved on the level of politics. Accordingly, his thought forms the basis of a new kind of cosmopolitanism, which resists the temptation of wanting to be a citizen of the world community, precisely because it prepares one to be a citizen of the cosmos, of that whole which is so much greater than humanity.

Further reading

Other works include: *Die religionskritik Spinozas* (1930); *Philosophie und Gesetz* (1935); *The Political Philosophy of Hobbes*, translated from German by Elsa M. Sinclair (1936); *On Tyranny* (1948); *Persecution and the Art of Writing* (1952); *Natural Right and History* (1953); *Thoughts on Machiavelli* (1958); *The City and Man* (1964); *Socrates and Aristophanes* (1966); *Liberalism Ancient and Modern* (1967); *Xenophon's Socratic discourse* (1970); *Xenophon's Socrates* (1972); *The Argument and the Action of Plato's Laws* (1975); and *Studies in Platonic Political Philosophy*, ed. Joseph Cropsey (1983). Strauss's early writings and many of his letters have been collected and edited by Heinrich Meier in three volumes under *Leo Strauss Gesammelte Schriften* (2001). For a general introduction to Strauss, see the entry on Strauss by Nathan Tarcov and Thomas Pangle in the third edition of Leo Strauss and Joseph Cropsey (eds) *History of Political Philosophy* (1987). For an account of his understanding of classical political philosophy see David Bolotin, 'Leo Strauss and Classical Political Philosophy', *Interpretation* (1994). For an account of his criticism of modern social science see Nasser Behnegar, *Leo Strauss, Max Weber and the Scientific Study of Politics* (2003). The best introduction to Strauss's later and obscure writings and their connection to his earlier theological reflections is Christopher Bruell, 'Strauss on Xenophon's Socrates', *Political Science Reviewer* (1984).

NASSER BEHNEGAR

STRAUSS, Richard George

1864–1949

German composer and conductor

Strauss was born in Munich, a true Bavarian. His father was Germany's foremost horn-player and his mother was of the Pschorr Brewery family. Richard was brought up comfortably and first showed signs of unusual talent when he composed a Christmas song at the age of four. He entered the Munich Ludwigs-gymnasium in 1874, went to Munich University in 1882 and thence to the Academy of Music in 1894. By the time he was sixteen he had mastered every aspect of composition, and in 1885 was given his first musical post as assistant to Hans von Bülow in Meiningen. After only a month, Strauss was left in charge of the Ducal Orchestra, where he learned the repertoire by having to play it. Between 1886 and 1889 he was third conductor at the Munich Court Theatre where he suffered under two seniors, both jealous because of the demand for Strauss to conduct his own works elsewhere. In 1887 his *Aus Italien* branded him avant-garde in Munich itself. In 1889 he became a musical assistant at Bayreuth and conductor of the Weimar Court Theatre where his revolutionary tone-poem *Don Juan* was first heard. In 1894 his first opera *Guntram* was a failure (it was too Wagnerian in concept) but he married the prima donna, Pauline de Ahna, daughter of a general and his former pupil. From then on she ruled Strauss and his life with iron discipline.

Further tone-poems added lustre to his reputation for variety and instrumental skill, and in 1896 he returned to Munich as principal conductor. In 1897 his only child, Franz, was born and in the following year the family moved to Berlin where Strauss became principal conductor at the Court Opera, a post he retained until 1918. So far his output, apart from considerable conducting engagements, was in two forms: songs (*Lieder*) and the tone-poems.

In 1901 he redeemed the failure of *Guntram* with *Feuersnot* (Dresden), a light and indelicate opera produced as a tilt against the Munichers. In 1903 Strauss received his PhD degree from Heidelberg as token of their esteem, an honour which he always cherished and wrote into every signature. The first important opera *Salome* (Dresden 1905) was to his own libretto from a German translation of **Oscar Wilde's** play. This fascinatingly barbarous score scandalized the Kaiser and Kaiserin and was censored by the church in Vienna. But it soon brought Strauss sufficient royalties to enable him to build his ideal house in Garmisch at the foot of the Bavarian Alps. Next came *Elektra* (Dresden 1909), another morbid one-act opera, this time to a libretto by the brilliant Austrian poet Hugo von Hofmannsthal. At this point Strauss may be seen as leader of European music, verging on the emergent achievements of the Second

Viennese School of composition (**Schoen-berg**, **Berg** and **Webern**). Had he pushed his thoughts beyond *Elektra* into complete atonality, Strauss would have aligned himself with them. But instead he quickly succumbed to a charmingly romantic libretto by Hofmannsthal who did not want to lose such a collaborator. This was, in avant-garde terms, a retrograde step, for the opera was *Der Rosenkavalier* (Dresden 1911). It made a fortune for both Strauss and Hofmannsthal, and immediately Strauss made or authorized many popular arrangements of its melodies. Hofmannsthal's next libretto was more complex: a new translation of Molière *Le Bourgeois Gentilhomme* (as a play with incidental music) followed by the one-act opera *Ariadne auf Naxos* (Stuttgart 1912). In this cumbersome form the hybrid work was scarcely viable and only after much recrimination between its two creators was the opera prefaced by a sung prologue to make an evening's entertainment (Vienna 1916), and the play was abandoned. But in between the two versions of *Ariadne*, Strauss and Hofmannsthal embarked upon their most ambitious project, a huge fairy-tale moral, very complex in its story and making heavy demands upon producer and theatrical effects. This was *The Woman without a Shadow* (*Die Frau ohne Schatten*, Vienna 1919). Before it had been half finished, the First World War intervened.

Strauss lost his entire fortune, banked in London, and had to postpone his intention to give up conducting altogether in 1914, when he was fifty years old, so as to devote his full time to composing. In 1915 he completed a vast symphony that told a day's adventure in the Alps (*Eine Alpensinfonie*, 'Alpine Symphony', 1915) but this was – had to be – the last composition conceived in massive terms.

In 1919 Strauss became co-director of the Vienna Opera with Franz Schalk (they did not get on), and began to work on a bourgeois comedy as an opera to his own libretto. *Intermezzo* (Dresden 1924) was conceived in a series of almost filmic scenes, scored in a new and economic manner; but the two former collaborators again worked on *Die*

aegyptische Helena (*The Egyptian Helen*, Dresden 1928), a less than satisfactory opera, and the partnership culminated with *Arabella* which attempted to be a later Viennese story in the *Rosenkavalier* vein. Hofmannsthal completed a difficult scene the day before his sudden death in 1929, leaving Strauss to finish composing, and to supervise the production (Dresden 1933) – a task which Hofmannsthal had always insisted upon undertaking.

In the same year Strauss returned to Bayreuth to conduct **Wagner's** *Parsifal* in the emergency of Arturo Toscanini's withdrawal on political grounds. This put him unintentionally into Nazi favour and helped to secure him the (unwanted) post of Head of the German Chamber of Music (Reichsmusikkammer) in 1934. Strauss was at a loss for an operatic partner until he found **Stefan Zweig** and his adaptation of Ben Jonson's *Epicoene*. Called *The Silent Woman* (*Die schweigsame Frau*, Dresden, 1935), the libretto suited Strauss admirably, and he quickly composed the complex, jovial score. But Zweig was Jewish and the Nazis were in full power in 1935. After four performances the opera was proscribed and, because of a politically tactless letter between Strauss and Zweig which the authorities intercepted, the composer was stripped of his office, reputation and all performances of his works in the Reich for a year.

Now unable to work any longer with Zweig, Strauss was recommended to a scholarly but extremely dull man called Joseph Gregor, whose three synopses (which all had their origins in previous ideas by Hofmannsthal or Zweig) were found to be acceptable. These operas, *Friedenstag*, *Daphne* and *Die Liebe der Danae*, were composed and were moderately successful between 1940 and 1946. By then the Second World War had begun and Strauss was again financially handicapped by lost royalties. He began to compose in an altogether fresh and economic manner as exemplified in the intellectual opera *Capriccio* (Munich 1942), and by several fragrant orchestral works of chamber proportions. He was mortified by the destruction of the principal German and Austrian opera houses in which his masterpieces had first been presented, and his *Metamorphosen for 23 Solo Strings* expresses his grief in music.

Strauss's Jewish daughter-in-law and his two half-Jewish grandsons came under his protection in Garmisch, and in order to secure their immunity Strauss was forced to abide by detestable political actions in order to save them – which he did. At the end of the war he was a sick man, almost penniless, and disgusted at the vanquished regime. Sir Thomas Beecham organized a Strauss Festival in London in 1947, where he was fêted and made to feel most welcome. He died in 1949, with his final composition *The Four Last Songs* (*Vier letzte Lieder*, London 1950) a perfect epitaph.

Strauss's composing career bridged sixty years, from *Don Juan* in 1889 to the *Four Last Songs* in 1948. This included contemporary romanticism, through a period of almost atonality (and certainly abrasiveness) and back to lush romanticism at a time when the so-called leading composers were treading harsher paths. A fervent admirer of Mozart, Strauss had an unparalleled skill with orchestral sound, a 'lifelong love-affair with the soprano voice' and the instant ability to create a theme to highlight words, then to get as much out of that theme as he possibly could. As a first-rate conductor he came to minimize his gestures to a flicker, yet got enormous results thereby; and this practical ability not only earned him a great deal of money but put him constantly among working musicians, new works by others and the standard repertoire.

Further reading

Other works include: ballets: *The Legend of Joseph* (*Josephslegende*, Paris 1914); *Whipped Cream* (*Schlagobers*, Vienna 1924). Other tone-poems: *Death and Transfiguration* (*Tod und Verklärung*, 1890); *Thus Spake Zarathustra* (*Also sprach Zarathustra*, 1896); *Don Quixote* (1898); *A Hero's Life* (*Ein Heldenleben*, 1899). Concertos: Violin (1882); Horn No. 1 (1885); Horn No. 2 (1943); Piano

(1890); Oboe (1946); *Duet Concertino* for Clarinet, Bassoon and Strings with Harp (1948). Chamber music: two Suites for thirteen winds (1882, 1884); two Sonatinas for sixteen winds (1944, 1946). Songs: 197 songs for voice and piano; sixteen songs for voice and orchestra (1868–1950). About Strauss: *Strauss – Hofmannsthal Correspondence* (1952, trans. 1961); Norman Del Mar, *Richard Strauss: A Critical Commentary on His Life and Works* (1962, 1969, 1972); E. Krause, *Richard Strauss, Gestalt und Werk* (1956, *Richard Strauss: The Man and His Work*, 1964); *Richard Strauss. Correspondance. Fragments de Journal*, ed. R. Rolland (1951, *Strauss–Rolland Correspondence*, 1968); A. Jefferson, *Richard Strauss* (1973); Matthew Boyden, *Richard Strauss* (1999); Bryan Gilliam, *The Life of Richard Strauss* (1999); Michael Kennedy, *Richard Strauss* (2005).

ALAN JEFFERSON

STRAVINSKY, Igor Fedorovich
1882–1971
Russian composer

Born into a prosperous middle-class family, Stravinsky was a late starter as a composer. His father was a bass singer at the Maryinsky Theatre in St Petersburg, and Stravinsky had the Russian theatre, particularly ballet, in his blood. He attended St Petersburg University (1901–5), allegedly studying criminal law and legal philosophy, in fact developing his musicianship. It was not until 1902, with the death of his father, that he began to study composition, privately, with **Rimsky-Korsakov**. A close relationship thereafter developed between the young Stravinsky and this master, until the latter's death in 1908.

Stravinsky was twenty-eight when he was abruptly launched into international fame, which never left him, by *The Firebird* – the first of the glittering series of Russian ballets prompted and staged by his compatriot **Diaghilev**. But some of the works written prior to that date are of key importance, his *gradus ad Parnassum*. Starting with some derivative piano pieces, such as the *Scherzo* (1902) and the Sonata in F sharp minor (1903–4), his apprenticeship ends with the Symphony in E flat (1905–7). Three orchestral works follow which are of genuine artistic importance: the short fantasy *Fireworks* (1908), the *Scherzo Fantastique* (1907–8), and the lost *Chant Funèbre* (1908) in memory of Rimsky-Korsakov. The *Scherzo*, for instance, even allowing for the sense of orchestral colour handed down from his teacher, the scherzando element of Mendelssohn, and a dash of **Wagner** and **Tchaikovsky**, still contains music which is recognizably Stravinsky's own. And it was after hearing a performance of this work, together with *Fireworks*, in early 1909, that Diaghilev invited Stravinsky to be associated with his new Ballets Russes.

Until 1913, when he moved to Switzerland, Stravinsky lived with his wife Catherine at Oustilug, a small village about a hundred miles south of Brest-Litovsk. His family included two sons, Theodore and Soulima, and two daughters, Ludmilla and Milena. The outbreak of war in 1914 cut him off from Russia, and he did not return there until 1962, when an official visit brought him back to the city renamed Leningrad. But in 1920, after spending the years of the First World War in Switzerland, he settled in France. It was there, as he said, particularly in Paris that 'the pulse of the world was throbbing most strongly'. In 1934 he became a French citizen; the following year he published his memoirs – in French. He remained in France until 1939, when he emigrated to America, following several visits to, and commissions from, that country. That was a year of triple bereavement for the composer, when his elder daughter Ludmilla, his wife Catherine and his mother all died. Soon after his arrival in America he was joined by Vera de Bosset, who became his second wife in March 1940. The couple settled in Los Angeles. Here they stayed until September 1969, when, largely for medical reasons, they moved to New York. There Stravinsky died in 1971, at the age of eighty-nine.

His output falls into three phases, Russian, neo-classical and serial. The first phase consists primarily of works written for the stage, of which there were nine: *The Firebird* (1910),

Petrushka (1911), *The Rite of Spring* (1913), *The Nightingale* (1914), *Renard* (1916), *The Soldier's Tale* (1919), *Pulcinella* (1920), *Mavra* (1922), *The Wedding* (1923). The last of these was also the last to be written for Diaghilev, who produced all but one (*The Soldier's Tale*). Other works of this phase include some important songs, chiefly *Three Japanese Lyrics* (1913) – wrongly claimed by many as showing the influence of **Schoenberg**, whose *Pierrot Lunaire* had been heard by Stravinsky shortly before – *Pribaoutki* (short nonsense songs, 1914, for which no translation is possible), and the *Three Stories for Children* (1915–17); the cantata *The King of the Stars* (1912), which is a vision of the Last Judgement by the Symbolist poet Balmont; and the *chant funèbre* in memory of **Debussy**, called *Symphonies of Wind Instruments* (1920). It is assumed that this work contains similarities of scoring to the earlier piece written for Rimsky-Korsakov, unless and until that is discovered.

Stravinsky's second phase, which terminates with the opera *The Rake's Progress* (1948–51), is usually, and correctly, described as neo-classical. In the case of this composer, neo-classicism was not simply a retreat into the past, nor a form of academic pastiche, nor merely a series of quotations of other composers' ideas; rather, it was a re-thinking and a re-application of aesthetic principles of the classical period. Stravinsky's curiosity was insatiable, and it is interesting that as he moved forward and progressed, so his musical sources extended further into the past. Machaut and Gesualdo came to replace Bach and Beethoven. The majority of his neo-classical works are for the concert hall rather than the stage, and they culminate in the two great orchestral works, the Symphony in C (1940) and the *Symphony in Three Movements* (1945), first heard in Chicago and New York respectively. Indeed, after the Russian works of the first phase, the interest in Stravinsky's new compositions was stronger in America than it was in Europe – which was one factor in his deciding to emigrate to that country.

To this second phase belong some of Stravinsky's best-known and most performed works. Concert works include the *Symphony of Psalms* (1930), the Violin Concerto (1931), *Duo Concertant* (1932), and the *Mass* (1948); stage works include *Oedipus Rex* (1927), *Apollo* (1928), *Persephone* (1934), *Orpheus* (1947). It will immediately be obvious that these titles show a marked predilection for classical Greek ideals. The exception is *The Card Party* (1936), though this is imbued, from first note to last, with the vocabulary of classic dancing and the classic tradition of the theatre. The same may be said for the ballet based on arrangements of Tchaikovsky's music, *The Fairy's Kiss* (1928).

In his third phase Stravinsky exploits the possibilities of serialism, following the example of **Webern**. Beginning hesitantly with the *Cantata* (1952) and the *Canticum Sacrum* (1956), which mark the transition, Stravinsky's characteristic style gradually reveals itself as being chiefly appropriate for vocal, religious music in this last stage of his life. Representative works are *Threni* (1958), *A Sermon, a Narrative and a Prayer* (1961), *Abraham and Isaac* (1963), and *Requiem Canticles* (1966), which was his last important work. It should be heard together with the *Introitus* in memory of **T.S. Eliot** (1965), which contains the opening words of the Requiem. Other works of this phase include, for the stage, *Agon* (1957) and *The Flood* (1962) and, for the concert hall, *Movements* for piano and orchestra (1959) and *Variations* (1964) in memory of **Aldous Huxley**. One of the chief fruits of his exploration into the possibilities of the serial method is his discovery of a new form of choral polyphony, based on canon. The creative impulse behind this was religious. He was a man of profound faith; as he says in *The Poetics of Music* (1947), quite explicitly, his creative work is the product of his conscience and his faith; indeed, the Russian Orthodox Church gave him just that spiritual *ordonnance* on which his life rested. Since choral, polyphonic music is traditionally the music of the church, it was through choral music that Stravinsky realized his reli-

gious nature. Moreover, serialism, as a principle of composition, is as remote as it could be from subjective emotion; and in this respect Stravinsky saw his new polyphony as most truly reflecting the spiritual aspiration of the universal church.

Stravinsky is the most representative of twentieth-century composers. His career began when, in the wake of **Wagner**, Western music had forsaken a single, common language. The period between the wars witnesses a polarization, between the Austro-German school on the one hand, whose representative was Schoenberg, and the Franco-Russian school on the other, of whom the most prominent was Stravinsky. The final period of his life witnessed his bringing together these two streams, so long divided. In this sense his work may be seen as reuniting and revitalizing twentieth-century music.

He has exercised a mesmeric hold over successive generations of European musicians, who no sooner would become acquainted with a particular aspect of his style, and maybe reproduce it themselves, than they would be disconcerted to see that its creator had moved off into some fresh territory. With each successive phase Stravinsky altered the face of Western music. He was incapable of repeating himself. Born outside the Austro-German tradition, he was not subject to the ardent yet limiting nationalism of the Second Viennese School, which claimed so many casualties in the first half of the twentieth century; at the same time he had the liveliest curiosity about everything that affected the *materia musica*, and about all aspects of music, from that of his contemporaries right back to the pre-classical period.

The Russian works of Stravinsky's first phase have a chief identifying characteristic – the development of rhythm, and metre, as an entity in itself. The nineteenth century, the age of Romanticism, had singled out harmony as the most important factor in musical composition; it was regarded as the parent of melody, the source of music's structures;

rhythm was taken to be of subsidiary importance. *The Rite of Spring* abruptly changed that. Rhythm, as a separate structural element, was now emancipated – a fact which many later composers, notably **Messiaen** and **Elliott Carter**, have recognized as a turning-point in the evolution of Western music.

The neo-classicism of Stravinsky's second phase has frequently been criticized, even dismissed as irrelevant and reactionary, by the more radical avant-garde, particularly in Europe. **Pierre Boulez** may be taken as representative of this shade of opinion. But the criticism is usually based on a misunderstanding of Stravinsky's creative purpose, which was one of order, and the revitalizing of tradition. This feature is indeed a prominent one in works of all three phases, not least in his serial works. It was a view he shared with Webern. But whereas the latter interpreted the twelve-note laws of his teacher Schoenberg within the strict confines of the Viennese tradition, Stravinsky saw in **Webern's** technique the suggestion of something much broader; an entirely new concept of order, and fresh possibilities for the enrichment of the melodic/harmonic tradition of Western music as a whole. He discovered new areas of tonality beyond the limits of the major and minor keys. The range of the tonal spectrum appeared enormous, extending from, at the one end, primary chords and keys, to, at the other end, the most abstruse chromatic relationships. Serialism seemed to Stravinsky the means whereby this new resource, hitherto untapped, could be exploited. He said in 1958, which was the year of the *Threni* and *Movements*, 'My recent works are composed on the – my – tonal system' (in *Conversations*, see below). This fresh and latest discovery was to prove just as far-reaching and radical as his exploitation of rhythm in the works of his first phase.

Further reading

See: *Chroniques de ma vie* (1935, translated as *Chronicles of My Life*, 1936) and *An Autobiography* (1936). With Robert Craft: *Conversations with Igor Stravinsky* (1959); *Memories and Commentaries* (1960); *Expositions and Developments* (1962); *Dialogues and a Diary* (1963); *Themes and Episodes* (1966); *Retrospectives and Conclusions* (1969). By Robert Craft: *The Chronicle of a Friendship* (1972); *Prejudices in Disguise* (1074); *Stravinsky in Pictures and Documents* (1978). See also: N. Nabokov, *Igor Stravinsky* (1964); Francis Routh, *Stravinsky* (1975); R. Vlad, *Stravinsky* (1958, trans. 1960, 3rd edn 1978); Stephen Walsh, *The Music of Stravinsky* (1993) and *Igor Stravinsky* (2000, first of a two-volume biography); Charles M. Joseph, *Stravinsky Inside Out* (2001); Stephen Walsh (ed.) *The New Grove Stravinsky* (2004). Stravinsky's music is published by Boosey and Hawkes, B. Schott's Sohne, and J. and W. Chester Ltd.

FRANCIS ROUTH

STRAWSON, Peter Frederick

1919–

English philosopher

Strawson is the leading member of the later phase of linguistic philosophy at Oxford. He became a fellow of University College in 1947, Waynflete Professor of Metaphysics in 1967, and was knighted in 1977. Strawson's work develops austere and abstract arguments in a lucid and elegant fashion. His early writings form part of ordinary language philosophy in so far as they criticize orthodoxies of logical analysis by reference to ordinary use. His later writings are constructive, and have led linguistic philosophy back to metaphysics along Kantian lines. But there is an abiding concern, namely with describing the most general and pervasive features of human thought about the world, in particular the operations of reference and predication. The main influences on Strawson are Aristotle, Hume, Kant and **Wittgenstein**.

Strawson's early articles are collected in *Logico-Linguistic Papers* (1971). His first target was **Russell's** theory of descriptions. According to Strawson a sentence like 'The present king of France is bald' is *neither true nor false* rather than simply false; it *presupposes* rather than entails the existence of the present king of France, i.e. that existence is a necessary precondition of the statement being either true *or* false (an idea which had a significant impact in logic and linguistics). By trying to paraphrase away singular referring expressions of the form 'the so-and-so', Russell misconstrued their distinctive role. *Introduction to Logical Theory* (1952) demonstrated further that the subtle structures of natural languages are distorted by being forced into the Procrustean bed of formal logic.

In his master-work *Individuals* (1959), Strawson's concern shifted from ordinary language to *descriptive metaphysics*. This enterprise differs from *revisionary metaphysics* in that it 'is content to describe the actual structure of our thought about the world', rather than attempting 'to produce a better structure'. It seeks to 'lay bare the most general features of our conceptual structure'. These are not visible in the motley of ordinary use, but in fundamental functions of discourse, notably those of *reference* – picking out an individual item – and *predication* – saying something about it. The basic objects of reference must be spatio-temporal individuals of, i.e. material bodies, animals and people. Strawson further maintains that the concept of a person is 'primitive'. A person is not a combination of two one-sided things (a body and a soul), as Cartesianism has it, but a single two-sided thing, one to which both physical and mental predicates can be applied.

Individuals has been the single most important factor in rehabilitating metaphysics within analytic philosophy. By contrast to traditional metaphysics, however, descriptive metaphysics seeks to describe not the most abstract features of the *world* but the preconditions of our *thought* about the world. Strawson also revived Kant's idea of *transcendental arguments*, which are supposed to show that sceptical doubts are incoherent or self-refuting. In later years, he instead pursued a Humean strategy: sceptical arguments are idle; they cannot persuade us since we cannot help believing, e.g., in material bodies or other minds. A similar response is given to attacks on the possibility of free will. Reac-

tive attitudes to human action – resentment, gratitude, indignation – are neither rational nor irrational. Even if determinism were correct, they could not be abandoned, since they form an indispensable 'part of the general framework of human life'.

According to *Analysis and Metaphysics* (1992), philosophy aims to elucidate those concepts which are essential to human thought – space, time, object, mind and body, knowledge, truth, meaning, etc. Its method is *connective analysis* rather than the *reductive analysis* practised by logical atomists, logical positivists and scientist philosophers. Concepts are elucidated not by decomposing them into elements which are simple or less problematic, but by tracing their connections with other parts of our conceptual scheme. Although, unlike science, philosophy does not yield new knowledge about the world, it provides a positive contribution to our self-understanding.

Further reading

Other works include: *The Bounds of Sense* (1966) and *Skepticism and Naturalism* (1985). See: Z. van Straaten (ed.) *Philosophical Subjects: Essays presented to P.F. Strawson* (1980); P.A. Schilpp (ed.) *The Philosophy of P.F. Strawson* (1998); H.J. Glock (ed.) *Strawson and Kant* (2003).

HANS-JOHANN GLOCK

STRINDBERG, Johan August

1849–1912

Swedish playwright and author

Strindberg's father was a steamship agent who married his housekeeper in 1847, after she had already borne him three children. Her death when he was twelve left Strindberg feeling deprived. He was married three times to women who all put their own careers first, and did not want to mother him. He had a pietistic upbringing which marked him for life, and he was never at ease without God. Before he discovered his vocation as a writer Strindberg tried a number of occupations:

student, doctor, actor and journalist. He wrote his first masterpiece *Master Olof (Mäster Olof)* in 1872, a play about the Lutheran reformer of the sixteenth century, Olaus Petri, but in spite of its deep psychological insight and brilliant dialogue it had to wait nine years for printing and performance. This was to be the pattern of Strindberg's career as a dramatist in Sweden. He never had more than brief periods of success, chiefly because he was always in advance of his times.

Fortunately for him he could write other things than plays. His seventy dramatic pieces are contained in only seventeen of the fifty-five volumes of his collected works. The rest contain poetry, novels, history, essays, pseudo-scientific and alchemistic writings. He made his breakthrough in Sweden with a novel, *The Red Room* (*Röda rummet*, 1879), a biting but light-hearted satire, written in sparkling Swedish, about his experiences in Stockholm. His first really successful play, *Lucky Peter's Travels* (*Lycko Pers resor*, 1882), was also a satire about the folly of illusions, a favourite theme in his later plays. This was preceded and followed by works that made him so unpopular in Sweden that he went to live abroad. In Switzerland, hoping to reinstate himself, he wrote *Getting Married* (*Giftas*, I–II, 1884–5), two volumes of short stories about sex and married life. But the first volume precipitated a trial for blasphemy, engineered, as he thought, by the feminists whom, though he was acquitted, he attacked with great bitterness in the preface and in some of the stories of the second volume. 'The Breadwinner', the last story in the book, was seen as a slur on his first wife, the would-be actress Siri von Essen, and only served to increase his unpopularity. This was the first serious crisis in his life, mental and physical. Theatres were afraid to perform his plays, publishers to print his books. The second volume also established his reputation as a misogynist, later confirmed by the so-called 'naturalistic' plays, the only works by which he is widely known in this country. But though for a period Strindberg was fiercely anti-feminist, he was no misogynist. 'I love women and I adore children and, as a divorced man, I recommend marriage as the only commerce between the sexes,' he wrote in a letter of 1892. In many of his later dramas, including his historical plays, there is little trace of the woman-hater.

Strindberg was an omnivorous reader. Kierkegaard, Brandes, **Mill**, **Darwin** and **Spencer** were on his bookshelves before 1886; then, in order to understand the working of his own mind and the minds of others, he turned with enthusiasm to psychology and pathology, and studied among others the Frenchmen Jacoby, Ribot and Garnier, and the Englishman Maudsley, in whose book *The Pathology of Mind* he found a complete diagnosis of himself. It is difficult to say how far this reading coloured the self-portrait in his autobiographical work *The Son of a Servant* (*Tjänstekvinnans son*, 1886). He was an inveterate role-player, and what he says about himself must not be taken at its face value. He used his new knowledge to good effect when he wrote the three powerful plays which, in course of time, brought him international fame: *The Father* (*Fadren*, 1887), *Miss Julie* (*Fröken Julie*, 1888) and *Creditors* (*Fordringsägare*, 1889). These plays are called naturalistic, though they in no way resemble **Zola's** photographic naturalism. In his preface to *Miss Julie* Strindberg says: 'I believe I have observed that for modern people the psychological development is what most interests them, and that our inquiring minds are not satisfied with seeing something happen, we want to know why it happens.' *The Father* is a study of the effects of doubt and female oppression on a precariously balanced mind. The construction of the play is conventional but in its three acts every aspect of mental torture is portrayed, what Strindberg called 'psychic murder'. *Miss Julie* is another case history, a piece of brilliant analysis, acted in one continuous scene 'to maintain the author's magnetic hold over the audience'. This is not psychic murder. It is true that Jean and the absent father exercise a hypnotic influence at the end, but Julie commits suicide because she cannot face disgrace. In *Creditors*, another one-act play, Strindberg has introduced Max Nordau's idea that suggestion may be in dumb show: Gustav acts an epileptic fit, and Adolf has one and dies. Recognition of the greatness of these plays was slow to come everywhere except Paris and Berlin.

During this same period Strindberg wrote two of his most famous prose works: *A Madman's Defence* (*Le Plaidoyer d'un fou*, 1888) and *The People of Hemsö* (Hemsöborna, 1887). The first, written in French, and not meant for publication, is the vindictive story of his marriage to Siri, the second an amusing account of life in the Stockholm archipelago. In both the theme of sexual jealousy is prominent. Back in Stockholm he produced another important prose work, *By the Open Sea* (*I havsbandet*, 1890), a story about the disintegration of a human being when isolated from his intellectual equals, and persecuted by the masses. It was written during the period of his uneasy atheism, but is shot through with a longing for God. In 1892 he wrote seven plays, none of which were performed in Sweden though one, *Playing with Fire* (*Leka med elden*), has since gained international recognition. After this set-back and his divorce from Siri, which entailed the loss of his children, Strindberg again went into exile, first in Berlin, then in Paris. For the next six years he abandoned literature and turned to his own brand of science. His great plan was to write a work which would enable him to understand how the universe was governed. But he was no ordinary scientist. He was an artist, who believed in intuition, and though he did make some experiments he distrusted them. He was retreating into that inner world which became so real to him. This is the world of his novel *Inferno* (*Inferno*, 1897), the book that has always been taken as the clearest indication that he was mad. It is in fact a highly coloured account of what he called his 'occult' experiences in Paris from 1894 to 1896, the period known as his 'Inferno Crisis', though then, as always, Strindberg knew perfectly well what he was about. It is true that he experimented with

madness, as he did with other things, but he never crossed the border line.

He emerged from this period a changed man. Swedenborg had revealed to him the meaning of his self-induced, but often terrifying, experiences: they were a punishment for sins committed in a previous existence. From being an atheist he became a believer. He knew this belief was a subjective matter. He needed God and so he believed, but in a very individual way. In this spirit he wrote one of his greatest dramas, *To Damascus* I–II–III (*Till Damaskus*, 1898–1901). These plays were quite unlike anything that had gone before. The technique was expressionistic, symbolism was freely used, and the dramatic unities were not observed. *To Damascus* is a journey, in the Kierkegaardian sense of *Stages on Life's Way*, in search of the self and of God. Both frequently elude the Unknown One, the protagonist of the play, but he persists, for, as he comes to realize, if you cannot know you must believe. Like most of what Strindberg wrote, *To Damascus* was before its time in Sweden, both in content and scenically. It was a precursor of the German expressionist movement of 1912.

The years from 1898 to 1903 were enormously productive. He wrote over twenty plays, some of them among his best. His cycle of historical dramas is the most effective dramatization of history since Shakespeare. The most popular of these is *Erik XIV* (1899), the Hamlet-like character, whom Strindberg himself called characterless. With *The Dance of Death* (*Dödsdansen*, 1901) Strindberg appears to be taking a step backwards to naturalism, but this is an illusion. The characters in this play are not men and women, they are types, elemental personifications of evil. As with many of Strindberg's dramas, episodes in his own life had fired his imagination, but it is the use he made of his source, not the source itself, that is important. As Ollén has pointed out: 'the details may correspond with uncanny precision ... but the whole is fantasy ... By magnifying, distorting, and freely associating ideas, he has created characters who live a fantasy life entirely independent of their origins.'

For Strindberg the climax of his work came with *A Dream Play* (*Ett Drömspel*, 1902). Like *To Damascus* it is a journey of the soul towards disillusionment and release. As illusions are burnt in the flames of the Growing Castle, the symbol of human life, the bud that crowns it bursts into bloom as the world did when Buddha ascended into nothingness. The action of the play takes place in an inconsequent dream world where anything may happen, but the dialogue is often very matter of fact:

> *The Daughter*: People are pitiable
> *The Father*: They are indeed. And it is a riddle to me what they live on. They marry on an income of four hundred pounds, when they need eight.

In 1907 Strindberg wrote some one-act chamber plays for his own Intimate Theatre, among them *The Ghost Sonata* (*Spöksonaten*). It is often considered to be obscure; in fact it is a beautifully constructed play and demonstrates clearly that Strindberg knew exactly what he wanted to convey. The contending forces of good and evil are visually defined in the first scene, in the second the full extent of evil is revealed, both in the dialogue and in the setting, while in the third, in spite of the bright room in which it is set, darkness triumphs. The end is death, as it is in all but one of the chamber plays.

Strindberg was a great innovator; he had no more use for the well-made character than he had for the well-made play. 'Where is the self,' he wrote in 1886,

> which is supposed to be the character? It is neither in one place nor in the other, it is in both. The ego is not one unit; it is a multiplicity of reflexes, a complex of impulses, of demands, some suppressed at one moment, others let loose at another.

He showed that this complex self is more interesting than the straightforward character and, in his later plays, that the journey of the soul can be dramatically effective. He employed scenery in novel ways, and revolutionized dialogue by using everyday speech. His whole life was pilgrimage in search of himself. From the depths of his own experience he fashioned a new form of drama that gave expression to an inner world of trial and struggle, and his influence has been immense. Perhaps **Eugene O'Neill** springs most readily to mind, but there have been many others who could say with Strindberg: 'I find the joy of life in its fierce, cruel struggles, and my delight is in knowing something, in learning something.' People who can adopt this attitude will not find his plays depressing.

Further reading

See: *The Plays*, Vols I and II (trans. Michael Meyer, 1964–75); *The Vasa Trilogy* (trans. W. Johnson, 1950); *The Chamber Plays* (trans. E. Sprinchorn, 1962); *Twelve Plays* (trans. E. Sprigge, 1963); *The Red Room* (trans. E. Sprigge, 1967); *The Son of a Servant* (trans. E. Sprinchorn, 1967); *A Madman's Defence* (trans. E. Sprinchorn, 1968); *Getting Married* (trans. M. Sandbach, 1972); *Inferno and From an Occult Diary* (trans. M. Sandbach, 1979). See: Mortensen and Downs, *Strindberg, His Life and Work* (1949); Gunnar Ollén, *August Strindberg* (1972); G. Brandell, *Strindberg in Inferno* (trans. 1974); W. Johnson, *Strindberg's Historical Dramas* (1962); M. Lamm, *August Strindberg* (trans. 1971). John Ward, *The Religious and Social Plays of August Strindberg* (1980), has an excellent bibliography. See also: Michael Robinson, *Strindberg and Autobiography: Writing and Reading a Life* (1986); Harry C. Carlson, *Out of Inferno: Strindberg's Reawakening as an Artist* (1996).

MARY SANDBACH

SUKARNO, Ahmed (Bung Karno)

1901–70

Indonesian president

There is no ancient Indonesia as there is an ancient Japan and ancient China. It is a new entity which began its life as an idea, 'the product', as the historian John Smail wrote, 'of a great and difficult leap of the imagination', first conjured up by students studying in institutions of higher learning in the

Netherlands and the Netherlands Indies (or 'Dutch East Indies') in the 1920s who longed to rid themselves of Dutch colonial rule. The Javanese among them, of whom Sukarno was the most prominent, resisting the temptation to exploit the numerical preponderance of their own ethnic group, shared instead with their non-Javanese colleagues the civic ideal of a multi-ethnic nation whose boundaries would be coterminous with those of the Netherlands Indies. The Japanese occupation of the Indies during the Pacific War (1942–5) had the effect of transforming this idea of Indonesia from an aspiration in the minds of a few to a tangible goal widely shared by the population at large.

It was in the latter years of this occupation that Sukarno came into his own as an inclusive leader and nation-builder, and he continued to lead in this manner after proclaiming independence on 17 August 1945. In his famous *Panca Sila* (Five Pillars) speech of 1 June 1945, he spoke of the aspiration to build 'a state of "all for all", "one for all, all for one"', 'a state built on mutual co-operation'. In seeking to realize this goal he sought a compromise between Moslems and Christians in the form of a 'Theistic State' and suggested that a representative body would be an appropriate place for them to advance their respective claims.

In most of these activities the flamboyant, Javanese and nominally Moslem Sukarno was closely accompanied by the staid, Minangkabau and devoutly Islamic Mohammad Hatta, who served as both prime minister (December 1949–August 1950) and vice president (1945–9, August 1950–December 1956). Although very different people, they had worked closely and cordially together since the beginning of the Japanese occupation, and by 1949 had become known as the *Dwitunggal* (two-in-one). They fell out in the end with Hatta resigning the vice-presidency in December 1956. Thereafter Sukarno's inclusive leadership began to lose its plausibility as he came increasingly to be identified with ethnic and political groups within the nation rather than with the nation itself.

By 1956 Sukarno was seeking alternatives to the liberal democratic government, which was struggling ineffectually with regional disaffection and unrest in the army. In a major speech of February 1957 that laid down the organizing principles of Guided Democracy, he called for the formation of a cabinet of 'mutual co-operation' in which representatives of the major parties, including the Communist Party, would sit, suggesting that it was not practical to exclude a group from the processes of government which received six million votes in the recent elections (of 1955). He also proposed the establishment of a national council to serve as an advisory body to the cabinet. Revealing the recent influence upon him of corporatist ideas, he suggested that the membership of this body should consist of representatives of functional groups in society and, as he saw it, thereby reflect the composition of society just as the cabinet would reflect the composition of parliament.

Sukarno's proposals were still consistent with an inclusive approach to Indonesia's problems. But his claim in the speech of February 1957 that he was 'the mouthpiece of the Indonesian people' implied that he was more able than either of these two bodies to give accurate expression to the wishes of the people. This substitution of himself for representative institutions (even corporatist ones) boded ill for his continuing application of inclusive leadership in Indonesia.

Guided Democracy was inaugurated in July 1959, and in the following year Sukarno banned Masjumi, the modernist Islamic political party which had garnered almost eight million votes from a largely outer island constituency in the 1955 elections, on the grounds of its involvement in the regional rebellion of 1958. This may be seen as a turning point in the history of his domestic leadership of the Republic of Indonesia for, after this drastic act of exclusion, it no longer seemed accurate to describe it as inclusive. And a year later his foreign policy began to show signs of a comparable transformation. Prior to that time Indonesia had adopted a position of non-alignment between the two rival blocs in the Cold War and had even on occasion sought, together with like-minded countries such as India, a lessening of the tensions between them. However, from 1961 Sukarno recast his map of the world. Where previously Indonesia had found a place between two competing groups, it now saw itself as a leading member of the 'new emergent forces' locked in conflict with their neo-colonial and imperialist counterparts (or 'old established forces').

But if the President's style of leadership in the early 1960s became increasingly divisive in some respects, then in others it appeared to be recklessly broad in its embrace. Thus in 1960 he re-introduced into Indonesian politics his belief, first formulated in 1926, in the desirability of co-operation between Islamic, nationalist and socialist forces. At first, this idea, now cast as NASAKOM unity (the unity of Nationalist [*Nasionalis*], Religious [*Agama*] and Communist [*Komunis*] forces) served to underpin his efforts to build a close working relationship with and between the Indonesian National Party, the traditionalist Islamic Nahdlatul Ulama and the Communist Party as a way of balancing the power of the Indonesian army. Later, however, it acquired the status of a doctrine equal in importance to the state ideology of *Panca Sila*, and one which, he claimed, was held in high esteem by 99 per cent of the Indonesian people.

There is a debate about what precisely Sukarno's motives were in the late Guided Democracy years: some argue that he was deploying the doctrine of NASAKOM to integrate the Communist Party into the existing order, whereas others believed that he was trying to smooth its path to power. Whatever the case, he was certainly mistaken regarding the favourable reception of this doctrine by his fellow country-people, as the massacre in 1965 of up to 400,000 communists by nationalist and religious elements, with the incitement, support and direction of General Soeharto and the army, demonstrated. Indeed, to bring together groups of such diverse – indeed, antagonistic – interests

within an environment shaped by frantic political mobilization, soaring inflation and serious food shortages, and to persist in such efforts amid the violence stirred up in the villages of Central and East Java by the Communist Party's attempt to implement the Land Reform Law of 1960, seemed to be courting disaster. For all Sukarno's growing conviction that he was uniquely capable of giving voice to the aspirations of the Indonesian people, what is striking about him at this late stage of his political career is not his intuitive rapport with the Indonesian people but just how out of touch he really was.

Sukarno was appalled by the massacre of the communists, seeing in this event the undoing of his life's work as a nation-builder. It also deprived him of his principal political support, and he was only able to cling to power until 11 March 1966 when, under duress, he transferred substantial power to General Soeharto. He never recovered from this setback and was formally replaced by Soeharto in March 1968.

Further reading

Sukarno is the subject of a collaborative auto-biography: *Sukarno: An Autobiography as told to Cindy Adams* (1965); and three biographies: Bernard Dahm, *Sukarno and the Struggle for Indonesian Independence* (1969); Bob Hering, *Soekarno: Founding Father of Indonesia, 1901–1945* (2002); and J.D. Legge, *Sukarno: A Political Biography* (1972). Other secondary sources, invaluable for understanding his presidency in its historical context, are: Herbert Feith, *The Decline of Constitutional Democracy in Indonesia* (1962); Daniel S. Lev, *The Transition to Guided Democracy: Indonesian Politics, 1957–1959* (1966); J.A.C. Mackie, *Konfrontasi: The Indonesia–Malaysia Dispute, 1963–1966* (1974); and the chapters on Indonesia written by John Smail in David Joel Steinberg (ed.) *In Search of Southeast Asia: A Modern History* (1971).

ANGUS MCINTYRE

SULLIVAN, (Sir) Arthur

1842–1900

Irish composer

Sullivan has been one of the more conspicuous victims of English musical snobbery during the last hundred years. Those who lavish praises on the operettas of Jacques **Offenbach**, Lehar and **Johann Strauss** are given to wrinkling their nostrils at the suggestion, amply borne out by an examination of the scores, that the Savoy Operas display a far subtler and more varied musical palette than any of these masters of the lighter genre. Such, however, is undoubtedly the case: Sullivan's exceptional early gifts, excellent training and professional dedication, linked with a cosmopolitanism unique among otherwise heavily parochial Victorian musicians, make him the most interesting English talent between Arne and **Elgar**.

Some of this catholicity and eclecticism derived from his family background. His father was a well-travelled Irish military bandmaster and his mother, Maria Clementina Coghlan, was half Italian. The boy Arthur, as a Chapel Royal chorister, gave rapid evidence of considerable promise, and went on to win the Royal Academy's first Mendelssohn scholarship to enable him to study at the Leipzig Conservatorium, then the finest in Europe. Out of this came the symphonic incidental music to Shakespeare's *The Tempest*, first performed in England at one of August Manns's enterprising Crystal Palace concerts in 1862, when the composer was only twenty.

The Tempest was followed three years later by Sullivan's only symphony, the 'Irish' (from its use of folk melodies in the scherzo), the most accomplished English symphony before Elgar's in A flat (1908) and a perfect example of its composer's ability to dilute the Mendelssohn and Schumann of his Leipzig days with touches of the Italian and French operatic manner for which he had such an abiding affection. Greater popularity, however, was to be gained in England by the production of those large-scale choral works which provided the staple fodder of Victorian music festivals and which, with one or two notable exceptions (Parry's *Blest Pair of Sirens* and the three major examples by Elgar), are now totally forgotten. In producing works such as *The Prodigal Son* (Worcester, 1869)

and *The Light of the World* (Birmingham, 1873) Sullivan established a reputation as the most enterprising and distinctive of the younger English composers, enhanced by his sterling abilities as a conductor and his notable grasp of every aspect of practical musicmaking. He was especially respected for his enthusiasm in promoting the teaching of music and for his encouragement of younger musicians, including Elgar, several of whose early works he conducted and whose style bears traces of his influence.

Witty and convivial, his talents as a raconteur and his fondness for 'fast' living brought Sullivan a smart and influential circle of friends, including the Prince and Princess of Wales and members of the aristocracy. As the doyen of late Victorian musicians he made the acquaintance of **Liszt**, **Gounod**, **Dvořák** and **Saint-Saëns**. He was much in demand as a composer of effective incidental music, his best scores being prepared for *Macbeth* (with its eerily **Wagnerian** prelude) and *The Merchant of Venice*. The sparkle and verve of the latter shows the authentic vein of comedy he was to develop after his meeting with **W.S. Gilbert** in 1871.

Their subsequent collaboration lasted some fifteen years (ending with *The Grand Duke*, 1896) and wholly altered the pattern of Sullivan's professional life. In the eyes of many he was failing to fulfil his obligations as a serious composer, and **Queen Victoria** herself suggested that he turn to grand opera, a suggestion which produced *Ivanhoe* (1891, to a dismal libretto by Julian Sturgis), a fascinatingly over-ambitious project. There is no doubt, however, that he had found his true *métier* and a close collaboration with the almost neurotically painstaking Gilbert enabled Sullivan to demonstrate a kaleidoscopic range of moods and styles. The enormous success of the Savoy Operas, due in part to an inspired impresario, Richard D'Oyly Carte, was alloyed by a serious quarrel between Sullivan and Gilbert, which broke the series for four years between 1889 and 1893, and by Sullivan's failing health. An immense crowd attended his funeral in St

Paul's Cathedral, but perhaps the most impressive single tribute was Gilbert's, paid several years after his collaborator's death: his mournful response to the hint that he should find another composer was 'What use is Gilbert without a Sullivan?'

The charm and strength of the Savoy Operas (so called from D'Oyly Carte's theatre specially designed to house them) lies not only in the dazzling variety of Sullivan's polyglot style, but in his unique gift for affectionate parody. *Iolanthe* (1882), for example, is heavily marked by reminiscences of a visit to Bayreuth, with allusions to *Das Rheingold* and use of Wagnerian motifs. *Trial by Jury* (1875, the first collaboration with Gilbert) features, in the ensemble 'A Nice Dilemma We Have Here', what is in effect a brilliant reconstruction of the sextet 'D'un pensiero' in Bellini's *La Sonnambula*. An enduring fondness for Italian opera irradiates the score of *HMS Pinafore* (1878), and the whole of the second act of *The Pirates of Penzance* (1879) can be seen as a sustained homage to **Verdi**. Notable also are Sullivan's attempts, in such numbers as 'Prithee, Pretty Maiden' in *Patience* and 'Brightly Dawns Our Wedding Day' in *The Mikado*, to imitate native English folk and madrigal styles.

As an orchestrator, armed with a practical performer's knowledge of most instruments, Sullivan stands comparison with **Berlioz** and **Rimsky-Korsakov**. Following his discovery, with Sir George Grove in Vienna in 1867, of Schubert's lost *Rosamunde* music, he reflected a markedly Schubertian quality in the lightness and delicacy of his scoring. His most personal utterances are to be heard in the five works which best display the fluctuations of his rapport with Gilbert. *Patience* (1881), an inspired spoof of the Aesthetic craze spearheaded by **Wilde**, **Swinburne** and **William Morris**, and *Iolanthe*, satirizing the House of Lords and the legal establishment, show a mature command of musical form in their handling of ensemble and grandiose through-composed first act finales. *Princess Ida* (1884), a burlesque version of **Tennyson's** *The Princess*, triumphs over Gilbert's ungainly

blank verse text by virtue of the music's extraordinary refinement and seriousness of intention: its second act is perhaps the best demonstration of Sullivan's artistic powers. *The Yeoman of the Guard* (1888) once again subdues the banalities of its libretto, an appalling study in mock-Tudor, in what is unquestionably the finest English dramatic music of the nineteenth century. *The Gondoliers* (1889) represents, in terms symbolized by the nature of its comedy, an attempt by its creators to reconcile their differences, and stands as the perfect collaboration, welding Gilbert's inimitable wit to Sullivan's effervescently Italianate and often hauntingly romantic score.

As a serious composer Sullivan never overcame his self-consciousness in the face of contemporary English preference and prejudice, and works such as *The Golden Legend* and *The Martyr of Antioch* show the lack of conviction essential to his ultimate failure in this guise. His real talent, which finds its parallel not in the operettas of Offenbach and Strauss, but in the Italian *opera buffa* of Rossini and Donizetti, lay in his genius for applying his innate gifts as a melodist and an assured grasp of the techniques of serious music to the creation of a species of sophisticated comedy which has numbered among its innumerable devotees such apparently unlikely figures as **Nietzsche** and **Stravinsky**.

Further reading

See: Herbert Sullivan and Newman Flower, *Sir Arthur Sullivan: His Life, Letters and Diaries* (1927); Hesketh Pearson, *Gilbert and Sullivan: A Biography* (1935); Gervase Hughes, *The Music of Arthur Sullivan* (1960); David Eden, *Gilbert and Sullivan: The Creative Conflict* (1986); Philip H. Dillard, *Sir Arthur Sullivan: A Resource Book* (1996); Michael Ainger, *Gilbert and Sullivan: A Dual Biography* (2002).

JONATHAN KEATES

SULLIVAN, Louis Henry

1856–1924
US architect

Louis Sullivan's career rose with the evolution of the tall metal-framed commercial buildings, during the last decades of the nineteenth century. Through his talents, he showed that such structures could be artistically considered, and thus brought them within the realm of architecture. His efforts in bringing a new order and grace to this type of building were parallel with those of such as **Walt Whitman** and **Mark Twain**, who equally were searching for a true American voice, and to free their creative production from European influences. Born in Boston in 1856 of Irish and Swiss parents, both musical, Louis Sullivan's early architectural experience and training were restless and varied. He spent a short time at the École des Beaux Arts in Paris, and worked in many architects' offices, including the office of Frank Furness in Philadelphia. He arrived in Chicago in the 1870s, during the city's first great building boom. Shortly after arriving, Sullivan met and sufficiently impressed Dankmar Adler to be offered a partnership in the latter's established practice. Adler was to act as technician and trusted friend during the major part of Sullivan's career, from 1881 onwards.

Their early work was much influenced by the buildings of **H.H. Richardson**, particularly the exterior of their first major building, the Auditorium in Chicago of 1886. The interior, in its use of elemental geometry to organize the major spaces, was similarly influenced; the surfaces within, however, were extensively decorated, much of the decoration being remarkably inventive, derived from a combined use of geometry and natural form. Ornament in architecture was to be the most lasting theme in Sullivan's work. His use of it was organizational and metaphoric, to represent his deepest conviction in a natural law of form relating to function. Hating the Beaux Arts style, representing to him, as it did, Europe's tired decadence, he rejected the Beaux Arts principle of the dominance of the plan and its ancient role in carrying the meaning of the building, and consequently his work became increasingly elevational, to concentrate on the façade, the plans within seemingly wilfully indifferent. The finest examples of his ideas as applied to the new tall building form were the Wainwright Building of 1890–91 in St Louis and the Guaranty Building of 1894–5 in Buffalo. Sullivan's increasing facility with ornament can be traced developing through a series of tombs, the best of which, the Getty Tomb in Chicago of 1890 and the Wainwright Tomb in St Louis of 1892, are composed of sombre pure forms set alive by the application of running, vibrating decoration.

In his famous essay of 1896, 'The Tall Office Buildings Artistically Considered', he expounded his theories of the idea of the natural law as a basis of architecture. In doing this he was extending to buildings theories concerning fitness to purpose expounded earlier by Horatio Greenough, the American expatriate sculptor, and more generally, extending the essentially puritan New England natural Transcendentalism of **Thoreau** and **Emerson**. In so doing Sullivan was attempting to root this quintessential American spirit in the centres of the new booming cities. His conviction was that functionalism was a natural law, and that through a careful, ritualistic analysis of the needs that the building was to fulfil, by 'using nature's own machinery', the form would naturally emerge, like a plant from the earth. This belief allowed him to begin to form an architecture free from the wilful European formalism of the time. The poetry and potency of the idea is susceptible, however, to two major linked weaknesses. First, in its inability to recognize any conflict of interest, and in its dependence upon an intense spirituality for its fullness, the theory, through its workings as a conscious re-examination of the minutiae of requirement, could quickly decay into an unquestioning acceptance of the client's requirements, and a blindness to the larger social issues regarding, for instance, the relationship between the public and the private realms. It is, however, one of Sullivan's most lasting memorials that after him, the style of the American skyscraper remains to create public space within the building, adjacent to the street.

The second weakness revolves around the difficulty of defining any function clearly. One might confidently say of a bread knife what its purpose is, but such a straightforward implement might find itself being used purposefully, in, for instance, the hands of a murderer. Thus in the complexity of engagement with the living, where the rule of natural order should be most vivid, the idea of clarity of function becomes most endangered. With the less easily defined functions that the simplest building must accommodate, the idea tends to useless generalities, without some other, perhaps unspoken, controlling intention. One might feel some confidence in defining the functions of an office building, but what of a house? And yet Sullivan's edict that form follows function together with Le Corbusier's claim that the house was a machine for living in were to become the two major beliefs of the International Modern Movement in the early twentieth century, paradoxically because of the dependence of the central concept.

Clarity of function depends upon the larger idea of propriety of use, and its antithesis, abuse. In architecture, the idea becomes a concern with the correct use of space and this in turn depends upon a concern for the correctness of human behaviour. Thus a creed that would pretend to be essentially amoral is built upon and requires a necessarily determined morality. Thus functionalism is the unimpassioned mask of moral intentions and thus it was that the progressive European architects of the early twentieth century were able to engage with the idea of social programme, and in so doing created their plain white taut façades to contain the workings of an essentially nineteenth-century movement for social reform.

The hidden contradictions in Sullivan's thought concerning the programme for the tall commercial building has meant that the skyscraper remains enigmatic and challenging to American architects, unabsorbed as it is by either current theories, relating to the shingle style or the loosely termed postmodernist. The World Columbian Exposition, held in Chicago in 1893, represented a rejection by his adopted city of his thoughts and life's work. Apart from his own Transportation building, the predominant style was that of the Beaux Arts. Chicago had decided to appear, to represent its burgeoning wealth, as a *fin-de-siècle* mid-European city. Two years later, Adler withdrew from the partnership. This heavy double blow compounded his natural solitariness, resolved his path as that of the prophet alone, and ushered in the final phase of his life.

Sullivan's finest later works were a series of banks in small mid-west towns, notably in Owatoma, Minnesota, in Grinnell, Iowa, and in Sidney, Ohio, in which there is the finest realization of his style of ornament related to building. Despite the vagaries of available commissions, during a time of depression, which this was, it is difficult not to read in these late works a retreat from and disillusion with the city. During this period up to his death in 1924 he concentrated much effort on writing, exploring, notably in *Kindergarten Chats* (1901–2) and *Autobiography of an Idea* (1924), his deep concern for the relationship between democracy and the practice of his art.

In 1924 a series of large drawings under the title *A System of Architectural Ornament According with a Philosophy of Man's Powers* were published, which are the most beautiful accomplished exposition of his genius for marrying geometry and plant form. These undertakings, carried out in a period of apparent decline, represent his finest work, upon which, increasingly, his reputation will safely stand. It is a measure of his influence that his most brilliant assistant, Frank Lloyd Wright, would, in his mature work, carry further the major themes of Sullivan's life and work, the search for a democratic architecture, the relationship between ornament and building, and finally also, the retreat from the city.

Further reading

Other works include: *Kindergarten Chats and Other Writings* (reprinted 1918). See also: Hugh Morrison,

Louis Sullivan: Prophet of Modern Architecture (1935); Willard Connely, *Louis Sullivan as He Lived* (1960); H. Frei, *Louis Henry Sullivan* (1992); Mario Manierielia, *Louis Henry Sullivan* (1997).

FREDERICK SCOTT

SULSTON, (Sir) John Edward

1942–

English scientist

John Sulston was born in Buckinghamshire, to a schoolteacher and an Anglican minister. As a child, he was fascinated with mechanisms, whether manmade or natural. In his 2002 Nobel Prize autobiography, he describes himself as always having been 'an artisan, a maker and doer'. Although from his early years Sulston differed with his father about religious belief and traditional social hierarchies, he attributes his relative indifference to material wealth and strong impulses to strive for the common good which have marked his career to his father's influence.

After a relatively unremarkable middle-class childhood, Sulston received a scholarship to attend Pembroke College, University of Cambridge, where he studied natural sciences, specializing in organic chemistry. When an application to join the development charity Voluntary Service Overseas fell through at the last moment, he stayed on at Cambridge to do research and take his PhD, which focused on the synthesis of oligonucleotides (short segments of single-stranded DNA).

Sulston took a post-doctoral position at the Salk Institute in California with Leslie Orgel, a British theoretical chemist who was studying the origins of life, and there he 'discovered' the intersection of biology and chemistry. After two years at the Salk, Sulston met **Francis Crick** (co-discoverer of the structure of DNA), who interviewed him for a position at the Medical Research Council Laboratory of Molecular Biology (LMB) in Cambridge. Sulston was appointed staff scientist in 1969 in the laboratory group of Sydney Brenner. The LMB had been officially founded in the early 1960s, and hosted many important research projects to elucidate the basic mechanisms of molecular biology. By the late 1960s, Brenner had begun to study the small nematode worm *Caenorhabditis elegans* as a way to understand the basic mechanisms of genetics, development and neurobiology. Sulston was one of a few ongoing appointments to this research project, which was initially treated by many in the biological community with scepticism.

For nearly thirty years, Sulston worked on a range of phenomena in 'the worm,' as it is known, including neurotransmitters and mutations that interfere with normal development. In a task that many of his colleagues describe as monumental and which took nearly a decade, he used a light microscope with special interference optics to directly observe individual cells through an unfolding sequence of cell divisions in the transparent worm as it progressed from fertilized egg to adult, making an intricate series of hand-drawings to record the fate and position of each cell. Sulston and colleagues eventually mapped the entire cell lineage of the organism, making it the first such multi-organ organism to be so described. This research served as the basis for identifying the genetic controls that propel each cell towards its fate, including particular cells programmed to die as part of the normal processes of development. This process became recognized as a general and important biological phenomenon called 'apoptosis'. The last part of this project was the completion of the cell lineage of *C. elegans* embryo, for which Sulston was elected to the Royal Society in 1986.

Together with Robert Waterston of Washington University in St Louis (who had previously been a postdoctoral fellow at the LMB), Sulston and colleagues produced a physical map of the worm's six chromosomes, then sequenced its genes. The nematode's genomic sequence, the first of a multi-cellular organism to be completed, was published in 1998. This project served as a technological stepping stone to the major collaborative efforts associated with the international

Human Genome Project (HGP). Sulston was appointed as the first head of the Wellcome Trust's Sanger Centre in Cambridgeshire, named after his long-time LMB mentor Fred Sanger and established in 1993 to house worm, human and other genome projects. He led a research group of several hundred scientists who sequenced nearly one-third of the three billion letters in the human genome as part of an international consortium.

As the project progressed, Sulston was drawn into a dispute with Celera Genomics, headed by the charismatic Craig Venter, which in 1998 made an aggressive bid to take over the HGP for profit. Venter promised to finish the sequence much more quickly than the public project would, using alternative technologies. This debate put Sulston into the political position of promoting the 'open science' ethos that had come to govern the HGP, codified in the group's 1996 Bermuda statement, namely that DNA sequence data should be publicly disclosed every day, and the human genome itself should not be owned or subject to commercial investment. This principle echoed those that formed the foundation of the worm community, which is well recognized for its mechanisms of communication which promote the sharing of data. Sulston believed that the HGP had progressed rapidly in large part because everyone shared data on the genetic and physical maps; mechanisms had been developed to facilitate this open access while still giving credit to individual accomplishments.

Sulston argued that the information gained through genomic research (but not the inventions that might be derived from it) should be freely released so that work could proceed efficiently and all could benefit, rather than limiting access through patenting or restrictive licensing. He contended that genes are merely discovered, not invented. The press eagerly picked up on this power struggle and what came to be known as the 'race' to sequence the genome, with Sulston portrayed as saintly or merely a naïve hippy, in juxtaposition to 'Darth' Venter who was viewed either as a savvy capitalist or an opportunistic scientist, whose drive originated from war experiences in Vietnam. Sulston's advocacy kept the human genome, as well as those of key model organisms such as the mouse, in the public domain. This public–private debate accelerated the sequencing of the human genome, perhaps at some cost to the initial accuracy of the data, and secured resources from both the private and public sectors, particularly when Sulston briefly threatened to leave the public project (ironically enough to start a private company). The nearly complete sequence was released to great fanfare in a ceremony hosted by US President Bill Clinton and U.K. Prime Minster Tony Blair in 2000, nearly five years ahead of the schedule for completing a human reference sequence.

In 2000, Sulston resigned as director of the Sanger Centre, though he continued some work on the HGP and the worm genome; he was knighted in 2001. Sulston views the data-sharing and ownership issues that arose with the human genome as fundamental to the practice of science, and argued for greater attention to free release of information and global equality in science and medicine in his book *The Common Thread: A Story of Science, Politics, Ethics and the Human Genome* (2002), co-authored with UK science journalist Georgina Ferry. In 2002, he was awarded the Nobel Prize for Physiology or Medicine jointly with Brenner and Robert Horvitz for their work on understanding the development of the nematode and particularly the role of programmed cell death or apoptosis. A 2001 portrait of Sulston by the artist Marc Quinn hangs in the National Portrait Gallery, and it is composed of a sample of Sulston's DNA in agar jelly mounted in stainless steel, perhaps appropriate for a man known as 'a scientist's scientist'.

Further reading

See: Francis Harry Compton Crick.

RACHEL A. ANKENY

SUZUKI DAISETSU TEITARO

1870–1966

Japanese Buddhist philosopher

Since he was the son of Ryōjun Suzuki, a medical doctor and Confucian scholar whose family religion was Rinzai Zen, and Masu, who was an adherent of a mystic and unorthodox belief connected with the Shin sect (Jōdo Shinshū, or True Pure Land Sect), it is not a coincidence that Daisetsu Suzuki grew to become the greatest modern exponent of Zen and Shin, the two representative schools of Buddhist thought in Japan.

In his early twenties, while he was a student at Tokyo Imperial University, Suzuki dedicated himself to Zen meditation in Kamakura. At twenty-seven, he joined Paul Carus of La Salle, Illinois, to assist in translating Chinese Buddhist texts into English. While working on the editorial staff of the Open Court Publishing Company, he produced translations, including the *Discourse on the Awakening of Faith in the Mahayana* (1900). When he came to Europe in 1908, he was invited by the Swedenborg Society to translate *Heaven and Hell* into Japanese. After fourteen years abroad, he returned home to become a lecturer in English at Gakushū-in School, where he was later promoted to a professorship, and at Tokyo Imperial University. At forty-one he married an American, Beatrice Erskine Lane, and in 1921 moved to Kyoto to take the chair of Buddhist philosophy at Otani University. There he began publishing the *Eastern Buddhist*, one of the leading English-language Buddhist journals in the world. The rest of his life was dedicated to writing, translating and lecturing both at home and abroad. In 1936 Suzuki visited London to lecture on Zen at the First Convention of the World Congress of Faiths and also gave lectures on Zen at Oxford, Cambridge, Durham, Edinburgh and London Universities. At the age of ninety-five he resumed editorship of the new series of the *Eastern Buddhist* and died in July that year.

Suzuki's contributions to world spiritual culture are incalculable. The phenomenal popularity of Zen in the West after the Second World War is the direct result of his efforts. He was the first to write seriously about Zen in English, and he kept up his zeal and energy in introducing Zen to the West until his last days. It is also from his works that many Westerners have come to know about Shin teaching, which centres around Amida Buddha and emphasizes absolute trust in his power.

Suzuki's activity was not motivated by conventional religious fervour or mere evangelism. He really understood both Eastern and Western thought and endeavoured to make people of the East and West understand and appreciate each other's spiritual heritage. His Japanese translations of English works include Emanuel Swedenborg's *Heaven and Hell* (1910), *The Divine Love and the Divine Wisdom* (1914) and *The Divine Providence* (1915). *Mysticism, Christian and Buddhist* (1957) clearly shows his insight into world spiritual culture. His greatest contribution, however, lay in popularizing Buddhist concepts in the West. It is through his lucid explanation that one easily learns of the state called 'satori', where there is no subject–object confrontation and where one attains 'absolute freedom, even from God' (*Essays in Zen Buddhism, First Series*, 1927).

Further reading

Suzuki's other works include: *Outlines of Mahayana Buddhism* (1907); *Essays in Zen Buddhism, Second Series* (1933), *Third Series* (1934); *Studies in the Lankavatara Sutra* (1930); *The Lankavatara Sutra* (a translation from the original Sanskrit, 1932); *An Index to the Lankavatara Sutra* (1933); *An Introduction to Zen Buddhism* (1934); *Manual of Zen Buddhism* (1935); *Zen Buddhism and its Influence on Japanese Culture* (1938); *The Essence of Buddhism* (1947); *The Zen Doctrine of No-Mind* (1949); *A Miscellany on the Shin Teaching of Buddhism* (1949); *Studies in Zen* (1955); and *Shin Buddhism* (1970). See: Rick Fields, *How the Swans Came to the Lake: A Narrative History of Buddhism in America* (1981); Masao Abe (ed.) *A Zen Life: D.T. Suzuki Remembered* (1986); William LaFleur's article on Suzuki in Mircea Eliade (ed.) *The Encyclopedia of Religion* (1993).

HISAO INAGAKI

SWINBURNE, Algernon Charles

1837–1909

British poet

Swinburne was born into an aristocratic naval family and brought up largely on the Isle of Wight and in Northumberland, where he developed a passion for the sea and coastal landscape. He completed his education neither at Eton, where his latent algolagnia was elicited by the flogging block, nor at Balliol, where he studied classics under **Jowett** who later became a friend. In 1857, before leaving Oxford for unspecified reasons, he met the Pre-Raphaelites (**William Morris, Edward Burne-Jones** and **D.G. Rossetti**) who were decorating the Union building with frescoes on subjects from the *Morte d'Arthur*, and thereafter became associated with them. Notably important was the worldly influence of Rossetti with whom he shared a *ménage* in Chelsea in the early 1860s. Together they comprise 'the Fleshly School of Poetry'.

But more vital to Swinburne's growth as an artist was his discovery at Oxford of Gautier's *Mademoiselle de Maupin* and, several years later in France, of **Baudelaire's** *Les Fleurs du mal* which he reviewed for the *Spectator* in 1862. In the preface to Gautier's novel the idea of 'art for art's sake' makes its first appearance, and Swinburne's review of Baudelaire is the first declamation of this doctrine in England. Briefly, it held that since any subject might be redeemed by art, all subjects were therefore available to it. This ran counter to the prevailing belief, typified by **Ruskin**, that art was in the service of morality. The redemption of sin through incorporation in art soon became an obligation for the Decadent artist. By legitimizing the forbidden, Baudelaire taught Swinburne how to express in poetry the fundamental sado-masochism of his nature.

On the occasion of Baudelaire's death in 1867 Swinburne wrote one of his finest poems, 'Ave Atque Vale', published in *Poems and Ballads Second Series* (1878), a volume which also contains the beautiful Villon translations. But what was spiritual torment in Baudelaire became in Swinburne a Dionysiac paganism so pure that it lacked the capacity for growth. Yet Baudelaire's confrontation with the modern world was uncompromising, whereas Swinburne's narrower improprieties were couched, as such things always were in Victorian England, in classical and medieval myths.

His first important book was *Atalanta in Calydon* (1865). Of it Ruskin wrote, 'It is the grandest thing ever done by a youth, though he is a demonic youth.' Nothing comparable had appeared in England since Shelley's *Prometheus Unbound*. Its leaping anapaests and dactyls were quite unexpected (**Tennyson's** *Enoch Arden* had appeared the previous year) and its success was immediate. In style *Atalanta* is as close as English literature has come to the Greek tragedy, but this is the Greek world overshadowed by the Marquis de Sade. Swinburne had been introduced to his works, then difficult to obtain, by Lord Houghton who owned an erotic library of European reputation.

Poems and Ballads (1866), dedicated to Burne-Jones, turned fame into notoriety. These two books represent Swinburne's significance, though not his entire worth, as a poet. Without warning, bestiality, cannibalism, necrophilia, hermaphroditism, homosexuality, blasphemy, republicanism and, above all, sado-masochism had been released into the Victorian drawing-room in spectral and elusive but fully conscious forms. For a kiss to become 'the lips inter-twisted and bitten/Till the foam has a savour of blood' was new and very alarming. In consequence Carlyle is said to have described the poet as 'a man standing up to his neck in a cesspool and adding to its contents'. **R.W. Emerson** called him 'a perfect leper and a mere sodomite', although there is no evidence of sodomy in his life and he preferred to be whipped by women.

Swinburne is the poet of sensual intoxication and sexual pathology, of passion in its original sense of suffering, and of youth. No poet is more characterized by his physical constitution. He was very small, with steeply sloping shoulders and a large head, and his limbs jerked a great deal due to an excess of 'electric vitality'. So sensitive was he to stimuli that pleasure and pain, in the intensity of their registration, became indistinguishable in the overall afflatus. Sometimes, to the consternation of his family and friends, this extreme excitability led to clinical fits, especially when he drank brandy.

In making explicit the masochism inherent in the Romantic view of man as the victim of Nature, Swinburne created his presiding goddess from La Belle Dame Sans Merci and thus transmitted the *femme fatale* to the European psyche as a whole, just as through him flagellation came to be known as *le vice anglais*. But he was composed of self-abasement and revolt in about equal measure, so that there is nothing simpering or affected in his work and his aggressive, hooligan joy was constrained only by a classical education. His rhythms are stressed heavily and become the rhythms of coition. Specific meaning in the poems is secondary to the erotic abrasion they supply. They are incantations for a secret ceremony, designed to arouse the senses and overwhelm the mind. There is no economy in Swinburne, no shortage of time, and few shocks of the intellectual sort.

Caught in a spasm of endless adolescence, he was rescued from an engulfing alcoholism in 1879 by Theodore Watts-Dunton who supervised the last thirty years of Swinburne's life at their house in Putney. As the lust left it, his poetry degenerated into Wordsworthian pantheism and Turneresque swirl, but the nature of his original power was not forgotten and it is not surprising that he was passed over for the Laureateship on the death of Tennyson. He was the first English Decadent. His influence on **Pater**, **Wilde** and their followers was enormous. **D'Annunzio** said that in Swinburne 'there seems to live again, with incredible violence, the criminal sensuality which fills primitive dramas with wild cries and desperate slaughters'. His celebration of physical things comes with a glorious, screaming, swooning freakishness into High Victorian literature.

Further reading

Other works include: *The Complete Works of Algernon Charles Swinburne*, ed. E. Gosse and T.J. Wise (20 vols, 1925–7); *The Swinburne Letters*, ed. C.Y. Lang (1959–62); *Lesbia Brandon*, ed. R. Hughes (1952), a novel, his most candid algolagniac work. See: George Lafourcade, *La Jeunesse de Swinburne* (1928); *Swinburne: The Critical Heritage*, ed. Clyde K. Hyder (1970); Philip Henderson, *Swinburne* (1974); R. Rooksby and N. Shrimpton (eds) *The Whole Music of Passion: New Essays on Swinburne* (1993).

DUNCAN FALLOWELL

SYNGE, John Millington

1871–1909

Irish dramatist and prose writer

Synge was born into an old Anglo-Irish family recently passed from the status of landowners to that of middle-class professionals, and inclined in religion to low-church zeal. These transformations occurring in the generation immediately before his have both coloured his achievement and obscured a proper assessment of it. He was educated haphazardly at Trinity College, Dublin, but pursued independently his studies in natural history, music, European literature and philosophy. His journeys to the Aran Islands (County Galway) from 1898 onwards provided a setting for a great transformative prose work, *The Aran Islands* (1907), in which romantic philosophy, aesthetics, politics and self-scrutiny converge. Other important 'travel' writings have been collected as *In Wicklow and West Kerry*.

Synge is best known as a dramatist of the 'peasant' mode, but this is the result of a crudely 'naturalist' reception in part encouraged by **W.B. Yeats** for propagandist purposes in Ireland. Synge's debt to the architectonics of classical French tragedy is evident in *In the Shadow of the Glen* (1903), and his reading of **Marx** and **Nietzsche** informs *Riders to the Sea* (1904). *The Well of the Saints* (1905) is an important play in its portrayal of language as creative mediation, a direct assault on the naturalism of Synge's later enthusiasts. His best-known play, *The Playboy of the Western World* (1907), is moving towards self-parody and an exposure of the 'play' element in human identity.

Such a summary omits two less than completed plays, *When the Moon Has Set* (1901 onwards) and *Deirdre of the Sorrows* (1907 onwards). An intensive analysis of the interaction of the first play's **Ibsenism** and the last play's mythic tapestries would reveal much of the underlying *Tod und Verklarung* ('Death and Transfiguration') motif in Synge's cultural politics. A comprehensive assessment of Synge has been frustrated by Yeat's deployment of him as a peasant dramatist sacrificed to a riotous and philistine petty bourgeoisie, by Marxist neglect, and by delay in the full presentation of his oeuvre to the world. The four-volume *Collected Works* goes some way towards rectifying this aspect of things.

Further reading

Other works include: *Collected Works*, ed. Robin Skelton and Ann Saddlemyer (1962–8). *Letters to Molly; John Millington Synge to Maire O'Neill* (1971) are essential reading. Synge's nephew Edward Stephens left a voluminous memoir-cum-study which Andrew Carpenter has admirably edited, *My Uncle John* (1974). See also: Nicholas Grene, *Synge: A Critical Study of the Plays* (1975); Declan Kiberd, *Synge and the Irish Language* (1979); D. Gerstenberger, *J.M. Synge* (1990); W.J. McCormack, *Fool of the Family: A Life of J.M. Synge* (2001).

W.J. MCCORMACK

SYNGE, John Millington

See: HENRIK IBSEN; KARL HEINRICH MARX; FRIE-DRICH NIETZSCHE; WILLIAM BUTLER YEATS.

SZASZ, Thomas Stephen

1920–

US psychiatrist

In the 1960s and 1970s Thomas S. Szasz was a leading proponent of an 'anti-psychiatry movement' in America that sought to characterize the diagnosis of many kinds of mental illness as a social, not medical, activity which infringed basic human rights. In the worst-case scenario he warned against 'pharmocracy', where the state uses diagnosis as a means of control, not cure. His reputation damaged by a long association with the Church of Scientology, Szasz subsequently found himself wrongfooted as the clinical treatment of some mental disorders, now proven to be the consequence of hitherto undetected changes in the chemistry of the brain, improved dramatically. But if medical science has in some measure vindicated Szasz's critics, he remains important for the side-on contribution he made to a generalized re-evaluation of mental illness.

Born in Budapest, Hungary, Szasz emigrated to the United States and graduated in medicine at the University of Cincinnati in 1944. Following an internship at Boston City Hospital, and postgraduate training in medicine at Cincinnati General Hospital, he studied psychiatry at the University of Chicago from 1946 to 1948. Between 1949 and 1951 he was a research assistant at the Chicago Institute of Psychoanalysis and a member of its staff until 1956. In 1956 he was appointed professor of psychiatry at the State University of New York, Upstate Medical Center in Syracuse, New York, a post he kept until his retirement.

Professor Szasz's background in psychiatry was that of orthodox psychoanalysis. Indeed, he wrote a number of papers on the subject, one in particular, 'The Concept of Transference' (*International Journal of Psychoanalysis*, 1963), being regarded as a classic. However, it was for his celebrated insistence that mental illness is a myth that Szasz attracted worldwide attention. He argued that the notion of mental illness derives its support from such conditions as syphilis of the brain and states of delirium in which individuals may manifest certain disorders of thinking and behaviour. However, in Szasz's view these are more correctly termed diseases of the brain rather than mental diseases. The vast majority of what are termed mental illnesses did not then manifest any underlying physiological or chemical abnormality, and so in Szasz's view did not qualify as diseases but were better classified as 'problems of living' (*The Myth of Mental Illness*, 1961).

Mistaking the metaphor for fact, which Szasz believed is what orthodox doctors and psychiatrists continually do, was not a harmless mistake in his view. Rather, he saw the medical conceptualization of mental illness as a deliberate policy by the medical profession to obscure and indeed deny the ethical dilemmas of life and to transform them into medical and technicalized problems susceptible to 'professional solutions' (*Ideology and Insanity*, 1973). From such a philosophical base, Szasz conducted a fierce polemical campaign against orthodox psychiatry, comparing psychiatrists and psychoanalysts to medieval inquisitors searching for the signs and symptoms of non-existent illnesses, and to totalitarian thought-police, implementing socially approved methods of behaviour under the guise of therapy (*The Manufacture of Madness*, 1971).

Szasz was often bracketed with **R.D. Laing**, with both being seen as seminal thinkers in the anti-psychiatric movement. However, Szasz emphatically stated his opposition to Laing, whom he accused of merely inverting not only the logic but also the vocabulary of psychiatry and appropriating them to serve his own idiosyncratic theoretical principles and therapeutic methods. In Szasz's view, psychiatrists had borrowed the disease model from medicine and, on the strength of it, declared psychiatry to be a branch of medicine, whereas in fact it was a speciality based on the combination of a medical metaphor and the police power of the state. The anti-psychiatrists, on the other hand, had borrowed the model of exploitation – of colonialism, foreign invasion and plunder – from the Old Left and, on the strength of it, declared anti-psychiatry to be a branch of the New Left, i.e. a movement based on the combination of a martial metaphor and 'the persuasive power of apocalyptic promises and prophecies' (*Schizophrenia: The Sacred Symbol of Psychiatry*, 1979).

Szasz's views, despite his adoption by the left as a champion of radical anti-psychiatric opinion, were actually sturdily right-wing and individualistic. His insistence that mental illness is a myth led him to oppose the role of the psychiatrist in court and the notion of mental illness as an excusing condition in certain criminal situations. Instead of seeing the schizophrenic individual as a patient needing treatment, Szasz regarded him as a person disrespectful of the rights of others. The grandiose or paranoid individual, likewise, is seen as boastful and self-centred.

Szasz was also an uncompromising opponent of socialized medicine. Indeed, the only psychiatry that can be practised with dignity, in his view, was that in which a fee passes between the patient and the therapist, i.e. socalled 'contractual' psychiatry (*The Ethics of Psychoanalysis*, 1965). All other forms of psychiatry are coercive and paternalistic and maintain the individual patient in a submissive and passive position relative to the therapist.

Szasz publicized his views in a steady output of books and journal articles. There was, and in some quarters still is, support for his view that many life problems are in danger of being medicalized into disorders requiring medical diagnosis and treatment. However, there was considerable argument concerning his views of the more serious psychological disorders such as schizophrenia, manic-depressive psychosis and the more crippling neurotic conditions; and it is in respect of these that Szasz's critique of psychiatry has retreated.

Further reading

Other works include: *Law, Liberty and Psychiatry* (1963); *The Second Sin* (1974); *Ceremonial Chemistry* (1974); *Psychiatric Slavery* (1976); *Heresies* (1976); *Karl Kraus and the Soul-Doctors* (1977); *The Myth of Psychotherapy* (1979); *The Theology of Medicine* (1979); *Cruel Compassion* (1994).

ANTHONY W. CLARE
(REVISED AND UPDATED BY THE EDITOR)

SZYMANOWSKI, Karol

1882–1937

Polish composer

Karol Szymanowski came from a refined artistic family background, a child of patriotic minor aristocracy, born during the Polish partition in what is now the Ukraine. The legacy of a privileged upbringing on the borderlands of Europe, which reach from the Carpathians towards the heady cultural and racial mix of the Black Sea regions, remained crucial throughout his musical career.

Many of his earliest published works (for example, the Preludes Op. 1, 1900, and Etudes Op. 4, 1902) are piano pieces in the manner of Chopin and early **Scriabin**. He was soon drawn to the ideas of *Młoda Polska* ('Young Poland'), the dominant force in Polish modernism, where a neo-romantic engagement with metaphysics and symbolism, principally drawn from Schopenhauer and **Nietzsche**, opposed the positivism and realism which had prevailed in much late nineteenth-century art. Key figures were Stanisław Wyspiański, who sought cultural renewal through grand syntheses of mythological sources, and Stanisław Przybyszewski, who proclaimed a religion of art based upon an ecstatic and apocalyptic release of sexuality suggestive of a **Freudian** image of Eros as a generative yet also potentially cataclysmically destructive force.

In 1905, in direct emulation of *Młoda Polska*, Szymanowski, along with Gzegorz Fitelberg, Ludomir Różycki and Apolinary Szeluto, formed the 'Young Poland in Music' group. Their admiration for Nietzsche and Schopenhauer was coupled with enthusiasm for the music of **Wagner** and **Richard Strauss**. In his settings of Young Poland poets, especially Kazimierz Tetmajer (Op. 2, 1902) and Tadeusz Miciński (Op. 11, 1905 and Op. 20, 1909), Szymanowski developed a musical tone of melancholic yearning expressed in complex chromaticisms, frequently dense piano textures and vocal declamation. He also set German poets,

especially Richard Dehmel (Opp. 13 and 17, 1907), in songs where diatonic tonality is stretched by tortured counterpoint and high levels of dissonance. In large-scale works of this time (the Second Symphony Op. 19, 1910, and the Second Piano Sonata Op. 21, 1911) post-Wagnerian or (more often) post-Straussian monumentalism and late romantic apotheosis co-exist with dense motivic elaborations approaching the complexity of the early symphonic works of **Schoenberg**. Contrasts between the lyrical and the dramatic are extreme, and at times the music approaches hysteria or bombast.

In 1913 Szymanowski 'discovered' the liberating air of the Mediterranean (as had Nietzsche before him) and Russian and French modern musical idioms – later Scrabian, **Stravinsky**, **Debussy** and **Ravel**. He also developed a fascination for Middle Eastern cultures, which were an exotic source of erotic inspiration. Eros became a central symbolic figure in his creative imagination, resonating with post-*Tristan* Wagnerism, the Nietzschean Dionysian, Scriabinesque ecstasy and the abundance of Oriental arabesques. Within a deliberate stylistic pluralism Szymanowski sought a new synthesis, with Eros functioning as a post-Platonic binding agent. The project was profoundly imbued by his homosexuality, overtly so in an incomplete novel, *Efebos* (after Plato's *Symposium*), written during the turmoil at the end of the First World War and the political unrest which followed. Greek mythological figures (Narcissus, Orpheus, Dionysus) acted as mouthpieces for an aesthetic of 'deviant' or 'transgressive' erotic sensuousness which closely aligns him with **André Gide** and **Oscar Wilde**. He espoused a new freedom for an élite of cultured individuals in an aestheticism derived from his reading of **Walter Pater**. This erotic-exotic world is explored in works such as the *Love Songs of Hafiz* Op. 26 (1914), the Third Symphony Op. 27 (1916), and *Songs of an Infatuated Muezzin* Op. 42 (1918). He saw Sicily as a cultural crossroads and *locus eroticus* after the manner of **Thomas Mann's Venice**, and it is the setting for the opera *King Roger* Op. 46 (1918–24). Drawing upon Euripides' *The Bacchae* and the notion of the resurrection of old gods after Heine, Pater and the Russian symbolist Dimitri Merezhkovsky, the opera focuses on Roger's liberating encounter with the ephebic, androgynous Dionysus, and ends with a new dawn for the Modern Nietzschean hero. Szymanowski's musical eclecticism produces stylistic shifts between post-Wagnerian chromaticism, Middle Eastern exotica, and (in a new departure) Polish archaisms.

With Polish independence after the First World War the epicurean, sybaritic Szymanowski felt a stranger in his homeland. His desire to play a central role in the nation's cultural life led to him assuming prominent positions at the State Academy of Music between 1927 and 1932, but his stints were not successful. In his music he now sought a modern, 'Polish' national style, taking the culture of the Tatra region around Zakopane as his inspiration. Stravinsky's impact and the legacy of Chopin were once more reassessed, and both are clearly heard in the *Mazurkas* Op. 50 (1925). The Tatra-set ballet *Harnasie* Op. 55 (1931) incorporated a large body of folk materials and in the *Stabat Mater* Op. 53 (1926) he attempted to express a specifically 'Polish' religiosity. In the final large-scale instrumental works such as the Fourth Symphony Op. 60 (1932) and Second Violin Concerto Op. 61 (1933) there is an emphasis on vigour and rigour, on expressive vitality coupled with meticulous control of *métier* (to use one of the composer's favourite terms). Though anti-romanticism is strongly featured in many of his essays of the 1920s and 1930s, his music retained qualities of emotional or erotic ecstasy and strove to invoke a metaphysical or spiritual symbolism. The objectivity and distancing techniques which characterize musical neo-classicism in the 1920s and 1930s are little heard in Szymanowski's music, even where the influence of Stravinsky is overt. Szymanowski is the most important Polish composer of the early twentieth century, but though the impact of the Third Symphony on the young **Lutosawski** was powerful he had little direct influence on the next generation of Polish composers. His sensualism and refined sonorities have, however, found wider creative response in recent decades and his profile outside Poland has steadily become more prominent.

Further reading

See: Jim Samson, *The Music of Szymanowski* (1980); Alistair Wightman, *Karol Szymanowski: His Life and Works* (1999); Alistair Wightman (trans. and ed.) *Szymanowski on Music: Selected Writings* (1999).

STEPHEN DOWNES

T

TAGORE, Rabindranath

1861–1941

Bengali writer

A poet, novelist, dramatist, essayist, composer, painter and educationalist, Rabindranath Tagore was a modern-day Renaissance man, who dominated the cultural life of Bengal for the first half of the twentieth century. He was the seventh, and the youngest, son of Debendranath Tagore, a wealthy Brahmin landlord of Calcutta, who was a founder of the Brahmo Samaj, a reformist Hindu movement which emphasizes monotheism. He was tutored at home, and became proficient in Bengali, Sanskrit and English. At sixteen he was sent to England to study law, a subject that failed to interest him. After his marriage at twenty-three he left Calcutta to manage the family estate at Silaidaha. He did so for seventeen years, and then moved to Santiniketan (Abode of Peace), the family retreat near Bolpur, about a hundred miles north of Calcutta. Here he founded an experimental school for boys which blossomed into an international university, Visvabharati, twenty years later.

He began writing verses when he was in his teens, and published his first volume of poems at eighteen. Later, he was to find the running of the family estate artistically rewarding. The close contact with the enchanting Bengali landscape fired his poetic imagination, while the insight that he gained into peasant life served him well in his works of fiction. In the 1890s his considerable output of poetry was complemented by drama (*Chitrangada* and *Malini*) and fiction (*Chitra*). The sadness caused him by the deaths of his wife and two children, between 1902 and 1907, was to be reflected in the mellowed sharpness of his later work.

His poetic genius found its most accomplished achievement in *Gitanjali* ('Song Offerings'), which appeared in Bengali in 1910. The English translation published two years later, and praised by, among others, **Ezra Pound** and **W.B. Yeats**, won him the Nobel Prize for Literature in 1913. This, and the knighthood that came in 1915, made him an international celebrity. In his lecture tours of America, Europe, Japan and South-East Asia he stressed the need for blending the ancient heritage of the East with the material achievements of the West. His catholic humanism is well captured in *The Religion of Man* (1931), where he regards love as the key to human fulfilment and freedom, and the surplus energy that finds expression in creative art as the most outstanding characteristic of human nature.

Although he did not participate actively in the freedom struggle of his countrymen, he was not apolitical. He renounced his knighthood in protest against the Amritsar massacre, committed by imperial Britain, in 1919. India honoured him in 1947 by adopting 'Jan Gan Man' ('Mind of the People'), one of his songs, as the national anthem, as did Bangladesh, a quarter of a century later, with its adoption of his 'Sonar Bangla' ('Golden Bengal').

He left a deep mark on the arts of Bengal, and thus of India and Bangladesh. By releasing Bengali prose from the traditional form of classical Sanskrit he made literary Bengali accessible to the masses; and by introducing new types of metres he enriched Bengali poetry. His song-poems remain as popular with the Bengali elite as they do with the peasants. He also introduced the forms of short story and opera to Indian literature and theatre. By combining the classical Indian arts with the folk traditions, and encouraging a creative interchange between Eastern and Western artistic forms, at Visvabharati he blazed a new path in education.

Further reading

See: *The Collected Poems and Plays* (1936); *Hungry Stones and Other Stories* (1916); *Stories from Tagore* (1918); *My Reminiscences* (autobiography, 1917); *Sadhana: The Realization of Life* (essays, 1913); *Thought Relics* (essays, 1921); *The Religion of Man* (essays, 1931); and the novels *The Home and the World* (1919) and *Gora* (1924). *A Tagore Reader* (1961) is the best anthology. About Tagore: E. Rhys, *Rabindranath Tagore* (1915); E.J. Thompson, *Rabindranath Tagore: His Life and Work* (1921); S. Sen, *Political Philosophy of Tagore* (1929); H.R. Kripalani, *Rabindranath Tagore: A Biography* (1962); Edward John Thompson, *Rabindranath Tagore: His Life and Work* (1982); Kalyan Sen Gupta, *The Philosophy of Rabindranath Tagore* (2005).

DILIP HIRO

TAINE, Hippolyte-Adolphe

1828–93

French philosopher, critic and historian

Taine was born in the Ardennes. His father, a country lawyer, died when he was twelve. The family moved to Paris and in 1848 Taine was admitted to the École Normale Supérieure. There, attempting to compensate for the loss of his religious faith, he immersed himself in metaphysics – Spinoza and, later, Hegel. His 'pantheistic' views brought him into conflict with the contemporary philosophical and educational establishment which, especially after 1852, was clerical and reactionary.

After a brief period of school-teaching he abandoned this career and settled in Paris, publishing critical articles on a wide range of subjects. Collected, recast and prefaced, these became a series of influential books: *Les Philosophes français du XIXe siècle* (1857), an iconoclastic attack on the dominant *spiritualiste* philosophy and on Victor Cousin in particular; the *Essais de critique et d'histoire* (1858) and the *Nouveaux essais* (1865) in which he championed Balzac and Stendhal; and the *History of English Literature* (*Histoire de la littérature anglaise,* 1864, trans. 1872), an attempt to understand the English character through literature. He also published his thesis on La Fontaine (1853) and a book on Livy (1856).

The year 1862 was one of crisis, described in a rare diary entry published in the richly informative *Life and Letters of H. Taine* (*Vie et correspondance,* 1902–7, trans. 1902–8). At thirty-four he was the leading critic of his generation. But he still had unrealized ambitions as a philosopher and he now discovered a vocation as a creative writer; he had a liaison with the mysterious novelist Camille Selden; he was convinced that greatness comes only from the imagination. But he chose reason rather than risk. He broke with Camille Selden, abandoned his novel (the fragment, *Étienne Mayran,* was published in 1910) and, in 1868, married into a wealthy family.

The Commune of 1871 may have been responsible for the anti-Revolutionary emphasis of his major work, *The Origins of Contemporary France* (*Les Origines de la France contemporaine,* 1875–93, trans. 1885–94), but the decision to become a historian is the resolution of his 1862 conflict, a means of reconciling risk-free exposition and dangerous imagination or, to use the symbolical figures he himself created, of being in an attenuated form, both orator and poet.

The Origins, which occupied the rest of his life, is, as a result of this tension, a unique work, brilliantly combining narrative and philosophical history. It is an attempt to explain the whole development of modern

France, a history which for the first time recognizes the importance of the provinces and which, in a highly contemporary way, describes the power of ideology.

His philosophy found expression in a treatise on psychology, *On Intelligence* (*De l'intelligence,* 1870, trans. 1889), and he also produced *Lectures on Art* (*La Philosophie de l'art,* 1880, trans. 1896), based on lectures he gave at the École des Beaux Arts.

Taine was the spokesman for the new positivist, determinist, anti-clerical, anti-Romantic philosophy which was to influence **Zola** so much. **John Stuart Mill** played a role but it was the impact of contemporary scientific achievement which led Taine to his basic belief, expressed powerfully in his article on Byron: scientific method should no longer be applied only to the physical world; there should be a science of man – of literature, of art, of society.

Contemporaries saw him as a dogmatic positivist. Not until the publication of the correspondence and the early manuscript material was the Romantic, the metaphysician, the follower of Spinoza recognized and given full weight. Taine is relevant today because of the way he lived out the contradictions of science. His insistence on the need for limited, detailed observation, his concern for the individual, was in conflict with a heroic commitment to system, theory, law. His explanatory concepts are frequently obscure or inadequate, as when he claims to explain a writer or a society by three forces, 'race', 'milieu' and 'moment' and by 'contrariété' and 'concordance'. But his unremitting struggle to meet the simultaneous demands of dispassionate observation and of articulated understanding over a vast area of subject-matter is what makes him one of the precursors of modern historiography, critical theory and social science. He is a remarkable example of a thinker who strove to reconcile a rationalist, continental outlook with Anglo-Saxon empiricism, who believed in the value of data collection and objectivity but nevertheless recognized the primacy of the structuring imagination and of subjectivity.

Further reading

See: Leo Weinstein, *Hippolyte Taine* (1972), contains a list of works translated into English. See: Colin Evans, *Taine, essai de biographie intérieure* (1975); Colin Evans, 'Taine and His Fate', *Nineteenth Century French Studies,* Vol. VI, 1–2 (1977–8).

COLIN EVANS

TAKEMITSU TŌRU

1930–96

Japanese composer

Tōru Takemitsu was the most important Japanese composer of the twentieth century, and his importance stems in large part from the subtle ways in which Eastern and Western musical features combine and interact in his compositions. Fascination with Japanese and other idioms from the Far East was widespread in twentieth-century Western music, and in Takemitsu's time composers as different as **Benjamin Britten** and **Karlheinz Stockhausen** found inspiration in their experiences of No theatre and Gagaku court music. Works like Britten's *Curlew River* and Stockhausen's *The Course of the Years* (*Der Jahreslauf*) transcend mere exoticism in their original, penetrating responses to the similarities and differences between these distinct musical worlds. Takemitsu was not the only composer from the Far East to return the complement, but the subtlety and sophistication with which he alludes to Western traditions is exceptional, and all the more notable, since he did not actually travel to the West until his personal musical style was well established.

Takemitsu's determination to be a composer – he was in most respects self-taught – came from early encounters with Western music when he was working for the Americans as a teenager in post-war Japan: even before the decisive impact of his first hearing of works by **Olivier Messiaen**, he had sensed a special affinity with French music in general and **Debussy** in particular. Given the enthusiasm for the exotic and the

Orient in these and other French composers, it is understandable that Takemitsu should have been particularly attracted to the expressive and formal qualities of music in which flexibility of rhythm and richness of harmony count for so much. Nevertheless, he soon became aware of other more astringent Western radicalisms, including the fractured, atonal expressionism of **Webern** and **Boulez**, as well as **Cage's** openness to chance happenings.

Takemitsu was able to draw on these and other diverse elements, forging his own distinctive idiom in ways which a more self-conscious composer, deliberately aiming to synthesize Western and Eastern principles, might never have managed successfully. He argued that 'as a Japanese I want to develop in terms of tradition and as a Westerner in terms of innovation'. The last thing he wanted was to lose the 'fruitful opposition' between old and new. Yet his music is the more memorable for shunning the kind of opposition that finds expression in overtly turbulent struggles. His overriding ambition was 'to produce sounds that are as intense as silence', and this paradox, of a music whose presence intensifies as sound itself becomes more sparse and attenuated, provides a useful guide to the quality and effect of his most typical compositions, which seek to engage the listener directly through economy, intensity and the imaginative, non-coercive use of progressive compositional techniques.

One possible reason why Takemitsu attached such importance to gaining the listener's undivided attention was that much of his time was given over to writing scores for more than a hundred films, including collaborations with **Oshima** and **Kurosawa;** he also provided a considerable amount of incidental music for theatre, radio and television. Most of his concert works are orchestral or instrumental. Among the most memorable are *November Steps* (1967) and *Autumn* (1973), both scored for *biwa* (a relative of the Western lute), *shakuhachi* (the Japanese flute) and orchestra, and *To the Edge of Dream* (1983) for guitar and orchestra. He is equally absorbing in the poetic orchestral dreamscape of *A Flock Descends into the Pentagonal Garden* (1977) and the delicate patterns of solo piano pieces like *Les Yeux clos* (1979), *Les Yeux clos II* (1988) and *Rain Tree Sketch II – In Memoriam Olivier Messiaen* (1992). His concern to use traditional instrumental combinations in new and unexpected ways is evident in a work like *Garden Rain* (1974), scored for brass quintet, but quite without the brash rhetoric and showy gestures conventionally associated with the medium.

Particularly in his later years, Takemitsu was a frequent visitor to Europe and America, and many honours and prizes came his way, including the Grawemeyer Award in 1994 for *Fantasma/Cantos* for clarinet and orchestra. To the end his music maintained its delicate, penetrating balance between Eastern and Western characteristics, and his subtle feeling for the nuances of modal harmony and impressionistic instrumental colour ensure that his compositions remain a refreshing presence on the contemporary musical scene.

Further reading

See: Peter Burt, *The Music of Tōru Takemitsu* (2001).

ARNOLD WHITTALL

TANGE KENZO

1913–

Japanese architect

Tange's work is both national and international in flavour. Born on the island of Shikoko in the south of Japan, he began his architectural training in the Department of Architecture at the University of Tokyo in 1938 and after a short break continued his studies there from 1942 to 1945. He worked initially with two leading Japanese architects, Kunio Mayekawa and Junzo Sakakura, both of whom had worked in the Paris office of the influential European **Le Corbusier** and who had become the pioneers in post-war

Japan of the international style sparked off by his Marseilles Unité, begun in 1947 and completed in 1952. Often referred to as 'Brutalist', it is tough and uncompromising and built of exposed concrete.

Tange was an academic and continued to teach at the University of Tokyo, where he became Professor of Architecture, until his retirement. In 1989 he became President of the Japanese Architectural Association. His many writings on the theory of architecture include the well-known 1966 paper on 'Function, Structure and Symbol', in which he outlined his belief that between 1920 and 1960 there was a period of functionalism based on the complexities of form, whereas since 1960 architects have been concerned with structures based on systems of communication.

His most important contribution to Japanese cultural life is his 1949 competition-winning design for the Peace Centre at Hiroshima, the city devastated by the first American atomic bomb four years earlier. The Peace Centre is one of the world's great symbols and Tange's design (made in collaboration with Takashi Asada and Sachio Otani) is based on a co-ordinated arrangement of three basic elements: a Community Centre, the Memorial Museum which houses the documentation of the bombing and its effects, and a Peace Plaza. It was Tange's first large-scale scheme and it established him as one of the most important international architects of the post-war years.

His thinking on the larger urban scale made him a major influence in CIAM (Congrés Internationaux d'Architecture Moderne) and in 1961 he founded his famous URTER (Urbanists and Architects Team) based on the early Bauhaus thinking of the German **Walter Gropius** who was later instrumental in forming the Architects' Collaborative in America.

Twenty-five young architects, including his own students at the university, jointly involved themselves in all aspects of specific projects, focusing particularly on the environmental needs of human beings rather than on any abstract problems of architectural style.

A student of ancient Japanese vernacular building, Tange is well aware of the tradition he has inherited and his concern with a vision of an integrated balance between the new technology and the needs of ordinary people has rightly earned him the professional esteem in which he is held.

Further reading

See: Kenzo Tange and Udo Kulterman, *Kenzo Tange* (1970). See also: Charles Jencks, *Modern Movements in Architecture* (1973); James Philip Noffsinger, *Kenzo Tange: Modern Japan's Genius Architect* (1980); Botond Bognar, *Contemporary Japanese Architecture* (1985).

JOHN FURSE

TANIZAKI JUNICHIRŌ
1886–1965
Japanese novelist

Tanizaki was born to a declining townsman family in Tokyo and his schooling was not without its difficulties and uncertainties as a result of his father's constant business failures, but in 1908 he managed to enter the Japanese literature department of Tokyo University. He was already inclined towards a literary career but he had little taste for the Naturalist type of fiction that dominated Japanese letters at the time and he preferred the exotic and decadent writings of Nagai Kafū, who later helped to establish Tanizaki as a novelist in the public eye. In 1910 he was forced to withdraw from the university for non-payment of fees and he then set out on a lifetime of literary activity by helping to found a new literary magazine.

Among the pieces he published in the magazine was 'Shisei' (1910, 'The Tattoo') in which a tattooer inscribes a giant spider on the back of a beautiful woman. When the tattoo is complete she is more imperious and confident and looks upon the tattooer as the first of the many men she will subjugate with the help of the tattoo. The element of the grotesque in this short piece is more characteristic of his early works, but the piece also contains the germs of a theme that runs through much of his oeuvre, and that is the abasement of the male before the female, often with incestuous or masochistic connotations. Other lasting characteristics of his work that appear in 'Shisei' and such early works as *Fumiko no Ashi* (1919, 'Fumiko's Feet') are his foot-fetishism and notorious lavatorial obsession.

During these years Tanizaki was a thrall of the West and its exotic attractions and held Japan in contempt. However, he began to alter his opinion and recognize the value of the Japanese tradition after the great earthquake of 1923, which devastated much of the Tokyo–Yokohama area, and after his subsequent move to Kansai, the area of Japan that centres on Osaka and Kyoto and is a repository of traditional culture. This shift came to the fore in *Some Prefer Nettles* (*Tade Kuu Mushi*, 1929, trans. 1955), in which the hero is fascinated by Western visions of feminine beauty but is at last drawn to the traditional charms of a Kyoto woman.

For much of the war Tanizaki worked on *The Makioka Sisters* (*Sasameyuki*, 1943–8, trans. 1958), a major work which seeks to recapture and preserve the atmosphere of Kansai before the war and the passing of the old ways, and which depicts in the troubled circumstances of one family both the confusion of the traditional and the modern in contemporary Japan and the difficulties of maintaining a balance between the two. In *Shōshō Shigemoto no Haha* ('The Mother of Captain Shigemoto', 1950) Tanizaki once again took up the theme of an idealized, remote and dominant female figure and combined this with incestuous undertones and imagery associated with the eleventh-century classic *The Tale of Genji*, which he translated into modern Japanese several times during the last thirty years of his life.

In later years Tanizaki came to recognize the inevitability of Westernization and the dilution of the Japanese tradition. In *The Key*

(*Kagi*, 1956, trans. 1961) and *The Diary of a Mad Old Man* (*Fūten Rōjin Nikki*, 1962, trans. 1965) he put aside his interest in the well-worked but ever popular theme of the tension between tradition and modernity in Japan and turned to the subject of sexual desire in the aged, which he treated with some humour and structural experimentation.

Tanizaki has sometimes been seen as a writer to whom aesthetic considerations were more important than ideas. Ethereal notions of beauty do indeed have a part to play in many of his works. But it belittles his work to pass over his interests in tradition and the effects of beauty on the behaviour of men, or to place undue emphasis on the obsessions that feature in his writings.

Further reading

H. Hibbett (ed.) *Seven Japanese Tales* (1963) is a collection of Tanizaki's shorter works, including 'The Tattooer'. See also: D. Keene, *Landscapes and Portraits – Appreciations of Japanese Culture* (1971); J.T. Rimer, *Modern Japanese Fiction and Its Traditions* (1978); Gwenn B. Petersen, *Moon in the Water: Understanding Tanizaki, Kawabata and Mishima* (1986).

PETER KORNICKI

TÀPIES, Antoni

1923–

Spanish artist

Antoni Tàpies was born in Barcelona to Josep Tàpies i Mestre, a lawyer, and Maria Puig i Guerra, whose father was the mayor of the city and a Catalan nationalist. Brought up in a liberal and intellectual environment, the young Tàpies was introduced to the European avant-garde in 1934 through a special edition of the journal *D'Ací i D'Allá*. Although he pursued his interest in drawing and painting throughout his adolescence and early adulthood, at Barcelona University he studied law but never completed the programme.

In 1947, Tàpies befriended the poet Joan Brossa, through whom he met **Jóan Miró**.

Along with a group of young artists and writers, Tàpies and Brossa founded the review *Dau al Set* in 1948, which published articles on many leading Surrealist artists, the occult, jazz and modern psychology. Steeped in the culture of Surrealism espoused by the *Dau al Set* group for whom Surrealism was an explicit critique of the repressive **Franco** régime, Tàpies began exploring Surrealist ideas of liberty and alternative modes of representation. His work of this period, such as *Dibuix* (1948) was heavily influenced by **Miró**, **Max Ernst** and **Paul Klee**, and experimented with unconventional materials such as thread, paper collage and thick pigment.

Around 1949, under the influence of João Cabral de Melo, the Communist consul from Brazil who advocated a more explicit connection between culture and politics, Tàpies began to reconsider the relevance of abstract art and began making more explicitly political work. Although Tàpies did not continue in this mode, his engagement with the political during this period contributed to his later attempts to articulate a language of painting that could at once embody the political goals of realism and the expressive ambitions of abstraction.

In 1950, Tàpies was awarded a scholarship through the French Institute of Barcelona, which enabled him to move to Paris. There, he developed his experiments with materials and calligraphic picture writing in the context of an international community of artists working to define a new mode of expression for the post-war period. Rejecting the traditional vocabulary of European painting as a moral and philosophical failure, these artists, among them **Jean Dubuffet**, Jean Fautrier and **Antonin Artaud**, defined Lyric Abstraction or Informel as a richer form of representation that incorporated the bodily and matter into painting. Tàpies' work from this period such as *Blanc et jaune* (1954) is fixated on the notion of the wall as silent witness, a material record of history, and through graffiti the place of clandestine expression. It was during the 1950s that Tàpies' artistic career took flight; he won the Carnegie Prize in 1950, showed at the Venice Biennale in 1952 and 1958 (where he won two prizes), won a purchase prize at the São Paolo Bienal in 1953, and participated in the Pittsburgh International in 1950, 1952, 1955 and 1958.

Tàpies has continued to produce strong, metaphysically charged work obsessed with matter, calligraphy and graffiti up to the present day. In the late 1960s and early 1970s, the artist became again more politically engaged, challenging the space of painting by making objects such as *Armari* (1973). In the 1980s, after the end of the fascist régime, Tàpies returned to the canvas. In 1993, he was chosen as the featured artist of the Spanish pavilion at the Venice Biennale, and had a one-person show at the Pace Wildenstein Gallery in New York in 2003.

Such European critics as Giulio Carlo Argan and Michel Tapié received Tàpies as an important voice in International Lyric Abstraction, and his work was seen as an existentialist project. In the USA, however, where the Cold War injected a politics of nationalism into International Lyric Abstraction, Tàpies was framed as a proponent of the 'Spanish school' in two important group exhibitions from 1960: *New Spanish Painting and Sculpture* at the Museum of Modern Art in New York and *Before Picasso After Miró* at the Solomon Guggenheim Museum. More recently, scholars such as Robert S. Lubar and Manuel S. Borja have attempted to rectify this perspective by situating his work in the international dialogue of Lyric Abstraction, of which it was such an integral part.

Further reading

See: Anna Agusti, *Tàpies, the Complete Works* (1989).

MING TIAMPO

TARKOVSKY, Andrei Arsenevich
1932–86
Russian film director

Tarkovsky was born in Zavrazhye on the Volga, into a cultured family, representative of the old Russian intelligentsia, his father a poet and translator, his mother an editor at a Moscow publishing house. His parents separated when Andrei was four, the future filmmaker brought up in the city by his working mother interspersed with infrequent stays with his father. The teenager rebelled against his mother's high cultural ambitions for him, but her persistence paid off. Tarkovsky, now in his twenties and quite a dandy, began to take seriously the study of classical literature, music and art. Following a short-lived stint at the Institute for Eastern Studies and a geological expedition to Siberia, he was handpicked by the gifted teacher Mikhail Romm for entry to the directing class at VGIK (the State Cinema Institute), where he studied until 1960. Following a relatively unremarkable short film *The Steamroller and the Violin*, rather typical of the liberal 'thaw' films of the 1950s Soviet Union, Tarkovsky the great artist emerged fully formed with his first feature *Ivan's Childhood* in 1961.

Although in parts highly influenced by the visual poetry of Alexander Dovzhenko and showing traces also of recent popular war films like the internationally successful *The Cranes are Flying* (Mikhail Kalatozov, 1957), in cultural terms *Ivan's Childhood* was released at a moment when it was no longer tenable for innovative young directors to work with the presuppositions and aims of their masters. An entirely new idea of what the essence of cinema involved was coming to the fore in the wake of **Welles**, **Dreyer**, Antonioni and the writings of film theorists such as Bazin. Most notably **Resnais** in the West and Tarkovsky in the East came to perceive that, as the Russian would later write in his theoretical manifesto *Sculpting in Time* (1986), 'the cinema must master a completely new material: time'.

Tarkovsky often gave the appearance of being a late Romantic, a contemporary **Dostoyevsky**, a man out of his time: a tendency that often clashed with his Modernist aesthetic preferences. Whereas Antonioni, for instance, asked how contemporary man can easily recognize technological obsolescence but not outmoded morals and beliefs, for Tarkovsky the issue remained the struggle within man between spiritual idealism (often misguidedly distilled into technological advancement) and moral entropy, a schism which may account for his obsessive creation of a fractured and palpable sense of temporality. In order to look beyond the image's representational aspect, Tarkovsky believed film makers should render narrative, action, character and psychology subservient to what he called 'the pressure of time in the shot'. For Tarkovsky, time is a non-chronological, multi-rhythmic phenomenon which, when encapsulated in the shots of a film, dictates its own pace, opposed to the artificial rhythms created by montage and editing in general. Thus the cinematic image becomes a temporal reality as if (in his words) 'crystallized in a drop of water'.

This approach to filmmaking is already found in a mature state in *Ivan's Childhood*. Its most striking departure was the director's success in severing the traditionally psycho-pragmatic links between dream and reality: one now no longer knows what is dream, what reality. As **Sartre** wrote a propos of Tarkovsky's film, 'the truth is that the entire world is an hallucination, and that in this universe the child is an hallucination for others' (*Jeune Cinéma*, Vol. 42, 1969). This also perhaps explains why newsreel footage are so readily incorporated into the fictional worlds of *Ivan's Childhood*, as well as some of Tarkovsky's later works, for example *Mirror* (1974). One of the first principles of Tarkovsky's 'cinema of time' involves the dismantling of traditional representations of space. Contrary to convention, and already in *Ivan's Childhood*, locations become unspecified and the linkages between individually framed spaces are loosened and often abandoned. The distinctions which were traditionally used to focus the spectator's interest – that is, distinctions between what is principal in the image and what is accessory, what is 'figure' and what is 'ground' – undergo a process of decomposition, and it is by way of this that Tarkovsky expresses his osmotic world out of which emerge fleeting but vaguely recognizable forms and objects. His cinema is often one of autonomous sensible qualities unattached to particular objects. In two important scenes in his debut feature, we perceive first Ivan's emergence from and later disappearance back into a foggy swamp – his human form reduced to a mere ripple on the water's surface.

Tarkovsky repeatedly uses many other cinematic devices to produce the idiosyncratic effect of his films. Such techniques, many already present in *Ivan's Childhood* but exploited more fully in his later work, include: the slow protracted shots over the earth, water and material objects (a *parti pris* he may have borrowed from **Mizoguchi's** *Ugetsu Monogatari*); the unhurried dilation of time infusing everything the camera sees with spiritual life (in particular in the so-called 'dream' sequences in *Ivan's Childhood* but also in the reconnaissance scenes and elsewhere); an abandonment of perspective and the promotion of a flat image (in the manner of Dreyer); and the changed function of high- and low-angle shots which cease to be psychological or expressionistic (as in early Welles), becoming instead a means of subsuming the human figure in a near-geometrical construct.

Time for Tarkovsky is a multi-faceted ground from which the spiritual dimensions of existence emanate. It is important to grasp that the Russian's ideas, which often seem to verge on the mystical (especially in his interviews), find their foundation in a particular philosophical approach towards the relationship between the 'spiritual' and the 'material': these are two lines of development emerging out of the cosmic or primeval 'swamp' that is Time; hence the literal appearance of swamps in *Ivan's Childhood*, cesspools in *Stalker* (1979), the dredged swimming pool in *Nostalgia* (1983) – images which should be appreciated in their full and intense materiality rather than interpreted metaphorically.

Correspondingly, throughout Tarkovsky's seven feature films, from *Ivan's Childhood* through to *The Sacrifice* (1986), there are at least two image-series within a film's structure: on the one hand, images of nature or the 'non-human' very often portraying indetermination or dissolution, the unexpected or inexplicable; on the other, a human series conveying a more deterministic universe, the characters often driven by a colossal burden or destiny which cannot be shaken off (men or women trapped in war or exile, in apocalyptic or messianic zones or events). When indeterminate nature encroaches upon or envelopes this human world (the rain that falls inside a house in *Mirror*, the snow inside a church in *Nostalgia*, holy icons encased in a river-bed in *Stalker*, the flooded battlefields of *Ivan's Childhood*), then life can no longer be thought of in terms of the 'real' as opposed to the 'dream' or the 'appearance', but only in terms of an indiscernibility between series or sides of the multi-faceted temporal crystal that, for Tarkovsky, defines reality.

Tarkovsky was a true cinematic philosopher who invented images instead of concepts. Although often the object of censorship by neglect, Tarkovsky was hardly the martyr some believe him to have been: he was usually allowed the final cut on his films, and was frequently permitted to travel abroad before his defection in July 1984. Having finished filming *The Sacrifice* in Sweden in late 1985, he was diagnosed with terminal cancer and died a year later. His influence has been enormous the world over, not only for his intransigence as an artist, his hopes that the cinema could be the equal of great literature and his ability to articulate its philosophical importance, but above all for his haunting images. He has come to represent the belief in what cinema might have been, and for some, what it might yet be.

Further reading

Other works include: *Andrei Roublev* (1966); *Solaris* (1972). Other writings that have been translated: *Time Within Time: The Diaries 1970–86* (1991); *Collected Screenplays* (1999). See: Mark Le Fanu, *The Cinema of Andrei Tarkovsky* (1987); Maya Turovskaya, *Tarkovsky: Cinema as Poetry* (1989); Vida T. Johnson and Graham Petrie, *Andrei Tarkovsky: A Visual Fugue* (1994).

FERGUS DALY

TARSKI, Alfred

1902–83

Polish/US mathematician, logician and philosopher

Tarski was among the most important mathematician-logicians of the twentieth century. He studied mathematics and philosophy under Leśniewski and Kotarbiński in Warsaw, where he taught between 1926 and 1939. Later he held positions at Harvard, Princeton and Berkeley. Tarski worked on algebra, geometry and set theory. But his most seminal contribution has been to metamathematics and semantic theory, especially through his definitions of logical consequence and of truth. Although his major writings are highly technical, he could also present complex logical issues with great clarity.

Tarski sought a 'methodology of the deductive sciences' which elucidates the axiomatizability, consistency and completeness of formal systems like that developed by **Russell**. This required an analysis of logical consequence (the relation which obtains between the premises of a deductive argument and its conclusion): a sentence s is a consequence of a given set of sentences X if and only if there is no way to reinterpret the non-logical terms in such a way as to render all members of X true and s false. This definition provided a foundation stone for *model theory*, the systematic study of the semantic rather than merely syntactic properties of formal systems ('O Pojcia Wynikania Logicznego', 1936).

For any given formal language, Tarski also needed to compare the class of its *true* formulae with the class of formulae that can be *proven* in it. For this purpose, he developed his famous *semantic theory of truth* ('Der Wahrheitsbegriff in den formalisierten Sprachen', 1935). It provides a way of systematically specifying the extension of 'true' for a specific formal language L. Tarski regarded such an account as a definition of 'true' for L, and insisted that it must meet two conditions.

First, it must be 'materially adequate', i.e. capture the 'classical' or 'correspondence' conception of truth. The conditions for particular sentences being true according to that conception are stated in so-called 'T-sentences', e.g. (1) 'snow is white' is true in English if and only if snow is white. By providing a definition of 'true' in its application to the particular sentence 'snow is white', (1) also provides a 'partial definition' of the term 'true sentence in English'. If the number of English sentences were finite, one could give a complete definition through conjoining all these partial definitions. Unfortunately, that number is potentially infinite. Consequently we have only reached a criterion for the material adequacy of such a definition, known as 'Convention T': any definition of 'true sentence in English' must entail all equivalences of form (T). (T) s is true in English if and only if p where 'p' can be replaced by any English sentence, and 's' by a name of that same sentence.

The requirement of 'formal correctness' comes into play because some instances of (T) give rise to semantic paradoxes like that of the liar. Consider (2). Sentence (2) is false. By substituting (2) in schema (T), one can derive a contradiction: (3). Sentence (2) is true if and only if sentence (2) is false.

The problem is that natural languages allow for the formation of self-referential sentences like (2). Tarski's solution is to confine the definition of truth to artificial languages that do not contain semantic terms like 'true'. In such cases we can distinguish between the 'object-language' L for which we define 'true', and the 'meta-language', M of our theory, in which that definition is couched. Finally, M fulfils the requirement of materially adequacy by providing a recursive procedure that allows the derivation of a T-sentence for any sentence of L from axioms that assign semantic properties to a finite set of semantic primitives.

In spite its technical brilliance, it is a moot question whether the semantic approach succeeds in *defining* truth. Tarski himself doubted that it can be extended to natural languages, since these contain semantic vocabulary and lack a formally precise structure. Furthermore, a Tarskian theory only specifies the *conditions* under which sentences of a *particular* language *L* are true. This is not the same as to define *what it is* for sentences in any language to be true, just as specifying the conditions under which contracts are valid in English law is not the same as to define what it is for a contract in any legal system to be valid. Nevertheless, by blocking the semantic paradoxes Tarski convinced **Carnap**, **Popper** and **Quine** of the legitimacy of semantic notions like truth. **Davidson** has suggested ways of constructing Tarskian theories for natural languages, and has claimed that they can do service as theories of meaning (rather than of truth) for such languages. Finally, naturalistic philosophers have built on Tarski's ambition to explain truth in purely physicalist terms.

Further reading

The Collected Works of Alfred Tarski (4 volumes, 1981) contains all of Tarski's published works, including two philosophical accounts of the semantic theory, 'The Semantic Conception of Truth and the Foundations of Semantics' and 'Truth and Proof'. The articles mentioned in the text are also included in Tarski's *Logic, Semantics, Met mathematics* (2nd edn, 1983). See: J. Wolenski (ed.) *Alfred Tarski and the Vienna Circle* (1998); American Mathematical Society, *Proceedings of the Tarski Symposium* (1990); W. Künne, *Conceptions of Truth* (2003); A. and S. Feferman, *Alfred Tarski: Life and Logic* (2004).

HANS-JOHANN GLOCK

TAWNEY, Richard Henry

1880–1962
British economic historian

In so far as egalitarian ideas form part of the culture of British society, we can discern the influence of men like R.H. Tawney, distinguished economic historian, social philosopher and passionate enemy of privilege. He was born in Calcutta in 1880, the son of an Oriental scholar in the Indian Educational Service. After his family returned to England, he trod the well-travelled path from Rugby School to Balliol College, Oxford. There were many in Oxford at the turn of the century who helped inculcate in Tawney and others what has been called the 'politics of conscience'. He did not remain content, however, with charitable attempts to better the life of the urban poor. A two-year period in the East End of London helped deepen further his indignation at the extent of social inequality in Britain. The most formative experience of his early life, though, was his work as first tutor and perennial inspiration of the Workers' Educational Association (WEA). This organization grew out of an attempt to prise open the gates of the ancient universities to give to working people educational opportunities monopolized by elites. This objective was never realized, but nonetheless Tawney was instrumental in the emergence of a movement in adult education in which his egalitarian Anglicanism found its most complete expression. This we can see in the moving *Commonplace Book* (1972) which he kept while travelling between WEA classes in the Potteries and Lancashire before the First World War.

The same set of moral commitments that made Tawney a pioneer in adult education led him in 1914 to join the British army as a private soldier. His two-year period of service in the Manchester Regiment was abruptly ended on the first day of the Battle of the Somme when he was severely wounded. On his return to England, he recuperated at the home of the Bishop of Oxford, Charles Gore. He joined other prominent Anglicans, such as William Temple, later Archbishop of Canterbury, in an attempt to formulate more clearly the social message of the Church of England and to alter its form to meet the challenge of war and its aftermath. He took up a Fellowship at his old college, Balliol, at the end of the war, and returned to work on the ethical and historical problems which were to occupy him for the rest of his life.

The academic distinction between moral philosophy and history, which many take for granted today, was one which made no sense to Tawney. Largely through his teaching for the WEA and after 1921 at the London School of Economics, his life-long academic home, he developed a concept of economic history of significant influence today. In his view, the subject entailed the retrieval of the resistance of groups and individuals in the past to the imposition on them of capitalist thought and behaviour. It is apparent, therefore, why conservative historians lament his influence and why liberal and socialist historians celebrate it. In his first book, *The Agrarian Problem in the Sixteenth Century* (1912), written to provide his WEA classes with a suitable textbook, he examined patterns of agricultural development, protest and litigation which surrounded the movement to enclose land in Tudor England. A decade later he developed the arguments which were to emerge in his best-known book, *Religion and the Rise of Capitalism* (1926). This famous study showed how alien to the tradition of the Reformation was the assumption that religious thought had no bearing on economic behaviour. Tawney captured in unforgettable Miltonic prose the clash within religious opinion that preceded the abnegation of the social responsibility of the church, and suggested that 'religious indifferentism' was but a phase in the history of Christian thought which could and ought to be ended.

No one who read Tawney could miss the present-mindedness of his history. Indeed, it was that very quality which made his work so attractive to a generation of students. He taught them that the study of economic history could raise fundamental questions concerning human behaviour and moral values. The same desire to speak to major social issues and to avoid the desiccation of academic specialism can be seen in his more speculative essays in social philosophy, *The Acquisitive Society* (1919) and *Equality* (1931).

The unifying theme of his work on educational policy for the Labour Party over forty years, his published and professional writing, and his teaching was a belief in equality that stemmed from his Anglican convictions. To appreciate the full extent of his influence, we must set his contributions in the contexts of the history of the socially committed wing of the Church of England and of the history of that part of the British Labour Movement which came to socialism through a belief that capitalism was sin.

Further reading

Other works: *Land and Labour in China* (1932); *The Attack and Other Papers* (1953); *Business and Politics under James I* (1958); *The Radical Tradition* (1964); *History and Society* (1978); *The American Labour Movement and Other Essays* (1979). See also: R. Terrill, *R.H. Tawney and His Times* (1973); J.M. Winter, *Socialism and the Challenge of War* (1974); B Elsey, 'R.H. Tawney: "Patron Saint of Adult Education"', in P. Jarvis (ed.) *Twentieth-Century Thinkers in Adult Education* (1987); Anthony Wright, *R.H. Tawney* (1987).

J.M. WINTER

TCHAIKOVSKY, Peter Ilich

1840–93

Russian composer

One of the most celebrated composers of the late Romantic musical period, Tchaikovsky was born at Votkinsk in central Russia where his father held a prominent position as a mining engineer. From an early age he showed great musical interest and was encouraged to learn the piano by his mother, to whom he had become neurotically attached. Her death when he was only eleven set the seal on an idealized view of women for the rest of his life. In 1855 the family moved to St Petersburg and the youth was sent to the prestigious School of Law, where he later graduated with honours. Accordingly he obtained a post in the Ministry of Justice where he remained for four years. However, the pull of music became so strong that he decided to enrol at the Conservatoire. Here he pursued full-time studies under Anton Rubinstein who had a high opinion of his composition exercises. Tchaikovsky's relinquishing of regular employment, just as he had become accustomed to a rather flamboyant lifestyle, meant a drastic drop in his living standards. He had to survive by giving lessons and acting as an accompanist for singers while writing his first compositions. Success in this field brought him a professorship of harmony at the new Moscow Conservatoire under Nikolai Rubinstein in 1866, and this enabled him greatly to increase his creative output. Compositions of this particularly fruitful period include the first three symphonies, the first piano concerto, three operas as well as *Romeo and Juliet* and the ballet *Swan Lake;* in addition, he was to produce articles for periodicals and become acquainted with many artistic contemporaries.

By his mid-thirties Tchaikovsky had met with sufficient acclaim both at home and abroad to fulfil short concert tours in Europe and purchase a house in the country for both rest and solitude. It is at this time that a curious correspondence was started with his new patroness Nadejda von Meck who over the thirteen years of their communications never made personal contact with the composer, though she did contribute greatly to his material needs. This, in contrast to his disastrous and shortlived marriage at the time, was to provide both platonic companionship and a secure income. In 1877, after recovering from a nervous breakdown and pathetic suicide attempt, he embarked on a travel programme which took him to Switzerland and Italy. Dissatisfied with his position at the Moscow Conservatoire he resigned in the following year and devoted more time to composition. New works soon included three orchestral suites, two symphonies, the second piano concerto, the violin concerto, *Sleeping Beauty*, the symphonic poems *Manfred*, *Hamlet* and *Voyevode*, together with four more operas.

Tchaikovsky spent his remaining five years touring Europe and promoting performances of his new scores. By the time von Meck had terminated their friendship he had directed concerts in Paris, Geneva, London, Leipzig, Berlin, Cologne, Hamburg and Prague. In 1891 he went to America and conducted concerts in New York, Baltimore and Philadelphia. A final move to a country house at Klin enabled him to complete the sixth symphony, subtitled 'Pathétique'. The award of an honorary doctorate by the University of Cambridge in 1893 was made immediately before the mysterious circumstances of his death which occurred in St Petersburg. His death from cholera has only very recently been disputed by the appearance of Russian sources which give the impression that he was directed to take his own life because of a homosexual affair with the relative of a high member of state.

Although Tchaikovsky's musical fame rests upon relatively few works, his output was of sizeable proportions and embraced most forms of the late nineteenth-century period. Compared with his colleagues in 'The Five' (**Balakirev**, Cui, **Borodin**, **Mussorgsky** and **Rimsky-Korsakov**), who chose to write strongly nationalistic works, Tchaikovsky's style was designed to appeal to international audiences. Inevitably such influences do appear, as can be heard in his frequent use of long modal melodies and sequential repetitions reminiscent of folk song and Orthodox Chant. However, the fact that the infections of French and Italian cantilena figure strongly in his style and also that he adored the operatic works of Mozart, Rossini and **Verdi** contributes much to an understanding of his melodic characteristics. A great admirer of **Bizet's** *Carmen* and the ballets of Delibes, Tchaikovsky drew upon these models, injecting his own personal brand of hysteria, and evolved a style which placed much less emphasis on the constraints of traditional architectural form. Though his most famous compositions have a tendency to be theatrical, he had no interest in the romanticism of Beethoven or **Wagner** despite the fact that his contemporaries **Bruckner** and **Brahms** drew extensively from such influences for their symphonic writing.

Tchaikovsky's orchestral works can be divided into two groups: those with a definite programme and mostly cast as single movements, and the symphonies based on more traditional forms. In this first group can be placed the tone-poems *Romeo and Juliet* (1869), *The Tempest* (1875), *Francesca da Rimini* (1876) and *Hamlet* (1888). Taking *Romeo and Juliet* as reasonably representative of the composer's formal layout we can see that he invariably commences a work with a slow introduction and follows with a fast sonata section of two contrasted themes; these are treated freely both within the exposition and development sections. Again in this tone-poem, three stylistic elements are evident: the first theme is vigorous and frequently agitated while the second is mournful but eloquent. The whole is held together with extended running passages of a forceful nature. The second category includes the abstract works, namely the mature works for solo instrument with orchestra and the three late symphonies. Here the composer's first movements again employ much developmental material within the expositions, and frequently introductory themes recur in later movements also. In this procedure the over-emphasis of the same thematic materials tends to wear rather thin in long movements. However, the use of rhythmic devices such as syncopation or alternatively adept instrumental colouring frequently minimize any formal miscalculations on the part of the composer. Though the three early symphonies, No. 1 in G minor ('Winter Daydreams', Op. 13, 1866), No. 2 in C minor ('Little Russian', Op. 17, 1872) and No. 3 in D major ('Polish', Op. 29, 1875), show him grappling with just these problems, they are worthy predecessors to the more mature works. Much of their colourful orchestration is derived from Mendelssohn and Schumann who, like Tchaikovsky, were inspired by country scenes and local village dancing. Symphony No. 4 in F minor (Op. 36, 1877), which was written soon after his abortive marriage and dedicated to his new-found friend von Meck, represents a new depth of expression with its 'fate' motive on fanfare brass and melancholic waltz theme: the whole work could be termed auto-biographical, though the composer had no wish to be explicitly programmatic. The Symphony No. 5 in E minor (Op. 64, 1888) is more philosophical in its emotional attitude: the first three movements are Tchaikovsky at his best, while any formal weaknesses in the finale are mollified by the work's universal popularity. The same can be said for the sixth symphony in B minor (Op. 74, 1893), the 'Pathétique'. Written close to his death, this work shows him to have transcended the difficulties of form as well as present programmatic elements which bring the 'fate' theme to a convincing conclusion. Once again he draws from his palette feelings of utter despair as in the outer movements, and contrasts these with a balletic *valse à cinq temps* as the centrepiece.

Recently, much more acclaim has been given to the lengthy and programmatic *Manfred* symphony (Op. 58, 1885), based on the life of Lord Byron: the composer was ambivalent towards this symphony for it presented him with the problem of providing themes capable of thematic transformation similar to those of **Berlioz** and **Liszt**.

Though there are several works for solo instrument with orchestra, only the first piano concerto in B flat minor (Op. 23, 1875) and the violin concerto in D major (Op. 35, 1878) have had any great following. Such works follow a narrower expressive range than the symphonies, though the latter is one of the finest written for the instrument since the death of Beethoven. Mention may also be made of the light-hearted *Variations on a Rococo Theme* (1876) for cello and orchestra which show an interest in pastiche later to be taken up in the opera *The Queen of Spades* (1890), and in *Mozartiana* (1887).

Tchaikovsky's three ballets – *Swan Lake* (1877), *The Sleeping Beauty* (1890) and *The Nutcracker* (1892) – provided the Russian ballet with a new kind of musical material with which to work. Prior to this audiences had to make do with French-style *divertissements* written by second-rate musicians who had been used to providing lightweight dance scores for operatic interludes or pageants for high society. Tchaikovsky built on this tradition by adding symphonic materials to the well-known folk forms of the polonaise, mazurka and minuet as well as drawing on such foreign dances as the tarantella and bolero. Within the first two ballets these, together with the concert waltz, are subjected to extensive development. His expertise in the portrayal of fairy tales via the use of scintillating orchestration can best be seen in the vignette-like miniatures of *The Nutcracker*, which owes a great deal to Delibes's *Sylvia* and *Coppélia* of twenty years earlier.

Of the dozen or so operas that Tchaikovsky wrote, only the Pushkin-inspired *Eugene Onegin* (1878) and the later *Queen of Spades* are regularly staged. The former is a masterpiece written at the time of crisis and owes more to the tragic lyricism of Bizet's *Carmen* than to the nationalist works of Glinka. The latter, with its biting satire and rococo style, can be traced to Mozart's treatment of the medium, though here the composer adds his own chromatic spice to the rather formal proceedings while ideally balancing lyricism and dramatic expressiveness.

For a long while the inflated popularity of a mere handful of orchestral compositions detracted from a wider appreciation of Tchaikovsky's complete oeuvres, particularly the beauty of the early quartets, many songs and piano pieces. These chamber works often achieve artistic greatness in their Slavonic individualism. It was this lighter side which was taken up by his successors Glazunov (1865–1936) and Miaskovsky (1881–1950): whether by way of *déjà-entendu* in **Rachmaninov's** symphonies or in the made-to-order 'socialist realism' of **Shostakovich's** ballets, the lilt of the Tchaikovsky concert waltz is instantly recognizable. Like many Romantic composers, his music contains many characteristic traits that have been copied. If the unstable side of his temperament frequently outweighs thematic and formal considerations, the humanity and sincerity of Tchaikovsky's artistry shines through.

Further reading

See: R. Newmarch, *Tchaikovsky* (1907); H. Weinstock, *Tchaikovsky* (1943); Gerald Abraham, *The Music of Tchaikovsky* (1945); E. Evans, *Tchaikovsky* (1966); John Warrack, *Tchaikovsky Symphonies and Concertos* (1974); Vladimir Volkoff, *Tchaikovsky* (1975); John Warrack, *Tchaikovsky Ballet Music* (1979); Alexander Poznansky, *Tchaikovsky's Last Days: A Documentary Study* (1996); Leslie Kearney (ed.) *Tchaikovsky and His World* (1998); Edward Garden, *Tchaikovsky* (2001).

MICHAEL ALEXANDER

TENNYSON, Alfred (Lord)
1809–92
English poet

Alfred Tennyson, first Baron Tennyson, was born in Somersby, Lincolnshire. His father was an emphatically gloomy country rector from whom the poet inherited a temperamental melancholy and from whom he received his early education, the rectory being well stocked with books. He began to write when he was eight years old. When he was eighteen, he and his brother issued *Poems by Two Brothers*. The next year Tennyson went to Trinity College, Cambridge, where he met Arthur Hallam. His discussions with the extremely clear-minded and sympathetic Hallam helped Tennyson to clarify his ideas about the nature of form in poetry and about poetic language. *Poems Chiefly Lyrical* (1830) and *Poems* (1833) established Tennyson in the eyes of Leigh Hunt, who had 'discovered' Keats, Shelley and Byron and set about promoting Tennyson. Hallam's death in 1833 marked Tennyson's life and affected his development as a poet. His most original and distinctive work was in a sense produced out of his dialogue with Hallam. He never had such another reader or friend. For nine years he published very little but was writing *In Memoriam* (published in 1850). *Poems* (1842) included earlier work but also 'Locksley Hall', 'Ulysses', 'Morte d'Arthur' (a prototype for the *Idylls of the King*) and other important work. *The Princess: A Medley* (1847) includes some of his best lyrics in a rather dull blank-verse flow from which they can fortunately be rescued to stand alone.

Fame was – for one of his temperament – a necessary burden. *Maud: A Monodrama* (1855) and the first four *Idylls* (1859) brought him much fame. *Enoch Arden* (1864) marked a decisive falling-off – not that Tennyson wrote badly after that date, only that he wrote dully, with a few vigorous exceptions. He became Poet Laureate in 1850 and held the post for forty-two years. His poetic 'working life' was among the longest in English literature – sixty-five years. His excursions into verse drama, as into narrative, were unconvincing, though he devoted his later years to them. His later collections were *Ballads and Other Poems* (1880), *Tiresias and Other Poems* (1885), *Demeter and Other Poems* (1889) and *The Death of Oenone* (1892). The 1885 collection took its title from an early poem he recovered and revised for publication.

His virtues as a lyric poet are essentially prosodic rather than conceptual. His narrative and dramatic limitations are clear from *Maud,* with its immediately memorable local passages and its eminently forgettable and sometimes absurd larger designs. Tennyson bases his dramatic procedure in the plays on what he takes to be Shakespeare's, but he is unable to give distinctive dictions to his speakers. His mimetic talents do not include the kind of self-effacement required of a dramatist nor the sense of thrift and pace which Shakespeare might have taught a brisker poet. Tennyson will talk through his characters: they reveal general states of feeling, not states of mind in specific context. The characters do not speak *in* character.

Even excluding the plays, Tennyson's output is huge. The good poems rise to the surface far more readily than they do in the work of a more integrated imagination – **Hardy's**, for instance – or of a more artificial one – for instance, **Browning's**. Tennyson had the desire and compulsion to write, but what he wrote did not always have the additional compulsion of emotional or psychological necessity. We distinguish the poems of feeling from the poems of conventional sentiment, but even they have prosodic merits. In some poems he thinks; in some he adopts, unimaginatively, other people's thoughts or the liberal sentiments of the age. As the 'Representative Voice', his politics and his religion are rooted in an idealizing memory of the past and a fear of the future.

Matthew Arnold discerned in 1860 that the Laureate, despite his vast accomplishments, 'is deficient in intellectual power'. This, of course, is one reason for the power of his lyric poems: they are not governed by ideas but by exquisitely held and apprehended feelings of a kind that 'intellectual power' might distrust, discard or ironize (as was the case with Browning, who – though one would hardly call him intellectually powerful – was no doubt clever, too clever to be seen to be sincere). Tennyson's poetic weakness is the narrowness of his register. He was technically omnicompetent; but he is truly accomplished only in a small area of his competence. His was a refining style which, when he tried to escape it, produced such disastrous work as 'Dora'.

Part of Tennyson's originality is in his mimetic conception of poetic language: sound and syntax could create, he believed, equivalents to motion and image, as 'The Palace of Art' and 'The Lotus Eaters' very differently demonstrate.

His idealization of the past provides him with epic and legendary figures, the best of them old men (whom he fleshed out in his youthful poems) – Tithonus and Ulysses especially. Those poems express – or seem to – through the vehicle of a *persona* Tennyson's deepest feelings and resolutions. The mask was for Browning a way of escaping the 'self'; for Tennyson it was a means of approach which suitably generalized the experience presented. No young poet has ever more effectively donned the mask of age.

His best long poem, *In Memoriam,* succeeds in part because it is an anthology of short poems arranged to follow the cycles of years and the gradual transformation of grief at the death of a friend into a kind of forced spiritual optimism. The lyrics – especially the melancholy ones – stand up well to reading out of context, as do the lyrics from *The Princess*. Organic units have been marshalled by Tennyson into mechanical structures. It is no wonder the structures do not hold; but the units retain unique force, the sum of the parts exceeding the whole. The language of *In Memoriam* is, for the most part, plain and direct with that refinement of sincerity which rejects the evasions of irony on the one hand and those of exaggeration in 'contextualizing' on the other.

The success of *In Memoriam* is its fragmentariness. Each section is an elegiac idyll. As one critic said, the faith is flimsy while the doubt is potent poetry. Tennyson was 'the voice of his age' in various ways – not least in a kind of nostalgic and intransitive eloquence, pure of designs on the reader beyond the design to pleasure and to move him – but not to impel him to action, rather to reflection. It is a poetry that – at its best – cannot be used, can only be valued.

One of the most rewarding contexts in which to set Tennyson's work is that of the first and second generation French Symbolists. The analogies are numerous and underline the freshness of his poetic intelligence and original imagination, his prosodic resourcefulness, whatever may have been the limitations of his more cognitive intellect.

Further reading

Other works include: *The Poems of Tennyson*, ed. Christopher Ricks (1969). See: Sir Charles Tennyson, *Alfred Tennyson* (1949); *Critical Essays on the Poetry of Tennyson*, ed. John Killham (1960); *Tennyson: The Critical Heritage*, ed. John D. Jump (1967); A. Sinfield, *Alfred Tennyson* (1986); D.S. Hair, *Tennyson's Language* (1991).

MICHAEL SCHMIDT

THATCHER, (Lady) Margaret Hilda (née ROBERTS)

1925–

British stateswoman

Nothing about Margaret Thatcher marked her out for leadership of the Conservative Party. Born the second daughter of a Lincolnshire greengrocer, state-educated, a science graduate (chemistry at Oxford), wife of a divorcee ten years her senior, Methodist, she seemed destined at best to occupy the outer fringe of the inner party. Yet by the time she was bundled out of office in 1990 as the longest-serving prime minister of the twentieth century she had decisively changed the terms of trade of British politics. Hated and respected in equal measure at home, regarded with awed incredulity abroad, Thatcher challenged and overthrew Britain's post-war political consensus. In Ronald Reagan she found an ideological and occasionally exasperating soul-mate, even if her relentless energy and mastery of detail (she had to be dragged kicking and screaming on holiday and hated every minute away from the office) were sometimes frustrated by the American president's more relaxed approach to high office.

Margaret Thatcher never forgot her Grantham origins: the spirit of middle England gave her much of her force. The hardworking civic virtues of Albert Roberts, her father, were her model. In her eyes the challenges of running a country were fundamentally those of running a household budget. And the elocuted assertiveness of her views drew their strength from the unshakeable belief that she was right. That she was susceptible to male charm, and perhaps even coquettish, did nothing to temper the categorical certainty of her views.

She broke the mould because she was Britain's first woman prime minister, successfully challenging Edward Heath for the leadership of the Tory Party after its 1974 general election defeat. Until then her main political job had been as Secretary of State for Education under Heath. This is where she earned the first of many sobriquets – for abolishing the provision of free school milk she became Thatcher the Milk Snatcher.

Thatcher brought to politics a strong ideological conviction which drew on Friederich-August von Hayek's *The Road to Serfdom* (1944) and the Chicago school of **Milton**

Friedman interpreted through her own gut instincts and belief in her own common sense. Her more immediate mentor was the fastidious, somewhat unworldly Tory political thinker Keith Joseph. She was also unashamedly sectarian, condemning post-war politics as largely a contest to see which party would manage a national decline accepted as inevitable. She did not coax or cajole Britain into change – she confronted and hassled the nation into change. The fact that the Labour Party reacted to its defeat at her hands in 1979 by reverting to 'dotty' left-wing policies gave her ideas an intellectual free-run which added to her dominance of the political agenda.

Margaret Thatcher was fiercely and proudly nationalistic – Gaullist in Europe, firmly but sometimes critically placing Britain alongside the US in global issues. She thrived on confrontation and conflict. The unsure start to her first term as prime minister was transformed by the most famous conflict of all – the Falklands War of 1982. Britain fought to re-conquer the islands occupied by Argentina. War was Mrs T's apotheosis – it brought out her determination, ability to withstand adversity in the shape of the early naval losses, leadership (ordering the sinking of the Argentine battleship *General Belgrano* even though it appeared to offer no immediate threat to the expeditionary force) and patriotism ('Rejoice,' she instructed the nation at the taking of South Georgia, 'Rejoice.')

Conflict also marked her second term – arguably a more important conflict. When Arthur Scargill led Britain's coal miners on strike without a ballot in 1984 both sides dug in for one of the most bitter industrial conflicts of the post-war period. For Mrs Thatcher this challenged the government's ability to govern. It also gave her the chance to put to rest the weary record of giving in to strikes (characterized under Harold Wilson as tea and sandwiches at No. 10) which had so undermined the country's economic competitiveness and turned it into the sick man of Europe. The conflict was all the more violent

because dissident miners set up their own union and continued to work, running the gauntlet of picket lines.

The government held out. The miners were forced back to work after a strike lasting a year. Given the totemic position of the miner in British industrial folklore it was a huge psychological and political victory for the government.

The reform of the British economy was a slower process, but this is what really changed the rules of British politics. The privatization of nationalized industries such as telecommunications, gas, electricity, coal, British Airways and, sociologically most important of all, the sale of municipal housing to their tenants at huge discounts both responded to public exasperation at the seemingly incessant needs of state-owned industry for subsidy and created a new popular capitalism. Coupled with tax-cutting, the curtailment of trade union powers (unions weakened by the demise of 'sunset' industries and the privatization programme) and the abolition of foreign exchange controls (almost the first act of the Tory government), these supply-side changes laid the foundations for the emergence of the UK as one of the strongest European economies.

But Thatcher's premiership was not without its internal conflicts. Both Geoffrey Howe and then Nigel Lawson, her longest-serving chancellors of the exchequer, were attracted by the European system of managed interest rates as ways of curbing the inflation which had been the curse of the British economy and of imposing discipline in public spending. Lawson shadowed the exchange rate mechanism without the Prime Minister's knowledge. She finally sanctioned British membership against her instincts, demanding an unwise interest rate cut as sweetener. Britain's calamitous and humiliating withdrawal from the ERM under the premiership of John Major, her successor, was to destroy the Conservative Party's unity and reputation for the best part of a generation.

The Prime Minister was accused of becoming progressively more domineering and of depending increasingly on her own instincts. Michael Heseltine, a political showman with long-nourished ambition and an instinct for creating policy-making, literally walked out of the Cabinet in a row over helicopter procurement. He became her nemesis when his leadership challenge brought about her resignation.

Margaret Thatcher had an ambiguous and even contradictory relationship with Europe. Her initiative to create 'the real common market' and introduce much greater use of qualified majority voting inside the European Union to make it happen was, arguably, the most integrationist programme of the 1980s. But she disliked and distrusted the 'federalist' ambitions of EU President Jacques Delors (being French and a socialist did not help his case!) and found West German Chancellor **Helmut Kohl** incapable of discussing issues in the detail she demanded. Ironically she was charmed and flattered by François Mitterrand, France's socialist president (he described her as having the mouth of Marilyn Monroe and the eyes of Caligula). She hated the vague inspirational rhetoric of European destiny. **Gorbachev** she recognized as 'someone we can do business with'. It is one of the ironies of Mrs Thatcher's personality that this most ideological of British leaders sought above all pragmatism in her interlocutors.

Her doughty handbag-wielding − and successful − battle to win a budget rebate for Britain ('I want my money back') helped seal her reputation as 'the Iron Lady' (a Russian description). But it was Europe which brought her down. Already weakened by the hostility to a new 'flat-rate' system of domestic property taxation (the poll tax), her increasingly strident opposition to European policies for integration ('No, no, no,' she proclaimed in the House of Commons) precipitated the palace revolt of her own party in November 1990. Failing to garner a decisive vote in the first round of a forced leadership contest and warned that she could lose the second to Michael Heseltine, she resigned.

For many in the party it was matricide. Indeed, arguably the party is still working out the catharsis of the assassination, not at the hands of the opposition or the electorate but by her own colleagues, of a leader with three election victories under her belt. The government of John Major, having scraped a majority in the 1992 general election, was destroyed by civil war over Europe, with Mrs Thatcher aiding and abetting the 'Euro-sceptics'.

Margaret Thatcher owed much to her husband Denis. He became a legendary figure at her side, reputedly always in search of a drink and a round of golf and calming Margaret down. The 'Dear Bill' letters in the satirical magazine *Private Eye* − a fictional series of missives from Denis to his golf and drinking partner Bill Deedes − remain classics of political humour illuminated by insight.

Few politicians have provoked so many epigrammatic summaries. The true believers (and the party was an uncharacteristically sectarian place under Mrs T) were 'one of us'. She was termed 'The Blessed Margaret' and 'She Who Has to Be Obeyed'. Her mantra in the matter of economic reform was 'there is no alternative', while her determination − and the perceived 'wetness' of some of her colleagues − led to her characterization as 'the only man in the Cabinet'.

Was Margaret Thatcher a Thatcherite? It is a real question. She was more pragmatic than her assertions led to believe. Her acolytes were perhaps more royalist than the queen. She did not privatize the railways − that was left to Major. She stopped short of the Post Office. She presided over a strong pound sterling − and over *de facto* devaluations. On the personal level she was unfailingly kind and considerate: her legendary mastery of detail included personal knowledge about people who would be surprised to learn that she could even remember their face. By the public at large − a huge generalization − she was respected but not loved. 'You always know where you stand with Maggie' was perhaps the most fulsome tribute.

Thatcherism, especially tax-cutting and privatization, has proven eminently exportable as part of the liberal economic model, nowhere more so than in the former Communist states of Eastern and Central Europe which are now part of the European Union. 'Old Europe' of France and Germany complain about the Continental invasion of Anglo-Saxon ideas. Given Thatcher's steadily growing antipathy to Europe's political construction it would be wonderfully ironical if the 'common market' ultimately delivered her biggest triumph.

Further reading

Other works include: *The Downing Street Years 1979–90* (1993) and *The Path to Power* (1995). See also: Margaret Thatcher: *Statecraft: Strategies for a Changing World* (2002); Robin Harris (ed.) *The Collected Speeches of Margaret Thatcher* (1998). About Thatcher: Hugo Young, *The Iron Lady* (1989) and *One of Us: Life of Margaret Thatcher* (also 1989); Alan Clark, *Diaries* (1993); John Campbell, *Margaret Thatcher, The Grocer's Daughter* (2001) and *Margaret Thatcher, Volume Two: The Iron Lady* (2003); John Sergeant, *Maggie: Her Fatal Legacy* (2005); John Clarke and Subroto Roy (eds) *Margaret Thatcher's Revolution: How It Happened and What It Meant* (2005).

DAVID CURRY

THESIGER, Wilfred

1910–2002

English traveller and writer

'I craved the past, resented the present and dreaded the future,' wrote Wilfred Thesiger, who saw himself, with sorrowful pride, as the last of his kind. He knew the past at first hand. He was born in 1910 in Ethiopia (then Abyssinia), where his father was ConsulGeneral. At the age of six he watched the victorious armies returning to Addis Ababa at the conclusion of a civil war, the chieftains in lion's mane headdresses and velvet robes stiff with silver embroidery, the warriors 'screaming out their deeds of valour'. The 'barbaric splendour' of the spectacle stayed with him all his life. He wrote about it repeatedly, and ascribed to its influence his lifelong compulsion to seek out violent people in remote places, to place himself in situations where he

could feel, as he had that day, that he was a part of a scene from the *Iliad*.

Thesiger came from the British imperial ruling class. His uncles included a high court judge and a viceroy of India. But although he served in the Sudan Political Service in his twenties, and subsequently accepted various other official appointments as pretexts for getting into countries closed to casual visitors, he had no appetite for power or taste for public service. He travelled for his own personal satisfaction. His autobiography was aptly entitled *The Life of My Choice* (1987).

Immediately after leaving Oxford he embarked on a journey through the Danakil country of eastern Ethiopia, territory forbidding not only because it was so physically inhospitable but because its inhabitants killed people for sport. He survived, making his name as an explorer. His stint in the Sudan followed, with Thesiger using his every leave to travel into the country's remotest mountains and deserts, riding mules or camels and living on equal terms with his African guides. During the Second World War he was with the irregular force invading Abyssinia under Orde Wingate, and subsequently with the SAS in the desert. Afterwards he travelled in Arabia, on and off for five years, crossing the sands of the Empty Quarter (he was the first European to do so twice), and adopting the dress, manners and allbutlethally rigorous lifestyle of the small group of *bedu* whom he hired to be his guides and companions. He repeatedly came close to death, either from drought or starvation, or at the hands of hostile tribesmen, but he had found exactly what he sought. These journeys form the material for his masterpiece, *Arabian Sands* (1959).

Other travels followed. Thesiger lived for most of five years among the Marsh Arabs of southern Iraq and he travelled extensively in the remoter parts of central Asia before settling to live for sixteen years with various African 'fostersons' in Kenya. But it was his Arabian adventures that thrilled him and his readers, largely because of the intensity of his love for the nomadic people he knew there. They seemed to him both splendidly primitive, in the sense of being uncorrupted by outside influences, and 'the lineal heirs of a very ancient civilisation'.

That he should be so entranced by ferocity and hardship while using the word 'civilized' as a term of the highest possible approbation is only one of the many paradoxes of Thesiger's life and writing. Intensely resistant to change and passionately deploring the intrusion of Westerners into previously unvisited parts of the world, he spent much of his life visiting such places, despairingly conscious that the maps he made, the books he wrote, the personal celebrity which he enjoyed, would all encourage others to follow him. But there is a final, benign paradox. Our present, the future he so dreaded, has recognized that his warnings about the deleterious effects of Westernization on third-world cultures were sadly prescient. The man who killed seventy lions over a period of five years (three of them in one morning) is read and admired by conservationists for the accuracy of his perception of the fragility of traditional social structures, as well as for the austere beauty of his prose and the sentimental power of his evocation of a murderous people 'whose spirit once lit the desert like a flame'.

Further reading

Other books by Wilfred Thesiger include *The Marsh Arabs* (1962), *Desert, Marsh and Mountain* (1979) and *Kenya Days* (1994). *Visions of a Nomad* (1987) is a selection of his superb black-and-white photographs. There is also an anthology, *My Life and Travels* (2002) ed. Alexander Maitland, Thesiger's authorized biographer, whose *Wilfred Thesiger* was published in 2006. See also Michael Asher, *Thesiger* (1994) and *Mark Cocker, Loneliness and Time: British Travel Writing in the Twentieth Century* (1992).

LUCY HUGHES-HALLETT

THOM, René

1923–

French mathematician

René Fréderic Thom was born in 1923 at Montbéliard (Doubs), and educated at the Lycée Saint-Louis and at the Ecole Normale Supérieure in Paris. After taking his doctorate he was Maître de Conférences at Grenoble and Strasbourg, before taking a chair in the Faculty of Sciences at Strasbourg in 1957. From 1964 he was a professor at the Institut des Hautes Études Scientifiques at Bures-sur-Yvette. Thom was awarded the Fields Medal in 1958, the equivalent of a Nobel Prize in mathematics. He became a member of the Académie des Sciences in 1976.

Thom's most influential work has been his 'Catastrophe Theory', an attempt to explain why certain surprises occur in systems which are known to be fully predictable. The key to understanding Thom's problem is the idea of a 'continuous' process in which a small change in the controls produces a small change in the effect. For example, as the petrol level in the tank of a car goes down by one millimetre the needle on the dashboard moves a tiny distance towards 'Empty' on the dial. The smaller the movement of the petrol level, the smaller the movement of the needle. There are many situations in which several such continuous processes act simultaneously to produce a composite result. For example, a painkiller pill may contain x mg of aspirin and y mg of codeine. The net effect of this is that it has a certain potency in quietening a painful tooth, say. We may express such an effect in terms of a number z, the number of pills or part pills needed to reduce the experienced pain of the tooth to zero. It is natural to expect the control variables x and y to control the potency of the pill – as expressed by the number z – *continuously* in the sense described above, namely that small changes in x and y produce only small changes in z. However, there are some situations in the sciences and in technology where the processes are known to be both fully predictable and continuous and yet, when operating simultaneously, produce a strange result: every now and then the effect variable (i.e. corresponding to z above) suddenly flips from one value to a different value. It was the occurrence of these situations which Thom set out to study, explain and classify. How does it come about that certain systems turn predictable continuous inputs into evidently predictable, but surprisingly *dis*continuous outputs? Thom showed that if we limit our attention to systems in which there are five or fewer control variables the number of patterns in which these 'flips' can occur is strictly limited too. In fact, Thom identified eight basic cases which he named the 'simple minimum', 'fold', 'cusp', 'swallow tail', 'butterfly', 'hyperbolic umbilic', 'elliptic umbilic' and 'parabolic umbilic'.

Thom's theory presented in full in his book *Stabilité structurelle et morphogenèse* (*Structural Stability and Morphogenesis*, 1972, trans. 1976) spread rapidly around the mathematically educated world. Professor Christopher Zeeman acted as Thom's **T.H. Huxley**. In impact Thom's theory had the characteristics of a cultural phenomenon. The reason for this seems to lie partly in the unique choice of the name 'Catastrophe Theory', partly in the way in which the theory was illustrated with an extraordinary variety of examples chosen from biology, psychology, industrial relations and medicine, as well as the more classical examples in engineering and control theory, and partly because it was a reflection of Thom's depth of insight as a new kind of philosopher-mathematician.

In assessing Thom's theory there are certain tendencies to misconception which have been amplified by the 'cultural phenomenon' mentioned above. First, there is no intrinsic reason why the theory should have been styled a 'catastrophe' theory. It is concerned with sudden flips occurring in continuous systems, but it is quite arbitrary whether one regards such flips as 'up' or 'down'. In a less deeply pessimistic age it might have seemed natural to call Thom's theory a 'breakthrough' theory or a 'take-off' theory. Second, many of the more exotic examples which have been given of Thom's theory, e.g. in accounting for the condition of *anorexia nervosa* or the biting behaviour of angry-frightened dogs, are really more like suggestive general analogies than precisely verifiable applications of the mathematics. Third, if the

theory seems to give us a certain limited degree of comfort that only a certain finite number of types of catastrophe can occur, this is an aspect whose practical significance is effectively nil. (Thom's classification still allows an infinite variety of catastrophes to occur, and does not, in any case, offer a complete theory of all possible catastrophes.) Fourth, Thom's theory, though a remarkable mathematical triumph, does not do anything to underwrite a generally deterministic model of the universe. The mathematics does not and could not establish the validity of this essentially metaphysical view of things.

Further reading

See Yung Chen Lu, *Singularity Theory and an Introduction to Catastrophe Theory* (1976); Christopher Zeeman, 'Catastrophe Theory', *Scientific American*, Vol. 236, No. 4 (April 1976).

CHRISTOPHER ORMELL

THOMAS, Dylan Marlais

1914–53

Welsh poet

Dylan Marlais Thomas was born on 27 October 1914 at 5 Cwmdonkin Drive in Swansea, where his father D.J. Thomas taught English at the grammar school and harboured unrealized ambitions to be a poet. D.J. gave his son the consciously literary names Dylan (the 'sea son' of the *Mabinogion*) and Marlais (a Welsh river adopted as bardic name by D.J.'s uncle) and encouraged him to read and recite poetry. Dylan stayed in his father's house until he was nineteen, referring to himself as 'the Rimbaud of Cwmdonkin Drive'.

If his home was excessively bookish, Dylan had no inclination for academic pursuits and liked to escape from 'splendidly ugly' Swansea. Near his house was Cwmdonkin Park, where he played and observed such unforgettable figures as 'The Hunchback in the Park'. Even more exciting were the summer holidays spent at Fern Hill dairy farm in north

Carmarthenshire, the home of his aunt Ann Jones. Dylan drew on his adolescent experiences in poems like 'After the Funeral' (in memory of Ann Jones who died in 1933) and the ecstatic 'Fern Hill' in which he recalled how he 'was young and easy under the apple boughs'.

Dylan left school in 1931 and spent his time acting with the Swansea Little Theatre, reporting for the *South Wales Daily Post* for fifteen months, and hanging about bars and cafés. He cultivated a romantic poetic persona but it was no sartorial pose; in the three years between leaving school in 1931 and leaving Swansea for London in 1934 he produced more than 200 poems including all the *18 Poems* (1934), most of the *Twenty-five Poems* (1936), early versions of many later poems and ideas that would subsequently be used in such works as *Under Milk Wood* (1954). It was the most creative period of his life and, by contrast, he wrote only eight poems in the last seven years of his life.

Thomas's poetry made an immediate and rather sensational impact on the public. His style was an individual mixture of the sensuous elements in poetry (as practised by Keats and **G.M. Hopkins**) and the linguistic experiments of **Joyce** and **Eliot**. When 'Light breaks where no sun shines' was published in the *Listener* of 14 March 1934 it provoked a storm of protest from readers who found the imagery obscene. However, Thomas's revitalization of the romantic tradition gained the admiration of Stephen Spender, Eliot, Edwin Muir and Edith Sitwell, who described the work *Twenty-five Poems* as 'nothing short of magnificent'. Thomas's early poetry was astonishingly dense in metaphor and treated sexual matters with surrealist manners. In a letter to Pamela Hansford Johnson – with whom he conducted an epistolary affair – he wrote in November 1933 that 'every idea, intuitive or intellectual, can be imaged and translated in terms of the body'.

Thomas had moved to London in 1934 and met Caitlin Macnamara, a twenty-two-year-old dancer who had been dismissed from the chorus line of the London Palladium.

The couple spent a holiday together in the Welsh fishing village of Laugharne and returned there after getting married in July 1937 in Cornwall. Despite the great critical success of his poetry and the income derived from wartime film work and post-war broadcasting, Thomas was unable to control his domestic destiny. His drinking was reaching epic proportions and the marriage was punctuated by frequent periods of despair. In 1949 Margaret Taylor, wife of the historian A.J.P. Taylor, obtained for the Thomases the Boat House on the estuary of the River Taf in their beloved Laugharne and for the remaining four years of his life this was home for Dylan and Caitlin and their three children.

The cliffside house had a magnificent view of the bay, and in his garden shed, which he called 'the shack', Thomas composed poems like 'Over Sir John's hill', 'Author's Prologue' and 'Poem on his birthday'. Perhaps because he was suspicious of the apparently effortless precocity he had once enjoyed – or perhaps because he could no longer respond so readily to his insights – Thomas evolved an excruciatingly painstaking method of composition. He would retire to his shed in the afternoon after the pubs had closed and endlessly revise his poetry, sometimes making as many as 200 work-sheets for one poem. As a result Thomas's mature poetry became more and more formally intricate so that the finished product contained a complex of cross-association and a delicate embroidery of interweaving internal rhymes. Thomas was still an inspirational poet but the source of his poetry was no longer anatomical but natural; he was also anxious to live up to the Welsh tradition of technical expertise and to become a master of 'my craft or sullen art'.

In 1950 Thomas made, at the invitation of John Malcolm Brinnin, the first of four trips to America. His public performances of poetry delighted American audiences, for Thomas's incomparably rich delivery conformed to their expectations of a bard drunk on the music of words. His private performances as an obstreperous drunk scandalized his hosts who constructed, out of a few indiscreet incidents, a monument to Dylan as an outrageous artistic clown. He was depressed by the malicious gossip that surrounded him in America, exhausted by the demands of extensive reading tours, and dismayed by the alcoholic pace his American admirers imposed on him. Yet he returned in triumph for his third trip in 1953. The previous year Thomas's *Collected Poems* (1952) had appeared to a crescendo of critical applause and he surpassed that with the New York reception of the stage version of his radio play *Under Milk Wood* (1954). The wit and brilliant linguistic invention of the play were enthusiastically appreciated and Thomas was well on the way to becoming an American institution; Boston University invited him to collaborate with **Stravinsky** on an opera on the re-creation of the world.

Thomas had earned substantial sums of money in America but had saved none of it so that life back in Laugharne, the setting of *Under Milk Wood*, became intolerable, and he embarked on his fourth and final visit to the USA to direct an expanded version of his play. His alcoholic decline was by this time complete and he suffered from *delirium tremens* and constant anxiety. When Thomas became uncontrollable his American doctor injected him with morphine; probably the effect of the drug, plus the intake of alcohol, proved fatal. On 4 November 1953 he was taken in a coma to St Vincent's Hospital, New York, and died five days later. The cause of death was diagnosed as 'Insult to the brain'. The poet's body was brought back to Wales to be buried in St Martin's Churchyard, Laugharne. Since then an academic industry has grown up around Thomas and his legend has been exhaustively examined; his poetry remains as the work of a virtuoso who created some of the finest lyrical works of the twentieth century.

Further reading

Other works include: *The Poems* (1971, revised 1974), ed. Daniel Jones; his broadcasts and stories

can be sampled in *Quite Early One Morning* (1954) and *A Prospect of the Sea* (1955). See also: John Malcolm Brinnin, *Dylan Thomas in America* (1956); Caitlin Thomas, *Leftover Life to Kill* (1957); Constantine FitzGibbon, *The Life of Dylan Thomas* (1965); and Paul Ferris, *Dylan Thomas* (1977); Caitlin Thomas with George Tremlett, *Caitlin: Life with Dylan Thomas* (1996); James A. Davies, *A Reference Companion to Dylan Thomas* (1998); Caitlin Thomas, *Double Drink Story* (1999); Paul Ferris, *Dylan Thomas: The Biography* (2000); Andrew Lycett, *Dylan Thomas: A New Life* (2003).

ALAN BOLD

THOMAS, Philip Edward
1878–1917
British poet

Edward Thomas was born on 3 March 1878 in Lambeth and, although he was to make his reputation as a writer concerned chiefly with the countryside, he spent most of his early life in London. Occasional holidays, however, were taken with relatives near Swindon, and these encouraged his admiration for Richard Jefferies, who had lived nearby. Jefferies's work and personality were to exercise a strong influence on his own. While he was still a schoolboy at St Paul's, Thomas's early essays brought him to the attention of the critic James Ashcroft Noble, who arranged for several of them to be published in the *Speaker* and the *New Age*. Others were included in his first book *The Woodland Life* which was published in 1897, and when Thomas went up to Oxford as a non-collegiate student later the same year he was already considering a career as a writer. He had also fallen in love with Noble's daughter Helen. In 1898 he won a history scholarship to Lincoln College, Oxford, where he continued to produce journalism and essays – now in a style much influenced by **Walter Pater**. It was one of the most carefree periods of his often unhappy life, but its freedoms were restricted when Helen found she was pregnant. In spite of their professedly Shelleyean attitude to their relationship, the couple were quickly married and their son was born in

January 1900. That summer Thomas disappointed himself and his friends by gaining only a second-class degree.

In spite of his father's advice to join the Civil Service, Thomas remained firm in his decision to live by his pen. His tenacity cost him increasingly dear. Before his death in April 1917 he was to introduce sixteen editions and anthologies, produce over a million and a half words of review, and write thirty volumes of topography, biography, criticism and belles-lettres. Many of these were on uncongenial topics, nearly all had to be produced very quickly, and their effect was almost literally soul-destroying. Between 1901 and 1916 he and his family (two more children were born in 1902 and 1910) moved house seven times in attempts to create a new start. But although he came to regard himself as a 'doomed hack', and although the quality of his prose work is uneven, its large bulk describes a sustained attempt at self-discovery. In a broader perspective, it may be seen as the struggle of a distinctly modern sensibility to emerge from the constraints of the nineteenth century. Thomas's prose is written in a gradually simplifying style and the best of it – his life of Jefferies, for instance, or his topographical books *The Icknield Way* and *In Pursuit of Spring* – combines clear judgement with close observation. In several cases, though, its chief interest lies in the fact that it anticipates the scenes, preoccupations and sometimes even phrasing of his poems.

At various times a number of Thomas's friends had tried to persuade him to write poetry – to no avail. But **Robert Frost**, whom Thomas met in 1913, slowly wore down his resistance, partly by force of personality and partly by sympathetic example. Frost's verse theories were extraordinarily similar to those Thomas himself had evolved independently in his reviews and criticism. Where Frost spoke of 'the sound of sense' Thomas used the phrase 'thought moments' to describe the rhythmical plain speech he admired. This quality is evident in his own poems, the first of which, 'Up in the Wind', was written on 3 December 1914. It is

important to stress that all Thomas's poems were written after the outbreak of war. The conflict sharpened his (always keen) feelings of dignified, organic patriotism and – more practically – the long periods of training which followed his enlistment in 1915 gave him time to write. In the twenty-five months between finishing 'Up in the Wind' and his death in the battle of Arras he produced 142 poems. The war is openly mentioned in relatively few of these – 'As the Team's Head-brass' is a notable exception – but its pressures and dangers helped to shape them all. Characteristically, they describe a cautious search for a sense of Englishness which, if found at all, can only be glimpsed fleetingly. In this they recall the work of several earlier Romantic writers, Wordsworth pre-eminently, but the fastidious pausing rhythms and intent particularity of his pastoralism are entirely individual. The natural world is always unsentimentally seen for what it is, as well as being used to contain and enact his pursuit of stable identity. The war, the decay of the old rural order and his own melancholic self-doubt continually threaten his quest, and the result is poetry of much greater formal interest and emotional complexity than that written by the Georgian contemporaries with whom he is sometimes bracketed. Other more recent poets seem not to have overlooked this, if his influence on the young **W.H. Auden** and the mature **Philip Larkin** is taken as evidence. But more popular acclaim has been slower to come. Only a century or so after his birth did he become widely admired for using what one of his critics called 'the minor modes' to write poetry of 'major psychological subtlety'.

Further reading

Other works include: *The Collected Poems of Edward Thomas*, ed. R. George Thomas (1978). Selections from the prose: *Edward Thomas on the Countryside*, selected by Roland Gant (1977); *The Selected Prose of Edward Thomas*, ed. Edna Longley (1981); *Edward Thomas: Selected Poems and Prose*, ed. David Wright (1981). Biography: Helen Thomas, *As It Was and World Without End* (1956);

Eleanor Farjeon, *Edward Thomas: The Last Four Years* (1958); John Moore, *The Life and Letters of Edward Thomas* (1939). Letters: *Letters from Edward Thomas to Gordon Bottomeley*, ed. R. George Thomas (1968). Criticism: *William Cooke, Edward Thomas: A Critical Biography* (1970); *Edward Thomas: Poems and Last Poems*, ed. Edna Longley (1973); Andrew Motion, *The Poetry of Edward Thomas* (1980).

ANDREW MOTION

THOMAS, Ronald Stuart

1913–2000
Welsh poet

As a young boy growing up on the farthest tip of the Welsh island of Anglesey, R.S. Thomas was captivated by the magisterial silhouette of distant Snowdonia. For him, deprived (in his view) of the Welsh language by his parents' snobbish choice, it represented the inaccessible, aboriginal, authentic Wales. Later, as a turbulent priest of the Church in Wales, he was to approach the Welsh geo-cultural heartland by cautious degrees, while attempting to gain full admission to it by becoming fluent in Welsh and substantially mastering the Welsh literary tradition. Yet, even when he finally settled on the Lleyn Peninsula, the psychic wound which, he was convinced, had been inflicted by the mother to whom he remained resentfully attached, failed to heal. Later in life, he was to concede that the powerful poetry he had written in what he regarded as the alien, and therefore self-alienating, English tongue had flowed from this wound. Echoing the words of **William B. Yeats**, who along with other 'Celtic' writers had been a considerably influence on his younger pan-Celtic self, he recognized that poetry proceeded from one's quarrel with oneself.

In Thomas's case, that quarrel took many different forms. It was encapsulated in the mesmerically contradictory figure of Iago Prytherch, the Welsh upland 'peasant' of his early poetry, and voiced as an obsessive, one-sided dialogue with a silent, deaf and implacably absent God throughout the last thirty years of his long life. Present in Thomas's railings against the 'Anglo-Welsh' it also erupted in fierce jeremiads against the modern world of technology and the 'Machine'. And it materialized in his aggressive support for direct political action on behalf of the Welsh language, his ambiguous attitude towards arson attacks on English holiday homes, and his championing of environmental causes.

The anguished concern at the plight of Wales that filled the poetry of Thomas's early decades found expression in poems some of which are classics of political engagement, but many of which are marred by shrillness, and disfigured by ugly hatreds. For Thomas himself, his defence of Wales (based on **Saunders Lewis's** nationalist vision) was only a local reaction to the threat of globalization, whose most powerful exponent was the US and which eroded the environment and unique cultural systems around the world.

In the latter years of his life, Thomas acted as the **Solzhenitsyn** of Wales – the uncomfortable, always extreme and at times bigoted voice of conscience of a Welsh people whom he despised as supinely acquiescing in the process of colonial assimilation by England. However, his dark charisma was based not only on his compelling public presence and sometimes scandalous utterance but also on his commanding stature as a poet. The equal but opposite of **Dylan Thomas**, the South Walian whose boyo personality and matching garrulity he affected to dismiss, Thomas produced a verbally austere poetry, apparently narrow in scope but correspondingly intense in focus. Repetitive in ways that seem claustrophobically restricting to many, his poems may also be seen as fruitfully obsessional, the frugal work of a profoundly meditative imagination. He was lastingly influenced by English Romantic poetry and continues to be viewed by some critics as an old-fashioned Georgian. But it can be argued that at his best he succeeded in refashioning traditional modes and discourses to produce a self-scrutinizing discourse capable of addressing the contemporary social, political and spiritual condition.

Although Thomas's first collection was published in 1946, it was only after the publication of *An Acre of Land* (1953) that the praise of **John Betjeman**, **Kingsley Amis** and others brought him to wide attention. The image of him that was fixed in the English imagination at that time – a Welsh country parson of attractively conservative style and subject – has unfortunately tended to recur in many circles. He has continued to serve as convenient example of one stubbornly persistent English stereotype of the Welsh – as rural, ruggedly remote, faintly exotic, and culturally reactionary. This is partly why token inclusion of Thomas's poems in anthologies of twentieth-century poetry almost always takes the form of Iago Prytherch. This remarkable psycho-mythic figure – 'just an ordinary man of the bald Welsh hills', his clothes 'sour with years of sweat', and by wholly unpredictable turns naturally wise and bestially ignorant – has been mistaken for social reality ever since Thomas first introduced him in *The Stones of the Field* (1946). In fact, Prytherch is a grotesque, born of Thomas's own deepest compulsions and pliant to his every obsession. He served his creator well for almost two decades as conduit for the vortex of his self-bewilderment.

So powerful did Prytherch ultimately become that he overshadowed the sensitive other poems that the earlier Thomas wrote about his wife, his mother and his son. During the last three decades of his life a like fate befell the fine painting poems and the powerfully original autobiographical sequence *The Echoes Return Slow* (1988), marginalized as they were by the poetry of repeated spiritual research. Most critics have condemned this poetry as rhythmically slack and imaginatively inert, lacking in the passion and linguistic impasto of the early writing. Alternatively they may be regarded as daringly innovative, seeking to pioneer a new discourse adequate to modern spiritual concerns, and uncannily attuned to the music of what mattered to the ageing and aged Thomas. Frequently turning on models and metaphors drawn from modern science, these spiritually sophisticated, self-cancelling poems constantly emphasize the provisional nature of their own conclusions and the incorrigible mortality of their would-be metaphysical language.

Despite its many palpable drawbacks, Thomas's *Collected Poems* made it evident that his lifetime's achievement had been as monumental as, to some, his poems seemed anorexically thin. While he was nominated for a Nobel Prize and admired in countries as distant as Japan, he remained a figure about whose literary stature there remained doubt and there raged dispute. It is, perhaps, the fitting legacy of a poet of unquiet spirit and unappeasable imagination. Echoing words uttered after **Matthew Arnold's** death, there were those who murmured at his passing: 'Poor old Thomas. He won't like God.'

Further reading

Collected Poems: 1945–1990 (1993) remains the standard text, but should be supplemented with *Collected Later Poems: 1988–2000* (2004). *Selected Poems* (2004) was Thomas's final selection. For the prose, see Sandra Anstey (ed.) *R.S. Thomas, Selected Prose* (1995) and Jason Walford Davies, *Autobiographies* (1997). Justin Wintle, *Furious Interiors* (1996) is a fine first critical biography. Selected criticism includes M. Wynn Thomas (ed.) *The Page's Drift* (1993) and Damian Walford Davies (ed.) *Echoes to the Amen* (2003).

M. WYNN THOMAS

THOREAU, Henry David
1817–62
US author

Where Thoreau was known at all during his brief New England lifetime, it was essentially as an oddity, a figure of quirks and eccentric opinion. To many fellow New Englanders, in Boston and the surrounding townships of Cambridge and his birthplace, Concord, he seemed the very reverse of the gainful, purposive Yankee. He was a Harvard graduate but had settled to no recognizable occupation, as minister, lawyer or businessman. Though perceived as a minor ripple in the larger Transcendentalist current, he was nonetheless literally closer than any to the master, **Emerson's** personal friend and protégé, and later a boarder and general handyman with the family. Then, despite the apparent outward severity of his character, a trait commented on not only by Emerson ('Henry is with difficulty sweet') but by **Hawthorne**, Thoreau's one-time neighbour in Concord, he was a committed family man, but as the life-long bachelor who was a favourite uncle and loved brother. Though indubitably 'literary' in interests, he was also an alert and eloquent naturalist. No one knew better, or more first hand, the topographies of New England, its geology and Indian relics, the farms, ponds, flora and fauna. Above all, Thoreau confirmed his supposed oddness when he refused to pay his poll tax in protest at the unjust foreign war he believed his country was conducting in Mexico, having taken up residence in the summer of 1845 in the hut he built by Walden Pond, on land owned by Emerson, and stayed there for nearly two years, the action of a man who, apparently in earnest, talked of 'significant living'.

Given a reputation which, true to Thoreau's contrary style, now exceeds that of Emerson, his Transcendentalist mentor, perhaps the saddest paradox is that his age barely noticed him for the two full-length works published in his lifetime, *A Week on the Concord and Merrimack Rivers* (1849) and *Walden* (1854), or for the essays which have subsequently become classics in the literature of political dissent, 'On the Duty of Civil Disobedience' (1849) and 'A Plea for Captain John Brown' (1860). Yet these writings, *Walden* most especially, were no less than cornerstones in the American Renaissance, the mid-nineteenth-century efflorescence which includes **Melville**, **Whitman**, Hawthorne and a run of minor Transcendentalists, and which Emerson heralded in *Nature* (1836) and 'The American Scholar' (1837).

Further, if Thoreau's published output looks scant, he was also the author of nearly forty journal notebooks, extraordinary notations of a mind taking cognizance of its own inclinations and powers, and of a number of posthumous 'travel' books. As befits a writer who sought to hone down existence to 'essence', or as he puts it in *Walden* 'to drive life into a corner and reduce it to its lowest terms', Thoreau also evolved a literary idiom of rare distinction, aphoristic, wonderfully spare, layered with congenial Yankee wryness and wit.

Something of Thoreau's contrariness was recognized by **George Eliot** when she reviewed *Walden* for the *Westminster Review* in 1856. She saw his lakeside sojourn as 'a bit of pure American life', but retold 'through the medium of a deep poetic sensibility'. She testified to his 'unworldliness' yet also to his tempering 'sturdy sense'. Not unexpectedly, one of the most revealing estimates of Thoreau was offered by Emerson in the obituary essay he published in *Atlantic Monthly* in 1862. He emphasized, no doubt as much from personal knowledge of the daily routines of his so-called 'practical disciple' as of his writing, the obdurate, Spartan and as he termed it 'military' element in Thoreau, making reference to his 'inexorable demand on all for exact truth'. Emerson thought him 'a born protestant', who 'chose to be rich by making his wants few, and supplying them himself'. This radical self-sufficiency, which lies behind Thoreau's politics, and behind his wish to dissent from the prevailing orders of American capitalism and 'society', is everywhere reflected in his writing. Thoreau, according to *Walden,* wanted 'the flower and fruit of man', but only if seen and tested for himself. His bid for 'simplicity' thus was always highly complex, self-reliance not in the interests of conventionally defined rewards – material profit, possessions, social esteem – but as the path to higher 'essential' truths. Emerson was equally right to detect the 'Transcendental' ends to which Thoreau put his naturalism, the habit of seeing in nature's fine detail abiding spiritual meanings.

Born of English Channel Island and New England storekeeper stock which had gone bankrupt, Thoreau was educated at Concord Academy (1829–33), then Harvard (1833–7), where he read widely. After a brief interlude in Concord's public schools, he set up a school venture of his own with his brother John (1838–41), with whom also he travelled the Concord and Merrimack rivers in 1839. In 1840, he had his first essays and poems published in the Transcendentalist journal the *Dial*; moved in with the Emerson family (1841–3); did some tutoring on Staten Island (1843); and on 4 July 1845, an 'Independence Day' dramatically different in kind from that celebrated by the majority of his compatriots, moved to Walden Pond and his self-constructed hut. In the interim, like his brother John he had been turned down in marriage by Ellen Sewall; perfected a graphite process for his father's one-time lead pencil enterprise; acted as messenger and handyman for various of the townships; and begun his all-important notebooks. But by Walden Pond, where he had gone 'to transact some private business' and where, among other things, he wrote *A Week on the Concord and Merrimack Rivers,* he began the most significant act of his life, his two-year experiment as a 'community of one'. In 1846, he was arrested and kept in prison overnight for non-payment of the poll tax (the tax, to his annoyance, was paid by 'friends'). He travelled in 1846 to the Maine woods; lived again with the Emerson family in 1847–8; lectured on 'Civil Disobedience' (1848), a year before *A Week on the Concord and Merrimack Rivers* was published; made a sequence of trips to Cape Cod (in 1850 with his great friend and first biographer, the poet Ellery Channing); visited Walt Whitman in Brooklyn in 1856 (he called the second edition of *Leaves of Grass* 'an alarum or trumpet-note ringing through the American camp'); and in 1859 lectured on 'A Plea for Captain John Brown'. In 1860, during a camping trip, he caught cold, which exacerbated his hitherto dormant tuberculosis. Despite an excursion to Minnesota with Horace Mann Jr in hopes of recuperation, he died in Concord on 6 May 1862.

Ostensibly, *A Week on the Concord and Merrimack Rivers* re-creates the canoe journey Thoreau made with his brother into New Hampshire's White Mountains in 1839. Under his transforming design, however, it becomes also the transcript of another dimension of journeying, a diary of contemplation and thought and of Thoreau's testimony to nature as the repository of Emersonian-Transcendental spiritual 'laws'. He explains the metaphoric implications of his up-river, seven-day travel thus: 'True and sincere travelling is no pastime, but is as serious as the grave or any part of the human journey, and it requires a long probation to be broken into it.' This notion of figurative travel anticipates Thoreau's later, equally equivocal and teasing utterance, 'I have travelled much in Concord.' His 'week', in fact, is his version of the Genesis week, the Creation, as it were, retold in terms of a New England river expedition. The geography of the two rivers, and of the surrounding banks and ecology, not only yields a vivid, engaging portrait of nature itself, it acts for Thoreau as the means to his search for higher, ultimate meanings. *A Week* offers journey-narrative, thus, of a profoundly double kind, travel both outward and inward, into which Thoreau imports not only precise natural observations but a range of learning ancient and modern, different vignettes, maxims and aphorisms ('The traveller must be born again on the road, and earn a passport from the elements, the principal powers that be for him'), and various illustrative poems, including his own notable 'I am a Parcel of Vain Strivings'. Beginning from the Saturday and departure from river-source, each separate day is annotated in full, until the brothers re-arrive at the stiller waters of the port of Concord, home-coming as a time for retrospection and reflection. A line of comparable 'philosophic' nature writing might include John Aubrey's *Natural History,* or Gilbert White's *Natural History and Antiquities of Selborne,* or, closer to Thoreau's own time, Wordsworth's Lake poems.

As he used the emblematic span of the Genesis week for his first book, so in his masterpiece, *Walden*, Thoreau refashions the actual time he spent at Walden Pond into a cyclic representative year, another chronicle of 'awakening' which occurs to the rhythm of the seasons, summer, autumn, winter and the rebirth of spring. The heart of his endeavour is given in Chapter 2, 'Where I Lived, and What I Lived For':

> I went to the woods because I wished to live deliberately, to front only the essential facts of life, and see if I could not learn what it had to teach, and not, when I came to die, discover that I had not lived.

> I did not wish to live what was not life, living is so dear; nor did I wish to practise resignation, unless it was quite necessary I wanted to live deep and suck out all the marrow of life ... to drive life into a corner, and reduce it to its lowest terms.

By this Thoreau intended no hermit-like avoidance of the world, but an exemplary act of self-realization, the individual life seeking to fulfil its best, most encompassing, possibilities. The attacks on the 'cost' of insignificant work, on mere money profit, and on the unneeded intrusions of state and society, Thoreau makes as the authentic anarch, a preserver and defender of self-acquired values. As the pond and its associated natural life turn, so Thoreau documents the turns of his own evolving consciousness, the self as a separate but complementary world. Most aspects of the pond – its changing seasonal colours, patterns and temperature, even its herbiage and fish – suggest to him analogies with basic human growth and change. And just as he develops, even more surely than in *A Week,* a magnificent account of nature, he insists on the need to be 'expert in home-cosmography', the scholar of the inner individual human landscape. The culminating point of his 'experiment', having taken his plumb-line to measure the pond and by clear implication his own being, lies in the arrival of the spring: 'As every season seems best to us in turn, so the coming in of the Spring is

like the Creation of Cosmos out of Chaos and the realization of the Golden Age.' As nature awakens in springtime, so each self, to Thoreau's perception, can awaken from past dormancy. Throughout *Walden,* and *A Week,* and in prose always subtly dual in angle, Thoreau adapts his observations of nature – and of 'economy' and 'profit' – to ends which are both moral and deeply existential. Typically, he writes at the conclusion of *Walden*: 'Let every one mind his own business, and endeavour to be what he was made.'

Thoreau's insistence upon the imperatives of unfettered selfhood equally marks out his essays. In 'Civil Disobedience', to which **Gandhi**, the pioneers of the British labour movement and a line of political 'resisters' have paid handsome acknowledgement, the ostensible object of attack is American slavery – but slavery not only as an actual historic and unconscionable indignity, but as the wider expression of how government always 'enslaves' its citizenry. Thoreau's spirited polemic seems to indict all statist systems, almost all imposed curbs on the claims of human liberty. Counter-arguments can, of course, be made. But the passion and controlling clarity of Thoreau's style make for one of the great, memorable formulations of dissent. Equally, Thoreau's espousal of John Brown in his famous 'Plea' is the argument of a philosophical radical to whom emancipation can, as at Harper's Ferry, justify murder. The other essays, and Thoreau's posthumous 'travel' pieces – *Excursions* (1863), *The Maine Woods* (1864), *Cape Cod* (1865) and *A Yankee in Canada* (1866) – have not had the currency of the earlier work, but they again underline his acute observational power and his principled insistence on individualism, the need for distinct, separate spheres of human consciousness.

Thoreau's 'eccentricity' is far less the expression of a man simply out of joint with his age, or with the American state and his inherited culture, but rather of a pragmatic, wholly undeferential, seeker after his own 'earned' truths. For him life was nothing if not lived in the particular, weighed and measured by individual inspection. The danger was always of solipsism, the self as all. But Thoreau's informed, radical respect for nature, and for the order of things as seen in his beloved New England forests and landscape, kept him mostly free of that impasse. Like Emerson he sought a 'transcendental' dimension, but only if gained through careful, meticulous personal experience. Here, as in almost every aspect of his life, he was the truest of Yankees, listening always, and never without irony, to his own drummer, the call of his own mind and conscience.

Further reading

See: Ellery Channing, *Thoreau: The Poet Naturalist* (1902); F.O. Mathiessen, *American Renaissance: Art and Expression in the Age of Emerson and Whitman* (1941); Joseph Wood Krutch, *Henry David Thoreau* (1948); *Thoreau: A Century of Criticism*, ed. Walter Harding (1954); R.W.B. Lewis, *The American Adam: Innocence, Tradition and Tragedy in the Nineteenth Century* (1955); J. Lyndon Shanley, *The Making of Walden, with the Text of the First Edition* (1957); Sherman Paul, *The Shores of America: Thoreau's Inward Exploration* (1958); *Thoreau: A Collection of Critical Essays*, ed. Sherman Paul (1962); *Twentieth Century Interpretations of Walden: A Collection of Critical Essays*, ed. Richard Ruland (1968); *The Recognition of Henry David Thoreau: Selected Criticism since 1848*, ed. Wendel Glick (1969); Raymond R. Borst, *Henry David Thoreau: A Descriptive Bibliography* (1982); Henry S. Salt, *The Life of Henry Thoreau* (1993); Edmund A. Schofield and Robert C. Baron, *Thoreau's World and Ours* (1993); Harmon D. Smith, *My Friend, My Friend: The Story of Thoreau's Relationship with Emerson* (1999); M. Sperber, *Henry David Thoreau: Cycles and Psyche* (2004).

A. ROBERT LEE

TILLICH, Paul

1886–1965

German/US Lutheran theologian

Tillich, a contemporary of **Karl Barth** and **Rudolf Bultmann**, was educated in the universities of Berlin (as were Barth and Bultmann), Tübingen and Halle. Ordained to the Lutheran ministry, he served as an army chaplain in the First World War. His initial university teaching was done at Marburg, Dresden (the Technische Hochschule) and Leipzig, and in 1929 he was appointed Professor of Philosophy at Frankfurt. Tillich had been from his early days a committed and practising Religious Socialist, and in response to his criticisms of the Nazi regime he was dismissed from his chair and forced to leave Germany. Through the good offices of **Reinhold Niebuhr**, he was invited to join the faculty of Union Theological Seminary in New York City, where he eventually became Professor of Philosophical Theology, a post which he held until 1955, when he was made a University Professor at Harvard. Shortly before his death he moved from Harvard to the Divinity School at the University of Chicago.

Tillich's thought (an amalgam of philosophical ontology, existentialism, depth-psychology and Christian theology) is both difficult and immensely complicated, and almost impossible to summarize succinctly in a short space, but it is arguable that his main life's work is his three-volumed *Systematic Theology* (1951–63) and that the fundamental principle of this is his 'method of correlation', whose influence overflowed into many of his other writings. There are, in his view, two 'poles' of Christian theology – the 'situational' and the 'revelatory' poles. Other styles of theology which obscure the former of these, like Barth's, are harshly criticized on the grounds that their emphasis on the latter is grotesquely distorting. Central to Tillich's thinking is the notion that the basic structure of theology is that of 'question and answer'; man, just because he is essentially the creature of God, continually asks existential questions; systematic theology scrutinizes such questions and gives them technical form; these questions receive the answers formulated by theology from the divine self-manifestation under the guidance of the questions which lie at the heart of human existence itself. No man, in Tillich's view, can receive answers to questions which he has never asked! In his investigation of the 'existential' questions Tillich does not, of course, ignore existentialist philosophy; but he insists that their sources are to be found in human 'culture' in a wide sense – in poetry, drama, novels, films, the plastic arts, therapeutic psychology and sociology. The influence of modern psychoanalysis comes out in *Systematic Theology* II in his study of the process of salvation: included in his analysis of human 'fallenness' (an existential category) are estrangement, suffering, loneliness, doubt, despair, the tendency to suicide, and meaninglessness. Correspondingly, the salvific work of 'Jesus as the Christ' is formulated so that these elements are abolished and replaced by the essential elements of 'the new man'. In his work Tillich is at pains to overcome criticisms that he is a subjectivist or a mere psychologizer or that he is vulnerable to the charges of subjectivism traditionally levelled at existentialism. Hence, he refused to be labelled as an 'existentialist' and preferred the descriptive title 'ontologist'. The background to his investigations, he insisted, is the notion of 'Being'; God is for him 'Being-Itself'; sinful man is estranged from his genuine 'being'; Jesus as the Christ brings 'New Being' to the world.

In *The Protestant Era* (trans. 1948) Tillich gave expression to his scepticism about the viability of that era which was begun by the sixteenth-century Reformation. But he is convinced that the fundamental principle of that Reformation should not and will not die, because of its fundamental importance for all Christian churches – the principle of prophetic protest against every power which claims divine character for itself. The prophetic protest, he insists, is necessary for every church and for every secular movement if it is to avoid disintegration – it has to be expressed in every situation as a contradiction to man's perennial attempts to give absolute validity to his own thinking and acting. This kind of thinking was influential not merely within the American churches, but inspired many of the religiously based protests against American social and foreign policy characteristic of the late 1960s, protests rooted in

that pragmatism and activism which have always been characteristic of American religion as a whole.

Tillich's theological system and writings have inevitably evoked much disagreement. More orthodox theologians protested that his theology was grotesquely biased towards the twentieth-century 'situational' pole to the detriment of the 'revelatory' one in Scripture and tradition; others complained that his translation of traditional religious symbols into the abstract terminology of idealism, psychoanalysis and existentialism evacuated the latter of their essential meaning. Be that as it may, his thinking and writing did have a widespread effect upon the post-war American intelligentsia.

Further reading

Other works include: *Love, Power and Justice* (1954); *Morality and Beyond* (1963). See: Wilhelm and Marion Pauch, *Paul Tillich: His Life and Thought* (1977); Alastair M. McLeod, *Tillich* (1973); J. Heywood Thomas, *Tillich: An Appraisal* (1963); Kenneth Hamilton, *The System and the Gospel: A Critique of Paul Tillich* (1963).

JAMES RICHMOND

TINBERGEN, Nikolaas

1907–88

Dutch ethologist

Niko Tinbergen was born in The Hague into an exceptionally talented family: his elder brother Jan later won the Nobel Prize for Economics and his younger brother Lukas did important biological work before dying young. As well as his biological skills, Niko Tinbergen was a hockey player of international standard. He studied biology at Leiden University and later returned there after a visit to Greenland. During the 1930s he studied many problems in animal behaviour (ethology) with a multiplicity of students and collaborators. In the war he was among many academics imprisoned by the Nazis for denouncing their treatment of the Jews; after his release he briefly joined the Dutch 'underground'. Soon after the war Tinbergen moved to Oxford University, where he remained. In 1973 he shared the Nobel Prize with **Konrad Lorenz** and Karl von Frisch, making the Tinbergens the only pair of brothers to have received this prize.

Tinbergen was an enthusiastic observer and photographer of natural history from an early age and in 1930 collaborated on a book of such observations and photographs of birds, *Het Vogeleiland* ('The Bird Island', 1930). However, it is for the ingenious design of experiments that Tinbergen is particularly famous. During the 1930s he studied many problems of how animals, mainly insects, find out about their environment (for example, navigation, locating food). He met Lorenz in 1936 and used Lorenzian terminology for a while. When imprisoned, Tinbergen wrote two children's books about animals and his important *Social Behaviour in Animals* (1953), which summarizes some of his earlier work. His ethological classic *The Study of Instinct* (1951) has the same structure as modern ethology; he suggested that there are four main areas of ethological inquiry: development, physiological mechanisms, survival value and evolution of behaviour.

By moving to Oxford Tinbergen introduced ethology to the English-speaking world; and, in part stimulated by the many evolutionary biologists at Oxford, Tinbergen's own research changed increasingly to the problem of survival value. He worked particularly on sea-birds; for example, he discovered (again by simple experiments) a suite of behavioural adaptations in gulls to reduce predation on eggs and young. His work on gulls is described in *The Herring Gull's World* (1953) and in *Signals for Survival* (1969, based on one of his award-winning television films). His autobiographical *Curious Naturalists* (1958) enchantingly relates his work on gulls as well as the earlier work on insects.

Tinbergen's films and popular books did much to popularize ethology; but unlike many popularizers he did not prognosticate on the human predicament. In later years Tinbergen became more interested in humans. He studied ethologically a kind of autism ('Kanner's syndrome', concerning children who are excessively withdrawn from society) which he interpreted as resulting from a conflict between the child's apprehension and his or her frustrated desire for society. This study illuminated Tinbergen's claim that ethology can contribute methodologically as well as theoretically to the study of man.

Further reading

Other works include: *Eskimoland* (1935); *Inleiding tot de Diersociologie* ('Introduction to Animal Sociology', 1946); *Kleew* (1948); *The Tale of John Stickle* (1954); *Bird Life* (1954); *Animal Behaviour* (1965); *Tracks* (1967); and two volumes of papers, *The Animal in Its World* (1972 and 1973). See also the biography, H. Kruuk, *Niko's Nature: The Life of Niko Tinbergen and His Science of Animal Behaviour* (2004), and the more general study, R.W. Burkhardt, *Patterns of Behavior: Konrad Lorenz, Niko Tinbergen, and the Founding of Ethology* (2005).

MARK RIDLEY

TINGUELY, Jean

1925–91

Swiss sculptor

Born in Fribourg, and trained during World War II at the Kunstgewerbeschule in Basle, where he was also apprenticed as a window-dresser, Jean Tinguely went on to create a body of sculptural works that, combining movement and junk materials, and sometimes auto-destruction, was intentionally fascinating, withholding from the eye any invitation to relax, and which made a main contribution to the development of Kinetic Art.

An important early influence was the Dada artist Kurt Schwitters, whose recycling of the detritus of everyday life Tinguely greatly admired. Briefly he tried out painting, but returned to sculpture, which had interested him since childhood. Spurred on by the Romanian emigré Daniel Spoerri, Tinguely began evolving his own innovative approach, undertaking stage design for the ballet involving moving sets. In 1953 he relocated to Paris, where he constructed his first meta-mechanical devices – the sculptures with moving parts for which he is celebrated.

Tinguely's role as a kinetic artist was established by his inclusion in *Le Mouvement*, an exhibition of kinetic works at the Galerie Denise René. As the decade progressed he became increasingly interested in viewer-participation, producing a series of *Meta-matic* machines that enabled members of the public to produce their own abstract art-works automatically. At the same time he began incorporating small electric motors into his own assemblages.

The year 1960 witnessed a fresh departure, when Tinguely was invited to exhibit at the Staempfli Gallery in New York City. Prior to his arrival, the curator, Pontus Hulten, had written to an engineer, Billy Klüver, suggesting that the two men collaborate. Tinguely's response was to design an enormous self-destructing machine 'in reverence' to the freedom and innocence of modern life, which Kluver's technical expertise helped him realize. Initially Tinguely's machine-sculpture was to demolish itself in a large hall, but instead the Museum of Modern Art made available its gardens. The destruction, entitled *Homage to New York*, lasted only twenty-seven minutes, but attracted considerable press attention, not all of it sympathetic.

In the same year, through his friendship with Niki de Saint Phalle, Arman, Yves **Klein**, **Christo** and others belonging to a group of artists centred round the critic Pierre Restany, Tinguely helped found the Nouveau Réalisme movement, which had as its common denominator an emphasis on materials taken from quotidian urban life. Through the use and exploration of such materials the widely divergent works of Nouveau Réalisme artists can be seen as a response to the spread of an American-style consumer society in Europe, and also a reaction against abstractionism, having similarities with the work of **Jasper Johns** and **Robert Rauschenberg**.

Tinguely's own output fitted in comfortably with this understanding of *Nouveau*

Réalisme. He continued making progressively more elaborate, motorized constructions, and in 1961 and 1962 realized two further large-scale destruction works: *Study for the End of the World No. 1* (in Denmark) and *Study for the End of the World No. 2* (in Las Vegas). Like the earlier *Homage to New York*, these involved vast quantities of junk material and explosives, creating short-lived but spectacular effects.

Later in the 1960s Tinguely sometimes collaborated with other artists, including Saint Phalle and Rauschenberg, and remained innovative. To mark the ten-year anniversary of the founding of Nouveau Réalisme he exploded an enormous gold phallus in front of Milan Cathedral. During the same period he created fountains and walk-in sculptures, and his imagery became more figurative. Yet the essence of his work changed little in his later career: his use of motion remained chaotic and random, rather than orderly and progressive, so that overall Tinguely embodies an often comical critique of technological culture.

Further reading

See: Heidi E. Violand-Hobi, *Jean Tinguely: Life and Work* (1995) provides an excellent introduction to Tinguely's art. See also: Pontus Hulten, *Jean Tinguely: A Magic Stronger than Death* (1987); and the *catalogue raisonné* of Tinguely's sculptures and reliefs compiled by Christina Bischofberger (1990).

ANNE K. SWARTZ

TIPPETT, (Sir) Michael
1905–98
English composer

Michael Tippett received an orthodox musical education, but developed late as a composer. It was only after two periods of study at the Royal College of Music in London (1923–8, 1930–2) that he began to assemble the elements of his personal, mature style. The sinuous rhythms of Tudor polyphony, the exuberant syncopations and inflected harmonies of jazz, **Stravinsky's** avoidance of regular accentuation and traditional diatonic progressions, would all contribute to a distinctive energy and vitality. But it was the synthesis between fugue and sonata, between elaborately unified and intensely dramatic formal principles, so powerfully achieved in the music of Beethoven, which fired Tippett's imagination most decisively. His first completely characteristic and successful work, the *Concerto for Double String Orchestra* (1939), belongs to a series of symphonic compositions – four piano sonatas, five string quartets, four symphonies, a piano concerto, a concerto for string trio and orchestra and a concerto for orchestra – in which the energy of interacting contrapuntal lines often supports only occasional hints of traditional harmonic or modal thinking. And in the later works, for all their reliance on easily detectable thematic and textural recurrences, even that degree of tonal chordal practice may be dispensed with.

Tippett's early teaching and performing activities with amateurs, and his radical political sympathies, led to a permanent adherence to pacifism, for which he was briefly imprisoned in 1943. His oratorio, *A Child of Our Time* (1939–41), is his most politically explicit work, dealing with the murder of a German diplomat by a young Jew in 1938. But it was only when Tippett turned away from such documentary concerns to explore the symbols and themes of **Jungian** psychology in his first opera *The Midsummer Marriage* (1946–52) that he released a flow of inspired lyricism whose conviction and formal coherence triumphantly compensate for any obscurities or oddities in either plot or libretto. His later operas, *King Priam* (1958–61), *The Knot Garden* (1966–70), *The Ice Break* (1972–6) and *New Year* (1986–8), as well as the major choral works *The Vision of St Augustine* (1963–5) and *The Mask of Time* (1980–2), all explore human aspirations, stressing the need for individuals to comprehend the psychic as well as social forces within, around and beyond them. By writing his own texts (or choosing appropriate

extracts, in the case of *The Vision of St Augustine* and *The Mask of Time*) Tippett revealed an idiosyncratic way with words, but an instinctive sense of the formulations needed to set his elaborate melodic lines in motion. In spite of the more naturalistic aspects of his later operas, and of the texts set as part of the Symphony No. 3 (1970–2), as well as in *The Mask of Time*, it is the exploration of myth and creative energy which remains most crucial. This is shown with particular clarity in his late setting of **Yeats's** *Byzantium* for soprano and orchestra (1989–90).

Tippett succeeds in communicating so forcefully because the importunate melodic eloquence and exhilarating superimpositions of his most characteristic textures are controlled by clear formal outlines, with easily perceptible repetitions and variations. Even in the absence of traditional tonal structures, there is a clear distinction between fundamental and ornamental aspects. Tippett's highly original style is always intensely coherent.

Further reading

Tippett's music is published by Schott. For his writings, see *Tippett on Music*, ed. M. Bowen (1995), and his autobiography *Those Twentieth-Century Blues* (1991). Important critical studies are Ian Kemp, *Tippett: The Composer and His Music* (1984) and David Clarke, *The Music and Thought of Michael Tippett* (2001).

ARNOLD WHITTALL

TOCQUEVILLE, Alexis de

1805–59

French political sociologist

Tocqueville, politically liberal, temperamentally conservative, was born in Normandy of aristocratic family, but through all his writings sought to persuade his fellow aristocrats to accept the legacy of the French Revolution, to accept that a growing equality was inevitable but to study how liberty could be preserved in an egalitarian age. A contemporary described him as like 'pious

Aeneas setting forth to found Rome though still weeping for abandoned Dido, *"Mens immota manet, lacrymae volvunter inanes'"* – the mind held firm but the tears flowed down. 'Despotism,' he was to write, 'appears to me peculiarly to be dreaded in democratic times. I should have loved freedom, I believe at all times, but in the time in which we live I am ready to worship it.'

In 1831 he and a friend, Gustave de Beaumont, accepted a commission from the French government to visit the United States and to write a report on reformed prison systems. From this resulted a published report in 1832 but also Tocqueville's great two volumes, *Democracy in America* (1835 and 1840). We now know that the broad idea was in his mind before going to America, indeed was largely the reason why he went: 'I confess that in America I saw more than America. I sought there the image of democracy itself in order to learn what we have to fear or hope from its progress.' Moreover, the main themes of his equally great and long laboured work, *L'Ancien Regime et la Revolution* (1856), were also forming. The two works must be seen as part of a single grand design: to establish how the old aristocratic order came to collapse; to persuade people of the inevitability of democracy (by which he meant equality of condition); and by studying actual democracy, the United States, where these tendencies had gone furthest, to see, as it were by comparative method, the future of Europe and learn how to safeguard its liberties against the unfinished work of the French Revolution. 'The nations of our time cannot prevent,' he concluded the first book of the *Democracy*, 'the conditions of men from becoming equal, but it depends upon themselves whether the principle of equality is to lead them to servitude or freedom, to knowledge or barbarism, to prosperity or wretchedness.'

In his *Recollections* (*Souvenirs*, 1893, trans. 1896), Tocqueville was to mock both the view of the politicians that all great events occur through 'the pulling of strings' and that of the philosophers that events can be traced to 'great first causes'. He spoke of tendencies rather than 'iron laws' and said that nothing occurs other than in the context of these tendencies, but that however ripe the time, nothing occurs by itself without the free actions of particular men. Thus he steers between determinism and voluntarism. There is an inevitable historical tendency towards equality, but the form it will take depends on unpredictable human action; however, the success of such actions depends on understanding historical tendencies and sociological circumstances, although no amount of understanding can replace (rather than guide) political action. Thus Tocqueville can appear to strike an almost perfect balance between sociological and political explanation, neither giving too much nor too little to the influence of abstract ideas on historical events; but some have said that his examples are picked to suit his argument, rather than that the argument follows from the evidence. Certainly his America is an abstract model, full of brilliant hypotheses and theories relevant to all modern societies, rather than an empirical investigation of a particular country; but equally certainly the archival research that went into *L'Ancien Regime* was not merely original and impressive, but is still of great value.

From work in provincial archives, he was able to formulate theories of lasting importance: that the actual revolution only speeded up a process of centralization long under way; that the time of maximum danger to an old order is when it tries to reform itself, and that the revolution occurred at a time of economic improvement, not at a time of peculiarly great hardship. He summed up the last two propositions by saying that men suffer hopelessly under despotism; they only stir when there are grounds for hope and signs of improvement.

Basic to both his great works is a distinction between liberty and democracy. He uses democracy in the classic sense as simply the rule of the majority which in turn implies an ever-increasing equality of social condition (he treated America as if it was a kind of middle-class classless society). Democracies may or may not encourage freedom of expression and individual choice in political action. Tocqueville thought that they could lead to greater liberty than ever before, both for general reasons that he states in *Democracy in America* and because of some institutions peculiar to America; but on the other hand many things in democracy uniquely threaten freedom and individualism: 'the tyranny of the majority', the intolerance of public opinion and the worship of uniformity and mediocrity, the distrust of eccentricity and excellence. Reading Tocqueville convinced **John Stuart Mill** that the main danger to liberty in our times would come from democracy, not from (they both optimistically believed) rapidly fading autocracy. Tocqueville feared the emergence of a wholly new form of government that he called 'democratic despotism', the rule of a small executive over a vast number of equal but isolated individuals, removed from all intermediary institutions which create (as well as inequities and anomalies) structures for political action. This has often been glibly read as a prophecy of twentieth-century totalitarianism, but it is more like a Conservative's view of the modern welfare state: he speaks of a 'benign and tutelary despotism' that will do everything for the physical well-being of people, so long as they sacrifice their freedom. Louis Napoleon seemed to embody many of Tocqueville's fears: the deliberate corruption of a nation rather than naked terror.

Two things could prevent 'democratic despotism'. First, intermediary institutions between the state and the individual must be preserved, indeed pressure groups of all kinds tolerated and positively encouraged: Hobbes, Rousseau and Bentham had all denounced such groups as 'worms within the entrails', 'divisive of the General Will' and 'sinister interests' respectively; but Tocqueville argued that freedom was too great a price to pay for rationalizing away all such traditional or commercial inequities and anomalies. Second, beyond questions of social structure, the individual must act like a free citizen, even if the odds of the moment are against such actions – as Jack Lively has written: 'he posed the essentially classical idea of the free man as an active participant in communal affairs'.

Tocqueville was internationally famous in his day and elected a member of the French Academy. He was elected from his own district in Normandy to serve in the Chamber of Deputies from 1839 to the *coup d'état* of 1851. His *Recollections* covers the political events of those days, but he was a better author and theorist than politician, finding it hard to mix with the bourgeois politicians whose emergence on the historical scene he regarded as inevitable and on the whole salutary. **Daumier**, in a memorable cartoon, gave him an intelligent but aloof and cynical face, showed him carrying many papers but clearly impatient with the Assembly and eager to be off. After the *coup* he worked in retirement on *L'Ancien Regime* and the *Recollections* and travelled in England and Ireland. After his early death, his beloved but pious wife claimed him as a good Catholic while French radicals elevated him to the secularist pantheon: even his silences were read both ways. Indeed, his explicit views were generally honoured, rarely attacked but often expropriated by almost all different camps in French politics, except the socialists. Liberals saw him as anti-aristocratic and as taking the best from the French Revolution without the excesses; and Conservatives saw his doubts about democracy as repudiation of the principle itself. Both his doctrines and his methods have been more often praised than understood. The first English translation of 1835 for instance, by Henry Reeve, was a fine piece of prose, but the Tory journalist heightened all Tocqueville's fears for democracy and America and toned down his hopes. Nonetheless, his influence on subsequent sociology and political theory was immense. He can now be seen to stand as the greatest figure, as **Raymond Aron** has claimed, in a distinctively French school of political sociology which from the time of Montesquieu to a modern exponent like Aron himself has blended sociology with history in a comparative perspective with an openly moral concern both to understand and preserve free institutions.

Further reading

See: Alexis de Tocqueville, *Oeuvres Complètes* (18 vols, 1951–98): *Democracy in America: And Two Essays on America*, ed. Isaac Kramnick (2003); *Democracy in America*, a new translation by Arthur Goldhammer (2004). See also: George W. Pierson, *Tocqueville and Beaumont in America* (1938); Jack Lively, *The Social and Political Thought of Alexis de Tocqueville* (1962); Raymond Aron, *Main Current in Sociological Thought*, Vol. I (1965); Robert E. Nisbet, *The Sociological Tradition* (1967); André Jardin, *Alexis de Tocqueville* (1986, trans. Lydia Davis and Robert Hemenway as *Tocqueville: A Biography*, 1988).

SIR BERNARD CRICK

TOLKIEN, John Ronald Reuel

1892–1973

British writer and philologist

J.R.R. Tolkien was born in Bloemfontein, South Africa, but on his father's death in 1895 his family moved to Birmingham, at first to a cottage at Sarehole Mill outside the town, later into the city itself. He was educated at King Edward's School, Birmingham (with a short spell at St Philip's Grammar School), and went to Exeter College, Oxford, as a scholar in 1911, reading Honour Moderations in classics and English language and literature, in which he was awarded a first class. His academic career was interrupted by military service between 1915 and 1918; after leaving the army he rapidly established himself as a distinguished philologist and successful academic, being appointed Reader in English Language at the University of Leeds in 1920 and Professor in 1924. In 1925 he was appointed Rawlinson and Bosworth Professor of Anglo-Saxon at Oxford, where he remained for the rest of his academic life. He became a friend of C.S. Lewis and was a member of the 'Inklings' circle.

The mythical fictions for which Tolkien became famous clearly grew from the same root as his professional and personal absorption in language (a talent he showed from an early age, not only becoming proficient in Anglo-Saxon and Gothic as a schoolboy, but also inventing languages at the same age). His imaginary world derived partly from a 'made-up' language, based on Finnish, begun in 1915, which needed a history to explain it (this language eventually became 'Elvish'). He began writing the poems and stories which eventually became *The Silmarillion* as early as 1916. His first published book of fantasy was, however, a children's book, *The Hobbit* (1936). The publishers, Allen & Unwin, expressed interest in a sequel, which finally emerged as a far more serious creation: *The Lord of the Rings*, written between 1939 and 1945, and published as a trilogy in 1954 (*The Fellowship of the Ring* and *The Two Towers*) and 1955 (*The Return of the King*). This, his most important work, achieved at first a respectable *succès d'estime* but went on to become a best-seller on both sides of the Atlantic and, on the face of it surprisingly, to become a campus cult particularly among the radical 'alternative culture' of the late 1960s. It was followed by the publication of slighter pieces, notably *Tree and Leaf* (1964) – a reprint of the well-known lecture 'On Fairy-Stories', and the short story 'Leaf by Niggle', both of which illuminate Tolkien's methods and intentions in *The Lord of the Rings*. *The Silmarillion*, a collection of legends and histories narrating the story of his imaginary world 'Middle-Earth' and 'Elvenhome' from its creation down to the end of its 'first Age', was published posthumously in 1977; it became a best-seller and was quickly followed by *Unfinished Tales of Numenor and Middle-Earth* (1980), both being edited by his son Christopher Tolkien. The popularity and continuing marketability of *The Lord of the Rings* and its largely fragmentary 'prequels', together with an accompanying 'Tolkien industry' of illustrated editions, guides to 'Middle-Earth', calendars, etc., were enormously increased by Peter Jackson's award-winning trio of films *The Lord of the Rings* in 2001–3 (the film titles following those of Tolkien's own trilogy). These were shot on location in New Zealand, with brilliant computer animations to represent the supernatural elements, the big battle-scenes and the monsters, including a finely grotesque and pitiful Gollum. The principal characters were played by leading actors, including Ian McKellen as a splendid Gandalf, Elijah Wood as Frodo, Ian Holm as Bilbo (a brilliant cameo role) and Orlando Bloom as a heroic Legolas. Although Jackson's films inevitably condense and to some extent simplify Tolkien's narrative, they remain remarkably faithful to their original, their dialogue even including some exchanges in Elvish (helpfully subtitled); they succeed particularly well in their portrayal of the set-piece battle-scenes and of the relation between Frodo and Gollum the corrupted hobbit. The enduring appeal of Tolkien's fantasy world is proved by Jackson's huge box-office success (not to mention the subsequent massive sales of role-playing computer games based on the film version of Tolkien's characters).

Tolkien believed in the making of fantasies as not only a legitimate and vital but a high form of art in which, as he wrote in the lecture 'On Fairy-Stories' (1939), man resembles God in the divinely granted faculty of 'sub-creation' of secondary worlds – as opposed to the primary world created by God. Consistent with this was his habit of referring to his stories as 'discoveries', rather than inventions; and his imaginary Middle-Earth is, unsurprisingly, structured on firmly Christian lines.

Why what began as the spare-time hobby of a professor of Anglo-Saxon should have enjoyed such enduring and versatile popular success is an interesting question. In the first place, Tolkien's imagined world both feeds and stimulates a public appetite for myth, for heroism and for imaginary marvels, while presenting these with a novelist's attention to detail and privileged entry into the characters' consciousness. Tom Shippey has shown in his

book *The Road to Middle-Earth* (by far the best critical study of Tolkien's writings) not only that *The Lord of the Rings* was profoundly influenced by its author's wide and deep knowledge of Dark Age and medieval Germanic literature, but also that although Tolkien's themes and imagery may be drawn from a wide variety of Old English, Old Norse and medieval sources, his narrative conventions are the familiar ones of realist fiction. Second, on a thematic level, *The Lord of the Rings* fits into a still-strong tradition of Romantic ruralist attacks on the evils of industrialism: Tolkien's insistence on the need for reverence towards non-human forms of life held a strong and continuing appeal to ecologically minded people alert to the threat posed to the biosphere by technological progress. Third, his world has the attraction of completeness; it has its own cosmology, mythology, history, variety of species, languages, literatures, scripts, maps, genealogies and even calendar. This world has also the ambiguous appeal of simplicity: there is hierarchy but no class, love-stories but no passionate sexuality, village life among the hobbits but no labour (unless you count Sauron's dimly glimpsed slaves) – in other words, a world without most of the problems which complicate human existence, dominated by a satisfactorily simple conflict between Good (the Elves and other 'Free Peoples') and Evil (Morgoth, Sauron and Mordor). Finally, the elegiac mood of Tolkien's writing – *The Lord of the Rings* is set almost at the end of the imaginary era of Middle-Earth, and readers are constantly referred back to a vanished past still more remote and wonderful – increases the same nostalgic appetite for myth and remoteness on which it feeds.

Further reading

Other works: *Beowulf, the Monsters and the Critics* (1936); *Farmer Giles of Ham* (1949); *Adventures of Tom Bombadil* (1962); *Smith of Wootton Major* (1967); *Letters of J.R.R. Tolkien*, ed. Humphrey Carpenter (1981). See also the first of the authoritative twelve-volume *History of Middle-Earth*, ed.

Christopher Tolkien (1983–96), beginning with *The Book of Lost Tales* (1983) and ending with *The Peoples of Middle-Earth* Vol. 12 (1996); this multiple edition contains all of Tolkien's fantasy writings, including early drafts of *The Lord of the Rings* and of *The Silmarillion*. See also the biographical studies by Humphrey Carpenter, *The Inklings* (1973) *J.R.R. Tolkien* (1977); *Letters of J.R.R. Tolkien* (1982). For a hostile view, see Edmund Wilson, 'Ooh, Those Awful Orcs!' in *The Bit Between My Teeth* (1956); for a strong defence, see Tom Shippey, *The Road to Middle-Earth* (1981), revised and reissued as *J.R.R. Tolkien: Author of the Century* (2000).

JANET MONTEFIORE

TOLSTOY, (Count) Lev Nikolaevich

1828–1910

Russian writer

Born in Yasnaya Polyana, near Tula, he was the fourth son of an aristocratic family of five children who were orphaned early by the death of their mother when Tolstoy was only two years of age. Given over to the guardianship of their Aunt Tatyana and their paternal grandmother, the children formed a close-knit group with their own nursery lore of an Ant Brotherhood and the legend of a little green stick on which the secret of happiness was written. The close intuitive understanding born of such relationships and the closed, protected world of Yasnaya Polyana itself, an estate supported by 800 or so serfs, were to influence profoundly Tolstoy's view of the world by leading to his insistence on the importance of the family as the basis of the social contract and the moral superiority of the country to the city, of the rural peasantry to the urban masses. The death of his father when Tolstoy was only eight contributed to the family's desire to close ranks, but Tolstoy's own curiosity about life, brilliantly conveyed in his first semi-autobiographical work *Childhood* (*Detstvo,* 1852), was unorthodox in its directness and clarity. The conventional education by tutors offered him little, just as his years at the University of Kazan (1844–7) ended without his completing the course. His own rich inner life impelled him into making encyclopaedic plans for self-education, while his passionate masculine nature led to successive fruitless attempts at moral self-improvement, as his diaries testify. By the time he was twenty he was living the typically licentious life of a young Russian nobleman.

In 1849 he moved to St Petersburg with the intention of entering the university, but at the time of the arrests in connection with the Petrashevsky affair he appears to have returned hastily to Yasnaya Polyana. A superficially aimless lifestyle was soon interrupted when, in 1851, Tolstoy accompanied his brother Nikolay to the Caucasus and found himself involved in the Russian colonial wars against the hill tribesmen. The effect on him was of incalculable significance. It not only spurred him to write, but it also forced him to examine the nature of human motivation in war, the meaning of courage and the role of vanity in determining behaviour even at the limits of endurance. Such studies of Caucasian military life as *The Raid* (*Nabeg,* 1852) and *The Woodfelling* (*Rubka lesa,* 1855) supplied the groundwork for his masterly examination of war at its most brutal and senseless in his *Sevastopol Sketches* (*Sevastopol' v dekabre,* 1855; *Sevastopol v avguste,* 1856). Experience of the Crimean campaign in 1854–5 taught him that war was never glamorous, but that its only hero 'is he whom I love with all the strength of my spirit, whom I have striven to depict in all his beauty and who always was, is and will be beautiful – truth'. Simultaneously he was completing the remaining parts of his autobiographical trilogy, *Boyhood* (*Otrochestvo,* 1854) and *Youth* (*Yunost',* 1856).

By the end of the Crimean War he had become famous and he was lionized in the salons of St Petersburg during the winter of 1855–6, being cultivated particularly by **Turgenev**. It was with Turgenev as his companion for part of the time that he went to Europe in 1857. A public guillotining which he witnessed in Paris and the vulgar behaviour of English tourists in Lucerne (which gave rise to the first of his philosophical works, *Lucerne*, 1857) reinforced both his distaste for European standards and his sense of moral outrage. Upon his return to Russia, though he published *A Landowner's Morning* (*Utro pomeshchika*), *Three Deaths* (*Tri smerti*), *Albert* and the novella *Family Happiness* (*Semeynoye schast'ye*) during the following three years, he was gradually being drawn towards an interest in peasant education. The dilemma of conscience which faced so many members of the Russian nobility as the emancipation of the serfs approached (February 1861) took the form in Tolstoy's case of a desire to be of practical assistance to the peasants on his estate. This interest took him abroad again for the second and last time in his life between July 1860 and April 1861, when he studied educational practice in many European countries, visiting London, for example, where he attended a reading by Dickens and is supposed to have met Matthew Arnold. Back in Russia, he threw himself into the work of the peasant school which he established at Yasnaya Polyana and produced a dozen issues of an educational journal. Yet, at the age of thirty-four in 1862, he suddenly altered the pattern of his life by marrying Sonya Bers, sixteen years his junior, and settling down to raise a family.

In the following years the need for money obliged him to complete and publish *Polikushka*, his powerful study of peasant life, and his longest work to date, *The Cossacks* (*Kazaki*), which had been ten years in the writing. Probably during the summer or autumn of the same year he began writing the monumental work about the Napoleonic invasion of Russia upon which his reputation still principally rests, though it was originally known simply as *1805* or *All's Well That Ends Well*. *War and Peace* was written over a period of seven years and was completed late in 1869. The immense effort involved may have brought him close to a nervous breakdown, for it is thought that he experienced a horrific vision of death while staying in a hotel in Arzamas at this time (described in *Notes of a Madman*, *Zapiski sumasshedshego*, 1897). In the ensuing decade his thinking,

like his writing, showed a growing preoccupation with the purpose of life and ways to combat the apparent meaninglessness of death. Whether through his ABC book for schoolchildren or the writing of his great novel *Anna Karenina* (1873–7), he aimed to show the universal moral norms at work in society and the need for the educated and privileged to learn the true meaning of goodness from the peasantry.

The last pages of *Anna Karenina* point the way to the religious conversion which Tolstoy described in his *Confession* (*Ispoved'*, 1882). For the remaining three decades of his life he devoted himself chiefly to writing tracts which expounded the fundamental tenets of his religious philosophy. This philosophy, while outwardly concerned with non-resistance to evil by violence, the virtues of work, vegetarianism and abstinence from alcohol and sex, was basically a prolonged attempt by Tolstoy to reconcile through religious precept the gulf between rich and poor, especially the gulf between the intelligentsia and the peasantry, which divided Russian society. His outspoken attacks upon the church and the state undoubtedly brought him enormous moral authority, but also led to his excommunication by the Holy Synod in 1901. He also placed his immense powers as a writer at the service of his philosophy and, apart from writing a great many simple, edifying tales for the people, he turned such fine works as *The Death of Ivan Ilyich* (*Smert Ivan Il'yicha*, 1886), *The Kreutzer Sonata* (*Kreytserova sonata*, 1889) and *Resurrection* (*Voskreseniye*, 1899) into illustrative tracts. In the 1880s he also began writing for the theatre with his sombre study of peasant greed and murder, *The Power of Darkness* (*Vlast' t'my*, 1886), and his comedy about spiritualism and peasant guile, *The Fruits of Enlightenment* (*Plody prosveshcheniya*, 1889), though probably his most original work for the stage was *The Living Corpse* (*Zhivoy trup*, 1900). In his last years two works demand special mention: his treatise on art, *What is Art?* (*Chto takoye iskusstvo?*, 1897), in which a case is made for the idea that art is a kind of emotional infection, and his remarkable short novel drawn from his early experience of war in the Caucasus, *Hadji Murat* (completed 1904, published posthumously).

The contrast between his high-minded advocacy of a religious life and the fact that he remained in the relatively comfortable circumstances of Yasnaya Polyana naturally caused tension between himself and his family, especially his wife. She was concerned for the future security of his nine surviving children and less eager than her husband to renounce all earthly wealth. There was the added complication that she felt she had been replaced in his affections by the Tolstoyanists or cult followers surrounding him, with the result that their relations became clouded by suspicion, enmity and open feuding. In despair Tolstoy finally left home in November 1910 and was taken ill at the railway halt of Astapovo on the Ryazan–Ural railroad, where he died, aged eighty-two.

If Tolstoy's later renown as the founder of Tolstoyanism and an arbiter of morals for his time has faded to vanishing point since his death, his fame as a novelist has steadily increased. The reason for this is due largely to the fact that his religious and philosophical views were outdated even for the nineteenth century, deriving so clearly from an over-simplified, Enlightenment view of human capabilities and purposes, whereas his supreme gift as a writer was an outstanding clarity and freshness of viewpoint in depicting the world. His writer's vision had the straightforward, illustrative quality of photography, and he tended to represent life with all the kinetic vitality of the cinema. He deliberately avoided such artifices as plot-structure, narrated biographies of character or the domination of fiction by a single central portrayal, preferring to evoke the multiplicity of experience by offering successive and varied viewpoints through a multiplication of central figures with whom the reader can identify. Deliberately concealing his own authorial role in the fiction for the greater part, he dared to assume that fiction could represent life pictorially, always governed by

a strict chronology, and that human nature changed with the passage of time and even discovered means to self-improvement. Probably the most daring of his achievements in this respect was his depiction of history and historical characters in *War and Peace* as relating to the same dimension as his fictional creations, so that the historical Kutuzov, the Russian commander, can be seen to know the fictional Pierre Bezukhov's wife, for example, and we as readers can appraise and appreciate Kutuzov through Pierre's eyes. Fiction and history here coalesce into a Tolstoyan truth which seems manifestly more real than the historian's.

For all the apparent breadth of vision and olympian skill with which Tolstoy moves us from a St Petersburg salon to the battlefields of Austerlitz or Borodino, from Pierre Bezukhov's world to the family world of the Rostovs, there are always certain limits of viewpoint and manner circumscribing the fiction and certain moralistic limitations or norms. In *War and Peace* the historical motivation imposes its own fatalism upon the lives of historical and fictional characters alike. Just as Napoleon is shown to be no more than a puppet of dynamic processes over which he can exert no real power, so Prince Andrey Bolkonsky can be seen to be predestined to act the role of doomed hero. There is perhaps a similar element of predestination about the evolution of the delightful Natasha Rostov into the matronly figure of the first epilogue. But the greatness of the fiction lies not in such fatalism, nor in the theory of history that turns its final pages (of the second epilogue) into a rather bullying tract; it lies in the assertion of the vital and positive ideas permeating the characters' lives. The role of the family, for instance, as exemplified by the Rostovs, is one that suggests stability, shared love and an instinctive hostility to all that threatens such an ethos, meaning chiefly the French invaders. Similarly, it is a search for a positive meaning in life that inspires Andrey Bolkonsky to replace his Napoleonic ideal by a faith in the boundlessness of love and equate such love with a divine force, or makes Pierre Bezukhov seek in freemasonry and numerology an answer to life's purpose that is finally revealed to him, in a simple equation of God with life, by the peasant Platon Karatayev. The epic size of *War and Peace* is therefore assessable both in terms of its enormous range of characters, its variety of locales and its timespan, and in terms of the profundity of the religious and philosophical ideas which concern the central characters.

Anna Karenina, though less ambitious in its scope, is no less daring as a novel in its portrayal of Anna herself – one of the most remarkable female characterizations ever achieved by a male author – and in its exploration of the manifold pressures in Russian society of the 1870s. A novel about marriage, female emancipation, the contrast between urban and rural life, between reason and faith, between suicide and religious purpose, *Anna Karenina* presupposes that there are certain norms, as rigid perhaps after their fashion as the railway lines which bring Anna into the fiction at the beginning and kill her at the end (of Part VII), and these norms point the way, so Tolstoy seems to be saying, either to personal fulfilment or to futility and suicide. Though a tragic mechanism may perhaps determine Anna's decision to leave her husband and son and give herself to Vronsky, the processes are so gradual and so subtle that her vitality seems always to outpace them. The extinguishing of the vital candle of her life is an act of immolation that indicts all the pretensions, hypocrisies and falsehoods of the society to which she has fallen victim. In compensation for her tragedy, the parallel story of Konstantin Levin's marriage to Kitty and final discovery of an intuitive law of right and wrong known only to the peasantry is magnificent in its own right, but it scarcely prevails in its optimistic message against the darkness that finally engulfs Anna herself.

Tolstoy's realism is of a controlled richness in its detail, with emphasis always upon appearance and action, but at its heart is an awareness of both the physicality of experience – the sense, in short, that his characters inhabit bodies – and of the rational processes by which they may discover for themselves new truths and beliefs. However seriously he may have taken himself (and his work is not noteworthy for its humour), he was by nature the least pompous of men, and the gleam which shines from his eyes in so many of his portraits bespeaks a man who enjoyed life's peculiarities while recognizing its sinfulness and its grandeur.

Further reading

Other works include: *Twenty-Three Tales*; *What Then Must We Do?*; *On Life and Essays on Religion: Recollections and Essays*; *Tales of Army Life*; *The Kingdom of God and Peace Essays*; *The Snow Storm and Other Stories*; etc. A selection of his letters translated by R.F. Christian has recently been published in two volumes (1978). About Tolstoy: the two-volume biography by A. Maude, *The Life of Tolstoy* (1930), has been largely superseded by E.J. Simmons, *Leo Tolstoy* (1960), and H. Troyat, *Tolstoy* (1968). Recent critical works on Tolstoy (in alphabetical order) include an excellent work by J. Bayley, *Tolstoy and the Novel* (1966); the famous study of Tolstoy's theory of history by I. Berlin, *The Hedgehog and the Fox* (1953); T.G.S. Cain, *Tolstoy* (1977); R.F. Christian's 'critical introduction' to Tolstoy's work, *Tolstoy* (1969); a chapter devoted to *War and Peace* in R. Freeborn, *The Rise of the Russian Novel* (1973); E.B. Greenwood, *Tolstoy: The Comprehensive Vision* (1975); F.R. Leavis, *Anna Karenina and Other Essays* (1967); G.W. Spence's study of the dualism in Tolstoy's thought, *Tolstoy the Ascetic* (1967); E. Stenbock-Fermor's valuable, if eccentric, *The Architecture of 'Anna Karenina'* (1975); and E. Wasiolek's opinionated, but stimulating, *Tolstoy's Major Fiction* (1978). Two recent collections of critical essays on Tolstoy should also be mentioned: *Leo Tolstoy: A Critical Anthology*, ed. H. Gifford; and *New Essays on Tolstoy*, ed. M. Jones; John Bayley, *Leo Tolstoy* (1997).

RICHARD FREEBORN

TOULOUSE-LAUTREC, Henri de

1864–1901
French artist

Born near Albi in the south-west of France into one of the most aristocratic of families, Toulouse-Lautrec's full physical growth was retarded as a result of injuries to his legs. He remained permanently self-conscious with regard to his handicap until his death from alcoholism in 1901.

His artistic career started formally in Paris, first at the studio of Bonnat and then at that of Cormon where he met Émil Bernard, **Vincent Van Gogh** and Louis Anquetin, with whom he remained on friendly terms for many years, painting their portraits and corresponding when he or they left Paris.

Lautrec's work developed starting with influence from Bastien Lepage, then from the Impressionism of **Pissarro**, finally to his own personal style which took its main impetus from subtle and direct line drawing. This he at times adapted for the purposes of lithography. His subject-matter remained almost entirely that of people.

In 1884 Lautrec set up his studio in Montmartre where he spent hours in cafés and cabarets drawing the people who worked there and the patrons who gave them their living. At first he drew mostly those who came to Aristide Bruant's café cabaret, Le Mirliton, opened in 1885. Bruant wrote and sang many of the ballads performed at Le Mirliton himself. Before 1885 when he worked in a more expensive quarter of Paris his songs were light-hearted, at times amusing. Montmartre had the effect of providing more tragic themes. It was these later ballads, based on the lives of the people in the locale of Le Mirliton – prostitutes, pimps, dancers, actresses, the homeless, forlorn or drunken – that provided Lautrec with subjects. Many of his paintings of the middle and late 1880s have titles taken from Bruant's ballads. *At Montrouge, Rosa la Rouge,* a single portrait of a girl of 1888, is a case in point.

It was at this time that Lautrec also adopted something of **Degas's** style and subject-matter, painting ballet girls with a light directional brush-stroke and achieving some acclaim for the work he exhibited. The brushwork then became less even and more open in handling and line began to separate itself from and dominate the colour areas. These portraits he carried out quickly but only after knowing

and observing the person well. Generally he worked from memory and only rarely for commissions over which he was immensely conscientious, asking the sitter to pose dozens of times.

By the 1890s much of Lautrec's effort was directed towards lithography, in particular poster design. The most famous posters of this era must be those of La Goulu, can-can dancer at the Moulin Rouge.

In 1896 Lautrec painted and made lithographs entitled *Alone.* A prostitute is sympathetically portrayed resting on a bed. Other such pictures show moments of intimacy, of women combing their hair, tightening their corsets or waiting in a salon for customers.

Shortly before his death, while spending the summer as usual in Bordeaux, Lautrec became enchanted by opera as well as operettas and some of his last works are evocations of the mood of moments from *Messaline* or *La Belle Hélène.*

Lautrec's very early drawings as a child show a liking for caricature. Later in life this preference takes the form of feeling for character so that the essential elements not only of an individual's personal appearance, but also the objects that suggest his or her personal tastes and role or profession in life are included.

Often Lautrec's view is cynical, but frequently it is also compassionate as he surveys the difficulties with which the most vulnerable in Parisian society had to cope.

Many later artists, such as those of the German and Belgian Expressionist movement, owed as much to Lautrec as to Van Gogh. One can see La Goulu in Felicien Rops's skeletal women, fat clients of the brothel houses more sharply criticized by George Grosz in scenes of corruption in Berlin. The decadence of the 'Gay Nineties' then becomes the despair of the early 1920s and Lautrec's cynicism the paramount attitude.

Further reading

See: Jean Adhémar, *Henri de Toulouse-Lautrec: Complete Lithographs and Drypoints* (1965); Eduouard Julien, *The Posters of Toulouse-Lautrec* (1966); M.G. Dortu and J.A. Méric, *Toulouse-Lautrec: The Complete*

Painting (1981). See also: Henri Perruchot, *Toulouse-Lautrec: A Definitive Biography* (trans. 1969); André Fermigier, *Toulouse-Lautrec* (trans. 1969); Douglas Cooper, *Henri de Toulouse-Lautrec* (1981); Julia Frey, *Toulouse-Lautrec: A Life* (1994); David Sweetman, *Toulouse-Lautrec and the Fin-de-siècle* (1999).

PAT TURNER

TOYNBEE, Arnold Joseph

1889–1975

British historian

Toynbee's family background and marriage (in 1913) to Rosalind Murray, daughter of the classicist Gilbert Murray, seemed to presage an academic career, but in the First World War Toynbee was employed in the Political Intelligence Department of the Foreign Office. He observed the Versailles peace conference at close quarters, and out of his experiences as correspondent on the war between Greece and Turkey came *The Western Question in Greece and Turkey* (1922). Its success led to a professorship in history at the University of London held conjointly with the post of Director of Studies at the British Institute of International Affairs.

Work on the yearly volumes of the influential *Survey of International Affairs* and his magnum opus *A Study of History* proceeded simultaneously; the destructive national passions of the 1930s analysed in the *Survey* were transcended in Toynbee's world history by the rise and fall of civilizations.

The first six volumes of *A Study of History* published in the 1930s compared twenty-one civilizations, seven of them extant, and all subject to a rhythm of growth and decay. Toynbee thought that civilizations developed as responses to challenges imposed by their environments, although the nature of these responses was not predetermined. Subsequent growth depended on the creative efforts of an elite whose culture was imitated by the rest of society. But when the creativity of the elite waned, and the majority withdrew their assent to the values of the minority, a loss of social unity and sense of direction followed.

This waning of creative power and failure of response Toynbee detected already in Western civilization of the twentieth century, and manifested in such strategies of withdrawal as 'archaism' and 'futurism'. The most likely end to this process of disintegration, as in previous cases, was the formation of a universal state by a dominant coercive minority. But the intermingling of peoples and religions might yet provide the preconditions for the emergence of a new universal religion, on which Toynbee pinned his hopes of ending the secular rhythm of rise and fall.

After a further spell of service in the Foreign Office as Director of the Research Department in the Second World War, Toynbee resumed his work on *A Study of History* and published four more volumes in 1954. These volumes served as appendices to the first six rather than breaking new ground; but it became clear that the chief purpose of history is the distillation of the higher religions. A one-volume abridgment in 1947 gave Toynbee the status almost of a prophet in America, yet Toynbee's aims and methods came increasingly under fire. Apart from factual errors serious criticism has focused on Toynbee's inclination to make history a stalking-horse for religious ideas, and on his penchant for scientific laws. In these ways, as in others, Toynbee's work has more in common with that of the great Victorian polymaths than with that of modern specialist historians, but it served to articulate twentieth-century doubts and hopes for Western civilization.

Further reading

Toynbee's prodigious output included: *Greek Civilization and Character: The Self-revelation of Ancient Greek Society* (1924); *The World and the West* (1953); *An Historian's Approach to Religion* (1956); *East to West: A Journey Round the World* (1958); *Acquaintances* (1967). See: M.F. Ashley-Montagu (ed.) *Toynbee and History* (1956); Pieter Geyl, *Debates with Historians* (1958); Roland N. Stromberg, *Arnold J. Toynbee* (1972); William H. McNeill, *Arnold J. Toynbee: A Life* (1989).

PETER JONES

TROLLOPE, Anthony

1815–82

English novelist

All authors may take courage from the extraordinary fortunes of Anthony Trollope, who enjoyed arguably even greater respect a century after his death than ever he did at the height of his Victorian success. His eminence is the more remarkable as resulting from a critical recovery after nearly half a century of contemptuous neglect, exacerbated at the outset by the publication, a year after his death, of his extremely blunt and straightforward *Autobiography* (1883), a plain statement of his aims and achievements as a man of letters and a professional employee of the Civil Service. Such frankness on the part of an artist was intolerable to an age which cherished artifice and performance: indeed, it was scarcely admissible that Trollope was an artist at all. His novels became swiftly relegated to the ranks of those relished rather guiltily by readers in search of a comfortable nostalgia. A work like *Framley Parsonage* (1861), fourth in the famous 'Barchester' series, was enjoyed almost solely for its superb characterization and neatly arranged plot, while its profounder and more abstract issues, dramatized to such ironic effect in the marital manoeuvres of Lucy Robarts, Griselda Grantly and Miss Dunstable, were totally ignored.

Writing was an inalienable part of the Trollope family heritage. Anthony's elder brother Tom produced a long and turgid set of works on Italian subjects and their father, a hopelessly unsuccessful barrister, made several attempts as a historian. The miserable childhood of the Trollope children, reared in an atmosphere of shabby gentility and feckless Micawberish optimism, was somewhat lightened by their indomitable mother, Frances, who gained considerable fame as a novelist dealing with social questions of the day and produced, after an unsuccessful attempt to carry culture to Cincinnati, the amusing and highly readable *Domestic Manners of the Americans* (1832).

Trollope was educated at Harrow and Winchester, and was eventually pushed into a Post Office clerkship at the age of nineteen. His careful cultivation of a bluff, even boorish exterior manner seems to have been designed to mask the acute sensitivity developed in him during his unhappy adolescence, and we can find traces of such characteristics in the awkward, gangling protagonists of certain of the novels. He appears to have put much of himself, for example, into Johnny Eames of *The Small House at Allington* (1864), and into Josiah Crawley, the gloomy curate hero of *The Last Chronicle of Barset* (1867).

The turn of his fortunes occurred in 1841 when he was transferred to Ireland to supervise postal operations in the central district. Here he was able to show a truly Victorian capacity for hard work and initiative, by which he soon won the respect of his superiors and sufficient funds to enable him to marry Rose Heseltine, the daughter of a Rotherham bank manager. He is almost exceptional among nineteenth-century novelists in having made a happy and successful marriage.

Ireland, its people and its problems offered him the material for his first and last novels, *The Macdermots of Ballycloran* (1847) and *The Landleaguers*, left unfinished at his death, and provided subject-matter elsewhere in his work. He returned to England to maintain the two careers in tandem throughout the 1850s and 1860s, fuelling each with the prodigious physical and mental energy which allowed him to indulge his other consuming enthusiasm, hunting. Thus his fiction is permeated throughout with an exactness of topographical detail acquired from journeyings across England on Post Office business, and several of his finest stretches of writing, notably in *Phineas Redux* (1874), *The Eustace Diamonds* (1873) and *The American Senator* (1877), are concerned with scenes in the hunting field.

His private and professional life was never marked by any especially dramatic events. As a thoroughly dependable official, despite a certain tendency to quarrelsomeness wherever

he felt he was being overborne by bureaucracy, he was sent to Egypt, the Caribbean
and the Pacific on postal assignments, and
wrote an interesting account of post-Civil
War America after visits to the principal
eastern cities. It was on his last voyage to
New York that he was seen by **Henry
James**, whose account of the man and his
work in *Partial Portraits* is one of the best of
contemporary treatments. Trollope had a
wide and loyal circle of friends, including
George Eliot, **Browning** and the popular
journalist George Augustus Sala, and died in
the guise of a respected, if distinctly conservative, mainstay of the circulating library
three-decker novel readership.

Few writers have been more honest in
their assessments of personal achievement and
few have done themselves a greater disservice
by being so. Only during the last thirty years
has the literary public recovered sufficiently
from being told by Trollope himself that he
made £68,939 17s 5d from his novels and
that it is not necessary to wait for inspiration
before writing, and distanced itself enough
from the Victorian era for us to have begun a
wholesale and much-needed reappraisal of his
work. Such a revaluation has brought him
the attention of committed scholarship and
placed him very high indeed among the
English novelists of his age. Instead of viewing him as a mildly entertaining chronicler of
clerical indiscretions in an English country
town, we have been taught to see him as the
quietly complex and admirably tolerant analyst of the strains imposed upon quintessentially normal people and societies by the
conventions they accept. He is never, in any
of his books, hysterical, dogmatic or pompous, and it is by virtue of what Henry James
called his 'complete apprehension of the
usual' that he so frequently triumphs.

His transcendent humanity prompts him to
invoke our compassion for even the most
transparently duplicit of his characters: the
ironic solution which drives us to sympathize
with Ferdinand Lopez in *The Prime Minister*
(1876), with the impossible Lizzie Eustace in
The Eustace Diamonds, with the unregenerate

fin-de-ligne Sowerby of *Framley Parsonage*, or
with gold-digging Arabella Trefoil as she
prepares to marry Mounser Green in *The
American Senator*, is always wholly acceptable.
By the same method, other characters are
made antipathetic by their unscrupulous cultivation of social orthodoxy: few are more
chilling than the glacially correct and heartless
Griselda Grantly of the Barchester novels or
the monomaniacal Mr Kennedy in *Phineas
Redux,* an offshoot of that profounder study
of marital obsession, Louis Trevelyan in *He
Knew He Was Right* (1869).

Pessimism, neurosis and the nightmare of
social disgrace are always splendidly handled
by the mature Trollope. His most perceptive
treatment of these themes appears in *The Last
Chronicle of Barset* and *The Way We Live Now*
(1875). The first of these is, despite formal
imperfections owing to an otiose sub-plot, an
acknowledged masterpiece, in which the
comic creations of the earlier Barchester
novels are fleshed out with an impressively
tragic dignity. The Lear-like figure of Josiah
Crawley, learning survival through rejection
and adversity, is cleverly opposed by the
almost demonically self-destructive Mrs
Proudie, the circumstances leading to whose
death give the event a convincing pathos
rarely equalled elsewhere in Victorian fiction.
The second, the most ambitious work Trollope ever attempted, a mercilessly satirical
indictment of debased values in the society of
the 1870s, creates a comparable balance to
the earlier book in counter-pointing the
buccaneering financier Melmotte with the
pillar of antique squirearchical virtue Roger
Carbury.

Trollope does not wholly underwrite Carbury's standpoint and, as if in acknowledgment that his exalted moral standards are
too lofty for most of us, makes the heroine
Hetta reject him in favour of the far more
doubtful but ultimately more full-blooded
Paul Montague. There is no doubt, however,
that Roger Carbury speaks for much of what
Trollope admired, and a succession of the
novels creates for us a consistent view of
the English gentleman culminating in the

fascinating figure of Plantagenet Palliser, whose appearances with his wife Glencora serve to link together a series of six books beginning with *Can You Forgive Her?* (1864) and concluding with *The Duke's Children* (1880) some sixteen years later.

Just as the Barchester series dealt in detail with the manners and trials of rural clergy and landowners, so the Palliser novels, with an equally sharp scrutiny, approach the world of politics and government. Though there is no evidence to suggest that Trollope planned either set through from start to finish, it is noteworthy that each is governed by the aura of a moral human presence – in the first case, that of Septimus Harding, hero of *The Warden* (1855), whose death in *The Last Chronicle of Barset* seems to ordain the sense of finality in the book rather than be ordained by it; in the second, those of Plantagenet and Glencora. The latter, by a master-stroke, is made to die before *The Duke's Children* opens, and the power of her often anarchic influence is felt through the behaviour of her children.

As a stylist Trollope is among the plainest of Victorian writers. His handling of dialogue has been admired to the point of declaring it the best among nineteenth-century novelists and his comprehensive and refreshingly unsentimental treatment of female characters contrasts favourably with most of the other male fiction writers of the age. In his early work the influence of Thackeray can be felt too heavily, especially in the tiresome invocations to the reader in novels such as *Barchester Towers* (1857) and *The Three Clerks* (1858), and several of his later novels, such as *Kept in the Dark* (1882) and *The Fixed Period* (1882), show how fallacious was his reliance on a daily quota of written words. He is nearly always, however, a master of plotting, a talent displayed at its best in *The Eustace Diamonds* (though the structure has also been criticized for relying too heavily on sensationalism), the exuberantly comic *Ayala's Angel* (1881) and the nowadays critically lauded *Mr Scarborough's Family* (1883).

Unlike **Dickens**, **Hardy** and **George Eliot**, Trollope seldom attempts to write within a consciously historical perspective, though, like each of them, he attempted a historical romance and, as in each case, it is not considered the equal of his other books. Whereas works such as *Great Expectations*, *Middlemarch* and *The Mayor of Casterbridge* rely for their effect on our awareness of the tensions between a recently vanished world and our vivid memories of its existence, novels such as *Orley Farm* (1862), *Phineas Finn* (1869) and *John Caldigate* (1879) rely on our sense of them as taking place within the ordinary world of the mid-Victorian reader. It was Trollope's achievement to have dissected that world within its own frame of reference, in a manner often severe but invariably humane. Recognition of this achievement has been belated but wholly sincere. Yet perhaps the best tribute ever paid to him by another writer was in the form of a note written by **Tolstoy** during the composition of *Anna Karenina,* with its many Trollopian features: 'Trollope kills me, kills me with his excellence!'

Further reading

See: N.J. Hall (ed.) *The Letters of Anthony Trollope* (2 vols, 1983). See also: Michael Sadleir, *Trollope: A Commentary* (1928, rev. 1945); A.O.J. Cockshut, *Anthony Trollope: A Critical Study* (1955); P.D. Edwards, *Anthony Trollope* (1968); *Trollope: The Critical Heritage*, ed. Donald Smalley (1969); R.H. Super, *Trollope and the Post Office* (1981); V. Glendinning, *Trollope* (1992).

JONATHAN KEATES

TROTSKY, Leon
1879–1940
Russian revolutionary

Born Lev Davidovich Bronstein into a moderately prosperous Jewish farming family in the southern Ukraine, Trotsky early became active in the Russian workers' movement and embraced **Marxism**. He was arrested in 1898 for political activity in the town of Nikolayev, imprisoned, and deported to Siberia. Escaping in 1902, he travelled to

London where he met **Lenin** for the first time and he began, with Lenin's encouragement, to write for the journal *Iskra* and to argue for its political standpoint – the building of a centralized Russian workers' party – in lectures and debates within Russian émigré circles in Europe. From the first he displayed a powerful literary and oratorical talent.

Present in 1903 at the Second Congress of the Russian Social-Democratic Party, at which the historic schism between Bolsheviks and Mensheviks occurred, Trotsky sided with the Mensheviks against Lenin. Though he would soon distance himself from them to stand outside both factions for more than a decade, on this issue he felt, and wrote, that Lenin's theory of organization was undemocratic, aiming to substitute the efforts of a revolutionary elite for the initiative of the workers themselves.

Trotsky returned to Russia in 1905 to play a prominent part in the revolution of that year as a leader of the St Petersburg Soviet of Workers' Deputies. The lessons he drew from this experience included reflections on the nature of workers' democracy and the theory, identified with his name, of permanent revolution: he formulated this now in the argument that the Russian proletariat, contrary to any orthodox Marxist expectation held by Bolsheviks and Mensheviks alike, might embark upon socialist revolution before the workers of the more advanced capitalist countries.

For his part in the work of the Soviet, Trotsky was again imprisoned and condemned to exile in Siberia. In 1907, making another escape while under escort into exile, he returned to Europe to settle in Vienna until the First World War. During that conflict, which he spent in Paris and, briefly, New York, his was a leading voice in the revolutionary opposition to the war by the internationalist wing of European socialism.

After the February revolution in 1917, Trotsky again returned to Russia and at once made common cause with Lenin, eventually joining the Bolshevik Party. This had now, following a change of political position by

Lenin, adopted a perspective essentially identical with Trotsky's own conception of permanent revolution. Trotsky became one of the Russian revolution's main leaders: brilliant orator, publicist, organizer, political strategist, President of the Petrograd Soviet. He prepared and led the October insurrection which delivered power into the Bolsheviks' hands. As Commissar of Foreign Affairs in the first Soviet government, he conducted the peace negotiations with Germany at Brest-Litovsk; as Commissar of War, supervised the construction of the Red Army through civil war and hostile foreign intervention; played a key role in the foundation and early congresses of the Communist International. Throughout these post-revolutionary years, he spoke and wrote on all important political issues, domestic and international, as also on literary, cultural and scientific topics.

From 1923 onwards, and especially after Lenin's death, Trotsky bent his efforts towards opposing the increasingly bureaucratic and authoritarian regime in the Communist Party, the rising power of **Stalin**, the latter's internal and foreign policies and the doctrine of 'socialism in one country' which he had begun to put forth. In this connection, Trotsky now developed and generalized the theory of permanent revolution. Defeated by Stalin, he was expelled from the Party in 1927, sent into remote exile near the Chinese border, and in 1929 deported from Russia altogether. During the next decade he would inhabit one brief and insecure refuge after another, in Turkey, then France, then Norway, finally Mexico. Isolated, beset by difficulties, bereft by family tragedies, he continued to write prodigiously: history, autobiography, diagnosis and warning concerning the danger of Nazism, analysis of the nature of Soviet society, defence of the authentic Leninist heritage, as he construed this, against its Stalinist despoliation, argument for the formation of a new revolutionary International. At work on a biography of Stalin, he was murdered in his home by one of Stalin's agents.

As political thinker and writer, Trotsky's importance is threefold. His work is one of the best examples of the creative application of Marxism in the area of political and historical analysis; between the time of Lenin's death and his own, Trotsky was in this respect without peer. His best writing, a clear, compelling and imaginative prose combining objectivity with the deepest commitment, achieved a standard of literary excellence first set by Marx himself and matched since by Marx's followers too rarely. Finally, he came to stand – against the currents dominant in the European workers' movement, gradualist and reformist on the one hand, Stalinist, authoritarian, on the other – for a socialism in which proletarian revolution and workers' democracy must sit side by side.

Trotsky's early analysis of the configuration of Russian society, and his prognosis about the character of the revolution that would emerge from it, provide one of the most striking instances of a Marxist theoretical projection confirmed in its broad outline by the immediately ensuing course of events. From 1905 onwards, he challenged the prevalent Russian Marxist belief that, in a backward country with a huge peasant majority, revolution could only mean bourgeois revolution, with its issue the extension of capitalist economy and the establishment of bourgeois–democratic political rule. In *Results and Prospects* (1906) and then *1905* (1910), Trotsky argued that, owing to the specific features of Russia's history in which capitalist development was fostered by the state and based largely on foreign capital, the indigenous forces of the Russian bourgeoisie were too weak, and Russian liberalism insufficiently bold, to lead a revolutionary assault against Tsarism. The Russian working class was small but highly concentrated. Like the compact, relatively advanced capitalist sector which had produced it, it was an expression of what Trotsky was later to call the 'law of combined and uneven development': as capitalism from its heartlands projected its consequences over the globe, heedless of traditional and national boundaries, so the features of modes of production that were, in the classical Marxist schema, distinct, would be found fused together within one social reality; so Russia now combined a modern industrial proletariat with pre-capitalist agrarian and political structures. A successful revolution here, Trotsky asserted, would have to be led by this small, militant proletariat, carrying behind it the land-hungry peasants, and because of this it could not remain a bourgeois revolution. The Russian workers once in power would not be able or willing to leave capitalist property relations intact. Establishing the first dictatorship of the proletariat, they would initiate the transition to socialism. But they could not complete this on their own without linking up with successful socialist revolutions in the West. Confined to a backward country, the enterprise would be doomed to defeat.

The main tenets of this conception were part also of the outlook of Bolshevism by the time it led the Russian proletariat to power in 1917. Later, when revolutions to the west had failed, leaving the young Soviet state isolated, Stalin asserted first the possibility, then the reality, of a socialism constructed in Russia alone. In *The Permanent Revolution* (1930) and other writings, Trotsky reaffirmed and developed his original conception. He insisted that the fate of Russian socialism still depended on the outcome of the revolutionary process elsewhere. He extended to the analysis of this process in other backward societies the framework first applied in his treatment of Russia; arguing, in anticipation of much subsequent discussion of 'underdevelopment', that such societies could not reproduce the path followed by the first capitalist nations.

The geographical reach of Trotsky's writings on these and related themes was long, covering Britain and China, Germany, France and Spain, the Soviet Union itself. So extensive an output could not be wholly even in strength. Two of its notable achievements, however, were his analyses of fascism and of the character of the Soviet state, historically novel phenomena still to be assimilated within Marxist understanding. With growing urgency Trotsky warned against the Comintern's complacency towards the Nazi threat in Germany. Nazism triumphant, he predicted, would install not just one reactionary variant of capitalist rule among others, but a qualitatively distinct form catastrophic for the working class, predicated on the destruction of its organizations and its means of political self-defence through the mass mobilization against it of petty-bourgeois strata. The Soviet Union, he proposed in *The Revolution Betrayed* (1936), was neither socialist, as Stalin and his apologists claimed, nor some new type of class, or even capitalist, society, as some critics averred. It was a transitional formation in which the chief economic conquest of the October revolution, socialized property relations, was still extant despite the fact that a privileged bureaucracy had fashioned for itself a monopoly of political functions. To advance to socialism the workers would have to overturn this bureaucratic group by a political revolution. On both these issues Trotsky's contribution was original, level-headed and penetrating.

Trotsky was one of the great writers of his time. Keenly interested in literary and cultural subjects to which he devoted a significant part of his output and, in particular, the theoretical study *Literature and Revolution* (1923), his own literary achievement was considerable. It was built upon a lucid and incisive style and the ability to present ideas, persons, events in a complex and vivid way. It encompassed pages of cogent political argument, historical and literary interpretation finely integrating abstract theory with concrete perception, sketches of contemporaries acutely observed; an impressive account of the year *1905*, an autobiographical work, *My Life* (1930), unusual in the Marxist canon and remarkable by any standards, and an outstanding work of Marxist historiography, *The History of the Russian Revolution* (1931). This was his masterpiece, an epic, in which individuals and masses moved against the vast backdrop of Russia's history to transform the destiny of the whole world.

On questions of socialist democracy and organization, Trotsky's record over forty years was neither uniform nor unblemished. He opposed at first the Leninist party concept, representing it in *Our Political Tasks* (1904) as an attempt to hold the working class in tutelage. After 1917 he rejected out of hand all such interpretations of it, upheld it consistently against the charge of having begot the crimes of Stalin. His strictures of Lenin he came to see as unjust and mistaken. *Our Political Tasks* spoke in the name of a democratic socialism open to the struggle between different tendencies; *1905* depicted the soviet form, the workers' council, as the very embodiment of this democratic principle, born of direct proletarian action and expressing as directly as possible the diverse voices within the working class. Though he would share in the necessities, the expediencies and the errors of the Bolsheviks in power, Trotsky was later to return to and develop these themes in his struggle against Stalinism, arguing for the right of tendencies inside revolutionary organizations and, beyond, for a united front within which different currents in the workers' movement could openly compete. Taken all in all, across the inconsistencies, Trotsky's final record was clear: for a socialism both revolutionary and democratic in an atmosphere uncongenial to this synthesis, thus in lonely, but for this very reason vital, continuity with the best traditions of Marxism and of Leninism.

Further reading

Other works include: *The Permanent Revolution and Results and Prospects* (1962); *1905* (1972); *The Revolution Betrayed* (1965); *The Struggle Against Fascism in Germany* (1971); *Literature and Revolution* (1960); *My Life* (1960); *The History of the Russian Revolution* (1965); *Our Political Tasks* (1980). On Trotsky: Isaac Deutscher, *The Prophet Armed, The Prophet Unarmed* and *The Prophet Outcast* (1954, 1959 and 1963); Louis Sinclair, *Leon Trotsky: A Bibliography* (1972); Baruch Knei-Paz, *The Social and Political Thought of Leon Trotsky* (1978); Irving Howe, *Trotsky* (1978); Ernest Mandel, *Trotsky: A*

Study in the Dynamic of His Thought (1979); Alex Callinicos, *Trotskyism* (1990); Antonovich Volkogorov, *Trotsky: The Eternal Revolutionary* (1996).

NORMAN GERAS

TRUFFAUT, François

1932–84

French film director

> I believe in communication and understanding. Things *can* be communicated. You *can* describe what you are feeling. You can talk.

Such concern with the spoken, or written, word is not normally associated with the cinema, but François Truffaut confessed to a feeling that he belonged more to the nineteenth century, and perhaps to a literary, humanist tradition that has its roots in Rousseau, Goethe and Balzac.

Under the paternal guidance of André Bazin, Truffaut, in his reviewing days for *Cahiers du Cinéma*, was a rigorous proponent of the 'auteur' theory, which credited directors with personal as opposed to collaborative responsibility for their films. The cinema of François Truffaut bears an uncompromising novelist's signature. Where **Godard** uses literary references, they are part of his rag-bag of multi-media quotation. Godard is a radical and dramatic essayist – impatient, didactic and innovative. Truffaut is a traditionalist. His films deal with love, friendship, loss: with human relationships. Plots exist in order for characters to interact, not to relate an A–Z narrative. Only the tone and the preoccupations are constant.

Truffaut was unabashed by stylized 'voice-over' commentary. For him the first-person confidential tone not only imposes unity on often very disparate material, but more importantly invites emotional complicity from each individual in an audience.

This intense personal involvement produced over twenty years a unique auto-biographical testament. Truffaut's first full-length film, *The Four Hundred Blows* (*Les 400*

coups, 1959), was based strongly on his own childhood experience in a reformatory. The hero, Antoine Doinel (always played by the same actor, Jean-Pierre Léaud), has reappeared at various stages of his *éducation sentimentale*, from the *Antoine and Colette* episode in *L'Amour à vingt ans* (1962) through *Stolen Kisses* (*Baisers volés*, 1969), *Bed and Board* (*Domicile conjugale*, 1970) and to the last in the sequence, *Love on the Run* (*L'Amour en fuite*, 1979).

Doinel cannot be interpreted simply as Truffaut's fictional *alter ego*. There is an extraordinary sympathy and identification between actor and director, but Doinel/Léaud, despite the passing years, has remained curiously frozen in perpetual adolescence.

Les 400 coups was an international success. With his *Cahiers* friends, Godard, Rivette, **Robmer** and Chabrol, Truffaut launched the 'Nouvelle Vague'. At a time of depression on shoe-string budgets these young film makers dragged the cinema out of the studios and into the streets. With portable lightweight cameras, free wheeling cinéma-vérité techniques, a regular company of actors, writers, composers and technicians, they made a virtue of improvisation.

But Truffaut's films, from the very beginning, reveal a genuine concern with cinematic vocabulary. His second feature *Shoot the Pianist* (*Tirez sur le pianiste*, 1960) adapted 'B'-feature Hollywood gangster motifs into a daringly uninhibited tragi-comic *jeu d'esprit*. 'It was a genuine experiment ... If I felt like shooting a particular scene I just did it, and then followed it with another that was completely different.' The film was a commercial flop.

But with *Jules et Jim* (1961), Truffaut's international reputation was confirmed. The romance, humour and pathos of an impossible *ménage à trois* is described with compassionate irony and lyrical charm.

As a reviewer Truffaut always attacked makers of 'serious subject' films like Stanley Kramer. 'If you have something to say, say it. Don't make a film about it.' With *Fahrenheit 451* (1966), Truffaut demonstrates the truth of the dictum. Based on Ray **Bradbury's** futuristic fantasy of the destruction of the written word, Truffaut's picture, despite all its emotional commitment, remains stilted and theoretical.

Like his 'Nouvelle Vague' comrades, Truffaut was nurtured on the cinema. At the age of fifteen, he had started his own ciné-club, called Le Cercle Cinémane. 'What first attracted me to the cinema was my love of fiction and what led me to want to make films was my desire to structure a fictional story.' But where Truffaut's preoccupation with style and structure lead him towards imitation (as with his **Hitchcock**-influenced 'thrillers' *The Bride Wore Black* (*La Mariée était en noir*, 1967), and *Mississippi Mermaid* (*La Sirène du Mississippi*, 1969), he can be awkward and remote. Where he pays direct tribute to the cinema, however, as in *Day for Night* (*La Nuit américaine*, 1973) he is assured, affectionate and romantically involved.

Truffaut reveals his supreme artistry when he focuses on the intimate paradoxes of human behaviour. In *The Wild Child* (*L'Enfant sauvage*, 1969) Truffaut himself took the role of Dr Itard, teacher of the Wild Child of Aveyron. The film is quite literally about language and communication, about the relationship between teacher and pupil, director and actor. The deceptively spare, almost documentary style is elegantly sensitive to psychological nuance and contains images of breath-taking beauty.

In his best films, Truffaut's presence whether as writer, actor, director (or all three) informs every frame. His insistence on individual values rejects all Bond-age blockbuster formulae. It may mean that his work can be flawed, miniaturist, sometimes casual or even too subjective, but it is never slick or pontificating. With all due modesty, the source of Truffaut's inspiration is always himself. He remained sceptical about patriotism, existential pessimism, politics (he never voted) and religion. 'My religion is the cinema. I believe in **Charlie Chaplin** . . . I make films to realize my childhood dreams, to make me feel good, and to make others share in that feeling.'

Further reading

Other works include: *Silken Skin* (*La Peau douce*, 1966); *Anne and Muriel* (*Les Deux anglaises sur le Continent*, 1972); *The Story of Adèle H* (*L'Histoire d'Adèle H*, 1975). See: François Truffaut, *Hitchcock* (1967); Graham Petrie, *The Cinema of François Truffaut* (1970); Don Allen, *Truffaut* (1974); François Truffaut, *The Films in My Life* (1979).

PAUL SIDEY

TURGENEV, Ivan Sergeyevich
1818–83
Russian writer

Born in Oryol, he was brought up on his mother's estate of Spasskoye-Lutovinovo. His parents were cultured members of the Russian nobility, but his mother was the richer and more domineering; his charming and accomplished father remained aloof from the family commitments (as Turgenev's portrayal of him in *First Love, Pervaya lyubov'* (1860) demonstrates so brilliantly). The growing boy received frequent beatings at his mother's hands and a generally tyrannical atmosphere in domestic affairs contrasted with a Frenchified, cultured taste in books and pretensions to elegance which prevailed at Spasskoye. The young Turgenev early realized the disparity between his privileged status and the servile condition of the peasantry. He was later to swear what he called 'a Hannibal's oath' against serfdom. Educated by ineffectual tutors, he was to grow into a giant of a man, both physically and intellectually, and was to attend the Universities of Moscow and St Petersburg before, in 1838, aged twenty, going abroad to complete his education at the University of Berlin. In Germany he first formulated his ideas on the need for Russia to learn from the West and grew to realize how important and precious was his own generation of young Russians who were to comprise the first generation of the Russian intelligentsia. When he returned to his homeland in 1841 he made attempts to gain a university chair and worked for a time in government service, but in 1843 his future seemed to be decided for him through the publication of a long poem, *Parasha*, which met with critical success, and through his meeting with the famous singer Pauline Viardot. After his fashion he was to remain devoted both to Pauline Viardot and to literature for the rest of his life, though he never became completely wedded to either.

In the mid-1840s, to a great extent under the influence of V.G. Belinsky, the critic, he turned from imitative poetry to the writing of prose sketches of rural Russian life whose originality lay in their portrayal of peasant types. These *Sketches from a Hunter's Album* (*Zapiski okhotnika*) began appearing in the *Contemporary* in 1847 and first appeared in a separate edition in 1852. Although mostly written while Turgenev had been abroad, he had returned to Russia for their publication in a separate edition and largely on their account, though also due to an obituary notice he had written on Gogol, he was arrested, imprisoned for a month and then exiled to his estate.

The enforced isolation made him take stock of his career. His efforts to become a playwright had ended with the banning of his only full-length play *A Month in the Country* (*Mesyats v derevne,* 1850), and though he wrote such famous stories as *The Diary of a Superfluous Man* (*Dnevnik lishnego cheloveka,* 1850) and *Mumu* (1854) at this time, he was beginning to feel his way towards the larger form of the short novel. At the height of the Crimean War he wrote his first novel *Rudin* (published 1856) in recognition of the need both to expose the weaknesses of his own generation and to justify its role in face of the mounting criticism from a younger generation. The same concerns dictated the elegiac tone of his second novel *Home of the Gentry* (*Dvoryanskoye gnezdo,* 1859), but with the approach of the emancipation of the serfs he acknowledged that the younger generation's desire for change was more assertive and radical and he portrayed it in Yelena's rejection of her past (in his third novel, *On the Eve, Nakanune,* 1860). His refusal to depict a

Russian revolutionary in this novel (the hero is Bulgarian) caused a critical storm in the radical press. He responded by offering his own objective diagnosis of the nihilism of the period in the masterly portrait of Bazarov, the hero of his fourth and finest novel *Fathers and Children* (*Ottsy i deti,* 1862). The result was a further critical uproar which produced grave misinterpretations of the novel and persuaded Turgenev to turn his back on Russia.

For the rest of his life he chose to reside abroad, returning to his own country only for periodic visits. During the 1860s he lived in Baden-Baden, close to Pauline Viardot's retirement home. His attitude to Russia became one of resentment and pity, expressed in his extremely caustic picture of the Russian intelligentsia in his fifth novel *Smoke* (*Dym,* 1867). He also tended to develop themes concerned with superstition, the supernatural and the occult in 'tales of mystery' which he wrote in the final two decades of his life. At the time of the Franco-Prussian War he and the Viardots moved temporarily to London and then later settled in Paris. He had by now achieved an international reputation and was so closely identified with the French literary scene through friendships with **Flaubert**, the **Goncourts** and **Zola** that he was regarded by the young **Henry James**, who met him in Paris, as a writer to be included under the heading of 'French Poets and Novelists'. He had become more highly esteemed in Europe than he was among the younger generation of Russians. His last novel *Virgin Soil* (*Nov',* 1877) was a bold attempt to win the sympathy of the revolutionary young in his own country, though his own liberalism and his scepticism about the revolutionary potential of the peasantry led him to suggest in his novel that the revolutionary movement in Russia was doomed. However, recognition of his services to Russia came from other quarters, notably from the University of Oxford which awarded him an honorary doctorate of civil law in 1879, much to his delight. Serious illness, which turned out to be cancer of the spine, afflicted him towards the end of his life. His last works took the form of 'mystery' tales like *The Song of Triumphant Love* (*Pesn' torzhestvuyushchey lyubvi*, 1881) and *Klara Milich* (1883) as well as a large cycle of *Poems in Prose* (*Stikhotvoreniya v proze*, 1882 and posthumously) which, if of uneven quality, offered a recapitulation in miniature of many of his favourite themes. He died in Bourgival in 1883.

Generally acknowledged to have been the first Russian writer to have achieved a major international reputation, nowadays he is thought of as a novelist who stands somewhat in the shade of his great contemporaries, **Dostoevsky** and **Tolstoy**. By temperament and talent Turgenev felt at home with such less extensive prose forms as the sketch, short story and short novel. In his studies of peasant Russia he created masterpieces of condensed, poetic description which conjured into brilliant and fleeting life types ranging from the practical, self-made Khor and the sensitive Kalinych (of his first *Sketch*) to the freedom-loving Kasyan, the inspired singer Yakov or the saintly Lukeria stricken by paralysis. His sardonic portrayals of Russian landowners revealed by their attention to detail and their scrupulous observation where the true evil of serfdom lay. He was similarly penetrating in his examination of the Hamletism and pretentiousness of the Russian intelligentsia. His early short stories and sketches are dotted with acute insights into the social and psychological aberrations in Russian life, though the urbanity and deftness of his style, accommodating both lyrical nature description and naturalistic dialogue, may seem on occasion to outshine all else in his work.

In his novels, upon which his fame now chiefly rests, he blended his expertise as a master of the love story with his capacity for social-psychological portraiture. His novels consequently became realistic appraisals of the evolution of the Russian intelligentsia in the 1840s, 1850s and 1860s. Always very sensitive to the changing political atmosphere in Russia and in Europe, he believed nonetheless that life enshrined certain permanencies – the permanency of nature and eternity, for example – and that man's role was at best ephemeral, that his hope of happiness was slight save through love and that when love failed his only destiny was a decent death. His recognition of the conflict between head and heart which so crippled his own generation of the intelligentsia led him to divide humanity into Hamlets and Don Quixotes (in his lecture of 1860 'Hamlet and Don Quixote'), the tragic egoism of the former being balanced against the comic altruism of the latter. His greatest fictional creation, the portrait of the nihilist Bazarov in *Fathers and Children*, can arguably demonstrate how the hero's Quixotic desire to serve the people is flawed and perhaps tragically foredoomed by the Hamlet-like weakness, the introspection and romanticism, which he discovers in his own nature.

Turgenev differs from Dostoevsky and Tolstoy in his rejection of all religious solutions to life's problems. An agnostic, he viewed life realistically and with faintly amused detachment, representing it most successfully in the confined, theatrical form he chose for his novels, but there is no doubt that as he grew older his pessimism became more marked and he seemed to seek answers in the exploration of psychic themes. Probably his most memorable writing is to be found in his love stories, particularly *Asya* (1858) and *First Love* (1860), both of which have an autobiographical basis and depend for their effectiveness on romanticized nostalgia for a poignant but lost happiness. His evocative lyricism in depicting summertime and young love is unequalled.

As a man he was unpunctual, often hypochondriac, depressive, linguistically of outstanding gifts, a delightful conversationalist, an indefatigable letter-writer and, above all, charming. He charmed many of the leading celebrities of his day throughout Europe and it is his appreciative understanding of European sensibilities, preserved for posterity in his letters and numerous memoirs about him, that has greatly contributed to his enduring popularity.

Further reading

Of recent translations Leonard Schapiro, *Turgenev's Spring Torrents* (1972), and Marion Mainwaring, *Youth and Age* (1968, containing 'Punin and Baburin', 'The Inn' and 'The Watch'), are noteworthy. Most of his other shorter works are available in Constance Garnett translations, though not generally outside libraries. About Turgenev: the recent biography, L. Schapiro, *Turgenev, His Life and Times* (1978), must now take precedence over earlier works by Yarmolinsky and Magarshack because it makes use of much new material, mostly letters, which has only become available in the last decade. Of recent critical studies relating to Turgenev the following are valuable (in alphabetical order): I. Berlin, *Fathers and Children* (1972), a study of Bazarov's Jacobinism; R. Freeborn, *Turgenev, the Novelist's Novelist* (1978), a study of Turgenev's novels; E. Kagan-Kans, *Hamlet and Don Quixote: Turgenev's Ambivalent Vision* (1975); V.S. Pritchett, *The Gentle Barbarian* (1977). A. FitzLyon, *The Price of Genius* (1964), is a biography of Pauline Viardot which pays particular attention to Turgenev's relations with her; and two detailed studies by Patrick Waddington illuminate aspects of Turgenev's relations with the West: *Turgenev and England* (1980) and *Turgenev and George Sand: An Improbable Entente* (1981). See also: Glyn Turton, *Turgenev and the Context of English Literature, 1850–1900* (1992).

RICHARD FREEBORN

TURING, Alan

1912–54

English logician

Alan Turing was born in London and was educated at Sherborne and King's College, Cambridge. A fellowship at King's College (1935) led to two years (1936–8) working with Alonzo Church at Princeton. During the war Turing worked in the Communications Department at the Foreign Office, and in 1945 he joined the National Physical Laboratory to work on their early computer, known as ACE. In 1948 he took the post of Reader at Manchester University, again working on problems associated with computers. He died of poisoning, possibly accidental, in June 1954.

It is astonishing that Turing's famous paper on computable numbers was published in 1937. In it he performed an historic thought experiment: he postulated a computer which could take its instructions from a paper tape containing a sequence of 1s and 0s, could print new sequences of 1s and 0s, which would then, if necessary, join the sequence of instructions. In this way it would modify its own program. Turing showed that any machine which was capable of doing this much was, in a certain sense, the match of any other machine which could do this much. He called a machine of this kind a 'Universal Automaton'. (This is usually called a 'Turing Machine' today.) A small, slow Turing Machine will be capable of doing anything which can be done by a larger, faster Turing Machine, assuming that there are no physical limitations on the storage of the program. Essentially the smaller machine can always be programmed to plod on and to get there in the end.

The earliest steps in the development of computers were diverse, unco-ordinated, and mixed up with interests in tabulation, statistics, ballistics, telecommunications. Yet out of this somewhat confusing mêlée a wise strategic decision emerged: to build general-purpose machines capable of modifying their own programs. The hardware would be as flexible as possible: programs punched on paper tape would supply the specialist features required to meet any specific difficulty. The result was that most of the computers subsequently made embodied a potentially limitless computing facility: there was no knowing what they might be brought to do. This maintained the essentially 'magic' feeling of the machine, and acted as a sustained intellectual stimulus for programmers and analysts. Such machines were, in effect, the Universal Automatons Turing had foreseen in 1937.

It could easily have been otherwise. That it was not was largely due to the efforts of Alan Turing and **John Von Neumann**.

Further reading

Alan Turing's main papers were as follows: 'On Computable Numbers ... ' (1937); 'Systems of

Logic Based on Ordinals' (1939); 'Computing Machinery and Intelligence' (1950); and 'The Chemical Basis of Morphogenesis' (1952). Unpublished in his lifetime, they can be found in *Collected Works of Alan Turing* (4 vols, 1992–2001). See also: S. Turing, *Alan M. Turing* (1959); Andrew Hodges, *Alan Turing: The Enigma* (1993); B.J. Copeland (ed.) *The Essential Turing* (2004); *Alan Turing's Automatic Computing Engine* (2005).

CHRISTOPHER ORMELL

TURNER, Frederick Jackson

1861–1932

US historian and teacher

Turner was born in Portage, Wisconsin, when that state had barely emerged from the frontier, and his thought can be viewed as a vindication of that birth. He attended the state university between 1880 and 1884 and, after a year as a journalist, taught in Madison until he moved to Harvard in 1910. For a year, 1888–9, he ventured east to Johns Hopkins University in Baltimore, then the foremost seminar for historical research in the United States. He was there versed in the stern exigencies of German historical method and irritated by the laconic indifference of easterners to the contribution of the West to American society. The Hopkins seminar, personified by Herbert Baxter Adams, preached the 'germ' theory of Anglo-Saxon constitutional development, whereby the democratic institutions of the United States – best exemplified on the East Coast – had evolved via England from the medieval tribes of Germany. In his decisive 1893 essay, 'The Frontier in American History', Turner accepted the evolutionary perspective (also represented at Baltimore by Woodrow Wilson and Richard T. Ely) but displaced German woods for American forests, rancid-buttered Ostrogoths for frontier Jacksonians. It was, Turner claimed, the sociology of the American frontier that had created the American predilection for democracy, that 'the existence of an area of free land, its continuous recession, and the advance of American settlement westward, explain American

development'. For the frontier initially drove the settler back upon the primitive and stripped away his European inheritance, impelled individualistic self-reliance and created the American temperament, coarse but inquisitive, inventive and materialist, exuberant and individual.

This essay was immensely influential, both in breaking the eastern stranglehold on the vision of the American past and, not in creating a myth of the American character, but in fashioning its first plausible sociological explanation. It was the more persuasive, since it appealed to a culture vanishing and regarded with nostalgic affection by Americans. Nothing else matched its influence, though Turner did venture other theses, notably an argument for the historical importance of geographical sections and even a plea for an urban interpretation of American history. But he was essentially an essayist, if he can be deemed a willing writer at all, and only one editor, Albert Bushnell Hart, ever managed to extract a full-length narrative from him. Turner was entranced by research, the accumulation of fascinating if unassimilated note cards, and his writing is notable for long passages of tedious detail, interspersed with paragraphs of lucid – if not always related – insight. He was perhaps most successful and most content as a teacher. At the University of Wisconsin he established one of the best graduate programmes in history at a state university. His students were some of his greatest assets, for they collected his essays, published several posthumous volumes, tidied up and defended the frontier thesis decades past its author's demise and wrote his definitive biography. In Carl Becker, Ray Allen Billington, Avery Craven, Herbert E. Bolton and Frederick Merk, Turner left a legacy wider than his own thought.

Further reading

Works include: *The Rise of the New West, 1819–1829* (1906); *The Frontier in American History* (1920); *The Significance of Sections in American History* (1932); *The United States, 1830–1850: The Nation and Its Sections* (1935). About Turner: R.S.

Billington, *Frederick Jackson Turner* (1973); Carl Becker, *Everyman His Own Historian* (1935); Wilbur R. Jacobs (ed.) *The Historical World of Frederick Jackson Turner* (1968); Richard Hofstadter, *The Progressive Historians* (1968); R. Hofstadter and S.M. Lipset, *Turner and the Sociology of the Frontier* (1968); Allan G. Brogue, *Frederick Jackson Turner: Strange Roads Going Down* (1998).

MICHAEL O'BRIEN

TWAIN, Mark (Samuel Langhorne CLEMENS)

1835–1910

US novelist and essayist

When Twain was five the family moved within Missouri to Hannibal, the rich cultural location of his Tom Sawyer and Huckleberry Finn fictions. Brief schooling ended in apprenticeship on the Missouri *Courier*. In 1853 he worked his way east to New York and Philadelphia and back west to Iowa as journeyman printer. In 1857 he exchanged that life for apprentice and journeyman Mississippi riverboat pilot, vividly described in *Life on the Mississippi* (1883). Twain here has one of his very few cultural heroes without serious blemish, Horace Bixby, the dandy master pilot, the only acceptable heroic authority Twain acknowledged, and juxtaposes him with the bogus glories of 'the absolute South', with its aristocratic humbug and grotesque belief in itself as a civilization. But the Civil War closed the river. For about two weeks Clemens became second lieutenant in the Confederate army – his family were confirmed Unionists – and was then released for vague 'disabilities' (the affair is parodied in 'The Private History of a Campaign that Failed'). Discovering that being secretary to his brother Orion, secretary to Nevada State, entailed no work and no pay, he unsuccessfully tried prospecting, turned to reporting, and in 1862 became city editor on the Virginia City (Nevada) *Enterprise*, using for the first time his pseudonym (a fathom call on the Mississippi boats but curiously indicative of the future schism in his character).

After an absurd duel (personal journalism proving a liability) he worked for newspapers in San Francisco, where he met **Bret Harte** and published 'The Celebrated Jumping Frog of Calaveras County', the just-about-funny story which made him famous and which he rightly did not value highly. The Sacramento *Union* assigned him travel reports in Hawaii, the Mediterranean and Palestine; the resulting *Innocents Abroad* (1869) combines the brash superiorities of the confident American tourist with a certain wariness of time and decay in monuments prior to America, largely brought on by the Sphinx gazing at Twain. The later tensions are already latent here: the overwhelming sense of time and eternity reducing men to transient data. With popular success and the editing of the Buffalo *Express,* he could marry Olivia, and their combined finances enabled him to buy a place in Hartford, Connecticut. His impulsive impracticality lost him a fortune in a typesetting machine already out of date, and in a publishing house which profited from General Grant's memoirs and then went bankrupt within ten years. Twain then wrote and lectured to pay debts and restore his finances. But inside national and international fame – between 1872 and 1900 he produced twenty-five books at least – private tragedy undermined him. A beloved daughter died, his only son died in infancy, his wife died in 1904 and another daughter in 1909. University honours were laid thickly upon him but, as he said, 'I take the same childish delight in a new degree that an Indian takes in a fresh scalp.' He finally left Hartford for Redding – still in Connecticut – and, having anticipated he would die with the return of Halley's comet, which had appeared at his birth, did so, of *angina pectoris*.

Twain's wit and humour constitute a balancing act, a controlled hysteria in the face of a contradictory and violent world, an edging towards the void of hopeless behaviourism and dehumanized determinism. Inside a witticism that the symbol of man ought to be an axe since 'every human being has one concealed about him somewhere, and is always seeking the opportunity to grind it', lies a sense of possible unbridled rapacity. The genteel fears of bourgeois society forced him to costume criticism and pain in ironic comedy, satire that excoriated cruelty, ignorance and hypocrisy, and farce resulting from the gap between established moral standards and the truth. *The Gilded Age* (1874), written in collaboration with Charles D. Warner, contains the exemplary figure of Colonel Beriah Sellers, epitome of the success ethic operating in the speculative corruptions of Washington, where his energies become a danger to youth by perpetuating a myth beyond practicality.

Shocks of recognition come through as nervous hilarity. His finest works retain an astonishing balance between buoyancy and despair. *The Adventures of Huckleberry Finn* (1884) is a pattern of duplicity and disguise, with a twelve-year-old boy, technically dead, discovering the adult hypocrisy of slavery, feuding Southern aristocrats in full stupidity, the confidence trickster who exemplifies capitalist fraud, the parent who exploits his child to extinction, and the training of another boy (Tom Sawyer) to believe in the competitive aggressions and romantic violence of the age. Huck's revolt against Christian society and the Fugitive Slave Law is one of the most moving and valuable moments in literature, a beacon of sense in a darkness of characteristic apologetics. But the brief days he and Nigger Jim spend on a piece of broken raft on the Mississippi cannot constitute a possible society, however idyllic and educative. Huck learns to respect a Negro and reject the shore societies, but can only then 'light out for the Territory', get clear of American lies by heading west. His inventive, explorative language – Twain created a rich vehicle from his memories of Hannibal – carries him to articulate understanding which is useless in 'sivilized' America. In *A Connecticut Yankee at King Arthur's Court* (1889) the technology that Hank Morgan brings from the Colt factory to medieval feudalism, in order to transform serfdom, the chivalric order and a bigoted church into a reasonably

humanitarian technocracy, turns to a violence which reflects American Civil War weaponry and the technological potentialities for aggression in the Philadelphia Exposition of 1876. A factory-colony is to turn 'groping and grubbing automata into men'. The revolution 'must *begin,* in blood, whatever may answer afterward. If history teaches anything, it teaches that.' Training is 'all there is *to* a person'. But the novel concludes with the nineteenth-century American mechanic roasting an army of knights on an electrified wire defence system. *Pudd'nhead Wilson* (1894) is one of the most savage and accurate exposures of racism and slavery ever written, but Twain also incorporates an analysis of American subservient snobbery before European aristocrats, the ruin of a young lawyer whose first mild joke is mistaken for stupidity by a stupid townspeople, and the lawyer's rehabilitation as a detective – a figure that will obsess American fiction in the following century and which Twain neatly mocked a few years later in *The Double Barrelled Detective Story* (1902). In 'The Man that Corrupted Hadleyburg' (1898) derision is the response to a town's untested reputation for honesty, or vanity disguised as self-righteous uprightness, the classic Christian social sin. Wealth attacks a society which believes that all things are ordered, including corruption; it is left praying: 'Lead us into temptation!'

These masterpieces manage, as works of art, to exhilarate the reader with wit, humour, skilled plots and critical vision, while impregnating him with recognitions of human cruelty and stupidity. But increasingly the famous novelist and much demanded after-dinner speaker began to lock manuscripts away from public scrutiny, in order to retain fame and fortune, to be honest with himself while entertaining the public who, as usual, demanded what it approved of. Mr Clemens divided from Mark Twain; the humorist's art could not fulfil the embittered conscience; the well-meaning censorship of his wife, **W.D. Howells** and others only exacerbated the schizoid life. The white-clothed public figure concealed the dark final phase of his genius. *What Is Man?* (1906) yields the creative impulse to mere training, behaviourism and a cynical equation of Shakespeare and a machine or a rat. Human nature is always content with its condition 'no matter what its religion is, whether its master be tiger or house-cat'. 'Everything has been tried, without success', so do not waste feeling on the possibility of social change. In 1878, Twain wrote that 'To man all things are possible but one – he cannot have a hole in the seat of his breeches and keep his fingers out of it.' The later work explores the impulsive and irrational to the point where Twain can say, 'Fleas can be taught anything a Congressman can.' Man's boasted '*intellectual* superiority' to the contrary, 'the fact that he can *do* wrong proves his *moral* inferiority to any creature that cannot'. In *The Mysterious Stranger* (1916) the archangel Satan visits medieval Austria to reassure young Theodor that human history accurately reflects the vileness of mankind, especially in wars which religion and philosophy support. The rest is void:

> There is no God, no universe, no human race, no earthly life, no heaven, no hell. It is all a dream. Nothing exists but you. And you are but a thought, a useless thought, a homeless thought, wandering forlorn among the empty eternities!

Twain, like his contemporary **Henry Adams**, is a sceptical index of the twentieth century, prophetic of its state of continuous emergency and creedless hypocrisy. 'Two or three centuries from now it will be recognized that all the competent killers are Christians; then the pagan world will go to school to the Christian – not to acquire his religion, but his guns': such is the chilling message to the modern world in *The Mysterious Stranger*. Angels, Satan adds, can only love each other; if they loved the human race, that love 'would consume its object like ashes. No, we cannot love men, but we can be harmlessly indifferent; we can also like them sometimes.' *Letters from the Earth* (1942) ridicules the inconsistencies and authoritarianism

of Old Testament lore: 'The Biblical law says: "Thou shalt not kill". The law of God, planted in the heart of man at his birth, says: "Thou shalt kill".' Twain opened the way to American 'black' humour of the 1960s and the comedian of despair, **Lenny Bruce**.

Further reading

Other works include: *The Writings of Mark Twain,* ed. Albert Bigelow Paine (37 vols, 1922–5); *Letters from the Earth,* ed. Bernard de Voto (1942); *The Complete Humorous Sketches and Tales,* ed. Charles Neider (1961); *Notebooks and Journal of Mark Twain,* ed. Frederick Anderson, Michael B. Frank and Kenneth M. Sanderson (2 vols, 1976); *Mark Twain and the Damned Human Race,* ed. Janet Smith (1962). See: Walter Blair, *Mark Twain and Huck Finn* (1960); Henry Nash Smith, *Mark Twain: The Development of a Writer* (1962); Justin Kaplan, *Mr Clemens and Mark Twain* (1966); J.M. Cox, *Mark Twain: The Facts of Humour* (1967); Robert Keith Miller, *Mark Twain* (1983); Henry B. Wonham, *Mark Twain and the Art of the Tall Tale* (1993); Fred Kaplan, *The Singular Mark Twain: A Biography* (2003); Karen Lystra, *Dangerous Intimacy: The Untold Story of Mark Twain's Final Years* (2004); Louis Budd and Peter Messent (eds) *A Companion to Mark Twain* (2005).

ERIC MOTTRAM

TYLOR, (Sir) Edward Burnett
1832–1917
English anthropologist

Tylor was the dominant figure in anthropology in Britain for at least thirty years after the publication of his *Primitive Culture* in 1871. Today his position within the subject can only be assessed historically, but

> for his period he had remarkably few philosophical, religious or racial obsessions; and as the first great synthesizer and sifter of ethnological knowledge it was he who largely created the universe of discourse inherited, through **Frazer** and **Malinowski**, by the senior living generation of British anthropologists.
>
> (Lienhardt, 1969)

How Tylor attained this position is both interesting of itself and also illuminates the characteristics of anthropology as it developed in the second half of the nineteenth century.

Tylor was the third son of a Camberwell brass founder, and, as a Quaker, was educated until he was sixteen at a nonconformist school at Tottenham. He then joined the family business until consumptive symptoms compelled his resignation four years later. Thereafter he possessed sufficient means to concentrate on his scholarly interests as a member of an intellectual group emerging from successful nonconformist and Evangelical families.

In 1856, while on an American tour, he met Henry Christy, a banker, fellow Quaker and archaeologist, 'in an omnibus at Havana', as Tylor somewhat romantically described it in his first book, *Anahuac: or Mexico and the Mexicans Ancient and Modern* (1861). Their four-month visit to Mexico followed, which set in train the process whereby Tylor became an anthropologist. Although primarily a travel book, *Anahuac* portrayed the author's interest in Mexican culture for its own sake. However, it was the intellectual history of the late 1850s and 1860s which profoundly influenced Tylor's anthropological attitudes, demonstrated in his books *Researches into the Early History of Mankind* (1865) and *Primitive Culture*. The latter was his most important work, and led to his election as a Fellow of the Royal Society in the year of its publication. His last book was *Anthropology* (1881), an introductory text, and his only major subsequent publication was the paper 'On a Method of Investigating the Development of Institutions: Applied to Laws of Marriage and Descent' (*Journal of the Anthropological Institute*, Vol. 18, 1888).

Tylor did not enter academic life until 1883, when he was appointed Keeper of the University Museum, Oxford, in order to lecture on the subjects embraced by the collection given to the university by General **A.H. Pitt Rivers**. Tylor became Reader the next year and a titular professor in 1896. He lectured regularly until his retirement in

1909, and was knighted in 1912. During his Oxford years he devoted much time to the organizational aspects of anthropology. Twice president of the Anthropological Institute, he was also the first president of the Anthropology Section of the British Association for the Advancement of Science. Ironically, despite Tylor's sustained efforts, Oxford refused to accept his proposals for a degree examination in anthropology.

Tylor was primarily a cultural evolutionist with a rather generalized view of human progress. According to Joan Leopold, the *Early History* and *Primitive Culture* show influences extending from the Enlightenment and positivism to the German historical school and the Humboldtians. She has identified the themes in these works: (1) the interpretation of evolution; (2) the explanation of similarities by independent invention, inheritance and diffusion with the assumption of psychological and environmental unity; (3) the analysis of 'survivals'; (4) methodology; and (5) the concept of culture.

From these elements Tylor developed a view of culture as an entity, embracing the past as well as the present:

> Culture or Civilization, taken in its wide ethnographic sense, is that complex whole which includes knowledge, belief, art, morals, law, custom and any other capabilities and habits acquired by man as a member of society. The condition of culture among the various societies of mankind, in so far as it is capable of being investigated on general principles, is a subject apt for the study of laws of human thought and action.
>
> (*Primitive Culture*, p. 1)

Tylor saw the history of culture as one not of degeneration but of a general gradual progression from a natural condition. Although there were local, and explicable, retardations, it was possible to reconstruct scientifically the details of this progress, where it lay beyond historical facts, by means of the comparative method. Contemporary human institutions could be arranged sequentially in terms of their likeness or otherwise to the society of his day.

Aside from his stress on the study of culture, Tylor became famous for his interest in 'survivals' and his elaboration of the theory of animism. For example, magical belief was a 'survival', itself resulting from the very simple mental law whereby primitive man confused external phenomena with his own perception of them. Therefore animism was a primitive universal belief in the existence of spiritual beings, which provided a common basis to all religions, and so a means of comparing them. Methodologically, 'survivals' were as much vestigial clues to past attitudes and practices as were prehistoric artefacts. It was consistent with these views that Tylor saw anthropology as 'a reformer's science' (as he wrote at the end of *Primitive Culture*) in that one of its roles was to expose as irrelevant those remains of ancient thought which impeded the development of society.

Tylor's breadth of vision and rational attitude towards all forms of evidence have helped his influence to survive. His definition of culture retains a modern ring, as does his interest in words apart from their etymology. Certainly his concept of culture lacked theoretical integration and his evolutionism implied an attitude of racial superiority. But his insistence that anthropology was fit to help tackle the analysis of the great moral and social issues of his time is still significant.

Further reading

Tylor's *Collected Works* were published in 1994; and *Anthropological Essays Presented to Edward Burnett Tylor in Honour of His 75th Birthday, October 2nd, 1907*, ed. N.W. Thomas (1907), contains a bibliography of Tylor's works. See also: R.R. Marett, *Tylor* (1936); George W. Stocking, 'Tylor, Edward Burnett', *International Encyclopedia of the Social Sciences*, Vol. XVI (1968); Godfrey Lienhardt, 'Edward Tylor', in *The Founding Fathers of Social Science*, ed. Timothy Raison (1969); Joan Leopold, *Culture in Comparative and Evolutionary Perspective: E.B. Tylor and the Making of 'Primitive Culture'* (1980).

PETER GATHERCOLE

TZARA, Tristan (Samuel ROSENSTOCK)

1896–1963
Romanian/French writer

A Romanian by birth, Tzara adopted the French language and in later life French nationality. His career as a cultural terrorist began in 1916 when, in neutral Zürich, he joined other refugees like Hugo Ball, Richard Huelsenbeck and **Jean Arp** to mount that brief but savage assault on Western cultural values known as Dada. Tzara was in his element as the ebullient impresario of this most anarchic of movements in the arts, contributing to the recitation of wild multilingual poems at the Cabaret Voltaire, setting up provocative exhibitions of Dada paintings, organizing stage performances at which the Dada group would, by their incoherent proclamations and insults, goad the audience into frenzied protest, and spreading the Dada message of subversion across Europe by way of publications and tireless correspondence with other avant-garde leaders like **Apollinaire**, **Marinetti**, Haussmann and **Breton**.

In 1920 Tzara settled in Paris, joining forces with André Breton and his Littérature group to launch a further series of outrageous spectacles. Eventually, though, bourgeois audiences began to enjoy being insulted and Dada scandal became a cultural commodity like any other. While Breton led the group into the new adventures of Surrealism, Tzara stuck to his individualist path, eventually to join up with the Surrealists again in the early 1930s, when he produced some of his best poetry. Later, Tzara's emergent **Marxist** concerns led him out of Surrealism: an active member of the Resistance during the Occupation, he entered the French Communist Party in 1947.

Tzara's most prized texts are his Dada manifestos, written to be performed in public and full of rumbustious tomfoolery and astringent wit. His is the language of a sophisticated savage, by turns silly, aggressive, and truculently paradoxical: 'I am writing a manifesto and there's nothing I want, and yet

I'm saying certain things, and in principle I am against manifestos, as I am against principles ... I won't explain myself because I abhor common sense.'

The poems of the Dada period are characterized by extreme semantic and syntactic incoherence: improvised nonsense statements are interspersed with random slogans or headlines, with puns, invented words and printer's errors tossed into the mixture. The resultant texts exhibit a staccato singularity, a kind of sublime inarticulacy. 'Dada is an anti-nuance cream,' Tzara drily observed.

The remarkable thing is that Tzara persisted in this experiment in linguistic deviancy, maintaining a studied inconsequentiality until, by a mysterious reversal, his style modulated from unreadable gibberish into a seductive and fertile surrealist idiom. *L'Homme approximatif* (1931) is his best-known poem, an extended meditation on mental and elemental impulses in which the obscure play of words gives rise to felicitous lyrical passages with images of stunning beauty: 'sweet utterance at rest within my hand magic freshness/deep down in the cormorant at its breast flying spinning like an astral sign/light when expressed forfeits its petals.'

Essentially Tzara's poetry exemplifies the principle of new insights being generated through the exacerbation of singularity, as he indicated in an early aphorism:

> To concede to each element its identity, its autonomy, is the necessary condition for the creation of new constellations, since each has its place in the group. The thrust of the Word: upright, an image, a unique

event, passionate, of dense colour, intensity, in communion with life.

Passing from Dada spontaneity through Surrealist automatic writing, Tzara arrived at a mature style of transparent simplicity in which disparate entities could be held together in a unifying vision.

In retrospect, harmony and contact had been Tzara's goals all along. The 'great destructive negative work' of Dada was a prelude to the renewal of mental perspectives, and the rampant nihilism of the *Dada Manifesto 1918* was counterbalanced by a desire to lay hold of the jostling realities of existence:

> Abolition of logic: DADA ... abolition of memory: DADA; abolition of archaeology: DADA; abolition of prophets: DADA; abolition of the future: DADA ... Liberty: *DADA DADA DADA*, the roaring of contorted pains, the interweaving of contraries and of all contradictions, freaks and irrelevancies: LIFE.

Further reading

Other works include: *Vingt-cinq poèmes* ('Twenty-five Poems', 1918); *De nos oiseaux* ('Of Our Birds', 1929); *L'Antitête* ('The Anti-head', 1933); *A haute flamme* ('Flame Out Loud', 1955). In course of publication: *Oeuvres complètes* (Vol. I, 1975; Vol. II, 1977). In English: *Seven Dada Manifestos and Lampisteries* (trans. B. Wright, 1977). On Tzara: René Lacôte, *Tristan Tzara* (1952); Mary Ann Caws, *The Poetry of Dada and Surrealism* (1970); Sadie Plant, *The Most Radical Gesture: The Situationist International in a Postmodern Age* (1992).

ROGER CARDINAL

U

UNAMUNO, Miguel de

1864 – 1936

Spanish writer

Born in Bilbao into a bourgeois family, Unamuno studied philosophy and letters and became a professor of Greek at Salamanca. Already famous as an essayist in his early thirties, he was made into a European celebrity when his deportation to the Canary Islands by the dictatorship of Primo de Rivera aroused a storm of protest well beyond Spain (1924). Unamuno went to Paris for a while, but soon was chosen as rector of his old university. He died in Salamanca shortly after a characteristic clash with a nationalist general at the beginning of the Spanish Civil War.

Unamuno belonged to the critical '1898' generation, a brilliant group of writers deeply engaged in national soul-searching. His first major work of essayism, *En Torno al Casticismo*, 1895, endeavours to raise the conception of the hispanic above its cheap 'exotic' overtones while at the same time musing over the right way to tackle a national tradition. He sets out to grasp the 'intra-historical' below the merely historical: the inner historicity, that is, of a culture, a task which he starkly distinguished from the contemplative disquisitions of German-like historicism as philological scholarship. The moral of the essay is that Spanish purity (*casticismo*) must be valiantly sought in a renewed contact with modern Europe, not in parochial isolation. For a time, Unamuno's thought tried to reconcile the irrational and instinctive with logic and analysis (e.g. in *Amor y Pedagogía*, 'Love and Pedagogy', 1902), but before long he turned against science and the 'biological values' of modern culture and asserted himself as an uncompromising vitalist in a strong irrationalist sense, not uninfluenced by his reading of Kierkegaard, **Nietzsche**, **William James** and **Bergson**. All vital values were for him irrational, and everything rational contrary to life.

In 1905, the tricentennial of the first part of *Don Quixote*, Unamuno published his most original book, the *Vida de Don Quijote y Sancho* 'commented' by him. He cast himself in the role not of a Cervantist, but of a Quixotist. For him, the squire Pança is foolish – in fact, more foolish than the knight – and 'Our Lord Don Quixote' is rescued from the comical light of Cervantes's novel in order to impersonate a crusade of faith against reason. Truth is not an object of thought but a driving force in conduct, a matter of guts, not of intellect. Unamunian 'misologism' reaches its consummation. What the wise, prudent Sanchos of our own world never understand is that we should inveigh against our dead machine civilization just as Don Quixote did against the windmills. While positivism, empiricism and naturalism are condemned out of hand, Don Quixote's passion for a justice beyond law receives praise, as does his strenuous search for glory, his 'hunger for immortality'. In his beautiful interpretation of the cave of Montesinos episode, the hispanic theme comes back in full: like his hero, Unamuno wants to cut his way to the genuine core of tradition through the useless jungle of stale traditionalisms.

His best poetical and fictional output also dates from the first two decades of the twentieth century. If his unmusical philosophical poems (*El Cristo de Velásquez*, 1920) are seldom reckoned among his best, his main novels, *Niebla* ('Fog', 1914), *La Tía Tula* ('Aunt Tula', 1921), and novellas (*Tres Novelas Ejemplares y un Prólog*, 1921) set Spanish story-telling on a new track, deliberately opposed to naturalist models. However, Unamuno was above all a master of the essay, as confirmed by his most accomplished work as a moralist, *The Tragic Sense of Life in Men and in Peoples* (*Del Sentimiento Trágico de la Vida, en los Hombres y los Pueblos*, 1913, trans. 1921). Following Nietzsche, Unamuno holds that there are no philosophies, just philosophers: thought springs from existential attitudes. Now man is eternally resisting his own nature as a finite being. Catholicism, i.e. Christianity, gave this tragic resistance its best rationale in the idea of a God who renders us immortal, thus maximizing our will-power before the unacceptable reality of death. Faith as a tragic sense of life is in a constant fight against despair. It is less a creed than an absurd hope. The 'sweet, redeeming uncertainty', anguish, becomes for Unamuno as for Kierkegaard the truest religious feeling and the basis for the inner leap from extreme denial to extreme assertion. Like its faith, the life of the Christian is bound to be restless: it is an *agon*, for as a Christian he must combat in himself the husband, the father and the citizen (hence the title of his reprise of *Del Sentimiento Trágico*, *La Agonía del Cristianismo*, 1924). The paradigm can be nothing less than Christ's own passion: the Golgotha is the goal. Unamuno's 'dolorismo' is the other face of his agonism.

Modern scholarship on the history of Christian thought has detected a curious Lutheran temper in Unamuno, who nevertheless always extolled Catholicism, even above Christianity. The tragic view of life and the upholding of a faith which is no 'creed' and is born of despair sounds indeed like Luther's own religiosity. Yet unlike Luther's, and unlike the thought of other antirationalist 'philosophers of life' (e.g. Bergson), Unamuno's piety evinces no mystical inclination: his religious outlook is fundamentally ascetic. Spanish catholicism seems to him most authentic precisely because it is highly ascetic and agonistic, whereas Roman catholicism lost its spiritual strength in a facile, erroneous attempt to marry the Gospel to Roman law (in the canon law). At bottom, however, the Unamunian agony is not confessional: it eschews every church, and aims at the perfect solitude of the individual in his yearning for eternity.

Unamuno's essays are couched in a terse style made of humourless fragments bristling with paradoxes: the blunt preaching language of a lonely prophet, of 'the Spanish Carlyle', 'don Miguel', the proud Basque who shook Spain up by the scandal of his burning prose. He was one of Europe's greatest individualists, who wrote that 'the only vital problem is the problem of our individual, personal destiny' – and as such, and in so far as he is much less of a believer than Kierkegaard, perhaps the most typical among proto-existentialists. Yet this fierce anarchic personality loved his country with all his heart, and only a true Spaniard could have written his briefest description of the human condition: 'Life is bullfighting.'

Further reading

Other works include: a collected; modern edition by the publisher Aguilar, Madrid. The best study of his thought is by Julián Marías, *Miguel de Unamuno* (1943). See: Ernst Robert Curtius, *Kritische Essays zur europäischen Literatur* (1954), José Luís Aranguren, *Catolicismo y Protestantismo como formas de existencia* (1952); Martin Nozick, *Miguel de Unamuno: The Agony of Belief* (1982); Gayana Jurkevich (ed.) *The Elusive Self: Archetypal Approaches to the Novels of Miguel de Unamuno* (1991).

See also: Henri Louis Bergson; William James; Fredrich Nietzsche.

J.G. MERQUIOR

UPDIKE, John Hoyer

1932–

US novelist and poet

John Updike was born in Pennsylvania and educated at Harvard and the Ruskin School of Drawing and Fine Art at Oxford. Critical opinion has always been sharply divided over his literary status, many seeing him as the archetypal *New Yorker* short-story writer, producing mannered, vivid, yet vacuously descriptive prose concerned primarily with the banalities of fornication. However, beneath this exterior dwells a religious writer who has created a series of commonplace characters – especially 'Rabbit' Angstrom of *Rabbit Run* (1960), *Rabbit Redux* (1971), *Rabbit Is Rich* (1981) and *Rabbit At Rest* (1990) – muddled and incapable of controlling their lives or loves, yet whose very failure or incompetence has its roots in their perceptions of the inevitability of our solitude, frailty and death. This awareness cuts them off from identifying themselves with the roles they are asked to play, plunges their lives into chaos and cuckoldry, due to their paralysing sense of horror and compassion, and yet makes them the embodiment of value in their environments.

Many of these figures are conservatives, like George Caldwell in *The Centaur* (1963), an idealistic teacher fascinated by knowledge, Piet Hanema in *Couples* (1968), who is inwardly pious, and who tries to preserve old-fashioned skills and perfectionism in the building trade, or Thomas Marshfield in *A Month of Sundays* (1975), who is a Christian minister and eschews existentialist, ritualist and humanist revisions of his religion. However, this conservatism is not seen as a defence or protection against experience, nor an ethical straitjacket keeping their actions within the conventional, but rather a refusal to accept the easy solutions of American optimistic pragmatism, and instead to preserve a sense of the mystery out of which we seek to relate to others and our circumstances by words and actions which are always inadequate and misleading. Out of this, Updike creates both comedy and pathos, especially from the essential strangeness of the confrontation with another's body and the meanings it has for us.

Updike himself has summarized his literary quest as being 'to give the mundane its beautiful due'. A consummate craftsman, this most thoughtful of contemporary American novelists has also been the most consistent – hardly a year goes by without another Updike offering, quite apart from his collections of poetry, literary essays and art criticism. Only rarely, however, does he step outside the parameters he seems so carefully to have set himself. *The Witches of Eastwick* (1984), while still set in suburbia, is a vamp, in which a group of women are seduced by no less a figure than Satan, brilliantly played by Jack Nicholson in a film version of the same title. *Brazil* (1994) is a retelling of the Tristan and Iseult story. Only in *Gertrude and Claudius* (2000) – a sort of prequel to Shakespeare's *Hamlet* – does he stray into recognizably modernist territory. Little of his recent work has excited positive critical attention, but for Updike, whose essentially Christian faith is brought out into the open in his semi-confessional memoir *Self-Consciousness* (1989), sales and acclaim are clearly not everything that matter.

Further reading

Other works include: *The Carpentered Hen and Other Tame Creatures* (poems, 1958); *The Poorhouse Fair* (novel, 1959); *Pigeon Feathers and Other Stories* (1962); *Telephone Poles and Other Poems* (1963); *Of the Farm* (novel, 1965); *Mid Point and Other Poems* (1969); *Bech: A Book* (episodic novel, 1970); *Museums and Women and Other Stories* (1972); *Marry Me* (1974); *Buchanan* (play, 1976); *The Coup* (1978); *Roger's Version* (1988); *Memoirs of the Ford Administration* (1992); *Collected Poems* (1993); *Villages* (2004); and two volumes of art criticism, *Just Looking* (1989) and *Still Looking* (2005). Joyce B. Markle, *Fighters and Lovers: Theme in the Novels of John Updike* (1973); Edward P. Vargo, *Rainstorms and Fire: Ritual in the Novels of John Updike* (1973); George W. Hunt, *John Updike and the Three Great Things: Sex, Religion and Art* (1985); James Plath, *Conversations with John Updike* (1994).

DAVID CORKER
(REVISED AND UPDATED BY THE EDITOR)

UTRILLO, Maurice

1883–1955

French artist

Born in Paris in 1883, Utrillo celebrated the city in his art throughout his life. The son of the painter Suzanne Valadon, Utrillo inherited the rich traditions of Impressionist and Post-Impressionist painting, yet his attitude to painting was personal and idiosyncratic in the extreme.

His early years were difficult and by the age of eighteen he was an alcoholic. In the beginning, painting was a therapeutic exercise and through this he discovered a commitment and talent that were born into him. He underwent no formal art education but emerged fully fledged with a mode of painting inspired by the Impressionist painter **Pissarro**, but which came naturally to him and which varied comparatively little throughout his life.

Utrillo's work presents an enigma for it is a unique combination of the sophisticated and the naive. He has often been referred to as a naive artist, yet his cityscapes, views of Parisian streets and buildings, show great competence and integrity. They are finely resolved works with no suggestion of slightness, incompetence or incompleteness. On the other hand Utrillo's subjects and style scarcely develop and on occasions he would paint from postcards. His technique was direct and decisive and his pigments were sometimes thickened with plaster.

In 1905 Utrillo found support from the dealer Sagot and his recognition began. He was increasingly respected until his final years, when taste moved away from his art somewhat. He exhibited at the Salon d'Automne in 1909 and four years later had his first one-man show. The apogee of his public recognition came in 1950 when he was chosen to represent France at the Venice Biennale. He died at Le Vesinet in 1955.

The Basilica of St Denis (1909) exemplifies the dense matted texture of his most powerful portraits of areas central or peripheral to Paris. While the frontal composition may derive from a postcard, Utrillo has given the image a gravity and grandeur appropriate to the subject; it is solemn, asymmetrical and decisive.

Further reading

See: A. Tabarant, *Utrillo* (1926); P. MacOrlan, *Utrillo* (1952); P. Pétrides, *Maurice Utrillo: L'Oeuvre Complète* (1959–62); W. George, *Utrillo* (1960); A. Werner, *Utrillo* (1981).

See also: Camille Pissarro.

JOHN MILNER

V

VALÉRY, Paul

1871–1945

French poet and thinker

Of mixed Italian and Corsican blood, Valéry was born in Sète, a Mediterranean port which was to inform his whole imaginary world as a poet. Already by the age of nineteen he had written between two and three hundred poems, was engaged in painting and fascinated by music (in particular that of **Wagner**) and architecture. Then, as a law student at the University of Montpellier, he added mathematics and physics to his interests. Moving to Paris he continued to write poetry until 1892, assiduously frequenting the milieu of the Symbolists, who, with **Mallarmé** as their focal point, sought to make poetry as pure, abstract and evocative as music. In his late teens Valéry also came under the spell of the aesthetic theories of Edgar Allan Poe, according to which the poet must always be aiming at the effect that he is going to create on the reader. But neither Poe nor the Symbolists offered Valéry a satisfactory account of the world of the emotions, and it became his credo that the intellect should take control. Giving up poetry he decided to devote himself to a rigorous exploration of the way in which 'the closed system that is the mind' functions.

To this end he read widely not only in philosophy but also in the sciences. Believing that it was physicists and mathematicians who held the key to an understanding of consciousness, he endeavoured to discover algebraic formulae which would express the constants and the variables of human reactions. But the main source for his researches was his own self. Abandoning all received ideas, his enquiry focused on the question 'Que peut un homme?' – 'Of what is a man capable?' Une Soirée avec Monsieur Teste (1894) presented a dialogue between Valéry and the strange character of Monsieur Teste, a fictional shadow employed to represent the intellect at its most abstract. Using a constant and constantly reflected self-awareness as his method, Teste attempts to transform even the inevitable weaknesses of the flesh and the knowledge of death into what he calls geometrical figures.

In his concern to establish a method of thinking Valéry next turned his attention to Leonardo da Vinci, whom he took as an exemplar of the universal mind. The Introduction à la méthode de Leonardo da Vinci (1895) establishes three stages of thought: a detailed observation of nature and man; the development of mental imagery, including the processes of induction and analogy; and, finally, construction. However, the core of his explorations into human possibilities was the famous Cahiers (2 vols, 1973–4), the notebooks to which, from 1894 until the end of his life, Valéry consigned the observations and ideas that he worked on in the early hours of each morning. Beside this formidable and perhaps unique enterprise, Montaigne's labyrinthine testings of himself, or **Gide's** fictional projections, seem digressive and self-indulgent. Valéry is not concerned with the contingent, surface individuality, but with what he calls *le moi pur*, later described in mathematical terms as the universal invariant, the pure functioning of the consciousness.

The author himself said that the *Cahiers* represented the best of him. Since they have been readily accessible to the public only since 1973, the full scale and portent of Valéry's activity is still being assessed. Before, it was widely accepted that between 1895 and 1912, when he again began to write poetry, there was a 'silence' broken only by one or two brilliant essays (including 'La Conquête allemande' of 1899, which prophesied the rise of German power). But the long poem which eventually emerged, and which immediately established Valéry as a leading poet, can now be seen in relation to a continuous intellectual activity. Working within the constraints of traditional form (which Valéry regarded as a necessary challenge), 'La Jeune Parque' (1917) – like the two collections that followed it, *Album de vers anciens* (1920) and *Charmes* (1922) – couples an intense cult of abstraction with an equally intense, palpitating sensuality. It is this, rather than any technical innovation, that marks Valéry's finest achievements as a poet.

With regard to 'La Jeune Parque', he claimed that the prolonged struggles with the combinatory qualities of language, the manipulation of the multiple possibilities of sound and sense inherent in words, were an important aspect of his understanding and mastery of himself. Although he insisted that his prime concern had been to exploit the musicality of verbal patterns, the poem is a profound examination of the working of consciousness in his symbolic human creation ('the young Fate'), its awakenings as she emerges from sleep, the gradual construction of her sense of identity, the physiological awareness of her sexuality and her simultaneous psychological reactions, and her recognition of recurrences and flux within her own being which reflect those of nature and interact with them.

Valéry's standing as a major poet was put beyond doubt with the publication of *Charmes*, which contained one of the most impressive pieces of the twentieth century, 'Le Cimetiére Marin'. Like 'La Jeune Parque', this poem springs initially from formal, musical preoccupations, but in this case it is the consciousness of a mature man at the height of his powers which is examined. Inserted into a diamantine Mediterranean setting, he experiences a fusion with nature which takes him to a peak of transcendence; but then, obeying the inevitable cyclical rhythms of nature, he drifts from the midday dazzle into a shadowed sense of mortality, until finally the lifting sea winds coincide with an invigorated acceptance of the limits of the human condition. The same coming-to-terms with the psyche through nature is sought elsewhere in the volume. 'Aurore' enacts the awakening of the poet in a garden at dawn; 'Le Rameur' brings together a rower's movement over water with his passage through time; and 'La Platane' and 'Palme' use trees as symbols of growth, of patience, and of the dual 'earth-rooted' heaven-seeking tendency of man.

Although there is evidence to suggest that Valéry continued to write poetry of a more experimental kind after 1922, he did not publish any. Instead he made his living as a critic and an essayist, the extraordinary breadth of his interests being attested in collected volumes such as *Variétés* (1924) and *Autres Rhumbs* (1927) and *Tel Quel* (1941). In 1925 he was elected to the French Academy, and in 1937 was appointed Professor of Poetics at the Collège de France. As a literary critic he was particularly forward-looking in his insistence on the impossibility of distinguishing between form and content, on taking a poem as an object – a view that has become a central tenet of much modern criticism. But if aesthetics were his profession, his relentless pursuit of his original question – '*Que peut un homme?*' – took him into widely different spheres. In this context three works, written in his favoured dialogue form, are of note. In the first, *Eupalinos* (1922), the shades of Socrates and Phaedrus evoke the architect Eupalinos as a model of the thinker-constructor who is obliged to pit himself bodily against intractable matter, and then shape it according to the laws of his own mind. Thus, by constructing out of nature the creator learns how to construct himself. In the companion *L'Ame et la danse* (1922), Valéry discovers in the dancer's art a further aspect of creativity: the capacity of the human being to transcend apparent limitations, to go beyond the self. The third, *L'Idée fixe* (1932), reintroduces Monsieur Teste, and reflects Valéry's attempt to understand the new physics of **Planck**, **Einstein**, **Schrödinger** and **Heisenberg**. Numbering several of the leading French physicists of the day among his friends, including Paul Langevin and Louis de Broglie, he hoped that the theories which had so revolutionized man's way of looking at the world would be applied to the complex living organism itself. Thus, Monsieur Teste, using his familiar *tabula rasa* technique, interrogates a doctor on a number of crucial issues in psychotherapy: the function of the senses, of memory, of suggestibility, the differences between group and individual behaviour, how to account for the individual's appetites and repugnances, the nature of dreams, which he finds more interesting for their formal structure than for any apparent symbolism; and throughout sees man as a being turned always to the future with a potential which is always capable of development. Interestingly, at the end of the dialogue, it is Einstein who is introduced as a modern example of the universal thinker idealistically seeking the secrets of the unity of nature.

If, summing up Valéry's varied achievements, one had to pin-point his exemplary importance in the modern world, it would be his role as a *maître à penser*. 'I work for those who come after me,' he said. His method was to formulate those precise, unequivocal questions which are at least capable of precise, unequivocal answers. He teaches, by example, how to think, the what to think being constantly ahead.

Further reading

Other works include: *Oeuvres I & II* (1957 and 1960); and, in translation, *The Collected Works of*

Paul Valéry (15 vols, 1956–75). See also: J. R. Lawler, *Lecture de Valéry* (1963); J. Robinson, *L'Analyse de l'esprit dans les Cahiers de Paul Valéry* (1963); Emilie Noulet, *Paul Valéry* (1950); W.N. Ince, *The Poetic Theory of Paul Valéry* (1970); Christine Crow, *Paul Valéry: Consciousness and Nature* (1972); C.G. Whiting, *Paul Valéry* (1979); Suzanne Guerlac, *Literary Polemics: Bataille, Satre, Valery, Breton* (1997); William Kluback, *Paul Valery: A Philosopher for Philosophers, the Sage* (1999).

MARGARET DAVIES

VAN DER POST, (Sir) Laurens
1906–95
South African author and traveller

Laurens van der Post came from a respectable Afrikaner family in South Africa's Orange Free State. He moved to Britain and became internationally famous as a best-selling writer, an authority on **C.G. Jung** as well as the Bushmen of the Kalahari Desert, a confidante of the British prime minister **Margaret Thatcher**, the heir to the British throne (Prince Charles) and also the leader of the Zulus, and a patron of the 'Wilderness' and environmental movements. He influenced and inspired countless men and women around the world.

After his death it was realized that he had always been a compulsive fantasist and mythomaniac. He was a superb storyteller, both on the page and in lecture halls, yet the stories he told were frequently either exaggerations, distortions or lies. Need this matter? His positive role was to lead people – Prince Charles was the perfect example – into areas they might not otherwise have explored, and this is one reason why in old age he was often described as a 'guru' or a mystic. He had a wide circle of devoted friends and followers who loved him dearly and never questioned his wisdom or his veracity.

His early years, as a journalist moving between South Africa and Britain, were unsuccessful, both professionally and personally. It was the Second World War which seems to have transformed him. After playing a part in the Allied liberation of Abyssinia (as always, the true details of van der Post's life as described by him are 'unreliable'), he was sent to the Far East where he spent more than three years in Japanese prison camps in Indonesia, somehow carrying off the deceit that he was a lieutenant colonel. He volunteered to stay on in Indonesia for two years after the war, trying to reconcile the Dutch to their imminent loss of empire.

After returning to Europe, he was sent by the British government on a modest research mission to Nyasaland (today Malawi) in Central Africa. This inspired an immensely successful book, *Venture to the Interior* (1952), which established his name and demonstrated his particular 'tone of voice', combining elegant prose, a sense of the exotic, and the exposition of high moral and spiritual values (which were not always evident in his own life).

This triumph led directly to his involvement with the Bushmen of Bechuanaland (today Botswana). He travelled there on several official missions, and then led his own expedition to 'find' this fast-declining and 'primitive' people, whom he chose to see in extreme Romantic terms: there was, he proposed, 'a cruelly denied and neglected first child of life, a Bushman, in each of us'.

These journeys eventually produced two travel books, two novels, a fantasized memoir and a television series, all of them enormously successful. Only after his death did it emerge that he was grossly exaggerating his expertise on, and experience of, the Bushmen.

In the meantime van der Post was writing fiction – again, very successfully – some of it based on his war experiences. He had first visited Japan as a cub reporter, in the company of his close friend the distinguished writer William Plomer, and after the war he bravely urged that the Japanese should be forgiven for their conduct.

His next influential role was to attach himself to the Swiss psychologist C.G. Jung, whom he admired unreservedly. His biography of Jung did much to introduce many people to a profound thinker whom they might otherwise have ignored (Prince Charles is again a good example).

From this eminence, van der Post's confidence knew no bounds. He travelled frequently (particularly in America and South Africa), fêted wherever he went. He ventured into politics, though remaining in the shadows. South Africa was of course his preoccupation, and though he hated apartheid and always spoke out bravely against it, he passionately opposed any suggestion of sanctions against his homeland. He undoubtedly was an influential friend of Mrs Thatcher.

He had no time for the African National Congress or **Nelson Mandela**; indeed, he was in many ways a typical South African white paternalist. He had never imagined that South Africa would embrace majority rule in his lifetime.

He attempted to play a part in the settlement of Rhodesia's UDI, but his claims of influence are not founded on fact. In old age his political meddling became more dangerous when he took up the cause of the Zulus and their leader Chief Buthelezi, whom he encouraged to defy the newly emerging South African state.

In these same last years, and as he identified himself with various environmental movements, his books became more 'mystical' and less effective, and their sales declined. He would be remembered above all for bringing to the attention of the world the plight of the Bushmen – in whose company he had in truth spent less than a fortnight and whose wonderful myths he had gathered not from them, as he claimed, but from a book written many years before by a German scholar.

Further reading

Other works include: *The Lost World of the Kalahari* (1958); *A Portrait of Japan* (1968); *A Story like the Wind* (1972); *Jung and the Story of Our Time* (1976); and *Yet Being Someone Other* (1982). See also J.D.F. Jones, *Storyteller: The Many Lives of Laurens van der Post* (2001).

J.D.F. JONES

VAN GOGH, Vincent

1853–90

Dutch artist

Son of a pastor, the young Van Gogh was placed in 1869 in the Dutch branch of the art dealers' firm, Goupil and Co., in The Hague. During the next seven years he journeyed variously to Paris and London carrying out his duties until finally dismissed for rudeness to his employers.

If Van Gogh was a man of sorrows it was because the abnormalities of his behaviour rendered him by turn violently excitable and then melancholically withdrawn. Those people who befriended him had extreme difficulty in maintaining their relationship so that the painter constantly found himself to be a social outcast. It is thought that the cause of his unacceptably intense moods derived from a lesion in the brain occurring at his birth. As his life progressed the problems became more acute until at the age of thirty-five he suffered his first attack of insanity.

Highly intelligent, an avid reader with a good command of four languages including English, Van Gogh had decided prior to his dismissal by Goupil that he would follow a higher calling, similar to that of his father. In 1877 he entered a small Evangelical College in Brussels, completing his training the following year but, because of his peculiar personality, failing the course. Of his own initiative he settled in that bleak part of Belgium known as the Borinage. In this coal-mining area reminiscent of that in **Zola's** book *Germinal*, Van Gogh became a lay preacher. At the same time he began frequently to make drawings of the people in the area. He was much influenced in this activity by his collection of engravings cut from contemporary English magazines, such as the *Graphic*, which commented upon the social problems of the working poor in industrial areas of Britain. Soon after, in 1882, while at Nuenen, Van Gogh painted the famous *Potato Eaters* which portrays a poor family at the meal table. The dramatic contrasts of light and dark required only a low

colour key and there is no hint of the colourist that the painter was to become.

By this time Van Gogh had realized his lack of aptitude for divine counselling and that he was better suited to the life of an artist. He left the church and settled for a time in Antwerp where he studied, among other works, those of Rubens. The appeal of these Baroque works probably lay in their warm colouring and lively movement. A further pleasure for the painter was his discovery of Japanese prints which he began to collect while at Antwerp. Their grace of line and simplicity of composition were as important to Van Gogh as they were to **Gauguin**.

It was not until the following year, 1886, when Van Gogh joined his brother Theo in Paris, that he finally met not only Gauguin but **Cézanne**, Bernard, Anguetin and **Pissarro** as well. While studying at Cormon's studio, Van Gogh, undergoing an immensely stimulating year, became interested in the flower paintings of Adolphe Monticelli, a Marseilles artist. Van Gogh experimented with flower pieces himself at this time, setting blues against complements of orange and playing with other such oppositions. These in conjunction with the use of an impasto technique strongly suggest a Monticelli influence. During the winter, however, Impressionism finally became apparent to the Dutchman who, in the spring of 1887, lightened and unified his palette while working out of doors with Bernard on the banks of the Seine at Asnières.

Nonetheless, Van Gogh still had the idea of starting a society of painters with a lifestyle he imagined to be like that of the Japanese: simple, homogeneous, warm and gracious. He travelled south in February looking for a suitable place and decided upon Arles in Provence. Here he painted some glorious spring pictures of orchards while he prepared a small house for the arrival of Gauguin. He had hopes that the master of the school of artists in Brittany could be induced to set up a similar arrangement in the south. Throughout the summer he corresponded with Gauguin urging upon him all the good reasons for complying with his request. At the same time he painted some remarkable pictures, arriving at expressive solutions with non-naturalistic colour as an important poetic element. He wrote of his interior *The All-Night Café* (1888) that he had 'tried to express the idea that the café is a place where one can ruin oneself, go mad or commit a crime'. The use of powerful reds, assertive blue greens and hot orange yellows gives the work an almost painful intensity. It was also during the summer that Van Gogh painted a series of views of the public gardens at Arles. He said he felt there the presence, along with that of other famous figures of the past, of Petrarch, who had lived not far away at Avignon. These paintings called the *Poets' Garden* were to hang in Gauguin's own room to express the idea of the master of today meeting in Arles with the masters from history.

Short of money, induced by the funds provided by Theo Van Gogh and perhaps preferring to winter in a warmer climate, Gauguin consented to Vincent's proposal and arrived in Arles in October. However, the relationship between Vincent and Gauguin proved no happier than previous ones and in December Gauguin acknowledged that he would have to go north again. At this point the Dutchman's sanity finally gave way and he entered the asylum at St Rémy. Between bouts of manic violence he continued to paint with acute control of colour and tone but with an increasing wildness of shape and form. Rolling mountains, waving cypress and olive repeat the whirling of sun and stars. The whole of nature, seen through the ferment of Van Gogh's temperament, takes on a tumultuous aspect.

To be nearer the ever comforting Theo, his new wife and small baby, also named Vincent, the painter entered another hospital, near Paris, at Auvers. Here he painted and wrote as long as he could. His last important painting was of black crows flying against a strip of sky, so dark in its blueness that it is almost black. It lowers heavily over a corn-field the colour of bile. The work expresses not only a psychological state of being but also the physical sensations resulting from extreme anxiety. At the same time Van Gogh felt it to be a projection of the energy of nature. A short while later, after these terrifying hours, Van Gogh wrote a letter to Theo stating that 'painters themselves are fighting more and more with their backs to the wall'. He finally could no longer face the notion of continued insanity and, according to a letter found in his pocket after his suicide, had come to accept the inevitable end with comparative tranquillity of mind. He shot himself in the chest, dying later from the wound on 29 July 1890.

Further reading

Other works include: *Le Pont de Langlois* (1888); *Pink Peach Trees* (1888); *Café at Night Arles* (1888); *The Postman Roulin* (1888); *Van Gogh's Chair* (1888–89); *Sun Flowers* (1888); *Starry Night* (1889); *Yellow Cornfield* (1889). See: *The Complete Letters of Van Gogh*, trans. J. Van Gogh-Bonger and C. de Dood (1958); Meyer Schapiro, *Vincent Van Gogh* (1950); A.M. Hammacher, *Vincent Van Gogh* (1961); *Selected Letters of Van Gogh*, ed. Mark Roskill (1963); J. Meier Graefe, *Vincent Van Gogh: A Biographical Study* (trans. J. Reece, 2 vols, 1922), Nagera, *Vincent Van Gogh: A Psychological Study* (1967); J. Hulsker, *The New Complete Van Gogh: Paintings, Drawings, Sketches: Revised and Enlarged Edition of the Catalogue Raisonné of the Works of Vincent van Gogh* (1996).

PAT TURNER

VARÈSE, Edgar Victor Achille Charles
1883–1965
French/US composer

Varèse was born in Paris, educated partly there and in Turin (his father was Piedmontese), then entered the Schola Cantorum in Paris in 1904. At the Schola he studied composition and conducting with d'Indy, counterpoint and fugue with Roussel, and Medieval and Renaissance music with Charles Bordes. In 1905 he was admitted to Widor's composition class at the Paris Conservatoire. From 1907 to 1913 Varèse lived in

Berlin where he earned his living mainly as a copyist, and met **Busoni**, Hofmannsthal, **Richard Strauss** and Romain Rolland. This period also coincided with his first marriage, which ended in divorce. He returned to Paris in 1913 and in 1915 was mobilized, but within the same year he was invalided out of the army. At the end of the year he sailed for New York, where he lived for most of his subsequent life, except for a period in Paris (1928–33), other trips to Europe and stays lasting a few months in New Mexico and Los Angeles. He married again in 1921 and became a US citizen in 1927.

Varèse spent a considerable amount of time and energy in activities related to music other than composition. From 1921 to 1927 he helped run the International Composers' Guild, which he founded with Carlos Salzedo. Varèse chose the works for the concerts of new music which the Guild organized. The following year (1928) Varèse founded the Pan American Association of Composers with Henry Cowell and Carlos Chavez. Most of his life Varèse conducted (and actually founded more than one choir), but he never made a career of conducting. He also gave lectures, classes and lessons from time to time, but he seems to have had only three serious students of composition: André Jolivet, Chou Wen-chung and Marc Wilkinson. He never earned much from his compositions and his output was small. At various times he received money from patrons (including the conductor Stokowski), but in 1933 he was refused a Guggenheim grant for research and the same year he applied unsuccessfully to the Bell Telephone Company for a post to research acoustics, film and radio. Varèse also submitted proposals elsewhere for research and technical collaboration but it was not until the 1950s, when he was already in his seventies, that he won practical co-operation and was able to produce his last two major works, *Déserts* and *Le Poème électronique*. For *Déserts* he recorded tapes in Philadelphia factories, then worked on these tapes in the studio of French Radio in Paris (1954). And in 1957–8 he worked in the

Philips studios at Eindhoven, Holland, on *Le Poème électronique*, commissioned for **Le Corbusier's** Pavilion for Philips at the Brussels World Fair in 1958.

It is a cliché to say that Varèse was ahead of his time and that he could not realize his intentions fully before the availability of tape and the development of electronic studios after the Second World War. But his works of the 1920s (notably the three pieces for various ensembles – *Hyperprism*, 1922–3, *Octandre*, 1923, and *Intégrales*, 1923–5) are perfectly realized in their medium, even if the instrumentalists are expected to be mechanically precise and brilliant rather than pliant or expressive. Certainly Varèse had a sense of artistic isolation, but it is easy to suspect that he wrote relatively little for personal rather than for strictly musical reasons. He suffered prolonged bouts of depression: *Déserts* is, among many other things, the document of his despair after a period of fourteen years when he completed no work at all. Yet as a man he was popular. He charmed people and seems to have enjoyed the effect he could have on them. In Greenwich Village, New York, as well as in international musical circles, he was known as a generous and hospitable man.

Varèse believed that genius was romantic: a work was only classic after it had been accepted. He told people that he was not a musician but that he worked 'with rhythms, frequencies and intensities'. Yet he was opposed to all systems and despised the twelve-note method of **Schoenberg**. He admired **Debussy** for 'balancing with almost mathematical equilibrium timbres against rhythms and textures – like a fantastic chemist'. Varèse's own music epitomizes an analytic perception of sound, in which not only pitch and duration, but attack, decay, dynamic and timbre are all detached from traditional conceptions like melody, harmony and orchestration, and are made equivalent subjects of compositional or 'artistic' choice. The most precise control of these factors could be achieved by electronic means. Yet it may be argued that all art necessitates compromise, and in works like *Hyperprism*, for nine wind instruments and percussion, or *Ionisation* (1931), for thirteen percussionists, there is no feeling that instruments or instrumentalists are being used as substitutes. Chou Wen-chung observed that there seems to be a fundamental difference between Varèse's works for instruments and those which include voices. The atmosphere of picturesque mystery and threatening drama in *Ecuatorial* (1934) for bass voices and ensemble, and in his final work, *Nocturnal* (1961, completed by Chou Wen-chung) for solo soprano, bass voices and orchestra, harks back to the world of Debussy and French symbolism, which is found in *Offrandes* (1921) for soprano and chamber orchestra, and in an even earlier song, 'Un grand sommeil noir' (1906).

Most of Varèse's music before 1920 was lost or destroyed; much of it is supposed to have been burnt in a fire in 1918, but Varèse suppressed some works himself. The huge orchestral piece *Amériques* (1920–1, revised mostly by 1929) already shows the essentials of Varèse's musical character. *Intégrales*, for eleven wind instruments and percussion, was the first work to be described as 'spatial'. In 1929, if not earlier, Varèse said that he wanted his music to be projected, literally, in space, like beams of light coming from different sources. He achieved this vision once – in *Le Poème électronique*, which was relayed through over 400 speakers placed along the parabolic and hyperbolic curves of the Philips Pavilion at the Brussels World Fair in 1958. Composers like **Boulez**, **Messiaen**, **Stockhausen** and **Xenakis** have long acknowledged Varèse as one of the seminal influences on developments in music since the Second World War. In 1950 Varèse lectured at the Darmstadt holiday courses, which set the latest fashions in avant-garde music. Of the Darmstadt composers, it was perhaps Luigi Nono whose music related most specifically to Varèse's in its austere and rugged surface, as well as the way attention shifts among different musical elements, so that one in particular (whether rhythm, timbre and so on) is selected for attention while the others are relatively inactive. In America in the 1950s Varèse became a rediscovered hero. But his individuality – sometimes rebarbative – has generally deterred composers from drawing from his example, and the more recent return to expressive melody and lyrical qualities in new music are far from Varèse's heroic stance. Yet his concept of music as 'organized sound' is likely to prove one of the most significant musical ideas of the last century.

Further reading

Other works include: *Arcana* (1926–7) for large orchestra; *Density 21.5* (1936) for solo flute. See: F. Ouellette, *Edgar Varèse* (1966, trans. 1968); Louise Varèse, *Varèse: A Looking-Glass Diary, Volume 1: 1883–1928* (1972). Analysis of Varèse's work has appeared in: *The Score*, No. 19 (Marc Wilkinson, March 1957); *Perspectives of New Music* (Gunther Schuller, Spring 1965; Milton Babbitt, Spring 1966; Chou Wen-chung, Fall 1966; John Strawn, Fall 1978); *Musical Quarterly*, Vol. 52, No. 2 (Chou Wen-chung, 1966); *Music Review*, Vol. XXVIII, No. 4 (Arnold Whittall, 1967); *Music and Musicians* (Adrian Jack, November and December 1975); J.W. Bernard, *The Music of Edgar Varèse* (1987); Alan Clayson, *Edgard Varèse* (2002).

ADRIAN JACK

VARGAS LLOSA, Mario

1936–

Peruvian novelist, playwright and critic

Mario Vargas Llosa was born in Arequipa, Peru, but was educated in Cochabamba, Bolivia, from 1937 to 1945 after his parents separated. He then moved to Piura in northern Peru. When his father returned to family life, Vargas Llosa was sent to the Leoncio Prado, a military academy outside Lima, to become a man, which would become the background to his scandalous first novel. Vargas Llosa always wanted to become a writer, but began as a journalist and broadcaster while studying at Lima's San Marcos University. In 1958 he won a scholarship to study for a doctorate at Madrid University, which he finally published in 1971, a meticulous study of his erstwhile friend **Gabriel García Márquez's** fiction (Vargas Llosa has refused to republish *García Márquez: historia de un deicidio*, and it hasn't been translated into English). He moved to Paris and then London, where he wrote and taught in different colleges at London University. He still lives part of the year in London, with his second wife, while their three grown-up children live around the world. Vargas Llosa has dual Spanish–Peruvian citizenship (with a flat in Madrid and a house in Barranco, Lima), and often teaches at prestigious universities. He is a brilliant lecturer, a wide-ranging columnist and continues to write immaculately crafted novels.

His first story appeared in 1956, collected in a book *Los jefes*, 1958 (*The Cubs and Other Stories*, 1980), but it was his first novel *La ciudad y los perros*, 1962 (*The Time of the Hero*, 1966) that catapulted Vargas Llosa to literary fame, winning the prestigious Bibliotecta Breve prize in Spain in 1962. A thousand copies were burnt in public by the military because he had defamed the military academy. The title refers to cheating and murder in the Leoncio Prado where the pupils are called *perros* (dogs). There are local characters from all Peruvian social classes, from a budding cowardly poet to a sensitive provincial officer to the slum-kid-turned-leader called El Jaguar. Most impressive is the unidentified monologue that traverses the novel. Combined with brilliant realism of place and dialogue, Vargas Llosa had written a formidable critique of *machismo* in Lima society. The first edition had a map of Peru, and a photo of the actual school. He had written this novel from abroad, and had sought the controversy it generated.

Vargas Llosa began writing with a Sartrian concern; fiction was serious and should explore what Peruvian society repressed. This earnest politicized writing, based on meticulous research and fine functional prose (Vargas Llosa has penned a study of **Flaubert**, *The Perpetual Orgy*, 1986), emerged in a critical realist vein that lasted until the late 1970s. This period mirrors his involvement and then

rejection of **Castro's** revolution, and a general drift to the neo-liberal right. There's a discernible shift in tone, but not in teasing technique and realism, to more humorous novels. In the 1990s he reverted to his more serious phase, moving beyond Peruvian topics. Behind all his writing is a seamless crafting of the novel in terms of plot, character and suspense. He has combined readability, with serious concerns that few have matched in Latin American fiction.

The first earnest phase includes his second novel, *La casa verde*, 1965 (*The Green House*, 1968), a tour de force of technical innovation and realism about the setting up of a brothel, the Green House, in Piura, with long sections in Peru's Amazonian jungle region. An overlapping time-scheme throws characters back and forwards in unidentifiable ways where an Indian girl ends up as a whore and a Japanese trader a leper. It won the prestigious literary prize, the Rómulo Gallegos, in 1967. It was followed by a political analysis of the Odría dictatorship in Peru called *Conversación en La Catedral*, 1970 (*Conversation in the Cathedral*, 1975), which refers to bar conversations about political corruption. A later epic work about a rebellion in northern Brazil, *La guerra del fin del mundo*, 1981 (*The War of the End of the World*, 1984) debated Latin American utopianism and fanaticism.

Vargas Llosa's second but equally realistic mode began with a farce, *Pantaleón y las visitadoras*, 1973 (*Captain Pantoja and the Special Service*, 1978), set in the jungle near Iquitos, about furnishing whores to sex-starved soldiers. This lighter tone took off with his 1983 best-seller based on his own affair when eighteen years old with his thirty-two-year-old aunt, *La tía Julia y el escribidor*, 1977 (*Aunt Julia and the Scriptwriter*, 1982). It revolves around a soap-opera broadcaster, with many samples of his mad plots. Further novels in this vein involve his recurrent character Lituma, a policeman from *La casa verde* with common sense but not much culture, in *¿Quién mató a Palomino Molero?* (1986, *Who Killed Palomino Molero?*, 1987). Around a sadistic murder of a half-caste (*cholo*) bolero singer, Vargas Llosa brilliantly recreates Peruvian racism and coastal life in Piura. Lituma re-appears in *Lituma en los Andes*, 1993 (*Death in the Andes*, 1993), delving into Andean Peruvian identity during the bloody Sendero Luminoso revolt. *Historia de Mayta* (1984, *The Real Life of Alejandro Mayta*, 1986) explores a homosexual revolutionary who fails (Vargas Llosa often fictionalizes fanatics). Most amusing is his 1988 *Elogio de la madrastra* (*In Praise of the Stepmother*, 1990) where a boy seduces his stepmother, told with full accounts of their fantasy lives and coloured illustrations of paintings by Titian and **Bacon**. A follow-up in 1997 was *Los cuadernos de Don Rigoberto*, (*The Notebooks of Don Rigoberto*, 1998).

In 1990 Vargas Llosa stood as presidential candidate in Peru and was defeated by the fugitive Alberto Fujimori. Vargas Llosa's entry into politics as a neo-liberal failed, but led to his account of his life as a writer with political ambitions, *El pez en el agua: memorias* (1993, *A Fish in the Water: Memoirs*, 1994). He has always chronicled Peruvian and Latin American life from this independent angle, ruffling many feathers. He speaks his mind, and cares little about being ostracized by the left. His best essays can be read in *Making Waves* (1996).

He returned to his more serious mode in the late 1990s with a detailed exposure of the Trujillo dictatorship in *La fiesta del Chivo* (2000, *The Feast of the Goat*, 2001). More recently, he has explored, in alternating chapters, **Gauguin's** last years and his grandmother, the revolutionary feminist Flora Tristan, in *El paraíso en la otra esquina* (2003, *The Way to Paradise*, 2003). He is also a playwright, and has written an untranslated study of Peru's great writer on indigenous matters, *La utopía arcaica: José María Arguedas y las ficciones del indigenismo*, 1996.

Further reading

See: Charles Rossman and Alan Warren Friedman (eds) *Mario Vargas Llosa: A Collection of Critical Essays* (1978); Dick Gerdes, *Mario Vargas Llosa* (1985); Efraín Kristal, *Temptation of the Word. The Novels of Mario Vargas Llosa* (1998).

JASON WILSON

VAUGHAN WILLIAMS, (Sir) Ralph
1872–1958
English composer

Vaughan Williams was slow to make an impression as a composer. His first published work, the very successful song 'Linden Lea', did not appear until 1902, and as late as 1908–10 he went to Paris to complete his studies under **Ravel**, having been previously the pupil of Parry and Stanford in London and of **Bruch** in Berlin. However, by the time he went to Paris the main features of his style were already formed. He had for some years been collecting English folk songs – his volume of *Folksongs from the Eastern Counties* was published in 1908 – and he had made use of this material in such utterly characteristic pastoral impressions as the orchestral *In the Fen Country* (1904). What he learned from Ravel was certainly not technique, for he could never boast anything like Ravel's precise craftsmanship, but confidence to continue along the path already mapped out. The Paris period saw not only his first important chamber work, the String Quartet in G minor (1908), but also his first symphony, *A Sea Symphony* with soloists and chorus (1909), and three other important compositions: the song cycle *On Wenlock Edge* setting Housman for tenor and piano quintet (1909), the inventive overture to *The Wasps* (1909) and the *Fantasia on a Theme of Thomas Tallis* (1910).

This last work was remarkable for its rich interplay of different string groups – two orchestras and a quartet – and also for its use of Tudor music, which Vaughan Williams had come to appreciate as musical editor of the *English Hymnal* (1906). He made a more direct return to the world of Tallis and Byrd in his Mass in G minor for unaccompanied chorus (1920–1), but the pervasive influence of Tudor music is to be found in his very distinctive harmonic style, which had its origins also in the folk music he continued to collect, to arrange, and to use in such works as *A London Symphony* (1913) and *A Pastoral Symphony*, with soprano or tenor soloist (1921).

From this point his style was more or less fixed. He produced occasional surprises, notably in the aggressive and forceful manner of his Fourth Symphony (1931–4), but generally his music is marked by a flowing melodic ease, by his unusual handling of consonant harmony, and by moods of pastoral rambling or religious serenity. After **Elgar's** death in 1934 he was regarded as the outstanding British composer of his day and he produced a large quantity of the expected choral music, ranging from festival oratorios to psalms and anthems for the Anglican church. There were also five more symphonies, among which the *Sinfonia antartica* for wordless female voices and orchestra (1949–52) was derived from music he had written for the film *Scott of the Antarctic* (1948). In addition, he turned during this later period to the composition of opera, beginning with *The Shepherds of the Delectable Mountains* (1922), a one-act treatment of an episode from Bunyan which was eventually incorporated in his full-length 'morality' *The Pilgrim's Progress* (1906–51). This major testament was found undramatic when it at last reached the stage in 1951, and neither of Vaughan Williams's other big operas, *Hugh the Drover* (1924) and *Sir John in Love* (1924–8, after *The Merry Wives of Windsor*), has proved successful. His setting of **Synge's** *Riders to the Sea* (1925–32), in which he found a subject better suited to the slow speed of his music's movement, is the most effective of his operas.

Vaughan Williams enjoyed a close friendship with **Holst** from 1895 until the latter's death in 1934, and each of them profited from criticism and understanding offered by the other. During his lifetime Vaughan Williams also had a great influence on younger English composers, but since his death he has been probably more realistically estimated as a curious offshoot from the tree of music and not a main branch.

Further reading

Other works include: *The Lark Ascending* for violin and orchestra (1914–20); *Job*, ballet (1930); *Fantasia on 'Greensleeves'* for orchestra (1934); *Five Tudor Portraits* for soloists, choir and orchestra (1935); *The Poisoned Kiss*, play with music (1936); *Dona nobis pacem* for soloists, choir and orchestra (1936); *Serenade to Music* for sixteen voices and orchestra (1938); Symphony No. 5 (1938–43); Symphony No. 6 (1944–7); Symphony No. 8 (1953–5); Symphony No. 9 (1956–7). Writings: *National Music* (1934); *Heirs and Rebels* (1959). See: Michael Kennedy, *The Works of Ralph Vaughan Williams* (1964); Ursula Vaughan Williams, *R.V.W.: A Biography of Ralph Vaughan Williams* (1964); Roy Douglas, *Working with R.V.W.* (1972); A. Frogley (ed.) *Vaughan Williams Studies* (1996); L. Foreman (ed.) *Ralph Vaughan Williams in Perspective* (1998); S. Heffer, *Vaughan Williams* (2000).

PAUL GRIFFITHS

VEBLEN, Thorstein Bunde
1857–1929
US economist and social critic

Despite his assumption of a guise of scientific detachment and objectivity, Veblen's writings form an excoriating critique of American society between 1870 and 1925 and, more generally, document the triumph of 'imbecile institutions' over reason in human affairs.

Veblen was born on a farm and was brought up in highly insular Norwegian communities in Wisconsin and Minnesota. In 1884 he received his doctorate from Yale, but his agnosticism debarred him from teaching philosophy and it was not until 1892 that he received a fellowship in economics at the University of Chicago, where he remained until 1906. Subsequently, Veblen taught at Stanford and Missouri and in 1918 moved to New York where for a year he was a contributing editor to the *Dial* and taught at the New School for Social Research until 1924. The last years of his life were spent in isolation and near-poverty in California.

Although he was formally an economist, Veblen was actually a true inter-disciplinary scholar who drew on a wealth of archaeological, anthropological, sociological and linguistic knowledge. His students pointed him out as 'the last man who knows everything' and **Einstein** described him as one of the world's great political writers, but despite much acclaim he did not receive an academic rank in any way commensurate with his reputation.

Veblen's departure from both Chicago and Stanford resulted from a combination of his scorn for academic boosterism and his refusal to cover his extramarital affairs with the conventional blanket of secrecy. For most of his life he resolutely avoided formal political commitments, but he twice became a cult-figure of the liberal left and, during the 'Red Scare' of 1919–20, was listed by governmental agencies as a dangerous radical. However, with the economic recovery and boom of the 1920s, Veblen's gleeful warnings of possible economic collapse appeared wrong-headed and irrelevant. Ironically enough, Veblen, the master of incisive irony, died complaining of neglect a few months before the stock market collapse of 1929 ushered in the world depression he had long predicted.

Veblen was a **Darwinist** in that he felt that both biological and social evolution were characterized by blind, purposeless change or drift. Given this conviction, he rejected the **Marxian** interpretation of historical development as teleological and hence unscientific and utopian, and charged mainstream economists with dealing in neat abstractions while resolutely avoiding consideration of the real factors impinging on the working of the economy. Economic writings were underpinned by conceptions of such putative 'natural' rights as the right to the indefeasible ownership and use of property. These outdated metaphysical conceptions were inappropriate in an era of machine production and their employment by economists served to legitimate and sanctify the economic dominance of businessmen and financier tycoons – the captains of industry – who, in Veblen's view, actually produced little but waste, corruption and exploitation.

Veblen's first two books, *The Theory of the Leisure Class* (1899) and its more specialized economic coda, *The Theory of Business Enterprise* (1904), provided a mordantly witty empirical documentation of these processes. Economic production in capitalist societies was governed by considerations of profit rather than of the usefulness or serviceability of the goods produced. Such production of fripperies and inessentials catered to the appetite for wasteful, conspicuous consumption produced by individuals' desire to win repute by vainglorious display and emulation of the style of life of those above them. Veblen drew a sharp distinction between socially useful 'industrial' occupations and non-productive, 'pecuniary' occupations. He deplored the permeation of American society by the spirit of business enterprise – expressed in chicanery, fraud, self-aggrandizement and predation – and in *The Higher Learning in America* (1918) castigated this spirit as manifested in the 'businesslike' conduct of American universities.

From 1914 Veblen's writings became more topical and more overtly political. In *Imperial Germany and the Industrial Revolution* (1915) and *An Inquiry into the Nature of Peace* (1917) he analysed the causes and implications of Germany's rapid emergence as an industrial and military giant and attempted to assess the possibility that the world war might end in a settlement conducive to lasting peace. His conclusions were pessimistic and perceptive, indeed he forecast that the newly industrialized, militaristic, dynastic nations of Germany and Japan would join forces and provoke an even greater world conflict. The Bolshevik Revolution in Russia led Veblen to hope that the 'vested interests' might similarly be overthrown in America, and the tone of his later writings became more rancorous as his hopes in this direction were dashed.

In personal encounters Veblen was generally extremely uncommunicative and he resolutely refused to subordinate himself to authority, conventions, personal attachments or dogmatic systems of thought. Almost inadvertently he made disciples, but he established no 'Veblenian' school. The institutional economists, who insisted on studying the real-life working of the economy, came closest to being such. Nonetheless, his influence was far-ranging, and is acknowledged in the works of (among many others) the economist **J.K. Galbraith** and the maverick sociologist C.W. Mills. To employ a term which Veblen coined in a different context, his reputation has to some extent suffered 'the penalty of taking the lead' – many of his ideas and concepts have passed into common intellectual parlance and have been borrowed by others with scant, or no, acknowledgment.

Further reading

The *Collected Works*, ed. Peter Cain, were published by Routledge in 1994. Other individual works include: *The Instinct of Workmanship* (1914); *The Vested Interests and the Common Man* (1919); *The Place of Science in Modern Civilization* (1919); *The Engineers and the Price System* (1921); *Absentee Ownership* (1923); *Essays in Our Changing Order* (1934). See: Joseph Dorfman, *Thorstein Veblen and His America* (1934); David Riesman, *Thorstein Veblen* (1953); Douglas F. Dowd, *Thorstein Veblen* (1966); John P. Diggins, *The Bard of Savagery* (1978); John M. Whitworth, *The Insubordinate Mind* (1981); Michael Spindler, *Veblen and Modern America: Revolutionary Iconoclast* (2002); Rick Tilman (ed.) *The Legacy of Thorstein Veblen* (2003).

JOHN WHITWORTH

VELDE, Henri van de

1863–1957

Belgian architect and designer

One of the most influential of Art Nouveau designers and theorists, van de Velde was outstanding for his versatility and style in many fields: architecture, interior design, furniture, painting, typography, dress and ceramics. Trained as a painter, he achieved recognition in Belgium during the 1890s through his typographical designs for the magazines *Van Nu en Straks*, developing a revolutionary linear abstract style that was to be widely imitated. It was at this time that he conceived a strong admiration for the work of **William Morris**, whose ideals inspired

him to abandon painting for the applied arts. In 1893 he embarked on the self-taught study of architecture. The completion of his own country house, the Villa Bloemenwerf, at Uccle near Brussels, two years later gave him an international reputation. The building exemplified many of his ideas: the straightforward use of materials with the constructional methods revealed, the rejection of historical styles in favour of an unornamented vernacular manner (comparable to buildings by the Arts and Crafts architects in England), and the organization by the architect of every detail within the building, including the furniture, kitchenware and even, in this case, the lady of the house's clothing. This care sprang from his belief that the quality of daily life was to a great extent shaped by the standard of design of ordinary artefacts, and from his determination to make his art socially useful.

'Art,' he declared, 'must conquer the machine.' In common with many other designers and architects working in an increasingly technological culture van de Velde doubted whether mechanical means of production could be reconciled with the maintenance of artistic individuality and excellence. Morris had been stimulated to return to archaizing designs and hand-craftmanship, but he and his followers, generally sympathetic to socialist ideas, were then faced with the inevitable costliness and inaccessibility of their productions. Van de Velde, a supporter of the Belgian Workers' Party, encountered the same paradox. Although he criticized the English Arts and Crafts movement for the narrowness of its potential market, and wanted to make his work more widely available, most of his architectural designs, both before and after his move to Germany in 1898, were executed for wealthy patrons. These included four rooms for Samuel Bing's Galerie de l'Art Nouveau (1896), the Havana Cigar Store, Haby's Barber's Store and other work in Berlin around 1900; the Art School at Weimar (1904–11), where he was the first director, the Villa Hohenof (1908) and the Werkbund Theatre in Cologne (1914). In 1917 he moved to Switzerland, and in 1921 to Holland, where he designed the Kröller-Müller Museum, Otterlo (1937–54), another private foundation. In 1925 he returned to Belgium.

In his Berlin designs van de Velde moved towards a more ponderous manner, with the slow curving forms and elaborately original decoration associated with Art Nouveau. In his later German work he experimented with a sparer functional style, with much use of white in interiors, and, although he was always distinguished by a feeling for consciously decorative elegance, in his final work he approached the spirit of International Modern. Two principles, however, constantly guided his teaching (apart from Weimar, in 1925 he founded the School of Architecture in Brussels, and taught at the University of Ghent between 1926 and 1936) and his designs. First, the importance of line, which, he insisted, must express the internal structure and 'force' of the object of which it is part, and must alone constitute the work's decorative quality; and, second, the need for the artist to invent a wholly original art from his own sensibility, rather than to re-use the language of the past.

Further reading

Other works include: *Jéblaiement d'art* (1894); *L'Art futur* (1895); *Kunstgewerbliche Laienpredigten* (1902); *Die Renaissance in modernen Kunst* (1901); *Les Formules de la beauté architectonique moderne* (1916); *Story of My Life* (1962). See also: K.E. Osthaus, *Van de Velde, Leben und Schaffen des Kunstlers* (1920); *Henri Van de Velde* (Brussels, Palais des Beaux Arts Catalogue, 1963); A.M. Hammacher, *Die Welt Henry van de Velde* (1967); H. Kreistl and G. Himmelleber, *Die Kurs des deutschen Möbels* (Vol. III, 1973); Klaus-Jurgen Sembach, *Henry van de Velde* (1990).

GILES WATERFIELD

VERDI, Giuseppe

1813–1901

Italian composer

The son of an innkeeper and a spinner, born in the tiny hamlet of Le Roncole, near Busseto in Parma, Verdi always stressed his humble origins, sometimes at the expense of the truth: the humbler his birth, the more dramatic would seem his ascent to spectacular success. He also insisted throughout his life that he had enjoyed no regular education. In actual fact he received a basic humanistic training at the Busseto *ginnasio*, formerly the local Jesuit school, which reopened in the year of Verdi's enrolment (1823); the teaching of the humanities was entrusted to Canon Pietro Seletti, who was also an amateur musician. Verdi was taught the rudiments of music, and organ playing, in his native village but regular music lessons began only in the autumn of 1822 with Ferdinando Provesi, a leading figure in Busseto's musical life. Soon Verdi was able to assist and deputize for his teacher in his various capacities as organist and head of the local Philharmonic Society (founded in 1816 jointly by Provesi and Antonio Barezzi, a rich Bussetan merchant). For this institution Verdi composed vocal pieces (arias, duets, trios), *sinfonie* (in the Italian sense of that term), virtuoso piano pieces and, on his own (perhaps somewhat mocking) later admission, 'marches for brass band by the hundred'. Also from this period came various pieces of church music, including a *Stabat Mater*.

By 1830 it was clear that the young musician's talent required further, less provincial teaching. An application to the Milan Conservatory was rejected, mainly on the grounds that Verdi was over-age and not a citizen of the Lombardo-Veneto kingdom, although the examiners' report bears witness to his talent for composition. But with financial support from Barezzi – who had in the meantime become Verdi's benefactor – private lessons were begun with Vincenzo Lavigna, former *maestro al cembalo* at La Scala, Milan. These, according to Verdi, consisted mostly of exercises in strict contrapuntal writing, although we learn from contemporary documents that *composizione ideale* (free composition) was also part of the training. At the same time Verdi established connections with a group of amateur musicians, mostly from the Milanese nobility, called the Philharmonic

Society. Pietro Massini, who taught singing and was director of the society, soon detected talent in the young man, and under his guidance Verdi prepared performances of Haydn's *Creation* (April 1834) and Rossini's *Cenerentola* (April 1835). In July 1835 Verdi returned to Busseto to become, the following March, the town's music master, a job which was alien to his temperament and inclinations, now decidedly turned towards opera.

Between January and September 1836 Verdi wrote an operatic work, originally entitled *Rocester*, which after various revisions was eventually performed at La Scala in 1839 under the title *Oberto, conte di San Bonifacio*. This first opera reveals the various models (Donizetti, Mercadante, especially perhaps Bellini) to which the composer had been exposed during the – relatively long – period of composition and reworking. The moderate success of *Oberto* encouraged Bartolomeo Merelli, the impresario of La Scala, to offer Verdi a contract for two other operas, the first of which happened, of necessity, to be a comic one: *Un giorno di regno* (1840), based on the revision of an old libretto by Felice Romani, was one of Verdi's rare fiascos, and he returned to the comic vein only much later in his career.

But the next opera, based on a new libretto by Temistocle Solera, marked the beginning of Verdi's triumphant ascent. *Nabucco* (1842), realized through a few elementary contrasts and with an important role for the chorus, owes its success to a perfect match between the dramatic conception – a vast biblical fresco – and the musical language in which this is expressed. The next opera, *I Lombardi alla prima crociata* (1843), is based on the same pattern (though with a different plot articulation) and, not by chance, is also on a Solera libretto and first performed at La Scala. For the smaller, more intimate theatre of La Fenice, Venice, Verdi composed *Ernani* (1844), his first encounter with a **Victor Hugo** play. Here the drama centres on the conflicts between three male voices (tenor, baritone and bass) fighting for possession of a soprano; the 'abstract' quality of the characters and the action, developed almost exclusively through solo and ensemble set numbers, is emphasized by the absolute pre-eminence of the vocal writing.

With these operas Verdi established the basic patterns around which he worked in the following years. The immediate, enormous success of *Nabucco* and *Ernani* brought him to the forefront of the international operatic scene, and obliged him to fulfil demands for new scores from many of the most important theatres of Italy and abroad. In a period of about six years, from 1844 to 1850, he composed – or reworked – no fewer than twelve operas, gradually becoming aware of the necessity to realize a dramatic unity by musical means, of establishing relationships at the musical level between dramatically significant points in the action. He soon concluded that a motif announcing the appearance on stage of a major character (as in *I due Foscari*, 1845) was too simple and basically inarticulate; it was only on his encounter with Shakespeare, in the setting of *Macbeth* (1847), that we see the first successful attempt at solving the problem. From *Luisa Miller* (1849) until the end of his career, Verdi adopted a compositional procedure totally unknown in Italian tradition: he sketched the entire score on a small number of staves, notating only the vocal line(s), bass part and essential instrumental connective tissue. This 'continuity draft' helped him to establish musical connections between the various moments of the drama; in this way the set numbers, instead of being the basic dramatic unity (as they had been in previous Italian opera), became the means of establishing the duration of a section, a necessary tassel, outside of which, or even within which, the fundamental elements of the musical language were employed as powerful vehicles of dramatic conflicts.

Thus *Rigoletto* (1851) and *La traviata* (1853), based respectively on Hugo's *Le Roi s'amuse* and **Dumas** *fils*'s *La Dame aux camélias*, are directional music dramas in which the action evolves mainly through the characters' development, and particularly through their conflicts; set pieces (mostly duets) and freer musical structures (*arioso*, recitative and *scene*, variously articulated) alternate in equal proportions, forming a balanced, tensely poised whole. In *Il trovatore* (1853), on the other hand, Verdi for the last time builds his score almost exclusively through set pieces, a structure fully in accordance with the elusive nature of the plot and the characters' lack of development; structural symmetries and correspondences therefore dominate.

The central period of Verdi's output bears two distinct features: the relationships of his musical theatre to French *grand opéra* and the pre-eminence of political themes. (Concerning the latter, the development of political content in the operas parallels the composer's position in his country. The early works provided several choruses of a very 'singable' character which gained immense popularity and became vehicles of Italian patriotic feeling. As Verdi became an emblematic figure – as well as a member of the first Italian parliament, at Cavour's request – so political themes as such became central to his plots.) *Les Vêpres siciliennes* (1855) is a full-scale (though not altogether satisfactory) experiment with the French genre; *Simon Boccanegra* (1857; thoroughly reworked in 1881) is an opera where the amorous element has a decidedly secondary role, the plot being built on conflicts between classes and personalities struggling for power – hence the necessity to experiment with new kinds of musical language and, especially, new methods of structural articulation. *Un ballo in maschera* (1859), on a revised libretto by the famous French dramatist Eugène Scribe, combines and blends a basically Italian organization with certain essentially French characteristics and musical features; unity is achieved mainly through a masterful handling of the overall structure of the score, and through the composer's developing skill in fusing light and serious musical elements. *La forza del destino*, written for the Imperial Theatre of St Petersburg in 1862 and revised for La Scala in 1869, exploits a tendency – typical of *grand opéra* – for small, isolated episodes: the opera

contains, among other things, the first entirely comic character in Verdi's mature theatre, the monk Fra Melitone. Yet again *La forza* invents new types of musical organization for the set numbers, in particular employing articulation in the orchestral part rather than the voices. In *Don Carlos* (based on Schiller's play), written for the Paris Opéra in 1867 and much revised later, Verdi once again places the dramatic emphasis on conflicts of power and of political conception, the one influencing and eventually determining the other, thus creating the most complex of his dramatic structures. *Aida* (first performed at Cairo's newly opened opera house in 1871) is in fact an 'Italianization' of the *grand opéra* structure, a fusion of personal conflict and scenic display: the clash between individuals and power structures is again the unifying factor in the drama, and is matched at the musical level by an equally well-measured organization.

After *Aida* Verdi's increasing pessimism over the Italian musical scene, the influence of German music and consequent lack of national musical integrity, as well as his despair over the distortions which conventional performance practice caused to his precise view of music theatre, caused a halt in operatic composition.

In 1874, however, came the *Messa di requiem*, composed to celebrate the first anniversary of the death of Alessandro Manzoni. In this work Verdi's pessimistic vision of man in relation to his fellow beings is transferred to the problem of death and the hereafter. The *Requiem*'s remarkable blend of various influences (from **Berlioz's** *Grande Messe des morts* to 'classical' polyphonic forms such as the figue) creates a uniquely coherent conception which should not be underestimated: for many the *Requiem* contains some of Verdi's very greatest music.

A deepening contact with Arrigo Boito, encouraged by the publisher Giulio Ricordi, eventually gave rise to Verdi's final two Shakespearian masterpieces. In Boito, the composer at last found a collaborator with the perfect blend of musical awareness, theatrical understanding and ability to adapt (though not always passively) to his dramatic intuitions. After some intensive work together on the revision of *Simon Boccanegra*, the way was clear for *Otello* (first performed at La Scala in 1887). In comparison with the previous operas, *Otello* displays a simplified plot structure – although the decorative elements (basically the choral interventions) still perhaps lie rather uneasily in relation to the whole. But the force of the drama lies in the power with which the basic centres of attraction, the 'good' of Desdemona, the 'evil' of Iago, revolve around the protagonist as he inexorably plays out his tragedy. One of the many delights of *Falstaff* (also La Scala, 1893) is that the composer is summing up, consciously and ironically, the experiences of his operatic career. The opera, which begins with a pseudo sonata form and ends with a fugue sung by all the characters, is a constant, magnificent parody of the dramatic structures and problems of musical organization which Verdi had confronted during his long career. Verdi's final compositions were a series of religious choral pieces, the *Quattro pezzi sacri*, written between 1890 and 1896.

What mattered above all to Verdi was the creation of a musical object whose perfection of workmanship gave it a guarantee of contact, of direct relationship with the public; and in this he succeeded: the operas from *Nabucco* onwards have never left the repertoire of Italian theatres, and many of them are mainstays of the major opera houses of the world. Their extraordinary vitality comes primarily from their force as dramatic facts realized through the most suitable musical means, from the perfect functionality of the composer's musico-dramatic intuitions. It is this which explains the substantial unity of Verdi's oeuvre, from which many have learnt, but which none has attempted to intimate.

Further reading

Other works include: *Giovanna d'arco* (1845); *Alzira* (1845); *Attila* (1846); *I masnadieri* (1847); *Il corsaro* (1848); *La battaglia di Legnano* (1849); and *Stiffelio* (1850). See: Frank Walker, *The Man Verdi* (1962); Julian Budden, *The Operas of Verdi* (3 vols, 1973, 1978 and 1981); J. Rosselli, *Verdi* (2000); A. Latham and R. Parker (eds) *Verdi in Performance* (2001).

PIERLUIGI PETROBELLI

VERGA, Giovanni
1840–1922
Italian novelist

The dubious benefits of fictional realism came rather late to Italy, owing in part to the fragmented nature of its culture and society in the decades before the final achievement of nationhood in 1870, but when it did arrive it was avidly seized upon. Nowadays it is customary to regard the whole realistic trend in the Italian novel, a movement represented at its best by writers such as Luigi Capuana in *Il Marchese di Roccaverdina* and Vittorio Imbriani in *Dio ne scampi dagli Orsenigo*, as a species of melodramatic aberration culminating in the disastrous advent of Gabriele **D'Annunzio**, a figure as much invented as genuine. Yet, amid numerous second-rate imitations of **Flaubert**, **Daudet** and the Russians, Italy produced a single master of the genre, whose style and treatment of theme established a tradition which has received striking renewals during the twentieth century.

As with **Luigi Pirandello** and **Giuseppe Lampedusa**, his being Sicilian is crucial to our estimation of Giovanni Verga. He was born into a society still based upon feudal ideals dating from the days of the Arabs and the Normans, and into a world which, at the same time, had committed itself fervently to the cause of unification. The fact that Italy meant little to Sicily and that life after the **Garibaldian** liberation campaigns of 1860, during which Verga was a patriotic student in Catania, went on in much the same atmosphere of remote and inchoate corruption as it had before is reflected in many of his later stories and in his novel *I Malavoglia* (when the news of the Battle of Lissa, at which Luca

Malavoglia dies, is brought to the village, it is reported as 'a battle between our men and the enemy, but nobody knew who that was').

Verga's upbringing was typical of the education of a child of the upper bourgeoisie in the mid-nineteenth century. Liberal ideals implanted by revolutionary preceptors inspired a first novel, the almost unreadable four-decker *I carbonari della montagna*, published in Catania in 1861, which earned Verga a favourable notice in a Florentine newspaper. His heart set on a literary career, he left Sicily for Florence in 1865 and for the next fifteen years lived mostly in northern Italy, earning money as a journalist and reviewer, writing the overblown and sentimental *Storia di una capinera* (1873), *Eva* (1874) and *Tigre Reale* (1875) – novels based on his observation of upper-class life in Sicily and Milan and heavily tinged with Balzacian influences.

A return to Catania in 1876 marked the beginning of a gradual withdrawal from the brilliant world of Milanese salons, centred upon the circle of Countess Maffei, friend of **Verdi** and Manzoni, where Verga's youthful reputation had been established. During the early 1880s, while still based in Milan, he turned towards the creation of the series of tales and sketches of Sicilian peasant life, exemplified in *Vita dei Campi* (1880), *I Malvoglia* (1881, trans. Eric Mosbadier as *The House of the Medlar Tree*, 1953) and *Novelle rusticane* (1883), upon which his subsequent fame has been largely founded.

Much as Verga was admired as the leader of the Italian *veristi*, *I Malvoglia* met with a generally lukewarm reception, but notwithstanding this the author pressed ahead, in *Mastro-don Gesualdo* (1888, trans. **D.H. Lawrence**, 1928), with his idea for a set of novels, in **Zola's** *Rougon-Macquart* style, embodying the aspirations of *i vinti*, the conquered, those who, within a rigidly stratified society such as Sicily's, attempt to better their condition and ultimately fail. His thesis in this connection is set out at the beginning of *I Malvoglia* itself, though it was not destined to full accomplishment. A kind of meridional

indolence seems to have overcome Verga in his later years, and a tendency to repeat characters, situations and backgrounds marks the stories in *Vagabondaggio* (1887) and *Don Candeloro e compagni* (1894). During the last two decades of his life, in which he successfully assumed the pose of the distinguished man of letters, an established figure in Catania society, he composed practically nothing, and though honoured with an official funeral and the usual tributes paid to literary panjandrums, he was soon afterwards, for an interval at least, ignored.

The recent revival of interest in Verga, much of it owing to the spate of cheap reissues of his work, has brought his sterling qualities firmly to our attention, and he can now be seen as, at the best, a splendidly unsentimental yet tender and sympathetic chronicler of life among the Sicilian poor. It is precisely this quality of compassion which distances him from Zola, who after meeting Verga rejected him as a disciple because of his unwillingness to embrace the French novelist's credo to the full extent of its more absurdly 'scientific' reaches. In this respect Verga more resembles **Thomas Hardy**, whose *Tess of the D'Urbervilles* has a coincidental similarity of intention to several of the *Novelle rusticane* in its treatment of a character struggling against destiny.

In his stories, Verga rejects Zolaesque determinism, based on studies of environment and heredity, in favour of a quality of fatalistic resignation which is not simply Sicilian but quintessentially Italian in feeling. His famous objectivity, branching out into an extraordinary exactitude of detail with regard to background and location (the setting of his celebrated *Cavalleria rusticana*, 1884, source of Mascagni's opera, matters almost as much as the characters), is not so much an artistic cult as a natural gift for dispassionate observation. The essential superiority of his art to that of practically every other European realist (we may perhaps except **Eça de Queiroz** and **Pérez Galdós**) lies in the sincerity of its indulgence towards the weak, oppressed, erring figures it delights to portray.

Further reading

Other works include: *Little Novels of Sicily* (1925) and *Cavalleria Rusticana and Other Tales* (1928), both translated by D.H. Lawrence. See: T.G. Bergin, *Giovanni Verga* (1931); Alfred Alexander, *Giovanni Verga* (1972).

JONATHAN KEATES

VERLAINE, Paul

1844–96

French poet

Verlaine was inevitably an over-indulged child: his parents had been married for twelve years before his birth and his mother had suffered three miscarriages; there were no further children. In 1851, Verlaine's father, an army officer in the engineers, resigned his commission and the family moved to Paris. Verlaine's education here proceeded with a rapid loss of application, attrition of will, flirtation with illicit literature. Nascent alcoholism can be traced to 1862, the year he passed his *baccalauréat*. His father tried to draw him back to an ordered life and, in 1864, insisted that he take a job as a clerk, first in an insurance company and then in the Hôtel de Ville. Throughout this period, his literary interests and contacts had developed and 1866 saw the appearance of his first collection, *Poèmes saturniens*. The opening, in 1867, of the Salle Lacaze at the Louvre, with its collection of eighteenth-century canvases (Watteau, Fragonard, Boucher, Lancret) is one of the clues to Verlaine's second volume, *Fêtes galantes* (1869). It was in 1869, too, that he met the sixteen-year-old Mathilde Mauté whom he married the following year and to whom were addressed the poems of his third collection, *La Bonne Chanson* (1870).

His undiminished drinking habits intermittently led Verlaine to brutal treatment of both his mother and his wife. The early months of this marriage were further strained by the Franco-Prussian War, the Siege of Paris and the ensuing Commune; Verlaine's sympathies with the Communards lost him his job and made him something of a fugitive.

His attempt to re-install himself in the world of bourgeois respectability was dealt a final blow by **Rimbaud's** arrival in Paris in September 1871, a month before the birth of Verlaine's son, Georges. In July 1872, after more violence to his wife and son, Verlaine left with Rimbaud, first for Brussels and then for London. The months of wandering which followed and during which Verlaine sought both to reconcile himself with Mathilde and to keep Rimbaud came to an end on 10 July 1873, in Brussels, with Verlaine shooting Rimbaud in the wrist. Sentenced to two years' imprisonment, spent at Mons, Verlaine was converted to the faith in 1874, the year of the publication of *Romances sans paroles* and of Mathilde's legal separation from him.

Released from prison in January 1875, he returned to England to teach French and drawing at Stickney (Lincolnshire) and in 1876–7 was teaching French at Bournemouth. In October 1877, he returned to France and took up a teaching post at Rethel, where he struck up a relationship with one of his pupils, Lucien Létinois, a relationship which lasted through another visit to England, an abortive farming project at Juniville and until Lucien's death from typhoid in April 1883. In the meantime, *Sagesse*, containing the poems of his conversion, had appeared (December 1880). Having failed to be reinstated as a municipal employee, and after another short spell in prison for drunken attacks on his mother, Verlaine finally settled in Paris, in poverty and squalor. The last decade of his life, which, ironically, saw the steady growth of his poetic reputation, was a sequence of seedy lodgings, hospitals, bouts of drink, homosexual liaisons (principally with the artist Frédéric-Auguste Cazals) and affairs with prostitutes (particularly with Eugénie Krantz and Philomène Boudin). Lecture tours in Holland, Belgium and England, his election as Prince of Poets on the death of Leconte de Lisle (1894), the publication of more verse-collections of diminishing quality, preceded his death from bronchial pneumonia in January 1896.

Verlaine's finest poetry belongs to *Fêtes galantes*, poems using the *personae* of the *commedia dell'arte* and the pastoral tradition, in eighteenth-century park settings and inspired by the work of Watteau and others, and to *Romances sans paroles*, poems growing out of the Rimbaud adventure, caught between Rimbaud and Mathilde, backed by the cityscapes of Brussels and London. The *Poèmes saturniens* contain adumbrations of this flowering, but are given over largely to Parnassian and **Baudelairian** derivations. The early poems of *Sagesse* are also of the best vein; those of the conversion are more laboured and conventional.

Verlaine's is the poetry of a floating sensibility which operates in an ill-defined space between sensation and sentiment, self-surrender and anxious interrogation. His vocabulary is a vocabulary of etiolation (*blême, pâle, gris, vague, doux, incertain*), half-measure (*quasi, à peine, un peu*), of infantile diminutives, of locational uncertainty (*parmi, par, vers*), of oscillating or circular movement, pacifying and often mindless (*bercer, balancer, circuler, tourbillonner*). His is a world subject to reflexive or intransitive action, frequently evanescent (*s'évaporer, s'effacer, se noyer, se mêler*), a world of uncontrollable autonomies and apparently directionless motivations. All sense of causality is submerged, and the connections between things, between subject and object are scrambled by intervening barriers (mist, foliage, indeterminate noise). It is, then, a poetry of responses, of the almost imperceptible creations and transformations of temperamental conditions. It would be misleading to speak of feelings, in any Romantic sense of the word; the Romantics have confidence in the value of feeling and in their possession of feeling; they feel with purpose, because feeling is self-projection and self-assertion, born not of sensation but of ideology and moral imperative. With Verlaine, feelings are absorbed back into the more primitive state of sentience and a sentience peculiarly divorced from a sentient being. And repetition, so recurrent a habit in his work, situates the poem in a realm where obsession, hauntedness, ennui, self-hypnosis, formal self-consciousness cannot be put asunder. It is Verlaine's ability to capture the unfocused, almost undifferentiated ripplings of consciousness at its lower levels, the kinetics of the psyche, the flickering modulations of affective reaction, which gives his poetry its distinction. And the pleasure provided by his poetry is a pleasure in the act of reading rather than in subsequent reflection, a pleasure in the infinite resourcefulness and polymorphousness of his verse-art.

Verlaine's 'Art poétique', written in April 1874, appeared in *Jadis et naguère* (1884). Here he calls for music, an art that liberates response in a pure form and re-articulates the elements of semi-consciousness. This enterprise is aided by the use of the imparisyllabic line, which does not let verse-utterance settle, keeps it unstable, volatile, nervous, a safeguard against the portentous. He asks, too, that words be chosen with a certain carelessness, grammatical and semantic, so that precision and imprecision constantly shade into each other. The poet should prefer the nuance to the unambiguous colour, because nuance allows an unhindered trafficking between different kinds of dream, between different 'sonorities', the wistful and the resonant. He rejects satiric verse and the conceit, though the *Fêtes galantes* are given their peculiar alertness and textural crackle by a restless ironic undertone. Next, he attacks eloquence and rhyme. His own verse, with its familiar locutions, unfussy syntax, sudden changes of direction, never loses touch with common speech. What he faults in rhyme is its privilege, the way it monopolizes structural and semantic function, its exemplary conclusiveness. Verlaine seeks to reduce rhyme's prominence, to cast in doubt what it foregrounds, frequently by resorting to bold *enjambement*, by disregarding the traditional rules of rhyming (particularly the alternation of masculine and feminine rhyme-pairs, thus, paradoxically, liberating the expressive potentialities of rhyme gender), by reducing rhyme to assonance and by increasing line-internal music (alliteration, assonance, internal rhyme). Thus the way in which the reader locks into the verse is not rigorously coded; his attention is more uniformly and continuously engaged in a more uniform and continuous diversity. Verlaine's *vers libéré* is not, however, *vers libre*; whatever liberties he took, he stoutly refused to do away with rhyme and syllabic regularity, and mocked the *verslibristes* for doing so. Traditional prosodic structure, however masked, was a necessary anchorage (moral? psychological? aesthetic?); it acted as a verse-consciousness which could be constantly sunk in, and salvaged from, a highly mobile, hesitant, somnambulistic verse-texture.

Jadis et naguère is the uncomfortable miscellany of poems previously laid aside and new poems that Verlaine's unimpressive late collections often are. It was his intention to follow through the two fundamental strains of his experience, the spiritual and the orgiastic, in parallel volumes. *Sagesse* was succeeded by *Amour* (1888), *Bonheur* (1891) and *Liturgies intimes* (1892). Simultaneously, the erotic thread was taken up by *Parallèlement* (1889), *Chansons pour elle* (1891), *Odes en son honneur* (1893), *Élégies* (1893), *Dans les limbes* (1894) and *Chair* (1896). But these collections are without momentum, falling back on the sentimental, the anecdotal, the rhetorical. Verlaine's poetry in these later years leaves his weaknesses untransformed: the infantile need for refuge, for the total passivity of naive belief or the oblivion of sensual self-immersion, and a mechanical reliance on poetic techniques now too conveniently a part of his growing reputation. There are also volumes of occasional verse: *Dédicaces* (1890), *Épigrammes* (1894), *Invectives* (1896).

If, in his earlier verse, Verlaine is a Symbolist, it is not because his poetry involves itself with metaphysical curiosity – though there is existential inquiry – or with essentialism, or with any excavation of idea from object. It is because his poems present, through sensory encounter, the shifting, polyvalent facets of a mood which is inhabitable but not definable; the poem unifies mood by harmonizing its multiplicity, not by resolving it into singleness. And if these earlier collections can be called Impressionist, it is because they cast anthropocentricity in doubt with their impersonal constructions, because they provide no dominant and stable perspective, because they relativize experience, because they totally subject concept to perception in a world of effects without causes, because they give peculiar substantiality to the half-realities of shadow and reflection, because they depict the mutual interpenetration of objects and surrounding space, because they pursue fugitivity in the free handling of their medium.

Verlaine's influence was marked but short-lived. In France, the Verlainian mode, that kind of poetry which veers between the most delicately musical tone and the prosy, which weds lyric indulgence in evanescent moods of disquiet and vague loss, moods often teased by erotic impulses, with a quizzical, often ironic, vigilance, leads through **Laforgue** to **Apollinaire**, but not beyond. Some critics have found a Verlainian transparency in Éluard's verse, but Éluard's verse is altogether firmer; where Verlaine's poems are so often self-consolatory chantings, *berceuses* by nature, Éluard's poems exude a confidence in their own public efficacy and his utterance is more lapidary. The Surrealists looked to Rimbaud, at Verlaine's expense: 'the over-valuation of Verlaine was the great mistake of the Symbolist school' (**Breton**).

In the Anglo-American world, Verlaine enjoyed a cult among the Nineties poets before slipping from sight with the Imagists. It was the neurasthenic strain in Verlaine which caught the fancy of the Nineties poets, the attractions of an experience governed by an atrophied will, by the subdued vyings of the sensual and the mystical, animated by the almost inaudible pulse of the subtlest and most transient sensations. Verlaine was translated (and copied) by Ernest Dowson, John Gray, Arthur Symons and others. In sending his poem 'Vanitas' to Victor Plarr (1891), for example, Dowson wrote: 'It's an attempt at mere sound verse, with scarcely the shadow of a sense in it: or hardly that so much as a vague, Verlainesque emotion.' **W.B. Yeats** had most of his familiarity with Verlaine's verse through Symons, and though he was unable to measure the extent of his debt, he indicated Verlaine's presence in *The Wind Among the Reeds* (1899); perhaps his pursuit of 'those wavering, meditative rhythms, which are the embodiment of the imagination, that neither desires nor hates' ('The Symbolism of Poetry', 1900) had something to do with Verlaine. But **Ezra Pound** found Verlaine to be of no pedagogic use, because he had not taken poetic art forward, as Gautier and Gourmont had done (letter to Harriet Monroe, 1913), an opinion hard to endorse.

Further reading

Other works include: criticism: *Les Poètes maudits* (1888), contributions to the series *Les Hommes d'aujourd'hui* (1885–93); fiction: *Louise Leclercq* (1886), *Les Mémoires d'un veuf* (1886); autobiography: *Mes Hôpitaux* (1891), *Mes Prisons* (1893), *Confessions* (1895); poetry: *Verlaine: Selected Poems*, ed. J. Richardson (1974). See: C. Chadwick, *Verlaine* (1973); C. Cuénot, *Le Style de Paul Verlaine* (1963); O. Nadal, *Verlaine* (1961); N. Osmond, 'Verlaine', in J. Cruickshank (ed.) *French Literature and Its Background*, Vol. 5 (1969); J.-P. Richard, 'Fadeur de Verlaine', in *Poésie et profondeur* (1955); E. Zimmermann, *Magies de Verlaine* (1967).

CLIVE SCOTT

VERNE, Jules

1828–1905

French novelist

The reputation of this prolific, popular writer of adventure stories, a pioneer of science fiction, has undergone some startling fluctuations. The 'New Criticism' in France inaugurated a stimulating rediscovery of works that had become scorned as mere edifying children's literature.

The son of a lawyer, Verne resisted pressure to follow the paternal example, preferring, in the 1850s, to write lightweight plays for the popular stage. In 1863, with the tale *Five Weeks in a Balloon* (*Cinq semaines en ballon*) he began publication of his *Extraordinary Journeys in Known and Unknown Worlds*, whose aim was described by the didactic publisher Hetzel as 'to summarize all geographical, geological, physical, astronomical knowledge amassed by modern science'. The *Extraordinary Journeys* were to total a hundred volumes, constituting sixty-two novels, produced at the rate of two per annum. In a sense, they may be seen as imaginary compensation for Verne's own settled existence. The only science in which he had any expertise was geography: a member of the Société de Géographie, he worked on an *Illustrated Geography of France and Her Colonies* (1867–8). He also found time to act as municipal councillor in Amiens from 1884; despite the ambiguous suggestion of anarchist sympathies in novels such as *20,000 Leagues under the Sea* (*20,000 lieues sous les mers*, 1870), he followed a moderate, anti-radical line.

Verne's work may be said to belong to a tradition of imaginary journeys, for all the addition of nineteenth-century scientism. Indeed, the element of fantasy is supremely important. Verne criticism long took the form of 'prediction-spotting', but his science, we now know, was second-hand, culled from vulgarized sources; what we find in his work is not so much science as a mythology of science. 'Known worlds' shade disconcertingly into 'unknown worlds', science acts as threshold to myth. Overriding the paraphernalia of factual information are powerful recurrent images of mythic force, constituting what Michel Butor described as the essence of Verne's naive genius, 'the prodigious power to make us dream'.

A frequent theme is the quest for uncharted locations – the source of the Nile, the Pole (*Adventures of Captain Hatteras*, *Voyages et aventures du capitaine Hatteras*, 1866), the centre of the earth (*Journey to the Centre of the Earth*, *Voyage au centre de la terre*, 1864) – that take on quasi-mythical significance, suggesting to the modern reader something akin to the Surrealists' *point suprême* where all contradictions are resolved. In Verne's poetically powerful vision of the Pole ('that unknown point where all meridians cross'), snow and fire are united: Hatteras discovers a volcano there, and goes mad in the attempt, Empedocles-like, to enter it. Repeatedly the volcano is associated (unscientifically!) with initiation: it is through an extinct volcano that the protagonists of the mythologically rich *Journey to the Centre of the Earth* begin their descent into the underworld, and it is through a live volcano that they are expelled out of the earth's innards in a fascinating transcription of the trauma of birth. Fire is a recurrent theme, often refined and purified in electricity, 'soul of the industrial world', as in *Clipper of the Clouds* (*Robur le conquérant*, 1886). Electricity is even curiously united with the trappings of Gothic horror in *Carpathian Castle* (*Le Château des Carpathes*, 1892). Verne's fascination with caverns, volcanoes, labyrinths and islands attains its finest synthesis in *The Mysterious Island* (*L'Île mystérieuse*, 1874–5). It is clear that much in his work can be read in terms of **Jungian** archetypes. Equally clear is the predominance of the initiation-pattern, together with a taste for cryptograms and word-play: the quest of *Journey to the Centre* begins from a coded message left by an Icelandic alchemist. Verne's imagination has much in common with the alchemical tradition, itself poised between science and mythology – gold and fire are suggestively united in *The Golden Volcano* (*Le Volcan d'or*, 1906).

Not surprisingly, characterization in these tales is rudimentary and largely reduced to standard types: eccentric scientists, young novices, initiates, mysterious holders of knowledge and power (Captain Nemo), humorous servants. The element of humour, to be found in most of his works, no doubt played a large part in the success of *Around the World in 80 Days* (*Le Tour du monde en 80 jours*, 1873). In a sense, humour acts as a check on the initiatory scope of these works, for Verne holds back from 'excessive' initiation. Transgressors, such as Hatteras, are punished, whereas in general the characters

return to a settled bourgeois life after a hint, a vicarious thrill of revelation. **Roland Barthes** has commented (in *Mythologies*, 1957) on the bourgeois aspect of Verne's work: a cult of enclosedness, the desire to reconstruct, with the help of science, a comfortable universe in microcosm, whether submarine, island or lighthouse.

However, Verne is not simply a representative of the optimistic nineteenth-century ideology of science. His later novels show increasing doubts about progress – *Master of the World* (*Maître du monde*, 1904), *The Survivors of the 'Jonathan'* (*Les Naufragés du 'Jonathan'*, 1909). A final story, *The Eternal Adam* (*L'Eternel Adám*, 1910), completes the development into pessimism: human history now appears as absurdly cyclical. Having expressed the nineteenth century's dream of science, its mythology, Verne finally, on the threshold of a more sceptical age, passes judgement on that dream.

Further reading

Other works include: *From the Earth to the Moon* (*De la terre à la lune*, 1865); *The Children of Captain Grant* (*Les Enfants du capitaine Grant*, 1868); *Black Diamonds* (*Les Indes noires*, 1877); *The Begum's Fortune* (*Les Cinq Cents Millions de la Bégum*, 1879); *Mathias Sandorf* (1885). See: M. Butor, *Répertoire I* (1960); I.O. Evans, *Jules Verne and His Work* (1965); M. Moré, *Le Très Curieux Jules Verne* (1960); S. Vierne, *Jules Verne et le roman initiatique* (1973); Andrew Martin, *The Mask of the Prophet: Extraordinary Fictions of Jules Verne* (1990); Herbert R. Lottman, *Jules Verne: An Exploratory Biography* (1997).

DAVID MEAKIN

VERTOV, Dziga (Denis Arkadevich KAUFMAN)
1896–1954
Russian film director

Born into a Polish family of librarians, Kaufman moved to Petrograd during the First World War. Changing his name to Dziga Vertov (thought by the French film historian Georges Sadoul to signify the notion of 'perpetual motion'), he attended the Institute of Psychoneurology and the University of Moscow, where, anticipating his later interests in sound, he invented a miniature 'laboratory of hearing' based on a gramophone recorder. After the Revolution he was recruited into the newsreel film work of the Committee of Cinematography, where he worked on titling and editing footage from the Revolution and Civil War. He soon took over the *Cine Weekly* series (1918–19), organizing a widespread network of newsreel cameramen, and travelling on the Civil War agit-train *The October Revolution* with his feature-compilation *The Anniversary of the Revolution* (1919). In addition to other shorts, he also completed the feature-length *History of the Civil War* (1922).

It was against this background that Vertov emerged as the major champion and theoretician of radical Soviet documentary and newsreel film. His two main subsequent series, *Kino Pravda* (1922–5) and the *Goskino Journal* (1923–5), extended Vertov's formal experiments in montage and in titling, and continued to be supported by polemical and theoretical writing on the cinema. His output in the later 1920s went on to include two films sponsored by interests outside the film industry – *Stride, Soviet* (1926) commissioned by the Moscow Soviet as an informational film for the 1926 election, and *A Sixth of the Earth* (1926), an advertisement of Russia's resources and capabilities on behalf of the trade agency, Gostorg. These were followed by *The Eleventh* (1928), a celebration of the ten years since the Revolution, and *Man with a Movie Camera* (1929), Vertov's feature-length experimental documentary about life in the city and about the practices of film-making.

The hardening of economic and cultural policy in the later 1920s augured badly for Vertov's cinematic radicalism, with its outspoken challenges not only to the cinema of fiction but to the traditional 'neutrality' and 'transparency' of documentary. By the time of the last-named film Vertov was out of favour, and subsequently found few outlets

for his work in a period when he was attacked for his formal extravagance and castigated even by **Eisenstein**. In the 1930s he was able to complete only three films: *Enthusiasm* (1930), his first sound film, an intricate documentary or 'symphony' as it was sub-titled on the efficiency of the miners of the Don Basin; *Three Songs of Lenin* (1934), a monument composed of a trio of films based on folk songs from Uzbekistan in Central Asia; and *Lullaby* (1937), a film on the women of the Soviet Union and of Spain. He was subsequently not fully employed, although he spent the period from 1944 until his death in 1954 regularly contributing to the newsreel *Daily News*.

Vertov's importance lies in his radical rethinking of the practices of documentary and newsreel cinema. His work in the aftermath of the Revolution led him to formulate, as his contribution to the Soviet critique of culture, and particularly of cinema, an emphasis upon the importance of documentary as opposed to fictional cinema, a position emphasized by the title of his major newsreel of the 1920s, *Kino Pravda* ('Cinema Truth') and spelt out in contributions to the journal *LEF* by Vertov on behalf of the 'Council of Three' set up in late 1922 with his wife Elizabeth Svilova, who collaborated on the scripting and editing of much of his work, and his brother, Mikhail Kaufman.

This led to a psycho-social redefinition of the function of cinematography under the rubric of the 'Camera Eye' (and, in parallel, the 'Radio Ear'). This notion entailed a new liberated conception of the function of the camera – which was to function more rather than less freely than the human eye – and of the camera-operator as himself/herself not merely a passive viewer but a liberated participant in the social processes being filmed. The former notion involved Vertov and his collaborators in an extension of the traditional range of the cinematographic process, from candid-camera shooting to complex editing experiments and special effects. The second led him to campaign for an active social application of work with documentary and newsreel film, including an ambitious but abortive attempt, during 1923–4, to establish a mass organization with clubs and correspondents throughout the USSR.

Vertov's virulent rejection of theatrical film (even including Eisenstein's 'acted films in documentary trousers'), together with his remodelling of the documentary mode through exploration of the complex materiality of film language and through visible insistence on the role of the film camera, editor, projection and audience as agents in the activity of producing film meaning, are most readily seen in Vertov's key work of the 1920s, *Man with a Movie Camera*, a dynamic and bravura homage to the city documentary genre and to the creative work of the camera-operator Kinok.

Vertov's legacy has been complex. First, he strongly influenced the European avant-gardes of the 1920s and 1930s, with his problematic and contradictory mixture of 'realist' and 'formalist' preoccupations; second, the notion of 'Cinema Truth' (*Kino Pravda*) became the key term for the French and American filmmakers of the early 1960s working under the translated rubric of 'Cinéma Vérité'; third, the politics of Vertov's work, together with his examinations of ideology at the level of film form prompted **Jean-Luc Godard** and his collaborator Jean-Pierre Gorin to rename themselves the Dziga Vertov Group in their attempts to found a new kind of political and social cinema following the May Events of 1968; fourth, the intricacy of Vertov's formalism strongly influenced certain branches of the 1960s and 1970s international avant-gardes, particularly the school of Structural-Materialist film.

Further reading

See: *Statyi, Dnievniki, Zamysly* ('Selected Writings', 1966); *Articles, Journaux, Projets* (1972); N.P. Abramov, *Dziga Vertov* (1965); Luda and Jean Schnitzer, *Dziga Vertov 1896–1954* (1968); Georges Sadoul, *Dziga Vertov* (1971); Stephen Crofts and Olivia Rose, 'An Essay Towards "Man with a Movie Camera"', *Screen* (Spring 1977); see also Jay Leyda, *Kino: A History of the Russian and Soviet Film* (2nd edn, 1973); Yuri Tsivian, *Lines of Resistance: Dziga Vertov and the Twenties* (2005).

PHILIP DRUMMOND

VICTORIA and ALBERT
1819–1901 and 1819–61
British monarch and prince consort

Queen Victoria, who ascended the British throne in 1837 and married Prince Albert of Saxe-Coburg-Gotha in 1840, is the only monarch who has given her name not only to an adjective, 'Victorian', but to a noun, 'Victorianism'. The adjective, apparently first used in 1851, has been applied to people, tastes, styles, institutions and values: the noun, apparently first used after her long reign was over, has usually been applied to a cluster of values, individual and social. Both usages frequently involve misconceptions. The very length of Victoria's reign meant that it saw many cultural changes, so that to apply the same adjective to all the shorter periods within it can be confusing: in addition, however, there was always a great variety of Victorian voices in any given period and it is impossible to select a number of them and treat them as typical of the whole. The noun, pointing to shared moral codes as well as shared convictions (e.g. belief in the gospel of work, in self-help, thrift, duty and character), was coined not by Victorians but by their successors, reacting against what were felt to be obsolete and restrictive rules and conventions, not to speak of cant and hypocrisy: already, indeed, in the last decades of her reign such reactions can be traced. Yet later generations reacted in their turn against the first rebels, and there have been many subsequent swings of fashion, both in interpretations of 'Victorian' and 'Victorianism' and in the acquisition of Victorian objects ('Victoriana') and the conservation of Victorian buildings.

Victoria herself had no sense that she was a culture-bearer, though she had strong tastes of her own, for example an early passion for opera and a more persistent interest in painting, and held firmly also that after the reigns of the four Georges and William IV she had an obligation to set a moral example. It was a personal tragedy for her that her devoted husband, who was a dedicated culture-bearer, died so early in her reign. Albert was deeply interested both in the arts and the sciences and in the relationship of both to social morality. As early as 1841 he was appointed chairman of a royal commission concerned with the promotion and encouragement of the fine arts in Britain, and ten years later he was personally responsible for much of the success of the Great Universal Exhibition, held in the newly built Crystal Palace. Through such activities, which were part of a pattern which also included concern for social reform, Albert was brought into close touch with a number of people inside and outside political circles, who were interested in what has come to be thought of as 'Victorian culture', the culture of the middle years of the Queen's reign: they included Charles Eastlake, Henry Cole, Lyon Playfair and, from overseas, Felix Mendelssohn and Gustav Waagen. It was a non-specialist culture with provincial as well as international ramifications, and with a built-in recognition of market forces as well as patronage. Albert commanded respect within it less because of his position as Prince Consort than because of his personal abilities and interests. Yet he had to face considerable political and social opposition and was often the target of the press. His most lasting contribution to posterity, apart from the controversial Albert Memorial, built to commemorate him, was the South Kensington complex of educational, artistic and scientific institutions, financed from the Great Exhibition surplus. Outside London the royal homes at Balmoral and Osborne were very much of his own conception: he also made significant changes at Windsor Castle.

Victoria was desolate when Albert died and spent years of her reign in deep mourning. Yet there was a final Victorian fling in the two royal jubilees of 1887 and 1897. Between the two jubilees an area of land forty times the size of Great Britain was added to Victoria's empire, of which India, over which she was declared empress in 1876, had been described as the brightest jewel in the crown. This overseas commitment ensured that Victorian tastes and styles are in evidence throughout the whole world: indeed, some of the most characteristic Victorian buildings can be seen in Bombay, Melbourne and Toronto. The adjective and the *ism* have also been used in relation to the United States.

The historian G.M. Young, whose *Victorian England, Portrait of an Age* (1934) marked the beginning of a change in attitudes to the Victorians, pushed further soon afterwards in relation to the visual arts by **John Betjeman**, insisted that the awkward terms 'Victorian' and 'Victorianism' should be applied, if they were to be applied at all, to other non-English-speaking societies also, where the terms have not usually found root. Downgrading the influence of Victoria, though not of Albert, he argued forcefully that ways and habits, fashions and prejudices, doctrines, ideas and even phrases which we think of as typically Victorian are really part of a general European cultural pattern. Albert, whose German education led him to Italy, was strongly European in his sympathies and aspirations, and Victoria, through her relatives, was closely linked to European courts. It was from the industrial north of England, however, that an address to Albert in 1857 thanked him for introducing a popular dimension into high culture: it spoke of Albert's 'encouragement ... to whatever tends to promote the material comfort of the people or to foster in them a taste for intellectual pleasure'.

Further reading

See: John Steegman, *Consort of Taste* (1950); Elizabeth Longford, *Queen Victoria* (1964); Winslow Ames, *Prince Albert and Victorian Taste* (1967). For contemporary colouring – and restraint – see the official *The Life of the Prince Consort*, ed. Sir Theodore Martin (5 vols, 1875–80), and *The Letters of Queen Victoria* (3 vols, 1908).

See also: Margaret Homans and Adrienne Munich (eds) *Remaking Queen Victoria* (1997); Christopher Hibbert, *Queen Victoria: A Personal History* (2000); Stanley Weintraub, *Uncrowned King: The Life of Prince Albert* (2000); John Plunkett, *Queen Victoria: First Media Monarch* (2002); Helen Rappaport, *Queen Victoria: A Biographical Companion* (2002).

ASA BRIGGS

VIDAL, Gore

1925–

US novelist and essayist

Gore Vidal was born in 1925. He graduated from Phillips Exeter College in 1943, joined the maritime branch of the Army Transportation Corps and served in the Aleutian Islands (off the coast of Alaska). This experience provided the material for his first novel, *Williwaw* (1946), written at the age of nineteen. The next few years saw a rapid succession of novels, including the *succès de scandale*, *The City and the Pillar* (1948, revised 1965), a matter-of-fact account of homosexual pursuit and disillusion. In the 1950s and early 1960s Vidal also wrote a number of plays for Broadway and television as well as doing film work, including an uncredited share in the script for *Ben Hur* (1959). Linked with the **Kennedy** dynasty, descended from a political family (his maternal grandfather was an Oklahoman senator and a cousin is Al Gore, Bill Clinton's vice-president and a presidential candidate in his own right in 2000), Gore Vidal has always displayed an ambivalent attitude towards power and politics while contriving to remain on the margin of that world. But since Vidal seems to have known everyone – as shown by his highly entertaining and anecdotal memoir *Palimpsest* (1995) – it is a very glittering margin.

Impatient or dismissive of his national culture and its parochialism – America is 'the civilisation whose absence drove **Henry James** to Europe' is one of many agreeable asides in *Two Sisters: A Memoir in the Form of a Novel* (1970) – Vidal has for many years lived in European exile (in Ravello). Provokingly describing the great US authors as 'minor provincial writers', he has been influenced by European or classical models. Little indication of Vidal's development therefore was provided by *Williwaw*, a story he himself described as 'written in the national manner ... a bit simple-minded but useful'. The 'true voice and pitch' which the novelist has to discover are partially to be heard in *The Judgement of Paris* (1952), the account of a self-regarding odyssey made by a young American in Europe, and in the apocalyptic *Messiah* (1954), which describes the growth of a worldwide death-cult. Vidal's elegant, sombre and world-weary voice found its perfect pitch in *Julian* (1964), the story of the apostate Roman emperor who belatedly tried to substitute Hellenism for Christianity.

Vidal's status as an adroit, even outrageous satirist was confirmed by *Myra Breckinridge* (1968), the eponymous heroine of which is a film buff and sex-change who recovers his masculinity and a belief in Christian Science in the parodic happy ending. Other satires of this middle period include *Kalki* (1978), in which the author once again brings the world to an unlamented end, with a few survivors cavorting in an empty White House, the target of so much of his polemical writing and fiction. During the final third of the twentieth century, Vidal produced seven historical novels dealing with the American experience under the collective title 'Narratives of Empire'. These are serious and carefully researched fictions, whose tone veers between the iconoclastic and the elegiac. Chronologically, the sequence begins with *Burr* (1973) – an earlier work, *Washington D.C.* (1967) was later incorporated into the series – and concludes with *The Golden Age* (2000). In this final novel, Vidal himself emerges as a (marginal) character and, during a postmodern epilogue, dismisses his creations in gentle Shakespearian fashion. If the series can be said to have a single preoccupation it is, at least in its closing volumes, the inadvertent way in which America acquired an empire, subsequently justified through a messianic sense of destiny. *Empire* (1987) is the title of one of the finest books in the sequence. In their mingling of fictional characters with historical figures, and with their privileged-seeming insights into politics and power, these 'Narratives of Empire' look set to be Vidal's principal fictional legacy.

The George W. Bush presidency and the US response to the 9/11 attacks have amply confirmed Vidal's long-standing belief in governmental duplicity and conspiracy, and produced some of his most polemical work. There is no loss of cynical zest in his work. In his writing Vidal continues to circle like an urbane bird of prey round a society in decline; the refined mixture of regret, relief and anger is all his own.

Further reading

Other works include: *Homage to Daniel Shay: Collected Essays 1952–72* (1972); *Myron* (1975); *1876* (1976); *Creation* (1981); *Lincoln* (1984); *The Decline and Fall of the American Empire* (2002); *Imperial America: Reflections on the United States of Amnesia* (2004) See: Bernard F. Dick, *The Apostate Angel: A Critical Study of Gore Vidal* (1979); Fred Kaplan, *Gore Vidal: A Biography* (1999).

PHILIP GOODEN

VIOLA, Bill

1951–

US artist

Bill Viola has brought the visionary into video art. In his videotapes and in the installations, making up the largest part of his oeuvre, in which video plays the key role, he has shown that it is possible to use a medium normally associated with entertainment to approach afresh the big existential questions of birth and death, of self and other, of humankind and nature, of what it means to be alive. While his work has always been of the highest technical quality and at the cutting edge of technological development, he is not interested in technology *per se* but rather for the images it makes possible. Belying the postmodernist contention that images can only be recycled, he has consistently created startlingly new ones – 'pictures never seen before', as the title of one of his exhibitions put it – awakening a sense of poetic and philosophical wonder.

Viola graduated from the Experimental Studios of the College of Visual and Performing Arts at Syracuse University in 1973. His works of the early 1970s were largely exercises exploring the properties of video as a medium, in a manner analogous to structuralist film, but his real concerns were already much closer to those of probably the greatest of all American avant-garde film makers, **Stan Brakhage**: exploring 'vision' in the widest sense, in a spirit deeply informed by Romantic poetics. Writers who have been important to Viola include **C.G. Jung**, **Mircea Eliade**, Jalal al-Din Rumi, St John of the Cross, William Blake and **Walt Whitman**. Along with other spiritual traditions, Zen Buddhism has been, as it has for a number of Western artists of his generation, an especially significant source of inspiration. While his work from around 1975 began to reflect these concerns, the real breakthrough came with a visit to a salt lake in the Tunisian Sahara where mirages regularly form, and the resulting videotape *Chott-el-Djerid (A Portrait in Light and Heat)* (1979). Entirely non-narrative and containing images at the extreme edge of perceptual legibility, this work is both extraordinarily beautiful and, for the first time ever in video, genuinely metaphysically unsettling.

The desert was to become a central motif in Viola's work. As well as actual deserts, he has used other landscapes of solitude, including mountain ranges and abandoned urban spaces, not only to evoke feelings of isolation and non-being but also to suggest the possibility of revelation and self-knowledge – notable instances being the black-and-white videotape *The Passing* (1991) and the film he made in 1994 to accompany live performances of **Edgar Varèse's** *Déserts*. *The Passing* was strongly influenced by the recent death of his mother, and contains footage of her lying on her deathbed and from the last years of her life, including at his first son's birthday party. Punctuated and given structure by images of the artist himself fitfully sleeping and waking, it is one of his most powerful meditations on time, consciousness and memory. The final image is of Viola lying motionless under water, presumably drowned.

A human figure, male and usually naked, immersed in water – sometimes floating, sometimes diving into it and sometimes apparently rising up from it – is another recurring motif in Viola's work, undoubtedly influenced by his experience of nearly drowning when he was a child. It forms the central section of the *Nantes Triptych* (1992), the two wings of which show, with literal matter-of-factness, the death of his mother and the birth, nine months later, of his second son. The naked figure in water was used again in the massive installation *The Messenger* (1996) in Durham Cathedral and in the even more ambitious *Five Angels for the Millennium* (2001), in both cases suggesting death and re-birth.

Two other, closely connected, recurring motifs are reflections in drops of water and in the pupils of eyes. One of his earliest installations, *He Weeps for You* (1976), contained a copper pipe at the end of which a tiny drop of water slowly grew, until it fell on to an amplified drum causing a loud booming sound – sound has continued to play a major role in many of Viola's works – whereupon a new drop would form, starting the cycle again. A magnified image of each drop was projected on to a large screen, showing clearly that it functioned like a fish-eye lens reflecting everything in the room, including the viewer. In a memorable sequence in the videotape *I Do Not Know What It Is I Am Like* (1986), the camera zooms in incredibly slowly on the eye of an owl, finally revealing the reflection of the artist and his camera. Again and again, he has successfully used phenomena of sense perception to point to correspondences between macrocosm and microcosm, the whole universe and the smallest object, the inner world of the self and the outer world of the other.

Much of Viola's work since 2000 has been concerned with the direct portrayal of emotion, previously only present implicitly, and with making links with art of the past. In a series of works collectively referred to as 'The Passions', very slow-motion videos showing actors portraying extreme emotional states, drawing inspiration partly from Old Master paintings, are displayed on flat LCD panels hung on the wall. The installation *Going Forth by Day* (2002) contains five panels using state-of-the-art high definition video each lasting 35 minutes, which again present themes of birth, death and re-birth, this time in a style paying explicit homage to Italian Renaissance fresco painting. His interest in extreme emotion, together with an abiding interest in music and the performing arts, led him in 2005 to collaborate with the Los Angeles Philharmonic, and director Peter Sellars, to produce a multi-disciplinary re-interpretation of **Wagner's** opera *Tristan und Isolde*.

Since 1981, Viola has been based in Southern California, with his wife and collaborator Kira Perov. In 1995, he represented the USA at the 46th Venice Biennale; and since 1997, when the Whitney Museum of American Art, New York, organized the exhibition *Bill Viola: A Twenty-Five-Year Survey*, his reputation as one of the most important artists working consistently with video has been secure.

Further reading

See: Viola's own website, www.billviola.com, is quite helpful, and contains links to other relevant sites. Extremely helpful is the collection of his writings, edited by Robert Violette and himself, *Bill Viola: Reasons for Knocking at an Empty House* (1995). Most critical writing is still to be found in catalogues and periodical articles. Among the most useful catalogues are Marie Luise Syring (ed.) *Bill Viola: Unseen Images/Nie gesehene Bilder/Images jamais vues* (Düsseldorf Kunsthalle, 1992); Alexander Pühringer (ed.) *Bill Viola* (Salzburger Kunstverein, 1994); and *Bill Viola: A Twenty-Five-Year Survey* (Whitney Museum of American Art, New York, 1997).

GRAY WATSON

VIOLLET-LE-DUC, Eugène

1814–79

French architect, historian, engineer and teacher

Viollet-le-Duc, a man with a deep understanding of French Gothic architecture, was a highly influential figure in the development of late nineteenth-century and early twentieth-century building, not only in his own country but throughout Europe and America. His importance is as a theorist and writer rather than as a practising architect and his ideas can usefully be seen in the context of the English Gothic revival led by A. Pugin. The English movement had a different motivation and reached higher standards than the French.

Born in France in 1814, le-Duc became a pupil of A.F. Leclere, himself a student of Durand. Therefore le-Duc was thoroughly grounded in methods of construction and use of materials as well as knowledge of Greek, Roman and Renaissance style. His thought arose from a rationalist functionalist background and only after these aspects had been fully absorbed was he encouraged, through his association with Labrouste, a brilliant innovator, to produce imaginative ideas. Labrouste, in one of his most famous buildings, the library of Sainte-Geneviève, Paris (1840), used, in the interior, exposed ironwork structures. This factor was important for the theories of le-Duc.

Despite time as a student in Greece, Rome and Sicily, it was finally to French Gothic that le-Duc was drawn. He studied with immense care not only its style but also the methods used for its construction. By 1854 he was able to publish the first of ten volumes forming the *Dictionnaire raisonné de l'architecture française* (eleventh to sixteenth centuries). The final volume appeared in 1868 and the whole was translated into several languages; consequently it was read widely and became influential throughout Europe and America.

The significance of these books was in part that they encapsulated much which architects interested in revival were laboriously seeking by travelling to the sources. The main thrust of revival came from England where a Catholic religious movement was making itself strongly felt in intellectual circles in the 1840s. This necessitated the building of churches, not simply in imitation of Gothic but in the true spirit of the original French Catholic Gothic. This aspect became an important emotional element for those revivalist architects such as Pugin, himself a Catholic. The passion with which these men re-interpreted the early builders gave their work an authority and brilliance, lacking for the most part in France, where revival was in new church building largely an empirical matter.

Le-Duc, in spite of his many commissions to restore and at times reconstruct old cathedrals, such as those at Carcassonne and Vezelay, nonetheless was interested in contemporary developments in industrial technology, more especially in the use of iron. There is little evidence of this knowledge in his Paris building, though. From 1846 to 1848 he built a block of flats in the rue de Liège and circa 1860 he built another in the rue de Douai. Both buildings are adjoined on either side by others, and each adapts to them, retaining a traditional, even slightly dour quality with evenly spaced long windows. The development in those years between the two blocks is slight. Le-Duc leaves out the shutters in the Douai block and, instead of recessing one small balcony with straight iron railings, projects one full width at the top with a smaller one lower down, and faces them both with decorated iron railings in an organic rather than geometric style.

During the later 1850s le-Duc, with his friend Lassus, was restoring and refurbishing Notre Dame in Paris. While engaged upon this immense task Lassus died and the year after, in 1858, le-Duc allowed himself his only High Gothic extravaganza, the decorations for the tomb of the Duc de Morny.

Already famous for his *Dictionnaire*, le-Duc assured his continuing success by publishing his *Entretiens sur l'architecture* in 1863 with plates appearing by 1872. In these volumes he makes clear his theoretical position with regard to the architecture of the future. One illustration suggests a church interior wherein the roof is supported by rectangular girders resting on thin rounded metal columns. These iron supports project diagonally upwards from the walls, as a type of buttress or large bracket. The effect is ungainly but later designers incorporated this type of structure into a more satisfying aesthetic.

Hector Guimard, the architect of many Art Nouveau domestic dwellings as well as Paris Métro stations, undoubtedly took up le-Duc's ideas. The sloping metal pillars appear as supports for overhanging façades and the charming decorative metal plant designs appear on houses and stations alike.

Le-Duc wrote that architects should find 'resources furnished by manufacturing skill' and that they ought to be 'making use of these means with a view to the adoption of architectural forms adapted to our times'. By this he meant that metal could be used not only for ornament but as structure, either as free-standing supports or as verticals and horizontals between infilling of masonry and glass.

In England these ideas were anathema to those who supported **Ruskin** and **Morris** in their condemnation of industry as immoral, through its degradation of labour. Nevertheless, in America le-Duc's proposals made rapid progress. In *Discourses on Architecture*, published in Boston in 1875, he wrote: 'A practical architect might not unnaturally conceive the idea of erecting a vast edifice whose frame should be entirely of iron, enclosing that frame and preserving it by means of a casing.' One Chicago architect, William Jenney, did exactly that and completed in 1885 the first skyscraper, ten storeys high. It took the invention of the Bessemer lightweight steel beam, unknown in le-Duc's lifetime, to make the top four storeys possible, but it was essentially le-Duc's proposition.

In England, despite lack of interest in his modern ideas, le-Duc received considerable recognition for his restoration work, as well as some criticism. He was invited to write for the *Ecclesiologist* and to visit Britain to tour Gothic buildings. When he came he pronounced the Houses of Parliament a 'frightful monstrosity', but later commended the work of the architect Burges. The RIBA saw fit to award him their Gold Medal although the École des Beaux Arts, of which le-Duc was Professor of Art and Aesthetics, caused him to resign as a result of its reaction to his ideas in *Entretiens*.

He continued to practise his architectural designing nonetheless and built some new churches, including by 1867 one at St Denis on the Seine, which is a pleasant, sturdy, traditional Gothic building with vaulted ceilings throughout, a tower minus a spire and some delicate decoration.

It was left, however, to the future architects to make le-Duc's dreams materialize. The brilliant engineer Contamin was to build the Halle des Machines for the Paris International Exhibition of 1889. This huge building with wall and roof in one was made of exposed metal ribs infilled almost entirely with glass. The same engineer was to provide the metal structure for the first ferro-concrete building of modern design, the Church of Saint Jean-de-Montmartre, built between 1897 and 1904 and designed by J. de Baudot.

The new materials introduced into building at this period made possible architecture with a more simple design. This knowledge, together with the understanding of basic structures inherent in early large-scale historic buildings, was an important factor in the development of twentieth-century International style architecture. In this respect Viollet-le-Duc can be considered one of its most important progenitors.

Further reading

See: *From the Classicists to the Impressionists: Art and Architecture in the Nineteenth Century*, ed. E. Gilmore Holt (1966); N. Pevsner, *Pioneers of Modern Design* (1970); H.R. Hitchcock, *Architecture: Nineteenth and Twentieth Centuries* (1971).

PAT TURNER

VISCONTI, Luchino

1906–76

Italian film maker and theatre and opera director

Born into an aristocratic Milanese family, and brought up with a dilettantish interest in music and horses, Luchino Visconti was drawn to the cinema and to an involvement with left-wing politics when **Coco Chanel** introduced him to **Jean Renoir** in 1935. After a short period working with Renoir in the France of the Popular Front, he returned to Fascist Italy and made an extraordinary first film, *Ossessione* (1942), which was a direct challenge to the official culture of the period and was widely hailed, on its release after the war, as a precursor of neo-realism. In 1947 he made the mammoth *La terra trema,* an epic about a Sicilian fishing family, loosely inspired by **Giovanni Verga's** classic novel *I Malavoglia.* If *Ossessione* was a precocious forerunner of neo-realism, *La terra trema* equally precociously outran it. Shot on location, with non-professional actors speaking their own lines in incomprehensible dialect, *La terra trema* emerged, paradoxically, as closer in style to grand opera than to the documentary realism that it originally aspired to. With *Senso* (1954) Visconti attempted a historical spectacular which would be realist in the **Marxist** or at least **Lukacsian** sense of producing a narration that enabled the spectator to grasp the nature of historical reality. Set in the Risorgimento, *Senso* tells a complex story of betrayal and counterbetrayal, in which the personal and political are closely but ambiguously intertwined.

The historical process recounted in *Senso* is one of 'passive revolution' (in **Gramsci's** phrase) and of muted change achieved by accommodations and compromise. The same process also figures in *The Leopard* (1963), an adaptation of Giuseppe Tomasi di **Lampedusa's** novel. In both these Risorgimento films the mechanism of the plot works through betrayal, whether sexual or political, while the underlying thematic concern is with the survival or otherwise of class and family groupings in a context of historical change. In *Rocco and His Brothers* (1960) the same mechanisms are returned to a modern setting – the life of a family of southern immigrants in Milan during the 'economic miracle'. The peasant family is torn apart under the pressure of urban life and its destruction is seen as both tragic and necessary and as the price to be paid if the individuals composing it are to survive. In *Vaghe stelle dell'Orsa* (1965) (known in the US as *Sandra*) a family is also destroyed, but the forces motivating its destruction are more internal. The story of *Vaghe stelle* is that of the *Oresteia,* and in particular of Electra, the daughter dedicated to avenging her father's death at the hands of her mother and stepfather. Again betrayal plays an important role. The daughter Sandra suspects her mother of having betrayed her father, a Jewish scientist, to the Nazis, resulting in his death in Auschwitz. Sandra in turn plays on her brother's (incestuous) love for her and betrays him, leading to his suicide. Sandra, however, survives and there is a sense at the end of the film that a future exists not only for her but for other survivors as well. History continues despite or even because of the family's destruction.

In his later films, however, Visconti shows himself more and more sceptical about history as a progressive development. In *The Damned (La caduta degli Dei,* 1969), the story of a German capitalist family destroyed by Nazism, there are no survivors. Nor are there in *Ludwig* (1972), where the mad king is incarcerated by his ministers leaving nothing behind him. Both these films are set in a recognizable history, whose development is cataclysmically blocked. In *Death in Venice* (1971) and *The Intruder (L'innocente,* 1976), on the other hand, there is no history at all. The films are set in their own present, which is our past. They have neither a future of their own nor any connection forward, even implicit, to our present. This cutting off of the past from the present goes along with an increasing interest in deviant sexuality. The protagonists of these late films are the last of their line and can only live in the present, knowing it to be the end. Significantly, few children are procreated, and none survive. This contrasts sharply with the world of *Rocco* or *La terra trema,* where the break-up of the family leaves behind children who are free to grow and develop. How much this involution of Visconti's concerns connects with his own homosexuality and his approaching death (during the making of *Ludwig* he had a severe stroke from which he never fully recovered) and how much it has to do with political disappointments is hard to determine. Suffice it to say that the later films, for all their splendours, lack the urgent forward-looking drive that characterizes the early ones.

Visconti's film output was not very great – some fourteen features in thirty years – but each of his films is in some way remarkable. Throughout his filmmaking career he was also busy with theatre and opera productions, in London and Paris as well as in Italy. Among his finest opera productions were **Verdi's** *Traviata* and *Don Carlo* for Covent Garden. In the theatre he directed Shakespeare, Goldoni, Beaumarchais and **Chekhov** as well as contemporary plays and (as these names imply) his work in the theatre included a lot of comedy, generally treated in a realistic vein. Although he soon abandoned realism as an aesthetic, he retained a gift for incidental realistic touches, both in theatre and cinema, helping to give substance to productions which would otherwise occasionally seem to be merely spectacular.

Further reading

Other works include: *Bellissima* (1951); *White Nights* (1957); *Lo straniero* (1967; from Camus's *L'Etranger); Conversation Piece* (1975). See: Monica Stirling, *A Screen of Time* (biography, 1979); Henry Bacon, *Visconti: Explorations of Beauty and Decay* (1998); Geoffrey Nowell-Smith, *Luchino Visconti* (2003).

GEOFFREY NOWELL-SMITH

VON FOERSTER, Heinz

1911–2002
Austro-American cybernet cian

Heinz von Foerster, the eldest of three children, was born to a successful Viennese family that had built the Ring, planned the new expansion of the city, and was well connected in Viennese cultural life. **Ludwig Wittgenstein** was a regular enough visitor to be called 'uncle' by the children, even though not strictly a relative.

Von Foerster was precocious. He reported he was a poor student, easily bored by traditional schooling (years later he became a friend of **Ivan Illich** whose sympathy for such educational experience is celebrated). An enthusiastic climber and skier, he and his cousin Martin Lange (the distinguished actor) funded their sporting escapades by becoming a magic double act. What interested von Foerster was not how the tricks were done, which he considered trivial, but the presentation that allowed the sense of wonder the audience enjoys. He later studied physics at the technical university in Vienna and attended the Vienna Circle, thus being the only member of both the Vienna Circle and the Vienna Magic Circle.

Von Foerster married the actress Mai Sturmer. They moved to Berlin where he subverted the Nazis by proposing and being funded to work on proposals that were quite impossible. He completed a PhD on microwaves (his work is seen as leading to the invention of the microwave oven) at the University of Breslau (now Wroclaw). After the war he returned to Vienna where he worked as both a broadcaster (as the famous interviewer of intellectuals, Dr Heinrich, on the American-funded RWR station) and (with Siemens and Erikson) in re-establishing communications networks.

In 1948 he went to the USA with little English and a theory of memory. The neuro-epistemologist Warren McCulloch adopted him, taking him to the Josiah Macy Jr Meetings (held in New York City between 1946 and 1952) on 'Circular Causal and Feedback Mechanisms', which meetings are becoming understood to have been perhaps the main source of cybernetics: indeed, the Macy title is probably a better description of the field than **Wiener's** 'control and communication in the animal and the machine'. Von Foerster had found his place. To improve his English **Margaret Mead** and Gregory Bateson suggested he be made secretary and editor of the proceedings. Thus he became part of the group that worked on the new, cybernetic, view of the world.

He became a professor at the University of Illinois and, in the later 1950s, he founded the Biological Computer Laboratory. This became the most active centre of 'contemplative' cybernetic research, employing **Ross Ashby** and providing a home from home for **Gordon Pask** and **Humberto Maturana**, among others, On his retirement to California, he moved the BCL with him. There he gave courses in local universities, and pursued a career as a lecturer (where his genius as a communicator and performer made even the most difficult clear).

The story thus far was of a successful man with much achieved. But his most remarkable work was to come – his reinvention of cybernetics in the reflective mode as 'second-order cybernetics', taking the circularity of cybernetic systems as a new starting point.

Second-order cybernetics involves cybernetics as the subject of its own investigation. The emergence of a 'cyber-culture' with cyber this and cyber that, and a persistent confusion with cryogenics (freezing stuff) makes the second-order approach (in which cybernetics is studied cybernetically) even more important, for what cybernetics is is often not well understood. Cybernetics is essentially concerned with circularity: the notion of feedback, evoked to provide a mechanism for error regulation and for many synonymous with cybernetics, ensures this circularity. But circularity has no effect unless an observing element observes what occurs as a result of some action and sends back (to the activator) a message about this which allows a

change in some aspect of the action calculated to bring what occurs more in line with what is intended. Thus there are two cybernetic observers: the one observing the system (sending the information back to the activator), and the one observing in the system (i.e. the one who defines and examines the whole system, including what is intended). Are these two observers significantly different? In classical cybernetics, the observer in the system was not understood as an observer, while the observer observing the system was an external observer, of the traditional scientific kind. In this explanation, the cybernetic observer is the one in the system: his role is to take part: to modify the behaviour of the system so that it achieves some goal.

But is this not what the observer observing from outside actually does? In which case our understanding of the scientific observer should be changed to the cybernetic understanding, and we should be concerned with the cybernetic observer. Von Foerster crystallized matters thus: first-order cybernetics – the cybernetics of observed systems; second-order cybernetics – the cybernetics of observing systems.

What is achieved by this shift? Responsibility for observations is returned to the observer. Some questions (such as whether there is any world independent of observations – or experiences) become explicit, and must be characterized as undecideable in principle. (Therefore, if we wish there to be a decision, we must make it and take responsibility for having made it.) Essentially the world is re-addressed so that experience, difference and involvement, for so long excluded, are reinstated. The status of knowledge, and our role in knowledge, is changed – radically – and we become active in our knowing as **Gordon Pask** would have us be.

Von Foerster's work within this new understanding concerned three themes. First, the power of recursive computation (which he particularly related to **Piaget's** object conservation); then, the shift from ontology to a genetic epistemology, which connected him with his friend Ernst von Glasersfeld's radical constructivism; and, finally, the ethical obligations that arise. He saw these as examples of wonder. For von Foerster, the magic of living in such a world is that it produces a sense of profound awe, which is at the heart of the human experience and condition.

Von Foerster spent most of his life unrecognized in his own land and his own tongue. Shortly before he died, the German-speaking world, and Vienna in particular, awoke to him. He was created honorary professor in the University of Vienna at the age of eighty-five. At ninety, he was given the city's key at a formal ceremony in the Vienna Rathaus. He was the first recipient of the Viktor Frankl medal: an honour that touched him greatly He liked to say, 'I am a Viennese.' At the end of his life, the Viennese finally concurred.

Further reading

See: Heinz von Foerster and Bernhard Poerksen, *Understanding Systems* (2002), compiled from a series of interviews; and Heinz von Foerster, *Understanding Understanding* (2003), von Foerster's own late selection of papers.

RANULPH GLANVILLE

VON NEUMANN, John
1903–57
US mathematician

It is often thought that the electronic computer was invented by mathematicians *mainly* for the benefit of mathematicians. This is far from being the case. In fact it is probably true to say that there was *less* demand from mathematicians for the facilities rendered by the machine in the early years than from physicists, chemists, engineers and technologists.

The electronic computer emerged by degrees from the electro-magnetic computer during the decade 1935–45, and it was the United States Army which built the first wholly electronic machine (ENIAC) towards the end of the war. It contained about 20,000 thermionic valves. The key idea which

opened up the possibility of an efficient automatic computer was the development of switch logic; and this in turn was a natural extension of the idea of **Wittgenstein's** Truth Tables. It was not until solid-state devices (initially transistors) were used in the 1950s, however, that the computer became a reliable instrument.

While professional mathematicians as a body showed surprisingly little interest in the early development of computers, there were two mathematician-logicians of exceptional talent who did contribute to the work: **Alan Turing** and John Von Neumann. Their unique contribution was a rigorous analysis of the potentialities of the new machine: their long-sighted, semi-philosophical papers provided the theoretical backing without which the development might have easily floundered. Commercial expediency, military security, technical obsolescence, training deficiencies – each of these was a factor which could have brought development to a standstill if it had not been felt that there was a strong theoretical basis for sustained progress.

Von Neumann was a mathematician of wide, all-round interests: an example of a type of generalist mathematician that has become progressively less common as mathematics has become an increasingly formidable labyrinth of complex and highly abstract ideas. He was born in Budapest when the Austro-Hungarian Empire was at its height as a cultural and intellectual power. He was educated at the universities of Berlin, Zürich and Budapest. After teaching for a time at the University of Berlin, he emigrated to America, where (in 1930) he took a chair in mathematical physics at Princeton. Later he moved to the Institute for Advanced Study at Princeton.

At Princeton Von Neumann worked in various areas of mathematics: mathematical logic, set theory, theory of continuous groups, ergodic theory, Quantum theory and operator theory. He was co-author (with Oskar Morgenstern) of a particularly influential and germinal book *The Theory of Games and Economic Behaviour* (1947). For many students of mathematics in the immediate post-war period this book had a profound effect. As the Pythagoreans had shown the surprisingly mathematical character of music, Von Neumann and Morgenstern showed the surprisingly mathematical character of games such as Matching Pennies, Three Boxes, Two Generals: they were also able to show how the concepts needed to analyse games could be applied to economics. (Von Neumann's interest in this area had first evidenced itself nearly twenty years earlier when, in 1928, he read a paper to the Mathematical Society of Göttingen on the mathematical theory of Matching Pennies which he had recently discovered.)

Von Neumann's essay 'The Mathematician' (in *The World of Mathematics*, 1956) expounded his general view of the state of con-temporaaneous mathematics. He was not entirely happy with what he saw. He draws a striking contrast between the professional research world of mathematics and that of physics. In the latter the effort of thought, analysis and research is highly concentrated 'on no more than one or two sharply cir-cumscribed fields', whereas the former is essentially diverse, being split into 'a great number of sub-divisions, differing from one another widely in character, style, aims and influence'. He felt there was a grave danger implicit in such a wide dispersal of effort: a risk that advanced work in mathematics would become 'more purely aestheticizing, more and more purely *l'art pour l'art*'.

Von Neumann's own work was never this: he maintained his *mathematical* interest in fields outside mathematics throughout his life: in games, physics, economics and, not least, computers. With Turing he must share much of the credit for the fact that the com-puter industry developed in a far-sighted, rather than in a narrowly commercial, way: particularly in the decision to build powerful, general-purpose hardware, supplemented by specific-purpose software (programs) to adapt the machine to any particular task required. Of course, in the end utility favoured the powerful generalized machine, but this was far from obvious at the beginning and short-term utility could all too easily have won the day.

Further reading

Other works include: 'The General and Logical Theory of Automata', in *The World of Mathematics*, Vol. IV (1956). See also: Leonid Hurwicz, 'The Theory of Economic Behaviour', and S. Vajda, 'The Theory of Games', in *The World of Mathematics*, Vol. II (1956). See also: William Aspray, *John Von Neumann and the Origins of Modern Computing* (1991); Norman MacRae, *John Von Neumann* (1996).

CHRISTOPHER ORMELL

VON STERNBERG, Josef
1894–1969
US film director

Josef Sternberg was born in Vienna in 1894. He moved to New York at the age of seven for three years, then returned to Vienna before settling permanently in the United States in 1908. Leaving school to work for a milliner and then a lace firm, he entered the film industry in 1911 as apprentice to a film-stock handler before moving to a job at the World Film Corporation in 1914. During the war he produced training films and was a Signal Corps photographer. Afterwards he worked as a cutter, writer, editor and assistant director in the United States and in Europe, ennobling his surname by the addition of 'von'.

His Hollywood career took off in the sec-ond half of the 1920s, following the prestige of his low-life (and low-budget) drama *The Salvation Hunters* (1925), which led to a con-tract with MGM, and, via *The Exquisite Sinner* (1925, now lost), to work for **Chaplin** on Edna Purviance's comeback picture, *The Sea Gull* (*A Woman of the Sea*, 1926), a film sub-sequently suppressed by Chaplin. The enor-mous success of Von Sternberg's *Underworld* (1927), one of the first gangster pictures, marked the beginning of his long relationship with Paramount and led to five films in the next three years, as well as re-editing work on Von Stroheim's *The Wedding March* (1927). The year 1928 saw *The Last Command*, the story of a Tsarist general reduced to the role of a Hollywood extra after the Revolution, *The Drag Net*, now lost, a follow-up to *Underworld*, and a further gangster picture, *The Docks of New York*. In 1929 Von Sternberg made *The Case of Lena Smith*, now lost, dealing with illegitimacy and class-relations in *fin-de-siècle* Vienna, and *Thunderbolt*, a 'gangster fantasy' (Weinberg) exploring the early possibilities of the sound cinema.

In 1930 Von Sternberg went to Europe to produce both English language and German versions of *The Blue Angel* (based on **Heinrich Mann's** novel *Professor Unrat*), the story of a schoolmaster who is bewitched and destroyed by a night-club singer. The film introduced Von Sternberg's new discovery, Marlene Dietrich, who then came to Hollywood to provide the cool and often mocking eroticism at the centre of Von Sternberg's love-dramas of the period, commencing with the North African romance *Morocco* (1930) and the spy story *Dishonoured* (1931). In 1931 Von Sternberg punctuated the Dietrich cycle with *An American Tragedy* – replacing the visiting Soviet director **Sergei Eisenstein** – before continuing with the 1932 Dietrich vehicles *Shanghai Express* and *Blonde Venus*. After *The Scarlet Empress* (1934), a sumptuous and grotesque account of the rise to power of Catherine the Great, came the last of the Von Sternberg/Dietrich collaborations, the Spanish caprice *The Devil is a Woman* (1935).

Von Sternberg's break with Dietrich and with Paramount led to a mixed bag of projects and associations. *Crime and Punishment* (1935) was followed by his version of an operetta on the life of Elizabeth of Austria, *The King Steps Out* (1936), and the unfinished *I, Claudius* (1937) for Alexander Korda. He moved on to the crime-drama *Sergeant Madden* (1939), followed by his return to oriental intrigue in *The Shanghai Gesture* (1941). After only one completed wartime project, the documentary short *The Town* (1943–4), Von Sternberg's career dwindled in the 1950s with the Cold War comic-strip *Jet Pilot* (1951) and the jewel-smuggling intrigue *Macao* (1952), both of which passed beyond his control. His last film, *The Saga of Anatahan* (1953), his most personal of the period, provides an oneiric account of a group of Japanese sailors who hide on an island for several years beyond the end of the Second World War, caught up in a cobweb of honour and desire with a man and woman from the island.

Von Sternberg is remembered for four main contributions to film history. First, for his totalizing attitude to film authorship, his ambitions in the direction of total creative control sometimes extending beyond mere perfectionism into the realms of sheer autocracy. Second, for his skills in intense pictorial stylization of frequently banal dramatic material through elaborate *mise-en-scène* and virtuoso cinematography. Third, for his contribution, in films like *Underworld*, *The Drag Net*, *The Docks of New York* and *Thunderbolt*, to the early evolution of the crime-film, a contribution later nuanced in such literary adaptations as *An American Tragedy* and *Crime and Punishment*. Finally, and above all, he is remembered for his representations of female eroticism through the figure of Marlene Dietrich in his middle-period Paramount films such as *The Blue Angel*, *Morocco*, *Dishonoured*, *Shanghai Express*, *Blonde Venus*, *The Scarlet Empress* and *The Devil is a Woman*.

Further reading

Other works include: *Fun in a Chinese Laundry* (1965); Andrew Sarris, *The Films of Josef von Sternberg* (1966); Herman G. Weinberg, *Josef von Sternberg* (1966); John Baxter, *The Cinema of Joseph von Sternberg* (1971); Carole Zucker, *The Idea of the Image: Josef von Sternberg's Dietrich Films* (1988); Gaylyn Studlar, *In the Realm of Pleasure: Von Sternberg, Dietrich and the Masochistic Aesthetic* (1993).

PHILIP DRUMMOND

VONNEGUT, Kurt, Jr

1922–

US novelist

Vonnegut's hip, breezy, atraditional style probably accounts for much of his enormous popularity, particularly among young adult readers. However, it is the tension between this light, humorous style and the seriousness of his themes and motifs that draws widespread critical acclaim. In general, each Vonnegut novel asks this question: In a world where technology, power, and greed inevitably produce war, where wealth and prestige have replaced love and kindness, where society's goals have replaced the individual's, where free will has become an obsolete notion, is it possible for human beings to have purpose and to live according to meaningful values? The fourteen novels, three collections of stories, seven stage plays and other miscellaneous writings represent the search for an answer. Vonnegut is variously labelled a science-fiction writer, a fantasist, an absurdist and a visionary. He is perhaps best understood as a black humorist, although Vonnegut prefers to see himself as an 'old fart with his Pall Malls'.

Vonnegut began writing for the *Daily Sun* while he was an undergraduate at Cornell. His formal education, mostly in the sciences and anthropology, was cut short by the Second World War; in 1943 he enlisted in the army. A year later, he was captured by the Germans and sent to a POW camp in Dresden. There he somehow survived the tragic Allied firebombing, and this experience obviously changed his view of modern man. Nevertheless, he returned to the United States and worked for the Chicago City News Bureau while attending the University of Chicago. In 1951, after working as a publicist for General Electric for four years, he quit to write full-time. For many years he was able to support himself and his family only by publishing popular stories (many have been reprinted in *Canary in a Cat House*, 1961, and *Welcome to the Monkey House*, 1968), but since the mid-1960s his novels

have been financially successful, a fact that seems to embarrass him.

It is no surprise that the first two novels, *Player Piano* (1952) and *Sirens of Titan* (1959), are stylistically more traditional than the later works. *Player Piano* is a reworking of *Brave New World* and *Sirens of Titan* is, at first glance, a somewhat ordinary science-fiction journey through space. However, these two books are seminal in the Vonnegut world. The main characters, Dr Paul Proteus and Malachi Constant, struggle to find lives worth living. Proteus fights valiantly against a technological, machine-dominated society only to find, in the end, that most people are happy being automatons. Proteus's rebellion fails to save society, but he finds personal satisfaction and, perhaps, salvation in his effort. Constant, in *Sirens of Titan*, is transformed from debauched mogul into a loving, contented and sensitive man. It is no coincidence that he first finds this happiness on Titan; the implication is, of course, that love and peace are difficult in the chaos on Earth. During his journey, Constant discovers that all human evolution occurs in order to rescue a stranded Trafalmadore space traveller. So man has no universal purpose other than this mission and, therefore, humankind has absolutely no free will. Even with this discovery, Constant returns to Earth and asserts that human beings should live and love those around them. From these early novels, we learn that it is good, although futile, for the individual to struggle against inhumanity; at the same time, it is necessary for the individual to remain gentle and loving.

The next three novels, *Mother Night* (1962), *Cat's Cradle* (1963) and *God Bless You, Mr Rosewater* (1965), build on the discoveries made in the first two. For many critics, *Slaughterhouse Five* (1969) is Vonnegut's most significant work. Twenty-five years on, the author writes about his Dresden experiences, and it is just this aesthetic distance that makes the novel so powerful. War and death are, of course, classic themes, but Vonnegut approaches these from a new perspective. Billy Pilgrim, survivor of Dresden, finds that he has no control over time, that he comes 'unstuck' and slips in and out from one moment to another. The Trafalmadores (space travellers) suggest cosmic detachment and advise Billy to cope with his chaotic world by enjoying the good moments and ignoring the bad. When catastrophe strikes, simply say, 'So it goes.' Then ignore it. Vonnegut clearly does not believe in this cosmic shrug; he illustrates, by the very act of writing this book, that the horrors of life are too important to ignore. However, one should not collapse into nihilism or withdraw into cosmic detachment under the weight of chaos; instead, one should face the bad (war, atrocities, greed, death, etc.) with grace, compassion and humour. *Slaughterhouse Five* is Vonnegut's testament to these values.

The same values inform much, if not all, of Vonnegut's subsequent work, which has had a tendency to become self-absorbed, even eccentric – for example *Breakfast of Champions* (1973) and *Slapstick* (1976). The last novel to be published was *Timequake* (1997), though this was followed by *Bagombo Snuff Box* (1999), a collection of stories. In 2000 a serious fire broke out in the East Side Manhattan house where Vonnegut had lived with his photographer wife, Jill Krementz, since 1970. Narrowly surviving acute smoke inhalation, and losing his library and papers, Vonnegut abandoned New York for a safer haven in Northampton, Massachusetts. That asteroid number 25399 is named after him is a touch straight out of his own imagination.

Further reading

Other works include: *Happy Birthday, Wanda June* (1971) and *Between Time and Timbuktu* (1972) are both plays; *Wampeters, Foma, & Granfalloons: Opinions* (1974) and *God Bless You, Dr Kevorkian* (1999) are collections of essays. The later novels include *Jailbird* (1979); *Deadeye Dick* (1982); *Galápagos* (1982); *Bluebeard* (1987); *Hocus Pocus* (1990); and *A Man Without a Country* (2005). See: Richard Giannone, *Vonnegut: A Preface to His Novels* (1977); Jerome Klinkowitz and Donald Lawler, *Vonnegut in America* (1977); James Lundquist, *Kurt Vonnegut* (1977); William Rodney Allen, *Conversations with Kurt Vonnegut* (1988); Lawrence R. Broer, *Sanity Plea: Schizophrenia in the Novels of Kurt Vonnegut* (1994); Thomas F. Marvin, *Kurt Vonnegut: A Critical Companion* (2002); Donald E. Morse, *The Novels of Kurt Vonnegut: Imagining Being an American* (2003).

GARY THOMPSON
(REVISED AND UPDATED BY THE EDITOR)

W

WAGNER, Richard

1813–83

German music dramatist

Wagner's work has often been described in terms of its paradoxes. Yet the fact that these paradoxes reveal so much about the nineteenth century is due to Wagner's having been a dramatist as much as a composer. He championed a socialist Utopia free from financial cares where the pursuit of art could be held as the highest ideal: yet subtly he reinforced the Christian-bourgeois morality of his day. He was an idealist and, for the most part, an optimist, yet death cast the longest shadow over his work. He unleashed in his music a liberating new sensuality and energy, while arguing dramatically that redemption could be achieved only through sublimation, renunciation and self-sacrifice. He worked on a massive scale, but was celebrated for his unprecedented sensitivity to detail. As an artist, he was particular to the point of pedantry, but used his art to preach anti-intellectualism and a recognition of nature as the teacher of spontaneity. And while his operatic reforms and innovations were radical and international in their influence, they were, at the same time, rooted in a vast cultural and philosophical learning, and in mythic sources that were conspicuously German. Nowadays these opposites may readily be understood as interdependent. But earlier judgements of Wagner have, not surprisingly, been characterized by significant contradictions: he has been seen both as the high priest of love and as a dangerous, even malevolent, theatrical wizard.

Something of this critical perplexity owes to a further apparent dichotomy: between the high seriousness and tenacity of his work on the one hand, and the rash impetuosity of his personal and financial affairs on the other. This became evident even at an early stage of his life. Born in 1813, he matriculated from Leipzig University as a music student in 1831, at which time he studied composition privately with Theodore Weinlig (lessons recalled, perhaps, in *Die Meistersinger*). It was the epiphanies of this time, in drama (the plays of Shakespeare) and music (Beethoven's Ninth Symphony, Weber's *Der Freischütz* and (allegedly) Wilhelmine Schröder-Devrient singing Leonora in *Fidelio*), that were to lead in due course to the synthesis of the two arts into a 'higher' form. Also no less important for the development of his impeccable sense of theatre and stagecraft was the early and extensive first-hand knowledge he gained of the operatic repertoire as music director in Riga (1837) and Dresden (1843), and his experiences as a resident in Paris (1840), the operatic capital of Europe. As a consequence, his first three operas showed diverse influences: *Die Feen* (1833), *Das Liebesverbot* (1836) and the highly successful *Rienzi* (1840) owe as much to the examples of Bellini, Mehul, Auber, Meyerbeer and Spontini as they do to those of his German contemporaries. But these were also turbulent years privately. In 1836, he married Minna Planer whose early, but brief, elopement with a Königsberg merchant boded ill for the couple's future. In 1839, debts compelled him to flee Riga. After travels to Russia and England he settled in Paris, where his extravagance landed him for a short time in debtor's prison.

There was a similar pattern to the next decade. With *Der fliegende Holländer* (*The Flying Dutchman*, 1841), *Tannhäuser* (1847) and *Lohengrin* (1848), he found his own voice, took Romantic opera to its peak, uncovered most of his later dramatic concerns and provided a vital transition from sectionalized opera to operas where entire acts were unfolded as unbroken musical textures. He was also deeply absorbed in the socially iconoclastic Young Germany movement (which inspired his belief in free love), the Young Hegelians and the anti-Christian philosophy of **Ludwig Feuerbach**. Yet his participation in the Dresden uprisings of 1848–9 forced him to flee Saxony (**Bakunin** said he was too much of an idealist to be an effective revolutionary), and in the following financially unstable years he derived his income from concert-giving (he later wrote a monograph on conducting), which entailed further travels to Italy, England and France (his notorious pamphlet deploring the Jewish influence on music appears to have been triggered by Meyerbeer's refusal to promote his work).

In the 1850s, the affairs with Jessie Laussot and Mathilde Wesendonck that led eventually to Wagner's separation from Minna were evidently bound up with the great effort of gestation demanded by the music drama format that engaged him for the rest of his life. At this time his principal sources were Grimm's *German Mythology* and Greek drama in general (though Aeschylus especially), sources central to his attempt to restore to the theatre a lost communal consciousness (the argument was further developed in *The Birth of Tragedy* by Wagner's protégé, the philosopher **Friedrich Nietzsche**); and in *The Artwork of the Future* (*Das Kunstwerk der Zukunft*, 1849) and the comprehensive *Opera and Drama* (*Oper und Drama*, 1851) he described

how traditional technical features would in future have to be newly balanced and blended in order that music at all times could illumine the drama and not vice versa (this is what he meant by the *Gesamtkunstwerk*).

The main fruit of this undertaking was *Der Ring des Nibelungen*, a music drama in three evenings (*Die Walküre*, *Siegfried* and *Götterdämmerung*) preceded by an introductory evening, *Das Rheingold*. The libretto was begun in 1848, the music completed in 1874, and the whole performed in 1876. In the meantime, he composed two other works motivated to a greater or lesser extent by biographical concerns. Of *Tristan und Isolde* (1859) he had written to his life-long friend Ferencz **Liszt**: 'As I have never in life felt the real bliss of love, I must erect a monument to the most beautiful of my dreams ... *Tristan and Isolde*.' And the extent to which he had absorbed the exotic nihilism of Schopenhauer's *The World as Will and Representation* emerges from his remark that 'freedom from all our dreams' – in other words, extinction – 'is our only salvation'. In the comedy *Die Meistersinger* (1867), however, he offered a defence of his own position as a German artist through the words of Hans Sachs and projected his aesthetic attitudes to the nature and function of high art.

But the end of the 1860s saw Wagner in changed circumstances. The publication of the poem of *Der Ring* had been prefaced by an appeal to an enlightened patron. In 1864, the young King of Bavaria, Ludwig II, declared himself ready and willing to respond. He eased Wagner's debts, promised him a regular income, and supported his projects – albeit intermittently – for the rest of his life. In 1861, Wagner had seen Minna for the last time (she died five years later); and two years after he had settled in Villa Tribschen near Lucerne, he was joined permanently by Cosima Liszt, at the time the wife of the conductor Hans von Bülow and daughter of the composer (according to whom she revered Wagner with a Senta-like devotion). Her diaries were to yield absorbing biographical information on Wagner's later years, following on from his auto-biography (which had extended only as far as the mid-1860s). In 1871 Wagner moved to Bayreuth, and the last twelve years of his life were devoted to founding a specially designed festival theatre (which opened in 1876), to building his own house (Wahn-fried, in 1874), to composing and producing his final music drama *Parsifal* (in part an idealization of Ludwig II), and to writing extensively on practical, musical and philo-sophical issues of the day. The organizational strain aggravated a heart condition (angina), and he died in Venice in 1883.

Although Wagner's art evolved extra-ordinarily during his lifetime, most of the main issues are essentially present in his first three mature works. In his transformation of Heine's account of *Der fliegende Holländer*, Wagner laid a special emphasis on the role of Senta. It is her self-sacrifice that redeems the Dutchman who had been destined to wander the seas eternally in punishment for his Pro-methean defiance of divinity. In the ballad that forms the kernel of the work, she reveals (with what **Thomas Mann** described as the 'lofty hysteria' of all Wagner's heroines) not merely love, but a deep, abnormal bonding with the more-than-human, timeless hero. On the other hand, his love for her is both a yearning for redemption and a longing for death (without her love, he is tragically doomed 'never to die'): her sacrifice is part of his self-fulfilment. But through it, they are both transfigured, and in a conclusion that reveals an essentially Christian morality, love emerges triumphant. Although the work is organized into discontinuous groups of scenes (Wagner soon came to prefer unbroken con-tinuities in each act), it is powerfully homo-geneous from a harmonic point of view – a feature of all Wagner's subsequent works.

If the Dutchman's quest for Senta repre-sented part of the nineteenth century's (and Wagner's) quest for Goethe's *ewig Weibliche* (eternal womanhood), then the examination in *Tannhäuser* (a significant conflation of two sources from *Das Knaben Wunderhorn*) of car-nality (the court of Venus) and sublime purity

(the Wartburg, the Minnesingers, Elizabeth and the pilgrims) established two poles important for Wagner's work generally. Their musical treatment through unstable harmony on the one hand, and pseudo-archaisms on the other, were to lead to the most characteristic sounds of *Tristan* and *Par-sifal*. In the libretto, the two worlds are to a certain extent interdependent. Tannhäuser, a singer with whom Wagner identified closely, recognizes that through Venus 'every sweet wonder stems', but nevertheless proclaims that 'in the midst of joy, I crave pain'. On the other hand, the gravity of the saintly Eliza-beth is at least partially sexually achieved: he has awoken in her 'emotions I had never experienced, longings I had never known'. Yet in its first version, the music (as with Senta's in *Der fliegende Holländer*) had not fully realized the feminine aspect of the text (Venus especially): and the post-Tristan revi-sions that developed the work's latent eroti-cism also unbalanced it stylistically. At the end of his life it remained the one work with which Wagner was still dissatisfied.

On the other hand, *Lohengrin* (derived from Wolfram von Eschenbach) is within its own terms consummately achieved. Here, humanity itself is put on trial, with only the divine and the superhuman exalted. Wagner saw in Lohengrin, a fearless emissary from the holy land of the Grail, a symbol of the artist, demanding unquestioning adherence to, and love for, his visions. Lohengrin agrees to defend and marry Elsa as long as she asks neither his name nor his origin. Inevitably, she is set upon by doubters, and after the wedding ceremony presses the forbidden question (why can't he trust her with his secret? she asks rather persuasively; how can love be ideal if she can't even address him?). Sadly, Lohengrin returns to the Grail, Elsa dies of shock and disappointment, and the moral is to be drawn – as **Gustav Mahler** put it – that 'the capacity for trust is masculine, suspicion is feminine'. More still, the audi-ence is left to realize, as Kant had already done, that moral law is not achievable in this world but only in the transcendence of death.

It was to become the dominant message of Wagner's oeuvre. But however two-edged Lohengrin's authoritarianism may be, there were three striking musical developments here: the impressive tableaux that portray an idealized medieval community are skilfully woven into a newly continuous texture; the music has a fresh synaesthetic splendour (**Baudelaire** revelled in the Lohengrin-Grail music); and the art of slow transition from one dramatic extreme (in Act III, festivity and private joy) to another (rupture, desolation and death) is effected by a large-scale control of harmony that adds a new dimension to the meaning of words.

Indeed, Wagner's theorizing in the early 1850s led to a new interdependence of word and music. Whereas previously, large-scale operatic continuity had been in part achieved by the use of 'reminiscence motives' – thematic entities that recurred with the effect of self-conscious quotations – Wagner now developed a constantly evolving orchestral web of thematic fragments, themselves significantly interrelated, which were symphonically developed in an 'unending' melodic flow according to dramatic circumstances. Over these 'leitmotives' (the term employed by Hans von Wolzogen) the voice sang in a heightened recitative (*Sprechgesang*), occasionally taking up the orchestral fragments to give them definitive meaning. This practice was also extended through new uses of harmony and versification. The orchestra thus assumed a narrative role similar to that of the chorus in Greek tragedy: the humans are the playthings of the gods, and the gods are subject to the force of destiny.

These new techniques are central to *Der Ring*, the quasi-Shakespearian complexity of which has attracted such a range of interpretation. The work opens with the depiction of original sin: the dwarf Alberich's seizure of power (symbolized by a ring) through the renunciation of love. He cruelly exploits his fellow dwarfs and places the curse of death on all the ring's future owners (the capitalist analogies here are what fascinated **G.B. Shaw**). Conversely, it is dread of the

loss of power that motivates Wotan, the all-too-human ageing head of the gods, to build Valhalla as a 'fortress against fear'. The cycle shows his fight against impending death, his acquiescence in it, and finally his combustion as flames consume Valhalla.

Importantly, however, there are two aspects to Wotan's personality, just as there were to Faust's. The male, mortal side schemes to perpetuate his power through the creation of a perfect hero, who, while being independent of himself, would represent a new and higher breed of being, capable of winning and guarding the ring. (Being fearless, Siegfried would be exempt from the curse: he is a cousin of Friedrich Schiller's fearless William Tell.) *Die Walküre* shows the failure of the hero's prototype, Siegmund; *Siegfried* shows the eponymous hero's schooling (from nature, not from received wisdom), and his winning of the highest prize, his bride Brünnhilde. *Götterdämmerung* reveals the truth of the comment made in *Das Rheingold* by Wotan's wife Fricka (the goddess of marriage and symbol of a legalistic, repressive society) that the god's eugenic plans are mere dreams: the 'tragic' destruction of Siegfried by Hagen (Alberich's son) is inevitable in a loveless world.

On the other hand, Wotan has a feminine, immortal side shown in two ways: first, in relation to Erda (the earth goddess), who represents the wisdom of the universe and his own deepest conscience. It is she who reminds him of the inexorability of destiny, and her decline matches his. Second, in relation to his daughter by Erda, the Valkyrie Brünnhilde. As his 'wish-child', she guards his deepest interests and intuitions. When the incensed Fricka insists that Wotan destroy his illegitimate child Siegmund (who is the lover of his own sister, herself the wife of another man), Brünnhilde refuses to execute the command as being contrary to Wotan's inner desires and a denial of the love Siegmund feels for Sieglinde. Wotan's strips her of her divinity, a punishment that gives her the independence to perform the Senta-like 'world-redeeming' act of self-sacrifice that atones for the sins committed against Sieg-fried: she casts herself on to the hero's funeral pyre. This act, together with the return of the ring to the Rhinemaidens, forms the basis for the underlying musical optimism with which the work ends (the conclusion, in fact, gave Wagner much trouble): the spirit of love remains if all else has perished.

What is so striking about this vast under-taking is the imaginative richness of its sur-face, especially in its use of the mythic, the elemental, the supernatural and the dynastic; in the complexity of its psychological situa-tions (notably in *Die Walküre*); in the force of its dramatic parallelisms; in its energy (above all in the superlative third act of *Siegfried*); and not least in the invention and variety of the music at every level.

In *Tristan und Isolde*, an essentially private 'action', extinction is seen as the only true consummation of love: as Carl Dahlhaus observes, the love-potion which the maid-servant substitutes for the intended poison, is, in a metaphysical sense, also a death-potion. But this nihilistic stance is not all that Wagner learnt from Schopenhauer. The life-enhancing eroticism of the music, so pre-eminent in Act II, derived its impetus from the key analogy drawn by the philosopher between the qual-ity of music and the quality of the 'Will'. For he describes the 'Will' as the dynamic essence of things, the motivating energy of life before it has been refracted through, and tempered by, consciousness. The merging of the iden-tities of the lovers in the duets is thus a shared return to the well-springs of nature, a redis-covery of what is usually found only in the night-time world of dreams. On the other hand, Wagner was too much of a moralist not to invest the day-time world of social contracts, embodied in the figure of King Marke, with its own dignity (Tristan appears to break honour in his love for Isolde); and the unification of the lovers in death – rather than in life – also offers a social answer to an illicit love (Marke's post-mortem absolution of Tristan and Isolde begs all kinds of ques-tions). Technically, the work is notable for two reasons: first, while Wagner adopted a

more flexible treatment here than in the *Ring* of leitmotif and *Stabreim* (the creation of poetic continuity through the incantatory use of internal alliteration rather than end-rhyme); and second, the music derives new, complex and revolutionary means for obscuring its traditional tonal anchors with-out renouncing them, as a way of mirroring the language of the 'Will'.

Just as *Tristan* reinterprets human energy in erotic terms, so does *Die Meistersinger* see the justification of art in the need to sublimate aggression and promote itself as the highest activity of all. In this work – a comic appen-dage to *Tannhäuser* – the central figure is no longer the impetuous young knight (in this case Walther), but the cobbler Hans Sachs (alias Wagner). Sachs is now the older man who declines to play King Marke to Eva's Isolde. His advice is mellow and wise: art, he says, must be rooted in dreams and not rules (his teaching Walther how to compose *Stol-len*, stanzas, has nothing to do with the impotent criticism of Beckmesser: he merely tames the socially disruptive aspects of Wal-ther's earlier song); the older artist must learn to re-create the impulsive spontaneity of youth; and new art must build on the achievement of the old (here, the German masters, symbolizing the spirit of Germany itself). Accordingly, the musical language of not just the trial song but the entire opera does just this: its 'archaic' harmonies, its newly clarified tonality, its transparently articulated form, and the precision of its details have all benefited from Wagner's ear-lier innovations.

Wagner's final work, the 'sacred festival play' *Parsifal*, provoked a virulent attack from the estranged Nietzsche. The denial and sub-limation of sexuality into Christian ritual (shown at its most theatrical), the covert misogyny, the obsession with the purity of blood (at this time Wagner cast doubt on Christ's Jewishness), the focused anti-intellectualism (Parsifal means 'so-pure-a-fool') and the invasion of pathology (the Knights' protection of animals reflects the composer's vegetarianism), all contributed to what Nietzsche saw as a denial of the important elements in the earlier music dramas. Certainly, its winnowing, enervate sexuality is that of an older man, and its central premise – that redemption may be won through pity (for Wagner, the highest love; for Nietzsche, a form of contempt) – was indeed new. But for all that Nietzsche's Zarathustran ideals (as presented, for example, in the *Genealogy of Morals*) were, in part, founded on a self-conscious refutation of the *Parsifal* philosophy, the criticisms represented only a half-truth. For in this work, as in the *Ring*, the kinship relations touch extraordinary depths (especially the Oedipal temptation of Parsifal by Kundry), and the music (orchestrated with a wonderful diffused light) is no less resourceful than that of *Tristan*'s in pursuit of new extremes of expression. Moreover, Wagner was reviewing here the worlds of *Tannhäuser* and *Lohengrin*, albeit with a Sachsian mellowness.

While the refutation of *Parsifal* contributed to the emergence of existentialism and the exploration of the consequences of 'the Death of God', both Nietzsche and Wagner were seen by Thomas Mann as part of a chain of German thinking that extended back through Mann's own stories and the writings of **Freud** to Schopenhauer and Kant. It was this tradition that also provided a foundation for so much of the thought of **D.H. Lawrence**. In France, on the other hand, it was chiefly the musical and synaesthetic effects of the music dramas that exerted so powerful an effect upon composers (**Debussy**, and later **Messiaen**), painters (**Renoir** and **Cézanne**) and writers (**Baudelaire**, **Mallarmé** and **Proust**). **James Joyce** argued that the 'musical effects' of his Sirens chapter from the novel *Ulysses* were superior to those of *Die Walküre*, and in Molly's final monologue he created a literary equivalent for the perorations of Isolde and Brünnhilde, albeit cast in a demotic language. Indeed, female protagonists are central to the immediately post-Wagnerian German operas that take psycho-sexual disorders to their extremes: **Schoenberg's** *Erwartung* (1909), **Richard Strauss's** *Salome*

(1905) and *Elektra* (1909), and **Berg's** *Lulu* (1928–35). The technical innovations in harmony, melody and instrumentation introduced in these and other works derived their impetus directly from the most advanced, rootless aspects of the music in *Tristan* and *Parsifal*, and led in due course to the formulation by **Schoenberg** of the twelve-tone method. This method, and the line of development supporting it, did not pass unchallenged, though the challenges (as with Nietzsche) derived strength from their opposition: even **Stravinsky's** no less controversial 'neoclassicism' was rooted in a refutation of the Wagnerian aesthetic.

In the years since the Second World War, scholarship has had to address the dark side of Romanticism that undoubtedly underlies Wagner's work in general and his life-long anti-Semitism in particular. Some scholars have left no stone unturned to reveal the scale of Wagner's hatreds; others have sought explanations; others still (including performers) have concentrated on the musical merits in their attempt to disassociate Wagner's name from the use to which it was put by Houston Stewart Chamberlain and the leaders of the Third Reich. Even **Theodor Adorno**, writing in 1963, advocated 'corrections' in modern productions. Thus today the paradox of Wagner is at its most acute: performances of Wagner's music in Israel arouse the strongest indignation, while opera houses and private companies around the world vie with each other to mount ever more outspoken interpretations. That is to say, Wagner's ability to transfigure the lives of his audiences remains entirely undiminished.

Further reading

See: *Wagner on Music and Drama* (1970). Still the best biography is Ernest Newman's *The Life of Richard Wagner* (4 vols, 1933–47), though Robert Gutman's *Richard Wagner, The Man, His Mind and His Music* (1968) is stimulating. G.B. Shaw's *The Perfect Wagnerite* (1922) is a classic study, and Robert Donington's *Wagner's Ring and Its Symbols* (1960) is intriguing in its application of Jungian ideas. Carl Dahlhaus's *Richard Wagner's Music*

Dramas (1971, trans. 1979), is a thoughtful recent introduction to the works. Barry Millington's *The Wagner Compendium* (1992) and U. Müller and P. Wapnewski's *Wagner Handbook* (1992) are both full of fascinating information, as is Michael Saffle's *Richard Wagner: A Guide to Research* (2002). The Jewish question is explored in Paul Lawrence Rose's *Wagner: Race and Revolution* (1992) and Michael Weiner's *Richard Wagner and the Anti-semitic Imagination* (1995). Other important writers on Wagner include Theodor Adorno, Dieter Borchmeyer, Warren Darcy, Martin Gregor-Dellin, Thomas Mann, Patrick McCreless, Jean-Jacques Nattiez, Friedrich Nietzsche and Curt von Westernhagen. The two volumes of *Cosima Wagner's Diaries* were published in English in 1978–80.

CHRISTOPHER WINTLE

WAJDA, Andrzej

1926–

Polish film director

The son of an army officer, Andrzej Wajda spent most of his childhood in the provinces. After the war he studied fine art, then moved on to the newly established film school at Lodz. His student films were unremarkable, but he entered the film industry in the early 1950s.

Wajda was only thirteen when the war broke out, but his first three films show a desire to come to terms with the recent past and form a trilogy of war stories. All were scripted by writers with first-hand experience of the events recounted. *A Generation* (1955) – the title is indicative of Wajda's ambition – was made at a time when notions of 'socialist realism' and 'the positive hero' reigned supreme and is the most conventional of the three in its telling of the political education of a young worker. *Kanal* (1957), a bitter tale of the failure of the Warsaw uprising, established Wajda's reputation abroad, but is surpassed by *Ashes and Diamonds* (1958), a work of enormous subtlety and complexity, set at the moment of the German surrender and benefiting from a dazzling performance by Zbigniew Cybulski. All three films show the richness of Wajda's visual style, which is carried to extremes in his first colour film *Lotna* (1959), an episodic tale built around a horse and set in the period of 1939 when the Polish cavalry found itself confronted with German tanks.

In the 1960s Wajda tried, less successfully, to broaden his style by tackling comedy and epic subjects, only to reach disaster with the unreleased international co-production, *Gates to Paradise* (1967). *Everything for Sale* (1968) was a self-examination prompted by the death of his close friend, the actor Cybulski. A delicate interweaving of fiction and actual events, it remains one of Wajda's major achievements. But despite this success, there is an uncertainty of tone and unevenness of quality in Wajda's subsequent work, as he moves constantly between cinema, the theatre and television. While he has worked on German, British and French co-productions, much of his work is specifically Polish in meaning, as in the series of literary adaptations begun with *The Wedding* (1972). Wajda's finest work of the 1970s is *Man of Marble* (1977) which, like *Everything for Sale*, is a complex reflection on the nature of film-making, as well as a look back at the **Stalinist** era in which the director began his career.

Man of Marble was matched, and arguably excelled, by *Man of Iron* (1981), which treats of the tensions between the individual and the state on an epic scale, set firmly within the emergent Polish Solidarity movement. It won Wajda the *Palme d'Or* at the Cannes Film Festival, but also forced him into exile. His next film *Danton* (1982), about the French revolutionary and starring Gérard Depardieu, was made in France, where Wajda remained until 1989, only returning to Poland once the communist state had been dismembered. Such was his standing among the Polish peoples that he was swiftly elected to the new parliament in Warsaw.

Wajda has continued to direct but, back in his homeland, his later work has generally been slow to find an international audience, being narrowly national in its patterns of meaning. His early work shows a fusing of the heritage of Italian neo-realism and an indigenous Polish taste for highly wrought visuals, complex symbolism and paroxysms of violence. His name will always be associated with his war trilogy which did much to establish Eastern European film making as a force in world cinema.

Further reading

Wajda's other films include: *Innocent Sorcerers* (1960); *Samson* (1961); *Siberian Lady Macbeth* (1962); one episode of *Love at Twenty* (1962); *Ashes* (1965); *Roly-Poly* (1968); *Hunting Flies* (1969); *Landscape after Battle* (1970); *The Birch-Wood* (1970); *Pilate and Others* (1972); *The Promised Land* (1975); *The Shadow Line* (1976); *Rough Treatment* (1978); *The Young Ladies of Wilko* (1979); *The Possessed* (1988); *Pan Tadeusz* (1999) and *Zemsta* (2002). *My Life in Film* (1987) is an autobiography. See also: Boleslaw Michatek, *The Cinema of Andrzej Wajda* (1973); Boleslaw Sulik, *A Change of Tack: Making the Shadow Line* (1976).

ROY ARMES
(REVISED AND UPDATED BY THE EDITOR)

WALCOTT, Derek

1930–

Caribbean poet, painter and dramatist

Derek Walcott was born in the town of Castries in St Lucia, one of the Windward Islands in the Lesser Antilles. The breathtaking beauty of the Caribbean landscape, with its immensity of sky and sea, has had a powerful shaping effect on his work, but so, too, has the painful colonial legacy of the place, with its disparate linguistic, cultural and religious traditions. Much of Walcott's poetry has been inspired by his profound sense of being 'divided to the vein' by his African and European ancestry. The English-speaking son of a Methodist family in a French-speaking Catholic community, Walcott quickly acquired an astute awareness of both the potential artistic fruitfulness and the personal and social conflicts that came with a complex multicultural inheritance. In his life and in his work, he has often been drawn by the compelling image of the castaway, caught between different places, cultures and

languages. Since the early 1980s, he has divided his time between the United States, working as Professor of Creative Writing at the University of Boston, and Trinidad, his new home as a Caribbean poet and dramatist.

Although Walcott made an impressive early debut with *25 Poems* in 1948, it was *In a Green Night* (1962) that brought him recognition worldwide. The title, echoing Andrew Marvell's great poem of religious exile, 'Bermudas', is one of many rueful reminders that the Renaissance was a green age of learning, but also a time of colonial darkness and oppression. That troubling contradiction informs Walcott's 'Ruins of a Great House', a magnificent subversion of the English country house poem, in which 'men like Hawkins, Walter Raleigh, Drake' appear as 'Ancestral murderers and poets'. Ironically citing John Milton and William Blake, the poem laments the lost paradise and the green fields of the Caribbean, but it closes with a moving and forgiving reminder of John Donne's *Devotions* and his famous declaration that 'No man is an island'. 'A Far Cry from Africa' has a more urgent contemporary political relevance and stretches Walcott's allegiances to breaking point as he contemplates the Mau-Mau insurrection against British rule in Kenya in the 1950s: 'I who have cursed/The drunken officer of British rule, now choose/Between this Africa and the English tongue I love.'

Displacement and dislocation are abiding themes in Walcott's work, and are palpably evident in the titles of such volumes as *The Castaway* (1965) and *The Gulf* (1969). He attempts to come to terms with the psychological effects of the African diaspora by finding parallels in the epic poetry of Homer, with its powerful images of voyage and exile. At the same time, Walcott is sensitively aware of what opponents might see as an elitist Eurocentrism. 'The classics can console,' he once wrote, 'but never enough.' Even so, the idea of the epic journey persists in his work, especially in *Omeros* (1990), with its punning emphasis on the Greek name for Homer and the circular quest for home. In several poems he imagines the Middle Passage, the sea journey that brought African slaves to the Caribbean, as a nightmarish odyssey. The epic journey also provides the structural underpinning for his long biographical poem, *Another Life* (1973), which both alludes to great autobiographical works in the English tradition (William Wordsworth's *Prelude* and **James Joyce's** *Portrait of the Artist as a Young Man*) and sets out to rediscover and repossess a distinctively Caribbean cultural inheritance. 'My generation,' he said, 'had looked at life with black skins and blue eyes.' In his next volume, *Sea Grapes* (1976), he returns to the sights and sounds of his native St Lucia, and in the rapturous 'Sainte Lucie' he closes a long passage of French creole with a passionate outburst in English: 'Come back to me my language.'

Although Walcott has tended to write in standard English, one of his most ambitious linguistic efforts was in the Trinidadian creole of 'The Schooner Flight', another sea-faring odyssey that appeared in *The Star Apple Kingdom* in 1979. The speaker is a Trinidadian sailor-poet, Shabine, who speaks eloquently for his creator: 'I'm just a red nigger who love the sea,/I had a sound colonial education,/I have Dutch, nigger and English in me,/and either I'm nobody, or I'm a nation.' There is a resolute refusal of identity politics here, at a time when 'hybridity' was just a glimpse in the eye of aspiring postcolonial theorists. Walcott refuses any simple categories of selfhood and nation, giving Shabine the last word on the matter: 'I had no nation now but the imagination.' In his 1974 essay, 'The Muse of History', he argues against a literature of either revenge or remorse, polemic or pathos, insisting that 'the truly tough aesthetic of the New World neither explains nor forgives history'.

That 'truly tough aesthetic' continues to be worked out in successive volumes, including *The Bounty* (1997), with its moving elegy for the poet's mother. *Tiepolo's Hound* (2000) is a painterly evocation of the life of **Camille Pissarro**, accompanied by Walcott's own watercolours, while *The Prodigal* (2004) is an exploration of European culture and the impact of the Old World on the New. Walcott's efforts to establish a distinctive New World aesthetic in poetry have been paralleled and complemented by his equal determination to construct a distinctive Caribbean theatrical tradition. His first major play, *Henri Christophe* (1950), reflects on the liberation of Haiti through a sustained psychological study of the enigmatic accomplice of Toussaint L'Ouverture. *The Sea at Dauphin* (1954) shows the influence of the Irish playwright, **J.M. Synge**, while *Ione* (1957) seeks to blend Caribbean folk elements with the legacy of classical drama. Walcott's determination to find a dramatic language that went beyond mimicry and to create a theatre where 'someone could do Shakespeare or sing calypso with equal conviction' was to be realized in Walcott's work with the Trinidad Theatre Workshop and in the production of powerfully engaging plays like *Ti-Jean and His Brothers* (1958) and *Dream on Monkey Mountain* (1967). Walcott has also collaborated on musicals such as *The Joker of Seville* (1974) and *O Babylon!* (1976), both with Galt MacDermot, and *The Capeman* (1998) with Paul Simon. He was awarded the Nobel Prize for Literature in 1992.

Further reading

Other works include: *Collected Poems 1948–1984* (1986). Bruce King's biography, *Derek Walcott: A Caribbean Life*, was in 2000. For stimulating critical commentary, see Paula Burnett, *Derek Walcott: Politics and Poetics* (2000), J. Edward Chamberlin, *Come Back to Me My Language: Poetry and the West Indies* (1993), and John Thieme, *Derek Walcott* (1999). *Agenda* magazine dedicated a special issue to Derek Walcott, edited by Maria Cristina Fumagalli (Vol. 39, Nos 1–3, Winter 2002–3).

STEPHEN REGAN

WAŁĘSA, Lech

1943–

Polish workers' leader and politician

Lech Wałęsa was a key element in the destruction of the Soviet empire. While most

Western leaders had come to see it as an evil dictatorship, they lacked the arguments and images that could persuade the masses and the broad left, which clung to a belief in it as an essentially benign system. Wałęsa provided those arguments and those images. In the space of a few weeks he convinced the politically naive throughout the world that the dictatorship of the proletariat was a cruel fiction. By the same token, he stripped the Soviet system of its credibility, and the international left of a large part of its *raison d'être*.

Conceived in a Nazi labour camp and orphaned in childhood, Wałęsa grew up in the rural poverty of northern Poland. After school he qualified as an electrician, and took a job at the **Lenin** shipyard in Gdańsk. In December 1970 he took part in protests against gruelling conditions and poor pay, learning his first lessons in politics as he watched the demonstrations turn to riots, ending in a massacre by the army. His political education continued through his contacts with the intellectuals who had set up the Workers' Defence Committee (KOR) and other dissident groups; and his determination was strengthened by the visit to Poland in 1979 of the newly elected **Pope John Paul II**, who brought people together and talked of human dignity, freedom, respect for work and honesty in government.

On 14 August 1980 the Lenin shipyard went on strike over the politically motivated dismissal of a welder. Wałęsa prevented the workers from going out on to the street, where they would be at the mercy of the government's tanks; instead he turned the strike into a sit-in and founded an independent trade union, Solidarność ('Solidarity'). Other shipyards, mines and factories all over the country followed suit and sent delegates to Gdańsk. Since Wałęsa refused to go to Warsaw, the government was obliged to send negotiators to the shipyard. As branches of the union were founded in virtually every workplace in the country, rapidly bringing its membership up to ten million, the negotiations were in effect between the government and the active population of Poland. The accords signed at their conclusion covered far more than working conditions: one clause stipulated that Catholic Mass must be broadcast live on state television every Sunday. Solidarność was more of a national movement than a trade union, a coming together of the people in rejection of the atheistic and materialist politics and culture of communism.

On the night of 13 December 1981 Poland's new leader General Wojciech Jaruzelski arrested thousands of workers and dissidents, abolished Solidarność and declared a state of war. Over the following months, the communist Polish Workers' Party reestablished control in draconian ways in every sphere of life.

After keeping Wałęsa in solitary confinement for eleven months, the authorities thought it safe to release him. He was allowed to return to work at the shipyard. But his moustachioed face, instantly recognizable to television viewers throughout the world, had become an icon of the unjustly downtrodden worker. In 1983 he was awarded the Nobel Peace Prize. He had been identified by the United States, Great Britain and other Western powers as a critical outpost on the front line of the Cold War. The Pope, whom Wałęsa had first met in 1981 and whom he saw during the pontiff's subsequent visits to Poland, was the principal conduit of their support. The authorities spared no effort to smear Wałęsa, dissident intellectuals belittled his significance, and a younger generation of workers dismissed him as a broken man. But when a fresh round of strikes broke out in 1988, he reasserted his authority. He defused the crisis but called openly for a change of the political system. The government suggested 'Round Table' talks and, taking a huge political risk, Wałęsa agreed.

The talks, which began in January 1989, changed the political system, allowing non-Party candidates to stand for a quota of the seats in parliament. The resulting elections, in June 1989, were a humiliation for the communists, with the entire free quota falling to Solidarność candidates. Wałęsa, who had not stood for election himself, brokered an agreement with the defeated but nevertheless powerful authorities which resulted in the formation of the coalition government of prime minister Tadeusz Mazowiecki. Key ministries such as defence were left in the hands of communists, in order to reassure the Soviet Union as well as the local Party. But as neighbouring communist regimes began collapsing and the Party dissolved itself in January 1990, the need to accommodate Soviet sensibilities evaporated. Wałęsa, who had been sidelined by Mazowiecki, called for fresh, entirely free elections. Unwilling to give up power, the government stood firm. Wałęsa responded by standing for the presidency, and was elected on 9 December 1990.

Wałęsa was not presidential material. A clever operator with a genius for improvisation rather than an intuitive leader, he lacked gravitas and vision. Born of conflict with his natural allies, his presidency was marred by mistrust and jealousy, making life difficult for the governments that succeeded each other during his term. When this came to an end in 1995, he was ignominiously defeated.

In 1981 and 1989 the combination of Wałęsa's hard-nosed opportunism and personal charisma with the intelligence and expertise provided by intellectuals who came to the support of the workers had produced a winning formula. Its undoing was the intellectuals' instinctive tendency to push Wałęsa aside once victory had been achieved. The conflict stemming from this vitiated the evolution of a new political culture and paved the way for the come-back of the communists' successors. Wałęsa himself quickly became an irrelevance, not only in Polish politics but in national life as well.

Further reading

Wałęsa's autobiography, *A Path of Hope*, was published in London in 1987 (trans. from French original, *Un chemin d'espoir*, 1987); the best all-round biography is Roger Boyes, *The Naked President* (1994); see also *The Book of Lech Wałęsa* (1982); Neal Ascherson, *The Polish August* (1981); Timothy Garton-Ash, *The Polish Revolution* (1983); and Peter Raina, *Poland 1981* (1985).

ADAM ZAMOYSKI

WALEY, Arthur David

1889–1966

British orientalist

A celebrated and prolific translator from Chinese and Japanese literature who succeeded in opening up these areas to the general educated public in a way that had never been done before, Arthur Waley studied classics at Rugby School and at King's College, Cambridge. Waley was his mother's maiden name which he adopted by deed poll in 1914.

At Cambridge, Waley came under the influence of Lowes Dickinson, who had recently travelled to China and Japan; and in the Oriental Print Department of the British Museum, where he worked from 1913 to 1929, his official superior was the poet and Eastern art expert Lawrence Binyon. Waley also almost certainly owed something to the example of **Ezra Pound**, whose *Cathay* or poems based on Chinese originals was first published in 1915 and with whom he had an acquaintance about then. After he resigned from the British Museum, Waley lived off the income he earned from his writings. He never held a full-time post at a university because he preferred not to, but he frequently attended or gave seminars on Chinese poetry at the School of Oriental and African Studies, London University. A Londoner all his adult life, he lived in Bloomsbury and never travelled to the Far East.

Waley's knowledge of Chinese and Japanese was self-taught and from 1918 he published a very large number of books, the main scope of which was literature but which also took in Chinese philosophy and history. Translation from Japanese was, in terms of separate titles, much the smaller part of Waley's oeuvre, and he did not really continue with this side of his activities after 1933. On the other hand, his own favourite among his published works is said to have been *The Pillow-book of Sei Shōnagon* (*Makura no Sōshi*, 1928), and undoubtedly his greatest single feat, and not only from the point of view of length, was *The Tale of Genji* (*Genji Monogatari*), brought out in six substantial volumes (1925–33). The two other books from Japanese were *Japanese Poetry: The 'Uta'* (1919) and *The Nō Plays of Japan* (1921).

All these books can be regarded in one way or another as partial translations. That on classical poetry was by intent a rather narrow selection and amounts to some seventy-five smallish pages of actual texts; *Nō Plays* contains translations of nineteen of the dramas and summaries of sixteen more; the *Pillow-book* is another slender work of 160 pages and consists of what Waley regarded as choice excerpts with connecting passages supplied by himself; even *The Tale of Genji* has a chapter of the original unaccountably omitted, though it runs to some 1,100 pages in the one-volume edition of 1935. Furthermore, all these books have now to some degree been put in the shade by later works by other hands. Yet Waley's output, even in the circumscribed area of translation from Japanese, has had an enormously beneficial impact on several generations of scholars and students as an introduction to the field, and though he is not above criticism as a translator (he is often accused of misunderstanding the text or embellishing it), the charm, vigour and, in many places, the underlying veracity of his style will continue to appeal. In particular, his translations of Japanese poetry are accurate as well as attractive.

Waley's translations from Chinese, which are too voluminous to mention briefly, have yet to undergo a process of critical sifting and evaluation. No doubt they will, and no doubt much good, hard wheat will be left once the chaff has been blown away. The early *One Hundred and Seventy Chinese Poems* (1918), however, holds a special place in the history of English prosody. Instead of attempting to 'versify' his renderings, in strict metre and rhyme, Waley developed a system of stressed syllables without rhyme, independently, or so

he claimed, of the 'Sprung Rhythm' of Gerard **Manley Hopkins**, whose work was first published in collected form the same year. Consequently, while Waley's example of 'free verse' influenced many of his younger contemporaries, as well as **W.B. Yeats**, he has also been the target of those who regret the abandonment of traditional versification.

In answer to his critics Waley contended that as a translator his first loyalty was to the spirit of the originals. His writings were also aimed at the general reader rather than the specialist. In the sense that for many the flavour of Chinese and Japanese literature is the flavour he provided it with, he was almost entirely successful in his endeavour. In C.P. Snow's novel *The Light and the Dark* (1947) a nervous Lewis Eliot, on a risky wartime flight from Bristol to Lisbon, tries to pass the time reading *Genji*, and 'subtle and lovely though it was, I wished it had more narrative power'.

Further reading

See: *A Bibliography of Arthur Waley* (1968) by Francis Johns; and Ivan Morris, *Madly Singing in the Mountains* (1970); A. Waley, *A Half of Two Lives* (1982).

R.H.P. MASON

WALLACE, Alfred Russel

1823–1913

English biologist

A.R. Wallace was born into a poor English family residing in Usk, Monmouthshire. Receiving little formal education, he read voraciously and, after moving to London (1837), attended public lectures which led to his becoming an agnostic. He began to collect plants while working as a surveyor (1838–43) and a teacher (1844–5), and turned increasingly to the sciences, especially the works of T.R. Malthus, Charles Lyell and Robert Chambers. It was Chambers's *Vestiges of the Natural History of Creation* that convinced Wallace that species had evolved and had not been created.

In pursuit of proof for this belief Wallace and a friend set off for the Amazon to assemble evidence. He collected specimens and made notes for four years, but on his return to England (1852) lost almost everything in a shipwreck. Nonetheless he was able to publish *A Narrative of Travels on the Amazon and Rio Negro* (1853).

Wallace then spent eight years (1854–62) in the Malay Archipelago, exploring, studying and assembling a collection of over 125,000 biological specimens. He wrote to **Darwin** about his views on the mechanism of evolution, and on 1 July 1858 the latter presented a joint paper to the Linnaean Society outlining the conclusion each had reached independently – that evolution proceeded by *natural selection.*

On returning to England Wallace studied his collections and wrote and lectured profusely. He married in 1866 and had three children. In the 1860s he became a spiritualist and later adopted other unpopular causes, such as women's rights and socialism, which he promulgated as eagerly as his scientific ideas. He died in 1913 in Dorset.

Wallace wrote about twenty books and four hundred articles and reviews which established him as a major figure in natural history. Of special fame is his work on evolution, which he concluded was demonstrated in the geographical distribution of species, as he stated in an important essay of 1855. But that left him with the problem of *how* species evolve.

Like Darwin, Wallace had observed the wide range of variation among individuals of the same species and had seen that many of their distinctive traits were inherited by their offspring. In 1858, while suffering a severe fever in the East, he remembered Malthus's essay on population and his doctrine of the 'survival of the fittest'. With this in mind Wallace concluded that evolution proceeded by *natural selection* of the fittest from this pool of variations – those individuals most able to compete for a limited food supply – whose beneficial characteristics were then passed on to their offspring. This was also Darwin's

conclusion and the argument of the joint paper presented to the Linnean Society in London in 1858.

In *Contributions to the Theory of Natural Selection* (1870), Wallace reprinted these essays along with others elaborating his views, including those few points on which he differed from Darwin. Wallace laid more emphasis on protective resemblance: for example, the physical resemblance of one species of fly to a dangerous wasp. More important, however, was his view of man, whom Darwin had placed at the pinnacle of evolution. Wallace, by now a spiritualist, argued that at a certain point in time the human body had ceased to evolve; the brain and mind now started to evolve independently of any physical evolution, making man a creature quite different from the animals. This mental evolution required a mechanism beyond natural selection. In other words, Wallace attempted to reconcile evolution with the existence of a higher being. With his later *Darwinism* (1889) we encounter one of the best nineteenth-century accounts of evolution by natural selection, a work which – unlike Darwin's *The Origin of Species* – firmly rejects Lamarck's theory of the inheritance of acquired characteristics.

At least as important, however, is Wallace's work on zoogeography, which he greatly promoted through his classic *The Malay Archipelago* (1869), *The Geographical Distribution of Animals* (1876) and *Island Life* (1880). These books present the fieldwork and deductions on which his evolution theory was based. As well, they define 'Wallace's Line', which he discovered – the boundary between the Australian and Asiatic zoogeographical zones, which runs through the Malay Archipelago.

Though overshadowed by Darwin, Wallace too was a formidable controversialist who deserves to be remembered for his fundamental contributions to modern biology.

Further reading

Other works include: *Palm Trees of the Amazon and Their Uses* (1853); *The Scientific Aspect of the*

Supernatural (1866); *Tropical Nature, and Other Essays* (1878); *Natural Selection and Tropical Nature: Essays on Descriptive and Theoretical Biology* (1891); *Vaccination a Delusion, Its Penal Enforcement a Crime: Proved by the Official Evidence in the Reports of the Royal Commission* (1898); *The Wonderful Century: Its Successes and Its Failures* (1898); *Studies Scientific and Social* (1900); *Man's Place in the Universe: A Study of the Results of Scientific Research in Relation to the Unity or Plurality of Worlds* (1903); *My Life: A Record of Events and Opinions* (1905); *Alfred Russel Wallace; Letters and Reminiscences*, ed. James Marchant (1916). *Lamarck to Darwin: Contributions to Evolutionary Biology, 1809–1859*, ed. H.L. McKinney (1971), includes Wallace's major articles on evolution. About Wallace: H.L. McKinney, *Wallace and Natural Selection* (1972); Wilma B. George, *Biologist Philosopher: A Study of the Life and Writings of Alfred Russel Wallace* (1964); Loren C. Eiseley, *Darwin's Century* (1958); Peter Raby, *Alfred Russel Wallace* (2001); Ross A. Slotten, *The Heretic in Darwin's Court: The Life of Alfred Russel Wallace* (2004).

MICHAEL SCHERK

WARD, Mary Augusta
(Mrs Humphry Ward)

1851–1920
British novelist and social worker

Though Mrs Humphry Ward wrote twenty-five novels, she earns her place here by the celebrity and influence of one work: *Robert Elsmere* (1888). If Carlyle's *Sartor Resartus* (1833–4) was the first great Victorian fictionalization of religious doubt and J.A. Froude's *The Nemesis of Faith* (1849) the most scandalous example of the genre, *Robert Elsmere* was the most complete literary document of the various shades of Victorian faith and doubt. As **Sir Arthur Conan Doyle** commented, '**Trollope** and Mrs Ward have the whole Victorian civilization dissected and preserved.'

The granddaughter of Dr Thomas Arnold of Rugby and niece of **Matthew Arnold**, Mary Ward inherited their moral earnestness. Her father, Thomas Arnold, was an inspector of schools in Tasmania, where she was born, the eldest of eight children, in 1851. He gave up his job in 1856 on becoming a Roman Catholic. The family returned to England, where the girls were sent away by their embittered mother to be unhappy at Protestant boarding schools, while the boys were reared as Roman Catholics. Thomas Arnold was reconverted to Anglicanism in 1865, and the joyfully reconciled family settled in Oxford. Here Mary married a don at Brasenose College, Thomas Humphry Ward, in 1872. To the family's horror, her father rejoined the Church of Rome in 1876, on the eve of taking up an Oxford professorship. He later became Professor of English Literature at University College, Dublin. Mary herself read biblical criticism and rejected the miraculous element of Christian dogma, retaining a quasi-Christian theism and stressing the need for ethical social action. Her interest in religious questions is reflected in most of her novels.

Robert Elsmere analyses at length, but with skill and a sympathetic insight born of her family experience, the strains of a marriage in which the partners differ about religion. It is also a remarkable documentary of the life of conscientious intellectuals in Oxford during the mid-nineteenth century, when Tractarianism, **Newmanism**, Broad Churchism and atheism were the alternatives facing those whose faith in the established church was being undermined by biblical criticism, geological and evolutionary studies. Though not a *roman à clef*, *Robert Elsmere* contains portraits of intellectual types who resemble **Walter Pater**, Mark Pattison, T.H. Green, all of whom Mary Ward knew well during her life in Oxford. Robert Elsmere is a clergyman whose thirst for knowledge leads him to reject traditional Christianity. Tensions arise in his marriage to a staunchly Evangelical woman who has no intellectual curiosity. Elsmere resigns his orders, but practises a kind of Christian Socialism in a centre for the education of the working class in the East End of London.

Within three years the novel had sold 70,000 copies in Britain. According to **Henry James**, it was 'not merely an extraordinarily successful novel; it was, as reflected in contemporary conversation, a momentous public event' (1892). Even **Gladstone** reviewed it, calling it 'eminently an offspring of its time'. *Robert Elsmere* is an intellectual novel, but it also shows something of the descriptive power and imaginative sympathy of **George Eliot's** fiction.

During the 1870s Mrs Ward supported the movement for the higher education of women, becoming the first secretary of Somerville College. Paradoxically, she later campaigned against women's suffrage, insisting on the importance of female influence in the home rather than in public life. Yet she herself was a notable public figure. In 1890 she helped found an unsuccessful establishment for popular Bible-teaching (not unlike Elsmere's centre) at University Hall in London. During the 1914–18 war she published two propagandist works, *England's Effort: Six Letters to an American Friend*, with a preface by the Earl of Rosebery (1916), and *Fields of Victory*, letters based on a journey through the battlefields of France (1919).

Mrs Humphry Ward was a representative late Victorian – learned, earnest, less than Christian but more than agnostic – who encapsulated in a fine imaginative work the representative spiritual problems of the earlier Victorian generation.

Further reading

Other works include: *The Writings of Mrs Humphry Ward* (16 vols, 1911–12). After *Robert Elsmere* Mrs Ward's best novel is *Helbeck of Bannisdale* (1898). Biography: Janet Penrose Trevelyan, *The Life of Mrs Humphry Ward* (1923). Criticism: William S. Peterson, *Victorian Heretic: Mrs Humphry Ward's Robert Elsmere* (1976); and Robert Lee Wolff, *Gains and Losses: Novels of Faith and Doubt in Victorian England* (1977).

ROSEMARY ASHTON

WARHOL, Andy (Andrew WARHOLA)

1928–87

US artist, film maker

Often categorized as a pioneer and leading exponent of Pop Art, Andy Warhol was born of Czech extraction in Philadelphia. He is best known for his paintings and films, but his activities, almost unrivalled in their diversity and volume, included producing the rock group The Velvet Underground (in the mid-1960s), designing record covers (notably for the **Rolling Stones'** album *Sticky Fingers*, with its openable zipper) and writing books (some of them taped conversations, some actually 'written'). From the late 1950s until 1968, when he was near-fatally shot by Valeria Solanis for motives that were never been clearly ascertained, most of his output flowed from the Factory, the idiosyncratic name given to his studio in Manhattan.

Warhol's fame was established by his silkscreen paintings of Campbell's soup cans and other everyday household objects in 1961–2. The popular, commercial images were transferred mechanically from the 'original' photographs to the silkscreen web, and then applied to paper or canvas. A reaction to Abstract Expressionism, they were in almost every respect, when they first appeared, a challenge to normal notions and practices of fine art. To begin with they were exhibited on the West Coast of the United States, not the East. Their subject-matter was drawn provocatively from an area that by definition was segregated from 'serious' artistic endeavour. But more revolutionary still was the idea of using *unchanged* and therefore *unlaboured* original material, and, further, reproducing this through assistants. This constituted, as Warhol intended it should, the almost total self-effacement of the artist's individuality, although purposely minor infringements (random marks, hand-pressure variations, drips) remained to belie the purity of the endeavour.

Paradoxically Warhol's denial of individuality made him a central personality in modern art. This predictable but illogical outcome naturally attracted suspicion, and Warhol's developments often raised the consideration: how much is expression and how much is ploy? Given the apparently successful de-individualization of his work, it is difficult to see what prompted its production in the first place. An incorrect summary might suggest that his admirers have mistaken the real target of his aesthetic, which was not the consumer product so much as consumer marketing. On the other hand there can be little doubt that Warhol significantly contributed to the refashioning of our sensibilities. A Campbell's soupcan is intrinsically neither funny nor sad, nor does it command any other emotional response when set apart from all other objects. The process of de-individualization has not stopped short at the artist, but extends to the viewer. But: are we being ironically rebuked for our willing self-immersion in the surface world of advertisement and brand promotion, or are we being offered a chance to empty out? Both of these, it could be claimed, are legitimate, if not conventional, functions for an artist to pursue.

While Warhol had worked as a commercial illustrator for *Harpers* early in his career, perhaps the more decisive experience was his involvement with a Brechtian theatre collective at the beginning of the 1950s. Interpreting **Brecht's** theoretical writings, he composed stage-sets in which drawings of interior objects were pasted or hung on the 'real' artefacts (thus the image of a chair might be attached to the chair which had been used as a model). This was done not as a scenic economy, but as a deliberate re-evaluation of space, of proximity and distancation.

Not unlike Brecht, Warhol was concerned to undermine, wherever he could, illusionist representation, treating it as the ideology of truth and humanism which permeates, produces and is produced by Western cultural forms. In his paintings of Jacqueline Kennedy, **Elvis Presley**, Suicides and the Electric Chair, all major representational images during the 1960s, he offsets his highly charged subject-matter by a style that is wilfully mundane. These offer a critique of illusionist representation. For examples of non-illusionist representation we must turn back to the soupcans, or to Warhol's films, where he usually jettisons the identificatory processes of character, plot, drama, goal, fictive meaning and psychological truth.

Unavoidably making a film requires 'labour'. Unless the camera is used nothing can be accomplished, and just how it is used involves strategy and decision-making. Warhol's solution to this problem was complex, and perhaps only partial. He evolved two techniques that, by not denying the procedure and process of filmmaking itself, allow for no 'effects' except for those which will be immediately recognizable as such. One is the use of a rigid, unmoving camera, sometimes sustained for hours at a time, so that the work seems to approach a zero point of stylelessness. The other is a camera which arbitrarily zooms, focuses, changes angle and depth of field and light intensity and 'sound focus', without apparent purpose. Both these serve, or seem to serve, as a forcing of the audience to the medium itself as a materialist practice. Other techniques, or ploys, include the sudden incorporation of unexposed footage which comes out as a brilliant white on the screen. These cinematographic habits, contrasted to normal 'editing', undermine the audience's status as a cohesive, uncontradictory consumer of an uncontradictory, pre-structured 'knowledge' of the real. This is Warhol's central project in all his work.

Warhol's aim was to discard the suspension of disbelief which is so necessary for dominant narrative cinema. The epitome of his filmwork is perhaps *Chelsea Girls* (1967), a three-and-a-half-hour double screen movie originally arranged so that its seven half-hour reels could be projected in any sequence. Many of the most well-known 'Andy Warhol' films, e.g. *Flesh*, *Trash*, etc., were produced and directed by his colleague Paul Morrissey, and Warhol himself ceased being personally involved in his films after 1969, with the important exception of the camerawork for *Women in Revolt* (1972), a study of conflictual sexual disorientations. Most of the 'real' Andy Warhol films have been hidden in a vault, possibly to make the Warhol/Morrissey films more attractive to their audiences, possibly as an annihilation ploy which, of course, produces precisely the opposite effect.

By the mid 1970s Warhol was undertaking commissioned portraits of politicians and wealthy socialites. His later paintings re-incorporate much more the abstract-expressionist hand-involvement, the mark, the scratch, the presence of the producer. But very often, as in the case of the ten *Mao* portraits (1972), each in editions of 250, they were produced in series, and this imposes a blandness that cancels out any suspected eruption of the artist's self. As in the earlier silkscreens, where only minor differences of tonality were noticeable, the emphasis remains on the mechanized and distanciated gesture, and it is for this quality, after a period in which other artists attempted to 'paint psychology', that Warhol is likely to be remembered.

Further reading

Other works include: *Screen Test*, stills from his films (1966); *The Index Book*, with fold-outs, pop-up soupcans, a record, a balloon, etc. (1967); *From A to B and Back Again* (1975). Among his films are: *Blowjob* (1963); *Empire, Couch, 13 Most Beautiful Women* (1964); *Vinyl, Kitchen, My Hustler, The Shopper* (1965); *Four Stars* (1966); *Lonesome Cowboys* (1978); and *Fuck (Blue Movie*, 1969). His silkscreens, paintings and lithographs are generally identified by their subjects, viz.: fruit tins, Coca-Cola labels, soupcans (1961); *Marilyn* (Monroe), *Liz* (Taylor), more soupcans (1962); car crashes, lynchings, suicides (1963); Brillo boxes, Kellogg's cornflakes cartons, flowers, *Jackie, Elvis* (from 1964); self-portraits, *Marlon Brando* (1965). Most of these and similar subjects were used in succeeding years. Others include: girls, boys, Indians, torsos, transvestites (1974); the Paul Anka T-shirt (1975); Hammer and Sickle (1976). About Andy Warhol: John Coplans, *Andy Warhol* (1971); Peter Gidal, *Andy Warhol: Films and Paintings* (1971); Stephen Koch, *Andy Warhol: Stargazer* (1973); Victor Bockris, *Warhol* (1990); Philippe Tretiack, *Warhol's America* (1997).

PETER GIDAL

WASHINGTON, Booker Taliaferro

1856–1915

US educator and racial leader

Born into slavery in Virginia shortly before the Civil War, Booker T. Washington grew up in an age of unbridled capitalism, rapid economic expansion, and 'self-made' men. Washington entered this competitive environment with few assets; his mother was a slave, his father an unknown white man. After emancipation, he walked with his mother, brother and sister to join his stepfather who was employed in a West Virginia salt furnace. Booker and his brother soon began working in order to supplement the family's meagre income. Opportunities for the personal advancement of a poor black boy were few. Less than forty years later, however, Booker T. Washington was being applauded by political leaders and entertained by some of the world's wealthiest men. President Theodore Roosevelt invited him to dinner at the White House, **Andrew Carnegie** welcomed him as a guest at Skibo castle, and **Queen Victoria** invited him to tea during one of his two trips to Europe.

Washington's climb from slavery to celebrity involved the coincidence of his personal and racial philosophy with that of the controlling white society. One of Booker's earliest memories was 'an intense longing to learn to read', and he pursued every avenue in his small West Virginia town that might further his education. He learned that pleasing important whites would open the doors of opportunity, and he impressed everyone with his self-discipline and willingness to work long hours to achieve his goals. In 1872, at the age of seventeen, Washington returned to his native Virginia to attend Hampton Institute. No one at the school knew that he was coming; he had almost no money; and he had to walk a good part of the five hundred mile journey. Booker's entrance examination involved sweeping and dusting a recitation room, and the New England Lady Principal was so impressed with his thoroughness that she admitted him to classes, although he had no money for tuition and the school year had already begun.

At Hampton, Washington met the most influential person in his career. As principal at this industrial training school for coloured youth, Samuel Chapman Armstrong combined a sense of white missionary paternalism with a Puritan's devotion to clean living, discipline and individual responsibility. He represented that class of elite whites who felt it 'knew' what was best for the former slaves and who could help them most in their climb from the depths of depravity and ignorance.

Booker T. Washington internalized the Hampton message. His experiences as a youth affirmed Armstrong's views, and when Washington graduated in 1875 he was a disciple. He taught at a school in his home town for three years and spent a year at a Baptist seminary before returning to Hampton in 1879 as a night-school teacher and secretary to Armstrong. In 1881 Armstrong recommended Washington as principal of a new normal school for blacks in Tuskegee, Alabama. Washington took the position with every intention of establishing a Hampton colony in the deep South. Beginning, as he later described it, 'with forty students in a dilapidated shanty near the coloured Methodist Church', Booker T. Washington built Tuskegee Institute into the best-known black school in the United States. At the time of his death the school had an extensive industrial training programme in addition to the normal curriculum, more than fifteen hundred students, and an endowment of almost two million dollars. Washington's international fame, however, arose from a ten-minute speech he gave in 1895 before the Cotton States and International Exposition in Atlanta, Georgia.

The Exposition was a highly publicized event, but its timing had much to do with the appeal of Washington's message. On the one hand, the South was openly seeking to diversify its stagnant agricultural economy by attracting northern industrial investment. On the other hand, race relations were tense and black citizenship rights were eroding seriously under a torrent of hostile legislation. Washington made a simple recommendation for both of these situations, and for blacks and whites alike: 'Cast down your buckets where you are.' Americans should concentrate upon their nation's abundance and the opportunity

for self-advancement. Ideally, blacks should look to whites for jobs and leadership, and whites should look to blacks for loyal and competent labour. Washington felt that racial tension impeded economic progress, and he advised blacks to be patient, to exercise discipline and self-control, and to avoid agitation in the face of lynching, segregation and disfranchisement. Furthermore, Washington urged blacks to seek friendships with conservative white philanthropists, to reject labour unions and to allow racial differences to work themselves out over time.

Blacks generally greeted Washington's message with restrained support, but the public white response was overwhelming praise. The young black educator offered them a relatively painless solution to the 'Negro Problem' by placing most of the burden upon his own people. He advocated a safe approach and his efforts earned white assistance. Very quickly, Washington became a powerful man among black Americans. Although a growing black minority, headed by W.E.B. DuBois, criticized Washington for his 'Atlanta Compromise' of their civil rights, whites invested him with considerable influence. He became an adviser to presidents, philanthropists and editors. Black politicians and college presidents awaited his signal to their white benefactors. As a black leader, Booker T. Washington was sincerely respected by his own people, and most publicly supported his 'go slow' policies. Black support came partly because Washington produced some modest results, but perhaps more importantly his policies offered a natural course along the lines of least resistance. When he published his autobiography, *Up From Slavery*, in 1901, he presented his own life as an example of the success of his racial philosophy. It won him further acclaim at home and abroad.

Washington worked hard to implement his views. In 1900 he founded the National Negro Business League in order to promote pride in black businesses and to encourage economic independence. Most obviously, however, Washington used Tuskegee Institute as a model for industrial training and character building. His graduates represented the success of his conservative philosophy to the public, and faculty members such as the noted scientist **George Washington Carver** regularly conducted workshops at farmers' conferences and other black gatherings in the South. Booker T. Washington rejected the more aggressive demands for full equality by the National Association for the Advancement of Colored People as impractical and dangerous. Instead, he accepted 'half a loaf' as a step 'toward obtaining the whole loaf later'.

When Washington died in 1915 he left his widow and three children by two previous marriages. His legacy also included a conservative approach to race relations which dominated American thinking until the civil rights upheavals of the 1950s.

Further reading

Other works include: *The Future of the American Negro* (1899) and *My Larger Education* (1911). Major works about Washington include: Samuel R. Spencer Jr, *Booker T. Washington and the Negro's Place in American Life* (1955); *Booker T. Washington and His Critics: The Problem of Negro Leadership*, ed. Hugh Hawkins (1962); Louis R. Harlan, *Booker T. Washington: The Making of a Black Leader, 1856–1901* (1972); Louis R. Harlan and R.W. Smock, *Booker T. Washington in Perspective* (1989); Barry Washington, *Booker T. Washington: An Appreciation of the Man and His Times* (2005).

LESTER C. LAMON

WATSON, James Dewey

1928–

US biologist

In 1947 when J.D. Watson completed his bachelor's degree in biology at the University of Chicago, the science of genetics was well developed but little was known about the nature of the fundamental unit of that science – the gene. Watson's major contribution, in collaboration with the British-born scientist, **Francis H.C. Crick**, was to propose in 1953 a plausible structure for the chemical substance DNA, or deoxyribonucleic acid, and to show how it might account for many of the properties of the gene.

When Watson left Chicago to pursue graduate work at the University of Indiana he was only nineteen years of age. It was his acceptance by Indiana on condition that he study genetics or embryology which turned him from his intended career subject of ornithology.

Following upon his PhD research, Watson came to Europe and worked in Copenhagen and Cambridge, supported first by a Merck post-doctoral fellowship, and subsequently by the National Foundation for Infantile Paralysis. Returned to the United States in 1953 he continued as a research scientist in the California Institute of Technology, then he moved to Harvard where he became Full Professor in 1961. For eight years, beginning in 1968, he also directed the Cold Spring Harbor Laboratory on Long Island. He resigned from Harvard University in 1976 to devote all his energy to Cold Spring Harbor. The transformation that he made to this rundown, ailing institution has been perhaps his greatest achievement. As he expanded and modernized it he also preserved and enriched its history, opened up its educational potential and as opportunity permitted moved into fresh fields – first cancer research, then neuroscience. In 1988 he became Associate Director of the Human Genome Project, in 1989 until 1992 Director. On appointing a successor to the Directorship of the Cold Spring Harbor Laboratory he became its President in 1994, and in 2004 its Chancellor.

Watson's genetic research at Indiana concerned the effects of X-ray damage upon bacterial viruses. It was hoped that this approach might yield clues to viral multiplication, a process thought to be virtually identical with gene duplication. In the event, this indirect approach to the nature of the genetic material proved disappointing. By contrast the direct approach using the techniques of chemistry and physics upon the genetic material looked more promising for unravelling the secrets of the gene. Watson therefore studied the transfer of chemical constituents from infecting virus particles to progeny virus particles using radioactive tracers. Then, fired with enthusiasm after seeing X-ray diffraction pictures shown by the British biophysicist M.H.F. Wilkins, Watson altered his strategy yet again, turning to the study of molecular structure as deduced from X-ray diffraction pictures.

Using data obtained by Rosalind Franklin, Raymond Gosling and Maurice Wilkins at King's College, London, Watson collaborated in Cambridge with Crick. Having concluded that the genetic material was not a nucleoprotein but simply nucleic acid, they hoped that the structure of this substance would show how the gene works – how it duplicates, changes abruptly when it 'mutates', and expresses itself by giving rise to the heritable characteristics of organisms. Although their first attempt at a chemical structure was a failure, their second, just over a year later, was to be numbered among the most celebrated achievements of twentieth-century science. A preliminary description of their model was published in *Nature* in the spring of 1953, followed by a second paper on the implications for genetics suggested by the model. The third paper, almost entirely written by Watson, appeared in 1954. The rule book for the translation of the chemical sequence of the gene – the genetic code – had been discovered.

The idea, long discussed, that hereditary traits could be encoded in a specific chemical sequence was here identified with the sequence of 'bases'. Constancy of hereditary transmission, they suggested, was due to the faithful copying of the base sequence; changes or 'mutations' were due to errors in copying. The copying process itself was pictured as involving the opening of the two chains (the double helix) in such a way that new chains could be laid down on each of the originals. The sequence of bases on a new chain was dictated by specific pairing with the bases of the original chain.

Despite modifications to the Watson–Crick model for DNA, its basic principles have been greatly strengthened over the succeeding two decades. Its authors' suggestions regarding its implications for genetics have been followed and confirmed. The chemical sequence of the gene – the genetic code – has been discovered. The mechanism by which this code is expressed, however, proved a far more complex process than Watson and Crick envisaged. Only a broad research programme of biochemistry and structural chemistry sufficed to unravel its mysteries. This triumph in analysis was catalysed by the many theoretical insights which Crick provided between 1956 and 1970. Watson, who was but twenty-five years of age in 1953, received with Crick and Wilkins the Nobel Prize for Medicine in 1962. Three years later, his textbook *The Molecular Biology of the Gene* (1965) appeared. He presented his subject boldly, because he believed the basic concepts provided by the molecular approach were now sound; in short, biology had by 1965 as sound a basis as chemistry had enjoyed since 1932 thanks to the Quantum Theory. It was time, he claimed, to reorient the teaching of biology and give 'the biologist of the future the rigor, the perspective, and the enthusiasm that will be needed to bridge the gap between the single cell and the complexities of higher organisms'.

After many revisions and some hard feeling within the scientific community, Watson published *The Double Helix*, an account of the period of his life spent in Europe which had led to the model for DNA. This very candid, at times corrosive, picture of an ambitious young American research scientist thirsting for the big discovery and winning a share in a Nobel Prize has undermined the public image of the unworldly scientist who solves problems by dedicated industry and accumulated expertise. The Watson of the *Double Helix* views much of the research going on in scientific institutions with a sceptical eye. The Watson of Cold Spring Harbor Laboratory set high standards and made great demands in his reach for excellence. But more than a researcher he yearned to be a successful writer, and that he has achieved in two very different books: *The Double Helix* and *The Molecular Biology of the Gene*.

Further reading

Other works include *A Passion for DNA. Genes, Genomes, and Society* (2000). See: J. Cains, G. Stent and Watson (eds) *Phage and the Origin of Molecular Biology* (1968); R. Olby, *The Path of the Double Helix* (1974); J. Inglis, S. Sambrook and J. Wilkowski (eds) *Inspiring Science. Jim Watson and the Age of DNA* (2003); V.K. McElheny, *Watson and DNA. Making a Scientific Revolution* (2003).

ROBERT OLBY

WATSON, John Broadus

1878–1958

US psychologist

Watson's young days were spent in South Carolina. In 1899 he graduated from Furman University, and under the influence of the Furman philosopher Gordon B. Moore he moved to Chicago for a PhD in psychology and philosophy. There he came under the influence of **John Dewey**, Jacques Loeb, H.H. Donaldson and James Angell. After nine productive years Watson was appointed to a full professorship at Johns Hopkins University, Baltimore. His divorce from Mary Ickes and subsequent marriage to his research collaborator, Rosalie Raynor, led to his enforced resignation in 1920. His academic career closed, he moved into the business world, becoming Vice President of the J. Walter Thompson Company in 1924, and Vice President of William Esty and Company in 1936.

When Watson went to Chicago in 1899 the structural psychology of Wilhelm Wundt had been eclipsed in America by the functional psychology of Angell, William James and Dewey. This placed emphasis upon mental activity as an adaptive response to the environment. It brought Darwinian ideas into psychology and gave an impetus to the experimental study of animal behaviour, since the adaptive responses of animals should throw light upon those of man. But functionalism did not reject mentalist terms, nor deny consciousness to animals. Watson studied examples of instinctive behaviour, the migration of terns, and maze-running by the white rat. He became increasingly impatient with the failure of functional psychology to make a clean break with subjectivism. In the winter of 1912–13 Watson gave a series of lectures to Columbia University which he summarized in his famous paper 'Psychology as the Behaviorist Views It' in *Psychological Review* (Vol. 20, 1913). Here the main features of his more mature formulation of behaviourism – with the exception of the conditioned reflex – can be found.

As a comparative psychologist studying the instinctive and acquired behaviour of animals, Watson had become increasingly unhappy with the obligation that psychology placed upon him to relate such work to the body of knowledge gained from the study of consciousness in man. When he considered the confusion within psychology, the disagreements over the meanings of terms, the nature of conscious content, and the elements of the mind, he determined to 'throw off the yoke of consciousness' and define psychology as a purely objective experimental branch of natural science in which introspection finds no place, and no line divides man from brute. Each should be placed 'as nearly as possible under the same experimental conditions'. In such a system of psychology when fully worked out, 'given the stimuli the response can be predicted'. The aim of this psychology was the prediction and control of behaviour. Unlike the old structural psychology, therefore, it should be useful to the educator, jurist, businessman and physician.

In the programme which Watson sketched out in this paper and more fully in his textbook, *Psychology from the Standpoint of a Behaviorist* (1919), the psychologist's task was to investigate the responses to specific stimuli and to distinguish the acquired from the inborn. As his views matured he came to the following conclusions. There are only three basic inborn emotions, those of rage, fear and love. By 1924 he came to doubt the need for the concept of instinct at all. Instead he listed the baby's reflexes of grasping, kicking, sucking, crying and so forth. Other responses were due to the process of conditioning, which begins at birth if not before. While Watson rejected mentalist terms, he regarded speech, like any other motor response, as a series of muscular contractions, and thought as 'implicit speech'; some weak motor responses still occurred but no sounds were produced.

The concept of the conditioned reflex had been developed by the Russian physiologist I.P. Pavlov. Watson had discussed it in 1915, and in 1924 he made it the major feature of his system. By conditioning, the emotion of fear could be brought out in response to stimuli not normally associated with fear. Thus a white rat, for which the child had no congenital fear, could illicit fear by repeated introduction of a loud sound along with the rat. Such a response could be 'unconditioned' by substituting food for the bang and progressively reducing the distance of the rat from the child.

Although Watson recognized the therapeutic value of psychoanalysis he rejected **Freud's** psychosexual theories. From a study of the children of his second marriage he claimed to have demonstrated that no long-term memory of events in early childhood existed, that attachment to the mother could be so weakened by a spell away from home that the son did not rush to his mother's defence when his father attacked her.

Watson's opposition to psychosexual theories was part of his extreme environmentalism, which is seen in his opposition to the claims of the eugenicists, in particular to the results of twin studies, and his confident claims for the potential of conditioning from early childhood. Too much love and attention from the mother generates overdependence of the child upon her. 'Punishment,' wrote Watson, 'is a word which ought never to have crept into our language.' Deviant behaviour should be corrected by a process of untraining and retraining using the principles of conditioning. He looked to a future in which society would base its ethics upon the principles of behaviourism. He was not asking people 'to form a colony, go naked and live a communal life', but he was suggesting how the application of behaviourism could 'gradually change this universe'.

The response to behaviourism was not immediate. Watson's influence was felt in psychology both directly, through the work of men like K.S. Lashley, and indirectly through the impact of his writings in the popular press. In the 1930s a new generation of psychologists formulated more sophisticated versions of behaviourism – R.C. Tolman, C.L. Hull and **B.F. Skinner**.

Further reading

Other works include: *Animal Education. An Experimental Study on the Psychical Development of the White Rat . . .* (1903); *Behaviour: An Introduction to Comparative Psychology* (1914); *Behaviourism* (1925; 2nd edn, 1931); with Rosalie Watson, *Psychological Care of Infant and Child* (1928). His celebrated debate with W. McDougall was published as *The Battle of Behaviorism. An Exposition and an Exposure* (1928). See also: David Cohen, *J.B. Watson, the Founder of Behaviourism: A Biography* (1979).

ROBERT OLBY

WAUGH, Evelyn Arthur St John
1903–66
British novelist

The son of Arthur Waugh, publisher and literary critic, and younger brother of Alec Waugh, novelist, Evelyn Waugh was educated at Lancing and Hertford College, Oxford. After abortive attempts at schoolmastering and carpentry he turned to literature and in 1928 published a biographical study of **D.G. Rossetti**. His first novel, *Decline and Fall*, appeared later in the same year. Based loosely on his experiences as preparatory school teacher, it was a racy mixture of burlesque farce and social satire that brought him critical acclaim, a number of journalistic commissions, but little money.

Popular success came with *Vile Bodies* (1930), which caught, with seemingly effortless precision, the frenetic social atmosphere of young upper-class London in the 1920s: the Bright Young People, their language, their parties and their aimlessness. Both in literature and in society Waugh became a fashionable figure, but his happiness was bitterly affected by the break-up, after a few months, of his first marriage. The behaviour of his wife left a scar that is visible in many of his subsequent writings. More immediately, it hastened his reception into the Roman Catholic Church in September 1930 – an event that Waugh regarded as the most important in his life.

Between then and the Second World War he travelled extensively in Europe, Africa, South America and Mexico. To this period belong: *Labels: A Mediterranean Journal* (1930); *Remote People* (1931); *Ninety-Two Days* (1934); *Waugh in Abyssinia* (1936). These travel books were later abridged into one volume, *When the Going was Good* (1946). The novels of this decade, which draw on the same experiences, are *Black Mischief* (1932), *A Handful of Dust* (1934), perhaps the climax of Waugh's early writings, and *Scoop* (1938).

In the course of the war, during which he served in the Royal Marines and later the Royal Horse Guards, he wrote *Put Out More Flags* (1942) and *Brideshead Revisited* (1945). The second of these, though attacked for its luxuriance and snobbery, was a best-seller in England and in America, bringing Waugh a measure of financial security and also heralding the deeper concern with religious themes that characterizes his later work. His main achievement during the last period of his life was the trilogy based on his wartime experiences: *Men at Arms* (1952), *Officers and Gentlemen* (1955) and *Unconditional Surrender* (1961). In 1965 these were published in one volume, with some revisions, as *Sword of Honour*. When he died, on Easter Day 1966, he had produced one volume of his autobiography, *A Little Learning* (1964), and was beginning work on the second.

Waugh is primarily a comic novelist, whose books display an anarchic imagination and cast an acute satirical eye on the manners of upper-class society. From the outset he was stimulated by the borderlands where civilization and savagery meet, where the sublime shades into the ridiculous, sanity into lunacy, sadness into hilarity. These oppositions fuelled his sense of the absurd, but also lent substance to his more serious preoccupations. If his work has a central theme, it is the triumph of barbarism in a civilization that has lost touch with the values on which it was founded. Throughout his writings this nostalgia for the values of a happier age finds an image in the country house, beleaguered, encroached upon or destroyed by the agents of a graceless modern world. His growing disgust with 'the century of the common man' had a political and social complexion which many commentators have found repulsive. In later life Waugh developed an image of eccentric and extreme Toryism which is brilliantly portrayed by him in the opening chapter of his autobiographical novel, *The Ordeal of Gilbert Pinfold* (1957). But he was not a political figure; closer to the heart of both his life and his writings is a romanticism at odds with the conditions of his age and society.

The earlier novels use irony as their characteristic response. In a world of arbitrary cruelties and absurd injustices the novelist observes his creatures with a detachment that shields his own vulnerability. Later, the influence of religion begins to reveal the strain on his irony, making possible the achievement of the war trilogy, in which irony and despair are tempered by a kindling of religious charity that gives to the work an unaccustomed depth of humanity.

To Waugh the question of style was paramount: he looked on writing 'not as an exploration of character, but as an exercise in the use of language'. Hostile to the practices of most modernist writers, he developed a style that was elegant, lucid and precise, in which words were chosen with loving propriety and a strict regard for their etymology. Not surprisingly he was devoted to the works of **P.G. Wodehouse**, while another important influence on him was **Ronald Firbank**, about whom he wrote one of his best critical essays. Waugh remains, however, a writer who is difficult to identify with any particular school, and he has had no followers of note. He can be seen as an important cross-current to the dominant intellectual and artistic trends of post-war years. To be reactionary was in his view the necessary function of the artist in society. It is not a role that has endeared him to the arbiters of academic critical fashion, but he may yet be read for his humour and lucidity when writers of more importunate relevance and less embarrassing opinions have been forgotten.

Further reading

Other works include: *Edmund Campion* (1935) and *Ronald Knox* (1959), both biographies; *Helena* (1950) is a historical novel; *Scott-King's Modern Europe* (1947), *The Loved One* (1948), *Love Among Ruins* (1953) are short novels. *Work Suspended* (1942) is an unfinished fiction. The *Diaries*, ed. Michael Davie (1976) and *A Little Order*, a selection of his journalism, ed. Donat Gallagher (1977) appeared posthumously. About Waugh: M. Bradbury, *Evelyn Waugh* (1964); Alec Waugh, *My Brother Evelyn and Other Profiles* (1967); R.M. Davis (ed.) *Evelyn Waugh: A Checklist* (1972); D. Pryce-Jones (ed.) *Evelyn Waugh and His World* (1973); Christopher Sykes, *Evelyn Waugh: A Biography* (1975); Humphrey Carpenter, *The Brideshead Generation* (1989); Martin Stannard, *The Critical Heritage* (1984), *Evelyn Waugh: The Early Years: 1903–1939* (1986) and *Evelyn Waugh: No Abiding City: 1939–1966* (1992); Selina Hastings, *Evelyn Waugh: A Biography* (1995); Douglas Lane Patey, *The Life of Evelyn Waugh* (1998). His work is also discussed in Martin Green, *Children of the Sun* (1976).

IAN LITTLEWOOD

WEBB, Beatrice and Sidney

(Martha Beatrice WEBB 1858–1943, Sidney James WEBB (Lord Passfield) 1859–1947)

English social reformers and historians

Martha Beatrice Potter, the daughter of a wealthy railway promoter, described the awakening of her social conscience and her early interest in the problems of London poverty in her distinguished autobiography *My Apprenticeship* (1926), and in the posthumous second volume *Our Partnership* (1948). She drew upon her remarkable *Diary* (microfiche, 1977) to portray the first two decades of her marriage to Sidney James Webb, the talented son of London tradespeople, who gave up his career as a civil servant to devote himself to journalism, social research and political reform.

The Webbs, influenced by Positivist and Utilitarian ideas of public service, did much to shape modern social democracy and the welfare state; but their concept of reform was essentially elitist, for they believed that it was the duty of enlightened intellectuals to reconstruct society in the interests of social efficiency and to the benefit of the poor, the sick and the aged. To this end they put great stress on education and effective public administration. These views are reflected in the policies of the Fabian Society, in which the Webbs and **George Bernard Shaw** played a leading role, in their foundation of the London School of Economics in 1895, in their energetic campaign of 1906–11 to reform the archaic Poor Law, and in their launching of the weekly *New Statesman* in 1913.

In 1916, after many years in which the Webbs had sought with limited success to 'permeate' the Liberal and Conservative parties with their reformist policies, they turned to the Labour Party as the favoured means of social reconstruction. After Sidney Webb had helped to devise the party's constitution he drafted its notable 1918 election manifesto called *Labour and the New Social Order*. In 1922 he was elected as MP for Seaham Harbour, holding office in the Labour government of 1924 as President of the Board of Trade and in the government of 1929–31 as Colonial Secretary, but he proved to be an ineffective Cabinet minister. When he was created Lord Passfield in 1924 his wife declined to use the title and continued to be known as Mrs Sidney Webb.

Sidney Webb, a man capable of unremitting work, was a prolific journalist and pamphleteer, writing many of the celebrated Fabian tracts in the heyday of that society; and Beatrice Webb had gifts of imagination and literary style which only too rarely gleamed in their joint work as historians and social theorists. Their first work was *The History of Trade Unionism* (1894), and this was followed by *Industrial Democracy* (1897), *English Local Government* (9 vols, 1906–29), *The Consumers' Co-operative Movement* (1921), *A Constitution for the Socialist Commonwealth of Great Britain* (1921), *The Decay of Capitalist Civilisation* (1923) and *Methods of Social Study* (1932). After the fall of the Labour government in 1931, and affected by the economic depression and the rise of fascism in Europe, the Webbs became convinced that the USSR exemplified Auguste Comte's 'religion of humanity' and *Soviet Communism, A New Civilisation?* (1935) was an extended and for the most part uncritical account of the **Stalin** regime. At the instance of Bernard Shaw, who thus sought to commemorate the long partnership of the Webbs, their ashes were interred together in Westminster Abbey.

Further reading

See: M. Cole (ed.) *The Webbs and Their Work* (1947); Kitty Muggeridge and Ruth Adams, *Beatrice Webb* (1968); N. and J. MacKenzie, *The First Fabians* (1977); N. MacKenzie (ed.) *The Letters of Sidney and Beatrice Webb* (1978); J. MacKenzie, *A Victorian Courtship* (1979); Royden Harrison, *The Life and Times of Sidney and Beatrice Webb 1858–1905: The Formative Years* (2001).

NORMAN MACKENZIE

WEBB, Michael *see:* ARCHIGRAM

WEBER, Max

1864–1920

German sociologist

It is now generally recognized that sociology emerged as an important academic discipline not so much through the work of Auguste Comte, who first used the term 'sociology', but rather through the development of three traditions represented by the work of **Émile Durkheim** who wrote, it is true, in the tradition of Comte, of **Karl Marx**, whose work became one of the central intellectual and political facts in European history, and of Max Weber whose range of comparative and historical work approached from the intellectual standpoint of Neo-Kantianism was perhaps more comprehensive than either of the others.

Weber's father was prominent in the National Liberal Party during the **Bismarck** era. At Heidelberg his original studies were in law, but, by the time he came to write his doctoral and habilitation theses, his interest had shifted to economics and economic history. His first academic post was as a Professor of Economics in the University of Freiburg, but he moved to Heidelberg after three years in 1896. At Heidelberg he suffered a severe mental breakdown leading to total disablement for four years and to an inability to accept any academic appointment until 1917. His life during this period has been devotedly chronicled in one of the most dignified biographies ever written. The biography was by his wife, Marianne, with whom he is believed to have had an unusual marriage, which, though it may never have been sexually consummated, provided the basis for a remarkable intellectual and moral companionship.

Marianne Weber provided Weber with a home which served as the focus for the intellectual life of some of the greatest intellects of the time in the fields of history, philosophy, economics, politics and literature. He also worked within the *Verein für Sozialpolitik*, an organization concerned with the application of social science findings to politics, and for many years edited and wrote in its journal, the *Archiv für Sozialwissenschaft und Sozialpolitik*. He also participated very actively in German politics, even though the Kantian perspective which he shared with his intellectual companions led him to make a radical dissociation between what he conceived to be the tasks of science and those which he thought appropriate to the politician.

Weber's earliest writing was in economic history. One of his theses dealt with agrarian civilization in the ancient world and another with trading companies in the Middle Ages. His contribution in these writings were partly oriented to controversies in German historiography, but he also used these themes for the development of generally applicable sociological concepts and for the understanding of contemporary problems. His association with the *Verein für Sozialpolitik* led him to make investigations of such topics as the condition of agricultural labourers in East Germany and of the stock exchange. Informing these studies was a developing interest in studying the role of religious thought in shaping economic behaviour, and the nature of modern bureaucratic organization. Behind this lay a more far-reaching concern amounting to an implicit philosophy of history based upon a conception of the rationalization, secularization and disenchantment of the world. The best-known outcome of this concern was Weber's *The Protestant Ethic and the Spirit of Capitalism* (Vol. I of *Gesammelte Aufsätze zur Religionssoziologie*, 1920, trans. 1930), in which, stimulated by Ernst Troeltsch, he agreed that it was in Calvinism that the roots of capitalism were to be found, rather than in Judaism as had been suggested by Sombart. This work was supplemented by comparative studies of Chinese, Indian and Jewish civilization which set out to show the difference which religious thought made to economic behaviour, but which inevitably brought into focus many other structural variables which differentiated these civilizations one from another. Among many themes discussed were types of authority and administration, the relations between prophets, priests and administrators, the nature of urban settlements, guild and other occupational organizations, and class and status structures. These studies combined with Weber's early studies of ancient and medieval

Europe and his study of contemporary issues to provide him with a range of comparative and historical knowledge which has probably had no equal in modern times.

In 1909 the publisher Paul Siebeck invited Weber to edit a new series of books which would replace the by then dated 'Handbook of Political Economy' edited by Gustav Schonberg. Although eventually contributions to this series were published, including those of distinguished authors such as Joseph Schumpeter, Werner Sombart, Robert Michels, Karl Bucher and Alfred Weber, Max Weber grew impatient with the tardiness and the inadequacies of some of his proposed authors, and eventually decided to expand his own contribution on the social structures within which economic systems developed. The original title which Weber gave to his own contribution was 'The Economy and the Arena of De Facto and Normative Powers'. When this was eventually published, together with a new introduction, it was called simply *Economy and Society* (trans. 1967), but it is the original title which specifies Weber's exact intention. He attempts here to outline the basic types of economic action, their organization into alternative types of economic system, and the ways in which such systems operate within a context of legitimating idea systems and structures of power. There are thus book-length sections of the whole volume dealing with the comparative economic systems, the sociology of the world religions, the sociology of law, forms of legitimate authority and administration, and the city, as well as a number of minor themes such as domestic organization, village life and ethnic groups.

Economy and Society constitutes Weber's systematic sociology. No one who reads it could continue to give credence to the view widely held in the English-speaking world after the publication of *The Protestant Ethic and the Spirit of Capitalism* in translation that Weber was a bourgeois idealist anti-Marxist. Nor could it be maintained, as it sometimes is on the basis of Weber's methodological writings, that Weber held purely subjectivist views, believing that history had to be written only from limited value-laden perspectives. What is evident here is an almost brutal realism derived from a reading of history, which took violence and exploitation for granted. No volume in fact could more justifiably claim as its text Marx's assertion that 'All history is the history of class struggles' than Weber's volume on *The City*, which first appeared as a section of *Economy and Society*. Nonetheless there *are* also normative powers and these Weber treats both in terms of ideological content and in terms of their institutional embodiment in his sections on the Sociology of Religion and the Sociology of Law.

The perspective of *Economy and Society*, and still more the perspective of Weber's early writings, derives from a Kantian approach to history and the social sciences, which was shared ground between Weber and his colleagues who came to visit him. Weber never set out systematically to discuss this approach, nor did he have much to say about Kant. Nonetheless, in the sustained methodological polemics in which he engaged with contemporary authors in the pages of the *Archiv*, Weber's Kantianism is clear. The central Kantian notion which is taken for granted is that of the possibility of sustaining simultaneously a view of the world as consisting of phenomena organized in terms of the categories of space, time and causality, and an alternative view in which man lives in the realm of freedom, confronting the Moral Law, yet free to choose and to make value judgements for which he is responsible. It was from this perspective that Weber wrote about the notion of cause in history, about ideal types contrasted with empirical laws, about the relation between value perspectives and the discovery of causal sequences and about the tension between value freedom and value relevance in social science.

Probably the central idea which Weber has is that of 'relevance for value'. This idea, which he took over from Rickert and modified, suggested that there are a multitude of value starting points from which the manifold of social and cultural facts could be analysed, and it is necessary that every social science investigation should make its value starting points explicit, in order to distinguish these from the value-free investigation of the causal relations between social structures to which they subsequently lead. Unlike Rickert, Weber did not see any way in which an objective basis for value standpoints could be arrived at, and, in his determination to emphasize the responsibility of the individual for his own actions, he leaned towards almost maintaining that the basis of value judgements themselves was arbitrary. Weber himself, however, would argue that to claim that discourse about values is distinct from scientific discourse is by no means to assert that it is irrational.

The second unifying theme in Weber's methodological writings is what might be called an attempt to give an account of the sociological *a priori*. Recognizing that the natural science categories of causation did not apply in the human studies, he sought to give an account of the way in which entities called social relations and groups might be thought of as being constructed, and the way in which they affected individual behaviour. As Weber saw it, social relations could be thought of as arising in meaningful action in which one actor took account of the behaviour of another. Thus the entities, which appear as compelling human behaviour from outside, are seen as human creations, potentially capable of being changed by human beings. This perspective is sometimes called methodological individualism and leads to Weber saying that explanations which are causally adequate should be supplemented by explanations which are adequate on the level of meaning. It is an approach which stands in sharp contrast to Durkheim's assertion that social facts should be treated as things. In these terms Weber went on to develop concepts of social structure which he called ideal types. At first these were types which were very specific and related to his own values. In *Economy and Society*, however, they were more abstract and less relativistic.

Weber has often been contrasted with Marx, and has been said to have 'carried on a lifelong dialogue with the ghost of Karl Marx', or to be the 'bourgeois Marx'. In fact, in most areas, his work is complementary to rather than opposed to Marx. He has the advantage over Marx in not having to come to terms with a Hegelian philosophical vocabulary, and some have argued that restating Marx in a language free of metaphysics would lead to accounts of the mode of production, social relations of production, social classes and the state which are very close to Weber's. It is not true that Weber offered some kind of spiritual determinism which was at an opposite extreme to Marx's materialist determinism. He explicitly denied this. What he did do was to give a structural and methodologically individualist account of the full range of social institutions in history, which included the institutions of production, but also all those other institutions which Marx was inclined to refer to, having the critique of Hegel in mind, as mere ideas, or institutions of the superstructure. Where perhaps Weber did differ from Marx was in his theory of class. He certainly distinguished class from status, as Marx would have done, but he saw class conflict as bargaining going on in any market situation, and going on indefinitely, because he had accepted marginalist economics, whereas Marx, basing himself on the labour theory of value, saw the concept of class as leading, not to bargaining, but to revolution.

At the end of his life Weber was much involved in politics and wrote some quite ephemeral documents, including an account of socialism designed to stop its spread in the army. He also offered himself unsuccessfully as a candidate in the elections in the new Weimar Republic. More interesting from a sociological point of view were his last lectures, which have been preserved from student notes and which are published under the title *General Economic History* (*Wirtschaftsgeschichte*, 1924, trans. 1961). On the political level he remained unconvinced that a transition of advanced industrial societies to socialism would mean anything else but the extension of rationalism and bureaucracy to its ultimate point, a prospect which he viewed with horror. To the end he remained a Kantian seeking to the point of despair to find a way in which individuals could remain free of an increasingly reified society.

Further reading

Other works include: *Economy and Society* (3 vols, 1968). The best introduction to Weber's methodological ideas can be found in *The Methodology of the Social Sciences* (1949), a selection and translation of his essays by E.A. Shils and H.A. Finch, to be taken with *Roscher and Knies* (1976), trans. Guy Oakes. Other translations include: *The Religion of China* (1953); *Ancient Judaism* (1952); *The Religion of India* (1958) – all from the *Gesammelte Aufsätze zur Religionssoziologie; The Agrarian Sociology of Ancient Civilizations* (1974). See also *From Max Weber*, ed. H. Gerth and C. Wright Mills (1946). About Weber: Marianne Weber, *Max Weber* (*Max Weber, Ein Lebensbild*, 1926, trans. 1950); Reinhard Bendix, *Max Weber, An Intellectual Portrait* (1962); Julien Freund, *The Sociology of Max Weber* (*Sociologie de Max Weber*, 1966, trans. 1968); F. Ringer, *Max Weber: An Intellectual Biography* (2004).

JOHN REX

WEBERN, Anton von
1883–1945
Austrian composer

Born into the minor Austrian nobility, Webern studied music history with Guido Adler at the University of Vienna, and at the same time took private lessons in composition with **Arnold Schoenberg**, to whom he remained a lifelong 'friend and pupil', as did his fellow-student **Alban Berg**. In 1906 he was awarded a PhD for an edition of part of the *Choralis Constantinus* by Heinrich Isaac, a Flemish polyphonist of the late fifteenth century. Although he was to be busy for the rest of his life as a composer, he could never support himself financially by composing alone. Instead, he made up a living from conducting, private teaching (he never held an official teaching post) and work for his publishers. In the 1930s his music was vilified as 'cultural Bolshevism', and his later years were marked by an extreme withdrawal that nevertheless saw the development of an important friendship with the poetess Hildegard Jone. In September 1945 he was accidentally shot dead by an American soldier of the Occupation.

Webern's oeuvre is relatively small: apart from a sizeable quantity of early pieces, a few unpublished later works, and a number of arrangements, there are only thirty-one pieces that bear opus numbers. Over half of these are vocal, his talent being essentially lyrical rather than dramatic – indeed, Erwin Stein, another Schoenberg pupil, placed him in the line of Schubert and **Debussy**. His work divides into three periods: a tonal phase (until *c.* 1907), an experimental 'anti-tonal' and early twelve-tone phase (*c.* 1907–24), and a final phase in which he adopted Schoenberg's twelve-tone serialism. His development as a composer is inseparable from that of his teacher: in his early years especially he could seize upon and extend the radical elements in Schoenberg's music with an intensity that irked the older man. Unlike his teacher, however, he was a miniaturist by temperament, and few of his pieces last more than ten minutes. His individuality lay in the expressive concentration of his music, and his importance in the fastidiousness with which he refined and developed what he considered to be essentially traditional features of composition.

The works of the first, tonal period show an absorption of, on the one hand, the Classical formal principles of sonata and variation, and, on the other hand, the advanced melody, harmony, textures and instrumentation of composers such as **Richard Wagner**, **Richard Strauss**, **Hugo Wolf** and **Gustav Mahler**. Whereas the form of the *Passacaglia*, Op. 1, for example, may well have been suggested by the finale of **Brahms's** Fourth Symphony, the progressive transformation of its themes owes more, perhaps, to the practice of Strauss's tone-poems.

In the second phase, this principle of 'developing variation' gave way to that of 'constant variation'. Traditionally, music had proceeded through the statement, development and repetition of ideas. But now overt repetition was abandoned, leaving merely statement and continual development. This created a style analogous to written prose, and epitomized the predominantly negative virtues of this phase: nothing was to be too concrete. Directionally orientated harmony was replaced by 'wandering' harmony and a deliberate annulment of natural tonal hierarchies. The avoidance of familiar formal prototypes led Webern, as it had Schoenberg, to an 'expressionist' reliance on texts to determine the formal outlines of his music, which at this time was predominantly vocal. Indeed, the imaginative world of Webern's music was inseparable from the work of the poets he set: George (Op. 3 and Op. 4), **Rilke** (Op. 8), **Trakl** (Op. 14), **Strindberg** (Op. 12) and **Kraus** (Op. 13). He also set Goethe (Op. 12), folk texts (Op. 15) and sacred works (Op. 16).

The rootless subjectivity of this music probably derived from the sensitivity of the word-setting in Wagner's music-dramas – indeed, Webern's life-long fastidiousness in the observation of prosody would seem to owe to Wagner's *Sprechgesang* (speech-song, a heightened recitative). In Wagner the significance of the individual words could be enhanced through the inflexions of melody, harmony, rhythm and instrumental timbre. Similarly, a wide range of colour is the hallmark of Webern's second phase, particularly in his Mahler-like predilection for unusual combinations of solo instruments, and in the resourcefulness of his exploitation of individual instrumental effects. The increased intensity of Webern's music, however, lay in the use of frequently angular and wide-leaping lines, and in his dramatic juxtaposition of extreme contrasts in tempo, dynamics, texture and articulation. These features appear most notably in the instrumental works written between 1909 and 1914: *Five Pieces for String Quartet* (Op. 5); *Six Pieces for Large Orchestra* (Op. 6); *Four Pieces for Violin and Piano* (Op. 7); and the *Six Bagatelles for String Quartet* (Op. 9).

Of such brevity was this music that the publication of Op. 9 was accompanied by an apologia from Schoenberg: 'To express a novel in a gesture, joy in a single breath: such concentration can only be found where self-pity is lacking in equal measure.' In the years after the First World War, therefore, it was partly through an urge to create large structures, and partly through a wish to re-align himself with a musical tradition rooted in Bach, Beethoven and Brahms, that Webern chose to adopt his teacher's twelve-tone 'method'. By fixing the twelve notes of the chromatic scale into a series that was then unfolded in different versions and transpositions, a new formal classicism could be built out of the previous rootlessness. This neo-classicism extended into details of melodic structure and textural organization. After three exploratory vocal works (Opp. 17–19) we find that his new, predominantly instrumental music bears Classical titles: *Trio* (Op. 20), *Symphony* (Op. 21), *Quartet* (Opp. 22 and 28), *Concerto* (Op. 24), *Variations* (Opp. 27 and 30) and *Cantata* (Opp. 29 and 31; also *Das Augenlicht*, Op. 26, for chorus and orchestra).

Webern's understanding of the twelve-tone method was arguably more probing – and his use certainly more consistent – than Schoenberg's. Although Schoenberg combined series in a quasi-polyphonic manner, it was Webern who had a deeper grasp of what **Milton Babbitt** was to describe as 'combinatoriality'. His earlier procedure of developing small, motivic cells now led to the principle of 'derivation', the division of the chromatic scale into identically constituted cells. Webern also re-introduced – though at a remote level – pitch hierarchies based on the tritone, the diminished seventh or the augmented chord, to govern large-scale musical movement. His scholarly interest in Flemish polyphony had led in the second phase to an extensive exploration of canon, which assumed a greater significance in the twelve-tone works, especially through the exploitation of the harmonic properties of canon-by-inversion.

It was the radicalism of the aesthetic attitudes accompanying these works, however, that was to prove so influential, even though, or perhaps because, they were so deeply rooted in nineteenth- and early twentieth-century intellectual currents. Webern's account of music history was historicist and evolutionary: his own music was to be the latest, highest and most inevitable stage in the development of Western (German) music. It would render the need to study earlier theory 'obsolete'. He attempted a Bach-like integration of different ideas (polyphony, accompanied melody, etc.) with the newly conquered twelve-tone language. Above all he admired everything that led to the greatest possible structural unity, frequently citing Kraus's demands for a moral responsibility towards language, Goethe's work on colour theory and plant metamorphosis, and Bach's purely pedagogic work *The Art of Fugue*. The latter he described as the 'highest reality', on account of the 'abstract' complexities emanating from a single theme. In such works as the String Quartet Op. 28 he aimed at a comparable abstraction, convinced that 'composition with twelve-tone technique has achieved a degree of complete unity that was not even approximately there before'.

These attitudes, far from representing a *volte face* with respect to the preceding Expressionist works, merely redress the imbalance that these in turn had created with respect to his early music. Indeed, most of his later music retains something of the earlier spare, expressive urgency. In the post-1945 era, however, it was principally with abstraction, and less with expression, that Webern's name was associated. With the subsequent international movement towards the extension of the orderable domains of language, traditional concern with idea in Webern's music was deemed obsolete, and a complete schism with all but the most recent past was effected. While, since its inception, the adequacy of the twelve-tone system as a musical language has always been in dispute, the arguably deleterious effect of this schism on the composition, criticism, teaching and performance of modern music has only more recently been called into question.

Although it seems unlikely that Webern's reputation will ever again stand as high as it did in the 1950s, any revaluation can only emphasize the expressive qualities of some of his later music. Through setting the words of the nature-loving Hildegarde Jone (Opp. 23, 25, 26, 29 and 31), he developed a uniquely tender lyricism which finds its most perfect utterance in the second movement of the *Concerto* Op. 24. It was with such pieces in mind that **Igor Stravinsky** remarked: 'Whether there are great, or only new and very individual feelings in his music is a question which I can only answer for myself, but for me Webern has a power to move.'

Further reading

Other works include: *The Path to the New Music* (trans. Leo Black, 1963), and *Letters to Hildegarde Jone and Josef Humplik* (trans. Cornelius Cardew, 1967). Important books on Webern include: W. Kolnedar, *Anton Webern* (trans. Humphrey Searle, 1961); H. Moldenhauer and D. Irvine (eds) *Anton von Webern: Perspectives* (1966); H. Moldenhauer, *Anton Webern: A Chronicle of His Life and Work* (1978); K. Bailey, *The Life of Webern* (1998); and *Die Reihe*, Vol. 2 (periodical). Other, mainly analytic, articles occur in *Perspectives of New Music*, *Music Quarterly*, *Score*, *Tempo*, *Music Review*. See also: R. Leibowitz, *Schoenberg and His School* (1949); G. Perle, *Serial Composition and Atonality* (1962).

CHRISTOPHER WINTLE

WEDEKIND, Benjamin Franklin (Frank)

1864–1918

German dramatist and performer

Wedekind was born in Hanover, the second of six children, on the return from the USA of his parents, Dr Friedrich Wilhelm Wedekind, physician, former Man of 1848 and pillar of San Francisco society, and his wife Emilie, once an emigrant singer. Rejecting **Bismarck's** Germany, Dr Wedekind moved his family in 1872 to the castle of Lenzburg in Aargau, Switzerland. Frank showed an early talent for light satirical verse-making after the manner of Heine, and moved on to study French and, at his father's wish, law, at the universities of Lausanne and Munich. But devotion to literature and gaiety led to a grand quarrel with his father and an interim earning a precarious living, partly in the advertising office of Maggi in Zürich, publishing his first essays and short stories in the *Neue Zürcher Zeitung*. Most of these are far too confident and accomplished to be regarded as journeyman work. Two essays of this period, 'Zirkusgedanken' ('Circus Thoughts') and 'Der Witz und seine Sippe' ('Wit and Its Relations', 1887), can be regarded as programmatic for his subsequent work in drama.

Reconciliation with his father, and soon afterwards his father's death, gave him a modest inheritance which enabled him to spend the next six years travelling, writing, becoming the literary Bohemian of his reputation. His first dramas included *Children and Fools* (*Kinder und Narren*, 1891) which already broached what was to become his theme: the forms imposed on women's erotic lives by social pressure. It contained an attack on Gerhart Hauptmann both impersonal and personal, rejecting Naturalism as a dramatic mode, and denouncing the man who had drawn on Wedekind's private confession of his family tensions for material for his own play *Das Friedensfest*. There followed Wedekind's first major play, *Spring Awakening: A Tragedy of Childhood* (*Frühlings Erwachen: eine Kindertragödie*, 1891), which rapidly gained him the reputation of an important new talent. But it had to be published in Switzerland on account of difficulties with censorship in Germany, and was not performed until 1906, when **Max Reinhardt** put it on, heavily cut, at the Berlin Kammerspiel. It presented a generation of the young, variously maimed by the inadequacy of timid, authoritarian, hypocritical parents and teachers to help them into a sexually adult world. It was as innovatory in style, or styles, as in subject-matter: open-ended, episodic, moving by way of juxtaposition of scenes rather than by plotted sequence of acts; confronting the lyrical mode with the grotesque, the realist with the surrealist, it inaugurated a line of epic tragi-comedy which had progeny as various as the dramas of Dürrenmatt and **Brecht**.

The next four years Wedekind spent in Paris, with an interval of six months in London. His experiences there of cabaret, variétés, music hall, popular boulevard drama, Grand Guignol, the circus, gave sharper focus to his dissatisfaction with the confining imitativeness of Naturalist drama, and to his wish to recover the flamboyant theatricality of popular entertainment. His encounters with the metropolitan half-world, the easy sexuality of the grisette, the friendships of circus strong-man (Willi Rudinoff) and financial manipulator (Willi Gretor, whose secretary he was for a while) reinforced his outsider's criticism of the precarious stabilities of bourgeois values.

His next major work, the 'monster tragedy' he worked on for a number of years, was to emerge after many revisions, some as late as 1911 and 1913, as the dual drama *Earth Spirit* (*Erdgeist*, 1895) and *Pandora's Box* (*Die Büchse der Pandora*, 1902). This amalgam of farce, myth and Grand Guignol, perhaps his greatest achievement, presents the rise and fall of Lulu, the courtesan from the gutter – or from before the world began – in an exploitative social world: the ambivalent eternal-feminine, joyful, destructive, changing, immutable, her sexual delight finally destroyed by sexual brutality. A famous performance was the private one-night stand in 1905 at the Trianon-Theater, Vienna, organized by **Karl Kraus**, in which Kraus played the minor part of Kungo Poti, Wedekind himself Jack the Ripper, and Tilly Newes, who was to become his wife, Lulu.

On his return to Munich in 1896 he became a regular contributor to Albert Langen's recently founded satirical weekly *Simplicissimus*, under the pseudonym Hieronymus Jobs. His satirical poems on political issues of the day brought fame – and trouble. Two of them – on Wilhelm II's journey to the Holy

Land – provoked a prosecution for *lèse-majesté*, for Wedekind's pseudonym had been mysteriously broken – by Langen, he was convinced. At work on *Der Marquis von Keith* (1900, first performed 1901), Wedekind fled to Zürich. Once the drama was finished, he returned to face six months in prison. After the experimental forms of *Spring Awakening* and the Lulu-dramas, he adopted the classic conversation-piece for this presentation of the charlatan outwitted. The tables are ultimately turned on the extravagant imagination and enterprise of the swindling Marquis precisely by the philistine bourgeois whom he had set out to exploit. His vitality and sheer gusto, the theatrical version of the **Nietzschean** life-force, represent a major theme in Wedekind's dramas. So, increasingly, does its defeat. But: 'Life is a fair-ground slide,' concludes the Marquis, as he decides in the last line to live, rather than shoot himself.

Out of prison, Wedekind began a new career as performer, mainly to publicize his dramas, which audiences still looked at askance. He turned cabaret artist, reciting his own monologues, singing his songs to his own accompaniment on the guitar, joining the largely amateur group known as the Eleven Hangmen. Cabaret, the satirical bohemian import from France, was only just beginning in Berlin and Munich, and Wedekind was an innovator in a genre which has become a permanent feature of German fringe theatre. At the same time Wedekind turned actor. The sharpness of his dialogue, the *ad absurdum* extremity of his situations, the abstract caricature of his figures, was something unfamiliar to actors and producers as well as to audiences. By taking on his own major roles, his powerful presence overwhelming his lack of professional skill, Wedekind was able to show the theatre what was required by way of intensity, energy, hardness. At various times he played The Ringmaster, Dr Schön, Jack in the Lulu-dramas, the title role in *The Opera Singer* (*Der Kammersänger*, 1899), Casti-Piani in *Dance of Death* (*Totentanz*, 1905), Buridan in *Censorship* (*Die Zensur*, 1908), Tschamper in *Schloss*

Wetterstein (1910). After his marriage in 1906 to a first-class professional actress, he and his wife toured performing cycles of his works so successfully that, allowing for battles with local censors, his reputation as an abrasive, disturbing dramatist was established. His society had caught up with him, and he had found a role to play in it.

After *Keith*, a more argumentative, ideological note enters his dramas. Where Lulu is powerful as image – her richness lies in her ultimate irreducibility to ideology – later works are explicit, overt in their treatment of their themes: marriage, the battle between the sexes, the position of women, censorship: sometimes all at once. The situations are increasingly extreme and absurd, the comedy blacker, the figures and their relationships increasingly exemplifications of a case. There is general agreement on a decline in talent with an increase in stridency. Perhaps the Shavian *Hidalla* (1904) is the most successful. In it Wedekind puts into the mouth of the central figure, Karl Hetmann, his own attack on the 'feudalism of love': the prostitute for purchase, the virgin-bride for sale, the suffragette who denied her sexuality, were all distortions of the true vocation of woman. In the final scene the grotesque visionary is seen as fit only for a job as a circus clown, and so destroys himself. It makes a dark comment on Wedekind's own fate as a truth-teller acceptable only as an entertainer – especially as Hetmann was Wedekind's most successful acting role. He frequently uses events and figures from his own life in these later plays, less for self-expression than to exemplify a general issue by means of his own situation, though the distinction is not always clear. In *Hidalla*, Langen's betrayal of Wedekind is turned into the entrepreneur's betrayal of the intellectual. In *Censorship* Wedekind's own life-long battle with the authorities is stylized into the protests of the serious moralist against the bland paternalism of the highly placed priest, but the same play steers closer to the private wind when it also presents the tensions in the marriage between a controversial dramatist and an accomplished actress. In the one case the private issue is successfully generalized; not so in the other.

Wedekind criticized his world not in political but in social and human terms, and the attitude to sexuality was the touchstone. In his time the terror of the bourgeoisie, he became, as perhaps he was bound to, a Good Liberal Cause, the literary opposition in Germany never failing to rally to his defence. He was the definitive pioneer of twentieth-century developments in non-realistic drama: not only did he break taboos of subject-matter, but his drama was sensationally and self-consciously theatrical. Dürrenmatt has recognized his debt to Wedekind's tragicomic absurdism; Brecht to his didactic buffoonery and 'alienation-effects'; the open form, the grotesque concentration, the dramatic subjectivity can be found again in the later **Strindberg**; the comic abstraction of his situations – and some of his targets – can be traced in the expressionist comedy of Carl Sternheim. His parodistic use of established dramatic genres, and his rediscovery of the popular spectacle of circus and music hall have become widely diffused tricks in the modern dramatist's repertory. The power of the Lulu-dramas is perpetuated in **Alban Berg's** opera *Lulu* (1937, completed 1979). His cabaret chansons virtually founded the genre in Germany.

Further reading

Other works include: *Gesammelte Werke*, ed. Artur Kutscher and Joachim Friedenthal (9 vols, 1912–21): a good selection, including additional unpublished material, is *Werke*, selected and introduced by Manfred Hahn (3 vols, 1954). Letters: *Gesammelte Briefe*, ed. Fritz Strich (2 vols, 1924). Prose: *Minne-Haha oder Über die körperliche Erziehung der jungen Mädchen* ('Minne-haha, or On the Physical Education of Young Girls', 1901). Translations: *Five Tragedies of Sex*, trans. Frances Fawcett and Stephen Spender (1952, containing *Spring's Awakening, Earth-Spirit, Pandora's Box, Death and Devil, Castle Wetterstein*). Other dramas: *The Lightning Artist* (*Der Schnellmaler*, 1889); *That's Life* (*So ist das Leben*, (1902); *Musik* (1908); *Franziska* (1912); *Bismarck* (1916). Ballet scenarios: *The Fleas* (*Die Flöhe*, 1892); *The Empress of Newfoundland* (*Die Kaiserin von Neufundland*, 1897). Biography: Artur

Kutscher, *Frank Wedekind: Sein Leben und seine Werke* (3 vols, 1922–31); Günter Seehaus, *Wedekind* (1974). Secondary works: Klaus Völker, *Frank Wedekind* (1965); Sol Gittlemann, *Wedekind* (1969); Alan Best, *Wedekind* (1975); E. Boa, *The Sexual Circus: Wedekind's Theatre of Subversion* (1987).

JOYCE CRICK

WEIL, Simone

1909–43

French essayist

Simone Weil was born in Paris, where her father worked as a doctor. Like her elder brother André, she showed early signs of a precocious intelligence, fostered by her parents, who, though of Jewish origin, were free-thinking agnostics. André became a brilliant mathematician, an interest shared by Simone, one of her concerns being the problem of abstraction in modern science. She also possessed a facility for languages both ancient and modern. It was from this broad cultural base that her highly original and apposite commentary on the human condition was made.

At sixteen she studied under the philosopher Emile-Auguste Chartier Alain, whose cult of self-mastery and the individual moral will had a life-long influence on her. Other influences were Plato, Spinoza, Pascal, Rousseau, Kant and Descartes, whose Cogito she took as the starting point for her diploma dissertation at the École Normale Supérieure, which she attended from 1928 to 1931.

Simone Weil had a capacity for intense suffering, being prone to debilitating headaches and a conscience so sensitive to inequity that she drove herself inexorably both in her intellectual pursuits and in tearing herself away from them in order to experience the concrete affliction of industrial and agricultural labour. Repelled by the exercise of force, she nevertheless attempted to place herself in the thick of the action in the Spanish Civil War – and again in the French Resistance, this time without success. Her early death in England in 1943 was due to unwillingness to eat more than the rations she thought her compatriots were getting, which exacerbated her tuberculosis; but it undoubtedly also owed much to the exhausting tension of feeling herself to be cut off and ineffectual in the midst of a crisis.

Politically, she allied herself with the left, wishing to take the side of those against whom, she felt, the scales of justice were weighted. She wrote for various left-wing journals and was heavily involved with the trade unions even while working as a lycée teacher. She did not assume the conventional identity of either sphere, and attracted the opprobrium of both left and right for her outspoken advocation of radical change. For the root of her activism was her spiritual insight, which led her to criticize the materialist side of Marx and its Soviet embodiment, as much as the other manifestations of what she apocalyptically called the Great Beast, such as Ancient Rome and Israel. She believed that the Nazis were playing out the blood-stained legacy of exclusivity bequeathed by the very culture they now sought to oppress. Although she embraced the church in its esoteric aspect, the exoteric collusion of a vengeful Jehovah and Roman bureaucracy repelled her. Seeing as much spiritual validity in the religions of the East as in her own Western inheritance, Weil felt that she, like the Gnostics, must be anathema and therefore could not be baptized.

A sense of cultural heritage features prominently among the needs of the soul outlined in *The Need for Roots* (*L'Enracinement*, 1949, trans. 1952), which she wrote in London shortly before her death, as a programme for the spiritual regeneration of France. The rest of her writing consists of articles, notebooks and other fragments (including poems and an unfinished play), published in various arrangements after her death. She can in turn be mistaken for a Marxist anarchist or a conservative traditionalist, the prophet of tolerance and pacifism or the harbinger of a bleak, strife-torn vision. This has to be seen in the context of her attempt to effect a type of synthesis which is rare in the modern age:

following Plato, she held that genuine truths must of necessity be paradoxical in character. We are mesmerized by the cave of illusions in which we live, and to free ourselves from this is almost impossibly difficult.

However, sustained by the few occasions on which she herself experienced the presence of the divine, Simone Weil attests that, as long as we do not rush to fill it with short-term comforts, the void of disillusion can act as a channel for grace. Thus is born a motive for overcoming our alienation from the reality of our condition.

Further reading

Other works include: *Gravity and Grace* (*La Pesanteur et la grace*, 1947, trans. 1952); *Waiting on God* (*Attente de Dieu*, 1950, trans. 1951); *Oppression and Liberty* (*Oppression et liberté*, 1955, trans. 1958); *Seventy Letters* (1965); *First and Last Notebooks* (from *Cahiers*, 1956, trans. 1965). *Gateway to God*, ed. David Raper (1974) is an introductory selection of Weil's writings. A. Reynaud, *Simone Weil: Lectures on Philosophy* (*Leçons de philosophie*, 1959, trans. 1978) are reconstituted notes. See also: R. Rees, *Simone Weil: A Sketch for a Portrait* (1966); Simone Pétrement, *Simone Weil: A Life* (trans. 1976); Francine du Plessix Gray, *Simone Weil* (2001).

LÉONIE CALDECOTT

WEILL, Kurt

1900–1950

German/US composer

One of the outstanding composers for the theatre in the twentieth century, Weill, a German-born Jew, studied composition with Albert Bing in Dessau and Humperdinck at the Berlin Hochschule. After brief stints as a repetiteur in Dessau and kapellmeister in Lüdensheid, Weill returned to Berlin in 1920 as one of six pupils chosen for **Ferruccio Busoni's** master class at the Academy of Arts. Weill supplemented his training with counterpoint lessons from Phillip Jarnach, bolstered his income with earnings as chief critic for *Der deutsche Rundfunk*, and broadened his intellectual horizons through membership in Berlin's November Group. In 1933 Weill and his wife, singer-actress Lotte Lenya, both on the Nazis' blacklist, fled to Paris. Two years later they moved to New York, where Weill devoted his energies to the Broadway musical stage until his death in 1950.

Weill assimilated the innovations of the post-**Wagnerian** generation of German composers (especially **Mahler**, Max Reger and **Richard Strauss**) in his earliest mature works: String Quartet in B minor (1919), Sonata for Cello and Piano (1920), and Symphony No. 1 (1921). Although all remained unperformed and unpublished during his lifetime, stylistic elements revealed here became firmly entrenched in Weill's musical language: semitonal shifts between successive sonorities, employment of fifth-generated diatonic structures, continual vacillation between major and minor, textures animated by reiterated propulsive rhythmic figures, and the underlying 'romantic' premise that no amount of irony or self-conscious denial could camouflage.

Under Busoni's tutelage until 1924, Weill adopted classic and pre-classic models in composing 'absolute' music characterized by formal concision and clarity of texture. The most successful of these works are the String Quartet No. 1 (Op. 8, 1923) – the first of Weill's compositions accepted for publication – the song cycle *Frauentanz* (Op. 10, 1923), and *Quodlibet* (Op. 9, 1923) – the orchestral suite that Weill extracted from his first theatrical work, the ballet-pantomime *Die Zaubernacht* (1922). *Recordare* (Op. 11, 1923), an *a cappella* setting of the fifth chapter of Jeremiah, *Divertimento* (1922), and *Sinfonia sacra* (1922) perpetuate the religious symbolism so evident in Symphony No. 1, where the chorale idiom had first appeared.

Weill's operatic début, the one-act tragedy *Der Protagonist* (Op. 15, 1926), was the first product of his collaboration with the prolific Expressionist playwright Georg Kaiser. This stunning score established Weill's reputation as the leading composer for the theatre of his generation and already employed his own technique of 'aesthetic distancing'. Although still tonal, its musical language is rivalled in complexity only by the Violin Concerto (Op. 12, 1925), and its success inspired a companion comic one-act, *Der Zar lässt sich photographieren* ('The Czar has his Photograph Taken', Op. 21, 1928). After the Weill–Brecht collaboration had ended in 1931 with **Brecht** denouncing his colleague as a 'phony Richard Strauss', Weill again turned to Kaiser for his last work for the German stage, *Der Silbersee* ('The Silver Lake', 1933).

Although Weill is best known for his collaborations with Bertolt Brecht, the notion (implied by Brecht and echoed in much secondary literature) that Weill was merely a musical amanuensis and that the dramatist was responsible for stylistic shifts in Weill's music is spurious. In fact, Weill had already incorporated modern dance idioms and the instrumentation of jazz, which he called an international folk music, in the cantata *Der neue Orpheus* (Op. 16, 1927), and the one-act film-opera *Royal Palace* (Op. 17, 1927) – almost two years before he initiated the collaboration with Brecht. Weill found in Brecht a librettist whose sociological and theatrical goals were sufficiently similar to his own to yield six works for the stage, three cantatas, and a number of incidental pieces.

By far the most successful was *The Threepenny Opera* (*Die Dreigroschenoper*, 1928), which was translated into eighteen languages for more than 10,000 performances within five years of its premiere. Its unsuccessful imitator, *Happy End* (1929), contains some of Weill's best 'Songs', a genre created by Weill and Brecht from various popular models as the central structural unit of epic opera. The epic style with its aesthetic distance (*Verfremdungseffekt*) and gestic music was first tested in the *Mahagonny Songspiel* (1927) and then expanded to monumental proportions in *Aufstieg und Fall der Stadt Mahagonny* ('Rise and Fall of the City Mahagonny', 1930). Epic features are no less prominent in the *Schuloper, Der Jasager* ('The Yes-Sayer', 1930) and the didactic cantata *Der Lindberghflug* ('Lindbergh's Flight', 1929), both of which enjoyed numerous performances in German schools.

The third member of the artistic triumvirate of epic opera, Caspar Neher, wrote the libretto for *Die Bürgschaft* ('The Trust', 1933), which Weill hailed as his return to pure music-making after the Brechtian detour.

The Brecht–Weill partnership was revived briefly in Paris when both suffered the common fate of exile for *Die sieben Todsünden* ('The Seven Deadly Sins', 1933), a ballet with singing staged by Balanchine. During his two-year stay in France, Weill also completed his Symphony No. 2 (1934), *Marie galante* (1934) – a play by Jacques Deval – and the operetta *A Kingdom for a Cow* (1935). Although Brecht repeatedly attempted to renew the association in America, Weill was too successful in his 'second career' to retrace his steps.

With the expressed purpose of continuing his life-long devotion to musical theatre, Weill hoped to create a genuine American operatic tradition through the popular Broadway medium. To this end he recruited a long list of illustrious dramatists: Paul Green (*Johnny Johnson*, 1936), Maxwell Anderson (*Knickerbocker Holiday*, 1938; *Lost in the Stars*, 1949), Moss Hart (*Lady in the Dark*, 1941), Ogden Nash (*One Touch of Venus*, 1943), Ira Gershwin (*The Firebrand of Florence*, 1945), Alan J. Lerner (*Love Life*, 1948) and Elmer Rice (*Street Scene*, 1947). More than any of his compatriots, Weill was successful in establishing a new identity in his adopted culture. He maintained the craftsmanship and formal invention of his European works, yet depicted Americana in *Street Scene* and the folk opera *Down in the Valley* (1945) as vividly as he had mirrored the milieu of the Weimar Republic in his earlier works. Unfortunately Weill's ultimate goals for American opera were left unfulfilled when he was felled by a coronary while composing a musical version of *Huckleberry Finn*.

Further reading

See: *Über Kurt Weill*, ed. David Drew (1975); Helmut Kotschenreuther, *Kurt Weill* (1962); *Weill–Lenya*, ed. Henry Marx (1976); Gottfried Wagner, *Weill und Brecht: Das musikalische Zeittheater*

(1977); Kim H. Kowalke, *Kurt Weill in Europe* (1979); R. Taylor, *Kurt Weill: Composer in a Divided World* (1991); Foster Hirsch, *Kurt Weill on Stage: From Berlin to Broadway* (2002).

KIM H. KOWALKE

WEIZMANN, Chaim

1874–1952

Scientist, Zionist and first president of Israel

Chaim Weizmann was born in the village of Motol, near Pinsk, in the Russian Pale of Settlement, one of fifteen children of a timber merchant. His early education was at a traditional *Heder* (literally: room) studying with other Jewish boys. Aged eleven, he entered high school in Pinsk and later went on to study biochemistry first in Germany and later in Switzerland, where in 1899 he was awarded a doctorate with honours. In 1901, Weizmann was appointed assistant lecturer at the University of Geneva and, in 1904, he was made senior lecturer at the University of Manchester.

Weizmann's involvement with Zionism, the political movement which sought to establish a home for the Jewish people in Palestine, began at an early age. At the 8th Zionist Congress in 1907, Weizmann was the principal champion of 'Synthetic Zionism', which advocated concurrent action on both tracks: political activity and practical endeavour in Palestine. It also stressed Zionist activity in the Diaspora such as modernized education and active participation, on separate Jewish tickets, in national and local elections.

Weizmann's 'Synthetic Zionism' soon became the dominating strategy of the Zionist movement. Along with his Zionist activities, Weizmann also pursued his research in chemistry, and during the First World War he was credited with developing a method of producing acetone from maize, which was needed for the production of artillery shells. This achievement brought him into close contact with British leaders, enabling him to play a key role in persuading them to issue the Balfour Declaration of 2 November 1917 which stated that, 'His Majesty's Government view with favour the establishment in Palestine of a national home for the Jewish people'. In 1918 Weizmann headed the Zionist Commission which was sent to Palestine by the British government to advise on the future development of the country and the implementation of the Balfour Declaration. Two years later, at the London Zionist Conference of 1920, Weizmann was elected president of the World Zionist Organization (WZO) and in 1929 he was made president of the newly founded Jewish Agency to represent the Jewish people vis-à-vis the Mandatory government in Palestine.

After the publication of the Passfield White Paper of 1930, in which the British government retreated from previous commitments to the Jews, notably from the Balfour Declaration, Weizmann angrily resigned his office, returning to the presidency of the WZO only after British prime minister Ramsey McDonald sent him a letter in which he renewed Great Britain's commitments to the Jewish National Home. In the 1931 election to the presidency of the WZO Weizmann was not re-elected, but he continued to devote his energies to the Zionist cause, undertaking fund-raising trips and throwing himself into the work of rescuing Jewish refugees from Europe. In 1935, he was elected again as president of the WZO and during the years that led up to the Second World War, he invested much effort in establishing the Jewish Brigade, as part of the British army (it saw action in Italy in 1945).

An Anglophile, Weizmann believed in close working relations with Great Britain, but when after the war the Labour Party assumed power in Britain and failed to keep its pre-election promise to adopt a pro-Zionist policy, Weizmann's position as leader of the Zionist Movement came to an end; the 22nd Zionist Congress, in 1946, did not re-elect him to the presidency. Although Weizmann no longer held an official position in the Zionist Movement, he continued as principal spokesman of the Jewish national cause and he was instrumental in the adoption of the Partition Plan by the United Nations on 29 November 1947, which called for the division of Palestine between Jews and Arabs. Weizmann also played a leading role in persuading the US to recognize the state of Israel in May 1948. With the establishment of Israel, Weizmann was chosen as its first president, a role he filled until his death on 9 November 1952. He was buried in the garden of his home in Rehovot, which was named the Weizmann Institute of Science.

Further reading

Weizmann's writings include *Trial and Error: The Autobiography of Chaim Weizmann* (1949), which has been translated into several languages.

AHRON BREGMAN

WELLES, George Orson

1915–85

US film director

Revered by Modernists such as **Jean-Luc Godard**, Welles's work centres on themes remote from Modernist concerns. From his appearance as Death in the early short *The Hearts of Age* (1934), the processes of mortality, corruption and the erosion of innocence haunt his films. Even if the perspectives are altered, the blueprint of classical tragedy, of hubris and nemesis, determines the structure of Welles's dramas, which are played out somewhere between life and legend. Two other traditions also meet in Welles: the ancient art of the storyteller, and the more recent association of the cinema, viit Georges Méliès, with the **Barnum** skills of illusionism. Welles's delight in presenting himself as prestidigitateur is no peripheral eccentricity, but a reason for his exhilarated display of cinematic resources: 'This is the biggest electric train set any boy ever had,' he remarked of the set for *Citizen Kane* (1941).

The son of an inventor and a concert pianist, Orson Welles attended Todd School in Woodstock, Illinois, and there became active in theatre. After directing and acting in plays at the Gate Theatre, Dublin, he returned to America and founded the Mercury Theatre in 1937, and with its company presented a series of radio plays, including the notorious adaptation of **H.G. Wells's** *The War of the Worlds* which panicked many listeners into believing that a Martian invasion was actually taking place. This brought Welles a Hollywood contract that gave him an unusual degree of artistic and financial control, but also fuelled suspicion and dislike. His subsequent career casts light on the contradictions of an industry simultaneously demanding creativity and submission to standardized practices. Like Erich von Stroheim before him, Welles was frequently to discover that studios preferred him to be in front of rather than behind the camera.

His first still-born project was an adaptation of **Conrad's** *Heart of Darkness* (later the basis of **Coppola's** *Apocalypse Now*, 1979). *Citizen Kane* thus became Welles's astonishing début. Many of the stylistic devices of this deservedly famous film – deep-focus compositions, flashback structure, overlapping dialogue, chiaroscuro lighting effects, bizarre camera angles – had a clear lineage, and even the character of Kane himself can be seen as a hybrid of William Randolph Hearst, **Fitzgerald's** Gatsby, Howard Hughes and Welles himself; but Welles's massive achievement was to make all these elements entirely pristine as he found expressive use for what had frequently been mere decoration. Described by **Borges** as 'a centreless labyrinth', the film is built around a search for the key to the personality of the dead Kane. From a welter of recollections emerges a bleak tale of irremediable loss of innocence, betrayal of hope and love, and the misuse of great power. But because of Welles's exuberant visual style and the carefully woven web of symmetries and complexity, the impact of *Kane* is anything but bleak.

Following *Kane*, a critical success but relative financial failure, Welles directed *The Magnificent Ambersons* (1942), an elegiac evocation of the decline of a minor aristocratic family at the turn of the century, and his only completed picture in which he does not himself appear. New management at RKO led to its re-editing in Welles's absence and subsequent release in a version 45 minutes shorter than Welles's own. It was not the last time he was to experience such treatment. *Touch of Evil* (1958), a masterpiece of *film noir* which marked his return to Hollywood direction, was shrugged off by Universal without even a trade showing. Ostensibly a banal police story, *Touch of Evil* explores the contradictions between being 'a great detective but a lousy cop' in a meditation on the law that has the maturity to separate principles from their proponents. But, *Kane* apart, it was perhaps only in Shakespeare that Welles could find a physical space large enough for his characters. Three films based on Shakespearian drama (*Macbeth*, 1948; *Othello*, 1952; and *Falstaff*, or *Chimes at Midnight*, 1966), although uneven, project a personal vision without prejudice to the complexity of human nature. The increasing bitterness of his later works finds respite in *Chimes at Midnight,* hailed by some critics as a premature testament and product of a talent that had finally transcended the qualities that gave it birth.

Rejecting **Eisenstein's** practice of creating cinematic meaning through the juxtaposition of shots in montage and the isolation of images in close-up, Welles chose to organize his world through intricate camera movements, deep-focus compositions and long takes (the opening, three-minute tracking shot of *Touch of Evil* is a famous example). Such a style democratizes the image, allowing the audience to immerse itself in the dramatic reality of the scene, but the constant camera movement establishes a tension between involvement and distance, between compassion and irony – a tension that is central to Welles's work. Despite his troubled relationships with studio hierarchies, Welles has had enormous influence on both Hollywood and European directors through his demonstration of the expressive powers of cinema, particularly those that derive from large-scale production, and through the magnanimity of his vision. Welles was a hard act to follow, but Francis Coppola, **Martin Scorsese** and **Stanley Kubrick** must all be considered at least partial inheritors.

Further reading

Other works include: *The Stranger* (1946); *The Lady from Shanghai* (1948); *The Trial* (1962); *The Immortal Story* (1968); and *F for Fake* (1973). Welles also directed a film version (1955, *Confidential Report* in the UK) of his own novel *Mr Arkadin* (1954). See: Andre Bazin, *Orson Welles* (rev. 1958, trans. 1978); Joseph McBride, *Orson Welles* (1972); Simon Callow, *The Road to Xanadu* (1995).

NIGEL ALGAR

WELLS, Herbert George

1866–1946

British writer

Journalist, novelist, popular historian and sociologist, H.G. Wells was a considerable influence in encouraging the modern mentality which brought scientific scepticism to bear on social, moral and religious questions during the early twentieth century. The logical outcome of the long curve which ran from the Renaissance through the Encyclopedists to **T.H. Huxley**, a curve sustained by the conviction that man was a rational being, Wells believed that once enlightened education had become universal and scientific techniques widely accepted, half the problems of humankind would be solved.

His beginnings were in complete contradiction to these lofty preoccupations. His father ran a shop in Bromley, Kent, which combined chinaware with cricket accessories, and Wells was born in a small bedroom over the shop. His mother, a simple woman of lower-middle-class origin, reached the height of her ambitions when she became housekeeper to Miss Featherstonhaugh who owned a mansion known as Uppark. It was at Uppark that Wells met some of the characters later to appear in his novel *Tono-Bungay* (1909), 'her leddyship' being drawn as a vivid caricature of his mother's employer.

A scant education led to his becoming a draper's assistant, but the life so appalled him that he quickly ran away. After several false starts he became a chemist's assistant, a post which revealed his lack of Latin. However, he astonished his tutor at Midhurst Grammar School by mastering the greater part of Smith's *Principia* in five hours, and after that nothing could stop his educational advance. At eighteen he won a scholarship to study biology at the Normal School of Science in London, then dominated by T.H. Huxley. The three years he spent there provided the scientific raw material from which he distilled the first wave of his scientific fiction.

Living in near-poverty as a teacher of science, he married his first cousin, Isabel Mary Wells, in 1891: an unfortunate choice which merely increased his financial problems. The *Pall Mall Gazette* printed his first article 'On the Art of Staying at the Seaside', in the same year, and thus began his lifelong habit of emptying his mind on the printed page in journalistic form whenever some urgent question demanded quick expression. Any conflict between his scientific training and his journalistic outpourings, however, was resolved when he wrote his first science-fiction story *The Time Machine* (1895), on the appearance of which W.T. Stead described Wells as 'a man of genius'. Constructing a brilliantly symbolized Time Machine, the Traveller flashes forward to the year 802701 and enters a society divided into two classes, the Morlocks, living and working in caves beneath the earth, and the Eloi, a class of graceful decadent sybarites. 'Man had not remained one species but had differentiated into two distinct animals', the result of the widening of differences between Capital and Labour. *The Time Machine* was a social allegory written with a poetic intensity its author never recaptured. Close on its heel came *The Wonderful Visit* (1895), *The Island of Doctor Moreau* (1896), *The Invisible Man* (1897) and *The War of the Worlds* (1898). Wells knew just

how to unlock the imaginative worlds, the latent excitements, buried beneath dull scientific data, but behind the virtuosity lay a deep concern for man and society. There were many comparisons with the work of **Jules Verne**, but the heroes of Verne's novels were idealized creatures turning invention to their own private account with little concern for the social problems that preoccupied Wells. He saw that he could harness scientific discovery to revolutionize our lives in ways as yet unforeseen. He also realized that science might run off in Frankenstein abandon, gathering more and more power over nature while the ordinary human being had less and less power over himself. He understood his scientific implications to be highly romantic, but each story carried a message, and it was the message that mattered when the drama had exhausted itself. Indeed, his concern for social problems soon drove him to abandon science fiction in favour of his lower-middle-class comedies: *Love and Mr Lewisham* (1900), *Kipps* (1905) and *The History of Mr Polly* (1910). Unlike with **Dickens**, what people did for a living became vital in his books, reflecting the organization of society, its greatest evil, the future always more important than the past or present. However, it was no accident that *Kipps* and *A Modern Utopia* were published in the same year. Wells was simply unable to express all his ideas in fiction. The scientist in him tried to shake off the novelist with *A Modern Utopia*, while the artist clamoured for comic simplicities untroubled by any vestige of science. In *Kipps* and *The History of Mr Polly* Wells drew heavily on his own attempts to climb from lower- to middle-class life, and he became the spokesman for millions of inarticulate people whose frustrations had never achieved such realistic expression in fiction before. Similarly, *Ann Veronica* (1909) crystallized the desire for greater freedom of thousands of young women in the period when the book was written. Here was a middle-class daughter who defied her father, ran off and threw herself into the arms of the man she loved. Wells once again brought to the surface the rational attitude to sexuality latent in the minds of many of his readers. Implicit in these novels, his belief in revolutionary progress found modified expression in *A Modern Utopia*, a vision of the future where society was divided into four entirely new classes: the Samurai, a voluntary nobility; the Poietic; the Kinetic; the Dull and the Base.

Attempting to translate theory into practice, Wells had joined the Fabian Society (a London-based group founded in 1883 and dedicated to transforming Great Britain into a socialist state) in 1903. Having created a following among many of the younger members, he quarrelled with the Executive, which included the **Webbs**, and challenged **G.B. Shaw**. Finally he resigned with a burst of that invective which came so readily from his pen. Always impatient, a man who over-reacted to every situation, Wells now abandoned world-making to write what is perhaps his best novel, *Tono-Bungay*. This brought alive an ignorant little man, Uncle Ponderevo, a combination of Whitaker Wright (the financial fraud) and someone in the likeness of all ambitious shopkeepers, to foist on the world a patent medicine, following through its social and psychological consequences with a skill that impressed even **Henry James**. It was a devastating criticism of unfettered private enterprise in a capitalist society.

However, during the period of the First World War Wells's power as a novelist declined, and it was not until the 1920s that his reputation was restored when he took on the mantle of public educator with *The Outline of History* (1920), a massive survey of world history, and its altogether more successful 'introduction', *A Short History of the World* (1922). This was a vividly written account that traced the evolution of man from the biological beginnings to his technological incarnation. Already, in several of his novels, Wells had brought men together as a species, over-ruling national divisions and seeing them in the light of a common destiny. Now he set out to counteract the insidious distortions of national histories with the conception of One World, the outcome of one people and one history. Despite its journalistic shortcomings and lack of precision, it was a remarkable feat which reached an audience of millions. Wells followed it with a number of huge rambling books with all-embracing titles like *The Work, Wealth and Happiness of Mankind* (1932), compendiums of information intended to enlighten the average man.

His later work became repetitious, re-echoing his earlier messages and culminating finally in the despairing *Mind at the End of Its Tether* (1945), which pictured a jaded world 'devoid of recuperative power'. Written during the Second World War, its pessimism can also be attributed to the fact that Wells himself was under sentence of death: doctors told him he would not last another year, and on 13 August 1946 he duly died, aged eighty.

Born into a lower-class background, Wells might have remained a straightforward rebel against society, but it was in a voluntary nobility that he put his trust in the end. Devoted to the ways of science, his brave new worlds were more mystic than scientific. Since Wells was impatient when people were not driven to action by his plans, they were plans frequently incapable of practical interpretation. A devotee of collectivism, of the group, of the belief that the individual was only a biological device which would decline when it had outlived its use, he stood alone, himself against half the world, and spectacularly burst out of every group he joined. He was a prophet who expected to be honoured in his own land, a brilliant example of what the ordinary man could become with grave misgivings about the proletariat. As a science-fiction writer he alerted the world to the dangers and benefits of scientific technologies; as a novelist he brought enlightenment and entertainment to a very large audience; as a mass educator he opened areas of knowledge relatively unknown to his readers; as a prophet his predictions were sometimes true, sometimes false. If he never achieved academic respectability, that in his own eyes was a tribute to his powers.

Further reading

Other works include: science fiction: *When the Sleeper Wakes* (1899); *The First Men in the Moon* (1901); novels: *The New Machiavelli* (1911); *Mr Britling Sees It Through* (1916); non-fiction: *Anticipations* (1901); *New Worlds for Old* (1908); *The Open Conspiracy* (1928); *The Science of Life* (1931, with G.P. Wells); and the immensely readable *Experiment in Autobiography* (1934). About Wells: Geoffrey H. Wells, *H.G. Wells: A Sketch for a Portrait* (1930); Vincent Brome, *H.G. Wells* (1951); J. Kargalitski, *The Life and Thought of H.G. Wells* (trans. from the Russian, 1966); B. Murray, *H.G. Wells* (1990); P. Parrinder, *Shadows of the Future: H.G. Wells, Science Fiction and Prophecy* (1995).

VINCENT BROME

WHARTON, Edith

1862–1937

US novelist

Few writers have belonged so exclusively to the world described in their novels as Edith Wharton. Born in 1862, Edith Newbold Jones was the child of a rich and influential New York family settled in America since before the Revolution. The values in which she was reared during a dull and over-protected childhood were those typical of a society conscious of European cultural dominance – class, loyalty, respect for money and property and an almost slavish adulation of the old world. At twenty-three she married a socially acceptable Bostonian, Edward Wharton, and the pair spent the next few years travelling in Europe. Successful as the partnership was, Wharton's incipient mental illness produced increasing complications, and his wife's enforced solitude drove her to renew an earlier interest in fiction writing.

All her major novels are based on the New York and New England of her early years and are pervaded by an awareness of the rapid social change overtaking America during the closing decades of the century. The society portrayed in *The House of Mirth* (1905), her most successful book, is both rigidly entrenched and nervously aware of its own weakness. Thus the heroine Lily Bart, a genteel

orphan riding for a fall in her pursuit of luxury, seems to challenge the assumptions of smart New York as much as she stands in awe of them. Her satirical antetype is offered in Undine Spragg, whose extravagant career of fortune-hunting and excitement-seeking in *The Custom of the Country* (1913) has wider applications, in its glimpses of the flashy, the heartless and the trivial, to the new America as seen by the somewhat embittered Mrs Wharton.

Her favourite theme of the spontaneous defeated by the conventional dominates *Ethan Frome* (1911), a terse, rather **Hardyesque** tale of an erotic triangle against a New England farming background, and *The Age of Innocence* (1920), arguably her finest achievement, in which the 1870s are lovingly recreated as a setting to a wistful chronicle of love. This novel, and various of her short stories, underline the author's sense of awkwardness in relation to the important shifts in ethics and mores which had taken place simultaneously with her development as a writer. She was both too old to embrace easily a world in which a **Lawrence**, an **Eliot** or a **Scott Fitzgerald** were coming to maturity, and too young to turn her back on its novel significance.

As a writer she enjoyed considerable success, spending most of her later life in France, a country for which she had a truly American fondness. After her death her reputation underwent an inevitable slump, but with the post-war reappraisal of the work of her friend and mentor **Henry James** her novels were rediscovered and her role as one of the most discriminating of early twentieth-century writers of 'psychological' fiction was duly acknowledged.

James had the clearest influence on her development both in style and aim as a novelist, though she fails to rival him either in penetrative skill or verbal convolution. Like him she learned a great deal from the nineteenth-century French 'realist' school, and certain scenes in *The House of Mirth* read like less crudely sensational versions of Alphonse **Daudet** or **Zola**. Much also is owed in her work to English novelists such as Thackeray, whose Becky Sharp is an obvious model for Lily Bart and Undine Spragg, though there is no doubt that Mrs Wharton herself, as novelist and short-story writer, influenced the young Fitzgerald, writing warmly in praise of *The Great Gatsby* on its appearance in 1925. Thus she ranks, in her somewhat subdued, dignified fashion, as a crucial link between the Victorian and modern movements in American fiction.

Further reading

See: Irving Howe (ed.) *Edith Wharton: A Collection of Critical Essays* (1959); Millicent Bell, *Edith Wharton and Henry James* (1965); Grace Kellogg, *The Two Lives of Edith Wharton: The Woman and Her Work* (1965); Richard W.B. Lewis, *Edith Wharton: A Biography* (1975); Millicent Bell (ed.) *The Cambridge Companion to Edith Wharton* (1995); Janet Beer, *Kate Chopin, Edith Wharton and Charlotte Perkins Gilman: Studies in Short Fiction* (2005).

JONATHAN KEATES

WHISTLER, James Abbot McNeill

1834–1903

US artist

James Abbot Whistler was born in 1834 in Lowell, Massachusetts, USA. In later life he replaced Abbot with his mother's maiden name, McNeill. Much of his childhood was spent in Russia, where his father was employed as an engineer. Having spent three years as a cadet at the prestigious West Point Military Academy, he left the United States for Paris in 1855, entering the studio of Charles Gleyre as a student of painting. He mixed widely in Paris with young British and French contemporaries, and was himself profoundly influenced by the work of **Gustave Courbet**, whose manifesto of Realism had been published in the year of Whistler's arrival in Europe. Having friends and relatives in London, he frequently visited England, where he gradually settled in the late 1850s. He met **D.G. Rossetti** and the members of his entourage in 1862, and for many years his

name was associated with the declining Pre-Raphaelite movement. In England in the 1860s he moved away from his earlier Realist style in favour of an increasingly economic version of the prevailing climate of Symbolist painting, with its rejection of analytic Naturalism. He worked closely with Albert Moore in the late 1860s, and was also largely responsible for the revival of British etching.

Following a visit to South America in 1866 he commenced his series of *Nocturnes*, employing a musical as opposed to a literary metaphor in order to describe his pictures, a practice which was very much in keeping with the Aesthetic movement, of which he was a leading representative. In 1878 he sued the critic **John Ruskin** for libel, after the latter's momentously foolish remark that he had heard of cockney impudence, 'but never expected to hear a coxcomb ask two hundred guineas for flinging a pot of paint in the public's face'. Whistler was awarded only a farthing in damages and was in consequence bankrupted. Ruskin was discredited. Whistler's work in the 1880s became increasingly abstract. He was also active as an interior decorator, and published a number of highly polemical articles and essays which were eventually anthologized in 1890 under the title of *The Gentle Art of Making Enemies*. He continued to exhibit in England and France throughout the 1890s, his work being purchased by numerous state institutions. Whistler also sustained a high, and lucrative, reputation as a fashionable portrait painter. He was very badly affected by the premature death of his wife Beatrix in 1896, dying six years later, shortly after receiving *in absentia* an Honorary Degree of Law from Glasgow University, which possesses many of his finest paintings. He was buried at Chiswick cemetery.

The very ease with which Whistler moved between the avant-garde communities of London and Paris reveals the fundamental unity of concerns within the European Art For Art's Sake movement of the 1880s, and it is as a major international impresario and spokesman for Aestheticism that he will be best remembered. His reputation fell victim to Roger Fry's dogmatic Anglophobia, and his wildly over-simplified picture of the supposed relations between English and French art in the late nineteenth century, and has only been partially recuperated as the force and influence of that picture have gradually relaxed. For it was Whistler who stood between the historical figures of **Baudelaire** and **Oscar Wilde**, Whistler who reveals the shared cultural assumptions which lay beyond such ostensibly disparate tendencies as the influence of Japanese art and the Hellenism of the 1890s. A highly serious painter and art theorist, Whistler's entire career after his removal to England constituted an eloquent and provocative denial of the middle-class assumption that painting was a mere appendage to literature and morality, an attitude which was quite as prevalent in France as it was in England. As he argued in the Ten O'Clock Lecture of 1885, 'to say to the painter, that Nature is to be taken as She is, is to say to the player, that he may sit on the piano'. For such uncompromising attitudes he was not widely loved, and his subsequent reputation for maliciousness and personal animosity was perhaps the inevitable result of his uncomfortable historical position *vis-à-vis* the official art establishments of his day. Thus he was fated to be condemned as a 'Decadent' by many of his contemporaries, and those Post-Impressionists who, a few years later, were to repeat many of his arguments in defence of such painters as **Picasso** and **Matisse**. Whistler is undoubtedly a difficult figure to come to terms with in the late twentieth century. In his obsessive insistence on the quality of paint itself he clearly anticipated one major strand of Modernism, yet the very emphasis on close tonal values and his attendant vocabulary of 'daintiness' and the 'exquisite' sound as generally off-putting today as they did in 1914.

Whistler represents the *ne plus ultra* of what was a necessary response to the total epistemological confusion of late nineteenth-century aesthetics. His role in painting was strictly analogous to that of his friend **Mallarmé** in poetry, both men insisting on the specificity of the media in which they worked. He should also be regarded as a key figure in the genealogy of Romanticism across the threshold of Victorianism and into the twentieth century, with his absolute denial of any social role for art, and his insistence on supposedly timeless and universal criteria for aesthetic evaluation and pleasure. In this respect his position was not unlike that of his near exact contemporary **Cézanne**, although the narrowness of concerns in his own painting, and the tendency to miniaturism in his later work, ensured that he exhausted the potential possibilities for developing his own style in his own lifetime. It was his lapidary wit more than his much vaunted *'valeurs gris'* which has sustained his influence. Yet just as he struck an exemplary dandy's pose between the courts of Baudelaire and Wilde, so, faced by Ruskin at the Old Bailey, he continues to represent the dignity and independence of the visual artist, albeit an independence which he himself embodied ambiguously, and not without irony, in his studied persona as 'The Butterfly', the matinée idol of Aestheticism.

Further reading

See: Elizabeth R. and Joseph Pennell's, *The Life of James McNeill Whistler* (2 vols, 1908). The best general introduction to his work and times is Robin Spencer, *The Aesthetic Movement* (1972). See: Hilary Taylor, *James McNeill Whistler* (1978); R. Spencer, *Whistler: A Retrospective* (1989); N. Thorp (ed.) *Whistler on Art: Selected Letters and Writings, 1849–1903* (1994); Stanley Weintraub, *Whistler: A Biography* (2001); Sarah Walden, *Whistler and His Mother* (2003).

SIMON WATNEY

WHITE, Patrick Victor Martindale

1912–90

Australian novelist

Patrick White was born in London's Knightsbridge while his parents, members of the Australian squattocracy, were paying one of their periodic visits to Europe. After spending most of his childhood in rural New South Wales he was sent unhappily back to England to finish his schooling at Cheltenham College. After a couple of years' jackerooing (jackeroo: someone from a good background who works as a hand on a grazing estate) in Australia, he shuttled back again and read modern languages at Cambridge from 1932 to 1935. In the 1930s he tried his hand at plays, poetry including a slim published volume, short stories and novels. In 1939 a first novel, *Happy Valley*, was published in London, followed in 1941 by *The Living and the Dead*, both of them unremarkable works in the modernist *lingua franca*; significantly, the former was set in the snow country of New South Wales and the latter in London. He saw the country and the city as 'like two different races'.

During the Second World War White served as an RAF intelligence officer in North Africa, the Middle East and Greece. Although he found the war 'one long bore', it fed his imagination, first with desert landscapes, then with the depths of the Greek way of life and 'the perfection of antiquity'. In 1948 he published his first mature novel, *The Aunt's Story* (London), which remains the most experimental work of this structurally conservative novelist. He then returned to Australia with a Greek friend and they bought a farm at Castle Hill outside Sydney. Suburbia crept up on them, as it does on the Sarsaparilla of his novels, and they moved into the city in 1964. After long aloofness from public life, White became a strong supporter of E.G. Whitlam's Labour government (1972–5). He continued to believe in involvement in public life 'as everything grows rottener and rottener', but his novels eschewed political themes.

White's major fiction is primarily concerned with the protestant quest for individual salvation, but the characters through whom he presents this are not Christians, even if the patterning of his books is sometimes accomplished by means of Christian motifs. Theodora Goodman, heroine of *The Aunt's Story*, resembles many of her successors in her isolation, her social awkwardness, her asexuality and the incommunicability of her vision. The middle section of this tripartite novel is a marvellous rendition of Theodora's inner migration, the coruscating images bringing to life an individual and communal subconscious. She comes to the end of the book mad in the world's terms, but against the clarity of her presumed madness the world is judged.

The Tree of Man (1955) was the first novel White produced after his return to the peculiar vacancy of Australian life. He saw it as his task to 'suggest in this book every possible aspect of life, through the lives of an ordinary man and woman. But at the same time I wanted to discover the ordinary behind the ordinary, the mystery and the poetry.' In this large, slow, almost clumsy novel White offers us a sense of the moments of vision which are vouchsafed to inarticulate, working-class people of no especial glamour or talents. At the same time, he sees larger forces at work imposing their symbolic patterns on a whole community. By this point his vividly metaphorical and epigrammatic style was cutting both ways: creating epiphanies and pillorying the smug materialism of modern urban life.

In *Voss* (1957), his most majestic work, White delves back into Australian history, as into the history of romanticism. The central figure is a stiff, misunderstood yet charismatic German who leads a doomed expedition into the central deserts. Here for the first time we find a telepathic communication between illuminati, Voss and Laura balancing, even from afar, as Yin and Yang, or self and anima; here, too, is a large symbolic patterning, based upon the events and characters of Christ's Passion, which prefigures *Riders in the Chariot* (1961), a book in which the biblical parallels were to become undramatic, intrusive.

White is peculiarly eclectic about religious systems and their codes of symbolism. *Riders in the Chariot* draws heavily on Hasidic tradition for its portrayal of the Jewish martyr, Himmelfarb, while its quadripartite design owes much to the book of Revelation; the twins in *The Solid Mandala* (1966) incorporate a **Jungian dualism**; and so on. He saw that, although the religious systems have collapsed and become unavailable, their icons will still serve to image the quest after reality, the moments of vision which make life, even modern life, bearable.

His critics have frequently singled out the acid wit with which the novels lash suburban conformism. Yet his novels claim that a hunger for the truth behind appearances, an access to moments of insight, may be the lot of almost anybody, from the rich old dying lady in *The Eye of the Storm* (1973, the year of White's Nobel Prize for Literature) to the ruthless painter Hurtle Duffield in *The Vivisector* (1970), a book marked out by fierce self-knowledge, to a proletarian housewife or an idiot. Businessmen are excluded, however: the world of action frequently seems inimical to that of the spirit. Even an active hero like the explorer, Voss, has earned his Australia 'by right of vision', a vision that is asocial, even hateful.

A similar idiosyncrasy of view is to be found in White's two volumes of short stories and in his plays of which *The Season at Sarsaparilla* and *Big Toys* (first produced 1977) are perhaps the best regarded. Rhetorical uncertainty in the plays throws light back on an interesting aspect of the novels: that they are not psychologically penetrating or inquisitive, but seek, in the comic tradition, to portray complex truths by the development of fixed characters – figures in a morality, as it were. The vivacious historical narrative of *A Fringe of Leaves* (1976) brought White closer to conventional storytelling and characterization than ever before.

Further reading

Other works include: *The Ploughman and Other Poems* (1935); *The Burnt Ones* (1964) and *The Cockatoos* (1974), both short stories; *Four Plays* (1965); *The Night of the Prowler* (1978), story and film script; *The Twyborn Affair* (novel, 1979); and the autobiographical *Flaws in the Glass* (1981). See also: Barry Argyle, *Patrick White* (1967); R.F. Brissenden, *Patrick White* (1966); Patricia A. Morley,

The Mystery of Unity (1963); G.A. Wilkes (ed.) *Ten Essays on Patrick White* (1970); D. Marr, *Patrick White: A Biography* (1991). Alan Lawson's *Patrick White* (1974) is a substantial bibliography.

CHRIS WALLACE-CRABBE

WHITEHEAD, Alfred North

1861–1947

English mathematician and philosopher

Born in Kent, the son of an Anglican vicar, Whitehead went to school at Sherborne. In 1880 he entered Trinity College, Cambridge, where, as student, tutor and lecturer, he was to remain for the next thirty years. Although his only university 'subject' throughout this period was mathematics, he acquired extensive knowledge of many fields, including philosophy. After leaving Cambridge for London in 1910, he held various posts at University College, and later the professorship of applied mathematics at Imperial College (1914–24). Then, having reached normal retiring age, he accepted an invitation to start a new career in a new country as professor of philosophy at Harvard, a post he held until 1937. He died in Cambridge, Massachusetts.

Whitehead's early mathematical work culminated in the ten years of collaboration with his former pupil **Bertrand Russell** that produced *Principia Mathematica* (3 vols, 1910–13). In this they attempted to demonstrate, rigorously and in detail, that logic and pure mathematics are not, as commonly supposed, mutually independent disciplines, but that the characteristic concepts of pure mathematics can be defined in terms of – and its propositions deduced from – those of logic. And while their thesis is far from commanding universal assent, *Principia Mathematica* is, in spite of rivals and reservations, still recognized as one of the major landmarks in the whole field of logic and the foundations of mathematics.

Whitehead's most important philosophical writings came late in his career, starting with *The Principles of Natural Knowledge* (1919), and drew upon an unusually wide range of background knowledge. In particular, he was one of the few thinkers of his time able to discuss relativity on something like equal terms with **Einstein**; and in the *Principles* and its successor, *The Concept of Nature* (1920), an essential role is played by ideas borrowed from relativity theory – for example, that of nature as a four-dimensional structure of events, within which there are various different, and equally valid, ways of distinguishing its spatial from its temporal aspects. Whitehead's central problem in these works is one which dates a long way back in empirical philosophy: granted that nature is, as he says, 'that which we observe in perception through the senses', and that the task of science is to describe nature (or the more general features thereof), what is the function of such scientific concepts as those of points, lines, instants, elementary particles, etc., which are not, and could not be, instantiated in sense-perception? Whitehead uses his sophisticated technical apparatus to show how these concepts can be defined in terms of what *is* given in sense-perception – as sets of events progressively diminishing in content towards certain ideals of simplicity – and hence that the theories of exact science are not, as sometimes suggested, about something outside or underlying the world as we perceive it, but are actually descriptions (though of a logically somewhat complex kind) of that world.

In the last phase of his work, from *Science and the Modern World* (1925) onwards, Whitehead advanced from his philosophy of nature to an all-embracing cosmology in which ideas of growth and development became increasingly important. *Every* element of reality, every 'actual entity', whether in the field of biology, physics or psychology, is seen as organically related to its environment, like a plant to the soil in which it grows; it *is* literally a process of self-development or self-creation out of the material provided by its background, and then, the process completed, provides in its turn material for the self-creation of the next generation of actual entities. In his last major work, *Process and Reality* (1929), Whitehead develops this philosophy of organism into a complex system of categories by means of which he attempts to show the essential unity of reality, and present both sides of such time-honoured contrasts as flux and permanence, subjective and objective, God and the world, as mutually indispensable elements within a single totality. Because of its difficulty, and its remoteness in aims and methods from the main body of modern English-language philosophy, this last work received at first somewhat limited attention; but in recent years there has been, in several fields of interest, most notably that of philosophical theology, growing recognition of the relevance and potential value of its characteristic ideas.

Further reading

Other works include: *A Treatise on Universal Algebra* (1898); *The Principle of Relativity* (1922); *Religion in the Making* (1926); *Symbolism* (1927); *Aims and Education* (1929); *Adventures of Ideas* (1933). See: P.A. Schilpp (ed.) *The Philosophy of A.N. Whitehead* (1941), which includes Whitehead's autobiographical notes; and W. Mays, *The Philosophy of Whitehead* (1959); George A. Lucas, 'Outside the Camp', in *Transactions of the C.S. Peirce Society* (1985).

T.E. BURKE

WHITMAN, Walt

1819–92

US poet

Long Island – 'fish-shape Paumanock' – nourished Whitman's earliest childhood, and the old port of Brooklyn his young manhood: landscape and the sea, and the urban commerce of America, are the main spheres of his poetry. Following a short schooling he apprenticed at fourteen to a printer, beginning his career in printing, editing and newspapers, broken only by intermittent years of school-teaching – 'one of my best experiences and deepest lessons in human nature'. His journalism exposed the rough condition of New York society, the social unrest of the times, and the dirt of politics. His early poetry was as conventional and sentimental as his temperance novel *Franklin Evans* (1842); but he began to read philosophy and the literary classics, and practised as a well-known speaker for the Democrats. With these bases he moved into a seminal period for his maturity. New York newspaper jobs began to irritate him; reformism and the theatre preoccupied him; he knew nothing of the vast expanse of America. Discharged from the Brooklyn *Eagle*, partly for political reasons, in 1848 he obtained a job on the New Orleans *Crescent*, and the journey south, with his brother Jeff, opened up his American experience, taking him into the Mississippi heartlands. (Myths of Whitman's children – six in New Orleans, twins in Brooklyn, a silent-movie actor calling himself Walt Whitman and looking like him – develop from this period; but his deeper sensual interests were restricted to a few young men – in particular Peter Doyle, a streetcar conductor in Washington – and to himself.) He quarrelled with *Crescent*'s editor, and back in New York decided to cut a dandy figure – clothes, a cane, the theatre, Bohemian cafés – and edited the *Brooklyn Times*, helping to support his family and buying real estate. He practised his rhetorical abilities, wrote angry poems on liberty, and lectured on art theory. Important for his later poetry, he absorbed the *bel canto* lines of opera and the exhibition of the world's arts and crafts at the World's Fair of 1853. Then in 1855 he printed and published the first small edition of the eleven accumulative editions of *Leaves of Grass*. The title page carries no poet's name (it appears in the copyright) but a frontispiece shows the image of the new bard, self-named Walt, the persona of the twelve untitled poems within – a deliberately undignified pose in worker's dress, dark hat on cocked head, one hand in pocket and the other on his hip, open-necked shirt showing a dark vest (the engraver said it was red). The myth proclaimed itself: 'an American, one of the roughs, a kosmos,/Disorderly fleshy and sensual ... eating drinking and breeding', and not at all

what he later called the tea-drinking British poet the American genteel copied. The persona enabled him to transcend his social and personal self into an ideal inquirer, on the road, looking for a sharing companion – 'I was the man, I suffered, I was there.' The book is his manifesto – 'who touches this touches a man' – and touch became a key word for his sensuous sociality. To the *Boston Post* the poems were 'foul and rank leaves of the poison-plant of egoism, irreverence and lust'; as Whitman said, 'I expected hell, and I got it.' But **Emerson** found the book 'fortifying & encouraging', although he, too, hedged at the sexuality of later editions. Undoubtedly, the long-breathed paragraphic lines, the personal punctuation, the *bel canto* freedom of the basically dactylic measures, the passionate rhetorical mode, the unveiled presence of love and death, the unashamed exhilaration and reverence in the self was an offensive pattern to those who wished simply to be confirmed in the narrowness and timidity. *Leaves of Grass* is a democratic book in its invitation to share openness to the mental and physical opportunity to expand and break with the sets of convention. It refuses the authoritarian impositions of fixed metrics and dominant heterosexuality.

Whitman's working man's dress became a necessity when the depression of 1857 made him poor. But he continued. The 1860–1 third edition contained 'Out of the Cradle Endlessly Rocking', a more personal poem than the persona celebrations of 'Song of Myself'. The Long Island boy experiences his first intuitions of love and death through the loves of two mocking birds; the adult poet recognizes the main instigation of his poetic life as a 'singer solitary, singing by yourself, projecting me ... Never more the cries of unsatisfied love be absent from me'. The tension with Walt increased: 'before all my arrogant poems the real Me stands yet untouch'd, untold, altogether unreach'd'. The third edition contained poems on sex ('Enfans d'Adam') which, when Emerson wanted to introduce Whitman to the famous Saturday Club, caused **Longfellow**, **Oliver**

Wendell Holmes and others to refuse to meet him.

The frontispiece image of the great 1860 edition shows the poet now in bardic Byronic pose – large collar and large floppy cravat, curly hair, trimmed beard, jacket. But the double theme is still 'to make a song of These States' and to generate 'the evangel-poem of comrades and of love'. In Whitman's nationalist poems ('Chants Democratic') the poet accepts his responsibility for fusing the people into 'the compact organism of one nation'. In the love poems he speaks of 'my limbs, and the quivering fire that ever plays through them, for reasons, most wondrous'. He pursued this double fecundity as a myth of resources necessary to make the nation positive and powerful – a new moral and social standard. In the 'Calamus' poems, focused on a phallic-shaped flag growing in the eastern states, the sense of lonely longing 'adhesiveness', his peculiar word for the total bonding of man to man, is therefore both personal and social in its vision. The Civil War shattered that American dream. Photographs of Whitman in his forties show him changing into a prematurely old man under the onslaught of his experiences as a wound-dresser in hospitals where more young men died than on the battlefields. His journals contain a remarkable account of these terrible years and of his exemplary ability to look after the men, some of whom never forgot his kindness. In his wartime poems, *Drum-Taps* (1865), he included the great elegy for **Lincoln**, 'When lilacs last in the dooryard bloom'd', one of his most formally accomplished poems.

His job as Department of the Interior clerk ended when the Secretary of the Interior discovered *Leaves of Grass*. The Attorney General's office took him on, but the sacking was a sign of the public reception he could still expect. Whitman turned his attention to the healing of the split nation and a vision of universal peace under political and technological progress: 'My spirit has pass'd in compassion and determination around the whole earth,/I have look'd for equals and lovers and found them ready for me in all lands,/I think

some divine rapport has equalized me with them.' Living still in an unheated room, still managing to publish his work, he received surprising recognition from William Michael Rossetti in the 1867 London *Chronicle*, and, such was American genteel snobbery, this impressed local critics. And this year, the fourth edition of *Leaves of Grass* introduced him to Germany. He wrote articles – primarily in response to Carlyle's predictions that American democracy would destroy civilization – which became *Democratic Vistas* (1871), one of the few intelligent texts on the philosophy of democracy. Now magazines began to pay him for work. **Swinburne** praised the Lincoln elegy and compared him to Blake. A correspondence with Mrs Anne Gilchrist, widow of Blake's biographer, developed to the point where she proposed marriage in 1871. Whitman replied: 'I too send you my love ... My book is my best letter, my response, my truest explanation of all. In it I have put my body and spirit.' And later: 'Let me warn you about myself and yourself also.'

In 1871 the fifth *Leaves of Grass* appeared, reprinted in 1872 with 'Passage to India', a major visionary poem on the expansion of democracy westwards from America, across the Pacific into Asia, and so encircling the globe back to 'These States' (the poem is unaware of a possible imperialist interpretation of such an action). Now, through ill-health, emotional strain and a certain quarrelsomeness retained from his youth, Whitman declined. In 1873 he suffered a paralytic stroke. He left Washington for Camden, New Jersey, to live with his brother George. Bored and lonely, he turned to Columbus as a stubborn visionary hero with whom in part to identify ('Let the old timbers part – I will not part!') and the figure of exploration ('anthems in new tongues I hear saluting me'). The subscription list for the Centennial Edition of *Leaves of Grass* included **Tennyson**, the **Rossettis**, George Saintsbury and many other famous names: the old man had made it. Mrs Gilchrist arrived in America; the romance did not develop. Whitman visited

Colorado and St Louis (to see his brother Jeff), lectured in Boston, and had the seventh edition published by a prestigious Boston publisher (1881–2). **Oscar Wilde** visited him in 1887 ('like a great big, splendid boy', Whitman told a reporter). In 1884, he could afford a small house in Camden, where he held court and, on his deathbed, held the 1891 *Leaves of Grass*.

The preface to an early edition announced the essential image: the frontier poet – 'here are the roughs and beards and space and ruggedness and nonchalance that the soul loves', replacing 'old theories and forms' with fresh compositions opposed to European elitism: 'the attitude of great poets is to cheer up slaves and horrify despots'. The poetry therefore fuses the ideal body with an ideal society through the actualities of life in a huge space where the reader is invited to move freely as a rational and sexual creative being. 'Whatever satisfies the soul is truth' – 'One's self I sing, a simple separate person,/ yet utter the word Democratic, the word En-Masse' – 'The moth and the fish-eggs are in their place;/The suns I see, and the suns I cannot see, are in their place' – these are the bases of Whitman's poetic faith, his vision of 'the procreant urge of the world', a vision which encompasses a confrontation with death, in 'The Sleepers', as well as 'The Song of Sex and Amativeness, and even Animality' (1888). It includes an ability to let the body merge into nature which no other nineteenth-century poet possesses – 'Something I cannot see puts upward libidinous prongs;/ Seas of bright juice suffuse heaven' – and a willingness to present national events, for example, 'Song of the Exposition', for the Philadelphia Centennial show. He invented and endlessly developed a major and still influential verse method which demonstrates the controlled freedom of measure which best suits the form-making body. Whitman remains an inspiration to American poets in his forms, his fresh sexuality and his buoyant futurity in the face of pressing catastrophe: 'Solitary, singing in the West, I strike up for a New World.'

Further reading

See: *The Complete Writings of Walt Whitman*, ed. R.M. Buckle and others (10 vols, 1902–68); *The Collected Writings of Walt Whitman*, ed. Gay Wilson Allen and E. Sculley Bradley (from 1961). See: Gay Wilson Allen, *The Solitary Singer* (1955, rev. 1967); Roger Asselineau, *The Evolution of Walt Whitman* (2 vols, trans. 1960 and 1962); Ezra Greenspan (ed.) *The Cambridge Companion to Walt Whitman* (1995); J.R. LeMaster and Donald D. Kummings (ed.) *Walt Whitman Encyclopedia* (1998).

ERIC MOTTRAM

WIENER, Norbert

1894–1964

US mathematician

A child prodigy, Norbert Wiener was born in Columbia, Missouri, of Russian parentage. His early education was provided by his father Leo Wiener, Professor of Slavonic Languages and Literature at Harvard University. Norbert entered the Graduate School at Harvard, initially to study zoology, at the astonishing age of fifteen – having graduated in mathematics at Tufts College the previous year! In 1913 the young Norbert, still only eighteen, received his doctorate for a thesis on mathematical logic. The teenage Dr Wiener then travelled to Europe with the aid of a Harvard scholarship. In Cambridge **Russell** advised him to concentrate on mathematics – advice which he took, and which shaped his subsequent career. In Göttingen he studied briefly with the master mathematician David Hilbert. Returning to America at the beginning of the First World War, he tried his hand at various occupations before becoming an instructor at the Massachusetts Institute of Technology, in the mathematics department. Wiener remained at the Institute for the rest of his life as full professor from 1932.

During his career Wiener made significant contributions in various branches of mathematics, including Quantum Theory, Brownian motion and stochastic processes. His reputation and his importance, however, are linked with his work in cybernetics. It was Wiener who coined the term 'cybernetics' and, more importantly, put together the concepts which created a new and highly relevant science. His book *Cybernetics* (1948, revised 1961) caught the eye of the public and thereby exerted an influence far beyond the narrow professional circle of university mathematics.

Cybernetics was defined by Wiener as being 'the science of control and communication in the animal and machine'. That a tool or machine can be controlled by its user is a commonplace: that it could be given sensors or antennae to 'feel' its own environment and hence control itself was not – at least in 1948. This is what cybernetics is about: machines and biological processes which regulate themselves automatically, without the intervention of an intelligent agency. Wiener's conception of cybernetics developed out of his preoccupations with control theory, the mathematical analysis of information, and filtering theory (for example, how to get rid of random noise on a telephone line without losing the current message as well). The key impetus was probably some work which he undertook during the Second World War on how to point a gun to fire at a moving object. Cybernetics introduced a new terminology applicable alike to machines, robots, organic processes, biological populations, human groups and institutions. It consisted of words like 'stability', 'information control', 'input', 'output', 'prediction', 'filtering' and, above all, 'feedback'. Negative feedback occurs when a machine dampens its own activity to achieve a certain pre-selected performance. Positive feedback occurs when a machine stimulates its own activity: for example, a microphone picking up its own amplified output which is then amplified even more, thus producing a high-pitched shriek known as 'hunting'. The sensitivity with which a machine interprets or reacts to its own message poses many deep mathematical problems and it was in this area that Wiener made his specialist contribution.

By isolating the self-regulatory aspects of a machine as being something worthy of separate study, Wiener considerably accelerated the development of the more modern, sophisticated concept of a machine. Before cybernetics emerged, machines were designed for certain conditions, and if the conditions changed, they failed. The *Titanic* sank, the R101 crashed, the tanks of 1917 were virtually invincible, the industrial steam engines took hours to reach full speed and hours to come to rest. Such artefacts lacked flexibility. They were man-made leviathans harnessing vast power, yet subject to little real control. But with the emergence of cybernetics machines were increasingly provided with built-in mechanisms to help them stay 'on course' – for example, the auto-pilot of an aeroplane, the stabilizers on a ferry. Windscreen wipers now parked themselves, central heating held its temperature, rockets balanced on their tails.

The outcome of this revolution is automation; and with the arrival of the microchip, automation is rapidly taking over many a job previously performed by a skilled person. Wiener himself in his book *The Human Use of Human Beings* (1950) was among the first to recognize that, as machines gradually take over their own regulation, the number of tasks requiring minimal human judgement inevitably diminishes. Wiener emphasized the positive side of this: that the extinct jobs were only machine-like jobs after all: that we should re-think human priorities to create more jobs requiring genuinely human judgement. It is a measure of Wiener's percipience that he saw both the problem and the lines on which a solution may be sought so many years ago.

Further reading

Other works include: *God and Golem Inc.: A Comment on Certain Points where Cybernetics Impinges on Religion* (1964); and two autobiographical volumes: *Ex-Prodigy* (1953) and *I Am a Mathematician* (1956). For details of Wiener's specifically mathematical work, see *The Dictionary of Scientific Biography*, Vol. XIV (1976). For a general comment on Wiener's work, see Abraham Kaplan, 'Sociology Learns the Language of Mathematics', in James R. Newman (ed.) *The World of Mathematics* (1956), also the *Bulletin of the American Mathematical Society*, January (1966). See: Flo Conway and Jim Siegelman, *Dark Hero of the Information Age: In Search of Norbert Wiener* (2004).

CHRISTOPHER ORMELL

WILDE, Oscar Fingal O'Flahertie Wills

1854–1900

Anglo-Irish writer, dramatist and wit

Oscar Wilde was born in Dublin, the son of Sir William Wilde, the eye surgeon, and Lady Wilde, who wrote Irish nationalist verses under the name 'Speranza'. A godson of the King of Sweden, he possessed immense curiosity and a remarkable memory and was from the outset the opposite of the 'ghetto' or 'partisan' type. He always tended to the wider world, to the universal, and so gravitated naturally towards a study of the classics. After the Portora Royal School and Trinity College, Dublin, where he won the Berkeley Gold Medal for Greek, he went on to Magdalen College, Oxford, in 1874, eventually taking a double first in Mods and Greats. In the long vacation of 1877 he travelled to Italy and Greece and subsequently wrote the poem *Ravenna* which won the Newdigate Prize in 1878. At Oxford, despite his gregarious manner and bulky physique, he gained notoriety as an aesthete, became the disciple of **Ruskin** and **Pater**, **Swinburne**, **D.G. Rossetti** and **Baudelaire**, and was excited by the glamour as well as the substance of art.

In 1879 Wilde moved to London and with a vigour that was characteristically Victorian achieved metropolitan celebrity by caricaturing – and so detaching himself from – his early influences. This capacity for detachment was one of his greatest strengths because Wilde sought to occupy in relation to the impulses of his personality the position of ringmaster and thereby acquire an individual gravitas sufficient, when married to his sense of purpose, to reconstitute his environment.

This he increasingly managed to do but was finally dislodged from the creation of his own destiny by his love for Lord Alfred Douglas, which in Nietzschean style he interprets in *De Profundis* (the full text of this long letter to Douglas from prison was not published until 1962) as a failure of will. But Wilde himself set in motion the sequence of legal actions which led to his downfall, and when events were taken out of his hands he had established all the preconditions for the completion of his life as a perfect drama.

In 1881 Wilde published his first collection of poems, which are significant not so much as poetry as for the efficiency of Wilde's cannibalizing of his mentors. In 1882 he went on a year-long tour of the USA to lecture the Americans on beauty in connection with the performances there of **Gilbert** and **Sullivan's** *Patience*. This operetta, which had opened in London the previous year, was designed as a skit on Rossetti and Swinburne, but typically Wilde had turned it into an advertisement for himself. In 1883 he made the first of many visits to Paris, where he astonished and instructed its salons and leading literary figures. His pedagogic instinct, which repeatedly turned into parable, also operated in reverse. He parodied the teacher in himself and in this way he created a mask, as well as a vehicle, for his serious intentions.

In his espousal of a cause, from his preaching the doctrines of Aestheticism in the early 1880s onwards, high seriousness and high comedy always clash and flirt with each other. Wilde used ideas in motion, not at rest. That is to say, his relationship to his theories was always strategic, the very opposite of art for art's sake, and his method suggests the conceptual gymnastics of a Zen adept. Wilde's genius for contradiction permitted, for example, his hyperactive propagation of the cult of inaction; or the fervent individualism of a man who could function only in symbiosis (when, after his conviction for homosexual offences in 1895, he lost his audience, he lost also his motivation, writing nothing after his release from prison except *The Ballad of Reading Gaol*, 1898). This ambivalence disconcerted other artists, especially **Whistler**, and they resented the familiarity with which Wilde sometimes treated them. But society was fascinated by the brilliant talker who entertained with his epigrams and hypnotized with his stories.

In 1884 his travels and burlesque postures were curtailed by his marriage to Constance Lloyd. They moved into a house in Tite Street, Chelsea, and immediately had two sons (Cyril, 1885; Vyvyan, 1886). At the age of thirty he settled down to consolidate his position through journalism. This is Wilde at his most straightforward, the editor of *Woman's World* (1887–9), eliciting contributions from Marie Correlli, Sarah Bernhardt and the Queen of Roumania. At home he wrote for inspiration at a desk which had belonged to Carlyle, publishing short stories, essays, reviews and poems but only one book, *The Happy Prince* (1888). These fairy-tales catch something of Wilde's charm, mercuriality and freedom from malice, which Graham Robertson called an 'almost child-like love of fun' and Wilson Knight 'a boyish immaturity often difficult to distinguish from the integration of a seer'. In this he resembled Byron, as he did also in his androgynous nature and appearance.

Marriage organized Wilde but it also crystallized the deep conflict between social acceptance and self-betrayal, classical restraint and romantic passion, love of others and love of self. From this derive his most important works, beginning in 1891 with the publication of *Intentions* ('The Decay of Lying', 'Pen, Pencil and Poison', 'The Critic as Artist', 'The Truth of Masks', previously published essays much revised here), *Lord Arthur Savile's Crime and Other Stories, The Picture of Dorian Gray* (published the previous year in *Lippincott's Magazine* in a slightly less moral version) and a second volume of fairy-tales *A House of Pomegranates*. These books – indeed Wilde's entire oeuvre – are a complex and dangerous act of brinkmanship in which he attempts to subvert an entrenched world view without sacrificing his place in it. That is, he wished to affect humanity at large and not merely some convertible coterie. Hereafter, until his imprisonment and apart from a few poems and prose poems, he conducted his campaign exclusively in the theatre and in the real world.

Pater, in his essay on Coleridge, wrote 'Modern thought is distinguished from ancient by its cultivation of the "relative" spirit in place of the "absolute".' Wilde was the first man to enact this as well as think it, which exposed him to charges of shallowness but increased his range enormously. So on the one hand there is the voluptuous Byzantine Wilde of *Salomé* (written in French and first published in 1893), romantic in style but modern in content, in which all is flux and dispute and no one speaks with authority; on the other, the streamlined Mozartian Wilde of *The Importance of Being Ernest* (first performance 1895), classical in style, modern in content. The characters of this play well understand the provisional nature of a statement, the techniques of role playing and image games, governable only by a transcendental ego. *Salomé* is dark and tragic, steeped in superstition; *Ernest* is light and humorous in the realm of the sublime. Neither can provide an exhaustive truth. Both are facets of reality. For a nineteenth-century mind already made dizzy by **Darwinism**, Wilde made the vertiginous trauma of relativity tolerable by converting it into play: spectacle and symbol, insincerity and lying. This is why he wished to detach his message from conventional morality. But he knew that a prerequisite of lying (except for the insane) is an apprehension of the truth. So in his system insincerity becomes the opposite of delusion.

By 1895 Wilde's success was very great and the world as it stood offered no challenge. The too-integrated personality can separate itself from life and float off like a balloon – this was **Nietzsche's** fate. Wilde rejected self-enclosure and plunged low to reconnect and stay sane (Alfred Douglas was both a poet and the most beautiful male aristocrat in the kingdom, and therefore worthy of symbolic behaviour). The spiritual effect of Wilde's downfall, which was to preserve and intensify his power, was the opposite of the social one. This was his final triumphant paradox: disaster rehumanizes him at the same time as it immortalizes him in myth.

He wrote:

> Understand that there are two worlds: the one that *is* without one's speaking about it; it is called the *real world* because there's no need to talk about it in order to see it. And the other is the world of art; that's the one which has to be talked about because it would not exist otherwise.

This is Wilde's challenge to entropy and takes us beyond Nietzsche into the regions of Gurdjieff, Aleister Crowley, Castaneda's Don Juan. Wilde belongs here too in that his ultimate concern is not with art but with power and transformation. But he scorned occultism and ridiculed it in the emblem of the green carnation.

Wilde was the last Romantic in his special claims for the artist in pursuit of ecstasy, and the first Modern in his knowledge of the relative manifestation of absolute being. In him these two opposed rotations are housed. As the first was overcome by the second, the capacity of Wilde's intellect and Wilde's sympathies enabled him – and only him – to hold them for a moment in dynamic balance, to accommodate both Salomé and Ernest in a weightless reciprocity of opposites – then it is gone, and we are in the twentieth century.

Further reading

See: *The Collected Works of Oscar Wilde*, ed. G.F. Maine (1952), is convenient but untidy. See also *Letters*, ed. Rupert Hart-Davis (1962); Phillipe Jullian, *Oscar Wilde* (trans. 1969); Robert Hichens, *The Green Carnation* (1895); H. Montgomery Hyde, *The Trials of Oscar Wilde* (1948) and *Oscar Wilde: The Aftermath* (1963); Karl Beckson, *Oscar Wilde: The Critical Heritage* (1970); Richard Ellman, *Oscar Wilde* (1987); G. Woodcock, *Oscar Wilde* (1988).

DUNCAN FALLOWELL

WILLIAMS, Bernard Arthur Owen

1929–2003
British philosopher

Bernard Williams was one of the outstanding philosophers of his generation. Interest in Williams's philosophy was largely confined to the academy but Williams himself was an avid participant in public life. He served on the board of the English National Opera as well as government committees on gambling, drugs, pornography and public schools. His described his political service with characteristic wit: 'I did all the major vices.'

Williams's first major publications exposed problems with the view that the self consists in its psychological qualities, such that it would be possible for a person to switch from one body to another. The thrust of these papers is that personal identity consists in the continued existence of our bodies.

His book on René Descartes is notable, not only for its commentary on its subject's philosophy, but also for articulating what Williams called the absolute conception of the world. This involves an attempt to think of the idea of the world as it really is, apart from our ways of thinking about it. Williams maintained that this plays an important role in our concept of knowledge since we regard knowing as representing the way things really are and not merely as representing some other of our beliefs. He also held that the absolute conception underwrites the natural sciences' aspiration to describe the world in a way that is minimally dependent on our peculiar way of apprehending it.

Williams paid special attention to moral philosophy. He criticized the impulse to develop theories or doctrines in ethics and left behind none of his own. Instead, he insisted on the diversity of ethical values, both within and across individuals and cultures. He strenuously denied that human nature is uniformly ethical. Thinking about what matters depends on one's perspective and the elimination of variation should not be the aim of ethical thought. By contrast, the natural sciences do properly aim to minimize the influence of diverse perspectives that give rise to differences of opinion.

What perspectives should ethical thinking take up? It may seem trivial to say 'those of human beings'. But, in Williams's opinion, that perspective has been poorly understood by moral philosophers who build theories of what we must do on the basis of an artificially narrow set of beliefs and values. Specifically, Williams maintained, philosophy has paid too much attention to morality, voluntary action, obligation, guilt and reason. It has neglected broader questions of how to live, good and bad fortune, character, shame, integrity and emotions. For example, attending to our emotions reveals something obscured by the 'morality system', the importance of luck. I will feel relief if no one is hurt by my carelessness, even though my will was just as bad as it would have been had someone been hurt. Conversely, I will feel remorse if I choose one evil over another, even though the principle of 'ought implies can' means that I could not have been obliged to avoid evil in these circumstances.

The point of this critical work was to defend the propriety of our thoughts and feelings against dismissive philosophical theories. Success would mean that philosophy does no harm. Even so, we would be left with open questions. Which of the many human perspectives should we rely on and to what extent? If we are to rely on our own perspectives, who counts as 'us' and how much of our preconceived values do we take for granted? What should moral philosophers do with the richer set of materials that he recommended? Williams appreciated these questions and aspired to be more constructive. He wanted to write about morality in a way that would make it look 'strange and new', but he was uncertain about how to do so.

In his later works, he looked to history to accomplish this goal in two different ways. First, the study of historically distant cultures can reveal alternatives to our values. *Shame and Necessity*, his study of ancient Greek philosophy and literature, explored a culture that took fortune, character and shame more seriously than ours does. Second, the history of our values can help us to make sense of them. *Truth and Truthfulness* employed historical genealogy to explain both why the virtues of truth, sincerity and accuracy have universal value, and also how these virtues could take different forms in different cultures. The aim was to show us something new about these virtues that would vindicate them while allowing us to acknowledge their historical contingency.

Further reading

Morality: An Introduction to Ethics (1972) is a marvellous introduction to the field. *Utilitarianism: For and Against* (1973) develops objections to the moral theory of utilitarianism. *Problems of the Self* (1973) is a collection of essays including the work on personal identity as well as essays on equality and the emotions. *Descartes: The Project of Pure Enquiry* (1978) presents the 'absolute' conception. *Obscenity and Film Censorship* (1981) contains most of the relevant committee reports. The criticisms of 'the moral system' are most fully developed in *Ethics and the Limits of Philosophy* (1985). Williams also published two collections of essays, *Moral Luck* (1981) and *Making Sense of Humanity* (1995), a short book, *Plato* (1999), and the two books mentioned above, *Shame and Necessity* (1993) and *Truth and Truthfulness* (2002).

MICHAEL J. GREEN

WILLIAMS, Raymond

1921–88

Anglo-Welsh literary and cultural critic and novelist

Raymond Williams was the foremost British cultural critic and public intellectual of his generation. His work, a massive interdisciplinary achievement of teaching, writing and political action, was sustained for over forty years. In some thirty books and countless articles he redefined the idiom and priorities of literary criticism, determined much of the foundation and early formation of cultural and media studies, and generated new methodologies for a sociology of literature.

He was a central figure in successive political movements: a co-founder of the British New Left of the 1950s (from which sprang both the original, mass-movement Campaign for Nuclear Disarmament, CND, and the radical journal *New Left Review*); co-author of the programmatic *May Day Manifesto* of 1968; co-instigator of the Socialist Society in the 1980s, and revered mentor to further generations of radical critics. He was throughout his career a resolute and sophisticated political strategist and thinker, his writing insisting on – and elucidating – the necessary, complex interrelations of politics, economics and culture. Indeed, it was his framing of these interrelations, refusing conventional intellectual limits and definitions, posing new questions and articulating innovative theories, which so distinguishes Williams's contribution to contemporary thought. He made connections between areas of thinking held to be separate or unrelated, insisting in his ground-breaking work *Culture and Society* (1958), on a conception of 'the theory of culture as a theory of the relations between elements in a whole way of life'. His commitment to the writing of fiction was grounded in the belief that literary form permitted the most effective representation of these relations, and some of his finest criticism explores the traditions of the realism: *The English Novel from Dickens to Lawrence* (1970) remains a key text in debates not only about the importance of the novel, but also about how to study fiction. Williams himself published seven novels and described himself, simply, as 'a writer'.

Williams came to prominence with the publication of two major books, *Culture and Society*, and *The Long Revolution* (1961). In these works he set the agenda for contemporary literary and cultural studies, bringing informed historical and political analysis into the frame of literary criticism. In his works of the 1960s and 1970s, he filtered and refined the waves of continental European theory, producing masterly syntheses such as *Marxism and Literature* (1977), which develops a technical vocabulary and methodology for what he called 'cultural materialism', and the innovative *Politics and Letters: Interviews with the New Left Review* (1979), in which he ranges over his own career, and the intellectual currents of his generation, with extraordinary sophistication and insight.

Williams's biography was a crucial factor in his work. He drew particularly on the experience of growing up in the close working-class community of a Welsh border village through a period of industrial and political unrest in the 1920s and 1930s. The General Strike is a recurrent point of reference, and is powerfully treated in his novels, above all in *Border Country* (1960). Throughout his writing the pressure of the ethics and values instilled by this lived political education is evident. Williams fought in the 1939–45 war as a tank commander. On demobilization he pursued an academic career, teaching first in adult education during the 1950s, an experience which he maintained gave him the confidence and the sense of collective identity from which to challenge conventional accounts of literature and culture, and subsequently as lecturer, then professor, of drama at Cambridge University. Challenged as to his acceptance of a position seemingly at the heart of the British establishment, he refused to see a contradiction, maintaining that such institutions belong to ordinary people, and should not be surrendered to a particular class or political interest.

Williams will be remembered above all for his assertion, against prevailing definitions of culture as a body of art and letters ('High Culture'), or as a privileged form of education, that culture is 'a whole way of life', a definition which extends to include the great collective institutions and achievements of the working class, such as trade unions, mechanics' institutes and other expressions of community solidarity.

Further reading

Fred Inglis, *Raymond Williams* (1995) is the recommended biography. See also: Alan

O'Connor, *Raymond Williams: Writing, Culture, Politics* (1989); Terry Eagleton (ed.) *Raymond Williams: Critical Perspectives* (1989); John Higgins, *Raymond Williams: Literature, Marxism and Cultural Materialism* (1999).

SEAN MATTHEWS

WILLIAMS, Tennessee (Thomas Lanier)

1914–83

US playwright

Twice a Pulitzer Prize winner, with *A Streetcar Named Desire* (1947) and *Cat on a Hot Tin Roof* (1955), Tennessee Williams was a playwright of great popularity who utilized his own life and preoccupations to dramatic effect. He grew up, in Mississippi and Missouri, in an often poor household dominated by his mother, a former Southern belle making a difficult adjustment to the twentieth century, and coloured by the disturbing presence of a delicate and extremely neurotic sister. His father was almost always away. Masculinity and femininity, roles and relationships, the Old and New Souths, the individual and society, weak men and strong women, artists and outsiders, violence, maladjustment and alienation: these were the concerns of Williams's life and have become the themes of his plays. These can be read as documents and as analyses, but they also embody a perpetual quest for self-knowledge, on the part of Williams, his surrogates and the rest of his characters.

Williams's first important play, *The Glass Menagerie* (1945), deals movingly with that time of his life when his mother was struggling to keep the home together, his sister was withdrawing from the world and he himself was faced with the necessity, as an artist, of leaving his womenfolk and of working out his own destiny. Nostalgia and hatred for a once halcyon, now debilitating past; reaction against and a desire for the conventional ties of home and family; mixed feelings of guilt and responsibility; a sense of yearning for ecstasy and self-expression – all

were equally present in his next play, *A Streetcar Named Desire*, in which Marlon Brando so effectively created the role of Stanley Kowalski, the urban jungle brute, the 'Polack' who marries a genteel girl reared on a now bankrupt plantation and who is confronted, in a clash of cultures, by his wife's sister, Blanche Du Bois. Blanche is one of Williams's finest creations: a woman who feels she is virginal, sensitive and artistic, who in fact is promiscuous, selfish and superficially cultivated, yet who still represents, with pathos and power, whatever virtues may have accrued to civilization. In such later plays as *Summer and Smoke* (1948) and *Sweet Bird of Youth* (1959), Williams continued to represent the Old South as an aging belle and harsh contemporary reality as an aggressive young man. The two rarely come together, except with violence. Stanley rapes Blanche.

Williams admired **D.H. Lawrence** a great deal, and in 1951 he wrote a play dedicated to Lawrence, *I Rise in Flames, Cried the Phoenix*. But there is nothing as satisfying as the relationship between Lady Chatterley and her gamekeeper in Williams's plays. In fact, Williams consistently suggests not only that the times are out of joint but seems to subscribe, fatalistically, to a belief in the inevitably unsatisfactory nature of all relationships. Love is rarely returned. In *Cat on a Hot Tin Roof*, Big Mama loves Big Daddy, but the reverse is not true; similarly Maggie and Brick. Gooper and Mae are content with each other, but are unattractive to everybody else. Normality is unacceptable; but abnormality (Brick's homosexuality) offers no alternative.

Although obsessed with the isolation of the artist, with violence between individuals, with heightened sexuality, especially homosexuality, Williams is able to distance himself from his preoccupations. Few of his protagonists are unsympathetic, whether nymphomaniacs like Blanche or virgins like Hannah Jelkes in *The Night of the Iguana* (1961) or shy bachelors like Blanche's suitor Mitch. Only the cruel and perverting Sebastian of *Suddenly*

Last Summer (1959) and the monstrous Boss Finley in *Sweet Bird of Youth* are without redeeming features. But only *Night of the Iguana*, Williams's most philosophical play, suggests that the playwright is, on occasion, reconciled to the human condition. Only in that play is there a willingness on the part of all the main characters to admit and accept the limitations of themselves and their universe. Most of Williams's characters are too large for life. To act them requires strength, even flamboyance; but when the casting is right – Anna Magnani as the lusty, remorseful Catholic widow, Serafina, in *The Rose Tattoo* (1950), for instance – the effect is compelling.

Most often Williams worked to achieve social realism, though he uses symbols (the glass menagerie, the iguana, Blanche's lamp-shade), a poeticized language and even neo-expressionism to achieve his ends. *Camino Real* (1953), for example, is a fascinating and ambitious fable of love and death, and mixes the myths of Old World and New – Casanova and Don Quixote rub shoulders with Kilroy. Williams experimented with forms other than plays, publishing four collections of short stories – *27 Wagons Full of Cotton* (1946), *One Arm* (1948), *Hard Candy* (1956), *Eight Mortal Ladies Possessed* (1975). One of his novels, *The Roman Spring of Mrs Stone* (1950) is not unimpressive. *In the Winter of Cities* (1956) contains Williams's favourites among his poems. His *Memoirs* (1970) are frank; so are the prefaces to his plays and a book by his mother Edwina Dakin Williams (as told to Lucy Freeman), *Remember Me to Tom* (1963).

Further reading

See: Signi Falk, *Tennessee Williams* (1978); Jac Tharpe (ed.) *Tennessee Williams* (1977); and Richard Leavitt (ed.) *A Tribute to Tennessee Williams* (1978); John S. McCann, *The Critical Reputation of Tennessee Williams: A Reference Guide* (1983); M.C. Roundane (ed.) *The Cambridge Companion to Tennessee Williams* (1997).

ANN MASSA

WILLIAMS, William Carlos

1883–1963

US poet

The son of an Englishman and a Puerto Rican of French and Spanish extraction, Williams studied medicine at the University of Pennsylvania, where he began a lifelong association with the poet **Ezra Pound**, and subsequently practised as a doctor in Rutherford, New Jersey, until his retirement in 1951. He also befriended **Marianne Moore**, Hilda Doolittle, **James Joyce**, **W.B. Yeats**, **E.E. Cummings**, Charles Demuth, Marsden Hartley and many other writers and painters. The American critic Hugh Kenner asserted that 'American poetry groups itself around twin peaks, Williams and **Whitman**', while William Empson took the contrary view that Williams 'renounced all the pleasures of the English language, so that he is completely American; and he says only the dullest things'.

Williams is the poet of the particular, the American, the local and the fact. 'One has to learn,' he said, 'what the meaning of the local is, for universal purposes. The local is the only thing that is universal.' Like Pound, he journeyed to Europe and took stock of important movements in the arts, but unlike Pound he rejected Europe in favour of finding the character and reality of his own American environment: 'I couldn't speak like the academy. It had to be modified by the conversation about me.' He learned from such artists as **Henri Gaudier-Breszka** and **Wassily Kandinsky** both that emotions might be derived from the arrangements of surfaces (or words) and that by expressing his environment the poet might marry a sense of place and his imagination. Although he continually produced impressionistic and improvisatory work, Williams's own predilections were Cubist, as demonstrated in a short early poem 'To a Solitary Disciple'. He should in fact be clearly associated with a number of influential art movements, Expressionism, Constructivism and Dadaism, as well as with Cubism. In *Spring and All* (1923), for example, he employed Dadaist jokes, while *A Voyage to Pagany* (1928) illustrates his experiments in improvisation. Like **Charles Olson** after him, Williams's abiding concern with the representation of reality, of space and time (motion), led him to draw on the philosophy of **A.N. Whitehead** for a theoretical base to his inspiration. In *Science and the Modern World* (1948), for instance, Whitehead stated that 'The objectivist holds that the things experienced and the cognisant subject enter into the common world on equal terms.' Williams strove in his poetry, as Mike Weaver puts it, to see himself as 'a functioning perceiver observing himself in action'. Eschewing traditional theories of poetics, and deploring the monumental example of **T.S. Eliot**, he determined as far as possible to avoid abstractions in his own poetry, to dismiss any ideological content, and – taking an important lesson from the movement known as Imagism (in a narrow definition, 'picture-making without content') – to discover the resources of words themselves. It is a premise of his poetry that meaning is a product of form; the arrangements of words and images approximate to reality (the facts and objects of the world about us), and to rearrange words is to discover new meanings. Likewise, according to historians of Imagism, the image itself directly communicates sensation, and to appreciate that notion gives the reader a vantage for understanding Williams's aims and achievements. Williams was briefly associated with a group known as 'Objectivists' (1931), and for that group as for Williams himself the importance of Imagism was as much musical as visual. Williams experimented in his verse with pace, syllabic quantity and metre, and evolved his own theory of measure: 'Make a musical sequence ... Vary the pace as much as you feel impelled to give it a jagged surface.'

Early in life Williams discovered what he termed an 'inner security' from 'a sudden resignation to existence ... which made everything a unit and at the same time a part of myself'. Accordingly, in surrendering his ego, he determined that words themselves

might be readily assimilated to patterns, to ideas, to places and to people, so that the reality of the world should become available to fresh discovery, without pre-existing sentimental or linguistic associations. 'The words,' he wrote in a gnomic but refreshing phrase, 'had come to be leaves, trees, the corners of his house', and again, that 'A poem is a small (or large) machine made of words.' It is relevant to observe, however, that in clinging to real details, Williams was fighting a natural poetic tendency towards the subjective and the romantic, and towards established modes of poetic utterance.

In the American Grain (1925), a study of American history and its heroes, prefigures *Paterson* (1963), an epic in five books which he called an assertion 'of a new and total culture, the lifting of an environment to expression'. The long poem, though jumbled in structure, purposively explores the meaning of life in the city of Paterson, New Jersey, a place in which (typical of the American experience) language is discovered to be in a state of divorce from the real and from the imagination. The city, a male giant, assumes mythic proportions and is personalized in the figure of Doctor Paterson. The poem studies the locality, its history, its legends and its present shapelessness of soul, and builds to the possibility that life might be recognized and reintegrated, and that language and imagination might again be equal to the reality of life.

The basic endeavour of Williams's long career in poetry was to discover a foundation for his own identity and the reader's within the immediate environment, on the poet's own understanding that 'poetry is the antithesis of the academy'.

Further reading

Other works include: *The Autobiography of William Carlos Williams* (1951); *The Collected Earlier Poems of William Carlos Williams* (1951); *The Collected Later Poems of William Carlos Williams* (1963); *The Great American Novel* (1923); *I Wanted to Write a Poem* (1958); *Kora in Hell: Improvisations* (1920); *Pictures from Brueghel and Other Poems* (1962);

Selected Essays (1954); *The Selected Letters of William Carlos Williams*, ed. John C. Thirlwall (1957). See also: James E. Breslin, *William Carlos Williams: An American Artist* (1970); Walter Scott Peterson, *An Approach to Paterson* (1967); Mike Weaver, *William Carlos Williams, the American Background* (1971); Paul L. Mariani, *William Carlos Williams: A New World Naked* (1981); Brian Bremen, *William Carlos Williams and the Diagnostics of Culture* (1993).

JOHN HAFFENDEN

WILSON, Edmund

1895–1972

US man of letters

Son of an eminent lawyer, Edmund Wilson Jr was born and educated in New Jersey. After Princeton and service in France (as a hospital orderly) during the First World War, he settled in New York as journalist, editor and reviewer first for the *New Republic* and later for the *New Yorker*. His range was formidable. He participated as friend or associate with almost every significant literary figure of his age. Last of the great freelance critics (consciously modelling himself on Saintsbury in England, **Croce** in Italy **Taine**, or Sainte-Beuve in France), he aspired to a metropolitan role that operated no longer from Paris or Vienna or London, but from New York.

Wilson was not preoccupied with the work of other critics, however, nor with theoretical approaches to criticism. The mark of his style, rather, is a critical width and gusto. As scholar, he taught himself Hebrew, Russian, Hungarian. His ever-widening quest took in Haiti, the Zuñi Indians, the Iroquois, the Dead Sea Scrolls. As he himself came to realize (in 'The Author at Sixty'), he became something of an eighteenth- or nineteenth-century figure for whom literature necessarily implied an international community. His task, as he saw it, was to explain the world to America and America to itself. The task was possible, he insisted, because the American and the European intelligentsia spoke a common language. It was an essential task because American achievement might well be the key to the continuity of that internationalism,

already exploited (for an English-speaking public) by **Eliot** and **Pound**.

As a man of letters, he worked in every conceivable genre: as weekly journalist and reviewer (whose authoritative judgements were later collected in *Classics and Commercials*, 1950, chronicling the 1940s; *The Shores of Light*, 1952, chronicling the 1920s and 1930s; and *The Bit Between My Teeth*, 1965, chronicling the 1950s and early 1960s); as poet (*Note-books of Night*, 1942, and *Night Thoughts*, 1961); as playwright (*Five Plays*, 1954); as novelist (*I Thought of Daisy*, 1929); as short-story writer (*Memoirs of Hecate County*, 1946); as essayist and reporter (whose biggest scoop was *The Scrolls from the Dead Sea*, 1955); as literary executor (editing **Scott Fitzgerald's** *The Crack-Up*, 1945); as travel-writer in America, Europe and Russia (*The American Jitters*, 1932; *Travels in Two Democracies*, 1936; *Europe without Baedeker*, 1947; *Red, Black, Blond and Olive*, 1956); as autobiographer (*A Piece of My Mind*, 1956; *A Prelude*, 1967; *Upstate*, 1972); and finally as correspondent (*Letters on Literature and Politics 1912–1972*, 1977; *The Nabokov–Wilson Letters 1940–1971*, 1979).

Moving from the privileged literary perception of *Axel's Castle* (1931) to the Communist enthusiasm of *To the Finland Station* (1940), Wilson retreated eventually to the patrician aloofness of his ancestral home at Talcottville in upper New York State. After introducing **Proust** and **Joyce**, **Yeats** and Eliot and **Gertrude Stein** to America, he abandoned the symbolist 'decadence' of the 1920s (even visiting the Soviet Union in 1935) for the **Marxist** ideology of the 1930s. *To the Finland Station* remains one of the best guides to the Western sources of Marxism-Leninism. But Wilson turned next to psychological explorations (in *The Wound and the Bow*, 1941) and to his central texts on North American literature and experience: *The Triple Thinkers* (1938); *The Shock of Recognition* (1943); *The American Earthquake* (1958); *Apologies to the Iroquois* (1960); *Patriotic Gore* (1962); *O Canada!* (1965).

Though thoroughly at home in French, English and Russian literatures, Wilson rigorously excluded Spanish and German. In fact, he increasingly enjoyed his role as an opinionated, cantankerous Early American, engaging in quixotic battles with the US Treasury (over unpaid income tax) and with **Vladimir Nabokov** (over Russian verse forms and vocabulary). For he remained a tense man who may have resolved his early Marxism and his Americanism, but not his love-hate for contemporary English literature and English men of letters. Nor could he resolve his literary internationalism and political isolationism. Serene in his critical judgements, he felt threatened by contemporary pressures that undermined his national self-esteem. He never truly reconciled himself to **Roosevelt's** New Deal, let alone the interventions of the Second World War. He loved the Republic, but distanced himself from encroaching democracy. Cornered at last in Talcottville, as recorded in *Upstate*, he faced the ruins of the American dream.

Further reading

See: Sherman Paul, *Edmund Wilson: A Study of Literary Vocation in Our Time* (1965); Jeffrey Meyers, *Edmund Wilson: A Biography* (1995); Lewis Dabney, *Edmund Wilson: A Life in Literature* (2005).

HAROLD BEAVER

WINNICOTT, Donald Woods

1896–1971

British paediatrician and psychoanalyst

It was while recovering from a broken collarbone in the sick room at the Leys School in Cambridge that D.W. Winnicott decided to become a doctor. He studied biology at Jesus College, Cambridge University, and completed his medical studies at St Bartholomew's Hospital, London. In 1923 he was appointed a consultant at Paddington Green Children's Hospital – a post he held for forty years. In addition he became Physician at the Queen's Hospital for Children (until 1933), and Physician-in-charge at the London

County Council (LCC) Heart and Rheumatism Clinic for Children. Winnicott calculated that by the time he retired he had seen some 60,000 children and mothers in one clinic or another.

Winnicott's career stands out as one of the most convincing examples of a marriage between theory and practice. During the 1920s he began reading **Freud** and was immediately attracted towards psychoanalysis, in particular the new theories of child analysis being developed by Anna Freud and **Melanie Klein**. He became Klein's pupil, and later qualified as a psychoanalyst. Just as his teacher had extended classical theory (Oedipal, dwelling upon three-person relationships) by emphasizing two-person (mother and child) relationships, so Winnicott formulated his own conclusions, which were to some extent shaped by his experience as a clinician. Essentially his theory of infant care embraces three facts: (1) a baby needs its mother; (2) the mother enjoys taking care of her baby; and (3) this bond between the two is facilitated and protected by the presence of the father. Talks based on these ideas were broadcast by the BBC in the early 1940s. They also provided the material for two subsequent publications, *The Child and the Family* (1957) and *The Child and the Outside World* (1954). The most salutary aspect of Winnicott's approach was one of tone. In contrast to his theoretical predecessors, who emphasized patterns of trauma in childhood, Winnicott firmly insisted that child-raising can be an exciting and happy experience for all concerned.

Transitional Objects and Transitional Phenomena (1953) contains what is regarded as Winnicott's most original contribution to growth psychology. It concerns the child's first 'not-me' possession. The importance of the object is not what it is – it may be nothing more than a piece of cloth or a handkerchief – but how the child relates to it and uses it. Of particular note is that the object remains with the child at bedtime, as a defence against anxiety. Parents get to know the object's value, and often have to allow it to remain dirty and smelly. It was Winnicott's belief that this first specially loved object, whose pattern of usage appears within the initial year of infancy, enables the child to reach out beyond the mother to the outside world.

Winnicott sustained a dialogue between paediatrics and psychoanalysis across four decades, with a particular interest in the emotional aspects of physical illness. His ability to communicate with both children and their parents was a special gift, reinforced by his awareness of the need to understand young patients within their family and social settings. It was largely through personal example that Winnicott extended the application of what has become a standard medical precept, that care and cure should be synonymous.

Further reading

Other works include: *Clinical Notes on Disorders of Childhood* (1931); *Collected Papers: Through Paediatrics to Psycho-Analysis* (1965); *The Maturational Process and the Facilitating Environment* (1965); *Therapeutic Consultations* (1971); *Playing and Reality* (1971). See: Adam Phillips, *Winnicott* (1988); Michael Jacobs, *Donald Winnicott* (1993); Brett Kahr, *D.W. Winnicott: A Biographical Portrait* (1999).

DAVID STURGEON

WISTER, Owen

1860–1938
US writer

Owen Wister, one of the leading exponents of the romance and nobility of the American West in the second half of the nineteenth century, was born in Germantown, a then well-to-do suburb of Philadelphia, and never saw the West until he was twenty-five. His paternal ancestors were successful doctors and merchants while his maternal ones included the actress and author Fanny Kemble, and Pierce Butler who served at the Constitutional Convention. **Henry James** was a visitor in the home of Wister's youth. Wister attended a boarding school in Hofwyl,

Switzerland, Germantown Academy, and graduated from St Paul's School in Concord in 1878. He then went to Harvard where he majored in music, graduating *summa cum laude* in 1882. There he made friends with Theodore Roosevelt, **William Dean Howells**, Henry Lee Higginson and **Oliver Wendell Holmes**. After graduation Wister made the obligatory trip to Europe, but he carried letters of introduction to the likes of **Ferencz Liszt**, who much admired one of his compositions. Unfortunately, upon return there was nothing but the drab reality of a position computing interest at Union Safe Deposit Vaults in Boston. Only membership of the rather literary Tavern Club sustained him at this time. In 1885, his family and biographer agree, Wister made the most important trip of his life, a journey west to Wyoming for his health. As he wrote in his journal, 'I don't wonder a man never comes back after he has once been here for a few years.' But first he enrolled in Harvard Law School in the fall of 1885, graduating in 1888 and moving to Philadelphia, where he was admitted to the Bar in 1890.

But the trips west continued, and finally they became the reality and the law practice merely a sideline. In order to, as Wister put it, 'save the sagebrush' he began to write tales of the West he knew before it disappeared. His first stories 'Hank's Women' and 'How Lin McLean Went East' were published in *Harper's* in 1892. By 1894 his writing had become his main profession, with eight pieces in *Harper's* alone, and in 1895 his first collection of Western tales, *Red Men and White*, was published. Further collections followed in 1897 and 1900. Meanwhile in 1898 he married Mary Channing, who gave him six children before dying in childbirth in 1913.

During this period he wrote his first and most famous novel, *The Virginian*, published in 1902 and dedicated to Theodore Roosevelt. Subtitled 'A Horseman of the Plains' the novel told the now familiar story of a handsome, daring and rather chivalric cowboy, known only as 'the Virginian', in the rough and tumble days of the 1870s and 1880s as he wooed the young Vermont schoolteacher Molly and upheld justice and virtue in the days before civilization arrived. In his introduction Wister called his hero 'the cowpuncher, the last romantic figure upon our soil'. In pointed criticism of the trends of the day and capturing the heart of the bourgeois American dreamer, Wister continued, 'The cowpuncher's ungoverned hours did not unman him. If he gave his word, he kept it; Wall Street would have found him behind the times. Nor did he talk lewdly to women; Newport would have thought him old-fashioned.' Wister here has forsaken the realism of Howells's *The Rise of Silas Lapham* invoked in the novel's introduction. The 'horseman of the plains' is idealized into a chivalric knight who courts the schoolmarm leisurely and nobly and invokes knightly codes of battle with his enemies when he is not reading Shakespeare and Jane Austen or investing in land. In fact, the Virginian often evokes the **Alger** dream of self-help – 'The world did not beget you. I reckon man helps them that helps themselves.' The Virginian is both the rugged individualist, however, and the decorous gentleman who knows how to treat a lady. This knightly cowpuncher rises in the course of the novel from cowboy to foreman to ranch-owner, while still maintaining his heroic status by demonstrating his Western skill with horses and gun against rustlers and his longtime opponent Trampas. At the same time, unlike many other Western heroes in literature, the Virginian demonstrates his ability to survive and thrive in the twentieth century by courting the East embodied in New Englander Molly Wood's learning, ancestry and manners.

The Virginian unified many of the American myths for the American public; the Buffalo Bill-anglo-frontiersman, the Horatio Alger upwardly-mobile poor, the virtues of the natural life, and the moral righteousness of Roosevelt's bully pulpit. And for sixty years Americans relived the story from Dustin Farnum's stage version, through four motion pictures, and a long-running television series.

Although Wister would continue to write, it was *The Virginian* alone that achieved the cultural and mythic influence that makes him such a summation of late nineteenth-century dreams: the aristocrat as outdoorsman, joining Roosevelt and Frederic Remington as the great popularizers of an idealized West where virtue, nature and manliness were inextricably linked.

Further reading

Other works include: *Philosophy Four* (1903); *When West Was West* (1928); *Lady Baltimore* (1906); *Roosevelt: The Story of a Friendship 1880–1919* (1930). See: Edward G. White, *The Eastern Establishment and the Western Experience: The West of Frederic Remington, Theodore Roosevelt, and Owen Wister* (1968); Joe B. Frantz and Julian Ernest Choate Jr, *The American Cowboy: The Myth and the Reality* (1955); Frances K.W. Stokes, *My Father, Owen Wister, and Ten Letters Written by Owen Wister to His Mother during His First Trip to Wyoming in 1885* (1952); Richard Etulain, *Owen Wister* (1973); Darwin Payne, *Owen Wister: Chronicler of the West, Gentleman of the East* (1985).

CHARLES GREGORY

WITTGENSTEIN, Ludwig Josef Johann
1889–1951
Austrian/British philosopher

Ludwig Wittgenstein was born in Vienna, into a large and wealthy family; he was the youngest of five brothers and three sisters, and was educated at home until he was fourteen. He came to England at the age of nineteen to study aeronautics at the University of Manchester, but in 1912 he met **Bertrand Russell** and spent five terms studying logic under him at Cambridge. It was during the Great War (he volunteered for service in the Austrian artillery) that he completed the notes for his *Logisch-Philosophische Abhandlung*, a copy of which he sent to Russell from a prison camp in Italy. It was published first in 1921, and then in the following year, together with an English version, under the title *Tractatus Logico-Philosophicus*. The introduction, by Russell, described it as an achievement of 'extraordinary difficulty and importance'. Apart from one short article, it was to be the only work Wittgenstein published in his lifetime.

After completing the *Tractatus* Wittgenstein gave up philosophy; he also gave away a large inherited fortune. He qualified as an elementary schoolteacher and for several years taught in various remote villages in southern Austria. But in 1929 he returned to Cambridge, submitted the *Tractatus* (already an established classic) as his PhD thesis, and was elected to a research fellowship at Trinity College. During the following decade he became a legendary figure. His 'lectures', given to small groups of devotees, were periods of intense concentration during which Wittgenstein 'thought aloud'; impassioned questions to the students would alternate with agonized silences as the philosopher struggled to achieve a new insight. During this period he wrote the *Philosophische Bemerkungen* ('Remarks', 1964) and the lengthy *Philosophische Grammatik* (1969). He also began work on his most famous book, which was not to be completed until 1948 and was still not fully revised at his death. This was the *Philosophische Untersuchungen*, or *Philosophical Investigations*, which appeared posthumously in 1953.

Wittgenstein was appointed Professor of Philosophy at Cambridge in 1939, but he spent the war years working as a medical orderly in London and Newcastle. He returned to Cambridge in 1945 but found the life of a professor unendurable (he described it to a friend as a 'living death'), and he resigned his post two years later. He lived for a time in Ireland (in total isolation) and visited America; but on his return to England in 1949 it was discovered that he had cancer. He died in Cambridge.

There are three main reasons for the unique fascination of Wittgenstein. The austerity and deep seriousness of his life; his extraordinary writing style, which almost completely avoids 'philosophical argument' as it is traditionally understood; and the curious tension between his earlier work in the *Tractatus* and the later material of the *Investigations*.

This last point needs some qualifying. The myth of a near-total split between the 'early' and the 'late' Wittgenstein has been sharply eroded: a study of some of the more recently published posthumous works has shown a more gentle transition and some elements of continuity. But it remains true that Wittgenstein's later views represent a marked retreat from the position taken in the *Tractatus* on the nature of language and its relation to the world.

The *Tractatus* is essentially a thesis about the limits of language and the limits of philosophy. 'The boundaries of my language mean the boundaries of my world' (Proposition 5.6). The book consists of seven brief propositions, each – save the last – followed by many further propositions (numbered in decimal system) which elucidate and develop what has gone before. An almost obsessive brevity marks the style; the compression does not always make for clarity, and several critics have complained that bald assertion often takes the place of reasoned argument.

The background presupposed by the author is the 'new logic' developed by Russell and the German philosopher **Gottlob Frege**, which replaced the old Aristotelian system of inference with a new symbolism based on analogies with mathematical functions. Part of Wittgenstein's purpose was to show how the 'truth value' (truth or falsity) of compound propositions depends on, or is a *function* of, the truth value of the elementary propositions out of which they are composed ('the proposition is a truth function of elementary propositions' – Proposition 5). To show this he employed the technique of *truth-tables* (now part of every introduction to logic); and he developed a symbolic notation to express the general form of any truth-function.

Alongside this technical apparatus for dealing with a proposition goes a theory about the relation of language to the world of which the key notion is that of a picture (*Bild*). The 'picture theory of meaning', as it has come to be known, is in one way very straightforward. The world, Wittgenstein asserts, is simply a collection of facts; the most basic kinds of fact are called 'states-of-affairs' or *Sachverhalten*. The proposition (*Sach*) now gets its meaning by being a kind of picture or model of a state-of-affairs. Wittgenstein admits that

> at first sight a proposition – one set out on the printed page for example – does not seem to be a picture of the reality with which it is concerned. But no more does musical notation at first sight seem to be a picture of music, nor our phonetic notation (the alphabet) to be a picture of our speech. Yet these sign languages prove to be pictures, even in the ordinary sense, of what they represent.
>
> (Proposition 4.011)

In a proposition, Wittgenstein goes on to say, 'one name stands for one thing, another for another thing, and they are combined with one another so that the whole group – like a *tableau vivant* – presents a state of affairs' (4.0311).

At first sight this theory looks innocent enough. Meaningful discourse consists of statements which can be broken down into elementary propositions which correspond (or fail to correspond) with the states-of-affairs they depict. But the austerity of Wittgenstein's conception can soon be seen from the fact that it allows no place for, for example, ethical or aesthetic judgements: these cannot be genuine propositions, since they are not pictures of facts in the world. They are beyond the limits of the sayable. Even logic can assert nothing significant beyond empty tautologies, which 'say nothing', their truth being guaranteed simply by their internal structure (6.1). Indeed, the whole of philosophy now becomes strictly unsayable: 'the correct method of philosophy would simply be this: to say nothing except what can be said, i.e. the propositions of natural science – i.e. something which has nothing to do with philosophy – and then, whenever someone wanted to say something metaphysical, to show him that he had failed to give a meaning to certain signs in his propositions' (6.53).

The book ends with the famous warning '*Wovon man nicht sprechen kann, darüber muss man schweigen*' – 'What cannot be spoken must be passed over in silence.'

These conclusions anticipate in some important respects the Logical Positivist movement of the 1930s (which rejected as meaningless any proposition which could not be factually verified). A notorious difficulty with this type of philosophical position is that it seems to cut the ground from under its own feet: what is one to make of such philosophical claims as those in the *Tractatus* itself, since on the very theory which the book presents they must be meaningless? Wittgenstein himself admitted that 'anyone who understands me recognizes my propositions as nonsense'; but the nonsense was nonetheless supposed to be helpful nonsense – like a ladder one climbs up and then throws away (6.54).

For all that, Wittgenstein was convinced that the *Tractatus* represented the final solution to the problems of philosophy. What compelled him to return to the subject, after a gap of some ten years, was not so much the type of difficulty just referred to, as some more technical problems about the logical independence of elementary propositions. More important, Wittgenstein gradually came to see that the way in which language is meaningful is very much more complex than the simple picturing model of the *Tractatus* had suggested. Words, he wrote in the *Philosophische Grammatik*, cannot be understood simply as the names of objects; they have as many different uses as money, which can buy an indefinite range of different kinds of item. Language, he wrote there and elsewhere, is like a toolbag, whose components are as diverse in function as hammer, saw and gluepot.

We have now arrived at one of the key slogans of Wittgenstein's later philosophy: 'The meaning of the word is its use in language' (*Philosophical Investigations* § 43). A detailed examination of the actual working of language in all its variety and complexity was to replace the insistence on a single model to which all meaningful propositions must conform.

The most famous concept Wittgenstein employs in presenting this new view of language is that of the *Sprachspiel* or *language-game*. We understand the meaning of a word by seeing the role it plays in any one of a vast number of language games. The important notions here are multiplicity and diversity. There is no one common essence that explains meaning, any more than there is one common feature shared by all games. In a famous passage Wittgenstein tells us to 'consider the proceedings that we call *games*. I mean board-games, card-games, ball-games, Olympic games . . . What is common to them all? Don't say *There must be something common or they would not be called games*, but *look and see*.' The conclusion is that there is no one essential feature or set of features, but instead 'a complicated network of similarities overlapping and criss-crossing' (§ 66).

'Overlapping and criss-crossing' is in fact characteristic of the style of the *Investigations*, which makes no pretence to be welded into a set of precisely stated philosophical conclusions. The author describes the book in the preface as 'a number of sketches of landscapes . . . made in the course of . . . long and involved journeyings'. The topic which begins to predominate as the sketches proceed is that of the philosophy of mind, the analysis of mental concepts, and in particular sensations.

Here Wittgenstein makes his most original contribution when he takes on the long-standing philosophical tradition which regards words like 'pain' as names for private sensations. In attacking this view, Wittgenstein manages to avoid the crude Behaviourist position which reduces sensations to their physical manifestations. Instead, his argument turns to the impossibility of what he calls a *private language*: words, to have meaning, must be subject to public rules for their application; so the picture of a man understanding the concept of pain by attending to an inner sensation and then christening it 'pain' is a fundamentally misleading one.

The controversy over the interpretation and validity of the 'private language argument' is still far from over. But as presented by Wittgenstein – as a struggle to free ourselves from a deceptive picture of how sensation words operate – it is characteristic of his later view of philosophy as a 'battle against the bewitchment of our intelligence by means of language' (§ 109). 'What is your aim in philosophy? To show the fly the way out of the fly-bottle' (§ 309).

Wittgenstein's influence has sometimes been destructive of good philosophy. Some philosophers of religion, for example, have taken the smug and cosy position that religious discourse can only be understood within its own 'language-game', which is apparently supposed to make it immune from scientific or other outside criticism. Other Wittgensteinians, trading on the idea that philosophy is purely the activity of linguistic clarification, have put forward the obscurantist doctrine that philosophical work on, for example, memory should confine itself to examining how we ordinarily use the word, and need take no account of physiological discoveries about how our brains work.

Wittgenstein himself would probably not have welcomed these developments. He had a horror of disciples, and once observed, 'The only seed I am likely to sow is a certain jargon.' In fact the harvest of Wittgenstein's thought is large, rich and still to be fully digested. Above all, there can be no doubt of his pioneering and lasting contribution to the two issues which have become definitive of so much contemporary philosophy – the nature of language and the function of philosophy itself.

Further reading

See: *Tractatus Logico-Philosophicus*, which presents an original German with an English translation by D.F. Pears and B.F. McGuinness (1961); the *Philosophical Investigations* is translated by G.E.M. Anscombe (1953). The *Blue and Brown Books* (1958) contain useful introductory material to the latter. Other posthumous texts include: *Protractatus* (1971); *Zettel* (1967); and *On Certainty* (1969). On

Wittgenstein: G.E.M. Anscombe, *An Introduction to Wittgenstein's Tractatus* (1959); N. Malcolm, *Ludwig Wittgenstein: A Memoir* (1958); G. Pitcher (ed.) *Wittgenstein* (1971); P.M.S. Hacker, *Insight and Illusion – Wittgenstein on Philosophy and the Metaphysics of Experience* (1972); A. Kenny, *Wittgenstein* (1975); P.M.S. Hacker, *Insight and Illusion: Themes in the Philosophy of Wittgenstein* (revised edn., 1986); H. Sluga and D. Stern (eds) *The Cambridge Companion to Wittgenstein* (1996); M. McGinn, *Wittgenstein and the Philosophical Investigations* (1997).

JOHN COTTINGHAM

WODEHOUSE, (Sir) Pelham Grenville

1881–1974

English novelist

When Wodehouse left Dulwich College in 1900 he became a bank clerk. His career was not distinguished. He had an urge to write, and when he gained some success in journalism he left the bank. He had found his vocation. His first successes were his books for boys. For many years such works had been marked by pietism, mawkishness and an embarrassing sentimentality. Wodehouse, who never preached, wrote with humour, good sense and understanding of boys at school.

In 1909 he went to New York. For some time the publishers showed little interest in him. When he married Ethel Rowley, a young English widow, in 1914, they had just over a hundred dollars between them. But things changed. His collaboration in musical comedy with Guy Bolton produced plays which delighted audiences in America and England, and for fifty years Wodehouse wrote for the stage. His books, however, were more important, and he had a real triumph when his novel *Something Fresh* (1915) was accepted by the *Saturday Evening Post*. The paper had a vast circulation and an extremely high standard. He wrote twenty-one serials for it, and the English editions were snapped up as quickly as they could be printed.

In the following years he spent most of his time in England. His last visit was in 1939, when Oxford University conferred upon him the honorary degree of Doctor of Letters in recognition of his services to English literature. A little later, in France, the Germans interned him. In 1941 he delivered his broadcasts to neutral America. The reaction to this in England was hysterical and ill-informed. He was a traitor, a disciple of **Hitler**, and so on. In fact, the talks were a shrewd criticism of the incompetence of Germans in managing their prisons. In America they were looked on as models of anti-Nazi propaganda.

Before he returned to America in 1947 the animosity of his detractors in England had faded away. The sales of his books, far from falling, increased greatly, and there were many more to come.

He was always modest about his books. They might give readers an hour or so of amusement because of their absurdities and their remoteness from real life, but otherwise they were valueless. He had no message for the world. Intelligent readers will not agree. His characters and their situations arouse laughter not because they are out of this world but because they are plainly within it. He was one of the great writers of the English comic tradition, and for all their lightness his books expose the shortcomings of society and all that is pretentious and unreal.

For many readers the genius of Wodehouse is best revealed in his series of stories about Bertie Wooster, his valet Jeeves and those about Lord Emsworth and Blandings Castle. They are brilliantly written with a continuous felicity of diction and metaphor, and it is in them that the peculiar flavour of the Wodehousian manner can be most fully savoured. It is odd that Bertie, who was in his middle twenties when he was created in 1919, is still of that age, and Emsworth, who in the first story about him was said to have been at Eton in the middle sixties of the last century, is not a day older now. But perhaps it is not so strange. They are of the immortals.

Further reading

See: Richard Usborne, *Wodehouse at Work* (1961), *Wodehouse at Work to the End* (1976), *Sunset at*

Blandings (1977); R.B.D. French, *P.G. Wodehouse* (1966); Robert A. Hall, *The Comic Style of P.G. Wodehouse* (1976). *Performing Flea*, ed. W.T. Townend (1953), is a collection of letters sent to him by Wodehouse. See also: Robert McCrum: *Wodehouse: A Life* (2004); Brian Taves, *P.G. Wodehouse and Hollywood: Screenwriting, Satires and Adaptations* (2005).

R.B.D. FRENCH

WOLF, Hugo

1860–1903

Austrian composer

Wolf was born in Windischgraz, lower Styria (now part of Yugoslavia), the son of a tanner. He studied at the Vienna Conservatoire, where one of his fellow students was **Mahler**, with whom he later shared a room. His first important songs date from 1878; he had already composed piano and choral music. On leaving the conservatoire he supported himself mainly by teaching; a conducting post in Salzburg was abandoned after only three months. From 1884 to 1887 he was music critic of a fashionable Vienna weekly, the *Salonblatt*, where his outspoken criticisms made him notorious.

In 1888 he produced two of the great song-books on which his reputation rests; a third was begun in the same year. From now on he enjoyed increasing public success. His wish to write opera led to the composition of *Der Corregidor* (1895), his one completed work in that genre; a Hugo Wolf Society was established in 1897. But the same year saw a dramatic breakdown in his health, undermined by syphilis; insanity and paralysis followed; and he died in 1903.

Wolf is conventionally regarded, and rightly, as a major figure in the German *lieder* tradition, perhaps the last who is worthy of comparison with Schubert, Schumann and **Brahms**. Schubert and Schumann he venerated, so much so that he avoided setting poems already set to music by them. Brahms he detested with the passion of a true Wagnerian, though Brahms's influence can be heard in some of his very early songs. Wolf had come under the spell of **Wagner** in 1875, and had never escaped it; indeed, his greatest contribution to the *lied* may be the way he brings a Wagnerian intensity of emotion, and a Wagnerian harmonic language, to this miniature form. Other important influences were **Berlioz**, **Liszt** and Chopin.

Wolf's first great song-book was *Gedichte von Eduard Mörike* ('Poems of Eduard Mörike, for voice and piano, set to music by Hugo Wolf' – the emphasis on the poet is characteristic). The song entitled 'Lebewohl' is typical on several counts: its brevity (only twenty bars), its extreme dynamic range (from *pp* to *ff* and down again), its declamatory vocal writing (another Wagnerian trait), its chromatic texture (with a nod to Hans Sachs in bar 7), and its 'progressive tonality' (it ends in the dominant). The concept of the song-book, or collection, devoted to the work of a single poet seems to have evolved partly from the great speed with which Wolf always composed; one song followed another as if by chain reaction. It led to an idealization of the poet on the composer's part: at times Mörike himself seems to be the subject of the song-book.

Wolf's *Eichendorff* song-book was conceived as a companion-piece to Schumann's Eichendorff *Liederkreis*, concentrating on the humorous figures which Schumann had ignored. This delight in musical characterization, much admired by Reger, is seen again in Wolf's *Goethe* song-book, especially in his settings of poems from *Wilhelm Meister*, where he tried to realize in music the characters of the novel. Wolf's fourth major song-book, the *Spanisches Liederbuch* (1889–90), sets translations of Spanish poems from the sixteenth and seventeenth centuries. It is in two sections, 'Sacred' and 'Profane', and the erotic/religious imagery inspires some of his most daring harmony; the piano writing, too, tends to be harsher than before, some of the sonorities anticipating **Bartók**. By contrast Wolf's final collection, the *Italienisches Liederbuch* (two volumes, 1890–1 and 1896: settings of Italian poems in translation), returns to a suaver, more lyrical style; here the vocal writing is perhaps his subtlest. Wolf himself said that many of the songs in the volume could be played equally well by a string quartet, and it is no coincidence that his most successful instrumental work, the Serenade in G (1887), is for this medium: it was later orchestrated as *Italienische Serenade*. Wolf's last songs are three to poems by *Michelangelo* (1897), in which the linear tendency combines with a bleak dissonance reminiscent of some of the Goethe songs.

Der Corregidor, based on Alarcón's *The Three-Cornered Hat*, is notable for its Spanish subject – a more substantial Mediterraneanizing of music than that found in *Carmen*. Its 'song-book' style has caused it to be criticized as undramatic, but this very lyricism, the containedness of the set numbers, gives it a Neoclassical quality far in advance of its time. Wolf told a friend that in his next opera (*Manuel Venegas*, left unfinished at his death) he would orchestrate like Mozart; this remark may be a surer indication of his future development than the style of the Michelangelo songs.

Wolf's achievement lies in his mastery of a single medium, the *lied*, rather than in his versatility. His concern for truth of expression led to a style of declamation whose aims, at least, had something in common with those of **Mussorgsky** – and later with those of **Fauré**, **Debussy** and **Janáček**. At the same time the motivic concentration of his work – a predominantly German characteristic – links it with that of his detested Brahms. His influence has naturally been felt most strongly by other song-writers: by **Schoenberg**, **Webern** and Schoeck among the 'Austro-Germans', but also by the English composer Robin Holloway, while one of **Stravinsky's** last creative acts was to orchestrate two Wolf songs.

Further reading

Other works include: String Quartet in D minor (1878–84); *Penthesilea*, symphonic poem for orchestra (1883–5); *Christnacht* for soli, chorus and orchestra (1886–9). Wolf's works are published by

the International Hugo Wolf Society under the editorship of Hans Jancik (Vienna). See: Frank Walker, *Hugo Wolf: A Biography* (2nd edn, 1968); Eric Sams, *The Songs of Hugo Wolf* (2nd edn, 1982), and 'Hugo Wolf', in *The New Grove Dictionary of Music and Musicians* (1981). See also: *The Music Criticism of Hugo Wolf*, trans. and ed. Henry Pleasants (1979); S. Youens, *Hugo Wolf: The Vocal Music* (2000) and *Hugo Wolf and the Mörike Songs* (2002).

DERRICK PUFFETT

WOLFE, Tom

1932–

US journalist and novelist

With the increasing tendency of post-**Joycean** fiction to move away from public reality into private exploration, and with the general lack of artistic ambition among journalists, there arose in the 1960s a middle ground in which some of the techniques, liberties and high purposes of creative writing were appropriated for the presentation of magazine non-fiction. It was **Matthew Arnold** who coined the phrase 'the new journalism' to describe the sharp, individualistic form of reviewing which arose in the 1880s and whose great exponent was to be **George Bernard Shaw**. Critics, of course, have always published in periodicals and many creative authors have also been gifted journalists – **Coleridge**, **Dostoevsky**, **Baudelaire** come to mind. But probably the first writers to use journalistic space as an experimental space were Vasily Rozanov in St Petersburg and Max Beerbohm in London, both at the end of the nineteenth century. In the 1920s and 1930s Cyril Connolly found himself unable to work easily in book form and produced an inventive series of jazz-rococo entertainments in journals and newspapers.

But Connolly was famously self-hating. He thought that the writer's purpose was to produce a masterpiece and not waste his talent in opportunistic journalism. Tom Wolfe, by contrast, stepped forward in an entirely unapologetic way. He was far from alone as a 'new journalist' – **Truman Capote** weighed in by claiming that his own book-long murder investigation *In Cold Blood* (1966) had started the whole thing – but Wolfe was the most audacious, systematic advocate of the cause, a position he later confirmed by editing and introducing with a passionate manifesto an anthology of articles by various authors under the title *The New Journalism* (1973) which claimed that this sort of work represented 'the most important literature being written in America today'. The emphasis in such journalism moved from the collation and analysis of fact towards the examination of personality, including the personality of the journalist. This chimed with the growing cult of celebrity and the proliferation of vanity columns, and it is no accident that some of the New Journalism's finest moments were in the interview, with its opportunities for dialogue and personal engagement.

Wolfe's approach to his material was generally mocking, as was that of his most outrageous protégé, Hunter S. Thompson, whose *Fear and Loathing in Las Vegas* (1971), developed from articles in *Rolling Stone* magazine, is the New Journalism's outstanding book (Thompson invented a sub-style for it called 'gonzo journalism' in which the author becomes the Quixotic hero/victim of the events going on around him). Wolfe's panache in debunking was made acceptable by the loving care with which he organized the foibles of social life into a subtle thesis. He was also able to adapt the prosodic adventures of modern fiction in a way which reached a large audience by harnessing them to popular idioms and concerns. In this fertile overlap of high and low culture, the arts, the media and the market place, he was as characteristic of the 1960s as were Warhol's Pop Art and the **Beatles'** records.

His language is colourful, overloaded, fast and slangy, with an obsession for microscopic detail which roots the subject in actuality. This linguistic flair was enormously influential. It was a style established in the title of his very first book, *The Kandy-Kolored Tangerine-Flake Streamline Baby* (1965). The demotic and sometimes philistine character (viz. *The Painted Word*, 1975, an attack on conceptual art) of his writing saw it published largely in leisure magazines such as *Esquire*, *Playboy* and *Rolling Stone*, which were generous with their fees, expenses and above all their space, allowing room to build a long, atmospheric, non-fiction story or thesis. Wolfe himself was a reporter for ten years after taking a PhD in American Studies at Yale 1957, and from 1968 a contributing editor to *New York Magazine*.

Wolfe is at his weakest when polemical (as is Hunter S. Thompson), the arguments being sentimental and glib. His true gift is for the comic mythologization of America's consumer society. However, he demonstrated a growing seriousness and a wish to eliminate his overt personality from the play of events (viz. *The Right Stuff*, 1979, about the world of the astronaut). At the same time the New Journalism was losing ground, eventually killed off by a later generation of mostly female magazine editors averse to risk-taking. It was not surprising, therefore, that Wolfe turned to the novel or that, when he did, he chose to reject the current fashion in literary fiction of writing *faux* confessionally in the first person, preferring the authorial overview. *The Bonfire of the Vanities* (1987), a celebration of Reaganite Manhattan, was compared to **Dickens's** work in capturing London. It was enormously successful, though working as it did within a long-established form, it did not make its author more interesting. The novels *A Man in Full* (1998) and *I am Charlotte Simmons* (2004) have sustained his reputation without adding to it.

Further reading

See: *The Pump House Gang* (1968); *The Electric Kool-Aid Acid Test* (1968); *Radical Chic and Mau-Mauing the Flak Catchers* (1970); *Mauve Gloves and Madmen, Clutter and Vine* (1976).

DUNCAN FALLOWELL

WOOLF, Adeline Virginia

1882–1941

English novelist

While Virginia Woolf's claim, in 'The Leaning Tower', that English writers tend to be firmly rooted in the middle class might not be altogether true or useful, it is certainly essential to an understanding of her own development. Daughter of Sir Leslie Stephen, critic, man of letters and editor of *The Dictionary of National Biography*, Virginia grew up in a London household in which distinguished writers and intellectuals were familiar figures, in which books and ideas were everywhere. Denied the formal education which Sir Leslie felt was appropriate for his sons but not his daughters, Virginia was at least given free access to his vast library, whose resources helped compensate for her exclusion from the educational opportunities offered to her two brothers. While she always resented the crippling patriarchal assumptions of life at 22 Hyde Park Gate, its rich intellectual ambience also nourished her and helped shape her early resolve to become a writer.

Liberated by Stephen's death in 1904, Virginia moved with her two brothers and sister Vanessa into Gordon Square, and into a new social life built around the Cambridge acquaintances of the Stephen boys. These new friendships, which fashioned the nucleus of the much deplored and admired 'Bloomsbury circle', also brought her a husband in the person of **Leonard Woolf**, Virginia's 'penniless Jew', who married her in 1911 after his return from Ceylon.

With the solidity of her marriage helping her to deal with the spells of incapacitating and, at times, suicidal depression which constantly assaulted her (until she finally took her life in 1941), Woolf began her novelistic career in 1915 with the publication of *The Voyage Out*. But neither this nor the book to follow, *Night and Day* (1919), is particularly successful or indicative of what was to come. Both are basically pedestrian works, written in the narrative, realist tradition she soon came to realize was an artistic dead-end for

her. For Woolf, conventional techniques could produce only conventional fiction; and it was not until the publication of *Jacob's Room* in 1922 that she felt she had finally learned 'how to begin (at 40) to say something in my own voice'. Irrevocably breaking free with *Jacob's Room* from what she calls 'the appalling narrative business of the realist: getting on from lunch to dinner', Woolf devoted the next nineteen years to exploring the different possibilities of that newly discovered voice.

Woolf was not alone, of course, in rejecting traditional techniques. Such rejection accounts for the history of modern art in general and the modern novel in particular. But in many ways Woolf is a more radical innovator than even **Conrad**, Ford Maddox Ford, **Lawrence**, **Joyce** and **Faulkner**. More totally than the others, she cuts herself off from any vestige of narrative energy. It is almost impossible to speak of 'the action' of a Woolf novel. As an artist Woolf was always absorbed with formal rather than substantive concerns, with trying to embody, as she says, 'the exact shapes my brain holds'. While she has frequently been associated with the 'stream of consciousness' novel her writing cannot, in fact, be understood by reference to any single label or technique. The astonishingly different forms of each novel – from the minutely detailed street life of *Mrs Dalloway* (1925) to the totally artificial, internalized depths of *The Waves* (1931), from the tripartite structure of *To the Lighthouse* (1927) to the day-long pageant of *Between the Acts* (1942) – suggest the single-minded purpose with which she sought to find fresh ways to express what the experience of living is like.

Woolf's own attempt to create shapes that can make sense out of the fluidity of life is paralleled by the same sort of quest going on inside the novels themselves. If it is possible to generalize about the meaning of the human activity in Woolf's fictional world, we can say that the characters all try, through widely different means, to fashion for themselves from the chaos surrounding them some coherent grasp of their world. Lily's painting in *To the Lighthouse*, Bernard's novel in *The Waves*, Miss LaTrobe's pageant in *Between the Acts*, and Clarissa's party in *Mrs Dalloway*, for example, are all efforts to effect what Woolf herself is seeking in her fiction. The workings of the creative imagination shaping different visions of order is the single great theme in Virginia Woolf's novels.

While Woolf's position as one of the important and original modern novelists seems now to be securely established, it is only recently that such canonization has taken place. During her lifetime and extending until the late 1960s, her critical reputation was extremely uneven, a result of both the inherent difficulties of the fiction itself and her involvement with the notorious Bloomsbury circle of writers, artists and intellectuals. As the term 'Bloomsbury' was for years a highly pejorative designation, Woolf suffered from the same critical opprobrium generally lavished on all manifestations of the phenomenon. Snobbish, sexually effete, morally perverse, politically unaware – the charges brought against Bloomsbury by Sir John Rothenstein, **Wyndham Lewis** and the **Leavises**, among others, were also brought against Woolf, and she remained for years the most dismissible of the great modernists.

For reasons that are less literary than cultural, however, the metaphoric significance of 'Bloomsbury' and all its constituent parts – **Lytton Strachey**, Clive Bell, **E.M. Forster**, **Maynard Keynes** and the rest – has dramatically changed, so that what was once seen as trivial and pernicious is instead hailed as prophetic and socially redemptive. For a culture that is in the process of trying to divest itself of the rigidities of traditional sexual role-playing and masculine constraints, the value the Bloomsberries are seen to place on friendship and art, and their rejection of the use of power in personal relationships, bring them into the cultural mainstream from which they were so long excluded. And at the very centre of this rediscovery stands Woolf herself, the high priestess of Bloomsbury, embodying all the life-giving virtues attributed to it. In its denunciation of masculine oppression, her social criticism, most especially in *A Room of One's Own* (1929) and *Three Guineas* (1930), is revered by feminists and androgynists alike, and readers now find in her novels an anguished awareness of the plight of the creative woman trapped in a sexist society.

The cultic admiration surrounding Woolf is not altogether edifying. The arguments for her social relevance are grossly distorted, and her feminism is far more complicated than the polemicists of the women's movement make it out to be. Woolf's genuine achievement as a writer, however, should outlast the topical claims made for her. It is above all else in her ability to create the resonant forms of *Mrs Dalloway*, *To the Lighthouse*, *The Waves* and *Between the Acts* that her reputation will ultimately rest.

Further reading

Other works include: *Orlando* (1928); *Flush* (1933); *The Years* (1937); *Roger Fry: A Biography* (1940). The standard biography is Quentin Bell, *Virginia Woolf* (1972). See also: Avrom Fleishman, *Virginia Woolf: A Critical Reading* (1975); Phyllis Rose, *Woman of Letters* (1978); Michael Rosenthal, *Virginia Woolf* (1979); Hermione Lee, *Virginia Woolf* (1995); Regina Marler, *Bloomsbury Pie: The Story of the Bloomsbury Revival* (1997); Sue Roe and Susan Sellers (eds) *The Cambridge Companion to Virginia Woolf* (2000); Julia Briggs, *Virginia Woolf: An Inner Life* (2005).

MICHAEL ROSENTHAL

WOOLF, Leonard

1880–1969

Editor and political writer

Leonard's Woolf's reputation both as editor and political writer has been overshadowed by the fame of his wife, whom he sustained and helped over thirty years until her final breakdown and suicide. Woolf came from a professional middle-class secular Jewish background, attending St Paul's School as a scholar, then Trinity Cambridge for five years, becoming one of the circle of Apostles, so coming under the influence of **G.E. Moore** and befriending such as **Lytton Strachey**, Clive Bell and Toby Stephen (the son of **Sir Lesley**) through whom he met Virginia Stephen.

Financially straitened family circumstances led Woolf to join the Colonial Service, serving seven years in Ceylon where, like **Orwell** later, his initial sense of mission soon turned to a rooted dislike of imperialism. Resigning in 1911 and returning to England, he resumed Cambridge friendships, fell in love with Virginia and they were married in 1912. From the beginning he recognized her genius as a writer and also the neurasthenic problems that needed constant care.

By 1914 he had written two books on consumer co-operative socialism and, under the tutelage of Beatrice and **Sidney Webb**, became active in the Fabian Society. In 1916 he wrote two Fabian reports on international government which, together with **George Bernard Shaw's** advocacy, influenced among intellectuals and the press, support for the idea of a League of Nations. He wrote on socialism and international affairs for *The Nation* and many other journals, also novels and short stories. But perhaps his major achievement was founding, jointly with Virginia, the Hogarth Press in 1917. They were the first to publish **T.S. Eliot** and **Katherine Mansfield**. They went on to publish work by most of the Bloomsbury circle and other modernist writers, as well as political pamphlets and, the long-term venture, the then standard translation of the writings of **Freud**. But somehow this left him time to become an active secretary of both the Labour Party's and the Fabian Society's colonial committees. He was closely associated with the *New Statesman*, and when Kingsley Martin would vanish on American lecture tours he would drop into the office and edit it – among other activities.

In 1930, he was associated with the founding of *The Political Quarterly* (*PQ*) in partnership with William Robson of the London School of Economics, a prominent, rising authority on public and administrative law. It was a strange but close partnership as joint editors, lasting from 1931 to 1958. Woolf thought that Robson was the intermediary of the new social sciences. Robson thought that Woolf was the intermediary to all the intellectuals. They both believed in writing at the highest level of intelligence, but in plain English, without jargon. Their stance was reformist rather than orthodox Labour, as shown **John Maynard Keynes** and Harold Laski being on the early *PQ* Board. Their approach was unashamedly elitist; Woolf wrote in his autobiography that all new ideas trickled down from an educated class of about 3,000 people (a view now as political unpopular as it is historically and sociologically accurate).

Woolf put his heart into a trilogy on international relations, *After the Deluge*, retitled as *Principia Politica* in 1953, but it was too long and laboured for his fellow intellectuals and by then, lacking the specialized scholarship that the universities were demanding, it appeared as a rather old-fashioned well-meaning piece of *a priori* liberal rationalism. However, the strength and beauty of his writing and his moral honesty as a self-critical humanist appeared in the widely admired five volumes of his autobiography, beginning with *Sowing* (1960), *Growing* (1961), *Beginning Again* (1964), *Downhill All the Way* (1967) and *The Journey Not the Arrival Matters* (1969). He was the serious side of Bloomsbury, immune to attacks from **Levisites** and others for its alleged frivolity and extreme aestheticism. Sometimes the professed honesty and truth of Bloomsbury could appear as exhibitionism but with Leonard Woolf it was always a sad and self-critical humane fatalism.

Further reading

See: S.P. Rosenbaum, *Edwardian Bloomsbury* (1994); N. Rosenfeld, *Outsiders Together: Virginia and Leonard Woolf* (2000); J.H. Willis, *Leonard and Virginia Woolf as Publishers: The Hogarth Press, 1917–1941* (1992); and D. Wilson, *Leonard Woolf: A Political Biography* (1978).

DUNCAN FALLOWELL

WRIGHT, Frank Lloyd

1869–1959

US architect

The great American architect died leaving behind the fruits of a working life that spanned some sixty years: years of prolific and original thinking that revolutionized architectural design by introducing a very sophisticated method of composition based on the subtle interplay of geometric forms which link all the elements of a building and its immediate environment into one essentially organic whole.

His initial training was in the School of Engineering at the University of Wisconsin but this formal education seems to have had little obvious lasting effect and was certainly less important to his work than the years of practical experience of long working days on his uncle's farm or the purposeful play induced by his mother's discovery of Froebel learning methods. His love for the land and the expressive possibilities of natural materials dates from this time.

Dissatisfied with the restrictive atmosphere at Wisconsin he moved to Chicago where he formed a close friendly relationship with the architect **Louis Sullivan** in whose office he eventually worked. Wright never lost his admiration for Sullivan and his faith in an architecture freed from convention based on the supposed great European tradition. As a Mid-West American Wright had no Beaux Arts training and much of the work he did with Sullivan during the six years he spent in Chicago, particularly the designs for private houses, clearly influenced the first buildings he developed as an independent architect – his Prairie houses, designed and built between 1900 and 1909.

Typified by the Willetts House of 1902, his 'house of the future' is composed of dramatic masses set around an articulate internal spatial arrangement, the geometric form of which is governed by purely functional needs. Embedded in its leafy surroundings it merges into the landscape, giving a sense of safe shelter and durability.

The designs for private houses grow in confidence and daring, culminating in the Robie House built in 1909 on a long narrow site in a wealthy area of Chicago. With its continuous flow of interesting planes and volumes, every component in the design including the fittings combines to give that total unity which Wright called an 'inner order'.

This concentration on housing for a rich minority has brought the obvious criticism that Wright avoided the real social issues of the day, and this is undoubtedly true, though it is equally true that it was their willingness to accept his ideas and to be able to pay for them to be put into practice that consequently influenced the evolution of modern architecture.

The public works are equally impressive. The Larkin Building, built in an industrial section of Buffalo in 1904 (and demolished in 1950), was far more than a new architectural form. It was a radical concept of what an office building should be and Wright concentrated on letting as much light as possible into the working area, which was open-plan with a series of galleries running around it and an open vertical court in which the employees could work in uninterrupted space. The most internationally influential of the early works, double-glazing was first used in this building and, most interestingly, the first wall-hung latrines.

The year 1909 saw the end of the productive Prairie House phase, and dogged by personal pressures Wright left for Europe. In his immensely readable *An Autobiography* (1943) he gives an admittedly lurid account of the desperation he felt at the time and also of the tragic seemingly endless story of Taliesin and his attempts to start life afresh in Wisconsin where he had been so happy as a boy.

Taliesin 1 was built with a pioneer spirit of independence and a desire for self-sufficiency. Conceived as an integrated group of buildings and built into the hillside from which it took its form, the living accommodation meandered informally in marked contrast to the earlier Prairie houses. Random gardens and natural vegetation were allowed to flow freely, though hinting at ideas to be used later in the Kaufmann House known as Fallingwater.

Wright's concern for an ideal way of life for others was sadly doomed to failure. His Millard House, designed in 1923, is not unlike the box-like form associated with the European architect **Le Corbusier**, but there was an important difference in the social attitudes of the two men. Unlike Le Corbusier, Wright had no thoughts for mass-production and was still working for a wealthy elite.

Worldwide recognition came late to Wright and only in his last twenty years did large commissions come his way.

The Johnson Wax Factory is an office block with walls of brick and glass tubes and an interior with mushroom-like columns giving an air of pure fantasy. The laboratory block with its tree-like Research Tower added later is evidence of Wright's continuing inventiveness and versatility.

But it is his famous Fallingwater that is his masterpiece. Built in 1936 for yet another wealthy client, it is nothing if not dramatic, with its flat terraces poised precariously over the cascading waterfall, the cantilevering made possible by reinforced concrete. As Wright himself wrote:

> This structure might serve to indicate that the sense of shelter – the sense of space where used with sound structural sense – has no limitations as to form except the materials used and the methods by which they are employed for what purpose. The ideas involved here are in no wise changed from those of early work.
>
> (*Architectural Forum*, January 1938)

From the beginning, Wright's thinking had been concerned with the underlying structure of form and its subsequent meaning, and right until the end he stuck to his beliefs. Even the somewhat cumbersome and impractical Guggenheim Museum is not lacking in ingenious solutions.

His influence on others is complex, but in terms of the development of the Modern Movement the impact on J.J.P. Oud and the designers of the Dutch De Stijl group is probably the most significant. Wright's designs were published in Holland in 1910 and they were greeted with great enthusiasm for their strictly formal geometric rightness.

Frank Lloyd Wright was a complicated man with a simple approach to life, and with the ever-increasing awareness of the need for a unity between the new technology and a fundamental human self-sufficiency there is much still to be learnt from him and the utopian ideals of Taliesin.

Further reading

See: *Collected Writings of Frank Lloyd Wright*, ed. Bruce Brooks Pfeiffer (5 vols, 1992–5); Vincent Scully Jr, *Frank Lloyd Wright* (1960); H.A. Brooks, *The Prairie School* (1972); Patrick Joseph Meehan, *Frank Lloyd Wright: A Research Guide to Archival Sources* (1983); William Allin Storrer, *A Frank Lloyd Wright Companion* (1993); Joseph M. Siry, *Unity Temple: Frank Lloyd Wright and Architecture for Liberal Religion* (1996); Neil Levine, *The Architecture of Frank Lloyd Wright* (1996).

JOHN FURSE

WRIGHT, Richard
1908–60
US novelist and essayist

Richard Wright is the last great American Naturalist writer in the tradition of Norris, **Crane** and **Dreiser**. He himself had to overcome the great 'scientific' forces defined by Naturalism: heredity, environment and chance. Born on a farm in Natchez, Mississippi to a former schoolteacher and a sharecropper, Wright overcame his race and his impoverished environment to achieve even the barest of goals. At twelve, he was already rebelling against the strict regulations of his Seventh-Day Adventist school, his family and its religious strictures. *Black Boy* (1945) tells of these years, beaten by his grandmother and mother for being rebellious, and beaten by whites for being 'uppity'. Slowly, he escaped that environment through reading, graduating valedictorian of his ninth grade class, and moving north: first to Memphis, then to Chicago, where at twenty he worked for the postal service. He lost that job in the wake of the Great Crash and began work on a rejected novel – 'Cesspool', on black life in Chicago. By 1933–4 he had joined the radical John Reed Club and then the Communist Party. For the next several years he supported himself by working for the Federal Theatre Project and the Federal Writers' Project while publishing poetry and essays in left-wing journals, including Michael Gold's *New Masses*.

In 1937 Wright moved to Harlem where he became the Harlem editor for the Communist *Daily Worker*. A collection of novellas (*Uncle Tom's Children*, 1938) was published and he received two commendations: one a Guggenheim Fellowship, the other a condemnation from the chair of the House Un-American Activities Committee.

Astonishingly, *Native Son* (1940) became a Book of the Month Club selection despite its sensationalist themes and actions: an ignorant poor black youth kills a rich white young woman and is defended eloquently by a Communist lawyer. The opening chapter illustrated perfectly Wright's Naturalist techniques. The protagonist (Bigger Thomas) wakes up to a shrill alarm clock in a one-room flat also occupied by a younger brother, sister and mother. Packed into these tight quarters, the family prepares to dress in relative modesty when they sight a huge black rat. The whole family rallies to battle and Bigger kills the terrified animal with a thrown skillet. The fear of the beast and the family are palpable. Before Bigger is fully awake, he is fighting for survival. As the novel progresses, he in turn becomes the cornered rat. In 1942 a theatrical version opened in New York, starring Canada Lee and directed by **Orson Welles**.

In 1944 his essay 'I Tried to be a Communist' appeared in *Atlantic Monthly*. The FBI decided he needed watching, as usual a little late, a little wrong. After World War II he travelled to France where he established permanent residence in 1947. He became friendly with **Albert Camus** and **Jean–Paul Sartre** whom many believe to have been an influence on his novel *The Outsider* (1953). His rejection of Communism led him to such other alienated European ex-communist intellectuals as **André Gide** and **Arthur Koestler**, with whom he joined in the publishing of the notorious 1949 anti-communist manifesto *The God that Failed*.

His life in Europe was fruitful as it was for so many black writers of the time, like Chester Himes and **James Baldwin**. Continuing his explorations of politics and existentialism in both his fiction and his essays, Wright's *The Outsider* showed him exploring both French Existentialism and more modernist writing. It lacks the raw power of his earlier Naturalist fiction but is part of the writer's intellectual growth that would prove so influential to the next generation of black writers. While *Native Son* and some of the other fiction are obviously great in themselves, the amount of non-fiction that Wright published provides a dramatic story of intellectual growth from the inchoate rebellion against the heredity and environment of his teenage years to the years channelling that rebellion through the Communist Party and coming out the other side to new philosophical positions that were broader than the 'scientific determinism' of Naturalism.

All of Wright's work influenced profoundly the next generation of black writers. The rage in *Native Son* and in much of his short fiction and non-fiction provides an important transition from the modernist and folk-lore writings of the Harlem Renaissance to the post-World War II black writers. Wright's 'Blueprint for Negro Literature' manifesto from 1937 spells out his demands. He insists that earlier educated Negro writers were dialoguing with white America, not writing for black America, and therefore argued that the true strength of black literature should come from Negro folk tales and the Negro church. Black writers, however, should not limit themselves to such roots but also use the works of the majority and primarily modernist culture. To express fully a minority culture's identity, a writer must use whatever tools become available, including the tools of the majority. We can see these ideas consciously at work in brilliant first novels like Ralph Ellison's *Invisible Man* and James Baldwin's *Go Tell It on the Mountain*.

Richard Wright was born on a sharecropper's farm in Mississippi and died too young of a heart attack in Paris in 1960 at only fifty-two: a long, strange journey of enormous distances and achievements and unfulfilled possibilities to come.

Further reading

See: James Baldwin, *Everybody's Protest Novel* (1964); Ralph Ellison, *The World and the Jug* (1964); David Bakish Ungar, *Richard Wright* (1973); Henry Louis Gates Jr and K.A. Appiah (eds) *Richard Wright: Critical Perspectives Past and Present* (1993).

CHARLES GREGORY

WUNDT, Wilhelm

1832–1920
German experimental psychologist

Wundt's long career offers an interesting paradox for historians of science. He was a laborious but not a clever man who personally made no useful discoveries nor ever had any valid theoretical insights. He was an immensely hard-working systematizer who opposed and devalued the contributions of better scientists. He was touchy and reacted to imagined slights with personal attacks. Yet his life's work, more than that of gifted contemporaries, launched human experimental psychology as an academic discipline.

Until the eighteenth century it had been thought impossible (and perhaps blasphemous) to suppose that we may learn anything about the human mind by experiments or observations. Systematic theories related personality type (e.g. choleric, sanguine,

phlegmatic or melancholic) to physique and even to diet. But it was thought impossible to understand perception or memory, or to measure the speed of human thought processes, because these functions involved a non-material entity whose functions were, in principle, unmeasurable and unquantifiable. Two conceptual steps were necessary: the first was to bring techniques of measurement and mathematical modelling successfully to bear on the study of human thought, as they had been brought to bear on the movements of the stars of the physics of the everyday world; the second step was to relate these measurements to the physiology of the sense organs, and eventually of the brain, in order to discover what happens in the nervous system to produce the vivid world of our conscious experience. Most of the necessary work had been completed by people who taught Wundt.

By 1860 J. Muller and E.H. Weber had shown that people can very reliably indicate the relative magnitudes of their sensations (touch, brightness, loudness, etc.) and that sensory thresholds and difference thresholds were remarkably constant across different individuals. G.T. Fechner had added the idea of a regular 'psychophysical law' for sensation. The great **Herman von Helmholtz** had published the early volumes of a *Handbook of Physiological Optics*, and a work on audition which were to remain useful until 1950. Helmholtz had put forward a useful theory of colour vision and, in about 1850, had shown that the speed of nerve-conduction (on which the 'speed of thought' must depend) was not infinite, as had been supposed, but was rather a lethargic and easily measurable process. The philosophical implications of this are greater than we can now realize. The capacities of the mind were now suddenly seen to be limited by the efficiency of human neurophysiology. Helmholtz's father saw another important point, and brilliantly captured it in two significant errors, in a letter to his son: 'Dear Son, I would as soon believe your result as that we see the light of a star that burned a million years ago'. Indeed, both examples show that Helmholtz had discovered that humans never can experience the present but merely an immediate past which was dated by nerve-conduction, just as the finite velocity of light dates their knowledge of distant stars to the remote past.

Wundt's early schooling as a pastor's son was remote from these intellectual debates. He was an ungifted pupil whose social awkwardness further hindered his progress. He went to the University of Tübingen in 1851 and then to Heidelberg to study medicine. He abandoned medicine, it is said because he grew bored with his patients, and went to Berlin to study for a year in J. Muller's physiological laboratory. He returned, took his degree in 1856, and began to teach. His great stroke of fortune was to be offered an assistant's position in Helmholtz's laboratory. Partly to aid his teaching he produced textbooks on the physiology of sensory perception and of movement control, among a steady flood of other publications. These gained him the Chair of Inductive Logic in Zürich in 1874, the year when his textbook *Principles of Physiological Psychology* (*Grundzüge der physiologischen Psychologie*, 2 vols, 1893, trans. 1904) was produced. This, in turn, with the approval of Muller and Fechner, may have resulted in the further, unexpected, offer of the Chair of Philosophy at Leipzig in 1875.

Wundt settled at Leipzig for the rest of his long life and his career there offers a choice of years from which anniversaries of the foundation of experimental psychology may be dated. In 1875 he requested space for demonstrations of psychological experiments and in 1879 began, in a single room, the Institute of Psychology at Leipzig, the first psychological laboratory in the world. To publish work carried out there he founded the first journal of psychology (*Philosophische Studien*, later *Psychologische Studien*) in 1881. His phenomenal rate of publication never slackened and even in his seventies and eighties, blind in one eye and only partially sighted in the other, he published continual revisions of his monumental

Outlines of Psychology (*Grundiss der Psychologie*, 1896, trans. 1902), brought out a series of volumes on *Volkerpsychologie* ('Social Psychology and Anthropology') and published an autobiography which was published, with impeccable timing, in the year of his death. Like his life, this autobiography was devoted to his ideas and his work. His marriage and his family were disposed of in a single paragraph.

Wundt regarded psychology as the study of human consciousness, resting on the physiological study of the central nervous system and culminating in the study of man's social and technological achievements (*Volkerpsychologie*). This attitude committed him to experiments in which laboriously trained subjects would attempt precisely to describe their emotions, feelings and sensations, or to describe the 'mental events' they experienced while they responded, as fast as possible, to a light or a sound. We may now agree with his discovery that people cannot reliably do this. But we also know that the efforts he made are not worthwhile, since most mental events do not involve language and cannot be described in language, and the categorizations imposed by language or subjective experience may be irrelevant and misleading. But it is likely that these interests in subjective experience were the reason for the extraordinary success of his public lectures. These were encyclopaedic in coverage, and his contemporaries have described them as dull and badly delivered. But they must have left an impression of *total* coverage of a discipline, from the physiology of sense-organs through the taxonomy of human emotions, through introspective studies of consciousness, mental illness, social psychology, sociology and anthropology. He was fascinated by the precise description of *experience* rather than of *behaviour*; by attempts to make precise distinctions between qualities of emotions (on a 'three-dimensional' plot of 'pleasant–unpleasant, tense–relaxed and excited–calm'); by the nature of experience at the moment of death; by the phenomena of attention and of intellectual creativity. He tackled all these problems without wit or imagination, but with honest labour. He attracted students who were no longer interested in hearing more brilliant scientists produce convincing reasons why these problems should be avoided.

Possibly his main contribution to his subject lies in the careers of his students. Kraepelin dominated German psychiatry. Lehrman, Lange and Munsterberg were influential psychologists, and when **William James** wished to establish psychology at Harvard he persuaded Munsterberg to teach there. Wundt had some students like Kulpe, who set up a rival school at Wurzburg, who strongly differed from him. But collectively the people he trained achieved a curious phenomenon – the transformation of an area of personal intellectual interest into an established academic discipline. Wundt was even more influential in American universities. J. McKeen Cattell at Columbia, E.B. Titchener at Cornell and G.M. Stratton at California all went on to carry out far more important research than he ever achieved. He also taught G. Stanley Hall of Clarke and C.H. Judd of Chicago who, like himself, were formidably influential personalities rather than distinguished scientists. Some of his talent for systematization was passed on to H.C. Warren who produced the first dictionary of psychology.

Wundt's career shows the distinction to be made between science as an intellectual game and as a public, social phenomenon involving the acquisition of funds, the construction of buildings, the acknowledgment of academic colleagues on committees and the trappings of professional establishments. The steps from 'psychological phenomena' as a minority interest among physiologists to the status of the 'science of experimental psychology' was a very long one indeed. It could hardly have been made by a less learned, less totally respectable man, whose enormous personal output of publications covered and defined the entire field of investigations possible in his time. Among Wundt's younger contemporaries the brilliantly neurotic **Freud**

found a different kind of influence. Men of genuinely original ideas like Exner or Kulpe could not have pulled it off. Later workers like Koffka, Kohler and Wertheimer benefited from the security of the established academic position which Wundt had defined and continued to maintain.

Wundt is in some ways the paradigmatic comic scientist, the learned dullard, a Dr Strabismus (whom God Preserve) of Leipzig, a caricature of pedantic obsessionality. In other respects he is a most admirable figure: isolated by awkwardness, overcoming lack of capacity by sheer industry, and maintaining that industry through extreme old age and blindness long after all reasonable personal ambitions had been gratified. A man whose extreme, even heroic, absorption in a line of work he had chosen led him to no personal intellectual achievement but left behind the foundations on which his successors have built a science.

Further reading

See: *Volkerpsychologie* (10 vols, 1900–20). About Wundt: J.C. Flugel and D.J. West, *A Hundred Years of Psychology, 1833–1933* (1933); E.G. Boring, *History of Experimental Psychology* (1950); R.W. Rieber and David K. Robinson (eds) *Wilhelm Wundt in History: The Making of a Scientific Psychology* (2001).

P.M.A. RABBITT

WYETH, Andrew Newell

1917–

US artist

Andrew Wyeth is at once one of the most revered and most castigated painters at work in modern America. By seemingly turning his back on modernist procedures and obsessions, and by choosing instead to remain rooted in the definably provincial setting of his native rural Pennsylvania and nearby rural Maine, he has enraged the mainstream urban art establishment by consistently fetching the highest prices for his supposedly 'realist' and 'traditional' work. Yet such is the quality of his workmanship that his art if anything breaks down the divide between the provincial and the metropolitan; and that perhaps has been his real transgression. By sticking to his guns he has exposed the intolerance that nourishes the radical and the avant-garde in art, while always presenting his audience and his market with a vision of an alternative, now largely ignored America, that eschews the fashionable as much as it disdains the purely sentimental.

Wyeth was born, and grew up, in Chadd's Ford, Pennsylvania. His father, Newell Convers Wyeth (1882–1945), was a well-known illustrator, and it was from him that the young Andrew Wyeth learned his craft, in particular the craft of draughtsmanship. Because he was a sickly child he was schooled at home, though in his late teens he spent a season at art college in New York, and it was in New York that he enjoyed his first solo exhibition, as early as 1937, at the Macbeth Gallery. Within a day all his exhibits had been sold to an eager and responsive public. But Wyeth refused to be drawn in by the city, or by its values, and instead returned to Chadd's Ford. Later the family, which has included several other artists spread across three generations, acquired a property in Cushing, Maine, used as a summer residence. Throughout his professional life, Wyeth has oscillated between these two locations, deriving both his inspiration and his subject-matter from them, and has rarely stepped outside.

The term 'realist', applied to Wyeth, conceals more than it reveals. Although some of his work, in its even-handed attention to detail across a composition, is suggestive of realism's 'truth to life' imperatives, elsewhere his brushwork is more aggressive, hosting both impressionist and expressionist tendencies. While much of his best-known, and also best, work consists of either tempera or watercolour landscapes – characteristically broad, open and bare, touched but never dominated by the presence of humanity and its artefacts – he has also produced a volume of portraits, studies of flora and fauna, and rustic domestic still-lifes. His technical flair apart, his primary strength is compositional: Wyeth just knows how to re-invent a conventional rural aspect by reconfiguring both the point of view and, through the altered point of view, the weighting of its components. The root of a tree, or the corner of a boulder, thus becomes the true object, not an incidental, of the scene presented.

All of which is not to say that Wyeth never errs. In two of his most celebrated pictures – *Chill Wind* (1947) and *Christina's World* (1948) – human figures are pointedly exploited to encapsulate a raw romanticism: the reason, perhaps, for their popular appeal, as well as their critical rejection. Elsewhere Wyeth's romanticism is more carefully managed. The landscapes he depicts and the nature he pays homage to are seldom comfortable, either aesthetically or by narrative implication. Reared in the countryside, Wyeth knows the countryside's physical and social treachery, and comments on it in his art. There is, though, an insistence in his work that the bond between humankind and nature is something we abandon at our greater peril. In this he can be seen as a perpetuator of American transcendentalism, as articulated by **Henry David Thoreau** and **Ralph Waldo Emerson**, and also as a kindred spirit of **Walt Whitman**. Or, in his own words: 'I dream a lot. I do more painting when I am not painting.'

To the surprise of many, in 1999 it emerged that Wyeth had, since 1930, been engaged on a series of personalized portraits of black Americans, drawn from a local 'Little Africa' community in Chadd's Ford, some of them nude female work. These were assembled for a touring exhibition that visited Mississippi and other southern cities, where they were welcomed and admired by black art critics. In the most startling of them – *Dryad* – his naked model, Senna Moore, is depicted stepping out of the trunk of a storm-ravaged oak tree, a naturally resplendent figure for whom the politics of race relations is neither here nor there, as, it may be presumed, must also be the case with the artist himself.

In 1963 **John F. Kennedy** presented Wyeth with the Presidential Medal of Freedom, the first time an artist had been so honoured. Twenty-seven years later, in 1990, Congress followed suit, with a Congressional Gold Medal.

Further reading

See: Andrew Wyeth, *Andrew Wyeth: Autobiography* (with Thomas Hoving, 1998); Andrew Wyeth and Betsy James Wyeth, *Andrew Wyeth: Close Friends* (2001). See also: Richard Meryman, *First Impressions: Andrew Wyeth* (1991) and *Andrew Wyeth: A Secret Life* (1998); Anne Knutson *et al.*, *Andrew Wyeth: Memory and Magic* (2005).

SAMANTHA GOAT

Y

YEANG, Ken

1948–

Malaysian architect

Yeang pioneered a radically new climatically responsive architecture for the tropics which was to have a global influence on the debate about an ecologically responsible world architecture and which challenges the very notion of an 'international style'. *The Skyscraper Bioclimatically Considered* (1996) sets out his ideas for a climate-generated architecture and changed our preconceptions of appropriate high-rise building forms for the tropics.

There are two powerful pressures to introduce new building forms: the first is cultural, where an architecture related to the local climate engenders built forms more appropriate to the local way of life; and the second is climatic, where designing to optimize the ambient conditions also leads to low-energy structures.

Yeang revealed that imported Western high-rise building forms are fundamentally unsuited to a tropical climate. It can be argued that International Style Modernism is also ill suited to more temperate zones, but when transported to the tropics, design flaws become more obvious. Yeang's response was the development of the concept of the bioclimatic skyscraper as a more environmentally appropriate model which consumes less energy and also provides a better and more humane environment for its users and establishes a unique cultural identity related to the location. This led to his subsequent theoretical and technical work on ecological design.

Yeang studied architecture at the independent Architectural Association in London (1966–71) where there is a tradition of radical questioning and where international modernism had never been uncritically accepted. At that time there was a trend for departments of tropical studies in architecture to teach the climatic design of low-rise traditional structures rather than acknowledging the aspirations of countries in the tropical zones to also have a modern high-rise aesthetic. But Yeang appreciated the problem while still a student and started on his lifetime quest to develop alternatives and to consider wider environmental issues. Yeang's approach was influenced by **Buckminster Fuller's** ideas on synergy and his global approach to resources and energy, by **Cedric Price** for his ideas on choice and flexibility, by **Archigram** and especially **Peter Cook** for alternative ways of looking at architecture, and by Charles Jenks for his ideas on biomorphic architecture. Yeang's uniquely Asian perspective was encouraged by Kisho Kurokawa in addition to his ideas on biological analogies and on metabolism.

To develop a theoretical methodology Yeang enrolled for a doctorate at Cambridge University (1971–4) where sustainable architecture was a newly established area of research. Yeang's ideas rapidly expanded, influenced by Eugene Odum's work on ecosystems, by **Alfred North Whitehead's** work on the philosophy of the organism, by Ian McHarg's ideas of ecological land-use planning techniques, and by Ludwig von

Bertellanfy's systems theory. Yeang's newly formulated principles were first presented at the 1972 conference of the Royal Institute of British Architecture which took 'Designing for Survival' as its theme, echoing a growing public awareness of the major contribution of construction to environmental problems. The theoretical framework for an ecologically appropriate architecture which Yeang developed at this time underpinned his subsequent architectural practice and was the basis of several of his books, including *The Green Skyscraper* (1999).

He returned in 1974 to his native Malaysia, to form an architectural practice with Tengku Robert Hamzah. He researched the local vernacular and indigenous architecture and published books on the cultural aspirations of Asia: *The Tropical Verandah City* (1986), *Tropical Urban Regionalism* (1987) and *The Architecture of Malaysia (1992)*. He then developed a set of architectural bioclimatic design principles for the bioclimatic high-rise such as the location of the elevator core, the use of transitional spaces, solar orientation and shading, structural massing and vertical landscaping, publishing *Bioclimatic Skyscrapers* (1994) and *Designing with Nature* (1995), which established the initial theoretical bases for an ecologically sound architecture, later developed in *Ecodesign: A Manual for Ecological Design* (2005).

A number of dominant themes and concepts emerge: the integration of vegetation and vertical gardens, the use of sky courts and the influence of solar geometry to achieve self-shading structures. Yeang's practice maintains a strong research and development ethos, entirely funded out of real projects when the budget and enlightened clients allow.

Yeang's status as an innovator and international influence was clearly established by the mid 1990s, and is attested by many honours including the Aga Khan Award (1996) for his IBM Menara Mesiniaga project, the Prinz Claus Fonds Award (1999) for his work on bioclimatic high-rise design, professorships at leading world schools of architecture, and many other awards and international prizes.

Most important is Yeang's influence on others, not just in Asia and the tropics, but also in the West and more northern climes. **Richard Rogers'** Tomigaya Tower and **Norman Foster's** Commerzbank in Frankfurt are major projects cited by Ivor Richards as influenced by Yeang's thinking. And a new generations of students born into a world which is going to have to deal with the problems created by a previous generation of profligate energy design are increasingly learning of Yeang's pioneering work. His work is celebrated in *T.R. Hamzah and Yeang* in the *Master Architect* series (1999), where an introduction by Leon van Schaik demonstrates that in Yeang's vision ecological design need not be a retreating battle of sustainability, but can contribute positively to an ecologically responsible future through energy production.

Further reading

See: Robert Powell, *Ken Yeang: Rethinking the Environmental Filter* (1989) and *Rethinking the Skyscraper: The Complete Works of Ken Yeang* (1999); Ivor Richards, *The Ecology of the Sky* (2001).

JOHN HAMILTON FRAZER

YEATS, Jack (John) Butler

1871–1957

Irish artist and writer

Jack Butler Yeats was the third son of the Irish academic artist and portrait painter John Butler Yeats and brother to the poet **W.B. Yeats**. The wise father once shrewdly prophesied that one day he would be known merely as the father of a great painter. Born in London, but living in childhood with his grandparents in Sligo, a part of Ireland which affected and influenced him profoundly, he moved back to London in his teens and became a successful illustrator for magazines, the *Manchester Guardian* and for various books. A season ticket for Buffalo Bill Cody's Wild West Shows at Earls Court sparked a life-long passion for circuses, horses, fairgrounds, racetracks, etc., particularly once, after a few years in Devon, he established himself in Ireland. With his brother W.B. and his two sisters he was a pillar of the Cuala Press in Dublin created to publish books, broadsheets and broadsides devoted to Irish topics, and he also illustrated prose books by **J.M. Synge**.

His early style, while wholly distinctive, was orthodox (although never academic) and he was a member of the Royal Hibernian Academy. He was indubitably the most successful portrayer of the Irish landscape and character, notably in the paintings he made to illustrate George A. Birmingham's book *Irishmen All*.

He exhibited at the seminal 1913 Armory Show in New York, the first major exhibition in America of new tendencies in European art.

He was, like his brother, a staunch proponent of Irish independence but was never politically active, making his contribution to the cause by his art, including the great protest painting *Bachelor's Walk in Memory of 1915*.

In the mid-1920s he began to alter his style, switching from conventional oil painting to the increased use of impasto while preserving his subject-matter, both rural and urban, in which he depicted people in trams and trains and, notably, theatres whose romance possibly exceeded for him even that of the racetrack and the circus. Gradually the impasto became heavier and heavier and the once-flat colours became richer and brighter, so that at first glance his great painting s of the 1940s and 1950s, shortly before his death, seem abstract. Yet on close scrutiny their outlines are revealed and we see men shouting in celebration, a backstage workshop with a solitary flower in *The Scene Painter's Rose* (as early as 1927), a singer about to begin. We see the semiallegorical works like *In Memory of Boucicault and Bianconi*, a glorious tribute to the travelling theatre troupes of his youth, or *Tinker's Encampment: The Blood of Abel*.

Yeats's later work has much in common with **Oskar Kokoschka**, who knew and greatly admired him. Kenneth Clark once perceptively wrote that: 'Colour is Yeats's element in which he dives and splashes with the shameless abandon of a porpoise.' While, as a writer, he cannot compare with his brother, had he not been so gifted a painter he would certainly have figured more prominently in the annals of Irish literature. His memoir of Sligo is simple, elegiac and beautifully written, and he wrote several novels and plays which explored Irish life with much the same benign searchlight as the drawings, watercolours and oil paintings.

While there is a case to be made for **Francis Bacon** as the leading Irish painter of the twentieth century there is also one to be made for Bacon as a nihilistic explorer of the particular ills of the second half of the century. Yeats is surely the greatest painter in the last century, and possibly ever, of Irish life and character. His prodigious output (some thousands of paintings) provides the unique and wholly seductive vision of some six decades of a now vanished Ireland of horse fairs, travelling circuses, barnstorming actors, sharp lawyers, conniving politicians, grand rooms in mouldering country houses, small boats at sea, horses galloping along deserted beaches, all done with a ferocious energy in which, in the later years, the palette knife and the fingers made almost as powerful a contribution as the brush.

Further reading

See: Hilary Pyle, *A Catalogue Raisonné of the Oil Paintings of Jack B. Yeats* (1992); T.G. Rosenthal, *The Art of Jack B. Yeats* (1993); Bruce Arnold, *Jack Yeats* (1998).

T.G. ROSENTHAL

YEATS, William Butler

1865–1939

Irish poet and dramatist

W.B. Yeats was born on 13 June 1865, the son of the eccentric but highly articulate John Butler Yeats, who in 1867 gave up a rather half-hearted career as a Dublin lawyer to become an art student in London. In 1863 he had married Susan Pollexfen, the eldest daughter of a Sligo mill-owning family of Cornish descent. Though the marriage itself turned out rather unsatisfactory, the union of the charming and gifted Yeats strain with the brooding introspective Pollexfens was, in J.B. Yeats's phrase, to 'give a tongue to the sea-cliffs' and to provide in W.B. Yeats and in his younger brother, **Jack Yeats** the painter, two artists of world repute. It was with the Pollexfens that W.B. Yeats spent a great deal of his youth, and the effect of the dramatic landscape around Sligo, with its visible reminders of the legendary past, combined with the influence of the Pollexfen family, and in particular his uncle George Pollexfen, to arouse his interest in astrology and Irish mythology, and turned the Sligo countryside into the symbolic landscape of his early poetry. Yet, despite the many shortcomings of J.B. Yeats as a father, he gave to his children an example of dedication to art which encouraged them in their own efforts. Like many fathers of men of genius his considerable talent foreshadowed, though it could not discipline itself to attain, the artistic flowering of the next generation.

Certainly Yeats seems to have learnt little in his formal education, first at the Godolphin School, Hammersmith, and later at the High School, Harcourt Street, Dublin, and the Dublin School of Art.

The Yeats family moved back to Ireland in 1880 and remained in and around Dublin until they returned to London in 1887, moving finally into a house in Bedford Park in 1887. It was in 1889 that Yeats's first substantial major poem, *The Wanderings of Oisin*, was published. This year, 1889, was a significant one for him in other ways: it was at this time that he began to frequent writers and artists who were to be his friends and associates in the Rhymers Club in the 1890s, and it was in this year too that he met and fell in love with Maud Gonne, whose total dedication to the cause of Irish independence and powerful, uncompromising nature were to torture and stimulate Yeats to some of his

finest poetry. The year 1896 saw his meeting with another powerful feminine influence on his life, Lady (Augusta) Gregory, who collaborated with him in the collection and publication of Irish folk stories and in his work for the Irish theatre. Both she and **J.M. Synge**, whom he met in the same year, were inspired by him to write plays of Irish life and in 1904 the Abbey Theatre opened under his management. For the next six years he was engrossed in the job of producer and manager of the theatre. In 1917 he bought a ruined tower, Thoor Ballylee, near Coole Park, Lady Gregory's house in Galway, and the same year married Georgie Hyde-Lees. In 1922 he became a Senator of the Irish Free State and in 1923 was awarded the Nobel Prize for Literature. He died on 28 January 1939 at Cap Martin and was buried in Roquebrune. It was not until 1948 that his body was brought back to Ireland to be buried in the churchyard of Drumcliffe, near Sligo ('under bare Ben Bulben's head'), where his grandfather had been rector.

'I had,' wrote Yeats of himself as he was 'at twenty-three or twenty-four', 'three interests, interest in a form of literature, in a form of philosophy and a belief in nationality.' It was then that a 'sentence seemed to form in my mind ... "Hammer your thoughts into unity." These preoccupations remained with him for the rest of his life.

At first sight Yeats is a man of seemingly irreconcilable contradictions. One expects of a major writer opinions and a consistent philosophy, a recognizable standpoint in relation to his subject. Yet Yeats is disconcertingly ambiguous in his attitudes: it is the clash between opinions, the tension engendered by ambiguities, that excites him ('Opinion is not worth a rush'). Where many modern writers, such as **T.S. Eliot**, have resolved their doubts to their own satisfaction by struggling through to a philosophical position which, however subtle and ambiguous, is still a position to which they can give emotional or philosophical assent, Yeats maintains a state of non-commitment. It is the conflict itself that he responds to, the forging of a mythology which can accommodate all opposites ('We make out of the quarrel with others, rhetoric, but of the quarrel with ourselves, poetry'). 'Opinions are accursed' because they harden and embitter the personality, and it is only through the free play of the mind, unfettered by dogma, that the greatness of man can be expressed. It is this ambiguous attitude that characterizes his dealings with, for example, Irish nationalism.

> Have I not seen the loveliest woman born
> Out of the mouth of Plenty's horn,
> Because of her opinionated mind
> Barter that horn and every good
> By quiet natures understood
> For an old bellows full of angry wind?

Perfection of the life and of the work can be attained only by discipline. Thoughts are hammered, not moulded, into unity; the bird on the golden bough can sing of what is past, or passing, or to come because it has itself passed through the purifying fire. The ideal is the dance, the total fusion of body, mind and soul, a Unity of Being symbolized by the whirling movement of the universe, the spinning-off of one spool of life on to the other, the eternal recurrence of the cycles of history.

It is often said that Yeats's 'philosophy' is nothing but elaborate rubbish; but the great purpose of *A Vision* (1937) is to create a myth that can be believed and disbelieved simultaneously. The truth of *A Vision* is an entirely symbolic truth: it is certainly not the truth of philosophy, and not even the truth of religion as it is commonly held by believers. When the so-called 'instructors' appeared 'on the afternoon of October 24th 1917' in response to Mrs Yeats's attempts at automatic writing, they produced such disjointed sentences that Yeats offered to dedicate his life to piecing together their jumbled message. 'No,' was the answer, 'we have come to give you metaphors for poetry.' Poetry for Yeats, as for **Mallarmé**, and others before him, held the key to existence itself. To give metaphors for poetry was to provide a 'supreme fiction' – supreme *because* fictional.

Some will ask whether I believe in the actual existence of my circuits of sun and moon ... To such a question I can but answer that if sometimes, overwhelmed by miracle as all men must be when in the midst of it, I have taken such periods literally, my reason has soon recovered ... They have helped me to hold in a single thought reality and justice.

As with **Baudelaire**, all Yeats touched he turned into symbol: Ireland, Byzantium, Maud Gonne, the Easter Rising, the Tower, religion, history, magic are all part of the great dance:

> So the Platonic Year
> Whirls out new right and wrong,
> Whirls in the old instead;
> All men are dancers and their tread
> Goes to the barbarous clangour of a gong.

'The fascination of what's difficult', the unending search for a harder and more 'hammered' style, developed partly at the instigation of **Ezra Pound**, leads not only to the stark power of Yeats's last poems, but to the 'wild old wicked man' which was the mask which the sensitive youth of the 1890s had by the end of his life assumed, if only perhaps as another 'metaphor for poetry'. His life and his art became increasingly inseparable and both aimed at a powerful, unsentimental vision of things. As the vision of an Ireland that could in reality rival the imagined unity of being, represented to him by the image of Byzantium, receded from his mind, so the ideal country of the imagination became more significant.

Yeats thought of himself and his generation as the 'last Romantics', their theme tradition, their ideal community one in which craftsmanship and artistic creation could flourish, a state without politics; but 'Romantic Ireland' was for Yeats 'dead and gone'; modern society belongs to the politicians. Only in art can man move into a higher reality; only there is it possible that 'things can and cannot be'. Yet for all its rejection of the 'filthy modern tide', for all its prophecies of doom,

Yeats's poetry is not ultimately pessimistic. By its firm grasp of the reality of the imagination it has achieved and teaches serenity and freedom.

Since the publication of the *Collected Poems* in 1950 Yeats has found an ever larger audience. Not only has his poetry been increasingly admired, but his prose and his plays – particularly his plays for dancers – have been much more commonly read and acted. Yeats's plays are notable for their very successful use of poetic language in the theatre and for their perhaps rather unexpected power when well performed, but it is in his lyric poetry that he writes with full conviction and mastery, and it is as the writer of some of the finest poems in the language that his work seems certain to survive changes of literary fashion.

Further reading

Other works include: *Collected Plays* (1952); *Autobiographies* (1956); *Mythologies* (1959); *Essays and Introductions* (1961); *Explorations* (1962); *Memoirs* (1972). See also: *Letters from W.B. Yeats to Dorothy Wellesley* (1940); *The Senate Speeches of W.B. Yeats*, ed. Donald Pearce (1961). The standard biographies are Joseph Hone, *W.B. Yeats 1865–1939* (1942) and R.F. Foster, *W.B. Yeats: A Life* (2 vols, 1997–2003). See: Louis MacNeice, *The Poetry of W.B. Yeats* (1941); Peter Ure, *Yeats the Playwright* (1963); Richard Ellmann, *Yeats: The Man and the Masks* (1949) and *The Identity of Yeats* (1954); Norman Jeffares, *W.B. Yeats, Man and Poet* (1949); John Unterecker, *A Reader's Guide to W.B. Yeats* (1959); A.G. Stock, *W.B. Yeats, His Poetry and Thought* (1961); Denis Donoghue, *Yeats* (1971); Frank Tuohy, *Yeats* (1976); Brenda Maddox, *George's Ghosts: A New Life of W.B. Yeats* (1999).

JOSEPH BAIN

YEVTUSHENKO, Yevgeny Aleksandrovich

1933–

Russian writer

Yevtushenko was born in Zima (literally 'Winter'), a remote settlement on the Trans-Siberian railway, and brought up partly there, partly in Moscow. His surname is that of his mother's family, peasants who were originally exiled to Siberia from the Ukraine after an insurrection; his father by contrast was a Latvian and an intellectual. It would not be too fanciful to find these contrasts in his origins and upbringing reflected in a dichotomy in his personality between the simple and the sophisticated, in his work between the public and the private, the international and the provincially Russian.

He was a precocious versifier, publishing a volume as early as 1949 (*Prospectors of the Future*); *Third Snow* (1955) and particularly the long autobiographical poem *Stantsiya Zima* (trans. as *Zima Junction*, 1956) mark the maturing of his talent. His publications deflected him from his early intention of becoming a professional footballer, and he attended the Moscow Literary Institute (unruly as ever, he was expelled without graduating). Tremendous popular success began to come his way from the mid-1950s, the period of Soviet 'de-**Stalinization'**: it is hard to say whether it was the more intimate aspect of his work, with its fresh spontaneity, or his public voice, touching on the traumas of politics and history (both his grandfathers had disappeared in the Great Terror), that stirred the greater resonances in his contemporaries. It soon became evident that Soviet officialdom had no consistent way of reacting to a loyal subject with a sharply questioning approach, an unquenchable inclination to expand the bounds of the permissible in literature and a wide popular reputation (from *c.* 1962 in the West as well). Nikita Khrushchev, while calling him 'ungovernable', evidently came to respect him: he was never prevented from publishing, though sometimes hampered or censored, and travelled insatiably.

The high point of Yevtushenko's poetic career was doubtless the publication of *Babiy Yar* (1961), a powerfully emotional response to anti-Semitism, and its subsequent incorporation into **Shostakovich's** Thirteenth Symphony (with four other poems of his – a cumulative portrait of the mood of the times). During the Brezhnev 'era of stagnation', however, 'loyal oppositionist' writers were sidelined with the rise of out-and-out dissidents and *samizdat*. Yevtushenko's poetry continued to sell in huge editions, but its impact diminished and his restless talent was anyhow seeking other outlets (including films). Prose took a growing place in his work: two well-crafted novels *Berry Places* (1982) and *Don't Die Before You're Dead* (1995) are intimately connected with their times. His nearest approach to memoirs since his *Precocious Autobiography* (1965) has been *Marked Papers* (*Volchiy pasport*, 1988), full of beguiling anecdotes – a talent for anecdotalism, in a broad sense, has been one of his prime strengths.

With *perestroika* and the end of the Soviet Union he again came to occupy a prominent public position: member of parliament 1988–91, associated with several good causes (e.g. ameliorating the inferior position of Soviet women, countering the ecological threat to Lake Baykal). But though he kept one foot in Russia, the other was planted in the American mid-west, where he found he could earn a living by college teaching. Russian literature was never far from his attentions: he edited a huge anthology of Russian poetry, much of it little known, first in Russian, then in English. He was awarded various honours, but turned down the Order of Friendship in protest against the suppression of Chechnya.

What of the work itself? The image of the 'Soviet Angry Young Man' dies hard; it was never very appropriate, and long ago became ridiculous. What Yevtushenko developed early and retains is a voice particularly his own: 'voice' is no mere metaphor, since his work is characteristically rhetorical (presupposing a listener, showing, persuading), and in fact gains much from oral delivery – witness the remarkable phenomenon of the mass poetry-readings of the early 1960s. His rhetoric is most successful not when grandiloquent, rather (herein lies its originality) when 'conversational', a confiding dialogue on neither too highbrow nor too simple a level. When his work is reproached – not

unreasonably – for looseness of texture or lack of intellectual polish we should remember that the features occasioning complaint are also integral to his particular talents. He is not naive, however: despite weak moments (usually in the longer poems) he shows a professional's mastery of verbal wit, rhyme, varied diction and dramatic construction.

Controversy attended Yevtushenko to an extent surely unmatched by any poet of the Soviet era. Despite, or because of, his popularity he has been subject to a battery of attacks – literary, moral, political, from a wide variety of standpoints – that vary from the reasoned, to the malicious, to the unanswerable. Through them he has steered a steady course: enjoying life, relishing fame but not being besotted by it, refusing to let anyone twist his arm too far. Though often represented, in the East as in the West, as feather-headedly changeable, he was perfectly consistent in his stance of 'independently minded loyalist' (condemning, for example, the events of 1968 or the expulsion of **Solzhenitsyn** while refusing to become a 'dissident'). His work too has shown a consistency that makes the best of it look more substantial and durable than the often fugitive occasions that sparked it off might have led one to suppose.

Yevtushenko and his close colleagues performed an important service when they restored to post-Stalin Russia a sense of artistic community and purpose, a renewed consciousness both of national cultural pride and of belonging to the whole community of modern nations. The movement in English poetry of the 1960s towards popular accessibility and oral effectiveness owed a large debt to him (*Babiy Yar* was *the* poem of the decade, if there was one). His open-heartedness, appreciativeness towards others' achievements, and lack of spite have set a worthwhile example (especially when combined with his sharp and wily intelligence). But above all he has given back respectability to the political dimension of poetry: not in the narrow sense (his humanitarian ethic hardly represents a political programme) but more fundamentally –

in an awareness that a generation articulates its concerns through poetry, that literature stands at the crossroads of the public and the private.

Further reading

Other works include: *Selected Poems*, trans. R. Milner-Gulland and P. Levi (1962); and *The Face behind the Face*, trans. A. Boyars and S. Franklin (1979). Novels: *Wild Berries* (trans. A.W. Bouis, 1984); *Don't Die Before You're Dead* (trans. A.W. Bouis, 1995). Edited anthology: *Twentieth Century Russian Poetry* (trans. M. Haywood *et al.*, 1993). Yevtushenko's own *Precocious Autobiography* (1963, unpublished in USSR) gives a memorable account of his formative years. See: Robin Milner-Gulland in G.W. Simmonds (ed.) *Soviet Leaders* (1967); P. Blake, 'New Voices in Russian Writing', *Encounter* (April 1963); and P. Johnson, *Khrushchev and the Arts* (1965).

ROBIN MILNER-GULLAND

YOSHIHARA JIRO

1905–72

Japanese artist

Jiro Yoshihara was born in Osaka, to Ai and Teijiro Yoshihara, the owner of an edible oil company. Heir to the family company, Yoshihara had tremendous resources at his disposal throughout his career, but was prevented from seriously pursuing an art education due to family expectations that he would one day become company president. Despite juggling his artistic career with business responsibilities, Yoshihara was a dedicated young artist and showed prolifically. Unlike other ambitious artists of his generation, Yoshihara did not study in France (despite encouragement from the Paris-based artist Tsuguharu (Léonard) Fujita), but learned what he could of the European avant-garde from his large collection of foreign and domestic books and magazines. His earliest work focused on **Cézanne**-influenced still-lifes, but by the 1930s Yoshihara had begun painting in the Surrealist-influenced abstract style for which he became known before the Second World War.

Yoshihara was excused military service because of tuberculosis. He spent the war years quietly, mostly painting still-lifes and portraits. At the end of the Second World War he emerged as an active figure in the art world, organizing members of several artists' associations, writing art criticism, and painting. In 1951, Yoshihara and other leaders of the art world in western Japan founded Genbi (Contemporary Art Discussion Group), a forum for young artists interested in articulating an artistic identity that was both modern and Japanese, bringing together a diverse group of practitioners from calligraphers to potters. Through his art criticism and such paintings as *Origins* (1952), which experimented with calligraphic brush-strokes in dialogue with Lyric Abstraction, Yoshihara took a leadership role in the immediate post-war quest to syncretize tradition and modernity.

In 1954, Yoshihara formed the Gutai group, whose name means concreteness or embodiment. No longer seeking simply to fuse tradition with modernity, Yoshihara pushed the Gutai artists to create something entirely new and to rethink the definition of painting by organizing innovative exhibitions that took art outside the museum or gallery space. In 1955, he organized his first outdoor exhibition, the *Experimental Outdoor Exhibition of Modern Art to Challenge the Mid-Summer Sun*, which was installed in a pine grove on the banks of the Ashiya river. The site dwarfed traditional works of art, forcing artists to create works that were site-specific. Drawing on his interest in the theatre, for which he began designing stage sets in 1949, Yoshihara also organized the *Gutai Art on Stage* exhibitions, which compelled artists to engage with time in the same way that the *Outdoor* exhibitions encouraged artists to confront the exhibition space. In 1965, Allan Kaprow published photographs of Gutai activities in the book *Assemblages, Environments and Happenings* as precursors of his own work.

How Kaprow learned of the Gutai's activities reveals another of Yoshihara's insights. An avid collector of magazines, who kept abreast of foreign artistic developments through his subscriptions, Yoshihara saw the post-war art world as an international community connected by art magazines, which functioned as its stage. From the very inception of Gutai, Yoshihara's priority was to publish the paintings, performances and installations that the group created in the *Gutai* journal, which he then sent to prominent figures in the international art world. Issues 2 and 3 were found in **Jackson Pollock's** studio. It was through these journals that the French critic Michel Tapié learned of the Gutai group in 1957, beginning a decade-long association that resulted in exhibitions of the Gutai internationally. In 1962, Yoshihara built the Gutai Pinacotheca, which gave the Gutai an architectural and institutional presence internationally.

Although his main contribution was as a visionary and leader, Yoshihara's artistic career was highly distinguished and recognized both domestically and internationally. Yoshihara painted throughout his life, even while busy as the Gutai group's international advocate. In 1962, he began painting the well-known circle series, inspired by Zen painting, which he pursued until his death in 1972.

Further reading

See: *Yoshihara Jiro-ten* ('Yoshihara Jiro Exhibition'), an exhibition catalogue published by the Ashiya City Museum of Art and History (1992).

MING TIAMPO

Z

ZAMYATIN, Yevgeniy Ivanovich

1884–1937

Russian writer

Born into a middle-class background in Lebedyan', Tambov Province, Zamyatin attended the *gimnaziya* at Voronezh and then the Polytechnic Institute at St Petersburg, training as a naval architect. He graduated, despite imprisonment and exile for revolutionary activities on behalf of the Bolsheviks, travelled widely in connection with his work, and published his first short story in 1908. Best known of his early works was *A Provincial Tale* (*Uyezdnoye*, 1913). He continued his dual professions of naval engineering and literature up to 1931, with his mathematical training frequently influencing his literary work. In 1916–17 Zamyatin spent eighteen months in England, supervising the building of ice-breakers at Newcastle-upon-Tyne, and presenting a caustic picture of English life in his stories *The Islanders* (*Ostrovityane*, 1918, trans. 1978) and *A Fisher of Men* (*Lovets chelovekov*, 1922, trans. 1977). Returning to Russia just before the October Revolution, Zamyatin proceeded to question the direction of the revolution, and the future for literature under it, in a series of pungent stories and essays. His futuristic novel *We* (*My*, written 1920, published in English, New York 1924, and in Russian, New York 1952) was denounced as 'a malicious pamphlet on the Soviet government' and was never published in the Soviet Union. Under increasing attack as an 'inner émigré', culminating in the 'Pil'nyak-Zamyatin affair' of 1929, Zamyatin requested of **Stalin**, and was surprisingly granted, permission to emigrate. He settled in Paris in 1931 and died in poverty in 1937, leaving an unfinished novel on the Roman Empire and Attila the Hun, the subject of an earlier play.

We, Zamyatin's only completed novel, depicts an apparently unsuccessful uprising against a totalitarian, glass-enclosed city-state of the distant future. Built on extreme mathematical and collectivist principles, 'The Singe State', having reduced its populace to 'numbers', determines to eradicate all remaining individuality by imposing an operation of 'fantasiectomy', to remove the imagination. *We* is notable for its linguistic and stylistic innovation, combining grotesque and primitivist elements with striking systems of imagery, as well as being a statement of Zamyatin's main philosophical preoccupations: the role of the heretic in the progression of human affairs, the necessity for an endless series of revolutions to combat the stagnation and philistinism of each successive status quo, and the cosmic struggle between energy and entropy. Influenced in its anti-utopianism and promotion of the irrational by **Dostoevsky** (*The Devils* and *The Notes from Underground*), and in its depiction of the future by **H.G. Wells**, *We* can be interpreted as a prophetic warning against tyranny, a work of science fiction in advance of its time, and a penetrating study of alienation and schizophrenia. Its plot and futuristic detail have been assumed, probably erroneously, to have influenced **Huxley's** *Brave New World* (1932), but had an acknowledged impact on **Orwell's** *1984* (1949). Parallels can also be drawn with near-contemporary works by **Karel Čapek**, and Georg Kaiser, and with **Fritz Lang's** film *Metropolis*.

An experimental prose writer and originator of the literary style of 'neo-realism', seen as a dialectical synthesis of Symbolism and Naturalism, Zamyatin was a leading figure of Russian modernism and an important influence on the prose of the 1920s, yet was far better known in the West than in the Soviet Union, where, unlike most of his disgraced contemporaries, he remained totally unpublished and rarely discussed.

Further reading

See: *A Soviet Heretic: Essays by Yevgeny Zamyatin* (1970); *The Dragon and Other Stories* (1975); *Mamay*, trans. Neil Cornwell, *Stand*, Vol. 17, No. 4 (1976). About Zamyatin: Alex M. Shane, *The Life and Works of Evgenij Zamjatin* (1968); Christopher Collins, *Evgenij Zamjatin, An Interpretative Study* (1973); E.J. Brown, *'Brave New World', '1984' and 'We': An Essay on Anti-Utopia* (1976); Gary Kern (ed.) *Zamyatin's 'We': A Collection of Critical Essays* (1998); Brett Cooke, *Human Nature in Utopia: Zamyatin's 'We'* (2002).

NEIL CORNWELL

ZAWAHIRI, Ayman (Abu MUHAMMAD/ Muhammad IBRAHIM)

1950–

Egyptian Islamist

Son of a pharmacology professor at Cairo University, and grandson of Rabiaa Zawahiri, the Grand Shaikh of Al Azhar University, Ayman Zawahiri graduated as a surgeon from Cairo University's medical school in 1978. He was one of the founders of Al Jihad al Islami, a clandestine, radical Islamist organization formed in 1974 – when he was still a medical student – and led by Ismail Tantawi. It was so secret that the Egyptian authorities discovered its existence only during the Muslim–Christian riots in 1978. After

Tantawi's departure for West Germany, Zawahiri became Al Jihad's leader.

Al Jihad focused on recruiting middle-class students and young professionals in large cities, and infiltrating the military, other security forces, and intelligence agencies, believing that only they collectively could overthrow the secular system that prevailed in the country. Its leading tactic was to assassinate high-profile officials to illustrate the weakness of the existing social system.

Following the assassination of Egyptian President Muhammad Anwar Sadat in October 1981 by Al Jihad activists, Zawahiri was jailed for three years for participating in the assassination plot. Following his release, he quietly revived Al Jihad, which issued its first manifesto, 'The Philosophy of Confrontation', the combined work of several imprisoned Al Jihad militants. Borrowing heavily from the writings of **Sayyid Muhammad Qutb**, it refined his ideas. It urged those Muslims who wanted to revive the Islamic *umma* (worldwide Muslim community) to wage a *jihad* against the infidel state, the only acceptable form of *jihad* being armed struggle. Al Jihad's funding came primarily from the members donating 10 per cent of their salaries.

In 1986 Zawahiri travelled to Saudi Arabia and then to Pakistan. There, he joined the medical corps in Peshawar to serve the Islamist *mujahedin*, both Afghan and non-Afghan, fighting the Soviets and the Soviet-backed regime in Afghanistan. He established a branch of Al Jihad in Peshawar as well as a monthly magazine, *Al Ghazu* ('The Conquest'). He met **Osama bin Laden** and worked with him. Al Jihad members translated US army and Marines manuals and topographical maps into Arabic for use at the training camps in Pakistan run by the Pakistani Inter-Services Intelligence (ISI) and supervised by the US Central Intelligence Agency (CIA).

Zawahiri and bin Laden regarded the withdrawal of the Soviet from Afghanistan in 1989 as a victory for the *jihad* mounted by pious Muslims worldwide, ignoring the vital role the United States and the CIA had played – financially, militarily, diplomatically and intelligence-wise – in bringing about the Soviet pull-out.

In the early 1990s, Zawahiri sought and received asylum in Switzerland. With the return home of many Al Jihad members from Afghanistan after the fall of the leftist regime of Muhammad Najibullah in April 1992, the organization revived in Egypt. It targeted high officials, such as ministers, but its two assassination attempts in 1993 failed.

In 1994, soon after an exiled bin Laden made Khartoum, Sudan, his base, Zawahiri left Switzerland to join him. When, in November 1995, the truck bombing of the Egyptian embassy in Islamabad left eighteen dead, the Egyptian government blamed Zawahiri.

By now Zawahiri had become the mentor of bin Laden, whose earlier intellectual guru, Muhammad Azzam, a Palestinian Islamist ideologue, had been assassinated in Pakistan in late 1989.

In 1997, Zawahiri moved to Afghanistan to join bin Laden there. In February 1998, Al Jihad, led by Zawahiri, merged with the Al Qaida network of bin Laden as a prelude to forming the World Islamic Front for Jihad against Crusaders and Jews, with Al Jihad members concentrating on forging documents, transferring money and arranging communications, and Zawahiri emerging as the Front's principal ideologue.

Zawhiri's thesis, adopted by bin Laden, was that attacks undertaken by their followers would force America and its allies to change their policies in the Middle East, and that would fulfil the ultimate objectives of the World Islamic Front for Jihad of establishing fundamentalist regimes in all Muslim-majority countries and recreating the Islamic *umma* under the caliph, and demonstrate the weakness of present Arab and Muslim leaders.

On 4 November 1998 a US federal grand jury returned a 238-count indictment – covering 227 murders caused by the bombings of the American embassies in Nairobi and Dar es Salaam in August 1998 and eleven other charges – against bin Laden and sixteen others, including Zawahiri, and charging them with leading a terrorist conspiracy from 1989 to the present, working in concert with other terrorist to build weapons and attack American military installations.

Following the terrorist attacks on high-profile targets in New York and Washington on 11 September 2001, Zawahiri was named as one of the leading conspirators. He was sitting next to bin Laden when the latter broadcast a twenty-minute statement on Al Jazeera Television on 7 October 2001 after the US started bombing Afghanistan.

In December 2001, Zawahiri and bin Laden, along with several hundred armed fighters, escaped into Pakistan's tribal areas adjacent to the Afghan border. Since then he has issued taped messages which have been broadcast by Al Jazeera and other Arabic satellite television channels.

Further reading

See: Peter L. Bergen, *Holy Wars Inc.: Inside the Secret World of Osama bin Laden* (2001); Dilip Hiro, *War Without End: The Rise of Islamist Terrorism and Global Response,* (2002); Jason Burke, *Al-Qaeda: Casting a Shadow of Terror,* (2003); Montasser Al Zayyat, *The Road to Al-Qaeda: The Story of Bin Laden's Right-Hand Man* (trans. Sara Nimis and Ahmed Fekri, 2004).

DILIP HIRO

ZOLA, Émile
1840–1902
French novelist

Zola was a naturalized French citizen, his family origins being Italian on the side of his father, who left his native Venice in 1821 eventually to set up practice as a civil engineer in Marseilles. The future novelist was born in Paris and spent his working career there, but his attachment to the sunlit landscapes of his childhood in Provence contributes to the sense in his writing of the power and beauty of nature behind the artifices and constraints of urban and industrialized society. Equally, the combination of being a first-generation immigrant, of reported persecution at school and of poverty brought on the family by the death, in 1847, of the energetic Francesco Zola, seems to have left the only child with feelings of insecurity and an intense desire to succeed which are translated into his whole approach to novel writing and into the values contained in his major novel series, *Les Rougon-Macquart* (1871–93).

Zola's early novels, of which the best known are *Claude's Confession* (*La Confession de Claude* 1865, trans. 1888), *Thérèse Raquin* (1867, trans. 1962) and *Madeleine Férat* (1868, trans. 1957), reveal a characteristic preoccupation with sexual guilt and a taste for melodrama, though here can also be discerned the radical conception of the individual as a complex of physiological forces which will find complete expression in the *Rougon-Macquart* volumes of the next two decades. In the 1868 preface to the second edition of *Thérèse Raquin*, Zola shows that he is aware of the dangers of oversimplification inherent in the confined scale of his first attempts at fiction and, in the broad canvases and massed characters of novels such as *Germinal* (1885, trans. 1954) and *Earth* (*La Terre*, 1887, trans. 1954), he will develop a literary form more appropriate to his dramatic social vision. Concerned to give a philosophical framework to his art, the novelist is drawn, during the 1860s, to contemporary work in physiology and biology, absorbing the general spirit of **Darwinian** evolutionary thought and the emphasis accorded by the positivist movement to the methods and achievements of science. After consulting, among other writings, Michelet's essays on women (*La Femme, L'Amour*), the study of Prosper Lucas on heredity (*Traité de l'hérédité naturelle*) and **Taine's** work on the influence of cultural and environmental factors on societies (*Introduction à l'histoire de la littérature anglaise*), Zola prepares, during the period 1868–9, a plan for his *Rougon-Macquart* series which is conceived as a natural and social history of a family under the Second Empire, subjected to the determinants of descent and the impact of the contemporary social and physical milieu.

Appreciation of Zola's novels was, for many years, clouded by legend and misunderstanding. What was seen as his gratuitous delight in the sordid and brutal side of life became a source of constant controversy, from brushes with the public prosecutor over his early books to the famous *Manifeste des cinq* ('The Manifesto of Five'), a public statement of protest made in 1887 by a group of young writers against the admittedly earthy *La Terre*. The novels of the series which deal with the problems of the working class, particularly *L'Assommoir* (1877, trans. 1970) and *Germinal*, were seized upon as political commentaries by those who chose to find in Zola's portrait of the proletariat a condemnation of the prevailing social order or who, alternatively, detected a patronizing and unfeeling demonstration to a middle-class reading public of the bestiality of the lower orders. A whole group of religiously inspired or disenchanted writers, among them Brunetière, **Huysmans**, Vogüé, would help to typecast Zola as the representative of a pessimistic and crudely materialist view of man as part of their call for a morally or spiritually uplifting literature as the century came to a close. A more enduring critical viewpoint, however, is that which challenges Zola's consistency in the theory and practice of literary Naturalism, particularly when the lyrical passages to be found in many of his novels and their barely concealed mythopoeic substructure are set against the claims made in such theoretical essays as *The Experimental Novel* (*Le Roman expérimental*, 1880) that his fiction is modelled on the procedures of experimental science. The case that Zola is at heart a romantic poet posing as a writer of sobriety and detachment appears easily substantiated when readers are confronted with descriptions such as those of 'Le Paradou', the exotic garden in *The Abbé Mouret's Sin* (*La Faute de l'abbé Mouret*, 1875, trans. 1957), or in *The Beast in Man* (*La Bête humaine*, 1890, trans. 1958) of the railway engine *Lison*, with a personality of its own. The strong impression of unity offered by the series, as well as by individual novels, nevertheless belies the presumption of an incoherent aesthetic or a novelist of incongruous objectives.

It is notably misleading to think of Zola's social vision as primarily political or economic; nor, despite the context given to the *Rougon-Macquart* series, should it be thought of as authentically historical. A superficial chronological framework locates the events of the series between the coup d'état of 1851 and the fall of the Second Empire in 1870, but an element of anachronism is apparent, lending to the early books in the series such as *The Kill* (*La Curée*, 1872, trans. 1895) the immediate atmosphere of a society in decay and to the later ones, including the war novel *The Debacle* (*La Débâcle*, 1892, trans. 1972), a mood of optimism and regenerative hope. It is sometimes held that this change of tone may be related to Zola's liaison, after eighteen years of childless marriage, with Jeanne Rozerot, a mistress some twenty-seven years his junior, and the birth (1889) of the first of two children by her. Beyond this, however, Zola's whole conception of time, in contrast with the linear historical perspective on the present to be found in Balzac's *Comédie humaine*, is both evolutionary and cyclical in that it is governed by the rhythms of all-powerful nature – for Zola the ultimate reality and force in the universe. While developing towards perfection, men and societies are conceived as subject to the seasonal flux of plant and animal life, so that the period of the Second Empire assumes the character of a phase of sickness or sterility, eventually emerging from the blood-letting of the 1870 war into new or potential fruitfulness. The constant ambivalence of a novel series which opens in an ancient graveyard (*La Fortune des Rougon*, 1871, translated as *The Fortune of the Rougons*, 1898) and ends in a celebration of the birth of a child (*Le Docteur Pascal*, 1893, translated as *Doctor Pascal*, 1957) is found in the idea that life and death are eternally interdependent. The intervening books of the series reinforce the correspondence between the ebb and flow of the natural cycle and that of human moral and social behaviour, a link which Zola, following Michelet,

sees most clearly manifest in the biological cycle of woman, alternating between the destructively barren and the redemptively fertile. In Naturalism, instead of the environment of woman being man, the environment of man is woman, elevated through her association with the maternal deity, nature, to a representative of the space of man's world and a metaphor of human existence. For the individual, as for the microscopic seed, life is experienced as an arena of bewildering uncertainty, a vast uterine system, as suggested by the reiterated image of the labyrinth, whether formed by the vaults and avenues of the Paris market in *Savage Paris* (*Le Ventre de Paris*, 1873, trans. 1955), the 'terrible machine' of the department store in *Ladies' Delight* (*Au bonheur des dames*, 1883, trans. 1957) or, more obviously, the mine of *Germinal* with its endless passages and tunnels. Subject to nature's own experimental plan, humanity is faced with the uncompromising test of its capacity to fulfil a purpose which is unknown, apart from the characteristics revealed by nature herself. Energy, dynamism and fertility thus become the necessary qualities for evolutionary success by contrast with those which bring deceptive reward in an abortive society: sloth, self-indulgence, infertile lust. This stoical but fundamentally positive code of values is clearly very close to that adopted by the novelist in his personal cult of effort and self-discipline and one which, subordinating the struggles of politics and class to the spontaneous selection of the life force, is reflected in Étienne Lantier, still driving forward at the end of *Germinal*, as much as it is absent in his mother, the generous but passive and backward-looking Gervaise of *L'Assommoir*. Determinism vies with determination in Zola's thought. The thread of hereditary patterning connecting the members of his fictional family also represents for him the icy grip of the past, always threatening progress and natural fulfilment.

The philosophical vision behind Zola's Naturalism, embracing the individual, society and organic nature in a single whole, governs rather than is dictated by the mimetic considerations of his art. While Naturalism clearly derives many of its formal techniques from existing realism, Zola's literary theories and working notes tend to focus less on the problems of mimesis as an end in itself and to emphasize the importance of balance, logic and coherence as the instruments of a necessary verisimilitude. As his cycle of twenty books, each dealing with a separate social organ, may suggest, the novelist sets out to portray an integrated world, the validity of the picture being found in the whole rather than the individual constituents, in the combination of features which may appear in themselves distorted or exaggerated. Beginning with his boyhood friendship with **Cézanne**, who provided the inspiration for his novel *The Masterpiece* (*L'Oeuvre*, 1886, trans. 1950), Zola showed a keen interest in contemporary painting and particularly the work of the Impressionists. What Naturalism and Impressionism have most in common is that both represent a departure from academic realism in positing a phenomenological relationship between artist and subject, allowing eye or imagination to compose the perceived elements into a synthesis which is the sum of imprecise detail. 'We are all of us liars, more or less,' wrote Zola in an important letter of 1885 to his friend Céard, 'but what is the mechanism and the spirit of that falsehood? ... I consider my lies to be directed towards the truth.' It is here that the much questioned analogy with experimental procedures begins to have its meaning: even if, in *The Experimental Novel*, Zola can justly be accused of neglecting the specifically literary qualities of fiction in relation to science and its methods, the experimental is a definition of man's and the novelist's relationship to an enigmatic universe, forever seeking to advance, through trial and error, towards clarification and understanding.

It was perhaps as a natural conclusion to the inquiring stance of *Les Rougon-Macquart* that Zola should devote the last years of his life to writing novels concerned with advancing social solutions. Many of the values of these late works can be traced retrospectively to the twenty-volume series, but with a corresponding loss of literary and dramatic power as explicit statement and blatant moralizing replace the conflicts and suggestive imagery of the classic texts. The trilogy *Les Trois Villes* ('The Three Cities': *Lourdes*, 1894; *Rome*, 1896; *Paris*, 1898) represents Zola's affirmation of faith in scientific rationalism in the face of the mounting tide of contemporary religious reaction, the unfinished tetralogy *Les Quatre Évangiles* ('The Four Gospels': *Fécondité*, 1899; *Travail*, 1901; *Vérité*, 1903) the elaboration of his utopian vision of reform through prolific family life, the brotherhood of labour and enlightened education.

If such works have interest for the modern reader, it lies, as F.W.J. Hemmings suggests, in what they record of the prevailing social and intellectual climate at the turn of the century. It was this same climate which gave the novelist his final claim to public attention when in January 1898 under the title 'J'accuse', the editor of the newspaper *L'Aurore* published Zola's famous open letter to the president of the republic on the subject of the Dreyfus Affair. In an outburst of anger which was as uncharacteristic as the personal courage entailed was familiar, Zola denounced the conduct of the court-martial which, by acquitting Esterhazy of espionage in the face of all the evidence, served to confirm the trumped-up charge levelled four years before against the Jewish Captain Dreyfus. Zola himself was faced with a libel suit and forced to spend an uncomfortable year's exile in England to escape a prison sentence. He died in Paris in September 1902, poisoned by the fumes from a coal fire. The circumstances were judged accidental but, in view of his support for Dreyfus in a period of nationalist and anti-Semitic fervour, these have never been entirely free of suspicion.

Further reading

Other works include: *Oeuvres complètes*, ed. H. Mitterand (1966–9); *Les Rougon-Macquart*, ed. H. Mitterand (1960–7). Standard modern translations are referred to above. See also *Nana*, (trans. 1972) and *Zest for Life* (*La Joie de vivre*, trans. 1955). See: Angus Wilson, *Émile Zola: An Introductory Study of His Novels* (1952); E.M. Grant, *Émile Zola* (1966); F.W.J. Hemmings, *Émile Zola* (1966) and *The Life and Times of Émile Zola* (1977); P. Walker, *Émile Zola* (1968); G. King, *Garden of Zola* (1978); J.C. Lapp, *Zola before the 'Rougon-Macquart'* (1964); Joanna Richardson, *Zola* (1978); Frederick Brown, *Zola: A Life* (1995).

DAVID LEE

ZWEIG, Stefan

1881–1942

Austrian writer

One of the first writers to employ psycho-analytic concepts in literature, Zweig was born into an affluent upper-middle-class Austro-Jewish family of mill owners. From an early age he showed intellectual pre-cociousness but he was always introspective, fatalistic and without humour. He graduated from the Vienna *Gymnasium* into the university in 1899, but refused to apply himself as a protest against the narrow and rigid way of life in Austria. He sought 'Freedom' (his keyword) and found it in Berlin in 1901. His first collection of verse had been published in 1900 (*Silver Strings*, *Silberne Saiten*) and he was already sought after by editors of journals in Berlin and Vienna. Zweig went to Berlin University for a single term and spent most of his time there among the *Bierkeller* 'intellec-tuals'; it was here that he was overcome by hearing **Dostoevsky** read aloud. Although he loathed violence, Zweig was at one with the Russian's concern for human guilt and its expiation, for suffering and anguish of the soul. Zweig was beginning to live this (very Jewish) mental self-torture.

In his desire to improve his intellect so that he might meet and exchange views with the great writers and thinkers of the time, Zweig returned home and obtained his PhD in Vienna in 1904. He had already met the Belgian poet Emile Verhaeren, whose influ-ence for compassion Zweig eagerly absorbed; and he was already at work on translations of

Verhaeren into German – work full of ambi-tious and idealistic plans for establishing human love and friendship in a pan-Eur-opean community. Zweig became Verhae-ren's disciple, and with his own money was able to travel from country to country as he wished. He met **Romain Rolland**, Léon Bazalgette, **Rainer Maria Rilke**, **Auguste Rodin** and (later) **Sigmund Freud**. Until 1910, Zweig luxuriated in intellectual rapport with these men and found himself attached to most of them by an emotional longing. He was now fluent in four or five European lan-guages, and Paris became his second home. His visit to India in 1910, to meet **Tagore**, brought him into contact with real poverty and, disgusted, he returned hastily to Europe.

Zweig's biographies attracted great atten-tion in these early days of psychoanalysis for, as Zweig once stated, 'My main interest in writing has always been the psychological representation of personalities and their lives.' His novel, *Beware of Pity* (1939), was a best-seller and a film was made; but his female characters are especially untrue, for they are created and seen from a man's point of view. His 'critical biographies' also seemed authen-tic at the time, but they may now be con-sidered less so, more likely symptomatic of Zweig's self-analysis. His biographical char-acters exhibit complexes and neuroses attuned to the 1920s and 1930s (to Zweig), rather than, for instance, to the times of Erasmus or Queen Elizabeth I or Balzac. Zweig thus discloses his personal fears and instabilities while clearly suffering with every one of his characters.

His association with a married woman, Friderike von Winternitz, had begun with her 'fan-letters' in 1901; and thereafter an extremely complex relationship fluctuated until her determination to possess him – out of sheer admiration – reached marriage in 1914. This somehow compensated for his divorce from all the friends whom the war now made his 'enemies'; but it seems unlikely that it was a complete marriage in the physical sense.

The First World War was a shattering experience for Zweig, who eschewed active service, and worked instead in the Press Bureau and Archives of the Army in Vienna. His assignment to a battle area in 1916 set him angrily against aggressors and war profiteers, and inspired the pacifist play *Jeremiah*, produced in Zürich in 1917. It is an expressionist work constructed in tableaux, with Jeremiah–Zweig welcoming defeat so as to purify the heart and soul, and inspire brotherhood among everybody.

After the war, Zweig and Friderike – and the two daughters by her first marriage – lived together in an isolated house on the Capuchin Mountain in Salzburg. Here he worked in comfort, indulged his passion for silence, order and sometimes succumbed to bursts of emotional imbalance when he was disturbed. He also added to and enjoyed his magnificent art treasures that included Beethoven memorabilia and one of the finest European collections of autographs. He regarded himself merely as caretaker for them all, not their owner. Zweig was a musical amateur and enjoyed the company of musicians who came to Salzburg: Toscanini, Bruno Walter, **Ravel** and **Bartók** especially.

With the emergence of the Fascist dictators, Zweig's morbid fear for the future became more intense. He satisfied his frequent need for 'freedom' by escaping from Salzburg, and its female-orientated household, for the purpose of meetings with old and new personalities such as **Gorky** in Russia in 1928. The introduction of a secretary into the Salzburg household set off an unforeseen chain of events: Charlotte (Lotte) Elisabeth Altmann was selected by Friderike. But gradually another involved, one-sided intellectual romance developed until Stefan and Friderike's marriage was doomed. Zweig now saw **Hitler's** persecution of the Jews as a measure instituted directly against himself and became more and more introspective, often oblivious of the duel over him between the women in his house.

His happy collaboration with **Richard Strauss** was cancelled out by the Nazi insult to both of them when it was proscribed because of Zweig's Jewish blood. In 1937 friends began publicly to ignore him, then his books were burned, his house was searched by the police and, in 1938, Austria collapsed before the Nazis. Zweig gave up the unequal struggle and escaped to London with Lotte, whom he married in Bath in 1939. But Bath was still too near Hitler and again they fled – in 1941 – to Brazil. Although Zweig was as happy there as he could be anywhere, pessimism overcame reason and he committed suicide with the faithful Lotte at Petropolis in 1942.

The need for freedom, and pity for humankind, tortured Zweig to death. He had lived a comfortable life and escaped the terrible end accorded to others of his race; but the fact that such evil could triumph above the innate good levelled against it was more than he could bear.

Further reading

Other works include: *Adepts in Self Portraiture* (*Drei Dichters Ihres Lebens*, 1928, trans. 1928); *Three Masters* (*Drei Meister* – Balzac, Dickens, Dostoevsky – 1920, trans. 1930); *Erasmus* (1934, trans. 1934); *Maria Stuart* (1935, trans. 1935); novels: *Letter from an Unknown Woman* (*Brief eine Unbekannten*, 1922, trans. 1933) and *Beware of Pity* (*Ungeduld des Herzens*, 1939, trans. 1939); autobiography: *The World of Yesterday* (*Die Welt von Gestern*, 1944, trans. 1945). See: Elizabeth Allday, *Stefan Zweig* (1972); Randolph J. Klawiter, *Stefan Zweig: An International Bibliography* (1991); Donald Prater, *The European of Yesterday: A Biography of Stefan Zweig* (2003).

ALAN JEFFERSON

index

John Stuart Mill and 1049; Juvenal des Ursins and 773
Todd, James T. 1387
Todd, Mabel 392
Todd, Olivier 252, 979
Tokarczyk, Michelle M. 402
Tolkein, John Ronald Reuel: Mervyn Peake and 1172
Tolkien, Christopher 1504
Tolkien, John Ronald Reuel 61, **1502–4**
Toll, Robert C. 510
Tolley, A.T. 869
Toloudis, Constantin 1230
Tolstoy, Count Lev Nikolaevich 21, 803, **1504–7**; Aleksandr Solzhenitsyn and 1392; André Gide and 585; Ernest Hemingway and 669; Franz Marc and 1002; Georg Lukács and 944; Isaac Singer and 1381; Isaiah Berlin and 140; Ivan Turgenev and 1519; John Ruskin and 1313; Kenji Mizoguchi and 1059; Kropotkin and 847; Mahatma Gandhi and 556; Pierre-Joseph Proudhon and 1217; Stephen Crane and 329; William Dean Howells and 714
Tolstoyanism 1506; Boris Pasternak and 1162
Tomassoni, I. 1202
Tomkins, Calvin 248, 419
Tomlin, Lily 26
Tomlinson, Charles 1074, 1171
Tompkins, J.M.S. 822
Tompkins, Keitha 848
Toop, Richard 912
Toorop, Jan 959
topology 1195
Torczyner, H. 966
Torrance, T.F. 101
Torre de Collserola 508
Toscanini, Arturo 1672
Toscano, Alberto 79
totalitarianism 42
Töteberg, Michael 480
totemism 519
Toth, Emily 305
Totten, Samuel 891
Toulouse-Lautrec, Henri de **1507–9**; Aubrey Beardsley and 111; Charles Demuth and 379; Edgar Degas and 372; Edouard Manet and 984
Townend, W.T. 1640
Townsend, Kim 754–55
Toynbee, Arnold Joseph **1509**; Carl Gustav Jung and 784
tractarianism 1586
Traill, David 1347
Trakl, Georg: Anton von Webern and 1601
Tramp, Charles: Marcel Marceau and 1003
transcendentalism 461–65, 743
translators: Burton, Richard F. 238–40; Waley, Arthur David 1583–84; *see also* linguists
Trautman, Thomas R. 1078

Traux, C.B. 1292
travellers: Burton, Richard F. 238–40; Doughty, Charles Montagu 409–11; Livingstone, David 919–21; Stanley, Henry Morton 1412–13; Thesiger, Wilfred 1484–85; Van Der Post, Sir Laurens 1535–36; *see also* explorers
Travisano, Thomas 161
Treglown, Jeremy 619
Tremlett, George 545, 1488
Tretiack, Philippe 1589
Trevelyan, G.M. 562
Trevelyan, Janet Penrose 1587
Trevor, Meriol 766
Trevor-Roper, H.R. 693
Trianon-Theater, Vienna 1604
Trilling, Lionel 49, 508, 714, 822
tripartition 558
Troeltsch, Ernst 1598
Trollope, Anthony **1510–12**; Charles Dickens and 390; Elizabeth Gaskell and 564; Mary Ward and 1586; Rodrigo Dos Passos and 403; Wilkie Collins and 318
Trompenaars, Fons 698
Trotsky, Leon 11, 1410, **1512–16**; André Breton and 208; Anthony Burgess and 235; destruction of 224; Joseph Stalin and 1409
Trotskyism 834; George Orwell and 1146; Mary McCarthy branded of 1025
Troupe, Quincy 89
Troyat, H. 1507
Trudgian, Helen 733
Truffaut, François **1516–17**; Jean Renoir and 1258; Robert Bresson and 207
Tryman, Mfanya Donald 971
Tryphonopoulos, Demetres P. 1209
Tsivian, Yuri 1557
tuberculosis 832
Tuchman, Maurice 1397
Tucker, James 1211
Tucker, M. 461
Tuohy, Frank 1660
Turco, Alfred Jr 1371
Turgenev, Ivan Sergeyevich **1517–20**; Edmond and Jules de Goncourt and 600; Guy de Maupassant and 1019; Henry James and 747; Leo Tolstoy and 1504; Truman Capote and 257
Turing, Alan **1520–21**; Eduardo Paolozzi and 1153; John von Neumann and 1567
Turing, S. 1521
Turkey 15–16, 57–59
Turkle, Sherry 528
Turku, Finland 1
Turnbull, A. 495
Turner, Bryan S. 1158
Turner, E.M. 485
Turner, Frank 1112
Turner, Frederick Jackson **1521–22**
Turney, J. 931